EDMUND SPENSER

EDMUND SPENSER

 A Life

ANDREW HADFIELD

OXFORD
UNIVERSITY PRESS

OXFORD
UNIVERSITY PRESS

Great Clarendon Street, Oxford OX2 6DP,
United Kingdom

Oxford University Press is a department of the University of Oxford.
It furthers the University's objective of excellence in research, scholarship,
and education by publishing worldwide. Oxford is a registered trade mark of
Oxford University Press in the UK and in certain other countries

© Andrew Hadfield 2012

The moral rights of the author have been asserted

First Edition published 2012

Impression: 1

British Library Cataloguing in Publication Data

Data available

Library of Congress Cataloging in Publication Data

Data available

ISBN 978-0-19-959102-2

Printed in Great Britain
on acid-free paper by
Clays Ltd, St Ives plc

FOR WILLIAM TIMOTHY MALEY

Contents

Acknowledgements

I have enjoyed writing this book more than any other I have written. I have been astonished at the generosity of vast numbers of people who have given up their time to help me complete this biography and it has certainly reaffirmed my faith in human nature. I only hope that I can repay some of them if given the chance.

I first conceived the idea of writing a biography of Edmund Spenser when I was asked to contribute an entry on his life for the *Oxford Dictionary of National Biography* in 2000 by the late Brian Harrison. I had never thought of writing a biography before—and will almost certainly not write one again—so this was an important event in my life. I could not have written the life without a British Academy Research Development Award (BARDA) and a Leverhulme Research Fellowship, together totalling two years (2008–10), as well as a year's sabbatical from the University of Sussex, although I will add that that was a reward for having served as Head of Department. I was also the fortunate recipient of a short-term fellowship at the Folger Shakespeare Library, taken in the summer of 2009, where I had the great pleasure of working with a number of formidably learned colleagues in a congenial, scholarly atmosphere. A British Academy small grant awarded in 2011 enabled me to tidy up a large number of loose ends.

At OUP I have been more than fortunate in having had the opportunity to work with two outstanding editors, Andrew McNeillie, with whom I first discussed the project, and Jacqueline Baker, who has matched insight, enthusiasm, good sense, and tolerance to keep me on track. Rowena Anketell, Jacqueline Harvey, and Brendan Mac Evilly were exemplary and courteous professionals who saw the book develop from a messy typescript. I have also relied on a number of friends and colleagues for particular help: Andrew King in Cork has been a wonderful companion and host, driving me round all the Spenser locations we could find in his impressive red Alfa Romeo and discussing a vast number of Spenserian obsessions with jovial good humour, and he has been a rock during the inevitable emergencies that befall a field researcher ('Everyone loses their passport now and again'); Anne Fogarty and Ulf Messner, and Raymond Gillespie and Bernadette Cunningham have been equally generous and hospitable in Dublin; Howard Erskine-Hill put me up and put up with me at Pembroke College, Cambridge; Alan Bryson and Simon Healy have been kind, patient, and courteous in helping supplement my miserable palaeographic skills ('No, that should be transcribed as "Queen Elizabeth" but, you're right that difficult hand could have written "Edmund Spenser"'); Tarnya Cooper has been a fountain of knowledge about sixteenth-century portraits; Jane Grogan helped save me from a bull at Graney Abbey, while I impersonated Lucetta Templeman; Eric Klingelhofer has discussed a number of matters relating to the archaeological digs he has led at Kilcolman and elsewhere in Munster; John McGurk has advised me on Elizabethan military matters, especially musters; Kenneth Nicholls has shared his immense knowledge of life in sixteenth-century Munster; Elizabeth Evenden, Stephen Galbraith, and Steve May have educated me in the often confusing highways and byways of early modern books, texts, and manuscripts; Charles, Catherine, and Phoebe Harold-Barry, owners of Kilcolman Castle, were yet more people who were hospitable and most generous with their time to a stranger; Henry Woudhuysen talked me through a number of aspects of Spenser's early literary career and sent me some vital unpublished research; and Jim Shapiro has been a great friend, mentor, and guide. Chapters have been read by a number of colleagues and friends: Alan Bryson, Peter Boxall, Patrick Cheney, Alison Hadfield, Margaret Healy, Andrew King, Elizabeth Oakley-Brown, Neil Rhodes, Jennifer Richards, Abigail Shinn, and Bart Van Es. I have especially enjoyed discussing the project with Patrick Cheney, Brian Cummings, and Matthew Dimmock. Two anonymous readers were exemplary, meticulous, and astringent, not only saving me from more than a few errors, factual, stylistic, and narrative, but both made constructive suggestions that significantly improved the book. While I was finishing off the book my friend Kevin Sharpe died. I am sorry that I did not have the chance to thank him properly for his help over the years.

I should also add that this book would not have been possible without the pioneering research of many who have laboured hard in the archives uncovering numerous facts about Spenser's life, most significantly, Jean Brink, Douglas Hamer, A. C. Judson, and W. H. Welply. The research has been carried out in many locations and I have been more than grateful to kind and helpful staff at the Bodleian Library, Oxford; the British Library; Cambridge University Library; Castle Howard archives; the Codrington Library, All Souls College, Oxford; the Library of Gonville and Caius College, Cambridge; the Library of Pembroke College, Cambridge; Chatsworth House Archives; Chichester Cathedral Library; the Dutch Church, Austen friars, London; Folger Shakespeare Library; Guildhall Library, London; Hampshire Record Office, Winchester; the Huguenot Library, London; Lambeth Palace Library; London Metropolitan Archives; the National Archives, Kew; the National Archives of Ireland, Dublin; the National Library of Ireland, Dublin; the National Library of Wales, Aberystwyth; National Maritime Museum, Greenwich; the Royal Irish Academy Library; Saffron Walden Town Museum; Suffolk County Record Office, Bury St Edmunds; Trinity College Library, Dublin; the Library at University College, Cork; and Westminster City Archives. I have also been grateful to the staff at a number of churches, houses, monuments, and museums: Canons Ashby, Northamptonshire; Christ Church Cathedral, Dublin; The collegiate church of St Mary, Youghal; Dublin Castle; Farleigh House, Farleigh Wallop;

ACKNOWLEDGEMENTS

Hill Hall, Essex; Limerick Cathedral; Ormond Castle, Carrick-on-Suir; Rathfanham Castle, Dublin; Rochester Cathedral; St Margaret's church, Westminster; St Patrick's Cathedral, Dublin; and Saffron Walden Museum.

The following people also helped in large and small, but always significant, ways: Mrs Abray; Hugh Adlington; Gavin Alexander; Stephen Alford; Pat Aske; Norma Aubertin-Potter; Bruce Bailey; Carlo Bajetta; Ros Barber; Michael Brennan; Ian Donaldson; Eamon Duffy; Martin Everett; Andrew Foster; Tom Freeman; Barbara Fuchs; Jonathan Gibson; Lucy Gwynn; Catrina Hay; Thomas Herron; Ralph Houlbrooke; Maurice Howard; Richard Hoyle; Jane Hurst; Kathryn James; Brendan Kane; David Scott Kastan; Amy Kenny; John Kerrigan; Gerard Kilroy; C. A. Knook; Donna Landry; Naomi Conn Liebler; James Livesey; Anna Louise Mason; Michael MacCarthy-Morrogh; Natalie Mears; Julia Merritt; Susannah Monta; Hiram Morgan; Stewart Mottram; Mark Nicholls; Micheál Ó Siochrú; Leanne O'Sullivan; Ann Padfield; Sean Palmer; Helen Parish; Andrew Peppit; Andrew Pettegree; Lee Piepho; Nicholas Popper; Lady Annabel Portsmouth and her family; Anne Lake Prescott; Christopher Ridgway; Jayne Ringrose; Paul Rondelez; Richard Simpson; Daniel Starza-Smith; Naomi Tadmor; James Towe; Sara Trevisan; Malcolm Underhill; Norman Vance; Saskia Verwey; and Sarah Wheale.

I have also benefited from giving talks on material reproduced in the book at the Universities of Aarhus, Brighton, Cork, Exeter at Cornwall, Galway (Moore Institute), Hull, Kent, Lancaster, NUI Maynooth, Newcastle upon Tyne, Penn State University, Padua, Reading, Surrey, Sussex, University College London, Warwick, and at the Institute for Historical Research (twice); the 400th Anniversary Conference of the Londonderry Plantation (Derry); Dublin: Renaissance City of Literature (Marsh's Library); the Renaissance Society of America (Venice); and the Sixteenth-Century Conference (Geneva). Material that appears here has already appeared in earlier forms in 'Secrets and Lies: The Life of Edmund Spenser', in Kevin Sharpe and Steven Zwicker (eds.), *Writing Lives: Biography and Textuality, Identity and Representation in Early Modern England* (Oxford: Oxford University Press, 2008), pp. 55–73; 'Spenser's Rosalind', *Modern Language Review* 104/4 (October 2009), 935–46; 'Religious Affiliation in Elizabethan London: Richard Mulcaster, Edmund Spenser and The Family of Love', in Roze Hentschell and Kathy Lavezzo (eds.), *Laureations: Essays in Honor of Richard Helgerson* (Newark: University of Delaware Press, 2012), pp. 243–58; and 'Educating the Colonial Mind: Spenser and the Plantation', in Micheál Ó Siochrú and Eamonn O Ciardha (eds.), *The Plantation of Ulster: Ideology and Practice* (Manchester: Manchester University Press, 2012). I am grateful to Oxford University Press, the Modern Humanities Research Association, the University of Delaware Press, and Manchester University Press for permission to reproduce work here.

ACKNOWLEDGEMENTS

I need to pass on, as ever, my love and gratitude to my family, Alison, Lucy, Patrick, and Maud, for putting up with me while I have been researching and writing this book, although, if I say so myself, I feel I have been a bit less grumpy and irritable than in the past, one thing at least that I owe to my experience as Head of Department at Sussex, which has made me appreciate ordinary life rather more. I have dedicated this biography to my friend and comrade, Willy Maley, who has been a major influence on my work, unstinting in his generous help while I have been working on Spenser's life, and whom I would like to acknowledge as we approach the silver anniversary of our first meeting.

List of Figures

List of Plates

All photographs by the author. Every effort has been made to trace or contact all copyright holders, and the publishers will be pleased to correct any omissions brought to their notice at the earliest convenience.

Abbreviations

Acts of the Privy Council	*Acts of the Privy Council of England, 1542–1631*, ed. John Roche Dasent et al., 46 vols. (London: HMSO, 1890–1964)
AJ	*Antiquaries Journal*
Amoretti, ed. Larsen	*Edmund Spenser's Amoretti and Epithalamion: A Critical Edition*, ed. Kenneth J. Larsen (Tempe, AZ: MRTS, 1997)
Atkinson, *Bibliographical Supplement*	Dorothy F. Atkinson, *Edmund Spenser: A Bibliographical Supplement* (Baltimore: Johns Hopkins University Press, 1937)
BL	British Library
Bracken and Silver (eds.), *Book Trade*	James K. Bracken and Joel Silver (eds.), *The British Literary Book Trade, 1475–1700* (Detroit, Washington DC, and London: Gale, 1996)
Carew	*Calendar of the Carew Manuscripts, preserved in the Archiepiscopal Library at Lambeth. (1515–1624)*, 8 vols., ed. J. S. Brewer and W. Bullen (London: Longman, 1867–73)
Carpenter, *Reference Guide*	Frederick Ives Carpenter, *A Reference Guide to Edmund Spenser* (1923; New York: Peter Smith, 1950)
Chronology	Willy Maley, *A Spenser Chronology* (Basingstoke: Palgrave, 1994)
CL	*Comparative Literature*
CSPI	*Calendar of State Papers Relating to Ireland, 1509–1603*, 11 vols., ed. H. C. Hamilton (London: HMSO, 1860–1912).
CSPS	*Calendar of State Papers Relating to Scotland and Mary Queen of Scots, 1547–1603*, 13 vols. (Edinburgh: HMSO, 1898–1969)

Cummings, *Critical Heritage*	R. M. Cummings, *Edmund Spenser: The Critical Heritage* (London: Routledge, 1971)
DIB	James McGuire and James Quinn (eds.), *Dictionary of Irish Biography*, 9 vols. (Cambridge: Cambridge University Press, 2009).
EETS	*Early English Text Society*
EHR	*English Historical Review*
ELH	*English Literary History*
ELR	*English Literary Renaissance*
ES	*English Studies*
Fiants	*The Irish Fiants of the Tudor sovereigns during the reigns of Henry VIII, Edward VI, Philip & Mary, and Elizabeth I*, 4 vols. (Dublin: Burke, 1994)
FQ	*The Faerie Queene*
Harvey, *Marginalia*	*Gabriel Harvey's Marginalia*, ed. G. C. Moore Smith (Stratford-upon-Avon: Shakespeare Head Press, 1913)
Harvey–Spenser, *Letters*	Gabriel Harvey and Edmund Spenser, *Three proper, and wittie, familiar letters: lately passed betvveene tvvo vniuersitie men: touching the earthquake in Aprill last, and our English reformed versifying With the preface of a well-willer to them both* (London, 1580)
HJ	*Historical Journal*
HLQ	*Huntington Library Quarterly*
HMC	Historical Manuscripts Commission
HMSO	Her Majesty's Stationery Office
House of Commons	P. W. Hasler (ed.), *The House of Commons, 1558–1603*, 3 vols. (London: HMSO, 1981)
HR	*Historical Research*
HSNPL	*Harvard Studies and Notes in Philology and Literature*
IHS	*Irish Historical Studies*

IUR	*Irish University Review*
JCHAS	*Journal of the Cork Historical & Archaeological Society*
JEGP	*Journal of English and Germanic Philology*
JHG	*Journal of Historical Geography*
JKAS	*Journal of the County Kildare Archaeological Society and Surrounding Districts*
JMEMS	*Journal of Medieval and Early Modern Studies*
Johnson, *Critical Bibliography*	Francis R. Johnson, *A Critical Bibliography of the Works of Edmund Spenser printed before 1700* (Baltimore: Johns Hopkins University Press, 1933)
JRSAI	*Journal of the Royal Society of Antiquaries of Ireland*
Judson, *Life*	A. C. Judson, *The Life of Edmund Spenser* (Baltimore: Johns Hopkins University Press, 1945), vol. xi of *Variorum.*
JWCI	*Journal of the Warburg and Courtauld Institutes*
MFCJ	*Mallow Field Club Journal*
MLN	*Modern Language Notes*
MLQ	*Modern Language Quarterly*
MLR	*Modern Language Review*
Moody et al. (eds.), *New History of Ireland*	T. W. Moody, F. X. Martin, and F. J. Byrne (eds.), *A New History of Ireland*, 10 vols. (Oxford: Clarendon Press, 1976–)
MP	*Modern Philology*
MRTS	*Medieval and Renaissance Texts and Studies*
N&Q	*Notes and Queries*
Nashe, *Works*	*The Works of Thomas Nashe*, ed. R. B. McKerrow and F. P. Wilson, 5 vols. (Oxford: Blackwell, 1966)
ODNB	*Oxford Dictionary of National Biography*
OED	*Oxford English Dictionary*
P&P	*Past and Present*

Patent and Close Rolls	*Calendar of the Patent and Close Rolls of Chancery in Ireland*, ed. James Morrin, 3 vols. (London: Longman, 1862–3)
PBA	*Proceedings of the British Academy*
PMLA	*Publications of the Modern Language Association of America*
Printers	R. B. McKerrow et al. (eds.), *A Dictionary of Printers and Booksellers in England, Scotland and Ireland, and of Foreign Printers of English Books, 1557-1640* (London: Bibliographical Society, 1968)
PQ	*Philological Quarterly*
PRIA	*Proceedings of the Royal Irish Academy*
PRO	Public Record Office
RC	Irish Record Commission (1810–30)
RES	*The Review of English Studies*
Riverside Chaucer	*The Riverside Chaucer*, ed. Larry D. Benson (1987; Oxford: Oxford University Press, 1988)
RQ	*Renaissance Quarterly*
RS	*Renaissance Studies*
SB	*Studies in Bibliography*
SCJ	*Sixteenth-Century Journal*
SEL	*Studies in English Literature, 1500–1900*
Sh. Stud.	*Shakespeare Studies*
SJ	*Sidney Journal*
SLI	*Studies in the Literary Imagination*
SP	*Studies in Philology*
SP	State Papers
Sp. Enc.	*The Spenser Encyclopedia*, ed. A. C. Hamilton (Toronto; London: University of Toronto Press; London: Routledge, 1990)
Sp. Handbook	*The Oxford Handbook to Spenser*, ed. Richard A. McCabe (Oxford: Oxford University Press, 2010)

Sp. St.	*Spenser Studies*
Spenser Allusions	William Wells (ed.), *Spenser Allusions in the Sixteenth and Seventeenth Centuries* (Chapel Hill: University of North Carolina Press, 1972)
Spenser, *Faerie Queene*	Edmund Spenser, *The Faerie Queene*, ed. A. C. Hamilton (Harlow: Longman, 2001)
Spenser, *Letters*	Edmund Spenser, *Selected Letters and Other Papers*, ed. Christopher Burlinson and Andrew Zurcher (Oxford: Oxford University Press, 2009)
Spenser, *Shorter Poems*	Edmund Spenser, *The Shorter Poems*, ed. Richard A. McCabe (Harmondsworth: Penguin, 1999)
SR	*Studies in the Renaissance*
Stationers	Edward Arber (ed.), *A Transcript of the Registers of the Company of Stationers of London, 1554–1640*, 5 vols. (London: privately printed, 1875)
Stern, *Harvey*	Virginia Stern, *Gabriel Harvey: A Study of His Life, Marginalia and Library* (Oxford: Oxford University Press, 1979)
TCD	Trinity College Dublin
TLS	*The Times Literary Supplement*
TNA	The National Archives
TRHS	*Transactions of the Royal Historical Society*
UJA	*Ulster Journal of Archaeology*
Variorum	*The Works of Edmund Spenser: A Variorum Edition*, ed. Edwin Greenlaw, Charles Grosvenor Osgood, Frederick Morgan Padelford, and Ray Heffner, 11 vols. (Baltimore: Johns Hopkins University Press, 1932–45)
Victoria County History	*Victoria County History* (London: Institute for Historical Research, 1933–)
YES	*Yearbook of English Studies*

Introduction: Writing the Life

EDMUND SPENSER's life will probably always be shrouded in a certain mystery. We cannot be sure about his ancestry and immediate family. As is usual for writers of the sixteenth century, no personal letters survive, and there are no significant literary manuscripts in Spenser's hand, only legal documents and secretarial works.[1] We know very little about Spenser's relationships with most of his patrons, friends, or the social superiors to whom he was connected. It was assumed for a long time that Spenser must have been an intimate associate of Sir Philip Sidney because they were both poets who had Irish connections, and that Sidney must have eased his entry into court society, but many have questioned how well they could have known each other, given their obvious difference in class and status.[2] We do not really know how close Spenser and Sir Walter Ralegh, with whom he is invariably depicted, really were in the 1580s and 1590s, especially if we bear in mind that their relationship survives principally in the form of literary works (Plate 1).[3] We do not know whether he was a close friend and confidant of Lord Grey, the Irish patron with whom Spenser has most frequently been associated, nor what his relationship was with Gabriel Harvey after he left for Ireland in 1580. In fact we do not know why Spenser left for Ireland in that year.[4] There are many people referred to in his poetry or related to his life, who may or may not really exist, most notably Rosalind and E. K. in *The Shepheardes Calender* and the careless servant who supposedly lost the later books of *The Faerie Queene* in Wales.[5] We do not know how Spenser died.[6] There is nothing of Spenser's opinions, comments, or even many details of his life outside his writings.

The most obvious reason for the lack of information we have about Spenser is that in the sixteenth century lives of even quite prominent people only really mattered when they told a useful, moral story that could be applied with profit to the reader's own case. Reading was often pragmatic and goal-oriented, a skill that Spenser's tutor and friend, Gabriel Harvey, practised, publicized, and made a cornerstone of his career.[7] Lives were made to fit obviously useful patterns, and it should not surprise us that so many seem to conform to familiar narratives, such as the parable of the prodigal son, a particular favourite in Elizabethan England.[8] The most spectacular example was that of Robert Greene (1558–92), who expired, according to his principal detractor, Gabriel Harvey, and his friend and ally, Thomas Nashe, after a 'fatall banquet' which involved 'a surfeit of pickle herringe and rennish wine'.[9] Greene's eventful life and death were represented in various works which have proved hard to attribute to any author with certainty.[10] However, they all construct his life in terms of a particular narrative structure, that of the repentant prodigal, who is able to save his soul after an agonizing deathbed confession enables him to atone for his previous sins. We cannot, of course, be sure that either Harvey or Nashe is actually telling the truth about Greene's death: significantly enough, no one knows who was at the fatal banquet, apart from the unknown Will Monox (who may be invented) and, perhaps, the publisher Cuthbert Burby.[11] Harvey is eager to expose the disgusting behaviour of an enemy who has been vigorously defended by his allies and so tells the story with considerable glee; Nashe exploits the detail as a means of showing that even if it were true (Nashe comments in parenthesis, '(if thou wilt needs haue it so)'), Greene was still a better man and writer than Harvey could ever hope to be.[12]

Most lives written in sixteenth-century Europe had a didactic religious purpose. As Irena Backus has pointed out in her study of life writing in Reformation Europe, whatever authors might claim, 'the early *Lives* of Luther, Calvin, Beza and the Swiss reformers were sui-generic', detail is included to tell a particular story, hagiographic or hostile.[13] Philip Melanchthon's biography of Luther is a case in point: 'Melanchthon ... announces what his biography is not: a biography in the sense of a chronological account of an individual's life. It is an account of Luther as instrument of divine providence, which also praises a selection of his extraordinary human qualities.'[14]

We now have a very different perception of biography, one that assumes that there can be a separation between the recorded details of the subject's life and his or her achievements. The two exist separately: after we have gathered together the life from the surviving life records (family records, legal documents, personal effects and objects, wills, and, above all, letters), we can then read the works and the life in terms of each other, so that the life helps to explain the works.[15] Ideally, an author writes details of his or her own life, an autobiography, that can be read with or against the grain.[16] Such assumptions lie behind the great recent literary biographies of men and women of letters from the eighteenth century onwards, such as Walter Jackson Bate's life of Samuel Johnson; Michael Meyer's Henrik Ibsen; Leon Edel's Henry James; Hermione Lee's Virginia Woolf; or Michael Holroyd's Bernard Shaw.[17] But things are more complicated when we try to reconstruct the lives of men and women in the early modern period, especially those born outside the aristocracy, who were not employed by the church, who did not live in a notably saintly or evil manner, and who were not engaged in politics or diplomacy, e.g., writers of the middling sort such as Spenser. It is notable that while a number of life records do survive that have enabled scholars to reconstruct the life of Sir Philip Sidney in considerable detail, virtually nothing relates to his literary activities. Sidney is represented in contemporary accounts as a Protestant saint and as a politician, notably in the life written by his friend, Fulke Greville (1554–1628), which makes no mention of his literary achievements, even though Greville edited the *Arcadia* after Sidney's death.[18] Sidney's literary works only became read in terms of his life a long time after his death.[19]

It is worth reminding ourselves that although English biography did exist in an earlier form than has often been recognized, biographers were not 'interested in minute and even apparently trivial information about remarkable persons' until the second half of the seventeenth century.[20] As is widely recognized, it is no accident that 'Milton is the first English author for whom we have so much in the way of biography'.[21] The first biographer who appears to have taken a proper interest in the apparently inconsequential details of lives is John Aubrey (1626–97), whose *Brief Lives* remained in manuscript until 1813. Only after such a development could a biographer really hope to assemble the sort of material that we think of as essential to the construction of a life. Paradoxically, the serious work of biography, one of the key genres of writing that we depend on today, could only begin with a desire to document superfluous, ephemeral details, a sign that lives were being read in rather less serious ways than when they were perceived in moral and theological terms. The history of biography and the history of gossip are intertwined.[22]

The problem that needs to be addressed is how we deal with this apparently fundamental division. Biographers invariably want to look back beyond the middle of the seventeenth century and find life records and narratives of lives that resemble those found later. But, such evidence does not often exist. This lacuna helps to explain why so many strange conspiracy theories have developed about the life of Shakespeare in particular, as, frustrated at the lack of surviving material, biographers with little experience of late sixteenth-century England imagine that a gap in the biographical record signals an aberration that needs to be explained, and so are able to conclude that Christopher Marlowe did not really die in Deptford but was resurrected as Shakespeare, or that William Shakespeare of Stratford was a front for another writer, Sir Francis Bacon, Edward de Vere, earl of Oxford, and, as has recently been suggested, Sir Henry Neville.[23] Indeed, it should not really surprise anyone interested in questions of early modern biography that a lengthy case has been made that Bacon wrote all of Spenser's works—as well as those of Shakespeare.[24]

But even a superficial trawl through the new *Dictionary of National Biography* will reveal how little we know about so many important figures, making the gaps in the biographical records of Shakespeare and Spenser seem typical rather than unusual and therefore in need of explanation. Thomas Nashe (bap. 1567, d. *c.*1601) was among the most significant literary figures of the 1590s, having forced the authorities to close the theatres and then censor the press within the space of two years, surely a unique achievement.[25] Yet, no one saw fit to record the date, let alone the cause, of his death.[26] Gabriel Harvey (1552/3–1631), his bitter opponent, and a writer who did leave behind a large number of clues about his whereabouts and opinions, nevertheless disappeared into relative obscurity in Saffron Walden for the last thirty years of his life.[27] The same might be said of John Lyly (1554–1606), a major court poet and dramatist. His *ODNB* biographer, G. K. Hunter, notes that 'The only expression of Lyly's literary talent in the last sixteen years of his life appears in the begging letters he wrote to Elizabeth and to the Cecils.' The case is no different if we turn to Thomas Lodge (1558–1625), another prominent literary figure, whose work had a major impact on the course of Elizabethan literature. His *ODNB* biographer, Alexandra Halasz, is also clear about the frustrating gaps in our knowledge: 'Although Lodge was occasionally recognized by his contemporaries, his name occurs less frequently than might be expected from the range of his work and the length of his life,' adding further, 'Some of the mentions, moreover, are not easily understandable in relation to what is taken to be Lodge's *œuvre*.' Almost nothing is known about the life of Abraham Fraunce (1559?–1592/3?), a key figure within the Sidney circle, who was among the first to appreciate the importance of Spenser's work. Even when a life can be chronicled rather more fully, such as that of Ben Jonson (1572–1637), there are frustrating gaps in the narrative.[28]

If we turn to dramatists who largely relied on the stage for their income, the picture is, if anything, even worse. It is especially hard to determine the canon of Thomas Middleton (bap. 1580, d. 1627).[29] Only recently has the important play *The Family of Love* (pub. 1608) been removed from the list of his known works, and, despite the recent interest in his life and work, many gaps remain in our knowledge of both.[30] The life records of John Webster (*c.*1578/80–1638?) are even more obscure.[31] Unless there is a reason to record lives because the narrative will tell the reader as much as a seriously learned book, or details are preserved through the records of state or other official mechanisms, evidence invariably does not survive. What are left are scraps, fragments, and clues in parish registers, court records, and probate offices.[32]

It is hardly surprising, given the state of the evidence, that often a great deal is made of one or two facts, which, read in particular ways, determine how a whole personality—and more—might be seen in relationship to their work. Again, the case of Shakespeare indicates how problematic such interpretations often are.

As there are virtually no literary remains left behind by Shakespeare outside his published works, and most of the surviving records deal with property and legal disputes, a revisionist impulse has attempted to correct the familiar picture of Shakespeare as a wild and untutored genius by representing him as a hard-headed provincial citizen with an eye for personal gain.[33] Moreover, a whole scholarly sub-industry hinges on what we might understand by the gift of the second-best bed to Anne Hathaway, whether the gesture signals the contempt of a husband trapped in a loveless marriage, or a sign of intimate affection because the second-best bed was the one the couple slept in.[34] The life and the works are then read as a symbiotic whole, with Shakespeare's plays and poems compensating for what he did not get at home; revealing his contempt for women; or, expressing a fulfilled and happy love as he saw it.[35]

The same problems of interpretation shadow Spenser's life and the ways in which it has been narrated. It was often assumed that because he wrote about the queen he must have been a devoted royalist and enjoyed a special relationship with the monarch. In Thomas Fuller's *Worthies of England*, published posthumously in 1662, the following story has pride of place in the brief entry:

There passeth a story commonly told and believed that Spenser, presenting his poems to Queen Elizabeth, she, highly affected therewith, commanded the Lord Cecil, her treasurer, to give him an hundred pounds; and when the treasurer (a good steward of the queen's money) alleged that sum was too much, 'Then give him,' quoth the queen, 'what is reason,' to which the lord consented, but was so busied, belike, about matters of higher concernment, that Spenser received no reward; whereupon he presented this petition in a small piece of paper to the queen in her progress:

> I was promis'd on a time,
> To have reason for my rhyme;
> From that time unto this season,
> I receiv'd nor rhyme nor reason.

Hereupon the queen gave strict order (not without some check to her treasurer) for the present payment of the hundred pounds she first intended unto him.[36]

The story has long been treated with some scepticism, and is undoubtedly based on confusion with Thomas Churchyard's complaint about his belated royal reward.[37] However, Spenser's biographer, A. C. Judson, argued that even if it 'sounds on the whole, rather like the work of a court wit', the story 'may indeed have a core of truth'.[38] The anecdote can only have a 'core of truth' if it is assumed that Spenser was a poet admired by the queen but treated with disdain by her other courtiers, in this case, William Cecil, Lord Burghley. The recently discovered 'Tresham letter' corroborates the widespread assumption that Spenser's portrayal of the 'fox' in *Mother Hubberds Tale* did indeed offend Lord Burghley, led to *The Complaints* being 'called in' after their publication, and placed the author in serious trouble.[39] However, it is unlikely that the queen took a personal interest in the poem and the anecdote seems to owe much to Fuller's own temperate support for the royalist cause and faith in the insight and efficacy of the monarch rather than his or her advisers.[40] The idea that monarchs enjoyed the cheeky wit of court poets is also perhaps partly proverbial wisdom, partly based on Spenser's own self-representation in his poetry.[41] On the other hand, it is documented that Elizabeth enjoyed jest books, and had courtiers read episodes from *A Hundred Merry Tales* (1526) to her on her deathbed.[42]

Fuller's anecdote, repeated in numerous subsequent lives of the poet throughout the eighteenth and nineteenth centuries, indicates how certain key details are seen to encapsulate a life in miniature.[43] The whole narrative, which is barely five hundred words long, is the first life of Spenser in the seventeenth century and so set the tone for much of what followed.[44] For Fuller, Spenser was a scholar who loved poetry, had a court career, then went to Ireland, where he fared badly (and did not really want to be), was burned out by the rebels, before 'dying for grief' in London, where he was buried in Westminster Abbey at the expense of Robert Devereux, second earl of Essex. In essence, this is the story that has been told ever since.

John Aubrey's brief life, as we might expect given his role as a 'hint-keeper', recording details for others to develop, is a mass of tempting but unconnected scraps, many of which only assume an importance in the story of Spenser's life later when they were published (1813).[45] Aubrey is the first to provide any details of Spenser's appearance, commenting that 'Mr Beeston sayes, he was a little man, wore shorte haire, little band and little cuffs.'[46] The description is not especially vivid or helpful and probably reached Aubrey at one remove, the Mr Beeston being William (1610/11?–82), son of the impresario and actor manager Christopher (1579/80?–1638), who could have seen Spenser in London but died when Aubrey was 13.[47] Nevertheless, the details may have some importance, as they suggest that Spenser was a man of modest attire, and habitually wore the clothes of the middle classes, as well as keeping his hair short, not a flamboyant courtier, as he is represented in the Kinnoull portrait, reproduced on the cover of this book. The 'little band' would have been of the same style as that worn by Ben Jonson in the portrait by Abraham van Blyenberch, painted in 1617, or by Shakespeare in the Flower portrait.[48] The story is a sign of Aubrey's desire to preserve apparently irrelevant detail, realizing that it might take on much greater significance later, or, simply be of interest to readers. In revealing his sources he also shows how much work he did in recording details and trying to preserve living memories of the dead. Aubrey reproduced details which originated in correspondence or conversations, again showing the close relationship between biography and gossip, and the accidental nature of the genre, details preserved because of who the author happened to know or encounter.

Aubrey's next paragraph provides a series of details that cannot simply be taken at face value, but which provide important clues about how Spenser was perceived in the later seventeenth century, as well as pointing us towards important facts:

Mr Edmund Spencer was of Pembroke-hall in Cambridge; he mist the Fellowship there, which Bishop Andrewes gott. He was an acquaintance and frequenter of Sir Erasmus Dryden: His Mistris Rosalind was a kinswoman of Sir Erasmus Ladys. The chamber there at Sir Erasmus' is still called Mr Spencers chamber. Lately, at college takeing-downe the Wainscot of his chamber, they found an abundance of Cards, with stanzas of the *Faerie Queene* written on them.[49]

The story of the competition for the fellowship at Pembroke with Lancelot Andrewes is wrong. Andrewes (1555–1626), like Spenser, was a pupil at Merchant Taylors' School, and then Pembroke College, Cambridge, matriculating two years after Spenser in 1571, so they must have been acquainted, especially as both were star pupils of the educational reformer Richard Mulcaster (1531/2–1611).[50] However, it was not with Spenser that Andrewes competed and won, but his exact contemporary Thomas Dove (1555–1630), who had been with him at Merchant Taylors' School, and then gone up to Cambridge at the same time. Each future divine was funded from the same bequest by Thomas Watts (1523/4–77), a notable benefactor of the school, whose funds had also helped Spenser's educational progress.[51] Aubrey is not far away from the truth, which suggests that the detail probably comes from a faulty memory by his source.

What the story illustrates is that from the middle of the seventeenth century, if not earlier, Spenser was seen, undoubtedly based in part on his self-representation in his writings, as a disaffected and disappointed man who was perpetually overlooked by the authorities. Certainly, the story of the failed fellowship was repeated in many of the lives written in the seventeenth and eighteenth centuries, until disproved by the historian and biographer Thomas Birch (1705–66) in his life of the poet for the 1751 edition of Spenser's works, the first that contained a properly critical and sceptical biography.[52] The confusion is understandable, but it also suggests that evidence was read in terms of the perception of the life, as much as it determined how that life was reconstructed.

The detail about Rosalind's connection to the Dryden family is, if anything, even more tantalizing. Aubrey or his source would again appear to have transposed details. In the course of his exhaustive research into Spenser's family, W. H. Welply discovered that Spenser's second wife, Elizabeth Boyle, was a niece by marriage of John Dryden, great-grandfather of the poet John Dryden

(1631–1700), and, therefore, a first cousin of Sir Erasmus Dryden (1553–1632), the eldest son of John.[53] If we assume that Aubrey has confused the literary figure, Rosalind, with Spenser's real wife, then the connection of Spenser with an exact contemporary is strengthened rather than weakened, as is his connection with Northamptonshire, the county of both the Spensers and Drydens.[54] Therefore, the existence of the Spenser chamber at the Dryden family home of Canons Ashby (Plate 2) need not be dismissed out of hand.[55] Dryden's particular interest in Spenser is not necessarily explained by this family connection, and he does not refer to any link between them, but it might have played a part.[56]

Aubrey produces two other significant details, both of which would appear to have some basis in reality:

Mr Samuel Woodford (the Poet who paraphras'd the Psalmes) lives in Hampshire neer Alton, and he told me that Mr Spenser lived sometime in these parts, in this delicate sweet ayre: where he enjoyed his Muse: and writt good part of his Verses . . .

Sir John Denham told me, that Abp Ussher, Lord Primate of Armagh, was acquainted with him; by this token: when Sir William Davenant's *Gondibert* cam forth, Sir John askt the Lord Primate if he had seen it. Said the Primate, Out upon him, with his vaunting Preface, he speakes against my old friend Edmund Spenser.[57]

Samuel Woodford (1636–1700) was another of Aubrey's witnesses who could have had no first-hand knowledge of Spenser. The tradition that Spenser spent some time in Alton has persisted into modern times, and there is a plaque on a house in the town's main street (1 Amery Street, see Plate 3) which bears the legend, 'Here lived Edmund Spenser Poet—1590'.[58] However, it is unlikely that Spenser stayed in this particular house, which would have been a small and uncomfortable dwelling next to a marketplace in the 1590s. Aubrey's story was revived in late Victorian times and the detail, 'neer Alton', transformed to 'in Alton' and then to the address in question. The owner placed the plaque on the house when he purchased the property in c.1900 on the authority of Revd John Vaughan, whose lecture, 'Some Local Celebrities of Alton', had a considerable impact in the town after it was delivered in January 1890. It certainly helped to save the house form the threat of demolition in the mid-1930s.[59]

Nevertheless, it is possible that Spenser did visit Hampshire, as Aubrey suggests, even if he did not stay in Alton. The estates of Sir Henry Wallop (c.1531–99) are nearby at Farleigh Wallop, and it is likely that Woodford was referring to this impressive manor house when recalling his knowledge of Spenser's visit.[60] Spenser was certainly closely acquainted with Wallop, who worked, somewhat reluctantly, as under-treasurer in Ireland in the 1580s, arriving in 1579, a year before Spenser.[61] Spenser might well have visited Wallop at some point during his long visit back to England (1589–90). If so, then Woodford, who lived near Alton, being rector

8

of Shalden and of Hartley-Malduit from 1673 until his death, could well have been repeating local knowledge to Aubrey.[62]

The final detail may be the most important of all. The first printed edition of Spenser's *A View of the Present State of Ireland* was published by Sir James Ware in 1633, possibly based on an extant manuscript which had been in the possession of James Ussher, now in Trinity College Dublin, perhaps another, now lost or destroyed in the publication process, that Ussher had.[63] If Aubrey is right that Ussher knew Spenser and had an especially high regard for him, then we have some evidence that the published work might have had some form of authorial approval. Moreover, Ussher's decision to tone down certain aspects of the work because 'if hee had lived to see these times, and the good effects which the last 30 yeares peace have produced in this land, both for obedience to the lawes, as also in traffique, husbandry, civility, & learning, he would have omitted those passages which may seeme to lay either any particular aspersion upon some families, or generall upon the Nation', could seem to be a more informed judgement that many of Spenser's critics have imagined.[64] Ussher (1581–1656) would only have been 17 when Spenser died, but it is possible that they met in Dublin where Ussher grew up. Ussher's father, Arland, worked in the same office as Spenser, although it is just as likely that Ussher refers to Spenser as a 'friend' because he admired him.[65] Certainly, the reported conversation has an air of authenticity. William Davenant (1606–68) was a figure who was extremely knowledgeable and voluble about the affairs of the many writers that he knew, and he was highly critical of Spenser's poetic methods and diction in his preface to his own epic poem, *Gondibert* (1651).[66] Sir John Denham (1614/15–1669), poet and courtier, was the son of Sir John Denham (1559–1639), attorney general for Ireland, and so perhaps had some obvious connection to Ussher's circle, and was eager to defend an esteemed writer they all respected.[67]

The principal work of any biographer of Spenser will be to sort out what are the known pieces of information from false leads, which then have to be placed in context. It was perhaps Alexander Grosart, notorious for his flights of fancy, whom W. H. Welply had foremost in mind in 1941 when he asserted that 'An authentic life of Edmund Spenser has yet to be written, a life, that is, which will purge away the dross heaped up around the career of this great poet by Todd, Grosart, Church, Hales, De Selincourt and others'.[68] Reconstructing the life of Spenser has proved almost as much a process of clearing away key misconceptions and false emphases as of establishing new facts. The major work in the first half of the twentieth century was carried out by Welply himself, as well as Douglas Hamer and Alexander Judson. Indeed, important parts of Welply's research into Spenser's family in Ireland, and, to a lesser extent, his ancestors, cannot be checked because the documents were destroyed in the fire that consumed the Irish Public Record Office in Dublin on 30 June 1922 during the Irish Civil War, hours before the surrender of the Anti-Treaty IRA.[69] Even so, certain key facts and pieces of information have emerged in the last ninety years which have changed our understanding of Spenser's life: details of his marriages; documents that he wrote and others that enable us to chart his movements in Ireland; details of land purchases; some annotations in books; and details of his descendants.[70]

However, writing a biography is as much about establishing the contexts in which that life was lived as it is about startling archival discoveries.[71] Contextualizing a life involves placing any figure within the respective social, political, and cultural contexts that they inhabited, in order to determine which choices they made, what influenced them in particular, what factors determined what they did, and to understand the significance of their actions.[72] The process will inevitably be circular because, in order to achieve this, one has to be able to reconstruct the contexts from the scraps of information that one has, and these then explain the information on which they depend.[73] The point is not that the process of writing history becomes impossible, as has sometimes been assumed.[74] Rather, context always remains a contingent entity constructed by the historian/biographer and never something that can exhaust or definitively end enquiry, an issue that the work of Frank Ankersmit and Marshall Sahlins explores.[75] We can never be entirely satisfied with, or rely on, contexts, which will never have a cast-iron authority, but we cannot ignore them if we wish to write about the past.

The same might be said of the most vexed of biographical concepts, speculation. Many professional academics would like to expunge such a concept from serious inquiry. Alan Downie, in his analysis of the lives of Christopher Marlowe, has argued that

The temptation to try to extrapolate Marlowe's artistic intentions not only from the text of his plays and poems, but from the little that is known about his dramatic career, continues to lead those who write about his life down blind alleys. This tendency to make use of what I like to describe as the 'must-have' theory of biography, according to which Marlowe *must have thought* this or *must have known* that, is widespread. [Downie's emphases][76]

And, of course, unfettered speculation invariably leads to bizarre and unsustainable conclusions, especially when produced by authors not familiar with the subject, who do not understand the limitations of the surviving records. But, again, there is no absolute means of policing the boundaries between the concrete and the flimsy, especially when we are dealing with biography. Some biographies are more rigorous than others, but rigour and speculation should not be seen as polar opposites. If we refuse to speculate, to join the dots up between fragmentary pieces of information when there is a plausible context that can be used, we risk the naivety of scepticism. In doing so we distort and warp the historical record, dismissing plausible interpretations through an over-reliance on the need to verify what evidence we have:

the concept of a speculation-free biography that simply relies on the facts is almost as much a fantasy as the far-fetched and distorted work that collapses fact and fiction. There is no solution to this conundrum and a biographer will inevitably be caught between the Scylla of speculation and the Charybdis of the limited archive.[77]

The point is neatly illustrated in Natalie Zemon Davis's speculative biography of Leo Africanus/Al-Hassan al-Wazzan, the author of the first history of Africa written in Europe, who was captured by Christian pirates and became a scholar in the papal palace before returning to obscurity in Morocco. There are numerous gaps in the historical record, which, if we want to read the life at all, have to be filled by speculation. In contrast to scholars approaching more mainstream lives that have been the subject of fanciful readings, Davis defends the use of the past conditional: 'Throughout I have had to make us of the conditional—"would have," "may have," "was likely to have"—and the speculative "perhaps", "maybe." These are my invitations to the reader to follow a plausible life story from materials of the time.'[78] While Downie thinks that the life of Marlowe requires less speculation and more evidence, Davis shows that the life of al-Wazzan can only be constructed from a series of traces and contexts. Different biographies require different approaches and methods. The central issue is how we reconstruct our picture of the early modern world. For Downie, we simply do not need yet another speculative biography that delves into the murky world of Elizabethan spying and tries to work out the circumstances of Marlowe's death: the genre has become too well established, its paradigms accepted, and it is not producing anything new or insightful for readers.[79] However, for Davis, the refusal to write a biography that requires speculation is more problematic than indulging in such apparently unscholarly practices, as it would deprive us of the knowledge of the life of a key figure who played a vital role in the central area of the early modern world, the Mediterranean, the subject of one of the most important studies of the period in the last century.[80] Reconstructing the early modern world, as we see it now, with the Mediterranean dividing Europe and the Ottoman Empire and North Africa, demands that the neglect of al-Wazzan cannot continue.[81]

The same logic, I would suggest, needs to be applied to the biography of Spenser. About as much is known of his life as is known of Shakespeare's, perhaps even a little more. Yet, what has inspired boldness in Shakespeare biographers has led to timidity in would-be biographers of Spenser.[82] Spenser's life is important in similar ways to al-Wazzan's. He was the most significant literary figure of all the many English colonists, settlers, officials, and soldiers in Ireland in the sixteenth century, in itself a distinguished cast list, which includes John Bale, Richard Beacon, Lodowick Bryskett, Sir John Davies, John Derricke, Geoffrey Fenton, Barnabe Googe, Meredith Hanmer, Sir John Harington, Fynes Moryson, and Barnabe Rich.[83] Ireland inspired his work in significant ways more than any other Elizabethan writer, yet he remained aware of his English identity, a legacy he was constantly rethinking and re-evaluating.[84] Spenser was both a major colonial thinker and bureaucrat and the most important Elizabethan non-dramatic poet. He bequeathed a complex, diverse, and, above all, dominant legacy of subsequent notions of literature and national/ethnic identity in the British Isles for the whole of the seventeenth century and beyond.[85] The context, as we have constructed it, and as we understand it, demands a biography of Spenser.[86]

The fact that no recent biography of Spenser exists means that our understanding of the early modern period is distorted, as other writers who have had their lives written, have dominated our perception of English Renaissance Culture.

There have been numerous recent biographies of Shakespeare, Ralegh, Marlowe, Milton, Jonson, Donne, Aemilia Lanyer, Mary and Philip Sidney; as well as political figures such as Sir Francis Walsingham; intellectuals such as Richard Hakluyt; political power players and patrons, such as Bess of Hardwick (Elizabeth Talbot); as well as a deluge of studies of various monarchs.[87] In contrast, there has been none of Spenser since A. C. Judson's pioneering work in 1945.[88] This lacuna has effectively removed Spenser from most discussions of life writing and political intrigue and patronage, so that he is invariably seen as a remote and unattractive figure, the poet's poet, or the brutal spokesperson for a savage colonial order in Ireland.[89] He is certainly regarded as less familiar and knowable than his contemporaries, even when their life records are as sketchy as his. The irony is that Spenser writes more extensively than most about his life in his work, encouraging readers to think about his work in terms of his life.[90] We are presented with a fundamental dilemma: either take what appears in the literary works as evidence of the poet's life or abandon any quest for that life and declare that it is unwritable. This *might* be a coherent position to adopt, but it appears somewhat less tenable if we consider how much Spenser represents himself in his writings and how often he urges the reader to read the work in terms of a life behind or beyond the printed page. There is a cat-and-mouse game established between author and reader about how much can be assumed and reconstructed from the text.[91]

How, then, can such a life be recovered? The first step is to piece together the surviving bits of information, and to sweep away any false leads, and so uncover the bare bones of Spenser's life.[92] The second is to work out how the life relates to the work and what each tells us about the other. This symbiotic process involves making decisions not only about the relationship between the individual writer and his work, but also how sixteenth-century lives were perceived. Research on infant mortality rates has led to vigorous debates between historians about attitudes to the sanctity of life and whether parents, prepared for the deaths of numerous offspring, had a more robust and less sentimental attitude towards their children than we do now.[93] In short, such research forces us to wonder whether life was perceived in a different way in early modern England. It has generally been assumed that Spenser's death at the age of 45–7 must have been caused by his traumatic departure from Ireland, but we should bear in mind that life expectancy at birth was about 35, that Spenser's lifespan was not unusually short, especially compared to those of people living in large cities such as London, and that many of his contemporaries, notably Fraunce, Greene, Marlowe, Nashe, and Sidney, for one reason or another, died much younger.[94] Privacy was much harder to obtain than we take for granted now, households rarely organized to give even quite wealthy people much time alone, hence the importance for a wealthy few of the one private room in the house, the closet.[95] People often slept in the same bed to keep warm or because there was little available space in a crowded household, an arrangement that Spenser and Harvey exploit in their published letters.[96] Household space undoubtedly had an impact on how people conceived their identities and so lived their lives. The same might be said of family groupings, much more extended than many experience now in Britain, and kinship ties, an important consideration when we cannot discover as much as we would like to, as is the case with Spenser.[97] Walter J. Ong suggested long ago that the commencement of teaching in Latin functioned as a puberty rite, bonding groups of boys together as they entered the phase of early manhood.[98] It is important, therefore, to think about the impact of education on a writer such as Spenser and how his early training might have made him think differently from us, in terms of his chosen career and the life for which it prepared him.[99] The list can, of course, be extended almost indefinitely, as we need to think about attitudes to sex, marriage, death, patterns of work, old age, and so on, and whether these should force us to see the lives that we reconstruct as radically different from how people experience life now.

Seen in practical terms, the task of reconstructing a life can never be satisfactorily completed, in itself a minor problem, although the lack of dialogue between practising biographers and theorists of historical change has undoubtedly limited our understanding of this fundamental issue.[100] Spenser lived at a point in European history which some have seen as a pivotal moment, one which witnessed the birth of modernity and modern consciousness, as men and women developed a sense of their interiority and an understanding of themselves as private individuals. The description of the period 1500–1700 (or 1800) as 'early modernity' implicitly endorses this teleological narrative.[101] Reflecting on a famous, pioneering study of impersonation, *The Return of Martin Guerre*, whereby the imposter Arnaud du Tilh ('Pansette') assumed the identity of the supposedly dead Martin Guerre, occupying his house and his wife's bed until a property dispute with Martin's uncle led to his exposure and execution, Stephen Greenblatt has argued that we witness a world that is not yet quite modern: 'For what most matters in the literary texts, as in the documents that record the case of Martin Guerre, are communally secured property rights to a name and a place in an increasingly mobile social world, and these rights seem more an historical condition that enables the development of psychoanalysis than a psychic condition that psychoanalysis itself can adequately explain.'[102] The argument is subtle and nuanced, but this case of impersonation and fraud in south-west France, which took place in the early years of Spenser's life, can be read in another way. As Greenblatt argues, the case is about property rights and identities, but do we need to add a grand, overarching narrative to place the story in a larger context? Natalie Zemon Davis's narrative can, *pace* Greenblatt, be read in straightforward terms as her interim conclusions frequently demonstrate. Martin Guerre probably left the village and abandoned his wife because of tension with his father, fears of his sexuality, and a dislike of women; Pansette probably impersonated Martin because he coveted Martin's larger inheritance, having learned about his life when two men confused him with Martin; Martin's wife, Bertrande de Rols, who was undoubtedly not fooled by Arnaud, probably found life with him preferable to life with Martin, a man who clearly generated antagonism and conflict; and the equal split of the villagers during the trial might be explained by their genuine confusion, religious divisions, or opportunist allegiances.[103] The largest mystery is probably why Martin decided to return after an absence of twelve years. Davis speculates that Martin probably found out what was going on and decided that he needed to act: 'Who am I, Martin Guerre might have asked himself, if another man has lived out the life I left behind and is in the process of being declared the heir of my father, Sanxi, the husband of my wife, and the father of my son? The original Martin Guerre may have come back to repossess his identity, his persona, before it was too late.'[104]

The story is indeed unusual, but what it reveals is perhaps not, and probably has little to do with mankind on the verge of discovering a new sense of identity. The motives that the actors involved reveal are familiar enough to any historian of everyday life throughout the late Middle Ages, the sixteenth century, and beyond: sex, jealousy, village rivalry, and, above all, the desire for property in a society that held virtually all wealth in the form of land and buildings.[105] There is no need for any particularly bizarre explanation to help us understand why Arnaud pretended to be Martin, why Bertrand accepted his duplicity, or why it ended so tragically. Indeed, the fact that a second film based on the events, undoubtedly inspired by the critical and commercial success of the first, could be transposed to the American Civil War, probably tells us less about the historical licence of film-makers, than about the ease with which the story of Martin Guerre can be transported in time and place.[106]

The life records and stories of English men and women in the sixteenth and seventeenth centuries do not, of course, suggest that people living four to five hundred years ago thought and acted just like us all the time.[107] Nevertheless, *The Autobiography of Thomas Whythorne* (c.1528–96), the most extensive life-writing narrative from the late sixteenth century, reveals him to have been an anxious man on the make; eager to record his sexual adventures; a callous exploiter of women; and desperately unsure of his own social status.[108] The same might be said of the greatest diarist of the next century, Samuel Pepys (1633–1703), especially as regards his relationship with women. It is also worth noting that the more substantial records left by prominent women, inspired by the chaos of the Civil War, Lady Anne Clifford (1590–1676), Lucy Hutchinson (1620–81), Margaret Cavendish, duchess of Newcastle (1623?–73), Anne, Lady Halkett (1623–99), Ann, Lady Fanshaw (1625–80), reveal a clear understanding that society was held together by property and marriage.[109] Spenser, a poet of marriage whose life was defined by a quest for property, frequently acknowledged, as often as not actually highlighted, the forces that he felt determined and shaped his life in his work. Spenser's life and work cannot be conflated, and his poetry has a significance that travels well beyond his individual circumstances. However, we also need to acknowledge that they cannot be irrevocably prised apart and that the poet's representation of himself in his work forms part of its significance, which is why his life matters, as well as his poetry.

Origins and Childhood

ALTHOUGH Spenser's origins are not easy to determine, he provides us with three details in his writings that we have no reason to doubt: his mother was called Elizabeth; he was about 40 in 1594; and he came from London. *Amoretti* 74, a sonnet published in 1594, reads:

> Most happy letters fram'd by skilfull trade,
> with which that happy name was first desynd:
> the which three times thrise happy hath me made,
> with guifts of body, fortune and of mind.
> The first my being to me gaue by kind,
> from mothers womb deriu'd by dew descent,
> the second is my souereigne Queene most kind,
> that honour and large richesse to me lent.
> The third my loue, my liues last ornament,
> by whom my spirit out of dust was raysed:
> to speake her prayse and glory excellent,
> of all aliue most worthy to be praysed.
> Ye three Elizabeths for euer liue,
> that three such graces did vnto me giue.[1]

Given that Spenser makes a similar reference in the second edition of *The Faerie Queene* (1596), describing Elizabeth Boyle, his second wife, as a fourth Grace whose beauty has eclipsed that of Elizabeth Tudor (VI.x.28), we can be confident that the details provided are true. Here, in the sonnet, the Graces refer to 'the second lesson at morning prayer for Saturday 6 April, Acts 3, in which Peter blesses the three-fold God of glory who has upheld Christ'.[2] The two carefully constructed frames of reference and the intra-textual relationship between the works of the poet ensure that the alert reader of Spenser's work detects the verisimilitude, a technique that Spenser employed throughout his career. The poet's origins, his family, and his ruler are cited to anchor the sonnet in a reality beyond the text.

Another sonnet in the sequence provides us with evidence of his birth and age:

> They that in course of heauenly spheares are skild,
> To euery planet point his sundry yeare:
> in which her circles voyage is fulfild,
> as Mars in three score yeares doth run his spheare.
> So since the winged God his planet cleare,
> began in me to moue, one yeare is spent:
> the which doth longer vnto me appeare,
> then al those fourty which my life outwent.
> Then by that count, which louers books inuent,
> the spheare of Cupid fourty yeares containes:
> which I haue wasted in long languishment,
> that seemd the longer for my greater paines.
> But let my loues fayre Planet short her wayes
> this yeare ensuing, or else short my dayes. (sonnet 60)

The astronomical knowledge revealed in this sonnet is detailed and precise, which is why we need to take its relationship to Spenser's life seriously.[3] Spenser has chosen the penultimate day of the year to celebrate the year's passing, principally because, as Kenneth Larsen has pointed out, 'the final day, was the feast of Palm Sunday in 1594 and required a festive sonnet', which Spenser duly provides in sonnet 61, 'The glorious image of the makers beautie'.[4] The sonnet has been used to date Spenser's birth, traced to 1554, if we assume that the *Amoretti* was written or revised in 1594 and accurately records the year of his second marriage, which took place on St Barnabas Day, 11 June 1594.[5] The correspondence between the dates of that year and the relevant church festivals indicates how carefully the sonnets were written to coincide with dates in the liturgical year and the correct Bible readings assigned for each day, a recognizable feature in a period when the calendar played an especially important role in establishing identities and communities.[6] The detail that Mars has run his course in 'three score years' (i.e., 60), alludes to the return of a planet to its original position in the heavens when its cycle is complete, demonstrating that the rule of Mars is now over and the time dominated by Venus can begin, as sonnet 74 indicates.[7] Given the precision of the numbers provided in the sonnet, a significant feature of Spenser's poetry, Spenser is surely referring directly to his birthday as 23 March, the day before the end of the year in the Julian calendar.[8] If so, he is telling us that he reached the age of 40 or 41 (depending on how we read the lines, 'the which doth longer vnto me appeare, | then al those fourty which my life outwent') while courting Elizabeth, the little world of the lovers mirroring the larger world of the heavens in its intricate numerical patterning.[9] The fact that he mentions his age twice, in lines 8 and 10, making his own life and his period of lovelessness coincide, confirms a reading of this poem as one that marks his actual birth date.[10]

Elsewhere, Spenser tells us that he originated from London. At the start of section 8 of the *Prothalamion* (1596), the betrothal hymn for the two daughters of Edward Somerset, fourth earl of Worcester, Elizabeth and Katherine, an event which took place on 8 November 1596, Spenser writes:

> At length they all to mery *London* came,
> To mery London, my most kindly Nurse,
> That to me gaue this Lifes first natiue sourse:
> Though from another place I take my name,
> An house of auncient fame. (lines 127–31)[11]

The lines unequivocally state that Spenser was born in London. The movement of the bridal procession is in contrast to the stasis of the poet. The use of 'sourse' in a poem which is based on a river journey, the origin of which, as a historically literate man like Spenser would have known, was disputed by contemporary historians, clearly places heavy emphasis on that word and locates his origin in the city.[12] Spenser's work refers time and again to the importance of rivers in early modern life, suggesting that this detail, like those representing time, cannot be accidental.[13] Here, arguments about the source of the Thames stand as a pointed contrast to the certainty of his own knowledge of his birthplace.

The other important personal detail is more nuanced and provides the reader with more problematic details. The reference to 'another place' and 'An house of ancient fame' which has provided him with his name, can only really be that of the Spencers of Althorp and Wormleighton, who had risen to prominence relatively recently, through their successful sheep farming.[14] Wormleighton was the Spencers' chief residence until it was badly fire damaged by Parliamentary forces in 1645, so if Spenser had any contact with the family he would have visited this manor house and not the large seventeenth-century house at Althorp.[15] By the time that he wrote *Prothalamion* Spenser had already dedicated four poems to daughters of Sir John Spencer of Althorp. Spenser suggests, in the dedicatory letter to Lady Compton and Mountegle prefacing *Mother Hubberds Tale*, that he may be related to her in some capacity: '[I] am bound to beare to that House, from whence yee spring', a hint that he is dedicating the poem to her from an understanding of their shared ancestry.[16] Lady Compton and Monteagle was Anne Spencer, the fifth of Sir John's eight daughters. In dedicating *The Teares of the Muses*, also in *Complaints* (1591), to Lady Strange, Spenser praises the lady's virtues and generosity, and refers to some 'priuate bonds of affinitie, which it hath pleased your Ladiship to acknowledge'.[17] Lady Strange was Alice Spencer (1559–1637), countess of Derby, the youngest daughter of Sir John, who married Ferdinando Stanley, Lord Strange, fifth earl of Derby (1559?–94), in secret in 1579/80. She gained a formidable reputation as a patron of poets and writers, including Thomas Nashe, Robert Greene, John Marston, and John Harington. Milton wrote *Arcades* for her, and *A Masque at Ludlow Castle* for her stepson and son-in-law, the earl of Bridgewater. She later married, rather unhappily, Sir Thomas Egerton (1540–1617), the Lord Chancellor, who also had connections to Spenser.[18] A third daughter, Elizabeth Spencer (1557–1618), received the dedication for another poem in the same volume of *Complaints: Muiopotmos, or The Fate of the Butterflie*, which again celebrates their name. Spenser claims that he is honouring her, not 'For name or kindreds sake by you vouchsafed, beeing also regardable; for that honourable name, which yee haue by your braue deserts purchast to your self, and spred in the mouths of al men: with which I haue also presumed to grace my verses, and under your name to commend to the world this small Poëme'.[19] All three ladies are then praised in verse, in *Colin Clouts come home againe* (1595, but probably first written in 1591):

> Ne lesse praiseworthy are the sisters three,
> The honor of the noble familie,
> Of which I meanest boast myself to be,
> And most that unto them I am so nie. (lines 536–9)

These five references need to be read together and they certainly look like a concerted campaign to gain aristocratic favour from female patrons by claiming kinship, especially as Spenser moves from dedicatory letters to placing the link in actual poems, a progression that looks carefully calculated.[20] The question is whether they amount to a convincing case for assuming that Spenser was, in fact, related to the Spencers of Althorp.[21] Certainly Spenser is keen to advertise his links to the Althorps, and it is hard to imagine that he could have done so if there was no evidence of a connection, although it is worth remembering that Sir John Spencer was fabulously wealthy. When he died in 1610 his fortune was 'estimated at between £300,000, and £800,000', making him one of the richest landowners in England.[22] However, Spenser only appears to have become seriously interested in advertising his connections to the Spencers after meeting his second wife, Elizabeth Boyle, who was related to them by marriage.[23] The lines, when placed together, do assert that there is a familial link, especially the 'priuate bonds of affinitie' that Lady Strange has acknowledged, and, the climax of the campaign, the statement in verse that Spenser is the meanest member of a noble family invites acceptance or contradiction.

The key phrase may well be Spenser's reference to a 'house of auncient fame'. Many families which had risen to prominence in the sixteenth century and recently been ennobled were eager to establish their lineages, making them as ancient as possible, in order to assert their aristocratic status and rights to land. Accordingly, people worked hard to trace relatives and connections and so make themselves a crucial part of the history of Britain.[24] Few families were more eager to do this than the Spencers, who had spectacularly risen to prominence in the early sixteenth century, making them the only great family who owed their success to farming, not to trade or the wealth of the disestablished monasteries.[25] The family, in an attempt to establish their pedigree and to fit in with aristocratic norms, applied for the rights to bear the arms of the ancient Norman family, the De Spencers, in 1504, but research proved that that ancient family had died out and the application was denied.[26] Nevertheless, despite the lack of evidence, the family claimed to be descended from the Norman family in 1595, the year before Spenser flattered the family by publicly praising their historical roots.[27]

Such evidence cannot solve the issue of Spenser's family, especially as Spenser was a common name in early modern England and there were more than ten Edmund Spensers who lived during Elizabeth's reign.[28] The poet may well have seen a chance to link himself to a wealthy family and taken the opportunity to invent a lineage that served both parties, perhaps with the agreement or encouragement of the Spenser ladies. Or, he may have been exploiting a real connection. Whichever way we read the information that he has placed in the printed record, the suggestion is that Spenser was not a new supplicant to the Spencer ladies, but a poet they certainly knew of, and probably knew personally. It is therefore likely that his immediate family came from the Northamptonshire area, and not Lancashire as used to be claimed.[29] Furthermore, Spenser's second marriage to Elizabeth Boyle provided him with an obvious connection to the county. Elizabeth was from Bradden, North-amptonshire, a village only a few miles from the Althorp estate.[30]

Edmund, having met Elizabeth in Ireland, might have used his name to claim kinship with the local magnates. Given that most marriages originated from estab-lished connections, however, it is more likely that there was a connection between the two that led to their meeting in England or Ireland, suggesting that Spenser had family links to Northamptonshire, and, possibly, of course, the Spencers of Althorp.[31] One of the defendants in a later dispute involving the will of Elizabeth's father, Stephen Boyle, John Matthew, made his answer to the charges on 18 January 1597 at Canons Ashby, the home of the Drydens, before Erasmus Dryden and Edward Cope, proving that Spenser must have known the Drydens, as Aubrey suggested (even though he mistook the exact nature of the connection).[32] Both Cope and Dryden were first cousins of Spenser's second wife, Elizabeth Boyle, which further suggests that he had family in this particular area of Northamptonshire and returned here on occasions.[33] Certainly there is more to link Spenser, in terms of family connections, movements, and circumstantial evidence, with the area around the Althorp estate than any other region in England.

Spenser's father may have been a John Spenser, a 'free journeyman', connected to the Merchant Taylors' Company in 1566, as Spenser attended the school founded by the guild, one of the twelve great livery companies of the city, which was granted its charter in 1408.[34] It is likely that John moved to London, like many others, because of the growing importance of trade, which determined the expansion of the capital.[35] A John Spenser, a relative of the Spencers of Althorp, sold the manor house of Hodnell, Northants, to Thomas Wilkes, in 1550, perhaps then migrating to London where his son, Edmund, was born, although it is unlikely that these two John Spensers are the same person.[36] Furthermore, there is no real evidence to suggest that this was Spenser's father.[37] We know that his mother was called Elizabeth, but no one has managed to trace her, or discover if a John Spenser married an Elizabeth who could have produced Edmund in 1554, along with his siblings.

Evidence about Edmund's brothers and sisters is equally elusive. Spenser probably had at least one brother but no details survive of any. There was another John Spenser who was admitted to the Merchant Taylors' School on 3 August 1571, but it is unlikely that he was the poet's brother.[38] However, we do know that he had a sister, Sarah, who also went to Ireland where she married John Travers. Travers, whose pedigree and descendants can be reconstructed with some accuracy, was from a distinguished Anglo-Norman family who had settled in Ireland in the twelfth century soon after the invasion.[39] Sarah's marriage, like those of Edmund's sons, shows that the family were often eager to establish connections outside New English circles. Travers was related to many of the leading Anglo-Irish families in the English Pale surrounding Dublin: the Fitzgeralds, the Barnwalls, the Eustaces, the Cusacks, and the Nagles (into whose family Edmund's son, Sylvanus, may have married).[40] Travers also appears to have been liked by both Richard Boyle, first earl of Cork, and Geoffrey Fenton.[41] The match was certainly an advantageous one for the family, as Travers was related through marriage to a number of figures who played a part in the land deals that Edmund made, notably his purchase of the estates at Renny for his son Peregrine.[42] Travers also appears, like Spenser, to have been notably successful at acquiring property.[43] Moreover, Travers had at least three sons who survived into adulthood.[44]

We do not know much about the relationship between Edmund and his sister, but there is a tradition which states that he gave her two ploughlands, Ardenbane and Knocknagappel, from his estates at Kilcolman to ensure a substantial dowry in 1587/8 and that she lived in Kilcolman, looking after the estate at various points.[45] It is likely that the two were close in some way, as they both emigrated to Ireland, lived near each other, and appear to have strengthened the position of the family through the matches they made.

Spenser probably grew up on the east side of London. George Vertue, who claimed to have discovered the first portrait of Spenser, was interested in the poet's life, and recorded in his notebooks: 'East Smithfield, near the Tower London the birth place of Edmund Spenser the Famous Poet, and our Second Chaucer.—a View of London—printed—by Hollar. 1647.'[46] Vertue's knowledge appeared to have been corroborated by the annotation made by William Oldys (1696–1761), who wrote 'in East Smithfield' in his copy of William Winstanley's (d. 1698) *Lives of the Most Famous English Poets* (1687) next to the date of Spenser's birth. However, as A. C. Judson discovered: 'Oldys supplied Vertue with a list of pictures at Wentworth Woodhouse, Yorkshire', demonstrating a direct link between the two and providing Vertue with an obvious source for his information.[47]

East Smithfield was part of Portsoken ward, a village beyond the Tower of London on the outskirts of the city, surrounded by fields until well into the seventeenth century.[48] Only a street name now survives of what was once a distinct area, formed when thirteen knights petitioned the Saxon King Edgar (943–75) to grant them the wasteland outside the city's eastern gate (Aldgate), as is recorded in John Stow's *Survey of London*.[49] The area was given the status of a liberty, independent of the central government of London. It was notable for a number of religious foundations, which were distributed to prominent nobles after the dissolution of the monasteries, as well as the hospital of St Katherine founded by Queen Matilda in 1148. If he did grow up in East Smithfield, Spenser would have witnessed the destruction of the Cistercian Abbey of St Mary, which was largely demolished when the crown acquired the land to build the Royal Navy victualling yard in 1560, the first mass catering factory in London.[50] Many of the buildings would have been little more than ruins by that time, but actual demolition, especially to replace religious foundations and a church with practical, secular institutions, would have been unusual, a sign of a growing, changing city, as well as the transformation of spiritual life in England.[51] Spenser, so concerned with ruins throughout his work, must have been aware of the significance of the change. The area also contained a number of mass burial sites dating from the Black Death, 1347–51, which were also recorded by Stow and so were probably obvious to inhabitants.[52] Most importantly, perhaps, aliens were not permitted to unload their cargoes in the city, so St Katherine's docks were used instead.[53] As a result, the area contained a large number of Dutch and French settlers, 'where foreigners seem to have enjoyed a separate community life to a much greater extent than they did elsewhere around London'.[54] In East Smithfield foreign adult males stood at over 20 per cent of the settled population.[55]

Whatever our scepticism about the nature of Vertue's evidence, the family were probably based somewhere in that area or nearby. Spenser must have lived relatively near the site of the Merchant Taylors' School, for him to be able to walk to school easily.[56] Lancelot Andrewes, a fellow pupil, was born in nearby Tower Street, according to Thomas Fuller.[57] We do know that Spenser lived in locations in central

London—principally, Westminster—which suggests that he was most obviously at home in the heart of the capital. The significance he invests in the Thames—and other rivers—in the *Prothalamion* and elsewhere in his writing, suggests that he felt a direct link to the city's principal river.

Spenser attended the Merchant Taylors' School before he went to Cambridge in 1569. The school was founded in 1560 when the company decided that it would establish a grammar school, one of many that would transform the educational opportunities of many young Englishmen in the sixteenth century.[58] It was established in Suffolk Lane, in the parish of St Laurence Pountney, in part of the manor house, the Rose, a building which had belonged to a series of aristocratic families, the street taking its name from the De La Poles, or Suffolks.[59] There would have been about 250 boys there in the school's early years.[60] The school was generously endowed by Richard Hills, 'a leading member of the court', who contributed £500, and it opened on 24 September 1561, when its statutes were published and the new headmaster, Richard Mulcaster, began work.[61] The school register shows that Spenser's fellow students would have largely been from the middle classes, with no offspring from the aristocracy or gentry. The records reveal the sons of bakers, carpenters, chandlers, clothworkers, drapers, fishmongers, goldsmiths, grocers, hosiers, husbandmen, innkeepers, ironmongers, leathersellers, mariners, milliners, plumbers, saddlers, silk-workers, scribes, scriveners (one being Thomas Kyd's father), skinners, and weavers, as well as a few sons of members of the company who had become citizens, and others described as merchants and schoolmasters.[62] The school statutes reveal that one of the principal concerns of the founders was to ensure that there was a fair and competitive process to select scholars and to avoid corruption so that elaborate procedures were established to distribute scholarship funds properly.[63] The social composition and the ethos of the school increases the likelihood that Spenser was the son of John Spenser, or a man of similar rank and wealth.

Indeed, it is likely that Spenser's understanding of the forms of civic identity that London merchants fostered had a great significance in fashioning his own sense of himself and his place in the social hierarchy of England, not least because of the money that he was paid for publishing his work.[64] Even though this made up a relatively small part of his income, it helped him identify with the merchant class who had founded the school he attended.[65] In the *Amoretti* Spenser represents his new bride among the 'tradeful merchants' at Youghal, deliberately contrasting her status to that of the court; in the *Prothalamion* he rediscovers a pride in his home city, part of a bid to return and escape the perils of war-torn Ireland; and in both editions of *The Faerie Queene* he provides us with an epic vision of the Tudor capital, a more stable entity than the monarch who lived and ruled there.[66] Although he was most frequently thought of as a court poet from the early seventeenth century onwards, Spenser's literary identity was by no means straightforward; it consisted of a number of different elements, and was rooted in both the city and the country.[67] But a key element was undoubtedly an identity established at a school in London for the 'middling sort'.

Assuming that Spenser did grow up in East Smithfield, his route to school would have been straightforward. He would have walked along Posterngate, past the Tower of London, and up Tower Hill, where the scaffold stood 'for the execution of such Traytors and Transgressors, as are deliuered out of the Tower', into Tower Street, notable for its churches, monuments to the wealthy citizens and merchants whose goods were unloaded in the docks immediately below the street next to the river, and pubs.[68] Passing the parish church of St Andrew Hubberd, he would have entered Eastcheap, through the great London markets, and into Candlewick Street, then left into Bush Lane and, finally, left again into Suffolk Street (Figure 1).[69] Spenser would have walked from the outskirts of the city, looking out over green fields and woodland, into the centre of the fastest growing capital in Europe.

London more than doubled in size during Spenser's lifetime, having a population of roughly 70,000–80,000 in 1550 and 150,000–200,000 in 1600—the overall population of England increasing at a slower rate in the same period, from about 2.8 to 4 million—causing massive social upheaval and bringing a predictable series of urban problems, in particular crime, poverty, and disorder.[70] There was, of course, a concomitant increase in the need for goods and services, many of which were supplied by the vast immigrant population, whose restricted opportunities encouraged them to concentrate on well-defined trades: brewing, the silk industry, and the silver trade.[71] London was a city in apparently constant change, as commentators frequently noted, with deaths outnumbering births, its population increased by migration to the capital, as many as one in six of the population spending some of their lives in London.[72] There was a significant influx of foreigners, especially French and Dutch, into the capital, many of whom settled in the east central areas of London, where the Spensers lived.[73] One estimate suggests that between 1550 and 1585 40,000–50,000 foreign refugees from the Wars of Religion, mainly from the Netherlands, came into London.[74] Perhaps a third of the city's population was made up of Dutch and Walloons in the 1580s.[75] As Donald Bruce has pointed out, 'The churchyard of St. Laurence Poultney, alongside the school, was traditionally the meeting place of immigrant Flemish weavers', and in 'the next lane eastwards Huguenots worshipped at the Church of St. Martin Orgar'.[76] Down towards the river was the Steelyard of the Hanseatic League, 'the largest establishment of any single group of traders', made up of merchants from northern Germany and the Baltic, many of whom settled in the surrounding areas.[77] Spenser grew up in a cosmopolitan urban community in which exiles had an obvious presence, and it is undoubtedly no accident that his first two published works are eager to demonstrate his sophisticated knowledge of Dutch and French literature.

(a)

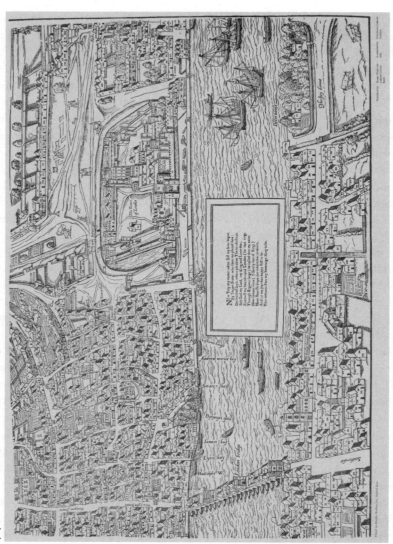

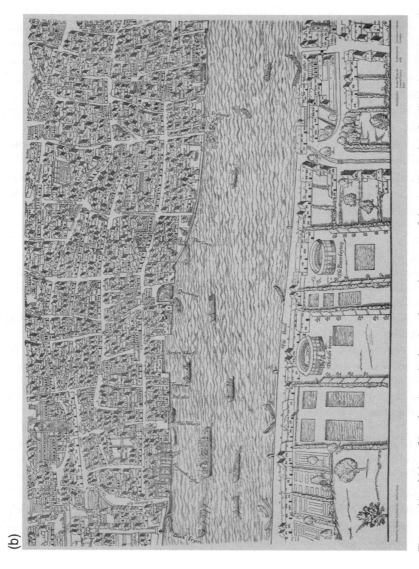

Figure 1. 'Agas' Map of London (c.1563), showing the south-east area of the city. Reproduced with kind permission of the Guildhall Library, London.

Spenser would have been taught to read by his parents or another literate adult, perhaps the parish priest, as pupils were expected to learn to read before they started their formal education.[78] Children usually started 'petty school' at the age of about 4, sometimes 5, according to William Kempe, before moving on to grammar school about two years later.[79] Petty schools were usually run by a local educated person, often a cleric, with children in a single room in groups of fewer than ten, where they were taught to read better, sing, and recite verses.[80] He would undoubtedly have learned from a hornbook, 'which consisted of a page of text attached to a wooden paddle and covered with a translucent layer of horn', for the boy to write on and so learn to copy the letters. The first words that Spenser would have written out would have been 'Our Father which art in Heaven', before he graduated to ABC primers.[81]

The statutes of the Merchant Taylors' School made it clear that the boys would be worked hard, be expected to pray frequently, and receive extensive religious instruction. They would not have been allowed to waste time, but would have been carefully monitored and looked after well, in line with other institutions recently established in London and throughout the home counties:

27. The Children shall come to the Schoole in the Mornyng at *Seaven* of the clock both Winter and Somer, and tarry there until *Eleaven*, and returne againe at *One* of the clock, and departe at *Five*. And thrice in the day, kneeling on their knees, they shall say the Prayers appointed with due tract and pawsing, as they be, or shalbe hereafter conteyned ina Table sett up in the Schoole, that is to say, in the Morning, at Noone, and at Evening.

28. In the Schoole at noe tyme of the yere, they shall use tallow candle in noe wise, but wax candles only.

29. Also lett them bring no meate, nor drinck, nor bottles, nor use in the Schoole no Breakfasts, nor drincking in the tyme of learning in no wise. If they need drinck, then lett it be provided in some other place.

30. Nor lett them use noe cock-fighting, tennis-play, nor *riding about of vectoring*, nor *disputing abroade*, which is but foolish babbling, and losse of tyme.[82]

The school's statutes show that the school day was comparable to that of others established in the same period, such as the nearby St Paul's School, set up by John Colet in 1509, whose own plan of an 'austere' school day has 'clear echoes of monastic practice'.[83] Erasmus had written the instructional manual *De Copia*, which showed readers how to take 'a sentence or an idea and make it more impressive', for Colet to use to instruct the boys in his charge, and this text would also have featured prominently in Mulcaster's curriculum.[84] Indeed, it should not surprise us that many sixteenth-century schools resemble each other, as often they were either founded by the same people or copied each other's statutes. The influence of Alexander Nowell (*c*.1516/17–1602), dean of St Paul's, who played a key role in the running of Merchant Taylors', as did his brothers, is especially prominent in the surviving documents of many schools in London, Middlesex, and Kent.[85] The long hours that the boys were expected to study, the regular interludes for prayers, the control over their consumption of food and beverages, and the surveillance of their leisure activities are all replicated elsewhere, and it is likely that the founders of Merchant Taylors' copied the statutes of St Paul's School.[86]

That school also stated that only expensive wax candles should be used in the classroom, not the cheaper tallow form, presumably because the smell of burning animal fat would have had a deleterious effect on the educational experience of both teachers and boys.[87] More significantly, each school sought to prevent needless dispute and 'foolish babling', evidently because the efforts of the boys were to be channelled into their studies, which did involve disputation and argument, but in a more productive way than they managed in the playground. Dialogue, debate, and the ability to argue eloquently were central ideals of Elizabethan education—and beyond—from the early sixteenth century onwards, as the influential dialogues of the Spanish humanist and educational reformist Juan Luis Vives (1492/3–1540), friend of Catherine of Aragon and tutor to Princess Mary, demonstrate.[88] The antiquarian John Stow (1524/5–1605), who dedicated a book to Spenser and certainly knew of the poet, if he did not know him personally, recalls how he witnessed grammar school boys, including those at Merchant Taylors', engaging in competitive public debates in Smithfield:

The arguing of Schoole boyes about the principles of Grammar, hath beene continued euen till our time: fo I my selfe in my youth haue yearely seene on the Eve of *S. Bartholomew* the Apostle, the schollers of diuers Grammar schooles repayre vnto the Churchyard of *S. Bartholomew.*, the Priorie in Smithfield, where vpon a banke boorded | about vnder a tree, some one Scholler hath stepped vp, and there hath apposed and answered, till he were by some better scholler ouercome and put downe: and then the ouercommer taking the place, did like as the first: and in the end the best apposers and answerers had rewards.[89]

The relationship between private study and public culture was made clear to London schoolboys. As Mulcaster argued in one of his treatises on education, *Positions* (1581), 'For how can *education* be *private*? It abuseth the name as it abuseth the thing.'[90]

A grammar school education would have been conducted primarily in Latin and would have taught the boys to be able to imitate a variety of forms of writing, literary, historical, rhetorical, and forensic, enabling them to produce imitations of the classics (more Latin than Greek), as well as to construct and conduct dialogues and argument.[91] Once boys had mastered basic fluency in reading and speaking Latin, taught from *Lily's Grammar*, they would have gone on to study Greek, Hebrew, and the Bible (although how much remains a matter of dispute).[92] It was especially important that the boys learned to use the style and argument of writers such as Cicero in particular, whose works were extensively prescribed in all schools, but also

Aesop, Caesar, Horace, Livy, Ovid, Sallust, Terence, and Virgil from the ancients, and often Erasmus and Buchanan from the moderns, all in selections, alongside the study of grammar and key religious texts (the New Testament, the Catechism, the Psalter, and Book of Prayer).[93] They would also have been taught from manuals of letter-writing and tropes and figures, and would have learned geography from reading Strabo, and possibly looking at some maps.[94] The school did not have a formal library until *c.*1661, but there probably was a room put aside for books, as records survive showing that books were bought. An inventory of 1599 suggests that it would have included works by Erasmus, a dictionary, commentaries on Latin works, but mainly guides to mythologies and classical texts, such as Natalis Comes' *Mythologiae*, the standard work on classical mythology in Europe, and a book that Spenser knew and used frequently.[95]

The aim of education was to train useful, learned citizens who would serve the commonwealth in a variety of productive ways: as functionaries; members of local government; magistrates (the term has a wider resonance in early modern English, meaning any civil officer charged with upholding the law, and not specifically 'a civil officer exercising local judicial power', *OED*); secretaries; ministers and clerics; Members of Parliament; teachers; record keepers; and so on. The problem was, as ever since, that there were not enough suitable positions to go around, leaving many over-educated young men with no obvious outlet for their talents or mounting frustrations, something that became an *idée fixe* for social commentators, culminating in Thomas Hobbes's famous argument that the road to revolution had been started by the over-educated who only half-understood the importance of the classics.[96] An expert knowledge of the classics could indeed be put to excellent subversive use, as the career of Christopher Marlowe indicates.[97] Spenser's career, which saw him achieve a number of prominent secretarial posts in the houses of great men and in the English civil service in Ireland, as well as produce a number of confrontational works that offended great men in authority, illustrates both aspects of the effects of such an educational system.[98]

Richard Mulcaster, the headmaster of Merchant Taylors' School, was an influential educationalist who wrote two important treatises on educational theory, and clearly ran the school in innovative and unusual ways. Although no girls went to the school, Mulcaster was one of the few educational theorists who favoured the education of young women.[99] Pupils at Merchant Taylors' 'read the same books, memorized the same kinds of rules, and wrote the same kinds of speeches' as those at other schools in the capital. However, Mulcaster placed unusual emphasis on the methods and modes of the delivery of speeches, paying close attention to sound and dramatic gestures. Mulcaster's expertise was acknowledged, as he wrote speeches for the Lord Mayor to deliver in the Lord Mayor's Show in 1568, while Spenser was in his charge and old enough to understand the significance of the commission, and he was respected for so long that he wrote speeches in English and Latin for the coronation entries into the city of both Elizabeth and James I.[100]

Drama played an important part in the Merchant Taylors' curriculum, alongside physical activity, in particular, wrestling and dancing, as Mulcaster had an integrated understanding of what a child should study, believing that the body had to be controlled and developed alongside the mind, and that both aspects of teaching had to be carried out by the same master.[101] Mulcaster was also known as a severe taskmaster, intolerant of idle pupils and, like many other Tudor schoolteachers, he argued that the rod was a key part of a teacher's equipment.[102] He was famous enough to feature, along with Spenser, in Thomas Fuller's *Worthies of England*, where he is represented as a dedicated, irascible eccentric, a law unto himself and his own rules and regulations:

His method in teaching was this. In a morning he would exactly and plainly construe and parse the lessons to his scholars; which done, he slept his hour (custom made him critical to proportion it) in his desk in the school; but woe be to the scholar that slept the while. Awaking, he heard them accurately; and Atropos might be persuaded to pity, as soon as he to pardon, where he found just fault. The prayers of cockering [indulgent] mothers prevailed with him as much as the requests of indulgent fathers, rather increasing than mitigating his severity on their offending child.[103]

His methods function outside any prescribed rules of education, and his own reflections on teaching emphasize the special bond between teacher and pupils.[104] Despite Mulcaster's desire to produce general principles for education in *Positions*, Fuller's comments are designed to show that he succeeded principally through his own efforts and force of personality, breaking rules and conventions in order to spur on his charges. This gap between the theory and the practice of education was undoubtedly common.[105] The fact that his employers, the Merchant Taylors' Company, 'finding his scholare so to profit, intended to fix Mr Mulcaster as his desk to their school, till death should remove him', is a further testimony to the myth of Mulcaster. Whether he really taught and behaved in this manner, or whether the incredible success of his pupils meant that it was then assumed that he must have taught in a demanding and odd way, is hard to determine. But, as a teacher, he clearly stood out from his peers.

Probably Mulcaster's most important contribution to Spenser's education was the emphasis he placed on learning languages, most notably Greek. Mulcaster matriculated at King's College Cambridge in 1548, the same year that John Cheke (1514–57), the great Greek scholar and the first Regius professor of Greek at the university, assumed the position of provost of the college.[106] Cheke may not have taught Mulcaster, as he was often absent from his academic institution, but his insistence on the need for Greek to play a central role in the university curriculum undoubtedly contributed towards Mulcaster's facility for classical languages.[107] It is, therefore, perhaps no accident that Spenser gravitated towards Gabriel Harvey, a protégé of Cheke's principal collaborator, Sir Thomas Smith (1513–77), when he went to Cambridge, nor that he was later described by Lodowick Bryskett as 'perfect in the Greek tongue'.[108] Indeed, Greek culture and thought were to play a major role in Spenser's career: he translated the pseudo-Platonic dialogue *Axiochus*, perhaps while still at school (at least it has been attributed to him, a sign that he was associated with Greek learning and culture); he based much of *The Faerie Queene* on Aristotle's *Nicomachean Ethics* and Xenophon's *Cyropedia*, as he outlines in the Letter to Ralegh; and he later returned to Platonism (or, at least, Neoplatonism) in the *Fowre Hymnes*. Mulcaster's influence was undoubtedly the key to Spenser's discovery of these particular intellectual coordinates.[109] It is also probable that Mulcaster ensured that Spenser had a solid grounding in Hebrew.[110]

Such an effect on a star pupil is hardly surprising, because Mulcaster, as Richard De Molen has shown, had an extraordinary influence on Elizabethan and Jacobean culture. Schoolboys were often close to their teachers, as they spent so much time together in an era when life expectancy was relatively short, and teachers often had a decisive influence on their charges. Indeed, the relationship was the subject of numerous sly references to pederasty.[111] Even so, Mulcaster appears to have had more impact than most. His students included Thomas Kyd and Thomas Lodge, as well as Spenser; seven bishops, the most significant of whom was Lancelot Andrewes, whose schooling in the arts 'of oratorical declamation in the performance of plays and [in] musical theory' left 'indelible marks' on his sermons; a number of prominent academics, including John Spenser (no relation), president of Corpus Christi College, Oxford, and John Peyrn, Regius professor of Greek at Oxford; scientists, including Thomas Heathe and Thomas Hood; Edwin Sandys, the colonial entrepreneur; Sir James Whitelock, justice of the Common Pleas and King's Bench; and Samuel Foxe, the diarist.[112] Mulcaster was also important enough to be involved in the production and recording of royal entertainments, and he produced a pamphlet detailing the verses and orations recited at Elizabeth's coronation in 1558, something that could have had an impact on Spenser's understanding of the panegyric function of public poetry in the April eclogue in the *Calender*, and much later verse.[113]

An especially interesting pupil, whose path seems to have crossed with that of Spenser at a number of points, was Gregory Downhall (*c*.1555–1614), schoolmaster, secretary, scribe, and MP for various Cornish boroughs. Downhall—his name is spelled in various ways, making absolute identification in a number of cases problematic—was one of the six scholars at the school given cloth as a result of Robert Nowell's will, alongside Spenser.[114] Downhall also studied at Pembroke College, Cambridge, matriculating in 1572 and graduating in 1575, overlapping with Spenser, who had started his studies there three years earlier.[115] Downhall must have established a good relationship with his alma mater, as he left the college £100 to establish a scholarship in his will.[116] He became a schoolmaster at the Crypt School, Gloucester, probably in 1576, where he was paid, like Spenser as secretary to Grey, the reasonably handsome sum of £20 per annum.[117] If he is the 'C. Downhalus' (the 'C' a mistranscription of 'G' by the compositor) who wrote a Latin poem prefaced to Thomas Watson's *Hekatompathia*, the first sonnet sequence in English, then he moved in the same literary circles as Spenser in the 1570s and 1580s, was interested in the same forms of poetry, and was, like most successful Mulcaster pupils, a trained linguist eager to plead the case for the translation of literature in modern European languages.[118]

Downhall later became a combative MP through the patronage of Lord Burghley, again suggesting that he had yet more connections in common with Spenser. In the tenth parliament of Elizabeth's reign (October–December 1601) he spoke with some vehemence against Sir Walter Ralegh on the subject of monopolies.[119] In the late 1590s he acted as Sir Thomas Egerton's secretary, working alongside John Donne.[120] Downhall had earlier worked for Egerton's predecessor, Sir John Puckering, who was linked, like Egerton, to the Chancery case that Spenser helped Elizabeth Boyle bring against Ferdinando Freckleton in 1597.[121] He married the daughter of Adriaan Vierendeels of Antwerp, a wealthy widow, who 'was probably one of the Flemish community gathered around the church of the Austin friars, London', which suggests that, like Spenser, he was connected to exiles from the Low Countries.[122] Furthermore, he was related to William Downhall, a lawyer who was secretary to Robert Dudley, earl of Leicester, and to the Downhall family in Geddington, north-east of Northampton, and owned property in Heathencote, Northamptonshire, about five miles from Bradden, the home of Elizabeth Boyle's parents.[123] How close Downhall was to Spenser is hard to determine, but the story of his life provides further evidence of the interrelationship of patronage systems, and the closely interlinked lives that those in the orbit of the good and great invariably led.

Mulcaster's wide network of connections was undoubtedly just as important in considering who Spenser might have known as the pupils he actually taught, and gives us some indication of how close to the centre of the intellectual nation Spenser's schooling took him. In particular, Mulcaster and the school were associated with the generation of Protestants who had been exiled under Mary in Geneva and who were directly influenced by Calvin. One of the school's principal patrons was Robert Nowell, whose brother, Alexander, was the author of the distinctly Calvinist catechism that dominated Church of England education in the late sixteenth and early seventeenth centuries.[124] The catechism was translated into English by Thomas Norton (1530/2–84), also the translator of Calvin's *Institutes* (1561). Norton acted as solicitor for the Merchant Taylors' Company, and was the son-in-law of Thomas

Cranmer (1489–1556), the archbishop of Canterbury, Marian martyr, and architect of the English Reformation.[125] Cranmer's printer, Reyner Wolfe (d. c.1574), a Dutchman who came to England via Strasbourg, left many of his papers to John Stow, who then dedicated a collection of miscellaneous medieval poems, *Certaine Worthe Manuscipt Poems of great antiquitie* (1597), 'To the worthiest Poet Maiser Ed. Spenser', presumably in the wake of the publication of the second edition of *The Faerie Queene*. This was one of only two works dedicated to Spenser in his lifetime (the other being the sonnet sequence *Chloris* by William Smith, published in 1596, which pays homage to Spenser throughout).[126]

Alexander Nowell was closely connected to Edmund Grindal (1516/20–83), briefly the archbishop of Canterbury, who was known for his particular interest in Calvin's theology, and who had corresponded with the great man during the reign of Edward VI.[127] Grindal was in charge of an inspection of the school on 16 August 1562, when Spenser was probably present.[128] Spenser vigorously defended Grindal in *The Shepheardes Calender* after the archbishop had been rusticated by the queen in June 1577 for defending the practice of training ministers through the use of 'prophesyings', a distinctly Protestant mode of education of clergy whereby the clergy gathered, often with members of the congregation, to discuss doctrine.[129] Elizabeth wanted the practice suppressed, even though most of her bishops supported its use.[130] The school was inspected by another former exile, the aged Miles Coverdale (1488–1569), biblical translator and former bishop of Exeter, also linked to the circle around Grindal.[131] Moreover, Spenser later worked for another Grindal associate, John Young (c.1532–1605), bishop of Rochester, and he refers to Thomas Drant (c.1540–78), Grindal's chaplain, twice in his correspondence with Gabriel Harvey.[132] The *Calender* was published by Hugh Singleton (d. c.1593), who was closely associated with John Foxe (1516–87) and had published some of his work. Foxe had been the room-mate of Alexander Nowell at Oxford.[133] Spenser would not have met Cranmer, who died when he was 2, and he may not have met Grindal, but he obviously did meet, however briefly, all the other figures in this list. It is hardly surprising that the progress of the English Reformation is so central to his work, as his schooldays involved such frequent contact with so many influential reformers.

In the opening chapter to his treatise on writing in English, *The First Part of the Elementarie* (1582), Mulcaster explains why it is necessary to begin the reform of teaching and learning as early as possible, a description that would appear to have wider resonance than its immediate context:

Good things finde hard footing, when theire ar to be reformed after a corruption in vse, bycause of that enormitie which is in possession, and vsurpeth on their place, which hauing strengthened it self by all circumstances, that can moue retaining, and with all difficulties, that can dissuade alteration, fighteth sore for it self, and hard against redresse, thorough the generall assistance of a preiudicate opinion in those mens heds, which might further the redresse... the nature of euills, not naturallie euill, which will neuer be better, but euill by abuse, which right vse will better, is so loth to be amended, and so long ear it harken to the voice of redresse, as at the first attempt to haue som redresse, the partie attempter is more wondered at for the wish, then esteemed of as wise. *Homer* the great Greeke poet deuiseth a monster, which he nameth Até, and giueth her for surname the Ladie of harm... This Até, saith he, is so swift of wing, so strong of bodie, so stirring to do il, as she flyes far before, & harmeth where she ligteth.[134]

Mulcaster is clearly thinking about more than simply the reform of spelling or the principles of educating children in arguing that delaying reform has drastic consequences and makes the goal of transformation harder, even impossible. If hard work is neglected at the start, then matters may well get out of hand, and resistance to reform steadily accumulate, as corruption sets in and changes the undesirable or limited into something thoroughly evil. The reference to Homer's *Iliad* indicates that Mulcaster is keen to get back to the foundation of Western literature and so establish proper models of art: the reference to Ate, daughter of Zeus and 'personification of blind folly' who was thrown out of Olympus by her father to dwell in the world of men, shows that his fear is a force of unreason and chaos that cannot be controlled if reform of language and education are ne-glected.[135] Ate must be controlled and circumscribed if education—or any reform—is to work.

This striking passage may well have had an impact on Spenser, probably looking back on it at some point during the 1590s. In one of the most frequently cited passages from his prose dialogue, *A View of the Present State of Ireland*, Spenser has Eudoxus baulk at Irenius' radical suggestions for the transformation of Ireland and affirm that surely stability is to be preferred because reform should be carried out by using the existing laws. Irenius explains that things have simply gone too far to trust in the statutes as they stand:

Iren: verye Trewe, *Eudox*; all chaunge is to be shonned, wheare the affaires stande in suche state as that they may continue in quietnes or be assured at all to abide as they are. But that in the Realme of Irelande we see muche otherwise, ffor everye daie we perceaue the trowbles growinge more vppon vs and one evill growinge on another, in soe muche as theare is no parte now sounde or ascerteined, but all haue theire eares vprighte, waytinge when the watchewordge shall Come That they shoulde all rise generallye into Rebellion, and Caste awaye the Englishe subieccion... And therefore where ye thinke, that good and sounde lawes mighte amende and reforme thinges theare amisse, ye thinke surelie amisse. ffor it is vaine to prescribe lawes where no man carethe for kepinge of them nor fearethe the daunger for breakinge of them. But all the Realme is firste to be reformed and lawes are afterwardes to be made for kepinge and Continewinge in that reformed estate/

Eudox: Howe then doe ye thinke is the reformacion thereof to begonne, yf not by Lawes and Ordinaunces/

Iren: Even by the sworde. for all those evills muste firste be Cutt awaie by a stronge hande before anie good Cane be planted, like as the Corrupte braunches and vnholsome boughes are firste to bee pruned and the foule mosse clensed and scraped awaye before the tree cane bringe forthe anye good fruite.[136]

The force of the law no longer operates in Ireland, so the power of the sword must be introduced and the island reduced to subjection before anything positive can be achieved. The logic of the paragraph has shocked generations of readers, especially in the twentieth century, who have resisted its brutal argument that the Irish have simply gone too far to be saved and so must be exterminated.[137] But the idea that dangerous times result when evil has become so entrenched that it cannot be removed or reformed would appear to look back to what Spenser learned from Mulcaster. Furthermore, it is worth noting that Ate plays an important role in Book IV of *The Faerie Queene*, appearing alongside Blandamour, Duessa, and Paridell to represent 'false friendship in contrast to the tetrad of true friendship: Cambina and Cambell, Canbacee and Triamond', provoking discord between a number of knights, including Britomart and Scudamore.[138] It is not possible to prove that such parallels stem directly from Mulcaster, but they do suggest that Spenser inhabited an intellectual world which recognized the effects of his old headmaster's thought, educational methods, and teaching and that what he was taught had a direct influence on his writing.[139]

The teacher and the pupil had other connections, which indicate how close they must have been. Mulcaster named one of his sons Sylvanus, having the child christened on 12 March 1564 in St Lawrence Poutney, the parish church of Merchant Taylors' School, just around the corner.[140] Spenser subsequently gave his own first-born son, probably born in the early 1580s, the same unusual name, a sign of homage to someone he saw as a key figure in his development.[141] Spenser's daughter was named Katherine, also the name of one of Mulcaster's five other children.[142] The poet pays further homage to his teacher in *The Shepheardes Calender*, representing Mulcaster allegorically as 'Wrenock'. In the December eclogue Colin Clout, an identity borrowed from John Skelton to represent Spenser himself, reflects on his upbringing and education:

> And for I was in thilke looser yeares,
> (Whether the Muse, so wrought me from my birth,
> Or I tomuch beleeued my shepherd peres)
> Somedele ybent to song and musicks mirth,
> A good olde shephearde, *Wrenock* was his name,
> Made me by arte more cunning in the same.

Fro thence I durst in derring doe compare
With shepheardes Swayne, what euer fedde in field:
And if that *Hobbinol* right iudgement bare,
To *Pan* his owne selfe pype I neede not yield.
For if the flocking Nympphes did folow *Pan*,
The wiser Muses after *Colin* ranne.[143]

The verses tell the story of an education, one in which the young Colin is trained to write well by Wrenock (Mulcaster), his proficiency then being recognized by Hobbinol, Gabriel Harvey, Spenser's friend and mentor at Cambridge.[144] Spenser is publicly acknowledging his two most important teachers. Reading Spenser's allegory literally is often a dangerous and fraught exercise which can reduce the poem to dull, often meaningless, source hunting, especially when searching for historical parallels.[145] However, too many critics have thrown the baby out with the bathwater and have failed to see that personal details lodged in the text have a definite relationship to the world outside it.[146] Following the narrative of the poem itself forces us to think of the poem in terms of the poet's life, even if we are resistant to the ingenious reading which argues that 'Mast. Wrenoc.' is an anagram of 'Mowncaster'. Mulcaster, who was from Carlisle, would have pronounced his name this way, and this is how it was spelled in the text of John Fletcher's play *The Knight of the Burning Pestle* (published 1613, first performed 1607/8), when the citizen's wife asks a boy, 'were you never none of Master Monkester's scholars?' (further testimony of the impact of Mulcaster's educational ideas).[147]

As well as his connections to a distinct section of the leading Edwardian reformers, Mulcaster also had well-known links to important Dutch figures and exiles in Europe and in England. In 1586, just after he had resigned from the Merchant Taylors' School following a dispute about salary, the distinguished Dutch scholar and statesman Janus Dousa (Johan van der Does) (1545–1604) dedicated a Latin ode to Alexander Nowell, in which he asked, 'from what imaginable retreat may the delightful Mulcaster be enticed?'[148] Mulcaster existed as part of a wider circle of international intellectuals, centred around an Anglo-Dutch axis, which included many figures who would prove especially important for Spenser in his early career, Mulcaster undoubtedly proving the link between Spenser and this vital international network. Mulcaster was probably also Spenser's link to Sir Philip Sidney, through his connections with Dousa, and with the key figure in many Anglo-Dutch diplomatic exchanges, Daniel Rogers (c.1538–91).

Dousa appears to have been at, or near, the centre of this circle, which was based in Leiden and had especially close connections to the philosopher and academic Justus Lipsius (1547–1606), a group that was especially important from the 1560s up to the death of Sidney in 1586. Dousa's Ode on the Queen's Birthday to Alexander

Neville (1544–1614), editor of poems on Sidney's death and closely connected to Grindal and Drant, refers to ten scholars linked to Sidney (and Rogers), who include Mulcaster; the historian William Camden (1551–1623), another important writer for Spenser; Abraham Ortelius (1527–98), the most celebrated geographer in the world; the Scottish Calvinist and university principal Andrew Melville (1545–1622); and many others.[149] Rogers, who was connected to the same figures, was the son of the Protestant martyr John Rogers (c.1500–55), another figure closely linked to the Marian exiles, and his Flemish mother, Adriana de Weyden (or Pratt), was related to the Antwerp printer Jacob van Meteren, who sponsored Coverdale's translation of the Bible in 1535.[150] Jacob's son, Emmanuel van Meteren, a scholar, historian, and merchant, was one of the leaders of the Dutch community in London while Spenser was at school. Mulcaster wrote a poem of friendship to van Meteren included in van Meteren's 'Album Amicorum'.[151]

Rogers, one of the key figures in the development of English antiquarianism, was among the best connected men in Elizabethan London.[152] He was a friend of Philip Sidney, having written the first poem addressed to him, and he was later sought out by Gabriel Harvey through the intervention of Christopher Bird, who lived in Saffron Walden, his letter of introduction reproduced in the first of Harvey's *Fowre Letters* (1592).[153] Rogers also had links with Laurence Nowell (1530–c.1570), a mapmaker and the cousin of Alexander Nowell; with Sir John Norris in Holland, another important figure later in Spenser's career in Ireland; and was especially close to George Buchanan (1506–82), a vital influence on Spenser's intellectual development.[154]

Like Rogers, Mulcaster was as familiar with French literature as he was with Dutch, an intellectual context that played a major role in Spenser's development as a poet.[155] *The First Part of the Elementarie*, Mulcaster's treatise on spelling reform and its importance to education, is heavily indebted to Joachim Du Bellay's *La Deffence et Illustration de la Langue Françoyse* (1549).[156] Mulcaster made the most of his opportunity as the principal source of Du Bellay's influence in England.[157] Given these connections, it must have been through Mulcaster's influence or direction that Spenser received his first poetic commission while still at school, a translation of several sonnets from 'Un Songe ou Vision' appended to Du Bellay's *Les Antiquitez de Rome* (1558), included as part of Jan van der Noot's important work, *A Theatre wherein be represented as wel the miseries & calamities that follow the voluptuous worldlings as also the greate ioyes and plesures which the faithfull do enioy* (1569), a significant combination of Dutch and French literature.[158] Translation was to be a major element of Spenser's writing throughout his career, and his work was always open to the influence of a wide variety of poetic traditions, which he absorbed and adapted.[159] The lengthy and elaborate text of some 130 folio pages consists of a series of sonnets and epigrams, each accompanied by an appropriate woodcut, followed by a prose 'declaration' of the author explaining his visions, 'taken out of holy scriptures, and dyvers Orators, Poetes, Philiosophers, and true histories'.[160] Spenser's translations appeared anonymously, and it was only because some of the sonnets were later published in *The Visions of Bellay* and *The Visions of Petrarch*, sections in *The Complaints* (1591), that we can be sure he was one of the translators of this complex and elusive work.

Jan van der Noot (*c.*1539–*c.*1596) is one of the most important poets in the history of the Netherlands, whose work had a crucial impact on the progress of Dutch literature.[161] His early sonnets determined the development of the lyric form; his later epic, *Olympia*, had the same effect on longer poetry.[162] Van der Noot was forced to leave Antwerp in 1567, along with many of his fellow Flemings, and accept a life of exile in London, where he lodged at Botolph Ward, between London Bridge and Billingsgate, within easy walk of the Merchant Taylors' School.[163] Here, he appears to have become an important figure. A work of medical history, *The Governanace and Preservation of Them That Fear the Plague* (1569), which was probably written by an earlier exile of the same name, was attributed to him, suggesting that the publisher, William How, wished to 'capitalize on the later writer's fame'.[164]

Van der Noot is a complex figure. *A Theatre* is certainly compatible with a Calvinist reading of European history, and it has often been assumed that van der Noot was a Calvinist author, or, at least, a committed Protestant.[165] However, like many major intellectuals in the Low Countries, including Lipsius, Ortelius, and the publisher Christopher Plantain (1520–89), he was associated with the Family of Love, a short-lived but important sect, who flourished in the 1560s, were still influential in the 1590s, but whose impact was on the wane by the early seventeenth century.[166] They were effectively extinct by 1635, their lack of a longer tradition being one reason why so little was known about them until relatively recently.[167]

The Family of Love were founded by Hendrik Niclaes (*c.*1501–*c.*1580), a visionary who claimed that he had direct access to the word of God. His idea of a religion based on the principles of unity, harmony, and universal brotherhood proved immensely popular during the extensive wars of religion that ravaged Europe in the second half of the sixteenth century, especially in those countries directly affected. Niclaes told his followers that they had to obey whatever authority was in power and never resist, marking them out from Calvinists and Catholics in the Low Countries. The Familists were Nicodemans, permitted by their church to lie about their faith, as they possessed an understanding of spiritual matters that went beyond the constraints of earthly values. As a result they were rarely persecuted, most state authorities having other more bellicose citizens to worry about, although there was considerable conflict between the Dutch Church in London and the Familists in exile.[168] Unsurprisingly, they are also hard to detect, leaving behind few explicit clues of their identity and affiliation, as well as attracting a number of fellow travellers who may have simply flirted with Niclaes's doctrines, perhaps more interested in the obvious practical advantages of Familist belief.[169] A large number of Niclaes's tracts were translated into English and published with the distinctive icon of the sect, and they had a significant impact on the development of alchemy in England, and, perhaps, radical ideas before the Civil War.[170]

Van der Noot was a client of Henry Howard, earl of Northampton (1540–1614), a leading Catholic nobleman and later secret correspondent of Mary Stuart. Howard was the son of the executed poet Henry Howard, earl of Surrey (1516/ 17–47), who had a significant influence on Spenser's development as a poet, especially in his use of blank verse and elegy.[171] Van der Noot prefaced his collection of poems, *Het Bosken*, with an ode to the Protestant William Parr, marquess of Northampton (1513–71), indicating that he was certainly prepared to hedge his religious bets in England.[172] Van der Noot later left England for Antwerp, via Paris, where he reconverted to Catholicism in 1578, having been an exile for eleven years.[173] In fact, van der Noot was known as a writer who would alter his works to suit his audience, removing anti-Catholic sections when selling to Catholic readers.[174] Moreover, he had changed his mind about religion before his formal conversion when he returned to the Rhineland in 1571, because in the German language edition of the *Theatre*, 'the original fierce attack on the Roman Catholic Church in the commentary has been reworked into a tirade against the devil'.[175]

Spenser must surely have met van der Noot, given the wealth of the connections they had in common beyond the obvious link through Mulcaster. Furthermore, van der Noot wrote a poem in praise of one of the many prominent members of the Gorges family, Blanca, providing yet another link to Spenser, as *Daphnaïda*, Spenser's elegy for Douglas Howard, was written for Arthur Gorges. That poem was dedicated to Northampton's widow, Helena, who later became the wife of Thomas Gorges, Arthur's uncle.[176] *Het Bosken* was published by Henry Bynneman (c.1542–83), an important printer and bookseller who worked with Reyner Wolfe and acquired his devices, ornaments, and initials after Wolfe's death in 1573.[177] Such evidence provides further links to the circles of writers and publishers around Spenser, as Bynneman was later to publish the Harvey–Spenser letters in 1580, all of which suggests that there may well have been connections that led Spenser from van der Noot to Harvey.[178] Furthermore, Bynneman was a client of Sir Christopher Hatton (c.1540–91), who also supported Spenser's future patron, Arthur, Lord Grey de Wilton (1536–93), and later became an undertaker on the Munster Plantation (although he never visited his estate at Knocknamona, Waterford), demonstrating that, as with the Norris brothers, there is a continuity in Spenser's friends, supporters, intellectual contacts, and patrons.[179] The evidence also shows that Elizabethan patronage networks were intertwined and overlapping and that a bright young man on the make might well find a wealth of different opportunities opening out for him.[180]

What is also clear is that *A Theatre*, which has been described as an example of the generic form 'muted apoclypse', is a work of exile, growing out of the sophisticated, cosmopolitan culture of the Dutch and French immigrants who had recently come to live in the centre of the English capital.[181] Spenser began and ended his literary career wrestling with the same phenomenon.[182] W. J. B. Pienaar's judgement that 'Spenser's association with a refugee poet, who, an eye-witness and a victim, had barely escaped the unspeakable tyranny in the Netherlands, must inevitably have made a lasting impression on the youth's mind', may be hard to prove, but it is also hard to dispute.[183]

The genesis of van der Noot's text is complex, given its existence in Dutch, French, and English, the fact that all three versions were published in England, and that it is unclear whether the French or the Dutch version was written first. These two foreign language versions of the *Theatre* were produced by John Day (1521/2–84), a publisher who had risen to prominence during the reign of Edward VI. Day was closely connected to the Geneva exiles and published many of the works of Calvin. He was immersed in the culture of the Dutch and French exiles in London, and, most importantly, his major achievement was the publication of John Foxe's *Actes and Monuments of the Christian Church*. Day was responsible for all the editions produced in his lifetime, in 1563, 1570, 1576, and 1583, providing further evidence of the influential circles to which Spenser was connected while still at school.[184]

Spenser, probably working with an assistant who knew Italian and Dutch, seems to have translated seven of Petrarch's sonnets into French by Clément Marot (1496–1544), titled 'Epigrams'; the eleven sonnets from Du Bellay's *Songe*; and the last four sonnets written by van der Noot himself (although these do not appear in the *Complaints* and so may not have been his work).[185] The long prose commentary on the poems, 'A Briefe Declaration of the Author upon his visions, taken out of holy scriptures', which emphasizes the fleeting nature of the world and the need for humankind to put greater trust in God's grace and judgement, was translated by Theodor Roest, another Dutch exile, but one who, unlike van der Noot, had probably been in London for a considerable time, given his excellent English.[186] It is likely that Mulcaster, because of his close connections to the exiled Dutch community—in particular, the pivotal figure of Emanuel van Meteren—was asked if he could find someone to help translate the sonnets from the French so that a book by a major Dutch writer had a proper impact in England.[187]

A Theatre was an expensively produced work, which made careful use of different fonts, roman typeface for the long introductory epistle dedicating the work to the queen, which praised her as an expert linguist (sig. A4ʳ), and the poems; black-letter (often called 'Old English') for the commentary, so combining production techniques that signified a juxtaposition of European and English culture, relevant to a translated work produced in exile.[188] The twenty woodcuts were produced by another Dutch exile in London in the late 1560s, Lucas de Heere of Ghent (1534–84).[189] De Heere was a friend of van der Noot, who was keen to establish a Dutch vernacular tradition. He had worked in France and was a poet as well as an artist, and had extensive experience of working with emblem books and other illustrated printed material. De Heere's involvement is an indication of the importance of the volume, and of the labour that went into producing the work.[190] The illustrations are a combination of biblical and classical themes, and were perhaps based on an illustrated vellum manuscript of Marot's *Visions de Pétrarque*.[191] This combination of text and image was pioneering in conception, and the form of *A Theatre* undoubtedly had an influence on Spenser's first major poem, *The Shepheardes Calender*, a work that, like van der Noot's, was multi-layered in style and conception, and that was eager to highlight its careful combination of different traditions and translations.[192] As has often been pointed out, Spenser's imagination was notably visual in style.[193]

Spenser's involvement in such an important project suggests that he was singled out at school as a precocious poetic talent with a great facility for languages, intellectual gifts which would have caught the attention of the headmaster, and which he was eager to parade when he began his career in earnest ten years later. It also probably indicates that he had ambitions to become a poet from a relatively early age, and used other forms of employment to ensure that he achieved his aim, rather than drifting into a vocation.[194] Certainly, he was familiar with a series of key European poets, Petrarch, Du Bellay, and Marot, and undoubtedly many others, while still a teenager. He was also a teenager extraordinarily well connected to a large number of significant European intellectuals and potential patrons, a sign of his precociousness and how hard Mulcaster was prepared to work on his behalf.

Spenser renders Du Bellay's sonnets in a straightforward and accurate manner, as befits a young apprentice translator, and as is appropriate for a volume designed to express van der Noot's apocalyptic vision of the fall of imperial cities, a form of reverse *translatio imperii*, as a message of doom crosses the Alps and the ages on its way to Britain.[195] Du Bellay's complex Petrarchan rhyme schemes are rendered without rhyme, clearly a deliberate decision that enabled the translator to produce a more accurate version as well as a coherent and plausible poem.[196] The interlaced abba abba ccd eed of Du Bellay's opening sonnet—

> C'estoit alors que le present des Dieux
> Plus doulcement s'écoule aux yeux de l'homme,
> Faisant noyer dedans l'oubly du somme
> Tout le soucy du jour laborieux,

Quand un Demon apparut à mes yeux
Dessus le bord du grand fleuve de Rome,
Qui m'appelant du nom dont je me nomme,
Me commanda regarder vers le cieux:

Puis m'escria, Voy (dit-il) et contemple
Tout ce qui est compris sous ce grand temple,
Voy comme tout n'est rien que vanité.

Lors cognoissant la mondaine inconstance,
Puis que Dieu seul au temps fait resistence,
N'espere rien qu'en la divinité.[197]

—is translated by Spenser as:

It was the time when rest the gift of Gods
Sweetely sliding into the eyes of men,
Doth drowne in the forgetfulnesse of slepe,
The carefull trauailes of the painefull day:
Then did a ghost appeare before mine eyes
On that great riuers banke that runnes by Rome,
And calling me then by my proper name,
He bade me vpwarde vnto heuen looke.
He criede to me, and loe (quod he) beholde,
What vnder this great Temple is contained,
Loe all is nought but flying vanite.
So I knowing the worlds vnstedfastnesse,
Sith onely God surmountes the force of tyme,
In God alone do stay my confidence. (sig. B8^r)

Spenser's rendition is designed to follow the lines of Du Bellay, and is conspicuously more accurate than most of the relatively free translations of European works produced by English poets in the sixteenth century, many of which are adaptations rather than translations.[198] Spenser is able to follow Du Bellay's syntax and so preserve the structure of the sonnet (he is conspicuously less successful when translating Marot's twelve-line epigrams, and producing the central *volta*, a much more difficult feat).[199] The translation divides naturally and easily into two quatrains making up the octave, and two tercets making up the sestet. Like most English translators, Spenser would have found this task extremely difficult if he had tried to match the rhyme scheme of the original, given the paucity of possible rhymes in English, an analytic language, unlike Italian, which is synthetic.

The same can be said of the subsequent sonnets. Sonnet 2, with an accompanying woodcut showing a large Doric temple 'an hundred cubits hie', about to be destroyed in an earthquake, describes the insubstantial nature of human achievements when confronted by natural forces controlled by God. The final tercet concludes:

> O worldes vainenesse. A sodein earthquake loe,
> Shaking the hill euen from the bottome deepe,
> Threwe downe this building to the lowest stone.

The third sonnet, accompanied by a woodcut showing an Egyptian obelisk covered in hieroglyphics about to be destroyed by a tempest, concludes with an equally straightforward moral.[200] The fourth sonnet represents a Roman triumphal arch with a chariot on top, and places more emphasis on the eyewitness, concluding:

> Le me see no more faire thing vnder heauen,
> Sith I haue seene so faire a thing as this,
> With sodaine falling broken all to dust.

The opening sonnets outline the contrast between the world's vanity and heavenly glory, emphasizing that we need to trust in God not man's works, and then show the destruction of the three ancient civilizations that early modern Europeans saw as the cultural and historical foundation of their modern world. The interrelated themes of ruin and destruction were to haunt Spenser's writing throughout his literary career.[201] What are probably his last verses, the fragmentary, 'imperfect' sections of canto viii that supposedly made up a part of the Legend of Constancy, the subject of the never published Book VII of *The Faerie Queene*, suggest that there may have been a deliberate return to his origins as a poet.[202]

The remaining seven Du Bellay sonnets are variations on the theme of God's constancy and man's mutability, although the message becomes more subtle and pointed in places. Sonnet 8—corresponding to sonnet 10 in Du Bellay's sequence—represents a weeping nymph beside a river who laments the fall of her city from harmony to discord. The sestet reads:

> Alas, suffisde it not that ciuile bate
> Made me the spoile and bootie of the world,
> But this new Hydra mete to be assailde
> Euen by an hundred such as Hercules,
> With seuen springing heds of monstrous crimes,
> So many Neros and Caligulaes
> Must still bring forth to rule this croked shore.

This is probably the most important poem in the sequence. Here we move away from the straightforward contrast between God and man. The Nymph, bemoaning her fate beside the Tiber, stands for ancient Republican Rome, and her lament is for the loss of its ancient liberties and the advent of the tyranny of the Julio-Claudians

Nero and Caligula. Perhaps we should read the nymph as foolish in trusting in earthly systems of government, and not being aware that even their best forms cannot last for ever.[203] It is equally likely, however, that the poem also has a republican message, transferring Du Bellay's attack on the Roman Empire and papal supremacy directly to the situation of Dutch exiles such as van der Noot, forced to flee their country, notable for its respect for the liberties of its diverse peoples, in the face of a tyrannical Spanish threat.[204] The combined force of religious and political oppression is pointedly condemned, an analysis expanded in van der Noot's prose commentary.[205] The sonnet also looks towards Spenser's future exploration of republican themes in his writings, an intellectual interest for which his early education undoubtedly prepared him, as well as his personal interest in the issue of exile.[206]

The sonnet has fifteen lines, the sestet of Du Bellay's original expanded to seven lines and the tercets run on, achieved through expanding the line 'Si cet Hydre nouveau digne de cent Hercules' into two, 'But this new Hydra mete to be assailed | Euen by an hundred such as Hercules.' As Anne Lake Prescott has pointed out, this is hardly likely to be an accident, given Spenser's sustained and sophisticated interest in numerology, and it is a deliberate change from Du Bellay.[207] The number fifteen 'represents spiritual ascent', following the fifteen steps to the Temple. It is also, as St Augustine, the central church father for Protestants, stated, a combination of the numbers seven, symbolizing Old Testament law, and eight, referring to 'the New Testament, resurrection, and the New Law'. Together 'they show the harmony of the two Testaments, and since the waters of the Flood rose fifteen cubits above the mountains "fifteen" also indicates baptism, a mystery beyond the learning of the proud'.[208] On the one hand the structure of the poem symbolizes a sense of harmony and unity; but on the other, its subject matter represents a fractured world in turmoil, a contrast that Spenser used extensively throughout his life.

The poem is extraordinarily precocious in its intellectual range and significance, indicating that Spenser was a potentially major poet from his youth, and was recognized as such by many whose opinion mattered; it also provides us with an insight into the intellectual environment in which he grew up. We would expect Mulcaster's pupils to be lively, intelligent, and learned. What Spenser's poem suggests is that they were exposed to a vast range of classical and Christian ideas, which they were able to use as building blocks for later careers. Mulcaster's influence can also be seen in different ways in other major Elizabethan and Jacobean figures, such as Lancelot Andrewes, who used what he had learned about acting and gesture from Mulcaster in his sermons, and Thomas Kyd, who also displayed a sophisticated understanding of rhetoric, theology, and stage conventions in *The Spanish Tragedy* (*c.*1589–92).[209]

One other poem deserves some comment, as it also prefigures themes in Spenser's later writing. Sonnet 10 (12 in Du Bellay), accompanied by a woodcut of aggressive fauns appearing from the left of the picture destroying the *locus amoneus* in a grove around a fountain and driving out the nymphs towards the right foreground, is, like sonnet 8, an eyewitness account of the event:

> I saw a fresh spring rise out of a rocke,
> Clere as Christall against the Sunny beames,
> The bottome yellow like the shining land,
> That golden Pactol[210] driues vpon the plaine.
> It seemed that arte and nature striued to ioyne
>
> There in one place all pleasures of the eye.
> There was to heare a noise alluring slepe
> Of many accordes more swete than Mermaids song,
> The seates and benches shone as Iuorie,
> An hundred Nymphes sate side by side about,
> When from nie hilles a naked rout of Faunes
> With hideous cry assembled on the place,
> Which with their feete vncleane the water fouled,
> Threw down the seats, and droue the Nimphs to flight.

It is hard not to read this translated poem as another reflection on tyrannous invasion and the pains of exile. Spenser refers to similar images frequently throughout his work, notably in *The Faerie Queene*, Books II, III, and VI. Book II concludes with Guyon's intemperate vandalism of Acrasia's Bower; Book III contains the brutal image of Hellenore ravished by satyrs while her watching husband, Malbecco, is transformed into an allegorical abstraction of Jealousy; while Book VI is structured around the image of the civilized settlement within the woods overrun by hostile, savage forces. Moreover, the destruction of Ireland is precipitated in 'Two Cantos of Mutabilitie' when Faunus, imitating Actaeon, insists on seeing Diana naked.[211] The description of the spring proving alluring to 'all pleasures of the eye' prefigures Spenser's exploration of the problem of the seductive delights of the visual imagination—again, encapsulated most obviously in Guyon's last significant act—and whether images lead us to truth or falsehood, one of the key debates throughout post-Reformation Europe.[212]

The sequence of poems culminates in van der Noot's somewhat undistinguished sonnets on his visions of the apocalypse, poems which are far less nuanced than those of Du Bellay immediately preceding them, and have probably helped to obscure his significance for later readers.[213] Nevertheless, although they acknowledge their emergence from a Protestant context, the poems in *A Theatre* are not obviously Calvinist in orientation. The use of visionary poetry suggests a time out of joint and the need for observers to look beneath the surface of things to discover their true significance within the universe. *A Theatre*, although clearly anti-Catholic, is not really a history of spiritual oppression and salvation as the world approaches its last days in the manner of John Bale (1495–1563) or John Foxe, authors frequently seen as the key influences on Spenser's understanding of Christian eschatology.[214] According to Anne Lake Prescott, 'It was not for an enraged or bigoted partisan that Spenser translated the sonnets by Du Bellay, but for a man of fairly tolerant temperament deeply attached to the most advanced literature of his time'.[215] Bearing in mind van der Noot's later conversion to Catholicism—in name, at least—and his association with the Family of Love, this is probably what might be expected. An awareness of this dimension to Spenser's connections seriously complicates our understanding of him as the Protestant poet he is often assumed to have been.[216] Spenser was exposed to more varied forms of religious thought than is generally realized—exactly what might have been expected, however, given his origins and schooling.

There is a further piece of evidence which suggests that Spenser's thought was notably syncretic and synthetic. In *Fowre Hymns*—published in 1596—Spenser tells us that he has combined some of the last poetry that he wrote with some of the earliest, again suggesting that he looked back to his early works for inspiration towards the end of his life. In the dedicatory epistle to the sisters, Lady Margaret Clifford (née Russell), countess of Cumberland and Anne Russell, two immensely powerful patrons of poets who played an important role in Spenser's later career, the poet explains the genesis of the four poems:

Hauing in the greener times of my youth, composed these former two Hymnes in the praise of Loue and beautie, and finding that the same too much pleased those of like age and disposition, which being too vehemently carried with that kind of affection, do rather sucke out poison to their strong passion, then hony to their honest delight, I was moued by the one of you two most excellent Ladies, to call in the same. But being unable so to doe, by reason that many copies thereof were formerly scattered abroad, I resolued at least to amend, and by way of retraction to reforme them, making in stead of those two Hymnes of earthly or naturall loue and beautie, two others of heauenly and celestiall.[217]

The dedication has an intimate tone, resembling that of Spenser's published correspondence with Harvey and dropping hints about his life beyond the page. There is a clear joke in the use of the phrase 'call in', the term for a work being seized by the authorities and subjected to post-publication censorship, as this is what had happened to *Mother Hubberds Tale* five years earlier, as the Tresham letter testifies.[218] Here, one of the ladies is jokingly equated—in print—with the team of state censors led by the archbishop of Canterbury, who oversaw all material submitted to the Stationers' Register, the body that regulated printing in London.[219] Of course, far from being designed to insult the lady in question, the reference expresses a shared joke, one that is at the poet's expense. The dedicatory letter deliberately hints at much greater knowledge between the three interlocutors, a characteristic strategy of

Spenser.[220] The style of the letter is also designed to verify the details contained within it, so we have no reason to doubt the statement that the poems were composed in the 'greener times' of Spenser's youth, or that they had circulated widely. We know that he revised his poetry because he frequently tells us that he does, and other testimonies from Lodowick Bryskett (c.1546–1609/12), Abraham Fraunce, and Gabriel Harvey provide corroborating evidence.[221] Hence, it seems most likely that the story we have here is true and that the first two hymns did circulate in manuscript and were then revised to fit into a coherent whole.[222]

When, specifically, were the poems written? The letter suggests that they were very early works, and perhaps dated from his schooldays, as juvenile poetic experiments that have survived as a late work.[223] In formal terms the hymns are conspicuously less experimental than most of Spenser's other work published in the 1590s. They are written in rhyme royal (ababbcc), a form introduced into English by Chaucer in *Troilus and Criseyde*, but common in sixteenth-century English poetry.[224] Chaucer's poem had a conspicuous influence on *The Shepheardes Calender*, whereas Spenser engaged more thoroughly with *The Canterbury Tales* in *The Faerie Queene*, especially in Book IV, which further supports an understanding of the first two hymns as early works.[225] Furthermore, we should note that the *Hymnes* were published together with an imitation of another Chaucerian work, *Daphnaïda*, which rethinks and rewrites the *Book of the Duchess*, although not necessarily successfully.[226] In terms of their content, the hymns are unusual in their easy and unchallenging reproduction of Neoplatonic ideas. The hymns represent the body as an imperfect form of the soul, itself an imitation of the true form of the divine. Such ideas were found throughout the works of Marsilio Ficino (1433–99), Baldassare Castiglione (1478–1529), and a host of related Neoplatonic works.[227] Although Platonic ideas were often challenged by Aristotelian notions of poetic composition at the end of the sixteenth century, there was a major revival of interest in Neoplatonic thought and hermetic philosophy, which had a particular impact on literature.[228] Harvey was especially interested in new developments in scientific and alchemical thinking.[229] Even so, the hymns would appear to be at odds with the much more sophisticated work that Spenser published in the 1590s, as well as witty and sardonic adaptations of Neoplatonic ideas of love in poems such as John Donne's 'The Extasie'.[230] Such evidence suggests that the first two hymns should be read as early works as Spenser states, reproduced for a new audience and for a specific purpose.[231]

'An Hymne in Honour of Love' argues that beautiful mortal forms are imitations of heavenly glories and will send the alert observer into a state of rapture:

> For sure of all, that in this mortall frame
> Contained is, nought more diuine doth seeme,
> Or that resembleth more th'immortall flame

> Of heauenly light, then Beauties glorious beame.
> What wonder then, if with such rage extreme
> Fraile men, whose eyes seek heauenly things to see,
> At sight thereof so much enrauisht bee?[232]

'An Hymne in Honour of Beautie' laments that 'many a gentle mynd | Dwels in deformed tabernacle'.[233] However, such discrepancies are ironed out in the spiritual sphere of love:

> For Loue is a celestiall harmonie,
> Of likely harts composed of stares concent,
> Which ioyne together in sweete sympathie,
> To worke ech others ioy and true content,
> Which they haue harbourd since their first descent
> Out of their heauenly bowres, where they did see
> And know ech other here belou'd to bee. (lines 197–203)

It is hard to believe that Spenser, an ironic, witty, and confrontational poet, well versed in telling nuances and subtle references, took such work seriously towards the end of his life, and the dedicatory letter can be read as an embarrassed apology for his refigured juvenile efforts. Certainly, there is little else in his mature work that indicates an unqualified enthusiasm for such effusions.

There is, however, a readily identifiable link between the young Spenser and Neoplatonism.[234] The Family of Love were notable for their particular interest in Neoplatonic thought, and they were instrumental in reviving many of its forms in the 1560s and 1570s, 'stimulated by the spectacle of religious discord' in the Low Countries.[235] Niclaes was inspired by Thomas à Kempis's mystical treatise *The Imitation of Christ*, with its attacks on the fruitless labours of scholastic theology, and desire to escape from the constraints of the world in order to penetrate the mysteries of heaven.[236] As already stated, his writings and ideas had a significant impact on intellectuals and poets throughout the Low Countries, in France, and in England from the 1560s to the 1580s.[237] It is at least arguable that one major English writer had intellectual links to the sect throughout his life.[238] Spenser, via Mulcaster, van der Noot, Rogers, and the Anglo-Dutch writers exiled in London, was well acquainted with the Family of Love in the late 1560s. He undoubtedly knew some members personally as well as van der Noot, and read their writings, even if it is hard to uncover such links directly, given the close secrecy with which Familists guarded their identities, and their belief in the doctrine of Nicodemism, 'hypocrisy in the cause of self-protection'.[239] Familists held that God's decree and Nature were indistinguishable, that human nature was perfectable, and that the Holy Ghost and the devil were real and could be located 'inside the self'.[240] These are all ideas that are compatible with Neoplatonism, especially as derived from a work such as Pico Della

Mirandolla's *On the Dignity of Man*, a work that Spenser undoubtedly read and knew well.[241] If the first two hymns are early works, written while Spenser was still at school, they indicate just how seriously he was interested in developing a poetic career, and how he was eager to experiment with new ideas. What seems odd and rather anachronistic for a mature poet writing in the mid-1590s was undoubtedly bold and innovative for a young man in the late 1560s, whether or not Spenser really adhered to the beliefs of the Family of Love. Of course, Spenser's late Neoplatonic poetry may bear no significant relation to any particular belief system, but it undoubtedly provides an insight into the intellectual coordinates of his youth.

Spenser Goes to College

IN THE sixteenth century various funds from foundations and charities were available for bright young scholars to help their school and university education.[1] Spenser was the recipient of a number of bequests at the Merchant Taylors' School, all from the fund of the wealthy and well-connected London lawyer Robert Nowell, who left significant sums of money to the school when he died on 6 February 1569. The bequests were carried out by Robert's brother, Alexander, dean of St Paul's.

In total, there are records of thirty-one scholars from London schools receiving a gown and a shilling each at Nowell's behest. Along with 254 poor men, the boys were paid to take part in the funeral procession, six of the scholars coming from the Merchant Taylors' School: Edmund Spenser, Richard Bitese, George Hunte, Thomas Curley, Henry Ive, and Gregory Downhall, along with pupils at St Paul's, Westminster, and St Anthony's, normal practice at funerals of the good and the great.[2] The fact that Spenser heads this list suggests that he may well have been the senior boy in the school.[3] On 28 April 1569 Spenser was again recorded in Nowell's account books: 'To Edmond Spensore of the m'chante tayler scholl, at his gowinge to penbrocke hall in chambridge—10s.'[4]

Such evidence has been used to argue that Spenser must have been an impoverished scholar in need of assistance, and to support the assumption that his father was the journeyman tailor John Spenser.[5] However, neither conclusion necessarily follows. Spenser is unlikely to have come from a rich family, and was, like most students, undoubtedly able to spend what money came his way without difficulty. Even so, he received only one small payment while at school, which does not suggest that his family was especially impoverished. The largest payment he received from Robert Nowell's fund was when he matriculated at Cambridge, which was a substantial sum. Undergraduates incurred a number of costs throughout their academic career, and the money from the Nowell bequest was evidently designed to offset these. In addition to accommodation, subsistence, books, and other living costs and expenses, a graduating Bachelor of Arts would be expected to pay over 15s. to receive his degree.[6] At Cambridge Spenser then received further payments of 6s. (along with Richard Laugher, another student at Pembroke) on 7 November 1570; of 2s. 6d. on 24 April 1571, making a total of 19s. 6d., along with the gown. These payments added up to a significant amount of money, certainly helpful for a young student, when the average wages of a skilled worker was about 11d. to 12d. per day, and an official university position, such as bedell, who was employed to enforce university discipline, paid just under £3 per annum.[7] Therefore, we cannot safely conclude that Spenser was in particular need or that he must have come from a poverty-stricken background. Similar sums are recorded as having been distributed to scholars, as well as the poor, throughout the record book, along with gifts of cloth.

Cambridge was, as it is today, much smaller than the only other university city in England, Oxford. William Camden, very much an Oxford man, pays it a rather backhanded compliment in *Britannia* (1586, 1610). Having praised the town's 'faire streetes orderly raunged', and the colleges as 'sacred mansions of the *Muses*', Camden comments:

Neither is there wanting any thing here, that a man may require in a most flourishing *Vniversitie*, were it not that the ayre is somewhat unhealthfull arising as it doth out of a fenny ground hard by. And yet peradventure, they that first founded an University in that place, allowed of *Platoes* iudgement. For he being of a verie excellent & strong constitution of bodie chose out the *Academia*, an unhollsome place of *Attica*, for to studie in, that so the superfluous ranknesse of bodie which might overlaie the minde, might bee kept under by the distemperature of the place.[8]

The Fens were notoriously unhealthy and it is perhaps little wonder that Cambridge suffered particularly from outbreaks of the plague, especially as it was also acknow-ledged that the city provided perfect breeding grounds for disease because the streets where the poor lived were so close together.[9] Spenser was absent a number of times from the college between 1571 and 1574, and received *aegrotat* payments (a certificate of illness excusing the student's absence). In total, he was absent for eleven and a half weeks in 1570; seven weeks in 1571; and six weeks in 1573, a considerable amount of time to be away from the university. Each time college records show that he received an allowance of 10d. per week.[10] Such payments were usually granted for sick leave, although commentators have assumed that there were probably other explanations.[11] It is quite likely that there is a hidden story to these payments, and there is evidence to suggest that '*aegrotat* allowances during Lent were an established custom', enjoyed by fellows and students alike, enabling them to pursue their studies or more lucrative employment elsewhere.[12] In addition, it is also an odd coincidence that the Watts Greek Scholars, who started to attend university in 1571, and of whom there were four at Pembroke, were also apparently ill a great deal, and were paid at the same rate, 10*d.* per week.[13] Moreover, the payments were all made while John Young, later to be bishop of Rochester (and Spenser's employer), was master of the college.[14] But, given the city's contemporary reputation for the ill health of its inhabitants, it is also possible that Spenser either suffered from debilitating bouts of disease or stayed away through an understandable fear of infection.

Cambridge during Spenser's time there was an exciting but troubled place, characterized by almost constant religious disputes. University life was dominated by the prolonged effects of the Elizabethan Vestarian controversy, as the archbishop of Canterbury, Matthew Parker (1504–75), struggled to impose uniformity on preachers who were required to wear the cope and surplice.[15] Many saw this as a denial of Reformation principles and refused to conform, led by Thomas Cartwright (1535–1603), sometime fellow of Trinity who was appointed Lady Margaret chair of divinity in 1570. Cartwright, who effectively became leader of the Elizabethan Presbyterians in the 1570s, opposed the hierarchical structure of the established church and argued that archbishops and bishops should be replaced by bishops and deacons who would possess spiritual rather than institutional authority.[16] He favoured a return to the principles of the primitive church and argued that the Elizabethan church should be stripped of its subsequent trappings and additions, claiming that very little of what was accepted practice—vestments, the altar, images, Latin Prayer Book—were *adiaphora*, or 'things indifferent', as his opponents alleged. While they asserted that these conventions had no effect on the proper nature of religious devotion, Cartwright and his followers argued that were diabolical practices introduced by the corruption of the Pope.[17] When Cartwright was deprived of his chair for preaching against established religion, as outlawed by no. 45 of the 1570 university statutes, 164 protesters opposed the enforcement of the statutes, equating the defence of Cartwright with an opposition to changes in university structure and forms of authority.[18] The Vestarian dispute soon led to protests about the forms of church service.[19] There were also objections to the use of Latin prayers (1568–9), and a host of disputes about the election of fellows who were deemed unsympathetic to the large groundswell of sympathy for 'Puritanism'.[20] In the face of such onslaught, Parker, backed by Lord Burghley, held firm, imposed the statutes, and issued a warrant for Cartwright's arrest, causing him to flee to Germany.[21]

In such a feverish climate Catholics and suspected Catholics were afforded the most hostile treatment. Dr John Caius (1510–73), master of the College that after 1557 bore his name, had his room ransacked on the orders of Edwin Sandys (1519?–88), bishop of London, whose instructions were then passed on to the vice-chancellor, Dr Andrew Byng (d. 1599). Byng wrote to Burghley on 14 December 1572, explaining what had happened:

I am further to geve your honor advertisement of a greate oversight of D. Caius, who hath so long kept superstitious monuments in his college, that the evil fame thereof caused my lord of London to write very earnestly to me to see them abolished. I could hardly have been persuaded that suche thinges had been by him reservid. But causing his owne company to make serche in that college I received an inventary of muche popishe trumpery, as vestments, albes, tunicles, stoles, manicles, corporas clothes, with the pix and sindon, and canopie, besides holy water stoppes, with sprinkles, pax, sensars, superltaries, tables of idolles, masse bookes, portuises, and grailles, with other such stuffe as might have furnished divers massers at one instant. It was thought good by the whole consent of the heades of houses, to burne the bookes and such other things as served most for idolatrous abuses, and to cause the rest to be defaced; which was accomplished yesterday with the willing hartes, as appeared, of the whole company of that house.[22]

Caius retired to his London house and died soon afterwards (29 July 1573).[23] The fact that this raid took place soon after news of the St Bartholomew's Day Massacre (23 August) reached England, when as many as 50,000 Huguenots may have been killed in France, probably explains its ferocity.[24] A year before the Massacre, on 30 August 1571, Elizabeth had completed a progress to Audley End, near Saffron Walden, accompanied by the French ambassador, Paul de Foix, sent to try and secure a match between Elizabeth and Henri, duc d'Anjou, the brother of the king of France, Charles IX. Sir Thomas Smith played a key part in the events, which culminated in a dinner at Trinity College, accompanied by a series of public disputations.[25] Such pleasant formal events must have seemed ancient history two years later. The representation of ecclesiastical practices, differences, and disputes in *The Shepheardes Calender*, Spenser's first major work, developed out of an understanding of the links between the local and the continent-wide impact of religious conflict, and the sudden twist and turns of political life. Spenser's religious beliefs were undoubtedly complicated and, probably, somewhat unorthodox and syncretic, made up of a variety of traditions and strains of belief (although this was hardly unusual).[26] Nevertheless, just as the diverse range of native and Continental forms of religion that he was exposed to at school left their mark on his work and thought, so did the equally complex mixture of factionalism, innovative theological and ecclesiological practice, and reaction to major European events, which he witnessed while a student, help to determine the course of his intellectual career.

Spenser would have been 15 when he began university, a relatively young age to start, but not exceptional. Many other precocious scholars started at the same age, including Sir Philip Sidney, born the same year as Spenser, who matriculated at Christ Church, Oxford, also in the same year.[27] Pembroke Hall was an obvious choice for Spenser, as it had well-established links to the Merchant Taylors' School and to the circle of intellectuals attached to it. Edmund Grindal had been a student, then fellow, at the College in the 1530s, before taking over as president in 1549, later becoming absentee master in 1559 for three years.[28] The College had a particular reputation for its commitment to the reformed faith, and many of its students and fellows were associated with the radical ideas that developed during the reign of Edward VI.[29] The first Marian martyr, John Rogers, father of Daniel Rogers, had graduated from Pembroke in 1526, and Nicholas Ridley (c.1502–55), one of the most prominent churchmen of his generation, whose heroic death is a key event in Foxe's *Actes and Monuments*, was student, fellow, and then its master between 1540 and 1553.[30]

Pembroke was not one of Cambridge's wealthiest colleges, and, with fewer than a hundred members, was among the smaller ones (Plate 4).[31] Caius, in his history of the university written four years later, stated that Pembroke College had 87 members: the master, 24 fellows, 6 minor fellows, 7 inferior ministers (i.e., servants), 36 pensioners (paying students), and 13 sizars, out of a university total of 1,813 students, fellows, ministers, and masters.[32] It was made up of a pleasantly situated series of buildings, most of which dated from the fourteenth century when it had been founded, off Trumpington Street in the heart of Cambridge. The college acquired further lands and buildings in the fifteenth and early sixteenth centuries, but it would have appeared as a pre-Reformation college to any new student coming to study during Elizabeth's reign, a striking reminder of England's medieval past. It also had its own orchard, and was designed, like all Cambridge colleges, to exist as a self-sufficient educational institution within the town.[33] Pembroke's social composition appears to have been largely from the middle ranks of society, many of the students supported by newly established scholarships, such as the Watts scholarship, established by Thomas Watts (1523/4–77), archdeacon of Middlesex, which provided funds for seven Greek scholarships at Pembroke. Two of the first recipients were Spenser's contemporaries at Merchant Taylors', Lancelot Andrews and Thomas Dove.[34] Indeed, it was a natural home for a schoolboy from the Merchant Taylors' School, having a similar social and intellectual composition, as well as housing a number of Spenser's former schoolmates.

Spenser entered Pembroke as a sizar in 1569, studying at Cambridge for the next seven years, until he graduated as an MA on 26 June 1576.[35] The term derives from 'size', an allowance of board and lodgings that was granted in return for duties that were otherwise performed by college servants (waiting at tables, running errands, working in the college kitchens), and is only used for students at Cambridge or Trinity College Dublin (founded 1592). Sizars were allowed to eat what was left over after the college fellows had dined, making them, like Oswald in *King Lear*, eaters of 'broken meats'.[36] Sizars were assigned to a fellow, shared the same room, and slept beneath the high bed of the fellow in a truckle or trundle bed, often with other students.[37] There would have been a series of tiny studies attached to the main communal bedroom, with desks and a few bookshelves. The atmosphere would undoubtedly have been rather claustrophobic, especially if the fellow and the students did not get along well, although there was also the opportunity for lifelong friendship between young men—fellows were invariably only just older than their students—of similar interests.

Compared to other students, sizars were needy, relatively poor scholars eager to find ways of supplementing their funds, a reality that may well explain many of Spenser's absences from college, as it would be surprising if he had not attempted to find employment when opportunities arose, despite the funds he received from various sources.[38] Thomas Middleton, in his clever response to Thomas Nashe's *Pierce Penilesse His Supplication to the Divell* (1592), provides a short description of the humiliatingly servile life of a sizar, designed to characterize what Middleton imagined was Nashe's experience at St John's College in the 1580s, a decade after Spenser:

Pierce Penilesse, exceeding poor scholar, that hath made clean shoes in both universities, and been a pitiful batteler all thy lifetime, full often heard with this lamentable cry at the butt'ry hatch: 'Ho, Lancelot! A cue of bread and a cue of beer,' never passing beyond the confines of a farthing nor once munching commons, but only upon gaudy-days [holidays].[39]

The description exaggerates and distorts the reality of a sizar's life but it does contain more than a grain of truth. Universities, as Hugh Kearney has demonstrated, were 'instruments for social mobility', and, even if there were still rigid divisions between the gentlemen and the rest, the two universities were transforming the social fabric of key elements of the nation as more students from moderate social backgrounds graduated.[40] The register which classifies the 13,569 students who attended the University of Oxford between 1567 and 1622 lists 6,635 as 'sons of plebeians', or just under half, and 3,615 as 'sons of gentlemen', just over a quarter.[41] There were numerous and clear signs of differing social status inscribed in the structures and practices of the universities, partly in order to offset what was perceived at the time as a serious social change.

The major relationship that Spenser established at Cambridge, at least as it was made available to a wider reading public through published works, was with Gabriel Harvey. It is quite possible that Spenser served as Harvey's sizar after Harvey was elected to a fellowship at Pembroke on 3 November 1570. Harvey had achieved this position through the offices of his patron, Sir Thomas Smith, having failed to achieve a fellowship at Christ's, where he graduated.[42] Not only did Harvey and Smith have previous connections—almost inevitably, through Daniel Rogers—but in their published letters (1580) Spenser asks Harvey what he thinks of a new Anacreontic epigram with the insouciant comment, which seems designed for a third party, 'Seeme they comparable to those two, which I translated you *ex tempore* in bed, the last time we lay together in Westminster?'[43] The lines seem to hint at a sexual relationship between the two men, even as it is denied, but they also suggest that their nocturnal intimacy had a long history.[44] The fact that Spenser provides this particular detail might suggest that he is placing himself in the role of supplicant—albeit cheekily—a reminder that, although the two men were almost exactly the same age (Harvey was probably born in 1552/3), Spenser had been, and perhaps still was, the apprentice.

Spenser would have studied the arts curriculum at Cambridge, designed to prepare an educated elite for service in government, national and local, the rapidly expanding civil service, as well as the church. The medieval arts degree had been planned to lead star students towards the study of theology, once they had completed their Bachelor's and Master's degrees, a path still followed by many who entered the church. However, universities throughout Europe were changing to meet the demands of a new social order that opened up a wider series of roles for graduates.[45] The complete course in the arts—which included what we now define as sciences—started with the trivium, the study of grammar, logic, and rhetoric; proceeded to the quadrivium, which covered arithmetic, geometry, astronomy, and music; and was completed by study of the three philosophies, moral, natural, and metaphysics.[46] There was also some study of mathematics, which, given its role within the arts curriculum, might explain where Spenser's much discussed interest in numerology originated, as well as geography, another subject that Spenser clearly valued.[47] By the later sixteenth century this basic structure was still in place—much less rigidly at Cambridge than at Oxford—but with important variations. Elizabeth produced a series of statutes for the university in 1570, which set out what should be taught by university lecturers, the forms of examinations, as well as the government and organization of the university. The university lecturer in rhetoric was required to teach Cicero, Quintilian, and Hermogenes; the lecturer in Greek, Homer, Demosthenes, Isocrates, and Euripides; and the lecturer in philosophy, Aristotle, Pliny, and Plato, every author to be taught in the original language. All examinations were oral disputations, and students were expected to argue with their teachers at least twice a year, as well as declaim in class a set number of times, the results decided by faculty present.[48] At Cambridge, the statutes of 1570 stipulated that candidates for the BA had to dispute twice in public, and twice in college during their four years of study; MA candidates had to respond to a teacher three times, dispute twice in hall, and deliver one oration.[49] The student would act as respondent and the examiner as opponent, debating a series of formal questions on the set texts. The student would be tested on his ability to argue logically as he either accepted or denied the propositions. The aim was to 'ensure that he neither contradicts himself, nor by implication denies the proposition that he is meant to be upholding, nor lets himself be reduced to confusion'. If the student maintained his position for a specified period of time, he passed.[50] Disputation was the key feature of the early modern university curriculum, and explains why so many writers—Spenser, Bacon, Milton—were able to write as they did.[51] Students were required to attend all lectures, morning and evening prayers, and there were punitive fines for non-attendance, and for other transgressions such as wearing prohibited dress (sleeves and ruffs of the wrong material or with excessively ornate cuts and styles), and leaving college without permission.[52] Life was as hard and regimented at university as it had been at school, students often working from four or five o'clock in the morning until ten at night, the day a mixture of lectures, private study, and devotions.[53]

The Cambridge degree demanded that the student concentrate on rhetoric, dialectic, and philosophy in the four years for the BA, with the statutes requiring the study of rhetoric in the first year, logic in the second and third, and philosophy in the final year. The MA required the study of philosophy, optics, astronomy, and Greek.[54] Under the inspiration of Quintilian and Erasmus, great emphasis was placed on the student's ability to argue a case, and undergraduates had to participate in a number of public debates, making university a natural progression from grammar or public school, especially for a student who had been taught by a teacher like Richard Mulcaster, who trained his charges in precisely this way.[55] There was also a new emphasis on the study of modern languages alongside Latin and Greek, as the universities realized that they had to train graduates to suit the needs of society outside college.[56] By the time Spenser completed his studies he would have read and attended lectures on Aristotle, Plato, Pliny (philosophy); Strabo, Ptolemy, Pomponius Mela (mathematics); Cicero, Quintilian (dialectic/rhetoric); Virgil, Horace (grammar); Euclid (geometry); Boethius (music); and many other classical authorities.[57] He would not have had access to the university library until he became an MA student—although it was in a notoriously poor state in the early 1570s. The Pembroke College library, however, was well stocked with classical and theological works.[58]

English and Continental books were often absent from institutional libraries, which concentrated largely on works in Latin and Greek.[59] Extracurricular reading was often encouraged, notably by tutors such as Harvey, who pursued his own course of reading and recommended numerous modern authors to his students.[60] Harvey noted in his *Letter-Book* that students were especially keen on recent works of controversial political history:

You can not stepp into a scholars studye but (ten to on) you shall litely finde open other Bodin de Republica or Le Royes Exposition upon Aristotles Politiques or sum other like Frenche or Italian Politique Discourses.

And I warrant you sum good fellowes amongst us begin nowe to be prettily well acquayntid with a certayne parlous booke called, as I remember me, Il Principe di Niccolo Macchiavelli, and I can peradventure name you an odd crewe or tooe that ar as cuninge in his Discorsi sopra la prima Deca di Livio, in his Historia Fiorentina, and in his Dialogues della Arte della Guerra tooe.[61]

Harvey had, undoubtedly, encouraged students to read these books himself, as they reflect his taste in modern political theory, and he certainly owned copies of Bodin, Guicciardini, and Machiavelli, which he probably lent to students.[62] Student wills also reveal that these were the sort of books they owned, along with Castiglione's *Book of the Courtier*, Camden's *Britannia*, and Buchanan's *History of Scotland*.[63] Given Spenser's relationship to Harvey it is hard to believe that Spenser was not one of the students about whom he was writing, and that Spenser did not also read these works along with his tutor, as they all had a significant influence on his later writings. It is surely no accident that *A View of the Present State of Ireland* refers to Aristotle and Machiavelli's *Discourses*, and is informed by the reading of Bodin and Guicciardini.[64] That Spenser would have been a voracious reader given his education at the Merchant Taylors' School and Cambridge is hardly surprising, but he would also have been exposed to Harvey's particular theories of careful, targeted reading, which may well have helped form his particularly scrupulous habits.[65] He would have begun learning to read Italian while he was at Cambridge, if he had not already acquired a working knowledge before.[66] Harvey's library contained a number of language manuals many of which he annotated, and it is likely that Spenser was able to use these throughout his long association with Harvey.[67] Spenser clearly knew French before he left school, and may well have used his knowledge of that language to help him learn Italian, translating texts as a means of acquiring the language. Often students were advised to learn through the use of an intermediary language, and John Florio suggested that a new language could be absorbed in three months, a claim that frustrated Harvey.[68]

Perhaps the most significant change to student experience in the early modern university was in the teaching of rhetoric and logic. Students were still taught complicated scholastic logic, as they had been throughout the Middle Ages, and heavy emphasis was placed on Aristotle's 'rigorous demonstrative logic'.[69] Certainly, the scholastic nature of much of the curriculum, especially the sciences (metaphysics, physics, and mathematics), was evident well into the seventeenth century.[70] Nevertheless, traditional methods and approaches were challenged, circumvented, and modified by some tutors, led by Harvey, and later by his brother, Richard, another fellow at Pembroke, who turned to the work of the controversial modern logician Peter Ramus (1515–72).[71] Ramus' logical method owed much to 'the topical logic of Agricola', which, in effect, 'abandoned a tool capable of dealing with scientific problems for a humanist dialectic of little use beyond merely literary pursuits'.[72] Furthermore, Ramus had perished in the Massacre of St Bartholomew's Day, and so was associated with Protestantism, an important factor in a college of a reformed character such as Pembroke.[73] Ramus' *Logic* was translated in 1574, just before Spenser took his MA, and a collection of other works followed in the years immediately afterwards, including Ramus' works on grammar (1585), geometry (1590), and arithmetic (1592).[74] By the early 1570s Ramus' works were already well known and owned by a wide circle of readers, his status rising even higher after he was made a Protestant martyr.[75] He was to have a significant influence on virtually every aspect of English culture in the next half-century, from science to law, from history to the science of memory, and, above all, in enabling Calvinist divines to develop a system of logic that explained how they saw God's plans for the world and the choices that he presented to mankind.[76]

The impact of Ramist reforms on the teaching of logic and rhetoric has probably been exaggerated, and it is clear that many humanists throughout Europe thought that Ramus' methods were not sophisticated enough to deal with complex epistemological matters. Nevertheless, Ramus did have a major influence on a general trend towards teaching rhetoric, alongside logic and a concentration on the art of persuasion, as central to the study of the humanities.[77] Ramus is sometimes caricatured as if he 'reduced rhetoric to style and delivery', whereas in fact he insisted that 'rhetoric and dialect be studied together'.[78] What Ramus achieved was to simplify logic so that it was based on a method of practical reasoning that could deal with any situation and could be transported easily enough from one situation to another. Rhetoric and logic were no longer seen as divergent fields, but ways of thinking and arguing that complemented each other—two similar methods of argument that could be combined and deployed as the user saw fit. M. Roll's translation of Ramus' *Logic*, which argues for the need to have such works in the vernacular and is printed in black-letter (English) type, opens with a characteristically lucid statement outlining divisions for the reader to follow:

Dialecticke otherwise called Logicke, is an arte which teachethe to dispute well.

It is diuidyd into two partes: Inuention, and iudgement or disposition.

Inuention is the first parte of Dialecticke, which teachethe to inuente arguments.

An argumente is that which is naturally bente to proue or disproue any thing, suche as be single reasons separately and by them selues considered.

An argumnte is eyther artificial, or without arte.

Artificiall is that, which of it self declare and is eyther first, or hathe the beginning from the first.

The first is that which hathe the beginning of it self: is eyther simple or compared.

The Symple is that, which symplie and absolutelie is considered: and is eyther agreeable or disagreeable.

Agreeable is that, wich agreethe with the thing that it prouethe: and is agreeable absolutely, or after a certaine fashion.

Absolutely, as the cause and the effecte.[79]

Ramist logic involved carefully dividing up different definitions and opposites, often leading to the construction of charts that show how any one concept can be split into two, two into four, and so on, with the hope that the reader will be able to see the apparently complex but actually straightforward relationship between a host of ideas and forms.[80] Alexander Richardson's *The Logician's School-Master* (1629), a posthumously published work based on his lectures and circulating among Cambridge students in the 1590s, gives a clear sense of the separation of logic and rhetoric derived from Ramus' distinctions, which was now widespread at the university:

[B]ecause things that are reported, are not so easily receuied, as those which are seene by our eye of *Logicke*...it was requisite that there should...be...a fine sugaring of them with Rhetoricke, for the most easie receuing of them...

Now because speech is an inartificiall argument, and so not easily receuied, therefore Rhetoricke serues to deliuer the matter more soberly and grauely; and Poetry yet makes it more fine, where all things must be done by measure and sweet sounds.[81]

Rhetoric serves to make the conclusions of logic palatable as well as accessible to a wider audience, in the same way that poetry serves philosophy in Sidney's *Apology*, an obvious influence on Richardson's text.[82] Such arguments post-date Spenser's time at Cambridge, but they do indicate what was starting to happen when he was there, inaugurated in large part by Harvey.

Ramist logic as an actual method was probably less revolutionary than either its proponents or its detractors claimed, certainly for the majority of non-specialist students taught at Cambridge, where it took root more sturdily than at Oxford.[83] Often the forms of argument described and recommended were the same as those of the scholastic logic they were supposedly replacing, although stripped of the sophisticated levels of content and forms of proof.[84] The basic building block of logical analysis was still the syllogism, derived from Aristotle's statement, 'discourse in which, certain things being posited, something else necessarily follows', but which by the Middle Ages had become more obviously formulaic, involving three categorical propositions, with the third (the conclusion) following from the first two (the premises).[85] The basic form of syllogistic logic was represented as 'All men are mortal; Socrates is a man; therefore, Socrates is mortal.' Although Ramists attacked such logical forms as tautologies, and a simple exercise in exploiting the definitions of words, they, nevertheless, invariably relied on syllogistic reasoning.[86] Dudley Fenner's explicitly Ramist *The Artes of Logike and Rhethorike*, for example, an attempt to outline a usable manual for Protestants, establishes a series of Ramist charts to outline the options available for logical investigation. He classifies the syllogism with a series of relevant examples:

The Affirmatiue generall:

All the iustified shalbe saued:
Al the iustified shal raigne with Christ. Therefore
Some that raigne with Christ, shalbe saued.

The Negative with the Proposition generall:

No hypocritical caller vpon God shalbe saued.
All hypocritical callers vpon God, say, Lorde, Lorde. Therefore
Some that say, Lord, Lord, shal not be saued.

Affirmatiue speciall:

Some who fel in the wilderness heard the word.
Al who fell in the wilderness, tempted God. Therefore
Some that heard the word, tempted God. Heb. 6. 3.[87]

The Calvinist nature of Fenner's examples, demonstrating to readers that outward signs of God's grace will not necessarily place them among the elect, is clear enough, as he forges a link between forward thinking in method and doctrine.[88]

The example of Fenner's influential text illustrates the importance of the Ramist revolution, especially in Cambridge (Fenner had studied at Peterhouse and was a protégé of Thomas Cartwright).[89] Ramism was most significant in the ways in which it transformed what mattered in education, the relationship between logic and rhetoric and the teaching curriculum, and its universalizing nature and style were strongly connected to puritanism—a significant reason why it flourished in Cambridge rather more than Oxford.[90] Logic now became a series of topics, which could be employed by the student in order to make a case. Logic itself might have been denuded of its significance in scholastic terms, but arguments could now be made in all sorts of ways using a variety of examples instead of being restricted to formalized academic debate. The syllogism was no longer seen in absolute terms, but as a tool for debating, an aid to dialectic designed to persuade an audience.[91] Accordingly, intellectual debate was highlighted as a major component of the strategies that could be employed by the orator to persuade an audience, in line with humanist preoccupations.[92] Arguments were not merely supplemented by a host of examples from other areas of the curriculum, most frequently literary, placing emphasis on the formal nature of the dispute; rather, the proper use of material became the *raison d'être* of debate, the art of persuasion assuming greater importance than the formal properties of logic itself. Ramus' *Logike* justifies its existence through the use of examples from Virgil, not through using them merely as supplements to the main argument. Ramism also had a significantly 'anti-hierarchical' thrust, which added to its appeal in the stratified world of the early modern university.[93]

Late sixteenth-century Cambridge became a university with 'an aggressively liberal approach to the curriculum', with teaching based on the wide reading of students in all areas of the arts held together by a textbooks of dialectic, most frequently by Rudolf Agricola as well as Ramus.[94] Such a system naturally precipitated the advance of charismatic star teachers, the most ambitious and significant of which in the early 1570s was Harvey, who rose rapidly from his fellowship at Pembroke, becoming university lecturer in Greek in October 1573 and university praelector of rhetoric in April 1574.[95] Harvey deliberately established himself as the leading exponent of Ramism in a time of Ramist revolution.[96] In *Ciceronianus* (1576), Harvey's Easter-term oration of 1575, printed by Henry Bynneman, publisher of *A Theatre for Voluptuous Worldlings* and, in the future, the Harvey–Spenser *Letters,* Harvey wittily but rather pompously argues his case in the form of an overarching syllogism: Ramus was a Ciceronian; Harvey is the true follower of Ramus; therefore, Harvey is the true heir of Cicero.[97] *Rhetor,* the text of the opening two orations that Harvey delivered as praelector (1574), also published by Bynemann (1577), represents the speaker as the modern manifestation of the great orator of the Roman Republic, persuading the audience that eloquence in argument is what matters most.[98] Harvey's influence on Spenser was principally through his command of rhetoric.[99]

Either Spenser gravitated towards Harvey because of his reputation, which developed rapidly after 1570, or they were introduced through mutual acquaintances and networks. A number of connections might have facilitated their academic relationship and friendship. Harvey was linked to Daniel Rogers and Sir Philip Sidney; he knew members of the circle around Lord Burghley, as Spenser did, through his tutor at Christ's College, William Lewin, a client of Burghley's, and tutor to his daughter, Lady Anne Cecil; and he cultivated Dutch connections, in particular Jan van der Does. Spenser, through Mulcaster, was also linked to the same circles.[100] It is also possible that Harvey, who had a keen eye for what was happening at the university, was able to put Spenser in touch with some of the other star students at Cambridge at the time: Abraham Fraunce, Robert Greene, Christopher Marlowe, and Thomas Nashe, perhaps through a shared interest in Lucian, the subject of a book-wager between Harvey and Spenser.[101] Whatever the background to their encounter, it is clear that Harvey shaped Spenser's educational experience at Cambridge and afterwards, and that his work would have developed in a different way—perhaps been rather less logical and less assured—if they had not met.

Harvey looked backwards and forwards in his hopes for a glittering academic career that would take him beyond the confines of the university and enable him to make his mark in the world of politics and at court. Harvey was heavily indebted to Sir Thomas Smith when he first met Spenser. Smith guided Harvey's career in the later 1560s, and Harvey looked up to him as an intellectual mentor, a role Harvey wanted to play for Spenser.[102] Harvey corresponded extensively with Smith in the early 1570s, and he is cited in the Harvey–Spenser *Letters* as an authority on orthography and prosody.[103] Smith dedicated his Latin work on the pronunciation of Greek, *De Recta et Emendata Linguae Graecae Pronuntiatione* (1568), to Harvey.[104]

Harvey records in a letter to John Young, then master of Pembroke, that he visited Smith at his house, Hill Hall, Theydon Mount, Essex, a further twenty-five miles away (a day's travel).[105] Smith also had a large town house in Saffron Walden, almost next door to one of the properties owned by the Harvey family.[106]

Smith was an immensely influential figure in England from the 1550s until his death in 1577. He had emerged as one of the key thinkers about the nature of English government under the radical Protestant regime of Edward VI (1547–53), like his younger contemporaries William Cecil (1520–98) and Sir Henry Sidney (1529–86).[107] The careers of all three were intertwined throughout Edward's regime and the first half of Elizabeth's reign.[108] Smith served as secretary of state during the dominant years of his patron, Edward Seymour, duke of Somerset (c.1500–52), and worked closely with Thomas Cranmer, who had—mainly indirectly—a number of connections to Spenser.[109] After Somerset's execution Smith disappeared into the political wilderness until rehabilitated by Elizabeth, for whom he served as ambassador to France in the 1560s, and then as secretary of state (1572–7). During his time as ambassador in France Smith wrote one of the key works of Elizabethan political theory, *De Republica Anglorum*, not published until 1581, four years after his death.[110] The work classifies the various forms of government, institutions, political offices, and the people who constitute the state of England, explaining how the various hierarchies in England work, the network of strands of government, and defines England as a monarchy ruled by the king or queen in parliament, which is 'The most high and absolute power of the realm of Englande'.[111] Spenser read this work in manuscript, undoubtedly at Harvey's bidding, and a commitment to the ideal of the sovereign only able to rule with the consent of parliament is certainly evident in his later writings, indicating that Smith's ideas stayed with him throughout his life.[112] The gloss to the word 'couth' in *The Shepheardes Calender* links Smith and Harvey and informs the reader that the latter lent the writer the former's book:

couthe) commeth of the verbe Conne, that is, to know or to haue skill. As well interpreteth the same worthy Sir Tho. Smith in his book of gouernment: whereof I haue a perfect copie in writing, lent me by his kinsman, and my verye singular good freend, M. Gabriel Haruey: as also of some other of his most graue and excellent writings.[113]

Of course, the notes to the *Calender* are attributed to 'E. K.', but given Spenser's very public relationship with Harvey, this certainly suggests that Spenser wrote many, if not all, of them, probably with the help of others.[114] The note is a deliberate advertisement of the intimate intellectual circle established around Smith, echoes of whose work have also been discovered in Spenser's *View*.[115]

Since Smith was one of the leading humanists of his generation, Harvey looked to emulate his career and establish himself as Smith's intellectual heir. Harvey was responsible for a series of Latin elegies composed after Smith's funeral (August 1577), which were published by Bynemann in January 1578, *Smithus; vel Lachrymae Musarum*. These works later influenced both the style and form of Spenser's *Teares of the Muses*: just as Harvey proclaimed that it was up to him as the author to seize the intellectual agenda in order to shape the future, so did Spenser, even more presumptuously and cheekily, in assuming the mantle of the deceased earl of Leicester.[116] Smith acquired a manor house, Hill Hall, through his second wife, Philippa Wilford, after their marriage in 1554, and he started to transform it into a major intellectual centre which represented humanist ideals (Plate 5). He assembled a carefully catalogued library, one of the largest in Elizabethan England, with works on civil law, theology, mathematics, history, philosophy, medicine, literature, including not only classical texts but many contemporary works of topical interest, such as Castiglione's *Book of the Courtier* and Machiavelli's works.[117] Like many of his wealthy neighbours, Smith was a keen student of architecture, and he redesigned Hill Hall as a classical palace, complete with impressive façades and allegorical frescos, in imitation of the French chateaux he had visited and the Italian houses he had read about.[118] Most significant of all, Smith may have used Hill Hall as an alternative university, encouraging scholars to meet and discuss important issues and problems in order to advise politicians, the logical culmination of his attempts to marry intellectual and practical endeavour, in line with the Aristotelian humanist ideal of combining the active and contemplative lives.[119]

One particular debate took place in late 1570 or early 1571, as Harvey recorded in his copy of Livy, using a reading of the historian of the Roman Republic to think about Elizabethan military strategy:

Thomas Smith junior and Sir Humphrey Gilbert [debated] for Marcellus, Thomas Smith senior and Doctor Walter Haddon for Fabius Maximus, before an audience at Hill Hall consisting at that very time of myself, John Wood, and several others of gentle birth. At length the son and Sir Humphrey yielded to the distinguished Secretary: perhaps Marcellus yielded to Fabius. Both of them worthy men, and judicious. Marcellus the more powerful; Fabius the more cunning. Neither was the latter unprepared [weak], nor the former imprudent: each as indispensable as the other in his place. There are times when I would rather be Marcellus, times when Fabius.[120]

As Harvey's account demonstrates, the debate was designed to decide whether the ruthlessness of Marcellus or the more cautious strategy of Fabius was better suited for the Elizabethan conquest of Ireland, Harvey indicating that he, and presumably many others, felt that the conclusion was finely balanced.[121] The debate, in front of an audience of 'several others of gentle birth', sounds very much like the sort of formal public exercises that students had to undergo in order to complete their degrees, further suggesting that Harvey and Smith saw events at Hill Hall playing a crucial role in bridging the gap between the university and public life. Spenser, of course, may have been present at this debate, given what we know of his close relationship with Harvey at this time, and he may have been working for Harvey in his role as a sizar. But even if he was not present, it is likely that such debates had an impact on his political awareness and interest in Ireland, especially given that Gilbert (1537–83) was the half-brother of Sir Walter Ralegh, a figure with whom Spenser was keen to be associated twenty years later.[122]

Gilbert had already made a name for himself as a ruthless exponent of martial law when military governor of Munster in late 1569, suppressing the Fitzgerald uprising and forcing the chief Irish lords who submitted to him to approach him through a lane of severed heads on poles, according to Thomas Churchyard (1523?–1604), a loyal soldier under Gilbert in the 1560s and 1570s.[123] Gilbert was also a keen advocate of the sort of educational reforms favoured by Smith, and wrote a short tract at about this time, *The Erection of an Achademy in London for Educacion of her Maiestes Wardes, and others the youth of nobility and gentlemen*, with another tract arguing the case for academies that bridged the gap between tertiary education and public life, especially in military matters.[124]

The immediate purpose of the debate at Hill Hall was to prepare Sir Thomas Smith's illegitimate son, also called Thomas, for his military expedition to Ireland to colonize the Ards Peninsula, the first stage of Smith's attempt to use the help of intellectuals to transform Ireland from the most rebellious and lawless of the queen's dominions to an ordered and settled society.[125] Smith published a pamphlet, *A letter sent by I.B. Gentleman vnto his very frende Maystet [sic] R.C. Esquire vvherin is conteined a large discourse of the peopling & inhabiting the cuntrie called the Ardes, and other adiacent in the north of Ireland, and taken in hand by Sir Thomas Smith one of the Queenes Maiesties priuie Counsel, and Thomas Smith Esquire, his sonne* (1572), clearly written in the wake of the Hill Hall debates. The pamphlet also published by Bynemann, provides yet another link between Harvey, Spenser, and Smith; written as a dialogue, it probably had some influence on *A View*.[126] It has the same practical but seriously informed approach to colonization, giving details of how much land each settler will need, what they should grow, how they need to protect themselves, and how they can rely on the native Irish churls to work for them, which will, in fact, lead to a problem: 'but I feare the sweetnesse which the owners shall find in the Irish Churle, giuing excessiuely, wil hinder the Countrie muche in the peopling of it with the Englishe Nation, making men negligent to prouide Englishe famours'.[127] Sadly and unsurprisingly, this optimistic assessment proved unfounded and the expedition ended in disaster, with the death of Smith Jr, his boiled carcass fed to the dogs by his Irish killers, according to Churchyard.[128]

Even before this debate Spenser had probably already entered this exciting but dangerous world between the academy and political/military action, the ideal of so many Elizabethan figures.[129] A bill dated 18 October 1569 confirms 'Edmonde

Spencer' as the bearer of letters from the English ambassador in France, Sir Henry
Norris (*c.*1525–1601), currently stationed in Tours, to the queen: 'Payde upon a bill
signed by Mr Secretarye dated at Wyndsor xviij. Octobris 1569 to Edmonde Spencer
that broughte lres to the Quenes Ma^{tis} from Sir Henrye Norrys knighte he Ma^{tis}
Embassador in Fraunce beinge then at Towars in the sayde Realme, for his charges
the some of vj^{li}.xiij^s.iiij^d. [i.e., £6. 13s. 4*d.*] over and besydes ix^{li}. [i.e., £9] prested
to hym by Sir Henrye Norrys.'[130] These are substantial amounts, in total over £15,
well beyond the sums that any scholarship could have provided a student. Could this
Edmund Spenser have been the poet? It is certainly plausible, even likely that he was,
even though he would have been very young, 15 or 16 at the time. Other students
had leave of absence from university to undertake important tasks, most notably
Christopher Marlowe; others, such as Ralegh, took leave from school to serve with
the Huguenots in France in the same month (October 1569) before matriculating at
university.[131] More relevant still is the connection with the Norris family, whose
interests seem to have been bound up with Spenser's from his schooldays. Spenser
had been singled out as an especially good French translator, which would suggest
that he had the right skills for the task of delivering letters in France itself,
and he was later to serve the sons of Henry Norris as the transcriber and bearer
of letters in Ireland.[132] Furthermore, Henry Norris, who was in regular contact
with the queen, Leicester, and Burghley, employed Daniel Rogers at this time as
a secretary, tutor to his children, and a spy to deal with Catholic conspiracies,
providing a further, perhaps key, link to Spenser.[133] The circumstantial evidence
that this Edmund Spenser was the poet is therefore strong. It would be a strange
coincidence if the Norrises and Rogers were connected to two letter-bearing
Edmund Spensers.

During Spenser's time at Pembroke John Young replaced John Whitgift
(1530/1–1604) as the master of the college. Whitgift, later archbishop of Canterbury,
enjoyed only a brief tenure as master, serving from April to June 1567, leaving to
become master of the much wealthier college, Trinity.[134] Young had the support
of Grindal, and was closely linked to Thomas Watts, archdeacon of Middlesex and
one of the chief benefactors of Pembroke, who had strong links to both Grindal
and the Merchant Taylors' School, which he had inspected when Spenser was there
as a pupil.[135] Young was appointed as master on 12 July 1567, nearly two years
before Spenser matriculated, and remained in the post until he was consecrated as
bishop of Rochester on 1 April 1578.[136] He served as vice-chancellor of the university
from 1568 to 1569.[137]

Young employed Spenser as his secretary when he became bishop of Rochester or
almost immediately afterwards.[138] He may not have known Spenser especially well
when he was an undergraduate, but Young clearly did know Harvey.[139] Spenser
probably achieved his position through Harvey's offices, although Young also knew

the divines connected to the Merchant Taylors' School: Grindal, Watts, and Nowell, who could have been a further source of information. Young accepted a variety of benefices in London, Cambridgeshire, and East Anglia throughout his career, undoubtedly in part to support him in his important roles, and he was frequently absent from Cambridge. This was not unusual at the time and seems to have produced no adverse comment. It is possible, of course, that Spenser's absences from Pembroke were looked upon sympathetically by Young, or may even have been connected to the master's own absences, given that Spenser worked for him later, but there is no evidence to support either conjecture. Spenser must surely have been grateful for the opportunity to work for Young, but, as his comments on Young in *The Shepheardes Calender* indicate, he may have had an ambivalent sense of Young as a bishop.[140]

Ill feeling and disputes between students and fellows were commonplace then as they are now. Harvey's *Letter-Book* opens with a series of letters relating to his problems in being granted his MA at Pembroke. He had already been denied a fellowship at Christ's, and had obtained one at Pembroke only after the intervention of Smith, so clearly he did not get on easily with all of his peer group. A long letter to Young of some eight thousand words, dated 21 March 1573, sought the support of the absent master against the other fellows, who were blocking the award of the degree.[141] Harvey's principal antagonists were Richard Osborn and Thomas Neville (*c.*1548–1615), younger brother of Alexander Neville, and a future master of Magdalene and Trinity colleges and vice-chancellor of the university in 1588.[142]

Harvey explains that there are three main charges levelled against him. First, that he was not 'familiar like a fellow, and that I did disdain everi mans cumpani', to which Harvey replied, rather defensively, that he 'was aferd les over mutch familiariti had mard al'. Nevertheless, he then asserted that, in fact, he really was a social animal: 'this I am suer, I never auoided cumpani: I have bene merri in cumpani: I have bene ful hardly drawn out of cumpani'.[143] The second accusation is that he has a low opinion of others and 'culd hardly find in mi hart to commend of ani man; and that I have misliked those which bi commun consent and agreement of al have bene veri wel thout of for there lerning'. Harvey repeats his recollection of their subsequent exchange:

I thout it mi duti to speak wel of those that deserved wel; and that he miht sundry times have harde me commend mani a on, but that it pleasd him now to wrangle with me. Whereuppon he tould me roundly, that that was mi fault indeed, and that I was evermore in mi extremities, ether in commending to mutch without reason, or dispraising to mutch without cause. To the whitch I gave him no other anser but this, that he ouht to give me and others as gud leave to use our iudgments in that behalf as I and others had givn him. Stil he harped upon that string, that I culd not afford ani gud wurd. And I made him aunser, that this were great arrogance and extreme folli.[144]

Neville's final accusation is that Harvey made 'smal and liht account of mi fellou-ship'. Harvey replied that he was stung by the accusation, that he had accepted the position to make money, retorting that he 'culd have made better shift without' one.[145]

The argument is a fascinating one and tells us a great deal about life in an Elizabethan university, as well as the protagonists. It is likely that Neville, as Virginia Stern surmises, while an upstanding pillar of Cambridge in later life, was 'less than exemplary in his youth'.[146] For Harvey, perhaps, the charges run deeper, and the accusation that he was a selfish, vain, and self-regarding man who was incapable of working with others is the basis of Thomas Nashe's attack on him two decades later.[147] But Harvey was clearly capable of making friends when he chose to, as his relationships with figures as diverse as Smith, Spenser, and John Wolfe indicate.[148] Harvey also appears to have been on good terms with such serious scholars as Dr John Still (c.1544–1608), master of Trinity College, who had been Harvey's tutor at Christ's College and who replaced Thomas Cartwright as Lady Margaret professor of divinity in 1572, and Thomas Preston (1537–98), playwright, civil lawyer, and later master of Trinity Hall.[149] In their published *Letters* Spenser asks Harvey to keep the poems contained in his first letter 'close to your selfe, or your verie entire friendes, Maister *Preston*, Masiter *Still*', which indicates either that the four discussed poetry together, perhaps with others as well, or that Spenser knew that Harvey was especially close to these two learned men. Harvey also mentions Still in the fourth letter in the series, arguing that a truly learned man able to assess the significance of the recent earthquake should be 'an excellent Philosopher, a reasonable good Historian, a learned Diuine, a wise discrete man, and generally, such a one as our Doctor *Still*, and Doctor *Byng* are in Cambridge'.[150] There was certainly a group of senior Cambridge academics who took Harvey seriously, discussed matters with him, and listened to his advice, unless we assume, rather implausibly, that Harvey and Spenser fabricated or misunder-stood the relationship.

The root of Harvey's quarrel with Neville may really lie in terms of what each antagonist considered the proper commitment to the university and college life. Neville accuses Harvey of not valuing his position at Pembroke; of not treating other fellows with proper respect; and of trying to use his fellowship to make himself rich, an accusation that Nashe made later when he represented the Harvey brothers as talentless and pedantic men-on-the-make.[151] Despite Harvey's outraged protestations of innocence, there was obviously much substance in the charges, enabling us to reconstruct how Harvey conceived of himself and how he operated at Cambridge.

Nashe, delving back into the history of Harvey's conduct at Cambridge in *Have With Yov to Saffron-Walden* (1596), makes a similar accusation:

so *Trinitie Hall* hath borne with him more than that, he being (as one that was Fellow of the same House of his standing informed mee) neuer able to pay his Commons [college bills], but from time to time borne out in almes amongst the rest of the Fellowes: how euer he tells some of his friends he hath an out-brothership, or beadsmans stipend of ten shillings a yeare there still coming to him, and a Library worth 200. pound.[152]

We do not know the identity of Nashe's anonymous informant, but the passage indicates that Harvey's selfish behaviour was still resented a decade later (Harvey qualified as Doctor of Laws at Trinity Hall in 1586 and probably left for London soon after this date, even though he remained a fellow of the college until 1592).[153] Nashe's story has Harvey acquiring books for his library and tactlessly boasting of its value, while neglecting to work for the common good of his fellow scholars.

Nashe's anecdote, when read alongside Harvey's representation of Neville's accusations, further suggests that Harvey placed more value in himself than his institution. The emphasis on his personal library also indicates that he was known for possessing a valuable and influential collection of books, a fact that he was keen to advertise as part of his status as a scholar and intellectual, confirming his particular value to others as an expert reader.[154] Harvey's negative reputation in Cambridge helps to confirm a suspicion that he was really more committed to the circle around Sir Thomas Smith than to his college. Smith's public relationship with John Cheke, in which the two sought to represent the interests of Cambridge to the court, appears to have been one that Harvey hoped to emulate in his relationship with Spenser, notably through the audacious act of publishing their correspondence in 1580.[155] By then Harvey had already positioned himself as the intellectual heir of Smith, asking Smith's advice about the value of civil law and then studying for a Doctor of Laws around the time of Smith's death, perhaps a symbolic act of intellectual patrilineage.[156]

Harvey clearly had plans for Spenser and we can see his influence in Spenser's early works. Harvey's involvement in *The Shepheardes Calender* and the publication of the *Letters* in 1580 indicates that their relationship was extremely close until Spenser went to Ireland in the November of that year. Therefore, Spenser must have been party to Harvey's educational methods, ideals, and goals. In the published letter dated 7 April 1580, the longest of the three sent by Harvey, which contains the discourse of the earthquake, Harvey concludes with some news from Cambridge. This section provides further evidence of Harvey's intellectual interests and approach to his work and life, as well as his familiar relationship with Spenser and student life at Cambridge.

Harvey starts by outlining the reading habits of undergraduates, who, he claims, do not read Cicero and Demosthenes as much as they used to, concentrating instead on the historians Livy and Sallust but neglecting Lucian, and treating the Greek philosophers with indifference and contempt: '*Aristotle* muche named, but little read: *Xenophon* and *Plato*, reckned amongst Discoursers, and conceited Superficiall fellowes.'[157] These reading patterns do suggest serious activity, and the list of Italian authors in the following paragraph—Machiavelli, Castiglione, Petrarch, Boccaccio, Guazzo, and Aretino—indicates that Harvey's desire to spread the study of modern languages is working well.[158] But, Harvey asks Spenser, 'The *French* and *Italian* when so highlie regarded of Schollers? The *Latine* and *Greeke*, when so lightlie?'[159] The implication is that, while many good things are happening at Cambridge, the fundamental problem is the neglect of the central humanist project of Cheke and Smith, who had sought to reform Greek orthography so that the language and its literature could be taught more effectively and widely.[160] Spenser is, of course, included within Harvey's circle of familiars, one who will understand how standards have slipped, which confirms that Spenser must have acquired a significant knowledge of Greek from Mulcaster.

Harvey caricatures the efforts of current undergraduates:

Much verball and sophisticall iangling: little subtile and effectuall disputing: noble and royall Eloquence, the best and persuasiblest Eloquence: no such Orators againe, as redhedded Angelles: An exceeding great difference, betweene the countenances, and portes of those, that are braue and gallaunt, and of those, that are basely, or meanly apparelled: between the learned, and vnlearned, *Tully*, and *Tom Tooly*, in effect none at all.[161]

In effect, Harvey is lamenting the failure of the university to listen to him and to organize teaching according to his ideas. Instead, students have the appearance of learning without the substance, the tricks of the trade without the knowledge that those tools were supposed to provide. Students look like they are arguing but they are not because they dismiss real debate as that of 'conceited Superficiall fellowes'. The attacks on Xenophon and Plato read suspiciously like those on Harvey by Thomas Neville, indicating that in Harvey's mind he has become the heir of true Greek scholarship, the intellectual son of Sir Thomas Smith, a sly reference surely designed for Spenser to enjoy. The students, meanwhile, have declined under the foolish charge of the Cambridge authorities, becoming 'redhedded Angelles' rather than skilled orators. The reference is to the story of St Augustine of Canterbury, the missionary sent to convert the Anglo-Saxons by Pope Gregory, who, on being told that the golden-haired English boys in the Roman marketplace were Angles, quipped that they should be called Angels not Angles.[162] Harvey uses the story to indicate that Cambridge has turned the clock back and transformed its once brilliant students, like Spenser, into ignorant English boys who cannot see the real value of reading Plato and Xenophon in Greek. One can distinguish undergraduates by the clothes they wear: the wealthy are able to flaunt their riches while the relatively impoverished are 'meanly apparelled'. But it is impossible to distinguish them in terms of their learning: a budding young Cicero (Tully) cannot be distinguished from a yokel (Tom Tooly).

Harvey addresses Spenser in terms that draw him into obvious agreement with the letter-writer, signalling to other readers that they share a series of jokes, and can easily read each other's references: both understand that things are not what they used to be and, in communicating at such an advanced level, are helping to restore proper humanist values. There is a familiar humour between the teacher and his former student, based on subtle references and deft puns, some obvious to any reader, others more difficult to discern, that define them as part of a university culture of wits, a corollary to their shared investment in the humanist educational project.

Harvey complains that the students now neglect Lucian, the most humorous and witty of Latin authors. As Harvey would have known, Lucian was the favourite author of Erasmus and Thomas More, a writer who lay behind their culture of banter and shared jokes and without whom the style and substance of *Utopia* and *In Praise of Folly* would have been impossible to achieve.[163] In Harvey's eyes, his exchange of witty and familiar letters with Spenser carries on the proper traditions of Cambridge learning, combining the skill and elegance of jests with serious intellectual substance, exactly what a humanist education demanded, making them the true heirs of Erasmus and More, as well as Cheke and Smith.[164] Harvey's copy of *A Merye Jeste of a man called Howleglas* (*c.*1528) contains a substantial annotation that provides further evidence of the importance of Lucian in Spenser and Harvey's culture of humanist wit (Figure 2):

This Howeletglasse, with Skoggin, Skelton, and L[a]zarill, given by me at London of Mr Spensar XX. Decembris 1[5]78, on condition [I] should bestowe the reading of them over, before the first of January [imme]diately ensuing: otherwise to forfeit unto him my Lucian in fower volumes. Whereupon I was the rather induced to trifle away so many howers, as were idely overpassed in running thorowgh the [foresaid] foolish Bookes: wherein methowgh[t] not all fower together seemed comparable for s[u]tle & crafty feates with Jon Miller whose witty shiftes, & practices ar reported amongst Skeltons Tales.[165]

It is possible that Spenser acquired these works as a schoolboy, as they were all printed by Thomas Colwel, who had a printshop near the Merchants Taylors' School.[166] The annotation shows how much Harvey valued Lucian, which is presumably why Spenser conceived the joke of forcing his teacher to read three books of more obviously popular culture and one recently translated and voguish novel, knowing it would stretch Harvey's literary horizons. Harvey's tone betrays an irritation at being taken away from more serious reading matter, perhaps with a hint of self-irony, indicating that Spenser already had the ability and the desire to goad his master, and probably resented Harvey's assumption of superiority and need to mould his charge in his own image. Harvey's comment appears to suggest that Spenser was eager to test the boundaries and limits of Harvey's Cambridge culture and to show him that humour did not begin and end with the classics. After all, More

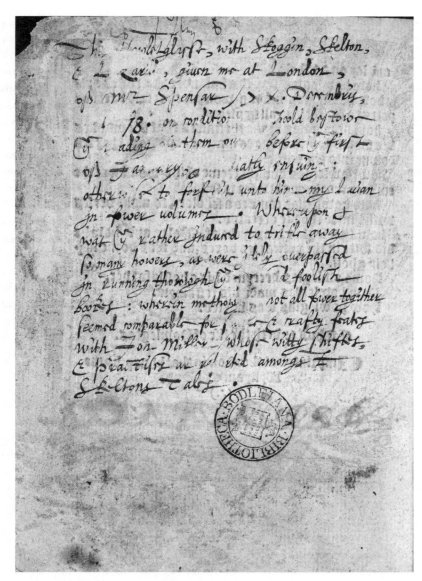

Figure 2. Gabriel Harvey's annotations in his copy of *Howleglas*. Reproduced with kind permission of the Bodleian Library.

and Erasmus enjoyed jest books like *Howleglas* and *A Hundred Merry Tales*, proving that popular culture was everyone's culture, especially when it came to humour, a lesson that Harvey appears to have resisted—at least, in part.[167] We get a glimpse of Spenser exploiting his status as Harvey's student, treating his mentor with a certain degree of gentle mockery in opening his eyes to a new world of bawdy and scurrilous jest books. Harvey records that he enjoyed the jests of Skelton best, perhaps because of their more conspicuously literary qualities, and because they were less hard-edged and grotesque in style, certainly in comparison to the scatological nature of Howle-glas's jests and the picaresque Spanish novel, *Lazarillo de Tormes*, as well as the hard-edged cruelty of Scoggin's jests.[168] Skelton's jests have particular significance because of Spenser's adoption of the persona of Colin Clout, appropriated from Spenser's poetry. Moreover, the rights to *Lazarillo* were bought by Bynemann in 1573—although it was not published until 1586 (by Abel Jeffries) and Spenser clearly read the work, probably with Harvey, and used phrases from it in *Mother Hubberds Tale*, providing some evidence that an early version of this work did exist.[169]

The copy contains a number of underlinings and a few notes, mainly on the table of contents at the end of the volume, indicating that, whatever he thought about the book, Harvey read it carefully. Next to the chapter headings, 'How Howleglas would fly from a house top' and 'How Howleglas wore a piece of cloth', Harvey has written 'Scoggins patterns', showing that he was able to make connections between the different jest books, so he had evidently taken Spenser's wager seriously.[170] One annotation is especially significant. Above the chapter title 'How Howleglas feared his host was a dead woulfe' Harvey has written 'great braggadocchio'.[171] The *OED* provides the definition of the word as 'An empty, idle boaster; a swaggerer', and gives the first citation as Nashe's *Unfortunate Traveller* (1594). Nashe was adopting the term from the first edition of *The Faerie Queene*, as the character, Braggadocchio, first appears near the start of Book II, and plays a minor but significant role in the next three Books.[172] Harvey's use of the term in 1578 provides further evidence that he read early drafts of the poem while Spenser was first writing it, and that he must have had a major influence on the poetic direction that Spenser took in this period. Harvey's main contribution, as we might expect and as the note implies, was undoubtedly in persuading Spenser to take a keen interest in Italian literature and culture, adding another layer to Mulcaster's French and Dutch influences.

Harvey's picture of Cambridge life also includes an attack on Andrew Perne (1519?–89), master of Peterhouse:

And wil you needes haue my Testimoniall of youre olde Controllers new behauior? A busy and dizy heade, a brazen forhead: a leaden braine: a wodden wit: a copper face: a stony breast: a factious and eluish hearte: a founder of nouelties: a confounder of his owne, and his friends good gifts: a morning bookworme, an afternoone maltworm: a right Iuggler, as ful of his sleights, wyles, fetches, casts of Legerdmaine, toyes to mocke Apes withal, odd shiftes, and knauish practises, as his skin can holde. He often telleth me, he looueth me as himselfe, but out lyar out, thou lyest abhominably in they throate.[173]

By the early years of Elizabeth's reign Perne was notorious as a turncoat, changing his religion to ingratiate himself with each new regime and each new change in religious policy. But Perne was also a powerful diplomatic figure, who 'served his university very well through a period of sustained danger to its very existence'. The qualities that Harvey lampooned were also those of a diplomat prepared to put the survival of the institution above the integrity of the individual.[174] Perne had his defenders, and Nashe attacked Harvey's words in *Have With You to Saffron-Walden*, referring to Harvey's 'impudent brazen-fac'd defamation of Doctor *Perne*', the echo of the word 'brazen' proving that Harvey's verbal assault was indeed understood to have been aimed at Perne.[175] Harvey had a sustained and unpleasant series of public quarrels with Perne, culminating in an unseemly dispute at Sir Thomas Smith's funeral about Harvey's acquisition of some manuscripts that had been in Smith's possession. Perne then successfully opposed Harvey's appointment as university orator in 1580, after Harvey had written to Burghley requesting the post. Perne persuaded the incumbent, Richard Bridge-water, to continue.

It is easy to see why Harvey and Perne disliked each other so much: Perne saw his task as preserving the intellectual health and success of Cambridge; Harvey felt the university's success was limited and was eager to transform it in his own image. Perne appears to have seen Harvey as Nashe saw him later, a brash and arrogant upstart. Harvey, as his comments indicate, saw Perne as a conservative time-server, dangerously unimaginative and ossified by the university's traditions. Yet again we have evidence of the clash of cultures, demonstrating that Harvey was clearly at odds with his fellows.

The rhetorical question that opens the description is intriguing. Harvey refers to Perne as Spenser's 'olde Controller', which enables him to suggest that he is, in fact, defending Spenser in providing him with a spirited attack on the character and behaviour of an old enemy. However, the evidence that we have suggests that it was Harvey who was Perne's real bête noire. Either Harvey is being especially tactless in transferring the opprobrium from himself to Spenser, or Spenser also fell foul of Perne at some point when he was a student.[176] The most likely explanation is a combination of the two, that Perne took against both men because they were flouting what he saw as the proper spirit of the university in establishing an alternative educational network. Harvey was clearly criticized for his comments on Cambridge, and later felt the need to apologize to 'that flourishing Vniversitie, my deere Mother' in *Fowre Letters and certaine Sonnets* (1592).[177] This is the first real evidence we have of Spenser antagonizing one of his superiors, a pattern that was to define his life and career.

Harvey was also attacked by other scholars.[178] He was satirized at the same time in a Latin play performed at Trinity College in 1581. Edward Forsett (1553/4–1629/30), a contemporary of both Harvey and Spenser, represents his central character in *Pedantius* as a ludicrous schoolmaster who speaks in an orotund Ciceronian style and argues using the most absurd chop logic.[179] He is also a vain dandy, ambitious and arrogant, with a self-professed Italian appearance: 'I shall comport myself so picturesquely that everyone shall say he perceives the very mirror of Tuscanism in this my Italian counternance.'[180] Harvey had been described by Elizabeth as having 'the face, the look of an Italian', when he was introduced to her on her progress to Audley End on 26 July 1578, suggesting that Forsett knew what was going on and that Harvey's reputation for self-regard and vanity was widespread.[181] Certainly Nashe made the connection, referring to *Pedantius* as a satire of Harvey in both *Fovre Letters Confuted* (1592) and *Have With You to Saffron-Walden*:

What will you giue mee when I bring him vppon the Stage in one of the principallest Colledges in *Cambridge*? Lay anie wager with me, and I will; or, if you laye no wager at all, Ile fetch him aloft in *Pedantius*, that exquisite Comedie in *Trinitie Colledge*; where, vnder the chiefe part, from which it tooke his name, as namely the concise and firking finicaldo fine School-master, hee was full drawn & delineated from the solar of the foote to the crowne of his head. The iust manner of his phrase in his Orations and Disputations they stufft his mouth with, & no Buffianisme throughout his whole bookes but they bolstred out his part with.[182]

The character Pedantius habitually argues in a careless, analogical manner, allowing connections that occur within his meandering train of thought to become what he thinks of as logical arguments, deluding himself in the process, but actually fooling no one. Pedantius is contrasted to his fellow academic, the scholastic and equally ludicrous Dromodotus, each representing equal and opposite forms of facile reasoning and the abuse of language. Pedantius starts to explain to Dromodotus why he is different from self-interested academics who wish to pursue careers at court:

As for myself, I don't care a fig for those snooty judges of whom you speak. I don't care a groat's worth, I scorn 'em, I despise 'em. Is it not the case that your academics now dress up and play at being courtiers, though there are not to be compared to me in point of genius or authority? And furthermore, 'when in Rome do as the Romans do,' where one's life is measured by one's dress, diction, manner of eating and drinking, and so forth. And the Court is a kind of Rome, and I a courtier, a sort of Roman. (III.v, lines 1–7)

Pedantius argues in such a loose manner, entirely without rigour, that he is able to end up at the opposite point where he started, initially denying that he has any interest in a public career but concluding that he would make a better courtier than his rivals. The spurious connection is provided through the link made in Pedantius' confused mind between the court and Rome, and his citation of the proverb, 'When in Rome do as the Romans do', which justifies his elevation to the court because he values himself more highly than his rivals. This speech, like so many others, satirizes Ramist logic and its use of appropriate places or topics to make a case via a series of analogies so that dialectic becomes a tool of a predetermined argument rather than a real one.[183] It also exposes Harvey as a hypocrite and shows how well known his aspirations were throughout Cambridge.

Pedantius has two pupils, Ludio and Bletus. Ludio is clearly the superior student, and the first to appear in the play, later in the same scene:

Lud: Here I am, most learned receptor.

Ped: Ah, see! Ludio, you sweetly eloquent lad, although I am in truth your most learned and most learning-dispensing preceptor, now, now I say, after I have been raised to higher and loftier station of dignity, you must henceforth address me in this wise: 'most honourable master, most worthy Maecenas', and 'if it please your highness'. These are the amplicative formulae of the rhetoricians. Procede.

Lud: Most honourable master, my worthy Maecenas, I shall always satisfy my every duty, or rather my pious obligation, towards you, in which I can never do enough to satisfy myself.

Ped: What a most Ciceronian young man! (One must employ a vocabulary of super-Latin super-latives, to keep the child happy). Now do you grasp the importance of garthering some more than familiar phrases from Cicero's letters to his familiars? (lines 53–66)

It is more than likely that Ludio is a satire of Spenser, who would have been associated with Harvey in 1581 after the publication of the *Letters*, which looked back to their Cambridge days together.[184] Forsett casts Spenser as a precocious, sycophantic student, ever eager to please his ridiculous master. Harvey is, yet again, shown to be unable to understand the advice he so desperately wants to hand out in order to further his own designs and status. Not only does he have a poor grasp of what Cicero actually says and simply uses his name as a means of recommending endless amplification—the common critique of Ciceronianism—but he fails to understand the allusions he makes.[185] Harvey demands that his recent success entitles him to the title of Maecenas, but he does not know that Gaius Cilnius Maecenas (70–8 BCE) was a wealthy nobleman in Augustan Rome, chiefly remembered for his patronage of major poets, and his close friendship with Horace. If Pedantius was really the great classical scholar he claimed to be, he would have known this, simply from reading Horace's *Satires* and Tacitus' *Annals*, hardly obscure volumes in Elizabethan England.[186] Failing to read satire makes one all the more likely to fall victim to it. Pedantius, like Harvey it is implied, wishes to be celebrated for his patronage of a talented young poet, but has forgotten—or simply failed to understand—the limitations of his own role and his dependency on the ability of his younger charge.

Casting Spenser as an enthusiastic schoolboy further suggests that the aspiring poet is equally naive and does not realize the extent of his talent. For now, his speech has become infected with the sub-Ciceronian verbiage that he has learned from his incompetent master. In the next scene Pedantius continues his suit for Lydia with Ludio faithfully supporting his master in ways that only diminish his chance of success, presumably a sardonic assessment of the malign effect that Spenser and Harvey's relationship had on each other. When Pedantius is rebuffed, Ludio comments: 'Honourable Maecenas, it would seem this woman is slanderous and chatterous. Since this does not suit your nobility, do you wish me to heap her with insults culled out of Cicero and Terence?' (III.vi, lines 25–7). He contributes a number of rather inept insults, which are really attacks on Lydia's inability to see Pedantius' true worth, culminating in 'If you were aware what manner of children he could beget, you would never refuse him. From Day One his son will be a pure Cicero, a pure Terence; in the first hour of his birth he will cry for his book' (lines 111–13). Lydia shows herself to be a better satirist than Pedantius and his supporters, a master of the appropriate insult when she eventually retorts, 'Was your mother accustomed to eat paper, that you would suck books out of her tits?' (lines 117–18). For all their learning, Pedantius and Ludio are unable to wield language as they would wish, and as Pedantius boasts he can.

Pedantius shows how Spenser and Harvey were seen by their critics in Cambridge, partly motivated, no doubt, by the insults delivered to the university in the recently published *Letters* and Harvey's attempts to establish alternative means of educating the serious youth of England under his auspices. Harvey is seen warping and distorting Spenser's intellectual gifts, and, simultaneously, dependent on his talents for all his assumption of mastery, a criticism repeated several years later by Nashe, who alleged that Harvey would never leave his 'olde trickes of drawing M. *Spenser* into euerie pybald thing' he did—exactly what Pedantius does when he allows his pupil to accompany him when out courting.[187] The play undoubtedly had a significant influence on a generation of students who attended the production, many of whom would have played an important role in English civic and cultural life, and it certainly helped to cement the reputation of Harvey as a myopic, pompous pedant, unable to perceive the heart of any matter. The *Parnassus Plays*, performed at Cambridge a generation later (1598–1602/3), written in the wake of the Nashe–Harvey quarrel, satirize Ramism, and appear to contain a number of sharp references to Harvey, who may be allegorically represented by the figure Luxurio. Interestingly enough, however, they display an intimate knowledge of Spenser's works, imitating phrases and refrains, and heap scorn on characters foolish enough to criticize him. Spenser is now seen as a touchstone of literary merit, suggesting that by the time of his death he was no longer identified as Harvey's stooge.[188]

Of course, this negative assessment of their relationship ignores what Harvey probably did help Spenser achieve. Harvey clearly stimulated and expanded Spenser's interest in rhetoric, literature, and languages. In 1592 a translation of *Axiochus*, a pseudo-Platonic dialogue, was published by Cuthbert Burby, about to play an important role in English literary history as the publisher of many of Robert Greene's works. *Axiochus* was his first book.[189] Attached to the dialogue in a separate printing was 'a sweet speech or Oration, spoken at the Tryumphe at White-hall before her Maiesties, by the Page to the right noble Earle of Oxenforde'. Why the two works were produced together is a mystery, especially given Spenser and Harvey's sniping at Oxford in the *Letters*, although it is possible that the speech was included 'at a late stage as a supplement to bulk out a short pamphlet'.[190] It is most likely that Burby, who had links with Oxford and his literary clients, notably Robert Greene, acquired the first part of this broken-backed volume from Spenser's major publisher, William Ponsonby (1546?–1604).[191] The translation was attributed to 'Edw. Spenser' and dedicated to Benedict Barnham (1558/9–98), a wealthy member of the Drapers' Company and alderman from Eastcheap, past the Tower of London where Spenser probably grew up.[192] Spenser's authorship has been vigorously disputed and a case has been made for Anthony Munday (1560–1633), who was at school with Barnham, both being members of the Drapers' Company. The mistake with the name does not serve as real evidence, as Spenser's full name had not yet been produced in print, and was often cited as 'Edward' elsewhere.[193] The author of the dedicatory letter to Barnham does refer to their 'younger yeeres' when they 'were Schollers together', but he was probably not the translator.[194] Moreover, there are echoes of *Axiochus* in Spenser's description of Acrasia's Bower which would seem to affirm his authorship beyond any reasonable doubt.[195] It is possible that the volume was a work of literary piracy, given Burby's eagerness to flout the control of the Stationers' Company, along with John Wolfe, Gabriel Harvey's friend and ally in the publishing trade.[196] Or, it might have been passed on to Burby by Ponsonby, as Ponsonby often had good relations with other publishers, but this is unlikely, given Ponsonby's investment in Spenser. Burby later published Richard Johnson's *Seven Champions of Christendom*, a prose epic which told the legend of St George (among others), clearly designed to exploit Spenser's popularity for a new, more middlebrow, audience, which suggests an interest in and knowledge of the commercial possibilities of Spenser's work, and even, perhaps, some knowledge of the writer himself.[197] The work was partly printed by John Charlewood (d. 1593), and partly by John Danter (*fl.* 1589–99), both associated with Ponsonby, but also well known as literary pirates (Charlewood, who was singled out by the Stationers' Company as a persistent offender against literary privileges, along with John Wolfe, printed the first unauthorized edition of Sidney's *Astrophil and Stella* for Thomas Newman in 1591).[198] Spenser had become famous—and notorious—in the wake of the publication of the first edition of *The Faerie Queene* and the *Complaints*, and the publication of *Axiochus* was probably a scheme to make use of his fame, the bookseller having acquired what was either believed to be, or, possibly, could have been passed off as, his work. The 'speech spoken at the Tryumph before the Queen', printed by Charlewoood, also included in the volume, is almost certainly transcribed, remembered, or written by Munday, an Oxford client.[199]

Axiochus was translated into French by Philippe du Plessis Mornay, and then appeared as the first treatise in *Six Excellent Treatises of Life and Death collected (and published in French) by Philip Mornay, sieur du Plessis; and now (first) translated into English*, published by Matthew Lownes in 1607, a publisher with a keen interest in the works of Sidney and Spenser, who had entered *A View* into the Stationers' Register in 1598 and later published the first folio edition of *The Faerie Queene*.[200] Lownes was also responsible for the reprint of a separate edition of Mornay's *A Discourse of Life and Death: written in French by Phil. Mornay. Done in English by the Countesse of Pembroke* in 1606, first published by Ponsonby in 1592, suggesting that *Axiochus* was closely connected to the Sidney circle, and had associations with both of Spenser's printers.[201] Even if *Axiochus* was not translated by Spenser it was certainly perceived as a work that he could have produced, an indication that he was regarded as a writer who had emerged from an intellectual culture at school and university that valued Greek as well as Latin.[202]

Assuming that *Axiochus* was translated by Spenser rather than Munday, the dialogue reads like a relatively early work, and would date from Spenser's schooldays or from his period at Cambridge, perhaps produced as an educational exercise.[203] Either way, it seems appropriate to link the text to Spenser's education and to suggest that the translation either led him to Harvey, one of the tutors at Cambridge most eager to disseminate Greek literature—especially, of course, in his role as lecturer in Greek—or was produced as a result of Harvey's tuition.[204]

Axiochus is not a remarkable work and shows the wise Socrates leading the confused and terrified protagonist towards an acceptance that death, far from being an end, leads the individual to a higher form of existence. It stands as a commonplace example of Christian Stoicism, popular because of the attempt to link such classical figures as Seneca and Socrates to Christian doctrines and values, as well as an intellectual and cultural counterpart to the *Fowre Hymnes*.[205] Towards the end of the dialogue Socrates explains to Axiochus how lucky he is to be dying:

Wherefor nowe O *Axiochus*, thou art not in the way to death, but to immortality, neither shalt thou (as thou didst seeme right now to feare) bee bereft of all good, but shall hereby enioy true and perfect good: Neither shalt thou perceiue such durty pleasures as are these, beeing mingled with the puddle of this sinfull body, but most pure and perfect delight being deuiod of all contagious trouble. For beeing loosed and deliuered out of the darksome dungeons of this body, thou shalt passe to that place where is no lacke nor complaint, but all things full of rest, and deuoid of euill.

Moreouer there is calme and quiet liuing without all knowledge of vnrest, peaceable and still occupied in beholding the course & frame of Nature, and studying Philosophy, not to please the idle ignorant and common sort, but with vpright and vndeceiuable truth.[206]

Socrates shows Axiochus that true philosophy will lead to an understanding of both natural and supernatural worlds, equipping the thinker with true wisdom and so ready to accept death as a release from the pains of life. The dialogue leads the reader towards this Christian Platonic ideal, in which Nature is a bad copy of divine forms, alluding to the famous shadows in the cave in the *Republic* and the awareness that the truth can only be perceived after death.[207] Axiochus is suitably grateful to Socrates for drawing him closer to enlightenment, and he states that he is no longer dreading his demise, but actually looking forward to it:

O Socrates with this gladsome speech thous hast now brought mee into a cleane contrary minde, for so farre am I nowe from dread of death, that I am euen set on fire and burne with desire thereof. And that I may stay my selfe in the steppes of them which are counted workemasters of speech, I will say thus much more excellently, Now I begin to behold those high matters, and doo ouerlooke that aeternall and heauenly course of things, hauing now raysed vp my selfe out of my weaknes, and being as it were renued and refreshed of my former malady.[208]

Such Neoplatonism sounds more like Ficino, or even the *Eroici Furori* of Giordano Bruno (1548–1600), who was well known to the Sidneys and their circle, than Plato, indicating that the *Axiochus* was a later work, perhaps a neo-Pythagorean work of the first century BCE.[209] Moreover, Charlewood was also the London printer of Bruno's works in English and Italian, possibly suggesting a further link between the circle of authors and printers.[210] A true Socratic work would have consisted of a much more rigorous dialogue which would not have led to such a straightforwardly consoling conclusion, one that no reader is likely to challenge.[211]

Axiochus' burning desire to confront death and to understand the mysteries of life, and his belief that there is a hidden reality that lies behind the surface of the natural world, resembles nothing so much in Spenser's work as the first two of the *Fowre Hymns*. The translation of *Axiochus* should probably be dated to a similar period in Spenser's literary career, the product of either a precocious school-boy or a talented and intellectually curious undergraduate. How seriously Spenser took the mixture of Neoplatonic philosophy and commonplace wisdom of *Axiochus* is hard to tell. Certainly it is difficult to imagine that he had anything to do with its publication, undoubtedly some years after it was written, suggesting that the publishers found an old copy and saw an opportunity that they could exploit, now that Spenser was an established literary name.[212]

Spenser graduated as a Bachelor of Arts in 1573. To graduate, a candidate had to have spent twelve terms at the university (usually a period of four years), and to have passed the college examinations in *responsiones* and *oppositiones* and the university's examinations, in the form of a series of philosophical disputations.[213] At this point the praelector (at Cambridge, a college fellow who formally presents students to the university at matriculation and graduation) submits a supplicat, asking for the degree to be conferred before the vice-chancellor and university senate. The process took place before Ash Wednesday (in 1573, this was 4 February, the earliest possible date), and the degree was then conferred during the six and a half weeks of Lent, before Palm Sunday. Spenser graduated eleventh out of the supplicats for the BA, third among those from Pembroke, a position that may have some reflection on his academic achievements.[214] Nine more terms of study later (usually three years) the Bachelor of Arts could answer questions from Aristotle's *Posterior Analytics*, complete other suitable exercises, and submit to become a Master of Arts, generally in early July. Spenser applied in July 1576, numbered sixty-seven in the list of seventy supplicats, and graduated as an MA.[215] His position in the list has led to some scepticism as to whether the list orders were based simply on merit, and certainly the list in the Grace book makes it clear that the Pembroke graduates were examined late in the examination period (26 June), which would explain why they came near the end of the list.[216] It is possible that Spenser left Cambridge in January 1574 and was already employed for much of the period he was registered, as there is evidence that the formal requirements for residency for an MA were not strictly applied at this time. Moreover, it is possible that Spenser did not return to Cambridge after 1573 when an *aegrotat* shows that he was absent for the last six weeks of the academic year owing to a severe outbreak of plague during which the university was 'practically disbanded'. The vice-chancellor, Andrew Perne, wrote to Burghley expressing his concern about the effects of the university on the poor people in the town, as the disease spread most quickly in areas of narrow streets, a noticeable feature of even the more affluent areas of the town. Fellows and students were advised to stay away from Cambridge, or to stay inside and shut their doors.[217] It is also possible that Spenser applied for but was not elected to a fellowship at Pembroke or another college, perhaps because of his association with Harvey, but there is no evidence for this.[218] Spenser may have left the university a long time before he graduated for the second time and was already employed elsewhere.

3

Lost Years

IT IS HARD to pin down Spenser's exact movements in the years immediately before and after he left Cambridge. This is certainly the case before April 1578 when John Young became bishop of Rochester and Spenser became his secretary. It used to be thought that Spenser must have travelled north, probably to Lancashire, where he fell in love with Rosalind, a country lass who bewitched him before leaving him for another man. The only evidence we have that he did travel north is E. K.'s gloss to line 18 of the June eclogue of *The Shepheardes Calender*, a passage which does require some further analysis, as E. K.'s notes encourage the reader to see the poem in terms of Spenser's life. The eclogue consists of a dialogue between Colin and Hobbinol, figures we know invariably stand for Spenser and Gabriel Harvey. Hobbinol is content where they are, but Colin is eager to move away:

COLIN

O happy *Hobbinoll,* I blesse thy state,
That Paradise hast found, whych *Adam* lost.
Here wander may thy flock early or late,
Withouten dreade of Wolues to bene ytost:
Thy louely layes here mayst thou freely boste.
But I vnhappy man, whom cruell fate,
And angry Gods pursue from coste to coste,
Can nowhere fynd, to shroude my lucklesse pate.

HOBBINOLL

Then if by me thou list aduised be,
Forsake the soyle, that so doth thee bewitch:
Leave me those hilles, where harbrough [refuge] nis to see,
Nor holybush, nor brere, nor winding witche [witch elm]:

And to the dales resort, where shepheardes ritch,
And fruictifull flocks bene euery where to see.
Here no night Rauens lodge more black than pitche,
Nor eluish ghosts, nor gastly owles doe flee.[1]

We learn that Colin's restlessness has been caused by his troubled suit for Rosalind, who has betrayed him for Menalcas, misleading her into inappropriately flighty behaviour, so that 'she the truest shepheardes hart made bleede' (line III).

E. K.'s notes to the poem explicitly direct the reader towards a biographical reading of the eclogue. Commenting on the words, 'Forsake the soyle' (line 18), E. K. asserts that 'This is no poetical fiction, but vnfeynedly spoken of the Poete selfe, who for speciall occasion of priuate affayres (as I haue bene partly of himselfe informed) and for his more preferment remouing out of the Northparts came into the South, as Hobbinol indeede aduised him priuately.'[2] In the note to 'The Dales' (line 21), E. K. is more specific still, referring to them as 'The Southpartes, where he nowe abydeth, which thoughe they be full of hylles and woodes (for Kent is very hylle and woodye; and therefore so called: for Kantish in the Saxons tongue signifeth woodie) yet in respecte of the Northpartes they be called dales. For indeede the North is counted the higher countrye.'[3]

That the June eclogue encourages us to relate its story to Spenser's life is clear enough; exactly how we are to do this is not.[4] What can be taken as a direct allusion to the poet's life and what is a literary fiction needs to be unravelled by the reader, who is in part directed by 'E. K.', in part misled, making the poem an intricate series of riddles and overlapping mysteries. Indeed, the decoding process is one of the key features of this ambitious work.[5] The long dedicatory epistle 'To the most excellent and learned both Orator and Poete, Mayster Gabriell Haruey, his verie special and singular good friend E. K. commendeth the good lyking of this his labour, and the patronage of the new Poete', does not seem to have prevented E. K. from failing to realize that Hobbinol is Harvey until relatively late in the sequence. In a note to line 176 of the September eclogue, in which Hobbinol names Colin Clout as Roffyn's boy, E. K. comments:

Nowe I thinke no man doubteth but by Colin is ever meante the Authore selfe, whose especiall good friend Hobbinall sayth he is, or more rightly Master Gabriel Harvey: of whose speciall commendation, aswell in Poetry as Rhetoricke and other choyce learning, we have lately had a sufficient tryall in diverse of his workes, but specially in his Musarum Lachrymae, and his later Gratulationum Valdinensium which boke in the progresse at Audley in Essex, he dedicated in writing to her Majestie. Afterward presenting the same in print vnto her Highnesse at the worshipfull Maister Capells in Hertfordshire. Beside other his sundrye most rare and very notable writings, partely vnder vnknown Tytles, and partly vnder counterfayt names, as hys Tyrannomastix, his Ode Natalia, his Rameidos, and especially that parte of Philomusus, his diuine Anticosmpolita, and diuers other of lyke importance. As also by the names of other shepheardes, he couereth the persons of diuers other his familiar freendes and best acquayntaunce.[6]

This comment surely cannot be serious and meant to be taken at face value. The wealth of detail indicates that the author of the note cannot be who he says he is. If he knows this much about Harvey then how could he possibly only have realized at this late stage that Hobbinol was Harvey? And why the sense of discovery in the notes, as if E. K. was reading them for the first time, especially as the detail that Colin is now Roffyn's boy (Spenser working for the bishop of Rochester) has already been revealed in the June eclogue? Here, the purpose is to provide a list of Harvey's poetic achievements, a rhetorical ploy whose surface innocence draws attention to the elaborate joke, as well as reiterating the game that the reader has to play when reading the eclogues in the last sentence.[7] While reading Spenser's works, especially when searching for details that reveal deliberately placed information about his life, we must be aware of the need to pay careful attention to the apparatus and form of the work, and to cross-reference sections, ensuring that the work has to be read in whole rather than parts.[8]

Therefore, June can be read, like January, as an exploration of Virgil's first eclogue, the second eclogue qualifying our understanding of the first and showing that the sequence evolves and changes as it develops.[9] In Virgil, the old man, Tityrus, is envied by the young shepherd, Meliboeus, because he has to leave the pastoral idyll and 'be dispersed— | To Scythia, bone-dry Africa, the chalky spate of the Oxus, | Even to Britain—that place cut off at the very world's end.'[10] This literary context is crucial to a decoding of the biographical information combined in the text and notes of the *Calender*. The June eclogue witnesses Hobbinol/Harvey staying put and Spenser/Colin leaving for the south. The most plausible explanation is that this tells us that Colin eventually had to move away from the Cambridge area, where Harvey spent his whole academic life, in part because he had found a new job, in part because of his personal life, something that is corroborated elsewhere in his published work but which is not quite what it seems to be.[11] The stubborn detail that does not fit this explanation is the note from E. K. which appears to indicate that Spenser and Harvey were living in the north of England. But surely this is another joke, suggesting that, for a Londoner like Spenser, Cambridge, and the counties immediately north of the capital, did indeed seem like the north. The lack of hills and rugged country in East Anglia, the flattest area of England, would then be part of a related personal joke, or simply a warning to the reader that not everything can be taken as read. Yet again, 'Northparts' may be a reference to Spenser visiting family in Northamptonshire. Harvey was certainly keen to refer to the queen's quip that he looked Italian, and perhaps E. K./Spenser/Harvey are playing with the idea of his being rooted far from his own intellectual home in southern Europe.[12] There may be further humour in the representation of Harvey as a man besotted with and rooted in the country, given his eagerness to be perceived as a modern man sweeping away stale and outdated traditions.[13] Moreover, the etymology that E. K. produces for Kent meaning 'woody' is wrong, which indicates a further deliberate confusion of identities and places. William Lambarde (1536–1601), the great expert on Kent and someone Spenser possibly encountered in this period, traces the root of the county's name, via Julius Caesar, as British not Saxon.[14]

There is no evidence that Harvey and Spenser ever made a journey to the north of England, something that would have been unusual and eccentric unless it had a specific purpose.[15] What the *Calender* does suggest is that leaving the Cambridge area at some point in the later 1570s was a significant wrench for Spenser, one he was eager to highlight in the January and June eclogues, casting himself as the exiled, dispossessed, and unhappy shepherd, rejected in love and, like Virgil's Meliboeus, afraid that he will end up cut off from all the world. There is, of course, deliberate and self-parodic exaggeration in these inflated claims—especially given what looks like Harvey's deserved reputation, noted by Nashe and others as well as providing a mainspring of the plot in *Pedantius*, for making ridiculous advances to women.[16] But they also contain an important grain of truth in letting the reader know how painful it was for Spenser to leave the company and influence of Harvey. In the January eclogue Colin represents his new-found love for Rosalind as a definitive break with his mentor, one that the slightly older man fails to accept:

> It is not *Hobbinol*, wherefore I plaine,
> Albee my love he seeke with dayly suit:
> His clowinish gifts and curtsies I disdaine,
> His kiddes [toys?], his cracknelles [light biscuits], and his early fruit.
> Ah foolish *Hobbinol*, thy gifts bene vayne:
> *Colin* them gives to *Rosalind* againe.
>
> I loue thilke lasse, (alas why doe I loue?)
> And am forlorne, (alas why am I lorne?)
> Shee deignes not my good will, but doth reproue,
> And of my rurall musick holdeth scorne.
> Shepheardes deuise she hateth as the snake,
> And laughes the songes, that *Colin Clout* doth make. ('Januarye', lines 55–66)

The poem represents Colin/Spenser's exile as a puberty rite. Colin has traded the security of male–male relationships for the insecurity of life in the marriage market.[17] He finds himself bitten by a female snake, perhaps a reversal of the gender roles and phallic norms that he expected; Hobbinol/Harvey, immediately deflated from his exalted role as patron in E. K.'s dedicatory epistle, is left bereft as Colin rejects his suit and, as he admits, cynically uses Hobbinol's gifts to court Rosalind.

It is hard to avoid the conclusion that this is a richly comic episode, especially if we remember that Spenser was at least 26 when the *Calender* was published, a rather advanced age to be experiencing the rites of passage into the adult world. But it was also the age at which most men got married and the eclogue charts, in a manner that is more humorous than has often been realized, Spenser's entry into the adult world and the state of matrimony.[18] What the eclogue also deliberately reveals is how close Spenser was to Harvey in the period before his marriage (1574–9), a time of his life about which we know virtually nothing.

It is likely that Spenser spent much of those years employed in a variety of tasks for different patrons—probably introduced to him by Harvey—and working away on the *Calender*, an astonishingly erudite and sophisticated poem which must have taken years to research and write given the range of its references and the number of poetic traditions that the poet has read, absorbed, and imitated. Such a work, clearly designed to transform the nature and culture of English verse, would have taken a long time to plan. Furthermore, 26 was also a relatively advanced age to produce a first work, however major: indeed, it is a sign of Spenser's immense confidence and ambition that he started his literary career in earnest with such a groundbreaking literary achievement. The generation of English poets writing immediately before Spenser usually started writing younger and certainly did not venture into print with a first work anything like as ambitious as the *Calender*. Barnabe Googe (1540–94) produced a translation of Marcello Palingenius Stellato's *Zodiac of Life* at the age of 21 in 1561 and his *Eclogues, Epitaphs and Sonnets* two years later, each important sources for the *Calender*.[19] George Turbervile (1540?–1610?) produced three works in 1567 when he was about 23 or 24: *Heroycall Epistles*, a translation of Ovid's *Heroides*; a translation of Mantuan's *Eglogs*; and, *Epitaphes, Epigrams, Songs and Sonets*, a collection that owed much to Googe's pioneering work. This last book, like Googe's collection, was a direct source for the *Calender*, as was the translation of Mantuan.[20] Nicholas Breton (1554/5–c.1626) published his miscellany, *A Smale Handfull of Fragrant Flowers* (1575), when he was 21.[21] Poets who had pursued military careers, such as Thomas Churchyard and George Gascoigne (1540–77), often started to publish, if not to write, a bit later and it is possible that Gascoigne's publication of his major collection of diverse works, *A Hundreth Sundrie Flowres*, in 1573 was an inspiration to Spenser, showing him what sorts of writing could be achieved by an English writer, and what a diverse range of poetic forms could be included in a volume. Certainly he is praised by E. K. in the *Calender* as a precursor to its author, although there is a clear attempt to indicate the superiority of the later writer. In a note to the November eclogue on the fate of Philomela, who was transformed into a nightingale after she had been raped and had her tongue cut out by Tereus, E. K. refers the reader to Gascoigne's *Complaint of Phylomene*, included in his later collection, *The Steele Glass* (1576), commenting that

[The Nightingale's] complaintes be very well set forth of Ma. George Gaskin a wittie gentleman, and the very chefe of our late rymers, who and if some partes of learning wanted not (albee it is well knowen he altogyther wanted not learning) no doubt would haue attained to the excellencye of those famous Poets. For gifts of wit and naturall promptnesse appeare in hym aboundantly.[22]

Gascoigne is an important poet, but Spenser is far better, superseding Gascoigne's native wit and learning, and transforming what the earlier poet had written into much more authoritative and significant verse.

The point is that Spenser's early career appears to have been carefully planned, a further indication that, as the *Calender* clearly states, especially when read in terms of the Harvey–Spenser *Letters*, Spenser worked closely with Harvey in the years after his graduation. Their separation when Spenser became secretary to John Young and got married in the year immediately before the publication of the *Calender* (1578–9), signalled an irrevocable break for both men. Harvey, as his *Letter-Book* demonstrates, appears to have changed various letters that were written to Spenser, probably planned as public letters in the manner of their published correspondence, readdressing them to John Wood, Sir Thomas Smith's nephew.[23] However, Harvey failed to establish a friendship that compensated for the loss of that with Spenser—at least, in terms of its public impact—and he drifted out of academic life in the early 1590s and by 1593, after his quarrel with Thomas Nashe, permanently retired to Saffron Walden.[24] Spenser still wrote poems with Harvey in mind, both as Hobbinol (although we need to be careful in assuming that the two can always be straightforwardly equated) and directly addressed to him, notably the Spenserian sonnet, 'To the right worshipfull, my singular good frend, M. Gabriell Harvey, Doctor of the Lawes', which was dated from Dublin, 18 July 1586, and published as a commendatory sonnet at the end of Harvey's *Fovre Letters and certaine Sonnets* (1592).[25] It is also likely that Spenser visited Harvey in his extended trips back to England in 1589–90 and 1596. But they were clearly never as close again, even though they would surely have corresponded frequently, and both men were acutely aware that Spenser moving to Kent signalled the end of an era.

Immediately after leaving Cambridge, Spenser probably spent a great deal of time with Harvey, as the close friendship advertised in the *Letters* suggests.[26] As these were published in 1580, it is clear that Harvey and Spenser were close throughout the 1570s. It is most likely that, at least intermittently, Spenser lived with Harvey in Saffron Walden, where the family owned a number of houses, as well as some in the nearby village, Wimbush. John Harvey, Gabriel's father, had risen to prominence in the town as a prosperous rope-maker and became the treasurer of the council.[27] The most likely location is a substantial town house in what is now Market Street, which later became a pub, the Bell, although Harvey could have lived in another house in Gold (formerly Gowle) Street (Plate 6).[28] Sir Thomas Smith's house in the town was only two doors away on the main square. The Harvey house was demolished in the nineteenth century to make way for a cattle market, before a building belonging to Saffron Walden Building Society was erected on the site. There is a splendid fireplace with a mantelpiece displaying the art of rope-making, which was removed from this property and which is now in the town museum (Plate 7). This impressive piece of furniture could have been commissioned by Harvey for his father during his lifetime, or after his death as a memorial. John Harvey's trade was celebrated by his son, in part to emphasize his own social progress through education, as well as his father's success, although his pride was cruelly mocked by Thomas Nashe.[29] The intricate designs on the chimney-piece make 'a moral statement about the value of labour and effort' rather than celebrating the family's name and genealogy.[30] The style of the artefact is clearly based on the fashionable emblems of Andrea Alciato (1492–1550), whose work had a major impact on English emblem books in the second half of the sixteenth century and influenced Spenser's emblematic style of poetry in the *Complaints* and the *Amoretti*.[31] The pictures derive from his work; the mottoes are variations on 'Sic Vos Non Vobis' ('Thus do you (but) not for yourselves'), 'an anaphoric verse attributed to Virgil . . . well known to sixteenth-century Continental and English impressa writers', further increasing the likelihood that Harvey commissioned the fireplace, as he was probably recalling what he had learned at Saffron Walden Grammar School.[32] The fireplace provides circumstantial evidence that this was the house that the family valued most, so would have been where Harvey probably lived and where he would have kept his large library. The family also owned a house in Hill Street—mentioned in a chancery case of 1608—just off the town square, which, with the house in Gold Street, may have been part of the same complex of buildings (a carved beam displays the initials of John and Alice Harvey over the doorway).[33] Somewhere the family would have owned buildings to contain a 'rope-walk,' which had to be 1,000–1,400 feet long, providing workers with the necessary space to wind and twist hemp bundles into a strong rope.[34] No trace of this has survived.

Spenser would undoubtedly also have known a number of Harvey's friends, including Arthur Capel of Hadham Hall, Hertfordshire, to whom Harvey loaned books and who is mentioned in the *Calender*, and, more importantly, George Gascoigne, where the recollection of him as 'a wittie gentleman, and the very chefe of our late rymers', suggests familiarity with his conversation as well as his writing.[35] Most significantly still, Spenser would have met Sir Thomas Smith, whose house in Saffron Walden he would have visited, perhaps a number of times in the 1570s before Smith's death in 1577 (Spenser probably attended the funeral with Harvey).[36] Hill Hall was the most important example of a purpose-built French-humanist house in Elizabethan England. Smith transformed the medieval building into a Renaissance palace in a series of stages, the most important of which was probably after his return from France in 1567, where he had been Elizabeth's ambassador. Smith was clearly influenced by his stay at a number of French chateaux, as he followed the court of Charles IX around the country, able to pursue his intellectual and cultural interests because there was little for him to do after the Treaty of Troyes (April 1564) had reconfirmed the standing agreement that both England and France had rights to Calais.[37] There are significant echoes of the architectural designs of the Chateau of Bournazal and the Hôtel d'Assézat in Toulouse, where Smith, whose library contained six editions of the works of the Roman architect and engineer Vitruvius, spent a long time recovering from a serious illness, as well as of Fontainbleau.[38] He also appears to have been influenced by the Castle of Écouen in Paris, built for Anne de Montmorency and his wife Madeleine de Savoie (1538–50), which was notable for its spectacular series of wall paintings and tapestries, as well as containing a series of windows depicting the story of Cupid and Psyche. The palace was a favourite haunt of Charles IX, and the court stayed there while Smith was part of the entourage.[39]

Smith was keen to recreate the neoclassical Renaissance splendour of the French court in Essex, establishing his home as a centre for culture and learning. Accordingly, he covered every possible space of Hill Hall with a series of magnificent wall paintings and tapestries, as well as commissioning an expensive collection of stained glass and floor tiles, all designed to narrate a series of important moral stories which would influence the considerable number of people who viewed them.[40] These ambitious sequences were unique in England in the 1560s and 1570s, and would have had a considerable impact on Spenser, the most visual of all Elizabethan poets, who had no opportunity to see any Renaissance art outside the British Isles (although he would undoubtedly later see the wall paintings representing the story of Jeroboam from 1 Kings 13 which appeared at the Drydens' home at Canons Ashby in the 1580s or 1590s, which closely resemble those of Hezekiah at Hill Hall).[41] Smith had a series of wall paintings and painted glass panels erected in 1568–9, with allegorical Protestant scenes.[42] The paintings preserved represent a variety of allegorical themes; one sequence tells the well-known story of Cupid and Psyche (Plate 8), who overcame the jealousy of Cupid's mother, Venus, to marry, a common theme in Renaissance literature and a work that demonstrated Smith's interest in Neoplatonism; another narrates the story of King Hezekiah, the religious reformer who helped unite the Israelites and who resisted the Assyrian tyrant King Sennacherib (2 Kings 18–19); as well as a figure of Magnanimity, part of a lost longer sequence on the cardinal virtues.[43] The stained glass has an image of *superbia* or pride, part of a sequence of the seven deadly sins.[44] *The Faerie Queene*, which also tells the story of Cupid and Psyche (III.vi.50–2), who produce a daughter, Pleasure, has a number of key moments which rely on the impact of carefully coded lavish visual material, often representing astonished figures who enter grand halls covered with a variety of pictures: the House of Pride (I.iv), Acrasia's Bower (II.xii), the Garden of Adonis (III.vi), and the Castle of Busirane (III.xi–xii) being only the most obvious examples.[45] Furthermore, the poem includes a masque of the seven deadly sins, who are paraded in the House of Pride (I.iv.20–36).[46] These are largely passages from sections of the poem that Spenser was probably working on relatively early in the poem's history, and may well have been influenced by what Spenser saw at Hill Hall, which would probably have been the most spectacular visual encounter of his early life.[47] Few poets have been as interested in tapestries as Spenser, whose visual imagination was undoubtedly also stimulated by his time at Leicester House in the same decade, as Leicester had an outstanding collection of pictures and wall hangings.[48] Moreover, if, as has been suggested, Lucas de Heere was the artist who painted the Hezekiah and Cupid and Psyche sequences, it is possible that there is a direct link to Spenser's work, as de Heere almost certainly produced the woodcuts for van der Noot's *Theatre*.[49]

What Spenser actually did after leaving Cambridge is as hard to determine as his movements and locations. We know that he was in Leicester House in 1579, but there is some circumstantial evidence that Spenser worked for Leicester rather earlier than has generally been assumed, information which may well change how we conceive his problematic relationship with Elizabeth's favourite. Spenser was friendly with Robert Salter, chaplain to Edmund Sheffield, third Baron Sheffield and first earl of Musgrave (1565–1646). Salter comments in a printed marginal note in his eccentric study of the Book of Daniel, *Wonderfull Prophecies* (1627): 'Mr Edmund Spenser. The great contentment I sometimes enioyed by his Sweete society, suffreth not this to passe me, without Respectiue mention of so trew a friend.'[50] We do not know when or for how long this friendship lasted, and it is likely, as the book was published nearly thirty years after Spenser's death, to have been rather later than the 1570s unless Salter was in his seventies or eighties, a considerable age in this period.[51] But Salter's comments do, nevertheless, provide us with a link between Spenser and the Sheffield family.

Sheffield's mother, Douglas, née Howard (1542/3–1608), had been abandoned by Leicester after they had an affair in the late 1560s and early 1570s, as the anonymous Catholic libel *Leicester's Commonwealth* (1584) detailed with considerable glee.[52] The story was then repeated in Thomas Roger's poem, *Leicester's Ghost* (c.1604).[53] As late as the mid-eighteenth century an expanded version of the story appeared in Arthur Collins's study of noble families. Collins, repeating a commonly understood version of the story, stated that Douglas was debauched by Leicester, who then planned to poison her husband. Unfortunately for him, the letter in which he stated his plan fell into the hands of her sister, who, understandably enough, passed it on to Lord Sheffield, who then threatened to do the same to the adulterous couple.[54] It is also possible that what was seen to have been a seduction was the basis for the plot of George Gascoigne's prose fiction, *The Adventures of Master, F. J.* (1573).[55] Lady Sheffield later claimed under oath that she had married Leicester secretly at some point between 11 November and 25 December 1573, their son, Sir Robert Dudley (1574–1649), being born on 7 August 1574. This had not prevented Leicester from marrying Lettice Knollys and Douglas marrying Sir Edward Stafford.[56]

Salter's comments provide evidence that Spenser probably worked for Leicester in the 1570s when Leicester and Sheffield were a couple and, most importantly, it might help to explain the slighting reference to Lettice Knollys in the *Calender*, as she had taken Douglas Sheffield's place. The dedicatory sonnets to *The Faerie Queene* include two with Sheffield connections: one is dedicated to Thomas Butler, tenth earl of Ormond, the husband of Douglas's daughter, Elizabeth, and another to Douglas's brother, Charles, Lord Howard of Effingham.[57] Spenser appears to have felt far more loyalty to the Sheffields than to the Dudleys, and, given the Sheffield family's understandable resentment at Leicester's behaviour, he may have weighed in to support them in the *Calender*.[58]

Another acquaintance of Spenser's at this time was the prolific poet Nicholas Breton, who dedicated what was probably his first collection to Lady Sheffield, *A Smale Handfull of Fragrant Flowers* (1575).[59] Breton later wrote an elegy for Spenser, the only poem for a named person published in his volume, *Melancholike Humours* (1600), perhaps one of the poems that Camden described being thrown into Spenser's grave, which appears to be based on personal affection for the best of his peer group.[60] Even more intriguing is the possibility that Spenser's link with Breton provides us with evidence of one of his lost works. BL Add. MS 34064, an undated poetic miscellany in a series of hands, contains a large number of Breton's poems.[61] A section in a distinct hand, however, contains extracts from *The Ruines of Time*—the sections relating to Leicester—and *Mother Hubberds Tale*—mainly the satires of the church.[62] Some of these extracts look as if they might have come from a separate manuscript from that used by Ponsonby to print the *Complaints*, which then raises the question of whether the opening section of this manuscript (fos. 1–4), in another hand, contains original unpublished works by Spenser. One poem, 'Ffrom the heavenes there hath descended' (sig. 4ᵛ), is attributed to 'Edward Spencer' (like *Axiochus*), but does not look at all authentic. However, two sonnets in alexandrines (sig. 3ᵛ) may possibly be experiments from the early 1570s and part of the lost *The Dying Pelican*, which, if so, would then have been a sonnet sequence:

The pretie Turtle dove, that with no little moane
When she hath lost her make, sitts moorninge all alone
The swanne that always sings an houre before her deathe
Whose deadlie gryves do give the grones that drawe awaie her breathe
The Pellican that pecks the blud out of her brest
And by her deathe doth onlie feed her younge ones in the nest
The harte emparked cloase: within a plot of grounde
Who dare not overlook the pale for feare of hunters hounde
The hounde in kennel tyed that heares the chase goe by
And bootles wishing foote abroade, in vaine doth howle and crye
The tree with withered top, that hath his braunches deade
And hangeth downe his highest bowes, while other hould upp heade
Endure not half the deathe, the sorrowe nor disgrace
That my poore wretched mind abids, where none can waile my case.

Ffor truth hath lost his trust, more dere than turtle dove
And what a death to suche a life; that such a paine doth prove
The swan for sorrow singes, to see her deathe so nye
I die because I see my deathe, and yet I can not dye.
The Pelican doth feed her younge ones with her bludd
I bleed to death to feede desires yt doe me never good
My hart emparked rounde within the grounde of greif
Is so beset with houndes of hate: yt lookes for no relief
And swete desire my dogg is clogged so with care
He cries and dies to here delightes and come not wher they are
My tree of true delight, is rokde with sorrow soe
As but the heavenes do soon helpe, wil be his overthrowe
In summe my dole, my deathe, and my disgrace is such
As never that ever lyvde knewe ever halfe so muche.

It is hard to judge whether these are authentic, but it does seem a strange coincidence that *The Dying Pelican* should be mentioned as a lost work by Ponsonby in his preface to the *Complaints*, when extracts from that collection also appear in this miscellany. The sonnets contain verbal and intellectual quibbles that may be Spenserian, especially the extended metaphoric use of the dog as a frustrated component of the hunt, a clever variation on the standard conceit of hunting the hart/heart. The central conceit, that the deluded speaker suffers more in love than the pelican who pecks her own breast to feed her children and then bleeds to death, would also seem to be characteristic of Spenser's ability to produce ironic dramatic monologues.[63] Moreover, it would also be odd if Spenser had not attempted to produce some sonnets in the 1570s, given the central importance of the form for Elizabethan poets.[64]

Another writer connected to the Sheffield family was Thomas Rogers of Bryanston (1574–1609), an eccentric poet and the uncle of John Donne through marriage.[65] Rogers was a lawyer, a graduate of the Inns of Court, and an MP in the 1590s.[66] He dedicated a number of mythological poems to the memory of the recently deceased Frances Howard, countess of Hertford, which appeared in his volume, *Celestial Elegies* (1598).[67] Frances was the sister of Douglas and it was in defence of her that he produced his manuscript poem, *Leicester's Ghost*, soon after the accession of James. The work was based on the libel, *Leicester's Commonwealth* (1584), but it owes a conspicuous debt to Spenser's *Complaints*, especially *The Ruines of Time* and *The Ruines of Rome*.[68] Such evidence only shows that Rogers knew and was influenced by Spenser's work, but, given their mutual connections to the different branches of the Effingham family, a connection that Spenser acknowledged and used when producing the dedicatory sonnets to *The Faerie Queene*, it is possible that they were acquainted in the 1570s.

We know from evidence in Spenser's first major publications that he started work on a number of poems and plays in the 1570s, many of which have not survived, or which are probably incorporated into other published works. In the epistle to Harvey which prefaces the *Calender*, E. K. hopes that 'Immerito' (Spenser) will be persuaded to publish 'divers other excellent works of his, which slepe in silence, as his Dreames, his Legendes, his Court of Cupide, and sondry others'.[69] In the preface to the October eclogue E. K. claims to have a 'booke called the English Poete, which booke being lately come to my hands'; and in a note to line 90 he refers to a sonnet which contains the lines, 'The siluer swanne doth sing before her dying day | As shee that feeles the deepe delight that is in death &c.'.[70] In the *Letters* Spenser refers to '*My Slomber*, and the other Pamphlets', which he may dedicate to Edward Dyer, *My Slomber* perhaps being the same as 'Dreams', and which is surely the work referred to as 'A senights slumber' in Ponsonby's prefatory letter to the *Complaints*.[71] The *Letters* also contain references to a book, *Epithalamion Thamesis*, which undoubtedly became the marriage of the Thames and the Medway in *The Faerie Queene*, Book IV, canto xi, and the *Stemmata Dudleiana*, all indications that Spenser was constantly writing and that he refigured, rethought, and rearranged his poetry throughout his life. Harvey also provides evidence of lost works when he refers to Spenser's 'nine Englishe *Commodies*' in the *Letters*, supporting Ponsonby's list in the preface to the *Complaints*, probably an attempt to create intrigue and drum up business for his charge.[72] It is likely that Spenser did produce partial or complete translated versions of the biblical *Ecclesiastes* and *Canticum Canticorum*; religious poems such as *Purgatory* (is this a sly reference to Dante, and evidence that Spenser did know the great Italian poet's work?), *The Howers of the Lord*, and *The Seven Psalms*; *The Hell of Lovers* (perhaps refigured as the masque of Busirane at the end of *The Faerie Queene*, Book III).

The comedies—assuming they were plays—may have been performed at college while he was a student, Spenser planning to revise them but never managing to complete the task.[73] But there is an impressive range of material in the 'lost works' that signals—and advertises—serious literary ambition: poetry, ranging from sonnets to capacious historical and topographical works; pamphlets; translations; and a treatise on poetry, perhaps one to rival Sidney's, which was circulating in manuscript but which had not yet been published. It is impossible to imagine that a man who had not spent a great deal of time reading, experimenting, and writing could have produced an incredibly complicated work such as the *Calender* by the time he was 26. Moreover, to write so much, Spenser needed access to significant supplies of paper, which was expensive in this period, costing between 2s. and 7s. a ream.[74] When he worked as a secretary in Ireland Spenser was granted £15 per year for supplies, including paper, a sum that a provincial parson would have earned in the same time.[75] Some of the money needed he may well have earned himself, but it is likely that he had another source, probably Harvey's access to the relevant materials as a Cambridge tutor. Furthermore, the *Calender*, as well as Spenser's later works, is informed by the books that were contained in Harvey's library, exactly what might be expected given Harvey's eagerness to assemble a significant collection of relevant books that would equip a scholar for an active life, and his desire to direct the reading habits and practices of those he taught and those he served.[76]

Harvey's library, which he told his students in 1576 was kept in his 'Tusculan villa' in Walden, was a mixture of ancient and modern books.[77] Harvey's collection, which he apparently boasted had cost him £200 at some point in the 1590s, was much more wide-ranging in subject matter than the inventories of books that survive in the wills of Cambridge tutors and students from the 1560s and 1570s.[78] These reveal a variety of libraries for different purposes, some working libraries for busy teachers, others much more comprehensive and capacious, such as the famous library of John Caius, now in his old college. However, even the extensive library of William Lyffe, who died in 1569 when Spenser started his Cambridge studies, contains mainly works of rhetoric, classical literature, history, and philosophy, including Isocrates, Plato, Aristotle, Ovid, Sallust, Hesiod, Euripides, the one modern author being Rudolf Agricola's works on dialectic; and theology and biblical commentary, notably Calvin (who appears in almost all inventories of books), Melanchthon, and Peter Martyr. Other libraries generally contained works by major authors such as Erasmus, Quintilian, Augustine, Josephus, Terence, Virgil, Cicero, Homer, Aesop, Bede, Lucan, and others, all authors that Spenser would have read in this period if he had not already done so.

Harvey's library was different because it contained so many modern works in French, Italian, as well as English, and because his works were so heavily annotated, which would have further helped to define Spenser's own reading habits. Harvey also had a keen interest in what seemed to many to be obscure subjects, such as Scottish literature. He established connections with Thomas Vautrollier, an Anglo-Huguenot printer who dominated the Anglo-Scottish book trade and was largely responsible for James VI's supply of French books.[79] Vautrollier's daughter married his apprentice, Richard Field, who later printed *Fowre Hymnes* for William Ponsonby, and who took over his business in 1588, indicating that the connections between authors and printers were sustained.[80] Moreover, he had published both Mulcaster's educational treatises, *Positions* and *The First Part of the Elementarie*. Harvey's link to Vautrollier provided him with knowledge of Scottish politics and culture. He was especially interested in the works of James VI, and was surely the source of Spenser's knowledge of Scottish political developments and his particular fear of the accession of James as king of England in the late 1590s.[81]

In addition to works which were in the libraries of many of his contemporaries and their Cambridge colleges, from surviving copies and evidence in other books, we know that Harvey possessed modern works of English literature, such as *A Mirror for Magistrates*, Gascoigne's poetry, and Sidney's *Arcadia*; Italian works, one of the largest collections in the library, including Baldassare Castiglione's *Book of the Courtier*, in Italian and English, Stefano Guazzo's *Civil Conversation*, Guicciardini's reflections on modern political practice, and, crucially, those of Machiavelli, John Florio's Italian dictionary, William Thomas's *History of Italy*, and Tasso's works; a large collection of works of French literature and politics, including works detailing the St Bartholomew's Day Massacre such as *Vindiciae Contra Tyrannos*, Rabelais's *Gargantua and Pantagruel*, and the poems of Sylvester Du Bartas; key historical works such as Olaus Magnus's *History of the Northern Peoples*; topical works such as George Buchanan's political treatises against Mary Queen of Scots, and John Cheke's *Hurt of Sedition*; a host of topographical and geographical works, including Humphrey Lhuyd's *Breviary of Britayne*, translated by Thomas Twyne; up-to-date works on science; and, of course, a number of Peter Ramus' works, as well as Thomas Wilson's *Art of Rhetoric* and his influential *Discourse upon Usury*.[82] These are only the works the details of which have survived, as Harvey possessed far more volumes, calculating himself that he had nearly four thousand.[83] A library of a few hundred volumes was unusual in this period, and the university library at Cambridge estimated that it had about 451 books and manuscripts in 1582. John Dee was one of the few bibliophiles who possessed a more extensive private collection of books than Harvey, although many of his were volumes of special scientific interest.[84] Harvey was probably inspired by the library of Sir Thomas Smith, kept at Hill Hall: the partially preserved inventory for Smith's library reveals a similar mixture of ancient and modern books, including works by Ramus, Machiavelli, and

Castiglione, as well as Sebastian Münster's *Cosmographia*, Olaus Magnus's *History*, and the literary works of Petrarch, Du Bellay, and Dante.[85]

That Spenser made extensive use of particular volumes in Harvey's library can be demonstrated, even if specific examples cannot be proved. Guazzo's *Civil Conversation* undoubtedly had a major impact on Spenser's intellectual horizons, and the opening stanza of Book VI of *The Faerie Queene* defines courtesy as the 'roote of ciull conuersation' (line 6).[86] We also know that Spenser made extensive use of Olaus Magnus' *History* in writing a *View*, and that George Buchanan's hostile portraits of Mary Queen of Scots played an important role in the representation of Duessa in Book V of *The Faerie Queene*.[87] It is likely that Spenser learned a great deal about close and careful reading from Harvey's habit of systematic and directed annotation, shown in such heavily annotated works as his copies of Livy and Castiglione.[88] Harvey also undoubtedly continued to develop Spenser's interest in the study of modern foreign languages, given his own keen interest in reading widely in ancient and modern works not written in English.[89] Spenser's education clearly went beyond what was provided for him at Cambridge.

From the published evidence of the *Letters* and surviving annotations in books, we know that Spenser and Harvey also exchanged and discussed particular books, a sign of their intimacy, as well as an indication that Spenser had the means to acquire books of his own. Such actions were not simply a means of sharing ideas—although they were that—but part of an elaborate game which explored their master–student relationship. The annotations and comments that survive also provide a wealth of information about Spenser's life in this period.

The most extensive evidence of this practice occurs in Harvey's copy of *Howleglas*, which suggests the growing independence of the student from the master, but is also a fond record—at least on Harvey's part—of their friendship.[90] The annotation tells us that Spenser and Harvey met in London after Spenser had started work as secretary for John Young in Rochester, presumably during the Christmas holiday, a further sign that their relationship had continued throughout the 1570s. We cannot know whether Spenser finally felt able to make some subtle digs at Harvey—which, in fact, corroborate the portrait of Harvey in *Pedantius*—because he now had an independent position; whether their relationship had always had this element of give-and-take; and whether Harvey was slightly irritated by Spenser's attitude or took it in good part.

What the annotation also makes clear is that Spenser was exploring the relationship between high and low forms of culture, and thinking about types of humour. Harvey compares Spenser to Ariosto:

To be plaine, I am voyde of al iudgement, if your *Nine Comedies*, wherevnto in imitation of *Herodotus*, you giue the names of the *Nine Muses*, (and in one mans fansie not unworthily) come not neerer *Ariostos Comoedies*, eyther for the finenesse of plausible Elocution, or the rarenesse of Poetical Inuention, than that *Eluish Queene* doth to his *Orlando Furioso*, which notwithstanding, you wil needes seeme to emulate, and hope to ouergo, as you flatly professed your self in one of your last Letters.[91]

The comment suggests that *The Faerie Queene* quickly evolved into a hybrid form that adapted Ariosto's *Orlando Furioso* rather than simply imitated it, a sign that Spenser was experimenting with poetic styles and genres from the very start of his literary career. The mention of Ariosto and comedy may well be a direct reference to George Gascoigne's adaptation of Ariosto, *Supposes*, written in 1566, and staged at Gray's Inn, so it is possible that Spenser saw a performance of the play, or, at least, heard an account of it.[92] Spenser, according to Harvey, was also writing works that adapted comic forms in new and unusual ways, producing a (now lost) work that combined a study of the nine muses with material from Herodotus' *History*, in essence, every form of literature (epic, lyric, tragic, dance, and so on) with the foundational text of Western historical writing.[93] Harvey's judgement—confirmed by his marginalia to his copies of Gascoigne's play, which was published in the collection *A Hundreth Sundrie Flowres* in 1573.[94]

At the same time Spenser also gave Harvey a copy of Jerome (Hieronymus) Turler's *The traueiler* (1575), a translation of the popular manual of advice for travellers by William How.[95] Harvey's copy bears the Latin inscription 'Gabrielis Harveij.' 'ex dono Edmundi Spenserii Episcopi Roffensis Secretarii. 1578' (a gift from Edmund Spenser, secretary of the bishop of Rochester). The inscription on the last page, 'Lege pridie Cal. Decembris. 1578. Gabriel Harvey', shows that it was probably received with the jest books.[96] Turler's work was a manual of instruction for the would-be traveller, the first, longer, book describing what he would need to consider and know; the second, a description of his own visit to Naples. Turler's opening chapter defines travel, following Cicero, and distinguishes between citizens and strangers (p. 2), before asking the key question, 'whether traueyling do a man more good or harme?' (p. 4). Turler concludes that travel is a positive experience and outlines why:

Traueill is nothing else but a paine taking to see and searche forreine landes, not to bee taken in hande by all sorts of persons, or vnaduisedly, but such as are meete thereto, eyther to the ende that they may attayne to suche artes and knowledge as they are desirous to learne or exercise: or else to see, learne, and diligently to marke suche things in strange Countries, as they shall haue neede to vse in the common trade of lyfe, wherby they maye profite themselues, their freindes, and Countrey if needed require. (p. 5)[97]

The passage stands out in italic script in a book mainly in black-letter typeface. Travel, according to Turler, serves a serious purpose and travellers acquire real knowledge of great use to themselves, their immediate circle, and their country. In a later chapter Turler states and answers common objections to travel, citing Claudian (as well as Horace and Ovid) on the unhappiness of exile and the envy the displaced feel towards the settled:

> O Happie hee that spent his daies
> In natiue soyles delight,
> Whom one self house hath seene a child,
> And eke an aged wight.
> Who limping with his staffe wher once
> He played the little Mouse:
> Can count the manie yeeres which hee
> Hath past in one poore house. (p. 92)[98]

Turler makes the obvious point that what 'they call Deportation or exile is one thing, and traueill an other' (p. 93). Nevertheless, it is interesting that Turler spends so much time refuting the fear that travel will become exile. In doing so he was surely highlighting the connection between the two after the wave of religious exiles in the wake of Mary's accession in 1553 and Pope Pius V's bull against Elizabeth, 'Regnans in Excelsis' (25 February 1570), stating that Elizabeth was a heretic and those Catholics who obeyed her would be excommunicated.[99] Given the strict restrictions on travel in the sixteenth century, with travellers requiring a licence to leave the country, many travellers were exiles, and the two forms of journeying were closely linked in the public imagination.[100]

Why did Spenser give this particular book to Harvey? The answer must surely be that Spenser had been on or was planning a journey; that Harvey was in the same situation; or that both of them had travel on their minds. This last situation was indeed the case. Early in 1578 Harvey was due to take part in an English deputation to the conference of Protestant princes at Schmalkalden in Germany, through the intervention of the ubiquitous Daniel Rogers, but the plan came to nothing.[101] Spenser himself may well have already travelled to Ireland if we can take the account that Irenius provides of the execution of Murrogh O'Brien in a *View* as an accurate testimony. The rhetoric of the 'I' witness lends credence to a point about the ancestors of the Irish (the Gauls), marking them out as a primitive people with ancient, primitive urges:

Allsoe the Gaules vsed to drinke theire enemies blodd and to painte themselues therewith So allsoe they write that the owlde Irish weare wonte And so haue I sene some of the Irishe doe but not theire enemyes but friendes blodd as namelye at the execution of a notable Taitour at Limericke Called murrogh Obrien I saw an old woman, which was his foster mother, take up his head, whilst he was quartered, and sucked up all the blood that runne thereout, saying, that the earth was not worthy to drinke it, and therewith also steeped her face and breast, and tore her haire, crying out and shrieking most terribly.[102]

Here, the fact that the event was witnessed is central to the argument, which differentiates the Irish from other savage peoples, suggesting that here we are justified in assuming that Irenius was Spenser and that he was present at the execution which took place in Limerick on 1 July 1577. The execution is also described in a letter from Sir William Drury to Robert Dudley, earl of Leicester. Drury compares O'Brien to James Fitzmaurice, the cousin of Gerald Fitz James Fitzgerald, earl of Desmond, the leader of the serious uprising in Munster which began in 1569, and which Sir Henry Sidney was struggling to suppress. He describes him as 'a second pillar of James FitzMorisch's late rebellion and a practiser of this new combination [i.e., rebellion], a man of no less fame than James himself', and comments that he was 'orderly indicted, arraigned, condemned, and judged for late offences ... He was amongst the people in great estimation; he was holden the best and forwardest horseman of Ireland; he was greatly of the good feared. His death was far better than his life, and he confessed he had deserved death', the ideal end for a traitor.[103]

The execution was clearly a major event and would have made a significant impression on any young English observer, given O'Brien's status and the setting among his own people hostile to English law, who saw him as a martyr.[104] It is probable that Spenser was in Limerick in July 1577, given his connections with Leicester through Harvey in the 1570s.[105] There may also have been another connection to the Lord Justice, Sir William Pelham (d. 1587), who refers frequently to his brother, Spenser, in the State Papers.[106] Pelham's brother was his brother-in-law, Captain James Spenser (d. 1590), who had been Master of Ordnance in the Northern Rebellion (1569–70) and then provost marshal in the Tower of London, and was married to his sister, Mary. He may have been a relation of Edmund's, although more likely he was related to the Spencers of Althorp, especially as Pelham's second wife, Dorothy, was the daughter of Dorothy Spencer, herself the daughter of Sir John Spencer of Althorp.[107] More significant still, Pelham named the only son from this marriage Peregrine, the same name that Edmund gave to the only son of his second marriage to Elizabeth Boyle (herself related to the Spencers of Althorp by marriage).[108] Clearly Spenser had a series of connections, however loose, that would have proved further reasons for him being in Ireland before he actually settled there.

Indeed, Spenser may have been the bearer of the letter cited above, from Sir William Drury (1527–79), the President of Munster and, later, the Lord Justice of

Ireland, to Leicester, dated 8 July. Drury also sent a 'cast of falcons of the best eyrie in this province' for Leicester.[109] Great attention was paid to the post system after Shane O'Neill's Rebellion in 1565, as officials in London sought to ensure that they received news quickly from the most exposed part of the territories ruled by the English monarch.[110] Spenser, as a servant of Leicester in the late 1570s, might have been sent as part of this process of improvement and the desire to control the circulation of information.[111] Even at this early date Spenser could have realized that his skills as a secretary would lead him to a life of exile in the Irish civil service.

Travel was evidently on the minds of both Harvey and Spenser in the late 1570s. As his published collection *Gratulationes Valdinensium* demonstrates, Harvey was especially eager to enter Leicester's service in the late 1570s, and the Harvey–Spenser *Letters* witness him openly discussing travelling abroad for the earl.[112] In the last section of his first letter (15 October 1579), dated from Leicester House, Spenser states that he is about to travel abroad in Leicester's service, which is why he has not been able to send Harvey some poetry, as he had hoped:

> I was minded to haue sent you some English verses: or Rymes, for a farewell: but by my Troth, I haue no spare time in the world, to thinke on such Toyes, that you knowe will demaund a freer head, than mine is presently. I beseeche you by all your Curtsies, and Graces, let me be answered, ere I goe: which will be, (I hope, I feare, I thinke) the next weeke, if I can be dispatched of my Lorde. I goe thither, as sent by him, and maintained most what of him: and there to employ my time, my body. My minde, to his Honours seruice.[113]

Spenser is using language that Harvey will understand and appreciate, that of the deserved rewards of loyal service to a public ideal, catapulting the intellectual into an exciting public world. Whether Spenser really thought that such opportunities were as exciting as he appears to suggest here is debatable, but his scarcely contained enthusiasm is deliberately set against his neglect of his poetry.[114] The journey he is referring to must have been to France, an anticipated return visit in Leicester's entourage to secure the marriage of the queen and François, duc d'Alençon, who had departed for France on 25 August after a long stay, involving a great deal of public celebrations, which had begun on 5 January.[115] Unfortunately, Alençon's visit also attracted a great deal of criticism, principally from courtiers and subjects anxious about their monarch being made subservient to the French, most spectacularly in the form of John Stubbes's *The Discouerie of a Gaping Gulf* (1579), as well as Sir Philip Sidney's open letter to the queen, and, of course, *The Shepheardes Calender*.[116] All were closely associated with Leicester.[117] In the face of opposition from the Privy Council, outlined by Burghley in a minute dated 6 October entitled 'Cause of misliking of the marriage', the possibility of marriage fizzled out, principally due to opposition orchestrated by Leicester.[118] Unsurprisingly, the visit abroad that Spenser refers to never took place, given the state of the negotiations in the autumn of 1579 and the key

(a)

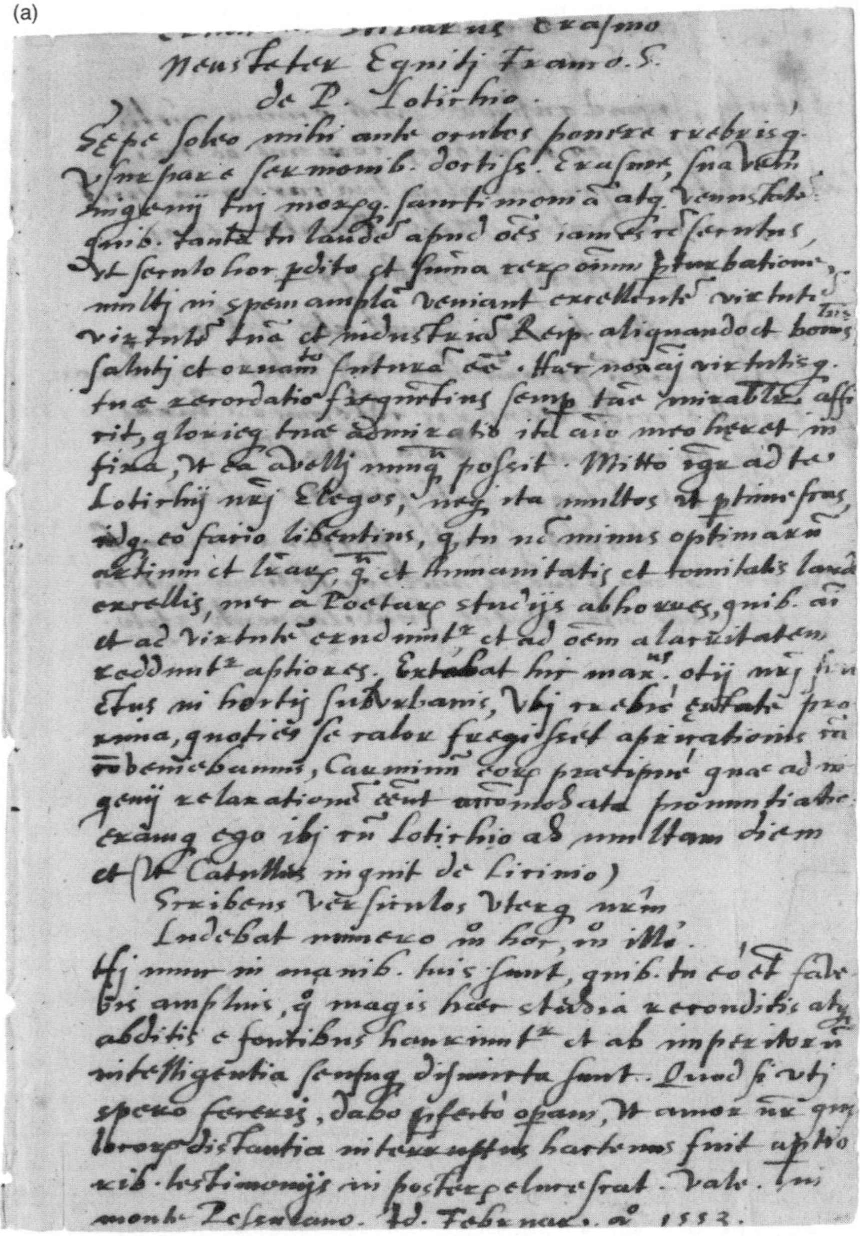

Figure 3. Spenser's annotations in his copy of Petrus Lotichius Secundus and Georgius Sabinus, *Poemata* (1576). Reproduced with kind permission of the Folger Shakespeare Library.

Joannes de Sylva...
Lotichium...

Lotichi, siquid rapida sint omnia metis
 Non opus in tenebris rorem met oc tom
Atq, aliquis spectans olim tua carmina dicet:
 Venator vates Miles Amator, erat.

 Fr. Artifex Athensis.

Lascivi, molles, teneri, simul, atq, salaces,
 Thespiadu prorul hinc vos iubet ira thorens,
Aet quue drondi Veneris obscenuxa luxas,
 Atq, sphaeretraty spurula saeda Dei;
Hos legitote Elegos, mihi pretate refectos
 Casta placent sanctii pectora mmminita,
Dulce poema fluens medioq thebicome petiti
 Exhibet hic Vates suavi loquente stylo.

103

role of Spenser's own patron—evidence, if any were needed, of his and Harvey's distance from the corridors of power.

We also have evidence of books that Spenser acquired himself, such as the copy of the work of the German humanist poets Petrus Lotichius Secundus (1528–60) and Georgius Sabinus (1508–60), which were bound together and published as one volume in 1563.[119] The book is inscribed 'Immerito', and contains a number of markings and underlinings, but no annotations, although some might have been destroyed when the book was later cropped. On the flyleaf Spenser has copied out a letter about Lotichius by Erhard Stibar, a student of Sabinus, as well as two poems in praise of Lotichius' poetry (Figure 3).[120] As Lee Piepho has argued, while we cannot be sure exactly when Spenser had the volumes, most likely he 'acquired them at a time when he was still learning the craft of poetry'.[121] The two collections were probably bound together in 1576, so Spenser probably obtained them in the late 1570s when he was working on the *Calender*.

The volumes are wide-ranging works by poets with major European reputations, containing a diverse collection of skilfully written poems, elegies, songs, and eclogues. In itself the book demonstrates just how capacious and catholic Spenser's literary taste was, especially when placed alongside his interest in Turler's *Traueiler* and the jest books.[122] They also demonstrate that German neo-Latin literature was important for English readers, German poets corresponding with their contemporaries throughout Europe.[123] It is quite likely that Lotichius in particular had an influence on Spenser, given the number of eclogues he wrote describing his suffering in love, and his invention of a number of fictitious women, devices, tropes, and modes that are on obvious display in the *Calender*.[124]

Spenser's interest in neo-Latin poets such as Sabinus (who was rumoured to have responded to Ovid's *Heroides*, a work that also attracted Spenser) probably tells us a great deal about early modern English intellectual culture and the range of interests of poets eager to establish poetry of European significance in the vernacular, one of the key aims of the *Letters*.[125] Indeed, Spenser was writing Latin poetry at the same time as he was preparing the *Calender* for publication, as his earliest letter to Harvey, dated 5 October 1579, demonstrates. Included here is a poem of 123 lines 'Ad Ornatissimum Virum', a partly tongue-in-cheek praise of his tutor written as he thought he was about to sail to France. The poem can be related to a number of verse epistles in praise of friends, patrons, and scholars written by humanist poets like Lotichius and Sabinus and was obviously influenced by Spenser's reading (he probably shared his copies of their books with Harvey, who would have seen no reason to use his resources on buying duplicates).[126] Spenser writes to Harvey as one poet to another ('Poëta Poëtam'), praising him because he values true fame above worldly success.[127] He argues that Harvey has triumphed over scorn and mockery, but that he ought not to neglect life's pleasures, which might include obtaining a wife (line 70), as well as offers of gold (line 72), suggesting that Spenser had in mind his own impending nuptials three weeks later and the separation of the friends after many years together.[128] He then refers to the journey that he thought he would have to take, wishing that he had Harvey's ability to understand what is useful as well as what is delightful, concluding: 'Ibimus ergo statim: (quis eunti fausta precetur?) | Et pede Clivosas fesso calcabimus Alpes' (We shall go then at once (who wishes me Godspeed at going?); | We shall press our worn feet up the jagged defiles of the Alps') (lines 98–9). As John Hale notes, 'It is difficult to exaggerate the broad sense in which the Alps were felt to divide a northern, transalpine world from a southern, temperamentally and culturally conditioned Mediterranean one', so Spenser's sense of the significance of the journey is easy to understand.[129] He never travelled outside the British Isles.

Presumably Spenser brought forward the date of his wedding when he learned that he was not going abroad to France: perhaps the opportunity to go to Ireland in 1580 had already arisen. The poem concludes with a lament that the two friends will not be able to exchange letters as easily in the future, and a confirmation of their lasting friendship:

> Harueiusque bonus, (charus licet omnibus vnus,)
> Angelus & Gabriel, (quamuis comitatus amicis
> Innumeris, geniûmque choro stipatus amæno)
> *Immerito* tamen vnum absentem sæpe requiret,
> Optabitque, Vtinam meus hîc *Edmundus* adesset,
> Qui noua scripsisset, nec Amores conticuisset,
> Ipse suos, & sæpe animo, verbisque benignis
> Fausta precaretur, Deus illum aliquando reducat, &c. (lines 105–12)

> [My good Harvey (howbeit equally dear to us all,
> And with reason, since alone almost sweeter than all of the rest),
> Angel and Gabriel both,—though surrounded by friends

> Who are countless, attended by a gracious circle of talents,
> Yet for Immerito, the only one absent, will often inquire
> And murmur the wish, 'Would Heaven my Edmund were here.
> He would have written me news, nor himself have been silent
> Regarding his love, and often, in his heart and with words
> Of the kindest, would bless me. May God guide him hither once more.' Etc.]

Spenser's poem values and celebrates the enduring friendship between the two men and is a public record of his gratitude to Harvey. It is also—as there is throughout the interrelated volumes the *Letters* and the *Calender*—a recognition of the end of its most intimate stage, as the lives of the two men are about to change. Male friendship was often represented in terms of marriage, and the two relationships were explored together in a number of influential treatises.[130] Accordingly, Spenser imagines Harvey pining for him even when immersed in the good fellowship of other close friends.

Books of neo-Latin literature, which circulated among the tightly knit circles of poets and learned societies, and their reflections on how to transform the poor state of literature in English owed much to a desire to emulate the sophistication of European poetry in Latin. Spenser, as we know from the *Letters*, claimed to be a member of a group called the Areopagus who held such discussions. In the letter to Harvey dated 15 October Spenser stated that

> The twoo worthy Gentlemen, Master *Sidney*, and Master *Dyer*, they haue me, I thanke them, in some vse of familiarity: of whom, and to whome, what speache passeth for youre credite and estimation, I leaue your selfe to conceiue, hauing always so well conceiued of my vnfained affection, and zeale towards you. Ane nowe they haue proclaimed in their ἀρείω πάγω, a general surceasing and silence of balde Rymers, and also of the verie beste to: in steade whereof, they haue by authoritie of their whole Senate, prescribed certaine Lawes and rules of Quantities of English syllables, for English Verse: hauing had thereof already greate practise, and drawen mee to their faction.[131]

The description is characterized by the familiar, intimate tone of the letters, designed to please and flatter Harvey, and with a considerable element of exaggeration. No one could imagine that the small band of poets discussing matters really had a 'whole Senate' whose advice they sought, especially as only two poets are mentioned—although claims have been made that others, notably Sir John Conway (d. 1603), occasional poet, and father of John Donne's friend, Sir Edward Conway (c.1564–1631) played a part in the group.[132] Furthermore, it is likely that Spenser is exaggerating his relationship with Sidney, especially given the following sentences: 'Newe Bookes I heare of none, but only of one, that writing a certaine Booke, called *The Schoole of Abuse*, and dedicating it to Maister *Sidney*, was for hys labor scorned: if at leaste it be in the goodnesse of that nature to scorne. Suche follie is it, not to regarde aforehande the inclination and qualitie of him, to whome wee dedicate oure Bookes.'[133] This allusion to Sidney's anger at Stephen Gosson's foolish dedication, the ostensible reason for writing the *Apologie for Poetry*, has the appearance of personal knowledge—which may, of course, be real—and the link between the two sections of the letter is indeed the figure of Sidney.[134] But the letter, which is our only real knowledge of the existence of the Areopagus, might perhaps be read best as a mirror image of Harvey's efforts to ingratiate himself into the favours of the good and the great, or, more likely still, a gentle parody of Harvey's behaviour, Spenser realizing that discussions between poets were nowhere near the formal level of a classical society.

It is true, however, that both Sidney and Sir Edward Dyer (1543–1607), a courtier poet central to the Leicester circle and close to Sidney and Fulke Greville, were present at Audley End on 26–7 July 1578 when the queen made her progress, where she was entertained by her subjects.[135] Prominent among them was Gabriel Harvey, who did already know Sidney, having read through three books of Livy with him, so he must have been the link between Spenser and the courtier poet.[136] Harvey made the most of his opportunity at Audley End, taking part in two philosophical disputations in Latin and presenting four manuscripts of his Latin verse to a series of powerful figures. Book I is addressed to Elizabeth; Book II to Leicester; Book III to Burghley; and Book IV to Oxford, Hatton, and Sidney. The volume was published as *Gartulationes Valdinenses* in September by Henry Bynemann, who had published the *Theatre for Voluptuous Worldlings* nine years earlier, as well as a host of other works by Harvey.[137] It is therefore likely that Spenser did have some conversations about poetry with Sidney and Dyer, as he states later in his second letter to Harvey of 2 April 1580:

I would hartily wish, you would either send me the Rules and Precepts of Arte, which you obserue in Quantities, or else followe mine, that *M. Philip Sidney* gaue me, being the very same which *M. Drant* deuised, but enlarged with *M. Sidneys* own iudgement, and augmented with my Obseruations, that we might both accorde and agree in one: leatse we ouerthrowe one an other, and be ouerthrown of the rest. Truste me, you will hardly beleeue what greate good liking and estimation Maister *Dyer* had of youre *Satiricall Verses*, and I, since the viewe thereof, hauing before of my selfe had speciall liking of *Englishe Versifying*, am euen nowe aboute to giue you some token, what, and howe well therein I am able to doe: for, to tell you trueth, I minde shortely at conuenient leysure, to sette forth a Booke in this kinde, whyche I entitle, *Epithalamion Thamesis*, whyche Booke I dare vndertake wil be very profitable for the knowledge, and rare for the Inuention, and manner of handling.[138]

Spenser openly advertises his connections to Sidney and Dyer, emphasizing their close relationship. The comment about Harvey's satirical verse receiving praise from Dyer again reads as if the pupil is showing the master that he is in charge. The praise of Harvey needs to be read in terms of Spenser's claim that he received Sidney's copy of Thomas Drant's work on art and quantitative metre, annotated by Sidney himself, an exchange of books that mirrors the Harvey–Spenser exchanges.[139] Perhaps this was Drant's well-known translation of Horace's *Art of Poetry*, *Satires*, and *Verse Epistles* published in 1567; more likely it is a lost work.[140]

It is hard to read the evidence and to assume that there was a close-knit circle of writers given the ways in which we need to read the public pronouncements of both Spenser and Harvey. The situation is made more complex because there was a group called the Areopagus in Florence earlier in the sixteenth century, referred to by William Thomas and cited by Harvey.[141] Therefore, it is possible that this group of English writers did meet on occasions in 1579—and perhaps earlier—probably as a result of their first meeting at Audley End. On 14 January 1579 Daniel Rogers, who may again have played a key role in facilitating this group, sent a poem to Sidney describing Sidney's friends as 'a happy band of like-minded fellows', perhaps seeking admission to the group.[142]

The group was probably a casual symposium of individuals that Spenser made seem more formal, perhaps even leading to its dissolution by making it public in the *Letters*, or acknowledging that its work was done, although possibly the term was used facetiously to mean 'any group of persons which exercised judiciary authority'.[143] What seems to have united the group is an interest in avant-garde verse, a desire to move English literature forward particularly through experiments with quantitative metre.[144] Certainly the *Letters* had a significant impact in terms of this mode of writing poetry, because in his pioneering translation of Virgil in quantitative metre, Richard Stanihurst refers the reader to Harvey's comments, having read them, even though he does not know who Harvey is.[145] Again, this might suggest that the Areopagus really existed in the terms exchanged between Spenser and Harvey.

Spenser's earliest letter to Harvey contains Spenser's only known poem in quantitative verse, 'Iambicum Trimetrum', a work which advertises its experimental function and which can be scanned as follows:

Unhappie Verse, the witnesse of my unhappie state,

Make thy selfe flutt[e]ring wings of thy fast flying

Thought, and fly forth unto my Love, wheresoever she be:

Whether lying reastlesse in heavy bedde, or else

Playing alone carelesse on hir heauenlie Virginals.

If in Bed, tell hir, that my eyes can take no reste:

If at Boorde, tell hir, that my mouth can eate no meate:

If at hir Virginals, tel hir, I can heare no mirth.[146]

Derek Attridge notes that this is the sole poem in quantitative metre by either Harvey or Spenser that 'is of any value . . . perhaps because . . . it imposes less severe restraints than most quantitative metres'.[147] Even so, the lyric, which consists of twenty-one unrhymed lines, is much less sophisticated than poetry Spenser had published a decade previously, and it is hard to believe that he saw this poem as an important work or anything other than a formal exercise. The verse, with its conspicuous and rather clumsy rhetorical patterning, employing the device of anaphora (repeating the sequence of words at the beginning of clause), reads like the parodic rhetoric

employed by Thomas Kyd, another of Mulcaster's famous pupils, at key points in
The Spanish Tragedy (*c.*1589). Responding to the terrible news of his son's death,
Hieronimo laments:

> O eyes, no eyes, but fountains fraught with tears;
> O life, no life, but lively form of death;
> O world, no world, but mass of public wrongs,
> Confus'd and fill'd with murder and misdeeds;
> O sacred heavens! If this unhallow'd deed,
> If this inhuman and barbarous attempt,
> If this incomparable murder thus
> Of mine, but now no more my son,
> Shall unreveal'd and unrevenged pass,
> How should we term your dealings to be just,
> If you unjustly deal with those that in your justice trust?[148]

If there is any link between these two passages, perhaps they each originate in a
common education in rhetorical practice, as well as dramatic performance, both of
which were particular interests of Mulcaster.[149] Perhaps Spenser's poem is far less
serious than has been realized, even a cheeky tilt at the principles of the master,
although it was reproduced in full in Abraham Fraunce's *Arcadian Rhetoric* (1588),
one of the earliest serious studies of Spenser's poetry by a member of the Sidney
circle.[150] Fraunce, who seems to have had access to a manuscript copy of *The Faerie
Queene* in 1586–7, was eager to show how English poetry was in line with and
reproduced the principles of Ramist logic.[151] According to Fraunce, Spenser's
poem illustrates the combination of iambic and spondaic metre.[152]

Distinct signs in the *Letters* suggest that neither writer any longer believes in the
quantitative verse project. In his reply, Harvey subjects Spenser's poem to a long
critique, starting with the unpromising opening comment, 'Your Englishe *Trimetra*
I lyke better, than perhappes you will easily beleeue', which indicates that neither
student nor master was confident that they were producing fascinating, significant
literature. Harvey's critique is based on his understanding that the metre is faulty:
'I finde not your warrant so sufficiently good, and substauntiall in Lawe, that it can
persuade me, they are all, so precisely perfect for the Feete, as your selfe ouer-partially
weene, and ouer-confidently auoche.'[153] Harvey concludes that, unfortunately,
proper poetry runs like 'A good horse, that trippeth not once in a iourney', and
quantitative metre cannot work like this, so 'perhappes the Errour may rather
proceede of his Master, *M. Drantes* Rule, than of himselfe [i.e., Immerito]'.[154]
The signs are that the quantitative verse movement was a serious discussion in the
late 1570s, especially in the wake of the commitment to the reform of orthography
and the correct teaching of ancient languages proposed by Smith and Mulcaster, the

two most influential intellectual influences on Harvey and Spenser.[155] Indeed, Smith and Mulcaster possibly knew each other and argued about the merits of the preservation of custom versus programmatic reform of spelling. It is likely that Stubborn, the good-natured but wrong-headed disputant who defends customary usage in Smith's *De Recta et Emendata Linguae Anbglicae Scriptione* (*A Dialogue of the Correct and Improved Writing of English*) (1568), is a representation of Mulcaster, who would therefore have been debating with Smith while teaching Spenser.[156]

The most successful quantitative verse experiments are those of Sidney, because he had such a keen interest in the pronunciation of Latin and its effect on metre.[157] But it was also clear—perhaps less so to Stanihurst—that the movement had run out of steam before 1580 and that other ways of writing English verse had to be tried if English literature was to move forward and rival the ancients and other European countries with more established poetic traditions and reputations, such as France and Italy, and, to a lesser extent, Spain and Germany. Straightforward imitation and direct reproduction of style and metre would not translate easily from one language to another. In any case, even if the loosely affiliated group had wished to continue discussing matters, events were about to intervene that broke them up, as they undoubtedly realized would be the case with a number of ambitious and restless men with an eye open for an opportunity, as well as the simple need to make a living.

Indeed, whilst these debates were taking place Spenser's life changed. He probably moved to north Kent to work for John Young at some point in 1578, perhaps joining his new employer when he was consecrated as bishop of Rochester on 16 March 1578.[158] Spenser remained in the bishop's service until the middle of the following year when the correspondence with Harvey indicates that he had entered—or returned to—the service of Leicester, signing his address as 'Leycester House'.[159] This marks out the period of employment as especially important for Spenser, who was at work on the *Calender* while he was in Young's service. The work could even have been written and conceived in the year or so that he worked for Young: certainly it bears the stamp of that experience.[160] The two works are designed to be read together, part of a literary game that works through the pretence that they were independent when they were nothing of the sort.

Young's official residence was in Bromley, the nearest town to London in the diocese of Rochester, the second oldest diocese in England after Canterbury, chosen to give the bishop access to the capital as well as his parishioners (Plate 9).[161] In Tudor times Bromley was a small town surrounded by woods and countryside only ten miles from London with a population of about 700, which as late as 1797 could be described as a 'pleasant market town' with 'two principal streets'.[162] Young also held other benefices, including a prebend in Westminster (a position which would have provided him with an income from the cathedral estates but did not involve onerous duties), and the income from the rectory at St Magnus the Martyr church in London, a building Spenser would have known, as it is near the Tower of London. Acting as a secretary to a bishop was a relatively good job—certainly Spenser was able to move on to another lucrative secretarial position soon afterwards. A cathedral, even one that was relatively small like Rochester, would have supported a community of clerics, administrative staff, and other employees, and working and living in one would have resembled living in an Oxbridge college.[163]

It is possible that Spenser may have considered a career in the church, like his college friend, Edward Kirk, and he later received a prebend in Ireland, which may have been more than a sinecure.[164] If so, he must have either changed his mind or found that a better opportunity presented itself when he had the chance to work as a secretary in Ireland. But, given the tone and style of the *Letters* in particular, it is more likely that Spenser was simply following a career at a time when means of support were few and far between and had to be taken when the opportunity arose, and that his real desire was for a literary career. Harvey, in *Rhetor*, assumed that his audience of Cambridge students would serve the goddess Eloquence as 'secretaries, scribes, priests, ambassadors, councillors, and in other noble and honored positions'.[165] The career of Anthony Harison (1563–1638), a well-documented case of an ecclesiastical secretary, for example, suggests that ordination was often the reward for good service, not the result of a vocation.[166] With limited career opportunities, joining the church would always be an option for anyone with a degree, if not necessarily a vocation, as the career choices of John Donne demonstrate.[167] Spenser certainly had an impressive knowledge of theology, church government, ecclesiology, and the practical importance of Christian ethics and practical living, but this probably came in part from his employment as well as his education, and it does not mark him out as different from many other highly educated writers, or suggest that he was a frustrated cleric.

As a bishop's secretary Spenser would have had to deal with civil law, derived from the Roman code of Justinian, which had largely replaced canon law after the Reformation, although civil lawyers were often the targets of attacks from puritans as administrators of 'Catholic' law.[168] The aim of civil law was always to provide a means of settling disputes through the formulation of general principles, rather than the study of previous cases, which was the basis of the common law. After 1545 doctors of civil law could exercise ecclesiastical jurisdiction.[169] Many senior ecclesiastical figures were, unsurprisingly, qualified civil lawyers.[170] Under Elizabeth, as had been the case in Henry's reign, the bishops were able to administer the ecclesiastical courts as long as they provided judgements in line with the royal supremacy.[171] The bishop would run a Consistory court for his diocese, which his secretary would help administer. The Consistory court dealt mainly with routine ecclesiastical matters, such as ordination, consecration, and the distribution of ecclesiastical property; questions of legitimate religious belief, and offences against religion, principally heresy; and offences against morals, which might include 'adultery, procuration, incontinency, incest, defamation, sorcery, witchcraft, misbehaviour in church, neglect to attend church, swearing, profaning the Sabbath, blasphemy, drunkenness, haunting taverns, heretical opinions, profaning the church, usury, ploughing up the church path'.[172] For many of these reasons ecclesiastical courts were frequently known as 'bawdy courts'. Prosecutions proceeded through inquisition and denunciation, and Spenser would have been directly involved in a number of such cases, giving him detailed knowledge of other peoples' behaviour, as well as marriage, inheritance, and legitimacy.[173]

It is unlikely that Spenser studied for a higher degree in civil law, which would have been time-consuming, and he probably acquired expertise in civil law as he worked. Such experience would have been of great benefit when he went to Ireland and might well have been an important reason why he was offered the post of secretary to Lord Grey. It also helps to explain why he was able to work for a number of different courts—including church courts—in Dublin, and why he took the lead role in his second wife's legal affairs in the 1590s. Trials in ecclesiastical courts, like Chancery, and unlike the general administration of the common law, were heavily based on the delivery of testimony. Spenser would have become used to hearing pleas and would therefore have learned how to present, as well as assess, the merits of a case himself, as is obvious from the legal documents with which he is associated and, more pertinently, his writing.[174] He would also have become familiar with the issues surrounding inheritance disputes, something that would concern his family in the 1590s.[175] Kent was one of the most organized and ordered counties in England and its legal officers had an acute understanding of their roles, not least because of the influence of William Lambarde, who became a justice of the peace in 1579.[176] The experience of working in the county would have provided Spenser with a thorough legal knowledge and understanding of local government.

Spenser never states where he lived in this period, but the fact that he returned to London to meet Harvey in December 1578 suggests that he was probably based mainly in Bromley. But he would also have spent some time in Rochester, about twenty-five miles away, especially in the magnificent Norman cathedral (Plate 10), and the castle, opposite, built as a defence of the Medway towns by Bishop Gundulf, who was also responsible for the plans for the Tower of London, in 1080.[177] The lost work *Epithalamion Thamesis* must have been begun in this period, inspired by the sense of the national and strategic importance of the two rivers joining as their estuaries opened out into the North Sea, just east of the capital.[178] The imposing estuary of the Medway as it opens out into the North Sea dominates the view of anyone looking north from the cathedral or castle at Rochester. Spenser refers to the Medway in the July eclogue of the *Calender*, a poem with a number of allusions to north Kent.[179] Furthermore, it is worth noting that the estate of

Penshurst, the Sidney family home, went up to the Medway, something acknowl-
edged in Ben Jonson's poem, 'To Penshurst' and noted by Camden in *Britannia*.[180]
Spenser dedicated the *Calender* to Sir Philip, a sign that he was looking to the
Sidney family for support in the late 1570s.[181]

In the July eclogue Spenser represents the river as the younger brother of the
Thames (lines 81–4), but in *The Faerie Queene* the river has changed sex and has
become a bride, the nuptials celebrated in a river-marriage poem, a genre established
by William Camden in his Latin work *De Connubio Tamae et Isis*, ultimately derived
from the use of lists in epic poetry.[182] The Medway's forthcoming union is an event
which symbolizes the establishment of a world order with England at the centre:

> It fortun'd then, a solemne feast was there
> To all the Sea-gods and their fruitfull seede,
> In honour of the spousalls, which then were
> Betwixt the *Medway* and the *Thames* agreed.
> Long had the *Thames* (as we in records reed)
> Before that day her wooed to his bed;
> But the proud Nymph would for no worldly meed,
> Nor no entreatie to his loue be led;
> Till now at last relenting, she to him was wed.
>
> So both agreed, that this their bridale feast
> Should for the Gods in *Proteus* house be made;
> To which they all repayr'd, both most and least,
> Aswell which in the mightie Ocean trade,
> As that in riuers swim, or brookes doe wade.
> All which not if an hundred tongues to tell,
> And hundred mouthes, and voice of brasse I had,
> And endlesse memorie, that mote excell,
> In order as they came, could I recount them well. (8–9)

When published in 1596 the apparent harmony of the marriage was shrouded with
fraught anxiety and ironies: England might have seemed the centre of the world to
many, but it was under siege from hostile Catholic enemies; its own future was
uncertain because of the queen's refusal to marry; holding the feast in Proteus'
house connoted terrifying, uncontrolled change rather than a positive transformation,
given that Proteus was the endlessly mutable sea-god who was impossible to pin
down; and, perhaps most pointedly, the numerous tongues that the narrator conjures
up seem to suggest a celebration but might also indicate cacophony and an absence of
unity and harmony, at odds with the purpose of the ceremony. Certainly, when
Spenser provides us with images of multi-tongued creatures elsewhere in his work
they are hostile creatures eager to undermine established order, like the barking

mouths of the Blatant Beast which first slanders Artegall, the Knight of Justice in Book V of *The Faerie Queene*, and later threatens to engulf the poet's words with a plethora of lies.[183] How the first version of the poem looked we cannot, of course, know, but it is unlikely to have been a straightforward celebration of England's glorious geography, given the tone and style of the *Calender*. Nevertheless, it is clear that Spenser, like most poets, made use of the immediate world around him, using the English landscape as he was later to use the Irish and, as in this example, often combining his observations of the two.[184]

During his time as Young's secretary Spenser would have made some new acquaintances. He may possibly have met Stephen Bateman (*c*.1542–84), the son of Dutch immigrants, who became the librarian for Mathew Parker, archbishop of Canterbury from 1558 until his death, when Edmund Grindal succeeded him.[185] Parker and Spenser's employer were closely allied within the church hierarchy. Bateman lived in Parker's household in Lambeth Palace and claimed that he had collected some 6,700 books for Parker, perhaps another library to which Spenser had access in this period.[186] Bateman was also the author of *The Trauayled Pylgrime* (1569), an allegorical religious romance of the life of a good Christian adapted to an English setting from the French of Olivier de La Marche (*c*.1426–1502), which concludes with the author's own death, once he has seen Elizabeth established as the champion of Protestantism against the papist Antichrist.[187] Bateman's work was the only 'significant nondramatic Protestant quest allegory before Spenser', and a work which had an obvious impact on *The Faerie Queene*.[188]

Family connections may also have been important. A case has been made that Spenser could have been related to another branch of the Spenser family, those at Wroughton in Wiltshire, one of whom was a cleric. A contemporary Spenser was Thomas Spenser, archdeacon of Chichester from 1559 until the 1570s, who was ordained by Grindal after he returned from exile, and who would have had a number of acquaintances in common with Edmund, notably Thomas Drant and Alexander Nowell. In a letter of 19 November 1567, Grindal recommended Thomas Spenser to Cecil as a possible bishop of Armagh.[189]

Thomas Spenser would have had considerable dealings with another key figure in Edmund Spenser's early career, Thomas Watts.[190] Watts had taken part in the visitations of the Merchant Taylors' School at least twice between 1562 and 1565.[191] He took a similar ecclesiastical line to Grindal, opposing the imposition of cape and surplice, but believed that church unity was more important than doctrinal belief, arguing that obedience to the crown had to come before individual conscience in this case.[192] He was also important as the benefactor who established the Watts Greek Scholarships financing the university careers of Spenser's fellow pupils, Lancelot Andrewes and Thomas Dove, probably through his close relationship to Grindal and Young.[193] Watts appointed Grindal as executor of his will with his wife, Grace, which he made on 23 May 1577, just before he died. Alexander Nowell was to be one of the overseers.[194] Watts cemented his close links to Pembroke by leaving the college his impressive library of Hebrew, Greek, and books in other languages, as well as copies of Erasmus' complete works, and histories by Polydore Vergil and Richard Grafton.[195]

In March 1578, soon after Watts's death, Grace married Young, a union that coincided with his consecration as bishop of Rochester, a relatively poor bishopric overshadowed by its neighbour, Canterbury.[196] Spenser, therefore, had a number of links to Young through his school and university friendship with Harvey, and, possibly, family connections.[197] He may even have attended the wedding. While the exact links that led to Spenser's appointment are probably impossible to untangle with any precision, it is clear that a tightly knit group anchored in educational and ecclesiastical institutions worked to procure a placement for one of their own when a position became available, exactly what we should expect in early modern England.[198]

It is hard to estimate how close Spenser was to Young. The published correspondence with Harvey indicates that both Spenser and Harvey knew a number of prominent academics. However, many of these were not a great deal older than either of them, whereas Young was about twenty years older than both, halfway between Harvey and Spenser and Sir Thomas Smith, and he had been master of Pembroke while Spenser was an undergraduate. It is hard to imagine that they were very close, and Spenser's representation of Young as Roffy in the *Calender* would appear to indicate, at best, qualified respect for an older man rather than warm friendship. In the September eclogue, Diggon Davie, a poor honest shepherd who has just returned from further afield where he lost his flock to rapacious 'Popish prelates', offers to tell Hobbinol what he has learned of Roffyn's recent adventures.[199] Hobbinol describes Roffyn as 'meeke, wise, and merciable' (line 174), but the anecdote suggests a more complex picture:

> Thilk same shepheard mought I well marke:
> He has a Dogge to byte or to barke,
> Neuer had shepheard so kene a kurre,
> That waketh, and if but a leafe sturre.
> Whilome there wonned a wicked Wolfe,
> That with many a Lambe had glutted his gulfe.
> And euer at night wont to repayre
> Vnto the flocke, when the Welkin shone faire,
> Ycladde in clothing of seely sheepe,
> When the good old man vsed to sleepe.
> Tho at midnight he would barke and ball,
> (For he had eft learned a curres call.)
> As if a Woolfe were emong the sheepe.

> With that the shepheard would breake his sleepe,
> And send out Lowder (for so his dog hote)
> To raunge the fields with wide oppen throte.
> Tho when as Lowder was farre awaye,
> This Woluish sheepe would catchen his pray,
> A Lambe, or a Kidde, or a weanell wast:
> With that to the wood would he speede him fast.
> Long time he vsed this slippery pranck,
> Ere Roffy could for his laboure him thanck.
> At end the shepheard his practise spyed,
> (For Roffy is wise, and as Argus eyed)
> And when at euen he came to the flocke,
> Fast in theyr folds he did them locke,
> And tooke out the Woolfe in his counterfect cote,
> And let out the sheepes bloud at his throte. (lines 180–207)

This praise of Roffyn is perhaps more double-edged than has been noted, and Diggon Davie's description of the relationship between Roffyn and his dog, Lowder, certainly makes them sound rather like Artegall and Talus in *The Faerie Queene*, Book V, rooting out dissent and opposition with ruthless efficiency.[200] Lowder was probably a reference to a real figure, most likely a chancellor or an archdeacon, the two church officers most closely related to the bishop and responsible for implementing his policies in the diocese, although the records for the Rochester diocese are poor for this period.[201] The episode perhaps refers to Spenser's experience of the ecclesiastical courts in Rochester.

The final line cited here seems ambiguous, suggesting that Roffyn cuts the wolf's throat, which then sprays out sheep's blood. It recalls an incident early on in *The History of Reynard the Fox*, a book Spenser would have known, as it was one of the sources for *Mother Hubberds Tale*, when Reynard, disguised as a priest, seizes Cuwart the Cat by the throat, while pretending to teach him the Credo.[202] On the one hand Spenser's tale might be read as triumphalist Protestant rhetoric, gloating over the fate of the true church's enemies.[203] This reading would certainly be in line with Young's own unqualified support of the queen's ecclesiastical settlement.[204] But on the other, the episode might suggest that even wolves are part sheep, indicating the complex post-Reformation world which so many people found hard to understand and negotiate, unsure who they could trust, which of their former neighbours and friends were now heretics and, worst of all, what was the truth and what was heresy.[205] The wolves are not quite what they seem, even when stripped bare.[206]

Neither is a shepherd who lets a dog with 'wide oppen throte' roam the fields at night hunting out those who threaten his flock. The description of Roffyn as 'Argus eyed' and prepared to do whatever it takes to root out heresy does not make him an obviously attractive character, despite the apparently positive description of him as a 'good old man'. It is also hard to square the final line cited above with Hobbinol's judgement that Roffyn is 'meeke, wise, and merciable', when he tears open the throat of the disguised wolf himself. The truth may be that perilous times demanded a vigilance that not everyone would understand or appreciate, and Spenser worked for Young nearly a decade after Pius' 'Regnans in Excelsis' had demanded violent opposition to Elizabeth. The Northern Rebellion (1569–70), the Ridolfi Plot (1570), and the execution of Thomas Howard, fourth duke of Norfolk (2 June 1572), had been followed by the first entry of Catholic missionaries into England in 1574, a campaign that was to become more concerted and threatening in the 1580s after the arrival of the first Jesuits.[207]

Perhaps a knowledge of and desire to suppress Catholic activity in Kent and the south-east of England, one of the more literate and obviously Protestant regions of England, lie behind Spenser's lines.[208] Another possibility is that Spenser is referring to Young's hostile comments on the Family of Love, published as a series of notes at the start of William Wilkinson's *A Confutation of Certaine Articles deliuered unto the Familye of Loue.*[209] Wilkinson's work appeared in 1579, the same year as the *Calender*, when Spenser left the Bishop's service. It was published by John Day and announced Young's contribution on the title page: 'Herunto are prefixed By the right reverend Father in God I. Y. Byshop of Rochester, certaine notes collected out of their Gospell, and answered by the Fam.' Young's comments had been written earlier and answered by a Familist, then reprinted by Wilkinson. Wilkinson (c.1551–1613), who had been a student at St John's College, Cambridge, while Spenser was at Pembroke (Wilkinson matriculated in 1571), was now a schoolteacher in Cambridge and fellow of his college.[210] He was clearly determined to root out what he saw as the dangerous heresy of the Family of Love because the sect undermined Christian doctrine through its belief in human perfectibility and toleration of Catholicism. English Familists mainly flourished in Cambridgeshire, but they also had a significant presence in many other parts of south-east England.[211]

Young's particular objection to the Familists was that they failed to make proper distinctions and so blurred and confused established boundaries: worst of all, they tolerated Catholics and did not perceive the real danger that the papacy posed to English religion.[212] In his comments Wilkinson makes a series of more sustained objections: the Familists believe that everyone can be a preacher whereas only a small number of the godly were called to serve Christ; they fail to distinguish between true and false brethren and so are prepared to tolerate heretics such as Anabaptists as well as Catholics; they insist on regarding marriage as a sacrament even though it was no longer an official belief of the reformed church; they disguise their true beliefs and so are untrustworthy; and they think that Adam committed no sin in eating the apple from the tree of knowledge, only Eve, which means that mankind can be perfected without God's intervention.[213] Young is particularly critical of the opinion that the Church of Rome is not Satanic:

First, he calleth the Church of Rome, the communion of all Christians, whereas it is but a particular Church fallen away from the universall Church of Christ...

But most plainly the Author showeth him selfe a frend to the Church of Rome, saying: that many, through contention and discorde did cast of the Church of Rome, and dyd blaspheme her with her ministeries, and of their owne, pretendyng the Scriptures haue brought in other ministeries and Religion: they spoke much of the word of God. Who doubteth that this is the voice and iudgement of Papistes against Protestauntes and true Christians.[214]

For Young, the Familists represent a real danger to Protestant England, and it is a priority to stop them infecting the nation's social fabric.

Others voiced this opinion throughout Elizabeth's reign—notably Hatton and Leicester—but no action was ever really taken against the Family of Love, even though many agreed that Familists held heretical views and were rather too close to Catholics in their beliefs.[215] The truth is that they simply never posed a real threat and there were far too many other aggressively oppositional groups to worry about—from Jesuits to puritans. Instead, the Family were left alone, and many of its members became respectable, often relatively affluent members of provincial society.[216] It is hard to imagine that Spenser does not have Young's comments on the Family of Love in mind for the September eclogue given when they were published (which may not, of course, tell the whole story). However, his representation of the bishop is far more nuanced than has generally been realized.[217] This suggests that despite the common background that Spenser, Harvey, and Young shared, or, even, the close friendship between Harvey and Spenser, they did not necessarily agree on everything, as the Harvey–Spenser *Letters* indicate. Spenser had known a number of Familists in London, and may have felt that Young's attack was harsh, misconceived, or even unwarranted. The image of the bishop as a shepherd with an aggressive dog, whose open jaws he imitates when killing the wolf in sheep's clothing, is not a comfortable one for the reader to appreciate and does not tally with the description of the bishop as meek and full of mercy. It also specifies how the *Calender* is a nuanced and provocative ecclesiastical work presenting the difficult nature of argument without providing easy answers—yet another reason why its publication was such a momentous event in the history of English literature, and why it needs to be read carefully and cautiously as evidence for Spenser's life in these lost years.

4

Annus Mirabilis

JULY 1579 TO OCTOBER 1580 was perhaps the most important period in Spenser's life. He was back in London in the summer of 1579, as an unpublished letter preserved in Harvey's *Letter-Book* demonstrates, possibly still in the employment of the bishop of Rochester, but had probably moved on to something else.[1] The second line of the poem, 'To His Booke', prefacing the *Calender*, refers to the poem as 'child whose parent is vnkent [unknown]', surely a reference to his having left the county and so being not in Kent any more.[2] By July 1580 he had got married, and published his first two major works, *The Shepheardes Calender* and his *Letters* with Harvey, before moving to Ireland as the secretary to the new Lord Deputy, Arthur, Lord Grey de Wilton, which was to become his permanent home until his death. While it would have been clear to many readers that Harvey was the author of his letters, which are addressed and signed 'G. H.' and 'G.', and give his residence as Trinity Hall, Cambridge, it would not have been immediately obvious to many readers that the unknown Edmund Spenser was the pseudonymous 'Immerito', the unworthy, or Colin Clout, the plain-spoken husbandman-poet represented in the works of John Skelton, the most important English poet after Chaucer.[3]

In part Spenser's anonymity was the familiar topos of the young author seeking approval before revealing his identity; in part it was a game played with the reader, teasing him or her to determine his identity from the information provided within the texts themselves.[4] Certainly, many early readers, including Sir Philip Sidney, to whom the *Calender* was dedicated, either did not know or chose not to reveal the author's identity.[5] Even an experienced writer such as George Whetstone (*c*.1550–87) thought that Sidney had written the *Calender* when he wrote his tribute to a fellow soldier-poet, *Sir Phillip Sidney, his honorable life, his valiant death, and true vertues* (1587).[6] Nevertheless, in the course of the year Spenser changed from an obscure figure, largely dependent on Harvey, to a married man with a steady income, prospects, and a serious track record as a writer. In fact, as the *Calender* makes absolutely clear, especially when read in conjunction with the *Letters*, Spenser believed he had the ability to transform English poetry and provide it with a range and substance it had hitherto lacked.

Although it is certainly topical in key places, the *Calender* is a complex and intricate book, and Spenser might have been working on it as a project ever since he left Cambridge, even if he did complete the writing relatively rapidly in the late 1570s. The *Calender* is one of the most innovative works in English literary history, something that suggests a long gestation in the 1570s, demonstrating a formidable knowledge of English, European, and classical books. The sophisticated balance of poetic text, notes, commentary, letters, with the critical apparatus reading like part of an exchange between equals, indicates that the poems have developed out of an intellectual milieu that looked back to the humanist ideal of the 'republic of letters', one the text itself has deliberately constructed. Spenser does not simply know what is contained within a wide variety of works, but has clearly worked hard on the form, style, and appearance of printed books, making use of his friendship with Harvey and Harvey's relationship to London printers and publishers, as well as literary patrons.[7] Each eclogue is prefaced by a woodcut, relatively crudely produced, but an integral and important part of the work that has to be related to the text. As Ruth Samson Luborsky has pointed out, no other poet had produced a text that had anything like such accompanying illustrations—apart, of course, from Spenser himself in *A Theatre*. Yet, given their poor quality, 'the cuts must have seemed quaint' to the first readers of the poem.[8] Was this a deliberate ploy? Or was it simply that the publisher, Hugh Singleton, was not an especially sophisticated printer?[9] There is a substantial commentary to every eclogue, a series of notes by the already mysterious E. K., which forces the reader to consider whether the notes are genuine, misleading, or a combination of the two. The text itself is carefully produced in a combination of typefaces: black-letter or English type for the poetry, roman for the paratexts, head-notes, notes, and commentary.[10]

In the prefatory epistle to Harvey, 'E. K.' explains that he has access to the intimate thoughts of the anonymous poet, and so is in an especially good position to write the notes to the poem:

I thought good to take the paines vpon me, the rather for that by meanes of some familiar acquaintance I was made priuie to his counsel and secret meaning in them, as also in sundry other works of his. Which albeit I know he nothing so much hateth, as to promulgate, yet thus much haue I aduentured vpon his friendship, him selfe being for long time estraunged, hoping that this will the rather occasion to him, to put forth diuers other excellent works of his, which slepe in silence, as his Dreames, his Legendes, his Court of Cupide, and sundry others; whose commendations to set out, were verye vayne; the thinges though worthy of many, yet being knowen to few.[11]

The supposed judgements of E. K. are clearly an advertisement, by way of a tease or challenge to the reader, for the value of the works of the anonymous author, attempting to create an audience for them when they are published. The author of the letter lets the reader know that he could describe the poems if he so wished, and does indeed recommend them to the reader as literature that should be more widely known, but to do so now would be 'verye vayne'. The modesty topos of dedications is wittily reversed and adapted to promote the *Calender* and future work.

There is no reason to doubt that the works described by E. K. did really exist: there are dreams in *The Faerie Queene*, notably those of Arthur and the Red-Cross Knight in Book I, and in the 'Letter to Ralegh' appended to the first edition, Spenser describes Arthur as having seen 'in a dream or vision the Faery Queen'.[12] The legends could be a number of works that were gathered together and eventually published in *The Complaints* (1591), or the British history sections in Books II and III of *The Faerie Queene*; the Court of Cupid must surely be the first version of the Masque performed for Amoret as the climax of Book III of *The Faerie Queene*. We know that Spenser was at work on his poetry throughout his life, through the testimonies of others such as Harvey and Lodowick Bryskett. Furthermore, if he had not been writing consistently it would have been impossible for him to have published so much work in the 1590s, when virtually everything he wrote apart from the *Calender* and the two short letters to Harvey was produced within the space of six years (1590–6).

Furthermore, E. K. provides a note that alerts the reader to the importance of the poet's unpublished work. Providing a gloss to the names Nectar and Ambrosia in the November eclogue, E. K. explains that they are 'feigned to be the drink and foode of the gods', adding that he has 'already discoursed that at large in my Commentarye vpon the dreames of the same Authour'.[13] Not only has Spenser produced a series of poems that deserve to reach a wider public through the medium of print rather than simply being circulated among a close circle of friends, he has an unpublished commentary already written on his work.

As was undoubtedly the case with the Areopagus, Spenser is placing a series of heavy hints that he belongs to a wider circle of serious writers and intellectuals who should be famous and influential, like, one suspects, the recently deceased Sir Thomas Smith. E. K.'s epistle to Harvey ends with a postscript that urges Harvey, inspired by Spenser's example, to publish his English poems so that he can receive the praise which is due to him and is currently stolen by others:

Trust me you doe both [the poems and Harvey's friends] great wrong, in depriuing them of the desired sonne, and also your selfe, in smothering your deserued praises, and all men generally, in withholding from them so diuine pleasures, which they might conceiue of your gallant English verses, as they haue already doen of your Latine Poemes, which in my opinion both for inuention and Elocution are very delicate, and superexcellent.[14]

Harvey had indeed published Latin poems, an elegy for Smith and a series of poems praising the good and the great which were first presented at the queen's progress to Audley End, both published by Henry Bynemann in 1578.[15] In 1579 he still had legitimate ambitions to be a poet and the careful state of the text of his English poems preserved in his *Letter-Book* suggests that he was seriously interested in publishing them at this time.[16] Here, the praise provided by E. K. in the dedicatory epistle suggests that the *Calender* was a promotional vehicle for Harvey as well as Spenser. Furthermore, the extensive references to Harvey's wealth of poetry, published and unpublished, in the notes, which expands on the comments in the epistle, reads as yet more promotion or advertising, with a certain amount of sly humour at carrying out such an obvious ruse.

But who was E. K., the mysterious promoter of these two writers? The initials are traditionally taken to stand for Edward Kirk (1553–1613), another sizar at Pembroke College, who matriculated in 1571, two years after Spenser, and who also received money from the Nowell funds.[17] Kirk received an MA in 1578, and became rector of St Giles church, Risby, Suffolk (Plate 11), through the offices of Sir Thomas Kytson, the uncle of the three Althorp sisters to whom Spenser refers in *Colin Clouts come home againe*. Kirk remained in Risby until his death at the age of 60 on 10 November 1613, as his monument in the church records.[18] He appears to have settled in Risby with other members of his family and later became friendly with the Gawdy family in Norfolk.[19] He probably wrote some Latin verses, ascribed to 'E. K.', prefacing an illustrated book by Everard Digby, published in 1587.[20] Kirk would have known Spenser and Harvey, probably very well, and the link to Sir Thomas Kytson, Kirk's patron, does not just indicate familiarity with Spenser himself, but suggests that the two men were part of an extended network connected to the Spencers of Althorp, providing more support for Spenser's later claim that he was related to the more wealthy branches of the family.[21] The Kytsons were conservative in religious leanings and later formed marriage alliances with the Catholic Gage family of Sussex, suggesting that Kirk was unlikely to have been the sort of forward Protestant that Spenser is often assumed to have been.[22] St Giles church in Risby was, like many East Anglian churches, distinctly high church in character.[23] Spenser, Harvey, and Kirk pursued three of the most obvious professions for graduates in early modern England: secretary, don, and clergyman. In the first letter of his published correspondence with Harvey, Spenser states that he visited—perhaps stayed with—a woman who might well have been Kirk's wife (or, possibly even his mother): 'Thus muche was written at Westminster yesternight: but comming this morning, beeyng the sixteenth of October, to Mystresse *Kerkes*, to have it delivered by carrier, I receuyued youre letter.'[24] In the *Calender* E. K. signs his epistle to Harvey 'from my lodging at London thys 10. Of Aprill. 1579'.[25] The very banality of the details would appear to confer authenticity. The two texts, the *Calender* and the letters, when taken together seem to be deliberately constructing a life relating to the text, one in which Spenser is a friend of Edward Kirk.

But can we actually believe that Edward Kirk wrote the notes and that they are what they claim to be, a serious commentary on the eclogues? E. K.'s notes have the appearance of comments made as the commentator is reading the text along with the reader, as the gloss to line 176 of the September eclogue indicates.[26] They often also read more as if they were familiar correspondence between friends, rather like the Harvey–Spenser letters, in fact, which is probably the illusion that they were attempting to create, as they provide the reader with teasing, often misleading insights into the exchanges between men of letters.

More plausibly, Harvey and Spenser wrote the notes—with the help of the relatively anonymous Kirk—constructing the *Calender* as a humanist book which resembled the great classical editions produced by leading European scholars, as a means of self-promotion but also as a self-regarding joke.[27] Readers are challenged to see if they can work out what is fiction and what is fact, so that the life of the poet is used as a game to promote the poetry, just as the poetry then serves to promote the poet in his life beyond the text. Even trying to solve this conundrum grants one unofficial entry into the world of the *Calender*. It is unlikely that any of the details of Spenser's and Harvey's lives provided in the text are false, but they have been selected to tell a particular story, one that is not obvious on first reading. We have the tantalizing detail, for example, that Harvey has written a number of works, 'sundrye most rare and very notable writings, partly vnder vnknown Tytles, and partly vnder counterfayt names', the reader not able to determine whether this is an advertisement of future publications or an enticing sign of impressive productivity that may always remain obscure and hidden.[28] The gloss to the first line of the October eclogue is deliberately misleading in casting E. K. as a reader who has not seen the text ever before: 'I doubte whether by Cuddie be specified the author selfe, or some other. For in the eyght *AEglogue* the same person was brought in, singing a Cantion of Colins making, as he sayth. So that some doubt, that the persons be different.'[29] These words are true, because Colin and Cuddie do not represent the same figure, and yet not true, because their author never thought that Colin and Cuddie were the same person. The *Calender* is nothing if not a self-reflective work, even when it appears to be straightforward and direct.

As many critics have noted in the wake of Richard Helgerson, Spenser saw the dizzying possibilities of promoting himself and his writing through the new medium of print, which in the 1590s held out the possibility of providing a career and an audience for the poet, freeing someone of his class from the need for an absolute dependence on patrons.[30] It was vital that poets who could not depend on the bounty of the rich and powerful found other ways of sustaining themselves and their literary career. Michael Drayton (1563–1631), a poet who was significantly indebted to Spenser as a role model, went much further than his predecessor and was actively rude to patrons who failed to support him as he felt was his due, using his prefaces to attack patrons and readers alike (the readers failed to buy *PolyOlbion*).[31] Drayton left no estate when he died but appears to have had a good career as a poet, exploiting the possibilities of constructing an audience in print, a path that Spenser had pioneered.

The *Calender* itself covers what was considered to be virtually the whole tradition of English literature as it was then known. The style and content of many of the eclogues contain numerous allusions to Langland and Chaucer, and the persona adopted by Spenser, as already mentioned, refers to John Skelton's most famous literary creation.[32] Skelton was significant as a trickster figure from the jest book that bore his name, and, more importantly, as the unofficial but universally recognized poet laureate, a title Spenser was also afforded without royal sanction by his contemporaries.[33] The style and form of many of the eclogues, which were written in dialogue and produced in black-letter type, make the text resemble the recently published eclogues of Barnabe Googe (1563) and George Turbervile (1567).[34] Spenser would have known their work, as well as the influential eclogues of Alexander Barclay (*c.*1484–1552).[35] The type used is also a conspicuous reference to Chaucer, whose poetry was always produced in black-letter type until the end of the seventeenth century.[36] While Googe and Turbervile produced straightforward black-letter poetic texts on the page, Spenser goes beyond what they have achieved in adding the elaborate textual apparatus. They wrote for students and graduates of the Inns of Court; Spenser deliberately recaptured the familiar and friendly style of their eclogues but looked to address a much wider audience.[37] The appearance of the book signals a new development in English writing and printing: its constituent elements were familiar enough, but the whole was more than the sum of the parts.

The *Calender* also provides a series of references that deliberately place it within the tradition of major European and classical pastoral poetry. E. K. remarks that the author is just learning to spread his poetic wings and follow the careers of the most celebrated poets: 'So flew Theocritus, as you may perceiue he was al ready full fleged. So flew Virgile, as not yet wel feeling his winges. So flew Mantuane, as being not full somd. So Petraque. So Boccacae; So Marot, Sanazarus, and also diuers other excellent both Italian and French Poetes . . . So finally flyeth this our new Poete'.[38] If the *Calender* has one obvious underlying model in terms of form, content, and the layout of the printed edition, it is Francesco Sansovino's 1571 edition of Jacopo Sannazaro's *Arcadia* (*c.*1489), a work that also exhibited a similarly important influence on Sidney's *Arcadia*, the other outstanding English literary work of the 1580s.[39] And, if we then consider that the work itself is designed to resemble a humanist edition of a work of Latin or Greek literature, we can see how provocative, unusual, and carefully placed Spenser's first volume truly was.

But the *Calender* has further semantic resonances, those of popular culture and contemporary politics. The book closely resembles the almanac, one of the best-selling forms of published work in the early modern period, and one closely linked to autobiographical writing.[40] The almanac was itself a diverse and varied form with an uncertain register, varying from cheap, disposable sheets aimed at a market of scarcely literate readers, to sophisticated and expensive books such as Marcellus Palingenius Stellatus' Neoplatonic calendar based on the signs of the zodiac, *The Zodiac of Life*, translated by Googe and dedicated to Burghley in 1576, a book Spenser could scarcely have avoided.[41] Almanacs were also intimately bound up with an understanding of the self, as individuals mapped the year in terms of their actions.[42] They were also closely linked to the popular and controversial discourse of astrology and the supposed influence of the planets on the world, a subject that was enthusiastically embraced by Gabriel Harvey's brothers, Richard (1560–1630) and John (1564–92), notably after the conjunction of the planets Saturn and Jupiter in 1583.[43] John Harvey, who was living in the Saffron Walden area in the early 1580s when Spenser was probably staying with Gabriel, wrote two almanacs in the 1580s, as well as a treatise about the value of prognostication after his predictions had proved to be false and had been publicly ridiculed.[44] It is never clear how seriously Spenser or Harvey took astrological predictions, especially when they became arguments for the apocalypse.[45] Harvey undoubtedly felt obliged to defend his brothers in public in the late 1580s and early 1590s, especially as they had written their books as if addressed to him, perhaps in imitation of his exchange of letters with Spenser.[46] Certainly it is difficult to imagine that Spenser and Gabriel Harvey had much time for Richard Harvey's pious diatribe, *A Theologicall Discourse of The Lamb of God and His Enemies* (1590), which launches an explicit attack on an author they both clearly admired. Richard Harvey describes Lucian as 'not worth a beane' before dismissing the wit and learning of the Greeks and Italians.[47]

Spenser was clearly exploiting this complex and divided heritage in the *Calender*, producing a book that was simultaneously gesturing towards a wider audience than most early printed poetry had reached and drawing attention to his mastery of the sources available. The *Calender* is conspicuously both an elite and a popular book. The author represents a version of himself as Colin Clout, another gesture of studied ambiguity that exploits an understanding of England's literary heritage as it was perceived in the 1570s. On the one hand, Colin was a voice of the people confronting the central authorities in the name of the popular will. On the other, he was the literary creation of John Skelton, who was seen to alternate between a court and a country identity, as well as adopting the guise of a fool.[48] Moreover, in making Colin Clout his own figure, Spenser was also signalling a debt to Chaucer, imitating

Chaucer's self-representation in his poetry, as well as taking on the mantle of Englishness.[49]

In short, the *Calender* is a work of literary pyrotechnics, one that forces a reader to think about every aspect of poetry: content, form, style, register, texts and emblems, printing, readership, distribution, audience, and so on.[50] It has traditionally been read as a project that was associated with the earl of Leicester, as Spenser appears to have been working for him—at least, intermittently—in the mid- to late 1570s.[51] It is indeed likely that Spenser had originally intended to dedicate the *Calender* to Leicester, but then changed the dedication to Sidney at a relatively late stage, at some point in October 1579, as the published *Letters* to Harvey indicate, probably because the Sidneys emerged as his new principal patrons, albeit for a brief period.[52] Furthermore, Spenser states that he was working on a Latin work, which has not survived, a verse history of the genealogy of the earl entitled 'Stemmata Dudleiana', one of the lost works referenced only in Spenser's own printed work, many of which were undoubtedly absorbed into Spenser's extant canon.[53] This suggests that Spenser was closely connected to the earl and his circle while he was working on the *Calender*, although the real link was perhaps through the Sheffield family.[54]

It is also likely that the *Calender* owed as much to Burghley as to Leicester. Although Burghley and Leicester had a complicated and often fractious relationship, one that has been used to interpret Spenser's life and allegiances, they were not consistently hostile towards each other. Moreover, they did have some connection, as Cecil had worked for Leicester's father, the duke of Northumberland, when he was cutting his political teeth during the reign of Edward VI.[55] The perceived division between the two men has as much to do with the contrasting ways in which they conducted themselves at court, as with any specific political and doctrinal divisions. Dudley assumed a flamboyance that was alien to the more taciturn Burghley. Yet each was a committed Protestant—Cecil had been Edward VI's principal secretary and had nearly been executed after his role in Northumberland's attempted coup before Mary was crowned as queen—and fervently anti-Catholic, eager to foster the progress of the Reformation in England, even if they had different ways of approaching the issue.[56] In the late 1570s both were involved in the marriage negotiations between Elizabeth and François, duc d'Alençon (later also duc d'Anjou), a match about which they both had reservations and which they came to oppose more forcefully as negotiations started to falter.[57]

Recent research has revealed how canny and underhand Burghley could often be in orchestrating opposition to policies and events of which he disapproved, and how he realized the power that the printing press could have in defining public opinion, a realization of the power of print that resembles that of Spenser. One of Burghley's most successful tactics was to carefully place works in print that looked as if they were simply the expression of a popular outrage at the dangerous mechanics of mighty figures. In fact, it is only now that some of Burghley's ruses are coming to light. Burghley was behind the 1572 publication of a supposedly Scottish publication of George Buchanan's *Ane Detection of the duinges of Marie Quene of Scots* (1572). This work played a decisive role in blackening Mary's character and helped to fix an image of her in English eyes as a treacherous murderess who had betrayed her people through her own intemperate lusts and who, accordingly, should be executed, even though this was against Elizabeth's wishes. Burghley had helped arrange that a supposedly authentic 'Scottified' version of the Latin text should appear with the false imprint of St Andrews and be made widely available in England.[58]

In 1579 John Stubbes published a lengthy pamphlet, *The Discouerie of a Gaping Gulf vvhereinto England is like to be swallovved by another French mariage, if the Lord forbid not the banes, by letting her Maiestie see the sin and punishment thereof,* which was a concerted attack on the marriage proposal. Stubbes, although professing his loyalty to the queen, had his hand publicly severed, while his publisher, Singleton, was only pardoned at the last minute, in part because of his advanced age.[59] Stubbes was a close associate of Burghley's secretaries, Michael Hicks and Vincent Skinner, with whom he had translated Matthew Parker's history of the archbishops of Canterbury.[60] There is no evidence that *A Gaping Gulf* was produced to order, like the carefully planted translation of Buchanan's attacks on Mary. Nevertheless, its publication at such a sensitive and important moment suggests that Stubbes either acted on his own initiative, imagining that his advice would be welcome in key quarters and would have been regarded as acceptable comment on public affairs, or that the pamphlet was part of a more concerted effort to put yet more pressure on the queen to abandon the projected marriage.[61]

Both *A Gaping Gulf* and the *Calender* were published by Hugh Singleton, providing a strong link between the two works.[62] Spenser and Harvey had no obvious connection to Singleton, having previously published their work with Henry Bynemann, a fact that further indicates that the circumstances of the *Calender*'s publication were deliberately contrived to link it to current political events. Singleton, who was evidently advanced in years in 1579, was a bookseller as well as a printer, and had begun his career selling the works of John Bale and John Foxe.[63] He was, as H. J. Byrom has pointed out, 'the last printer in London likely under ordinary circumstances to have been recommended to Spenser as a fit publisher for *The Shepheardes Calender*'.[64] He had not produced any literary work before and was a relatively poor craftsman without the means to cope with such a complicated and ornate work with different typefaces and woodcuts. Rather, Singleton, who had links in his early career to John Day, publisher of Foxe's *Actes and Monuments*, had been known principally as a printer of the devotional and theological works of leading reformers, including Calvin and Knox. An exile under Mary, he was not beyond subterfuge, having published John Bale's *Vocacyon . . . to the bishiprick of Ossorie in*

Irelande (Wesel, 1553) using a false colophon that he employed elsewhere with other works, 'Rome, before the Castell of S. Angell at the signe of S. Peter'.[65] That work would certainly have been known to Spenser, as would another of Day's major publications, one of his last, John Derricke's *The Image of Irelande with a discouerie of woodkarne* (1581).[66]

It is likely that Singleton, who had only one printing press, published the *Calender* in December 1579 when it was entered into the Stationers' Register, having worked on it in the summer, but then turned his attention to *A Gaping Gulf* and the subsequent trial. The *Calender* and *A Gaping Gulf* were set using different typefaces, 83 textura and 68 roman.[67] Spenser was probably working on the *Calender* from 1577, perhaps longer, given its elaborate format, and the carefully chosen illustrations.[68] A corroborating work claims that Spenser was flexible enough to make last-minute changes and was eager to advertise this ability in print. In the second of his two published *Letters* to Harvey (5 October 1579), Spenser discusses the uncertainty he has over the dedication of the *Calender*, apparently worrying that he risks irritating the dedicatee, or that the poem is 'too base' for 'his excellent Lordship', and so has to be dedicated instead to a 'priuate Personage vnknowne' (Rosalind).[69] Love elegies were not habitually dedicated to earls—but why discuss this matter unless a point is being made?

Given that the letter is signed from 'Leycester House', the 'excellent Lordship' can only be Robert Dudley, earl of Leicester, which makes the passage especially uncomfortable reading, as it puts the weighing up of dedicatory options openly on display, and advertises Spenser's fear that addressing a mighty personage in inappropriate terms would undoubtedly result in a rebuff. Discussing whether to dedicate the poem to a private person, who must be Spenser's wife-to-be, Machabyas Childe, whom he was to marry on 27 October, also indicates a pronounced contempt for the authority of the mighty, a gesture that prefigures the later reference to his second wife as an Elizabeth of greater quality than Queen Elizabeth when Colin Clout conjures up the Graces in *The Faerie Queene*, VI.x.25–8.[70] There is a calculated rudeness—or simply tactlessness—in Spenser deciding that he cannot dedicate his poem to Leicester because it is written in honour of a 'priuate Personage vnknowne', so that someone the poet knows personally proves more important to him than a great lord.[71] Certainly, the passage draws attention to itself and predicts what might be offensive and likely to attract 'some yl-willers', and, in doing so, articulates what it is supposedly erasing and avoiding. It is possible that the key to the origins of Spenser's career in Ireland can be found in the *Letters*, and that his relationship to Leicester is the key. The prefatory sections of the *Calender* show that, whatever pressures were placed upon him and whatever cross-currents led to the publication of the work, Spenser meant to be his own man.

On the one hand such discussion about the *Calender* is designed to place emphasis on the role of the poet as well as to encourage the reader to make obvious connections between the *Letters* and the eclogues, especially if we bear in mind that the later letter makes the tongue-in-cheek boast that in the poems there are 'some things excellently, and many things wittily discoursed of *E. K.* and the Pictures so singularly set forth, and portrayed, as if *Michael Angelo* were there, he could (I think) nor amende the best, nor reprehend the worst'.[72] This ludicrous claim must surely be a dig at Singleton's production values, as well as a further part of the pretence, exposed later in the volume, that E. K. was a mysterious figure unknown to the poet. It is also more evidence that the *Letters* were carefully prepared for publication because Spenser could only have written to Harvey in such terms as part of an elaborate joke.

In the end the poem was dedicated to Sir Philip Sidney, who had received the unwelcome dedication of *The Schoole of Abuse* from Stephen Gosson earlier the same year, an unfortunate event that Spenser discusses at some length, probably to advertise his own contrasting intimacy with Sidney, as the *Calender* was published before the *Letters*.[73] Perhaps, the discussion in the *Letters* is intended to mislead the reader and Spenser had always intended to dedicate the *Calender* to Sidney, although Sidney's comments on the work in the *Apology for Poesie* suggest that not only does he not know the author, but that he has not really understood the poem and why it was written the way it was: 'The *Shepherd's Calender* hath much poetry in his eclogues, indeed worthy the reading, if I be not deceived. That same framing of his style to an old rustic language I dare not allow, since neither Theocritus in Greek, Virgil in Latin, nor Sanazzaro in Italian did affect it.'[74] Sidney sounds very like E. K. complaining about other writers who have made English 'a gallimaufray or hodge-podge of al other speeches', a common complaint in early modern England.[75] The resemblance is, however, undoubtedly more apparent than real, given the obvious irony of E. K.'s remark, and the straightforward nature of Sidney's.[76] William Webbe, in his *Discourse of English Poesie* (1586), seems to be answering Sidney in describing the *Calender* as 'in my iudgement inferior to the workes neither of *Theocritus* in Greeke, nor *Virgill* in Latin, whom he narrowly immitateth'.[77]

It is equally possible that the work was hastily revised to accommodate a new patron, or because it was no longer appropriate to dedicate the poem to Leicester, probably through the recently established political role of the poems in the Alençon affair (it might have been too obvious, if Burghley was involved in the printing of the *Calender*, to have the book dedicated to Leicester, another opponent of the match close to the queen). The poem 'To His Booke', an imitation of Chaucer's envoy to his greatest poem, *Troilus and Criseyde*, published on the first page of the volume, appears to address a more high-born subject than Sidney:

> Goe little booke: thy selfe present,
> As child whose parent is vnkent:
> To him that is the president
> Of nobleness and of cheualree, . . .
> And when his honor has thee redde,
> Craue pardon for my hardyhedde.[78]

According to William Ringler, the phrase '*his honor*' had to refer to a nobleman such as Leicester, and could not have been adopted for a gentleman like Sidney, who, although not yet a knight, would have been addressed as 'your worship'.[79]

In fact, the *Calender* directly insults the earl elsewhere. The March eclogue is a debate about the impact of the seasons on young shepherds. While Thomalin laments the continuation of winter, Willye celebrates the coming of spring and summer with their attendant pleasures:

> Tho shall we sporten with delight,
> And learne with Letice to wexe light,
> That scornefully lookes askaunce,
> Tho will we little Loue awake,
> That nowe sleepeth in *Lethe* lake,
> And pray him leaden our daunce.[80]

Leicester had married Lettice Knolles, widow of Walter Devereux, first earl of Essex, in secret at Wanstead House on 21 September 1578.[81] The marriage appears to have been widely known from early on, with Thomas Ratcliffe, earl of Sussex, informing the French ambassador in November 1578. But the queen was furious, publicly rebuked the earl in August 1579, and banished him from court.[82] The publication of Spenser's poem later that year could certainly have done little to help the situation, as the light tone of the lines is scornful, suggesting that the marriage was a trifle, probably because Spenser felt more loyal to the spurned Lady Sheffield.[83] Furthermore, Sidney was Leicester's nephew, and his uncle's marriage and the consequent prospect of children (a hope realized in June 1581 with the birth of the short-lived Robert Dudley, Baron Denbigh (1581–4)), significantly reduced Sidney's chances of ever becoming earl of Leicester, drawing attention to the inappropriate form of address in the dedication.[84]

It is inconceivable that Spenser was ignorant of the significance of the marriage, especially if he was close to the Sheffield family, so his lines can only be read, like the debate over the dedication, as tactless, reckless, or deliberately confrontational.[85] Spenser had begun his literary career as he meant to continue it. In his gloss to the line E. K. writes as if he were attempting to disguise the significance of the name and to minimize any possible slight, while actually drawing attention to the insulting nature of the reference, a familiar Spenserian trick. He states that Lettice was 'the name of some country lasse'.[86] In the April eclogue Colin's love is named as 'the Widdowes daughter of the glenne, | . . . fayre *Rosalind*' (lines 26–7). But, in pointed contrast to the gloss to Lettice, E. K. is clear about her exalted status as 'a Gentle woman of no meane house', whose looks and virtue raise her above all other women.[87] While Lettice is simply 'some countrey lasse', Rosalind is the noblewoman who is more beautiful and cultured than the mistresses who inspired the world's greatest poetry. The purpose of the contrast might have been purely playful, especially if we consider that E. K., feigning ignorance of Colin's identity, has already suggested that he is probably the servant of 'some Southern noble man'.[88] Yet, we then need to remember that in the April eclogue Colin fails to turn up at the celebration of the queen, and has Hobbinol read out his poem, because he is too much in love with Rosalind, an absence that can be read as a further sleight of his patron and his monarch.[89] However we imagine the tone of these lines and notes, it is hard to believe that they were read with pleasure by Leicester, or indeed anyone at court.[90] The *Calender*, in line with other definitions of the pastoral, quite deliberately inverts the normal world order.[91] The poem is framed to suggest that Spenser was attempting to sever himself from the world of patronage politics and in doing so was asserting his independence as a poet.[92]

Perhaps the most important point that needs to be made is that such changes indicate how keen Spenser was to establish his control over the text. It is improbable that Singleton, an aged and limited printer with only one press and a small supply of type, would have been responsible for the varieties of type used in the production of the *Calender*; the woodcuts (Singleton had not produced an illustrated text for twenty years); the imitation of Sannazaro's *Arcadia*; or the apparent last-minute changes to the dedication.[93] The text of the *Calender* leaves us with a series of interpretive puzzles, suggesting that it is the product of divergent forces: on the one hand it appears to be a text in which the 'new poete', albeit anonymous (at least until the publication of the *Letters*, which tell the attentive reader who the author was) sets out his stall; on the other, it looks as if it was co-opted by someone on high to fight a political battle.

The *Calender* is an elaborate mixture of the political, the poetic, and the personal, carefully and deliberately relating all three and establishing the right of the poet to comment on contemporary events, advise rulers and their advisers, as well as the audience, who can read the printed text, and so establish Spenser as a key figure in English cultural and political life. If there was a serious attempt to create a 'public sphere' in Elizabethan England the *Calender* is probably its most important mani-festation, a natural development of the ideas of Smith and Harvey.[94] The eclogues contain extensive comment not just on Elizabeth as queen, but on the state of the Church of England. The April eclogue, if read superficially and as an isolated poem, appears to praise Elizabeth, but is actually highly critical of her and fraught with anxiety. The last poetic lines of March, Thomalin's Emblem, provide a pointed pun that overshadows the April poem: '*Of Hony and Of Gaule in loue there is store:* | *The Honye is much, but the Gaule is more*' (lines 121–2). The allusion is to the French match and the fear that the Gaul will assume control, the standard fear of the effect of queens marrying and having to obey their husbands, especially if they were foreign, like Mary's husband, Philip II.[95] There then follows a pointed contrast between the celebratory 'Argument' that prefaces the April eclogue, claiming that it is 'purposely intended to the honor and prayse of our most gracious souereigne, Queene Eliza-beth', and the gloomy words of Thomalin:

> Tell me good Hobbinoll, what garres thee greete?
> What? Hath some Wolfe thy tender Lambes ytorne?
> Or is thy Bagpype broke, that soundes so sweete?
> Or art thou of thy loued lasse forlorne?
> Or bene thine eyes attempred to the yeare,
> Quenching the grasping furowes thirst with rayne?
> Like April shoure, so stremes the trickling teares
> Adowne thy cheke, to quenche thy thirstye payne. (lines 1–8)

A poem in praise of the queen does not usually open with such a colloquial phrase, 'garres thee greete' (misfortunes torment you), quite at odds with the anticipated description of a royal triumph. The gap between the 'Argument' and the opening line of the poem immediately alerts us to the disjunction between the celebrations taking place at court in 1579 to greet the queen's potential husband and the despair that grips her humble subjects throughout her lands. Thomalin's speculations can, of course, also hint at broader issues, especially the fear in line 2, which is a direct reference to the terror of the godly flock being infiltrated by pernicious heretics, a staple image in Protestant anti-Catholic polemic, and one Spenser uses elsewhere in the *Calender*.[96] It also reminds us of the central focus of the eclogues and that what links them together is the figure of the shepherd protecting his sheep from wolves.[97] And, with Colin's absence from court, the queen should certainly get the message that her subjects are not happy. If we think that Colin is E. K., then he tells us in his opening epistle to Harvey that he is at his London lodging on 10 April 1579, a further piece of calculated rudeness.[98] In the eclogue Colin/Spenser places his relationship with his own lady far above that with the queen so that, despite the beauty of the song he has composed in her honour, its purpose as praise poetry is undercut by its context, within and beyond the poem.

Even details which appear to heap genuine praise on Elizabeth are undermined by a knowledge of their immediate relevance, often inverting their ostensible meaning in the poem. Colin celebrates the queen's face in terms that appear to reflect standard Renaissance concepts of female beauty: 'The Redde rose medle with the White yfere, I In either cheeke depeincten lively chere' (lines 68–9).[99] The gloss to the word 'yfere' draws our attention to the political relevance of the colours:

Yfere) together. By the mingling of the Redde rose and the White, is meant the vniting of the two principall houses of Lancaster and Yorke: by whose longe discord and deadly debate, this realm many yeares was sore traueiled, and almost cleane decayed. Til the famous Henry the seuenth, of the line of Lancaster, taking to wife the most virtuous Princesse Elisabeth, daughter to the fourth Edward of the house of Yorke, begat the most royal Henry the eyght aforesayde, in whom was the firste vnion of the Whyte Rose and the Redde.[100]

The gloss neatly brings us back to where we started in repeating the phrase from the verse, a pointed reminder that history can come full circle. The Tudors came to power to end a bloody civil war, but Elizabeth's reign would be the last of the dynasty and her death might lead to another upheaval. Either she will marry the duc d'Alençon, and so change the nature of the English crown, ending its independence, or she will die childless, in which case a new dynasty will assume the throne. It is most likely that this would be the Stuarts, perhaps even Mary Stuart, whom Elizabeth had suggested that she would name as her successor on various occasions, an action that terrified many of her chief advisers, including William Cecil.[101]

It was fear of Mary that had inspired Cecil to publish Buchanan's work, which strengthens the probability of a link between Cecil and Stubbes's *Gaping Gulf* and the *Calender*. Cecil was undoubtedly heavily involved in the events of 1571 which saw England's premier Catholic nobleman, Thomas Howard, fourth duke of Norfolk (1538–72) executed after his dangerous plan to marry Mary was revealed, and the exposure of the Ridolfi Plot, which further heightened a general consensus among Protestants and moderate Catholics that Mary was their chief enemy.[102] It is likely too that the reference to 'discord and ... debate' reveals a knowledge of Elizabeth's poem, 'The Doubt of Future Foes', written c.1571, but circulating widely enough for George Puttenham to be able to include a version in his *The Arte of English Poesie* (1589). Elizabeth describes Mary as 'The daughter of debate, that eke discord doth sowe I Shal reape no gaine where formor rule hath taught stil peace to growe'.[103] In a neat couplet and with a carefully targeted note Spenser encapsulates a precise sense of English past, present, and future as it was seen by many of his countrymen and women. While the *Calender* does not give an obvious answer to the question of whether Elizabeth should marry a foreign prince—unlike Stubbes who says no—or offer any solution that will ensure future happiness and prosperity, it does show, through an annual cycle that begins and ends with the poet conspicuously isolated and miserable, what has gone wrong and what dangers lie ahead.[104]

The November eclogue, closely linked to April, casts Elizabeth as Dido, the spurned queen of the ancient world whose glory is eclipsed as a new world order emerges, and so further makes the point that England is in serious trouble in relation to recent developments at home and in Europe.[105] The *Calender*, contrary to what is often asserted, is not a straightforwardly Protestant poem that sweeps away every legacy of England's past, eager to start afresh.[106] Rather, Spenser shows himself to be painfully aware of the delicate nature of the survival of the nation's history and the need to preserve it, one reason why the *Calender* is so hostile to papal forces eager to impose their version of religion on a complex, living entity. There is often much less difference between an English Catholic's and an English Protestant's understanding of the past and the radical impact of the Reformation than is assumed. After all, even John Bale, one of the harshest—and most repetitive—critics of monastic life, worked tirelessly to preserve the libraries, historical records, and literature of England that were in danger of being swept away by the dissolution of the ecclesiastical orders.[107]

In the February eclogue Thenot tells the story of the oak and the briar, in which the arrogant and myopic young briar persuades the woodman to cut down the aged oak which overshadows it, only to realize, too late, that the oak had protected it against the harsh winds and storms that eventually destroy the smaller and more vulnerable tree. The allegory is a traditional one of youthful pride receiving its just deserts, a warning to others to respect their elders and learn from the wisdom they have accumulated. But the poem demands to be read in terms of the Reformation. The oak is described as 'Sacred with many a mysterye, | And often crost with the priestes crewe, | And often halwed with holy water dewe' (lines 208–10). The phrase 'priestes crewe' is glossed as 'holy water pott, wherewith the popishe priest vsed to sprinkle and hallowe the trees from mischaunce. Such blindnesse was in those times, which the Poete supposeth, to haue bene the finall decay of this aunciente Oake.'[108] Yet again, the gloss is not what it seems to be and cannot be taken at face value, but functions within the wider context of the *Calender* as a book. It is not the oak's past which destroys it but the hostile intervention of the briar, forcing the reader to think carefully about what the *Calender* is actually saying. If the oak's past had been the cause of its downfall, then the briar would have been right to condemn it, not criticized as foolish in the poem. The point is surely that the Reformation must not forget its roots in the past and that all Christians need to think through what is good and what is pernicious about the legacy of the pre-Reformation. Thenot's fable ends abruptly: 'Such was thend of this Ambitious brere, | For scorning Eld' (lines 237–8). The omission of the full stop and the use of a half-line, a device Spenser uses elsewhere in his work to draw attention to a salient point, must be deliberate, and invests the conclusion with particular force.[109] Cuddie interrupts Thenot with particular rudeness, 'Now I pray thee shepherd, tel it not forth: | Here is a long tale, and little worth' (lines 239–40), before complaining that 'the day is nigh wasted' (line 246). Perhaps Thenot has overdone his tale, although Piers's fable of the kid in the May eclogue is a similar length. More likely what we see is the impatient 'Heardsmans boye' failing to listen to the wise words of the 'olde Shephearde', reinforcing the message that they exist in a society that is in danger of forgetting its past. Moreover, it is obvious that this fable is an adaptation of one by Aesop, demonstrating Spenser's eagerness to use and adapt the past himself.[110] The same message has to be applied to religion.

Does this mean that Spenser was really a Catholic sympathizer, arguing that traditional practices such as the sprinkling of holy water should be preserved by the church? It is hard to push this claim too far, although Spenser's poetry does contain a significant number of Catholic elements, such as the symbols and the rites practised when the Red-Cross Knight is healed in the House of Holiness (*FQ* I.x).[111] But the use of holy water, represented in the poem and highlighted in the gloss, should probably alert our suspicions, and indicate that we should not accept Thenot's comments uncritically. After a period of toleration, the liturgical use of holy water was forbidden in the Edwardian Prayer Book, which was largely designed and written by Thomas Cranmer, the father-in-law of Thomas Norton, who was closely involved in the Merchant Taylors' School.[112] Spenser's fable, framed within the eclogue, the sequence, and the whole book, does not indicate that there is a straightforward answer to the question of religion, religious belief, and religious practice. The fable cuts both ways, reminding readers not to ignore the legacy of the past, but also warning them that not everything can be tolerated and allowed, not least, because, as Cuddie argues, nothing would ever get done.

A similar, but inverted, balance can be detected in the more obviously Protestant fable of the fox and the kid in the May eclogue. The fable, also derived from Aesop, tells the story of the foolish kid, left alone by his mother, who is then kidnapped by the fox, disguised as a pedlar, lured away with a 'trusse of trifles . . . | As bells, and babes, and glasses' (lines 239–40). It is narrated by the Protestant Piers, whose name reminds readers of Piers Plowman, in order to refute the more Catholic Palinode.[113] The problem with the fable is that Palinode, far from being an aggressive Catholic, is mild, well behaved (unlike Cuddie, he does not curtail the lengthy speech of his interlocutor), and reasonable, significantly less combative in fact than Piers. Certainly Palinode bears no resemblance to Piers's description of the wolves disguised as shepherds who often 'deuouered their owne sheepe' (line 128). Although he thinks Piers's fears are vastly exaggerated, he concludes by asking him if he can tell his tale to 'our sir Iohn', because 'if Foxes bene so crafty, as so, | Much needeth all shepheardes hem to knowe' (lines 312–13). Sir John may well stand for an ignorant clergyman, or even one inclined towards Catholicism, as the gloss indicates: 'Our sir Iohn) a Popishe priest. A saying fit for the grosenesse of a shepheard, but spoken to taunt vulearned Priestes.'[114] However, the fact that Palinode is planning to warn him about the dangers to the church from the wolves suggests that Spenser is quite deliberately dividing Catholics into two groups.[115] There are native English, like Palinode, who may be complacent and naive, but are hardly enemies of the true church, and the foreign wolves—perhaps, even like Sir John—who seek to undermine and appropriate the English church for their own imperial designs. E. K.'s note only confuses matters further, seeming to undermine the figure of the good Protestant shepherd, Piers, even as E. K. professes scorn for Catholics. Palinode is now cast as the educator of the unlearned, even if he, like Piers, is a gross shepherd. This is precisely the sort of position one might expect from someone who had worked on van der Noot's *Theatre* and who had detailed knowledge of Spanish behaviour in the Low Countries. Religious belief and confessional allegiance involved difficult choices, rather like a queen deciding whether she should marry, and whom, both central and intimately related questions in the *Calender*.[116] Nevertheless, making sure that your country did not surrender its freedom to foreign powers was a principle that could not be violated.

The *Calender* pays some debts to major figures in Spenser's life, not just Richard Mulcaster, represented as the 'good olde shepharde' Wrenock in December (line 41). The poem also lends its support to the recently deposed archbishop of Canterbury, Edmund Grindal. Although Bishop John Young emerges as an ambiguous figure in the *Calender*, defending Protestant values in a rather excessive way that seems to resemble the actions of the wolves he opposes, Grindal, one of Young's patrons, is represented as a much more ecumenical figure capable of unifying the church.[117] While many of the shepherds in the *Calender* separate themselves from their flock through a sense of their superior status as men of the cloth, enjoyment of the church's wealth, or contempt for their flock, Algrind appears as a man of the people. In the May eclogue Piers quotes him to this effect, in lines which, nevertheless, contain their own important ambiguities:

> But shepheardes (as Algrind vsed to say,)
> Mought not liue ylike, as men of the laye:
> With them it sits to care for their heire,
> Enaunter [i.e., lest that] their heritage doe impaire:
> They must prouide for meanes of maintenaunce,
> And to continue their wont countenance.
> But shepheard must walke another way,
> Sike worldly souenance he must foresay. (lines 75–82)

The paradox that these lines express is Algrind's understanding that pastors need to be set apart from the laypeople they serve in order for them not to be cut off from society. Divines must not be seen to benefit from their privileged position as men of God so that they will be accepted by the communities in which they live. Spenser's account beautifully captures Grindal's understanding of ecclesiastical politics and that what mattered was the church and its authority to order society. Grindal is often cast as a moderate puritan, and his inclination was certainly towards the more austere end of church life and discipline. He opposed the wearing of the cap and surplice, appears to have had no objection to clerical marriage, was in favour of the Edwardian Prayer Book, and had close contacts with Calvin and Geneva.[118] Yet, he was prepared to enforce the agreed regulations when bishop of London, then archbishop of York and finally archbishop of Canterbury, insisting that the clergy put the good of the church before their own private integrity in matters of 'indifference' (adiaphora).[119] Grindal insisted that laws passed against Catholicism were upheld but was adamant that the church be as broad and tolerant as possible, the main reason why he stood up to the queen's demand that he suppress the 'prophesyings'.[120]

His sense of balance was probably also the reason why Grindal excited Spenser's particular imagination. He was a major cleric who had principles yet was also keen to make the church a place where most people could worship; he was a national figure who would not permit the nation to be undermined by aggressive foreign interests, yet who was also prepared to preserve as many diverse elements of the nation as he could. For many, commenting on events in the wake of the Grindal affair, the safety of the queen was intimately bound up with her inspiring the loyalty of her subjects.[121] The July eclogue contains a debate between Morrell and Thomalin, 'made in the honour and commendation of good shepheardes, and to the shame and dispraise of proude and ambitious Pastours. Such as Morrell is here imagined to bee.'[122] Despite their differences, both shepherds praise Algrind and lament his recent misfortune, a transparent allegory of Grindal's suspension as archbishop:

MORRELL.
But say me, what is *Algin* he,
That is so oft bynempt [named].

THOMALIN.
He is a shepheard great in gree,
but hath bene long ypent.
One daye he sat vpon a hyll,
(as now thou wouldest me:
But I am taught by *Algrins* ill,
to loue the lowe degree.)
For sitting so with bared scalpe,
An Eagle sored hye,

That weening hys white head was chalke,
    a shell fish downe let flye:
She weend the shell fishe to haue broake,
    but therewith bruzd his brayne,
So now astonied with the stroke,
    he lyes in lingring payne.

MORRELL.

Ah good *Algrin,* his hap was ill,
    but shall be bett in time. (lines 213–30)

Read one way, this might seem like a tactful representation of Grindal's unfortunate fate, but the story is really intensely critical of the queen, as well as complicating our understanding of the ways we should perceive the relationship between the two shepherds.[123] If the queen as the eagle did not mean to injure Algrind/Grindal, then she clearly does not know what she is doing and has no understanding of the effects of her actions; if she did mean to injure him, and Thomalin is merely being tactful in claiming that the shell was dropped on his head by accident, then Elizabeth has alienated her clergy, who unite in defence of Algrind/Grindal at the time when she most needs their support. Thomalin shows that he does not have the moral high ground in assuming the low ground in order to criticize Morrell for sitting on a hillock, as the woodcut and the Argument suggest. He uses the story of Algrind's fate to avoid high office, supposedly a policy in keeping with Algrind's principle that the clergy must not become too high and mighty and must always remain in touch with the people. The truth is the opposite, of course, as Grindal took high office in order to serve the church, seeing the institution as more important than he was, which suggests that Morrell's position is not as culpable as might appear from an initial reading of the Argument. Thomalin, in contrast, is serving his own agenda and living his life as he would like to, a parallel to Spenser's critical representation of Calidore, the Knight of Courtesy, who abandons his quest in *The Faerie Queene,* Book VI, to assume the life of a simple shepherd, a dereliction of his knightly duty which inevitably leads to disaster.[124] Like Piers, Thomalin rejects the trappings of worldly success and argues that they have no part in the church. But the poem does not necessarily adopt this position: Grindal's example demonstrated that high office within an episcopal structure did not inevitably involve self-indulgence.[125] The *Calender* indicates that Spenser's religious position is less doctrinal or confessional in emphasis and more based on a commitment to the institution of the church as a means of incorporating the diverse believers who constitute a nation. Spenser's concern in the eclogues is not to articulate a dogmatic position that needs to be followed, but an exploration of the rights and wrongs of various positions so that accepted wisdom can be challenged and rethought, and the boundaries of possible belief established.

It has usually been assumed that Morrell represents John Aylmer, bishop of London (1520/1–94), not without reason.[126] However, one passage, which has received little attention from commentators, presumably because it does not further this identification of Morell, might tell a different story, one closer to home. In defending his decision to remain high above Thomalin on a mound, Morrell tries to convince his interlocutor of its value and benefits:

> Here han the holy *Faunes* resourse,
>   and *Syluanes* haunten rathe [early].
> Here has the salt Medway his sourse,
>   wherein the Nymphes doe bathe.
> The salt Medway, that trickling stremis
>   adowne the dales of Kent:
> Till with his elder brother Themis
>   his brakish waues be meynt.
> Here growes *Melampode* euery where,
>   and *Teribinth* good for Gotes:[127]
> The one, my madding kiddes to smere,
>   the next, to heale theyr throtes. (lines 77–88)

As Louise Schleiner has argued, 'an idealized Kent is clearly the *Calender*'s mental locale, reflected in numerous references scattered through the eclogues', as well as the glosses.[128] Here, we have a direct link between Morrell and the Medway, the river that defines the geography of the county that Spenser knew, which then connects it to the Thames, the river that Spenser celebrated as one of the fundamental geographical features of London. The rivers flow into the sea and merge to form the Thames estuary, the Medway ending at Rochester, the bishop's see, which might suggest that there is a suppressed pun here and elsewhere in Spenser's writings.[129] Their union is celebrated in Spenser's description of the marriage of the Thames and the Medway, eventually published in 1596. Morrell, the keeper of goats, would seem to be a figure either of Spenser's now former employer, John Young, who is portrayed in ambiguous terms, especially if we read the description of him as Morrell alongside that of him as Roffyn in the September eclogue; or someone else in the ecclesiastical hierarchy of Kent. In the September eclogue Roffyn appears excessively vigilant against his enemies. If Morrell is Young, he here appears, if anything, rather lax in his approach, and his role as the shepherd of the goats suggests that he is either wasting his time in ministering to those who cannot be saved, or, more likely, spreading his net wide in order to make the church as inclusive as possible.[130]

Perhaps Spenser is showing that he witnessed both types of ecclesiastical abuse while he was in Kent, excessive vigilance and excessive tolerance; perhaps, neither can be avoided. The eclogues indicate that Spenser was using his experience in Kent to think about the issues that confronted the church—and the nation—in 1579. The *Calender* combines serious poetic experiment with comment on contemporary events, as well as providing a wealth of more directly biographical information, when read carefully.

After completing the *Calender*, but before it was published, Spenser married Machabyas Childe at St Margaret's church, Westminster on 27 October 1579 (Figure 4).[131] Machabyas, who was christened in the same church on 8 September 1560, may have been the daughter of Robert Childe of Westminster, who married Alice Lord on 18 October 1556.[132] A Robert Childe was buried on 25 February 1573, which, if Machabyas were his child, would have made her a widow's daughter, a fact that could be significant. Unfortunately, there is no extant record of the names of Robert Childe's children (although a number died in Westminster in the years after 1556), and he makes no mention of them in his will, so, unfortunately he cannot be positively identified as Machabyas' father.[133] More significantly, Machabyas is a highly unusual name. Two approximations that have been found are that of Megphias/Mackfias Ellis, baptized in 1545 and buried in 1581, and the nickname given to John Macalpine by Philip Melanchthon.[134] Macalpine was a Scottish reformer who married Agnes, the sister of Miles Coverdale's wife, Elizabeth Macheson (Coverdale had connections with the Merchant Taylors' School and Spenser would have encountered him).[135] This coincidence probably has little direct bearing on the first name of the first Mrs Spenser, although it might suggest that she had parents interested in the reformed religion, perhaps closely connected to the circle of Calvinist divines linked to the school. Her name would appear to derive from the apocryphal book of the Maccabees, which narrates the revolt of the Israelites led by Judas Maccabeus against the Seleucid Empire (167–160 BCE) and which established the feast of Hanukkah to celebrate the restoration of worship in the temple. It may well be that Machabyas came from a committed Protestant family, as some commentators have suggested, her name signifying the need to combat the oppressors of the true faith.[136]

But, unfortunately, the evidence is far from clear. No other example of the name has been discovered among either native English families or the immigrant communities of French and Dutch Protestants in London.[137] Moreover, the Book of Maccabees is not a book of the Bible extensively used by Protestants, even though the Apocrypha was included in the Geneva Bible. Calvin refers to it only twice in the *Institutes* and it does not feature in his Bible commentaries, nor do the Grindal circle make much use of the book.[138] Moreover, the book contains one of the key biblical examples of the idea of Purgatory (2 Maccabees 12:39–45), a description of Judas Maccabees praying for the souls of his dead soldiers, 'So hee made a reconciliation for

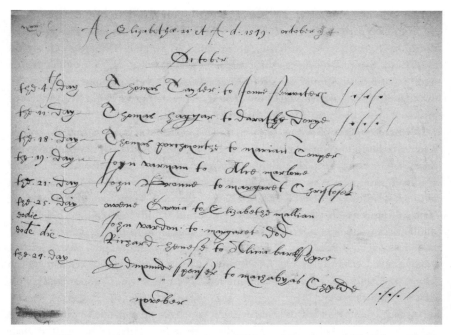

Figure 4. The entry in the marriage register of Edmund Spenser and Machabyas Chylde [Childe], 27 October 1579. Reproduced with kind permission of Westminster Abbey.

the dead that they might be deliuered from sinne' (45). The downgrading of the book after the Reformation was an important statement that the doctrine could not be sustained by Protestants.[139] Machabyas' origins are even more obscure than those of her husband, although the fact that she came from Westminster, a conspicuously wealthy part of London, probably suggests that her family had means.

Spenser, as he states at the end of his earliest published letter to Harvey, was at Leicester House in Westminster on 5 October 1579, three weeks before his wedding, and it is likely that he was living there, unless the instruction that Harvey needs to send letters to 'Mistresse Kerke', indicates that she was his landlady nearby.[140] Leicester had surely not yet had the contents of the *Calender* revealed to him. It was normal for marriage ceremonies to be conducted, as it is today, in the bride's parish (although, of course, most couples lived in the same parish anyway), so we can assume that the Childes also lived in Westminster, where their daughter was baptized.[141] St Margaret's was a distinctly conservative parish: wealthy and traditional in its outlook, often resistant to change, more so than its sister parish, St Martins. Returning to Catholic forms of worship after the Marian Restoration did not prove much of a problem. In late Elizabethan times the dominant elite tended to be from the parish itself, and although St Margaret's contained the palace of Westminster and the key government buildings in London, there was not always an obvious connection between the locals and the aristocracy.[142] If the Childe family were a vociferously Protestant group, eager to mark their religious commitment through the distinctive naming of their children, they certainly would have stood out in such a central parish.

We have no clear idea how Spenser met his wife, but it is likely that the couple were introduced in some way, and that the two families had made arrangements for their match, as virtually all early modern marriages were planned unions.[143] The dominant groups in Westminster were tradespeople, many involved in the production and distribution of food and drink. It is therefore likely that there was some form of connection between the Spenser and Childe families, given their potentially similar backgrounds as citizens of London, although, unfortunately, there is no hard evidence of their professions.[144] However the marriage came about, it was clearly a momentous decision for Spenser, as it closed off any chance of a career as a college fellow in Cambridge, a path he might have been expected to follow, given his relationship to Harvey.[145]

Spenser was more or less the average age at which men got married, being about 25 to 26, the mean age being 28, but Machabyas was rather young, being 19 rather than the average age of 24 to 26.[146] We know next to nothing about their married life, apart from the fact that they had two children, Sylvanus and Katherine, named after two of Richard Mulcaster's six children (three boys and three girls).[147] Spenser perhaps attended the christening of Mulcaster's son in March 1564, and the boy's funeral on 28 January 1573.[148] Machabyas died at some point before August 1590, probably not long before, as Spenser shares his own sense of grief with that of the bereaved Arthur Gorges in *Daphnaïda*.[149] It is likely that she conceived early in the marriage and was pregnant by the time that Spenser went to Ireland eleven months after the ceremony, or, possibly, had already given birth by then. Sylvanus was old enough in 1600–6 to mount a protracted legal challenge about the ownership of Kilcolman so he must have been born between 1579 and 1585.[150] And, Machabyas must surely have followed her husband to Ireland, but whether they left together immediately after his appointment as secretary to Lord Grey, or whether she joined him later is impossible to determine. Virtually nothing is known of her: given Spenser's comments on the subject elsewhere, Machabyas may have died in childbirth, or from resulting complications, a common cause of death for many women in the period.[151]

St Margaret's church, next to Westminster Abbey, was certainly a grand venue for a wedding: Milton and Pepys were married here in the following century, and St Margaret's is now the official church of the House of Commons. Newly rebuilt in early Tudor times (1482–1523), it is an imposing and spacious building, long and elegant, with magnificent high arches in the nave, leading straight to the altar at the east end.[152] The church witnessed a horrific event on Easter Day 1555 when William Flower, a disgruntled and deranged former monk, assaulted and stabbed the priest, John Cheltham, as he was about to take the communion service, his blood despoiling the consecrated host. When captured, Flower explained that he had a violent objection to transubstantiation. It is likely that he targeted St Margaret's church because of its proximity to Westminster Abbey, a monastic church which was about to be revived as a religious order, a symbolic target as the Catholic centre of the nation.[153] Flower was then burnt at the stake in the churchyard, having had his offending hand severed. John Foxe, while admitting Flower's crime, included him among the Protestant martyrs for his stand against transubstantiation.[154] The incident provides further evidence of the conservative nature of the social and religious world of late Elizabethan Westminster. One or both of Machabyas' parents would probably have witnessed the event, especially if they were Robert Childe and Alice Lord, who were married eighteen months later. At the very least, they would have heard about the shocking event from members of the congregation. It is hard, of course, to suggest that Flower's acts had any direct impact on Spenser's writing. Even so, knowledge of his assault and violent death may well have confirmed Spenser's understanding that the institution of the church was what really mattered, that it needed to be protected and supported, and that it should be able to accommodate a wide spectrum of belief, and not be dogmatically confessional in character.

Marriage, the act that was widely regarded as the proper transition into adulthood, was certainly a central feature of Spenser's writings, as C. S. Lewis famously argued, and Spenser's first two published works tell us a great deal about his first marriage.[155] In the *Letters*, Harvey concludes the first part of the correspondence with greetings to Spenser's new wife. In the letter dated from Saffron Walden, 23 April 1580 he states that 'Per tuam Venerem altera Rosalindula est' (through your love there is another (second) little Rosalind (?)) and describes her as 'mea bellissima Collina Clouta' (my most beautiful Mrs Colin Clout).[156] As Henry Woudhuysen has argued, 'The letters were issued to complement the publication of *The Shepheardes Calender* by describing the literary and intellectual concerns of those associated with Leicester House', which was where Spenser was living at the time.[157] There are numerous references in the *Letters* which explain and substantiate the meaning of the eclogues in the *Calender*, one of which is the figure of Rosalind, Colin's beloved.

Rosalind never actually appears in Spenser's poetry but she is named in six of the twelve eclogues in the *Calender* and later in *Colin Clouts come home againe* (1595). The first reference is in the opening eclogue, 'Januarie', when Colin confesses that it is pointless for the shepherd Hobbinol to give him 'clownish gifts and curtsies' because he 'giues them to *Rosalind* againe'.[158] E. K.'s long note explaining the significance of the name 'Rosalind' gives us a clear sense that the story is not quite what it seems to be:

Rosalinde) is also a feigned name, which being wel ordered, wil bewray the very name of hys loue and mistresse, whom by that name he coloureth. So as Ouide shadoweth hys loue under the name of Corynna, which of some is supposed to be Iulia, themperor Augustus his daughter, and wyfe to Agryppa. So doth Aruntius Stella euery where call his Lady Asteris and Ianthis, albe it is wel knowen that her right name was Violantilla: as witnesseth Statius in his Epithalamium. And so the famous Paragone of Italy, Madonna Coelia in her letters enuelopeth her selfe vnder the name of Zima: and Petrona vnder the name of Bellochia. And this generally hath bene a common custome of counterfeicting the names of secret Personages. (Spenser, *Shorter Poems*, p. 39)

The note achieves the opposite of what it claims to be doing, and actually draws attention to its cryptic nature even as it invites the reader to look for certainty. The use of 'wel ordered', meaning rightly lettered, sounds as if E. K. thinks that 'Rosalind' is an anagram, a false lead that has encouraged a number of bold readings. But, we must remember that this is the opinion of a commentator who is undoubtedly not what he appears to be. Therefore, instead of the clarity of a straightforward allegorical interpretation we are encouraged to think in terms of a series of complex and diverse literary texts, which hide as much as they reveal to the reader. The names that E. K. cites—Corynna, Asteris, Ianthis, Zima, and Bellochia—are literary, not familiar ones, and were invented for the texts in question as part of the literary games played by the authors to encourage their readers to speculate about the relationship between the text and an external reality.

More information is given about Rosalind in the April eclogue, when Hobbinol confirms Colin's story, telling Thenot that the 'Southerne shepheardes boye' (line 21) has rejected him and his gifts 'And woes the Widdowes daughter of the glenne', 'fayre *Rosalind*' (lines 26–7). E. K.'s note to line 27 showers extravagant, if somewhat facetious, praise on her:

The Widowes) He calleth Rosalind the Widowes daughter of the glenne, that is, of a country Hamlet or borough, which I thinke is rather sayde to colour and concele the person, then simply spoken. For it is well knowen, euen in spighte of Colin and Hobbinoll, that shee is a Gentle woman of no meane house, nor endewed with anye vulgare and common gifts both of nature and manners: but suche indeede, as neede nether Colin be ashamed to haue her made knowne by his verses, nor Hobbinol be greued, that so she should be commended to immortalitie for her rare and singular Vertues: Specially deseruing it no lesse, then eyther Myrto the most excellent Poete Theocritus his dearling, or Lauretta the divine Petrarches

Goddesse, or Himera the worthye Poete Stesichorus hys Idole: Vpon whom he is sayd so much to have doted, that in regard of her excellencie, he scorned and wrote against the beauty of Helena. For which his præsumptuous and unheedie hardinesse, he is sayde by vengeaunce of the Gods, thereat being offended, to haue lost both his eyes. (Spenser, *Shorter Poems*, p. 66)

The note is teasing and testing, allusive and elusive. It starts off by appearing to tell us that she is a young woman from a hamlet, a widow's daughter, which is then immediately denied as E. K. explains that this is a disguise and does not reveal her true identity. The words 'coloure and concele' hint at a possible pun on 'Rose', and even an anagram, but the last anecdote warns of Stesichorus losing his eyes as punishment for gazing on Helen too much, a sign that the reader needs to be careful and alert in reading the text. Colin and Hobbinol have been misleading the reader because she is in reality a gentlewoman, actually well suited to Colin, who should be proud to know her and to be able to write verses for her. The note accords with George Puttenham's well-known words on pastoral verse as a medium in which the poet is able 'under the vaile of homely persons, and in rude speeches to insinuate and glaunce at greater matters'.[159] E. K. concludes with a long series of flattering literary comparisons: Theocritus' Myrto, Petrarch's Laura, Stesichorus' Himera, and, best of all, Helen of Troy. Rosalind is a rare and inspirational beauty, as well as being more rooted in ordinary life.

The identity of Rosalind has inspired a large number of articles, many following Alexander Grosart, believing her to be a northern lass, whom Spenser met when he was in Lancashire, when he supposedly stayed at a house now called Spenser House, near Hurstwood Hall. Others have cast her as a Kentish maid he fell for when working for John Young in 1579.[160] Alexander Judson was speaking for many of his fellow scholars when he asserted that 'Rosalind was certainly a real person', even though 'Spenser took care that her identity should not be revealed'.[161] More recent studies have generally concluded that Rosalind is a figure standing for the queen (even though Elizabeth is represented in the April eclogue) or a more abstract poetic fiction.[162]

However, the identity of Rosalind is, I think, obvious enough if we read the *Calender* and the *Letters* together: she is clearly Spenser's new wife.[163] Therefore, when Harvey greets her in the letter of 23 April as 'alterea Rosalindula' and 'mea bellissima Collina Clouta' he is saluting Spenser's bride of six months and making sure that the alert reader understands who she is in the *Calender*. Harvey's Latin indicates that Machabyas is not like Rosalind or a second Rosalind as many have assumed, but she *is* Rosalind transformed into a real person. The drama of Colin, Hobbinol, and Rosalind is made clear for us, the joke of Colin rejecting Hobbinol for her revealed. Spenser can no longer write poems in bed with Harvey as the *Letters* tell us he did earlier because he is now a married man and shares his bed with

Rosalind/Machabyas. Critics have been eager to see Spenser sharing jokes in print with Harvey and other poets and writers, collaborating on the *Letters* and the *Calender*. However, they have not usually imagined that his wife might have been part of this circle and enjoyed the joke of her supplanting Hobbinol/Harvey in Colin/Spenser's affections. Colin transfers Hobbinol's gifts to Rosalind, a process that probably makes most sense if we think of it in terms of the poet's time and writing. Moreover, the literal description makes the actors in the apparent love-triangle appear pubescent, as Colin exploits Hobbinol's affection to further his suit for Rosalind, passing on the 'clownish gifts', toys, biscuits, and fruit, that Hobbinol gives to Colin.[164] This description of the exchange of gifts surely signals to the alert reader that a joke is taking place. Harvey's public acknowledgement of who she is in the *Letters* affirms her identity and her importance within the group around himself and Spenser. If Hobbinol, Colin, and, perhaps, E. K. bear a tangential relation to the names of the people they represent, why should Rosalind be any different? Critics have been curiously literal-minded in searching for her, or have chosen to sever her relationship to reality. The truth may be that identifying Rosalind as Machabyas is actually a straightforward task, which is part of the joke. Rosalind, like Machabyas, was an unusual name, a link that Spenser is surely exploiting.[165]

Spenser's representation of his new wife in his first major poem tells us frustratingly little about their life together. It does suggest, however, that Machabyas was party to her husband's literary jokes and extravagant references, showing that women were often involved in the literary coteries that were established through both manuscript circulation and print, even when they did not write anything. This is an important aspect of Spenser's literary career, especially given his later involvement with women patrons, and indicates that he always engaged with the women in his life, however he represented them in his poetry.[166] The *Calender* ends with Colin bereft and lonely, abandoned by Rosalind, who has left him for Menalcas, a figure first seen in the June eclogue in which Colin accuses him of stealing Rosalind: 'that by trecheree I Didst vnderfong my lasse, to wexe so light, I Shouldest well be knowne for such thy villanee' (June, lines 102–4). It is possible that the episode refers to a hiatus in Edmund and Machabyas' courtship. But, given the fictional representation of Spenser and Harvey's friendship in the *Calender*, no easy conclusion can be reached, especially as Menalcas is a name borrowed from Virgil's *Eclogues*. Furthermore, by the time the *Calender* was published, the couple were married, an outcome that was surely predictable when the work was submitted to the printer, sometime in April–May.[167]

We do not know where Edmund and Machabyas lived in London in the first year of their marriage. Marriages were usually delayed until the couple had acquired property, or, at least, the expectation of property and a reasonable income.[168] Perhaps Spenser knew that his prospects were good, being closely associated with, perhaps already in the employ of, the earl of Leicester. It is most likely that the couple continued to live in Westminster, the most expensive and fashionable area of the city, which would suggest that someone was looking after them, whether parents, relatives, or a patron such as Leicester or Burghley.[169] Spenser was probably searching for a job that would give him the means and the time to write, given the nature and style of the *Calender*. He could surely not have expected to have made his living directly from his writing. Accordingly, his first volume of poetry advertises his employability as a brilliant writer who had all the requisite skills to be a secretary: ability to work fast, mastery of a range of styles and registers, ability to keep secrets, loyalty. It is also a work that was designed to launch a literary career, and so to discovering a way of supporting that goal, not a means to an end, as has been suggested.[170] Moreover, being a secretary was a job that would have given Spenser and his wife the chance of living reasonably well: a place to live in a household; a range of important contacts; as well as access to paper and writing materials (secretaries often had generous allowances), even if the writer's time would be restricted. It was probably preferable to making a precarious living as a hack writer, producing a mixture of pamphlets, prose romances, and jointly authored plays, as the careers of such writers as Thomas Churchyard, Robert Greene (1558–92), and Henry Chettle (d. 1603–7) demonstrate.[171]

It is quite likely that Spenser planned to pursue a career as a secretary, and he may have acted in this capacity for Leicester in 1579, a possibility made more likely if we assume that he had already worked for Leicester carrying letters earlier in the 1570s (after the publication of the *Calender* it is unlikely that such a relationship could continue).[172] The most important book on being a secretary was Angell Day's *The English Secretorie*, which gives advice on how to write letters, forms of address, appropriate styles, tones and registers to use, but this was not published until 1586.[173] Spenser might have known Day in the late 1570s, as he was associated with the bookseller Cuthbert Burby, who published Spenser's translation of *Axiochus*, and they had a number of literary connections. Day knew Captain Nicholas Dawtrey, who was at Lodowick Bryskett's house in Ireland with Spenser in the early 1580s for the debate that prefaced *A Discourse of Civill Life;* both Day and Spenser published prefatory verses to William Jones's translation of Giovanni Battista Nenna's *Nennio, or A Treatise of Nobility* (1595); and Day also produced a version, via Jacques Amyot's French translation, of the Greek pastoral prose romance *Daphnis and Chloe* (1587), which may have been inspired by the success of the *Calender*, and clearly bears marks of its influence, as well as an elegy on Sidney's death (1586), as Spenser did a few years later.[174] There were indeed significant links between the two men, and it is therefore possible that Spenser might have seen or known about Day's book before it appeared. Working as a secretary was a plausible career opening for Spenser that might have enabled him to pursue his literary career, and an ambition entirely in keeping with the scholarly ideal of Gabriel Harvey to combine intellectual and political paths. In the late sixteenth century the conception and role of a secretary was changing rapidly to cope with the development of a national bureaucracy, as well as ordering the lives and papers of great men and women. Not only were there more jobs; there was also a great deal more writing about the secretarial office, as secretaries were imagined as both confidants and employees of the powerful.[175] Certainly, it was an attractive enough option for the classical scholar Henry Cuffe (1562/3–1601), who may have been the brother of Hugh Cuffe, Spenser's neighbour on the Munster Plantation, to abandon the Regius chair of Greek at Oxford, and join the secretariat of Robert Devereux, earl of Essex, alongside Henry Wotton and Anthony and Francis Bacon.[176]

However Spenser acquired income, he was still at work on his numerous literary projects. Years of study lie behind the *Calender*, but it is hard to know exactly how much work went into the planning and production of the published *Letters*, although it is fair to assume that they were not simply published as they were first written. Spenser's contributions are relatively short compared to Harvey's, most notably Harvey's lengthy treatise on the recent earthquake of 6 April 1580, the subject of a number of works by well-known London-based authors which draw the predictable conclusion that the natural event is a sign of God's wrath at the evil lives of Londoners.[177] The inclusion of Harvey's discourse on the earthquake and the subtitle to the first section of the letters, 'Three proper wittie familiar Letters, lately passed between two Vniversitie men, touching the Earthquake in April last, and our English reformed Versifying', suggests that Harvey and Spenser saw an opportunity to direct their work towards a wider audience and make a significant impact. The occasion of the earthquake was the spur to publish the letters in the form in which they appeared in print, the reverse order of the two sections, the first containing letters dated 2 (perhaps in error for 10) April (Spenser), April (Harvey), and undated (Harvey); the second, 5 October 1579 (Spenser) and 23 October 1579 (Harvey). The covering letter by a 'wellwiller of the two authors' is dated 19 June 1580, which suggests that the volume was hastily assembled and published soon after that date (it was entered in the Stationers' Register on 30 June).[178]

Much of the discussion between Harvey and Spenser concerns the need to reform English poetry, along the lines discussed by the Areopagus group, which the *Letters* define and undoubtedly exaggerate in significance and coherence.[179] The evidence of Harvey's *Letter-Book*, especially the section of letters addressed to Spenser, which are a mass of crossings-out and heavy revision, indicate that Harvey ushered the volume into print based on a series of original texts that he heavily altered, certainly his own. The volume, published by Harvey's printer, Henry Bynneman, looks as if it were designed by Harvey to promote his young protégé, advertising the two correspondents as equals on the title page, but then assuming the dominant role himself.

In doing so, Harvey was also promoting himself as the tutor of the great new poet with whom he discusses poetry as a learned authority, and lending weight to his satirical discourse against Cambridge contained in the discourse on the earthquake, the dullness of which contrasts to the brilliance of his own enterprise.[180] And, as most of the authors of treatises on the earthquake were linked to Edward de Vere, seventeenth earl of Oxford (1550–1604), Harvey's attack on pious, providential discourses about God's wrath also looks like a concerted verbal assault on the earl and his circle, especially when read alongside Harvey's poem 'Speculum Tuscanismi'.[181] The seeds for the bitter feud between Nashe and Harvey were undoubtedly sown here.

The correspondences between the *Letters* and the *Calender*, and the extensive comments that Harvey provides on the anonymous volume, suggest that Spenser was involved in the planning and production of the volume. The evidence of cordial relations between the two later suggests that Spenser did not feel aggrieved or exploited by Harvey's project, if that is what it was. We have little sense of Spenser's identity from his letters, which amount to a total of twelve pages (four of which are verse), compared to over fifty by Harvey. Spenser writes about quantitative metre; he lists what he is working on; he defers to Harvey and asks his advice and invites him to respond at great length on subjects, as a student would when writing to a tutor; he plays jokes, keeping up the pretence that E. K.'s commentary is by an unknown third party, for example. If we are to learn anything significant about him from his two letters we have to read between the lines, always a problematic exercise. Spenser is both elusive and eager to control the representation of himself that he helps present to the world.

This is especially noticeable in Spenser's discussion of the last-minute changes he claims he made to the *Calender* in the letter of 5 October 1579, so giving readers an apparent insight into the composition of the work, further evidence that these earlier letters would have come first had the opportunity of the earthquake not arisen:

You may perceiue how much your Counsel in al things preuaileth with me, and how altogether I am ruled and ouer-ruled thereby: I am now determined to alter mine owne former purpose, and to subscribe to your aduizement: being notwithstanding resolued stil, to abide your farther resolution. First, I was minded for a while to haue intermitted the vttering of my writings: leaste by ouer-cloying their noble eares, I should gather a contempt of my self, or else seeme rather for gaine and commoditie to doe it, for some sweetnesse that I haue already tasted. Then also me seemeth the work too base for his excellent Lordship, being made in Honour of a priuate Personage vnknowne, which of some yl-willers might be vpbraided, not to be so worthie, as you knowe she is: or the matter not so weightie, that it should be offred to so weightie a Personage: or the like. The selfe former Title stil liketh me wel ynough, and your fine Addition no lesse.[182]

In so many ways, this is an extraordinary passage and one that it seems hard to imagine was ever designed to be part of a published book. The letter appears to give us an insight into the private life of a writer, a rare and extremely unusual documentation of an author's thought process: certainly nothing like this had been published before in Tudor England. But is it what it seems to be, or has the letter been carefully prepared for us? Harvey saw the letter as a literary form that expressed the ideal of the 'Respublica literaria', the free exchange of ideas between equals in an otherwise hierarchical society. His *Letter-Book* shows that he altered letters that were probably never sent, replacing the addressee 'Immerito' with 'Benvolio', which, as Henry Woudhuysen has argued, was probably a change made when Spenser went to Ireland, Benvolio standing for John Wood, the nephew of Sir Thomas Smith, who had been at school with Harvey.[183] The *Letters* are hardly a simple record of the correspondence between Spenser and Harvey; they are shaped as literary works that represent the two writers as they themselves saw fit.

Spenser represents himself as subservient to Harvey and eager to take his advice on all matters. Harvey is credited with an addition to the title of the *Calender*, presumably the subtitle, 'Conteyning twelue Aeclogues proportionable to the twelue monthes', a detail that might have prevented readers from confusing the work with the popular *Kalender of Shepherdes*, one of the sources for Spenser's poems.[184] Spenser claims that Harvey has influenced how he has changed the *Calender* for the better in every way, and that he values his counsel so much that it always overrules what he thinks. It is impossible to believe that this is true, or that Spenser and Harvey cooperated in this way, especially given Harvey's rather facetious comments on the *Calender* in his final letter on versifying in the first part of the correspondence, where he designs a new emblem in praise of the queen to add to the March eclogue; cites Cuddie's opening speech from October to state how weary he is after working so hard (lines 7–18); and concludes that, while Colin is a good poet, Cuddie and Hobbinoll (i.e., Harvey himself) are not real poets, being 'as little beholding to their *Mistresse Poetrie*, as ever you wist'.[185] It is unlikely that either Harvey or Spenser deemed such comments sage counsel, and Harvey is deliberately undercutting his role as Spenser's superior. Spenser can therefore seem properly deferential to authority, and his tutor playful and self-deprecating, each assuming a role that is then refused by the other party so that they end up relatively equal in status. Like the *Calender*, the *Letters* deliberately construct an ideal image of a collection of intellectual equals who have produced the text working together, indicating that, while Harvey was the senior partner, it was a collaborative enterprise. Read together, both texts suggest that a republic of letters has been established, and that reading the work of its members—often in the form of their letters—is an ideal mode of learning, far better, as Harvey's satire indicates, than attending one of the established universities, which are riddled with false hierarchies, spurious learning, and gullible, unimaginative dons.

Why might Spenser and Harvey have assumed these positions and made this case? Could the *Letters* be read as an advertisement of their talents to anyone who wished to read them, suggesting that they have enough to offer any prospective employer? Neither Harvey nor Spenser was averse to self-publicity, or to confrontation.[186] But it is extraordinary, probably a unique case in literary history, to discuss the dedication of the work designed to launch your literary career. Perhaps the *Letters* mark the recognition that the earl of Leicester's support had either ceased or was about to end. The correspondence can be read to indicate that the writers are for hire to a prospective patron, showcasing their skills as letter writers whose achievements go beyond anything contained in one of the many letter-writing manuals freely available at the time, the first of which, William Fulwood's frequently reprinted *The Enemie of Idlenesse* (1568), had been published by Bynneman.[187] Leicester would surely have been affronted by such public discussions of patronage, and he would understandably have been offended by Spenser's behaviour. Spenser writes in his letter of 5 October that he expects to be going abroad in the earl's service: 'let me be answered, ere I goe: which will be (I hope, I feare, I thinke) the next weeke, if I can be dispatched of my Lorde'.[188] The information is already out of date. The journey never took place and the point of advertising it now can only be to show how close to the earl Spenser used to be and how much his work was valued.[189]

The *Letters* show that personal relationships are far more important than ones designed for gain and advancement: this may well be a double-bluff, designed to attract patrons impressed at the honesty and dexterity of the correspondents. More significantly, they are an ambitious attempt to fashion Spenser and Harvey as the English heirs of the great letter writers of the classical and humanist world, Cicero, Erasmus, and Vives.[190] Their irreverent cheek and self-regard probably did attract certain important 'yl-willers', among whom was the earl of Oxford, evidently angered by the portrait of him as the vain Italian earl in 'Speculum Tuscanismi', with his 'cringing side necke, Eyes glauncing, Fisnamie smirking, | *With* forfinger kisse, and *braue* embrace to the footewarde,' a description that was probably brought to his attention by his literary client, John Lyly.[191] Oxford's enmity eventually fed into that of Thomas Nashe and began the quarrel that ended Harvey's literary career, a neat irony, if we assume that the same volume helped to kick-start Spenser's career in the Irish civil service.[192]

5

To Ireland I

ARTHUR, Lord Grey de Wilton (1536–93) was appointed Lord Deputy of Ireland on 15 July 1580, with the explicit instruction that he establish government in Munster.[1] He was not, like many Lord Deputies, necessarily delighted by his appointment, which generally involved hard service and, in extreme cases, accusations of treason and even execution; the risk of illness; and inevitable penury, the crown often failing to remunerate the incumbent adequately, forcing the official to supplement military action through their own finances.[2] Certainly, Grey complained that he had not been given enough time to prepare for his demanding new role, and he had successfully avoided the job in the early 1570s when he was—or was pretending to be—ill.[3] Nevertheless, he had powerful support from Ralegh, Walsingham, and Leicester, and received a long letter of advice from Sir Henry Sidney, Leicester's brother-in-law, who had served as Lord Deputy three times in the 1560s and 1570s.[4]

Grey came from a military family. His father, William, had a reputation for ruthlessness and had played a prominent role in the bloody suppression of the 1549 rebellion in East Anglia.[5] Grey was appointed specifically because of his extensive military experience in France and Scotland to counter a serious threat to Tudor rule in Ireland, the second Desmond Rebellion (1579–83).[6] This particular revolt had broken out in part because the FitzGerald earls of Desmond had felt that their power and authority were threatened by the spread of Tudor rule and the attempt to make the ancient Irish lordships conform to English law, tenancy, and social expectation. Once the Act of the Irish parliament passed on 18 June 1541 had declared that Henry VIII was king rather than lord of Ireland and could command the unconditional obedience of his Irish subjects,[7] Irish lords had to surrender their titles and have them regranted under new terms and conditions by the English crown. They had, understandably, often resented this change in status and seen crown attempts to regulate them as part of a much more sinister campaign.[8] The revolt was also a result of the fractious rivalry between the Desmonds and the Ormonds, the two major dynasties in south-west Ireland, one that the Ormonds were always likely to win given their superior power at court and relationship to the queen.[9]

The revolt soon developed into a serious and well-supported rebellion that went beyond the last desperate actions of a dying dynasty.[10] In 1580 the situation looked like the Tudor regime's worst nightmare: the combination of local hostility with an international Catholic crusade, led by an impassioned zealot, James Fitzmaurice Fitzgerald, eager to draw Irish resistance into a larger assault on the realms of the usurping heretic queen. Although Fitzmaurice was killed in a skirmish on 18 August 1579, his uncle, Gerald Fitzgerald, the fourteenth earl of Desmond (c.1533–83), now reluctantly assumed leadership of the rebellion, and was duly proclaimed a traitor on 2 November 1579.[11]

Grey appointed Spenser as one of his secretaries immediately afterwards, with a salary of £10 per six months.[12] Spenser was probably recommended to Grey by Leicester and the Sidneys, who would have known him as a writer capable of acting as a secretary from his stay in Leicester House in 1579. It is possible that they had already met, given Grey's proximity to Leicester and the Sidneys, or even through George Gascoigne, the soldier-poet who was a client of Grey's and a friend of Gabriel Harvey's.[13] Presumably, Spenser was recommended as someone in need of work who was capable of performing secretarial tasks, especially scribal duties, and he had worked hard to represent himself as a capable writer for hire in his first two published works. Spenser probably worked as part of a larger team around the Lord Deputy, in the same way that other secretariats in England functioned, especially as it was the stated aim of many in the English Privy Council to reform Irish government and civil service and make them more like their English counterparts.[14] He was not Grey's only secretary, as by 1581 Grey also employed Timothy Reynolds, and undoubtedly had other clerks and secretaries in Dublin Castle working for him. Moreover, the consistent handwriting that survives in Grey's letters to the Privy Council and major political figures in England indicates that Grey had at least another two secretaries copying out documents.[15] Although no trace of his hand survives in any of Grey's letters, one of these would have been Geoffrey Fenton, who came to Ireland at about the same time as Spenser, and whose life was connected to Spenser's over the next few years (both were present at the Massacre at Smerwick and both married into the Boyle family), although Fenton soon moved on to higher office.[16] The evidence of the surviving letters suggests that Spenser soon became Grey's chief secretary and was trusted more than his other secretaries, often being the last to check and seal the Lord Deputy's letters.[17]

We will probably never know whether this was a great opportunity for the newly married poet in need of gainful employment or an effective banishment as a result of offending too many people in his early work, most significantly Leicester rather than the usual suspect, Burghley.[18] In fact, given Burghley's extensive and well-attested interest in Ireland—he carried Nowell's superb map of Ireland in his pocket—it is hard to see how Spenser could have obtained this position if he had incurred the hostility of the chief minister at this stage.[19] A secretary was, in fact, an extremely good job, coveted by many, especially writers, scholars, and intellectuals; Henry Cuffe gave up his Oxford chair for a salary of £20 per annum, the same wage that Spenser received for working for Grey.[20] Henry Chettle received £25. 5s. from playwriting in 1601–2, probably as large an income as an experienced writer for hire might expect to receive in London at the time.[21] In general professional salaries for schoolmasters, university lecturers, clergymen, the sort of professions that Spenser could have expected to pursue, ranged from about £10 to £20.[22] Lower down the social scale, a good servant, capable of overseeing others, would only have received about £2 per annum in the 1590s.[23] A secretary was also of considerable influence, as many collaborated with their masters in producing letters and documents, often acting as co-authors.[24] The role could be seen as a natural continuation of Spenser's relationship with Harvey, as well as entailing the sort of political influence that Harvey consistently argued that the intellectual deserved.

Spenser was probably made an offer he could not refuse, and, although it may not have been quite what he wanted, Ireland was a land in which fortunes large and small could be made, higher standards of living could be enjoyed, and there was access to property for those without any obvious means of obtaining it in England. Spenser's Irish career illustrates these possibilities as well as any, given his ultimate acquisition of the Kilcolman estate and marriage into the phenomenally wealthy Boyle family.[25] His own writings suggest that he was preparing himself for such a career and using his access to print to advertise his range of skills and availability. As a secretary he would have been able to acquire significant supplies of paper and writing materials. A document written out in 1581 lists payments to the clerks and secretaries, including Bryskett, Reynolds, and Spenser. Spenser received an allowance of £15 a year for 'paper, yncke and parchment', a large sum, as it was nearly the same as his annual salary.[26] Paper, which had to be imported from Europe, mainly Italy and France, as English paper mills were extremely limited, was relatively expensive.[27] A ream (500 sheets) cost between 2s. and 7s. at the end of the sixteenth century, and about the same in Ireland, which suggests that even if Spenser had to buy some expensive paper to send official letters, as well as ink and parchment, he still had a generous amount to spend on rough paper for his own purposes. The cheapest white paper available was about 2s. 6d. a ream in London, and approximately the same in Ireland, according to the Bristol port books accounting for trade with the south-west.[28] Nevertheless, Spenser published nothing for the next ten years, a significant lacuna in a writing career that had started with such aplomb. This hiatus can partly be explained by the significant demands that his working life placed upon him, and would further indicate that his work had caused offence in 1579–80 and that only when he had freed himself of the need for dependence on patrons did Spenser feel able to place his work before the public once again.

Grey travelled to Ireland from Beaumaris, Anglesey, about 10 August 1580. He had already been on the Welsh island for about a month, partly delayed by unfavourable winds, a common problem. Grey was also waiting for his army from Berwick to arrive and his army from Wales to assemble so that they could join with an army that had marched the 225 miles from London. There was an understandable swell of ill feeling, especially as shelter and provisions were inadequate for the soldiers and their families who had travelled with them, as was often the case.[29] The company sailed in the *Handmaid* and arrived on 12 August in Dublin where Grey took up his residence in Dublin Castle (Plate 12). Spenser would have been among the Lord Deputy's entourage and he would probably have started his new life taking rooms in the castle, just as he had lived in Leicester House when in the earl's service. Whether Machabyas sailed with her husband we do not know, but she either came with him then, or joined him later, perhaps when he finally acquired a house.

An Act of the Privy Council (29 August) records that Grey's wife was granted forty-two horses to help convey her belongings to port ready to travel to Ireland, so she clearly sailed after her husband, obviously in part due to the short notice of his appointment.[30] Moreover, there is a funeral monument in Christ Church Cathedral to two of Grey's sons, who died while the family lived in Dublin.[31] The Spensers' first two children, Sylvanus and Katherine, appear to have made their adult lives in Ireland and so would have lived there as children, which they would probably not have done had the Spensers remained apart. Nevertheless, the fact that the couple only had two children who lived into adulthood may be of significance. Possibly some did not survive long or Machabyas suffered a number of spontaneous abortions, as would have been common. England had a relatively low fertility rate compared to the rest of Europe, owing to prolonged practices of breastfeeding, but even so women tended to conceive nearly every year. Moreover, London women tended to make more use of wet nurses and so conceive more frequently than their provincial counterparts. The evidence suggests that either the Spensers lived apart or that Machabyas was not especially healthy, which a move to Ireland, notorious for a damp climate that often had a fatal impact on English settlers, would not have helped.[32]

Grey, noted for his decisive, often impetuous, style of commandment, decided to confront the rebel armies immediately. As his letters invariably reveal, he was a confident, straightforward man who saw the world in terms of black and white and who was unable to understand why anyone could see matters differently, reflecting his military training and outlook. As his later actions demonstrate, he had no time for opposition to the queen. Spenser saw the world in far more complex terms, but his loyalty to Grey probably reflects the fact that his employer was nothing if not consistent and was certainly keen to look after those in his employ whom he trusted, one of whom was Spenser.

Grey should probably have waited until he understood Irish conditions better before engaging the Irish in battle, but he decided that he should meet the threat of the O'Byrnes and O'Tooles to the south of Dublin in August.[33] Military campaigns were not like those fought against regular armies on the Continent, but messy skirmishes and ambushes. The Irish, used to raiding rather than fighting pitched battles, and less well equipped than their English counterparts, generally relied on speed and stealth to attack English forces. Irish armies largely consisted of kerns, on foot and on horse, lightly armed soldiers who fought without armour or helmets, and who were especially effective when their enemies had little room for manoeuvre, and gallowglasses, Scottish mercenaries, mainly from the Hebrides, also armed with axes, spears, and two-handed swords, who were especially effective against cavalry.[34] Sudden attacks took place in woods, which were especially dangerous places, and valleys. Grey's first engagement with the Irish was the disastrous defeat at Glenmalure in the Wicklow Mountains on 25 August when, after a tiring climb in full armour, the regimented English were easily picked off in the narrow glen by the mobile Irish enemy led by Fiach MacHugh, elected chief of the O'Byrnes and the most dangerous military figure in the O'Byrne and O'Toole lordships.[35] Out of a force of about 2,000 men the English suffered more than 100 casualties before retreating to Dublin—hardly a decisive defeat, but a costly and embarrassing setback against a force that numbered no more than 700. The battle merited a prominent description in the *Annals of the Four Masters*.[36]

Spenser undoubtedly accompanied Grey on his first military excursion. He refers directly to the defeat in his account of the marriage of the Thames and the Medway in *The Faerie Queene*, referring to the 'balefull Oure, late staind with English blood' (*FQ* IV.xi.44, line 5) (the river does look red because of the clay soil through which it flows) (Plate 13). In *A View* Spenser makes a characteristic quibble/pun, referring to 'the strengthe and great fastnes of *Glan malour*', an evil place and an evil time, which the rebel Hugh McShane used to build up his power: 'Adioyneth vnto his howsse of *Ballinecorre* drewe vnto him manye theves and Outlawes which fled vnto the succour of that glenne as to a Sanctuarye and broughte vnto him parte of that spoile of all the Countrie thoroughe which he grewe stronge and in shorte space got vnto himself a greate name therby amongst the Irishe.'[37] In the 1590s the enemy was the O'Neills so Spenser concentrates on their threat to the crown (Hugh McShane was the cousin of Hugh O'Neill). Nevertheless, the reference is also to Grey's defeat, the word 'balefull' in the poem providing a gloss for '*malour*' in *A View*, indicating that this first observation of Irish warfare imprinted itself on Spenser's imagination.[38] Given his trenchant defence of Grey in *A View*, it is hardly surprising that he does not discuss the defeat, surviving as little more than a ghostly presence, a reminder of what could go wrong.

The first recorded acts of Spenser's new job are copies of letters from Hugh Maginnis to the Lord Deputy complaining about the attacks on his lands in County Down by Turlough Luineach O'Neill and appealing for help, dated 29 August; and a letter dated 31 August containing similar appeals for help from Hugh O'Neill, Baron of Dungannon, warning that Turlough was planning to 'invade the pale' (Figure 5).[39] These apparently minor documents provide a sense of the murky and confused nature of Irish political life. Both O'Neill and Maginnis were clients of the crown who had sworn an oath of obedience to the queen and agreed to rule their tenants according to the English model, giving them established plots legally recorded, charging rents, and settling them in particular areas rather than permitting the more flexible Irish model of tenancy.[40] Here, they are also trying to exploit the crown forces in their own struggles with their neighbours, a tactic that must have been obvious to Grey. Spenser clearly worked as Grey's copyist in this early period of his service, a role that was menial, as befitted a new secretary, but also intimate, one reason why he was undoubtedly required to accompany his master on his various expeditions around Ireland and acquired a personal knowledge of the country's geography alongside his use of maps and other topographical aids.[41]

Spenser was trusted with the distribution of concordatum, 'a special fund at the disposal of the Lord Lieutenant and Council for payment of extraordinary expenditure'.[42] Between September 1580, soon after he arrived in Dublin, and August 1582, when his term as Grey's secretary ended, Spenser appears to have been responsible for the payment of nearly £600 to messengers, a huge sum, which indicates that he inspired the trust of his superiors, was a relatively senior figure already among the civil servants working in Dublin, and became used early on to seeing large amounts of money change hands. The task would also have sharpened his awareness of the topography and navigable routes in Ireland. The same document also records a payment to Spenser of £20 per annum, necessary for a secretary attending the Lord Deputy and Council.[43] It is hard to believe that such money was simply for travel expenses, as it was another year's salary. Probably Spenser had to buy clothes and conduct himself in a grander manner than he had been used to in provincial England, and the large sum was to enable him to fulfil his new status.

Grey had not yet been invested as Lord Deputy because his predecessor, Sir William Pelham, Lord Justice of Ireland, had not returned to Dublin from his ruthless campaign against the rebels in Munster. Pelham's actions, hanging scores of rebels, destroying crops and villages, and massacring the inhabitants of Carrigafoyle Castle on 27 March, created the terrifying wilderness that was unable to support its considerable population described in one of the most memorable passages in *A View*.[44] The *Annals of the Four Masters* saw Pelham's actions as a new departure in Irish warfare:

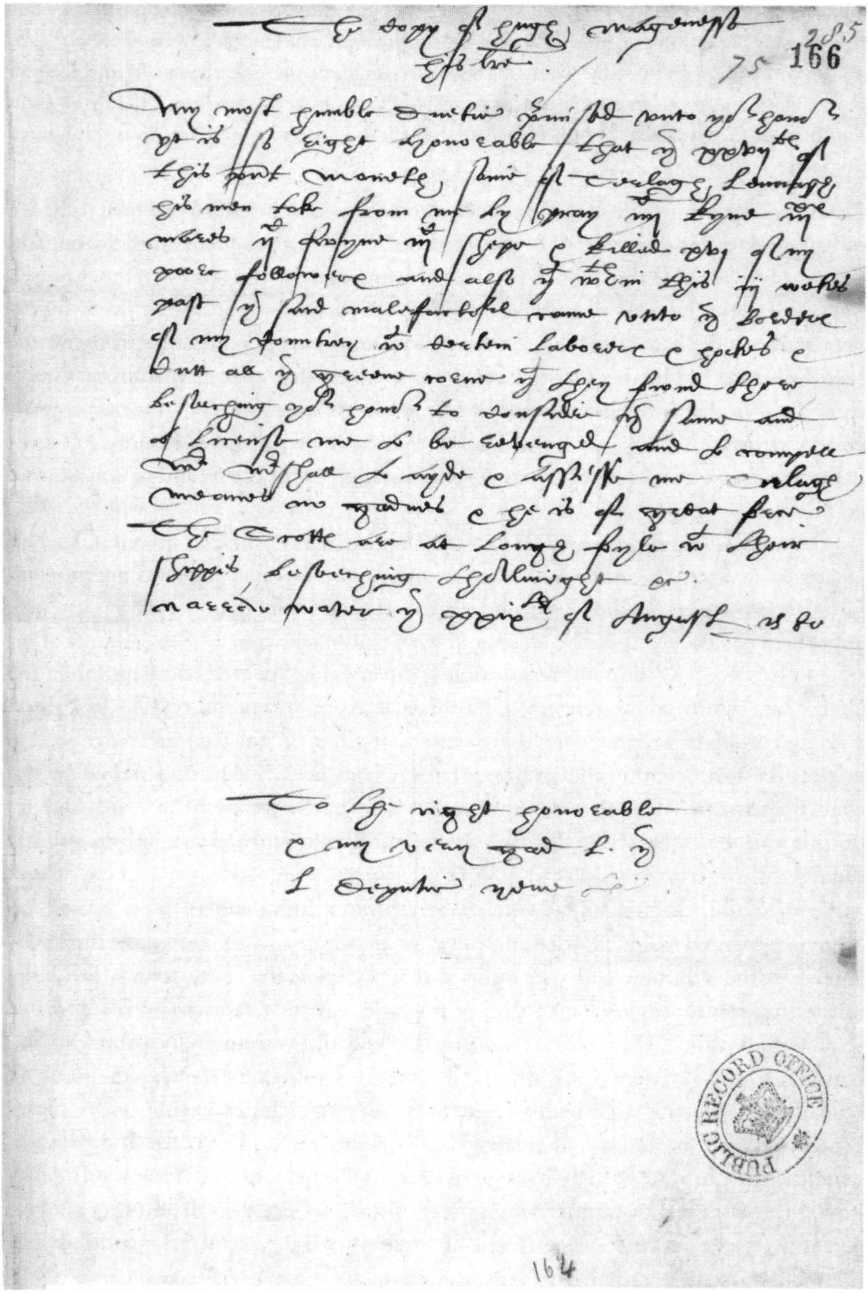

Figure 5. Hugh O'Neill to Lord Grey, 31 August 1580. Reproduced with kind permission of the National Archives.

The lord justice proceeded with all his forces . . . they gave no mercy to rich or poor that came in their way. It was not surprising to kill those who were able to make resistance, but they also slew the blind and infirm, women, sons, and daughters, the sick, the feeble, and the old; their wealth and properties were carried away to the camp where the lord justice was; great numbers of English fell by those who were endeavouring to recover their plundered property.[45]

Pelham's decision to refuse to let a rebel surrender unless he could produce evidence of having slain another rebel of higher rank became known as 'Pelham's Pardon' and set the style for the rest of the protracted campaign in the south-west, although Pelham's tactics were to be pushed to the limits by Lord Grey during his two-year deputyship.[46] Pelham eventually returned to Dublin on 6 September bringing the sword of state.[47] The day before he had complained that a letter written by Grey's secretary—probably Spenser, given his role in Grey's bureaucracy—was not 'considerately written', which was more likely a criticism of the Lord Deputy's lack of deference than a comment on Spenser's handwriting or his command of epistolatory etiquette.

The next day Grey was invested as Lord Deputy in St Patrick's Cathedral, Dublin (Plate 14), an event Spenser would have attended. The sword of state was presented to Grey by Sir Henry Wallop, the under-treasurer, another figure to whom Spenser appears to have been especially close, and with whom he worked from the start of his time in Ireland.[48] Wallop was responsible for overseeing Spenser's distribution of the concordata to official messengers.[49] Two days later, on 9 September, Grey set off on a second military excursion to the northern reaches of the Pale at Drogheda, to inspect the fortifications and to bring Turlough to heel, but he had retired by the time they reached the city. Spenser would also have attended the Lord Deputy on this journey. Meanwhile, Pelham was taken ill and returned to England in early October.[50]

Campaigning in Ireland was invariably a brutal affair which took its toll on even experienced soldiers used to physical discomfort and harsh conditions.[51] There was no standing army, so military forces depended on conscripts, levied by muster masters throughout the shires of England, which were each given a quota to recruit, and which they often made up by enlisting criminals, vagabonds, and masterless men.[52] There was a strict and efficient command structure, the result of reforms made during Elizabeth's reign, with the commander having under him a general of the foot and a lieutenant general of the horse. A marshal and provost-marshal (the position Barnabe Googe secured in Connaught and Thomond) determined the locations of camps and enforced discipline. Beneath them other soldiers performed specific tasks: the sergeant major-general assembled battle forces; the scout-master, reconnaissance operations; the forage-master, securing and distributing victuals; and the carriage-master, transport. But, despite this disciplined organization, transporting troops and equipment, especially large field guns for siege warfare, around a boggy, wet, and inhospitable country with a hostile population, was a major logistical problem. Artillery, which often proved ineffective in battle anyway, frequently sank and got stuck in the muddy Irish roads. Camps were primitive and uncomfortable, and it was invariably difficult to find food, the native population being sparse and exceptionally mobile. Pay, equipment, and supplies were invariably badly distributed, or purloined by corrupt officials, usually the captains in charge of each company, and impoverished soldiers tended to sell their uniforms for food. Although soldiers were supposed to be mainly English, and laws and ordinances were passed to allow only limited numbers to join the ranks, a large number of the English army were Irish. Desertion was a major problem, as was disease, the main cause of death for English soldiers unable to cope with the damp climate. Running even a relatively small-scale campaign in Ireland was incredibly expensive. While the crown complained of ever-increasing costs, the military felt that the army was not adequately supported, given the major tasks it was assigned.

In the autumn of 1580 the situation in Munster was reaching crisis point. Although ships had been sent to intercept them, a small armada carrying a force of perhaps as many as 800 Spanish and Italian papal troops landed in Smerwick Harbour in Dingle on 12–13 September, joining the Irish troops already there, who had established earthwork fortifications on a promontory on the west side of Smerwick Harbour, on the site known as Dunanoir, the Golden Fort.[53] Although protected from the elements and with good visibility, enabling the defenders to observe ships coming into the harbour as well as troops coming towards them using the only logical route over the Slieve Mish Mountains, the fort was conspicuously isolated and the expedition force was vulnerable if not supported by reinforcements from land or sea.[54] A contemporary Spanish map shows that its precarious position was well understood, the cartographer representing the fort as 'virtually an island except for a narrow neck of land connecting it with the mainland'.[55] An English map shows a similar picture with the fort vulnerable to a combined land and sea assault (Figure 6).[56] It had been noted earlier that year that the rebels were likely to try and establish a base there and Pelham had inspected the fort in early July. He found it, ominously for the later expeditionary force, 'a vain toy, and of little importance, in which place no man could hide himself but that in the hill adjoining he was subject to all shot, small or great'.[57]

Grey's response was, as might have been expected, immediate. If the papal troops could join up with local rebels the situation in Ireland could become desperate for its English rulers, given the unrest in Ulster and Leinster which threatened the borders of the Pale. A month after he had been installed as Lord Deputy, Grey marched down to Cork, leaving Dublin on 6 October. We can be sure that Spenser was with him, as there are letters in his hand, which were written while on the campaign.[58]

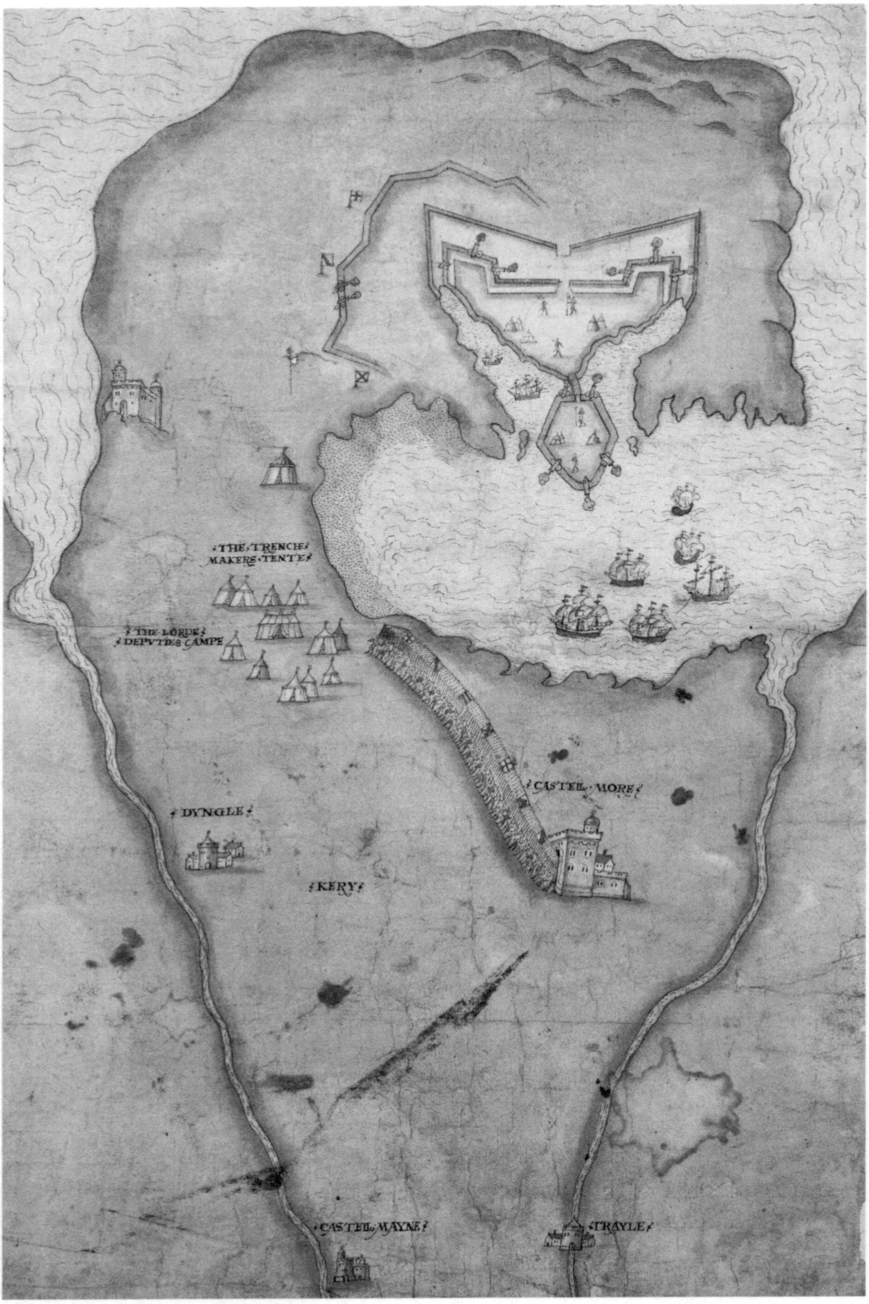
THE TRENCHE MAKERS TENTE
THE LORDE DEPUTIES CAMPE
CASTELL MORE
DYNGLE
KERY
CASTELL MAYNE
TRAYLE

Figure 6. Map of Smerwick Harbour, 1580. Reproduced with kind permission of the National Maritime Museum.

On 17 October the army left Cork, marched north to Limerick, and then on to Smerwick, arriving there on the 31st.[59] It must have been on this journey that Spenser first witnessed the effects of the wars on the local population in one of the key passages in *A View* written more than fifteen years later, although later he would have seen the even more terrifying effects of Grey's scorched earth policies in 1581–2, as witnessed by Warham St Leger, who Spenser knew well.[60] Irenius predicts that the military action he suggests is necessary to end Tyrone's latest challenge to crown authority will not last long because of the terrible effects of conflict:

The profe whearof I sawe sufficientlye ensampled in | Those late wars of mounster, for notwithstandinge that the same was a moste ritche and plentifull Countrye ful of Corne and Cattell that ye woulde haue thoughte they Coulde haue bene able to stande longe yeat ere one yeare yeat ere one yeare and a haulfe they weare broughte to soe wonderfull wretchedness as that anie stonie harte would haue rewed the same. Out of euerie Corner of the woods and glinnes they Came Crepinge for the vppon theire handes for theire Legs Coulde not beare them, they loked lkike Anotomies of deathe, they spake like ghostes Cryinge out of theire graues, they did eate the dead Carrions, hapie wheare they Coulde finde them, Yea and one another sone after, in so muche as the verye carcasses of water Cresses or Shamarocks theare they flocked as to a feaste for the time, yeat not able longe to Continve therewithal, that in shorte space theare weare non allmoste lefte and a moste populous and plentifull Countrye sodenlye lefte voide of man or beaste, yeat sure in al that warr theare perished not manie by the sworde but al by the extremitye of famine which they themselves had wroughte.[61]

This is an extraordinary passage, a rhetorical tour de force, that still has the power to shock, as it was obviously designed to when written in the 1590s. Spenser has deliberately crafted a series of details that authenticate Irenius' status as a privileged eyewitness to the terrible events: the crawling, the cannibalism, the desperate foraging for plants to sustain life in a once abundant and fertile area. And yet, even though he can accurately recall the carnage of the Desmond Rebellion, Irenius/Spenser defends the brutal tactics pursued by Pelham and Grey. The text is clear that the responsibility lies with the rebels themselves. Spenser was hardly the first to argue this way or to use terror to subdue the native population: Sir Humphrey Gilbert made visitors to his headquarters at Kilmallok approach him along a path marked by poles on which were placed the heads of rebels before they could surrender to him and John Derricke ended his defence of Sir Henry Sidney's period as Lord Deputy, *The Image of Ireland*, with a long lament by the dead Rory Oge O'More warning others not to threaten the crown or they too would find their severed heads mounted on the walls of Dublin Castle.[62] But Spenser is going a stage further than merely showing that it is important to take drastic measures *pour encourager les autres*. He is demonstrating the benefits of his humanist-inspired education, showing that he can think through serious, difficult, and disturbing problems. If England wants to maintain its hold over Ireland and to spread the benefits of its civilization to the Irish, then policies that might seem unthinkable to most English men and women will have to be pursued. In order to salvage the sa(l)vage island, a pun Spenser makes in both *A View* and *The Faerie Queene*, savage methods will prove necessary.[63] The longer-term benefits will outweigh the costs, but in the short term it might be hard to see the purpose of so much death or where the destruction will end.

Spenser had clearly read Erasmus' adage, 'Dulce Bellum Inexpertis' (war is sweet to the ignorant) and here outlines the full horror of war in order to show that the apparent victims are the ones who have failed to understand its grim reality.[64] Accordingly, Irenius can support the terror tactics of Pelham, actions that also make those of Grey seem more plausible and reasonable in contrast. The adage appears to have been appropriated by those around Grey as a means of defending their behaviour and tactics.[65] Earlier, Gascoigne had appealed to Grey for patronage as one old soldier to another in his poem founded on the same adage, which recounted his experiences with Grey in the Netherlands (1572–4).[66] The poem was based on the assumption that both men shared a distaste for war, but realized what had to be done, praising Grey as 'an universall patrone of all Souldiours'.[67] It opens with lines that claim that only those who know war can write about it with understanding, a deft appropriation of Erasmus' rather more obviously pacifist argument, later followed by Spenser: 'To write of Warre and wote not what it is, | Nor ever yet could march where War was made, | May well be thought a worke begonne amis' (lines 1–3). Spenser would have read Gascoigne's poem when it appeared in 1575, although Harvey noted in his copy of Gascoigne's *Poesies*: 'A sory resolution for owre Netherland Soldiours. A good pragmatique Discourse; but vnseasonable, & most vnfitt for a Captain, or professed Martialist.'[68]

Spenser's description of the massacre, especially if read alongside others in *A View*, further testifies to the profound impact that his first few months in Ireland had on his imagination.[69] Certainly the horror of the account of the famine is a world away from the irreverent banter of the *Letters* or the literary pyrotechnics of the *Calender*. Within three and a half months Spenser had been transported from the city of his birth, taken up residence in a foreign capital (at a time when few Englishmen outside the aristocracy and the military travelled at all), been present at a spectacular military disaster, and marched with an army some 300 miles through hostile territory laid waste, in which he had witnessed the terrible effects of early modern military operations. But worse was to come.

On 29 September an English naval detachment of nine ships led by Admiral William Winter set out for the Fort D'Oro.[70] The first ship of the flotilla, the *Swiftsure*, commanded by Richard Bingham, reached Smerwick Harbour on 7 November, the same day that Grey's army arrived. Some minor skirmishes were fought while the *Swiftsure* fired at the fort. During one of these, John Cheke, son of the Greek scholar John Cheke, was killed, the only English casualty, according to both Grey and Geoffrey Fenton.[71] The rest of the ships arrived on the 9th', and unloaded a number of heavy cannon. The fort was then bombarded from land and sea for a day.[72] The garrison commander, Colonel Sebasiano di San Giuseppi, realized that his position was hopeless, as it had been for at least a month in the absence of major reinforcements, and he started to entreat Grey for favourable terms of surrender on the 10th'. Grey accepted terms of unconditional surrender, which he clearly felt gave him the right to dispose of the inhabitants of the fort as he saw fit, whereas his enemies expected to be granted mercy and then imprisoned.[73] Grey's own account of his actions, in his letter to the queen (12 November), copied out by Spenser in his best italic hand, leaves few questions unanswered (Figure 7). When he learned that the troops had been sent by the Pope for the defence of the Catholic faith, Grey was incensed, claiming that if they had been sent by a prince who had declared war on Elizabeth, he would have, at least, understood their reasons for being in Ireland, but they have obeyed the orders of 'a detestable shaveling the right Antichriste & generall ambitious Tyrant ouer all right principalities, & patrone of the Diabolica fede'. Accordingly,

At my handes no condition of composition they were to expecte, other then that simply they should render me the forte, & yield theyr selues to my will for lyfe or death: with this answere he ['Alexandro their CampMaster'] departed; after which there was one or twoo courses two and fro more to haue gotten a certainty for some of their liues, but fynding that yt would not bee, the Coronell him selfe about Sunne setting came forth, & requested respitt with surceasse of armes till the nexte morning, & then he would giue a resolute answere; fynding that to bee but a gayne of tyme for them & losse of the same for my self, I definitely answered I would not graunt yt, & therefore presently either that he tooke my offer or elles retourne & I would fall to my business. He then embraced my knees, simply putting him self to my mercy, onely he prayed that for the night hee might abyde in the Forte, and that in the morning all should be putt into my handes . . . Morning come I presented my companies in battaile before the Forte: the Coronell comes forth with x or xij of his chiefe ientlemen, trayling theyr ensigns roled vp, & presented them vnto mee with theyr liues & the Forte: I sent straight certain gentlemen in to see their weapons and armures layed downe & to gard the munition & victaile there lefte for spoile: Then putt I in to certeyn bandes, who straight fell to execution. There were 600 slayne.[74]

'Grey's faith', his betrayal of the prisoners in his charge who believed that he would spare their lives, became notorious throughout Catholic Europe, and the dead priests and Catholic gentlemen, whose bones were broken on a blacksmith's forge before they were executed, were afforded the status of martyrs for the faith. For Philip O'Sullivan Beare, the act 'became a proverb for monstrous and inhuman perfidy', an indication of how the Protestant English treated the Catholic Irish.[75] There was a vigorous English defence of Grey's actions in print, probably written by Anthony

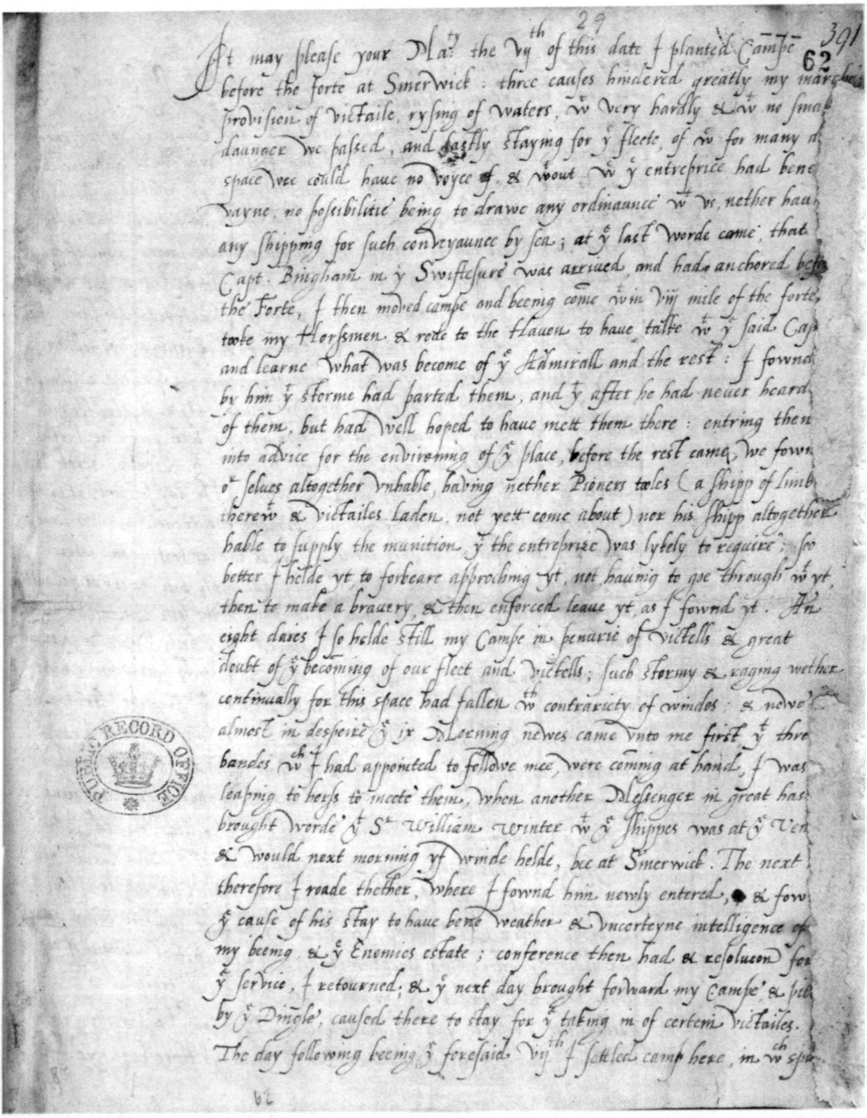
29 391 62

It may please your Matie the vijth of this date I planted Campe
before the Forte at Smerwick: three causes hindered greatly my marc
provision of victaile, rysing of waters, wch very hardly & wt no smal
daunger we passed, and lastly staying for ye fleete, of wch for many d
space wee could haue no voyce of, & wthout wch ye entreprice had bene
vayne, no possibilitie being to drawe any ordinaunce wt vs, nether hau
any shipping for such conveyaunce by sea; at ye last worde came that
Capt. Bingham in ye Swiftesure was arrived, and had anchored bef
the Forte, I then moved campe and beeing come wtin viij mile of the forte,
toke my Horsmen & rode to the Hauen to haue talke wt ye said Cap
and learne what was become of ye Admirall and the rest: I fownd
by him yt storme had parted them, and yt after he had neuer heard
of them, but had well hoped to haue mett them there: entring then
into advice for the enviroming of ye place, before the rest came, we fown
or selues altogether vnhable, hauing nether Pioners tooles (a shipp of timb
therewt & victailes laden, not yett come about) nor his shipp altogether
hable to supply the munition yt the entreprize was lykely to require; soo
better I helde yt to forbeare approching yt, not hauing to goe through wt yt,
then to make a brauery, & then enforced leaue yt, as I fownd yt. An
eight daies I so helde still my Campe in penurie of victells & great
doubt of ye becoming of our fleet and victells; such stormy & raging wether
continually for this space had fallen wth contrariety of windes; & neve
almost in despeire ye ix Morning newes came vnto me first yt thre
bandes wch I had appointed to followe mee, were comming at hand, I was
leaping to horss to meete them, when another Messenger in great has
brought worde yt Sr William Winter wt ye shippes was at ye Ven
& would next morning yf winde helde, bee at Smerwick. The next
therefore I roade thether, where I fownd him newly entered, & fow
ye cause of his stay to haue bene weather & vncerteyne intelligence of
my beeing & ye Enemies estate; conference then had & resolucon for
ye service, I retourned; & ye next day brought forward my Campe & pit
by ye Dingle, caused there to stay for ye taking in of certein victailes.
The day following beeing ye foresaid vijth I settled camp here, in wch spa

62

Figure 7. Lord Grey to the queen, 12 November 1580. Reproduced with kind permission of the National Archives.

Munday, followed later by a more general defence of English actions against papal threats to England and Ireland by Burghley himself, the existence of this propaganda war indicating how controversial such massacres were.[76]

Grey's explanation of his actions relies on three crucial points. First, did he ever really promise mercy to the occupants of the fort? Grey is quite clear that he did not and expected them to surrender on any terms. Certainly, his emphatic recall that he 'definitely answered' that he would not grant them mercy looks like an anticipation of future criticism, or a response to a condemnation already made. And, of course, it is possible that Grey is overly clarifying what was ambiguous at the time, although this is unlikely given the desperate surrender of Colonel San Giuseppi and the fact that there appears to have been serious opposition to his plan to trust to Grey's mercy.[77] Second, what were the 'one or twoo courses' that would have saved at least some of the lives of the papal and Irish forces? No evidence can tell us whether such a possibility was really communicated to the colonel, or whether Grey was serious that some form of action on the part of the defenders might have changed his subsequent response. Third, and most important, was this a legitimate act of war under the circumstances or should we label it, as we would now, a 'war crime'?[78]

There had been appalling massacres before this point, notably the slaughter of the Ulster Scots by Walter Devereux, earl of Essex and Sir John Norris on Rathlin Island in July 1575; and at Mullaghmast, in 1577, when Rory Oge O'More's supporters were lured into an ambush in County Kildare, an action celebrated in John Derricke's *The Image of Ireland*.[79] The Rathlin Island massacre, in particular, forms an almost exact parallel to that at Smerwick. The constable on the island 'came out, and made large requests, as their lives, their goods, and to be put into Scotland'. These were refused, the company surrendered unconditionally, and were then slaughtered, as were those found hiding in caves later.[80] Moreover, as David Edwards points out, Grey, despite his self-styled reputation as 'chief executioner of Ireland', had far less 'rebel blood on his hands' than Thomas Butler, tenth earl of Ormond (1531–1614), a cousin of the queen through the Boleyns, who was often at court, and, with the decline of the Geraldines, became unquestionably the most powerful magnate in Munster.[81] Indeed, it was Ormond who oversaw the defeat of the rebellion and the fall of the House of Desmond in 1583, events he helped to engineer.[82] Pelham, a ruthless commander himself, recommended Ormond as a suitable commander against Desmond.[83] Violence was becoming ever more endemic and pronounced in late sixteenth-century Irish society, as Spenser's record of Pelham's actions in Munster indicates, especially after the declaration of martial law in Munster on 11 January 1580.[84] This allowed crown officers to torture and execute suspected traitors without trial and to burn and destroy their lands.[85] One estimate of casualties in the wars in Munster between 1579 and 1583 puts them as high as 50,000, about a third of the Munster population and a tenth of the whole population of Ireland (Munster contained about a third of the population).[86] Grey's actions, horrifying as they were, can be seen on the one hand as one of a number of atrocity stories that make up Irish history; and, on the other, as an element of the increasingly brutal religious conflict that was developing in the wake of the Reformation, 'a deliberate act of exemplary terror, designed to discourage further incursions'.[87] The defence of and the attack on 'Grey's faith' needs to be seen in terms of the growing irreconcilable differences between confessional allegiances in early modern Europe.[88]

Spenser was certainly caught up in the verbal battles, and made vigorous public defences of his former employer in both *A View* and the second edition of *The Faerie Queene*. In the poem he represented Grey at times as Artegall, the Knight of Justice, distancing the Lord Deputy from his violent actions by portraying him restraining his loyal servant, the iron man, Talus; elsewhere as Zele, arguing for the death of Mary Queen of Scots, as Grey had done when serving as a commissioner for Mary's trial in 1586.[89] However, it is noticeable that there is no defence of Grey's actions at Smerwick in the poem, which may be an indication of how controversial these were still deemed to have been over fifteen years later. In *A View*, however, a work designed for manuscript circulation not publication, Spenser tackles the question directly in the passage immediately after the horrifying description of the Munster famine, which provides the crucial context for Grey's behaviour in Ireland. Spenser's description of the course of events tallies with that of the Lord Deputy, which is hardly surprising as Spenser wrote out Grey's original letter. In Spenser's account the colonel

Came forthe to entreate that they mighte parte with theire Armours like souldiours, at leaste with theire lives according to the Customes of war and lawe of nacions, it was strongelye denied him and tolde him by the Lord deputye him self that they Coulde not iustlye pleade either Custome of war or lawe of nacions, for that they weare not anie lawfull enemyes, and if theye weare willed them to shewe by what Commission they I Came thither into another Princes dominions to war whether from the Pope or the kinge of Spaine or any other... whearevppon the saide Coronell did absolutelye yealde himselfe and the forte with all therein and Craved onely mercye, which it beinge not thoughte good to shewe them bothe for dauger of themselues if beinge saved, they shoulde afterwards ioyne with the Irishe... theare was no other waie but to make that shorte ende of them which was made.[90]

Spenser's euphemistic final line serves as a pointed contrast to his more explicit references elsewhere, notably of the effects of the Munster famine. But it is noticeable that, apart from some minor confusion about names, Spenser's account tallies exactly with that of Grey.[91] Irenius even repeats for emphasis the fact that the 'adventurours' appealed to their status as lawful enemies under the law of nations, a claim Grey had rejected on the logical grounds that no war had been declared between England and Italy or Spain. Spenser follows suit. The implication of

Spenser's defence is clear enough: however unpalatable Grey's methods might seem, they are the right ones to use in times of crisis, and what Grey did in Munster in 1580 must be repeated against the even greater threat of Tyrone.[92]

Irenius also argues that Grey was harshly criticized for his actions: 'moste vntrewlye and malitiouslye do these evill tonges backebite and slaunder the sacred ashes of that most honourable personage', echoing his earlier praise of Grey as a wise pilot of state in a tempestuous storm. Eudoxus is relieved that Grey has at last been properly valued, as he has 'harde it often times maligned and his doinges depraved of some whom I perceaued did rather of malicious minde or private grevaunce seke to detract from the honour of his deds'.[93] The representation of Slander and Detraction attacking the Knight of Justice, Artegall, at the end of Book V of *The Faerie Queene* seems to echo this description of the maligned Lord Deputy.[94] Spenser is the earliest—perhaps the only—real source for our understanding that Grey was criticized and then recalled early from Ireland before his mission was finished, a claim later made more substantial by William Camden: 'Neuerthelesse, the Queen, who from her heart detested to vse cruelty to those that yeelded, wished that the slaughter had not beene, and was with much difficultie appeased and satisfied about it.'[95] In fact, it is more likely that Grey's office was terminated for reasons other than this particular incident in the campaign. When he was recalled, the queen made a point of thanking Grey for his services at Smerwick but expressing some concern over the financial wisdom of his tenure. And, it is more feasible that the number of executions he carried out after Smerwick would have caused her alarm as the queen was wary of her commanders assuming excessive executive power.[96] Grey's relatively brief period as Lord Deputy witnessed the first attempt to establish systematic plantations in Ireland in Munster, a costly enterprise, the significance of which only emerged later, and it is likely that this policy, which produced no obvious short-term results, irritated his masters as much as the slaughter of the Irish. The Spanish ambassador, Don Bernardino de Mendoza, condemned Grey's actions to Burghley, but, although Burghley, too, was critical of Grey in private, he stood by him in public.[97] It was the intervention of the most powerful figure in south-west Ireland that really undermined Grey's reputation at court and afterwards.[98]

The earl of Ormond had a long history of fractious relations with a succession of Lord Deputies, who were invariably eager to curb what they saw as his excessive power, but also resentful of his particular influence at court and with the queen.[99] Ormond wished to preserve 'the principles of aristocratic delegation and devolution', while the Deputies 'were inclined to interfere in the running of his territory [the significant county of Kilkenny, as well as the Palatinate in Tipperary] in order to reveal it as a place where forces hostile to the crown lurked and plotted under the earl's nose'.[100] Ormond's greatest achievement was his success in keeping the Butlers' vast lands in Kilkenny, Tipperary, Waterford, out of the conflict, and it is clear that he was prepared to act on behalf of the crown against his neighbours in order to secure peace and relative prosperity for his own people, the results of which are still visible today. The former Ormond lands still have their medieval village and land structures, in contrast to the rest of southern Ireland.[101]

Grey tried to undermine Ormond's reputation with Elizabeth, deliberately failing to forward details of Ormond's military successes so that the queen, as Ormond later complained, obtained 'false reports . . . of my slackness in service'.[102] The plan badly misfired. When Ormond eventually managed to reach the court he persuaded Elizabeth that he was the man to bring order to the province and that Grey's financial mismanagement and his taste for apparently random summary executions was undermining the queen's reputation for impartial justice.[103] The problem was that Ormond had such influence with the queen that he 'could break the government of lord deputies'.[104] Spenser's relationship with Ormond, expressed in his dedicatory sonnet to *The Faerie Queene*, was, predictably enough, somewhat wary.[105]

Spenser's defence of Grey is far more substantial and unequivocal than his defence of Bishop John Young, and forms a pointed contrast to his public pronouncements about Leicester and Burghley. Spenser, like many other New English settlers in Ireland, including his friend Lodowick Bryskett (c.1546–1609/12), was grateful to Grey as a Lord Deputy who defended their interests against more powerful lobbies at court—such as Ormond—and the encroachments of the native Irish. Another settler, Richard Beacon, praised Grey as a governor who forced the Irish to obey the English through his 'rare skill and knowledge in military discipline'.[106] Grey was also a generous patron of and friend to a number of writers, including George Gascoigne, George Whetstone, and Richard Robinson. Gascoigne, in particular, appears to have been close to Grey, and he dedicated a poem to him, but Gascoigne was from a significantly higher social class than Spenser—and, indeed, than Gabriel Harvey, Richard Mulcaster, and Sir Thomas Smith. His father was a substantial landowner of the Home Counties, and had served as almoner at the coronation of Edward VI, just as his grandfather had done at the coronations of Henry VIII and Anne Boleyn.[107] Spenser was probably more of a trusted servant than an equal. Nevertheless, Grey appears to have been especially successful at inspiring loyalty from those who served with him and, certain failures apart, was usually a successful commander and at ease in the martial world.

Spenser's defence appeared after Grey's death (1593) and was dictated by the more specific purpose of *A View*, so that it does not reveal an intimate understanding of his master's thoughts on any issue. We cannot infer from what Spenser writes that he personally liked Grey, or enjoyed his confidence, beyond his role as Grey's official letter writer. Spenser was connected to many men who espoused Grey's brand of ecclesiastical Protestantism, but it is not obvious from his writings that he adopted an identical religious position.[108] Moreover, his defence of Grey is careful to make no mention of religion. Certainly, Spenser's respect for Grey looks markedly different from his publicly advertised friendship with Harvey.

In Book V of *The Faerie Queene* Spenser makes an explicit connection between the poet and the soldier.[109] Having just defeated Malengin, the shape-shifter who represents crafty and devious subversion, specifically in Ireland, Artegall and Talus return to the court of Mercilla where they are greeted by blank incomprehension from the courtiers there.[110] They then encounter a particularly disturbing sight:

> They [the courtiers] ceast their clamors vpon them to gaze;
> Whom seeing all in armour bright as day,
> Straunge there to see, it did them much amaze,
> And with vnwonted terror halfe affray.
> For neuer saw they there the like array.
> Ne euer was the name of warre there spoken,
> But ioyous peace and quietnesse alway,
> Dealing iust iudgements, that mote not be broken
> For any brybes, or threates of any to be wroken.
>
> There as they entred at the Scriene, they saw
> Some one, whose tongue was for his trespasse vyle
> Nayld to a post, adiudged so by law:
> For that therewith he falsely did reuyle,
> And foule blaspheme that Queene for forged guyle,
> Both with bold speaches, which he blazed had,
> And with lewd poems, which he did compyle;
> For the bold title of a Poet bad
> He on himselfe had ta'en, and rayling rymes had sprad. (*FQ* V.ix.24–5)

Read superficially, these stanzas look like praise of the stability of the Elizabethan regime. But they are, of course, bitterly ironic. The courtiers are rendered speechless as the knights enter, obviously terrified of men in military uniform, and have no idea of who the knights are or what they do, not realizing that their safety depends on the actions of men like Artegall. They never speak about war, which enables them to imagine that it does not really exist, although the reader would have known that in 1596 a frightening and bloody war, the outcome of which was far from certain, was being fought in Ireland. Grey's defence of his actions was that the troops who landed at Smerwick were not legitimate enemies but rebels against the crown, i.e., they were waging war in an underhand manner and so risked forfeiting their lives. Such distinctions, vital for the protection of the realm, are lost on those at the court itself, so it is little wonder that they condemn Grey, that the queen is badly advised, and that she therefore acts to undermine rather than secure the safety of her realms.

Spenser is articulating sentiments similar to those of Gascoigne in his poem on Erasmus' adage where he asserts that soldiers do not wish to fight but recognize what has to be done; moreover, he is defining himself as an 'at war' poet, whose work is directly relevant to the current conflict.[111] The second half of the first stanza cited here is therefore openly sarcastic, representing the courtiers as self-interested creatures who take bribes and do not deal just judgements (how can they when they have no idea what really goes on in the world?). The contrast drawn between the useless indoor courtiers and the vigorous knights in the field, shows that the dangers suffered by the latter are exploited by the former. The ill-used knights find themselves caught between the ignorant Irish, who do not realize the perils of war, and the deluded courtiers, who do not even know what a war is.

The second stanza must surely be a self-representation, as Spenser had by this time been censured and censored for his publication of the *Complaints*.[112] In trying to tell the truth the fictionalized poet is seen as a figure of guile, like Malengin, whereas he is really a truth-teller trying to do the right thing. Courtiers are shown to be at odds with soldiers and poets, the former ruling without insight or reason, the latter united in their efforts to make their rulers see sense. Indeed, we also witness Mercilla/Elizabeth's court as a centre in disarray that has lost touch with reality. The magnificent porch through which the knights enter is guarded by Awe, whose job is to 'keepe out guyle, and malice, and despight' (22, line 7), providing an exact verbal link to the first line of headnote to the canto which informs us that 'Arthur and Artegall catch Guyle'. The court imagines that it is keeping out Guile but it fails to recognize or reward those who really do perform that difficult task. For Spenser, the court had no knowledge of war or understanding of literature, and he carefully links the two as activities that are treated with contempt by the court at a crucial allegorical point in his magnum opus. In his published work after he went to Ireland Spenser was always loyal to the military men with whom he worked, often seeing the world as they saw it, and setting his stall against powerful courtiers, aristocrats, and clerics. His Irish experiences changed his understanding of England and English society, and witnessing the Massacre at Smerwick—or, perhaps, having to defend it—played a pivotal role in his life.

Spenser would also have met Sir Walter Ralegh (1554–1618) at Smerwick, a figure who is usually assumed to have been a close friend and a major influence on Spenser's life, rivalling that of Harvey.[113] Ralegh was another military figure who, after a certain amount of experience in the Low Countries, had been placed in charge of carrying out the killing of Italian, Spanish, and Irish forces.[114] He had taken a commission as a captain in the army after a fractious time at court and, like Spenser, had just come over to Ireland.[115] Ralegh, from a family of seafarers and adventurers, was eager to obtain land in the Munster area, and later negotiated with Grey to receive confiscated lands there, although his wish was not granted until 1586 when he obtained the largest part of the confiscated Desmond lands.[116] Ralegh and Spenser were almost the same age and they had a connection through Sir Humphrey Gilbert, Ralegh's half-brother, who knew Harvey and Smith and had taken part in the Hill Hall debate in 1570/1.[117] How well Spenser and Ralegh actually knew each other is hard to determine, although they did obviously have a number of common interests.[118] Evidence of their relationship has largely been deduced from references made by Spenser in his printed works. However, it is significant that Ralegh makes no mention of Spenser in his published writings or in his surviving letters, although he did produce two dedicatory poems for the first edition of *The Faerie Queene*, the only author to write more than one poem, receiving one in return from Spenser.[119] Even so, 'literary familiarity of this kind does not of course confirm parallel processes of face-to-face conversation and debate'.[120] The answer may lie in Ralegh's well-established reputation as a fair-weather friend, always following his own interests, and this problem could explain Spenser's public disdain later.[121] It is only after Ralegh's death that we have evidence that Ralegh knew Spenser.[122]

Grey's army remained in south-west Ireland for another month, strengthening the garrisons at Limerick, Castelmain, Askeaton, Aherlow, and Kilmallock.[123] On 30 November they were still at Clonmel, Tipperary, reaching Dublin at some point in early December.[124] Spenser, when not on military expeditions, probably spent most of the next two years in the Dublin area, mainly in the capital itself, as nearly all of Grey's letters in his hand were written in the city and were presumably dictated or copied in Dublin Castle. There is a record of Grey attending a ceremonial feast at Cullenswood just outside the city walls, provided by the mayor and sheriffs of the city on Easter Monday (27 March) 1581, and presumably Spenser, as Grey's principal secretary, accompanied him as part of his household.[125] During this period he would have witnessed the arrest of the earl of Kildare and his son-in-law, Christopher Nugent, fourteenth Baron Devlin, in the Council Chamber, for treasonable contact with the rebels in the Pale on 23 December 1581.[126] The episode, which led to the imprisonment of both men and the execution of Christopher's son, Nicholas, on 6 April 1581, occupies extensive correspondence in Spenser's hand in the period between the two dates.[127] Spenser was able to watch the destruction of the noble family who had effectively ruled Ireland as viceroys from the mid-fifteenth century.[128] A member of the disgraced Nugent family, Richard, published a sonnet sequence, *Cynthia*, in 1604, a work that transposes the tradition of the sonnet sequence—including Spenser's own *Amoretti*—to English Ireland. The lady who inspires the narrator's affections is a combination of the queen and a 'local Irishwoman', implying 'that Cynthia simultaneously allegorises the poet's love of Ireland and his loyalty to the English crown'.[129]

Spenser would have continued to accompany Grey on most, if not all, of his military expeditions, such as the one into the midland counties, Leix and Offaly, in January 1581, and into Connaught against the O'Connors the next month.[130] On this expedition, if he had not already done so, he would have travelled through or around the Bog of Allen, the largest in Ireland and a noted problem for soldiers, which dominates the Irish midlands to the west of Dublin, an area that provided one of the better known personal reflections in his poetry.[131] Spenser compares the forces besieging the Castle of Alma to the insects that torment travellers in Ireland:

> As when a swarme of Gnats at euentide
> Out of the fennes of Allan do arise,
> Their murmuring small trompets sounden wide,
> Whiles in the aire their clustring army flies,
> That as a cloud doth seeme to dim the skies;
> Ne man nor beast may rest, or take repast,
> For their sharpe wounds, and noyous iniuries,
> Till the fierce Northerne wind with blustring blast
> Doth blow them quite away, and in the *Ocean* cast. (*FQ* II.ix.16)

This is yet another passage based on his personal experience, at one level humorous in its mock-heroic style. However, as Ireland was notorious for the illness it spread among the English, especially those newly arrived who fell prey to the 'country disease', and as disease was believed to be airborne, the stanza is double-edged.[132] Alma's Castle, an image of the healthy, temperate body, is under serious threat and all the careful regulation that has been carried out may not save it from the perils of life in Ireland.[133]

On 22 March Spenser was given another office when Bryskett was made controller of the customs on wines and passed on his position as the registrar or clerk for faculties in Chancery, a position he may only have held for a year before he was succeeded by Roland Cowyk.[134] Spenser would have worked for the new Lord Chancellor, Adam Loftus (1533/4–1605), archbishop of Dublin, puritan sympathizer, educational reformer, and first provost of Trinity College Dublin. Loftus was initially eager to make Dublin Protestant, although his enthusiasm soon waned and he was heavily criticized by Sir Henry Sidney for reducing the church to a lamentable state.[135] Loftus also had an unsavoury reputation for vigorously promoting his family's own interests, and for falling out with other powerful figures.[136] Unsurprisingly, his family became the leading landowners in the Dublin area by the mid-seventeenth century.[137] It is likely that Spenser formed a low opinion of Loftus during his time in the court and satirized him in *Mother Hubberds Tale*, yet another instance of Spenser attacking those he had worked for in print.[138] Given that Spenser benefited substantially from his patrons, notably Grey and Wallop, it is not clear how far such attacks were really based on noble principles, but there was enough hostility towards Loftus for Barnaby Rich's claims that Loftus was spectacularly corrupt to warrant an official enquiry in 1592.[139]

It is also unclear how extensive Spenser's duties in his new post would have been, or how many of them he actually performed, as it was common practice to regard offices as sinecures that could be passed on to more junior scribes for a lower fee, the officer pocketing the difference. Spenser was certainly allowed to employ a deputy, as his terms of employment stated.[140] The job was, however, a natural one for the Lord Deputy's secretary to undertake, given the powerful role that the Chancellor played alongside the vice-regent, and the incumbent would have been assigned documents to copy out and process for the Chancellor, much as he did for the Lord Deputy. It was also a job that would have suited someone who had worked as a bishop's secretary, with a knowledge of canon law.[141] The Chancellor 'had the custody of the Great Seal; all royal charters, letters patent and close and other public instruments issued out of the Chancery, and were enrolled there; his writs set in motion the courts of justice, and authorised the issue of money from the King's Exchequer. Thus he was at first an executive rather than a judicial officer.'[142] The clerk's duties would have involved overseeing a number of ecclesiastical issues, establishing who had the right to which benefice and which title, sorting out any resulting quarrels, distributing titles, goods, and money after the death of an incumbent, and other related tasks.[143] A record does indeed show that Spenser, in his role as servant to Lord Grey, appeared in person in the Court of Exchequer on official business, suggesting that his duties may have been extensive.[144]

Chancery was one of the principal courts of equity, but also oversaw some common law cases, causing friction with the common law courts.[145] It was notable also for making use of Brehon Law (native Irish law), despite the prohibition of its use in English areas in the Statutes of Kilkenny (1366), most significantly the practice of 'gavelkind' (dividing lands between sons) in inheritance cases, because legal practice relied on close personal communication with the plaintiffs.[146] This experience contributed to Spenser's comments on Brehon Law in *A View*.[147] The records for Chancery are—or, rather, were—among the most substantial historical archives for early modern Ireland, as they are in England. It is clear that plaintiffs involved in property disputes in particular sought redress in the Chancery courts because they felt they had little chance of success under the common law. The same is true in England in this period, as the extensive Chancery records in the National Archives demonstrate.[148] However, the problem was especially acute for the English in Ireland, not simply because of the number of disputed properties and land holdings, but because they had good reason to fear Irish juries. When the Munster Plantation was established in the mid-1580s, its architects managed to draft qualification rules for jurors that effectively excluded most English tenants. A juror had to be a 40s. freeholder for life and tenants on the Plantation were disqualified as they were simply tenants for twenty-one years. As a result most juries were Irish.[149] Spenser outlined what he saw as the issue in *A View*, where he complained that 'theare are more attainted Landes concealed from her maiestie then shee now hathe possessions in all Irelande', something he would have realized from his professional career. When it is objected that the honesty demanded by a fair trial would surely solve this problem, his mouthpiece, Irenius, explains that such assumptions cannot be made about the Irish because they are implacably opposed to the English:

Not onelye soe in theire verdites but allsoe in all other theare dealinges speciallye with the Englishe they are moste wilfullye bente for thoughte they will not seme manifestlye to doe it yeat will some one or other subtill headed fellow amongest them picke some quirke, or devise some evacion whereaf the rest will lightelye take houlde, and suffer them selves easelye to be led by him, to that themselues desired.[150]

Irish jurors are master of deception and duplicity, working against the interest of the settlers and the crown, a defining—but hardly surprising—feature of English experience in Ireland, according to Spenser.

It is little wonder that legal issues feature so prominently in *A View*. Spenser had a privileged insight into the workings of executive and legal power—in this instance, the relationship between the office of the lawmaker and his ability to override the established practices of case law to correct injustices, which could mean to protect the integrity of the executive itself. This would have been especially pronounced, as the late sixteenth century was a period of significant law reform during which the crown sought to expand its power over Ireland through the spread of legal as well as military means. The chief legal figures in Ireland, the Lord Chancellor, the Master of the Rolls, the two chief justices, and the Baron of the Exchequer, were all members of the Irish Privy Council, meaning that constitutional and legal power overlapped, a fact that would have been obvious to Spenser and undoubtedly influenced his conception of government.[151] The drive was begun in particular by the Lord Deputy Henry Sidney in the 1570s, and one of Spenser's key patrons, Sir Henry Wallop, who was known for his combative and partisan style of conducting himself, became a key figure in enhancing the power of legal institutions in Ireland in the 1580s and 1590s.[152]

The Irish Chancery court also received a significant number of appeals from women, often cases brought against their husbands, which may have been relevant when Spenser helped his second wife bring a case against her stepfather in 1596.[153] However, the court had a reputation for applying legal principles more rigidly than its English counterpart, and was often in conflict with the Irish Star Chamber, the Court of Castle Chamber, as each court sought to uphold its judgements to be endorsed by the crown.[154] The Chancery court's guiding principle, equity, its importance in defining sovereignty as well as its potential abuse, is a key concept in Spenser's later work, especially the second part of *The Faerie Queene*, suggesting that his experience in the Dublin courts had a profound effect on his conception of the law and his literary imagination.[155]

Dublin, in contrast to most of Ireland, had been successfully anglicized by 1580, and much of the surrounding area was dominated by old families, mainly Old English, the descendants of the Anglo-Norman colonists in Ireland who were being displaced by the Tudor settlers and gradually turning from loyalty to the crown and making common religious and political cause with the native Irish.[156] John Speed's map of 1610 shows a carefully planned walled town that resembles any number of equivalent provincial English towns.[157] However, the capital was obviously more militarized than its English counterparts, as the dominating nature of the huge square castle, where Spenser probably lived at first, demonstrates.[158] John Derricke's images of Sir Henry Sidney's riding out from Dublin Castle and his triumphal return into Dublin, where he is received by the grateful aldermen of the city, gives the same impression of the capital, the heads on the walls perhaps reminding viewers that justice was dispensed in Ireland as it was in London.[159] The capital was, nevertheless, a conspicuously Catholic city, with only a few significant families leaning towards Protestantism.[160]

Dublin was a city of about 6,000 people, slightly smaller than the populations of such major English provincial cities as Norwich, York, Bristol, Exeter, and Newcastle, which contained about 9,000–12,000 people. The city was run by a corporation consisting of a group of aldermen (*jurés*) who elected a mayor each year. Beneath them were a group of *demi-jurés* and a group of 'numbers', elected from the various trade guilds. Towards the end of the sixteenth century the administration of Dublin was dominated by merchants who had roughly the same concerns as their London counterparts: they were concerned to make trade flourish, and were eager to protect and promote their families. They did so through the promotion of a self-interested civic culture and calculated intermarriage. Overseas trade and the export of goods were important, but internal trade was probably the decisive factor in determining how successful any individual family was. The most important trades were wool and linen, as they were in England. Like London, Dublin suffered from serious epidemics and about 3,000 of its inhabitants died from the plague in 1575. Many aspects of Dublin life would not have seemed that much different from life in Westminster or Cambridge, especially if Spenser was staying in Dublin Castle as he had lived in Leicester House.[161] Each street had a particular character and role, as in London: the High Street contained meat stalls, shops selling leather goods, and places to eat; the fish market was in Fishamble Street; sheep were sold in Ship (Sheep) Street; and wine and beer were sold in Winetavern Street.[162] The Chancery courts were next to Christ Church Cathedral (Plate 15), so much of Spenser's life in the city would have been spent between the three dominating institutions, the Castle, Christ Church Cathedral, and, to a lesser extent, St Patrick's Cathedral, just outside the city walls.[163] Beyond the city there was relatively affluent farmland, which grew less wealthy the further one travelled from Dublin, but which was clearly able to support the large population of the Pale.[164]

Dublin does not appear to have had a commercial theatre until the Werburgh Street Theatre was established in 1635.[165] The corporation did, however, sponsor a number of public pageants performed throughout the year on key dates, and there was the annual riding of the franchises, in which civic officers and important figures in trade guilds processed around the city's boundaries, 'an expression of community, a reassertion of hierarchy, and a proclamation of collective privilege', very similar to the civic pageants in Elizabethan London.[166] These processions and public performances often expressed Dublin's complex sense of itself, caught between Gaelic Ireland and imperial England, uneasily negotiating a sense of identity between the two. They also suggest that Dublin would have seemed more obviously connected to the past than many English cities, and it is not clear how vigorously medieval practices were swept away.[167] On St George's Day (23 April) a pageant of the adopted English saint was performed, the actors processing through the streets, the event culminating with St George slaying the dragon.[168] We know that Spenser was at work on *The Faerie Queene* in the first few years after he came to Ireland. It may be that this pageant, the nature of its performance, and the overt or suppressed reactions to what Dubliners saw, representing the complicated and problematic relationship between the different communities of Old English, New English, and Gaelic Irish in Ireland, had an impact on his decision to write Book I, the story of the Red-Cross Knight, a section of the poem that was clearly not written first. Dublin also had a large number of musicians and the corporation sponsored frequent public events and spectacles, and there were a significant number of performances of plays and music in private houses.[169] Spenser, connected to the New English elite, even if not actually part of it, would have attended some of these. His cultural life in Dublin would have been almost as rich and varied as it had been in London, certainly more lively than it would have been had he lived in a number of substantial English provincial cities.

Even so, Dublin was a city acutely aware that it was under threat, not least because of the heavy taxes imposed on the citizens to maintain the army. These had become especially burdensome in the late 1570s, as Sir Henry Sidney had sought funds to pay for campaigns, most importantly in Connaught, and had levied a new tax, 'composition', without parliamentary authority. There were frequent delegations of Palesmen to the English court and parliament protesting against Sidney's actions, the conflict actually helping to establish the colonial Old English identity of Dublin and the Pale caught between the crown and Gaelic Ireland.[170] Spenser, as his later published work demonstrates, especially *Colin Clouts come home againe*, was acutely aware of the nuances of colonial identities, an understanding that would have dated from his first years in Ireland.

Spenser's acquaintances in this period would have been predominately other New English settlers, principally those working for the Dublin administration. We know that he was close to Lodowick Bryskett, who had first come to Ireland with Sir Henry Sidney and had subsequently worked for a number of Lord Deputies as clerk to the Council and clerk in Chancery, the position he passed on to Spenser.[171] Although Bryskett accompanied Sir Philip Sidney on his grand tour (1572–4), probably as a language tutor, there is no evidence that he was ever considered a friend by Sidney, a pointed contrast to his relationship with Spenser.[172] As he came from an Italian family and moved in Catholic circles, Bryskett also acted as a government spy, while his own extended family was extremely complicated in terms of its religious affiliations—rather like that of the next generation of Spenser's, in fact.[173] Spenser later followed Bryskett down to Munster, after Bryskett was disappointed that he did not get the post of secretary of state for Ireland, which went to Geoffrey Fenton, a defeat registered in his *Discourse of Civil Life*.[174] Bryskett had been petitioning Burghley for the post, when it was clear that the incumbent, John Chaloner, was in failing health.[175] Spenser later represented Bryskett as Thestylis, a shepherd friend of Colin's in Ireland, in *Colin Clouts come home againe*.[176] Spenser also addressed sonnet 33 of the *Amoretti* to his friend, lamenting his inability to finish off his magnum opus:

> Great wrong I doe, I can it not deny,
> to that most saced Empresse my dear dred,
> not finishing her Queene of faëry,
> that mote enlarge her liuing praises dead:
> But lodwick, this of grace to me ared:
> doe ye not thinck th'accomplishment of it,
> sufficient worke for one mans simple head,
> all were it as the rest but rudely writ.[177]

The sonnet concludes that the poem is too much for one man, so he will stop work on it until his 'proud loue' grants him some rest, a public acknowledgement that *The Faerie Queene* cannot be finished. But, through the carefully ambiguous use of pronouns, the reader is left unsure whether the love who is keeping him from his rest is Elizabeth Boyle or Elizabeth Tudor, hinting that the completion of the poem depends on proper government.

The reason why this sonnet was addressed to Bryskett was undoubtedly because Bryskett had been involved in debates about the poem during their time in Dublin, as his *A Discourse of Civill Life* records. This adaptation of Giambattista Giraldi Cinthio's *Tre dialoghi della vita civile*, the second part of *De gli hecatommithi* (1565), was not published until 1606 but was originally written in the early 1580s, probably 1582, and planned as a work for Lord Grey, to show off the intellectual culture that thrived under his leadership.[178] Spenser would have read the work in manuscript and it may have had a direct impact on *The Faerie Queene*.[179] The dialogue describes a real or imagined meeting of various intellectuals at Bryskett's house about a mile and a half from Dublin, possibly in the village, Rathfarnham, now a Dublin suburb, where Bryskett and, probably, Spenser, lived.[180] As well as Spenser, described as 'late your Lordship's secretary', the nine friends present were John Long, archbishop of Armagh (1547/8–89); Sir Robert Dillon (d. 1579), a judge, the only Old English member of the group, related to Bryskett by marriage; George Dormer, described as 'the Queenes sollicitor', probably working for the Irish judiciary under the Lord Justice; Sir William Pelham, the Lord Chief Justice, whose second wife was the widow of Sir William Dormer, clearly a relative of George; Captain Christopher Carleill (1551?–93), a naval commander, who travelled to Russia, saw action in the Low Countries, and served in Drake's fleet in the West Indies; Sir Thomas Norris (1556–99), the fifth of the Norris brothers who, like Sir John Norris, spent considerable time in Ireland and later acted as Spenser's superior in Munster; Warham St Leger (1525?–97), sometime president of Munster, colonial adventurer in Ireland, who later became a neighbour of Spenser's on the Munster Plantation; Captain Thomas Dawtrey; and Thomas Smith, no relation to the owner of Hill Hall, an apothecary, and the first medical practitioner in Dublin, according to Nicholas Malby (presumably the first English one).[181] All of this group either definitely were or could have been in Dublin in 1582.[182]

Bryskett's purpose in recording those present at the debate is to show how lively and varied the intellectual culture of the New English in Dublin was, perhaps as a means of promoting and defending Grey, but probably his real aim was to illustrate how civilized and sophisticated they were in trying to establish culture in an island best known to an English audience as a violent, savage outpost, and a graveyard for the English forces there. After all, although they are assigned speaking parts in the dialogues, the group are not really required to further the debate, which takes place over three days.

The first day concerns the ideal education of a young child; the second, the progress from youth to adulthood; and the third, the proper activities and pursuits of a mature man.[183] This group of diverse citizens from the civil service and the military, who have a wide range of interests from the conquest of Ireland and the establishment of colonies to treatises and poems on self-government and education (Spenser and Bryskett), closely resemble the group who met at Hill Hall about a decade earlier. Might that event have been a model for subsequent gatherings? Or did middle-ranking citizens frequently stage such intellectual debates? Bryskett's record of his symposium is probably a good guide to the aspirations of the more educated and studious English in Ireland in the late sixteenth century and it is likely that similar meetings took place later when Spenser and Bryskett moved south to Munster, although geographical factors undoubtedly limited their frequency. There was a need not only to stage such events but to make sure that they were recorded and duly noted.

Bryskett lavishly praises Spenser in the only passage devoted to him in the work. He describes Spenser as impressively well educated, a model of the sophisticated gentleman, who is 'perfect in the Greek tongue, but also very well read in Philosophie'.[184] Bryskett states that Spenser has been instructing him in Greek, and urges him to teach the company about 'the great benefites which men obtaine by the knowledge of Morall Philosophie, and in the making vs to know what the same is, what . . . be the parts therefore, whereby vertues are to be distinguished from vices' (pp. 25–6). The text may have been emended before it was published in 1606 to take account of the retrospective knowledge of the two published volumes of *The Faerie Queene*. But, even so, we are given a clear sense of Spenser's high standing within colonial circles, and his reputation as a serious thinker and teacher.

Spenser declines the invitation to 'open . . . the goodly cabinet, in which this treasure of vertues lieth locked vp from the vulgar sort' (p. 26), Bryskett's phrasing indicating that the event serves as a process of self-validation for the group. He asks to be excused because he has

Already vndertaken a work tending to the same effect, which is in *heroical verse*, vnder the title of a *Faerie Queene*, to represent all the moral vertues, assigning to euery virtue, a Knight to be the patron and defender of the same: in whose actions and feates of arms and chiualry, the operations of that virtue, whereof he is the protector, are to be expressed, and the vices and vnruly appetites that oppose themselues against the same, to be beaten downe & ouercome. Which work, as I haue already well entred into, if God shall please to spare me life that I may finish it according to my mind, your wish (*M. Bryskett*) will be in some sort accomplished, though perhaps not so effectually as you could desire . . . Whereof since I haue taken in hand to discourse at large in my poeme before spoken, I hope the expectation of that work may serue to free me at this time from speaking in that matter, notwithstanding your notion and all your intreaties. (pp. 26–7)

Instead, he urges them that they listen to a reading of Bryskett's translation of Giraldi, to which they assent, even though 'they had shewed an extreme longing after his worke of the *Faerie Queene*, whereof some parcels had bin by some of them seene' (p. 28).

Spenser's poem is used as a means of introducing Bryskett's translation and it is not clear whether this stands as a faithful record of the event or a retrospective reconstruction that, with some humour, promotes Bryskett's own status via his famous dead friend. Nevertheless, Spenser's clear, precise, polite, and familiar manner of speech bears a close resemblance to his surviving non-poetic works, the *Letters*, the Letter to Ralegh appended to *The Faerie Queene*, and sections of *A View* which establish the nature of the interaction between Irenius and Eudoxus. Perhaps we are genuinely hearing his voice here. We also learn that Spenser's work circulated widely in manuscript, as it did in England, which suggests that many apparent echoes of Spenser's work that appeared before the relevant text was printed are likely to be authentic.[185] The discussion of works and their circulation among colonists appears to have been a key method of constructing a shared series of reference points, even a common identity, notable features of a number of works Spenser published in the 1590s.

On 27 January 1582 Grey wrote to Walsingham that he was able to redistribute land and property confiscated by the crown after the rebellion of James Eustace, Viscount Baltinglass, who had fled to Spain in the wake of the Massacre at Smerwick in the vain hope of raising more troops to continue the revolt, a conspiracy 'motivated almost exclusively by religious concerns'.[186] Grey noted that he had rewarded Wallop, Raleigh, Thomas Lee, and others, and had granted 'the lease of a house in Dublin belonging to Baltinglass for six years to come unto Edmund Spenser, one of the Lord Deputy's secretaries, valued at 51 [£]', showing that Spenser was being handsomely remunerated for his valuable service as the Lord Deputy's secretary. This is probably where Spenser lived while he was in Dublin: undoubtedly the largest property he had occupied so far and a sign that he was moving up in the world towards the status of a gentleman. The Baltinglass estates were to the south of the city centre, based around the village of Rathfarnham, three miles from Dublin Castle on a good road which appears on John Speed's map of the city.[187] As already noted, Bryskett lived here, and it is possible that Spenser had moved to the area before he acquired this house. The principal beneficiary from the Baltinglass Rebellion was Adam Loftus, who acquired extensive lands at a nominal rent, cementing his position as one of the largest property owners in Dublin. He was able to build Rathfarnham Castle in the mid-1580s, probably the earliest example of a fortified house in Elizabethan Ireland.[188] The roots of Spenser's apparent hostility to Loftus appear to date from this period, and experiencing Loftus' rapacious acquisition of property at first hand and possibly suffering in a dispute, could have caused—or added—further fuel to his anger.

Spenser was also granted the lease of lands at Newland, County Kildare, near Naas, for an annual rent of £3, confiscated from James Eustace, presumably a relative of Baltinglass. He may not have enjoyed possession of these for long, and they were reassigned to Thomas Lambyn on 1 December 1590.[189] However, a Chancery Bill dated 9 July 1622, filed against Spenser's second wife, Elizabeth, and her second husband, Roger Seckerstone (then deceased), by Spenser's second son, Peregrine, designed to restore his rights to his father's lands, indicates that Spenser did retain connections with Kildare after he moved to Munster, including the ownership of land.[190] The deed states that two prominent landowners in the Dublin area, Sir William Sarsfield of Lucan (1520–1616), and Sir Garrett Aylmer (d. 1634), had 'granted lands and impropriate [i.e., ecclesiastical property that had passed to a layman] tithes in trust for the use of Roger Seckerstone and Elizabeth his wife' on 24 August 1600.[191] The lands had been bought by Spenser who had paid all but £25, which had then been paid by Seckerstone after Spenser's death. Peregrine claimed that they were really intended for his use. The details of the original document, destroyed in 1922, but copied out in the nineteenth century, provide further evidence that Spenser was a successful accumulator of property and wealth: he secured the livings associated with the rectories of Athnowen (Ovens), Rennyborough, Kilbride, Kilbrogan (near Bandon), Kilmainane, and Agneholtie.[192] Spenser also held 'parcels' of the lands of the Abbey of Graney, a nunnery, about fifty miles south-west of Dublin and ten miles north-east of Carlow, part of a prosperous area with a number of other religious and military settlements, some twenty miles south of New Abbey, Kilcullen. Graney had been in the possession of two Lord Deputies, Lord Leonard Grey and Anthony St Leger, before becoming part of the Kildare holdings.[193] The remaining livings are all in the Cork area, many of them appearing as part of his estate in other documents.[194]

Spenser continued to work hard for Grey, copying out a number of important documents which show that he was 'at the centre' of the 'intense political turmoil' in Ireland, including information of the killing of Captain James Fenton, the brother of Geoffrey Fenton, the secretary for state, on 23 March 1582.[195] However, it is likely that Spenser was acutely aware that the term of a Lord Deputy was likely to be relatively short, especially as so many were eager to be recalled. Grey left Ireland on 31 August, having finally been granted the recall he so desperately wanted, a desire frequently expressed in the letters to members of the Privy Council that Spenser copied out for him.[196] He was not replaced by another deputy until Sir John Perrot was appointed on 7 January 1584. For the intervening eighteen months Ireland was governed by Loftus and Wallop, who were appointed on 25 August. Spenser received his last payment as Grey's secretary that month—from Wallop—and now had to find other sources of income.

Spenser was involved in a number of land deals in the early 1580s and undoubtedly acquired a lot of property in this period. On 6 December 1581, he leased the manor of Enniscorthy in Wexford, a former Franciscan monastery, along with 'a ruinous castle, land, and a weir there, lands of Garrane, Killkenane, Loughwertie, Barrick-erowe and Ballinparke, and the customs of boards, timber, laths, boats bearing victuals, lodges during the fair, and things sold there, and fishings belonging to the manor, and all other appurtenances as well within the Morroes country as without' (Plate 16).[197] This was a substantial collection of lands and properties situated in a strategically important place, twenty miles north of Wexford on the River Slaney south of the Wicklow and Blackstairs Mountains. In his description of the Irish rivers present at the marriage of the Thames and the Medway, Spenser refers to 'The sandy

Slane, the stony Aubrain' (*FQ* IV.xi.41, line 2), linking together two waterways next to places which he owned (the Aubrain is the River Arlo, near Kilcolman, Spenser using a different name because he had already used Arlo to name the mountain, Galtymore, and the Vale of Aherlow).[198] Like other planters of relatively modest means Spenser was involved in major land deals that would have been beyond his imagination in England. The crown urgently needed to find loyal subjects to occupy the estates of those they had dispossessed and there were rich pickings available for anyone bold enough to risk being a settler. Spenser immediately sublet the property out (9 December) to Richard Synnot, sometime sheriff of Wexford, who had possessed it earlier. Synnot, who was probably acting as an agent for Wallop, then apparently passed the lands on to his master (4 November 1595), who had earlier written to Walsingham of his plans to develop them on 6 January 1586, suggesting that they were probably already in his possession.[199] Wallop, an assiduous acquirer of Irish ecclesiastical property, had been associated with the history of the monastery from early on: in 1582, acting in the queen's service, he had destroyed the house and killed the guardian and two others, when ordered to suppress what had become an illegal religious organization.[200] Lodowick Bryskett acquired one of the farms connected to the Castle, Maghmaine [Macmine], in the early 1580s, and spent the Christmas of 1594 with the Wallops, a further indication of how closely the Lord Treasurer was involved with his intimate circle.[201] The Castle remained as a possession of the Wallop family until the early twentieth century, though it had fallen into decay by the time it was sold in 1914.[202] That Spenser took part in such a land deal is an indication of his importance to Wallop, who probably assumed the role that Grey had previously played in his life. Wallop not only accumulated a great deal of land and property for himself, but was also eager to look after the interests of his clients, notably Bryskett and Spenser, through the generous distribution of Irish assets.[203]

The property commanded a substantial annual rent of £11. 13s. 4d. and the description of the lease to Wallop makes it clear that this was a valuable estate with an orchard and a mill.[204] Wallop later rebuilt the castle that survives today and it is a matter of conjecture whether he established a new building or added to the thirteenth-century structure badly in need of repair.[205] At the same time Spenser leased the former Augustinian friary at New Ross (Plate 17) about ten miles away, buying the lease from Lord Mountgarret of Ballyragget, Kilkenny, and, as with the estate at Enniscorthy, selling the lease on within a short time, this time to Anthony Colclough of Tintern, Wexford.[206] Both Enniscorthy and New Ross were key strategic sites in south-east Ireland, part of the southern corridor established by the English to prevent 'major regional alliances from being created or sustained between the Gaelic lords of the Midlands and those of the southeast'.[207]

Spenser, Wallop, and Synnot were behaving as most English settlers in Ireland behaved throughout the early modern period, acquiring land and property cheaply in order to make a quick profit.[208] In the sixteenth century substantial properties and estates were to be had for little after the dissolution of the monasteries, as was the case here, and the confiscation of the lands of rebel Irish lords. In many ways what happened was a replication of events in England in the first half of the sixteenth century, although in Ireland ecclesiastical property and rents were considerably less lucrative. Even so, Richard Boyle was able to amass what was probably the largest fortune in the British Isles by using his position to claim land for himself, one that perhaps exceeded that of the most successful English sheep farmers of the period, the Spencers of Wormleighton and Althorp, a sign of what was possible for New Englishmen on the make in Ireland.[209] Probably, even at this early stage, and whatever he thought about making a life in Ireland, Spenser planned to acquire a significant estate and so afford himself the status of a gentleman, with which came independence and the freedom to write with fewer restrictions, especially in Ireland. He would be free of the need to depend on patrons and away from the political intrigues and fashions of court.

Only when he acquired his estate in 1590 did Spenser start publishing again and he produced the bulk of his works in a frenetic outpouring of six years: part one of *The Faerie Queene* appeared in 1590, as did the *Complaints*; *Daphnaïda* in 1591; the *Amoretti* and *Epithalamion* in 1594; and *Colin Clouts come home againe*, along with *Astrophel*, in 1595; and part two of *The Faerie Queene*, the *Fowre Hymnes*, and the *Prothalamion* in 1596, an astonishing achievement.[210] Clearly Spenser had been writing throughout the 1580s and had made no secret of the fact that he was at work on a large project, as the testimony of Bryskett demonstrates. His day jobs would have taken up a significant amount of time, even if he farmed work out to deputies, as he was entitled to do. It is possible that he had considerable family duties after the birth of his son, which was probably at some point during his early years in Dublin, but childcare and the education of children were seen by most men as the exclusive responsibility of women.[211] The writer he most closely resembles is Shakespeare, whose priorities appear to have been similar. Shakespeare clearly valued his independence and security, and used his talents to acquire a number of houses in Stratford, which he achieved by becoming a shareholder in his acting company and limiting his writing to two plays a year. Each would have been anxious to avoid the fate of talented, over-prolific writers such as Robert Greene, who was only ever a writer for hire and so never acquired wealth and property. It is perhaps not a coincidence that Greene was involved in literary conflict with both writers.[212]

In the same month that Grey left we have a record of Spenser acquiring yet more property. On 24 August he was granted a twenty-one-year lease of the former friary, New Abbey, in Kilcullen, County Kildare, along with 'an old waste town, adjoining, and its appurtenances', also forfeited after the Baltinglas rebellion, all told another substantial acquisition which helped make him a landed gentleman.[213] Indeed, the abbey was significant enough to have its founding recorded in the *Annals of the Four Masters*, and its founder, Roland Eustace, Baron of Porchester (d. 1496), had been Lord Treasurer of Ireland and, briefly, Lord Deputy, further indications that Spenser was able to deal in land and property which would have been beyond his horizons in England.[214] Spenser probably made some use of this property, as it was only twenty-five miles from Dublin, and on 12 May 1583, he was appointed as one of the commissioners for the musters in the county, the entry recording New Abbey as his residence, part of the plans for strengthening the army in the wake of the Desmond Rebellion.[215] Spenser might even have secured the property in order to fulfil this role at a crucial time, rather than the other way round. The other commissioners were stationed at key places throughout the county, some being local gentry, others, like Spenser, citizens of Dublin who were chosen to oversee the armies gathered in England and Ireland; some volunteers, others pressed into service. The principal duty of a commissioner was, with the muster masters, to check on numbers and to oversee the payment of the troops.[216] Spenser had had extensive experience of the military in the previous three years, which would have made him an ideal candidate for the task, but it is also likely that there was a limited choice of suitable men available.[217] Along with largely the same group of men, he was appointed again on 4 July 1584.[218] Mustering was an especially important and fraught activity in the Irish wars, owing to the corruption of so many captains, who had to be closely watched by the muster officials. Frequently incomplete companies would be sent over from Chester, captains planning to pocket the difference in pay once they had claimed it. Maurice Kyffin, a translator and poet, who occupied the post of muster master in 1596 and who clearly knew Spenser, frequently complained to the Privy Council about the corrupt state of the musters in Ireland but despaired of the prospect of reform.[219]

Now that Spenser was no longer secretary to Grey it is harder to track his movements. Nevertheless, we can tell that he spent time in both the Dublin area and south-west Ireland probably because of his close link to Bryskett, who appears to have become, as Harvey was before, a patron or mentor, as well as a personal friend. Once again, we can see the vital importance of rank and status in the Elizabethan world, and how much easier it was to become friendly with equals than with superiors or inferiors.[220] Even at this early date, New English officials probably knew that there might be a chance of securing land in Munster. After Gerald Fitz James Fitzgerald, the fourteenth and last earl of Desmond had been proclaimed a traitor on 2 November 1579, his lands were forfeited by the 1582 Act of Attainder. It was clear what future plans the English government had for the area.[221] The commission of Sir Valentine Browne and others to survey the rebels' lands (19 June) and the appointment of the resolute Sir John Norris as president of Munster on 24 June 1584 would only have confirmed what many already knew. Spenser, perhaps via Bryskett, may well have felt that his future lay in south-west Ireland rather than the Dublin Pale. It is therefore likely that he was trying to make a profit on his land dealings in order to save up for an estate there. Information may have come from Wallop, who 'had been the first and most persistent of the commissioners [of the Munster Plantation] to press for the peopling of the escheated lands from England'.[222] The Irish and Old English frequently complained that the New English officials knew when land titles were likely to become available and tipped each other off.[223] The immediate problem that faced the English government was how to repopulate the devastated areas in the south-west and there was ample opportunity for English settlers to acquire an estate, exactly what Spenser must have wanted.

On 11 March 1583 Bryskett was promised the lucrative position of clerk of the Council of Munster (at £20 per annum the salary was about three times the salary of Bryskett's job as clerk of the Council in Dublin) upon the death of the incumbent, Thomas Burgate. Burgate duly died on 17 October and Bryskett obtained the necessary letters patent on 6 November.[224] The Council had been revitalized by Sir Henry Sidney, based on his experience of the value of the Council of Wales, as part of his attempt to impose a regional government in Ireland, a key strategy in anglicizing the country. The Council, under an English president, was expected to take an active role in bringing over-mighty feudal magnates to heel, and to spread English law and culture.[225] The Munster Council had jurisdiction over the five shires of Cork, Waterford, Limerick, Kerry, and Desmond: Tipperary, although nominally part of Munster, was overseen by the earl of Ormond as his palatinate. This included the forest of Arlo, the area to the north-east of Spenser's estate on the other side of the Ballyhoura Mountains, notorious as the refuge of Irish resistance to English government. The president had the power to oversee all military, civil, and ecclesiastical matters without reference to Dublin or London.[226] The administration of the province involved a combination of military and administrative skills, the former more vital in periods when martial law was established, the latter necessary to facilitate the everyday running of government machinery and the spread of control over the area.[227] This balance of concerns mirrored the experience of Bryskett and Spenser in Dublin.

As Raymond Jenkins has pointed out, it is unlikely that Bryskett spent much—if any—time in Munster between 1584 and 1588. Apart from the lure of his life in London, the Council rarely met because so many of its members were absentee landlords and the Norris brothers effectively ruled the province alone.[228] On 15 January 1584, the earl of Ormond, who, as the principal military leader in Munster, was responsible for mopping up the last vestiges of Desmond resistance after the earl was killed in November 1583, complained that Bryskett had gone to England trusting his duties to a servant, Henry Shethe.[229] Bryskett was bearing letters from Wallop and Loftus to Burghley—later he worked as Wallop's steward at Enniscorthy, which had first been granted to Spenser from Grey and immediately sold, yet another link between the two officials.[230] This transaction further reveals the closely interrelated nature of New English society in Ireland and indicates that Spenser deputized for Bryskett in Munster, just as he had used deputies in his work himself. The relatively well-paid job as clerk provided exactly the same income that Spenser had received as secretary to Grey and, even if he was not paid the full amount, living in Munster would have been cheaper than living in the Dublin area.[231] The clerk was entitled to 'diet money' and Bryskett stopped receiving this in April 1584, which would indicate that Spenser and his family moved down to Munster at this time.[232]

Spenser may have known his new employer, Sir John Norris, for some time as he was yet another figure connected to Daniel Rogers.[233] Norris, who remained as president until 1597 when his brother Thomas took over, became Spenser's principal employer until he secured the estate at Kilcolman, suggesting that their relationship was similar to the ones Spenser had with Grey and Wallop. Very few letters survive in Spenser's hand from his time in Munster. Either they have been lost or destroyed, or Spenser now undertook more responsible duties for Norris than he had done for Grey and, because he worked with Thomas Norris for a relatively long time, a case can be made that the Norris brothers became more important figures in Spenser's life than Grey had ever been.[234] Spenser undoubtedly accompanied Norris on a number of military expeditions in the next few years, as he had done with Grey. It is likely that he went with Norris and the new Lord Deputy, Sir John Perrot, first through Munster and Connaught in July, to establish the new presidents, Norris and Sir Richard Bingham (1527/8–99) in their posts. Bingham, another military man with a fierce reputation, later distinguished himself by massacring 2,000 Scots at Ardnaree on the River Moy, when they had tried to unite with the Mayo Burkes (22 September 1586).[235] They then headed north, after briefly stopping in Dublin, to Ulster in late August to campaign against the Antrim MacDonnells after Sorley Boy MacDonnell had landed on the Antrim coast with a large contingent of Scots, the crown forces eventually overrunning the MacDonnell stronghold, Dunluce Castle.[236] Spenser's impressive knowledge of the geography of the north of Ireland indicates that he must have been on this excursion, which further suggests that he would have been in attendance on his superiors in other places.[237] He then returned to Munster with Norris in November but was back in Dublin again in March 1585. Here he copied out letters to the Privy Council detailing, among other matters, the devastation that had been visited upon Ulster. Norris noted: 'The wasteness and general desolation of the province is such, as well for want of people as of cattle, being all consumed through the late wars, as that amongst them, which remain many stealths are committed to keep them in life, which are hard to be avoided through their extreme necessity.'[238] Norris's logic is not far away from that of Spenser when describing the Munster famine: the suffering is, unfortunately, the inevitable consequence of rebellion. On 31 March Spenser copied out another letter from Norris to Burghley from Clonmel, which provided similar details showing that much of Ireland was in a similarly desperate state: 'The wasteness of this province is so huge and universal for want of people that it will be very long before the inhabitants shall regain any ability of living.'[239]

Plans for the settlement of Munster were well underway and must have occupied both Spenser's professional and his personal life in the mid-1580s. Norris had made it clear that he saw one of his key tasks as 'planting' English settlers.[240] Given the ways in which land had been distributed by Grey and Wallop it is likely that Spenser hoped that he would gain from his service for John Norris, especially given the current situation after the Desmond Rebellion had been crushed. We have no actual record of where he was living at this time, but he probably stayed in Cork in order to attend the Lord President when they were not on the road. The president had no official residence and lived in either Cork or Limerick. John Norris spent two years (May 1585 to July 1587) campaigning in the Netherlands and ruled Munster through his brother, Thomas, who was appointed vice-president in December 1585, so Thomas would have spent more time in Munster and had a greater influence on the government of the province than his elder brother.[241] Thomas gravitated towards Cork, undoubtedly because his estate at Mallow was nearby.[242] One of the few surviving letters in Spenser's hand from this period is from Thomas Norris to the Privy Council, 22 January 1589, from Shandon Castle in the city.[243] Spenser was probably closer to Thomas than John, given the former's presence at the debate at Bryskett's cottage in 1582, and the fact that he owned the estate next to Kilcolman, including Mallow Castle (Plate 18). Whatever Spenser's precise relationship with the Norrises, we do not know whether his family, Machabyas, Sylvanus, and Katherine, joined him or whether they stayed on in Dublin until he took control of Kilcolman at some point in the late 1580s.

Nevertheless, Spenser would have been busy with official duties, as plans for the Munster Plantation were gathering pace. He worked with a large team of predominantly English officials in the area, many of whom may have become friends: the chief justice Jessua Smythes and, later, William Saxey, and the Irish deputy, James Goold; Richard Royser, the attorney general; Captain George Thornton, whose nephew, Warham St Leger, had been at the symposium at Bryskett's cottage; and Richard Beacon, attorney general after 1586, and author of *Solon His Follie* (1594), the only English treatise on Ireland that can rival Spenser's *View* in its sophisticated analysis of Ireland.[244] He also spent a great deal of time on the road between Cork and Dublin, travelling via either Limerick or Clonmel. Thomas Norris was in Dublin on 27 February 1586, and then again as Member of Parliament for Limerick, with its impressive Cathedral St Mary's, notable for its splendid misericords (Plate 19), for the session that lasted from 26 April to 14 May, and it is more than likely that Spenser accompanied him.[245] Spenser was back in Dublin on 18 July, either having returned by that date, or having stayed there for much of the first half of the year, indicating that he had not yet moved down to the Cork area. He dated a sonnet, 'To the Right Worshipfull, my singular good frend, M. Gabriell Haruey, Doctor of the Lawes', on this day, published on the last page of *Fowre Letters and certaine Sonnets* six years later:

> HARVEY, the happy aboue happiest men
> I read: that sitting like a Looker-on
> Of this worldes Stage, doest note with critique pen
> The sharpe dislikes of each condition:
> And as one carelesse of suspition,
> Ne fawnest for the fauour great:
> Ne fearest foolish reprehension
> Of faulty men, which daunger to thee threat.
> But freely doest, of what thee list, entreat,
> Like a great Lord of peerlesse liberty:
> Lifting the good vp to high Honours seat,
> And the Euill damning euermore to dy;
> For Life, and Death is in thy doomefull writing:
> So thy renowne liues euer by endighting.
>
> Dublin: this xviij: Iuly: 1586.
>
> Your deuoted frend, during life,
> EDMUND SPENCER[246]

It is easy to see why Harvey would have wanted to publish this sonnet in 1592. Spenser was starting to become famous as a writer once again after a long absence with the publication of the first edition of *The Faerie Queene* in 1590, along with the fourth edition of the *Calender*, the *Complaints*, and *Daphnaïda* the following year, which also led to the issue of *Axiochus*. Embroiled in the quarrel with Nashe and mindful of the need to defend his family's honour, Harvey launched an assault on the legacy of the recently deceased Robert Greene in *Fowre Letters*, as a vulgar popularizer, in pointed contrast to the serious work of his friend, Spenser. The sonnet stands as a reminder of the great literary friendship that had launched Spenser's writing career.

In 1586, the sonnet probably had a less defiant significance for its author. Spenser appears to be envying Harvey his life of quiet solitude and contemplation, a reminder of their time together in the 1570s; but it is also a mild rebuke, contrasting Harvey's settled life with his own itinerant existence serving the powerful in Ireland, constantly on the move, with little time to write and no home. There is an undisguised aggression in lines such as those describing Harvey 'as one carelesse of suspition, | Ne fawnest for the fauour great', that read as a bitter reflection on his own life in 1586. Spenser laments that he is unable to see a way beyond a life of enforced servitude rather than intellectual liberty, which makes it easy for us to see why he so valued a home, home life, and liberty so much in his later works. Nevertheless, the sonnet is one of remembered, affectionate friendship and indicates that Harvey and Spenser, even if they did not see each other often after 1580, kept in touch and had a high regard for each other. Harvey refers to 'Scanderbeg' in a sonnet published in *A New Letter* (1591), indicating that he knew about the forthcoming translation of that work by Zachary Jones (1596) for which Spenser wrote a dedicatory sonnet, further evidence that the two men were in contact.[247] As Steven May has suggested, the Dublin sonnet may have been sent as an accompaniment to a manuscript version of *The Faerie Queene*, which would explain why the text circulated among literary figures, such as Christopher Marlowe whom Harvey may have known at Cambridge, before it was published.[248]

Spenser probably already had plans to change his lot. On 8 December 1586 he was behind with a payment of £3 for the prebend of Effin, a parish near Kilmallock, with a substantial church, some ten miles north of the area in which he eventually settled (Plate 20).[249] The payment was due under the Act for First Fruits, decreed by Henry VIII in 1540, transferring the right of the pope to claim a percentage of the income derived from the first year of any ecclesiastical benefice to the king. Spenser's non-payment suggests that the prebend was a benefit to him rather than a sign of a serious religious calling.[250] A prebend provided a stipend drawn by a clergyman (a preben-dary) attached to a cathedral: usually the incumbent received an income from the cathedral's estates in return for duties performed, helping with the complex admin-istration of the cathedral and occasionally preaching. Most were distributed by the bishop, but a few were in the gift of the crown, which might explain the origin of Spenser's office. In Ireland, prebendaries were sometimes canons, senior clergy who formed the chapter that administered the cathedral, entitled to sit in designated pews during services, although there were also some lay prebendaries and the position was evidently used as a convenient means of supporting government officials, probably the most likely explanation for Spenser's role here. The practice inevitably reduced the effectiveness of ecclesiastical administration and resulted in widespread absentee-ism.[251] Possibly Spenser attended chapter meetings at Limerick Cathedral, but, as virtually no cathedral records survive, we have no means of knowing.[252] The Effin lands consisted of about 1,052 acres.[253] It is hard to believe that the possession of this prebend had any real significance for Spenser, especially given his obviously busy life and the fact that he was not ordained.[254] Probably Spenser was one of a number of English officials granted such a position after the queen decreed that no native Irish should 'be preferred to any ecclesiastical living in the cathedral church of Limer-ick'.[255] Despite his condemnation of cynical abusers of clerical positions in *Mother*

Hubberds Tale, Spenser undoubtedly did what he felt he had to do. In that poem the priest boasts:

> Is not that name [i.e., a clerk] enough to make a liuing
> To him that hath a whit of Natures giuing?
> How manie honest men see ye arize
> Daylie thereby, and grow to goodly prize?
> To Deanes, to Archdeacons, to Commissaries,
> To Lords, to Principalls, to Prebendaries;
> All iolly Prelates, worthie rule to beare,
> Who euer them enuie: yet spite bites neare. (lines 417–24)

We cannot be sure whether Spenser wrote this before or after he had taken up the position at Effin, nor whether he authorized Ponsonby's publication of the *Complaints* in 1591.[256] The lines might expose the poet's hypocrisy; point out his own virtue; have been written in advance of his decision to take the money; or be designed to express the spirit of the age. Perhaps Spenser was prepared to resort to accepting dubious government handouts for personal gain, or, most likely, felt that he, unlike others in England, had earned such benefits in Ireland.

There are more examples of possible sharp practice. In 1587 Spenser was clearly involved in the illegal seizure of a Spanish carvel full of Canary wines, which had been captured by the *Thomas Bonaventure*, a ship owned by the London merchant Thomas Cordell. Along with his fellow undertaker, William Herbert, and the Norris brothers, the *Thomas Bonaventure*, which had run aground on the Dingle Peninsula, was sailed to Cork under Spenser's command and looted of its cargo, which, unsurprisingly, led to a court case when Cordell and his fellow merchants found out what had happened. Piracy was common in south-west Ireland, perpetrated especially by crown officials who knew how hard it was for the law to touch them.[257] The English colony at Baltimore, west Cork, prospered through supplying pirate ships.[258] Spenser was perhaps forced to participate in the crime by the Norrises; equally, he may have felt that such booty was, like the prebend, the just deserts of hard-working, oppressed settlers transforming a dangerous land for the crown.[259]

Spenser still had a number of official duties but, by the end of the 1580s, these now appear to have been all in Munster. In March he must have been at the spring session of the Munster Council and in June and November at the summer and autumn sessions in Limerick. By October he was officially established as Bryskett's deputy as clerk to the Council of Munster and a note next to the payment to Bryskett on 31 March 1588 records: 'This is exercised by one Spenser as deputy to the said Bryskett.'[260] Spenser must have paid a deputy to do his job at the Court of Chancery in Dublin until the office was sold to Arland Ussher, on 22 June 1588.[261] Arland was the father of James Ussher, who later obtained a copy of *A View* and almost certainly passed it on to Sir James Ware who used it to produce the first printed edition of the work.[262] This personal connection increases the likelihood that the copy used has a particular connection to Spenser, and suggests that, again, there is some substance in Aubrey's anecdotes.[263]

The year 1588 witnessed the coming of the Armada and most of Spenser's official work would have been concerned with the panic induced first by the possibility of Spanish invasion and then by the wrecks of ships off the Munster coast. Four ships came to grief in the province: the *San Esteban* at Doonbeg; the *Anunciada* in the mouth of the Shannon; the *Sta María De La Rosa* on the tip of the Dingle Peninsula; and the *San Juan Bautista* on the Blasket Islands.[264] Thousands were drowned and those who made it ashore were invariably slaughtered, apart from a few who were worthy of a ransom.[265] As Sir George Carew (1555–1629), then Master of Ordnance, put it, 'There is no rebellion in the whole realm, so much terror prevails.'[266] Carew estimated that about 5,000–6,000 Spanish sailors and soldiers died in Ireland, and that off the Irish coasts, 3,000 of them were slain when forced ashore by desperation. The Armada had been launched in part as a reaction to the execution of Mary Stuart on 8 February 1587, a crusade directed against the heretic Protestant Jezebel on the English throne in defence of her persecuted Catholic subjects.[267] Certainly, this is how events were read by almost all English commentators, regardless of religious affiliation. By the late 1580s confessional battle lines were clearly defined.

Whatever the exact form of Spenser's religious beliefs, like many Englishmen he clearly had a particular fear of aggressive international Catholicism and interpreted events in the light of contemporary European developments. For Spenser, the execution of Mary had been a justifiable action, as she threatened to undermine the stability of the state and so endangered the queen's subjects. *The Faerie Queene* does not follow the chronology of recent historical events, but groups them thematically and in terms of their significance. In Book V, canto ix, we witness Mercilla/Elizabeth's reluctance to execute Duessa/Mary Stuart, until she is forced to act by the logic of her councillor, Zele, who reminds her that pity for her fellow monarch is not reason enough to pardon someone whose crimes are so heinous:

> First gan he tell, how this seem'd so faire
> And royally arayd, *Duessa* hight
> That false *Duessa*, which had wrought great care,
> And mickle mischiefe vnto many a knight,
> By her beguiled, and confounded quight:
> But not for those she now in question came,
> Though also those mote question'd be aright,
> But for vyld treasons and outrageous shame,
> Which she against the dred *Mercilla* oftn did frame. (40)

Zele wins the argument and Duessa, who has already escaped justice with a relatively light punishment, only to return to commit yet more crimes, is duly executed. Duessa, as Zele makes clear, has threatened the power of the prince and her representatives and so, like the Irish leaders who withstood the due process of English law, deserves to die.[268] The penultimate stanza of the canto makes an explicit verbal and thematic link between Zele and Artegall, as '*Artegall* with constant firme intent, | For zeale of Iustice was against her bent', at the same time that '*Zele* began to vrge her punishment' because 'was she guiltie deemed of them all' (49, lines 4–7). Lord Grey had been a commissioner at the trial of Mary and had defended William Davidson when he was publicly blamed for issuing the order to execute Mary by Elizabeth, on the grounds that Davidson 'preferred the saftie of his prince and contrie before his owne welfare . . . his zeale therein was in his opynion to be rewarded'.[269] The use of the word 'zeale' here might indicate that, on this issue at least, Spenser had some insider knowledge of public policy. In *The Faerie Queene* he links the demand for the execution of Mary to an effective policy in Ireland, representing the monarch as weak and feeble on each occasion, first in trying to prevent Mary's execution, and second in leaving Ireland exposed by recalling the successful hard-line Lord Deputy before his work is finished:

> But ere he could reforme it thoroughly,
> He through occasion called was away,
> To Faerie Court, that of necessity
> His course of Iustice he was forst to stay,
> And *Talus* to reuoke from the right way,
> In which he was that Realme for to redresse.
> But enuies cloud still dimmeth vertues ray.
> So hauing freed *Irena* from distresse,
> He tooke his leaue of her, there left in heauinesse. (V.xii.27)

The allegory at one level represents the fate of Lord Grey and the criticism of his policies noted in *A View*.[270] But it is far more flexible than this, working in terms of larger themes rather than merely historical events in line with Sir Philip Sidney's argument that poets were not tied to the tyranny of facts as historians were, a distinction repeated in the Letter to Ralegh.[271] Here, the 'poet historical' can reveal the underlying truth, that the real dangers to Ireland and its Irish and English population often have their origins outside as well as inside Ireland itself, as was the case with the earlier Fitzmaurice Rebellion, the effects of which Spenser saw first-hand. The failure to deal with aggressive and dangerous Catholic opposition within England leads to attempted invasions of Ireland to support local rebellion, which then, in turn, threatens the stability of England. While Spenser appears to have been interested in native religious traditions within England, which meant the

Catholic faith in its broader definition, he had no time for the papacy or Spanish-sponsored Catholic crusades. We should be careful to distinguish the two beliefs which have often been conflated and confused.

The failure of the Armada is represented in *The Faerie Queene*, but it appears as a relatively minor event, which has often surprised commentators.[272] The description of Arthur's defeat of the Souldan (V.viii.28–45) has been linked to the defeat of the Armada since it was first noticed in John Upton's edition of the poem (1758). The image of the Souldan in his chariot appears to refer to Philip II's representation of himself in his impresa.[273] Furthermore, the description of the Souldan's horses fleeing in panic when blinded by the reflection from Arthur's shield is tailored to refer to the scattering of the fleet by the fireships in the channel:

> The dredful sight did them so sore affray,
> That their well knowen courses they forwent,
> And leading th'euer-burning lampe astray,
> This lower world nigh all to ashes brent,
> And left their scorched path yet in the firmament. (40, lines 5–9)[274]

Spenser compares the aborted Spanish invasion to the rash attempt of Phaeton, son of the sun god Helios, to drive his father's chariot across the skies, a disaster ended only when Zeus destroyed the boy with a thunderbolt. The use of this particular classical myth shows that Spenser correctly understood that the Armada was a less threatening event than the serious rebellions within Ireland: perhaps he had in mind what he had witnessed at Smerwick, which features as a far more frightening prospect in his writing. It is also a sign that by the time the ships reached Munster the Armada was a spent force likely to cause little serious danger to the English in Ireland—although, as everywhere else in Elizabeth's dominions, there was a thanksgiving service in Cork Cathedral, with a victory sermon delivered by Bishop William Lyon (d. 1617), former chaplain to Lord Grey.[275] Perhaps Spenser was there. And, yet again, the placing of the representation of the event shows how flexible, in terms of both time and subject matter, Spenser's allegory invariably was.[276]

6

Spenser's Castle

As PART OF the survey of the forfeited lands of the earl of Desmond the estate of Kilcolman, derived from the Irish for 'Colman's Church', was preserved as a distinct unit.[1] The demesne consisted of an inhabitable tower house, perhaps built on the site of an existing Norman structure, with 3,028 acres of mainly pastoral land. There were some other buildings, a church, from which the estate took its name, probably ruined, and a limestone quarry. Kilcolman, although relatively small, was broadly similar to the other estates occupied by English settlers in Munster.[2] The estate itself consisted of three townlands, Kilcolman East (209 acres); Kilcolman Middle (233 acres); and Kilcolman West (751 acres). The rest of the land was made up from surrounding townlands: Rossgh, East and West, Kylnevalley, Lysnemucky, Ard Adam, Arden-reagh, Carrigyne, Bally Ellis, Kyllmack Ennes, and Ardenbane.[3] Spenser had acquired a large squarish block of land stretching down from the Ballyhoura Hills to the Awbeg River, which formed the eastern and southern boundaries of his estate; the western boundary was the Castlepook River, separating his property from that of the Synans.[4] The estate had first been owned by the De Rupe or Roche family, who had probably erected the castle at some point in the fourteenth century, a date that tallies with the archaeological evidence. It was briefly owned by Sir Henry Sidney in 1568 and was subsequently part of the lands confiscated by the crown after the Munster Rebellion, but was always claimed by the Roches as their own.[5]

The castle is situated on a rocky promontory overlooking a bog, commanding a view of the surrounding hills (Plate 21). Like many other Norman towers it would have been easy to defend from small raiding parties but was not designed to withstand more sustained assault.[6] In the 1580s the estate was extremely desirable, even though much of the land needed extensive labour if it were to become especially profitable. Moreover, the plot was relatively isolated, and would have been sur-rounded by woods, a common problem on the Plantation, where settlers were dispersed throughout the different parts of the 300,000 acres that the Desmonds had acquired piecemeal over hundreds of years.[7] A letter from Sir John Perrot to the Privy Council (25 October 1584) lists Kilcolman as one of the castles that are to be fortified, its strategic importance above the rich, fertile Blackwater Valley vital to guard the route between the Boggeragh and Nagle Mountains down to Cork.[8] Accordingly, Spenser's house was one of many small settlements established and developed along the valley in the 1580s.[9] Close to the towns of Buttevant and Mallow, it would have been a convenient site for someone who had to travel north to Limerick; south to Cork; and across country north-east to the midland fortresses of Clonmel, Kilkenny, and Carlow, on the route to Dublin. Spenser would indeed have had to travel frequently—as part of an armed convoy—along the established routes in the wide valleys between the Ballyhoura and Mullaghareirk mountains to Limerick; and between the Galtee and Knockmealdown mountains to the mid-lands.[10] Densely forested areas, in particular on the sides of the Ballyhouras and Galtees and in the Vale of Aherlow, would have been carefully avoided by the English settlers, who tried to clear away as much forest land as they could.[11] The most imposing site that he would have passed numerous times was the peak of Galtymore, the highest point in south Munster at 919 metres, between Limerick and South Tipperary, about thirty miles north-east of Kilcolman. The peak, Dawson's Table, is visible from virtually every position in the immediate area, which Spenser used as the setting for the debate between Mutabilitie and Jove to determine the fate of the universe in 'Two Cantos of Mutabilitie' (Plate 22). Spenser would also have made use of the waterways, in particular the Awbeg, which was navigable in this period, and the Blackwater, and would have taken him down to Youghal, probably a more natural port for north Cork settlers to use than Cork city would have been.[12]

Although the road system in Munster was not especially bad—in fact, land travel 'could be comparatively speedy' by European standards—virtually all maps of the province produced in this period place heavy emphasis on an extensive system of relatively deep waterways running into the River Lee and on to Cork, as well as the Blackwater, which Spenser celebrates in *The Faerie Queene*.[13] The Bristol port books record extensive trade in textiles, principally wool and cloth, hides, and wine (imported), as well as other commodities such playing-cards, metal implements, and paper.[14] However, the first stone bridge over the river was not constructed until 1600, after Spenser's death, leading to a period of bridge-building spearheaded by Richard Boyle, who saw the value of strategically placed bridges in the province, which then enabled the development of the road system.[15] A 'rough' map of Munster preserved in the National Archives, which belonged to Burghley, represents the province in terms of exaggerated, wide waterways, showing that they were seen as the principal means of communication in Munster, the passage along the Blackwater to Youghal being one of three main routes (Figure 8).[16] Spenser would have been

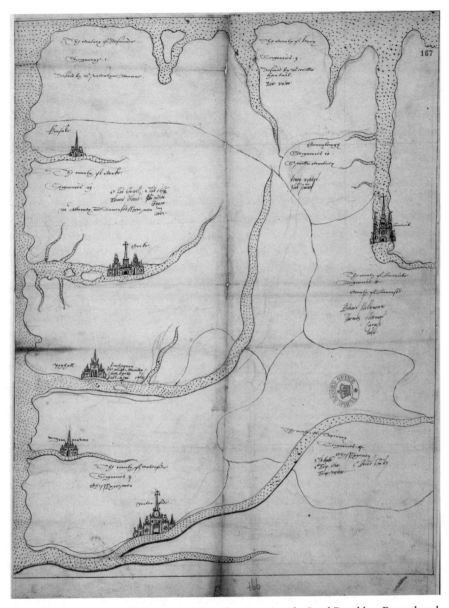

Figure 8. 'Rough' map of Munster (1586), with annotations by Lord Burghley. Reproduced with kind permission of the National Archives.

able to access the Blackwater from its tributary, the Awbeg, immediately south of his estate, which would further explain his expressed enthusiasm for rivers in his work, especially as this route would have connected him to Elizabeth Boyle, who would become his second wife.

Three thousand acres was a substantial estate, even though it was one of the smallest allotments, or seigniories, distributed to an undertaker, who signed the original treaty establishing the Plantation and who agreed to populate, run, and maintain the estate.[17] Land was first granted in divisions of 12,000, 10,000, 8,000, 6,000, and 4,000 acres, although, probably through a misunderstanding, Sir Walter Ralegh obtained a gargantuan estate of three and a half seigniories totalling some 42,000 acres to the south-east of Cork at Youghal, demonstrating his central importance to the enterprise.[18] There were clear rules about how the lands were to be farmed, although these were changed later on. In a seigniory of 12,000 acres the undertaker was to have 1,600 acres (later changed to 2,100); a chief farmer 400 acres; other farmers plots of 300 and 200 acres; fourteen freeholders 300 acres each; and forty copyholders 100 acres each—which left 800 acres over for mesne (i.e., held by the undertaker to distribute as he saw fit).[19] We know little about the actual running of Spenser's estate, although Spenser records in his return to the commissioners that he had six households there. It is likely that there was a similar structure to other working estates, with a pecking order among the farmers and tenants working for the undertaker. Although tenants were supposed to be English, the 1611 'Inquisition' found that many freeholders and farmers were Irish, undoubtedly given land by undertakers unable to fulfil their obligations.[20] Spenser's estate, however well run, would have been no different.

Kilcolman was granted first to Andrew Reade, an undertaker from Faccombe, Hampshire, a lawyer who was probably closely connected to Sir Henry Wallop, whose estates were about twenty miles away, and who was by far the most important local landowner in east Hampshire.[21] Reade's family, like the Wallops, were involved in numerous land deals, and one of Reade's family, Richard, dealt directly with their grander western neighbours. Andrew Reade seems to have been trusted by his social superiors, as Spenser was in Ireland, to take part in important land transactions. It is unlikely that Reade ever set foot on the Irish estate he acquired, and it is possible that he was involved in a speculative plan that was always designed to benefit Spenser.[22] This would explain why Spenser was prepared to move down to Munster while he still had to keep travelling back to Dublin, in contrast to Bryskett, who looked to get back to England as often as he could. Certainly, the acquisition of Kilcolman looms large in the documents that detail Spenser's life and his own representation of himself once his publishing career was reignited in 1590.[23] If so, Spenser may well have occupied the estate before the legal documents indicate that he did, perhaps as early as 1587, when it was assigned to Reade on 14 March.[24] Significantly enough, there are no records after this date of Spenser in Dublin, suggesting that his move to the south-west was now complete. Spenser and Reade had drawn up an agreement whereby Spenser would occupy the lands and assume control of the estate if Reade had not done so by 22 May 1589, a clear indication that Reade had never had plans to live there.[25]

Spenser provided a series of answers to a list of 'Articles of Instructions given in charge to the Commissioners for examining & inquiring of her Maiesties attained landes past to the vundertakers' in May–June 1589, further indicating that he and his family had probably occupied the estate some time before. Spenser's answer is preserved in the Irish State Papers alongside those provided by his neighbours and the other undertakers throughout Munster, a sign of how seriously such documents were taken by the authorities.[26] It was vital to have as much information about the area as possible so that it could be controlled and governed by the undertakers on behalf of the crown. It was their duty to use the legal system and raise an army in order to transform the land from a rebellious backwater into a flourishing, anglicized outpost, an expansion of England. This is the message of such treatises as Robert Payne's 'hugely optimistic tract', *A Brief Description of Ireland* (1589), which assured would-be colonists that the land was so much more fertile than in England (a common theme in descriptions of the province), the consequent yields of crops so much more abundant, and the Irish so loyal that only a fool would not take up the exciting new opportunity on offer to settle in Munster.[27] Indeed, the title of Payne's short treatise, which anticipates Thomas Harriot's *A Briefe and True Report of the New Found Land of Virginia* (1590), suggests a deliberate colonial rivalry, with Munster undertakers like Payne trying to persuade English tenants that they would be better off travelling within the British Isles rather than risking all by sailing across the Atlantic, however attractive that prospect might seem.[28] Harriot, a client of Ralegh's, had leased Molana Abbey near Youghal (Plate 23), in August 1589, part of Ralegh's extensive estates on the Munster Plantation, something that Payne undoubtedly knew.[29] Harriot may well have been living there soon after that date, and records show that he spent time in Ireland in the 1590s, as did another Ralegh client, the artist John White.[30] Spenser probably knew—or, at least, encountered— Harriot, a self-made intellectual commoner like Spenser, who lived close to the town where he met and wooed his second wife, as well as White.[31] If he travelled down the Blackwater to Youghal Spenser would have passed Molana. Spenser names the nymph who is tricked by Faunus into revealing the whereabouts of Diana in 'Two Cantos of Mutabilitie', Molanna, perhaps a glancing reference to Harriot's bold scientific explorations, which provided him with a contemporary reputation as a daring atheist.[32]

Spenser's answers to the commissioners give us an indication of the estate in 1589, which suggests that even if he had occupied it earlier than May 1589, Kilcolman was not yet up and running as an English concern.[33] In his seven responses Spenser confirms his desire to bring over settlers from England, as he was required to do, but states that he has at present only six 'householdes of English people vpon his land', because the patent had not yet been confirmed. However, he asserts that 'sondry honest persons in Eng[land] have promised to come ouer to in habit his land so sone as his pat[ent]' was granted. He had not yet divided the lands up for the tenants for the same reasons, and also states that he has not received the full complement of 4,000 he was granted, as 'there wanteth of his dew Proporcion m [1,000] acres as he supposeth at the least'.[34] It appears that he never received this last section of his promised estate. In a survey undertaken in late 1591 the estate is confirmed as 3,028 acres, and Spenser, like other undertakers, was to pay a reduced rent until 1595 of £15. 13s. 9d. per annum, and, after that, the larger sum of £22. 12s. 11d.[35]

Spenser had more pressing, immediate concerns than obtaining what he felt was his due. His right to the estate was immediately challenged by Lord Maurice Roche of Fermoy (d. 1600), from whose estate the lands had been escheated.[36] Roche had first complained about the loss of his lands on 3 September 1588, but had received no satisfaction.[37] He wrote a number of times to Ormond, Walsingham, and the queen throughout 1589, finally writing to Elizabeth and Walsingham on 12 October 1589, detailing the list of the injuries done to him by the undertakers, mentioning Spenser by name, as well as his neighbours on the Plantation: George Browne, Hugh Cuffe, Arthur Hyde, and Jesse Smythes.[38] Roche, an Old English gentleman, described by the Four Masters as 'a young man distinguished for his gentleness, personal figure, and learning in Latin, Irish, and English', was clearly convinced that he had a prior legal right to the lands.[39] In writing directly to the queen, Roche appears to have been hoping that he could appeal to their ancient lineage against the vulgar New English upstarts who had usurped his ancient rights, a common feature of Irish appeals to monarchs after the Reformation and Act of Kingship of 1541.[40] Roche makes a convincing case that he has been cheated of his rightful possessions by the New English who have appropriated his property and abused his tenants: 'Edmund Spenser falsely pretending title to certain castles and 16 ploughlands, hath taken possession thereof. Also, by threatening and menacing the said Lord Roche's tenants, and by seizing their cattle, and beating Lord Roche's servants and bailiffs he has wasted 6 ploughlands of his Lordships lands.' More specifically, Roche accuses Spenser of abusing his official position: 'by collo[r] of his office and by makinge of corrupt Bargaines w[th] certaine psons pretendinge falslie title to p[ar]cell of the L. Roches lau[n]des disposed the said L. Roche of certaine castles and xvi plough laundes'.[41]

Roche's case is entirely plausible and shows that he—or whoever was acting on his behalf—had a sophisticated knowledge of English law, as well as how he might best proceed by eventually bypassing the courts which, as his first attempt indicates, were unlikely to be sympathetic to his cause.[42] 'Waste' is a technical legal term, which seems to have been used in its precise meaning by Lord Roche. As Andrew Zurcher has noted, 'The crime of waste is basically one committed by the temporary custodian of an estate against its future possessor(s), and amounts to the stripping of that estate of its capital assets—timber, soil, mineral or metal deposits, and any buildings.'[43] Roche, showing that he was indeed the educated man that the Four Masters claimed he was, is arguing that Spenser and the other undertakers are guilty of the crime of abusing the land, razing to the ground what has been cultivated and built, and that they are plunderers not planters. Roche, an Anglo-Norman settler, claimed that he was the rightful owner of the estate and that the queen should recognize that her interests would be best served by returning it to him. Equally important is Roche's other claim that Spenser has abused his office and, together with his fellow under-takers, has made corrupt bargains to obtain false titles to the land. We know that this is exactly what many of the undertakers and government employees did, and that Bryskett, Fenton, and Richard Boyle, all working in government offices and closely associated with Spenser, made their fortunes this way. Either Roche knew that Spenser had been helped by Wallop—who was, after all, one of the commissioners assigned to deal with the 574,645 acres that had come into the crown's possession—and others to obtain his estates, as he had been by Grey some years before, perhaps because Roche had an informant in the Munster civil service,[44] or Roche was asserting that this was the general practice among the New English and so he was calculating that making such an accusation was almost certain to be vindicated in court.

Roche's testimony provides further evidence that Spenser's acquisition of Kilcol-man was carefully prepared and planned. The undertakers' bill against Lord Roche, submitted on the same day (which demonstrates how each party carefully crafted their formal suit), takes an entirely different tack:

Against the Lord Roche.

Imprimis the Lord Roche in Iuly 1586 and at sundry tymes before & after relieved & maynteyned one Kedagh Okelly a proclaimed Traitour being his fosterbrother & caused the Sessoures man [i. e., assessor], who had brought into the countrey, to bee apprehended And when the sayd Kedagh was sought for he convayed him away.

Iames birne

Item the said Lord secretly vpon the first report of the Spaniardes coming towards this countrey caused powder & munition to bee made in a privy place of his house, from the knowledge of his owne servauntes

mr Mc Hendry

Item the said Lord vseth in his grace to pray that god would take away this heavy hand from them and speaketh il of the gouernment, & hath vttered wordes of contempt of her Maiesties lawes calling them vniust.

mr Edmound Spencer
Iames byrne[45]

Only after these first three accusations do the undertakers start to list Roche's specific crimes against them (imprisoning tenants, stealing a cow, concealing lands from the queen). While Roche tries to make the case hinge on issues of lawful land possession and usage, the settlers try to move the case onto the question of loyalty and treason. The different approaches to the dispute indicate how far apart the mental and social worlds of natives and newcomers really were and how much Irish society would be transformed by the intrusion of New English settlers.[46] The dispute suggests that, whatever colonial writers like Robert Payne asserted, far from seeing Munster as an extended part of England, the undertakers were acutely aware that it was a hostile land that they had somehow to make civilized. English law may well be the means of achieving this aim, but the real issue was the fundamental loyalty of the region to the crown. It should not surprise us that as the case dragged on with no clear-cut solution, and as the Roche family stepped up their hostility to the colonists, Spenser should lose all faith in the wisdom of spreading English law to Ireland before the loyalty of the inhabitants had been secured.[47] Spenser's desire for an estate underpinned his literary aspirations, the pastoral retreat providing the material base for the epic poetry, though his quest also compromised his lofty ideals, a conflict he clearly understood. But he would not have been alone in placing such a high value on the acquisition of property in early modern England.

Nevertheless, just as Roche's case against the undertakers appears entirely plausible, so does the undertakers' case against Roche, if taken on their terms. Roche had, in fact, been indicted for rebellion in 1580, an act that had almost cost him his estate. In a long letter on miscellaneous matters dated 20 May, Lord Justice Pelham had informed the Council in England that Maurice Roche had joined with Viscount Barry's son in rebellion, but had changed his mind and given himself up. He blamed his father's severe parenting, for which the angry Lord Roche threatened to disinherit him. Pelham, however, claimed that it was in everyone's interests that the Roches be reconciled as they were such significant landowners in the Cork area.[48] Roche was therefore known to the English as a rebel who had supported the Fitzmaurice Rebellion, which helped to start the Desmond Wars and which, in turn, led to the establishment of the Plantation, a fact that could not have escaped an informed colonist such as Spenser. Furthermore, Roche's wife, Eleanor, was the niece of James Fitzjohn Fitzgerald, fourteenth earl of Desmond, and the sister of the 'arch traitor', James Fitzmaurice Fitzgerald, who had landed at Smerwick.[49] Again, Spenser must have been aware of this link between them, so the tactics employed by the undertakers make perfect sense as a means of achieving their desire of claiming their entitlement to Munster.[50]

The case between the undertakers and Roche was clearly a significant one: few other undertakers had their claims to land challenged as directly and forcefully as Spenser's was, with an opponent who had much better access to the queen and her advisers than he did. Although there were a number of surprises, cases usually went the way of the settlers.[51] Perhaps Spenser, coming from a society in which disputes over land and other matters were part of daily life, had been surprised at the level of resistance to his claims, given the stated aims of the government to make Ireland loyal and English.[52] When he was formally granted Kilcolman on 26 October 1590, Spenser's choice of the name for his new estate is a sign of his acceptance of the complicated and uncertain route by which he had acquired it. He was entitled to 'hold for ever, in fee farm, by the name of "Hap Hazard", by fealty, in common socage'.[53] The name, reflected the fact that the property was one he could not have expected to possess just over ten years earlier, as well as the current struggle with Lord Roche, which he knew would stretch into the foreseeable future.[54]

Spenser had to deal with other land disputes involving his Irish neighbours. An undated manuscript in Spenser's hand grants a portion of his lands to 'MacHenry', possibly Edmond MacHenry, an Irish landowner who pressed claims against Henry Billingsley, an undertaker who held an 11,800-acre estate at Kilfinny, Limerick, just above that of Spenser's immediate neighbour, Hugh Cuffe.[55] The document, in Spenser's secretary hand, reads:

Be it knowen to all men by these presentes that I Edmund Spenser of Kilcolman estate doe giue vnto mac Henry the keeping of all the woodes which I haue in Balliganim & of the rushes & brakes without making any spoyle thereof & also doe covenant with him that he shall haue one house within the bawne of Richardston for him self & his catell in tyme of warre. And also within the space of vij yeares to repayre the castle of Richardston afore sayd & in all other thinges to vse good neighbour hood to him & his

Edmund Spenser[56]

Richardstown is a mile immediately west of Doneraile, and the woods formed the most southerly section of Spenser's estate. The grant, probably made in 1589 when many claims were lodged against the newly established undertakers, raises several interesting issues about life on the Plantation and the part that Spenser played. The clause referring to 'spoyle' suggests that there was considerable conflict between undertakers and natives and the need for Spenser to establish a 'bawn' (a defensive wall) to protect MacHenry's cattle 'in tyme of warre' further implies that there was fear of future aggression. Perhaps these were standard clauses agreed by lawyers, but we do not have enough comparable documents available to be confident of this. It is possible that Spenser was a 'good colonist' and sought to return land that rightfully belonged to someone else, holding on only to what he felt was his, and that he was here correcting the excesses of his tenants.[57] More plausibly, I think, it suggests that either Spenser was coerced into acting against his interests, feeling that he had no choice but to comply with an irate neighbour, or that he wanted to win over MacHenry as a potential ally against a more powerful branch of the Roches. The

MacHenrys were related to the Roches, which shows that English settlers simply had to work with their Irish neighbours, as the history of the Spenser family's interactions with the Nagles, Roches, and Synans demonstrates.[58] Sylvanus Spenser married one of the Nagles who owned Ballynamona Castle on the banks of the Awbeg, only about six miles from Kilcolman, which surely explains how they met, and shows how closely local families interacted in Ireland, as they did in England (Plate 24).

Furthermore, Spenser did eventually lose two of his ploughlands to another Irishman of Anglo-Norman descent, Nicholas Synan [Shynan], also known as McShane and Shane Barry. The Synans were another long-established Anglo-Norman family whose base was in Kilbolane, near Charleville, on the northern side of the Ballyhoura hills. They had built Richardstown Castle, completed in 1291, as well as Castlepook (1380), fortified dwellings immediately bordering on the Kilcolman estates, but their adherence to Catholicism meant that their power was on the wane and that most of their lands were lost by the early seventeenth century.[59] The case brought before the Munster commissioners in 1592 shows that this dispute was of exactly the same nature as Roche's case against Spenser:

> Edmond Spencer deft. for Ardadam a plowe land & Killoyenesie, half a plowe land, Balliellicie a plo: lande & Ardgilbert dip lo: land.
>
> The p*ts* [i.e., the plaintive, Synan] tytle ys by discents from his auncestors. The defend*t* saith they were *p*cells of S*r* John of Desmondes landes, viz. *p*cell of Kilcolman and Rosacke to w*ch* her Ma*tie* is intitled.

The case was duly heard by the sheriff in Cork, either Florence O'Driscoll of Downshed or Hugh Cuffe, in front of a jury who weighed up the evidence and decided that 'Ardadam . . . the p*t* shall recover until better mater appeare for her Ma*tie* or for the defennd*t*', but that Balliellice 'ys passed to the defend*t* at one plowe land'. Moreover, 'the defend*t* ys abated the rent of two plo: landes, viz after the rate of 28 plowe landes to a Seignorie of xij*m* [12,000] acres, and after the rate of a C [100] marks to a seignorie of xij*m* [12,000] acres in the Countie of Corke'.[60]

The case—as well as the grant to MacHenry—shows the determination of the authorities in Munster to bring the due process of English law to the province even if individual cases went against the undertakers who had been recruited to plant English customs and practices in Ireland. This policy often had the unfortunate effect of leaving undertakers isolated and vulnerable as settlers surrounded by understandably hostile Irish landowners.[61] Indeed, as Anthony Sheehan has pointed out, English authorities were by no means always committed to supporting the New English in Ireland, and 'the government commission of 1592 was quite willing to consider cases against the undertakers and their tenants and to rule in favour of the native claimant'.[62] Synan was awarded the ploughlands because

Spenser and the crown could not prove that they were part of the confiscated Kilcolman estate so they reverted to the original owner's possession. To do otherwise was to create a dangerous precedent, which is why English officials were so keen to excavate records of landholding.[63] The rate of rent on the ploughlands was calculated in terms of the general principles of the Plantation so that all proceeded exactly as matters would have done had the case been heard in England by one of the Chancery courts which Spenser knew well and from which he later sought a judgement.[64] Given the finely balanced and problematic situation in which Spenser found himself he was undoubtedly prescient in naming his property as he did. Certainly, Nicholas Synan, like Lord Roche, was not always hostile to the English authorities and in 1594 cooperated in a land deal with Sir Thomas Norris, suggesting that even on the cusp of the Nine Years War, it was often business as usual on the Plantation.[65]

In the early seventeenth century Spenser's eldest son, Sylvanus, married Ellen Nagle, a daughter of David Nagle, from a powerful Catholic Anglo-Irish family who held extensive lands east of Kilcolman around the Nagle Mountains.[66] These Spensers brought their children up as Catholics so that by the 1630s both Spenser sons had become Catholic.[67] William, the second son who eventually inherited the Kilcolman estate, lost a significant part of the family lands in 1654 when they were confiscated by Cromwellian soldiers. This further complicates our understanding of the religious allegiances of the Spensers and it might further explain why A View makes so little mention of religion.[68] Either the Spensers had relatively cordial relationships with most of their neighbours, perhaps until the rebellion threatened to overthrow the Plantation in the mid-1590s; or English and Irish found it easier to marry after English power was secured in 1601; probably both. Perhaps the pressure for religious and social conformity after the effective collapse of the Elizabethan Reformation was simply too great to resist.[69] Certainly, by the early seventeenth century marriage between natives and incomers was common, especially in more stable areas.[70]

It is hard to imagine that this union of significant local families could have taken place without some form of negotiation, especially if we consider the extent of the property involved. Documents from the 1630s and 1640s show that Sylvanus and William Spenser were dealing in land with the Nagles, perhaps selling parts of the estate to cover debts, or perhaps the families were working together to establish the unity of their holdings.[71] Spenser's family were prepared to secure their future through intermarriage, although whether this was only possible after his death is not easy to determine. Nevertheless, both of Spenser's eldest grandchildren were known as Catholics: Hugolin, Peregrine's eldest son, and the heir to the other Spenser estates at Renny, either converting once he had left home or preserving his faith into adulthood and never seeing fit to renounce it, unlike his eldest cousin.

At the very least their stories suggest that it is possible that both of Spenser's sons found it easy to adopt local religious practices, something that became more obvious a generation later. That the Spenser household was religious we cannot doubt; what version of religion was practised—and, concomitantly, what sort of religion was forbidden—is much harder to ascertain.

The Kilcolman estate formed part of a nexus of seigniories immediately north of the Blackwater. Spenser's closest neighbour to the south was Thomas Norris, to whom Spenser appears to have been closely allied.[72] Norris had the 6,000-acre seigniory of Mallow, the nearest town of any significance, where he built a large castellated house, 'the only surviving house built by an undertaker on his demesne'.[73] The impressive structure was based around a number of polygonal towers to provide an imposing grandeur, and was probably intended for his daughter.[74] Mallow was a relatively small settlement with no more than 200 houses in 1641, although it did have two castles, one at either end.[75] To the east of Norris was Thomas Saye, about whom nothing is known, who had the seigniory of Carriglemlery, which occupied 5,778 acres. To the immediate north was Hugh Cuffe, who had the larger seigniory of Kilmore, a total of 12,000 acres, although he was dogged with legal disputes with his neighbours, Ellen Fitzedmond Gibbon and James MacShane, which eventually reduced the size of his holdings.[76] Cuffe was probably related to Henry Cuffe, Essex's secretary, and may have been his brother. Henry was executed in 1601 after Essex's failed coup, and notorious for teaching the earl how to use a classical education to ferment rebellion.[77] If so, then, given that the Cuffes were a West Country family from near Taunton, who had strong links with the Paulet family, it is possible that Cuffe acquired his estate through a Ralegh connection, as the Raleghs also had strong links to the Paulets, which might in turn have linked Cuffe to Spenser before they both took up their lands.[78] Cuffe, who often complained bitterly of the hardships that his Irish estates caused him, eventually sold his lands to the Audley family.[79]

It is also possible that Cuffe was the 'H. C.' who wrote the manuscript 'Dialogue of Peregrynne and Silvynnus', which was then presented to the earl of Essex, an attribution which would make sense in terms of the link between the undertakers and the fact that the author of that dialogue was influenced by *A View*. The opening of the work, when Silvynus encounters his brother, Peregryn, in London, having not seen him 'full one yeare and a half', resembles the start of Spenser's dialogue when Eudoxus meets Irenius, who has just returned from Ireland.[80] In his second speech Silvynus states that Ireland is 'a country of wrath', a pun that would appear to owe much to the often repeated pun that Ireland was a 'land of Ire', a quibble made in *Amoretti* 22, when the poet states that he needs to 'builde an altar to appease her yre', the possessive pronoun referring to his betrothed, but, also, in the form of a synecdoche, Ireland.[81] Unfortunately, it is difficult to prove that the author was Cuffe. Whoever wrote the dialogue had extensive knowledge of the political situation in the Irish midlands and may have acted as an Irish-speaking spy among the Irish community in London for Burghley, and we have no evidence that Cuffe acted in this capacity.[82]

Whatever the truth, Spenser is more likely to have had extensive contact with Cuffe than most of the settlers, especially given their common foe, Lord Roche, and what we can assume were their shared intellectual interests. Furthermore, Cuffe, like Spenser, served as sheriff of Cork (1592–3), indicating that they were regarded in similar terms by their peers and superiors and so may also have had contact through official circles.[83] It has long been acknowledged that Spenser would have had a number of like-minded friends and associates on the Plantation, notably Bryskett, whom he had known before, Ralegh, and Richard Beacon.[84] Beacon's seigniory of 6,000 acres at Clandonnell Roe was the furthest east of all the planters, beyond those of Ralegh and Sir Christopher Hatton, a hundred miles or so from Kilcolman; his other lands were in west Cork.[85] Ralegh's at Youghal was over sixty miles away, a considerable journey anywhere in early modern Europe, but especially in a country with such a limited system of roads (albeit one that Spenser must have often made).

Spenser knew how to ride, and would have learned by the time he left Cambridge, as it would have been the easiest way of travelling to Harvey's house in Saffron Walden. Riding would have been a skill that any aspirational gentleman would have had to master, its very familiarity, in this case, explaining a lack of references to horsemanship. More importantly, it would have been essential for the sort of work Spenser did, first as a carrier of messages, then as a secretary. The opening stanza of the first canto of *The Faerie Queene* advertises his familiarity with riding techniques, skills, and terminology:

> A Gentle Knight was pricking on the plaine,
> Y cladd in mightie armes and siluer shielde,
> Wherein old dints of deepe wounds did remaine,
> The cruell markes of many' a bloudy fielde;
> Yet armes till that time did he neuer wield:
> His angry steede did chide his foming bitt,
> As much disdayning to the curbe to yield:
> Full iolly knight he seemd, and faire did sitt,
> As one for knightly giusts and fierce encounters fitt. (I.i.1)

'[P]ricking' in line 1 is a multivalent pun, a brilliant way for Spenser to relaunch his career after such a long absence and to remind readers that a premier and unsettling literary talent was back in print.[86] There is a sexual reference, especially relevant to the knight, given his particular failings in Book I. More significantly here, 'pricking' meant both spurring a horse on, which is obvious enough, and writing, both because a pen had to 'prick' the paper, and because a secretary, or any other functionary eager to produce a neat document, would use a pin to make marks in the margin so that the document could be produced in straight lines across the page ('pricking'), as, for example, was the case with Grey's letter to the queen dated 12 November 1580, written out in Spenser's best formal italic hand.[87] One of the key meanings of the opening line is the connection made between Spenser's day job and his literary career: he has 'pricked' out his poem just as he has spurred his horse around Ireland in the service of the state. The Red-Cross Knight has to control his 'angry steede', which is champing at the bit, and not let the 'curbe', the strap passing under the lower jaw of the horse, lead him. He has to master the skill of horsemanship if he wants to get to where he needs to go.[88] Spenser is also telling the reader that it is only through acquiring this skill that he has been able to accumulate the means to enable him to write the poem, a further sign of the vital significance of horses in early modern England.

Spenser would have been able to ride out to see Ralegh and others on the Plantation, but it is unlikely that he did so very often, given the difficulties of early modern transport, the expense, the labour involved, and the fear of the dispossessed native population, a problem often signalled in Spenser's poetry. This might suggest that the image of the Red-Cross Knight on his charger was rather closer to the norm for English travellers in Ireland in this period than has often been realized.[89] He would have had to travel around the area when he was acting for the government, in particular to Limerick and Cork for the sessions of the Munster Council, and the main roads must have been usable because records show that trade, as well as military operations, took place at regular intervals and without obvious difficulty.

The most important commodity not produced locally was wine, imported from Bordeaux and northern Spain, but salt and iron were also significant staple imports. The major exports were hides, linen, and wool, and undertakers were also given licence to export corn to England and Wales, and many hoped that they could grow lucrative crops such as woad and madder, used in dying.[90] Woad was a cash crop that could be grown in Ireland free from duty and restrictions, a fact that generated considerable interest in the mid-1580s, not least from Sir Henry Wallop.[91] A Belgian bronze mortar discovered in the Cork area, probably acquired to be melted down and recast, further indicates a trade in metal for remanufacture with Europe.[92] Traders from the ports would travel into the interior selling wine carried in barrels on horses' backs, collecting hides and cloth for export.[93] Although isolated, Spenser would not have been cut off at Kilcolman and, in addition to his professional duties, he probably made a few extended visits to see other planters such as Ralegh, perhaps Beacon or Warham St Leger. But his closest relationships must surely have been with his nearest neighbours, Cuffe and Norris, as it was unlikely that he spent much time travelling for pleasure. Spenser's extensive knowledge of the immediate area would also have been acquired from the large number of maps that were available.

Map-making had improved dramatically in the late sixteenth century, facilitated in part through the establishment of the Plantation and the consequent need to survey and record the lie of the land and the waterways, to which information Spenser would have had ready access through the Munster Council.[94]

Many of Spenser's other English neighbours were significantly interconnected, as were most of the undertakers in one way or another.[95] To the north-east of Kilcolman, one of a ring of seigniories around Limerick, was Ballygibbon held by Richard and Alexander Fitton, totalling 3,026 acres; their brother, Sir Edward Fitton, held Knockainy (11,515 acres), immediately to the north. Sir Edward (1548/9–1606) was another figure who corresponded with Burghley about Irish affairs, many of his letters surviving in the State Papers. He was instrumental in promoting the Munster Plantation, bringing his two brothers over, one of whom, Alexander, was still in Ireland in 1598 acting as his brother's agent after Sir Edward had returned to Cheshire in debt and disillusioned with the project.[96] Sir Edward worked closely with the Kerry undertaker Sir Valentine Browne (d. 1589) in the 1580s, whose seigniory at Molahiffe, near Killarney, contained 6,560 acres, to uncover concealed lands for the crown and to help establish the legal basis for the Plantation. Browne, who was the effective leader of the Kerry settlers, was a 'reluctant mortgagee' and had to fight a difficult losing battle with the earl of Clanmore, MacCarthy-Mor, when it was revealed that the estate he occupied was made up of lands which had been seized by the earl of Desmond from the MacCarthys, who therefore had a prior claim. This was a common problem on the Plantation as lands that were often assumed to belong to the earl, especially in the 1584 survey, were often either seized by him from other Irish landowners or were 'chargable', i.e., the freeholders had been forced to pay him charges such as 'coyne and livery' [billeting soldiers free of charge], which affected their status and value.[97] The loyal earl, understandably enough, wanted them returned and the crown agreed that he had a better claim than Browne did, although a compromise was eventually reached.[98] East along the Blackwater were Arthur Hyde at the Carrignedy estate (11,766 acres) and Thomas Fleetwood and Marmaduke Redmayne at Cloghley (12,667 acres). Interestingly enough, Fleetwood and Hyde, as well as Sir Edward Fitton, were accused of Catholicism, probably because of family connections, although none of the charges could be substantiated. There was, nevertheless, a constant fear that some of those imported to prevent rebellion may actually have been secretly in sympathy with the native population, undoubtedly another influence on the creeping paranoia that characterizes Spenser's later writings, and may well have been a significant issue within his household.[99] Spenser's other acquaintance, Sir Warham St Leger, held the Carigaline estate (6,000 acres) in south Cork on the River Lee, west of that of Ralegh.[100]

Spenser must also have known in some capacity Sir George Carew. He was a cousin of the pioneering colonist Sir Peter Carew (1514?–75), a client of the

Cecils, and one of the chief military figures in Ireland, being especially active in Munster, where he inherited his cousin's contested claims to land made through the research of John Hooker, author of the Irish section in Holinshed's *Chronicles*, which Spenser knew well.[101] Carew's brother, also called Peter, had been killed at Glenmalure, an event Spenser witnessed, and, partly as a result, George was known for his bitter hatred towards the Irish, playing a key role in the defeat of Hugh O'Neill, after he became president of Munster in 1600, as his surviving papers demonstrate.[102] Carew translated part of Don Alonso de Ercilla's Spanish military epic describing the brutal conquest of Chile, *The Historie of Aravcana*, at some point during his time in Ireland, rendering sections of the first sixteen of the thirty-seven cantos in English prose. Carew's translation remained in manuscript, so would not necessarily have been seen by Spenser even if it was composed before his death (it was probably written when Carew was president of Munster), as Carew was unlikely to have socialized with a relatively lowly official, albeit an emerging major poet. But the work suggests another shared intellectual concern between Spenser and other English officials living in Ireland, perhaps part of a wider culture of martial literature used as a way of thinking about conflict and conquest.[103]

Spenser would have spent most of his time when in Munster either on official/state/council business, or on his estate. Probably, as he became more established and affluent, he spent less time involved in official duties but paid others to carry out tasks assigned to him, as others had once used him, and as he had done before. Given his extraordinary rate of productivity in his final years, Spenser must have spent a great deal of his time writing and preparing works for publication.[104] Also, bearing in mind that he made two extended visits to England, Spenser undoubtedly employed a bailiff to run his estate, making sure that he could concentrate on his other duties when he had them, and could carry on with his writing.[105]

Spenser was involved in yet another dispute over landownership with Robert Synan, around the claim to part of the Castlepook estate, the territory to the east of Kilcolman, which carried on upwards into the Ballyhoura Mountains. Castlepook was the ancestral home of the Synans, who owed allegiance and rent to the Roches, and was well known for its substantial cave, home to the benign giant, Phooka, who secretly ground corn for farmers at night.[106] The estates were separated by the Castlepook and Bregog rivers, which merged just over a mile east of Kilcolman Castle, the latter referred to in *Colin Clout* and 'Two Cantos of Mutabilitie'.[107] Spenser's claim was entered on 17 November 1596 through William Hiernane, husbandman, and it is likely that he was the man Spenser trusted to run his estate, so he was probably one of the farmers mentioned in the hierarchy of tenants in each seigniory.[108] Spenser would have left the everyday running of the estate to Hiernane, giving himself time to manage his own affairs.

How much contact Spenser would have had with Irish speakers, or whether he spoke or read much Irish, is controversial and difficult to determine. Assuming that he did employ someone to run his estate, there was no need for Spenser to have to deal with the many Irish speakers who made up the majority of the population. The Synans spoke Irish, as did the Roches, but they also would have spoken English, and, given the lawsuits that took place, it is unlikely that Spenser had that much direct contact with them. Very few English people appear to have mastered Irish, rare exceptions being Thomas Lee, but he spoke only what he called 'broken Irishe', and, interestingly enough, Roger Boyle, son of the earl of Cork, who had 'Irish sufficient to be his father's interpreter'.[109] Most, even experienced senior officials who had spent much time in the country, relied on interpreters, unless they married Irish women. The Irish vocabulary that Spenser uses in *A View* is relatively small and does not demonstrate that he had any real fluency in speaking the language. Furthermore, he often seems to cite words as he heard them rather than understanding their spelling.[110] Irenius uses only twenty-nine loanwords of Irish, and many of his derivations are wrong, relying on earlier English misunderstandings. John Draper's conclusion that Spenser had no more than 'a slight conversational [grasp of Irish] and some legal vocabulary', would seem to be accurate, as regards Spenser's spoken knowledge.[111] It was clearly possible to function effectively in the civil service, the army, or on a plantation, without an extensive knowledge of spoken Irish, especially if one lived as part of an English family. After all, settlers were not merely discouraged from mixing with the Irish: it was against the law.[112]

On the other hand, a case can be made that intellectuals like Spenser would have disguised the amount of Irish they knew for fear of exposing themselves to suspicion, and in order not to undermine the case that Ireland needed immediate help from England in order to transform a land hostile to English manners, customs, civility, and order. A certain amount of Irish was necessary for everyday purposes and, as Richard Stanihurst noted, inhabitants of towns 'speak English and Irish also because of their daily commerce with their Irish neighbours'.[113] In *A View* Irenius refers to the Irish bards on two occasions: first, to censure the type of false history that they have produced; and, second, to explain the nature of the poetry, which he finds skilful and admirable in form, but pernicious and subversive in content. Irenius, who must at this point be speaking as Spenser, although the fictional identity provides yet another layer of protection, explains that he has 'Cawsed diuerse of them to be translated vnto me that I might vnderstande them'.[114] The use of the passive ensures that the exact nature and circumstances of the translation cannot be recovered, a characteristic device enabling English speakers to distance themselves from Irish.[115] Spenser's work suggests that he had an extensive knowledge of Irish literature and history, however this was acquired.[116] For Richard McCabe, Spenser must have had a good reading knowledge of extremely difficult Irish in order to understand the Irish poetry that interested him, and *A View* acknowledges that he knew far more than he was admitting (although this does not prove that he could have spoken demotic Gaelic).[117] Arguments have been advanced that Spenser would have been taught by Irish Lord Roche's bard, Teig Olyve, or the earl of Ormond's brehon (Irish) lawyer, MacClancy, but there is no surviving evidence and such cooperation is somewhat implausible.[118] Yet the truth must be that either Spenser developed an advanced reading knowledge of Irish, or that he worked with Irish speakers who helped him read the works that he describes and those that he evidently used elsewhere. These would have included the *Leabhar Gabhála* (*The Book of Invasions*), a collection of Middle Irish poems and prose that chronicles the history of Ireland from the creation of the world to the Middle Ages, a work that owed much to Eusebius' *Chronicon*, the standard history of the world up to AD 325.[119]

The English translator of Eusebius' other major work, *The Ancient Ecclesiastical Histories* (1577), Meredith Hanmer (1543–1604), had moved to Ireland to take up a number of ecclesiastical livings in or before 1591.[120] Hanmer's patrons were the earl of Ormond and the Norris brothers, whom he served as chaplain in the early 1590s. Hanmer must have known Spenser through the latter connection—if not other ways, as he later became warden of St Mary's church, Youghal—and he provides a link between Spenser and Ormond, one of the recipients of a dedicatory sonnet in the first edition of *The Faerie Queene*.[121] Hanmer was a tenacious antiquarian, and he wrote to Burghley in 1594 to tell him that he was collecting as many of the country's surviving documents as he could find. His collection of historical notes and documents, accumulated between 1601 and 1603, is preserved in the State Papers and shows signs that he was attempting to understand Irish as well as preserving records. One undated passage contains a description of the story of Murrogh O'Brien's foster mother drinking his blood, surely taken from a manuscript of Spenser's *View*, a further sign of the links between the two men.[122] The fruits of his research were later published posthumously as *A Chronicle of Ireland* in James Ware's *Ancient Irish Histories* (1633), the volume that also contained the first edition of *A View*.[123] Hanmer's work suggests that there were Englishmen on the Plantation who were interested in Irish history and culture, however hostile they may have been to other aspects of Irish life (Hanmer had become well known as the chief crown opponent of Edmund Campion, so he is unlikely to have been ignorant of the course of the Desmond Rebellion, or especially sympathetic to the Irish Catholic cause). Perhaps Spenser acquired what knowledge he had of Irish from the same source as Hanmer, or even from Hanmer himself. Certainly they both had similar scholarly interests, as well as significant patrons in common.[124]

English representations of Ireland, including Spenser's own in *A View*, characterize Irish society as pastoral in character, the Irish living a nomadic life, following cattle herds around the country, a practice known as 'bolleying'.[125] In England, arable farming was regarded as inherently superior to pasture farming, which was one reason for the widely held perception that the Irish, as they were savages, could not practise sustained and settled agricultural practices.[126] But, while this may well have been the view of Irish society held by most people in England, settlers in Ireland would have known that this representation did not accurately describe the more sophisticated and complex reality of Irish agricultural and social practices. Spenser's description is a deliberate piece of propaganda, designed to reinforce English prejudices, and to persuade the queen and Privy Council to support the New English, who are represented as the only means of bringing Ireland into the modern world. Irenius' account of Irish customs opens with his description of their primitive economy, which he sees as a distinctly Scythian practice, inherited from the ancient ancestors of the Irish, via the Scots:

I will then beginne to Counte theire Customes... and firste with the Scithian or Scottishe manners Of the which theare is one vse amongst them to kepe theire Cattell and to live themselves the moste parte of the yeare in *Bollyes* pasturinge vppon the mountaine and waste wilde places and removinge still to freshe lande as they haue depastured the former The which appearethe plaine to be the manner of the Scythians... and yeat is vsed amongst all the Tartarians and the people aboute the *Caspian* sea which are naturallie Scithians to live in the Herdes As they Call them beinge the verye same that the Irishe *Bollyes* are drivinge theire Cattell Continuallye with them and feedinge onelye on theire milke and white meates/[127]

The passage is a carefully placed and nuanced representation with an obvious political purpose, designed to persuade statesmen with a wide knowledge of the modern and the ancient worlds and a clear series of reference points. The Irish are cast as an essentially primitive people, resembling those in the ancient world whom humanists would have read about in Strabo, Lucian, Herodotus, and others; they are also like the more savage peoples of the contemporary world, such as the Tartars, who would have been known from works such as Anthony Jenkinson's accounts of his voyages to Russia (1557–60), Giles Fletcher's more extended narrative of his experience as an ambassador there in 1588, and, perhaps most significantly, the recollections of Christopher Carleill, present at the gathering at Lodowick Bryskett's house.[128]

Accordingly, Spenser's dialogue would have looked to an engaged observer like a well-informed and serious piece of humanist scholarship. What is so pernicious about booleying for English observers is that it not only preserves the Irish as an ancient, primitive society, but enables them to rebel against the English who wish only to make them civil for their own good:

By this Custome of Bolloyinge theare growe in the meane time manye great enormityes vnto that Comon wealthe for firste if theare be any outlawes or loose people (as they are never without some) which live vppon stealthes and spoile, they are evermore succored and finde reliefe onelye in those Bollies beinge vppon the waste places, whereas els they shoulde be driven shortelye to sterve or to Come downe to the townes to steale reliefe wheare by one meanes or other they I they woulde sone be Caughte.[129]

Accordingly, it becomes clear that the description of Irish pastoralism has a key place within Spenser's argument, revealing the origins of the Irish and explaining why their way of life cannot be tolerated by civilized authorities. It is also worth noting, yet again, how central the concept of 'waste' was to an understanding of Irish land. In a striking parallel to Spenser's dispute with Lord Maurice Roche, Irenius here argues that Irish practice leaves land waste, in obvious distinction to the English desire to plant and improve the soil. The next topic that Irenius and Eudoxus discuss is the Irish mantle, also derived from the Scythians, and a means of enabling them to live in a primitive manner and to subvert settled English agricultural society.[130] Spenser, in accordance with the sound humanist principles he learned from Mulcaster and Harvey, is showing how book learning can be used to sort out serious problems if applied correctly to the matter in hand.

However, Spenser must have known that what he described in *A View* was a serious distortion of the truth.[131] If the Irish in Munster were following herds of cattle in the 1590s, it was in part because their agriculture had been so comprehensively destroyed in the late 1570s and early 1580s. Traditionally pastoralism had been a major component of the Irish economy, but, despite the frustrating lack of evidence, 'there is no doubt that tillage was practised on an extensive scale'.[132] The most common practice was a 'long fallow' system whereby part of the land was planted with crops using a team of horses rather than oxen as in England, which required the use of eight horses and meant that tenants had to cooperate and lend each other their horses in order to till the land. The rest of the land was used for pasture, the fields being rotated every few years, making sure that land was left as pasture for longer than it was tilled, a sensible process in areas with a low population. In places there was a three-course rotation system of winter-corn, spring-corn, and fallow, practised throughout the Pale in the sixteenth century, which had spread to other areas, perhaps including Munster.[133] The Irish economy was, unsurprisingly enough, less organized and developed than its English counterpart— there had not been any enclosure of land yet, implements for husbandry were less developed, and there were few if any of the early experiments in cross-breeding and other means of increasing yields—but it was far more sophisticated than English observers, eager to press their own claims to the land and to trumpet their abilities and achievements, suggested. Indeed, after about 1560, English farming was becoming more efficient and produced more crops and higher yields from the land specifically 'as a result of the reclamation of waste and the conversion of pasture', a process that explains why so many English observers reacted to the Irish countryside as they did.[134] The point is that Irish agriculture was not of a different order to that practised in England, whatever the settlers might have claimed at times.[135] Robert Payne's description of what could be grown in Munster makes this clear, as he tried to lure over his fellow Nottinghamshire farmers with a picture of abundance and a soft life:

Their soyle for the most part is very fertile, and apt for Wheate, Rye, Barly, Peason [Peas], Beanes, Oates, Woade, Mather [used to make red dye], Rape, Hoppes, Hempe, Flaxe, and all other graines and fruites that England any wise doth yeelde... There be great store of wild Swannnes, Cranes, Pheasantes, Partriges, Heathcocks, Plouers, greene and gray, Curlewes, Woodcockes, Rayles, Quailes, & all other fowles much more plentifull then in England.[136]

Payne adds that there is easy access to lead, iron, and timber from the Irish woods, which makes it easy to establish industry, and that everything is much cheaper in Ireland.[137] Supplies of wood were coming under pressure and it was widely agreed in England that Ireland could be exploited for timber to establish industrial production: which in turn, led to worries later that Irish woods were being destroyed.[138] The undertakers and settlers exploited Irish natural resources rather than face the 'difficult capital development of an agricultural economy', in pointed contrast to their counterparts in England.[139]

One of the principal transformations that Ireland experienced in the late sixteenth and early seventeenth centuries was the loss of its woodlands, which covered about an eighth of the island in 1600 and only a fiftieth in 1800.[140] Irish wood was used for coopering, shipbuilding, glassmaking, housebuilding, and ironmaking.[141] The first blast furnace in Ireland was probably established in Mogeely, County Cork, in 1593 by Spenser's employer and neighbour, Sir Thomas Norris, although a forge had been established at Enniscorthy in 1560, another area where Spenser had bought property.[142] It may have been a cooperative venture planned by Norris and Sir Walter Ralegh, using the tenants he brought over who lived on the small village on his land near the castle there, an attempt to establish a nucleated English settlement in Ireland.[143]

Spenser would have run an estate that combined Irish and English agricultural practices, especially as his property was divided up into a series of well-established and agreed townlands—Kilcolman East, Middle, and West, still visible on the Ordnance Survey map today—which determined how the land was used before and after his brief tenure. If the land had not been tilled for some years, probably because of the disruption caused by the wars and dispossession of the Geraldines, then it would be left fallow for long periods, altering the ideal balance between agricultural and pastoral fields, as happened in similar areas in England, or where the soil was poor in the northern counties.[144] The farm would have practised the three-crop rotation system, probably planting spring and winter barley, and oats. Oats were grown in England, especially in mountainous regions, and were vital for brewing beer—traditionally a woman's job—as well as making porridge and bread, but they were a more significant staple crop in Ireland before the introduction of the potato.[145] Oats, highly valued as a cereal crop to feed humans and animals in early modern Britain, were used to make flat cakes baked on a griddle, as well as porridge, which formed the diet of the Irish peasants, supplemented by milk and butter, and, when possible, beef or pork.[146] A number of grains were found at Kilcolman—wheat, barley, oats, and rye—probably used for brewing as well as making bread and porridge.[147] There was a working mill established by the time Sylvanus took over the estate, which he leased out to another undertaker: it had probably been functioning earlier.[148] On the pasture, cows, sheep, and goats would have grazed, guarded from the wolves which roamed in the forests up on the Ballyhoura Mountains, as Spenser frequently notes in his poetry.[149] In fact, according to Colin Breen, 'with the arrival of the English planters in the latter half of the sixteenth century, pastoral activity greatly increased across Munster', again exposing the false dichotomy of English agriculture against Irish pasturage. Sheep rearing, a more important part of economic life in Munster than the rest of Ireland, increased further in significance after the arrival of the English, where sheep were the main source of income for pastoral farms.[150]

Sheep were undoubtedly the most common animal on Spenser's estate.[151] The excavations at Kilcolman indicate that the sheep were of a variety of breeds, suggesting that both Irish and English breeds were bred.[152] Most specimens were about three years old, which would confirm that they were reared for wool production.[153] Irish breeds of sheep were not usually the heavy-wool-producing sheep found on English lowlands, evolved from longwool medieval breeds, but hair sheep, which resembled domestic sheep before woolly breeds were developed, and are now extinct. These sheep did not have wool, and were bred for their hides and their meat. They were also far more resistant to parasites and bad weather, and their hides could be used to make Irish mantles.[154] The wool and hides not used would have been exported via Cork city to England, France, Spain, and the Low Countries.[155] Sheep were especially important in the economy of southern Ireland and it is worth remembering that the Spencers of Wormleighton and Althorp, to whom Spenser later claimed to be related, had amassed an enormous fortune through sheep farming in Northamptonshire.[156] A further indication of the central importance that sheep had in the early modern English economy was that, as well as producing wool and meat, their milk would have been used to make cheese.[157] The farm would also have devoted some land to growing wheat, now the standard food crop of the Pale, and beans. The tenant farmers would have had their own plots and would have grown vegetables for their own consumption, as would the Spenser household. The estate, as Payne's description of economic life in Munster suggests, would also have taken part in the timber trade, cutting down trees to supply ironworks such as Mogeely, as well as supplying English demand for ship timber, charcoal, and barrel-staves, sending the hardwood harvested down the Blackwater and on to the port of Youghal.[158]

Spenser, like other undertakers, was evidently keen to improve his estate and to make parts of his house and gardens resemble those in rural England, transforming a military structure into a comfortable residence, converting some of its defensive features in the process by opening up walls to create large windows, establishing new rooms, and adding a series of attractive and colourful features.[159] The archaeological evidence suggests that he developed the Irish tower house along the lines of an English manor house, making it much less of a fortified castle than it had been in the late Middle Ages, as did most settlers who occupied existing castles.[160] The aim would have been to make the house more feasible as a substantial family residence and to provide the inhabitants with greater privacy, in line with architectural developments in England at the time.[161] Chimneys were inserted so that smoke now exited via a flue and not through holes in the centre of rooms, creating a feature that invited decoration. Indeed, 'chimneys were associated with improved living conditions... [and so] were celebrated as a status symbol'.[162] The walls were reduced in thickness so that more windows could be added, and more attention was paid to what the house was like to live in, in particular, its interior design, invariably the woman's domain.[163] Ceilings were raised to allow more ventilation. As interiors became more open to light so did the need for brighter and more detailed decoration become more obvious.[164] Kilcolman would probably have had mouldings on the wall, panels, tiling, and elaborate fireplaces with mantel-pieces above them.[165] Spenser may have shared Harvey's interest in iconographic design and installed an object like the fireplace celebrating Harvey's father's rope-making trade: perhaps, like many of his contemporaries, he wished to adorn his house with religious imagery, such as devotional wall hangings and alabasters, or images of St George.[166] There could have been biblical or classical inscriptions on and above the beams, especially if Spenser did feel that it was his duty to act as the overseer of a godly, isolated household.[167] Wallpaper was becoming more widely available in the period and it is possible that the walls of the house of a new member of the landed gentry were covered with this cheaper material instead of the more costly stone, velvet, or wall hangings.[168]

As in English house development in the sixteenth century, Kilcolman had rooms built over the Great Hall—in this case a stair tower with a garderobe (toilet) and another garderobe turret—floors were added and walls plastered.[169] Spenser would have had to use the hall for administrative and ceremonial functions necessary for a member of the local gentry.[170] There is evidence of a parlour added which was largely destroyed in a fire in 1598, undoubtedly the one that preceded the family's return to England.[171] The room was then repaired by Sylvanus when he took over occupancy of Kilcolman, at some point before the survey of 1622 (which also states that 'there was a fair stone house built by Edmund Spenser', providing further evidence that the poet significantly improved the castle).[172] In the same period, Sylvanus or Edmund had a cellar built, and wooden structures alongside the tower house, where servants would probably have lived.[173] There would have been a number of outbuildings essential for running a reasonably substantial estate, archaeological remains of which survive. These would have included 'stable, barn, forge, cart shed, well house, storage rooms, kitchen, servants' lodging, etc.'.[174] Such buildings were probably hastily constructed, as other archaeological evidence suggests that their plastered stone walls were often held together by clay rather than mortar, presumably because there was a lack of skilled masons in Ireland and buildings had to be erected quickly.[175] The more substantial buildings would have had wooden roofs, while the barns and sheds would have been thatched.[176]

Remains on the site suggest that the Spenser family led a relatively privileged existence, with a decent diet and time for leisure. It is unlikely that Machabyas had to cook and act as a housewife, although, like many women of her status, she would have known how to prepare food and would have overseen the household accounts.[177] Animal bones recovered from the site indicate that mutton and goat were the principal forms of meat consumed, pork being a rarity, suggesting that relatively few pigs were kept on the farm, as was normal in Ireland.[178] Rabbits, perhaps kept in cages, ducks, and geese were also reared. There was evidence that deer were consumed, indicating that hunting in the forests was a popular sport, as in England.[179] There are shards of north Devon gravel-tempered ware, found elsewhere on the Plantation, further evidence that there was a healthy trade between England and Munster. More significantly there was also a tuning peg for a lute, which we might well expect to find, given Spenser's interest in music in his poetry, and the verse attributed to him by Sir James Ware on the earl of Cork's lute, a sign that Spenser was associated with music, even if that poem is spurious.[180] Music was undoubtedly one of the leisure activities supported at Kilcolman. It is also likely that the Spensers spent some money on furniture, ornaments, and pewter, again, like other families in England and elsewhere on the Plantation, as the economy of the British Isles developed to enable families to acquire more goods and consumables.[181] William Herbert, one of the most vocal and innovative of the undertakers, who occupied the large Castleisaland estate (13,276 acres) about thirty miles west of Kilcolman in Kerry, brought over a wealth of items and materials from England: tapestries, linen, bedding, pewter, brass, plate, jewels, and cloth, a variety of items of furniture (bedsteads, table-boards, chests, stools, leather chairs, and a close stool), as well as iron, armour, and weapons (cannon and hand guns).[182]

Also among the animal bone assemblage unearthed at Kilcolman were the remains of shellfish, as well as chicken, goose, and rabbit.[183] Overall the waste reveals a varied and interesting diet, with considerable consumption of high status foods, indicating that the Spensers lived rather better than their counterparts in Cork city.[184] Fishing was an important industry in Munster and fish would have been an important part of the Spenser family's diet, especially as there is extensive evidence from the Plantation of fish being smoked and then stored in barrels for trade, and extensive fishing from the abundant supply in the local rivers. Fish were also kept in ponds and there may have been one at Kilcolman, although there is no surviving evidence.[185] The surviving inventory for Herbert's estate shows that his larder contained cheese, bacon, beer, bread, and spices, as well as soap and starch.[186]

There is also evidence that Spenser had a walled garden built north of the tower house, the east part of which was probably used as a kitchen garden to grow vegetables and herbs. If the Spensers had followed the advice given to English families then Machabyas would have been in charge of the gardens.[187] The west could have contained a pleasure garden, perhaps a knot garden with emblematic patterns of flowers and shrubs, as was the fashion for Elizabethan estates.[188] Planting gardens in Ireland, especially ones inspired by classical literature or Italian culture and styles, was seen as a key method of establishing civility and cultural superiority, as well as to provide an aspirational model for pliant natives to adopt.[189] William Herbert established a garden, hopyard, orchard, and carefully designed pathways for walking around his manor house, as well as a mill, brewery, kiln, and stables; Thomas Norris had two gardens and an orchard.[190] Spenser may not have been as ambitious or as affluent as Herbert, but the evidence that does survive indicates that he planned similar developments on his estate. Like Shakespeare, whose work shows how much he knew about horticulture and agriculture, Spenser's poetry indicates a profound interest in gardens and gardening.[191] A careful student of Virgil's poetic reflections on and instructions about rural activities, represented in his *Georgics*, Spenser's own literary output suggests that he thought carefully about the ways in which poetry can be used to think about such matters and, to a lesser extent, in the management of estates.[192]

Many questions remain in constructing the nature of everyday life on the estate. In particular, what was the relationship between Spenser, his wives, and their children? Life on the Munster Plantation may have forced women, who in other ways were conscious of their rising social status, to breastfeed their own children rather than to use servants, unless they brought over their own or recruited from English women living in Ireland. Families were much closer knit units than they would have been had they remained in England, because of their relative isolation.[193] Certainly there would have been little opportunity for the sort of male friendship that Spenser and Harvey had cultivated, and Spenser, having already thought about the institution of marriage and what it meant for two people to live together, would have been conscious of the need to ensure that the couple enjoyed spending time together. It is also likely that some of Elizabeth's relatives, who we know came over to Ireland, lived at Kilcolman, perhaps younger sons and daughters, like Peregrine

Spenser, who worked for Richard Boyle after his mother intervened to secure him gainful employment.[194] Children were often sent away from home in early adolescence to school or to work as part of their upbringing to ensure a successful transition from childhood to adulthood.[195]

Did the Spensers employ a tutor? Education and the provision of schools was an important topic in this period, in part through a desire to educate and so anglicize the Irish, in part through the need to provide for English settlers in Ireland.[196] If not, then they must have taught their children themselves, which would have been the case for many families on the Plantation. It is possible that they made use of an impoverished Anglican cleric in the area, co-opting one into their household as a 'life-cycle servant', which was common practice in England.[197] However, such figures were notoriously absent in Ireland, which had trouble attracting English clerics to poor benefices.[198] There is no record of a school being established in the Doneraile area.

The same issues apply to the question of daily worship. Would the Spensers and their children have attended a local church? If so, would they have travelled into Doneraile (about five miles) or Buttevant (about six miles), both situated on the Awbeg, which would have provided a natural link to either town? It is more likely that they had a chapel somewhere in the house, like many much grander houses in the area, such as Blarney Castle. If so, it would have been on the upper floor, the typical location, but no evidence has survived. There is a ruined church on the north side of Kilcolman bog, but whether it survived the Reformation, or was repaired and used, is not known. It is most likely that Spenser conducted everyday worship held in the house, using the 1559 Book of Common Prayer, as evidence in surviving contemporary copies indicates was the case when there was no church nearby or service available.[199] He would have led the family and servants in daily prayers and perhaps also took Sunday services, on the occasions when the Spensers did not travel into Buttevant or Mallow.[200] There were relatively powerful churches in both towns, Spenser having obvious connections to each. He worked for Thomas Norris, who lived in Mallow Castle, and he acquired the ruined abbey in Buttevant, probably in 1597.[201] Religious devotion was undoubtedly more varied and improvised than it was in England. Furthermore, although it is improbable that Spenser did not use the Book of Common Prayer, exactly what type of religion dominated the household is hard to determine. Spenser's own background and the evidence of his writings suggest an eclectic faith and, perhaps, change over time. Richard Boyle was a noted Protestant, 'theologically left of centre', so perhaps Elizabeth was too.[202] However, Sylvanus and Peregrine both became Catholic at some point in their lives, if the suspicions of the authorities are accurate, perhaps through expediency, while Katherine married a friend of the earl's, and went to live in Bandon, a noted

Protestant, planter town.[203] Perhaps the compromise of the Prayer Book held the family and household together.[204]

The description of the landscape in *Colin Clout* indicates that Spenser was familiar with the route to Buttevant, travelling there by means of the Awbeg:

> Old father *Mole,* (*Mole* hight that mountain gray
> That walls the Northside of *Armulla* dale)
> He had a daughter fresh as floure of May,
> Which gaue that name vnto that pleasant vale;
> *Mulla* the daughter of old *Mole,* so hight
> The Nimph, which of that water course has charge,
> That springing out of *Mole,* doth run downe right
> to *Butteuant* where spreding forth at large,
> It giueth name vnto that auncient Cittie,
> Which *Kilnemullah* cleped is of old:
> Whose ragged ruines breed great ruth and pittie,
> To trauailers, which it from far behold.
> Full faine she lou'd, and was belou'd full faine,
> Of her owne brother riuer, *Bregog* hight,
> So hight because of this deceitfull traine,
> Which he with *Mulla* wrought to win delight. (lines 104–19)

Mole is the name Spenser gives to the Ballyhoura Hills that overlook his estate from the north, and Mulla is the Awbeg, named here from the ancient name for Buttevant, Kilnemullah.[205] Here Spenser uses his knowledge of local topography to produce an aetiological fable which explains the creation of the rivers, the Mulla and Bregog, that mark the boundaries of his own lands, and that connect him to the key settlements in the area: in other words, the natural features that determine his life.[206] The Mulla wants to marry Bregog, but her father prefers Arlo, a tributary of the Blackwater.[207] To circumvent his wishes, the crafty Bregog flows underground and meets Mulla. In his fury Mole creates a landslide and blocks the course of the Bregog, so that the two rivers become one, 'so deare his loue he bought' (line 155). The Bregog is, as Spenser's myth represents it, 'for over a mile of its course dry for half the year' (Plate 25).[208] The myth used here, which shows that Spenser was engaged with local Irish folklore, whether he could read such legends in Irish or was simply repeating tales he heard, looks forward to the evocative, symbolic representation of his environment in 'Two Cantos of Mutabilitie'. Furthermore, in celebrating the Irish rivers on his land in this manner, Spenser is engaging in 'an act of substitution in which he play[s] the part of a rival Irish bard', replacing the natives he criticized so forcefully in *A View of the Present State of Ireland*.[209] In representing his close connection to his land—albeit with a certain amount of ambivalence—he is stating his right to be considered a local, a poet who can speak for the Ireland where he lives.[210]

What is also apparent here is the poet's lament for the destruction of Buttevant, a once impressive city now laid low. As ever in Spenser, the description is ambiguous. We do not know whether the poet is simply regretting the fact that time marches on, whether he is pinning the blame on foolish men for causing unnecessary destruction and, if so, whether the blame lies with the English or the Irish. Spenser's brief lament for Buttevant is expanded at the end of *The Faerie Queene* in the account of the ravages wrought by the Blatant Beast, when he despoils the monasteries:

> Into their cloysters now he broken had,
> Through which the Monckes he chaced here & there,
> And them pursu'd into their dortours sad,
> And searched all their cels and secrets neare;
> In which what filth and ordure did appeare,
> Were yrkesome to report; yet that foule Beast
> Nought sparing them, the more did tosse and teare,
> And ransacke all their dennes from most to least,
> Regarding nought religion, nor their holy heast.
>
> From thence into the sacred Church he broke,
> And robd the Chancell, and the deskes downe threw,
> And Altars fouled, and blasphemy spoke,
> And th'Images for all their goodly hew,
> Did cast to ground, whilest none was them to rew;
> So all confounded and disordered there. (*FQ* VI.xii.23 and 24, lines 1–6)

The British Isles were littered with the ruins of religious foundations in the late sixteenth century.[211] Even so, this is an astonishing image, especially for readers who want to see Spenser as a straightforward Protestant with low church leanings. Equally so, it complicates the arguments of those who want to see accounts of 'bare ruin'd quires' as evidence of a coded sympathy for Catholicism.[212] Many 'church papists' were nostalgic for the unified church of the late Middle Ages.[213] Ben Jonson was presumably referring to these stanzas when he remarked to William Drummond that 'by the blating beast the puritans were understood'.[214] Jonson's judgement is acute, indicating that he thought that Spenser, like so many others, deeply regretted the division of Christendom and the destruction it wrought, and, like Rome and Verulam (St Albans) in his own *Complaints*, looked back nostalgically to a more unified, happier past.[215]

Here, we are told, the Beast despoils the monasteries, ejecting the monks, before entering their cells where the narrator, using the rhetorical device of *occupatio*, describes what he claims he wishes to keep hidden: 'In which what filth and ordure did appeare, | Were yrksome to report.' What should be a sacred place for thought and study has become the hidden area where the bowels are evacuated, a suppressed pun on 'closet', an enclosed room that could also be a privy.[216] This confusion has predictably dire consequences for the church, although whether it is the Beast who defiles the monasteries, or the monks themselves, is left to the reader to decide.[217] The Beast then attacks the church and its furniture, rather as Kirkrapine did in the opening book of *The Faerie Queene* before he was dispatched by Una's lion.[218] While the allegory there looked like a traditional attack on the greedy abuse of the church—although it could easily be read to indicate a 'sympathy for traditional religion'—here it is rather more problematic.[219] The Beast robs the chancel, traditionally the most sacred part of the church which contains the altar, often behind a rood screen, separating the clergy and the church's valuable goods—plate, chalice, etc.—from the laity in the nave. Spenser's representation of this part as the 'sacred church' carefully conforms to the standard division of space in the late medieval church, distinguishing it from the post-Reformation Protestant church.[220] The Beast then fouls the altar himself, indicating that either he was guilty of the first offences in the monasteries, or that he has learned his appalling behaviour from the monks, before uttering blasphemy and destroying the images, which are described in notably positive terms. The use of the term 'altar' is significant, as more ardent reformers were replacing stone altars with wooden communion tables, and, as Brian Cummings has pointed out, 'an altar that was not stone was not an altar'.[221] Spenser's narrator speaks in a manner diametrically opposed to the concerns of reformers, certainly in its radical Edwardian form, and his words read like a strong defence of traditional religion.[222] We witness the growth of disorder and chaos, which engulfs and overturns order and hierarchy, a fear that shadowed Spenser's life and writing. Here, traditional pre-Reformation religion is the locus of stability, security, and culture.

Of course, this cannot quite be the case, although Spenser was associated with writers like the antiquarian John Stow who clearly did have Catholic sympathies and who was outraged at what they saw as the wanton destruction of the beliefs, values, and institutions of traditional English religion.[223] Sir Henry Sidney, to take another example, had books dedicated to him by prominent recusants Edmund Campion and Richard Stanihurst.[224] Nevertheless, it is the Beast's indiscriminate attack on all forms of religion which is the target of these lines, even if the religious institutions described are clearly late medieval. It was as a consequence of the Reformation that Spenser was able to achieve the rank of gentleman through the acquisition of property, which enabled him to write what he did. As Sir Thomas Smith noted in 1572, 'England was neuer that can be heard of, fuller of people than it is at this day, and the dissolution of Abbayes hath done two things of importance heerin: It hath doubled the number of gentlemen and mariages, whereby commeth daily more increase of people: and suche yonger brothers as were wonte to be thruste into

Abbayes, there to liue (an idle life) sith that is taken from them, must nowe séeke some other place to liue in. By thys meanes there are many lacke abode, and fewe dwellings emptie.'[225] Most of the properties and land that he acquired were disestablished religious foundations of various types, although mainly Franciscan: friaries at New Ross, New Abbey, and Enniscorthy; the prebend at Effin; a series of ecclesiastical livings mainly to the south-west of Cork city, and Buttevant Abbey, also a Franciscan friary. The Irish church was largely in ruins at the end of the sixteenth century.[226] These are substantial concerns that would have been acquired by people much higher up the social scale in England. Therefore, it is hardly surprising that ecclesiastical ruins in Ireland featured so prominently in Spenser's imagination, not least the one which he was to own a few years later and which he must have seen frequently, perhaps even once a week.[227] The Irish landscape, even more so than in England, and especially Munster, was devastated in the 1580s and 1590s, peppered with shells of once grand buildings, a catastrophe which was very much to Spenser's advantage—at least, at first—although he was painfully aware of the price others paid for his gain. What he had managed to create and build in his lifetime might eventually be ruined, perhaps sooner rather than later. Travellers to Ireland now witness Kilcolman as a ruin, just like Buttevant Abbey.

It is inconceivable that Spenser did not have a substantial library on his estate, given his isolated situation, how he appears to have planned his life, and the learned references throughout his works published after he had acquired Kilcolman.[228] The second half of the sixteenth century was a period in which many intellectuals started to assemble libraries as they realized the potential of early printed books, which were now being produced in larger numbers than in the first half of the century. The loss of the monastic libraries after their disestablishment was keenly felt and various attempts were made to establish libraries that could be used by a wider public.[229] Many individuals assembled large libraries because institutional ones that existed, such as those at the Inns of Court, were often limited and inadequate for the needs of most readers.[230] Moreover, Spenser had been provided with the example of two significant book collectors in Harvey and Smith, working in the library of one which was inspired by that of the other.

As Raymond Gillespie has pointed out, access to large numbers of books was possible for individuals in southern Ireland, given the records of the numbers imported and testimony from early readers, even those who could not assemble a significant personal collection.[231] Presumably, either Spenser's books did not survive, which is likely given the evidence of fire at his estate in 1598, or he left no obvious sign of ownership in his books and they were dispersed at some point in the seventeenth century. Evidence of a number of private libraries does survive, and, living in the same area, Meredith Hanmer certainly found it possible to acquire a substantial collection of books, as well as manuscripts. But most surviving libraries were possessed by gentlemen of much greater means than Spenser, whose families were not dispersed in the way that Spenser's was in the seventeenth century.[232] Books varied in price and cost anything between ½d. for a ballad to 42s. for a copy of Foxe's *Actes and Monuments*. In the same period a pair of shoes cost 6d., a hen 2d., a pig just over 1s., and beef was about 2d. a pound.[233] Hanmer probably funded his book-buying habit by acquiring various ecclesiastical livings, and it is likely that Spenser was able to use some of his considerable income from various official positions—which he farmed out to others—to purchase books needed for his real work.[234] The inventory of the earl of Kildare's possessions made in 1526 shows that he had imported a miscellaneous collection of books into Ireland. The inventory is divided up into Latin, French, and English books, and shows that as well as obvious classics and religious literature, he possessed copies of More's *Utopia*, Henry VIII's *Assertio Septem Sacramentorum* ('The kyng of Englond his answer to Lutter'), Mandeville's *Travels*, *Le Roman de la Rose*, Petrarch's works, 'Lanncelot du lake 3 volumis', Lydgate's *Siege of Thebes*, Chaucer's *Troilus*, a book simply entitled 'Arthur', and, most intriguingly, 'The Shepherdis Calender', the French work that Spenser also knew, showing just how widely read this work was in the sixteenth century.[235]

Just as Spenser was able to acquire an estate in Ireland that would never have been available to him in England, so, one suspects, he was able to collect enough books to make a library (although he may have been able to borrow books from such literate friends and contemporaries as Bryskett, Hanmer, and Thomas Norris). While it is impossible to know how large the library would have been and exactly what it would have contained, it is possible to make a number of educated guesses.[236] Some gentlemen, such as William Crashaw (1572–1625/6), lawyer and father of the poet Richard, were able to amass huge personal collections, which rivalled those of the university libraries. Crashaw's library consisted of some 200 manuscripts—possibly more—and 4,000 books, demonstrating how many works could be acquired by determined bibliophiles, and it is possible that Hanmer had an equally large library.[237] Certainly many bishops had collections well above 400 volumes in the early seventeenth century, as did some scholars at the two English universities.[238]

In England Spenser would have had access to books, as we know that he exchanged copies with Harvey, probably others as well, and he was undoubtedly able to use some larger collections, such as those of Sir Thomas Smith or the Bedford family.[239] Major collections would have been used by more than the owner. Crashaw's collection, which he left to the Middle Temple where he had been their preacher when he moved back to Yorkshire, was 'the resource centre of a working scholar, preacher, publicist, polemicist, and divine', and so would have been available for others.[240] Spenser must have acquired a few volumes while working in Dublin; he might have been able to buy books imported into Cork, Youghal, Waterford, and Limerick, although records show that most of those imported were for schools (horn books, grammar books, fables); and he would have bought some on his two visits to London in 1590 and 1596.[241] If he had any models in mind they were probably those of Harvey in Cambridge or Saffron Walden and Smith's library at Hill Hall.[242]

If Spenser had a number of books, he would have organized them into categories, arranged on 'sloping shelves set round the room at an angle to the wall', as contemporary library inventories and illustrations demonstrate.[243] There would have been sections on theology; history; liberal arts and philosophy; medicine; law; cosmography and geography; and music.[244] There would have been more books on theology, history, and rhetoric than other categories, and most books would have been in Latin.[245] There would also have been a number of works in Italian and French, and possibly Spanish and German, especially as Spenser had been a student of teachers so keen to instil in their charges the value of reading contemporary literature in foreign languages.[246] Accompanying these would have been the relevant dictionaries and guides, and there would have been a large number of standard reference books.[247] Spenser probably possessed rather more books of English poetry than many of his contemporaries, but, even so, these would have been a relatively minor section of his library.[248] Books on what we now think of as science would have been included in the sections on liberal arts and philosophy and cosmography and geography. While most book owners in England purchased loose sheets and bound their own books, it is unlikely that this service was readily available in Ireland, although someone might have bound some of Spenser's books in England on his behalf.[249]

There were obvious works that most educated gentlemen would have possessed: Virgil, Homer, Aristotle, Plato, Lucan, numerous volumes of Cicero, Erasmus, Ovid, Pliny, Herodotus, Seneca, Hesoid, Xenophon, Tacitus, Suetonius, Ptolemy, Caesar's *De Bello Gallico*, with a collection of commentaries, along with the Bible and its own attendant commentaries, the 1559 Book of Common Prayer, and other familiar works from any private library.[250] All such works would have been imported from English publishers.[251] There would have been a large collection of books of theology, ecclesiology, and religious devotions, especially given Spenser's work as a bishop's secretary. Spenser would have possessed Calvin's *Institutes*, as well as a selection of works by church fathers such as Augustine, Jerome, and Tertullian; major European Reformation figures such as Melanchthon, Luther, Bucer, and Bèze; and English theologians and thinkers such as John Jewel and Hugh Latimer.[252] There would also have been legal works such as Bracton's definitive study of English law, *De Legibus*, and Justinian's *Institutes*, and a number of works on rhetoric, probably including Thomas Wilson's popular manual, *The Arte of Rhetoricke* (1553), as well as a number of works on rhetoric and logic by Ramus.[253] It is also hard to believe that Spenser did not have works on farming and animal husbandry, such as Thomas Blundeville's *The Foure Chiefest Offices Belonging to Horsemanship*, which was frequently reprinted in the late sixteenth century, or even the two short treatises on horses by the governor of Connaught, Sir Nicholas Malby; the equally popular *Five Hundred Points of Good Husbandry* by Thomas Tusser, which was in Gabriel Harvey's library and which told husbandmen and housewives how to run their estate, and how to plan the farming year in an easily searchable array of devout verses; and Barnabe Googe's *Foure Bookes of Husbandry*, which told readers how to run an estate, plant a garden, and manage crop cycles. Googe spent considerable time in Ireland and makes it clear in his dedicatory letter to Sir William Fitzwilliam, Lord Deputy of Ireland (1571–5 and 1588–94), and his preface to the reader, that his translation is partly aimed at transforming a country such as Ireland from dearth and chaos to civility and order.[254] Ben Jonson had a volume which bound together Spenser's *Calender* with Tusser's guide to managing an estate, showing how close practical advice on husbandry was to georgic poetry, a genre that especially interested Spenser.[255]

We can also infer a great deal from Spenser's writings, especially those after 1590, which makes *A View* particularly valuable, because of the sources it cites.[256] It is likely, therefore, that Spenser possessed works of history, anthropology, and topography, including Buchanan's *History of Scotland*, which is referenced a number of times; Camden's *Britannia*; Holinshed's *Chronicles*; Strabo's *Geography*; Bodin's *Six Books of the Commonwealth*; Machiavelli's *Discourses*; Hector Boethius' *History of the Scottish People*; Johan Boemus' *The Fardle of Facions*, the first comprehensive survey of the origins of European peoples; Diodorus Siculus' *Universal History*; and others. There would have been works of more local history such as Richard Carew's history and topography of Cornwall and William Lambarde's work on Kent, and works on Wales and Welsh history.[257] Spenser may not have possessed many Irish books, but he clearly had access to them, probably from neighbouring collections, such as that of Hanmer. He would also have possessed other more modern works, especially if we bear in mind what we know about his reading tastes from his correspondence with Harvey.

Spenser must have had more popular works, such as almanacs, jest books, travel guides, collections and encyclopedias, such as those produced by Stephen Bateman; and, most importantly for his poetry, editions of old and recent works of European and English literature, such as Sidney's *Astrophil and Stella* and *Apology for Poetry*, and perhaps Puttenham's *Arte of English Poesie*, Chaucer, Langland, Gascoigne, Marlowe, Skelton, probably Nashe (given his antagonistic relationship with Harvey in the early 1590s), perhaps Churchyard and Chapman, Boccaccio (in particular, *De Claris Mulieribus*), Tasso, Ariosto, perhaps Dante, Du Bartas, Du Bellay, Ronsard.[258] There must also have been some manuscripts passed between poets, such as Ralegh's 'Ocean to Cynthia', which Spenser saw at various stages of its life, works by Drayton, Daniel, probably Mary Sidney, and other members of her circle to which Spenser was connected.[259] Moreover, given their availability in

Elizabethan England, Spenser might have possessed some medieval manuscripts, possibly even illuminated ones.[260] In total, his working library must have contained at least 200–300 volumes, probably rather more, a substantial collection that he would never have had the means to acquire had he stayed in England: perhaps he possessed as many volumes as John Donne, who often complained of poverty but acquired as many as a thousand books.[261] The same is true of Spenser's gaining an estate, and in England he would probably not have needed to accumulate so many books himself, as it would have been easier to use and borrow those owned by others.

7

Back to England

LATER in the year in which he obtained Kilcolman, Spenser returned to England for an extended visit, one of two that he was to make before his final crossing in 1598. An entry in the Irish Chancery Recognizances for 18 June 1589 states that Edmund Spenser of Cork was to provide security for the delivery of James Shropp to Newgate.[1] The entry further states that Spenser was bound for the sum of £100 to Richard Spence to carry out this and another obligation, the recovery of £30 owed by Richard Brysse to Richard Crowther, deceased.[2] We know nothing of any of these figures, only one of whom, Brysse, appears elsewhere in the State Papers, or why Shropp was being sent to Newgate, but the entry might suggest that Spenser left Ireland relatively early in the year, unless he simply stood security for the delivery of the prisoner.[3] It shows that he remained a trusted servant of the crown, which further suggests that he may have travelled to England on official business on other occasions. For this visit, Spenser passed over his duties as deputy clerk to the Munster Council to Richard Chichester, who had become the constable of Limerick Castle on 16 September 1588, and was, therefore, probably another figure associated with the Norris brothers.[4] The timing of the journey indicates that Spenser had probably already occupied Kilcolman for some time, had the estate in good running order, and was thus able to hand on responsibilities to a trusted team of settlers under a bailiff. His departure demonstrates that there were others who could undertake his duties for the Munster Council, and that this may have been a regular practice. It is also possible that he may have chosen to leave Ireland at this point because Machabyas had died, perhaps recently.

Spenser's visit is closely associated with his relationship with Ralegh, and the common image we have of Ralegh and Spenser discussing poetry over their pipes begins with the story that Spenser stayed with Ralegh at Myrtle Grove, next to St Mary's church, before embarking together for England, the two having spent the best part of the summer together at Kilcolman.[5] According to Francis Allen, Ralegh retreated to Ireland after he was chased from the court by the queen's new favourite, the earl of Essex.[6] However, the only solid evidence of Spenser's friendship with Ralegh is what Spenser tells us in his dedication to Ralegh prefacing *Colin Clouts come home againe*, and the Letter, dated 23 January 1589, appended to the first edition of *The Faerie Queene*. Nowhere in his own published and unpublished writings does Ralegh mention Spenser, outside the dedicatory poems which he contributed to *The Faerie Queene*.[7] It is only after Ralegh's death that we have evidence—albeit problematic—outside Spenser's writings that Ralegh knew Spenser, through the annotations made by Ralegh's widow, Elizabeth Throckmorton, in the 1617 folio of Spenser's *Works* owned by their son, Carew.[8] Lady Ralegh's bizarre claim that she was the object of Colin's fruitless devotion in *Colin Clouts*, writing 'E. Throkemorton his mistris' in the margin of the copy she gave to their son, Carew, next to lines 464–79, complicates rather than clarifies the evidence of a relationship between Ralegh and Spenser. The poem later reveals that the lady is actually Rosalind, a figure of Spenser's wife, rather than 'a fourth Elizabeth in Spenser's life'.[9] Lady Ralegh's marginal note suggests that she knew little of her husband's interaction with Spenser beyond rumour and hearsay, perhaps because she never went to Ireland. More significantly, the note provides further evidence that Ralegh's relationship with Spenser was not a friendship of much substance or longevity and Lady Ralegh was trying to show her son that his father and mother were immortalized by a famous poet. Had their marriage not been revealed at the point that it was, things might have been different and Ralegh might have been able to advance his client.[10] Certainly, Lady Ralegh's comments suggest that 1589–90 was the one time when the two men knew each other.

Spenser and Ralegh clearly had a literary relationship and read each other's poetry.[11] In 'A Letter of the Authors' (Letter to Ralegh), Spenser claims that he represented Queen Elizabeth as the Faerie Queene, in places 'fashioning her name according to your [Ralegh's] owne excellent conceipt of Cynthia'.[12] This statement suggests that Spenser read Ralegh's 'Cynthia' poems before he wrote his own major poem, although he clearly did not adopt Ralegh's courtly hyper-Petrarchanism wholesale, and was eager to distinguish his own work from that of Ralegh.[13] As Jean Brink has pointed out, the Letter should be dated, as it is in the first edition of *The Faerie Queene*, 23 January 1589, before Spenser set out for England and before he acquired official possession of Kilcolman.[14] The Letter then reads as an appeal for support from Ralegh, as well as a means of advertising Spenser's connection with a rising star at the court, which in 1589, Ralegh clearly was. Ralegh's rise had been meteoric in the 1580s, partly driven by the poems that he wrote for the queen—a major reason why he was such an astute choice for Spenser as an advocate in 1589.

Moreover, it looks as if Spenser was in urgent need of support for his work in the late 1580s, as his publishing career had ground to a halt—although he was undoubtedly involved in the second and third editions of *The Shepheardes Calender* in 1581 and 1586—and it was probably hard to place *The Faerie Queene* with a publisher.[15] Certainly the rather plain and uninspiring form in which the first edition of the poem appeared suggests that economy was an important consideration. The poem was published by John Wolfe for William Ponsonby in 1590, in a blockish quarto format, with no annotations, a form that does not seem appropriate for such an ambitious, innovative, and challenging work. Perhaps Wolfe was chosen as a matter of expediency rather than for his publishing skills, the deciding factor being the need to have Spenser proofread the work quickly before he returned to Ireland.[16] Certainly, there is a stark contrast between the 1590 *Faerie Queene* and the elaborate folio of Sir John Harington's translation of *Orlando Furioso*, published a year later by Richard Field, who was responsible for the significantly more ornate second edition of Spenser's poem in 1596, by which time Spenser had become a much more celebrated figure.[17] Field's printing—he also printed the *Arcadia* (for Ponsonby), and later Shakespeare's narrative poems, *Venus and Adonis* and *The Rape of Lucrece*—was far superior to that of John Wolfe.[18]

That Spenser and Ralegh encountered each other is clear enough; that they read each other's work is also evident; that they had mutual connections, common interests, and the opportunity to be closely acquainted, is also beyond doubt.[19] Whether they were ever really friendly is open to question, as the evidence that survives comes from only one of them. And, whatever relationship they had, whether it was friendship, or that of a patron and client, evidently went badly wrong later.[20] Were Ralegh and Spenser literary conspirators in the ways in which Harvey and Spenser had been? It is worth thinking about the two friendships together. Spenser had learned about the sly tactical use of the letter from Harvey, and the importance that many in high places gave to letters. The Letter to Ralegh sounds very like Harvey's letters to Spenser written a decade earlier, a resemblance that cannot be accidental. It should be no surprise that Spenser, more than any other late Elizabethan writer, made clever use of published letters and paratexts after the intellectual training he had received. Spenser's Letter is designed to give the reader the impression that he was closely connected to the courtier, discussed literature with him, and was treated as an equal as well as a client. Subsequent commentators have followed Spenser's representation of their relationship. Writing about his method, Spenser apparently provides an insight into the ways in which his mind functioned, a description that bears an uncanny resemblance to the level of intellectual discussion throughout the Harvey–Spenser *Letters* and Spenser's own comments on the dedication of the *Calender*:

By ensample of which excellente Poets [Homer, Virgil, Ariosto, Tasso], I labour to pourtraict in Arthure, before he was king, the image of a braue knight, perfected in the twelue priuate morall vertues, as Aristotle hath deuised, the which is the purpose of these first twelue bookes: which if I finde to be wel accepted, I may be perhaps encoraged, to frame the other part of polliticke vertues in his person, after that hee came to be king. To some I know this Methode will seeme displeasaunt, which had rather haue good discipline deliuered plainly in way of precepts, or sermoned at large, as they vse, then thus clowdily enrapped in Alegoricall deuises. (Spenser, *Faerie Queene*, pp. 715–16)

The Letter has an obvious function as an advertisement—again, much like the earlier *Letters*. As Richard McCabe has argued, the commentary 'is better understood as an attempt to generate rather than to provide exegesis'.[21] *The Faerie Queene* is shown to be an extraordinarily ambitious poem that attempts to combine the values of the best poets of the ancient and modern worlds, so going beyond their achievements and making English poetry the most sophisticated that has ever existed. What the *Calender* did for the history of pastoral poetry, *The Faerie Queene* will do for epic, combined with romance to produce a new hybrid form.[22] The author, while expressing some doubt as to whether the poem will prove too challenging and experimental for many readers, announces that he has a great deal more to come if readers find his work stimulating. And, like the *Calender*, Spenser tells the reader that the poem is full of games and surprises—exactly what Elizabethan readers enjoyed— not always meaning what it says.[23] Just as the *Letters* served in part as a showcase of the work and talents of Harvey and Spenser, so does the Letter to Ralegh, claiming that Spenser had perhaps as many as twenty-four books on moral virtues planned, a claim we should not take seriously as a statement of intent at this stage of his career. Altogether, the Letter shows what Spenser had learned about printing and publishing from the first stage of his writing life, forming a neat bridge between the two stages and providing further evidence that he had thought carefully about how to relaunch his poetry now that he had acquired an estate and obtained his independence. The Letter cannot, therefore, be taken as a direct statement of his aims and plans, or as irrefutable evidence of his intimacy with Ralegh.

Moreover, the Letter was placed after the poem, before the commendatory verses, one of which was by Ralegh, and the dedicatory sonnets, one of which was to Ralegh. The decision to place the Letter at the back was unusual, suggesting that, in Darryl Gless's words, 'Even if the Letter does represent an authentic formulation of Spenser's intentions . . . it could have influenced few actual readings.'[24] The position of these paratextual materials 'set this edition apart' among early modern books, suggesting moreover that Spenser was trying to assert his independence as a poet, placing the value of his work over and above that of the patrons and aristocrats to whom he had to dedicate the poem, deliberately challenging and correcting readers' expectations.[25] Placing the prefatory material last looks like yet another example of calculated rudeness by the poet, but also an attempt to show that direct communication between writer and reader was both possible and desirable.[26] The Letter was not included in the 1596 edition of *The Faerie Queene*. Ralegh had fallen from favour, but it had probably done its job and there was no longer a need for the author to correct readers' errors. Even so, it had probably caused some measure of offence, not least to its addressee.[27]

Spenser and Ralegh may well have sailed over to England together, but there is no corroborating evidence that they did so beyond Spenser's own claims. It is most likely that their relationship was one of convenience with an uncertain Spenser eager to attach himself to the rising star at court. Ralegh had come from a relatively humble background, like Sir Thomas Smith, wrote allegorical poetry, and was perhaps the only figure at court who could appreciate what Spenser was trying to do in his work.[28] Ralegh, in turn, may well have realized the value of Spenser's support, especially as he had already started to court Elizabeth Throckmorton and must have realized that trouble would be in store for him with the queen. The alliance of a brilliant poet, whom Ralegh could rediscover and relaunch, would help his cause (and the award of a pension to Spenser indicates that his instincts were indeed sound). Elizabeth jealously policed the private lives of her ladies-in-waiting and showed little tolerance for any who formed independent attachments, most significantly, when another favourite, Robert Dudley, earl of Leicester, married Lettice Knollys in 1578, an event to which Spenser had referred rather contemptuously in the *Calender*.[29] In pointed contrast, Spenser defended Ralegh with considerable—albeit ambiguous—vigour in the second edition of *The Faerie Queene*.[30]

There is also no real evidence that Spenser attended court and read his poetry aloud to the queen, as has commonly been assumed, although it is possible that he did do this.[31] The dedication of *The Faerie Queene* to Elizabeth does not tell us anything, given the vast number of books dedicated to the queen for a variety of motives.[32] It is clear, however, that the visit was a success in one important detail, in that Elizabeth awarded Spenser a life pension of £50 a year on 25 February 1591.[33] These were to be paid to him in four equal instalments on Lady Day (25 March); the Nativity of John the Baptist (24 June); Michaelmas (29 September); and Christmas Day. The first instalment was collected by one of Ponsonby's employees, Edward Blount, the son of a member of the Merchant Taylors' Company, who was to establish himself as a publisher in 1594, his most celebrated work being the first folio of Shakespeare's plays. The second was collected by Ponsonby himself, after which Spenser had various people pick up the payments in two half-yearly instalments, including a member of the Dryden family, relatives of Elizabeth Boyle after their marriage in 1594.[34]

We do not know what the pension was awarded for, but it was a significant sum, over twice the annual salary of most secretaries and government officials. Spenser may have been rewarded for his services to the crown, but this would seem unlikely, unless there is a secret career—spying?—waiting to be discovered. If not, then it is clear that *The Faerie Queene* did have an important impact when it was published at some point in early 1590, having been entered into the Stationers' Register by Ponsonby on 1 December 1589, soon after Spenser arrived in London. It is likely that Ralegh worked hard on Spenser's behalf, and that his efforts secured the funds from Elizabeth, who was notoriously parsimonious and only awarded one other pension to a writer in her reign, the aged Thomas Churchyard, a prolific and loyal writer. Churchyard was granted 18*d.* per day in January 1593, increased to 20*d.* in July 1597 (Spenser's pension was nearly twice Churchyard's, working out at 2*s.* 8¾*d.* per day).[35] Indeed, the story that has often been attributed to Spenser, complaining about the non-payment of his pension, is, in fact, the work of Churchyard.[36] It is also possible that Burghley was the other main influence on Elizabeth, perhaps seeing Spenser as a vital political figure in Munster. Certainly it is notable how seriously *A View* appears to have been taken by those close to power, and for such a long period of time, suggesting that Spenser already had a reputation as an astute commentator on Irish affairs by those in the know before he wrote the dialogue.

The evidence that Ponsonby had been in charge of collecting Spenser's pension shows that Spenser had a close working relationship with his publisher and probably spent a great deal of time in his company when he was in London. Ponsonby appears to have worked hard for Spenser, establishing relationships with varied clients. These included John Ramsey, born in 1578, a student at Peterhouse in 1601, later to be a lawyer, minor courtier, and a traveller, as well as the rather more grand Henry Percy, ninth earl of Northumberland, both of whom were eager to buy Spenser's works.[37] Ramsey's Commonplace Book, written between 1596 and 1633, reveals him to be an avid reader of Spenser, copying out three poems from the *Complaints*; imitating Spenser's lyric style in his own poems; and eager to obtain lost poems such as the 'Court of Cupid', a work that both he and Ponsonby believed to have existed in the late 1590s.[38]

This relationship was not unusual. Writers spent a lot of time with their publishers and printers, especially when they came from similar backgrounds. Thomas Nashe, for example, was so closely associated with his publisher, John Danter, that Harvey insulted him as 'Danters gentleman', implying that the one was a client of the other.[39] Spenser probably also spent time with the printer John Wolfe, who worked closely with Harvey, and encouraged writers to frequent his house and printing shop in Distaff Lane, south-east of St Paul's churchyard at the heart of the London publishing industry.[40] Harvey, who never married and lodged with various male friends at different points in his life, wrote his *New Letter of Notable Contents* (1593), addressed to and printed by Wolfe, while living at Wolfe's house.[41] Wolfe, who was living at Stationers' Hall in 1589, creates a neat link between Harvey and Spenser, suggesting that all three met up in London during this period. Wolfe's keen interest in publishing Italian books—he was responsible for printing various versions of sections of Tasso's *Gerusalemme Liberata*—shows that his printing shop would have been an ideal place to check and revise *The Faerie Queene* ready for publication.[42]

Ponsonby, who had previously published a number of literary works, including some by Robert Greene, as well as political and religious tracts, had shown a keen interest in publishing Sidney's *Arcadia*, a project that had not been strongly supported by the Sidney family. Nevertheless, Ponsonby pressed ahead, secured a licence in 1588 and published *The Countesse of Pembrokes Arcadia*, printed by John Windet, in 1590.[43] The work would have been with Wolfe's compositors or going through the press when Spenser was in London. Windet was another printer closely associated with Wolfe, who took over many of Wolfe's commissions when Wolfe gave up printing for bookselling in 1591, including Richard Carew's very literal-minded translation of Torquato Tasso's *Godfrey of Bulloigne* (1594).[44] Windet published the fourth edition of the *Calender* in late 1591 (it was entered into the Stationers' Register in October), using Wolfe's distinctive emblem.[45]

The evidence demonstrates that there was a close relationship between printers, booksellers, and writers, and points to a network more extensive than is obvious at first glance. Windet was from Exeter, and was related to the Vowell-Hookers, who were connected to the Carews. Sir Peter Carew employed John Hooker (*c.*1527–1601), the antiquary, who acted as Carew's legal adviser in Ireland.[46] The Carews were, in turn, one of the significant west country families who were connected to the Raleghs and the Gilberts.[47] Richard Carew (1555–1620), was later the author of *The Survey of Cornwall*, which was dedicated to Ralegh, further suggesting that he, as the first English translator of Tasso, must have been known to Spenser.[48] He was also the author of a short treatise, 'The Excellency of the English Tongue', first published by Camden in *Remains*, a work that cites Spenser—as well as Sir Thomas Smith—as examples of the proper use of sophisticated English that had absorbed foreign words and styles, and which demonstrates further shared interests with Spenser's more immediate circle.[49] It is likely that he was the R. C. who contributed a dedicatory sonnet to Zachary Jones's translation of *Scanderbeg* (1596), published by Ponsonby, as it was dedicated to his brother, George Carew (*c.*1556–1612). Carew's sonnet appears alongside Spenser's, providing yet more evidence that they moved in the same circles.[50] The central link between all these figures may well have been Gabriel Harvey.[51]

In securing the work of Spenser along with Sidney, Ponsonby was astute enough to realize what the immediate future of English literature was likely to be, as he now had a monopoly on the work of the two most celebrated poets of the 1590s.[52] Moreover, it is likely, given Ponsonby's preface to the *Complaints* volume, published in 1591, that Spenser either handed over a large part of his publishing duties to

Ponsonby, or collaborated closely with his publisher.[53] However we read the evidence, Ponsonby and Spenser appear to have become friends—much closer than Spenser and Ralegh could have been—and existed in London within a wider network of other intellectuals.

But it is implausible to imagine Spenser spending most of his time socializing. Given his output in the next two years when, in addition to the first edition of *The Faerie Queene*, Spenser published the *Complaints* and *Daphnaïda*, wrote *Colin Clouts come home againe*, and would also have been at work on the second edition of *The Faerie Queene*, he must have spent most of his time writing, as he had done when he lived with Harvey after leaving university.

It is also likely that Spenser visited Hampshire at some point in 1589–90, as Aubrey claimed he did based on the testimony—albeit second-hand—of people who had known Spenser over half a century earlier.[54] The estates of Sir Henry Wallop at Farleigh Wallop, only about fifty miles from central London, were within easy reach for someone who had travelled extensively in Ireland (the distance is shorter than from Cork to Limerick, which is just over sixty miles).[55] Wallop, miserable in Ireland and often petitioning Elizabeth's chief ministers to be allowed to leave the country so that he could sort out his affairs in England, sailed to England in April 1589 and remained in Hampshire until 1595, even though he was still employed as Irish treasurer. His brother, William, was sheriff of Hampshire, and is buried in the nearby village of Wield, and a handsome funeral monument still exists in St James church (Plate 26), which may provide us with some idea of what Sir Henry looked like, as no likeness of him survives. There were complaints about Sir Henry staying on his estates and in 1592 'the royal auditor Christopher Peyton . . . had to travel to Wallop's Hampshire home to clear his accounts', indicating that Wallop was extremely reluctant to move from his home and anyone who had to see him had also to seek him out.[56]

Spenser may have been sent to see Wallop on official business, perhaps because of the cordial relations they appear to have enjoyed; may have decided to visit him as a valued mentor; or may have been summoned by Wallop. Certainly, Wallop appears to have looked after Spenser, as they were involved in a significant number of mutually advantageous land deals. Spenser would have been closer to people he had worked with in Ireland, both those on the same level as himself, and his superiors such as Grey, Thomas Norris, and Wallop, than he was to many more obviously literary and cultural figures, especially those at the court, something that is evident in his published work in which he consciously fashions himself as an Englishman in Ireland. Now a large country house which once served as a school, rebuilt after a fire in 1661 and extensively renovated subsequently, Farleigh House would have been a substantial manor house in the late sixteenth century, big enough to house the queen and her courtiers in autumn 1591, when she visited the area on one of her many progresses throughout her kingdom.[57] Little remains of that building apart from the outline of a moat, a fireplace, and some Elizabethan windows in the north wing (Plate 27). Spenser might only have visited Farleigh House briefly, but it is also possible that he spent a few weeks staying with a significant patron, as he had done at Leicester House, and he may have written or revised sections of the *Complaints* in this period.[58]

We do not know how long Spenser remained in London, but his primary purpose would have been to see *The Faerie Queene* into print, as has usually been assumed.[59] Richard Chichester is recorded as acting as deputy clerk to the Munster Council on 10 July 1591, which suggests that Spenser was still in England at that point.[60] However, it is possible that he returned to Ireland at various points in this period, perhaps for brief stays. He was perhaps back in Ireland on 30 May 1590, as F. P. Wilson has suggested, to carry on his court battle with Lord Roche of Fermoy, as a bill of imprest (authorization to draw money in advance) is made out to him in person by Wallop.[61] It is also feasible, given Wallop's reluctance to leave his estates at Farleigh Wallop, that Spenser travelled there instead and that this was the occasion of his visit to Hampshire recovered by Aubrey. Wallop's account book is a large, neatly produced folio volume, clearly copied out by a scribe at the conclusion of his period of office, so it provides no real clue of his whereabouts while performing his duties. *Colin Clouts come home againe* was not published until 1595, but was dated in the dedicatory epistle to Ralegh as 'From my house of *Kilcolman* the 27. of December. 1591'. This makes it clear that Spenser had returned to Munster at some point before Christmas, probably in the autumn or early winter. The preface also suggests that Spenser meant to publish this work in early 1592, but waited until 1595. Why did he do this? The tone of his Letter to Ralegh provides us with some significant clues:

SIR, that you may see that I am not always ydle as yee thinke, though not greatly well occupied, nor altogether vndutifull, though vnworthie of your higher conceipt for the meanesse of the stile, but agreeing with the truth in circumstance and matter. The which I humbly beseech you to accept in part of payment of the infinite debt in which I acknowledge my selfe bounden vnto you, for your singular fauors and sundrie good turnes shewed to me at my late being in England, and with your good countenance protect against the malice of euill mouthes, which are always wide open to carpe at and misconstrue my simple meaning.[62]

There is a noticeable shift from the open, generous tone of the Letter appended to *The Faerie Queene*, in which Spenser negotiated between a friendly and a supplicating style in addressing the court figure. Here, Spenser is far more abrupt, the first line being familiar, even rude, in reminding Ralegh that he has, despite all appearances to the contrary, been hard at work in his interests. The change of style to a more deferential mode serves only to highlight the startling nature of the first sentence. Spenser is telling Ralegh off in public, an address, if anything, even more confrontational than the discussion of the non-dedication to Leicester in the *Letters* with Harvey.

Furthermore, the letter forces the reader to assume that this is a response to an irate letter castigating the poet for failing to support him properly, making it a public advertisement of their falling out. The poem, which is extraordinarily, aggressively dismissive of the court and courtly values, can hardly have been what Ralegh would have wanted to read and cannot have been much help to him in 1595.[63] While the first public letter made use of Ralegh's support to promote the poem, this second one makes clear to Ralegh that he is now dependent on Spenser's goodwill and that he cannot command the gentleman of Kilcolman. The letter also provides corroborating evidence that Ralegh had intervened in 1589–90 to gain Spenser preferment and material reward, as well as the familiar Spenserian theme that his work has been misinterpreted, a claim that was at least in part disingenuous, even as it became ever more self-fulfilling. *Colin Clout* now serves as a means of paying Ralegh back, a complicated return gift that asserts the giver's power more than warranting the receiver's gratitude.[64] Spenser's preface, a conscious inversion of the Letter to Ralegh placed after the poem, reminds readers that it is the poet who now has the power to represent his patron.[65]

What had caused the unusual delay in publishing a poem that advertised when and where it was first written? We know that the poem was revised between 1591 and 1595 as it refers to the death of Ferdinando Stanley, Lord Strange, husband of Alice Spencer, dedicatee of *Teares of the Muses*: 'Amyntas quite is gone and lies full low, | Hauing his *Amaryllis* left to mone' (lines 434–5). Both were noted literary patrons.[66] Furthermore, Spenser refers to Alice as 'highest in degree' (line 543), another addition, as she only obtained this status when her husband was made earl of Derby on the death of his father in 1593, and the reference to the husband of her sister, Anne (Charillis), post-dates their marriage on 4 December 1592 (lines 552–5).[67] Again, these revisions provide us with some clues about this (apparently) personal and autobiographical poem.[68] What is clear is that the poem, whatever traces it bears of earlier incarnations, was carefully revised to express Spenser's numerological concerns, the twelve poets and twelve ladies centred around the figure of the poet—yet another sign that Spenser was determined to show that he was the principal figure now, not his patrons or rivals.[69]

Ralegh's fall was indeed spectacular and Elizabeth's anger was much greater than even Ralegh had anticipated. In August both husband and wife were sent to the Tower. Ralegh remained in disgrace, banished from the court until 1597.[70] In another passage in Spenser's poem that must represent a revision to an original version, one of the shepherds, Thestylis (Bryskett), asks what song the 'shepherd of the ocean' (Ralegh) sang. Colin replies that

His song was all a lamentable lay,
Of great vnkindnesse, and of vsage hard,
Of *Cynthia* the Ladie of the sea,
Which from her presence faultlesse him debard.
And euer and anon with singulfs rife,
He cryed out, to make his vndersong
Ah my loues queene, and goddesse of my life,
Who shall me pittie, when thou doest me wrong? (lines 164–71)

Spenser had clearly read Ralegh's poetry, as this passage refers to the unpublished 'The Ocean, to Cynthia', suggesting that the story told in the poem of Ralegh seeking Spenser out and the two reading poetry together may have a basis in truth.[71] The lines also allude to Ralegh's well-attested penchant for self-regarding dramatic gestures, such as his staged attempt to escape from his guards in the Tower after he had seen Elizabeth in a barge, seize a rowing boat, shouting that he 'wolde disguyse hymselfe and gett into a pare of oares to ease his mynde butt with a syght of the Quene, or els, he protest, his harte wolde breake'.[72] The queen was not amused. Spenser's lines are perhaps not an entirely fair or serious comment on Ralegh's poem, which, if it was as Spenser represented, was at odds with the more critical tone of *Colin Clout*, serving to highlight the superior nature of Spenser's work and perhaps even hinting that Ralegh sounded rather like the insincere flatterers at court, described later in the poem. A 'lamentable lay', after all, could simply be a bad poem, not just a sad one.[73]

These events suggest that *Colin Clout* was first imagined as a poem that would be published in the wake of Spenser's return to Ireland later that year. It was probably conceived in the main as the confrontational and deliberately aggressive work that we now have, attacking the queen's lack of interest in her subjects in Ireland and complaining of their hard life surrounded by the hostile Irish. Cuddy, having listened to Colin's stories of Cynthia's land, asks, 'What land is that thou meanst . . . | And is there other, then whereon we stand?' (lines 290–1). This appears to be a disarmingly naive question that demonstrates his ignorance, before we realize that something is not right if the queen is not known by her subjects, a problem that the metropolitan authorities need to solve. More sustained is the ferocious attack Colin makes on the English court, a place where no self-respecting shepherd would want to live:

For sooth to say, it is no sort of life,
For shepheard fit to lead in that same place,
Where each one seeks with malice and with strife,
To thrust downe other into foule disgrace,
Himselfe to raise: and he doth soonest rise

That best can handle his deceiftull wit,
In subtil shifts, and finest sleights deuise,
Either by slaundring his wel deemed name,
Through leasings lewd, and fained forgerie:
Or else by breeding him some blot of blame,
By creeping close into his secrecie;
To which him needs a hollow hart,
Masked with faire dissembling curtsie,
A filed toung furnisht with tearmes of art,
No art of schoole, but Courtiers schoolery. (lines 688–702)

Perhaps the last line is the most cutting: the court has many arts, sophistication, and skill on display, but all of them are opposed to the 'art of schoole', the arts that Spenser had spent his life acquiring. The court is fundamentally at odds with the craft of the intellectual and so no one could ever hope to fulfil Smith and Harvey's ideal of the active academic participating in public life. The poet, instead of following Virgil's career path from shepherd to poet, must remain as a shepherd, and so save himself from the pernicious influence of the court in order to be able to write sensibly and to tell the truth. There were, of course, many criticisms of the court and its role in poetry and drama in the period, but few went quite as far as Spenser.[74] Nor did many re-emphasize the message, as Spenser does in *Mother Hubberds Tale* and *The Faerie Queene*, Book VI, echoing words and phrases such as 'leasings' and 'filed tongue'.[75]

This passage may post-date 1591, but it sounds as though Spenser's comments were a more immediate reaction to the experience of the court, which he may not have visited before 1589—unless he accompanied Leicester at some point in 1579–80, or attended in the 1580s on Irish business—and probably only visited twice again in 1596–7, and just before his death in January 1599. Therefore, it is safe to assume that the first draft of *Colin Clout* would have contained at least some of this hostile comment, articulating a clear sense of Spenser's identity as an Englishman in Ireland, a New English settler.[76] In pointed contrast, Ralegh probably spent little, if any, time on his Irish estates after 1591—he first visited them in 1588—eventually selling them off to Richard Boyle, first earl of Cork in 1602 for £1,500.[77] He did, however, make a lot of money from them, especially from selling timber for barrels, and developing the iron-mill at Mogeely.[78]

Colin Clout, while apparently praising Ralegh, looks as if it was always a poem that was critical of Ralegh's life and values as a courtier. Spenser affirmed his identity as an Irish settler and cast Ralegh, whose attention was elsewhere, focused on his marriage, and his colonial and privateering ventures across the Atlantic, as rather more frivolous, dependent on the goddess Cynthia, who neglects her distant subjects. The publication of the poem must surely have been delayed because of Ralegh's disgrace and the attendant dangers of dedicating a poem to him in 1591–2; through Spenser's own sense of events, based on the advice of friends in London; and because Ponsonby was too sensible to risk another scandal after the *Complaints* had been called in.[79] Spenser's expression of irritation with Ralegh in 1595 was surely a result of Ralegh's sense that Spenser had let him down in not defending him vigorously enough, in return for the favour that Ralegh had done him in securing him his pension. In addition, Spenser undoubtedly wanted the reader to read an extract from a correspondence in order to assert his own independence and power as a poet, a device derived from earlier attempts to make the Areopagus sound more substantial than it really was.

However we read the circumstances of the publication of *Colin Clout*, Spenser reminds the reader that he was associated with someone as powerful as Ralegh— perhaps as a counterweight to Burghley, whom he had offended so badly in 1591. And he does indeed defend Ralegh through the allegory of Timias and Belphoebe in Book IV of *The Faerie Queene*, published in 1596, albeit in terms that do not wholly endorse Ralegh's behaviour and which do not provide evidence of their close friendship. Ralegh is represented as a loyal courtier, even though his surrender to passion has provoked the 'deepe disdaine' of the queen.[80] In the poem Timias/ Ralegh is reconciled to Belphoebe/Elizabeth, enabling him to live 'An happie life with grace and good accord', even though this had not taken place when the poem was published.[81] Moreover, Spenser's apparent praise of Ralegh's colonial exploits may not be quite what they seem.[82] Spenser also reminds the reader who is in charge at this point, that Ralegh now needs him, although he has no more need of Ralegh. Moreover, Spenser is now adamant that he has made Munster his home, for which he has just acquired a new wife.[83] Living in the margins, Spenser was now able to place himself at the centre of his world.[84]

And he was, once again, with the publication of *The Faerie Queene*, the most important poet writing in English. Thomas Watson's pastoral elegy on the death of Sir Francis Walsingham (March/April 1590), written in imitation of the *Calender*, in particular the November eclogue on the death of Dido, acknowledges the pre-eminence of Spenser:

> sweet *Spencer* let me leave this taske to thee,
> Whose neuer stooping quill can best set forth
> such things of state, as passe my Muse, and me.
> Thou *Spencer* art the alderliest swaine,
> or haply if that word be all to base,
> Thou art *Apollo* whose sweet hunnie vaine
> amongst the Muses hath a chiefest place.[85]

Watson's homage tells us that for a significant poet like him (Watson), Spenser was seen as the unofficial laureate, probably because he had returned to the capital and had just published or was about to publish a major work.[86]

Thomas Watson (1555/6–92) was a writer best known as a friend of Christopher Marlowe, whom he helped in a brawl in Hog Lane in September 1589, killing William Bradley in self-defence, for which crime he was sent to Newgate until pardoned in February 1590.[87] Watson wrote primarily in Latin and had a particular interest in music. He dedicated the first English sonnet sequence, *Hekatompathia, or Passionate Centurie of Love* (1582), to Edward de Vere, seventeenth earl of Oxford.[88] The work is heavily indebted to Petrarch and other Italian and French poets and was published, appropriately enough, by John Wolfe, who was close to Gabriel Harvey, who cited Watson's work with approval.[89] Notably, the sequence contains a number of puns on the word 'prick', as written musical notation and penis, a quibble that Spenser could have borrowed for the first line of *The Faerie Queene*.[90] Both poets moved in many of the same circles in London; each read the other's work carefully, and publicly praised the other's poetry.[91] Accordingly, Watson, who was close enough to Spenser to see the manuscript of *The Faerie Queene* in 1588, selects Spenser as the poet best suited for recording Walsingham's life for the queen.[92] Spenser did transcribe letters to Walsingham from Grey in 1580, when Walsingham was most concerned with Irish affairs through his spy network, but there is no real evidence of any relationship between Elizabeth's principal secretary and Spenser, apart from their connection to the Sidney family.[93] Watson's plea that Spenser is fittest for the task in hand suggests either that he is using this opportunity to promote Spenser or that he has no real understanding that Spenser's relationship to the court was always problematic. Watson's praise pre-dates the publication of Spenser's praise of great men in the *Complaints*, further suggesting that some such works probably circulated in manuscript.

The first edition of *The Faerie Queene* does indeed leave much to be desired, a problem that was corrected in later, more handsome editions; the contrast between first and second editions is especially marked. But, as Jean Brink has argued, the plethora of dedicatory sonnets, commendatory verses, and the Letter to Ralegh at the end of the first edition makes this an unusual book, one that bears little resemblance to comparable works.[94] Perhaps these sonnets were intended to be given to individuals to accompany a gift of the poem, and were gathered up in the print shop by mistake and added to the text, which suggests that Spenser had less to do with the final stages of the printing of his poem than has often been assumed. Perhaps, after such a long absence from the public sphere, Spenser was eager to remind various influential readers of the significance of his work, which is why so many sonnets and poems were appended to the poem: he was always eager to forge a career as a literary innovator. The repetition of so many poems might also suggest a hurried production, not overseen by the author, as Brink suggests, although, as Marjorie Plant has argued, '[t]he close proximity between author and printer-publisher allowed for constant supervision of the press by the author'; indeed, 'this supervision . . . was expected'.[95]

Spenser may have been more keen to secure attention for his work than lucrative patronage. The production of both sets of dedicatory sonnets, with the second set of fifteen containing eight of the first ten, mixed in with the seven new ones, only serves to draw attention to who was omitted from the first list. These include Burghley, Walsingham, Mary Sidney, and Sir John Norris, suggesting that nothing binds this group together, as it is unlikely that Spenser would have forgotten to include Norris, then hastily included him, risking offence by showing that he was not one of the first list. The usual explanation that Spenser's friends, shocked at the exclusion of Burghley, urged him to quickly insert a sonnet to him, seems implausible.[96] Writing about the sonnets as the conclusion to *Pierce Penilesse His Supplication to the Divell* (1592) Thomas Nashe certainly saw the issue as an embarrassing example of the patronage system whereby authors had to appeal to the fickle favours of the high and mighty. Spenser, according to Nashe, had overreached himself, and Nashe, ostensibly helping the poet to correct yet another oversight, produced his own sonnet to the fictitious neglected peer, Amyntas, parodying the language Spenser had adopted in his sonnets:

> Perusing yesternight, with idle eyes,
> The Fairy Singers stately turned verse,
> And viewing after Chap-mens wonted guise,
> What strange contents the title did rehearse;
> I straight leapt ouer to the latter end,
> Where like the quaint Comaedians of our time,
> That when their Play is done do fal to ryme,
> I found short lines, to sundry Nobles pend;
> Whom he as speciall Mirrours singled fourth,
> To be the Patrons of his Poetry:
> I read them all, and reuerenc't their worth,
> Yet wondred he left out the memory.
> But therefore gest I he supprest thy name,
> Because few words might not comprise thy fame.[97]

The sonnet is a generic parody and is not aimed at any particular poem to a patron or, as the first lines indicate, a specific commendatory verse. In referring to the 'strange conceits' of the poem Nashe is, however, making a sly and cutting allusion to Spenser's apparent omission of Ferdinando Stanley, Lord Strange. Stanley, from an ancient Catholic family, had a significant claim to the throne (which may have led to his suspicious death).[98] The reference to 'Chap-mens' possibly alludes to George Chapman (1559/60–1634), the most significant poet patronized by Stanley, although Chapman's poetic career did not take off until 1594.[99] In doing so Nashe simultaneously insults Chapman and Spenser as poets who write for hire as producers of chapbooks, cheap works in print designed to sell to an undiscriminating audience, and as writers of occult works of Neoplatonic philosophy ('strange contents'), known to appeal to Lord Strange, as well as Spenser's patron, Sir Walter Ralegh.[100] Indeed, Spenser included the character Amyntas, 'a stock pastoral name descending from Theocritus', in *Colin Clout*.[101] His representation of Amyntas as a noble patron who could also write with some distinction himself ('Both did he other, which could pipe, maintain, | And eke could pipe himselfe with passing skill' (*Colin Clout*, lines 442–3)), suggests that Spenser felt obliged to respond to Nashe's taunt, either because he saw the need to protect his reputation and a possible source of income, or because he genuinely desired to defend Stanley and his family.[102]

Nashe appears to have known a great deal about Spenser and had a keen sense of the circles in which Spenser moved as well as the social and economic values they espoused. Clearly the worlds of both writers overlapped, and they would have known each other, even if circumstances placed them on opposite sides in a bitter dispute. Spenser had far more in common with a writer such as Nashe, from a similar background (Nashe's father was a minor cleric in Suffolk, often short of money), than with an aristocrat such as Lord Strange.[103] Strange, who had similar interests to Ralegh, and who was Nashe's patron from the late 1580s or early 1590s, allowed Nashe to live in his house and provided him with sustenance while he wrote *Pierce Penilesse*.[104] That Nashe dedicated his pornographic poem, *The Choise of Valentines*, generally known as 'Nashe's Dildo', to Strange in 1592, indicates a considerable degree of intimacy. Strange might have been interested in supporting Spenser; or, more to the point, would have been a potential patron to whom Spenser might have appealed for help. Nashe's cutting intervention, if taken at face value, appears to be an attempt to close off such links. However, the complicated and fluid nature of early modern patronage relationships could also indicate that this was an elaborate joke, and was actually making the possibility of Strange's support for Spenser more likely. Not everyone in Strange's circle got on, and not everything written for Lord Strange took his interests seriously.[105] Nashe was later patronized by the Careys, and he spent Christmas 1593 at Carisbrooke Castle on the Isle of Wight, 'and a great while after'.[106] The Careys also supported Spenser (Spenser dedicated *Muiopotmos* to Lady Carey, the eldest daughter of Sir John Spencer of Althorp, and wrote a dedicatory sonnet for her appended to the first edition of *The Faerie Queene*), further indicting connections between the two writers.[107] Certainly Nashe's later references to Spenser express great respect for his ability and achievements, and Spenser's representation of Lord Strange as Amyntas in *Colin Clout* indicates a significant degree of gratitude. Just because Harvey and Nashe were at odds does not mean that Spenser and Nashe were also always in conflict, even though Nashe aimed a few barbs at Spenser. Apart from the sonnet addressed to Harvey from Dublin, dated 1586, we have little evidence of Spenser and Harvey's friendship continuing on anything like their previously intimate terms after 1580, and it is possible that they grew apart or disagreed, although they never made any public statement to this effect. Certainly both were involved in numerous disputes, and it is notable that Spenser kept his distance from the Nashe–Harvey quarrel, in pointed contrast to the mutual loyalty of the Harvey brothers and Nashe's vociferous defence of his dead friend, Robert Greene.[108]

Nashe's insult is a good one and might even have been enjoyed by his victim, given Spenser's track record. Nashe notes the unusual placing of the paratexts, and then dismisses Spenser's work by claiming that he passed over the poem itself in order to reach them, suggesting, of course, that *The Faerie Queene* was too boring to read.[109] Nashe compounds the barb by pretending to be acting in friendship when his purpose is quite the opposite: 'Beare with me gentle Poet, though I conceiue not aright of thy purpose, or be too inquisitive into the intent of thy obliuion: for, how euer my coniecture may misse the cushion, yet shal my speech sauour of friendship, though it be not alied to iudgement.'[110] Nashe pretends that he would like to be Spenser's friend but claims that in order to do so he would have to separate his judgement from his amicability. The lines, when read alongside the sonnet, show that Nashe had been reading Spenser carefully, as might be expected from someone who was about to conduct a war in print with Spenser's most obviously public friend, Harvey, a quarrel that originated in the Harvey–Spenser *Letters*. Nashe refers to Spenser as a 'gentle Poet', a sly dig at his new status as a homeowner of substance, and, in alluding to friendship, refers back to the heavy weight placed on friendship in that epistolary exchange. The reference to 'Chap-men' in the sonnet further points out the gap between the pretensions of the dedicatory poems and the poverty of the actual book produced. Nashe's rudeness towards Spenser is either at odds with the sycophancy he detected in the dedicatory verses, something he ruthlessly exposes by pointing out how Spenser and Harvey had made such capital out of their relationship as equals, or an acknowledgement that Spenser, like Nashe, was another poet capable of spectacular rudeness to the powerful. Furthermore, given his later assaults on Harvey, Nashe may be showing that Spenser could, at his worst, seem very like his mentor.

The commendatory verses and dedicatory sonnets appended to the 1590 *Faerie Queene* are indeed a very unusual collection of poems, suggesting that the author was uncomfortable and slightly out of place, not quite knowing how to play the game, as Nashe's comments demonstrate with brutal accuracy. The first two sonnets are by Ralegh, as the initials 'W. R.' indicate, an identification confirmed by Lady Ralegh's

comment in her son's copy of the poem, 'bothe thes of your fathar's making'.[111]
Ralegh is the only definitely identified court figure among the poets, which further
confirms the suspicion that he was the one link between Spenser and the court. The
first poem, 'Me thought I saw the grave, where *Laura* lay', alludes to the claim that
the French poet Maurice Scève had discovered Laura's grave in Avignon in the
1540s.[112] Ralegh then claims to see a vision of Elizabeth as the Faerie Queene,
'At whose approach the soule of *Petrarke* wept' (line 7), casting Spenser as a loyal
Petrarch to Elizabeth's elusive but infinitely desirable and irresistible Laura.[113]
The second sonnet, 'The prayse of meaner wits this worke like profit brings',
hints strongly that the poet and his courtly patron are surrounded by enemies,
who will try to thwart their efforts. The reference to Philomena in the second
line would appear to allude to a factional struggle at court, most likely Ralegh's
conflict with Essex.[114] If the queen can read the poem she will see how Spenser has
written her virtues as models for all others to copy: 'If Chastitie want ought, or
Temperance her dew, | Behold her Princely mind aright, and write thy Queene anew'
(lines 7–8).

Ralegh's poem certainly seems written with the dedicatory Letter to him in
mind. The sonnet also suggests an attempt to transform Spenser into his client
and use him to promote his own courtly ambitions as the queen's chief champion
among so many doubters and hostile forces at court.[115] Ralegh's praise of Spenser's
poem has a clear agenda and it is not obvious that he has actually read much beyond
the Letter addressed to him.[116] Both Ralegh and Spenser take the idea of 'fashioning' seriously, but, for Ralegh, the monarch is the centre of all virtue, the poet
reflecting her glory: 'she shall perceiue, how farre her vertues sore | Aboue the reach
of all that lieu, or such as wrote of yore' (lines 9–10). For Spenser, the poet has
considerably more power to represent the monarch and to guide the reader.[117] It is
hard to square Ralegh's extravagant praise of the queen and the notion that if he can
get back to the centre then all will be well, with Spenser's subsequent assault on the
court and its values in a poem that describes the very circumstances that brought
The Faerie Queene into existence as a printed text. Perhaps this was another reason
why the confusing morass of paratextual material was moved to the end of the
volume.

The only other author that can be identified with any certainly is 'Hobbynoll',
Gabriel Harvey. Harvey's poem, 'And fare befall that *Faerie Queene* of thine',
indicates a much closer knowledge of Spenser's life and thought than Ralegh's two
self-serving poems do. Harvey concentrates on the theme of progress, of the poems as
a means to advance the poet, not to reflect on the monarch and the court. Having
accused Spenser of abandoning his flocks and the 'louely Rosalinde' (lines 7–8),
Harvey suggests that *The Faerie Queene*

Enfusing by those Bewties fiers deuyne,
Such high conceites into thy humble wits,
As raised hath poore pastors oaten reede,
From rusticke tunes, to chaunt heroique deedes. (lines 21–4)

Harvey, eager to ensure that readers remember that he and Spenser are still the
shepherds in the *Calender*, reflects on Spenser's literary progress, but also, in
describing the poet as a 'poore pastor' with an 'oaten reede', reminds the reader
that he was once a humble secretary to a bishop when he wrote his first poem, as well
as alluding to Spenser's practice of referring to poets as priests educating their flock in
his poetry.[118] While Ralegh seems to be using Spenser for his own ends, Harvey
shows Spenser what his poetry can do for him. Harvey also reminds the queen of her
duties. After noting that the poem sees the victory of the Red-Cross Knight in
fairyland, standing for Albion (England), Harvey states that Elizabeth in the guise of
the Faerie Queene 'shieldes her friends, and wares her mightie foes, | Yet still with
people, peace, and plenty flowes' (lines 29–30). The poem concludes with a warning
to Spenser to be careful of the court as a dangerously alluring chimera for a poet:

But (iolly Shephearde) though with pleasing style,
Thou feast the humour of the Courtly traine:
Let not conceipt they setled scene beguile,
Ne daunted be through enuy or disdaine.
Subiect thy dome to her Empyring spright,
From whence thy Muse, and al the world takes light. (lines 31–6)

We do not know when this poem was written, but the anxieties expressed coincide
exactly with those articulated in the first edition of *The Faerie Queene* and look
forward to the disillusioned mood and anti-court sentiments of *Colin Clout*. Harvey
warns Spenser to be wary of the attractions of the court, which will prove no friend to
him and which will impede his ability to write poetry. The queen's role is to protect
her subjects throughout her realm; the poet's, to ensure that he can write, which, for
a poet like Spenser, according to Harvey, almost certainly means working outside
the court. Again, the contrast to Ralegh's straightforward celebration of the queen
and courtly values is marked.[119] Ralegh claims that the poem can rise above the envy
of other courtiers; Harvey tells Spenser to avoid them.

The other four poems, by 'R. S.', 'H. B.', 'W. I.', and 'Ignoto', have not been
identified with any certainty—although 'R. S.' was probably Robert Salter—but it is
most likely that they are by other writers rather than courtiers.[120] They all praise the
serious value of the poem, H. B. making the obvious comparison to Virgil, W. I. an
equally obvious one to the *Iliad*, suggesting that just as Ulysses brought Achilles
(Thetis' son) from retirement into arms, so '*Spencer* was by *Sidneys* speeches
wonne'.[121] The comparison suggests that *The Faerie Queene* was seen in a military

context by some early readers, a poem that had grown out of an understanding of the need to inspire works of aggressive chivalric literature.[122] It also indicates that this contributor knew about Spenser and his claim to be connected to Sidney, rather than actually knowing Spenser. The poems urge the queen to reward the poet; Ignoto's last stanza describing how he will 'hang a garland at the dore', is perhaps an allusion to the garland of laurel presented to the laureate and a hint to the queen to present Spenser with a garland to wear.[123] The poems are relatively undistinguished, apart from Ralegh's and Harvey's, and these four, linked together by their classical themes, may have been assembled by Ponsonby rather than Spenser, as the Sidney comparison indicates.

The dedicatory sonnets pose even more of a puzzle.[124] There were initially ten on pp. 601–5, addressed to a miscellaneous variety of court patrons: Sir Christopher Hatton; Robert Devereux, second earl of Essex; Edward de Vere, earl of Oxford; Henry Percy, earl of Northumberland; Thomas Butler, tenth earl of Ormond; Charles, Lord Howard of Effingham; Arthur, Lord Grey de Wilton; Ralegh; Lady Elizabeth Carey; and the ladies at the court. But then after 'finis' and a list of errata, a list of seventeen sonnets was printed, the same ten with seven new ones addressed to Burghley; George Clifford, earl of Cumberland; Sir Henry Carey, Lord Hunsdon; Thomas Sackville, Lord Buckhurst; Sir Francis Walsingham; Sir John Norris; and Mary Sidney, countess of Pembroke. There is nothing that seems to connect this group of people, other than that they are all powerful and influential figures at court.[125] The sonnet addressed 'To all the gratious and beautifull Ladies in the Court' would appear to cement this conclusion, one that Nashe also reached. Spenser is likely to have known some of his addressees, including Grey and Norris, for whom he worked; the two with Sheffield connections, Ormond and Howard; probably Burghley; Mary Sidney, with whom he may have collaborated later; Sackville, who worked with Norton and so had a connection, albeit tenuous, to the Merchant Taylors' School; and, of course, Ralegh.[126] But being familiar with these courtiers is clearly not the principal issue here, especially if we recall that most works published in the late sixteenth century were dedicated to people of high status whom the author or publisher barely knew.[127] The problem is that there is no obvious logical order to the dedicatory sonnets, neither to the first list nor to the sonnets then added and mixed amongst the original poems. Important peers are included in the first list, but some obvious names, notably Burghley and Walsingham, are added later; the sonnet to Norris only appears in the second list; and sonnets to Irish nobles appear largely in the first list. It was unusual to have so many dedicatory sonnets to any work, especially after the poem itself, which might suggest that there was a plan that was later changed for some reason, perhaps connected to Ralegh, the only author to contribute two commendatory sonnets. A decision could have been made to move the prefatory material to an appendix and to expand it, perhaps related to Ralegh's impending fall, but we shall probably never know why the material appears as it does or whether Spenser played any part in what must have been, finally, a publisher's decision. It could not have been made at the last moment—like the inclusion of the second, expanded group of sonnets—as the page numbers would have to have been set first and the sheets printed and ordered with signatures. But, given the ways in which Spenser played with paratextual material before and after he published the first edition of *The Faerie Queene*, it is hard to believe that the plethora of appended sonnets did not serve some purpose, if only to remind potential patrons that they were less important than the poet.

To take one example: the sonnet to the court ladies, in its witty, knowing manner, flatters them but also reminds the ladies who is really in charge:

> The Chian Peincter, when he was requirde
> To pourtraict *Venus* in her perfect hew,
> To make his worke more absolute, desird
> Of all the fairest Maides to haue the vew.
> Much more me needs to draw the semblant trew,
> Of beauties Queene, the worlds sole wonderment,
> To sharpe my sence with sundry beauties vew,
> And steale from each some part of ornament.
> If all the world to seeke I ouerwent,
> A fairer crew yet no where could I see,
> Then that braue court doth to mine eie present,
> That the worlds pride seemes gathered there to bee.
> Of each a part I stole by cunning thefte:
> Forgiue it me faire Dames, sith lesse ye haue not lefte.

Spenser claims that in attempting to represent Elizabeth he is like the painter commissioned to paint Venus who thought that he ought to see the most beautiful women in the world first to make sure that he understood exactly what he had to produce. It is vital that Spenser follows the same course and observes the ladies of the court who are the fairest women alive. In doing so he steals a small part of each one and apologizes for having to do this. The sonnet fits into the familiar pattern of courtly banter and praise of ladies by poets, inevitably with a fairly clear agenda of the poet wanting something beyond the desire to simply serve without reward, i.e., advancement or sex.[128] But here, there is a barely disguised dissonance that sets it apart from lyrics written by courtiers who have a real chance of succeeding in the game.[129] Spenser casts himself as a court painter, perhaps even with a glance at the dreadful fate of the court painter in Sidney's *Arcadia*, mutilated and killed during a rebellion, when acting at the behest of the powerful for their benefit.[130] However, through his skill and ingenuity he is able to turn the tables and represent them as he wishes, taking away a part of them because they now become what he makes them through his representation. Art has the power to transform and go beyond nature, as Sidney argued in his *Apology for Poetry*.[131] The poet/painter is also cast as a voyeur, sizing up the ladies for his poem/picture, a freedom denied other courtiers, although they may, of course, like Ralegh, marry one of them. At one level the poem is a neat conceit, a compliment that is not quite what it seems to be, elegantly tossed off as a joke, as is appropriate for a dedicatory sonnet; at another, it points to the stratified and mercenary nature of an institution Spenser was to attack with such vehemence elsewhere.

Other poems have similar, deliberately constructed faultlines. The sonnet to Norris makes no mention of the court because Norris had little association with it, having spent his life as a soldier.[132] Instead, Spenser praises Norris's 'warlike prowesse and manly courage, | Tempred with reason and aduizement sage', qualities that are the very antithesis of those possessed by the ladies.[133] He then lists Norris's achievements, stating that his qualities 'Hath fild sad Belgicke with victorious spoile, | In *Fraunce* and *Ireland* left a famous gage, | And lately shakt the Lusitanian soile'.[134] This is an accurate description of Norris's career in the years immediately before 1590, mixing a representation of war as chivalric deeds, like those in the tiltyard with the mention of 'gage', and an awareness of the dreadful effects of war in referring to Belgium being now filled with 'victorious spoile'. The chief trading port of Belgium, Antwerp, had been the victim of a ferocious assault by the Spanish on 4 November 1576, 'the Sack of Antwerp'. This outrage had quickly become a European horror story and had helped sustain the 'Black Legend', which cast the Spanish as the evil villains of world affairs.[135] The horrific destruction of the city had been extensively described by George Gascoigne in *The Spoyle of Antwerpe* within a month of its occurrence; Norris served in the Low Countries in the late 1570s.[136]

The sonnet to Ormond might also be read as rather less celebratory than it seems on first reading, also placing the emphasis on the poet's ability to represent the dedicatee and fashion him as he saw fit. Spenser praises Ormond's mansion, undoubtedly referring to his house in Carrick-on-Suir not Kilkenny Castle, which Spenser must have visited on a number of occasions on official business, especially when travelling on to Dublin. He refers to it as a rare place where 'sweete Musses' can be harboured in an otherwise barbarous land, representing his poem as 'wilde fruit, which saluage soyl hath bred', and concluding with the exhortation that 'as the wasted soyl doth yield, | Receiue dear Lord in worth, the fruit of barren field'.[137] The ostensible message of the poem celebrates Ormond's success in spreading civility, the poet bringing him tribute from the otherwise barren land. It is indeed true that Ormond's stately home is a model of its kind, carefully designed to bring the values of the English country house to Ireland (Plate 28). The house has the earliest and longest long gallery in Ireland, one that matched those at contemporary houses in England.[138] It has impressive plasterwork throughout, the gallery decorated with emblems and icons of Elizabeth and Edward VI reminding visitors of the owner's loyalty to the English crown; rooms designed for public use; and was full of pictures, tapestries, and fine furniture.[139] But the sonnet is also written in the knowledge that the land in Munster was barren in part because of Ormond's actions: whether through killing large numbers of his fellow Irishmen on behalf of the crown, or as the chief obstacle to New English progress in the region, Spenser does not say.[140] The poem is studied in its ambiguity and works in negative as well as positive terms, listing what the province does not have before it singles Ormond's fortress as an exception to the rule, an outpost of civilization in an otherwise desolate landscape. Spenser witnessed the destruction in Munster and the poem is craftily evasive, leaving the reader to decide whether Ormond is part of the problem or the solution, helping to establish order amid chaos, or hoarding the land's goods for himself. When Spenser brings the poem to him, is it a form of praise for what he has done, or a rebuke from a besieged subject abandoned by those who should be protecting him?

The sonnet to Grey is more effusive, expressing the true gratitude of a loyal servant:

> Most Noble Lord the pillor of my life,
> And Patrone of my Muses pupillage,
> Through whose large bountie poured on me rife,
> In the first season of my feeble age,
> I now doe liue, bound yours by vassalage.[141]

Spenser makes it clear how much he feels he owes to Grey's patronage. He is not bringing him a poem out of the wilderness as tribute, but thanking him for supporting his writing when he was younger, further evidence that Spenser was at work on *The Faerie Queene* all the time he was in Ireland. Grey's support was material rather than intellectual and Spenser is thanking the former Lord Deputy for setting him on the road to obtaining Kilcolman, as acquiring his estate enabled him to be in London presenting his poem to the court.

If anything, the dedicatory sonnets show that Spenser's loyalties are easy to read: those who have helped him are fulsomely thanked; those who should help him are reminded of their duties; those who have not helped him are damned with faint, ambiguous praise. These are not the works of a poet eager for court patronage—which is not to say that Spenser might not have thought in these terms when he sailed over from Ireland—but someone with the confidence to tell others how things are and what to do.

The text of the poem itself raises few issues and it remained almost entirely the same for the second edition, indicating that the printing of the first edition was either overseen by Spenser, or that the text Ponsonby received was clear and clean.[142] *The*

Faerie Queene, like the *Calender*, is a unique poem, a new departure in English poetry that changed its course and nature. Everything about the poem is new: the combination of epic and romance; the mixture of high and popular cultural registers; its old-fashioned and archaic diction; the new stanza form (the Spenserian stanza), a complex Italianate development of the courtly rhyme royal, with a rhyme scheme, ababbcbcdd, consisting of eight pentameters followed by one alexandrine, that Spenser invented; its unfamiliar representation of St George; and the creation of Britomart, an Amazon in armour, as the culmination of the three virtues represented in the poem, Holiness, Temperance, and Chastity. It is at least arguable that *The Faerie Queene* was instrumental in establishing the pentameter as the dominant mode of English poetry.[143] The poem clearly challenged and confused many early readers, not least Ben Jonson, who remarked that '*Spencer*, in affecting the Ancients, writ no Language', an acknowledgement—albeit negative, as Jonson adds, 'Yet I would have him read for his matter; but as *Virgil* read *Ennius*'—of the innovative nature of the poem.[144] Ennius was a rough and unpolished poet who was admired by Virgil, even as he was irritated by his failings. Jonson cleverly turns Spenser's imitation of Virgil against him, casting himself as the chosen Augustan poet, and suggesting that reading Spenser was 'like sifting dung'.[145] A case can also be made that the style is a deliberate balance between high and low, creating a middle style between epic and pastoral, suited to a poet like Spenser, who was especially eager to appropriate and develop the georgic.[146] Other readers seem to have taken refuge in historical certainty as a means of making sense of the poem and establishing definite coordinates, their desire for security a sign of its unsettling complexity as much as a guide to how the poem was actually read.[147]

Given the torrent of work that Spenser published in the next six years it is clear that the first edition of *The Faerie Queene* had been chosen to secure his reputation as the most important English poet since Chaucer. While the production values of that book were not of the first order, Ponsonby evidently worked hard to ensure that subsequent works appeared in much more obviously impressive editions, showing that the plan succeeded, and that the significance of the poem was recognized.

We do not know how Spenser composed the poem, but it must have changed a great deal in more than a decade of interrupted composition. Harvey's description of the poem in 1580 as '*Hobgoblin* runne away with the Garland from *Apollo*' suggests that early versions were probably more romantic than epic in tone and style, based on Ariosto in particular.[148] The line suggests that sections of Books II and III were probably written before Book I, and the current shape of the edition took place when the first Book was written. This is an important point indicating that we need to think about how Book I relates to Books II and III, rather than how they fit into the pattern established by Book I, as has usually been the case. If Spenser did revise

254

The Faerie Queene a number of times, he would have needed the copious supplies of paper that his job as a secretary provided.[149]

Given Spenser's ambitions and desire to experiment it is likely that the Spenserian stanza was in place from the start. In appearance and form the poem owed much to Ariosto's *Orlando Furioso*, which was written in ottava rima (ababacbcc), as was Tasso's *Gerusalemme Liberata*, the two Italian models for the poem, along with Chaucer's *Troilus and Criseyde*, written in rhyme royal, a work that enjoyed a far higher reputation in the Renaissance than *The Canterbury Tales*.[150] Spenser worked from the Italian originals and it is a sign of his erudition and literary success that his poem then influenced Edward Fairfax's translation of Tasso (1600).[151] Combining elements of these poetic models was an extraordinarily ambitious feat, made gargantuan through Spenser's stated aim of also imitating the epics of Homer and Virgil, going beyond what any English poet had achieved so far—or, indeed, since.[152] Equally important was the *Cyropaedia* of Xenophon, singled out in the Letter to Ralegh, because it 'fashioned a gouernment such as might best be', a counterpart to fashioning a gentleman, and a contrast to Plato who had only 'formed a Commune welth such as might best be' (Spenser, *Faerie Queene*, pp. 715–16). The *Cyropaedia*, one of the most widely read books in Tudor England, told the life of Cyrus, the warrior king of Persia, whose exemplary restraint and temperance enabled him to conquer and maintain a vast empire.[153] The work, translated by the Catholic William Barker during Mary's reign, was reprinted in 1567, and was probably among the books that Spenser had in Ireland, as it had a tangible influence on *A View*.[154] It is odd, then, that *The Faerie Queene* has generally been read, even by many of its most able commentators, as if it were a rather straightforward panegyric of Elizabeth, perhaps because of the pension that the queen awarded him.[155] In fact, from the start, the poem advertises its confrontational nature, ensuring that readers have to understand that the poet controls the objects he represents, in pointed contrast to the claims of Ralegh's commendatory verse.

The Faerie Queene is dedicated to a virgin queen, but the thrust of its narrative is towards marriage and reproduction as the desirable goals of life. In this way, Spenser continues one of the most significant strains of the *Calender*'s multifaceted nature, forcefully reminding Elizabeth that she had failed to take her opportunity to marry, and had left her subjects facing an uncertain future.[156] The opening line of *The Faerie Queene* is a stark, even coarse, reminder of sexual desires and needs, something that undermines the pretensions and stance of the queen.[157] The first Book tells the story of the young St George, the Knight of Holiness, who needs to discover his true nature and so defeat the dragon who has imprisoned the parents of his bride-to-be, Una. The knight's ambiguous and multi-layered identity suggests that we need to see him as a Knight of the Garter, but also a pastoral figure who perhaps loses as well as gains through his transformation.[158] In the opening canto he is able to defeat a monster, 'Error', a victory that he complacently imagines marks a stage on his triumphal procession to victory. However, there are enough warning signs for the reader to realize that the knight is sorely mistaken and has little understanding of the nature of his quest. Before he kills Error, the knight holds her in a powerful grip so that

> Therewith she spewd out of her filthy maw
> A floud of poison horrible and blacke,
> Full of great lumpes of flesh and gobbets raw,
> Which stunck so vildly, that it forst him slacke
> His grasping hold, and from her turne him backe:
> Her vomit full of bookes and papers was,
> With loathly frogs and toades, which eyes did lacke,
> And creeping sought way in the weedy gras:
> Her filthy parbreake all the place defiled has. (I.i.20)

The carefully crafted description of Error's vomit centres around a particular dramatic irony: the monster reproduces books and papers amongst the collection of poisonous sludge, blind frogs and toads, and undigested lumps of flesh. Readers see this, but it soon becomes obvious that the Red-Cross Knight does not, and that he cannot distinguish between the different forms of Error's vomit. In other words, he cannot read. Even here, Spenser is reminding us that reading is a difficult process, and that texts are full of details that will lead the reader into error so that we have to be constantly on our guard.[159]

Within a few stanzas it becomes clear that we are one stage ahead of the knight when he fails to see the rather straightforward problems with the figure he encounters next:

> At length they chaunst to meet vpon the way
> An aged Sire, in long black weedes yclad,
> His feete all bare, his beard all hoarie gray,
> And by his belt his booke he hanging had;
> Sober he seemed, and very sagely sad,
> And to the ground his eyes were lowly bent,
> Simple in shew, and voyde of malice bad,
> And all the way he prayd, as he went,
> And often knockt his brest, as one that did repent. (29)

The description of Archimago is replete with clues that direct the reader's interpretation.[160] He looks like a monk or hermit, with his black robes, grey beard, and bare feet, which indicates that he belongs to a Catholic order. We do not know what book he carries. The initial assumption is that it is probably the Bible, but we learn a few stanzas later that he has a study full of magic books (36), so this may be one of them.

As the stanza progresses our suspicions, along with those of the travellers, are aroused. Archimago *seems* sober and sad, which implies that he may not be, and the appearance without the reality of sanctity is confirmed in the last two lines. Although he appears modest, he prays ostentatiously and repents in public, recalling the hypocritical publican in Luke 18:13 who 'would not lift up so much as his eyes to heauen, but smote his brest, saying, O God be mercifull to me a sinner'.[161] The stanza shows that the hermit 'parodies the contemplative life, the alternative to the active heroism' that the knight intends to demonstrate.[162] The Red-Cross Knight's grasp of reading is so feeble that he is not able to understand when he witnesses the signs of religion without the substance. He will have little chance with any complex allegory. Readers need to learn from his mistakes.

Of course, Archimago, the Catholic enchanter, is able to separate the Red-Cross Knight from Una with embarrassing ease, and by the start of the second canto the knight has been deluded into thinking that she has given herself to another knight—a devilish chimera that Archimago has conjured up from Hell—and, abandoning her in a fit of rage, the knight subsequently falls prey to the wiles of Duessa. The reader is in danger of falling into a trap like the knight, imagining that he or she is superior to the foolish protagonist. Archimago is a Catholic figure, but the sin that ensnares the Knight of Holiness is not obviously theological; it is lust. He is tormented and tempted by erotic dreams of Una—actually an incubus conjured up by Archimago—the night before he leaves her, an indication that his enemies, like the reader, know him better than he knows himself. But, even so, Spenser is challenging us to think about the more profound problems that he is representing in his narrative.

The story of the Red-Cross Knight's complicated quest raises a cluster of interrelated issues crucial for any one reader living in the British Isles in 1590. If the knight is a figure of Holiness, why is his downfall related to sex? What does this tell us about Holiness?[163] And, given that the knight is later revealed as St George, England's patron saint, how do he and Una represent the nation? Protestant attacks on the history of the pre-Reformation church were often heavily concentrated on the sexual repressiveness and hypocrisy of clerical celibacy, a fact of life that affected an enormous number of people when 'the medieval church was state', and, in a variety of guises, employed almost as many people as the secular authorities.[164] Monasteries in particular were attacked as dens of vice, notably in the widely available writings of John Bale, whose work Spenser would have known.[165] The problem was also recognized in more popular cultural literary forms. The jest book, *Merie Tales… made by Master Skelton*, which Spenser possessed and which informed his understanding of Colin Clout (the persona he adopted from the work of the Henrician poet), contains an especially relevant tale. Irritated by gossip about him, Skelton brandishes his child in front of his congregation while preaching a sermon on humanity after he has learned that they have complained to the bishop that he has been keeping a common-law wife. Skelton preaches on the text, 'Vos estis, vos estis—that is to say, You be, You be', and argues that because his child is not deformed then all is well and his flock ought to be more concerned that they are not cuckolded by him: 'If that you exalt yourself and cannot be contented that I have my wench still, some of you shall wear horns.'[166] Whether intentional or not, it is easy to see how this could be co-opted as a Protestant attack on papal celibacy, as the need to recognize human sexuality is central to the story. Priests, it was thought, could not resist the urge, whatever they had promised in their vows.

After the Reformation there was no longer a separate category of celibate clergy apart from the laity, which meant that marriage became the institution to which most people had to belong.[167] The key Reformation thinkers were quite clear about this and placed great emphasis on Paul's Letters to the Romans and Corinthians, especially his statement that if one could not abstain, 'it is better to marry then to burne' (1 Cor. 7:9).[168] In practical terms, for the few who could not live up to the ideal of celibacy, the most sacred state on earth was holy matrimony, a subject that Spenser represents enthusiastically throughout his poetry. The Red-Cross Knight seems to imagine his quest in traditional romance terms, as the defeat of dragons and rescuing of ladies: what he fails to realize is that he can pass such tests easily enough because the real problem is elsewhere, his relationship to women. The epic quest takes place in a romance, a subtle and complex literary development that places great demands on the reader.[169]

The Red-Cross Knight and Una are a spectacularly ill-matched couple. While the knight is out 'pricking on the plaine', Una is described as a chaste virgin, hardly an ideal basis for a marriage:

> A louely Ladie rode him faire beside,
> Vpon a lowly Asse more white then snow,
> Yet she much whiter, but the same did hide
> Vnder a vele, that wimpled was full low,
> And ouer all a blacke stole she did throw,
> As one that inly mourned: so was she sad,
> And heauie sat vpon her palfrey slow:
> Seemed in heart some hidden care she had,
> And by her in a line a milke white lambe she lad. (I.ii.4)

Una is associated with white, the colour of purity, being white herself, riding a white ass, and accompanied by a white lamb.[170] She wears a veil, described here as 'wimpled'. Wimple, as the *OED* entry indicates, has explicit associations with the church before the Reformation. It was often used by unmarried women to hide their hair and so preserve their modesty, as free-flowing hair was invariably a sign of available virginity.[171] But the word was more often associated with lifelong virgins, nuns, and the verb could mean to 'take the veil'. Most obviously, Spenser would have known Chaucer's Prioress, who wears a wimple.[172] The image of a modest woman in white riding an ass would seem in itself to suggest a saintly figure from the late medieval church, or, perhaps a pilgrim like Chaucer's Prioress.

The marriage of this couple is not necessarily doomed to failure, but it is clear that a great deal of work will have to be done before they can come to a mutual understanding. We should not really be surprised when, at the end of the first Book, they are betrothed but immediately separated, indicating that there is a way to go before they can be united.[173] In terms of his stated aim of 'fashioning a gentleman', Spenser shows that a gentleman needs to think about marriage in relation to Holiness in order to provide an answer to the question Aristotle poses of how one should live one's life.[174] On a related allegorical level Spenser makes a profound point about the progress of the Reformation in England, one in line with his comments about toleration in the *Calender*, probably influenced by his experiences as a youth in cosmopolitan London as well as the confessional and sectarian conflicts in Cambridge. The knight and Una, standing for England and its church, do not understand each other because they do not yet know who they are, how they should behave, and what the future will provide.[175] Spenser is showing how the Reformation was still a new concept in England, only sixty years old, a tiny part of the church's overall history of one and a half millennia. Those sixty years had proved complicated enough already, with Henry VIII's disquieting sequence of volte-faces, Edward's forward Protestantism followed by Mary's return to Catholicism, before Elizabeth's compromise church settlement.[176]

There had been waves of persecution that had seen many of Henry's principal counsellors executed; burnings and exiles under Mary, often carried out because of disagreements over the nature of the sacraments; and, in the wake of the threat of the Armada, a new wave of persecution of Catholics.[177] It was little wonder that ordinary people could not understand how they were supposed to worship, whether what they thought was tolerable or intolerable, orthodox doctrine or heresy, when their rulers could not decide and provide them with a consistent religious policy.[178] In representing the knight as an old-fashioned hero from a romance, and Una as a medieval religious figure, Spenser confronts his readers with the reality of the past as a living entity that has to be acknowledged and absorbed, not simply discarded.[179] The language of the poem is archaic for a reason, forcing readers to realize that the past still lives. *The Faerie Queene* is intensely hostile to the papacy and to the power of Spain, as the representations of Duessa as the Whore of Babylon, and, in the second edition, the Souldan, demonstrate.[180] But it is much more nuanced about the remnants of traditional religion in England than scholars once thought, in line with Spenser's earlier work.[181] The House of Holiness in which the knight is restored to physical and spiritual health in Book I, canto x, shows him passing through the traditional stages of penance, being 'exorcised, shriven, and ma[king] a confession of faith' before baptism in the Well of Life, all elements of traditional worship in England before the Reformation.[182]

The poem shows that there can be no premature hope for religious unity until the significance of the Reformation has been properly absorbed and thought through.[183] Book I sees the knight called away to serve Gloriana and our attention is turned to Guyon, the Knight of Temperance. Yet again, Spenser is making another confrontational narrative turn, showing the reader that Holiness—which is, after all, a term associated with purity, virginity, and the values of the traditional church—far from being the apex of Christian virtue, is a first stage only, something that has to be defined and fleshed out in the subsequent Books.[184] It is one of Spenser's sly ironies that he casts the hero of a book that sounds as if it will be about religious purity as a lusty bachelor. In attempting to deny his bodily needs and desires, Guyon only succeeds in provoking them. Temperance might seem to be a lesser virtue than Holiness, but in a world in which marriage is the logical choice for most people, regulating the passions is vital. Spenser's conception of Temperance conflates the Aristotelian distinction between Continence, the censorship of bodily pleasure, and Temperance, a more positive virtue that deals with the regulation, control, and proper functioning of the body.[185] Spenser carefully catalogues the forms of intemperance and incontinence that assault the individual, a panoply of weaknesses and vices that the Knight of Temperance resists with success. In the end, however, Guyon, the only one of the three protagonists of the first instalment of *The Faerie Queene* who does not have a marriage partner, is tempted by the sensual beauty on display in Acrasia's Bower and has no means of dealing with his response other than destroying everything:

> But all those pleasant bowres and Pallace braue,
> *Guyon* broke downe, with rigour pittilesse;
> Ne ought their goodly workmanship might saue
> Them from the tempest of his wrathfulnesse,
> But that their blisse he turn'd to balefulnesse:
> Their groues he feld, their gardins did deface,
> Their arbers spoyle, their Cabinets suppresse,
> Their banket houses burne, their buildings race,
> And of the fairest late, now made the fowlest place. (II.xii.83)

Guyon cannot control himself in the face of such sexual provocation and he lapses into fury, not the most serious form of intemperance, according to Aristotle, but a vice that renders reason impotent and so undermines a measured approach to life.[186] Moreover, as Anne Fogarty has argued, 'His act of regenerative violence akin to the military campaigns pursued by successive Elizabethan viceroys is designed to restore order and to obliterate the evil of this savage other world.'[187] Guyon's first victory was over the 'symbols of men's angry passions', Furor and Occasion and Pyrocles, so that in lapsing into anger himself, the wheel has come full circle and he has become what he was supposed to defeat, demonstrating the limitations of Temperance as a virtue.[188] Temperance is an advance on Holiness, which deludes the subject into thinking that he or she can simply ignore the dictates of the body, but it has to give way to the superior virtue, Chastity.

Book III provides a suitably provocative conclusion to the first edition of *The Faerie Queene*. We now follow the narrative of a female knight who is revealed as more morally alive and engaged than her two male counterparts. Nevertheless, Spenser uses the figure of Britomart to attack Elizabeth for what she had not done, marry and have children, in showing the female knight on a quest to find her husband, Artegall, the Knight of Justice, and so secure the future of her dynasty.[189] Guyon's destruction of the Bower can be read as an assault on the values of the Elizabethan court and the queen herself. Elizabeth, known for her love of costume, looks more like figures in Book I, Duessa and especially Lucifera, who lives in the gaudy House of Pride, than the triumphant figure in Book III who, as Merlin shows in his magic mirror, achieves everything that Elizabeth has not.[190] Britomart's quest pointedly exposes the failings of the real queen, serving as a negative commentary on the second half of her reign and, in doing this, Spenser neatly weaves the stands of the allegory together by the end of the Book. Britomart ensures the success of the Reformation, a feat that the virgin Elizabeth, according to Spenser, has failed to achieve. Britomart manages this through her political triumphs, but also her personal life and, in marrying Artegall, she fulfils the Reformation ideal of marriage, like Spenser himself. Elizabeth, as Gloriana, further hinders the course of the Reformation by prematurely recalling Artegall from the Salvage Island at the end of Book V, intervening in the fictional world to undermine proper government:

> But ere he [Artegall] could reforme it thoroughly,
> He through occasion called was away,
> To Faerie Court, that of necessity
> His course of Iustice he was forst to stay,
> And *Talus* to reuoke from the right way,
> In which he was that Realme for to redresse. (V.xii.27, lines 1–6)

The allegory is clear, especially as the next line informs us that the chief reason Artegall was recalled was envy of his success, illustrating the shifting cross-currents between the historical and fictional worlds of *The Faerie Queene*.[191] The true married queen who will lead England towards a glorious future has been usurped by an impostor who, like the Red-Cross Knight in the Wood of Error, has followed too many false paths. Had Elizabeth been chaste—rather than simply virginal (temperate)—like Britomart, Spenser argues, the future would probably look bright.

The first instalment of the poem ends with a complicated and disturbing image, later modified to ensure narrative continuity in the second edition, suggesting that this was a crux that was important to Spenser.[192] We witness Britomart staring at Scudamore and Amoret, the lovers she has helped to unite, as they combine to create a hermaphroditic form:

> Had ye them seene, ye would haue surely thought,
> That they had beene that faire *Hermaphrodite*,
> Which that rich *Romane* of white marble wrought,
> And in his costly Bath causd to bee site:
> So seemd those two, as growne together quite,
> That *Britomart* halfe enuying their blesse,
> Was much empassiond in her gentle sprite,
> And to her selfe oft wisht like happinesse,
> In vaine she wisht, that fate n'ould let her yet possesse. (III.xii.46; 1590 edn.)

This is a striking moment designed to stay in the memory, in line with the Horatian theory of poetry as *ut picture poesis* whereby 'the poet and the painter both think in visual images which the one expresses in poetry, the other in pictures'.[193] No source for the description of the statue has ever been identified—assuming there is one—so we cannot know whether what the rich Roman saw from his bath was high art or base pornography. Probably, that is the point. We then follow Britomart's mixture of jealousy (the description, quite deliberately, has her as 'half enuying' their joy), passion (inspired by great art or provoking a desire for intercourse?), and isolation (wishing that she could be part of a similar fusion). Spenser shows the reader the sort of emotions that a queen should have, the excitement not just at her much antici-pated future union, but also the prospect of securing her nation's future. In framing this concluding vision, Spenser brings us back full circle to the issues raised at the start of the Book I, showing that the future lay in thinking carefully and properly about sex.

Perhaps the key word in the stanza is the penultimate 'yet'. Britomart will have her day, even though it does not happen in the extant poem. She is a young, passionate woman who is on a quest that will lead her eventually to marriage. Seeing Amoret and Scudamore is simply part of the process of growing up, learning the mechanics of love-making as part-inspiration, part-horror.[194] Spenser pointedly reuses this scene in *Epithalamion*, a sign of just how important this image of the voyeur and the hermaphrodite was for him.[195] In the later poem he describes Cynthia/ Elizabeth's failed love for 'the Latmian shephard'. But instead of Britomart staring at Amoret and Scudamore with a mixture of guilt and excitement, we have the unedifying scene of Cynthia, the goddess of chastity, and a form of Elizabeth throughout Spenser's works, peeping through the window at Edmund and his

Elizabeth. Read one way this might seem innocent enough: the newly-weds live in Ireland and so require particular protection from their monarch and would surely welcome the knowledge that she will always be around to ensure their safety. Diana/Cynthia was chaste herself, but was the goddess of fertility and so was often asked to bless newly-weds with children. Read another way, Spenser draws attention to what the queen has missed and what she has not done, a somewhat cruel repetition of something that had appeared obvious to him in 1590.[196]

Even so, Spenser's sympathies may be more complicated than this account implies. At the start of *The Faerie Queene*, Book III, canto vi, the epicentre of the poem, as numerological studies have pointed out, Spenser gives us a description of a painless birth granted to Chrysogonee, the virginal nymph and mother of the twins, Amoret and Belphoebe:

> Her berth was of the wombe of Morning dew,
> And her conception of the ioyous Prime,
> And all her whole creation did her shew
> Pure and vnspotted from all loathly crime,
> That is ingenerate in fleshly slime.
> So was this virgin borne, so was she bred,
> So was she trayned vp from time to time,
> In all chast vertue, and true bounti-hed
> Till to her dew perfection she was ripened. (III.vi.3)[197]

The stanza is an affectionate and moving moment in the poem that seems to recognize the pains and perils that women go through when giving birth. Like Milton, who referred to this particular passage in Spenser when he was writing about childbirth, Spenser may have been indifferent to women's oppression but extremely sensitive to their suffering.[198] The Garden of Adonis serves a key function in Book III, the book of chastity (married sexuality). As the later cantos demonstrate, especially when Amoret is trapped in the Castle of Busiraine, adult sexuality is a dangerous and very painful game, albeit sometimes comically so. The Garden of Adonis is a fantasy within fairyland, a place where, for a brief moment, sexuality is suspended, Nature is fecund and reproduces without problem. It is, as the name implies, unstable and doomed, just as Venus' boy will be painfully taken from her before he has a chance to reach maturity.

Spenser shows that he was well aware that the real victims of sexual behaviour were often women. The most dangerous years for women were those of sexual maturity and childbirth when a huge percentage of women died. As Sara Mendelson and Patricia Crawford point out, 'During every pregnancy, each woman feared her own death.'[199] In one of the few extant sources recording the experience of early modern childbirth, Revd Ralph Josselin records just how much his wife suffered during her pregnancies and how frightened she was as her labour approached.[200] Women also had a long time to contemplate the forthcoming ordeal, increasing their anxiety, as most would have witnessed the death of other women through childbirth and seen many have their bodies distorted or deformed through the process.[201] It is little wonder that the successful deliverance of mother and baby after childbirth was an important religious event, celebrated by the ritual of churching, as women were joyfully welcomed back into the community.[202] If women survived these trying times, they had a good chance of living to a ripe age; many did not, as women ran 'a cumulative risk of dying in childbed of 6 to 7 per cent during their procreative careers'.[203] Spenser would appear to recognize this through his description of the lucky escape of Chrysogenee.

Is the poem telling us what happened to Machabyas Spenser? We can never be sure, of course, but Machabyas was probably dead before this point, as *Daphnaïda*, published the year after the first edition of *The Faerie Queene*, suggests.[204] As she died before the age of 30 she would have still been fertile and it is possible that the lack of children produced by the Spensers indicates a health problem as well as protracted periods of separation (or that she breastfed their children).[205] In normal circumstances couples would have produced about one child a year, but there might have been a number of stillbirths or cases of infant mortality. It seems likely that the tale of Chrysogenee bears some relationship to life and death in the Spenser household, a reminder that, for many, human reproduction came at a cost as well as bringing joy. Perhaps Spenser recognized that the queen's decision not to have children was reasonable, even if he saw it as a dereliction of her duty as queen.

8

1591

SPENSER'S next published work, the miscellaneous volume *Complaints*, caused a major international scandal in the English-speaking world. As a result it was 'called in', i.e., copies were seized and removed from circulation because the work was judged to be seditious.[1] A number of manuscript copies of complete or extracts from poems exist, testifying to the popularity of the volume, and indicating that readers were eager to preserve what they could of the prohibited text.[2] Some may have been produced for sale to fill a need due to the lack of a printed copy.[3] Spenser's sense of timing was either very good or very bad. Ponsonby had entered *Complaints* into the Stationers' Register on 29 December and Spenser had been awarded his pension on 25 February.[4] The volume went on sale at some point before 19 March 1591 when H. Cocke—quite possibly Henry Cocke, a figure loosely associated with the Sidneys—bought a copy for 2*s.* 6*d*.[5] The first payment of Spenser's pension was collected on Lady Day, 25 March, by Edward Blunt, an employee of Ponsonby's, which seems to indicate that Spenser had returned to Ireland by then, no doubt having some idea that his collection was likely to cause a stir when it appeared.[6]

All contemporary commentators agree that the basis for the decision was the inclusion of *Prosopopoia, or Mother Hubberds Tale*, a beast fable that satirized the court. Spenser's poem tells the story of an Ape and a Fox who exploit and abuse their fellow countrymen, eventually usurping the rightful monarch, a Lion, with the Ape assuming the regal position advised by the cunning Fox, the real power behind the throne. The Catholic exile Richard Verstegan [Rowland] (*c*.1548–1640) cited *Mother Hubberds Tale* as evidence of the evil designs of Lord Burghley in his diagnosis of the problems that beset England in the early 1590s:

And because no man dare frame an endytement against him [Burghley], I will here omit many other articles of highe treason, but yf any will vndertake to iustifie his actions in his course of gouernment, let him know, that there is sufficient matter of reply reserued for him, which is not extracted out of *Mother Hubberds* tale, of the false fox and his crooked cubbes, but it is to be vtered in plaine profe, and shal lay open to the world, his birth, his lyf, and perhaps his death, seing his detestable actions are such, as do aske vengeance of heauen and earth.[7]

Verstegan, the most important English Catholic historian of the period, was making the familiar case that Burghley was Elizabeth's chief anti-Catholic conspirator, whose underhand dealings had been responsible for the execution of Mary Stuart, against the queen's wishes, and who took every opportunity to persecute Catholics.[8] His statement is clear in singling out Spenser's poem as the chief source of information against Burghley's nefarious dealings, supplemented by his claim that he has other, corroborating evidence. Verstegan's book became known as 'Burghley's Commonwealth', after the spectacular success of the earlier Catholic libel, *Leicester's Commonwealth*, a work Spenser undoubtedly knew well.[9]

Spenser's fellow pupil at the Merchant Taylors' School, the Catholic Thomas Lodge, made extensive use of Spenser's poem in his scathing dialogue outlining the ills currently infecting the world, *Catharos, Diogenes in his Singularitie* (1591).[10] Lodge was just one among a considerable Catholic readership who enjoyed the scandal of Spenser's poem. The long-suffering loyal Catholic appellant Sir Thomas Tresham (1543–1605), who lived at Rushton, Northamptonshire, wrote a sizeable letter to an unnamed friend, perhaps one who lived abroad, on 19 March 1591, the same day that Henry Cocke bought his copy of the *Complaints*.[11] Tresham, who built the unusual Rushton Triangular Lodge in 1593 to celebrate his release from prison and to affirm his faith, knew of, but appears not to have known, Spenser, although he did know the Spencers of Althorp who lived about eighteen miles south-west of his estate.[12] Had he ever seen it, Rushton Lodge would certainly have appealed to Spenser with its complex use of numerological patterns and sequences, as well as the punning relationship between Tresham and triangle.[13] Tresham recounts his persecution at the hands of Burghley, before describing at some length the unfortunate impact of Spenser's poem:

Tales, I meane no Tayles, are nowe on the sodden in greate request; especiallie mother Hubburds tale, dedicated to the wydowe Lady Compton. The whole discourse of that ould weoman ys (as I heare reported) to showe by what chaunce the apes did loose their tayles. Thowghe this be a iest, yet is itt taken in suche earnest, that the booke is by Superior awthoritie called in; and nott to be had for anie money. Where ytt was att the first sould for vi d. it is nowe of redie money a Crowne. The bookebynders have allreadie gotten by the vent of this booke, more then al the Apes in Parys garding is worthe. I did never see ytt myselfe; neither would I read ytt nowe, yf I might have ytt, becawse yt is forbidden. Menne, I wene, are sett on maddinge, and madder then marche hares, that thus desire to be resolved howe apes did first forgoe their tayls: principallie when the discourse thereof proceedeth from mother Hubber that ould fooll.[14]

Tresham's rather gleefully punning account, notably the passage on mad March hares, suggests that he may have more idea either of the contents of the tale or Spenser's poetic style than he is admitting to his correspondent—especially if we note that the ending of the poem sees the Ape lose his tail, 'quight | Cut off' by the awakened Lion.[15] Tresham's comments also relish the discomfort that the poem has caused Burghley by, as he sees it, exposing his crafty dealings, as well as demonstrating that nothing sold a work like scandal. Authors and booksellers would clearly push the boundaries of what was acceptable to stimulate and feed the demands of readers, as Ponsonby and Spenser had done here, only for their efforts to exceed expectations rather spectacularly. What looked like a clever jest by March hares, eager to cock a snook at the authorities, has ended in them caught up in a beast fable they had not anticipated.

Tresham also shows that he has done some homework on Spenser and has been eager to find out who he was, a further indication of the importance that Spenser was starting to assume in public life after 1590:

He that writt this discourse is a Cantabrigian and of the blood of the Spencers. Yt is nott yett a yeare since he writt his booke in the prayse of the Quene, which he entitled the Fayrie Quene, and which was so well liked, that her ma:tie gave him ane hundred marks pencion for the of the Exchequer: and so clerklie was yt penned, that he beareth the name of a Poett Laurell. Butt nowe in medlinge with his paes tayle he is gott into Ireland: also in hazard to loose his foresaid annuall reward: and fynalie hereby prove himselfe a Poett Lorrell.[16]

Most of what Tresham states is accurate enough, so it is possible that there is some substance in his judgement that Spenser might have been in danger of losing his pension (which Tresham overestimates). Tresham provides testimony that Spenser was unofficially regarded as the poet laureate and confirms that the pension was awarded because of *The Faerie Queene* (or, at least, was assumed to have been). What is also significant is that Tresham knows that Spenser went to Cambridge University and claimed to be related to the Spencers of Althorp. He either learned these facts from his contacts, neighbours, or from attending court, or, despite his disclaimer, he had read Spenser's works.

The first place in which Spenser claims that he has a real connection to the Spencers of Althorp is in the dedicatory letter to *The Teares of the Muses*, the second of the *Complaints*, in which he states that, as well as the 'particular bounties' that she [Lady Strange] and her spouse bestow, they have 'priuate bands of affinitie' to the poet.[17] Perhaps Tresham had just read the dedication to Alice Spenser, Lady Strange, wife of Ferdinando Stanley, Lord Strange. The Stanley family were probably secret Catholics like Tresham—in itself further evidence of the wide-ranging religious connections of Spenser—and Ferdinando was approached by plotters in 1593 urging him to press his claim to the throne through Mary Brandon, the younger sister of Henry VIII. Tresham was clearly interested in the case primarily for religious reasons, hardly a surprise given his faith and his suffering at the hands of the authorities.

Even Gabriel Harvey appears to have been shocked by *Mother Hubberds Tale*, and he obviously felt that Spenser had gone too far with his criticisms of the good and the great this time. Writing against the fashion for excessive satirical raillery, a trend Spenser's poem may have helped to develop, Harvey notes that 'Mother Hubbard, in heat of choller, forgetting the pure sanguine of her sweete Feary Queene, wilfully ouer-shott her malcontented selfe', an analysis that corroborates Tresham's judgement of Spenser's transformation from poet laureate to poet lorrell (fool).[18] John Weever, in his epigram on Spenser's death and achievements published in 1599, concentrates on this unfortunate aspect of his literary career, not his poetic achievements, showing that the scandal certainly lingered:

> *Spencer* is ruin'd, of our latter time
> The fairest ruine, Faëries foulest want:
> Then his *Time-ruines* did our ruine show,
> Which by his ruine we vntimely know:
> *Spencer* therfore thy *Ruines* were cal'd in,
> Too soone to sorrow least we should begin.[19]

Accordingly, the poem spawned a host of imitations produced up to the Civil War, and determined the form of the satirical beast fable in English, a genre that from now on was characterized as distinctly Spenserian.[20]

It is easy to see why *Mother Hubberds Tale* caused such offence.[21] Evidence suggests that readers were eager to buy the poem on its own for a high price years after it was published, indicating that the work generated considerable interest because of its scandalous reputation.[22] The poem's aggressive and confrontational message must have been obvious to far less educated and sophisticated readers than Verstegan, Tresham, and Harvey. The Fox and the Ape, 'disliking of their euill | And hard estate' (lines 46–7), decide to better their fortunes through foul means and so travel upwards through society in a series of four episodes. They disguise themselves as a soldier (the Ape) and his servant (the Fox), persuading a gullible husbandman to trust them to guard his sheep, which, of course, enables them to consume most of the flock (lines 45–342). Leaving before they are caught they then disguise themselves as clergymen and take advice from a corrupt and incompetent priest, who tells them how to obtain ecclesiastical livings. They duly exploit their parishioners when they then assume the identities of a priest (the Ape) and a parish clerk (the Fox) (lines 353–574). Again leaving just before an official visitation, they then become courtiers, the Ape disguising himself as a gentlemen, the Fox as his servant, their natural dishonesty and sly craft serving them well, until even the courtiers find their behaviour too reprehensible to tolerate (lines 581–942). Finally, they wander into the forest, coming across a sleeping lion, steal his pelt, along with his crown and sceptre, which the Ape wears (after a brief dispute) and they rule the beasts as selfishly as they have done so far, until the gods lose patience and they are duly exposed and punished (lines 949–1384).[23]

The poem's satire is comprehensive and owes much to the medieval estates' satire of Chaucer's *Canterbury Tales*, as well as such medieval beast fables as *Renard the Fox*, and the well-established tradition of complaint, combining an attack on individual abuses with a more general understanding of the ills that have consumed contemporary English society.[24] In many obvious ways the poem seems to predict the vogue for satire in the late 1590s, which eventually led to the Bishops' Ban of 1599.[25] Yet again, Spenser is demonstrating that he is ahead of his contemporaries and that what he produced was imitated and adapted by other poets. Harvey would seem to be chiding Spenser for writing in a style that left him open to becoming embroiled in the aggressive literary conflicts of the 1590s that Harvey so bitterly resented.[26] Certainly the opening lines, with their description of the dog days of August, seem to look back to the astrological disputes of 1583 involving the Harvey brothers, John and Richard, when Jupiter and Saturn were in alignment:

> It was the month, in which the righteous Maide [Astrea, goddess of justice],
> That for the disdaine of sinfull worlds vpbraide,
> Fled back to heauen, whence she was first conceiued,
> Into her siluer bowre the Sunne receiued;
> And the hot *Syrian* Dog [the dog star] on him awaiting,
> After the chafed Lyons cruell bayting,
> Corrupted had th'ayre with his noisome breath,
> And powr'd on th'earth plague, pestilence and death. (lines 1–8)

Such apparently inconsequential lines may well have irritated Harvey, as they refer in a light-hearted, even dismissive, manner back to debates that his immediate family had taken seriously and that had indeed predicted plague, pestilence, and death as a prelude to the apocalypse. Furthermore, both John and Richard had suffered open ridicule for their false, incautious predictions.[27] As a result, John had subsequently written a treatise, dated 1587 but not published until 1598, his longest work by far, attacking false predictions and urging a more cautious approach to astrology. This work contained a short poem listing the attributes of beasts, facetiously claiming that they had more ability to predict the future than men did:

The Foxe in craftie wit exceedeth most men:
A Dog in smelling hath not his peere:
To foresight of weather if you looke then
Many beasts excell, as appeereth cleere.
The wittines of Elephants doth letters attaine:

But what cunning doth there in the Bee remaine?
The Emmet foreseeing the hardnes of winter,
Prouideth vittailes in the time of Sommer.
The Nightingall, the Linnet, the Thrush, the Larke,
In musicall harmonie passe many a clarke.
The Hedgehog of Astronomy seemeth to know,
And stoppeth his caue where the winde doth blow.
The Spider in weauing such Art doth shew,
None can him amend, or folow I trow.
When a house will fall, the Mice right quicke
Flee thence before: who can do the like.[28]

John concluded that often there were scientific ways of predicting some aspects of the future, but that much had to be trusted to the judgement of God. Gabriel was especially fond of John, referring to him often as a talented younger brother whose achievements would outshine his own if he were taught properly in his *Letters* to Spenser and he lamented his premature death in *Pierces Supererogation*.[29]

However, the real scandal of Spenser's poem must have been its aggressive attack on Burghley as the Fox, the man who was thought to secretly rule England in the interests of the small cabal that he controlled, as it was known to contemporaries, the *regnum Cecilianum*.[30] Spenser's poem played no small role in blackening Burghley's name for contemporaries and future generations of readers.[31] When the pair rule the animal kingdom, the Ape is represented as a tyrant:

No care of iustice, nor no rule of reason,
No temperance, nor no regard of season
Did thenceforth euer enter in his minde,
But cruelties, the signe of currish kinde,
And sdeignfull pride, and wilful arrogaunce. (lines 1131–5)

Readers would have recognized the caricature of a ruler who had no legitimate right to govern; who had no intention of obeying the law; who used the country only to satisfy his own appetites; and who enjoyed abusing the subjects he was supposed to rule with proper love, care, and attention.[32] The Fox is equally culpable, and his behaviour is highlighted in an extensive analysis:

But the false Foxe most kindly plaid his part:
For whatsoeuer mother wit, or arte
Could worke, he put in proofe: no practise slie,
No counterpoint of cunning policie,
No reach, no breach, that might him profit bring,
But he the same did to his purpose wring.
Nought suffred he the Ape to giue or graunt,
But through his hand must passé the Fiant.
All offices, all leases by him lept,
And of the al whatso he likte, he kept.
Iustice he solde iniustice for to buy,
And for to purchase for his progeny.
Ill might it prosper, that ill gotten was,
But so he got it, little did he pas.
He fed his cubs with fat of all the soyle,
And with the sweete of others sweating toyle,
He crammed them with crumbs of Benefices,
And fild their mouthes with meeds of malifices,
He cloathed them with all colours saue white,
And loded them with lordships and with might,
So much as they were able well to beare,
That with the weight their backs nigh broken were. (lines 1137–58)

Burghey's son, Robert (1563–1612), was a hunchback, heavily promoted by his father and widely perceived to have benefited from his protection and patronage.[33] Spenser's description of the Fox's cubs receiving so many gifts that their backs were almost broken must be a reference to Robert's congenital deformity. Certainly, Verstegan made the connection when he referred to 'the false fox [a description used in the poem] and his crooked cubs'. Moreover, it was only after Robert's death in 1611 that *Mother Hubberds Tale* appeared in some copies of Matthew Lownes's first folio of Spenser's *Works*, suggesting that the poem could now be republished as the main obstacle to its reproduction had been removed.[34] One of the two copies of the folio in Cambridge University Library has the poem inserted after the *Calender*. This was clearly a late inclusion, as the edition was made up from Lownes's existing unbound stock of Spenser's poetry, either a decision made by the publisher or, more likely, at the purchaser's request.[35] The other does not.[36] Furthermore, it is worth noting that Richard Niccols's imitation of Spenser's beast fable, *The Begger's Ape*, which also alludes to Robert's deformity, was written in *c.*1607, but not published until 1627, providing further evidence that the Cecil family bitterly resented Spenser's satire.[37]

Spenser had written satire before, and had made numerous biting topical references in the *Calender* and *Faerie Queene*, and the Harvey–Spenser *Letters* were hardly devoid of passing hits aimed at the high and mighty, which may have cost the authors dear. But *Mother Hubberds Tale* was unusually direct in its bilious attacks on Burghley as well as the corrupt court where few 'For vertues bare regard aduanced bee, I But either for some gainfull benefit, I Or that they may for their owne turnes be fit' (lines 638–40). Of course, this lesson applies to Burghley and his son more than anyone else. The representation of Burghley as a self-seeking politician who has torn apart the fabric of English social life simply for his own benefit chimes uncomfortably accurately with Catholic attacks on Burghley, one reason why two Catholic readers refer to the poem and why they were so astonished that a poet who had been awarded a pension by the queen should appear to share their vision of Elizabeth's most trusted politician.[38] It is not beyond the bounds of possibility that Verstegan actually made use of Spenser's poem when writing *A Declaration of the True Causes of the Great Troubles*, claiming that Burghley had overthrown traditional social hierarchies (p. 10); collaborated with other Protestants to pervert religion so that it depended simply on 'the will of their Prince' (p. 12); spoiled churches (p. 22); ignored national and international laws when it suited him (p. 27); undermined the legitimate rights of princes and peers (p. 38); paid more attention to the doctrines of Machiavelli than scripture and the teachings of the true church (p. 53); and secured his own domination of the English court (p. 63).[39]

The question remains why Spenser launched this assault on Burghley, one that has determined our biographical understanding of his place in the courtly hierarchy.[40] The prefatory letter to the *Complaints*, written by Ponsonby, argues that he was responsible for the volume, not Spenser:

SINCE my late setting foorth of the *Faerie Queene*, finding that it hath found a fauourable passage amongst you; I haue sithence endeeuoured by all good meanes (for the better encrease and accomplishment of your delights,) to get into my handes such smale Poemes of the same Authors; as I heard were disperst abroad in sundrie hands, and not easie to bee come by, by himselfe; some of them hauing bene diuerslie imbeziled and purloyed from him, since his departure ouer the Sea.[41]

Ponsonby then claims that he gathered these works together, including as much as he could find, but ends with a plea to the reader to help him secure copies of a number of works that are still missing: some new works, such as a translation of *Ecclesiastes* and *The hell of louers*, others, such as *The Dying Pelican*, were referred to earlier in the Harvey–Spenser *Letters*. Parts of these works, which were probably collections as well as individual poems, undoubtedly appeared in various locations as Spenser recycled and rethought much of his early verse, but some were never published and remain undiscovered.[42] Interestingly enough, Ponsonby claims that what unites one diverse group of poems, '*Ecclesiastes*, and *Canticum canticorum* translated, *A senights slumber*, *The hell of lovers*, his *Purgatorie*', is that they are 'all dedicated to Ladies', and may have been intended as a single volume, perhaps a sly attempt to build up a market for his client, who certainly targeted female patrons later.

Ponsonby was surely not spreading false rumours, given the information that can be gleaned from Spenser's paratexts elsewhere, and the games that Spenser himself plays with his texts. But, equally, it is not likely that this is the whole truth, especially given the number of dedicatory letters written by Spenser designed to accompany printed texts.[43] In either case *Complaints* would stand out as an anomaly. The dedications prefacing each poem, to Mary Sidney, countess of Pembroke (*Ruines of Time*); Lady Strange (*Teares of the Muses*); Leicester (deceased) (*Virgils Gnat*); Lady Compton and Monteagle (*Mother Hubberds Tale*); and Elizabeth Spencer, Lady Carey (*Muiopotmos*)—all, apart from Leicester, prominent women patrons, three daughters of Sir John Spencer of Althorp, the other Sir Philip's Sidney's sister and collaborator—do not read as if they were intended for private publication, but public declarations of the poet's affiliations and circle. The opening poem, *The Ruines of Time*, writes with deliberate paradox, acknowledging the '*worlds Ruines*', while the work is 'speciallie intended to the renowning of that noble race' from which Mary and Philip 'sprong'.[44] The same process of recovering an ancient lineage was especially important for the great families of early modern England, in particular the Spenser family, who were acutely conscious of their origins as sheep farmers, and the second poem, *The Teares of the Muses*, advertises Spenser's role as the poet and historian of his surname.[45]

The volume also shows signs that it was carefully revised for the press: sections of *Mother Hubberds Tale* refer back to the Alençon match and the politics of 1579–80 (which is why it was claimed, without any corroborating evidence, that the poem probably circulated in manuscript in 1580), suggesting that, like *The Faerie Queene* and *Colin Clout*, it had a long gestation period before it appeared in printed form; *The Ruines of Time* probably makes use of the lost early work *Stemmata Dudleiana* and perhaps some passages from *Dreams*; and the sonnets in *The Visions of Bellay* and *Visions of Petrarch*, the second of which had the subtitle 'formerly translated', are revisions of the sonnets first published in van der Noot's *Theatre for Worldlings*, transformed from blank verse to English sonnets.[46] It is hard to imagine that *Complaints* was thrown together by an unscrupulous printer searching for quick profits, as the volume bears all the signs of having been carefully produced to follow the success of the first edition of *The Faerie Queene*, a work that held out the promise of a sequel, encouraging the eager reader to expect more before too long.[47] Although some copies exist that suggest that readers selected which poems they wanted to preserve, such as the copy in Cambridge University Library which contains only *Muiopotmos* and the three *Visions*,[48] there are nevertheless clear underlying themes and connections that can be made between many of the poems, especially the three beast fables, *Virgils Gnat*, *Mother Hubberds Tale*, and *Muiopotmos*.[49] *Complaints* looks as if it was designed to accompany *Colin Clout* and *Daphnaïda*, flooding the literary marketplace with Spenser's achievements after a ten-year gap in the wake of *The Faerie Queene*. The responses to *Mother Hubberds Tale* indicate that there was clearly an appetite for Spenser's work, which either already existed or was cleverly created by poet and publisher at the start of the decade.

Even so, Ponsonby's prefatory letter seems designed to protect the author from the possible malign attention of the authorities, perhaps with the example of Stubbes's *Gaping Gulf* in mind, the work published alongside the *Calender*, which had seen the author mutilated and the publisher, Singleton, pardoned only at the last minute.[50] It is hard to judge why Spenser wished to attack Burghley so ferociously. Burghley had, after all, been close to Sir Thomas Smith and so was hardly the enemy of Harvey and Spenser—which might explain Harvey's reaction to *Mother Hubberds Tale*. Perhaps Spenser was genuinely shocked by what he saw at court, but this would seem an astonishingly naive reaction, as there was a long history of criticizing court behaviour, notably in John Skelton's satire *The Bouge of Court* reproduced in *Pithy, Pleasaunt and Profitable Workes of Maister Skelton* (1568), a volume Spenser must have read and almost certainly possessed, given the impact that Skelton had on his poetry. Moreover, Spenser had been the recipient of considerable favours from his employers in Ireland, receiving well-paid work, sinecures, and land in ways that closely resembled the practices for which he excoriated Burghley.

Perhaps Spenser objected to an aspect of Burghley's policies in Ireland. More likely, there was a more personal reason; perhaps Spenser had hoped for preferment when he returned to court and had found Burghley an obstacle; perhaps Burghley had objected to the ending of the 1590 *Faerie Queene*, seeing an allusion to the disastrous marriage of his daughter, Anne, to Edward de Vere, earl of Oxford, which would explain the reference to the 'rugged forehead' who has taken exception to his 'looser rhymes . . . | For praising loue . . . | And magnifying louers debate' (*FQ* IV, proem, i, lines 1–5). In his dedicatory sonnet to Oxford, Spenser writes that he has represented the earl allegorically in the poem: 'Vnder a shady vele is therein writ, | And eke thine owne long liuing memory' (lines 7–8).[51] It is possible that Spenser was connected to Oxford through his own links to Thomas Watson, a poet who makes much of his admiration for Spenser in his poetry.[52] If the dedicatory sonnet does indicate a substantial link to Oxford, then the story of Amoret and Scudamore could be read as a version—with a happy ending that was conspicuously absent in real life—of the marriage between Anne Cecil and Edward de Vere.[53] Given the explosive nature of this union and its far-reaching consequences for many important figures at the court, Spenser was perhaps guilty of—yet again—overstepping the mark, supporting the man who had caused Burghley's family more misery than anyone else alive.

Even so, the evidence is hardly overwhelming and we shall probably never know for certain why Spenser singled out Burghley as the representative of all that was wrong with court life. Nevertheless, Spenser's hostility to Elizabeth's chief minister is conspicuously on display in the *Complaints*. In *The Ruines of Time* Spenser praises the lost glory of Leicester, whose name will live on through Spenser's verse:

> Thy Lord [Leicester] shall neuer die, the whiles this verse
> Shall liue, and surely it shall liue for euer:
> For euer it shall liue, and shall rehearse
> His worthie praise, and vertues dying neuer,
> Though death his soule doo from his bodie seuer.
> And thou thy selfe herein shalt also liue;
> Such grace the heauens doo my verses giue.[54]

Leicester stands as a pointed contrast to Burghley as Spenser weighs the heroic figures of yesteryear against the petty-minded politicians of today. Lamenting the death of Walsingham (Meliboe), the narrator comments that 'his wisedome is disprooued quite; | For he that now welds all things at his will, | Scorns th'one and th'other in his deeper skill' (lines 446–8).

The comment indicates that Spenser was probably not party to the machinations at court, as Burghley and Walsingham were often allies in political matters and appear to have got on reasonably well personally, although there were inevitable differences of opinion and policy at fraught moments.[55] More significant is the fact that the poem itself is shrouded in layers of irony, which suggest that *Complaints* has a far more sardonic attitude towards Leicester than appears on a first reading and places heavy emphasis on the role of the poet as the real historian, in line with the Letter to Ralegh appended to *The Faerie Queene*. Leicester may well be preferable to Burghley but that might only be because he is dead and so the fit subject of poetry. The narrator, Verlame, the female spirit of Verulamium, originally a British town which was then colonized by the Romans and which became St Albans, chides Spenser in his guise as Colin Clout for failing to praise Leicester as he should have done:

> Ne doth his *Colin*, carelesse *Colin Cloute*,
> Care now his idle bagpipe vp to raise,
> Ne tell his sorrow to the listening rout
> Of shepherd groomes, which wont his songs to praise:
> Praise who so list, yet I will him dispraise,
> Vntill he quite him of this guiltie blame:
> Wake shepheardes boy, at length awake for shame. (lines 225–31)

The lethargy that irritates Verlame is a reference to the inactivity that overtook Colin in the December eclogue of the *Calender*, as he realized that the world was becoming a harsher and more hostile place. In itself, this self-absorption places the life of the poet over that of the political figures he supposedly praises and, yet again, it is hard to read these lines at face value. Why would Spenser criticize himself so publicly? Moreover, we would perhaps do well to remember the fate of Verulamium, which was destroyed by the Iceni under Boudicea, as Camden noted.[56] Verlame is well aware of her fate and she can be linked to the weeping female figure of Rome in the *Theatre for Worldlings*, one of the fallen cities of past empires that she refers to at the start of her complaint (lines 71–7), as well as the woman in Psalm 137 and Lamentations 1–2.[57] And, as she points out, Troynovant (London) was itself nearly destroyed when it was besieged by Uther Pendragon (lines 104–5), a pointed reminder of the perilous position that London found itself facing in 1591, from internal as well as external pressures.[58] Poets may well be more important than statesmen but they too could be overwhelmed by events beyond their control and were unfortunately dependent on forces that were hard to predict. Spenser is painfully aware in this first *Complaint* that the mutual relationship between poets and patrons could be complicated and problematic, just like the relationship between poets and the history they recorded. In the end, everything could be ruined by time.

On a more mundane level, Spenser is reminding his readers that he can choose how to represent Leicester rather than simply praising him. After all, Leicester had been subject to one of the most powerful and effective libels of Elizabeth's reign, *Leicester's Commonwealth*, a work that had a major impact on his subsequent reputation as a self-interested royal favourite who was unable to control his appetites and who had got away with murder.[59] Indeed, Leicester became the archetype of the corrupt royal favourite, Spenser's volume playing a major part in establishing and disseminating this reputation.[60] Thomas Nashe's 'Tale of the Beare and the Foxe', published the following year in *Pierce Penilesse*, is an attack on Leicester as the evil genius behind the rise of puritanism culminating in the Marprelate Tracts, clearly based on the praise of Leicester in *The Ruines of Time*, using the style of *Mother Hubberds Tale*, a further sign of how closely Spenser was read by his contemporaries and a testimony to the weighty impact of the *Complaints*.[61] Thomas Rogers of Bryanston's poem, *Leicester's Ghost*, also owes much to the tradition of complaint Spenser helped to develop, and its opening stanzas can be read as a witty refutation of Spenser's apparent claim that his verses would enable Leicester's fame to live for ever:

> I that sometime shin'd like the Orient Sun,
> Though *Fortuns* Subject, yet a puissant Lord,
> Am now an Object to be gazd vppon,
> An Abject rather, fitt to be deplored,

Deiected nowe, that whilom was adord,
Affected once, suspected since of manye,
Reiected now, respected scarce of anye.[62]

Later stanzas are clearly indebted to *The Ruines of Time* and *The Ruines of Rome*, showing that the *Complaints* was read as an attack on Leicester as well as Burghley, and was appropriated to dishonour the memory of Spenser's erstwhile patron.[63]

In *The Ruines of Time*, Spenser is asking his readers to judge the performance of contemporary leaders and heroes and how they have succeeded or failed in protecting the nation from external threats. Spenser knew how to exploit and manipulate the amorphous audience of a printed work, and his ambiguous representation of Leicester helped to cement his former patron's dubious posthumous reputation. The author knew that readers had the power to make up their own minds about what they had achieved and what was really taking place, especially if they were prompted by some subtle—and not so subtle—hints. Verlame's lament for the fallen civilizations, and, in particular Rome, is more than just an extended *ubi sunt* motif:

And where is that same great seuen headded beast,
That made all nations vassals of her pride,
To fall before her feete at her beheast,
And in the necke of all the world did ride?
Where doth she all that wondrous welth nowe hide?
With her owne weight downe pressed now shee lies,
And by her heaps her hugenesse testifies.
O *Rome* thy ruine I lament and rue,
And in thy fall my fatall ouerthrowe,
That whilom was, whilst heauens with equall vewe
Deignd to behold me, and their gifts bestowe,
The picture of thy pride in pompous shew:
And of the whole world as thou wast the Empresse,
So I of this small Northerne world was Princesse. (lines 71–84)

In 1591 these lines could not be anything but ironic. Any reader of the opening cantos of the first book of *The Faerie Queene* would have known the answer to the two questions posed in the first of these stanzas. Rome was anything but dead, and very much alive and threatening Protestant England. And, if the reader turned to the proem to the second book, a refutation of the third point would be made. Rome was pressed down by her vast wealth but this was an opportunity rather than a problem as Spanish gold promised to support international Catholicism's aggressive expansionist ambitions, which might include, the principal English fear, another Armada.[64] More pointed still, perhaps, the stanzas were written in the light of Spenser's first poetic composition, the sonnets lamenting the fall of Roman liberty, now rewritten and reproduced as the last two sections of *Complaints*, *The Visions of Bellay* and *The Visions of Petrarch*.[65] The beginning of Spenser's literary career now appears at the end of the volume, circling back to provide answers to the questions posed in the opening poem of the collection, a pattern that is in keeping with Spenser's interest in sequences, numbers, and repetition.[66]

In many ways, of course, Spenser could be seen, yet again, as regretting the overthrow of Rome and the dismemberment of Christendom that resulted in, and then from, the Reformation: neither Protestants nor Catholics can be regarded as broadly homogeneous groups who had consensual perspectives of the history of religion, and, as a recent historian has argued, 'there was in this period no such thing as a unitary English Catholicism at all'.[67] The same, of course, was true of Protestantism and its relationship to Catholicism. The problem that each side faced was what could be done about the division of European civilization, a reality that the opening poem acknowledges. Spenser's politics, along with those of many of his contemporaries, are invariably more ambiguous and complicated than has generally been assumed. He acknowledges a problem but does not necessarily provide the solution that might be expected. The second poem, *The Teares of the Muses*, laments the decline of the value of poetry in the modern world, concluding that Polyhymnia, the Muse of Rhetoric, while condemning the general decline of letters, celebrates Elizabeth as the only monarch to value poetry properly:

> One onelie liues, her ages ornament,
> And myrrour of her Makers maiestie;
> That with rich bountie and deare cherishment,
> Supports the praise of noble Poësie:
> Ne onelie fauours them which it professe,
> But is herselfe a peereles Poëtresse. (lines 571–6)[68]

Elizabeth is complimented for recognizing the value of poets, being one herself. But the praise is double-edged in a volume that invites readers to make up their own minds about the state of the nation and what should be done about the present crisis, and which again heaps scorn on the values of the court.[69] Elizabeth has clearly demonstrated astute judgement in rewarding Spenser, but in doing so, she has given him licence—or, rather, he now claims licence—to take his role as an unofficial laureate seriously and to write and publish what he feels is necessary, which includes satire such as *Mother Hubberds Tale*. Perhaps he was making liberal use of Skelton's example, as a jester/trickster figure in the *Merry Tales* and, more potently, as the scourge of the mighty, the courtly poet who savaged the court, in *The Bouge of Court* and *Why Come Ye Not To Court?* Furthermore, he may have made the connection between Skelton's attacks on Henry's chief minister, Cardinal Wolsey and his own on Elizabeth's, Lord Burghley.[70] Spenser could not have been ignorant of what he was doing in publishing such a provocative volume, nor in granting himself the power to determine how the monarch was represented, with her assumed approval.

The third complaint, *Virgils Gnat*, continues in the same mode of complaint in the dedicatory poem to Leicester, in which Spenser explicitly tells the reader that he fell out with the late earl:

> Wrong'd, yet not daring to expresse my paine,
> To you (great Lord) the causer of my care,
> In clowdie teares my case I thus complaine
> Vnto your selfe, that onely priue are. (lines 1–4)

These are astonishing lines, especially in a dedicatory poem to a recently deceased aristocrat (which was unusual enough anyway). Spenser informs the reader that there was a real falling-out between the poet and the earl, and makes it clear that their rift was Leicester's fault.[71] It may well be true that the exact cause was known only to Leicester, who has taken the secret to his grave, and that Spenser either has no plans to reveal what went on, or cannot explain his fate. There may be a connection to Leicester's failings as a commander in the Low Countries, especially as Sir John Conway, who had links to Spenser, had expressed a low opinion of the earl's military ability.[72] But it is also possible that the secret advertised here is not a real one and that the lines, yet again, mean the opposite of what they ostensibly state.[73] Spenser had, after all, published his deliberations over not dedicating the *Calender* to Leicester, and, almost certainly, publicly insulted the earl in the poem for marrying Lettice Knollys. If these were not sufficient reasons for Leicester's anger, it is hard to imagine what else Spenser had done over ten years earlier. There is also a clear joke in the disingenuous statement that the poet dares not express his pain when he had spent so much energy attacking those he felt merited censure, including, of course, Leicester himself. The dedicatory poem continues in ironic mode, claiming that only an Oedipus could unravel the cunningly hidden mystery of the poem, which will reveal exactly what went on if read right, and that if there is one out in the world, could he or she remain a silent sharer of the secret?

> But if that any *Oedipus* vnware
> Shall chaunce, through power of some diuining spright,
> To reade the secrete of this riddle rare,
> And know the purporte of my euill plight,
> Let him rest pleased with his owne insight,
> Ne further seeke to glose vpon the text. (lines 5–10)

There is an exhortation to resist or hide interpretation, the exact opposite of what a poet such as Spenser invariably demanded from his readers, another sign that this dedicatory poem is a sly joke, drawing attention to the poet's transgression (perhaps it was widely known?) with the safe knowledge that its dedicatee cannot reveal something that took place many years ago. However these details are read, and whether the poem was partially written in the early 1580s and then revised (which seems unlikely), the dedicatory verse cunningly represents Spenser as the loyal servant of an aristocrat who scarcely deserves such devoted service, another manifestation of the poet's power to represent his subject how he wished.[74] The poem might look like a poem seeking favours from the mighty, but it is a defiant assertion of its author's independence.

Virgils Gnat is an adaptation and expansion of the *Culex*, a Latin poem in hexameters, which was attributed to Virgil in the sixteenth century. It tells the story of a shepherd who kills a gnat which stings him, not realizing that the gnat has warned him of an approaching poisonous snake.[75] Spenser varies the style and substance of the original in line with grammar school exercises based on proverbs, whereby students altered a letter or word to transform the substance of a particular maxim.[76] The gnat then appears to the shepherd in a dream and reproaches him for his lack of gratitude.[77] The initial assumption of the reader must be that the gnat stands for Spenser and the shepherd, Leicester, although the title might be first read to suggest that the earl was no more than a gnat represented by the Virgilian poet, especially as Spenser was alive and Leicester dead. But the logical trajectory of the poem's allegory suggests otherwise, with Spenser being the gnat who was ill-treated by Leicester the shepherd—in itself surely an insult that belatedly matches Leicester with Lettice, 'some country lasse', as E. K. described her in the *Calender*. Spenser cannot be wholly serious in complaining of being wronged by Leicester, although it is possible that in lamenting his place in the underworld, 'this bitter bale', 'waste wildernesse' (lines 330, 369) where he has been outcast, the gnat is referring to Spenser's own situation in Ireland.[78] More important is the poet's sense that he has the power to represent others apparently more powerful than himself; to select which aspects of his personal experience he wishes to reproduce; and to make what looks like a wrong into a right. It is hard to think of another example of anyone of the rank of an earl being dressed down in public in quite this way until Michael Drayton took over where Spenser left off.[79]

Virgils Gnat is balanced by the Ovidian beast fable *Muiopotmos, or The Fate of the Butterfly*, the two works separated by translations from Du Bellay's sonnets, *The Ruines of Rome* (*Les Antiquitez de Rome* (1558)), poems which extend the comparison between London and Rome first made in *The Ruines of Time*, and a key motif throughout the volume.[80] Du Bellay's work, which Spenser had known since he was at school, as he was revising his earlier translations for the volume, had a pervasive influence on Spenser's style, vocabulary, and the themes of his major works, especially the dominant motifs of mutability, time, and imperial decline. Nevertheless, the two poets were not always in agreement. In his essay on the state of the French language, Du Bellay, although eager to defend the French language from criticism that it was a barbarous tongue, was clear that the modern language was manifestly less sophisticated than Latin or Greek and he was eager to see the language enriched through the adoption of classical vocabulary and style.[81] Spenser, as the *Calender* demonstrates, was much more eclectic in his approach to the English he wished to create, accommodating the use of native forms and the survival of remnants of medieval literature and culture, alongside Latin and Greek.

Du Bellay's project had been founded on the assumption that, however skilful and dedicated the poet, he could neither produce a perfect translation from work in other languages nor recapture the glories of the past, an understanding of the project of poetry that is implicit in Spenser's later work, even when he challenges his source texts.[82] Spenser's sonnet 7, for example, a relatively faithful rendition of the equivalent sonnet in Du Bellay's sequence, 'Sacrez costaux, et vous saintes ruines', reproduces the common Spenserian obsession with the slow destruction of magnificent ancient buildings:

> Ye sacred ruins, and ye tragic sights,
> Which only do the name of Rome retain,
> Old monuments, which of so famous sprites
> The honour yet in ashes do maintain:
> Triumphant arcs, spires neighbors to the sky,
> That you to see doth th' heaven itself appall,
> Alas, by little ye to nothing fly,
> The people's fable, and the spoil of all:
> And though your frames do for a time make war
> 'Gainst time, yet time in time shall ruinate
> Your works and names, and your last relics mar.
> My sad desires, rest therefore moderate:
> For if that time make ends of things so sure,
> It also will end the pain, which I endure.[83]

The sonnet shows what a good poet and translator Spenser had become, especially if it is compared with his first French translations more than twenty years earlier. Following Du Bellay, Spenser has an ambivalent understanding of the legacy of the past. As the final lines suggest, there is no point in bewailing what cannot be avoided, and the inevitability of the destruction of human artefacts simply has to be accepted (Spenser translates Du Bellay's 'vivez donques contents' as 'rest therefore moderate', an accurate translation of familiar, colloquial vernacular). This is a painful lesson to learn, but it also reminds English readers, if not their French counterparts, that new Romes can be built, like the new Troy ('Troynovant') in *The Faerie Queene*.[84]

Perhaps the sonnet, like so many other sections of Spenser's poetry, can be related to the situation in Munster as he saw it after his acquisition of Kilcolman, where what had once been a ruin, was now repopulated and rebuilt.[85]

Muiopotmos was dedicated to Lady Carey (1552–1618), another of the Spenser daughters, who had married Sir George Carey, Lord Hunsdon (1546/7–1603). She also received one of the dedicatory sonnets to *The Faerie Queene*, and was later clearly referenced in *Colin Clouts come home againe* as 'the floure of rare perfection' (line 544). Of all the Althorp Spencer sisters, she appears to have been the one whose support was most eagerly sought, perhaps because there was some personal connection; perhaps because her husband's family was particularly powerful; or perhaps because she was a noted literary patron and received dedications of works from a number of writers, including Thomas Nashe, Thomas Churchyard, Abraham Fleming, and John Dowland.[86] The dedication indicates that Spenser valued this poem highly. Adapting the *Metamorphoses*, it tells the story of a foolish butterfly who is ensnared in the web of a vengeful spider. The spider is eager to destroy the pretty creature after the labours of his ancestor, Arachne, have been outdone by the beautiful needlework of Minerva, who produces a butterfly that outshines her skilful picture of Jove as a bull ravishing Europa.[87] The poem means everything and nothing: it is a light fable with no real significance beyond its obvious message of the fate of those vain enough to trust in earthly beauty, and it can be read as an allegory of the soul.[88] In a volume replete with topical allusions and allegories *Muiopotmos* reads like an allegory, but resists allegorical interpretation, which would appear to be at the heart of its significance and value for Spenser, a characteristically Spenserian paradox and puzzle, like the relationship between the dedication to and text of *Virgils Gnat.*[89] *Muiopotmos* also stands as a counterpoint to the grand design of *The Faerie Queene*, and serves as a pointed contrast to the gloomy solemnity of many of the other *Complaints*, breaking up the otherwise relentless style and tone of the volume. The absurd descriptions of Clarion, the butterfly knight, might seem satirical but they are of a different order to the tale of the Fox and the Ape in *Mother Hubberds Tale*:

> Vpon his head his glistering Burganet,
> The which was wrought by wonderous deuice,
> And curiously engrauen, he did set:
> The mettall was of rare and passing price;
> Not *Bilbo* steele, nor brasse from *Corinth* fet,
> Nor costly *Oricalche* from strange *Phoenice*;
> But such as could both *Phoebus* arrowes ward,
> And th'hayling darts of heauen beating hard.
> Therein two deadly weapons fixt he bore,
> Strongly outlaunced towards either side,

Like two sharpe speares, his enemies to gore:
Like as a warlike Brigandine, applyde
To fight, layes forth her threatfull pikes afore,
The engines which in them sad death doo hyde:
So did this flie outstretch his fearefull hornes,
Yet so as him their terrour more adornes. (lines 73–88)

Clarion is, after all, a butterfly, a delicate creature not known for its robust and aggressive demeanour, or for striking terror into those who cross its path.[90] The bathetic nature of the poem continues with a number of mock-political references, notably the description of Aragnoll the spider as a 'greisly tyrant' (line 433) just before he kills Clarion. The point is that there are knights and tyrants, both real and allegorical ones, who inhabit the world beyond the poem. *Muiopotmos* cannot be pigeonholed as light relief—although it is that. Rather, it can be read in three interrelated ways: as a sign that *Complaints* is a serious volume and that Spenser's dark allegories are very deliberately designed; that Spenser was a major poet who would always place heavy demands on his readers; that he could write in any number of different ways, showcasing his ability to produce a range and quality of work that none of his contemporaries could rival.

Therefore, *Complaints* cannot have been compiled solely by Ponsonby, who, according to his letter, had hunted out various bits and pieces of Spenseriana that had fallen into the hands of random, unconnected readers in London. The volume, which was produced far more handsomely than the first edition of *The Faerie Queene*, gives every indication of having been carefully planned by author and publisher. This was a volume designed to make an impact, undoubtedly as a means of generating interest in the work that had recently been published, a relationship between texts that he had planned before with the *Calender* and the *Letters*. *Complaints* is central to Spenser's poetic career and his and our understanding of him as a writer. It cannot be seen as a sideshow or a detour, even though the volume encourages the naive reader to think that this is the case.[91] Material has been carefully revised, both in terms of its style (notably, *The Visions of Bellay* and *The Visions of Petrarch*), and, so far as we can tell, in terms of its topical and political comment (*Mother Hubberds Tale*, *Virgils Gnat*). Other works appear to have absorbed and refigured earlier poems (notably, *The Ruines of Time*); there is a deliberate balance between types and styles of poems (*Virgils Gnat* and *Muiopotmos*), as well as carefully placed allusions to major works of classical and European literature; and the conscious imitation of genres and individual works of literature (*The Teares of the Muses* refers back to Harvey's Latin elegy for Sir Thomas Smith, *Smithus; vel Musarum lachrymae*).[92] Spenser was following up the publication of the first part of his magnum opus with a coherent collection of shorter works designed to further his reputation as a poet of range, intensity, and depth. He was also, I would suggest, quite deliberately courting controversy, eager to be seen as a writer who would take risks and generate excitement. In this aim, he probably succeeded rather too well, although it is important to note that, in a litigious age, people were often pardoned after they had transgressed. Many who had done so went on to enjoy successful careers after they had accepted their punishment, as the lives of John Stubbes, and Henry Wriothesley, third earl of Southampton (1573–1624), forgiven for his central role in the Essex rebellion, indicate.[93] Spenser would certainly have been aware of the first case, given their interconnected printing history.

Spenser also published *Daphnaïda* in 1591, an elegy for Douglas Howard, the 19-year-old wife of Sir Arthur Gorges (d. 1625), who had died on 13 August 1590, after a dispiriting illness that had left her largely immobile for the last two years of her life. The poem has never been one of Spenser's most popular works, but it contains a number of suggestive clues about his life, especially his relationship to other writers and his friendships.[94] Gorges was a cousin of Walter Ralegh, and it has usually been assumed that Ralegh must have introduced the two men at some time in 1589–90 when they were both over from Ireland.[95] But it is equally likely that Spenser had prior connections to the Gorges family, met Ralegh in Ireland, and was then keen to advertise his relationship to the more important man. Gorges, although of ancient pedigree—as the poem points out at length—and descended from the Howards as well as being married to one, was relatively impoverished and not of an obviously higher status than Spenser in 1591.[96] Jan van der Noot had been a client of William Parr, marquess of Northampton, who was married to Helena Snakenborg (1548–1635), a Swedish aristocrat and intimate associate of the queen who had stayed in England to marry the marquess after coming over as a teenager in 1565 as part of the entourage of Princess Ceclia.[97] When the aged and infirm Parr died, Helena married Sir Thomas Gorges (1536–1610), the uncle of Arthur.[98] Arthur's father, William, Thomas's brother, who had commanded the *Lion* at Smerwick in 1580, built a manor house at Alderton, Northamptonshire, only a few miles away from the Boyles at Bradden, and the Spencers at Althorp.[99]

Spenser had a number of obvious connections with the Gorges family, familial and geographical, which suggest that there were probably links between the families earlier than any possible friendship between Spenser and Ralegh.[100] Gorges, who addresses a number of his poems to his wife as Daphne—hence the title of Spenser's poem—was a noted poet, later translator of Lucan, whose verse shows considerable influence of Spenserian style, especially pastoral.[101] Spenser praises Gorges as Alcyon in *Colin Clout*, and in the same poem represents the marchioness as Mansilia, one of the key female attendants of Cynthia, as contemporary readers noted:

Ne lesse praise worthie is *Mansilia,*
Best knowne by bearing vp great *Cynthiaes* traine:
That same is she to whom *Daphnaïda*
Vpon her neeces death I did complaine.
She is the paterne of true womanhead,
And onely mirrhor of feminitie:
Worthie next after *Cynthia* to tread,
As she is next her in nobilitie. (lines 508–15)[102]

As is his usual practice, Spenser cross-references his works, referring to the death of Helena's niece as he praises her virtue. The allusion would have been more striking still if *Colin Clout* had been published in 1591, as seems likely was the original plan, which would have publicly demonstrated that Spenser was on intimate terms with both the more powerful members of the Gorges family as well as Ralegh.

Spenser dedicated *Daphnaïda* to Helena, his letter dated 1 January 1591, but also took the opportunity to remind the reader of the impressive pedigree of the family and the current number of its far-reaching branches:

The occasion why I wrote the same, was aswell the great good Fame which I heard of her deceassed, as the particular goodwill which I beare vnto her husband Master *Arthure Gorges*, a louer of learning and vertue, whose house, as your Ladiship by mariage hath honoured, so doe I find the name of them by many notable records, to be of great antiquitie in this Realme; and such as haue euer borne themselues with honorable reputation to the world, & vnspotted loyaltie to their Prince and countrey: besides so lineally are the descended from the *Howards*, as that the Lady *Anne Howard*, eldest daughter to *Iohn* Duke of *Norfolke*, was wife to Sir *Edmund*, mother to Sir *Edward*, and grandmother to Sir *William* and Sir *Thomas Gorges* Knightes. And therefore I doe assure my selfe, that no due honour done to the white Lyon, but will be most gratefull to your Ladiship, whose husband and children do so neerely participate with the bloud of that noble family. (Spenser, *Shorter Poems*, p. 324)

The poem is designed to impress on the reader the lineage of the Gorges family in order to show that they had no need of any wealth or title other than their own—whereas the truth was that they were in urgent need of finances.[103] The mention of the Howard emblem, the white lion, is designed to elevate the Gorges to an almost equal status with the Howards, suggesting that they were really part of the same family. This was not simply a fawning compliment by a poet to his patron. Rather, it was part of an unpleasant struggle over the legitimacy and therefore the legacy of Arthur and Douglas's daughter, Ambrosia, who was 3 in 1591.

Arthur had courted Douglas in 1584 when she was 12 and in protective custody away from her abusive father who had been imprisoned for his mistreatment of his family. Her mother had agreed to the marriage but Henry Howard, second Viscount Bindon, had never granted his permission for the match. He brought a case immediately after the wedding against Gorges in the Star Chamber claiming Gorges had illegally abducted his young daughter. After Douglas's death Thomas Howard, Henry's brother and now third Viscount Bindon, tried to have Ambrosia declared illegitimate, and claimed that she was not Douglas's child. The legal battle was raging at the time the poem was written and published and was never really solved, continuing to inspire bitterness well into the early seventeenth century. Thomas Howard had conceded that he would accept Ambrosia's legitimacy, but then reneged on his promise; Gorges was still fighting off other claimants to what he felt was rightfully his daughter's property at the time of her untimely death in 1600.[104]

Spenser was in an ideal position to promote Gorges's case. Not only was he a poet whose work was starting to gain both sales and praise, but he had worked extensively in the Chancery courts in Ireland, and had learned something of civil law when working for the bishop of Rochester, and so would have understood the issues that faced Gorges as he sought to fight his opponents. *Daphnaïda* has sometimes been read as if it were a satire on Gorges's excessive grief for his dead wife, a reminder that he needed to curtail his desolate mourning, remember the fate of the godly, and get on with his life (although a case has also been made that the bleak representation of death anticipates Renaissance tragedy).[105] Given the close relationship between Spenser's poem and Chaucer's elegy for Blanche, duchess of Lancaster, *The Book of the Duchess*, which tries to draw her husband back from self-destructive lamentation to more measured grief, there is some substance to this reading.[106] Chaucer's poem was the first narrative poem in English to start with 'I', an appropriate detail that a writer planning an elegy that centres on the all-encompassing grief of the speaker was likely to notice.[107] However, Alcyon, originally the disconsolate widow of Ceyx in the *Metamorphoses*, never accepts any form of consolation in *Daphnaïda* and the narrator admits that he has failed to persuade him to see life more positively. The poem ends on a bleak note:

> But by no meanes I could him win thereto,
> Ne longer him intreate with me to staie,
> But without taking leaue, he foorth did goe
> With staggring pace and dismall lookes dismay,
> As if that death he in the face had seene,
> Or hellish hags had met vpon the way:
> But what of him became I cannot weene. (lines 561–7)

Instead Alcyon remains locked in his bitterness:

> I hate to speake, my voyce is spent with crying:
> I hate to heare, lowd plaints haue duld mine eares:
> I hate to tast, for food withholds my dying:
> I hate to see, mine eyes are dimd with teares:

I hate to smell, no sweet on earth is left:
I hate to feele, my flesh is numbd with feares:
I hate all men, and shun all womankinde;
The one, because as I they wretched are,
The other, for because I doo not finde
My loue with them, that wont to be their Starre;
And life I hate, because it will not last,
And death I hate, because it life doth marre,
And all I hate, that is to come or past. (lines 414–27)

Spenser's point cannot be that it is acceptable for Alcyon/Gorges to feel exactly like this, to be deprived of any form of consolation after his tragic loss. Indeed, Alcyon speaks of the fruit of his union with Daphnaïda left to him by his poor wife: 'a pledge . . . | Of the late loue, the which betwixt vs past, | My yong *Ambrosia*' (lines 288–90). As Jonathan Gibson has pointed out, Alcyon/Gorges is feminized in his grief, the 'monotonous lists' resembling the litany of complaints of female supplicants in the tradition of the *Heroïdes*, a genre Spenser had done so much to establish.[108] In doing so Spenser is not ridiculing the poem's speaker but pointing out how seriously he has been abused by the forces working against him, exactly the sort of tactic that might enlist sympathy for Gorges from readers, as well as help persuade a judge in Chancery that he had right on his side. Many supplicants to Chancery were women, far more than appealed to other legal institutions, and the court encouraged the submission of bills that were 'relatively informal in their language and structure', which emphasized the harsh fate of the petitioner and which appealed to the humanity and emotions of the reader.[109] Irish courts, modelled on their English counterparts, worked in similar ways, suggesting that Spenser knew what he was doing in representing Gorges as the heartbroken Alcyon.[110]

It is not known how well—if at all—the poem worked. *Daphnaïda* indicates that Spenser was very familiar with the sad circumstances in which the Gorges family found themselves in 1590/1, perhaps as a client of the family; possibly as a friend and supporter who was prepared to use his knowledge and talents on behalf of the Gorges; most probably a combination of both. *Colin Clout* suggests that Spenser knew Gorges's manuscript poetry well, and had seen much of it, so perhaps they were poets who exchanged their work, especially as Spenser clearly shared literary manuscripts with other writers and encouraged the manuscript circulation of his work.[111] Gorges's poem, 'A pastorall unfynyshed', referred to in *Colin Clout* where Spenser urges Gorges to complete the poem, can be read as a reply to *Daphnaïda*. In his later lament for the death of Henry, prince of Wales, *The Olympian Catasrophe*, Gorges casts himself in the role of Spenser's narrator in the same poem.[112] Certainly, there is more of a suggestion of intimate knowledge carefully applied in *Daphnaïda* than there is in the published correspondence with Ralegh. It is also more likely that

Spenser would have had a relationship on relatively equal terms with an impoverished member of the Northamptonshire gentry such as Gorges, than a grand, court figure likely to recover favour with the queen, however hard his times were in 1589–90. Both Spenser and Gorges were eager defenders of Ralegh in this period, Gorges being obviously closer to Ralegh in social rank than Spenser—although given Ralegh's somewhat modest provincial origins he was an unusual aristocrat with a more complicated patronage network than many at the court.[113] Furthermore, it is likely that Spenser empathized with Gorges because of the loss of his own wife. The appearance of the figure of Alcyon is preceded by the narrator's own reflections on his state: 'So as I muzed on the miserie, | In which men liue, and I of many most, | Most miserable man' (lines 36–8). If these do refer to the poet's own life, as seems likely, then he is informing the reader that he has experienced grief just as Gorges has, enabling us to date the death of Machabyas to some point in the later 1580s or even 1590. Fortunately, both Gorges and Spenser successfully remarried.[114]

9

More Lost Years and Second Marriage, 1592–5

THERE is little trace of what Spenser did in the next three years, a situation not helped by the loss of the Irish State Papers in 1922. We know from the reference in the dedicatory Letter to Ralegh in *Colin Clout* that he was back in Ireland over the Christmas season. He might have been absent again from his estates in August–September 1592, possibly back in England, but there is no record of him returning to London. A document in the Irish State Papers, 'A particular of the number of English tenants inhabiting under each several undertaker', endorsed by the Lord Chief Justice, Sir Robert Gardiner, and the Solicitor-General, Sir Roger Wilbraham, omits Spenser's name from the list of undertakers who have secured tenants on their estates—these include Sir William Herbert (thirty-five tenants); Sir Edward Denny (four tenants); Henry Billingsley (sixty-six tenants), adding up to a total of 245 tenants. The others are sternly reprimanded because they have not 'performed the plot of the habitation so well', especially in terms of 'any English building . . . each one excused his default, alleging that they have time of respite to perform Her Majesty's plot till anno 1594'. The failing undertakers are reminded that 'each undertaker of 12,000 acres is by his letters patents bound to erect 92 families, English, upon his seigniory before Michaelmas 1594; and so after that proportion rateably for other inferior seigniories'. However, 'few or none will accomplish that convenant'.[1]

The document, produced at the behest of powerful, central figures in the Irish civil service, shows that the authorities were starting to become worried about the status of the Plantation quite early in its history, placing the blame squarely on the undertakers. Perhaps they were also realizing that the task of making Ireland English would prove more difficult than they had first imagined. Clearly many undertakers did not have the time or the funds to erect English buildings and were finding it impossible to transplant English families to Ireland, undoubtedly through their lack of enthusiasm for a venture that was always likely to prove insecure and dangerous. They also faced the complex task of establishing their rights to the land and, consequently, their ability to evict existing Irish tenants and landowners. It suggests that Spenser's time in England had seriously reduced his ability to transform his Irish estates, and he may not have fully transformed the Norman castle into an inhabitable house by this point. It is possible that he had assumed that he would be able to return to England permanently in 1589, or had at least thought about this prospect, perhaps imagining that now that he had acquired an estate in one of the queen's kingdoms, he could exchange it for another elsewhere. This might have been his long-term plan all along and his other recorded long visit (1596–7) probably had the same aim, albeit in rather more desperate circumstances. If so, this would further indicate that he probably took his children, Sylvanus and Katherine, with him, and that Machabyas died before or during that prolonged visit.

The sections at the end of *Colin Clout* refer to his second marriage, although they probably survive from an earlier version of the poem before the marriage actually took place. Spenser must have met Elizabeth Boyle in England, or, more likely, at some point soon after his return to Ireland in 1590, perhaps staying the publication of that poem because of her, in addition to his complicated relationship with Ralegh— although it is more likely that he met her in the second half of 1592 or early 1593.[2] Without these last lines the poem seems like a hostile lament about his unlucky fate, a complaint in the manner of the volume he published in 1591; with them, even though he laments that Rosalind neglects his suit, a repetition of Colin's futile endeavours in the *Calender*, there is something to hope for and while prospects ostensibly look bleak in the poem, readers of the *Amoretti and Epithalamion*, published a year earlier, would have known that Spenser had remarried. But in 1589–91, especially if his first wife died in or just before this period, Spenser could have been eager to leave Ireland and been hunting for an English patron to support him, first seizing on Ralegh, and then searching for another when the prospect of Ralegh's help evaporated. The absence of such a figure may also have fuelled the aggressive style and tone of the *Complaints*.

Nevertheless, the same series of records compiled for Gardiner and Wilbraham note that Spenser was required to pay an annual rent of £17. 7s. 6½d. for the Kilcolman estate, and that he paid £5. 15s. 10d. to the crown in Easter 1592.[3] Another note records that his total landholdings were of 4,000 acres (the Kilcolman estate was 3,028 acres) and that the annual rent he paid to the crown was £22.[4] The extra 972 acres, assuming this figure is accurate and not just based on an assumption, indicate that Spenser held other lands that are unrecorded (assuming the document is not referring to the prebend at Effin and the lands that he may still have held elsewhere, such as those at New Ross).[5] If Spenser had been attempting to leave

Ireland in the late 1580s or early 1590s, he was evidently holding on to his lands (although he may have been unable to sell them).

Having produced such an impressive volume of published work in 1590–1, Spenser did not publish anything else until 1595. This hiatus indicates, as might be expected given the miscellaneous nature of the work that appeared in the wake of *The Faerie Queene*, that virtually everything Spenser had written that could be found and that he wanted to see in print appeared in those two years. He surely spent most of the next three years on his estate writing, working on the second edition of *The Faerie Queene*, *Astrophel*, and other shorter poems. Some of this body of material may have been written or planned earlier—Sidney had died in 1586 and sections of *The Faerie Queene*, Book IV, and possibly Book V, probably have earlier origins—but, if so, each was revised.[6] It is likely that he put *Colin Clout* to one side in 1591 and completed that later when an opportunity arose.

Spenser would also have spent significant amounts of time and energy fighting his legal battles with Lord Roche, although he would have relied on trusted servants to complete the documents and make the relevant appearances before judges. It was probably also in this period that the Kilcolman estate was transformed, given the strident tone of Gardiner and Wilbraham's document and what we know took place from the archaeological records.[7] Again, it is hard to judge how involved Spenser would have been in such developments: like many bookish Elizabethans, he was interested in buildings and architectural projects, as his poetry demonstrates, and he undoubtedly made some plans for the transformation of Kilcolman Castle.[8] But he probably left the actual building work to be supervised by his chief servant, perhaps William Hiernane. Spenser also appears to have further withdrawn as much as possible from more public duties, most likely in order to concentrate on his writing and his estate, which suggests that he now had enough income from his lands and—perhaps—his writing to support himself and his family. At some point in 1593 Spenser passed his office of deputy clerk of the Munster Council on to Nicholas Curtis, according to Lord Roche in his petition to Adam Loftus, in his role as Lord Chancellor.[9] In a letter to Robert Cecil written soon after Spenser's death, Curtis reveals that he had obtained the office through Spenser and Bryskett, providing further evidence that such positions were distributed as the holder saw fit and so remained within a small circle.[10] In another document submitted to the Irish Court of Chancery, Roche suggests that Spenser passed on the office to fight his legal disputes more effectively.[11] The truth is probably more complicated and less conspiratorial, as Spenser would have held on to the office if he had wanted direct access to and influence with the Council (although Curtis could well have served as his informant):

whereas, one Edmund Spenser, gentleman, hath lately exhibited suit against your suppliant for three plowe lands, parcel of Shanballymore (east of Doneraile), your suppliant's inheritance, before the Vice-President and Councill of Munster, which land hath bene heretofore decreed for your suppliant against the said Spenser and others under whom he conveied; and, nevertheless, for that the said Spenser, being clark of the council in the said province, and did assyne his office unto one Nicholas Carteys, among other agreements, with covenant that during his life he should be free in the said office for his causes, by ocacon of which immunity he doeth multiply suits against your suppliant, in the said province, upon pretended title of others.[12]

Again, Roche represents—accurately—the English settlers as a closed group eager to help each other against the Irish. Roche's petition also cites Joan Ny Callaghan, who had the 'supportation and maintenance of Edmond Spenser, gentleman', demonstrating that Spenser had Irish tenants on his land, hardly a surprise, given what took place elsewhere on the Plantation.[13] In a letter to Robert Cecil in February 1599, Curtis confirmed that he had taken over Spenser's post and had served 'in that poor and troublesome place of clerk of the Council of Munster', which he had received 'upon the trust of Lodowick Bryskett and Edmund Spenser (men not unknown to your Honour)'. He also describes Spenser as 'lately deceased, the mean and witness of our mutual trust and confidence'.[14]

Curtis's testimony indicates that, while Spenser may have railed against the English court and the ways in which offices were distributed in England, he was prepared to use his influence in similar—albeit more limited—ways in Ireland. Curtis's expression of support for Spenser to Robert Cecil might be read as somewhat ironic given Spenser's fractious relationship with Cecil's father, but is probably an indication of how rapidly disputes could be forgotten within a culture that tried to ensure that reconciliation between opposing parties could take place if at all possible.[15] Clearly officials and settlers were eager to assume lucrative offices if and when they became available, as Spenser's own career in Ireland demonstrates.

Although he probably spent much of his time writing, it is unlikely that Spenser was totally reclusive during this period and he must have visited other settlers, just as they would have visited him. The colonists probably made visits lasting a few days, given the complicated and difficult terrain in south-west Ireland, and the obvious dangers of travel. Given his interest in the culture of letters, Spenser would also have continued long correspondences with various friends, such as Harvey and Ponsonby, perhaps Mulcaster, or even Edward Kirk. He was probably also connected to other groups, resulting from his protracted visit to London in 1589–90, presumably a mixture of other poets such as Nicholas Breton and Michael Drayton, publishers, officials, administrators, and military men.

At a time in which dedicatory and commendatory verses, 'an innovation of the Renaissance humanists', were increasing exponentially, Spenser only wrote three, a sign of his relative isolation, perhaps the result of his obscurity and aloofness or of his pre-eminence.[16] These three sonnets all prefaced the books of writers, principally translators, with close connections who may have formed their own distinct group, a circle on the fringes of the Sidney circle who later gravitated towards Essex. In 1595, Sir William Jones published his translation of Giovanni Battista Nenna's treatise on nobility, *Nennio*, dedicated to Essex and prefaced by dedicatory sonnets from a formidable team of advocates: Samuel Daniel, George Chapman, Angell Day, and Spenser. Spenser advises the reader that 'Who so wil seeke by right deserts t'attaine | vnto the type of true Nobility' should give thanks 'To *Nenna* first, that this worke created, | And next to *Jones*, that truly it translated'.[17] Jones (1566–1640), from Caernarvonshire, finished his studies in Lincoln's Inn in the same year, having translated Justus Lipsius' *Sixe Bookes of Politickes or Ciuil Doctrine* a year earlier.[18] He later became an important judge.[19] Spenser would have read Jones's translation, given the neo-Stoic Lipsius' important role in articulating conceptions of temperance and self-control, and probably possessed a copy, given that Jones's translation was published by Ponsonby.[20] Jones may have been related to Zachary Jones, the translator of *The Historie of George Castriot, surnamed Scanderbeg* (1596), another work published by Ponsonby, for which Spenser wrote a second dedicatory sonnet, stating that Scanderbeg's achievements in defeating the Turks would be remembered when the vain monuments of princes had crumbled (linking this work to the *Complaints*, especially *The Ruines of Time*).[21] Spenser was a contemporary of Zachary's at Cambridge, who dedicated his translation from the French to George Carey, second Baron Hunsdon, the husband of Elizabeth Spencer, to whom Spenser had dedicated *Muiopotmos* and addressed a sonnet accompanying the first edition of *The Faerie Queene*. Spenser's links to Zachary are therefore significant and it is likely that they knew each other reasonably well.[22] Spencer's poem concludes that Scanderbeg was 'The scourge of Turkes, and plague of infidels', providing a neat link to Spenser's representation of Saracens in *The Faerie Queene*, and the connections he makes between them and the Catholic forces besieging Protestant England and Ireland.[23]

The final dedicatory sonnet was written to preface Lewis Lewkenor's translation of Gaspar Contarini's *The Commonwealth and Gouernment of Venice* (1599), published by John Windet, a printer closely linked to Spenser's circle of printers and booksellers. Maurice Kyffin and John Astley, future master of the revels, also wrote dedicatory sonnets suggesting that they may all have been clients of the countess of Warwick.[24] This sonnet is the most significant of Spenser's three poems. He praises Venice as the 'flower of the last worlds delight', replacing the vain beauties of the two great cities of the ancient world, Babylon and Rome.[25] While the other empires have fallen, recalling the descriptions in *A Theatre for Worldlings* and the *Complaints*, Venice 'farre exceedes in policie of right', a comparison that enables Spenser to indulge in a witty hyperbole that praises Lewkenor: 'Yet not so fayre her buildinges to behold | As *Lewkenors* stile that hath her beautie told.'[26] Lewkenor

(1560–1627), a relative of the Sidneys, was a Catholic who had left England in 1580 having studied at the Middle Temple, fearing persecution because of his faith.[27] He fought in the Spanish army and returned to England in 1590 after safe passage was guaranteed by Sir Robert Sidney, writing about his experiences in *A Discourse of the Usage of the English Fugitives by the Spaniard* (1595), a work designed to cover his tracks by professing his loyalty to the crown. Ponsonby 'acquired but never used the copyright' on the expanded version of this work.[28] Lewkenor put his linguistic skills to good use and produced a version of Olivier de La Marche's *Chevalier Déliberé* from the Spanish translation, Hernando de Acuña's *El Caballero Determinando*, entitled *The Resolved Gentleman* (1594). This work, like the translation of Contarini, was dedicated to Anne, countess of Warwick, a dedicatee of the *Fowre Hymns*, providing further evidence that Lewkenor and Spenser had a series of connections in common. Lewkenor praised Spenser in an obvious addition to his translation, commenting that the queen's rare virtue will

Drawe vp (as the heate of the Sunne doth vapours from the earth) the excellent wittes of her time to so high a pitch, that the following ages among millions of other noble workes penned in her praise, shall as much admire the writer, but farre more the subiect of the fairie Queene, as euer former ages did *Homer* and his *Achilles*, or *Virgill*, and his *Aeneas*, such worth, rare, and excellent matter, shall her matchless and incomparable virtue yeelde them to enoble their pennes, & to immortalize their fames.[29]

Spenser's compliment to Lewkenor reverses his trope, providing further evidence that the two men were on friendly terms. While Lewkenor places the object of Spenser's work, the queen, above the poem, Spenser places Lewkenor's translation above its object, Venice. There is no real evidence to link the two Joneses and Lewkenor, but they were connected to the Sidneys as well as Ponsonby, and had patrons in common with Spenser. It is worth noting that, yet again, Spenser was connected to people with differing religious views, one of whom was a well-known Catholic.

A final figure whom we know to have existed in Spenser's orbit in the 1590s is Maurice Kyffin (*c.*1555–98), who was 'on close and friendly terms with a wide circle of scholars and littérateurs, who numbered among them such celebrated figures as John Dee, William Camden, Edmund Spenser, Sir John Harington, William Morgan, Dr David Powell'.[30] Kyffin, another translator, was a Welsh author and soldier who translated John Jewel's *Apologia Ecclesiae Anglicanae* into Welsh in 1595, and whose career reveals a number of parallels with that of Spenser. He also translated guides to help students learn Latin, as well as one of Terence's plays, *Andria*, into English prose. This play was dedicated to Thomas Sackville, Lord Buckhurst, whose sons he had tutored in the early 1580s, and to whom Spenser had addressed a dedicatory sonnet in *The Faerie Queene*.[31] His poem in praise of Elizabeth, *The Blessednes of*

Brytaine (1588), was published by John Wolfe and dedicated to Essex, and he contributed another dedicatory poem himself to Lewkenor's *Resolved Gentleman*.[32] Furthermore, Kyffin was praised by Harvey in *Pierces Supererogation* (1593) as one of a number of writers in whose work 'many things are commendable, diuers things notable, some things excellent', and he later served as comptroller of the musters (1596–8) in Ireland, where he died and was buried in Christ Church Cathedral.[33]

Spenser's connections to such figures, whether they formed a distinct group or not, indicate that he had significant links with English writers in the early 1590s. All four writers produced important translations, suggesting that Spenser was especially eager to associate with intellectuals tuned in to contemporary developments in European culture. His three dedicatory poems promote a variety of translations from Italian, French, and Spanish. Moreover, Kyffin, along with John Eliot, whose work was published by Wolfe and who was a staunch supporter of Harvey during his quarrel with Nashe, was especially keen to write about the practice and theory of translation in order to encourage Englishmen to make works available for themselves and their fellow countrymen, a means of strengthening and opening out English intellectual culture, in line with Spenser's stated aims and practice in his poetry.[34] Two of the writers, William Jones and Kyffin, were Welsh, the latter especially important for his translations into Welsh.[35] As has often been suggested, Spenser was interested in Welsh history and culture and may have used correspondents, friends, and acquaintances to help him with Welsh literature and history, and perhaps even Welsh language texts.[36]

We cannot be sure what role, if any, Spenser played in the Nashe–Harvey quarrel, which lasted from 1590 to 1596, when Nashe published *Have With You to Saffron-Walden*. This dispute dominated a major strand of the literary scene in London, and was cited as a key reason for the prohibition of satire in the Bishops' Ban, 4 June 1599.[37] Nashe, who valued Spenser's work and praises him elsewhere, was notably sarcastic about the dedicatory and commendatory sonnets to *The Faerie Queene* in *Pierce Penilesse* (1592), probably because of Spenser's public association with Harvey.[38] Although Spenser must have corresponded with Harvey during this period, at no point did Spenser intervene in the quarrel, possibly because he was too remote from the fray. Moreover, he did not return to England until 1596, by which time the exchange of pamphlets had effectively ended.[39] Other explanations might be that he had started to distance himself from Harvey, whether through design or circumstance; that Spenser was not prepared to help Harvey, through fear of the consequences or because he was too preoccupied with his own issues; or, most likely, that he or Harvey agreed that he would stay out of the quarrel, because of the damage it might do his literary reputation, an explanation supported by Harvey's public criticism of the satirical nature of *Mother Hubberds Tale*.

Overall, we do not know enough about the quarrel to state how much was motivated by personal animus, intellectual issues, or even the desire for self-promotion and the promotion of the value of literature as a serious medium for debate in the wake of the Marprelate quarrel of 1588–9.[40] Therefore it remains difficult to judge why Spenser stayed aloof from a quarrel in which his mentor was involved. The combined effect of these interrelated disputes was clear enough. What emerged from both the Marprelate Tracts, the anti-Martinist campaign, and the subsequent Nashe–Harvey quarrel were not principles and positions but a scurrilous style of writing which all parties adopted, and a concomitant understanding that they had forged 'new ways of presenting...ideas to a public increasingly recognized as an entity that could be addressed in print'.[41] As Spenser spent his entire literary career addressing a public through the medium of print, and attempting to create new ways of exploring the possibilities that it produced, it was perhaps wise to remain apart from the fray. More likely, Harvey, whose position throughout was that scurrilous exchange was not the proper way for intellectuals to conduct their business, wanted his protégé to remain uncontaminated by what he felt he had to do to defend his honour and that of his brothers.[42]

It is equally unlikely that we will ever discover when Spenser met his second wife, Elizabeth Boyle, unless new evidence appears. But, as he married her on 11 June 1594, and he records the courtship in terms of a calendar year in the *Amoretti*, it is most likely that he met her in 1592–3, and she agreed to marry him at Easter 1593, as the sonnet sequence suggests.[43] The couple could have met through the offices of her relation, Richard Boyle, given the role he played in her life after Spenser's death, and because Spenser's daughter, Katherine, married William Wiseman, who was well known to the earl's family.[44] The fact that Elizabeth married three widowers in rapid succession would further support this conjecture and suggests that Boyle may have planned her life—and the lives of others within the family circle—perhaps rather more than she would have liked, as her surviving letters to him suggest. Boyle, who was closely acquainted with Geoffrey Fenton and who also knew Bryskett, would have known—or known of—Spenser, and would have realized that, as a widower with a family and an estate to run, he was probably eager to get married, as well as being a decent catch.[45]

Far more is known about Elizabeth than Machabyas, and a stone image of her survives (Plate 29). In 1636 Elizabeth's third husband, Robert Tynte, erected a monument with a stone effigy of himself and his two wives, one kneeling at his feet, the other at his head, in Kilcredan church, just over ten miles from Youghal, on the estates that Richard Boyle, earl of Cork, purchased from Walter Ralegh in 1602. Tynte established the church in 1636.[46] Elizabeth died in 1622, so we cannot know how accurate the image of her is, but, as she had four children with Tynte, it is probable that she is the 'more staid and matronly' lady at Tynte's head.[47]

Unfortunately the church was closed in 1917 and was vandalized, and the heads of Tynte's wives were knocked off, so that the once impressive monument is now a shadow of its original state, and has decayed beyond the possibility of proper restoration. One of the heads of the wives is visible in a photograph from 1927, although it has subsequently been lost.[48] This somewhat unclear and problematic image and Elizabeth's decapitated trunk are, unfortunately, the closest we have to physical likenesses of Spenser's immediate family.[49]

Elizabeth was the daughter of Steven and Joan Boyle from Bradden, North-amptonshire (Plate 30), a small village about six miles from the Dryden house at Canons Ashby, and so near to the large estates of the Spencers of Wormleighton and Althorp. Numerous branches of the Spencer family exist throughout the area, and there is an attractive plaque erected in 1606 to commemorate the lessees of the local manor, Thomas and Dorothy Spencer and their family in the church of St Mary, Everdon, about eight miles north of Bradden (Plate 31). If Spenser's family were from Northamptonshire, as seems likely, the couple could have met through mutual connections, and might have known each other before their courtship began in earnest, given the importance of kinship and evidence that 'members of the proper-tied classes took care during this period to maintain a fairly broad knowledge of their kindred, going well beyond those with whom they were on close terms'.[50] In fact Elizabeth was related to the Spencers of Althorp by marriage, through her mother, Joan, née Cope, whose grandfather had married Jane Spencer, granddaughter of John Spencer of Hodnell, Warwickshire, also the ancestor of Sir John Spencer, to whose daughters Spenser dedicated a number of poems. These three sisters were fourth cousins of his wife, a relationship that would have had some significance within Northamptonshire circles.[51] Elizabeth was also a distant relative of Richard Boyle, perhaps his cousin: she is not mentioned in his memoir of 1632, but he certainly showed a keen interest in her welfare.[52] Geoffrey Fenton, a rather more successful career civil servant than Spenser who had come to Ireland at the same time, became Boyle's father-in-law in 1603, when his daughter, Catherine, became the second wife of the earl.[53] English settlers intermarried, as would be expected, especially second time around, but we cannot be sure whether Edmund and Eliza-beth met in England or Ireland, although the *Amoretti*, which records a number of places and events in their courtship, makes no mention of a journey which would be expected if the couple had first met in England.[54] The most likely explanation is that Elizabeth moved to Ireland because of her relation's conspicuous success in acquiring wealth and lands. Two of Boyle's sisters settled in the Youghal area, and Elizabeth moved to Ireland with her brother, Alexander, indicting that emigration to Ireland was often a family affair.[55] It is further possible that Sir George Boyle, knighted in 1624, who practised iron smelting on the earl's estate, was yet another relative who made the journey over from England.[56] Records show that Elizabeth later rented a house owned by the earl in Kilcoran, west Youghal, near the strand.[57] If she occupied this or a nearby house before her marriage to Spenser, then the opening line of *Amoretti* 75, 'One day I wrote her name upon the strand', and another line in the *Epithalamion*, when the poet states that he will sing 'of the sea that neighbours to her neare' (line 39), can be read autobiographically (Plate 32).[58] Moreover, as Ralph Houlbrook has pointed out, 'Ties with relatives by marriage and maternal kinsfolk were often stronger than those with paternal kindred', providing further evidence that after his second marriage Spenser started to make use of his new connections within the wider Boyle family circle.[59] After all, some of his own family seem to have followed him over, notably his sister, Sarah, who married John Travers, another sign that members of the Spenser and Boyle families had moved over from North-amptonshire to Munster en masse.[60]

Boyle signed the agreement to buy Ralegh's estates for the knockdown price of £1,500 on 7 December 1602, by which time Ralegh had long lost interest in his Irish lands.[61] Boyle's family evidently had a significant presence in that area before then, suggesting that there may have been connections between the Boyles and the Raleghs, providing us with yet another context through which Edmund and Elizabeth could have met. Youghal, a well-established and relatively affluent town which had received its charter of incorporation in 1209 and had acquired walls by 1275, was nearly as important a port as Cork in the 1590s, as figures for customs receipts, wool exports, and livestock and cattle-hide exports demon-strate.[62] William Camden, although admitting that it was 'no great towne', nevertheless provided a positive description of an anglicized settlement that was recognized as important in England: 'the fruitfulnesse withal of the Country adjoining, draweth merchants unto it, so as it is well frequented and inhabited, yea and hath a Major for the head magistrate'.[63] Cork's rise to prominence took place in the wake of the lapse of the Navigation Acts in the late seventeenth and early eighteenth centuries, as the development of Atlantic trade transformed the region and placed the city centre stage, its population increasing from about 3,000 in 1600 to about 5,000 by the late 1620s.[64] Youghal's importance in this period owed much to the presence of the Boyles, in particular, Richard Boyle's ability to secure land for his followers, and his patronage of local merchants. It also benefited from an 'open policy towards prospective New English freemen (in contrast to the situation in Cork)', which helped to create its character as a loyal, Protestant city, and its strategic importance on the Blackwater made it a natural outlet for trade from the interior, especially from the Mallow area where Spenser lived (Plate 33).[65] The town had been a target of Desmond forces in November 1579, when it was sacked, and again in January 1583.[66] There was significant interaction with English towns, notably Bristol, where a number of Irish appren-tices went to learn their trades.[67] Spenser would have had more reasons to be in Youghal than any other local town so it was where he was most likely to encounter a wife in Ireland.

Elizabeth was clearly a lot younger than Edmund, probably in her early to mid-twenties, perhaps even younger, given the number of children she had with Robert Tynte, after they married in 1612.[68] A date of 1576 has been conjectured as her birthday.[69] She was not without some assets, as her father had settled about £250 on each of his children when he died in 1582, and may have had access to some of Richard Boyle's vast wealth.[70] Her parents were clearly people of some means, as Steven Boyle's will mentions four children, which would have involved them inheriting the not inconsiderable sum of £1,000 in total, to be paid when they reached maturity (21) or got married, whichever came first (if any died, as it appears one did, the money was to be divided between the surviving siblings). As Steven died when his children were still minors, and probably fairly young, the sum would have been based on projected income from his estates, suggesting that he was comfortably off by the standards of the time, rather than especially wealthy.[71]

Elizabeth was also well provided for after Spenser's death, with the earl leasing her a house in Kilcoran, at a nominal rent of 2s. 6d. per annum, perhaps one she was already occupying, when her second husband, Roger Seckerstone, died, probably in April 1606.[72] She then married Captain Robert Tynte (b. 1571), a member of the minor gentry from Wraxall, Somerset, also the original home of the Gorges family with whom Spenser was closely linked, suggesting that there may have been a further series of connections between the parties. Tynte later followed Spenser as sheriff of Cork (1625–6). The marriage ceremony took place at Richard Boyle's house in March 1612, as he records in a letter: 'Cap^{tn} Robert Tynte was married in my study in yoghall by my cozen Richard Boyle, dean of Waterforde, to my kinswoman Mrs Elizabeth Boyle, als. Seckerstone, widow; and I gaue her unto him in marriadge, and I beseech god to bless them wth good agreement and many virtuous children.'[73] Tynte was a friend or client of Boyle's, as was Seckerstone, and Boyle's relation was employed to carry out the ceremony.[74] One of seven commissioners of the town, he became very wealthy, as his financial dealings indicate, and was able to afford a grand monument to display his status when he died. The wording on the tomb indicates that it was erected in his lifetime, as was normal practice.[75] Tynte acquired the impressive tower house still standing in Youghal, known as Tynte's Castle (Plate 34), probably used as the trading base which secured the economic development of the family.[76]

Elizabeth wrote a number of letters expressing her gratitude to the earl for supporting her, showing that she was literate, a relatively unusual achievement for a woman of her status in the 1590s.[77] One dated 22 December 1615 states her 'thankfullness for your ever wonted kindness towards me', and, in the postscript, records a conversation Elizabeth had with Catherine Boyle in which she 'spake to your Lady conser[n]ing some bisnes which if you can do me the faviour I would put what monyes I can of my Childrine . . . conser[n]ing some estates to setell upon them'.[78] The letter makes clear how much Elizabeth had come to rely on the earl for welfare and well-being, along with that of her children. In another letter dated 19 November 1616 Elizabeth asks that Boyle keep her son—probably her son with Seckerstone, Richard, as her children with Tynte would have been too young, and Peregrine would have been grown up by now—'for his better edicacion' and she asks Boyle to 'show [his] louinge favour & countenance towards him & his childes accions to excuses in regarde of his youeth & want of exsperiance'.[79] Boyle took a great interest in Richard, who was his godson.[80] We do not know what the boy did, but the letter again shows Elizabeth's dependence on her benefactor and the Boyles working as an extended family in Ireland in a manner that was probably only unusual in terms of the wealth and power that they possessed.[81]

Elizabeth's mother, Joan, was widowed in 1582, and remarried Captain Ferdinando Freckleton the following year. He was probably the captain who came to Ireland in 1596, possibly earlier, and, as he served in Ireland until 1611, when the last record of him appeared in the State Papers, he probably brought his family over with him, assuming they were still alive at that point. Captain Freckleton was knighted in Dublin Castle in 1603 along with Richard Boyle by the Lord Deputy, Lord Mountjoy, to mark the coronation of James I, providing yet more circumstantial evidence that the larger Boyle family group stayed together and looked after each other. It is therefore likely that the Freckletons settled in the Youghal area.[82]

The Spensers undoubtedly behaved in a similar way. Edmund's sister, Sarah, moved to Ireland at some point in the 1580s, and married John Travers, from a family who had moved to Ireland at some point in the middle of the sixteenth century, registrar of the diocese of Cork, Cloyne, and Ross, in 1587 or 1588.[83] Furthermore, Peregrine Spenser married Dorothy Tynte, Robert's daughter in 1623, a year after his mother's death, and Spenser's daughter, Katherine, also married someone close to the earl, again showing how intricately interwoven the lives of settler families invariably were.[84] Indeed, the evidence suggests that Elizabeth was 'carefully controlled' by the earl, and he may even have arranged many of these marriages, which might explain why she married Roger Seckerstone so soon after Spenser's death.[85]

Elizabeth's continuing relationship with the earl probably suggests that during their marriage the Spensers had important contact with the Boyles and their circle after 1594. Spenser was by no means badly off, and neither was Robert Tynte, who was later ennobled, and Boyle was prepared to help out his family. Boyle's rapacious and self-interested pursuit of gain was the logical culmination of the colonial mentality that had made Spenser's principal patrons, Grey, the Norrises, and Wallop, so successful and popular among the New English they employed and supported. Boyle made sure that he had access to information about land titles and claims, through contacts such as Fenton; acquired rights to estates; and then took possession of as much land and property as he could. He carefully looked after those who mattered to him, his family, and a close circle of friends and retainers, exactly what Anglo-Irish lords such as Lord Roche of Fermoy alleged was normal practice among those whom the crown had entrusted to administer the law impartially. It is little wonder that there were competing communities in Ireland, different groups of Old and New English appealing to the authorities that they had the exclusive right to land and property and the force of law to protect them and trying to ensure that they had the largest share of what property and wealth was available.[86] Boyle was also conspicuously successful in marrying his children into the most important families in England, including the Clifford and Howards, and that of the rising star at the Stuart court, George de Villiers, duke of Buckingham; and in Ireland, the Barrys, earls of Barrymore, and Fitzgeralds, earls of Kildare.[87]

Boyle's behaviour was always likely to make enemies, and he earned the enmity of Adam Loftus, whom Spenser also appears to have detested, as well as the Lord Deputy, Oliver St John (1559–1630), who was viceroy from 1615 to 1622.[88] More significantly, the need to secure land led to disputes within the extended family itself, and Elizabeth and her new husband, Roger Seckerstone, were challenged by Sylvanus, who had probably just come of age, in 1602–3, for the rights to Kilcolman.[89] If Boyle controlled the family, Edmund and Elizabeth's married life may not have been without its tensions, and, as is all too often the case, stepchild and stepmother may have had different understandings of what was rightfully theirs. The Boyle family were certainly involved in a number of complicated financial and legal disputes— although this was not unusual in this period and anyone who acquired land expected to have to fight for rights of possession in the courts.[90]

The *Amoretti* appeared along with the *Epithalamion* in 1595, part of the second— and last—flurry of published work that Spenser produced (1594–6). As with the *Complaints*, the volume shows Ponsonby advertising his role in helping to make Spenser's work public. His dedicatory letter to Sir Robert Needham, who was knighted on 1 September 1594, just before he returned to England on 25 September, suggests that the sequence was finished at some point during the summer, after the Spensers' marriage on St Barnabas' Day, 11 June.[91] Sir Robert Needham of Shavington, Cheshire was yet another figure with a connection to the Spencer family, as his mother-in-law was Mary Spencer, another daughter of Sir John Spencer of Althorp.[92] Ponsonby's letter also shows his confidence in his own literary taste and judgement. Thanking Needham for bringing the manuscript over for him to publish, Ponsonby waxes lyrical in ways that make him sound far more like a contemporary literary critic than a publisher, demonstrating a significant change from the more technical and cautious letter that accompanied the *Complaints*.

I do more confidently presume to publish it in his absence, vnder your name to whom (in my poore opinion) the patronage thereof, doth in some respectes properly apertaine. For, besides your iudgment and delighte in learned poesie: This gentle Muse for her former perfection long wished for in Englande, nowe at the length crossing the Seas in your happy companye, (though to your selfe vnknowne) seemeth to make choyse of you, as meetest to giue her deserued countenaunce, after her retourne[93]

Ponsonby addresses Needham, a knight, and tells him how important his role has been in helping to produce a major literary work, which in itself suggests that normal assumptions of literary relations have been reversed. Needham is clearly—and publicly—cast as the willing, ignorant messenger who has worked to serve the writer and his publisher by bringing the manuscript over from Ireland, a sign that, in the Spenser circle at least, publishers and writers assumed equal relations and valued the outside world only in so far as it served their needs.

Sir Robert Needham may not have loomed large as a major figure in Spenser's life, but the volume does provide us with other clues of whom Spenser knew. Two dedicatory sonnets by 'G. W. Senior' and 'G. W. I.', the 'I' undoubtedly standing for 'Junior', were probably written by Geoffrey Whitney (1548?–1600/1), best known for his collection, *A Choice of Emblems*, published by Christopher Plantin at Leiden in 1586, and his father.[94] The identification is not certain, however.[95] Whitney Junior did have a number of significant links to Spenser, and, through his connections with Leicester, moved among Dutch artists and intellectuals in the Low Countries, providing us with some evidence that Spenser had maintained links he had established earlier in London when he was young, perhaps by correspondence.[96] He was also probably the brother of Isabella Whitney (*fl.* 1566–73), the first significant English female poet from outside the ranks of the aristocracy, and author of two miscellanies, who may, therefore, have been another writer of Spenser's acquaintance.[97] Isabella's work is notable for its unusually forceful style of female complaint, a 'unique representation of a woman's reaction against the tyranny of the masculine lyric tradition', as the speaker laments her fate at the hands of an inconstant male, which probably had an effect on Spenser's development of this particular genre of poetry and his adoption of female voices.[98] Her brother dedicated two of his poems to Alexander Nowell and Sir John Norris, important figures at different stages of Spenser's life.[99] Spenser had a particular interest in emblems and the relationship between word and image in printed texts, and he may well have had a copy of Whitney's book in Ireland.[100] Neither dedicatory poem is especially remarkable, but the opening quatrain of the first, 'Darke is the day, when *Phoebus* face is shrowded, | and weaker sights may wander soone astray: | but when they see his glorious raies vnclowded, I with steddy steps they keepe the perfect way', certainly suggests that it was written by someone well versed in emblem books.[101]

The sonnet sequence itself is best known as a celebration of Spenser's marriage, a new departure in the recently established genre, which, following Sidney's *Astrophil and Stella*, first published in 1591, had charted adulterous love or unrequited passion.[102] Yet again, Spenser's intervention was designed to transform the state of English culture: using a number of mainly French and Italian models and examples, he invented a new style of English sonnet, now known as the Spenserian sonnet, based on a 'very demanding rhyme scheme, at least as difficult as the Petrarchan scheme (ABAB ABAB CDE CDE)'.[103] The Anacreontic poems that join the two major works are also an innovation in both style and substance.[104] In the *Amoretti* Spenser tells the story of his courtship of Elizabeth, the sequence culminating in another new form of English poem, the marriage-hymn, the *Epithalamion*, as no one before had combined 'the roles of bridegroom and poet-speaker'.[105] Although there were well-known classical precedents in the works of Claudian and Statius, Spenser's poem had yet another innovative stanza pattern, 'derived from the Provençal and Italian *canzone*, which Spenser introduced to England'.[106] Furthermore, as Kenneth J. Larsen has demonstrated, 'The eighty-nine sonnets of the *Amoretti*, as numbered in the 1595 octavo edition, were written to correspond with consecutive dates, beginning on Wednesday 23 January 1594 and running, with one interval, through to Friday 17 May 1594: they correspond with the daily and sequential order of scriptural readings that are prescribed for those dates by the liturgical calendar of the Church of England.'[107] Spenser narrates the course of his courtship and marriage of Elizabeth in terms of the prescribed Bible readings used by the established church, a token of his allegiance to that church, as well as a manifestation of the establishment of English culture in Ireland. In 1594 Spenser's life had reached a high point of stability and renewed purpose through his second marriage, something he celebrates in this volume, and in the revised *Colin Clout*, published in the same year after a significant hiatus, perhaps also brought over by Needham. Ironically enough, it was to prove a brief and false dawn, his hopes for the future dashed by the outbreak of the Nine Years War, leading eventually to the destruction of the Munster Plantation, and Spenser's flight and death.

The volume shows that the Munster planters believed that they had established a civilized order in Ireland that could rival and even supersede the tired culture of the court. Spenser appropriates the language of the courtly lyric—in the main that of Sidney's sequence—in order to praise his bride-to-be, translating the tropes of courtiers to a conspicuously provincial, commercial scene:

> Ye tradefull Merchants that with weary toyle,
> do seeke most pretious things to make your gain:

and both the Indias of their treasures spoile,
what needeth you to seeke so farre in vaine?
For loe my loue doth in her selfe containe
all this worlds riches that may farre be found;
if Saphyres, loe her eies be Saphyres plaine,
if Rubies, loe hir lips be Rubies found;
If Pearles, hir teeth be pearles both pure and round;
if Yuorie, her forhead yuory weene;
if Gold, her locks are finest gold on ground;
if siluer, her faire hands are siluer sheene,
But that which fairest is, but few behold,
her mind adornd with vertues manifold.[108]

Elizabeth is as beautiful as any courtly lady, and Spenser's sonnet may well have Astrophil's ornate description of Stella's face in mind, transposing the elaborate ironies of that poem to a new, middle-class setting and a different series of literary coordinates.[109] Sidney's poem reads:

Queen Virtue's court, which some call Stella's face,
Prepar'd by Nature's choicest furniture,
Hath his front built of alabaster pure;
Gold in the covering of that stately place.
The door by which sometimes comes forth her Grace
Red porphyr is, which lock of pearl makes sure,
Whose porches rich (which name of cheeks endure)
Marble mix'd red and white do interlace.
The windows now through which this heav'nly guest
Looks o'er the world, and can find nothing such,
Which dare claim from those lights the name of best,
Of touch they are that without touch doth touch,
Which Cupid's self from Beauty's mine did draw:
Of touch they are, and poor I am their straw. (*Astrophil and Stella*, sonnet 9)

Sidney's poem asserts that his lady has all these marvellous possessions as part of her substance; in pointed contrast, Spenser claims that his is better than these things, establishing a distance between her (middle-class) virtues and the riches that the merchants bring back from far-flung lands, most of which, presumably, end up at court and in the possession of courtiers. Furthermore, Spenser's love is witnessed by merchants, not courtiers, and her commodified body serves to revitalize them, the real substance of society, not those at court who imagine that their actions run the country.[110] The opening quatrain, especially if read alongside the proem to Book II of *The Faerie Queene*, claims that foreign exploration is probably a waste of time, as more profit will be gained, financially and spiritually, by staying at home and securing England's possessions within the British Isles, a development that would involve the strengthening and proliferation of provincial society, not the spectacular voyages of explorers and empire builders which invariably disappointed investors.[111] In marrying Elizabeth, Spenser is achieving this aim, making him a better citizen than many of his more exalted counterparts. The sonnet may take another swipe at Ralegh, and is the sort of writing that would have done nothing to help the courtier regain his position at court or secure support for his transatlantic ventures, suggesting that Spenser felt betrayed by his erstwhile champion in some way, perhaps for abandoning Ireland.[112] The description is repeated in the tenth stanza of the *Epithalamion*, when the poet-narrator asks, 'Tell me ye merchants daughters did ye see | So fayre a creature in your towne before?' (lines 168–9), followed by a similar depiction of Elizabeth in terms of a blazon invariably applied to court beauties.[113] Spenser reminds his readers that his bride has a radiance that puts them to shame, marking the couple out as both part of the community and yet also separate from it. When read alongside *Colin Clout* the marriage poems express a recommitment to making a life in Ireland and an understanding that the Spensers were choosing to adopt an Anglo-Irish identity in doing so.

Spenser also repeats earlier works that place a high value on the religious significance of marriage as the holy state in which Christians were exhorted to live. Throughout the sequence the poet adopts the erotic language of the Song of Songs, most conspicuously in the 'garden sonnet' (64):

> Coming to kisse her lyps, (such grace I found)
> Me seemd I smelt a gardin of sweet flowres:
> that dainty odours from them threw around
> for damzels fit to decke their louers bowres.
> Her lips did smell lyke vnto Gillyflowers,
> her ruddy cheekes, lyke vnto Roses red:
> her snowy browes lyke budded Bellamoures
> her louely eyes lyke Pincks but newly spred,
> Her goodly bosome lyke a Strawberry bed,
> her neck lyke to a bounch of Cullambynes:
> her brest lyke lillyes, ere theyr leaues be shed,
> her nipples lyke yong blossomd Iessemynes,
> Such fragrant flowres doe giue most odorous smell,
> but her sweet odour did them all excell.[114]

Spenser celebrates his forthcoming union with his bride in terms of the description of the beauties of Nature employed to describe the marriage between the church and God in the Canticles. Although the church insisted that this book be read allegorically, there was a long tradition of it being read in more obviously literal, erotic terms.[115]

In the *Amoretti* Spenser represents his marriage as a sacred event, the impending first act of sexual intercourse as a holy rite of passage into the joys of Christian matrimony, the proper way of living and establishing the social order after the Reformation.

However, a dissonant note is struck in the concluding stanzas of the *Epithalamion*, just as the much anticipated act is about to take place. In bed the newly-weds look out of the window and spot an unsettled figure unable to find her own place of rest:

> Who is the same, which at my window peepes?
> Or whose is that faire face, that shines so bright,
> Is it not Cinthia, she that neuer sleepes,
> But walkes about high heauen al the night?
> O fayrest goddesse, do thou not enuy
> My loue with me to spy:
> For thou likewise didst loue, though now vnthought,
> And for a fleece of woll, which priuily,
> The Latmian shephard once vnto thee brought,
> His pleasures with thee wrought,
> Therefore to vs be fauorable now;
> And sith of wemens labours thou hast charge,
> And generation goodly dost enlarge,
> Encline they will t'effect our wishfull vow,
> And the chast wombe informe with timely seed,
> That may our comfort breed:
> Till which we cease our hopefull hap to sing,
> Ne let the woods vs answere, nor our Eccho ring. (lines 372–89)

It is not usually remarked when listing Spenser's poetic innovations that he appears to have been the first poet who imagined the queen looking into his bedroom on his wedding night.[116] The image relies on a conventional understanding of the monarch as Cynthia, the imperial moon, continually watching over her subjects in order to protect them from any ills.[117] But here she is the one looking through the window, staring in jealousy at her subjects, reversing the normal hierarchical relations. The poem also, as in Donne's lyric, 'The Sunne Rising', asserts that the lovers' bed is the centre of the world at the time of their holy union.[118] This can be read as a particularly offensive stanza, especially given Spenser's track record, designed to provoke the queen, should she or anyone close to her read it—a strident revision of the genre, deliberately striking a discordant note and asserting, once again, that the poet was the really important figure.[119]

The key word is 'envy', given Elizabeth's virginity, and the reminder that she once loved: *The Shepheardes Calender* had made a number of references to the projected Alençon match, so the 'Latmian shephard' may be François, duc d'Alençon, or, even,

Robert Dudley, earl of Leicester.[120] The queen is cast as a voyeur, peeping through the curtains, jealous of the joy of the lovers, an image that repeats the closing lines of the first edition of *The Faerie Queene* with Britomart gazing enviously at the joy of the hermaphrodite created by the lovers Amoret and Scudamore.[121] There, we know that Britomart will have her time when she marries Artegall, leading to a dynasty of mighty kings.[122] Here we are told that Cynthia/Elizabeth has had hers, and needs to bless the lovers and stop her envy. Spenser would appear to be commenting on her inability to rule effectively in Ireland, a theme he was developing in the second edition of *The Faerie Queene*, on which he would have been working at this time, and her failure as a ruler of men and women who have sexual desires, as Ralegh had discovered to his cost three years earlier.

It is possible, of course, that Spenser has this scandal in mind, as he celebrates his own marriage in a conspicuously bourgeois manner, as he was soon to publish an allegory of Ralegh's fate.[123] The stanza is also a *memento mori*, a cruel reminder that Elizabeth had failed to marry and produce an heir, when her duty, as Spenser clearly saw it, was to ensure the protection of her subjects. Instead they have to depend on her failing corpse-like body, wandering at night like a ghost, a parody of the true role that Cynthia should play.[124] Spenser has linked his own life and situation with that of the monarch, skilfully—and confrontationally—drawing together two of the main concerns articulated throughout his writing career. His personal life is seen at odds with, and as more ordered than, the larger political state of affairs. The newly-weds appeal to Juno, the goddess of marriage, to bless their bridal bed, and to enable it to remain:

> Without blemish or staine,
> And the secret pleasures of theyr loues delight
> With secret ayde doest succour and supply,
> Till they bring forth the fruitfull progeny,
> Send vs the timely fruit of this same night. (lines 400–4)

The *Epithalamion*, a poem written as a numerological artefact in order to represent the 365 days of the year, as a counterpoint to the 52 weeks represented in the *Amoretti*, has often been read as if it were a work that expressed the divine order of the universe.[125] In fact, the harmony of both of the poems' structures is distinctly at odds with the anxiety and, in places, hostility represented in the content, which is full of sly and skilful reversals of expected norms. Spenser hopes for a bright future for the couple with children and stability in their home, but has to acknowledge that this does not depend on themselves alone, counterpointing his domestic bliss with that of a threatening world outside his domestic sphere.[126]

Amoretti and *Epithalamion* also provide the reader with more mundane details designed to anchor the works in the realities of the poet's life. Again, Spenser's model was probably Sidney in *Astrophil and Stella*, who, using the rhetorical technique of *occupatio*, referred to his keen knowledge of political events while ostensibly denying any interest, and quibbled on the name 'Rich', the name of Penelope Devereux/ Stella's husband.[127] Sidney's death had been swiftly followed by his posthumous canonization and, as his works were printed, the conditions of writing were transformed, because secular lyric poetry in print became far more socially acceptable and popular.[128] Such lessons were not lost on Spenser, and Sidney's influence is especially apparent in the poetry he published immediately after the first edition of *The Faerie Queene*.

As already noted, in *Amoretti* 33 Spenser addresses his friend Lodowick Bryskett, who published poems alongside Spenser in *Astrophel* later that year. He explains that he has neglected his duties to the queen in failing to finish *The Faerie Queene*, because he has been so tormented in his pursuit of his proud mistress that he will be unable to continue work until 'she vouchsafe to grawnt me rest, | or lend you me another liuing brest' (lines 13–14).[129] When read in conjunction with sonnet 74, expressing his devotion to the three Elizabeths in his life—mother, queen, and wife—the sonnet again demonstrates that Spenser's primary devotion was to his wife ahead of his sovereign. In representing Elizabeth Boyle as a cruel, tyrannical mistress until she submits to his suit, Spenser is adapting conventional poetic imagery in an unfamiliar manner—although he may well be consciously adapting Dante's representation of Beatrice in *La Vita Nuova*—emphasizing the need he has for a partner in order to be able to live his life and work properly.[130] The *Amoretti* can be read as a critique of the 'pagan self-sufficiency' of Stoicism and a statement of the benefits of married life, casting the poet's wife in a more active role than that imagined for many unobtainable ladies in the poetry of Spenser's contemporaries.[131] The eventual union of the disdainful beloved and the desperate suitor, achieved at the turn of the year, 25 March, in sonnet 62, may or may not correspond exactly to a development in their romance. The last lines, 'So likewise loue cheare you your heauy spright, | and change old yeares annoy to new delight', are surely conventional and employ the traditional poetic theme that spring brought the awakening of new love, but they may chart the course of Spenser's suit from the 'long storms and tempests sad assay' to sight of the 'happy shore', as the next sonnet states.[132]

It is more likely, however, that in his most famous sonnet, 'One day I wrote her name vpon the strand', Spenser is recalling an event that he wants the reader to note, as Elizabeth did probably live near Youghal strand, a significant feature of the town, suggesting that he spent some time in the area, probably through connections to the Boyle family. If she did not live in the house in Kilcoran already mentioned, Elizabeth might have lived with her brother-in-law, Sir Richard Smith, in a house on the estuary where the River Blackwater flows into the sea, which suggests that the topographical exhortation in *Epithalamion* is another carefully placed detail: 'Bring with you al the Nymphes that you can heare | both of the riuers and the forests greene: | And of the sea that neighbours to her neare, | Al with gay girlands goodly wel beseene' (lines 37–40).[133] The marriage must have taken place in Youghal, or nearby, not in Christ Church, Cork, as is often assumed.[134] If so, the ceremony would have been conducted in St Mary's church, damaged in the Desmond Rebellion, but undoubtedly restored by 1594, where there is a large monument to Sir Richard Boyle and his family, of a similar style to the one in St Patrick's Cathedral, Dublin (Plates 33, 35).[135] The warden at Youghal was Nathaniel Baxter (*fl.* 1569–1611), a vociferous Calvinist minister whose long poem, *Sir Philip Sydneys Ouránia, that is Endimions Song and Tragedie* (1606), shows that he knew the Sidney family well and had taught Sir Philip Greek. The work is, unsurprisingly, heavily influenced by Spenser, whom he would have known in this period. Baxter would have attended the wedding ceremony.[136] Ralegh's house at Myrtle Grove was next to the church, although no evidence survives that he ever lived there.[137]

It would have made little sense to have travelled into Cork, which would have been an expensive and time-consuming journey. Moreover, it is not clear that either bride or groom had any significant reason to be in Cork. The marriage was far more likely to have been held in the bride's parish—or, less likely, the groom's parish or house, which would have meant either on the Kilcolman estate or in nearby Buttevant. Custom would have suggested the bride's parish, as had been the case with Spenser's first marriage.[138] *Epithalamion*'s plea that the couple be not disturbed by terrors of the night—goblins, witches, nightmares, owls, ravens, and so on—concludes with 'Ne let th'unpleasant Quyre of Frogs still croking | Make vs to wish theyr choking' (lines 349–50). The reference has a distinguished and obvious classical precedent in the *Georgics*, where Virgil describes the dangers and irritations that the farmer needs to be prepared to confront, culminating in the croaking of frogs:

> No, rain need never take us
> Unawares: for high-flying cranes will have flown to valley bottoms
> To escape the rain as it rises, or else a calf has looked up
> At the sky and snuffed the wind with nostrils apprehensive,
> Or the tittering swallow has flitted around and around the lake,
> And frogs in the mud have croaked away at their old complaint.[139]

In recalling this line in a marriage hymn Spenser situates bride and groom in a country setting, ready to run their estates together, suggesting that he now identifies himself and his future with his country estate at Kilcolman.

Given the ways in which Elizabeth is represented in the *Amoretti* as a beautiful, cruel tyrant, we might wonder whether she read Spenser's work. Most likely, she was party to his literary games and representation of their lives in fictionalized form, as it appears Machabyas was over a decade earlier, a privileged woman reader entering a male world of reading and writing together, shared books and manuscripts, and the deft use of print.[140] A copy of *The Faerie Queene* exists, now in private hands, which, if it is authentic (a big 'if'), was the volume that Spenser must have given to Elizabeth. At the end, beside the Letter to Ralegh, is an earlier version of the first sonnet of the *Amoretti*:

A sa mistresse

Happy ye leaves when as those lilly Hands
That houlds my life in hir deaddoing might
Shall handle yo^u and hold in Loves swete bandes
Like captives trembling at ye victors sight.

Happy ye liues when as wth stary light
Those lamping eies shall deigne on yo^u to looke
And reade the sorowes of my dieng spright
Written wth tears in harts close bleedinge book.

Happy ye rymes bathed in ye sacred brook
Of Helicon whence shee derived is
When as you shall beholde y^t angels looke
My soules longe lacked foode my heavens blisse.

Leaves, lines & rymes seeke her to please alone
Whome if yo^u please I care for others none/.[141]

The printed version of the sonnet has been lightly but carefully revised. In line 2 'That' has become 'which'; in line 3 'swete' has become 'soft'; line 5 has been changed to 'And happy lines, on which with starry light'; in line 6, 'shall' has become 'will' and 'on yo^u' has become 'sometimes'; in line 9 'Happy ye rymes' has been changed to 'And happy rymes' to parallel the structure of line 5; line 11 has become 'When ye behold that Angels blessed looke'; and in line 14, 'yo^u' has become 'ye'. The possible revisions are plausible, although as there are no Spenser holographs, we know very little about his writing practices, and the revised poem could well be a fake.[142]

But even if the inscription is fraudulent, the point may not be seriously affected. In both versions of the sonnet Spenser casts Elizabeth as the most important reader of his poetry, making it clear that the references to her bewitching eyes throughout the sequence signal not just her beauty but her ability to read the 'Leaues, lines and rymes' that he has written for her. Spenser claims that he is only happy when writing for her, anchoring his poetry in his private, domestic sphere, with the knowledge that in print the representation of that personal world takes on a different meaning as an alternative to the courtly mode that has dominated English poetry and that he has now appropriated and subverted.[143] The point becomes all the more obvious when read alongside the references to the merchant families as the community in which the couple exist. In inscribing the first edition of his magnum opus for Elizabeth to read and to become his reader, Spenser includes Elizabeth within his circle of readers, inscribing the book to mark their new life together. It is likely, then, that the sonnet to Bryskett describing his failure to complete the second part of *The Faerie Queene* because of his quest for Elizabeth's hand, was a shared joke between a married couple rather than simply an address to a male friend about the malign effects of his love life on his work.[144] After all, Spenser had represented his married life in this way before.

And an old flame was indeed revitalized in the same year. Rosalind appears again as Colin's love in *Colin Clout*. As in the *Calender* she is represented as a cruel mistress who has rejected poor Colin's advances by the shepherds Hobbinol and Lucid: 'Indeed (said *Lucid*) I have often heard | Faire *Rosalind* of divers fowly blamed: | For being to that swaine [Colin] too cruel hard, | That her bright glorie else hath much defamed' (lines 907–10). Exactly like Elizabeth Boyle in the *Amoretti*. Nevertheless, Colin vigorously defends her in the closing speech of the poem:

> Ah shepheards (then said *Colin*) ye ne weet
> How great a guilt upon your heads ye draw:
> To make so bold a doome with words unmeet,
> Of thing celestiall which ye never saw.
> For she is not like as the other crew
> Of shepheards daughters which emongst you bee,
> But of divine regard and heavenly hew,
> Excelling all that ever ye did see.
> Not then to her that scorned thing so base,
> But to my selfe the blame that lookt so hie:
> So hie her thoughts as she her selfe have place,
> And loath each lowly thing with loftie eie.
> Yet so much grace let her vouchsafe to grant
> To simple swaine, sith her I may not love:
> Yet that I may her honour paravant,
> And praise her worth, though far my wit above.
> Such grace shall be some guerdon for the griefe,
> And long affliction which I have endured:
> Such grace sometimes shall give me some reliefe,
> And ease of paine which cannot be recured.
> And ye my fellow shepheards which do see
> And heare the languours of my too long dying,
> Unto the world for ever witnesse bee,
> That hers I die, nought to the world denying,
> This simple trophe of her great conquest. (lines 927–51)

Even though he has not yet won her love, Rosalind gives Colin a reason for making Ireland his home, providing him with the 'grace' that renders the pains of living in Ireland bearable. The key lines in this speech are surely 'Unto the world for ever witnesse bee, I That hers I die, nought to the world denying'. Colin hints strongly that he desires a permanent union with Rosalind, which can only mean marriage, especially when written by a poet so obsessed with the institution. These lines appear to allude to those in the marriage ceremony that require the couple to live together 'forsaking all other', and to promise 'to love and to cherish, tyll death us depart'.[145] Therefore, Rosalind must now be Spenser's new wife, Elizabeth.[146] Even though we cannot be sure when these lines were written and whether they survive from a 1591 version of the poem, or a time closer to 1594, the poem points towards a new marriage in Ireland as a means of establishing the poet's sense of place and making him accept the hostile country as his real home, the debate over Spenser's 'home' and identity being a—if not the—key theme of *Colin Clout*. The ending, which looks forward to a marriage as a reason for making and staying in a home, also provides a neat link to the *Amoretti* and *Epithalamion*, and suggests that we should read these three poems as a group centred around Spenser's second marriage. Spenser seems to have revised *Colin Clout* in order to confirm his identity as an Englishman in Ireland. The poem cannot simply be read as an anti-court poem—although it is that. Spenser makes it clear that he is staying in Ireland because he has met and married Elizabeth, a second Rosalind who will transform his life as the first did. In dating and describing the poem as written 'From my house of Kilcolman, the 27. of December. 1591' Spenser connects it not just to Ralegh and their journey to London (1589–90), but also to its importance in his own life, as his estate and the home of his wife, linking the two as key events in his story. Both point him in the same direction, away from the court and towards Ireland with its community of shepherds and merchants, where he plans to remain rooted.[147]

Rosalind's new identity as Elizabeth is also confirmed in the second edition of *The Faerie Queene*, yet another example of Spenser cross-referencing his works with each other and with his life, his fictional creations reappearing throughout his career in different guises. As has often been noted, a fourth Grace, who 'seem'd all the rest in beauty to excell', appears on Mount Acidale before Colin Clout, a fictionalized version of the poet (VI.x.14, line 4). This Grace, Elizabeth, represents his new wife, who, despite her relatively humble origins, surpasses the queen and is the chief inspiration of Colin, the shepherd poet (VI.x.25–8).[148] Furthermore, Elizabeth is 'Crownd with a rosie girlond, that right well I Did her beseeme' (14, lines 5–6). 'Rosie girlond' is a reference to Rosalind, with the clear implication that Elizabeth is her new manifestation.[149]

Bound in the same volume as *Colin Clout* was *Astrophel: A Pastoral Elegy upon the death of the most noble and Valorous Knight, Sir Philip Sidney*, and dedicated to Sidney's widow, Frances Walsingham.[150] She had secretly married Robert Devereux, second earl of Essex, in the late 1580s, the union becoming public in 1590 when her advanced pregnancy could no longer be kept hidden.[151] This is probably the most mysterious volume which contains Spenser's work. There is no dedication prefacing the poems, not even a deliberately misleading one, providing us with clues as to its provenance, so we have no sense of who made the decision to publish the miscellaneous volume; what input the publisher, Ponsonby, had; whether Spenser—or someone else—collected poems by the other poets included in the volume; or whether the writers compiled the volume themselves. Perhaps Ponsonby was attempting to further exploit Spenser's fame, but, if so, the volume seems oddly placed as a hidden second part to *Colin Clout*.

In his dedicatory letter to Philip's sister, Mary, prefacing *The Ruines of Time*, Spenser states that he had started to write some poetry in memory of Sidney, which had not yet reached fruition. He acknowledged that when he was in England 'some frends of mine . . . knowing with howe straight bandes of duetie I was tied to him . . . haue sought to reuiue them [i.e., the poems] by upraiding me: for that I haue not shewed anie thankefull remembrance towards him' or his family.[152] Nevertheless, this does not explain why the volume did not appear for another four years, especially as the belated nature of the tribute had already been acknowledged. *Complaints* was published five years after Sidney's death, meaning that Spenser waited for almost a decade before commemorating the event, and, as the letter prefacing the *Ruines* acknowledges, the Sidneys do not seem to have been pleased by the long hiatus, which was perhaps inspired by a serious rivalry between the two poets.[153] Spenser's whole career is notable for gaps and delays as well as frenetic bouts of publication and there are probably a host of reasons why works did not appear smoothly and easily, not least because he offended so many important people throughout his life. But the explanation for the wait here may be the simple one that he only published the elegy when it was ready. After all, we know that he began his literary career at the relatively late age of 25, perhaps slightly older; revised a large number of early works, abandoning others; and worked on his magnum opus for at least twenty years. Spenser was not a poet who liked to publish work when others wanted it. He only produced his work when he was satisfied with what he had written.[154]

Astrophel contains other poems besides Spenser's: two elegies, 'The Mourning Muse of Thestylis' and 'A Pastorall Aeglogue Vpon the Death of Sir Philip Sidney Knight', which are attributed to 'L. B.', generally assumed to be Lodowick Bryskett, and which show him to be a more than competent poet; one by Mathew Roydon; an epitaph by Walter Ralegh; the volume concluding with another epitaph by Fulke Greville or Edward Dyer.[155] The whole volume was, according to Patrick Cheney, 'historic... the first book in English literature to feature the national poet as the center of a national community of fellow poets and civic leaders', further evidence of Spenser's role within an intellectual culture and his relationship to other writers.[156] These last three poems had already appeared in sequence as the first three poems in the collection of poetry and prose, *The Phoenix Nest* (1593), compiled by Richard Stapleton, a gentleman of the Inner Temple.[157] That volume was in part a collection of poems dedicated to the memory of Philip Sidney, in part a robust defence of the legacy of Leicester and his circle against the attacks launched by Nashe in particular, in *Pierce Penilesse.*[158]

The compilation of *The Phoenix Nest* sets in train a number of issues as we do not know who authorized the selection of poems, which includes work by Oxford, Dyer, Greene, and Peele, as well as writers with connections to Spenser: Breton, Lodge, and Ralegh.[159] The same problem applies to the *Astrophel* volume: unless we assume that Ponsonby imposed the selection on one of his greatest literary assets, then either Spenser must have agreed to the choice of poems, or made them himself. This then leads to the question of authorship. The poems that appeared in both *The Phoenix Nest* and *Astrophel* were clearly written by poets other than Spenser. However, evidence indicates that some of the other poems in *Astrophel* may have been jointly authored, notably Bryskett's 'Pastorall Aeglogue', which may have been partially written by Spenser, suggesting that the poem was written specially for the volume, perhaps making the whole enterprise a joint project.[160]

The poem is a dialogue between Colin (Spenser) and Lycon (Bryskett), which looks back to the debate eclogues in the *Calender*, especially 'November', in lamenting the death of the dominant literary force of the 1580s.[161] The two names stand as anagrams of each other, probably meaning to signal how closely the two men worked together, something that Bryskett, who probably knew Sidney much better than Spenser, having accompanied him on his grand tour, highlights in his *Discourse of Civil Life.*[162] Certainly Colin's voice sounds 'distinctly Spenserian' and, if it is not by Spenser, then it was ventriloquized by someone who was able to imitate the *Calender* and *Colin Clout* (which he must have seen in manuscript) perfectly.[163] Colin's opening speech begins:

> Ah *Lycon, Lycon,* what need skill, to teach
> A grieued mynd power forth his plaints? How long
> Hath the pore Turtle gon to school (weenest thou)
> To learne to mourne her lost make? No, no, each
> Creature by nature can tell how to waile.
> Seest not these flockes, how sad they wander now?
> Seemeth their leaders bell their bleating tunes
> In dolefull sound. Like him, not one doth faile
> With hanging head to shew a heauie cheare,

PLATE 1 'Spenser and Raleigh'.

PLATE 2   Canons Ashby, Northamptonshire.

PLATE 3   1 Amery Street, Alton, where Spenser is said to have lived.

PLATE 4   Pembroke College, Cambridge.

PLATE 5   Hill Hall, Theydon Mount, Essex.

PLATE 6   Gabriel Harvey's house, Market Street, Saffron Walden.

PLATE 7   Gabriel Harvey's fireplace.

PLATE 9   The Bishop's Palace, Bromley.

PLATE 10 Rochester Cathedral.

PLATE 11 St Giles church, Risby.

PLATE 12
Dublin Castle.

PLATE 13   Glenmalure.

PLATE 14   St Patrick's Cathedral, Dublin.

PLATE 15   Christ Church Cathedral, Dublin.

PLATE 16 Enniscorthy Castle, Co. Wexford.

PLATE 17 St Mary's church, New Ross, Co. Wexford, next to the site of the Augustinian friary.

PLATE 18   Mallow Castle, Co. Cork.

PLATE 19   Misericord in Limerick Cathedral.

PLATE 20   Effin church.

PLATE 21
Kilcolman Castle, Co. Cork.

PLATE 22   Galtymore, Co. Cork.

PLATE 23   Molana Abbey, near Youghal.

PLATE 24   Ballynamona Castle, Co. Cork.

PLATE 25   Bregog River, dry in summer, at Streamhill Bridge, part of Spenser's estate.

PLATE 26 Tomb of William Wallop, St James's church, Wield.

PLATE 27 Farleigh Wallop, Hampshire.

PLATE 28   Ormond Castle, Carrick on Suir.

PLATE 29   The Tynte monument, Kilcredan church, near Youghal.

PLATE 30   Bradden, Northamptonshire.

PLATE 31   The Spenser plaque, church of St Mary, Everdon, Northamptonshire.

PLATE 32   Youghal strand.

PLATE 33   St Mary's church, Youghal.

PLATE 35   The Boyle monument, St Mary's church, Youghal.

PLATE 34   Tynte's Castle, Youghal.

PLATE 36   Buttevant Abbey, Co. Cork.

PLATE 37   Buttevant Abbey (detail).

PLATE 38   Bridgetown Priory, Co. Cork.

PLATE 39   Kilbonane church, Co. Cork.

PLATE 40   Holy Trinity church, Templebreedy, Crosshaven.

PLATE 41   Confluence of the Beheena and the Fanchin rivers.

PLATE 42   The cave at Kilcolman.

PLATE 43   Christ church, Kilbrogan, Bandon, Co. Cork.

PLATE 44   Spenser monument,
Westminster Abbey.

PLATE 45   Chesterfield portrait of
Edmund Spenser.

PLATE 46   Kinnoull portrait of
Edmund Spenser.

PLATE 47   Plimpton portrait of
Edmund Spenser.

> What bird (I pray thee) hast thou seen, that prunes
> Himselfe of late? Did any cheerfull note
> Come to thine eares, or gladsome sight appeare
> Vnto thine eies, since that same fatall howre?[164]

The confident representation of dialogue, the use of brackets to insert parentheses, the concentration on Anglo-Saxon diction, the employment of carefully chosen repetition and parallels, and the skill in producing a consistent iambic pentameter with frequent enjambement, all point to Spenser's authorship of Colin's lines. It was only after his death that other poets, such as William Browne in *Britannia's Pastorals* (1613), consistently started to adopt Spenser's persona as Colin (although Harvey had addressed Spenser as Colin in his commendatory verse to *The Faerie Queene*, 'To the learned Shepheard'). In his lifetime Spenser forged Colin's voice as his own, which suggests that Spenser probably wrote these lines, and that we should read the poetic dialogue with Bryskett as a real one, perhaps composed together by the friends.

However, the most contentious and problematic issue in the volume has been the relationship between *Astrophel* itself and the poem that follows it, the 'Doleful Lay of Clorinda'. In the final stanza of *Astrophel* the speaker announces that the poet's sister, Clorinda, will deliver a 'dolefull laye' (line 214) to the assembled mourners. The monologue appears as a separate poem in this volume, divided by a printer's flower. Later in Matthew Lownes's edition of 1611 the two poems were merged and critics have been divided about the authorship of the 'Doleful Lay'.[165] Is Spenser ventriloquizing Mary Sidney; did they collaborate on the poem; or did she write it for inclusion in the volume?[166] As much recent feminist criticism has argued, it is almost impossible to extract authentic female voices from complex literary texts, which, directly or indirectly, involve collaboration, and we should modify our understanding of 'authorship' to include the person who shaped the work into its published form.[167]

Nevertheless, it is hard to imagine that Spenser or Ponsonby would have buried the poem so discreetly if they had secured a work by such a powerful figure, or that, given the differences of rank and status between the two, they would have cooperated on such a poem. There are few examples of such a collaborative practice—the 'Pastorall Aeglogue' being a potentially rare case, albeit a dialogue. Even Harvey and Spenser appear to have written alongside and in relationship to each other rather than composed passages together. More importantly, there was a long literary tradition of male writers imitating female voices, a significant example being Erasmus' *Praise of Folly* first printed in 1511, which, of course, Spenser would have known, as he would have encountered Erasmus at school, and of which he undoubtedly owned a copy, especially as it was discussed by Sidney in his *Apology*.[168] George Gascoigne, who was highly regarded by Harvey and Spenser, who dedicated a work to Lord Grey de Wilton and who worked on an entertainment to celebrate Elizabeth's progress to Kenilworth in the summer of 1575 with Richard Mulcaster, experimented with female voices and represented himself as a female supplicant, as well as a hermaphrodite, in *The Steele Glasse*.[169] A devotee of Ariosto, Gascoigne was an ambitious writer with a substantial output of diverse forms who had an impact on the poetic practice of many subsequent writers, including Spenser, and may well have had an influence here.[170] And, Nicholas Breton, a poet Spenser knew who attracted the countess's patronage, later assumed her persona in his poetry, notably 'The Countess of Pembroke's Love', published in 1592, and 'The Countess of Pembroke's Passion', probably written around the same time and perhaps inspired by Spenser's example.[171] The publication of the latter as *The Passions of the Spirit* (1599), addressed to another patron, Mary Houghton, the wife of a sheriff of London, appears, not surprisingly, to have gravely offended the countess, a sign of the high risk that such prosopopoeia ran, and an indication of how close to the wind Spenser was sailing in his poem.[172] One of Spenser's characteristic poetic strategies was to insert dramatic monologues into his works, a practice he followed throughout his literary career, and, in terms of rhetorical practice, as well as style and diction, the poem reads as if it were the work of one author.[173] Moreover, as Pamela Coren has argued, Spenser is not trying to pass his work off as that of the countess; rather, 'The *Lay* does what it should for *Astrophel*, completes the fiction with a "womanish" burst of feeling and orthodox otherworldly direction'.[174]

The suspicion that the *Astrophel* volume was designed by Spenser and Bryskett is further strengthened by a reference in Bryskett's other poem, 'The Mourning Muse of Thestylis', to the voice of Mary Sidney. Bryskett refers to 'His [Philip Sidney's] noble sisters plaints, her sighes and teares emong, I Would sure haue made thee milde, and inly rue her paine'.[175] Such lines could only have been written if the author had had access to the 'Doleful Lay' in manuscript.[176] It is somewhat less likely that 'Pembroke and Bryskett worked with Spenser to prepare *Astrophel* as a commemorative volume that would include a selection of works written by his friends', although by no means impossible, given the countess's role in seeing her brother's work into print.[177] Moreover, as her translations of the Psalms indicate, she was a close and careful reader of Spenser's *Ruines* poems, adopting his vocabulary and imagery to supplement biblical language in order to represent the pathos of mutability.[178]

A more significant issue that has not been addressed is Spenser's appropriation of an aristocratic female voice, a device traceable back to the *Heroides*, a major component of the classical tradition within which Spenser worked.[179] This is a sign of his confidence as a poet, as he 'places himself as leading the mourning' for Sidney, 'contain[ing] and control[ling] the figure of the countess of Pembroke with her superior claims to the position of chief mourner, by placing her in a relationship of dependency' within a text he controls.[180] Furthermore, given the countess's undoubtedly hostile reaction to Thomas Newman's appropriation of *Astrophil and Stella*, and her probable intervention to have the pirated volume impounded by Burghley in 1591 before being reissued with corrections, Spenser was, yet again, showing that he published as he pleased, and was prepared to take risks that few other poets would take.[181]

Astrophel appears, then, as a complex and integrated poem, with a number of European and classical sources, including Ronsard and Ovid.[182] Perhaps its most significant debt is to Moschus' *Lament for Bion*, enabling Spenser to emphasize his own role as the funeral poet speaking for a grieving nation.[183] While the join between the poem that we know to be Spenser's and the female complaint of the 'Doleful Lay' is not seamless, that poem is written in the same style as those produced by the melancholy female narrators in *The Ruines of Time* and *The Ruines of Rome*, making it hard to tell their voices apart:

> O vaine worlds glorie, and vnstedfast state
> Of all that liues, on face of sinfull earth,
> Which from their first vntill their vtmost date
> Tast no one hower of happines or merth,
> But like as at the ingate of their berth,
> They crying creep out of their mothers woomb,
> So wailing backe go to their wofull tomb. (*The Ruines of Time*, lines 43–9)

> Ay me, to whom shall I my case complaine,
> That may comparison my impatient griefe,
> Or where shall I vnfold my inward paine,
> That my enriuen heart may find relief?
> Shall I vnto the heauenly powers it show?
> Or vnto earthly men that dwell below? ('Doleful Lay of Clorind, lines 1–6)

It would have been almost impossible for readers to tell the style and tone of these works apart, which is presumably the point. Each female narrator begins with an apostrophe, which, in Quintilian's terms, is 'the diversion of our words to address some person other than the judge', i.e., an utterance with no particular addressee.[184] More specifically, each speaker employs the figure of ecphonesis (exclamation), an expression of 'extreme emotion'.[185] Both lament the vanity of earth's glory and urge the hearer to place their trust in heaven in an elegiac style that Spenser had adopted from the start of his literary career and had produced at length in the *Complaints* volume. The rhyme scheme of each poem is almost identical (*The Ruines of Time* has an extra fifth line), as is the diction (again, conspicuously Anglo-Saxon) and the predominantly end-stopped lines.

Yet again, the *Astrophel* volume is a work that risks offending the good and the great through its appropriation of their voices, and through deliberately revisiting the *Complaints*, a work still subject to censorship that Spenser also alludes to in the dedicatory letters to the *Fowre Hymnes* a year later. This tactic is in line with Spenser's conspicuous public self-representation as a middle-class poet, eager to show off his skills in opposition to the courtly centre, especially when read alongside its companion poem, *Colin Clout*.[186] Perhaps the fear of offending yet more courtiers explains why this volume, clearly designed to help foster the burgeoning legend of Sidney as the lost great aristocratic poet, was published in such an unusual, disguised manner.[187] As Danielle Clarke has pointed out, Spenser cunningly appropriates both the voice and the legend of the Sidneys, in having Clorinda's poem echo his own, 'thus overseeing the transition from Sidney to Spenser as the poet occupying the preeminent position' in England.[188] This changing of the guard was also acutely imagined, as it had to be, in terms of class.

The volume appears to have had a serious impact, significantly transforming the representation of Sidney from a soldier to a poet, which suggests that it did reach a wide audience, showing how eager readers were to consume Spenser's work in the mid-1590s and how carefully they read it.[189] Ponsonby might have held the volume back at the press, if he feared the consequences of publishing the work, and it is plausible that the *Astrophel* volume was completed soon after the *Phoenix Nest*, ready for publication in 1594. We will probably never know why *Astrophel* was published as an appendage to *Colin Clout*, but, especially given Spenser's complicated publication record and his fraught relationship with authority, the decision to bind the volumes together cannot have been taken lightly or be entirely devoid of significance.

Spenser's elegy is not uncritical of Sidney, who, in his warrior mode, is cast as a combination of the reckless Adonis and the terrifying Talus, the Iron Man of the second edition of *The Faerie Queene*, administering the violent side of the law.[190] Spenser describes Astrophel as a foolhardy and bloodthirsty soldier, who courts death and is appropriately rewarded:

> It fortuned as he, that perlous game
> In forreine soyle pursued far away:
> Into a forest wide, and waste he came
> Where store he heard to be of saluage pray.
> So wide a forest and so waste as this,
> Nor famous *Ardeyn*, nor fowle *Arlo* is.
> There his welwouen toyles and subtil traines,
> He laid the brutish nation to enwrap:
> So well he wrought with practise and with paines,
> That he of them great troups did soone entrap.
> Full happie man (misweening much) was hee,

So rich a spoile within his power to see.
Eftsoones all heedlesse of his dearest hale,
Full greedily into the heard he thrust:
To slaughter them, and work their finall bale,
Least that his tolye should of their troups be brust.
Wide wounds emongst them many a one he made,
Now with his sharp borespeare, now with his blade.
His care was all how he them all might kill,
That none might scape (so partiall vnto none)
Ill mynd so much to mynd anothers ill,
As to become vnmyndfull of his owne.
But pardon that vnto the cruell skies,
That from himselfe to them withdrew his eies.
So as he rag'd emongst that beastly rout,
A cruell beast of most accursed brood:
Vpon him turnd (despeyre makes cowards stout)
And with fell tooth accustomed to blood,
Launched his thigh with so mischieuous might,
That it both bone and muscles ryued quight. (lines 91–120)

The implicit comparison is to the legend of Adonis, gored to death by a boar; undoubtedly with Shakespeare's recently published poem (1593) in mind.[191] Sidney/Astrophel deserves his fate even more than Adonis did. Adonis was merely naive in his pursuit of the boar; Sidney is actively cruel in his desire to kill the enemy. He is happy in his role as an errant knight, failing to realize that he is neither performing at a tilt for his uncle, the earl of Leicester, whose estates bordered the forest, nor in an unavoidably dangerous situation, like Spenser, who lived near to 'fowle Arlo' and so had to defend himself from attack, as descriptions of the shepherds' life in Ireland in *Colin Clout* made clear. In that poem, Colin celebrates the stable life of rural England by means of a comparison with the dangers experienced in rural Ireland:

No wayling there nor wretchednesse is heard,
No bloodie issues nor no leprosies,
No griesly famine, nor no raging sweard,
No nightly bo[r]drags, nor no hue and cries;
The shepheards there abroad may safely lie,
On hills and downes, withouten dread or daunger:
No rauenous wolues the good mans hope destroy,
Nor outlawes fell affray the forest raunger. (lines 312–19)

Colin is talking about an area such as Arlo, the glen about twenty miles north-east of his estate, which, as 'Two Cantos of Mutabilitie' demonstrates, Spenser recognized as

319

one of the most dangerous areas in Ireland, a place that the English crown could not afford to ignore if it wished to govern Ireland effectively. The reference in *Astrophel* contrasts violence that has to be carried out, such as that at Smerwick Harbour, with the juvenile bloodlust of Sidney. It is no accident that he chances upon a forest that is 'waste', the description combining a romance motif with a technical legal term to demonstrate the extent of Sidney's misplaced valour.[192] Spenser shows that Sidney has cut himself off from any divine direction, the words used forcefully demonstrating his lack of care and knowledge of what he was doing: 'misweening', 'heedlesse', 'unmindfull'. More disturbing still is Sidney's eagerness to kill: he is represented as unable to control his martial vigour, greedy in his desire to slaughter as many of the enemy as he can, making himself as savage and as brutish as the enemy he hunts, a familiar motif in Spenser's writing, especially in the second half of *The Faerie Queene*.[193]

These lines should be read with a number of considerations in mind. Sidney's death on 17 October 1586 from the injuries sustained at Zutphen took place just before the recall of the commander of the forces, Leicester, in November. Towards the end of his life Leicester was extremely unpopular and was blamed for the failure of the war and the death of Sidney.[194] In pointing out that the dead Sidney had not been fighting in the Forest of Arden, Spenser was rather archly reminding readers that Sidney had perished in a disastrous campaign, led by his uncle, which had failed to achieve any of its goals, continuing his criticisms of the earl. The hostile comments further indicate that Spenser, for all his opposition to aggressive international Catholicism, was not necessarily an uncritical supporter of the war in the Netherlands, and that he was painfully aware of the costs of war, one reason why he was so eager to defend Lord Grey from the charge that he was a 'blodye man' in *A View*. In contrast to Grey, Sidney and, by implication, Leicester are represented as very bloody men. It is perhaps worth recalling that Spenser was certainly familiar with a large number of Dutch immigrants in London, many of whom, like van der Noot, had undoubtedly returned to their native land. A large proportion of them would have been eager to stay clear of the religious crusade that Leicester was eager to launch; some would have been members of the Family of Love; and others, like Jan van der Noot, would have reconverted to Catholicism out of either conviction or expediency. Spenser did support Elizabeth's right to intervene in the Low Countries as proper resistance to international tyranny in the Belge episode in *The Faerie Queene*, Book V, cantos x–xi.[195] But, as these lines in *Astrophel* demonstrate, he was clearly less than enthusiastic about Leicester's role.

Spenser was concerned to show that Sidney's real achievement was not as a soldier, or an aristocratic patron, but as a widely read poet.[196] In the poem we witness Astrophel/Sidney abandoning poetry for military glory (lines 67–72); Spenser returns Sidney to his true vocation, so recovering what he did best for a non-courtly audience.[197] In doing so he claims his legacy for the shepherds, 'all which loued him full deare' (line 200), figures who represent other poets, as well as ordinary readers away from the court. He quite deliberately makes Sidney seem like himself in *Colin Clout*, one of the 'shepheardes nation'.[198] And, following Sidney's conceit in *Astrophil and Stella*, Spenser stellifies the poet as his (Sidney's) fictional alter ego:

> The Gods which all things see, this same beheld,
> And pittying this paire of louers trew:
> Transformed them there lying on the field,
> Into one flowre that is both red and blew.
> It first growes red, and then to blew doth fade,
> Like *Astrophel*, which thereinto was made.
> And in the midst thereof a star appeares,
> As fairly formd as any star in skyes:
> Resembling *Stella* in her freshest yeares,
> Forth darting beames of beautie from her eyes,
> And all the day it standeth full of deow,
> Which is the teares, that from her eyes did flow. (lines 181–92)

If Stella is Penelope Devereux, then Spenser has deliberately obscured the complicated personal histories of Philip and Penelope so that they can be reunited after death. In joining them as a posthumous couple—even though Penelope Devereux did not die until 1607 and was famous in the 1590s for her scandalous affair with Charles Blount, Baron Mountjoy—Spenser is placing the literary relationship ahead of what happened in real life.[199] If Stella is Sidney's widow, Frances, then Spenser has used the name Stella in the same way that he used Rosalind in representing his own love life in poetry.[200] Either way, the end result is the same: Spenser is, in effect, rewriting Sidney's sonnet sequence as if it were his own story of happy, provincial marriage. The shepherd-poets, at least, have inspirational figures to follow. Meanwhile Clorinda is left to mourn her loss, in the familiar style of female complaint, a genre developed in this period by Spenser and Spenserian poets, most notably Daniel and later Drayton, which in effect proves Spenser's point that the aristocracy need to learn from the work of their social inferiors.[201] Having discounted any comfort from the heavens or men, she turns to the natural world:

> Woods, hills and riuers, now are desolate,
> Sith he is gone the which them all did grace:
> And all the fields do waile their widow state,
> Sith death their fairest flowre did late deface.
> The fairest flowre in field that euer grew,
> Was *Astrophel*; that was, we all may rew.
> What cruell hand of cursed foe vnknowne,

Hath cropt the stalke which bore so faire a flowre?
Vntimely cropt, before it well were growne,
And cleane defaced in vntimely howre.
Great losse to all that euer [did] him see,
Great losse to all, but greatest losse to mee. (lines 25–36)

Spenser has employed another of his favourite poetic devices, prosopopoeia, making Clorinda one in a line of female personae in Spenser's poetry, her words recalling the speeches of Verlame and Rome in the *Complaints*. Clorinda/Mary Sidney is desolate in her grief, experiencing Nature as a bleak reflection of her state of mind and seeing her own loss as the greatest of all. The universe provides her with no sense of purpose. The shepherd-poets, in contrast, remember Sidney as a fellow poet, who looks down on them from the heavens and so helps them produce their work. Spenser, who had first praised Sidney back in the 1570s, now 'can repudiate his precursor at the same time that he invents him', and, in doing so, glorify/stellify his own literary career.[202]

10

Return to London, 1596–7

THE YEAR 1596 was another major one in Spenser's life, although it proved to be a swansong rather than a new beginning. No one could have known at the time that it would be the last year in which he published anything: Spenser undoubtedly had a lot more to say that never materialized. By its end he had produced the second edition of *The Faerie Queene*, adding a further three books and changing the ending of Book III in order to link the narratives together; he had also published the *Fowre Hymnes*; and the *Prothalamion*, a spousal verse for the daughters of the earl of Worcester who were married on 8 November. He also probably started and perhaps finished his prose dialogue, *A View of the Present State of Ireland*, and returned to England with his wife Elizabeth. One aim was to settle an inheritance dispute, as well as to visit a number of significant figures throughout the country.[1] However, if 1594 had seemed an especially hopeful year for Spenser, and, one imagines, the other English inhabitants of the Munster Plantation, then 1596, with the rebellion of Hugh O'Neill gathering pace, was one overshadowed by impending disaster.

If Spenser's public declarations about his marriage are anything to go by, his relationship with Elizabeth was a happy one. Spenser was not an old bridegroom but he would have been aware that he was now well into middle age and may not have had a great deal of time left, which may have been one reason why he wrote and published with such regularity. He was almost certainly at least twice as old as his wife and they lived on his estate, which suggests that he dominated the relationship, as might have been expected. Sylvanus and Katherine would have been teenagers by 1596, so that the birth of Peregrine would have made the household acutely aware that it consisted of two different layers. Elizabeth might even have conceived on their wedding night or very soon after, so the *Epithalamion* may be referring to a fait accompli when it charges Cynthia to bless their union and 'the chast wombe informe with timely seed'.

323

It is possible that we can work out how the Spensers' marriage would have functioned by paying heed to the wealth of social history about early modern marriage and the family, the archaeology of south-west Munster, and what Spenser tells us in his writings. Writing about a slightly later period Alan Bliss has used the evidence of the influence of Irish on the English spoken by settlers to conclude that 'the planters must as babies have been cared for by Irish nurses, and in their childhood they would no doubt have fraternised with the children of their servants'.[2] Certainly there were numerous complaints about Irish wet nurses and foster mothers breastfeeding English babies and so transforming them into rebels.[3] This was a natural corollary to the commonly held belief that wet nurses could determine the character of the babies they suckled.[4] In *A View*, which was written when Spenser had a baby who was probably still being breastfed, Irenius comments that:

The Chief Cause of bringinge in the Irish language amongst them was speciallye their fosteringe and marryinge with the Irishe The which are two moste daungerous infeccions for first the Childe that suckethe the milke of the nurse muste of necessitye learne his firste speache of her, the which beinge the first that is envred to his tongue is ever moste pleasinge vnto him In so muche as thoughe he afterwards be taughte Englishe yeat the smacke of the firste will allwaies abide with him and not onelye of the speche but alsoe of the manners and Condicions for besides the younge Children be like Apes which will affecte and ymitate what they see done before them speciallye by their nurses they love so well. (*Variorum*, x. 119)

Quite a lot can be gleaned from this passage. Irenius casts himself as the man who really knows what is happening in Ireland and so is in a position to speak with authority to those back in England. Like many other commentators, he singles out the Irish practice of fostering children out to nurses as a central cause of Ireland's ills, one that has been imitated by the English, which has caused them to become Irish and which has to be stopped if Ireland is to be reclaimed under English authority.[5] The passage indicates that this was still common practice among colonists on the Munster Plantation, one reason why the settlement was such a dangerous place, lacking proper English authority, the problem beginning within the family unit.[6] Presumably, Irish nurses were chosen because they were available, and English parents acted as they would have if they had been in England; or, perhaps, as in England, the use of wet nurses was a sign of a rise in status, and many settlers were adopting practices and customs that would have been beyond their means in their homeland.[7] In late Elizabethan London parents often sent children out as far as forty miles away to be nursed.[8] In the provinces servants and former servants were used so that wet nursing 'was simply an extension of their previous role within the household'.[9] Such nurses tended to have their own domestic duties and rarely lived with the family for whom they worked, and were invariably chosen with great care.[10]

However, it is hard to imagine that, after Irenius' comments in *A View*, the Spensers would have used Irish nurses to rear Peregrine. This would suggest that either they made use of English servants or that Elizabeth breastfed Peregrine herself.[11] Both Richard Jonas's book on midwifery, *The Byrth of Mankynd* (1540) and Robert Cleaver's *A Godly Form of Household Gouernment* (1598) recommended that mothers breastfeed their children themselves in order to nurture and protect the Protestant family and there was a pressure from some puritan quarters to induce good Protestant mothers to feed their own children.[12] It is more likely that someone of Spenser's relatively new status would have preferred the former option and, possibly through the earl of Cork, who played such a central role in their lives and who influenced so many major decisions made by his extended family, they had access to English domestics who would perform the task. Like many men in the period, he might have objected to his wife breastfeeding and preferred the employment of a wet nurse.[13] Given the wealth of opinions about love, marriage, and reproduction that Spenser articulates in his work it is likely that we would have heard about breastfeeding if he had been a very early advocate of its practice. Peregrine, like his half-brother and half-sister, would have been breastfed for nearly two years, his diet probably supplemented by 'pap and pre-chewed bread or vegetables'.[14] A live-in English/Protestant wet nurse would have joined the array of servants living on the Kilcolman estate.

Most duties in the household would have been devolved to the chief servants of whom there must have been a number in a relatively large household like Kilcolman, especially if we bear in mind the ambitious building projects that were undertaken there in the 1590s.[15] The Spensers must have had at least a dozen servants to run the household, assuming that the tenant farmers played a role in running the estate. If Spenser spent most of his time writing, as his prolific output indicates, Elizabeth probably played a considerable role in overseeing what went on if her life was anything like that described in the diaries left behind by women who managed households in provincial England.[16] The archaeology of the estate suggests that Kilcolman would have been established in relatively similar ways to its English counterparts. Elizabeth, like Machabyas before her, would have tended the gardens near the house; she would probably have been involved in preserving and preparing food; she may well have taken part in brewing ale and, if the estate had beehives, mead, as many women did; she may have had to play some role in sorting out the accounts of the estate, as well as overseeing the servants if her husband was busy and wanted to be left alone to write.[17] She would have been expected to oversee the education of the children, who may have been taught by a private tutor, as no schools would have been available in the area for them to attend.[18] Unless, of course, the couple educated their children themselves. This is possible, as we know from her letters that Elizabeth was literate and articulate, whereas no evidence survives to attest to Machabyas' education. Whatever the arrangements, Elizabeth's life would have been as busy as that of her husband, as early modern marriage dictated that husband and wife were partners, albeit scarcely equal ones.[19] The circumstances of life on the Plantation would have made the Spensers a closer family unit than their English counterparts, especially if Spenser was travelling infrequently by this time.

All of which suggests that the couple probably spent a larger amount of their time with their children than they would have done had they lived in England, since the elder two would still have been at home in the mid-1590s, as they could not have been older than 13 or 14 in 1595. Spenser's work, however, while it shows great interest in marriage and reproduction, contains relatively little about childhood.[20] An exception is the much-discussed episode of the child with the indelibly bloodstained hands, Ruddymane, born to Amavia and Mortdant in Book II of *The Faerie Queene*, but this tells us little about Spenser's understanding of childhood and more about his willingness to explore the subtle nuances of theories of predestination.[21] Moreover, the little evidence we have about his children that survives does not tell us much at all: if anything, it points to an antagonistic relationship between Elizabeth and her sons, perhaps to be expected in a litigious age, but also a possible sign of a household that had been less harmonious than the parents had desired.

It is likely that the household was a godly one, given Spenser's interest in religion and the varieties of religious thought throughout his life, as well as the ways in which he represented his courtship and marriage in the *Amoretti* and *Epithalamion*, and that devotions structured the everyday experience of the house (after all, he had worked for a bishop immediately prior to his first marriage). A key feature of Protestant writers on marriage was that they placed more emphasis on religion as a family experience within the household than their Catholic predecessors and counterparts. Wives were supposed to defer to their husbands, who assumed the role as head of the household; public prayers would mark points in the day; and there would be time for private devotions.[22] Spenser's intimate and detailed knowledge of the Bible, which he undoubtedly read in the Geneva version (although he clearly knew other versions), and his desire to think about its relevance for everyday life suggest that his work was reflected in, and perhaps grew out of, his diurnal experience.[23] It is unlikely that the Spenser household was as pious and devoted as that of the devout Lady Margaret Hoby, who habitually prayed privately at least three times a day, but religious belief would have structured the life of the inhabitants of Kilcolman Castle.

On 20 January the second edition of *The Faerie Queene* was entered in the Stationers' Register.[24] Spenser had clearly been at work on Books IV–VI for much of the time since he had acquired Kilcolman. Parts of Book IV were probably written earlier and survive from an incarnation of the poem produced in the 1580s (although not the Timias/Belphoebe episode in Book IV, cantos vii–viii, which was written after 1592), but Books V and VI read like later works. It is possible, of course, that sections of

Book V were also written earlier than others, notably the story of Britomart and Artegall, but the ending of Book V refers to events in the mid-1590s and is clearly designed to be read alongside Book VI.[25] The new Books significantly widen the focus of the poem, so that the journey from Holiness to Chastity, centred on the individual self, now moves outward through Friendship and Justice to Courtesy. It will always be a matter of debate whether Spenser intended the published poem to end with Book VI, and had abandoned his apparent plan to write twenty-four Books, as he indicated in the Letter to Ralegh.[26] The quest of Calidore is impossible because courtesy is defined in series of contradictory ways, being the 'roote of ciuill conuersation' (VI.i.i, line 6) yet also buried 'deepe within the mynd' (proem, 5, line 8); emanating from the court (i.1, line 1) and imagined as a flower that grows on a 'lowly stalk' (proem, 4, line 3). It is little wonder that Calidore, who 'loathd leasing [lying] and base flattery, I And loued simple truth and stedfast honesty' (i.3, lines 8–9), feels that he has been forced 'To tread an endlesse trace, withouten guyde' (i.6, line 2).[27] Nor is it surprising that his quest seems peripheral to the narrative of the book, which comes to focus on the pastoral community of shepherds who need protecting from savages, brigands, and other hostile enemies, an allegorical continuation of the world that Spenser had established in *Colin Clout*.[28] The ending of the 1596 *Faerie Queene* could be read as a despairing comment on the nature of the project as outlined in the Letter to Ralegh, claiming that the poem was designed to 'fashion a gentleman or noble person in virtuous and gentle discipline'.[29] Now, circumstances contrive to thwart any such project since courtesy, the culmination of a gentleman's training, proves to be an impossible ideal, neither fashioning a gentleman nor enabling him to fashion himself, but actually preventing him from acting.[30] Perhaps the omission of the Letter from the second edition of the poem reflects Spenser's acknowledgement that his original purpose was now impossible—although the 1596 poem still promises twelve books—as well as a sign of his realization that there was nothing to be gained by being so publicly associated with Ralegh. Ralegh was no longer in disgrace in 1596, but he had not regained his original status and the allegorical representation of him as a courtier whose devoted love for Belphoebe exceeds the bounds of what is proper in Book IV of the poem is, at best, an ambiguous defence of a former patron and ally.[31]

The poem did acknowledge, however, the substance of Ralegh's achievements in taking over the patent for the first American colonies, in contrast to some rather sceptical comments about the value of transatlantic discovery that Spenser had made elsewhere. Spenser expanded the 1590 dedication of the poem to Elizabeth as 'Qveene of England, Fravnce and Ireland and of Virginia'.[32] In doing so he recognized the reality of England's overseas possessions, placing them on an equal footing with the multiple kingdoms she ruled within the British archipelago and the rather spurious claim to be the sovereign of the old enemy, France.[33] The edition, printed by

Richard Field who replaced John Wolfe, for Ponsonby, reproduced, in the main, the 1590 text, with a few corrections, and the addition of a stanza, I.xii.3, which had probably been omitted by a printer's error. The mass of commendatory and dedicatory verses were also omitted—along with the Letter—apart from the two sonnets by Ralegh and Harvey's poem, 'To the learned shepherd'. which now appears at the end of Book III and so between the two parts of the poem.[34] This indicates that the first edition had been seen as inadequate, and perhaps Nashe's scathing comments on the accompanying poems had hit home. The 1596 edition was also a far more impressive book, printed on better, more uniform paper than it had been in 1590, so that the print does not bleed as it does in places in the 1590 text, the volume having a more professional appearance, a sign of how much Spenser's stock had risen since his return to print in 1590.[35] The volume would have required three, perhaps four, compositors, a sign also of how carefully the work was printed. Moreover, revisions to the episode involving Sir Sergis, in V.xi.36–44, suggest that Spenser oversaw the production of the second half of the text, if not the first.[36]

The poem was revised to change the ending of Book III so that the story runs on into Book IV. The union of Scudamour and Amoret, who no longer form a hermaphrodite, now takes place in canto x of Book IV.[37] It is possible that Spenser changed the ending of the first edition because of opposition from Burghley, who perceived a reference to the disastrous marriage of his daughter to the earl of Oxford.[38] Book IV has usually been seen as the least successful of the new books, probably because it betrays rather too many traces of its complicated history and the changes that must have been made to it before publication.[39] The ending of the first edition is recycled and refigured, so that Scudamore now tells us how he led Amoret away from the Temple of Venus, having become a Petrarchan lover eager to impose himself on his lady, not an equal half of conjoined flesh. He displays his shield to Amoret 'On which when *Cupid* with his killing bow | And cruell shafts emblazond she beheld, | At sight thereof she was with terror queld, | And said no more' (IV.x.55, lines 3–6). He then seizes her hand and forcibly removes her from the Temple, seeing her as a 'warie Hynd within the weedie soyle', boasting that 'no intreatie would forgoe so glorious spoyle' (lines 8–9). In the first edition of the poem the union of the lovers had a clear purpose in showing a Platonic ideal of equal married love and looking forward to Britomart's realization of the true ideal of chastity. Here, the story is deferred once more, and no end is in sight. The virtue of friendship points us forward to the opening out of private values into a more obviously public world, but it is not always clear where we are heading.

In a sense, this is the point. Just as Calidore laments that he has to follow an endless trace without any real means of understanding where he is going or what he is doing, so does the narrator of Book IV exclaim towards the end of the book, 'O what en endlesse worke haue I in hand' (xii.1, line 1). It is significant that this complaint appears immediately after Spenser has told the story of the marriage of the Thames and the Medway, surely a revised version of one of his earliest lost poems, *Epithalamion Thamesis*, now incorporating his knowledge of the Irish rivers, especially those near his home, who are invited to the nuptials of the chief rivers of the queen's dominions.[40] Spenser is commenting not simply on the complexity of his task in trying to finish *The Faerie Queene*, already noted in *Amoretti* 33, but also on his life's work as a poet, one that could never be completed to his satisfaction. In representing the Irish rivers he makes three central points. First, he shows how vital the rivers are to Irish economy and society, in providing transport links as well as sustenance. Second, he emphasizes his own relationship to the natural world:

> There was the Liffy rolling downe the lea,
> The sandy Slane, the stony Aubrian,
> The spacious Shenan spreading like a sea,
> The pleasant Boyne, the fishy fruitfull Ban,
> Swift Awniduff, which of the English man
> Is cal'de Blacke water, and the Liffar deep,
> Sad Trowis, that once his people ouerran,
> Strong Allo tombling from Slewlogher steep,
> And Mulla mine, whose waues I whilom taught to weep. (IV.xi.41)

The list of rivers begins with the Liffey, which Spenser would have known well from his life in Dublin; it includes the Arlo (the Aubrian), which flows down from Arlo Hill (Galtymore); it notes that the English have named the Blackwater, the arterial waterway of south Munster and Spenser's route down to Youghal; and it concludes with a reference to his local waterway, the Awbeg, the tributary of the Blackwater, that flowed through his estate.[41] The inclusion of the Irish rivers also reminds the reader that all is not simply harmonious: why has Spenser taught the waves of the Awbeg to weep? Is it because he is seen as an intruder? Or has he told the sad stories of his life to his local river?

Third, Spenser shows how little control the English have over the Irish rivers, and how they are unable to record them all. The description begins: 'Though I them all according their degree, | Cannot recount, nor tell their hidden race, | Nor read the saluage cuntreis, thorough which they pace' (40, lines 7–9). The same applies to the 'saluage cuntreis', and also because they are not appropriate guests at a wedding. In mentioning the hostility of the country Spenser is reminding readers of the provisional nature of the celebration of the union, one that is still under threat from the combination of forces that he witnessed when he first came to Ireland. The sequence ends with more obvious signs of Irish resistance to English rule: 'The spreading Lee, that like an Island fayre | Encloseth Corke with his deuided flood; | And balefull Oure, late staind with English blood: | With many more, whose names no tongue can tell' (44, lines 3–6). Cork is enclosed because it is a walled city built to withstand assault; the Oure is a reminder of the bloody defeat of Lord Grey's troops in Glenmalure on the banks of the Avonbeg in the Wicklow Mountains. The list begins and ends with references to rivers that Spenser observed in his first few months in Ireland.

Book IV contains a number of different narrative strands that represent the complex elements of friendship and show how our understanding of the virtue is always related to other concerns. As James Nohrnberg has observed, 'Stories begun in III are dilated in IV, and even beyond.'[42] The story of the true friends Cambell and Triamond who, together with their two ladies, make up a group of four, a number that symbolizes concord, is interwoven with the tale of Scudamour, who has been separated from Amoret, and that of the discordant group of four false friends, which includes Duessa, Ate, goddess of Discord in the *Iliad*, and Paridell and Blandamour, as well as Braggadocchio, a word that Spenser added to the language. Also involved are Artegall and Britomart, although they disappear from the narrative halfway through the book. The unit of four is then often combined with other numbers to form yet more stable units, principally with the Telamond of the book's title, the three brothers Priamond, Diamond, and Triamond, and a series of other couples (Triamond and Canacee, Cambell and Cambina) and brother/sister pairs (Cambell and Canacee, Triamond and Cambina). The plot is loosely held together as the changing groups of knights and ladies attend a series of tournaments where the knights compete for the girdles of the true and false Florimells. However Book IV is read and whatever its high points, it appears far more episodic than the other five books of the poem.[43] Spenser continues his sustained interest in Chaucer through a continuation of *The Squire's Tale* beginning in ii.32–4.[44] He imitates the first line of *The Knight's Tale*, the first of *The Canterbury Tales*, 'Whilom, as olde stories tellen us', with his 'Whylome as antique stories tellen us' (IV.ii.32, line 1). Nevertheless, the different forces of amity are brought together at the end of the Book. The relationship between love and friendship is reconciled in a tour de force that pays further homage to Chaucer, the Temple of Venus, in canto x, followed in the next canto by the manifestation of cosmic order in the marriage of the Thames and the Medway.[45]

Books V and VI, works which make an obvious pair, are more clearly rooted in Spenser's experience in Ireland. This is not to deny that, as throughout his work, there are episodes in Book IV which can be related to patterns of imagery that are informed by Spenser's life in Ireland, such as the description of Lust as 'a wilde and salvage man', 'ouergrowne with haire' (IV.viii.5), which forms part of the debate about the nature of the savage in the second edition of the poem.[46] Spenser's representation of the savage can never be separated from, although it is not confined to, his understanding of the nature of Ireland.[47] Book V, for so long the least popular of the Books of the poem because of its brutal subject matter, argues that only if justice is imposed in Ireland can the British Isles flourish in peace and prosperity.[48] When Artegall, the Knight of Justice, is called away prematurely from the Salvage Island by the Faerie Queene, he is first attacked by the hags Envy and Detraction who claim that he has behaved with brutal disregard for the lives of his enemies in Ireland:

> Then th'other [Detraction] comming neare, gan him reuile,
> And fouly rayle, with all she could inuent;
> Saying, that he had with vnmanly guile,
> And foule abusion both his honour blent,
> And that bright sword, the sword of Iustice lent,
> Had stayned with reprochfull crueltie,
> In guiltlesse blood of many an innocent:
> As for *Grandtorto*, him with treacherie
> And traynes hauing surpriz'd, he fouly did to die. (V.xii.40)

The stanza alludes to Lord Grey's alleged treachery at Smerwick, in deluding the besieged Italian and Spanish soldiers, as well as the frequent attacks on his brutal tactics in restoring order, which represented him as a cruel and vicious commander, causing unnecessary bloodshed.[49] Here, Spenser provides a forceful defence of Grey's actions, dehumanizing the opponents of Grey as allegorical representations of related vices, akin to figures such as Malbecco, the envious husband who becomes a figure of jealousy near the end of Book III.[50] We do not learn what the consequences of this failure have been until we read Book VI, the legend of Courtesy, which represents its hero as bewildered and bemused, eager to abandon his quest and to become one of the shepherds he is supposed to protect. His desire may well be reasonable enough, but the consequence is that the shepherds are assaulted and overwhelmed by savages and brigands who are able to ambush them without fear of opposition.[51] The English pastoral world that Spenser created in the *Calender*, which was then transplanted to Ireland in *Colin Clout*, now stands for the rural, non-metropolitan fabric of the British Isles. The message is clear enough: the failure to deal properly with Ireland and to establish a platform on which to build Irish society anew, populated with English settlers who will be enabled to transform the island to an ordered and prosperous state, will lead to the destruction of English society. The forces of Grantorto, the Souldan, and others, representing aggressive international Catholicism led by Spain and the papacy, will overwhelm the English crown.[52] Others may attack Grey for his policies but the true knight of justice will be able to see the bigger picture and will know that he will have to supplement force with guile in order to defeat the forces of darkness. And, given his experience in Ireland, he will undoubtedly see this problem more clearly than the queen back in the capital.

In canto ix of Book V, probably the allegorical core of the Book, the reader can see why the quest of Book VI is doomed before it is begun. Here, at the court of Mercilla, we witness a body that is not fit to govern itself, let alone a nation, so that it should come as no surprise that Calidore's quest fails because he has no hope of defining what he does. Furthermore, there is no proper means of ruling, or even controlling, the country in which the Blatant Beast has been set loose by the actions of the crown itself. The failure of justice leads directly to the meaninglessness of courtesy in Book VI, as the one paves the way for the other.[53] Furthermore, we also witness the poet Bonfont, who has his tongue nailed to a post and his name changed to Malfont. This is a brutal iconic image that shows how impotent the poet, a proper counsellor of the monarch unlike the flattering, self-interested courtiers, is in the face of vicious suppression. There is no point in writing poetry for the queen and her court if no one is prepared to read it. Spenser weaves together a series of narrative threads which point towards an imminent disaster.[54]

Sections of the second half of *The Faerie Queene* were probably written earlier than 1595, as the poem looks back to events in the early 1580s, the defining moment of Spenser's political consciousness. Equally, Books V and VI appear to have been produced with the current events of 1596 very much in mind, applying the lessons of earlier years to the current situation. There is an awareness of a manifest threat to the settlers articulated at key moments in the *Amoretti* and *Epithalamion*, but nothing that compares to the level of anxiety articulated in Spenser's poetry published a year later, when the need for Talus, the iron man, is everywhere present, and when he is absent the isolated rural communities are invariably overwhelmed by secretive and hostile forces that he is designed to root out and destroy. It is hard to believe that the poem published in 1596 was ignorant of specific developments in Ireland, as the rebellion of Hugh O'Neill gathered pace. The extent of the direct challenge to the crown became obvious on 7 August 1594 when the English forces under George Bingham coming to the relief of the Enniskillen garrison were overwhelmed by Tyrone's forces.[55] The battle took place in Ulster, so may not have signalled an obvious transformation of the military state of the country, and probably had little impact on Spenser's composition of the sonnets and the wedding ode, when that was sent over to London soon afterwards. But there could be no mistaking what was happening by the time the manuscript of *The Faerie Queene* reached London in early 1596. On 16 February Tyrone's brother, Art O'Neill, burned the fort and bridge on the Blackwater that Walter Devereux, first earl of Essex, had established in 1575; English reinforcements were sent from Brittany and arrived in Waterford on 19 March 1595, followed soon after by Sir John Norris who was immediately appointed military commander for Ireland. In May Enniskillen, one of the key strongholds in Ulster, fell to Hugh Maguire of Fermanagh and Hugh Roe O'Donnell, two of O'Neill's closest allies, evidence that he was able to command the loyalty of the powerful Ulster lords. On 13 June O'Neill overwhelmed Sir Henry Bagenal's forces at Clontibret, County Monaghan, and he was duly proclaimed traitor on 23 June. The Lord Deputy, Sir John Russell, waged a summer campaign against Tyrone, who now received the promise of aid from the Scots, in Ulster, converting Armagh Cathedral into a garrison. On 22 August Tyrone indicated to Norris that he was prepared to seek a pardon, but a day later he offered the kingship of Ireland to the governor of the Spanish Netherlands, Archduke Albert, demonstrating that the rebellion had already gone further than any in the century, and that O'Neill had the realistic ambition of driving the English out of Ireland. On 17 September O'Neill and O'Donnell formally wrote to Philip II of Spain, asking for military aid in return for securing him the Kingdom of Ireland. A month later, on 18 October, Tyrone and O'Donnell submitted to the crown, and they were pardoned on 12 May 1596.[56]

Spenser, given his contacts in the Munster government, and his close relationship to the Norris brothers, would have known a great deal about these events and the seriousness of the threat to the Munster planters, especially after the surrender of O'Neill and O'Donnell, even though the rebellion had the appearance of being contained within Ulster. Of course, the move was designed to buy time, and by the end of 1596 the rebellion was spreading throughout the island as Tyrone urged the 'gentlemen of Munster' to join him (6 July) and Spanish ships landed in Donegal (17–18 September).[57] The gathering pace of the threat would explain the polemical urgency of the last two Books of *The Faerie Queene*, which signal a clear break with Book IV, as the poem displays a terrifying vision of English civilization, which had been in a fragile and semi-formed state at the start of the poem, engulfed by hostile forces it is unable to repel.

Spenser's knowledge of what was taking place might also explain why he risked yet another confrontation with one of the most powerful figures in the British Isles. The most hostile reader of the poem was James VI of Scotland, one of whose courtiers must have brought the poem to his attention. Correspondence preserved in the State Papers for Scotland shows that James was furious at what he correctly perceived were aggressive attacks on his mother, Mary Queen of Scots, who had been executed on 8 February 1587 for her alleged role in the Babington Plot to overthrow Elizabeth.[58] On 1 November 1596 the English ambassador in Scotland, Robert Bowes, wrote to Burghley to inform him that the king had refused to allow the second edition of *The Faerie Queene* to be sold in Scotland and 'further he will complain to Her Majesty of the author as you will understand at more length by himself'.[59] On 12 November Bowes followed his letter up with another, explaining that James was quite clear why the poem had aroused his anger, as it contained 'som dishonourable effects (as the king deems thereof) against himself and his mother deceased'.[60] Although, according to Bowes, he had persuaded James that the book had not been 'passed with the privilege of Her Majesty's Commissioners', and so did not have the royal approval that James suspected that it had, he, nevertheless, 'still desired that Edward [*sic*] Spenser for his fault be duly tried and punished'.[61] The affair did not end there. On 5 March 1598 George Nicolson, a servant of Bowes, wrote to Sir Robert Cecil that Walter Quinn, a poet later employed at the courts of James I and Charles I, was in the process of 'answering Spenser's book, whereat the king is offended'.[62] The work, assuming it was completed, has not survived, suggesting that while rancour remained in Scotland no further action was taken, although it is possible that Spenser's public connection with Ralegh did little to help the latter gain favour with the new monarch.[63]

If anything, this was an even more severe crisis for Spenser than that of 1591, and the strength and length of James's reaction demonstrates the seriousness with which he viewed Spenser's hostile representation of his mother as Duessa in Book V, canto ix.[64] There is a rather neat comic irony in Bowes writing to Burghley to assure his political master that he is defusing the crisis as best he can after Burghley's experience of Spenser's writing in 1591, and Burghley's own behaviour in stoking earlier, related aggression. Why had Spenser risked returning to controversial events and represented them in such a way that they were likely to provoke a hostile reaction? Perhaps he had simply miscalculated, or perhaps he did not really care what those in power thought about him. A more likely explanation is that he was drawing a comparison between the events of 1587 when the queen had to be persuaded by her counsel, led by the recently deceased Lord Grey, represented in the poem as Zele, to execute Mary before ever more dangerous plots against Elizabeth were hatched, which threatened not just her life but the stability of her subjects.[65] Certainly there was opposition to James in south-west Ireland when he did become king of England.[66] Perhaps Spenser knew about the submission of Tyrone and O'Donnell in late 1595 and was publicly warning Elizabeth not to repeat what he saw as her earlier error. More plausibly, the poem reminds readers of the dangers of Scotland and the treachery of the Stuarts, making clear that the threat to Protestant England came from Scotland as well as Ireland, especially if forces within the British Isles were supported by military aid from Spain and the papacy.[67] Spenser was eager to use the second edition of his historical allegory to demonstrate the nature and strength of the variety of forces confronting England and the New English in Ireland.

Spenser, accompanied by his wife, made another long visit to England in 1596–7. The dedicatory letter to *Fowre Hymnes* was written from Greenwich on 1 September and it is highly probable that the couple were still in England in Easter 1597, as they were fighting a complicated lawsuit concerning funds relating to Elizabeth's father's will.[68] However, it is likely that they came over earlier, perhaps in the early summer of 1596. Internal evidence suggests that *A View* was written in that year, probably finished at some point well before Christmas.[69] The most compelling evidence for this dating is that Spenser refers to the impending death of Daniel McCarthy-More, the earl of Clancarty, who was known to have been ill in late 1595 but who did not die until the end of 1596.[70] Moreover, there is an allusion to the rising star of Essex near the end of the dialogue.[71] Essex had enjoyed spectacular success in capturing and looting Cadiz in the summer of 1596, the fleet setting off on 1 June and the first ships returning on 1 August.[72] Irenius argues that Ireland needs to be ruled by a Lord Deputy, 'But thearewithall I wishe that ouer him theare weare also placed a Lorde Lietennante of some of the greatest personages in Englande, suche an one I Coulde name vppon whom the ey of all Englande is fixed and our last hopes now rest'.[73] Given the nature of the statement and the clear expectation that any reader would know who was meant, the reference must be to Essex, who was lauded for his success, became a national hero, and increased his standing at court when he returned to England. Indeed, the Cadiz expedition was the key event that precipitated the division that dominated court life in the last years of the century, that between the Cecils and Essex.[74]

It is easy to see why Spenser might gravitate towards Essex, as did many who felt that they had nothing to gain from the Cecils. Moreover, Essex was, and was seen to be, a generous patron of writers and intellectuals.[75] Whether Spenser was making a serious pitch to the earl, as he did in the *Prothalamion*, or had extensive dealings with his closer circle is impossible to determine without more evidence. But the trajectory of Spenser's dialogue suggests that he thought that Essex rather than Cecil could be persuaded to support the expensive military operations that *A View* argues are vital for the preservation of Ireland under English rule, an opinion which many would have shared in the summer of 1596. Spenser's erstwhile champion and rival, Ralegh, was also present in Cadiz and played a crucial part in ensuring the success of the raid.[76] But his role was eclipsed by that of Essex, at least in public.[77] Spenser's apparent change of sides might seem callous, but it was probably a move born out of a growing sense of the impending crisis in Ireland. It suggests that he was thinking pragmatically and it shows that he saw the earl as the right man for the job, a judgement that was cruelly exposed when Essex was actually made Lord Lieutenant on 12 March 1599.[78]

The opening of *A View* indicates that it was written, as it was set, in England:

Eudox: But if that Countrie of Irelande, whence youe latelye come be so goodlye and
   Commondious a soyle as yee reporte I wonder that no course is taken for the turninge
   thereof to good vses, and reducinge that salvage nacion to better gouernment and Cyvilitie/
Iren: Mary soe there haue byne diuerse good plotes devised and wise Councells cast alreadye
   aboute reformacion of that realme, but they saie yt is the fatall destinie of that Lande that no
   purposes whatsoeuer are mente for her good, prosper or take good effecte, which wheather it
   proceed from the *very Genius* of the soile, or influence of the stares, or that Almighty god
   hathe not yeat Appointed the tyme of her reformacion or that he reserueth her in this

vnquiet state still, for some secret scourge, which shall by her Come vnto Englande it is harde to be knowen but yeat much to be feared//[79]

It is hard to imagine a more dramatic opening to a political dialogue. Certainly, although there are a number of eloquent works preserved in the Irish State Papers, there is nothing that remotely resembles *A View*. Spenser was using all his literary, logical, and rhetorical resources to produce a work that would transform his English audience's understanding of the importance of Ireland so that they would realize that helping the beleaguered New English was not just a moral duty, but central to the survival of England. Eudoxus is a rational but ignorant humanist intellectual, unable to understand why Ireland cannot be made obedient and civil, as his education has indicated should be the case.[80] Irenius' subtly crafted opening speech, with its detached, forensic style, the product of considered rational reflection that matches that of Eudoxus, carefully built up parallel clauses, metaphysical imagery, leads towards a shocking conclusion: if Ireland is resistant to the application of humanist logic, perhaps this is because its recalcitrance is part of God's shocking plan to bring arrogant England to its knees. The reader knows after reading these two short speeches that *A View* is a work that cannot be ignored. The dialogue will explain that what must have seemed like a pressing and frightening prospect in the late 1590s was in fact a far more urgent problem than anyone had realized. The island requires immediate attention and only English people who live in Ireland will be able to explain the significance of the threat that is now posed to England. The message dovetails neatly with that of the last two books of *The Faerie Queene*. England is in mortal danger from what is happening in Ireland and the voices of the New English must be heeded.

A View did indeed have an enormous impact, and about twenty manuscript copies have been discovered, an unusually large number and a testament to the influence of Spenser and the seriousness with which his dialogue was taken as an analysis of the situation in Ireland. The Rawlinson copy in the Bodleian Library (B.478), which was submitted to the Stationers' Register in April 1598 by Matthew Lownes, is inscribed twice by John Panton, who wrote out the title and dated and attributed the work: '1596 by Ed: spenser gent.' (Figure 9).[81] Panton was in a good position to know who had written the text—he studied at Lincoln's Inn and moved in intellectual circles in London. He acted as secretary and confidential agent to Sir Thomas Egerton (1540?–1617), the Lord Chancellor, who had requested that Panton be admitted to the Inn in 1594. There was a close family connection as Egerton had employed Panton's father.[82] Egerton also had a sustained interest in Spenser's work as he owned and annotated the copy of the dialogue now in the Huntington Library, and employed the young John Donne alongside Panton.[83] Gregory Downhall, who had been at school with Spenser, also worked for Egerton.[84] Egerton's third wife (they married in October

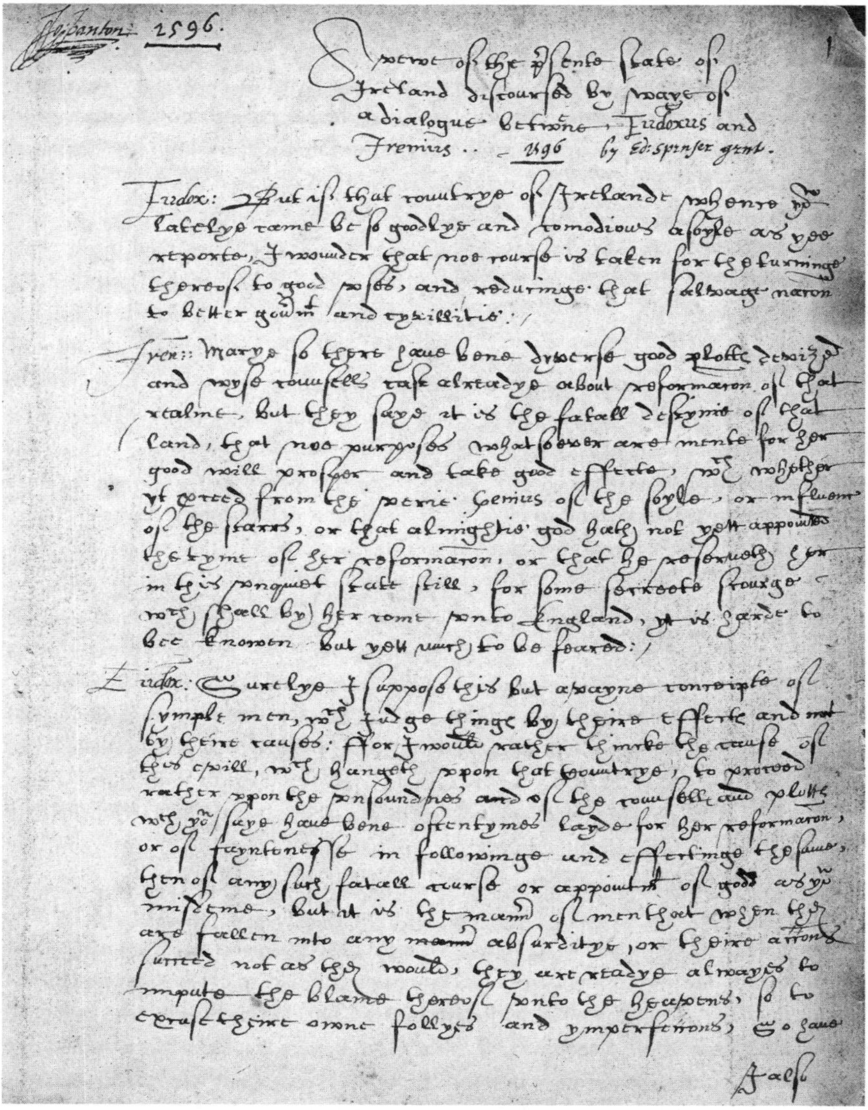

A vewe of the present state of
Ireland discoursed by waye of
a dialogue betwene Eudoxus and
Irenius. 1596 by Ed Spenser gent.

Eudox: But if that countrye of Irelande whereof ye
latelye came be so goodlye and comodious a soyle as yee
reporte, I wounder that noe course is taken for the turninge
thereof to good passe, and reducinge that saluage nacion
to better gouernment and ciuillitie:

Iren:: Marye so there haue bene dyuerse good plottes deuized
and wyse counsells caste alreadye about reformacion of that
realme, but they saye it is the fatall desteny of that
land, that noe purposes whatsoeuer are mente for her
good will prosper and take good effecte, whether
yt procede from the verie Genius of the soyle, or influence
of the starrs, or that almightie god hath not yet appointed
the tyme of her reformacion, or that he reserueth her
in this vnquiet state still, for some secrete scourge
whch shall by her come vnto England, yt is harde to
bee knowen but yet muche to be feared:

Eudox: Surelye I suppose this but a vayne conceipte of
symple men, whch iudge thinge by theire effecte and not
by theire causes: ffor I would rather thinke the cause of
this euill, whch hangeth vpon that countrye, to procede
rather vpon the confusednes and of the counsells and plottes
whch you saye haue bene oftentymes layde for her reformacion,
or of fayntenesse in followinge and effectinge the same,
then of any such fatall course or appointment of god as yow
misterme, but it is the manner of men that when they
are fallen into any manner absurditye, or theire actions
succede not as they would, they euermore alwayes to
impute the blame thereof vnto the heauens, so to
excuse theire owne follyes and ymperfeccions; so so haue

A als

Figure 9. MS Rawlinson B.478, title page. Reproduced with kind permission of the Bodleian Library.

1600), was Lady Strange, née Spenser, who had received a number of dedications of literary works from Spenser.[85]

A copy in the British Library has the name of Sir Arthur Chichester (1563–1625), Lord Deputy of Ireland from 1605 to 1616, inscribed on the top of the first page, indicating that Spenser was read by powerful and influential people a long time after the immediate significance of the text had passed. The copy is in neat secretary hand, has justified left-hand margins, and inscribes the names Irenius and Eudoxus in a slightly lighter coloured ink for ease of reference.[86] The copy preserved in the State Papers would also have belonged to a high profile figure, probably the Lord Deputy, either Sir William Russell (c.1553–1613), the incumbent when A View was written, who served from 1594 to 1597, or Essex himself.[87] Another copy, already noted, now in the Huntington Library, can be directly traced back to Egerton, 'who may have acquired it through his marriage to Alice Spencer [the dedicatee of The Teares of the Muses]...or to whom it may have been directly presented by Spenser himself'.[88] Clearly Sir James Ware had a copy, perhaps the one preserved in Trinity College Dublin. This manuscript, still in its original binding, is neatly copied out in secretary hand, and contains two marginal notes directing the reader to a passage on 'Religion' and another on 'St. Patrick', suggesting that the work was owned by someone particularly interested in ecclesiastical matters.[89] Other copies, such as that in Lambeth Palace Library, were small, and designed to be carried around easily, probably by those on campaign in Ireland or important statesmen in England. The text is copied out by a number of hands, perhaps the work of a secretariat producing a work for someone who needed it in a hurry such as a major official or military commander in Ireland.[90] A View could have been used to supplement a map of Ireland.[91] This Lambeth text, still in its original vellum wrapper, carries the date 'finish 1596' at the end of the manuscript, and consists of a series of approximately equal sections in different secretary hands, suggesting that the work was produced rapidly for immediate use. The Rawlinson copy has a similar appearance and, like the Lambeth Palace copy, also has its vellum wrapper, and was produced by a number of hands. It was the text that Lownes attempted to publish in 1598.[92] Copies in the National Library of Ireland, Gonville and Caius College, Cambridge, the Beinecke Library at Yale, and the one preserved in the State Papers, have also been copied out rapidly by a scribe or series of scribes, indicating that secretariats were put to work to produce copies of a major work that required immediate attention.[93] Also of note is the copy preserved as part of Folger V.b.214, a long collection of different works, many dealing with issues of treason and religious conflict, a significant number relating to Essex, which was probably compiled just after Essex's execution in 1601.[94] The volume later belonged to the Scott family, clients of Essex, further indicating a link between Essex and Spenser and strengthening a sense that the reference to Essex in A View was understood by Essex's inner circle.[95] What is significant is the care with which this elaborate and expensive book has been made. It still has its original calf binding, contains paper of 'heavy and of uniform quality', and has been carefully copied out by a skilled secretariat, a work designed for years of use.[96]

A number of readers clearly wanted to preserve *A View* for consultation at leisure in a library. What is undoubtedly the most handsome, carefully written copy, that preserved in the archives at Castle Howard, looks as if it might have been originally intended as a presentation copy for James I, perhaps written in the wake of the proposed union in 1607, as the material on Scotland and Ireland is highlighted on the title page. The manuscript is in a single, easily legible secretary hand, with even spaces between speeches and key words highlighted in italic, and still has its original velvet binding.[97] The Gough copy, which was probably produced during Spenser's lifetime or in the early seventeenth century, also seems to have been designed for use in a library and places great emphasis on the etymological sections of the text.[98] It is noticeably larger than the Lambeth and Rawlinson copies, has an added title for reference, 'Ireland's Survey', is carefully transcribed with wide margins, and has a number of marginal notes to help guide the reader. These refer to historical sections and explanations ('Spaniards arrival into the west pt. of Ireland'; 'Ireland had letters—before England long'); judgements about Irish life and culture ('The abuses of the Irish bards'); and practical and military matters, often highlighting the numbers of soldiers and horses needed or the number of ploughlands in any one region.[99] It is possible that this text was also designed to be published.[100] The Sloane copy in the British Library is in one, far neater, italic hand, has justified left-hand margins and *litterae notabiliores* (thick large script) to signal the beginning of every speech, also indicating that it was produced for consultation in a private library.[101] The same would appear to be true of Harley 1932, also in one neat italic hand throughout, a slightly smaller manuscript, which has a number of printed sections pasted in dating from the mid-seventeenth century, to provide the reader with lists of Lord Deputies, 'A Prognostication of Irish history', up to 1612, and 'A Brief Computation of times, and memorable things done in this kindgome of Ireland'. This copy suggests that its seventeenth-century owner—perhaps not the original— added information to update the volume.[102] Harley 7388 is another copy in neat italic hand suggesting similar usage.[103] The variety of types of copy of *A View* shows just how important the manuscript was seen to be when it was first written and that it retained its importance as an analysis of Ireland until well into the seventeenth century.[104]

A View is a response to an immediate, growing crisis, which manifests itself in a trenchant defence of the New English position in Ireland. Spenser either composed the dialogue just before he came over to England, or completed it after he had arrived, staying with his family in a patron's house or lodgings, probably somewhere in London. Therefore it is most likely that one of the purposes of his visit was to act as a spokesman for the Munster settlers and to persuade as many powerful English politicians and courtiers as possible to support their cause, a role he clearly assumed later when he came over for the last time in December 1598. The number of manuscript copies of *A View* that survive—and it is safe to presume that we have only a proportion of those that were made—suggest that the work was aggressively promoted and placed in the hands of influential figures by either the poet himself or his patrons and allies. After all, the evidence of the dedicatory sonnets appended to the first edition of *The Faerie Queene* indicates that Spenser was not averse to using whatever contacts he had when need dictated, and this time more was at stake than simply the revitalization of a moribund career. Spenser would surely have used a series of familiar names: Wallop, who had entertained the queen at his house in Farleigh Wallop; perhaps Ralegh, even though their relationship may have been problematic by this time; Sir Christopher Hatton; Harvey, who still had some connections to the great and the good; and, most important, Essex. As Spenser recommends Essex as the best man to oversee the pacification of Ireland, it is likely that he presented Essex with a copy during his time in London. This might even have been the main reason why he travelled over in 1596.

But it is also clear that *A View* is not simply a hurried response to a crisis, like so many other treatises preserved in the Irish State Papers.[105] The dialogue was the work of many years of study and thought, much of which must have been undertaken to produce Spenser's works on history, genealogy, and ruins, providing further evidence that he had access to a substantial collection of books in Ireland. Eudoxus' final words suggest that the work was not conceived in isolation but would be joined by a companion piece in due course (although this may have been a conventional trope, common in humanist dialogues): 'I thanke youe *Iren*: for this your gentle paines withall not forgettinge now in the shuttinge vp to put youe in minde of that which ye haue formerlye halfe promised that hereafter when we shall mete againe vppon the like good occacion ye will declare vnto vs those your observacions which ye haue gathered of the Antiquities of Ireland////.'[106] Eudoxus' request probably explains why Spenser was able to produce *A View* so rapidly. The conclusion suggests that he was working on a history of ancient Ireland and Irish antiquities, which, given his scholarly attention to English history, would have been a logical development of his intellectual ambitions and would explain why he had such knowledge of Irish historical writings.[107] It would also explain the somewhat hybrid form of *A View*, a work that has struck at least one commentator as unfinished.[108] The truth is probably that the material was adapted to suit circumstances, not that the text was simply uncompleted. Had Spenser lived longer it is likely that he would have produced more historical work on Ireland, and it is possible that Sir James Ware had some knowledge of his plans when he published *A View*, along with the histories of Campion and Hanmer—the latter was probably the source of much of the historical material that informed Spenser's dialogue—in 1633.[109]

A View can also be read both as a text that states what its author thinks needs to be spelled out in the desperate year, 1596, and in terms of longer and broader perspectives. Spenser notes how much money the queen has to spend to keep Ireland quiet, upwards of £20,000 a year, and argues that it would be better to send over a huge army of ten thousand footmen and a thousand cavalry to sort out any rebellion quickly than to continue to incur substantial long-term debts. The cost would be tremendous, of course, but, in the end, it would save considerable sums of money. Then, in his final recommendations as to how Ireland should be reformed, Irenius argues that the country needs to be levelled, flattened, and civilized:

and firste I wishe that order weare taken for the Cuttinge downe and opening of all places thoroughe wodes so that a wide waye of the space of C. yeardes mighte be laide open in euerye of them for the safetie of trauellers whiche vse often in suche perilous places to be Robbed and sometimes murdered Next that Bridges weare builte vppon all Riuers and all the fordes marred and split so as none mighte passe anie other wye but by those bridges, and euerie bridge to haue a gate and a smalle gatehowse set theareon. Whereof this good will Come that no nighte stealthes which are Comonlye driven in by waies and by blind fordes vnused of anie but suche like, shalbe Convaied out of one Countrye into another as they vse, but that they muste passe by those bridges, wheare they maie either be happelye encountred or easelye tracted or not suffred to passe at all by meanes of those gatehowses thereon. Allsoe that in all stretes and narrowe passages as between Two Boggs or thoroughe anie depe forde or vnder anye mountaine side theare shoulde be some little fortilage or woden Castle set which shoulde kepe and I Comaunde that streighte wheareby anie Rebelles that should come into the Coutrye might be stopped that waie or passe with great peril/

Moreouer that all higeh waies shoulde be fenced and shut vp on bothe sides leaving only xl fote breadth for passadge so as none shoulde be hable to passe but thoroughe the highe waies, wheareby theves and nighte Robbers might be the more easelye pursued and encountred when theare shalbe no other waie to drive theire stolen Cattell but therein as I formerlye declared:

Further that theare shoulde in sundrie Conveniente places by the highe waies be townes appointed to be builte the which shoulde be freeburoughes and incorporate vnder Bailifes to be by theire inhabitants well and strongeleye entrenched or otherwise fenced with gates at eache side theareof to be shut nightely like as theare is in manye places in the Englishe pale and all the waies aboute it to be stronglye shut vp so as none shoulde passe but thoroughe these Townes, To some of which it weare good that the priviledge of a market weare given the rather to strengthen and enhable them to theire defence for theare is nothinge dothe soner Cause Civilitye in anye Countrye then manye market Townes by reasone that people repairing often thither for their nedes will dailye see and learne Civill manners of the better sorte[.]

Spenser has clearly thought carefully about what needs to be done in Ireland and what he outlines is exactly in line with what happened when the Londonderry Plantation was established in the early seventeenth century with the removal of the great forests that once covered Ulster; the introduction of small farms and small towns; the construction of proper roads, crossings, and bridges; and, crucially, the building of well-fortified garrisons in strategic places throughout the north.[111] Spenser's comments are, of course, principally a comment on what had not yet happened on the Munster Plantation and amount to a desire to transform Ireland into what one contemporary treatise described as 'mearely a West England'.[112]

The conclusion is shocking, as is so much throughout *A View*, most famously, the description of the Munster famine with its provocative ending, 'which they themselves had wroughte'.[113] But there is a determined, pitiless, and rigorous logic to the dialogue, one that tallies exactly with the political arguments advanced about Ireland in *The Faerie Queene*.[114] However uncomfortable Irenius' arguments and conclusions might make the reader feel, he shows that he has superior logic and knowledge to his interlocutor, remaining one step ahead in the dialogue. Eudoxus' objections can always be countered effectively and provide Irenius with the chance to demonstrate just how far beyond the experience and understanding of even the most astute and adept English political thinkers England's Irish problem has become.[115] The same might be said of Irenius' claim that Protestantism cannot be advanced in Ireland because 'instruccion in religion nedethe quiet times and ere wee seke to settle sounde discipline in the Clergie we muste purchase peace vnto the Layitye for it is ill time to preache amongst swords'.[116] Other writers, notably John Hooker and Barnabe Rich, made the opposite case, claiming that Catholicism inspired the Irish to rebel against the crown and so it had to be tackled as a matter of urgency.[117] Irenius' comments justify the lack of emphasis on religion throughout *A View*, as well as warning an English audience that what they expect is never the case in contemporary Ireland.

Spenser's disturbing claims show why he was so widely read and why he was able, in Nicholas Canny's words, to 'set the agenda' for English policy in Ireland.[118] *A View* points back to the debates held at Hill Hall, when Ireland was the major topic of discussion among humanists eager to think about colonialism and colonial policy. It also advertises its origins in the Cambridge of Spenser's youth. The dialogue is a text that follows a straightforward logical argument, its form owing much to the educational system that Spenser had experienced as a university student and which had been augmented by Gabriel Harvey. Other public debates in Ireland and England were carried out with a conscious acknowledgement of the forms of logic and argument acquired through a university education.[119] The point is further cemented if we also note that the works of Sidney and Spenser—albeit not *A View*—were then employed by Abraham Fraunce to illustrate his books on Ramist rhetoric and logic, a case of *post hoc ergo propter hoc* logic.[120] Irenius constantly reminds Eudoxus that his propositions might seem reasonable in England, but have no chance of working in Ireland because of the unsettling and unclassifiable nature of the country, meaning that proper experience is required in order to argue logically about it. The argument between the two invariably takes the form that what Eudoxus states would be true if Ireland were what he thought it was. However, it is not and so the solution to the problems existing there has to be of a different order, a form of negative syllogistic reasoning. Hence, Eudoxus argues that the spread of the law should render Ireland loyal to the English crown, but is told by Irenius that his own experience qualifies his logic and renders it inadequate by itself to understand a strange land in which fundamental principles need to be re-established.[121] This is surely an argument based on Spenser's own experience of working with the law in both countries.[122]

Eudoxus is further staggered at the size and cost of the army that Irenius argues is needed to conquer Ireland, complaining that Irenius is recommending 'an infinite Chardge to her maiestie', but he is eventually persuaded that such expense has to be borne as it will save money in the long run.[123] The dialogue might be read as one large, provocative syllogism:

Ireland needs to be governed properly.
Proper government will involve methods that will seem shocking, but which are necessary.
Therefore:
Ireland requires methods that will seem shocking, but which are necessary.

A View is a humanist dialogue of the most sophisticated sort, building on the tradition established throughout the sixteenth century, notably by Sir Thomas Smith in the wake of Erasmus and More.[124] In the Letter to Ralegh Spenser had argued at length that the principal virtue of the 'Poets historicall' was to establish exemplary figures who would influence readers eager to learn how to govern, a key reason why the work of the poet could not be read in the same way as that of the historian, whose task was to remain faithful to the facts: 'For an Historiographer discourseth of affayres orderly as they were done, accounting as well the times as the actions, but a Poet thrusteth into the middest, euen where it most concerneth him, and there recoursing to the thingesd forepaste, and diuining of thinges to come, maketh a pleasing Analysis of all.'[125] In a dialogue Spenser can combine his literary and historical skills to produce a fiction that has a more obviously direct impact on policy-making than even so grand a poem as *The Faerie Queene*, an example of Harvey's ideal of the intellectual in public service. Furthermore, *A View* is an embattled defence of Spenser's right to possess the estate he had worked so hard to acquire in Ireland. The number of surviving manuscript copies is a tribute to the dialogue's success, as well as to Spenser's ability to craft an argument that could not be ignored by those who mattered.

Spenser was also over in England with his wife to fight a court case in Chancery, concerning the considerable sum of £100 that had been entrusted by Elizabeth's late father, Stephen, to two local men, John Mathew, from Elizabeth's home village, Bradden, and Thomas Emyly, from Helmdon, about five miles away.[126] We do not know how much of the proceedings Spenser attended in person, but it is likely that he felt the need to be over in Northamptonshire to instruct counsel about this suit. The case indicates that Elizabeth's late father, Stephen, who died in 1582, had left about £250 to his four children in his will, to be given to them when they came of age or got married, which, as the Chancery document records, did not take place until 1593–4. Three of the Boyle children survived into adulthood: George, Alexander, and Elizabeth, Alexander joining his sister in Ireland.[127] This was all quite normal practice and Stephen was behaving responsibly in ensuring that his children would be properly provided for and that his widow—or, more likely, her husband—could not appropriate their rightful legacy—a common, and in this case prescient, fear. Elizabeth's mother, Joan, now remarried to Ferdinando Freckleton, allowed £100 of her children's legacy to be lent to Edward Lucy, of Kingston, Warwickshire, a member of the powerful Lucy family from Charlecote, Warwickshire, whose surety was provided by Valentine Knightley, another member of a prominent local gentry family.[128] Both men sealed a penal bond of £200 to repay the capital and any interest to Thomas Emyly and John Mathew, who were named as trustees by the Freckletons, placing them in the role of *prochains amis*, trusted friends of the family who would act in their best interests.[129] Emyly and Mathew were probably quite close to the Boyle family: Mathew had witnessed Steven Boyle's will in 1582.[130] Emyly was probably older than many of the others involved in the case, having taken his BA at Magdalen College, Oxford, in 1555, so that he would have been about 60 in 1596.[131] He died on 29 March 1608. His will, granted probate on 15 September 1608, shows that he held extensive lands in Helmdon, including the local manor, Netherbury or Cope's manor, which he had bought from Sir Richard Knightley, further evidence of the close links between families with property in the area.[132]

Both Emyly and Mathew were lawyers. Mathew had studied at Gray's Inn, having been admitted under special circumstances in 1573.[133] As another Chancery document demonstrates, Emyly had chambers there and he appears in the pension records as a member of the Inn, helping to pay for a new gate (7 February 1593), but probably studied elsewhere as there is no record of his admission.[134] Emyly appears to have been the link between the Boyle family and Mathew, who was probably associated with him in London as a fellow lawyer at Gray's Inn. Mathew held extensive lands in Hertfordshire, and he was involved in a series of relatively high profile disputes in the years immediately prior to the case analysed here. The *Acts of the Privy Council* records two disputes with James Smyth and Thomas Crane, both over the sale of lands. Crane was especially incensed—or, at least, claimed to be—by Mathew's behaviour, and petitioned the Privy Council, complaining of the 'coolorable and craftie practises used by John Mathew . . . who by his circumventions and by wresting th'intencion of the law according to his own humour and subtiltie multiplieth sondrie suits without anie sufficient cause' against Crane. The Privy Council took Crane's side, deciding that he had been 'wronged by the craftie devises of the said attorney' and asked that both men appear before the archbishop of Canterbury so that Mathew could be commanded to 'conform himself to such severall orders as have formerlie been sett down eyther in th'Exchequier or els whear for the determining of the said variaunces, and to cease to vex or molest the said Mr Crane with anie frivolous suits'.[135] In the earlier case the Privy Council deemed that Mathew was the wronged party, although there was clearly less certainty than in the dispute between Crane and Mathew. The Council ordered both men, Mathew and Smyth, to appear before the Lord Mayor of London, 'to give such speedie order for the redress of the injuries by the said Mathew sustained', further adding that, 'if by the wilfulness of either parties their differences can not take end, then you certifie us in whome the default resteth'.[136] Disputes over property were common enough in early modern England and virtually every family who owned an estate of some value was embroiled in the intricacies and complexities of the legal system at some point, plaintiffs invariably turning to the Chancery courts for restitution, as they were designed to deal with such conflict.[137] However, the surviving legal records of Mathew's dealings suggest that he may have been involved in some dubious deals, having to sell off his lands to pay for something else or simply to manage his affairs. It is possible that at a time when moneylending was heavily restricted after the 1571 Usury Act, he was effectively arranging mortgages for his clients. There is no indication that Emyly was a party to Mathew's unusual legal affairs and he was clearly still prepared to work with Mathew while such matters continued (the Smyth dispute was not resolved until 24 June 1595). But the evidence that remains of Mathew's disputes indicates how fractious and confrontational property cases invariably were in early modern England, and suggests that families engaged experienced and hard-nosed lawyers to defend their interests even when other members of the immediate family unit were involved.

The demand for the return of the loan undoubtedly arose after 1594 when Elizabeth married Spenser, and the newly-weds were trying to put their affairs in order. The three children were also now over 21 and so were entitled to their legacy. The case first went before the Northamptonshire Assizes on 20 November 1596, but was unsuccessful. It was then lodged with the lawyer, Edward Heron, who filed a suit in Chancery. Spenser, who appeared as plaintiff alongside the three Boyle siblings, may have taken the lead in presenting the case, because of his age, education, and, more importantly still, because of his experience as a Chancery official and land speculator in Ireland. Moreover, Spenser had been involved in a similar case in Ireland. An entry in the Irish Chancery Recognizances dated 10 June 1589 records that Edmund Spenser and Richard Roche of Kinsale entered a bond of 100 marks for a case in Chancery between Spenser and Hugh Strawbridge (Strowbridge).[138] No details are given of the case, but as Strawbridge became clerk of the first fruits, charged with ensuring that taxes on ecclesiastical properties were paid, it is likely that the case had something to do with Spenser having failed to pay the £3 he owed as prebend of Effin.[139] It is also worth noting, however, that Strawbridge was a prominent servant of Lord Deputy Fitzwilliam who served in that office from 17 February 1588 to 16 May 1594, frequently taking messages from Fitzwilliam to the Privy Council.[140] Like Spenser and other New English settlers in Ireland he was connected with a number of significant land deals.[141] Strawbridge also fell out with Wallop, perhaps over one of these deals, and this connection suggests that Spenser's description of Fitzwilliam as an incompetent doctor who had actually made Ireland 'more dangerously sicke than euer before', may have had some basis in his own personal experience, recalling his sly digs at Loftus.[142] Whether Richard Roche was related to the Roches of Fermoy with whom Spenser had such bitter and lasting disputes is not known, but, if he was, then the case provides more evidence of how flexible early modern allegiances could be when interests of property were involved.[143]

The dispute between the Boyles and Freckleton was heard before the Lord Keeper of the Privy Seal, Sir Thomas Egerton, who had significant links to Spenser, although not ones which would have been regarded as improper by the standards of the age.[144] The most curious aspect of the Chancery case is that the defendants were not Lucy, who had borrowed Boyle's money, or Knightley, who had stood surety, but Emyly and Mathew, who were supposed to have been acting on behalf of the Boyle children. Their answers, which gain credibility from the fact it would have been easy to disprove their testimony, insist that they had both behaved in a responsible manner. Mathew, who filed an answer before Erasmus Dryden and Edward Cope, both cousins of Elizabeth, at Canons Ashby on 18 January 1597, acknowledged receipt of the money and bond from Lucy, but claimed that he had given the bond and the money to Emyly to pass on to Freckleton. In his answer on 20 February, Emyly denied any knowledge of the money himself, and claimed that he had given the money to Freckleton.[145]

We do not know the outcome of this fascinating case, nor what really happened about the money, but the paper trail leads to Freckleton as the guilty party, an interloper in the family, who has misappropriated the children's legacy. But matters may not be so straightforward. Such cases were, of course, common, and there was often conflict between children and stepparents over the rights to property as one party would be eager to establish their future while the other would be attempting to ensure security in their later years.[146] Indeed, in 1603 Spenser's eldest son, Sylvanus, disputed the right of his stepmother to occupy Kilcolman with her second husband, Roger Seckerstone, and he petitioned the Lord Chancellor for return of the title deeds, which he thought would prove his right to the property, a case that neatly mirrors Elizabeth and Spenser's dispute with Joan Boyle and Freckleton.[147]

Was Freckleton guilty of defrauding his wife's children? Not necessarily—if this was his intention, the plaintiffs would have expressed themselves in far stronger language in their bill. His own answer insisted that Lucy owed him a large sum of money, which had been settled with a land transaction. So the most likely reason Freckleton had not paid his stepchildren their legacies was because the cash was tied up in land. The plaintiffs' replication makes it clear that they believed that Freckleton was the party at fault, and that he could expect further proceedings. However, the language of the case does not indicate that an irreparable breach had torn the family apart; rather, that a paper trail was being established so that the rights to considerable assets could be fairly determined. Of course, a subsequent case, should one have been brought, might well have been far more explosive, but none is known to exist. The likeliest outcomes were either that Freckleton borrowed the money required to pay the outstanding legacies and end the lawsuit before it became too expensive, or that events in Ireland in the last two and a half years of Spenser's life overwhelmed the couple before they could file a fresh lawsuit.

We know relatively little about Freckleton, whether he might have been the villain of the piece, or whether this was simply the sort of difficulty that most families with property experienced.[148] But a number of pieces of evidence link him to the Boyles and the Spensers. Freckleton was presumably part of a Warwickshire family, making him a member of the gentry circles in the Northamptonshire–Warwickshire area, in which the Boyles and Spensers moved. The will of Walter Freckleton, 26 February 1606, leaves his son Ferdinando 20s., 'as a token of my last farewell'. The will also provides evidence that the Freckletons were a well-connected family, as some money is left to Walter's kinsman John Freckleton, who served Lady Puckering, widow of Sir John Puckering (1543/4–96), Speaker of the House of Commons, patron of Thomas Kyd, and Egerton's predecessor as Lord Keeper.[149] A Ferdinando Freckleton graduated from Oxford on 4 April 1573, the same year that Spenser graduated from Cambridge.[150] Assuming he is the same man, he later published a dedicatory verse to the clown/actor Richard Tarleton's *Tragical Treatises* (1578), a work published by Henry Bynneman two years before he published the Harvey–Spenser *Letters*. Freckleton's verse is not especially remarkable, but the classical allusion in the opening stanza

> If blinde men could of costlie colours iudge,
> and intermeddle with *Apelles* arte,
> Or were not fretting Enuie giuen to grudge
> the faith of him who places a freindlie paste,
> Or if my skill could see in causes deepe,
> I would reueale what nowe I secreate keepe

347

suggests literary ambition, a knowledge of the conventions of poetry, as well as an ability to play the game of advertising his skills to a potential employer.[151] Given his link to both Bynneman and Tarlton, Freckleton might have been known to Spenser from the late 1570s, and they both had an interest in jest books and merry tales. Spenser, through Harvey, was probably quite close to Bynneman, and may also have known Tarlton, a notable London figure at this point, who knew of the Harvey brothers and who was referenced by both sides in the Nashe–Harvey quarrel later.[152] Later, perhaps unable to secure a position in a significant household, having failed as a writer, or, simply cutting his losses, Freckleton became a captain in the army, where he enjoyed a conspicuously long and successful career. At the time of the Chancery case he was in Chester recruiting men ready to sail to Ireland where he was stationed in Newry and Dundalk.[153] In Ireland he started off with a reasonable command of a fifty men, rising later to a hundred, and he was knighted for his services on the coronation day of James I in 1603, by the Lord Deputy, George Carey, along with Richard Boyle.[154] Again, the intertwining with Spenser's life and career is notable, and it would be odd if this were not the same Freckleton who married Joan Boyle. Freckleton continued to serve in the army with distinction, before he was discharged at some point before 1610.[155] A monument was erected to his wife, Frances, at Nether Eatendon (Ettington) in Warwickshire.[156] She died aged 80 on 13 September 1633, demonstrating that Freckleton married another woman from the area after Joan died, although we do not know when this was. Freckleton had apparently died in Ireland and she had returned to her family.[157]

Therefore, Joan Boyle's second husband must surely have been the gentleman of Huntingdon who had taken part in an identical transaction to the one outlined here between the Drydens and the Spencers of Althorp in 1591–2, preserved 'in the Exchequer of George Dryden of Adson alias Adneston co. Northamp. gent.': 'Whereas Ferdinando Freckleton of Huntington gent became bound to me 25 October 28 Eliz. in 200 £to secure 100 £; and Whereas Sir John Spencer of Althorpe Kt is indebted to the Queen in divers sums of money—to assign Freckleton's bond on security in behalf of Sir John Spencer—28 April 34 Eliz. 1592.'[158] This is further evidence of a connection between the Boyle family and Freckleton, as the grandfather of Joan Boyle, née Cope, had married Jane Spencer, granddaughter of John Spencer of Hodnell, Warwickshire.[159] Freckleton may have been put forward as a husband for Joan after she was widowed as a means of keeping the family together and so preserving its property.

The Chancery case also raises a host of issues relating to Spenser's life. If nothing else, it shows that he now had—assuming he had not before—a vested interest in the Bradden–Canons Ashby area of Northamptonshire. It also suggests that he was now relied upon to take the lead in family matters by his wife and her brothers, as we might expect given his age, status, and legal knowledge. What we cannot know is for how much of the case Spenser and his wife were present; whether the case signalled a permanent break with the Freckletons; whether those family members who lived in Ireland travelled back to Northamptonshire to attend the various proceedings; nor, indeed, how many of them lived there anyway. It does provide yet more information about the social and familial networks in which Spenser existed, indicating that local contexts were especially important for him and that he lived at least one remove from the established gentry, as did the Northamptonshire Boyles. The case, as made practical sense, was heard locally, further evidence provided by the fact that the replication of the Boyles was lodged in Clapham, a village about twenty miles from Northampton. The documents also show that the Spensers were not—and probably could not be—careless with money and felt that he needed to ensure that they kept what they held.

They also indicate that Spenser may have fostered a link with Egerton, a powerful figure whose stock was still rising, as on 6 May of that year he was made Lord Keeper to succeed Sir John Puckering, probably as a result of the queen's intervention, retaining the Mastership of the Rolls.[160] The Egertons were Catholics, Sir Thomas only converting to Protestantism in the early 1580s, another indication of the close interaction of people on either side of the religious divide in early modern England. Egerton employed John Donne as his secretary (1597–8), after Donne had served with Egerton's son under Essex on the Azores expedition in 1597. However, Egerton then dismissed him after Donne secretly married Ann More, daughter of Sir George More, Egerton's brother-in-law, a further reminder of the need to respect distinct social hierarchies.[161]

Spenser was evidently busy at work in England, and it is unlikely that the property dispute with his wife's family took up too much of his time. He produced two more poems within the year, *Prothalamion*, to celebrate the bethrothal of the daughters of the earl of Worcester on 8 November 1596, an event he probably attended; and, *Fowre Hymnes*, the dedicatory letter to which was written from Greenwich, on 1 September 1596. Spenser was evidently advertising the fact that he was in attendance at court, which was held at the royal palace at Greenwich that summer, suggesting to readers that he was, at last, in favour.[162] Spenser would have witnessed Henri IV, king of France (ruled 1589–1610), invested as a Knight of the Garter on 29 August, a more opulent and elaborate ceremony than the investitures he had attended in Dublin.[163] His representation of the Burbon episode (*FQ* V.xi), which tells the story of the knight Artegall rescues from Grantorto and restores to his lady, Flourdelis, a transparent allegory of the besieged French king, could have been informed by personal observation of the monarch.[164] Spenser may well have been able to stay there and write *A View* under the patronage of Essex, or someone in his circle. Whatever the story, the fact that the place is cited is significant, as it suggests that Spenser was advertising his connections and angling for patronage, and, probably, a position away from Ireland, at least in the short term. *A View* was undoubtedly written to benefit its author as well as the settlers in Munster. Given Spenser's previous comments about the court there is a rather nice irony in his attempt to return and secure lucrative favours, and perhaps an inevitability about his failure to achieve these.

Fowre Hymnes occupy an uneasy position within the Spenser canon. They are elaborate poems, inspired by the Neoplatonic philosophy which had become modish in court circles since the 1570s. They suggest that Spenser had recently read a French or Italian translation of the *Symposium*, and had immersed himself in the writings of Ficino and the Platonic Academy in Florence, Pico della Mirandola, Castiglione, Pietro Bembo, and Jerome Benivieni's *Canzona della Amore celeste et divino*, which has been seen as a direct source for the *Hymnes*.[165] The poems might also provide further evidence that Spenser was reading such major Italian poets as Dante and Cavalcanti, as well as making use of the Neoplatonic French poetry of Ronsard and Du Bellay that he had learned from Mulcaster.[166] Probably these were all works he read throughout his life. The *Hymnes* are into two pairs, the first two describing earthly love and beauty, the second two recounting the far greater forms of heavenly love and beauty, of which the earthly forms are a pale shadow.[167] 'An Hymne of Heavenly Beautie' concludes with a plea for the reader to abandon the vain pleasures of earthly delights and to concentrate on the secure and everlasting value of God's love:

> And looke at last vp to that soueraine light,
> From whose pure beams al perfect beauty springs,
> That kindleth loue in euery godly spright,
> Euen the loue of God, which loathing brings
> Of this vile world, and thease gay seeming things;
> With whose sweete pleasures being so possest,
> Thy straying thoughts henceforth for euer rest. (lines 295–301)

Although the four poems have often been praised as the mature works of a major poet establishing a late style, and have been regarded as the culmination of Spenser's poetic career, bearing comparison to 'Two Cantos of Mutabilitie', they occupy a distinctly anomalous place in his *œuvre* and literary trajectory.[168] Perhaps, as has been suggested, they were an attempt to answer the criticism recorded in the proem to *The Faerie Queene*, Book IV, that Spenser was a 'loose' poet who had written indiscriminately on love.[169] Perhaps they were a response to the Jesuit martyr-poet Robert Southwell (1561–95), a keen reader of Spenser who had been executed the previous year.[170] As Terry Comito has noted, they 'do not wear their learning lightly', an observation that would support the judgement that they are not quite what they seem.[171]

The dedicatory letter to the countesses of Cumberland and Warwick makes a scarcely veiled joke about the censorship of the *Complaints*, which places the two ladies on familiar terms with the poet and demonstrates to the outside world that they can all share a highbrow literary joke.[172] Not only can the ladies appreciate the joke, but the reader can see that Spenser is on intimate terms with these powerful aristocrats, suggesting that the *Hymnes* may be a part of Spenser's strategy of securing patronage by advertising his literary skills. Ponsonby published the *Hymnes* in a neat quarto with expensive paper and handsome and clear roman type, along with *Daphnaïda*.[173] It was 'more carefully printed than any other of Spenser's works printed in his lifetime', further evidence of the close link between author and publisher, as well as a reminder that what is subsequently valued by readers may not have been what was thought important at the time.[174] The earlier poem had a separate title page, now reset from the original, so that the words 'An Elegy' were now in capitals and appeared on a line alone, standing out, before the reader notes for whom the poem is written.

The reproduction of *Daphnaïda* makes the volume look even more like an advertisement of the poet's skill. Two very different works, each conspicuously lofty literary forms, are contained within one small, handsome book, each written to order for aristocratic patrons. The dedicatory letter sees Spenser claiming that he had two works already written from 'the greener times' of his youth, and now he produces two more, challenging readers to try and see the join.[175] Given the complex and challenging nature of Spenser's poetry, which often links harmonious forms with disturbing subject matter, the *Hymnes* seem particularly slight as philosophical statements. Other poets who use Neoplatonic ideas in their poetry invariably do so in order to undermine the ostensible subject of their verse. Sidney's sonnet 'Who will in the fairest booke of Nature know' (*Astrophil and Stella* 71) has Astrophil claiming that in witnessing Stella's beauty he is inspired to behave more virtuously and to think about the perfect forms of Platonic beauty before the final line undermines his sentiment and exposes his true feelings:

> And not content to be Perfection's heire
> Thy selfe, doest strive all minds that way to move,
> Who marke in thee what is in thee most faire.
> So while thy beautie drawes the heart to love,
> As fast thy Vertue bends that love to good:
> 'But ah,' Desire still cries, 'give me some food.'[176]

Spenser would have known this poem, given his connections with Sidney, and it shows that even those with personal connections to European Neoplatonists did not necessarily treat them with unqualified respect.[177] John Donne also had an interest in Neoplatonic philosophy, but his major lyric, 'The Extasie', is based on the joke that because the union of the lovers is so pure and refined they ought to unite their bodies so that others can read the essence of their love, even though they do not need to:

> To our bodies turn we then, that so
> Weak men on love revealed may look,
> Love's mysteries in souls do grow,
> But yet the body is the book.
> And if some lover, such as we,
> Have heard this dialogue of one,
> Let him still mark us, he shall see
> Small change, when we'are to bodies gone.[178]

Indeed, Neoplatonic poetry in Italy and in England was full of sly, underhand references and was rarely what it seemed to be. Given Spenser's representation of his relationship with Harvey in the *Calender* it is possible that he knew that 'Socratic love' in many Italian poems exploited the ambiguity of the Greek texts and stood as barely disguised code for same-sex desire.[179] It is hard to imagine that the *Hymnes* were designed to be taken at face value. The last two hymns reject the earthly love in the first two, which would seem to be at odds with the relationship between sexuality and religion in *The Faerie Queene*.[180] Equally, it is hard to imagine that a poet as sophisticated as Spenser could take such ideas quite so seriosuly when his contemporaries were often sceptical about the significance and purpose of Neoplatonism and imaginative in their employment of the ideas and images it generated.

What might the two countesses have made of the *Fowre Hymnes* and why might Spenser have dedicated the work to them? They were Lady Margaret Russell, countess of Cumberland (1560–1616), and Anne Russell (1548/9–1604), widow of Ambrose Dudley, first earl of Warwick, who had died in 1590. They were younger sisters of Sir William Russell, the Lord Deputy of Ireland (1594–7), at the time when the poems were published. Spenser would have known, or, at least, met, Russell, although he may not have been especially close to him, as Russell had an openly fractious relationship with Spenser's patron, Sir John Norris.[181] Lady Margaret had lived with her aunt in Lilford Hall, Northamptonshire, for some years after her mother died in 1562, about forty miles from Bradden, so there would have been obvious connections between her and the gentry families that were linked to Spenser, and she certainly would have known the Spencers of Althorp.[182] She married George Clifford, third earl of Cumberland (1558–1605), one of the dedicatees of *The Faerie Queene*.[183] Her daughter, Lady Anne Clifford (1590–1676), on whom Lady Margaret doted after the early death of her two sons, later paid for Spenser's funeral monument in 1620, further indicating the close link between the family and Spenser.[184] The family home was Skipton Castle, Yorkshire, and it is possible that Spenser sought them out during this period in a bid to secure their support. Lady Anne was a noted reader and patron of English poetry, who knew a variety of major intellectuals, including John Dee and Aemilia Lanyer. She had a number of literary works dedicated to her and was tutored by Samuel Daniel.[185] Spenser perhaps knew Lanyer (1569–1645) through the Clifford family and so may had an impact on her poetry, just as he influenced the work of Mary Sidney.[186] Lady Anne had a portrait commissioned, the Belcamp triptych, when she was 53, showing her standing in her closet with her dog. On the shelves behind her are her books, which, along with biblical, classical, and philosophical works, include those of the major Elizabethan and Jacobean poets—Daniel, Sidney, Hall, and Spenser.[187] Moreover, she mixed with the Spencers of Althorp, the Wallops, and the Norris family, further indicating close links to Spenser's circles.[188] Spenser praised Lady Margaret in *Colin Clout* as 'Faire *Marian*, the *Muses* onely darling: | Whose beautie shyneth as the morning cleare, | With siluer deaw vpon the roses pearling' (lines 505–7).[189]

While Lady Margaret was a provincial figure of some significance, her sister, the countess of Warwick, was much closer to the centre of power, having been made a maid of honour to Elizabeth in 1559, becoming one of her favourites. She had other obvious links to Spenser as the stepsister of Lord Grey's wife, and correspondent with the wife of Sir Nicholas Malby (*c.*1530–84), a prominent figure in Ireland in the late 1570s and early 1580s, who became president of Connaught and was unusual because he had learned Irish well. Malby served with Grey at the defeat at Glenmalure, and so would have been known to Spenser.[190] The countess was also a female aristocrat who had a reputation as a major patron of writers and intellectuals and she had been instrumental in gaining John Dee favour at court. She had done what she could for her friends, the Sidneys, but had not been able to have Sir Henry relieved of his position as Lord Deputy of Ireland, demonstrating that her power had clearly defined limits.[191] Spenser had praised her more extensively than her sister in *Colin Clout*:

> Ne lesse praise worthie I *Theana* read,
> Whose goodly beames though they be ouer dight
> With mourning stole of carefull widowhead,
> Yet through that darksome vale do glister bright;
> She is the well of bountie and braue mynd,
> Excelling most in glorie and great light:
> She is the ornament of womankynd,
> And Courts chief garlond with all vertues dight.
> Therefore great *Cynthia* her in chiefest grace
> Doth hold, and next vnto her selfe aduaunce,
> Well worthie of so honourable place,
> For her great worth and noble gouernance. (lines 492–503)

The countess is celebrated as a wise widow, respected by the monarch as someone who merits her place at court and who is able to dispense good advice, eagerly sought out by those eager to secure their just deserts from the apex of power. The adjectives and nouns are carefully placed throughout this passage, designed to praise the countess as she probably wished to be seen by those around her. She is 'worthie' (a word used twice, along with the noun 'worth'), 'carefull', possesses great 'vertue', and is 'honourable' and renowned for her 'bountie' and 'noble gouernance'. Spenser had earlier praised her in *The Ruines of Time* as the wife of the earl, 'His noble Spouse, and Paragon of fame' (line 245), who had made her husband especially happy.

It is easy to see why Spenser, eager for support from those in high places, should have turned to these sisters at this time. He may have travelled to visit one or the other, met them through their family connections, or encountered them in Greenwich in 1596. Each had the means and the desire to ease the lives of writers like him; he had numerous connections to the families of each lady, had already praised them extravagantly in public; and they continued to promote his memory and fame after his death, indicating that a reciprocal relationship had been established. Moreover, given what he had written elsewhere and the stern reactions his words had provoked, Spenser probably had relatively few options. But it is likely that Spenser's links to the sisters were especially close. On the last page of an early fifteenth-century illuminated vellum manuscript of John Gower's *Confessio Amantis* belonging to Anne Russell, two lines from Ovid's *Tristia* are copied out, 'Tempore foelici multi numerantur amici | Cum fortuna perit nullus amicus erit' ('While you are safe, the friends you'll count are many; | If cloudy weather comes, alone you'll be'), bracketed next to the name 'Spenserus' in an Italian hand (Figure 10).[192] If this is by Spenser, and circumstantial evidence would suggest that it is—especially as Gower was an author he would have read, even though there is only one direct reference to his work in a gloss in the *Calender*—then he may well have had access to the Bedford family library in his youth.[193] Anne's father, Francis Russell, second earl of Bedford (1526/7–85), compiled one of the largest recorded Elizabethan libraries, which contained a number of important manuscripts, as well as printed books—including Mulcaster's *Positions*.[194] He was another noted patron of writers and had a large number of books dedicated to him.[195] Furthermore, the Russells may have played more of a role in patronizing Spenser than has often been realized, perhaps helping to secure his position in Ireland. The lines seem to express Spenser's gratitude to the family and sense of loss in being severed from their hospitality (assuming Spenser wrote them on a visit in 1596–7).[196]

Both Lady Anne and Lady Margaret had well-established reputations for running puritan households and for supporting puritan divines (as, indeed, did Lady Anne Clifford). The *Hymnes* would seem to be exactly the sort of poetry that such sophisticated readers would like. Written in Chaucerian rhyme royal, they

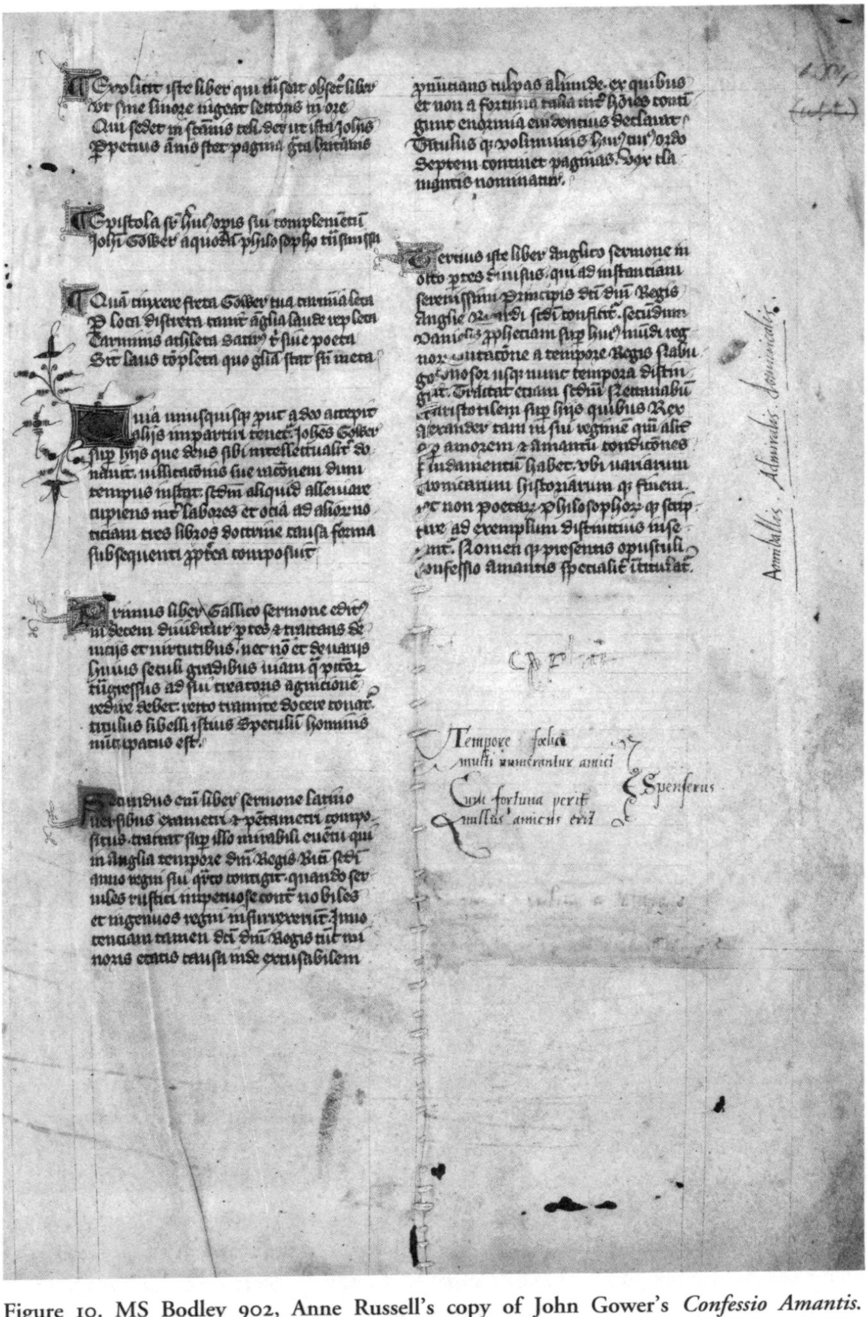

Figure 10. MS Bodley 902, Anne Russell's copy of John Gower's *Confessio Amantis*. Reproduced with kind permission of the Bodleian Library.

domesticate and anglicize Neoplatonic ideas and sentiments. Spenser would have known that both branches of the family knew John Dee and had an interest in alchemy, as her daughter noted, so that the *Hymnes* could easily be read as tailor-made for the sisters, merging mystical philosophy and orthodox Christian theology in an elegant, yet easily digestible form.[197] 'An Hymne of Heavenly Love' concludes by telling the enlightened that, once the reality of God's love has been realized and understood,

> Thenceforth all worlds desire will in thee dye,
> And all earthes glories on which men do gaze,
> Seeme durt and drosse in thy pure sighted eye,
> Compar'd to that celestiall beauties blaze,
> Whose glorious beames all fleshly sense doth daze
> With admiration of their passing light,
> Blinding the eyes and lumining the spright.
>
> Then shall thy ravisht soule inspired bee
> With heauenly thoughts, farre aboue humane skil,
> And thy bright radiant eyes shall planely see
> Th'Idee of his pure glorie present still,
> Before thy face, that all thy spirits shall fill
> With sweete enragement of celestiall loue,
> Kindled through sight of those faire things aboue. (lines 274–87)

Such poetic sentiments are not hard to understand, certainly not when compared to the intricacies of form and substance articulated in the *Calender* or *The Faerie Queene*, nor, indeed, even so apparently straightforward a poetic sequence as the *Amoretti*. The simple notion that we should despise our flesh and concentrate only on heavenly glory directly contradicts the thrust of the argument of *The Faerie Queene*, a work that is acutely sensitive to the dictates of the body and the need to accept, control, and govern them productively. But such a message would undoubtedly have pleased two aristocratic sisters of a puritan persuasion, especially one who was a widow and who had been publicly praised by the same writer for her discipline, self-control, generosity, and piety, and they would surely have been flattered by so eminent a poet publicly stating that he had revised work he had long forgotten at their behest. And the *Hymnes* are an astonishing technical accomplishment produced with Spenser's characteristic mastery of form and numerology, pitting the wilfulness of the blind Cupid against the infinitely powerful universal love of God.[198] Enough readers have heaped praise on the poems subsequently to suggest that *Fowre Hymnes* have always found an audience eager to read them as substantial literary achievements, so it would be something of a surprise if Lady Margaret and Lady Anne were anything but delighted with Spenser's offering. Lady Anne's subsequent support of

Spenser would indicate that they were a success, even if they did not produce the material reward for which the poet perhaps hoped.

In the same year Spenser produced a 'spousal verse' to celebrate the betrothals of Elizabeth and Katherine, the two daughters of Edward Somerset, fourth earl of Worcester (c.1550–1628) to Henry Guldeford and William Peter (although they would have been married by the time the poem was actually published).[199] Guldeford and Petre were both Catholics, further evidence, if any more were needed, that Spenser moved in diverse religious circles.[200] The *Prothalamion* would be the last work published in his lifetime.[201] Spenser's reasons for writing and publishing the poem would seem obvious enough. The wedding took place at Essex House, with three days of celebration, 8–10 November, but the betrothal ceremony, as the poem suggests, was probably in late summer or early autumn, as the court was at Greenwich until 1 October, most likely at some point between 7 and 29 September.[202] In writing a poem connected with this large, fifty-room house on the Strand Spenser was returning to the start of his career, because Essex House was Leicester House, which had become the property of the earl of Essex in about 1590. Spenser may well have stayed there, perhaps with his family, as he had done in 1580. Essex did have many guests to stay, setting aside rooms for frequent guests, such as Lady Penelope Rich (1563–1607), Essex's sister, when she came to London.[203] The interior of the house would have looked very different from 1579, however, as Leicester's family were forced to sell off the possessions, including the earl's extensive art collection, to pay off his debts.[204] Essex would have refurbished the house, at a time when the Strand witnessed the erection of ever grander palaces, each competing in splendour with the others. Soon after the betrothal, the great house-building family, the Cecils, close neighbours of Essex, started to build Salisbury House.[205] Worcester was a close ally of Essex, but the relationship was to turn spectacularly sour later on when Worcester was imprisoned by Essex during his coup after he was sent with other Privy Councillors to ask why so many men were assembling in Essex House, and then became one of the key crown witnesses at the trial.[206]

Spenser's poem is yet another innovative, technically sophisticated work, based on 'the Elizabethan dance-song stanza of three traces'.[207] In celebrating the espousal of the sisters, the poem follows what must have been their real journey upstream, recording the actual event as a brilliant memento. The poem was probably presented as a wedding present, and may have been financed by Essex.[208] The volume also looks like an attempt to secure the patronage of the earl, especially if read alongside the obvious reference to Essex in *A View*. Spenser had no clear connection to the family other than through Essex, so we must assume either that Spenser was asked to write the *Prothalamion* or offered it as an engagement present.[209] Essex receives extravagant praise for his heroic feats in Cadiz, the most important event of the summer, which the earl was trying his hardest to exploit to secure his position as the

pre-eminent figure at court, and to which Spenser had alluded, albeit indirectly, in
A View:

> Yet therein now doth lodge a noble Peer,
> Great *Englands* glory and the Worlds wide wonder,
> Whose dreadfull name, late through all *Spaine* did thunder.
> And *Hercules* two pillors standing neere,
> Did make to quake and feare:
> Faire branch of Honor, flower of Cheualrie,
> That fillest *England* with thy triumphes fame,
> Ioy haue thou of thy noble victorie,
> And endlesse happinesse of thine owne name
> That promiseth the same:
> That through thy prowesse and victorious armes,
> Thy country may be freed from forraine harmes:
> And great *Elisaes* glorious name may ring
> Through al the world, fil'd with thy wide Alarmes. (lines 145–58)[210]

If Spenser's neighbour Henry Cuffe was related to Essex's secretary, Hugh Cuffe, as
seems likely, Spenser would have had an obvious means of knowing about Essex's
attempts at self-promotion, as Cuffe collaborated with Essex to produce the pamphlets which made his case.[211] While Spenser celebrated his own position within the
social order in the *Amoretti* as akin to that of a merchant, Spenser here defers to the
earl as the 'flower of Cheualrie', referring to his elite status as a Knight of the Garter,
elected at the tender age of 22, an order to which Worcester also belonged.[212]

In the *Prothalamion* Spenser plays his hand with a clarity that would later seem
like reckless abandon, as the court started to crystallize into two factions surrounding
Essex, the heir of Leicester, and the Cecils. As well as openly backing Essex, he
laments his own status as an outsider in the capital, casting himself as a disgruntled
and poorly rewarded loyal servant who deserves far better than he gets. Spenser
contrasts his dark mood with the calm of the city on a pleasant day:

> Calme was the day, and through the trembling ayre,
> Sweete breathing *Zephyrus* did softly play
> A gentle spirit, that lightly did delay
> Hot *Titans* beames, which then did glyster fayre:
> When I whom sullein care,
> Through discontent of my long fruitlesse stay
> In Princes Court, and expectation vayne
> Of idle hopes, which still doe fly away,
> Like empty shaddowes, did aflict my brayne,
> Walkt forth to ease my payne
> Along the shoare of siluer streaming *Themmes*. (lines 1–11)

It is rare that early modern poets are as open about their failures and disappointments as Spenser is here, especially in an expensively produced slim volume.[213] Spenser casts himself as a discordant figure at odds with the relative harmony of the city, a position that enables him to celebrate the betrothal of the couples when he perceives the happiness of the event and is included as a guest.[214] He will be able to transform the world and give it meaning for the young lovers.[215] But the *Prothalamion* begins with the poet advertising the fact that he has been unsuccessful at securing anything from the court, ensuring that his presence there, which he had trumpeted abroad in the *Hymnes*, was no happier than his previous recorded visit six years earlier. Instead he shows that his success is tied to securing help from Essex. The *Prothalamion*, like the *Amoretti and Epithalamion*, pits commercial values against aristocratic ones, deliberately eliding the role of the poet in the early modern economy.[216] In producing this functional ambiguity, Spenser reminds us that his position as a hired writer is a precarious one and that he always risks returning home with nothing.

What cannot be disputed is the poem's celebration of the marriage as a definitive London event, one that sees the author begin as an exile but soon start to remember his place in the city and, therefore, his part in the marriage as an event in the capital. Although he takes his name from 'another place' and 'An house of auncient fame'— aligning him, for a moment, with the aristocratic values represented by Essex— Spenser takes the opportunity to remind readers that 'mery London' was his 'most kindly Nurse, | That to me gaue this Lifes first native sourse' (lines 127–31). These are, as usual, biographical details that are carefully and strategically placed in the poem, demonstrating that Spenser belongs to the city and so has a right to live and work there.[217] The refrain, 'Sweete *Thames* runne softly, till I end my Song', can be read as a declaration of Spenser's identity, and as a plea that he return to the city until his death, especially when produced by a poet who had written so often about rivers and defined his identity in terms of them throughout his literary career.[218] Spenser has deliberately produced his most London of poems at a late stage in his life, reminding readers of his origins and showing them where he thought he belonged. In doing so he has skilfully adapted a series of poetic traditions, most significantly William Vallans's *A Tale of Two Swans* (1590), a work that established the genre of the river poem and which had urged Spenser to publish his *Epithalamion Thamesis*.[219] Vallans probably did not know Spenser, but would have read about the early river poem in the *Letters*, a version of which had now appeared in Book IV of *The Faerie Queene*.[220] Vallans celebrates his own River Lee, a tributary of the Thames that runs through Hertfordshire, and establishes the boundary between Middlesex and Essex, before joining the Thames at Bow Creek, just east of Greenwich, where Spenser stated that he was staying. Vallans had clearly been influenced by Spenser to produce his poem.

He has his swans swim past Verulam, a key source of Christianity in the British Isles, 'albeit there be nothing left but the ruines and rubbish of the walles', in what must surely be a reference to his own *The Ruines of Time*, as well as the historical substance in Camden and Powell.[221] In writing the *Prothalamion*, Spenser outdoes his disciple, Vallans, celebrating London through the Thames and showing that he was the true poet of the capital.

It is noticeable that in the second edition of *The Faerie Queene* and *A View*, Spenser is at pains to promote his credentials as an expert on Ireland, attuned to its history and place within the British Isles, understanding the island's ancient culture as well as any antiquarian working in England, and, perhaps most significant of all, proving himself to be an astute commentator on contemporary Irish politics. Whether this was part of a subtle plan, designed to show that he would be best used as an expert on Irish affairs resident in London; whether he became more eager to demonstrate his allegiance to the capital as he realized that he would have to go back to Ireland; or whether he was simply articulating the two sides of his impressive literary career, is impossible to know.

Last Years, 1597–9

AT SOME POINT either just before Christmas 1596, or in early 1597, Spenser returned to Ireland. He may have planned to be back home at that point, or, more plausibly, found that it was impossible to obtain a position in London, perhaps because he had offended too many powerful people or because it was hard to secure lucrative employment. His estates in Ireland were far too valuable to abandon even for a short period and it was unlikely that he would have found a buyer willing to pay what they were worth, given how difficult it had proved to attract settlers to Ireland on even the most favourable terms.

In early 1597 the situation in Spenser's adopted homeland looked no better than it had a year earlier. Tyrone had been pardoned for his offences against the crown on 12 May 1596, after negotiations with Wallop and Gardiner, although he had made it clear that he was not happy with the manoeuvres of the crown to curb his power in Ulster, in particular through the establishment of a garrison at Armagh.[1] In November Tyrone had taken up arms again, besieging and blockading the Armagh garrison until January 1597. Tyrone's resistance was inspired by the positive response he received from the papacy and Philip II when he requested aid, and Spanish ships landed with arms and munitions at Killybegs, Donegal, on 17 September.[2] The O'Byrnes of Wicklow led by Feach MacHugh O'Byrne, who had surrendered in November 1595, also rebelled in that month, and a second Spanish Armada sailed into the channel.[3] Fortunately for the English the Spanish ships were dispersed by storms but the fleet was another potent reminder of how isolated England—and especially the English settled in Ireland—were.[4] In March 1597 a new Lord Deputy, Thomas, Lord Burgh, replaced Sir William Russell, and convinced himself that he had the military power and skill to overcome Tyrone. Burgh headed towards Tyrone's heartlands via Armagh and at the same time the new chief commissioner of Connaught, Sir Conyers Clifford, attacked the forces of Tyrone's chief ally, Red

Hugh O'Donnell, using the fort at Ballyshannon as a base. However, Burgh's campaign stalled when the fortifications he established at Blackwater were blockaded by Tyrone, and Clifford was forced to retreat when his powder ran out, the Irish sarcastically naming the point where he crossed back over the Erne the Ford of Heroes (Casan-na-gCuradh).[5] Burgh died of typhus in Newry on 13 October 1597, a few weeks after Sir John Norris died, his brother, Thomas, Spenser's neighbour, formally assuming the presidency of Munster. These events left English rule in a vacuum, placing 'civil and military authority in Ireland in the hands of a committee, with the inevitable consequences of indecision and procrastination'.[6] For the rest of Spenser's life there would be no chief governor in Ireland, as the next one was Robert Devereux, earl of Essex, who was granted the title of Lord Lieutenant in March 1599. Instead, Ireland was ruled by Archbishop Loftus and Chief Justice Gardiner, with the earl of Ormond in charge of the army. Ormond concluded a truce with Tyrone on 22 December 1597, but it was clear that, with none of Tyrone's demands agreed, it could only be temporary. A second attempt at a Spanish invasion had failed when Spanish ships were driven back by a storm in October and Tyrone's inclination was clearly to wait until a new opportunity presented itself.

Instead of Russell, a Deputy with whom he had connections, Spenser now saw power transferred to a man he had no reason to trust or support, Loftus; and with the death of John Norris, another sympathetic figure, authority passed to Ormond, whose principal loyalty was to his family's lands in central and south-east Ireland rather than the New English on the Munster Plantation. More significantly, by 1597 the 'situation in Ireland was critical'.[7] The Old English Catholics were still loyal to the crown and suspicious of the crusading forces led by Tyrone, but the English army was overstretched and ill-disciplined.[8] There were ominous signs that things could only get worse before they got better, especially given the new eagerness of the Spanish to get involved in the war.

Nevertheless, Spenser acquired more land at considerable expense on his return to his adopted land. He bought the castle and lands at Renny for the handsome sum of £200, for his infant son, Peregrine, as well as the disestablished Franciscan priory at Buttevant, which he must have also obtained in this period (Plates 36 and 37).[9] Both were important estates that, yet again, show how much wealth he had accumulated over the years—£200 was a sum that could only have been made through property dealing, as it was ten times Spenser's not inconsiderable salary as a secretary in 1580.[10] The purchase also confirms how much parents expected to spend on securing the future of their children.[11] The castle at Renny, now demolished, was a prime site on the Blackwater, about fifteen miles south-east of Kilcolman, and on the way to Youghal, a further thirty-five miles down the river. It was an ideal place for Spenser to obtain, and it is not surprising that anecdotes have developed suggesting that Spenser lived there and wrote parts of The Faerie Queene under a tree—'Spenser's oak'—overlooking the river.[12] Opposite the castle was the magnificent Augustinian foundation, Bridgetown Priory, the most significant religious complex in the area, dating back to the early thirteenth century, which had become the chief burial place of its founders, Spenser's bitter rivals for the land beneath the Ballyhoura Hills, the Roches of Fermoy (Plate 38).[13] This had become the property of Sir Henry Sidney in 1576, and had then been passed on to Lodowick Bryskett, again suggesting that Lord Roche's allegations that property deals were planned by the New English for their own gain had considerable substance.[14] Renny came with 395 acres, and could command a rent of £6. 8s. 11d. in 1668 when Hugolin Spenser, the poet's grandson, occupied the estate.[15]

Buttevant Abbey was an equally obvious property for Spenser to acquire as it was only about three miles from his house. The Abbey was built beside the Awbeg, just down from where the Bregog flows into it, both rivers having an important role in the mythological world of *Colin Clout* and 'Two Cantos of Mutabilitie', the work on which Spenser was probably engaged in 1597–8, further demonstrating what a significant role the landscape played in his imagination. They then flow on into the major navigable river, the Blackwater.[16] The Abbey had been confiscated from the Barry family, who had held it after the dissolution of the Irish monasteries, for their part in the Desmond Rebellion.[17] It came with a relatively modest plot of 30 acres.[18] A draft book of Orders of the Revenue side of the Exchequer of 1609 contains an entry that suggests that Spenser acquired even more land in his final years: 'Corke, Edmonde Spencer, Kilvrogan, Kilwanton, Backheliston, Neghwan, Balintegan, Rynny, in Conte Corke, sp'ualities and temp'alities.'[19] These ecclesiastical sites, from which Spenser clearly derived some income, cannot all be identified. However, a number can be traced which form a cluster to the south-west of Cork city: Neghwan (Ovens, and also Backbeliston, as an earlier grant to Anthony St Leger in the reign of Henry VIII makes clear); Kilbrogan (Kilvrogan), which is now part of Bandon, where Spenser's daughter, Katherine, lived, and surely refers to the church where she is buried; and Killountain (Kilwanton). Ballylegan is to the north-east of the city, while Ballinlegan (Ballintegan) remains unknown.[20] Peregrine passed on his estates to his son, Hugolin. These included, as well as Renny and Buttevant, tithes, parsonages, and rectories at Templebride (Kilbride), Brinny, and Kilbonane (Plate 39). Templebride is probably Templebreedy, Crosshaven, immediately south of Cork (Plate 40); the first two fit easily into the group of sites south-west of Cork. Spenser might well have acquired these at the same time that he acquired Renny and Buttevant, part of his efforts to secure a substantial portfolio of properties for his children.[21]

Nevertheless, this land grabbing clearly came at a price and it is unlikely that Spenser was ignorant of the gamble he was taking. He is recorded as having failed to pay his rent arrears on the Abbey, the only reason that we know that he acquired the valuable former religious institution: '7 mo Februar, 1597 [i.e., 1598], Mr Spencer by Mr Cheffe Barron's dirrecc'on under his hand hathe day ffor payment of the arreradgis of rnet due upon the Abbey of Buttevant until the beginning of Easter terme next, ffor that at this present, by reason of trouble in the way, he durst not bring downe anie monny.'[22] The ominous phrase, 'trouble in the way', suggests that normal life was breaking down on the Plantation by that point, and that English settlers who had not fled were afraid to leave their estates. Estimates indicate that by 1598 there were only 3,000 English settlers instead of the 8,000 planned, and that the English lived as isolated farmers in an overwhelmingly hostile environment, 'vulnerable to an uprising of the native population'.[23] Had Spenser lived a little longer and survived the Battle of Kinsale on 21 September 1601 his acquisition of so much Irish property would have seemed a sensible and far-sighted risk worth taking. Perhaps, he felt he had no choice but to remain in Ireland and believed that O'Neill would eventually be overcome so that accumulating property that was relatively cheap in the short term and valuable eventually was the best option for his family. The suits that his sons brought against Elizabeth Boyle's second and third husbands, Roger Seckerstone (Sylvanus) and Sir Robert Tynte (Peregrine), indicate that they thought that their father had intended that they should inherit the bulk of his Irish lands.[24]

Spenser was still embroiled in events in England, even if he was not directly party to them. The anger of King James appears not to have abated, which might explain why Spenser published nothing more once the scandal of the second edition of *The Faerie Queene* broke out. It would certainly have provided him with another motive to risk staying in Ireland. The fact that James was still attempting to commission a book answering Spenser's offensive comments two years after the second edition of *The Faerie Queene* had been published indicates just how angry the monarch was and how right Spenser was to feel in danger. James was not a man who forgave past insults and transgressions easily, as his—not unreasonable—objection to George Buchanan's hostile perception of the habitual role of the Scottish monarchy indicates.[25] James's fury at Spenser's representation of his mother as Duessa was also not without its reasons. Although James had not known her at all, his claim to the English throne depended on his descent from her. One of James's first acts when he reached England was to have a velvet pall sent to cover her tomb and, a decade later, he had her body exhumed and reburied in Westminster Abbey under a grand monument facing that of Elizabeth.[26] Spenser was unlikely to find a return to court easy, especially if James became king, which seemed likely, if not inevitable, in the late 1590s.[27]

Spenser found his way blocked in another way too, just over a month later, although this was probably an event over which he had no control and which he may never have wanted to happen. On 14 April the publisher and printer Matthew Lownes entered the Rawlinson copy of *A View* into the Stationers' Register, a means of asserting his sole right to reproduce the text. A note at the end of the copy from the Warden of the Company to the secretary makes it clear that the dialogue was generating a certain amount of anxiety: 'Mr Collinges / pray enter this Copie for Mathew Lownes to be printed when he do bringe other authoritie. Thomas Man.'[28] There are a number of reasons why any book might have needed other authority before it was printed: the copyright might have belonged elsewhere; it might have contained problematic religious references; it might have been offensive; or it might have included political references that the crown or authorities did not want to see circulating widely. Spenser, after all, had a history of producing transgressive works that courted controversy. The main reason why *A View* was probably refused a licence for publication was that it was a work containing details about Ireland at a particularly sensitive time. Indeed, the text, especially the second half, is full of information about the positioning of garrisons; military manoeuvres required to defeat the Irish; strategies and tactics that English generals should employ; and so on. It would have been a strangely lax system that allowed such a work, obviously designed for manuscript circulation, to enter the public sphere.[29]

At first sight it is surprising that *A View* was entered for publication by Matthew Lownes, a publisher and bookseller whose career was in its infancy, as he had only been granted his freedom to publish by the Stationers' Company in 1594, and had published his first book in 1595. He had, however, shown an interest in the poetry of Spenser and his literary imitators and fellow travellers, publishing Michael Drayton's *Mortimeriados: The Lamentable Ciuell Warres of Edward the Second and the Barrons* and Benjamin Griffin's *Fidessa, More Chaste Then Kinde* in 1596, a sonnet from which, '*Venus, and young Adonis sitting by her*', was reprinted in *The Passionate Pilgrime*, and passed off as Shakespeare's work.[30] Drayton was, by this point, often connected to Spenser by critics, and Griffin's sequence is based on the guise assumed by Duessa when she first encounters the Red-Cross Knight (I.ii.26), her name sounding as if it means faithful when it really means faithless.[31] Using a name from Spenser's romance-epic to write a sonnet sequence just after Spenser had published the *Amoretti* certainly indicates a keen interest in the master's work. Lownes's print shop was in St Dunstan's churchyard, Fleet Street, near the Inns of Court and it is likely that Lownes had connections with the Inns, where Griffin was a student.[32] Griffin had connections with Sir Thomas Lucy (*c*.1532–1600), a key figure in the Warwickshire–Northampton area, who was related to the Edward Lucy involved in Spenser's Chancery court case, a link that might explain why he had read and made use of *The Faerie Queene* in his own literary effort, supposedly the start of a writing career that never materialized.[33] Lownes also published an edition of Sidney's *Astrophil and Stella*, probably pirated, demonstrating that he had a keen eye on the contemporary poetry scene and was eager to make a name as a publisher who made such work available.[34]

The Rawlinson copy of *A View* was owned by John Panton, Egerton's confidential agent.[35] It is most plausible that Lownes acquired a manuscript of *A View* via his connections with the Inns of Court and law students and it is possible that there is a direct relationship between Egerton's copy of Spenser's dialogue and Panton's.[36] Lownes was probably taking a risk in imagining that he could have this work of Spenser's published, although it is possible—but unlikely—that he had no idea that the work was by the poet who had inspired the work of one of his publications a year earlier, as there is no clear sign other than the initials, 'E. S.', of the author.[37] The insistence of the warden, Thomas Man, that further authority was required before *A View* could be published is probably a reference to the fear that a work of this contemporary importance required explicit government approval.[38] The use of the term 'authority' indicates that Man's concern was with political censorship, not an early form of copyright, as then the term 'licence' would have been used.[39] The non-appearance of *A View* should not really surprise us, as relatively little was published dealing with Ireland in Elizabeth's reign—a pointed contrast to the wealth of manuscript material—apart from the Irish chronicles in Holinshed's *Chronicles* (1577, 1587), and these were written under the shadow of censorship; John Derricke's poem in praise of Sir Henry Sidney's government, *The Image of Ireland*, with its collection of expensive, carefully reproduced woodcuts; and works by Churchyard and Rich.[40] The only work that remotely compares to Spenser's dialogue is Richard Beacon's allegorical, Machiavellian-inspired analysis of Ireland, *Solon His Follie* (1594), dedicated to the queen, and perhaps published because it escaped the eyes of busy censors; perhaps because it was deemed too generalized in style and approach to cross accepted boundaries; perhaps because the situation was by no means as terrifying in that year, when Spenser published the *Amoretti and Epithalamion*, as 1598. Furthermore, it is worth noting that the Royal Charters that established the monopoly of the Stationers' Company and defined its duties to the crown did not include the university presses. Beacon was a Cambridge graduate and had no obvious connection with Oxford, so his choice of press looks odd unless he had particular connections, or was trying to avoid unwelcome attention.[41] Read in such light the publication of Beacon's work helps explain why Spenser's dialogue failed to appear in print.

Lownes's attempt to publish *A View* looks like a risky, probably doomed enterprise. It appears to have done him no harm in the short or long term as he continued to publish works of poetry, many of them obviously connected to Spenser, such as Edward Fairfax's translation of Tasso, *Godfrey of Bulloigne, or The Recovery of Ierusalem* (1600); Ralph Byrchensa's *A Discourse occasioned on the late defeat, given to the Arch-rebels, Tyrone and O'Donnell* (1602), which owed a great deal to *A View*; and, of course, the first folio of *The Faerie Queene*, including 'Two Cantos of Mutabilitie' in 1609; followed by Spenser's *Works* in 1611, each printed by his brother,

Humphrey.[42] Indeed, Lownes went on to enjoy a long and fruitful publishing career until his death *c.*1625, along with Humphrey, who was also a printer and produced a number of works, including many of his brother's publications. Lownes later became a senior warden of the Stationers' Company, at the same time that his brother became its master in 1620–1, and passed his business on to his son, Thomas, one of several Lowneses working in the printing and publishing business in the early seventeenth century.[43] Lownes published a significant number of other major poets, including Thomas Campion, Thomas Churchyard, Thomas Bastard, and Drayton's *Poly-Olbion*; plays, such as Ben Jonson's *Poetaster* and John Marston's *Antonio and Mellida* and its sequel, *Antonio's Revenge*; prose fiction, including Robert Greene's *Card of Fancie* and Sidney's *Arcadia*; music, including madrigals by John Dowland, and books by major composers such as William Corkine, Henry Lichfield, and Francis Pilkington; works of history, recent and classical, including William Fulbecke's digest of Roman history, Robert Chester's *Annals of Britain*, and Philemon Holland's translation of Suetonius; works relating to France; and a large number of religious works and sermons, including Richard Hooker's *Laws of Ecclesiastical Polity*. In short, Lownes was a major force in English publishing in the reigns of Elizabeth and James.[44]

Lownes clearly kept abreast of what Spenser was doing and probably had designs on his work, in whole or in part, from the start of his publishing career. It is clear from the number of works of Spenser that Lownes published after 1609 that Spenser was one of his showcase authors, and that he was keen to make the most of what he had—although he did wait for five years after obtaining the rights to Spenser, which might suggest that Spenser was not an obvious cash cow in the early 1600s, as has been claimed.[45] Or, it might suggest that Lownes was eager to make a big impact with Spenser and not simply reprint work inherited from Ponsonby, as he did with other works. The 1609 folio of *The Faerie Queene* was an expensively produced work, which must have taken time to produce, as it involved resetting the 1596 quarto text, which it follows closely, adding handsome new woodcuts as headings to each canto and elaborate ornamental designs to signal breaks in the text. Care was taken in setting the stanzas in large double columns, ensuring that pagination was right and margins were properly spaced.[46] Expensive paper had to be used to ensure that the ink did not run.[47] Literary works were not usually produced as folios before the appearance of the folio edition of Jonson's *Works* in 1616, an obvious inspiration for Heminges and Condell's production of Shakespeare's first folio in 1623—an indication of how significant a writer Spenser was deemed to have been by his contemporaries. The most obvious inspiration for Lownes's edition was Sir John Harington's *Orlando Furioso*, first produced by Richard Field in 1591, and reprinted for John Norton and Simon Waterston in 1607, although there were folios of Sidney's *Arcadia*, printed by Windet for Ponsonby in 1593 and Samuel Daniel's *Works*, published by Waterston in 1601, showing that folios of literary works were produced by those connected to Lownes.[48] As Jason Scott-Warren has pointed out, 'To set the 1591 *Orlando* alongside Spenser's 1590 *Faerie Queene* is to confront the oddity of branding the writer of the former an amateur. While Spenser's book is a barely-adorned quarto, the *Orlando* is one of the finest productions of the Elizabethan printing-house. Harington did not merely "english" the text; he englished the book.'[49] This must have occurred to Lownes, who had published Tasso, the other major Italian influence on Spenser's poem according to the Letter to Ralegh.[50] Now, the publisher ensured that the two works, *Orlando Furioso* and *The Faerie Queene*, existed as equals and Spenser clearly started to sell. Lownes was able to produce folio editions of the works 'made up by issuing as a single volume a number of separate sections which had been printed independently at periods often several years apart'.[51]

It is inconceivable that Spenser would not have known about Lownes, and he would surely have encountered Lownes at the start of his career when he stayed in London in 1596. When Ponsonby died in January 1604, his major copyrights were purchased by the half-brother of his wife, Joan, Simon Waterson, who also drew up the inventory of Ponsonby's estate.[52] Waterson then sold on a number of these rights to Lownes, who started to publish titles that had originally been produced by Ponsonby. Sir Clement Edmondes's *Observations Upon Caesar's Commentaries* (1604), which was a partial translation of *De Bello Gallico*, with a commentary based on military matters, was published in two editions dated 1604, one by Ponsonby and one by Lownes. *A Discourse of Life and Death: Written in French by Phil. Mornay. Done in English by the Countesse of Pembroke* (1606) was a reprint of a work first published by Ponsonby, which Lownes republished a number of times in the next few years. Most significantly, Lownes's 1609 first folio edition of *The Faerie Queene* had been first assigned to Simon Waterson after the death of Ponsonby. That Waterston published Ariosto in 1607 suggests that the two publishers had a clear sense of what the other was doing, and that they might have been working in tandem, especially as Richard Field, who published Ariosto first in 1591, was also linked to Ponsonby and had been the publisher of a number of Spenser's works subsequently, including the 1596 *Faerie Queene* and *Fowre Hymnes*.[53] There are other links that indicate connections between Spenser and Lownes or, at least, significant acquaintances in common. Lownes employed the printer John Windet, who worked with Ponsonby, Humphrey Lownes, and Harvey's publisher and close friend, John Wolfe, of whose estate he was executor in 1601.[54] Lownes also published Zachary Jones's translation of Pierre Le Loyer's *A Treatise of Specters or Straunge Sights, Visions and Apparitions Appearing Sensibly Vnto Men* (1605) (Jones had translated *Scanderbeg*, published by Ponsonby, for which Spenser had written a dedicatory sonnet).

Did Spenser know anything about Lownes's first attempt to publish his work? It is quite likely that he did, given the interest he took in designing his works as books and overseeing them through the publication process. For Spenser to have authorized the publication of *A View* would have been reckless in the extreme, especially given his track record of offending the good and the great. However, passing responsibility over to a publisher, especially one who was at one remove from his major publisher, might have been a calculated gamble. The subterfuge surrounding the publication of the *Complaints*, a volume that all parties surely realized might well cause a stir, was probably repeated here. On the other hand, it is equally possible that Spenser turned a blind eye to an unscrupulous move by Lownes; or, at least, accepted that such was the norm in the entrepreneurial publishing world, with its relatively small profits. After all, Cuthbert Burby seems to have leapt on the chance to publish a juvenile translation, indicating that by the mid-1590s Spenser was known to be an asset for publishers and his works must have sold well enough to make a reasonable profit.

In the first half of 1598 we have virtually no record of Spenser's activities in Ireland. This was a period of relative calm before O'Neill's attempt to eject the English from Ireland moved into its final stages. It is most likely that Spenser was back at Kilcolman—the claims that he was at Renny are hard to credit—at work on his poetry, albeit with a growing sense of unease, even doom. However, the only fragment that we have from this period is 'Two Cantos of Mutabilitie', published by Lownes ten years after Spenser's death, and it is likely that whatever he did produce in this last year of his life has not survived. The Cantos make a number of references to the current situation in Ireland, suggesting that even if they are a revised version of an earlier Ovidian work, Spenser reworked them in the years—if not months—immediately prior to his death.[55] Moreover, it is likely that the Cantos contain a reference to an eclipse that took place in April 1595, a likely topical reference to a notable event, especially if we bear in mind the discussion of the earthquake in the *Letters*, and Spenser's sustained interest in astrology and astronomy.[56]

Nevertheless, much about the Cantos remains a mystery, especially their relationship to the rest of *The Faerie Queene*; whether they survive as Spenser intended; whether they are as he left them or there were more passages that were lost; and how they found their way into Lownes's print shop. When he left Ireland for the last time Spenser must surely have brought over some papers, which found their way into Ponsonby's hands either directly or after his death.[57] We can never be sure whether the Cantos were authorized or whether there is indeed some substance in James Ware's claim that Spenser had, in fact, finished *The Faerie Queene*, but that it 'was soone after unfortunately lost by the disorder and abuse of his servant, whom he had sent before him into *England*'.[58] But it is most likely that Lownes inherited them from Ponsonby's papers.

'Two Cantos of Mutabilitie' have an anomalous appearance, consisting of two complete cantos and two stanzas of a third. The whole bears the publisher's advertisement: 'Two Cantos of Mutabilitie: Which, both for Forme and Matter, appeare to be parcell of some following Booke of the FAERIE QUEENE, ( ) VNDER THE LEGEND OF *Constancie*. Neuer before imprinted.'[59] The title has clearly been given to the fragment by the publisher, Lownes, and it is likely that he was making sense of a manuscript he found among Ponsonby's papers. It is therefore almost certain that a version of the Cantos circulated in manuscript before it appeared in print, and there is further evidence to suggest that this was the case.[60] The text was probably set from a manuscript in secretary hand, a script that may not have been Spenser's own, and would have consisted of about thirty pages. The last two cantos, printed as 'The VIII. Canto, vnperfite', were probably intended as the conclusion to canto vii.[61] This would make sense of what otherwise seems a confusing mess. There is no quatrain describing the forthcoming canto, as there is for every other canto in the poem. Furthermore, the stanzas provide a logical and satisfying conclusion to the judgement of Nature at the end of canto vii as it stands, that Mutability has no right to rule the universe, which does have, *pace* the Titaness, a logical order ruled by God:

> When I bethinke me on that speech whyleare,
> Of *Mutability*, and well it way:
> Me seemes, that though she all vnworthy were
> Of the Heav'ns Rule; yet very sooth to say,
> In all things else she beares the greatest sway.
> Which makes me loath this state of life so tickle,
> And loue of things so vaine to cast away;
> Whose flowring pride, so fading and so fickle,
> Short *Time* shall soon cut down with his consuming sickle.
>
> Then gin I thinke on that which Nature sayd,
> Of that same time when no more *Change* shall be,
> But stedfast rest of all things firmely stayd
> Vpon the pillours of Eternity,
> That is contrayr to *Mutabilitie*:
> For, all that moueth, doth in *Change* delight:
> But thence-forth all shall rest eternally
> With Him that is the God of Sabbaoth hight:
> O thou great Sabbaoth God, graunt me that Sabaoths sight. (viii.1–2)

Nature, as Gordon Teskey has pointed out, has been speaking about 'the Christian doctrine of the resurrection of the dead' recounted in 1 Corinthians 15, when God shall return to earth and history will end.[62] Here, in the narrator's response to her words, there is a profound pun in the last couplet, emphasized by the repetition of 'Sabboath' meaning both 'host or armies' and, as Sabbath, 'rest'.[63] Spenser's poem appears to have reached a real conclusion, pointing away from earthly matters towards the peaceful rest promised for the faithful after death. If these are Spenser's final lines then they assume a haunting melancholy, a clear recognition that his own end is near and that he needs to think about the afterlife.[64]

However, such a conclusion would appear to be rather too neat and too easily assimilated into his biography. We know from Camden that Spenser's funeral was an event; that his death affected a number of powerful people; and that a mythology of Spenser as the lost poet of Elizabethan England developed quickly among those eager to follow in his footsteps.[65] It is more likely that a manuscript which proclaimed that these were Spenser's final verses circulated than that he for a poet's final words left behind an authorized fragment that others then recognized as his last thoughts. Besides, we are no nearer to explaining why the Mutability Cantos were designated as the six, seventh, and eighth cantos of a new lost book. If the numbers have Spenser's authority then he was clearly intending to write, or had already written, more books, some of which are now lost. If a scribe, Lownes—or someone else in his print shop— added the numbers then they must also have read them as sections from the middle rather than the end of a book. Either way, the Cantos do not seem like the middle of other books in the poem, which usually contain narrative episodes based on romance motifs ready for Arthur to appear and influence the course of the action in canto viii, signalling that the problems outlined in the first half of the book will start to be solved.[66]

It is more plausible that the Cantos are part of a book exploring the legend of Constancy, as, presumably, the poet signalled, and scribe and editor recognized. A characteristic strategy of *The Faerie Queene*, as of Spenser's poetry in general, is to provide the reader with what look like concluding statements which are then qualified by later stanzas.[67] The same would surely have been the case with the Mutability Cantos. On one level they provide the obvious wisdom that men and women should always have one eye on 'last things'. The abolition of the medieval doctrine of Purgatory 'engendered a crude foreshortening of the eternal perspective of Christianity' and many Protestants 'refocused their own hopes on the end of time, an end which some at least did not believe to be so far away'.[68] The Mutability Cantos certainly follow this pattern, and express the fear of an accelerating conclusion to world history common to both Protestants and Catholics after the Reformation.[69] Nevertheless, the representation of the impending apocalypse in the poems is more subtle, double-edged, and troubling than straightforward resignation in the face of God's terrible judgement on sinful mankind.

The Cantos are written with the painful awareness that there can be a profound separation between earthly and heavenly concerns, a division that does not necessarily support the assumption that the universe is, in its final essence, constant. Moreover, this is a perspective that is consistent with Spenser's thinking about religion throughout his life, from his contributions to the *Theatre for Worldlings* to the comments on the spread of religion needing quiet times in *A View*.[70] Nature, after all, had vanished in the lines immediately preceding the narrator's reflections on her judgement, 'whither no man wist' (VII.viii.59, line 9). Moreover, can we really take her judgement of the dispute between Jove and Mutability at face value? Her words sound much more like the quibbling of poetry than a serious philosophical argument based on the rigorous application of logical principles:

> I well consider all that ye haue sayd,
> And find that all things stedfastnes doe hate
> And changed be: yet being rightly wayd
> They are not changed from their first estate;
> But by their change their being doe dilate:
> And turning to themselues at length againe,
> Doe worke their owne perfection so by fate:
> Then ouer them Change doth not rule and raigne;
> But they raigne ouer change, and doe their states maintaine.
>
> Cease therefore daughter further to aspire,
> And thee content thus to be rul'd by me:
> For thy decay thou seekst by thy desire;
> But time shall come that all shall changed bee,
> And from thenceforth, none no more change shall see.
>
> (VII.vii.58 and 59, lines 1–5)

The words sound comforting and conclusive, the argument being that change itself becomes a principle of steadfastness because everything will, in the end, change back to its first state. Such an atomist principle could well have been taken by Spenser from Lucretius' *De Rerum Natura*, a work in vogue in late sixteenth-century Europe that Spenser would have read and probably possessed.[71] We are made up of tiny pieces of matter and will return to our constituent elements when we die, as matter is indestructible, unlike us.[72] Death is not something that we should be afraid of, according to Lucretius, as the universe has a natural order that can be understood.[73] On one level the narrator's conclusion is therefore right, and in line with the ideas of Christian Stoics such as Justus Lipsius, who was associated with many of the Dutch figures close to Mulcaster, and whose *Two Bookes of Constancie* was translated into English just before Spenser started writing—or revising—the Cantos.[74] Nevertheless, it is hard to accept that drawing the conclusion that God therefore rules over everything can be read as the final message of *The Faerie Queene*, or that Nature's argument effectively destroys the claims of Mutability.[75]

The Cantos confront the reader with a stark and terrifying political message, which has to be balanced against the narrator's pious hope that as God rules the universe, all will be well. Read in the context of the possibility of an impending apocalypse, this might well have been true, but it also meant that a great deal of effort had to be expended in the last days.[76] Mutability's challenge involves a confrontation with Cynthia, installed by Jove as rightful ruler in the 'Circle of the Moone' (VII.vi.8, line 1). Mutability thinks that she is entitled to all the kingdoms of Cynthia (18), a belief which casts her as the Stuart claim to the English throne, as Cynthia is a representation of Elizabeth, an identification made clear in the Letter to Ralegh.[77] Mary Queen of Scots was long dead, but her claim lived on through her son, James VI, the Scottish king, who had taken such exception to the representation of his mother as Duessa in Book V.[78] Cynthia/Elizabeth, as the poem makes clear, was near to death and would not be able to escape the sands of time for long. Indeed, he sits at her gates, 'an hory | Old aged Sire, with hower-glasse in hand' (8, lines 5–6) and, if this is not a clear enough message, in the following canto Mutability turns to address the queen directly:

> And first, concerning her that is the first,
> Euen you faire *Cynthia*, whom so much ye make
> *Ioues* dearest darling, she was bred and nurst
> On *Cynthus* hill, whence she her name did take:
> Then is she mortall borne, how-so ye crake;
> Besides, her face and countenance euery day
> We changed see, and sundry forms partake,
> Now hornd, now round, now bright, now brown & gray:
> So that *as changefull as the Moone* men vse to say. (vii. 50)

Cynthia/Elizabeth is forcefully reminded that death is waiting for her and that her body is preparing itself to make the natural change to its new state. The final line also reminds her that her capriciousness has not been a benefit for her subjects; that her changefulness has resulted in chaotic policies; and that no one knows what will happen when she dies as there is no clear successor, apart from the figure of Mutability.

Mutability's claim that she has the right to rule is therefore true and she will govern according to her principles and ideals, bringing in chaos and endless change.[79] The episode is a nicely judged rewriting of Artegall's encounter with the Giant with the Scales, in which Artegall, who rules in Jove's name, tries to uphold the rulers of the universe against its challengers. Artegall wields Chrysaor, the sword that Jove used against the Titans, and here he is confronted by a Giant, presumably a Titan, one of the race whom Jove defeated, but who return to threaten the established order.[80] The Giant's claim that the universe should be based on more equitable principles has generally received short shrift from commentators, who have supported Artegall's assertion of the hierarchy established by those in power, using words that sound distinctly Lucretian:

> Likewise the earth is not augmented more,
> By all that dying into it doe fade.
> For of the earth they formed were of yore;
> How euer gay their blossome or their blade
> Doe flourish now, they into dust shall vade.
> What wrong then is it, if that when they die,
> They turne to that, whereof they first were made?
> All in the powre of their great Maker lie:
> All creatures must obey the voice of the most hie.
>
> They liue, they die, like as he doth ordaine,
> Ne euer any asketh reason why.
> The hils doe not the lowly dales disdaine;
> The dales doe not the lofty hils enuy.
> He maketh Kings to sit in souerainty;
> He maketh subiects to their powre obay;
> He pulleth downe, he setteth vp on hy;
> He giues to this, from that he takes away.
> For all we haue is his: what he list doe, he may. (40–1)

The lines have often been accepted as a statement of Spenser's political beliefs.[81] What is generally omitted from an assessment of them is Artegall's claim that the natural order simply happens and is decreed by God, a belief that the poem quite clearly does not uphold. In fact, Artegall has to act to end the debate, which he achieves by pushing the Giant off the cliff in a shocking epic simile:

> Like as a ship, whom cruell tempest driues
> Vpon a rocke with horrible dismay,
> Her shattered ribs in thousand peeces riues,
> And spoyling all her geares and goodly ray,
> Does make her selfe misfortunes piteous pray.
> So downe the cliffe the wretched Gyant tumbled;
> His battred ballances in peeces lay,
> His timbered bones all broken rudely rumbled:
> So was the high aspyring with huge ruine humbled. (50)

The stanza is important for what it tells us about Artegall's role in the poem, and, as he is acting for Jove, like Cynthia in the Mutability Cantos, the relationship of his actions to the claims of the Titaness and the judgement of Nature. The stanza is disturbing, just as the condemnation of the poet, Bonfont, is later in that book, and the heresy hunting of Roffy and Lowder had been in the September eclogue of the *Calender*. The simile of the destruction of the Giant does not make for pleasant reading, especially if the reader remembers what was done to serious criminals, and serves as a reminder of the need for brutality in the age of iron.[82] What is more significant here is the narrator's pointed contrast between the natural act of a tempest wrecking a ship, and Artegall's conscious actions in deciding on and then carrying out his act of destruction. Artegall claims that there is a natural order to human government, and that what humans have created mirrors what is ordained in the world in which they live. In terms of Artegall's ferocity reflecting a state of nature the analogy holds. However, he has to intervene in order to neutralize a threat to the order he wishes to uphold, a potent reminder to the reader that mankind has to be responsible for what it produces and achieves. The merits of the argument between the Giant and Artegall, each of whom claims that their position is supported by an appeal to the natural world, are probably less significant than the need for Artegall to take drastic action in order to support his belief in the inevitability of hierarchical order.[83]

Such an episode complicates our understanding of the Mutability Cantos and their ostensible meaning, preventing us from taking them at face value. Spenser's careful reading of Chaucer's *Parliament of Fowls* transforms Artegall's argument on a cliff top to an elaborately staged debate on a mountain summit.[84] Spenser locates his dispute on Arlo Hill, or Galtymore, the highest peak in the Galty Mountains near his house, and visible for miles around. It is inconceivable that he would have climbed the peak, which would have been an extremely dangerous undertaking in a hostile land, a waste of time and resources, and not a leisure pursuit that Elizabethans enjoyed, because 'no one who thought themselves civilized had any positive feelings about an actual steep mountain'.[85] Nevertheless, Spenser would have passed Galty-more every time he travelled north of his house to Limerick or towards Carrick and Dublin, and also seen it when he travelled south-east towards Youghal. The local setting is a timely reminder that the metaphysical conclusions of Nature are one thing, but what really mattered to most people were their immediate surroundings, especially in Ireland.[86] Nature can declare that Jove has the right to rule, but his rights are meaningless without force to implement them. Artegall has the power to destroy the Giant, but Jove is not backed up by Nature, who simply disappears, leaving Cynthia to fight Mutabilty in Ireland on her own. As with the debate between the Giant and the Knight of Justice, winning the argument may be of dubious value and irrelevant to what actually takes place afterwards. What Spenser has achieved in his poetry is a sophisticated understanding that the obvious may be true. Where characters in his work make errors it is usually in assuming that because there is a divine or natural order it is automatically manifested in the sublunary human world.[87] Spenser shows us a world in which there is a radical separation of the human and the divine, entirely consistent with his religious thought throughout his writing career. The fact that God has a plan for the world does not mean that we have the ability to understand it. Rather, we have to act and govern ourselves as best we can, and to try and make sense of the situations we find ourselves in, which is probably one of the qualities that especially appealed to Spenser's most important seventeenth-century reader, John Milton.[88]

The Mutability Cantos remind us that, as the Gods debate on Galtymore, looking down on the divided inhabitants below, the future of the known world is at stake. Spenser provides the reader with an aetiological Ovidian myth, one that combines his close local knowledge of the area and the legends of the physical features of the Irish landscape with an acute sense of their wider significance.[89] Spenser retells Ovid's story of Actaeon, combined with other secondary myths to represent the fate of his adopted homeland.[90] Ireland, we learn, was once a beautiful place, the fairest of the British Isles, justly revered by the Gods, especially Cynthia (Diana), who used to come with her nymphs to Arlo Hill to enjoy the pleasure of the woodland retreat (37–9). However, once she had been seen naked by Faunus, the 'Foolish God' who corrupts her nymph, Molanna, and then laughs at the sight of her naked body, she curses the whole island, having first punished Faunus by making him dress as a stag to become the prey of his own hounds. In the last stanza of canto vi, immediately before the Gods assemble for their debate, we learn that

> parting from the place,
> There-on an heauy haplesse curse did lay,
> To weet, that Wolues, where she was wont to space,
> Should harbour'd be, and all those Woods deface,
> And Thieues should rob and spoile that Coast around.
> Since which, those Woods, and all that goodly Chase,
> Doth to this day with Wolues and Thieues abound:
> Which too-too true that lands in-dwellers since haue fou[n]d. (55, lines 2–9)

Spenser represents Ireland transformed from a 'holy-Island' (37, line 7) to a cursed land, echoing a pun he makes in *A View* where he describes Ireland as '*Sacra Insula*, taking *sacra* for *accursed*'.[91] Ireland has now become the dangerous land that oppresses the shepherds in *Colin Clout*, one in which he has made his home.

What does Spenser claim has happened to Ireland? Spenser's myth is flexible and works in terms of several time schemes at once. Read most simply, the allegory tells us that Elizabeth used to enjoy the benefits of rural Ireland but now she has abandoned it to its harsh fate because she has been seen there for what she really is, an old unattractive lady with no clothes, subject to the scorn of smutty fauns who want to see her naked, as the Mutability Cantos are at pains to demonstrate. Who is Faunus? He has often been read as an abstract allegorical figure, 'our human sexual appetites', 'every fool in the world', when he has not been given a specific, topical Irish reference.[92] However, Faunus is another name for the god Pan, the god of flocks and shepherds who was always represented with his pipe.[93] Given Spenser's representation of himself as Colin Clout—like Pan, always with his pipe—it is hard not to think that Faunus is a version of the poet himself.[94] Like Spenser he is loquacious and in trouble with the authorities and perhaps there is a reference to Tresham's comment that Spenser was a poet 'lorrel' rather than a poet laureate, assuming that the comment or something like it got back to him.[95] Spenser would appear to be saying that he is the one who has seen the queen naked and exposed her as a fraud, unable and unwilling to protect her true subjects from the ravages of time and mutability, a problem exposed most cruelly and dangerously in Ireland. But perhaps he is the real fool, for when exposed she flees and leaves the land to its unhappy fate. As ever, the poetry is studied in its ambiguity: are the true fools those who live in Ireland, or those in England who do not realize the danger their fellow subjects of the crown face and who fail to protect them properly?

In the Cantos Spenser refers back to the story of the union of Bregog and Mulla in *Colin Clout*, yet another self-reference structuring his poetry in terms of his larger poetic designs. One of Diana's nymphs is called Molanna, Spenser's name for the Behanna (Beheena), a small river which flows down the slopes of Galtymore, and becomes a tributary of the Funsheon, called the Fanchin in the Cantos.[96] They join about fifteen miles east of Kilcolman at Kilbeheny, a place Spenser would have known as it was on the main route to Caher, a fortified town and stopping point on the route to Dublin (Plate 41). Molanna loves Fanchin, just as Mulla loves Bregog. It is easy, therefore, for Faunus to corrupt her with gifts of 'Queene-apples and red Cherries from the tree' (43, line 6) and the promise of facilitating her desired union with Fanchin, in order for her to betray her mistress and reveal where Diana bathes naked.[97] Faunus achieves his aim, with predictably disastrous results.

We are reminded that the relationship between the human and the natural worlds is complex. At times, Nature is unaffected by the ravages wrought by the contingencies of the human. Faunus is dressed as a deer and chased by his hounds, but he is allowed to go free, and the nymphs turn their hostile attention to Molanna:

> So they him follow'd till they weary were;
> When, back returning to *Molann'* againe,
> They, by commaund'ment of *Diana*, there
> Her whelm'd with stones. Yet *Faunus* (for her paine)
> Of her beloued *Fanchin* did obtaine,
> That her he would receiue vnto his bed.
> So now her waues passe through a pleasant Plaine,
> Till with the *Fanchin* she her selfe doe wed,
> And (both combin'd) themselues in one faire riuer spred. (53)

377

There is a delicate balance between men and women and their environment. The river can be blocked off and its course diverted, but this will result in it following a different course, not in its destruction. Here, the actions of the angry gods help the lovers achieve their aim rather than separate them, and, as locals would have known, the stones were carried down by the river itself.[98] In the next stanza, when Diana curses the land, we are told that much remains the same despite her actions: the forests in the Vale of Arlo survive, as do the salmon in the Shure (Suir) that runs through Tipperary to the east of Spenser's estate. However, Spenser is also painfully aware that the opposite of what he states can also be true. He would have known that forests can easily be cut down and that they were disappearing at a phenomenal rate in early modern Ireland. He would also have known that fish can equally easily be removed from rivers unless they are protected and that the main reason why salmon were abundant in the Suir was through the ability of the earl of Ormond, whose principal residence was at Carrick-on-Suir, to protect his estates in the Palatinate of Tipperary.[99] What seems like the consequences of human action in the stanzas is actually natural and what looks as if it is a natural process is at the mercy of the human.[100]

At one level the episode is humorous, reminding us that just as we do not always understand what we do, neither can we control the consequences of our actions: Spenser can narrate the myths of the natural world but he cannot circumscribe the meanings of what he writes. But, yet again, Spenser is showing off his local knowledge of the terrain, deliberately separating those who would know the topography he is describing from those for whom these are simply names in a poem, as they do not appear on contemporary maps.[101] This, of course, is a key point, as the rhetorical question inscribed within the verse at the start of the myth demonstrates. The Gods are due to meet:

> Eftsoones the time and place appointed were,
> Where all, both heauenly Powers, & earthly wights,
> Before great Natures presence should appeare,
> For triall of their Titles and best Rights:
> That was, to weet, vpon the highest hights
> Of *Arlo-hill* (Who knowes not *Arlo-hill?*)
> That is the highest head (in all mens sights)
> Of my old father *Mole*, whom Shepheards quill
> Renowmed hath with hymnes fit for a rurall skill. (36)

For some Arlo-Hill has a real meaning, as do the rivers and mountains in the area, and they will understand the significance of the poem, which is another reason why it is likely that the Mutability Cantos did circulate in manuscript before they were published. But for others there will be anxiety and confusion as to whether they should know about a terrain that is alien to them. On one level, Spenser is exposing the difficulty of chorographical poetry and its accompanying aetiological myths: either you already know why the myths are there, or the poem seems oblique and self-obsessed, a problem that anyone who seeks to give advice to a large audience has to face.[102] More importantly, it is no accident that Spenser refers back to *Colin Clout*, the poem which transported the English shepherds of the *Calender* to Ireland, and showed that the English in Ireland were irrevocably separated from their counterparts in England. In the Mutability Cantos we learn that they know the myths, dangers, and importance of the land where the battle for the right to rule the British Isles will be fought. The myth and its framing casts Spenser as a Cassandra figure: he knows enough to warn people of the perils they face, but his very knowledge obscures the value of that knowledge. He will undoubtedly be able to persuade those already in the know, but those outside this inner circle will either be resistant to what they are being told, or will not recognize its importance. One reason why the story of Faunus is narrated in the way that it is, is to entice readers to find a way to unlock its secrets and so to understand just what is at stake in south-west Ireland. The apparently trivial and obscure holds the key to the great questions, a truth that those at the centre invariably fail to grasp. Furthermore, Faunus' tale tells us, those who do have access to the secret knowledge in Ireland are struck by the terrible absurdity of what they find, and so are punished, not rewarded.

By the summer of 1598 the Nine Years War had reached an even more dangerous stage for the English in Ireland. A series of truces had been agreed between Tyrone and the Lords Justices and Ormond, which finally expired on 7 June, and, perhaps under pressure from his followers, Tyrone divided the forces he had built up. One division attacked the Blackwater Fort; a second confronted Ormond in Leinster, planning to inspire the O'Mores, Kavanaghs, and O'Byrnes to rebel; and Tyrone himself led the attack on Cavan Castle. Substantial reinforcements were sent over from England and Sir Henry Bagenal, the marshall of the army, set off to relive the Blackwater Fort.[103] The fort had been resented for a long time by Tyrone as an aggressively situated outpost on the boundary of his lands, threatening the main routes into Ulster. For the crown it was valuable only as long as it served a serious military purpose and had become an exposed, expensive, and dangerous outpost, hard to supply and protect.[104] Tyrone surrounded the fort and Bagenal marched towards them with a well-equipped large army of 3,901 foot soldiers and 320 on horseback. At the Battle of the Yellow Ford Bagenal's forces were skilfully ambushed between Armagh and the south shore of Lough Neagh at the Callan River by the slightly larger Irish forces (over 4,000 foot soldiers and some 600 on horseback), who, although more lightly armed, had considerable advantages in terms of mobility. The English forces were dogged by a combination of bad tactics, incompetence, and bad luck, finding their field cannon useless in the boggy ground, and suffering an explosion of a powder cart which enabled their assailants to rout the central section of the army.[105] Bagenal was killed, along with about 900 of his troops. It was—and remains—the worst defeat the English suffered in Ireland, a much more serious reverse than Grey's defeat at Glenmalure.

Most significantly it left English settlers exposed and open to attack without a central force to defend them.[106] The English crown responded and, eventually, a massive army was dispatched under the command of the earl of Essex, consisting of 16,000 foot soldiers and 1,300 horse, the largest ever to be sent to Ireland. But this did not reach Ireland until 15 April, some three months after Spenser's death.[107] In the meanwhile the fate of English settlers was perilous in the extreme, exactly what Spenser would have feared when he was in London two years earlier.

On 30 September Spenser was nominated for the post of sheriff of Cork by the Privy Council in a letter to the Lord Justices of Ireland, Loftus and Gardiner:

Though we doubt not but you will without any motio[n] from us have good regard for the appointing of meete and great importance, especially at this tyme, when all parts of the Realme are touched with the infection of Rebellion, yet wee thinke it not amisse sometyme to recommend unto you such men as wee hold to be fit for that office. Amonge whom we may justly reckon Edmond Spencer, a gentleman dwelling in the Countie of Cork, who is so well known unto your Lordships, for his good and commendable parts (being a man endowed with good knowledge in learning, and not unskilful or without experience in the service of wars) as wee need not use many words in his behalf. And therefore, as wee are of opinion that you will favour him for himself, and of your own accord, so we do pray you that this favour for him may increase his credditie so farre forth with you, as that he may not faile to be appointed Sheriffe of the Co. of Cork, unless there be by you known some important cause to the contrary, we are persuaded he will so behave himself in the place, as you shall have just cause to allow of our commendation and his good service. And so, etc.[108]

Sheriffs in Munster were seen as absolutely vital to the preservation of control over the province and 'were of greater importance than in England, especially in times of martial law', the situation in 1598.[109] Sir James Croft, Lord Deputy from 1551 to 1552, had placed heavy emphasis on their crucial role, arguing that if the right people were appointed and they functioned well, conflict could be avoided and there would be no need for the imposition of martial law.[110] An anonymous document sent to Robert Cecil by William Saxey, Chief Justice of Munster, on 5 December, 'Imperfections in the State of Munster', argues that the inability to root out corruption and treason is what has fatally undermined English rule in Munster. The author recommends that judges become more active and help redress wrongs to keep many loyal, and to prevent the inevitable delay in reaching a judgment if cases are referred to Dublin. He has especially harsh words to say about sheriffs, who he alleges 'within the Province are oftentimes the most dangerous persons, and such as procure the office only to enrich themselves by extortion and oppression. And it is thought there is no Sheriff that payeth not for his place, and therefore they make an ordinary trade to unlawfull means to the subversion or interruption of justice.'[111] The author recommends that the process of appointing sheriffs be centralized, overseen by the 'State at Dublin', and the Privy Council's intervention in the process appears to be an attempt to achieve this aim and to cut out local practice.

As the letter demonstrates, these were obviously desperate times. Spenser's name does not appear in the official list of sheriffs of Cork, unlike that of his wife's third husband, Sir Robert Tynte, who served from 1625 to 1626.[112] Spenser would have succeeded Richard Barry (1597–8) or Edmund Newman (1598–9), neither of whom appears in official records outside the list of sheriffs.[113] It is also possible that he was never appointed, perhaps because the letter was ignored, through the hostility of officials (perhaps Loftus), or because someone else had filled the position.[114] A letter from Captains Thomas Southwell and Timothy Cottrell to the Privy Council on 8 December informs them that the sheriff of Cork, along with the Lord President (Thomas Norris), the bishop of Cork, Clyne, and Ross (William Lyon), and the provost-marshall (George Thornton), as well as most of the undertakers and their wives and children, had been in Cork city since the start of the rebellion.[115] Unfortunately the name of the sheriff is not given. Spenser must have either taken refuge in the security of the walled city of Cork two or three weeks earlier than he is generally assumed to have done, or stayed in his house to help defend the Plantation. Settlers were leaving their farms; only a few remained, such as the courageous Captain Francis Barkley, who defended his castle at Askeaton, Limerick, protecting 500 English settlers who had taken refuge there, until the arrival of Ormond's forces—a rare exception.[116] Sir Henry Oughtred's Castle at Mayne near Rathkeale, south-west of Limerick, was burned on 8 October when he failed to guard it.[117] At some point before 6 October Hugh Cuffe, Spenser's neighbour to the north, had abandoned his estate and there was a general fear that the whole Plantation would soon be left waste by the settlers.[118] In a series of letters to the Privy Council, Sir Robert Cecil, and the queen from Youghal on 21 October, the earl of Ormond, who felt that he had defended the Plantation as best he could, was savage in his criticisms of the undertakers who had left their castles and houses:

I may not omit to acquaint your Lordships that, at my coming into this Province, I found that the greatest part of the undertakers had most shamefully quitted and forsaken their castles and houses of strength before even the traitors came near them, leaving all to their spoils, whereby they furnished themselves with the arms and other munition that before served against them, to Her Majesty's dishonour, and the increasing of the traitors' pride.[119]

He also sent on an extensive list of the tenants of undertakers who had abandoned their estates, including those of Warham St Leger, Phane Beecher, Sir William

Herbert, Nicholas Browne, and Sir Walter Ralegh.[120] There is no mention of Spenser. The undertakers in turn blamed the poor military tactics and cowardly behaviour of the Lord President, who retreated ignominiously when the enemy advanced at Kilmallock, and fled to the relative safety of Cork in the middle of October.[121] Presumably some of these tenants had started to reach England and were spreading alarming stories.

The Privy Council's letter is clear that the manner of Spenser's appointment is unusual, and it is hard to determine whether it is an attempt to impose a measure of control on an outlying and exposed area, or, more likely, a realization that a man on the ground had to be found. It shows that Spenser was held in great esteem in official circles, notwithstanding his past transgressions. The emphasis placed on his learning and knowledge echoes Spenser's self-representation in *A View*, suggesting that the recommendation was probably based in part on key officials having read the dialogue.[122] The judgement that he had experience of war probably refers to Spenser's role as Grey's secretary, which involved travelling around Ireland and observing conflict zones, as well as his part in overseeing the musters. Moreover, the duties of a sheriff involved apprehending criminals and incarcerating prisoners, and ensuring that the chain of command functioned properly, actions Spenser had carried out when escorting a prisoner to London and in overseeing the post.[123] Sheriffs also had to collect taxes and fines, and a sheriff could be imprisoned himself if he failed to collect and send on the relevant sums, which is probably what the author of 'Imperfections in the State of Munster' was referring to when he expressed his lack of faith in the current incumbents.[124] The phrase 'wee need not use many words in his behalf' also tells us that in London Spenser was thought to be a significant and well-known figure in Ireland, and it is evident that by 1598 he was, as his poetry informs us, considered to be an Englishman whose home was in Ireland.

By early October, the English authorities in Ireland realized that the Irish were planning a major assault on the Munster Plantation and that they had very little chance of resisting a serious assault. The Lord President, Sir Thomas Norris, had hardly any troops available to defend the planters, records suggesting that he had no more than 142. His forces were supposed to be supplemented by about 800 from the settlers, but, as the Plantation was under-populated, this imperative had been neglected.[125] In a letter dated 4 October from Kilmallock, about fifteen miles from Kilcolman, north of the Ballyhoura Mountains, Sir Thomas Norris, who may have recommended Spenser as sheriff of Cork, James Goold, second justice of Munster, and George Thornton, the provost-marshal of Munster, three of the most powerful men in the region, wrote to the Privy Council informing them that they had information that the O'Mores were about to invade Munster, but that this intelligence had been ignored by the Dublin authorities. Such evidence of internal divisions and inefficiency in the English ranks further helps to explain the Privy

Council's actions in attempting to appoint Spenser directly from London. The letter states:

And now those traitors, taking advantage of the Lord Lieutenant's long absence in the north and other places far distant, with all the forces heretofore appointed to prosecute them in Leinster, (finding no impediment) are entered the borders of this Province with two thousand men, and have taken several castles and preys of cattle, intending (as we understand) to march forward and to possess themselves of Connello or Arlough, and so of the whole country at their pleasures.[126]

The O'Mores were heading straight towards the Plantation through the Vale of Arhelow, intending to link up with local opposition to English rule. As the letter makes clear, they had overwhelmed castles so would not find the limited defences of a tower house such as Kilcolman a significant obstacle. Inspired by these developments and supported by local leaders on 10 October James Fitzthomas Fitzgerald declared himself earl of Desmond using the authority of Hugh O'Neill as earl of Tyrone.[127] He was known as the 'súgán' or 'straw-rope' earl because of the weak nature of his claim to the title, but his role was to serve as the figurehead of the revolt, a local leader to rally opposition to the crown.[128]

The letter also expresses the obvious fear that the invaders will receive substantial support from the local population. The authors state that they have done what they can to offset this danger: 'Upon the first suspicion of these troubles, we took pledges of most of the better sort of the Province, and are in good hope that none of them will join with these traitors.' However, the second half of the sentence acknowledges that this is more in hope than expectation. Not only might even the loyal Irish join with the rebels if 'they be permitted to prevail above expectation', a recognition that self-interest will determine individual behaviour, but many are eager to join the rebellion anyway: 'yet are we well assured that many idle discontented young men are combined, and will adhere unto them'.[129] These dangerous men would have included the extended family of Spenser's neighbours and antagonists, the Roches of Fermoy. On 23 October Sir Thomas Norris wrote to Sir Robert Cecil from Cork advising him that the son of Lord Maurice, David, had joined with the rebel forces, although his father remained loyal until a little later and later repented of his actions in belatedly joining the revolt.[130] The same letter also noted that some of Spenser's neighbours to the south-west, the Barrys, had also joined the rebel forces.[131] In their letters of submission after the rebellion, the local Irish landowners invariably claimed that they had been forced to rebel out of expediency.[132]

This must have been a terrifying time for the Spensers and their children, whether they took refuge in Cork, or, worse still, remained in Kilcolman. A letter of 26 October from Saxey to Robert Cecil paints a grim picture of murder and destruction based on a series of atrocity stories that point forward to those circulating after the rebellion of 1641.[133] Saxey informs Cecil that

These combinations and revolts have effected many execrable murders and cruelties upon the English . . . infants taken from the nurse's breast, and the brains dashed out against the walls; the heart plucked out of the body of the husband in the view of the wife, who was forced to yield the use of her apron to wipe off the blood from the murderers' fingers; [an] English gentleman at midday in a town cruelly murdered, and his head cleft in divers pieces; divers sent into Youghal amongst the English, some with their throats cut, but not killed, some with their tongues cut out of their heads, others with their noses cut off; by view whereof the English might the more bitterly lament the misery of their countrymen, and fear the like to befall to themselves.[134]

There is perhaps something rather formulaic about this account, with the description of the bloody family scene and its combination of neatly paralleled horrors.[135] Saxey was writing to Cecil requesting military aid, giving him every reason to stress the dire straits of the English settlers and the wickedness of the Irish. But the wealth of testimony means that we cannot doubt that such events took place. The description of the mutilated English entering Youghal shows just how vulnerable Spenser's extended family were in Ireland. On 21 October Ormond also wrote of the exposed position of the town because of its extensive city walls, which were hard to defend.[136] Such stories must have circulated around the Plantation and spread terror and panic.[137]

Saxey appeals to a common bond of Englishness against the perfidious Irish:

Besides, the manifold spoils, thefts, and violences daily done unto the English, the sight and consideration of which miseries would force any Englishman to bleed in the common calamity of the English, who in manner all are utterly undone, and every one after the rate of his fortune doth smart exceedingly. And these execrable parts are performed by the Irish tenants and servants of the English; and those that but the last day were fed and nourished by the English, are now the thieves that violently before their faces take from them their corn, cattle, and other goods; and the party spoiled thinketh himself happy, if he escape without loss of life, or other shameful villainy to himself, his wife, or children; whereby it seemeth that it is a plot laid down by the traitors, that every Irish next inhabiting should kill and spoil his English neighbour.[138]

Saxey's words form an instructive counterpoint to the legal depositions of Lord Roche against Spenser in which he accuses the English of plotting to defraud the Irish of their legitimate land titles. Saxey, in casting the English as one unified race, exposes and reinforces the boundaries between settlers and natives in Ireland. He also reveals that the theory and the practice of the Plantation was widely divergent, a fact clearly so commonly known that there was little point in hiding it. The Plantation was supposed to have been populated with English tenant farmers and servants, not Irish ones. Given the failure to attract English servants over to

Ireland, the Plantation would not have worked without Irish tenants and servants, who now became the principal reason for its destruction. What was only a few days earlier a prosperous region able to support a large number of people has now become a terrifying wilderness, from which the inhabitants are glad to escape with their lives. The destruction wrought on the province only a generation earlier, and which the Plantation was designed to remedy, threatens to return.

In many ways Saxey's description of the outbreak of the rebellion bears out what Spenser had foreseen in the last few years in *A View* and Book VI of *The Faerie Queene*. In Book VI Spenser represents the shepherds living in a clearing in wooded areas, always under threat from hostile savages and brigands, who become ever more dangerous as the poem progresses until, eventually, they raid and destroy the settlement.[139] The failure to protect the hapless shepherds allows the dangerous situation to develop until it is impossible to stop.[140] In *A View* Spenser argues that until Irish society is transformed by the English the Irish can never be trusted. Unless the English assume control, there will always be forces at work to make the English Irish, the most dangerous inhabitants of Ireland being the Old English who have 'degenerated', gone native, and become more Irish than the Irish.[141] What Spenser—and others—had feared and predicted had now become a reality.

By the time that Ormond reached Mallow on 14 October the town had been destroyed by the rebel forces.[142] At some point soon after, Kilcolman was attacked and burned, as the archaeological evidence demonstrates.[143] A note dated 15 October lists the spoils committed by Onie O'More, James FitzThomas, and Captain Tyrell in the barony of Buttevant, immediately next to Spenser's estate. Lord Barry, Viscount Buttevant, was said to have lost fifty-four towns which were burned down; 9,400 cows; 4,800 horses; 58,800 sheep and pigs; and corn and other 'household stuff' to the value of £8,200, a colossal fortune.[144] Even allowing for some considerable exaggeration, this gives an idea of the scale of the destruction in Spenser's immediate area: in the early seventeenth century the wealthiest English peers could count on a rental income of some £4,000–6,000.[145]

Ben Jonson told Drummond 'That the Irish, having robbed Spenser's goods and burnt his house and a little child new-born, he and his wife escaped'.[146] This suggests that the story of Spenser's dramatic flight from Ireland was still doing the rounds as an oral tradition among educated Londoners at the end of the second decade of the seventeenth century, although it is possible that Jonson was one of the poets described by Camden who attended Spenser's funeral, and so would have had more privileged information. Certainly what Jonson claims is possible. There is an underground passage beneath Kilcolman, recorded on an estate map made for the owners of the castle, the Harold-Barrys, in 1857.[147] The cave where the tunnel re-emerges in an old quarry, undoubtedly the source for the castle's stone, is still accessible and could have been the escape route (Plate 42).[148] The Spensers were not an especially large family by early modern standards and we do know that Elizabeth Boyle produced more children with her second and third husbands, so it is possible that one was lost when the castle was overwhelmed. But we cannot trust everything that Drummond claimed that Jonson said, especially as this statement comes in a sentence alongside his other intriguing claim that Spenser died 'for want of bread'. The story of the escape adds colour to Spenser's last days in his adopted homeland, and has assumed a significance in versions of his life in post-romantic times. However, it is more likely that the truth is rather less dramatic and that the Spensers were holed up in Cork when Kilcolman was destroyed.

Troops were now pouring into the southern Irish ports: Cork, Kinsale, and Waterford. Sir Thomas Norris acknowledged the arrival of 2,000 men in a letter to the Privy Council dated 9 December.[149] Life would have been cramped, uncomfortable, rather frugal, and undoubtedly insanitary for the English flooding into the walled towns. On 9 December Spenser left Ireland for London, sent over by Norris to deliver the letter in question, along with other documents, to the Privy Council.[150] Given the backing he had recently received from that body, his extensive working relationship with Norris, as well as his intimate knowledge of life in Ireland, Spenser was the logical choice to act as a messenger to plead the case for the support of the New English in Ireland. He was surely accompanied by his wife and children, who would all return to Munster after Spenser's death.

Spenser also brought with him three documents outlining the dire situation of the planters and their sketchy suggestions for the recovery of English rule in Ireland. These survive in a document probably in the handwriting of Dudley Carleton, Viscount Dorchester (1574–1632) in the State Papers.[151] Carleton worked for Thomas Norris's brother, Edward, in 1598, and so was likely to have known about the provenance of the manuscripts, although if he did copy out the documents, he probably did so in the early seventeenth century.[152] There are also two other surviving copies of the last section of the documents, one of which was owned by the Yelverton family, and which survives as one sheet in a large miscellany of political, literary, and historical works now in All Souls College, Oxford.[153] The Yelvertons were a family of prominent lawyers with significant Northamptonshire links, living at Whiston, twelve miles south of Althorp. As the miscellany, which is mainly of seventeenth-century works relating to Sir Christopher's later career, contains nothing else on Ireland, it is likely that they acquired the text through a local connection and that Sir Christopher (1536/7–1612), judge, MP for Brackley, and Speaker of the House of Commons, who had written the epilogue for Gascoigne's *Jocasta* when it was performed at Gray's Inn in 1566, and his son, Sir Henry (1566–1630), judge and MP, knew Spenser in some capacity.[154] Unfortunately the sole attribution, 'A briefe discourse of Ireland, by Spenser', in Carleton's copy, is in a later hand.[155] It is difficult to judge whether all or only part of the documents which now go under this general title are by Spenser. The documents are miscellaneous in purpose and style. They may have formed part of a larger collection brought over by Spenser on 9 December, which might have included one of the surviving copies of *A View*, or they may have been assembled later and so not be as closely connected as has often been assumed.[156] The first is a summary of Ireland's current economic state and value, listing the towns, ploughlands, bogs, woods, as well as the money to be made from fishing and wardships, concluding that Ireland could be of great profit if it were run properly, because in Edward IV's reign 'it yielded the Crowne of England 14146.^{li} sterling'.[157] The second is a long formal letter addressed to the queen outlining the desolation of the undertakers, and blaming their fate on the wiles of Hugh O'Neill.[158] The third, another short document, 'Certaine pointes to be considered of in the recovery of the Realme of Ireland', outlines a series of issues that need to be addressed if Ireland is to be recovered.

None of the documents is signed and, given their diverse nature, it is hard to determine whether they were written by the same person or by a group of people. The most likely explanation is that the letter addressed to the queen is a hastily produced co-authored work. It opens with a strident and aggressive opening line, a lengthy and convoluted sentence clearly designed to catch the attention of the addressee, with its striking, quasi-apocalyptic imagery alluding to the dead left trapped underground needing to rise from their graves:

Out of the ashes of disolacon and wastnes of this your wretched Realme of Ireland. vouchsafe moste mightie Empresse our Dred soveraigne to receive the voices of a fewe moste vnhappie Ghostes, of whome is nothinge but the ghost nowe lefte which lie buried in the bottome of oblivion farr from the light of your gracious sunshine which spreeth it selfe ouer Countries moste remote to the releeving of their destitute Calamities and to the eternall aduancement of your renowne and glorie yet vpon this miserable kand being your owne iuste and heritable dominion letteth no one little beame of your large mercie to be shed either for vnworthinesse of vs wretches which no way diserue so great grace, or for that the miserie of our estate is not mae knowne vnto you but rather kept from your knowledge by such as by concealement thereof think to haue their blames concealed.[159]

There is nothing in *A View* that resembles the biblical rhetoric of this plea for relief, which seems to have been written with an implicit comparison between the New English in Ireland and the Israelites in exile in Canaan and Egypt uppermost in the author's mind. That comparison is developed in another tract written slightly later in the wake of the destruction of the Plantation.[160] The work that the letter resembles most is *The Supplication of the blood of the English, most lamentably murdred in Ireland, Cryeng out of the yearth for revenge*, which begins:

To the high and mightie Princesse, ELIZABETH, by the grace of god Queene of Englande, ffraunce, and Irlande, defender of the faith etc. ffrom the face of that disloyall and rebellious yearthe of Irland, Crieth the bloode of yo^{re} Ma:^{ties} subjects, whose bodyes dismembered by the tyranie of traytors, devowred by the merciless laws of ravenous wolves, humblie Craveth at the hands of yo^{re} sacred Ma:^{tie} (unto whom god hath committed the sword of Iustice to punishe the offender, and upon whom he hath imposed a care and charge for the maintain[a]nce and defence of the innocent) To revenge the monstrous rapes of many poore forlorne widdowes, and the bloody murders of many yo^{re} faithfull subiects.[161]

In the former work, the English cry out of the graves; here their blood cries out for revenge. In the one they were cut off from the sun; in the other, they are surrounded by wolves. If the former referred to Exodus, here the biblical subtext is surely Genesis, and the murder of Cain, who is told by God that the 'voyce of [his] brothers blood cryeth vnto me from the earth' (Genesis 4:10, Geneva translation). The *Supplication* survives in the same batch of State Papers as the 'Brief Note', and it was undoubtedly composed in Cork in November–December 1598.[162] The proximity of the two texts, their similar, complementary styles and argument, suggest that, as Ciaran Brady has noted, they may have been part of a 'concerted propaganda effort'.[163] The link might be pushed further to suggest that the campaign was one coordinated in Cork by the dispossessed English, who would certainly have had the motives and the time to conduct one. Spenser could well have had a hand in such works and have brought over the *Supplication* in December 1598.[164] Certainly, Ralph Byrchensha, writing in 1602 on the defeat of Tyrone and O'Donnell at Kinsale, appears to connect Spenser's *View* and the *Supplication*, indicating that works on the situation in Munster in the 1590s were read together soon afterwards.[165]

The letter is, however, critical of Sir John Norris, and records a damning judgement from some settlers. Writing of the opposed policies of Norris and the Lord Deputy, Sir William Russell, the author(s) argue that the growing power of Tyrone was augmented through 'the faintnesse of those which were sett here to followe him', as well as 'through occasion of the devision of the gouernment here betwixt S.^{r} willm Russell and S^r. Iohn Norris'. While Norris sought to defeat Tyrone through military means, Russell 'thought by good treatises rather wynn him to make fair wars'. The author(s), who generally favour Norris's approach to O'Neill, nevertheless repeat a common criticism of Norris: 'But by some it was thought that the onely purpose of S^r. Iohn Norris in handling things after that sorte was to obtaine the absolute gouernment to him selfe./'[166] Given Spenser's close relationship to Thomas Norris it is unlikely that he was the author of such a statement.[167] Spenser's adult life was punctuated by disputes with many influential figures, but he was invariably loyal to strong military figures such as Grey, Wallop, and the Norrises, and it is hard to imagine him authoring this damning verdict, especially at a time when his belief in the value of the army was clearly vindicated.

There is a stronger case to be made for the third paper, 'Certaine pointes'. It is attributed to Spenser twice, as the Harley manuscript is entitled 'Spensers discours briefly of Ireland', a description that suggests it was copied from the National Archives copy, or the source of that text.[168] A six-line poem at the end of this copy asserts that Tyrone will be defeated by Essex. This enables the document to be dated as earlier than September 1599 when Essex left Ireland in disgrace, and, probably, at some point between December 1598 and March 1599 when Essex left for Ireland, and provides further evidence of Spenser's impact on official English thinking about Ireland.

The text, which is only about 800 words long, consists of a series of logical propositions which mirror the more extended dialogue of *A View*. The work is obviously designed for rapid reading, presumably to persuade busy officials that they need to act quickly. The opening proposition and answer make it clear that immediate, concerted military action is required:

Question The question is whether be better and easier for hir Maiestie to subdue Ireland
 thoroughly and bring it all vnder or o reforme it and o repaire hir beyond decayed partes/

Of these two that must	*charge*
needes be better and also	*peril*
easier which may be done	*tyme*
with less	

Reason The assumption then is that it will be lesse charge, lesse peril and lesse spending of
 tyme to subdewe it altogether then to go about to reforme it / If you seeke to reforme it then
 you must retaine and saue the partes that seeme sounde and afterward recouer the partes
 that are vnsounde./[169]

Proofe of the
Reason

Here, in a nutshell, is the argument of *A View*. It might seem that spending a great deal on military intervention in Ireland is a course to be avoided, but it is actually far cheaper in the long run to invest early on in men and arms. Reform looks like a good option but it is, in fact, expensive, dangerous, and ineffective. This simple argument is repeated and reinforced throughout the two pages of the document. The author argues that 'the greater force will finish all in one yere or 2.° yeres which the lesse will not do in 4 or .yeres./'[170] The text gives precise recommendations of numbers of soldiers, places great emphasis on the strategic advantage of stationing garrisons throughout Ireland, and advocates the extensive use of famine to force the Irish into submission, all policies advanced in *A View*. The text concludes by anticipating opposition to its arguments, asserting that if 'the resolution to subdue Ireland wholly with stronge force is too blouddie and crewel', this is to be offset by a general proclaimation offering pardons. Again, this is exactly what was claimed in *A View*, providing further evidence of Spenser's authorship. Moreover, the style is economical and always to the point, something that could not easily be said of the Letter to the Queen. Sections of the text are designed as gnomic statements of practical wisdom, with Spenser's habitual punning and quibbling:

Lesse losse of tyme by menaes of the spedie finishing of the enterprise

Great force must be the instrument but famine must be the meane for till Ireland be famished it can not be subdued/.

But if the reformacion shall neuertheles be intemded then these proposicions are therein to be considered and obserued/.

That there can be no conformitie of gouernment whereis no conformitie of religion/.

That there can be no sounde agreement between twoe equall contraries viz: the English and Irish./

That there can be no assurance of peace where the worst sorte are the stronger.[171]

Again such lines read very much like a careful distillation of *A View*, in style as well as content, explaining at a glance why the situation in Ireland has reached a dangerous stage that is beyond reform and control. The first two points state what the author thinks has to be done; the following three look as if they are weighing the evidence for reform against military action carefully and judiciously. In reality, they undermine the notion that reform might be possible. The author then argues that there can be no proper government before religious divisions are sorted out, a recommendation in line with the judgement in *A View* that reform of religion 'needeth quiet times', and it is clear that the absolute division between the English and the Irish is based in part on their difference in religion. The final proposition might be taken as the fundamental message of *A View*: that there can be no hope of reform when the very elements that most urgently need to be reformed dominate the island and constitute its character. The devastating logic of these statements is in line with Spenser's stated views elsewhere and 'Certaine pointes' reads like a carefully targeted summary of ideas the author has been working hard to convey elsewhere and that he has at his fingertips ready to repeat.

Spenser would have arrived in England two to three days after sailing from Cork, assuming all went well. He would have landed in Bristol and then travelled up to London, one of the key routes that defined transport systems in England.[172] The journey could be completed in about twenty hours by a post horse, but which would probably have taken somewhat longer, especially if Spenser was with his family— although they may have travelled a bit later.[173] Spenser probably arrived in London at some point between 14 and 16 December. We have no reason to doubt Ben Jonson's statement that Spenser died in King Street, Westminster, even though some of his other assertions might need qualification.[174] Spenser had lived in Westminster earlier and his first marriage had taken place at St Margaret's church. King Street was the main thoroughfare through Westminster, and is now replaced by the government offices in Parliament Street. It ran from the south end of Downing Street to Westminster Abbey.[175] Spenser either found lodgings himself; stayed with relatives; or was supported by a patron, possibly the earl of Essex, who might have been at least one voice behind the attempt to appoint him sheriff of Cork. Rents in Westminster, especially at so fashionable an address, were undoubtedly high, which probably rules out the first possibility.[176] As King Street was so near the Palace of Whitehall, it is most likely that Spenser was being supported by a patron, eager to have him nearby to plead the case of the Irish settlers to the queen, Privy Council, and court. However, it is also worth noting that there was an Elizabeth Spenser, widow, possibly a relative, who died in August 1588 and left her daughter, Elizabeth Palmer, a tenement, the Castle, in King Street.[177]

Spenser was undoubtedly in contact, perhaps indirectly, with the Privy Council immediately, as he had been sent over by Norris to deliver letters to them. He may well have attended the court in session at Whitehall on 24 December, but he probably completed his business before this point, given the gravity of the situation in Munster.[178] A document in the State Papers confirms that Spenser had delivered the letters from Norris as he was paid for his labour: 'To Edwarde Spencer [*sic*] gent upon a warr^r. Signed by Mr Secretarie [i.e., Robert Cecil] dated at Whitehall xxx^{mo} Decembris 1598 for bringing lres. For her ma^{te} speciall service from Sir Thomas Norrys Lo: President of Mounster viii. li.'[179] The common mistaking of his Christian name suggests that Spenser was often referred to as 'Edward', and it further indicates that he was not especially close to many on the Privy Council, even though he had dedicated a number of sonnets to them.[180]

The payment also suggests that Spenser was not as poor as Jonson alleged when he claimed that he 'died for lack of bread', unless for some reason he was unable to pick up such payments. Perhaps he was already ill, facing a winter in London that would have been far more bitter than that in the shelter of Kilcolman (London is on average 10 °C colder in winter than south-west Ireland); perhaps he was exposed to the diseases of the city after a long time in a relatively healthy country environment; perhaps he was traumatized by his sudden departure from his estate, enforced sojourn in Cork, and a bad sea-crossing; or he may have been simply getting on a bit.[181] The year 1598 was not a good time to have to stay in the city. After four bad harvests in a row there was considerable dearth and poverty, the wages–price index being at its worst in 1597, and, although 1598 was by no means as bad as the previous year, London's infrastructure was struggling to cope with the influx of impoverished rural labourers who had migrated to the city in the vain hope of relief.[182] Spenser might have been bed-ridden during this period, or, at least, incapacitated in some way, which would have added to the general sense, articulated by Jonson among others, that he was never given his due reward by the authorities.

We do not know what Spenser did in the last month of his life. As Jim Shapiro has pointed out, Spenser was in Westminster for the court's Christmas festivities and he was likely to have seen some of the plays staged at Whitehall (if not too ill). These would have included two by the Lord Chamberlain's Men, one of which was Shakespeare's *The Second Part of Henry the Fourth*, a play that attacks local corruption and deals with the problem of conscription, two central issues in a *View*.[183] It is quite possible, of course, given what appears to have been a mutual admiration, tinged with more than an edge of competitiveness, in their respective writings, that the two writers met, as many later writers and artists imagined.[184] If Spenser were well enough he would have met up with poets, publishers, courtiers, administrators, and military men in his circle in London, although he probably did not travel further afield in the middle of winter. He must surely have met Ponsonby, who had made arrangements to collect his pension over the years.[185]

Spenser was now widely recognized as the most important living English poet and he was widely praised by a large number of poets in 1598, including Richard Barnfield, George Chapman, Edward Guilpin, and Thomas Rogers; and playwrights, including Samuel Brandon and John Marston.[186] Thomas Lodge, who referred to Spenser as 'reuerend Colin' in his collection of eclogues, verse epistles, and satires, *A Fig for Momus* (1595), had already gone into exile by this time, but may have been in contact with him.[187] Spenser was also cited with approval in Francis Meres's important overview of the state of English poetry, *Palladis Tamia: Wits Treasury. Being the second part of Wits Commonwealth*, playing a central role in the revival of English letters as 'our famous English Poet *Spenser*', who had helped enrich English as Greek had been transformed by Homer, Sophocles, and Aristophanes, and Latin by Virgil, Ovid, and Horace. Meres also stated that he knew 'not what more excellent or exquisite Poem may be written' than *The Faerie Queene.* [188] The author, a writer and translator who later worked as a schoolmaster, had a number of links to Spenser: he appears to have known Sir Thomas Egerton; he graduated from Pembroke College (albeit a decade after Spenser); and *Palladis Tamia* was published by Cuthbert Burby.[189] Spenser was also cited with approval in Thomas Speght's edition of Chaucer, as one of two contemporary writers who had understood the significance of the most important English poet of the Middle Ages. Speght praised Roger Ascham for his prose, and Spenser for his verse, each being 'two of the purest and best writers of our daies'.[190] Speght, who had developed an interest in Chaucer from a young age, had been at Cambridge at the same time as Spenser, and worked with Chaucer's previous editor, John Stow, another learned figure with Spenser connections.[191] Spenser would have seen some of these writers, nearly all of whom would have been in London in late 1598, and many must have attended his funeral less than a month later.

Spenser's life may have been financially restrained: certainly most commentators on his last days writing soon after his death emphasize his poverty. But was Spenser really so badly in need of ready cash? Or was the general perception of him based on a more widespread understanding that he had been unfairly treated in his lifetime and never afforded the recognition that he deserved, a reputation that his own work had done so much to foster? It is hard to believe that Spenser was in dire straits in London, which is not to suggest that he was comfortably off. As the Privy Council records indicate, a payment of £8 was made out to him on 24 December: not a huge sum, but nearly half a year's salary for many educated men.[192] However, there is no record of him receiving his pension, which he had had others collect for him in half-yearly amounts of £25, one payment due at Christmas. This was probably held over until 28 February when it was collected, undoubtedly on behalf of his widow, by Henry Vincent, gentleman, probably the son of an Elizabeth Spenser of North-amptonshire, and so a relative of Edmund's, perhaps even a half-brother if this Elizabeth was Spenser's mother.[193] Moreover, Spenser would surely have been able to borrow money from friends and relatives in advance of receiving his pension.[194] The truth appears to be that Spenser was not near the breadline, but that he had been burned out in Ireland, had lost his estate, and was now the victim of more financial restrictions in London than he had expected.

Writing to his friend Dudley Carleton on 17 January 1599, the enthusiastic correspondent John Chamberlain (1553–1628) noted that 'Spencer, our principall poet, coming lately out of Ireland, died at Westminster on Satturday last'.[195] Chamberlain's testimony confirms that Spenser died on 13 January.[196] Chamberlain is a good recorder of court gossip and a barometer of what interested the upper echelons of London society. His letters demonstrate a detailed knowledge of life at court, as well as current political events, notably with regard to Spain and Portugal, and Ireland. Spenser's death is reported at the end of a letter listing the marriages and deaths of people they both know. Chamberlain's description of Spenser as 'our principall poet' indicates that neither he nor Carleton were especially close to Spenser personally—although Carleton may have copied out parts of a 'Brief Note' soon after Spenser's death—but knew him as a poet, Irish settler, and government official. We have no idea what led to Spenser's death. The few accounts we have of his last days, all of which are brief and limited in detail, fail to provide clues of his state of health or mind. The trouble is that different explanations are equally plausible. Spenser's circumstances might have had an impact on the timing of his death, or he might simply have died of natural causes, being neither especially young nor particularly old to die in an era of relatively primitive medical practice, bad diet, and the absence of comfort when winter weather was extreme. The most striking fact is that he died within three weeks of leaving Ireland in grim circumstances.

Spenser was buried a few days later in Westminster Abbey. William Camden has provided the best account of what must have been a moving and significant event. Camden, like Jonson, provides evidence in his short sketch of Spenser's life and death that Spenser was perceived to have been harshly treated in life and that he died in poverty, a belief shared by most who commented on the last months of Spenser's life in the early seventeenth century.[197] Concurring with Speght and Meres that Spenser was the best English poet since Chaucer, Camden writes:

But by a Fate which still follows Poets, he always wrastled with poverty, though he had been Secretary to the Lord *Grey*, Lord Deputy of *Ireland*. For scarce had he there settled himself in a retired Privacy, and got Leisure to write, when he was by the Rebels thrown out of his Dwelling, plundered of his Goods, and returned into *England* a poor man, where he shortly after died, and was interred at *Westminster*, near to *Chaucer*, at the Charge of the earl of *Essex*; his hearse being attended by Poets, and mournfull Elegies and Poems with the Pens that wrote them thrown into his Tomb.[198]

Many of these elegies would have reappeared in print, such as the unknown M. L.'s *Enuies Scourge, and Vertues Honour* (*c.*1605), a poem which imitates the style and substance of its subject's work, and that by the young Cornish poet Charles Fitzgeoffrey (1593–1636), who had already praised Spenser as the heir of Homer in his long lament for Sir Francis Drake (1596), and who now cast him as the English Virgil in a series of Latin tributes published in 1601.[199] There were poems from more established writers such as Nicholas Breton, whose 'An Epitaph upon Poet Spencer', with such memorable lines as 'Sing a dirge on *Spencers* death, | Till your soules be out of breath', was published as the last poem in the volume *Melancholike Humours* (1600).[200] It is also likely that another elegy written for the occasion was the unpublished Latin epigram by William Alabaster (1567–1640), 'In Edouardum Spencerum, Britannicae poesios facile principem', which does sound as if it were designed for the funeral:

> Fors qui sepulchre conditur siquis fuit
> Quaeris uiator, dignus es qui rescias.
> Spencerus istic conditur, siquis fuit
> Rogare pergis, dignus es qui nescias.

[If you ask who's buried here, passer-by, you deserve to hear. Spenser is buried here. If you go on to ask who he is you don't deserve to know.][201]

Another was surely that by John Weever (1575/6–1632), published in his youthful volume, *Epitgrammes in the Oldest Cut, and Newest Fashion* (1599), written while he was an undergraduate at Cambridge:

Epig. 23 In obitium Ed. Spencer Poetae prestantiss.
Colin's gone home, the glorie of his clime,
The Muses Mirrour, and the Shepheardes Saint;
Spencer is ruin'd, of our latter time
The fairest ruine, Faëries foulest want:
Then his *Time-ruines* did our ruine show,
Which by his ruine we vntimely know:
Spencer therefore thy *Ruines* were cal'd in,
Too soone to sorrow least we should begin.[202]

Weever's poem, with its quibbling on 'ruins', is clearly the work of a young man on the make who may not have been especially close to the dead poet, although he does appear to have been connected to poets in the wider Spenser orbit, such as Michael Drayton, and publishers such as Cuthbert Burby.[203] But this perhaps tells us more about Spenser's reputation and contemporary significance than marks Weever's poem out as a work written by a writer closer to the poet. The epigram indicates that the volume that Weever really knew well was the *Complaints*—perhaps he possessed a copy—although he manages to include references to both the *Calender* and *The Faerie Queene*, suggesting that he also understood the trajectory of Spenser's career. The cunning reference to the ruins being 'cal'd in' combines a pun on Spenser's death with a reminder of his brush with the authorities in 1591, demonstrating that, even as late as 1599, the scandal of *Mother Hubberds Tale* was still in the public mind.[204]

Camden also provides evidence that Spenser worked in order to make time to write, and that the crucial event in his writing career, if not his life, was the acquisition of a home. The description of Spenser's funeral as a major event attended by poets who felt they owed much to his example and who lamented his demise, must surely be based on fact. Many of the writers who had even the most tenuous association with him appear to have been there, and the number would probably have included Nathaniel Baxter, Nicholas Breton, George Chapman, Thomas Churchyard, Samuel Daniel, Michael Drayton, Sir Edward Dyer, Arthur Golding, Sir Arthur Gorges, Fulke Greville, perhaps Jonson himself, John Lane, Lodowick Lloyd, John Lyly, Thomas Sackville, William Warner, and John Weever.[205] There may even have been figures such as Anthony Copley (1567–c.1609), still a loyal Catholic at this point, who had produced the first poetic response to *The Faerie Queene* in 1596.[206] Sadly, a search for Spenser's grave, conducted on 2 November 1938 with the hope of finding some poems, pens, and the names of the poets who had attended the funeral, yielded no results.[207] Also present would have been some of the soldiers and administrators with whom Spenser had worked in Ireland, as well as his family, friends, and patrons. If they had been able to attend, these would surely have included Lodowick Bryskett, Gabriel Harvey, Edward Kirk, Sir William Russell and the Russell sisters, Anne and Margaret, Sir Henry Wallop, and, perhaps, courtiers such as Ralegh and Robert Devereux, second earl of Essex, who, according to Camden, paid for the funeral.

The decision to bury Spenser near to Chaucer was a first step towards defining the collection of graves of writers in the south transept, Poets' Corner. The area was not formally designated as the resting place for the nation's most celebrated writers until the eighteenth century, but Spenser, generally accepted as the natural heir of Chaucer, was buried next to his most illustrious predecessor, a decision that started a trend.[208] By 1723 the site contained the graves and monuments of a number of illustrious poets: Samuel Butler, Abraham Cowley, Michael Drayton, John Dryden, Thomas Shadwell, and others.[209] According to John Lane (*fl.* 1600–30), a poet who conspicuously modelled his career on Spenser and who was an important friend of John Milton, Sr, the earl of Essex paid for Spenser's funeral only after he was prompted by another poet, Lodowick Lloyd.[210] Lloyd (*fl.* 1573–1607) published poems in the miscellany, *The Paradise of Dainty Devices* (1595), alongside verse by (probably) Francis Meres, and a host of other writers, providing further evidence that many of the poets who looked up to Spenser were connected to each other and existed within small, overlapping groups.[211] Unfortunately, the poems attributed to E. S. in that volume are, as the editor suggests, unlikely to have been written by Spenser.[212]

Lane produced a long manuscript poem, 'Triton's Trumpet' (1621), based on the *Calender*, consisting of 206 folios, which was handsomely bound as a presentation copy, and dedicated to Prince Charles. In the November eclogue, modelled on Spenser's lament for Dido's death in the *Calender*, Lane rather grudgingly acknowledges Essex's role in honouring Spenser but takes the opportunity to berate aristocratic patrons for their neglect of poets. On learning that Spenser is dying and is too modest to seek proper restitution, Essex, according to Lane, tried to help him:

> Natheless of pining griefe, and wants decaid
> hee may thank that stout Earle, yet this him said,
> the medicine comes too late to the pacient!
> he died. And so woold I, if thither went!
> Alas! was that his ende, quoth Damus, tho,
> I pittie him, yet heare of this I know,
> he ha on him bestow'd a funeral
> after the rites of Laureat Coronal
> At that tripova laugh'd, naie swore these serive
> To dandle poets dead, yeat leave a live
> ne had that rose vppon bin implode,
> but for my loving frend *Lodowick Lloyd*.[213]

Lane's story is valuable on many accounts and it does suggest that he had some detailed knowledge of the events surrounding Spenser's death. Lane provides more evidence that Spenser was struggling financially in his final days and was in failing health. Most usefully, perhaps, Lane suggests that Spenser existed as part of a community of poets in London and was seen by his fellows as their champion, a worthy laureate, perhaps a bridge between them and the upper echelons of society.[214] Michael Drayton, in an oblique tribute, appears to have had a portrait of himself painted, crowned with a laureate crown and dated 1599, indicating that he now thought of himself as Spenser's heir.[215]

A different story is provided in William Browne's *Britannia's Pastorals*, although Browne's account does not sound authentic. Browne claimed that the queen had planned to erect a magnificent monument to Spenser, but that, unfortunately, the agent she employed was overcome by Avarice who 'rob'd our *Colin* of his monument'.[216] Browne's lines look rather like special, Spenserian pleading, as well as a self-validation of his own work as a fitting monument to the work of the master, and they are part of an attack on the dire fate of England under James and his wilful neglect of the past.[217]

A monument was eventually erected by Lady Anne Clifford (Plate 44). Clifford, who had been taught by Samuel Daniel, and was later pictured alongside her books, which included Spenser, was clearly eager to advertise her role as a reader and patron of English poetry.[218] The monument was built by Nicholas Stone (1585/8–1647), who noted in his account book, 'I also mad a mroument for Mr Spencer, the pouett and set it up at Westmester for which the contes of Dorsett payed me 40£'.[219] Stone was a distinguished master mason, 'the best English sculptor of his generation', who later designed John Donne's tomb in St Paul's Cathedral, helped build the Banqueting House in Whitehall from Inigo Jones's designs, as well as Goldsmith's Hall and a number of other funeral monuments and prominent country houses.[220] His son was important enough to visit Bernini in 1638.[221] The inscription on the now destroyed monument, gave erroneous dates for the poet's birth and death, although, at least, his Christian name was spelled correctly:

> HEARE LYES (EXPECTING THE SECOND
> COMMINGE OF OVR SAVIOUR CHRIST
> JESVS) THE BODY OF EDMOND SPENCER,
> THE PRINCE OF POETS IN HIS TYME;
> WHOSE DIVINE SPIRIT NEEDS NOE
> OTHIR WITNESSE THEN THE WORKS
> WHICH HE LEFT BEHINDE HIM.
> HE BORNE IN LONDON IN
> THE YEARE 1510. AND
> DIED IN THE YEARE
> 1596.[222]

End of the life Vol. 1.　　　　　　　Lud Du Guernier in et Sculp. 7

Figure 11. Engraving of Spenser's monument, Westminster Abbey, *The Works of Mr. Edmund Spenser*, 6 vols., ed. John Hughes (London, 1715), vol. i, facing p. xxii. Reproduced with kind permission of the British Library.

The original monument does not survive. According to the antiquarian John Dart (d. 1730), it was not an impressive edifice, a pointed contrast to its replacement.[223] Recommending a tour of the poets' monuments in the south transept, Dart notes that

[T]he first Tomb you come at is a rough one, of coarse Marble and looks by the Moisture and Injury of the Weather, and the Nature of the Stone, much older than it is. This, whose Form is here erected to the Memory of Mr. *Edmond Spencer*, a Man of great Learning and such luxuriant Fancy, that his Works abound with as great Variety of Images (and curious tho' small Paintings) as either our own or any Language can afford in any Author.[224]

Dart, citing Camden as an authority, reproduces a Latin epitaph that was supposedly on the original tomb, although it is now no longer visible. Dart translates it as:

Here lies Spenser next to Chaucer, next to
him in talent as next to him in death. O Spenser,
here next to Chaucer the poet, as a poet you are
buried; and in your poetry you are more permanent
than in your grave. While you were alive, English
poetry lived and approved you; now you are dead,
it too must die and fears to.[225]

None of this remains and Dart and Camden are the only witnesses to the original.

It is likely that 1510 was an error for a date of 1550 in manuscript, but the lack of interest in the exact details is a sign of how little Spenser's life mattered to contemporaries, as the description of him as 'the prince of poets *in his time*' (my emphasis) suggests.[226] Even so, the monument was important enough to feature in John Hughes's edition of his works, in an engraving by Loius de Guernier.[227] The edition, the first illustrated edition of Spenser's works, included a picture of four well-dressed figures, two men and two women, discussing the inscription on Spenser's tomb, obviously in the absence of a portrait of the poet (Figure 11).[228] Poets' Corner was taking shape as a place in the public imagination, started through the union of Chaucer and Spenser, usually regarded as the nation's two greatest writers throughout the seventeenth century.[229] The monument decayed and crumbled away and was replaced in 1778 by a more durable marble structure in the same style, built by William Mason (1725–97), the poet and garden designer, who had been a fellow at Pembroke College.[230] Mason also gave the college a copy of the Chesterfield portrait which hangs in the hall.[231] Now, there was a clear desire to know what Spenser had looked like, unfortunately a long time after any evidence could be recovered.

Afterword

SPENSER is an elusive writer, even by the standards of the early modern period. If he had the same presence outside the academy as his younger contemporary, William Shakespeare, many would doubt that he was the author of many of the works attributed to him. Indeed, this process has started to happen in some discussions over *A View*, although momentum does now seem to be waning. But if linking the poet to a life manifested outside his works is not an easy task, it is one that cannot be ignored because Spenser conspicuously refers to his life throughout his work, albeit in invariably oblique terms. In Richard McCabe's words, 'He was constantly auto-referential but seldom autobiographical.'[1] As a result Spenser's subsequent reputation has been complicated and divergent. On the one hand he occupies a central place within the English poetic canon, so that he can be praised as an author who makes us 'grow in mental health', or who is especially adept at making the reader think.[2] On the other hand, Spenser is often remembered as a morally flawed, self-interested sycophant, complicit with a brutal policy of extermination that he articulated with great skill in order to protect what he had gained as a colonist in Ireland.

Spenser makes a couple of fleeting appearances in Brendan Kennelly's powerful sequence of short poems, *Cromwell* (1983). In one he is imagined being praised by Cromwell for his talent and for having 'devoted nights and days | To pleasuring his fellow-countrymen'. The deliberately sexualized nature of the utterance describes an auto-erotic fantasy that has nothing to do with the reality of the island and its people. Kennelly probably has in mind Cromwell's letter to the Irish Council about William Spenser's right to inherit Kilcolman, based in part on his grandfather's poetic prowess, as well as Edmund's own descriptions of sterile sexuality in the Bower of Bliss, the most celebrated section of *The Faerie Queene*.[3] Cromwell then reflects on the harsh nature of the world, which he thinks is populated by murderous 'bloody apes', projecting the violence of the English onto the Irish, the familiar colonial trope of 'blaming the victims'. He concludes:

> Aren't we lucky, then, to have such a skilled
> Poet, one who has truly learned his trade
> Of delight, delight, delight?[4]

Again, the poem is aware of contemporary literary developments, as well as of the history of Spenser criticism. The reference to 'delight' is a recollection of Sidney's dictum that poetry should both 'teach and delight'.[5] Spenser, according to Cromwell's escapist understanding of poetry, can only delight his English readers and teaches no one anything. Kennelly is also surely referring to W. B. Yeats's famous essay on Spenser, which praised the poet's ability to write symbolist poetry but regretted his penchant for allegory, lamenting that if only he could have engaged with the beauties of Ireland, Anglo-Irish literary history would have been different and better.[6] Kennelly is therefore acutely aware of the history of Spenser criticism and its relationship to the perceived nature of the poet's life. Who Spenser was is a question that has been caught up with his subsequent critical reputation so that the two have become inextricably intertwined. Spenser is still, in Marx's words, 'Elizabeth's arse-kissing poet', a man on the make who aspired to be at court and who was prepared to exploit the Irish to get what he wanted and felt he needed.[7] The fact that he was such an intelligent man and such a skilful poet only makes his craven complicity seem worse.

Re-reading the life records and the literary works qualifies this picture, if anything placing the moral and political problems in even starker relief. Spenser was not a court poet. He clearly attended the court on occasions, probably three times, and may have aspired to a place there at certain points in his life. But he was not really a courtier in any meaningful sense and cannot have been the man with a ruff represented in the Kinnoull portrait and adapted on frequent occasions in the last two hundred years. That picture, along with the Chesterfield portrait, has undoubtedly contributed to the illusion that Spenser looked and dressed like men assumed to have been his close friends and fellow poets, Walter Ralegh and Philip Sidney. Spenser was often an acerbic writer, and was astonishingly rude to the good and the great throughout his life, his list of insulted victims including Elizabeth, James VI, Lord Burghley, the earl of Leicester, and Sir Walter Ralegh, as well as (arguably) Bishop Young and Archbishop Loftus, a distinguished collection of names. And, as this list also demonstrates, he had little compunction about biting the hands that fed him. Spenser came from that amorphous category, the 'middling sort', and he associated largely with social equals throughout his life: writers, publishers and printers, bureaucrats, soldiers, academics, secretaries, and clergymen, rather than the mighty and the powerful who moved in their own circles. The significance of his social status has often been ignored because of what he wrote and who he was, therefore, assumed to have been. His apparent aspirations to acquire property and rise in status makes him no better nor worse than most of his peers who were also eager to join the gentry and afford themselves the status of a gentleman.[8]

Perhaps thinking in counter-factual terms might help us understand who Spenser really was. His life would have looked very different if he had never had the opportunity of going to Ireland. Life in Ireland eventually made Spenser into a very rich man, one who acquired far more wealth and property than he would have done if he had stayed in England. It may also have distorted his career so that his poetic output involved two, scarcely related, spectacular bursts of productivity. If he had never gone to Ireland it is likely that Spenser would have become a divine, a Cambridge don, a soldier, a hack writer for hire, or, most likely, a functionary of sorts in a substantial household. Perhaps his literary career would have proceeded at a rather steadier pace. Perhaps, the key decision he made, and which changed his life most dramatically, was to get married in 1579, and he placed a heavy emphasis on the significance of marriage, especially his own, ever afterwards. It is also probable, given his origins and what we can understand of his opinions and views from his early works, that he would have seemed more tolerant and open-minded than brutal and bigoted and that the full extent of his poetic experiments would have been even more obvious. Despite all the efforts to prise apart the colonial administrator and the poet, the image of the former, a civic functionary in England's first overseas imperial possession, has dominated the perception of the latter, casting Spenser as a man who, exiled from court, really wanted to be there, a key element of the seventeenth-century biographies. If we try to understand why a man like Spenser would have gone to Ireland in his mid-twenties, our picture of him changes, even if our sympathies remain the same.

It is also likely that Spenser's religious beliefs, which have been cast as those of a low church Protestant, eager to purge the British Isles of Catholics, would have looked very different too. Spenser's early work suggests that he was wary of narrow doctrinal belief, adhered more to the institution of the church itself, had an acute understanding of the pains and tribulations generated by sudden ecclesiastical and theological change, and realized the terrible effects of the Wars of Religion in France and the Low Countries. Furthermore, that notably intolerant work, *A View*, is significant for its lack of interest in religion. Spenser clearly felt the danger of the international Catholic threat to the independence of the English-dominated British Isles, but that does not mean that he was a blinkered Protestant or that he hated all Catholics. Certainly his sons appear to have had no serious issues establishing homes which encompassed diverse forms of worship, evidence that has probably not been accorded its due importance. They may have married out of expediency and felt the need to protect their lands and to fit into Irish colonial society, but, even so, it is clear that their upbringing did nothing to hinder any such pragmatic aim.

English colonization of Ireland can be seen in at least three interrelated contexts: that of an English desire to dominate the British Isles; that of an expansion westwards towards America; and that of the expansion of the more powerful states within European to colonize their neighbours.[9] Spenser was part of this process, which shaped his life and work as a colonial civil servant and a writer. But we should not, I think, assume that he was the enthusiast for Irish genocide for which he has often been taken. Spenser may well have been present at the Hill Hall debates about colonial warfare, and, if not, would surely have known about them from Harvey. His descriptions of Ireland in 1594–5, in the *Amoretti* and *Colin Clout*, are hardly flushed with unqualified enthusiasm for the land and people, but the argument for spectacular violence only really occurs in works written a year later as the Nine Years War became ever more dangerous for English colonists. Spenser was clearly caught up in processes and events that he could scarcely control and which he assumed that he could influence only in a limited and futile way, hence the terrified allegory of 'Two Cantos of Mutabilitie' in which he imagines the struggle for universal supremacy happening only a few miles from his house. The irony, of course, is that, while it could not prevent the disastrous events of 1598–9, *A View* may well have set the agenda for subsequent colonial practices.

Is Spenser's Irish experience the key? We also need to understand that it is possible that had Spenser not gone to Ireland his poetry would have remained largely recognizable as what we have today, while his life would not have. The relationship between the life and the poetry would have changed, of course, which shows that Spenser's Irish experience is crucial to an understanding of the man and his work, but is not the only thing that we need to know about him. We also need to consider his origins; his class; his education; his wives and children; his friends and patrons; his reading; and the host of forces that shaped the possibilities, prospects, achievements, and course of his life, some of which he would have understood, much of which he would have been unable to control as he might have wished.

The truth is that Spenser was undoubtedly not an especially savage or violent man, at least, according to the standards of Elizabethan England, and a careful study of his work reveals a profound understanding of the effects of violence.[10] To single out one particular episode already covered in this biography: it is worth remembering that George Gascoigne used Erasmus' most famous dictum, 'Dulce Bellum Inexpertis', as the title of a long poem that he dedicated to Arthur, Lord Grey de Wilton, a work that, paradoxically, defends the duty of the true warrior, rather than condemning the futility of war. Gascoigne defines war in familiar terms that condemn the ambition of the tyrannical ruler who cannot be confined by the laws of nations:

> And for my parte my fansie for to wright,
> I say that warre is even the scourge of God,

Tormenting such as dwell in princelie plight,
Yet not regarde the reaching of his rode,
Whose deedes and duties often times are odde,
Who raunge at randon jesting at the just,
As though they raignde to do even what they lust.[11]

Grey, the duplicitous author of 'Grey's faith', is cast here as a privileged reader who, like Gascoigne, realizes that war is bloody, futile, and to be avoided if possible. Only a tyrant who has failed to listen to good advice will energetically pursue military conflict. The message is that both Gascoigne and Grey will only wage war if they have to, obeying a monarch, who may or may not have sufficient reasons to fight the enemy.

Like Gascoigne, who had been present at the siege of Antwerp, Spenser witnessed terrible slaughter, which had a significant impact on his imaginative powers, manifested throughout his writing. And also like Gascoigne, he distances his patron from the effects of his actions, representing Grey as Artegall restraining the excessive violence of Talus, rather than being its perpetrator.[12] Spenser's later writing emerges from its context, his personal experience working to determine the course that his work took, even if it is only formally manifested in an auto-referential mode. It is not only Spenser's work that makes us think—so does its relationship to his life.

Appendix 1
Spenser's Descendants

Spenser's family stayed in Ireland after his death. Assuming that Elizabeth fled to London with him, as seems most likely, she probably returned at some point in the early 1600s. She appears as 'Mrs Spenser' in a list of undertakers, appended to a letter written by Hugh Cuffe to Sir Robert Cecil in February 1601.[1] Cuffe states that he himself 'never more intend to dwell in Ireland, having had so many crosses'. He had lost his son in the defence of Kilmallock (fifteen miles north of Kilcolman over the Ballyhoura Mountains) at the start of the insurrection, and his seigniory was now reinhabited by his two daughters and his bailiff. Cuffe places the blame for the destruction of the Plantation squarely on the shoulders of the other undertakers and demands that they now return and populate the devastated lands, 'Otherwise myself and some few others that are desirous to do her Highness service shall lose our labour, as hitherto we have done.' Perhaps with some significance, Sir Walter Ralegh heads the list of both Cork and Waterford undertakers: Mrs Spenser is fourth from last in a list of twelve, after Cuffe himself.

Munster remained in turmoil until Sir George Carew's campaign in summer 1600 started to clear out rebel strongholds in Limerick and Kerry. After this, settlers started to return, and the government was eager to repopulate the Plantation. A few appear to have stayed throughout parts of the crisis, such as Hugh Cuffe (although he clearly had abandoned his estate at one point), but as late as 1603 there was concern that sixteen of the undertakers were still absent.[2] Elizabeth was obviously in the first wave of English settlers to return, most likely because she had too much to lose in staying away and had to take the risk. Eventually, the Plantation was re-established and became a much more obviously anglicized settlement, with swift transport links to England and Europe.[3] This is where the family lived until the eighteenth century.

The family's principal home, Kilcolman, had been badly damaged in the rebellion, and must have been in a state of disrepair in the first years of the seventeenth century. It is hard to know whether Renny was in a similar state, but it is possible that it had survived the years rather better and may have been where the family lived at first. At some point between Spenser's death and 20 August 1600, Elizabeth married Roger Seckerstone, as proved by a deed that grants 'Roger Seckerton and his wife' the right to 'Rennyborough' and various rectories that must have been associated with the castle. The Seckerstone family, like so many other settlers (including the Spensers), appear to have become Catholics by the middle of the seventeenth century.[4]

It is possible that Sylvanus and Peregrine stayed in England and only returned to Ireland later, as we know that Peregrine was in London on 15 May 1618, when Richard Boyle sent him £5.[5] Sylvanus would have been almost at the age of majority when his stepmother remarried; Peregrine would have still been quite small, and could not have been older than 5. At some point in the early 1600s, Sylvanus's sister, Katherine, married William Wiseman of Bandon, the most significant new town in Ireland some twenty miles south-west of Cork city.[6] Spenser had income from a number of ecclesiastical properties in the area in the late 1590s, notably at Kilbrogan, where Katherine was eventually buried. More relevant still, Bandon was a Protestant planter town owned, planned, and developed by Sir Richard Boyle, to show that settlements in Munster could rival those in Ulster, such as Londonderry.[7] Wiseman, son of Simon Wiseman, an original colonist, was described by Boyle as a 'verie loving friend'.[8] He was escheator for County Cork, a lucrative position which involved the inspection of the property resulting from people who had died intestate, to see whether it could be transferred to the crown.[9] Richard Boyle had been the deputy escheator, which would explain how the couple met.[10] They lived in Kilbeg Castle, just outside Bandon. Boyle made his fortune through appropriating land in this manner, and the Wisemans clearly did well for themselves, as his will indicates.[11] William remarried in 1635, so Katherine was dead by this point, probably at some point in the 1630s. She was buried in the grounds of Christ Church, Kilbrogan, the oldest Protestant church in Ireland, about a mile from her house (Plate 43).[12] Wiseman died on 11 February 1635, his funeral entry confirming that they had no children who survived into adulthood.[13] A Lawrence Spenser of Kilpatrick, near Bandon, who died in 1653 and was also buried in Christ Church graveyard, was a yeoman father and not the poet's son, as was once claimed.[14]

Nothing is really known about Seckerstone. He was another acquaintance of Sir Richard Boyle's as references in the Lismore Papers demonstrate, and he may have been descended from a merchant who was either Irish or who was English and had lived in Ireland for a long time.[15] Elizabeth, a vulnerable widow in a difficult situation, was probably persuaded that remarriage was desirable.[16] Widows in late sixteenth-century England generally remarried after nine months so Elizabeth appears to have followed a well-established pattern, probably waiting slightly longer than the norm.[17] The union produced one child, Richard, who was the godson of the earl. Seckerstone was dead by April 1606, probably dying in that month, as an indenture between Elizabeth Seckerstone and Richard Boyle of 3 May 1606 describes her as a widow. The document was drawn up to lease a house in Kilcoran, Youghal (near the strand) to her for sixty-one years at an annual rent of 2s. 6d., presumably the house where the couple had been living.[18]

Elizabeth now remained as a widow for a relatively long period, perhaps because she had no immediate need to remarry now that the situation in Ireland had stabilized, perhaps because she was well looked after by her wealthy cousin. She eventually remarried Captain Robert Tynte in 1612, becoming his second wife and assuming the title 'Lady Tynte'. The couple had four children before Elizabeth died on 23 August 1622.[19] She may have been in ill health before this, as a letter to Richard Boyle written on 5 January 1615 indicates.[20]

In the intervening years the complicated nature of the Spenser family had led to a series of legal disputes about property that resemble those brought by Edmund and Elizabeth against the previous generation. In 1603, Sylvanus, who had probably just come of age, petitioned the office of the Lord Chancellor for access to the title deeds to Kilcolman which were held by Roger and Elizabeth Seckerstone. The document, now destroyed, stated

Whereas your Petitioner's father, Edmund Spenser was seized in his demense in ffee of Kyllcolman and divers other lands and tenements in the county of Corke, which descended to your petitioner by the death of his said father, so it is right honourable, the evidences of the sayd inheritance did after the decease of the petitioner's father cum to the hands of Roger Seckerstone and petitioners mother which they unjustly detayneth; which evidences forasmuch as your petitioner can have no accion at common lawe, he not knowing theire dates and certainty, he is driven to sue in consideracion before your Honourable Lordship, and avoweth that the said Roger Seckerstone, his mothers now husband, unjustly detayneth the said evidences, to your petitioners damage of one hundred pounds, where in he prays remedy.[21]

These words indicate a serious conflict between heir and widow, as was often the case with English inheritance laws.[22] Sylvanus was obviously successful, perhaps through an amicable settlement with his stepmother, as he is recorded as an undertaker in 1603.[23] In 1605/6 Sylvanus was embroiled in disputes about death duties (heriot and relief) and he was summoned before the Exchequer court, after which the estate was seized on the sheriff's orders.[24] Sylvanus evidently paid the duties and reoccupied the estate in 1606.[25] Like his father, he was involved in disputes with his neighbours over the extent of his land, Sir Allan Apsloe, Kt. and John Power of Doneraile, but also had some rent abatements as his father had sold two ploughlands to the Synans.[26] He was indicted in 1611 for being an absentee landlord, most of whose tenants were 'mere Irish'.[27]

Sylvanus would have occupied Kilcolman at some point in the early seventeenth century, animal remains indicating that the castle was inhabited at this time, when a number of architectural innovations took place, including the raising of the floor in the parlour that his father had established.[28] However, it is likely that Sylvanus abandoned the tower house in 1620, when a fire destroyed much of the building and he had a manor house constructed on the estate as the Plantation Survey of 1622 records.[29] In c.1630 Sylvanus married Elinor, one of David Nagle's nine daughters.[30] Nagle was a powerful Anglo-Irish neighbour of the Spensers, who held lands in Monanimy, near Killavullen, about eight miles east of Mallow, the marriage being a sure sign that the Spensers now envisaged themselves as part of the minor gentry in south Munster.[31] More significantly, David Nagle also owned Ballynamona Castle, only a few miles from Kilcolman. Elinor was the granddaughter of William Roche, who was related to Lord Maurice Roche, a sign of how complex family relationships and legal disputes could be in the early modern British Isles.[32] The first wife of Edmund's nephew, Sir Robert Travers, was Katherine Nangle, who may have been from the same family.[33] The Nagles were a prominent and distinguished Catholic family who controlled the area around Monanimy, before they were dispossessed after the leading role that Sir Richard Nagle (1636–99), Sylvanus's nephew, played as a Jacobite in the Williamite Wars.[34] The marriage of Sylvanus and Elinor suggests that either the Spenser family had changed or that they had always had good relations with their Catholic neighbours.[35] Neither story would be surprising, as many undertaker families—notably the Audleys, the Brownes, the Cullums, and the Thorntons—had become Catholic by the second quarter of the seventeenth century.[36] Sylvanus and Elinor probably lived in Ballygriffin, near Killavullen for a part of their twenty-odd years of married life.[37] Sylvanus died in 1636, having produced two sons who survived into adulthood, Edmund and William, Edmund being his heir and assuming the rights to the estate.

Peregrine, Spenser's son from his second marriage, appears to have suffered from the general affliction of second sons, lack of means of support. He appears in the Lismore Papers, writing a rather self-pitying letter to Richard Boyle on 2 October 1618 for help to secure a living. Claiming that his health has prevented him from effective study, Peregrine apparently pleads for guidance—'But if yo[r] charity wil vouchsafe to be a meanes to direct my youth in a path that my age may liue to pray for you in all the zealous offices that so obliged a kinsman as my self may be acceptable, I wil conforme my industry to yo[r] disposing'—before asking the earl if he knows what has happened to the £5 he has heard from his mother that he sent him, one of what looks like a number of payments made to him by the earl.[38] The earl appears to have looked after his relative, as he had his mother, which was surely another reason why the family returned to Ireland. An earlier letter (19 November 1616) from Lady Tynte to Boyle pleads with the earl to overlook some unstated 'childes accions to excuses in regarde of his youeth & want of exsperiance' and thanks him for offering to allow Peregrine to stay with him 'for his better edicacion'.[39] Peregrine was clearly regarded as something of a problem child, worried his relatives about his development into adulthood, and does not appear to have followed their plans. Like his brother, Peregrine had to fight against what he saw as the appropriation of his rightful property by his mother and stepfather, lodging a bill on 14 January 1623, after Elizabeth's death, against Francis Marshall, who had presumably acquired Renny and its accompanying lands from Roger and Elizabeth Seckerstone.[40] Peregrine married Dorothy Tynte, the daughter of Elizabeth's third husband, Sir Robert Tynte, from an earlier marriage, in 1623.[41] They had four children, and the eldest son, Hugolin, inherited the Renny estates. Hugolin's sister, Catherine, married Ludovicus O'Cahill, son of Daniel Duffe O'Cahill, the harper of Queen Anne of Denmark, James I's wife.[42] Peregrine died in February 1641/2 fighting for Charles I in the Civil War.[43] Hugolin lodged a claim with the Court of Claims in the early 1660s and had to deny suggestions that he and his father were Catholic, indicating that the family, like many others, had been under suspicion for a long time. The court concluded that they were innocent.[44] Dorothy lived on for many years and may well have possessed the copy of *The Faerie Queene* that Spenser gave to Elizabeth, as the initials 'D. S.' are written on the title page.[45]

Sylvanus's son, Edmund, who appears to have been rather argumentative and confrontational, died on 28 August 1640, when he broke his neck falling from his horse in Dublin and was buried in St James's churchyard, next to his maternal grandfather David Nagle.[46] As he had no heirs, Kilcolman passed to his younger brother, William (1634–1713). William was a Catholic, and it is evident that Elinor had brought their children up as adherents of the traditional faith, clearly with the agreement of Sylvanus. Accordingly part of the estates, Kilcolman, Lisnamucky, and Knocknamaddery, totalling 1,599 acres, were seized by Cromwellian troops led by Captain Peter Courthope in 1654.[47] William appealed to Oliver Cromwell on 27 March 1657 for the return of his lands, as is recorded in Cromwell's letter to the Irish Council:

A petition hath been exhibited unto us by William Spencer, setting forth that being but seven years old at the beginning of the Rebellion in Ireland, he repaired with his mother, his father being then dead, to the City of Cork, and during the Rebellion continued in the English quarters, that he never bore arms or acted against the Commonwealth of England, that his grandfather Edmund Spencer and his father were both Protestants, from whom an estate of lands in the Barony of Fermoy and County of Cork descended on him, which during the Rebellion yielded him little or nothing towards his relief, that the said estate hath been lately given out to the soldiers in satisfaction of their arrears, only upon the account of his professing the Popish religion, which since his coming to years of discretion he hath, as he professes, utterly renounced; that his grandfather was that Spencer, who by his writings, touching the reduction of the Irish to civility, brought on him the odium of that nation, and for those works and his other good services Queen Elizabeth conferred on him the estate which the said Wm. Spencer now claims. We have also been informed that the gentleman is of civil conversation and that the extremity his wants have brought him to have not prevailed over him to put him upon indirect or evil practices for a livelihood; and if, upon inquiry, you shall find his case to be such, we judge it just and reasonable, and do therefore desire and authorise you that he be forthwith restored to his estate, and that reprisal lands be given to the soldiers elsewhere, in the doing whereof our satisfaction will be the greater by the continuation of that estate to the issue of his grandfather, for whose eminent deserts and services to the Commonwealth that estate was first given him.[48]

The Council resolved matters swiftly and issued a final judgement on 11 August 1657.[49] Despite Cromwell's intervention, William had to surrender the lands to the soldiers, although he preserved the rest of the Kilcolman estate, and he was transplanted to Connaught, albeit with a reasonably substantial portion of land, 1,011 acres in the Ballinasloe area, about twenty miles south-west of Athlone, on either side of the Galway/Roscommon border.[50] In 1660 he was restored to his Kilcolman estate and appears to have kept his lands in Galway and Roscommon.[51]

This document tells us a great deal.[52] William's petition was clearly cunningly crafted and his description of the hostility of the Irish towards his grandfather's 'writings touching the reduction of the Irish to civility', looks like a deliberate echo of the opening lines of *A View*, providing further confirmation of Spenser's authorship of the dialogue.[53] However, what Cromwell records that William Spenser claims is certainly problematic, although it may have a basis in reality. William argues that he was only ever a Catholic out of youthful ignorance, and that his father was always a Protestant. This would indicate that his mother dominated the character of the household, including the religion that the children would follow. Sylvanus, according to his son, maintained his faith in opposition to what was happening in the rest of the house, something that is possible but unlikely to be the whole story of the family's religion. William's own convenient renunciation of his Catholicism was the basis of his claim that he be restored to his estate. Certainly the Spenser household as represented by William seems to have been at odds with the norm in England where '[t]he husband was expected to be the dominant partner in the religious life of the household'.[54] Moreover, the deposition of Richard Gettings of 10 May 1642 asserts that 'the heirs and executors of Edmond Spenser late of Kilcolman' were among the rebels, which would appear to refer to Sylvanus's branch of the family, and would suggest that William and his brothers were out in rebellion.[55] Gettings could, of course, be mistaken or lying, but his testimony indicates that the Spensers were not thought of as an especially loyal family. Certainly other settlers, assumed to have been 'British Protestants', joined the rebels, among whom was one Walter Spencer of Ballinalty.[56]

William Spenser had clearly exaggerated his loyalty in order to reclaim his property. Cromwell's account suggests that he probably believed what William had told him, perhaps also out of convenience, as he probably wanted to retain a loyal subject in the area and thought that more land could easily be taken from other places to compensate his soldiers. It is also obvious from reading this that Cromwell had a high regard for Spenser and thought that he had been rewarded by the state just as he planned to reward his soldiers and Spenser's grandson. Cromwell's comments on *A View* indicate that he had read the text, undoubtedly in preparation for his campaign in Ireland.[57] For Cromwell, the opprobrium that it had generated in Ireland was a sign of its author's virtue for which his family deserved to keep their land.

William met his wife, Barbara Edwards, daughter of William Edwards of Loughrea, about twenty-five miles south-west of Ballinasloe. She brought a number of new lands in her dowry so that the couple owned about 2,000 acres in the region and, once they had recovered Kilcolman, they seem to have alternated between the two estates. The couple had two children, Nathaniel and Susanna.[58] Nathaniel, like his great-grandfather, appears to have become a prebendary of a church in the diocese of Limerick Cathedral.[59]

Hugolin had an equally fraught and complicated existence, and an indenture dated 9 August 1673, shows that he had to mortgage many of his lands.[60] He is mentioned in the 1641 depositions as living at Renny.[61] Like William, he had become a Catholic, perhaps converted after he had left home, unless both of Spenser's sons became Catholics when they married and passed their faith on to the next generation. Hugolin and Dorothy were dispossessed of their impoverished estate, although they were later reinstated as 'Innocent Papists'.[62] The two cousins fought on opposite sides in the Williamite Wars (1689–91), Hugolin taking the side of James and the Catholic Irish Confederacy, while William supported William III, a division that reflected the experience of many English families in Ireland in this period.[63] William suffered particularly badly, complaining that he lost 300 head from his herd of black cattle, 1,500 sheep, and that his houses were ransacked and burnt down and his family abused. Hugolin was declared an outlaw for high treason at Mallow on 15 August 1694, his estates forfeited and transferred to William in compensation for his services to Ireland. The formal transfer was approved by the king on 23 April 1697, and the Renny lands passed on to William's son, Nathaniel, on 14 June. William was later dispossessed by an Act of Parliament which negated all such grants, but he was reinstated when he travelled to London to appeal against the decision by a private Act.[64]

However, Hugolin had already mortgaged the Renny estates to his daughter Dorothy's husband, Pierce Power, whose family had married into the Boyle family before Edmund had married Elizabeth, for £300, to be raised to £500 if Hugolin died without male issue, which he did.[65] William and Nathaniel mortgaged all their lands, the Kilcolman and Renny estates, for £2,100 on 24 December 1697. When William died in April 1713 Nathaniel was forced to sell a large part of his lands to pay his debts. In 1738 mortgage documents amounting to £2,000 belonged to Elizabeth, the widow of Sir Richard Meade, the great-grandson of Sarah Spenser, Edmund's sister (her son, Sir Robert Travers, had married the daughter of Sir John Meade).[66]

The male descendants of Peregrine died out with Hugolin; Sylvanus's line lived on through Edmund Spenser the third, son of Nathaniel, making him the great-great-grandson of the poet. He finally disposed of the remnants of the original Spenser estates in 1733 and the Connaught estates in 1748.[67] Edmund the third appears to have left to live in Dublin, where he planned to write a life of his ancestor for an edition of his works, which, unfortunately, never appeared.[68] Spenser's descendants through his female heirs survive today in the Cahill, Fitzgerald, Power, Ryan, and White families in Ireland.[69]

Appendix 2
Portraits of Spenser

Unfortunately there is no reliable image of Spenser, or of his wives or descendants. This is not really surprising: there are no positively identified images of many of his contemporaries. We have no real idea what Thomas Deloney, Robert Greene, Gabriel Harvey, Thomas Lodge, Christopher Marlowe (arguably), Thomas Middleton, Thomas Nashe, Robert Southwell, and John Webster looked like. We cannot be sure about Shakespeare, although the funeral monument in Stratford-upon-Avon is probably based on observations drawn from life.[1] In any case, Shakespeare died late enough to have caught the vogue for producing civic portraits of writers.[2] We have a number of reliable portraits of early seventeenth-century authors, including George Chapman, Samuel Daniel, John Fletcher, and Ben Jonson. However, only a few unusual examples survive from the late sixteenth century, most significantly the portraits of John Donne and Michael Drayton, who had himself painted as poet laureate in 1599, the year that Spenser died, the clear message to the knowledgeable viewer being that Drayton was claiming Spenser's garland.[3]

No printed portrait of Spenser appeared alongside work published in his lifetime. But in the mid-seventeenth century an imaginary engraved portrait appeared alongside other portraits of writers on the title pages of John Cotgrave's survey of the written achievements of the English gentry, *Wits Interpreter, the English Parnassus* (1655) (Figure 12). The title page also includes thumbnail portraits of Geoffrey Chaucer, William Camden, Francis Bacon, and others, several of which are based on authentic known portraits of these sitters. The shadowy figure identified as Spenser shows a generic seventeenth-century long-haired man with a moustache, wearing costume from the 1640s. As this date is forty years after Spenser's death, it is clear that the likeness could not be based on an authentic image and that the motive was largely an illustrative device; simply a shorthand means to associate the work with some major literary figures. Another similar portrait also identified as Spenser was reproduced on the frontispiece to the second edition of Edward Phillips's *The New World of English Words, or A General English Dictionary* (1658).[4] This portrait was probably inspired by the earlier print and shows a more clearly rendered man between two pillars with the same long hair and moustache (Figure 13), again one portrait as part of an ensemble of other renowned writers.

The first portrait of Spenser appeared soon after the publication of Jacob Tonson's (1655/6– 1736) edition of Spenser's *Faerie Queene* in 1715, nearly a hundred and twenty years after the poet's death, when the painter George Vertue (1684–1756) claimed to have discovered one in 1719 in the possession of John Guise (1682/3–1765) (Plate 45).[5] Guise left his collection of 250 paintings to Christ Church, Oxford, but there is no record of any being of Spenser.[6] The original has disappeared, but Vertue made what appears to have been a copy in 1727, which is of the same type later identified as the Oxford/Chesterfield portrait of Spenser, of which numerous copies exist, so this 'original' may well have been simply a copy of that painting or another version of it.[7] The timing of the discovery is suspicious and, as David Piper has argued, the relationship of the portrait 'to Spenser himself remains doubtful—not only because of its late emergence, but because of the clash of inscriptions of date and age that the versions bear'.[8] Another copy, painted by Benjamin Wilson (1721–88), was given to Pembroke College by William Mason (1725–97) in 1771, the year his great friend, another fellow of the college, Thomas Gray, died.[9] In fact, it seems clear that the surviving versions are later seventeenth century or even eighteenth century in origin. Therefore, it is possible that no original ever existed, but instead that the portrait type is a fabrication, perhaps like that of the so-called 'Soest' portrait of Shakespeare which dates from c.1667 and which shows Shakespeare as a handsome and notably romantic figure.[10] Moreover, the style of dress in the Spenser portrait (particularly the doublet with wide shoulder guards) dates from c.1615–20 which clearly indicates that the original could not have been produced during Spenser's lifetime. Therefore, the portrait type was either based upon a portrait of a Jacobean man whose likeness became associated with Spenser at an early date, or was an invented portrait to create a suitably sensitive portrait of Spenser at an opportune moment.[11]

The desire to find a picture of Spenser was clearly acute in the early eighteenth century, fuelled no doubt by Tonson's own interest in the subject. Tonson, who almost single-handedly changed the nature of publishing by producing quality editions of the finest authors of his age to help bestow dignity upon the writing profession, had himself portrayed holding his own volume of Milton by Sir Godfrey Kneller.[12] Along with Sir John Somers (1646–1723), he helped to revitalize Spenser's reputation through publishing finely produced editions of his poetry.[13] Tonson dedicated his edition of Spenser's *Faerie Queene* to Somers, who was then painted by Kneller for the Kit-Cat Club holding the book in 1715 or 1716, as soon as it appeared.[14] The Kit-Cat Club was named after the mutton pies of Christopher Catling, which the group of artists, writers, intellectuals, and politicians who met in central London taverns to discuss matters of importance, consumed during their meetings. It had been founded by Tonson and other intellectual Whigs eager to use their influence to transform the cultural politics of the nation. They held Spenser, seen as a Protestant, Whig poet, in especially high regard. Tonson's edition of Spenser did not include a picture of the poet, but showed a group of gentlemen and ladies staring avidly at Spenser's tomb in Westminster Abbey, a sign of his growing celebrity in the period and the need to have tangible remains of the famous dead (Figure 11). This lack of a secure image of the poet undoubtedly fuelled the need to find a portrait, especially as ones of Milton were relatively easy to procure. We should, then, not be surprised that a portrait turned up soon after Tonson's edition, especially as it was found by the antiquarian George Vertue, who was close to the family of one of the central members of the club, Robert Walpole (1676–1745), whose son, Horace (1717–97), purchased many of his pictures.[15]

The first biographer to be able to locate a portrait of Spenser was Thomas Birch, author of a substantial life as a preface to his 1751 edition of the *Works*. Birch declares that 'An original picture of him is still in being, in the neighbourhood of his seat, at Castle-Saffron [just east of Doneraile], the House of JOHN Love, Esq.'.[16] A letter published in the *Gentleman's Magazine* in March 1818 confirms that the picture was removed at some point in the late eighteenth century.[17] It has never been recovered and we have no knowledge of whether Mr Love had a copy of an existing portrait or a new one that has now been lost.

In 1776 the discovery of another supposed likeness of Spenser was announced by the traveller Thomas Pennant (1726–98), when he visited Dupplin Castle, near Perth. This was the 'Kinnoull' portrait, named after the earls who then owned the estate (Plate 46). There was no obviously immediate reason for a picture at this time, as there had been in the aftermath of the

The Muses

Witts
INTERPRETER
Or
The New Parnassus
Severall New Songs,
Fancies, Epigrams,
Drollery, Letters.
&c.

Spencer

Shakespeare

Johnson

Randolph

S.ʳ T. More

L.ᵈ Bacon

Sydney

Strafford

Richlieu

Dubartis

Drollery

Figure 12. John Cotgrave, *Wits Interpreter, the English Parnassus* (1672 edition), title page. Reproduced with kind permission of the British Library.

Figure 13. Edward Phillips, *The New World of English Words* (1658), frontispiece. Reproduced with kind permission of the British Library.

Tonson edition. It is worth noting that Spenser's role as the inspiration behind the Gothic revival of the later eighteenth century had been cemented by the publication of William Kent's startling illustrations in Birch's edition of *The Faerie Queene* and, immediately before that, James Thomson's Spenserian tale, *The Castle of Indolence* (1748).[18] Moreover, Pennant was a close friend of the naturalist Gilbert White (1720–93), White's letters to Pennant making up a substantial part of White's extraordinarily popular *The Natural History of Selbourne* (1771). White had a spaniel called 'Fairey Queene', a sign of how significant Spenser was in so many diverse ways to such groups of cultural gentlemen, and how he helped to form their intellectual horizons.[19] Spenser was more popular in the second half of the eighteenth century than he had been at any time before, his work, in particular *The Faerie Queene*, appealing to Augustans and Romantics alike.[20] The absence of a portrait of Spenser was, if anything, even more frustrating for readers when Pennant announced his find.

The 'Kinnoull' sitter inspired flights of Victorian fancy: G. W. Kitchin, who edited *The Faerie Queene*, Book I, characterized this image of Spenser as 'A refined, thoughtful, warm-hearted, pure-souled Englishman'.[21] The 'Kinnoull' portrait shows a man in his middling years wearing a white ruff edged with fine lace and a black cloak in a three-quarter pose facing right. The ruff probably dates from the first decade of the seventeenth century, but could conceivably be very late 1590s.[22] The painting may date from around 1600, although dendrochronology would be needed to be certain of its date. The identification of Spenser, rather than any other well-to-do member of the middling sort, gentry, or a minor courtier, lacks any evidential basis, other than tradition, and the elaborate lace ruff would seem to indicate a sitter rather more wealthy than the poet.[23] There is also little to be said for the case of the Fitzhardinge miniature, attributed at one time to Nicholas Hillyard, but clearly not his work. Little is known about the provenance of this portrait, but it is extremely unlikely to be Spenser.[24]

The evidence of portraits of Spenser existing after the early eighteenth century does not add much to our knowledge. Thomas Birch does not provide any details of the portrait that was discovered at Castle Saffron and we do not know its location now.[25] Attempts to track it down in the early nineteenth century proved fruitless. There is a record of another portrait, perhaps the same one, in the possession of Edmund Spenser the third, the great-great-grandson of the poet, which was then passed on to a Mrs Sherlock, his granddaughter. This has also disappeared.[26] An exchange between interested parties in 1850–1 led a correspondent, 'Varro', to claim that he was 'well acquainted with an admirable portrait of the poet, bearing the date 1593, in which he is represented as a man of not more than middle age'.[27] When challenged to produce his evidence by the original correspondent, 'E. M. B.', he failed to reply, but it is most likely that he was referring to the Chesterfield portrait.[28] The exchange further reveals the history of uncertainty surrounding portraits of Spenser and the lack of confidence that a true likeness exists. When working on his biography of Spenser in the 1940s A. C. Judson had to work hard even to find the Fitzhardinge miniature as well as the Kinnoull portrait, more evidence that images of the poet do not have a definitive status.[29]

There are some later portraits but these are all oddities. A small canvas in the Plimpton collection at Columbia University, with the name 'Spencer' written beside the head and shoulders of the figure, is clearly a crude work based on the Chesterfield portrait, showing the poet at a slightly younger age. It was probably painted in the early nineteenth century (Plate 47).[30] Another, a mid-Victorian work held in the National Portrait Gallery, shows Spenser greeting Shakespeare, each bowing with great formal reverence to the other. The painting is part of a general effort of the nineteenth-century imagination to think of the great writers of

Elizabethan England in productive conversation with each other. As well as Shakespeare, Spenser is most commonly imagined in conversation with Sir Walter Ralegh, as in the charming print in H. E. Marshall's *English Literature for Boys and Girls* (Figure 1). A tradition has developed in which Spenser is represented as a small man, with a neat beard, resembling the figure in the Chesterfield portrait rather than the more angular-featured man in the Kinnoull portrait. Unfortunately, this image has no serious claim to authority, although it is in keeping with the most authentic description we have of Spenser: 'a little man, wore shorte haire, little band and little cuffs'.

Appendix 3
Spenser's Lives

As the brief biographies of Spenser by Fuller and Aubrey outlined in the Introduction indicate, some facts were available about Spenser's life based on the testimony of his contemporaries even as late as the Restoration. However, Aubrey's gleanings remained hidden from view until the pattern of Spenser's life had already been established, at which point they were reintroduced into a familiar story rather than having the impact they might have done had they appeared at a more formative time. The first analyses of Spenser's life were a few brief comments in Robert Johnson's *Historia Rerum Britannicarum* (1655), slightly expanded and refined in Edward Phillips's compilation of the lives of poets ancient and modern, *Theatrum Poetarum Anglicanorum* (London, 1675).[1] Phillips (1630–c.1695) was Milton's nephew, providing another link between the two pre-eminent early modern English poets.[2] Phillips refers to Spenser as 'the first of our English Poets that brought Heroic Poesie to any perfection' (p. 34), judging *The Faerie Queene* to be only just inferior to the epics of Greece and Rome and the modern romances of Italy. He acknowledges, however, that it was the *Calender* that first 'brought him to Esteem'. The life is structured around the conflict of art and bureaucracy that was to become familiar. Sidney brought Spenser to Elizabeth's attention and then secured him a job with his brother, Henry [*sic*] in Ireland. When his employment ceased he came back to England but lived in poverty. Eventually he appealed to the queen, who, impressed by Spenser's skill, was about to award him £500 when Lord Burghley, still smarting from Spenser's hostile comments in *Mother Hubberds Tale*, exclaimed 'What all this for a Song?' and the sum was promptly reduced to £100. Spenser lapsed into melancholy and died. Sketchy as it is, the two and a half pages are quite substantial for a modern poet (Sidney only merits half a page), suggesting Spenser's significance for Phillips as the English poet who defined modern writing. Furthermore, he defends Spenser from the charge of flattery, arguing that at times praise of the monarch is necessary and, besides, Elizabeth was a great queen (p. 36).

The first serious life of the poet, one that has therefore probably had a greater influence than critics eager to correct falsehoods have recognized, was the anonymous 'A Summary of the Life of Mr Edmond Spenser' that prefaced the 1679 folio of Spenser's works, an account of the life that was twice as long as any earlier version.[3] This life, which makes use of Ware's comments on Spenser, claims that Spenser was born in London in 1510 (based on the dates on his monument), and was 'by his Parents liberally educated'.[4] Spenser then went to Cambridge; was defeated in the fellowship competition by Lancelot Andrewes; travelled to the north of England, where he fell in love; returned to London, and decided to introduce himself to Sir Philip Sidney, 'then in full glory at *Court*'. Spenser's plan works rather well:

To that purpose [Spenser] took an occasion to go one morning to *Leicester-House*, furnish'd only with a modest confidence, and the Ninth *Canto* of the First Book of his *Fairy Queene*: He waited not long, e're he found the lucky reason for an address of the Paper to his hand; who having read the Twenty-eighth *Stanza of Despair*, (with some signs in his Countenance of being much affected, and surpris'd with what he had read) turns suddenly to his Servant, and commands him to give the Party that presented the Verses to him Fifty Pounds; the Steward stood speechless, and unready, till his Master having past over another *Stanza*, bad him give him an Hundred Pound; the Servant something stagger'd at the humour his Master was in, mutter'd to this purpose, That by the semblance of the Man that brought the Paper, Five Pounds would be a proper Reward; but Mr *Sidney* having read the following *Stanza*, commands him to give Two Hundred Pounds, and that very speedily, least advancing his Reward, proportionately to the heighth of his Pleasure in reading, he should hold himself oblig'd to give him more than he had.[5]

After this encounter, Sidney becomes both patron and friend of Spenser, showing that great art breaks down social barriers, even if those involved in any transaction are obliged to respect them. It also helped to make Spenser's description of Despair one of the key descriptions for later readers, especially the Romantic poets.[6]

The length of this description, which amounts to nearly a quarter of the whole biography, emphasizes the importance of the relationship between Spenser and Sidney for late seventeenth-century readers. The story is also told independently in Aubrey's life of Sidney, without the specification of the passage read, or the incremental increase in the amount of the reward (Aubrey simply states that Sidney ordered Spenser to be given 'so many pound in gold').[7] Although apocryphal, this repetition may suggest that the tale has a basis in fact, perhaps like the tale of Burghley's hostility to the poet.[8] Ever after Spenser and Sidney have been linked as the two major non-dramatic Elizabethan poets, *The Faerie Queene* and the *Arcadia* read as parallel projects, even though Sidney only mentions Spenser once in his extant writings, in the *Apology for Poetry*, and does not even mention his name.[9]

The story of Burghley's hostility and parsimony is then repeated from Fuller, with the comment that the '*great Councellour*...studied more the Queen's Profit than her Diversion'. The biographer also asserts that the lines in *The Teares of the Muses* (they are actually from *The Ruines of Time*), which he cites as

> O Grief of Griefs! O Gall of all good Hearts!
> To set that Vertue should despoiled be
> Of such, as first were rais'd for Vertue's parts,
> And now broad-spreading, like an aged Tree,
> Let none shoot up that nigh them planted be!
> O let not those of whom the Muse is scorn'd,
> Alive, nor Dead, be of the Muse adorn'd! (lines 449–55)

are a direct reference to Lord Burghley, and urges the reader to consult *Mother Hubberds Tale* to gauge the full extent of Spenser's hostility to Elizabeth's chief secretary.[10] The last paragraph runs through a series of points that define Spenser's life and work. He was esteemed and rewarded by many of the nobility, whom he then praised in his poetry, but unsuccessful in love, as the episode with Rosalind demonstrates, when he lost out to the unscrupulous Menalcus. Spenser did well in Ireland and was handsomely rewarded by the queen for his services, but lost all in the rebellion, as well as the second half of *The Faerie Queene*, which disappeared through the 'abuse of his Servant, whom he had sent before him into *England*', a story taken from Ware. Spenser, learning that his friend and patron Sidney had died soon before, yielded 'to the impressions of a Fortune obstinately adverse to him, he died, without the help of any other Disease save a broken Heart'. He was then buried in Westminster Abbey next to Chaucer at the expense of the earl of Essex.

This first thumbnail sketch of a biography is worth citing at some length because it establishes the narrative that subsequent biographers have largely followed.[11] Spenser's life is punctuated by paradoxes: he is a man of humble birth who rises to greatness through his talent, but while he is successful in his chosen career, he is unlucky in love; the queen and her courtiers love him, but the chief minister blocks his path to advancement; his mind is set on the court, but he has to make his way in Ireland; he has a great capacity for friendship, but is continually undone by bad luck and treachery.[12] Spenser's life may not have a moral as direct as those of saints and reformers, but it certainly tells a tale of the inverse relationship between poetry and worldly success.

The pattern is largely followed in Jacob Tonson the elder's important edition of Spenser's *Works*, the first to contain illustrations, published in 1715.[13] The life in Tonson's edition, written by the editor, John Hughes (1678?–1720), expands that of 1679 to some twenty-two large pages, without producing a great deal more evidence.[14] Hughes duly notes that 'The Accounts of his Birth and Family are but obscure and imperfect', one reason why they are assumed to have been humble, which then leads to the judgement that, although related and connected to the wealthy, 'his Fortune and Interest seem at his first setting to have been inconsiderable'.[15] Hughes repeats the details, established in 1679: that Spenser lost out to Andrewes for a fellowship and was forced to leave Cambridge; that in the north he was ditched by the cruel Rosalind, but produced some good poetry; that he returned south, persuaded by Gabriel Harvey, and was helped to preferment by Sidney who became his 'judicious friend and generous patron' (p. iv) after he had read the Despair episode; and that at court he became the unofficial laureate, until Burghley thwarted his progress (the pension story is repeated) (pp. vi, x–xi). Hughes adds that Spenser would have been saved from Burghley's designs had Sidney not been abroad (p. viii). Hughes was astute enough to read some of Spenser's published work and so worked out that the *Letters* to Harvey published in 1580 indicate that Spenser was planning to go abroad at this point, but the evidence does not tell us whether he ever went (p. xi). In Ireland Spenser prospered, principally because he was good at his job as *A View* indicates (again, Hughes makes judgements based on the published work) and had sound ideas about government (p. xii). The grant of Kilcolman led to a friendship with his neighbour, Sir Walter Ralegh, as shown in *Colin Clouts come home againe*, resulting in the restoration of his favour with the queen after their joint visit (p. xiv). He finished *The Faerie Queene*, half of which was lost by the careless servant. Eventually Spenser, plundered in the Desmond Rebellion (Hughes conflates this with the Nine Years War), returned to England, where heartbroken on learning of the death of Sidney, he died in the same year as his nemesis, Burghley, and was buried next to Chaucer in Westminster Abbey (p. xv).

The similarities to the 1679 life are striking. For all his careful reading, Hughes follows the pattern set by his predecessor, showing Spenser's broken fortune in life, and establishing the pointed irony that he and Burghley expired in the same year.[16] Hughes shows the value of reading Spenser's published work carefully for clues about his life, and the need to weigh up what is stated with considerable scepticism. Spenser tells us a great deal about his life in his work, but it is not information that can be taken at face value and there are always traps for the unwary.

Spenser's great-great-grandson, Edmund, planned to produce an edition of his works in 1744–5, which never appeared owing to a failure to interest enough subscribers and to the advent of the Jacobite Uprising. He claimed that he was planning to write a definitive life but his surviving letters do not indicate that he had any new information and his main motive appears to have been financial.[17] The next substantial life, written by Thomas Birch (1705–66) as a preface to his 1751 edition of the poem, follows the now established narrative (although Birch thinks that Spenser was of noble descent), with more details added.[18] Birch corrects the error derived from Fuller that Spenser competed with Andrewes for a fellowship at Pembroke, and rightly names Thomas Dove as Andrewes's unsuccessful rival.[19] Spenser had left for the North before where he was treated badly by Rosalind (Birch follows Hughes), but returned south and was attached to a nobleman in Kent or Surrey (p. iv). Birch is sceptical of the Despair story (p. viii), but this is because he argues that Sidney played a significant role in the earlier development of Spenser's literary career, persuading him to turn from pastoral to heroic verse (pp. viii–ix). Birch notes that Sidney commends Spenser in the *Apology*, as does William Webbe in his *Discourse of English Poetry* (1586) (p. vi).[20] He also assumes, from reading Spenser's 'earthquake letter', that Spenser did go abroad in 1579, which is undoubtedly an error, but an understandable one, which, again, shows how keen Birch was to read the works and establish the facts (pp. ix–x). Birch provides comment on the allegorical figures represented in *The Shepheardes Calender*, identifying Algrind as Grindal and Morrell as Aylmer (p. vii), and follows Hughes in commenting on the lost works in the Harvey–Spenser *Letters* (from which he quotes substantially) (pp. x–xii). He expresses doubts about Fuller's stories of Burghley's animosity and Spenser's role as court laureate (pp. xii–iii), but he accepts that the evidence of *The Teares of the Muses* and *The Ruines of Time* show that Spenser felt neglected by the great and the good, while, in *Mother Hubberds Tale* he imitated Chaucer in satirizing the court (pp. xiv–xv). In citing Spenser's dedicatory sonnet to Burghley, prefaced to *The Faerie Queene* in 1590, Birch shows that he has an astute understanding of the complexities of patronage networks and the dangers of assuming that relationships can be read straightforwardly, and that they stayed constant throughout people's lives. Birch suggests that Burghley probably disliked Spenser because of his proximity to Leicester and Essex, not for any particular fault of his own (p. xvi).

Birch also did some research on Spenser's Irish career. He was aware of Spenser's sense of debt to Arthur, Lord Grey de Wilton, expressed in the sonnet prefacing the first edition of *The Faerie Queene*, but also saw that his career was linked to other powerful officials in Ireland, Adam Loftus, archbishop of Dublin, and Sir Henry Wallop, an insight that has not always been followed by subsequent biographers eager to stress the relationship between Spenser and Grey. Birch was also able to state correctly that Spenser had acquired his Irish estate at Kilcolman when it was acquired by the crown after the Desmond Rebellion, and was able to provide a description of the estate (p. xviii).

Following Hughes again, Birch confirms that Spenser found a new love who was much more amenable than Rosalind, and that he visited London with Ralegh, adding that Ralegh was in Ireland because of his feud with Essex (Birch again shows a nuanced understanding of court politics and the volatile nature of patronage networks) (pp. xviii–xix). Birch states that Spenser met the queen and then developed his own usage of Cynthia after Ralegh's poem 'The Ocean to Cynthia', referred to in *Colin Clouts come home againe*, also astutely decoding many of the names in that poem (Astrophel is Sidney; Urania is Mary Sidney; and, Mansilia is the Marchioness of Northampton).[21] Spenser then published a second edition of *The Faerie Queene*, failing to correct some errors from the first edition, even though many were noted. Birch follows Elijah Fenton in arguing that the extant version of the poem is all there was, Spenser not having been robust enough to complete it.[22] Birch also endorses Fenton's notion that the story was copied from Suetonius Tranquillus, author of the life of Terence, who repeated the rumour that Terence's death had resulted from the understandable grief he felt when he lost a bag containing 108 plays adapted from Menander in a shipwreck (pp. xxiii–iv).[23] Spenser biographers have not always been so careful at spotting the uncanny resemblances between literary anecdotes, or in recognizing that early modern lives often appropriated or imitated stories found in other life stories, or were modelled on other lives.[24]

Birch concludes that Spenser must have been in England in 1596 where he wrote *Fowre Hymnes* and oversaw the publication of the second edition of *The Faerie Queene*, again showing his ability to make connections and use the published material to support his judgements (p. xxv). His reading of *A View* is also more informed and astute than any that had gone before, linking the work's logic and conclusions to Sir John Davies's *A Discoverie of the true causes why Ireland was never entirely subdued* (1612). Birch argues that Sir James Ware used Archbishop Ussher's copy of *A View* for his printed edition, repeating Ware's judgement that Spenser would have mollified his opinions had he lived in more tranquil times (pp. xxv–vi). Birch also demonstrates a robust sense of humour and refusal to be intimidated by his subject in arguing that

in the History and Antiquities of the Country he is often miserably mistaken, and seems rather to have indulg'd the Fancy and License of a Poet, than the Judgment and Fidelity required for an Historian; besides his Want of Moderation. If this Character be a true one, we have the less Reason to regret his not finishing another Treaties, which he promised at the Conclusion of his View, expressly upon the Antiquities of Ireland. (pp. xxvi–xxxii)

Here, Birch may not have been fully alive to the wit and etymological play of Spenser's work, but his understanding of the dangers and, implicitly at least, the power politics of taking such liberties with the truth show an astuteness that needs to be imitated.[25] Birch notes that we cannot be sure how long Spenser stayed in England, but he was back in Ireland by 1598 (pp. xxxviii–xxxix). He estimates that Spenser was 45 or 46 when he died, and confesses that, despite extensive searches in the London Prerogative Office, he could find no will (p. xxxix).

Birch's biography is a clear advance on its predecessors. He reads the works carefully for any clues; has laboured extensively in all the relevant areas (Elizabethan London, the poet's family, life in Ireland); is resolutely sceptical about the reliability of anecdotes; always provides his sources; admits when he does not know the answer so that future researchers know where to look; and makes the best of the sources that he has available. None of the lives produced for the next 150 years—those of Henry John Todd (1805), J. C. (1840), George L. Craik (1845), F. J. Child (1855), J. Payne Collier (1862), J. W. Hales (1869), R. W. Church (1879), and, especially Alexander Grosart (1882)—improve significantly on Birch's account of Spenser's life.[26]

Of these lives, only that by Grosart warrants analysis, principally because of the errors and unfounded suppositions that it introduced, misleading notions that are often repeated in recent works, although there are also some important new discoveries too.[27] Grosart did all Spenser scholars a great service in uncovering the Townley Manuscript, which laid out the money spent by Robert Nowell, and provided crucial evidence of the resources provided for Spenser at school and university. But, as even his admirers admitted, he often allowed his enthusiasm for research get the better of him and spoil his hard work. His friend, Ernst Dowden, remarked of Grosart's life of Spenser, 'I have Grosart's wild wilderness of a Life, which of course contains some valuable things', which, as Arthur Sherbo noted, was clearly 'damning with faint praise'.[28]

Grosart's main aim was to prove that Spenser originated from Lancashire: to be precise, the Burnley area. The link had not originated with Grosart, and had been proposed on a number of previous occasions in the nineteenth century, in the lives by Craik and Child, as well as articles in the *Gentleman's Magazine*.[29] But, Grosart pushed the evidence as hard as he could in order to demonstrate that Spenser's family had lived in Lancashire for generations.[30] Grosart, to his own satisfaction, proved that Spenser was a member of the Pendle Forest Spensers, and that returning home to see his parents after leaving university he fell in love with Rose Dineley of Downham, 'at the foot of the Pendle, in the north-west, about three miles from Clitheroe', only for her to leave him for a local yeoman called Charles Aspinal (allegorically represented as 'Menalcas' in *The Shepheardes Calender*, an anagram in which a 'C' makes up 'C Asmeral', i.e., Aspinall).[31] Exhibiting none of Birch's caution over a century earlier, Grosart asserted that when Spenser writes in his first published letter to Harvey from Leicester House, 5 October 1579, 'Et pede Clibosas fesso calcabimus Alpes' ('We shall press our worn feet up the jagged defiles of the Alps'), there can be 'no question' that he is referring to the Pendle Hills and his recent visit to Rosalind (*Works*, ed. Grosart, vol. i, p. lvi).[32] And, if this does not quite prove the case on its own, he adds that the publisher of the *Calender* was Hugh Singleton, a Lancashire man, and, given the prominence of briars in the poem, Spenser must be referring to Burnley where they proliferate (*Works*, ed. Grosart, vol. i, pp. lvi–ii, lx).

Elsewhere, Grosart is over-confident in his judgements and makes irritating mistakes. He claims that Spenser must have had a penchant for 'fair women'; that Lord Grey was gentle but stern in Ireland; that the two hymns that Spenser refers to as works written in the 'greener times of my youth', which he has been persuaded to publish, reluctantly, in 1596, were the love songs spurned by Rosalind; that Diggon Davie in the *Calender* is Jan van der Noot; that Robert Dudley, earl of Leicester was Philip Sidney's brother-in-law (in fact, he was his uncle); that Lord Burghley was crooked and ugly (Grosart is confusing him with his son, Robert) (*Works*, ed. Grosart, i. 124, 136–7, 81, 25–7, 85, 77). The point is not simply that Grosart misleads the reader: rather, the issue is also related to his frustration at the lack of evidence available and his desire to establish a proper Victorian biography of his subject and so place Spenser alongside the dominant figures of his age: Elizabeth, Drake, Mary Queen of Scots, Shakespeare, Ralegh, Sidney, all of whom were the subjects of substantial biographies in the second half of the nineteenth century. Their personalities, however shaky the evidence that enabled writers to reconstruct them for their readers, dominated an understanding of the English Renaissance after studies of the period had been revivified in the wake of Jacob Burkhardt.[33] In many ways Grosart's instincts have been proved correct. A. C. Judson's 1945 biography was a tremendous achievement, especially in his analysis of Spenser's life in Ireland, even though it probably did not receive adequate praise in contemporary reviews.[34] One reviewer concluded, rather harshly, 'this life of Spenser, in spite of its goodwill, its research, its patient industry, because it illuminates neither the poet nor his works, fails to extend our understanding'.[35] But, perhaps owing to questions of space and the fact that it was commissioned as part of the *Variorum* edition, it did not comment adequately on the works, omitting the reason why a reader might care about the life in the first place.[36] Moreover, it fits within the familiar paradigm of Spenser as an ambitious would-be courtier, eager for patronage, whose goal in life was to shower praise on the queen.[37]

Notes

Introduction

1. Peter Beal (ed.), *Index of English Literary Manuscripts*, i/2. *Douglas to Wyatt* (London: Mansell, 1980), pp. 523–31. John Donne is a notable exception as many personal letters do survive.
2. Donald Cheney, 'Spenser's Fortieth Birthday and Related Fictions', *Sp. St.* 4 (1984), 3–31; S. K. Heninger, 'Spenser and Sidney at Leicester House', *Sp. St.* 8 (1990), 239–49.
3. H. E. Marshall, *English Literature for Boys and Girls* (London: T. C. and E. C. Jack, 1910), opposite p. 252. On Spenser and Ralegh see Robert Lacey, *Sir Walter Raleigh* (London: Sphere, 1975), pp. 155–9; Judson, *Life*, pp. 135–42; Andrew Zurcher, 'Getting It Back to Front in 1590: Spenser's Dedications, Nashe's Insinuations, and Raleigh's Equivocations', *SLI* 38/2 (2005), 173–98.
4. The literature on this issue is substantial. The most influential article has been Edwin Greenlaw, 'Spenser and the Earl of Leicester', *PMLA* 26 (1910), 535–61. Another series of speculations is provided in Muriel Bradbrook, 'No Room at the Top: Spenser's Pursuit of Fame', in John Russell Brown and Bernhard Harris (eds.), *Elizabethan Poetry* (London: Arnold, 1980), pp. 90–109.
5. On Rosalind, see Richard Mallette, 'Rosalind', in Hamilton (ed.), *Sp. Enc.*, p. 622; Paul E. McLane, *Spenser's Shepheardes Calender: A Study in Elizabethan Allegory* (Notre Dame: University of Notre Dame Press, 1961), ch. 3, 'Elizabeth as Rosalind'; Andrew Hadfield, 'The Fair Rosalind: What's in a Literary Name: Disguise and the Absent Beloved in Spenser and Shakespeare', *TLS*, 12 Dec. 2008, pp. 13–14. On the servant, see Edmund Spenser, *A View of the State of Ireland*, ed. Andrew Hadfield and Willy Maley (Oxford: Blackwell, 1997), p. 5.
6. Ray Heffner, 'Did Spenser Die in Poverty?', *MLN* 48 (1933), 221–6; Josephine Waters Bennett, 'Did Spenser Starve?', *MLN* 52 (1937), 400–1.
7. William Sherman and Lisa Jardine, 'Pragmatic Readers: Knowledge Transactions and Scholarly Services in Late Elizabethan England', in Anthony Fletcher and Peter Roberts (eds.), *Religion, Culture, and Society in Early Modern Britain: Essays in Honour of Patrick Collinson* (Cambridge: Cambridge University Press, 1994), pp. 102–24; Lisa Jardine and Anthony Grafton, ' "Studied for Action": How Gabriel Harvey Read His Livy', *P&P* 129 (1990), 30–78; Eugene R. Kintgen, *Reading in Tudor England* (Pittsburgh: University of Pittsburgh Press, 1996).
8. Richard Helgerson, *The Elizabethan Prodigals* (Berkeley and Los Angeles: University of California Press, 1976).
9. Gabriel Harvey, *Fovre Letters and certaine Sonnets, especially touching Robert Greene and other parties by him abused (1592)*, ed. G. B. Harrison (1922; Edinburgh: Edinburgh University Press, 1966), p. 13; Nashe, *Works*, i. 287–8.
10. Henry Chettle and Thomas Greene (attrib.), *Greene's Groatsworth of Wit, Bought with a Million of Repentance (1592)*, ed. D. Allen Carroll (Binghamton, NY: MRTS, 1994); Robert Greene, *Greenes vision vvritten at the instant of his death. Conteyning a penitent passion for the folly of his pen* (1592); Robert Greene, *The repentance of Robert Greene Maister of Artes. Wherein by himselfe is laid open his loose life, with the manner of his death* (London, 1592). For discussion, see *ODNB* entry; Kirk Melnikoff and Edward Gieskes (eds.), *Writing Robert Greene: Essays on England's First Notorious Professional Writer* (Aldershot: Ashgate, 2008).
11. Charles Nicholl, *A Cup of News: The Life of Thomas Nashe* (London: Routledge, 1984), pp. 123–4.
12. Nashe, *Works*, i. 288. For analysis, see Andrew Hadfield, ' "Not without Mustard": Self-Publicity and Polemic in Early Modern Literary London', in Healy and Healy (eds.),

Renaissance Transformations, pp. 64–78. On Greene's life, see also Brenda E. Richardson, 'Studies in Related Aspects of the Life and Thought of Robert Greene, with particular reference to the material of his prose pamphlets', unpublished DPhil thesis, University of Oxford, 1976, ch. 1.

13. Irena Backus, *Life Writing in Reformation Europe: Lives of Reformers by Friends, Disciples and Foes* (Aldershot: Ashgate, 2008), p. xxxiii.

14. Ibid. 4.

15. For discussion see John Bachelor (ed.), *The Art of Literary Biography* (Oxford: Clarendon Press, 1995).

16. For astute reflections, see Laura Marcus, *Auto/biographical Discourses: Theory, Criticism, Practice* (Manchester: Manchester University Press, 1994).

17. Walter Jackson Bate, *Samuel Johnson* (New York: Harcourt Brace, 1977); Michael Meyer, *Ibsen: A Biography* (London: Hart-Davies, 1967–71); Leon Edel, *The Life of Henry James*, 5 vols. (London: Hart-Davies, 1953–72); Hermione Lee, *Virginia Woolf* (New York: Knopf, 1997); Michael Holroyd, *Bernard Shaw*, 4 vols. (London: Chatto and Windus, 1988–92).

18. Fulke Greville, 'A Dedication to Sir Philip Sidney', in *The Prose Work of Fulke Greville, Lord Brooke*, ed. John Gouws (Oxford: Oxford University Press, 1986), pp. 3–135. For recent lives, see Katherine Duncan-Jones, *Sir Philip Sidney, Courtier Poet* (London: Hamish Hamilton, 1991); Alan Stewart, *Philip Sidney: A Double Life* (London: Pimlico, 2001).

19. On the creation of the myth of Sidney, see Jan Van Dorsten, Dominic Baker-Smith, and Arthur F. Kinney (eds.), *Sir Philip Sidney: 1586 and the Creation of a Legend* (Leiden: Brill, 1986); Gavin Alexander, *Writing After Sidney: The Literary Response to Sir Philip Sidney, 1586–1640* (Oxford: Clarendon Press, 2006).

20. Alan Pritchard, *English Biography in the Seventeenth Century: A Critical Survey* (Toronto: University of Toronto Press, 2005), pp. 7, 181.

21. Nicholas von Maltzahn, 'John Milton: The Later Life (1641–1674)', in Nicholas McDowell and Nigel Smith (eds.), *The Oxford Handbook of Milton* (Oxford: Oxford University Press, 2009), pp. 26–47, at p. 26.

22. Roger Wilkes, *Scandal! A Scurrilous History of Gossip, 1700–2000* (London: Atlantic Books, 2002); T. H. White, *The Age of Scandal: An Excursion through a Minor Period* (London: Cape, 1950); Keith Thomas, *The Ends of Life: Roads to Fulfilment in Early Modern England* (Oxford: Oxford University Press, 2009), 98–9, 220–2, *passim*. Michael Mascuch makes the analogous point that the use of private notebooks appears to have been a new phenomenon after 1600: *Origins of the Individualist Self: Autobiography and Self-Identity in England, 1591–1791* (Cambridge: Polity, 1997), p. 72.

23. The literature on this subject is depressingly voluminous: on Shakespeare as Marlowe, see A. D. Wraight, *In Search of Christopher Marlowe: A Pictorial Biography* (1965; Chichester: Hart, 1993); on Shakespeare as Sir Henry Neville, see Brenda James and William D. Rubinstein, *The Truth Will Out: Unmasking the Real Shakespeare* (Harlow: Longman, 2005). For overviews of the anti-Stratfordian claims, see Scott McCrea, *The Case for Shakespeare: The End of the Authorship Question* (Westport, CT: Praeger, 2005); James Shapiro, *Contested Will: Who Wrote Shakespeare?* (London: Faber, 2010).

24. Edward George Harman, *Edmund Spenser and the Impersonations of Francis Bacon* (London: Constable, 1915).

25. For discussion, see Hadfield, ' "Not without Mustard" ', pp. 66–8.

26. Nicholl, *Cup of News*, pp. 269–70.

27. Stern, *Harvey*, ch. 7.

28. Ian Donaldson, *Ben Jonson: A Life* (Oxford: Oxford University Press, 2011).

29. MacDonald P. Jackson, 'Early Modern Authorship: Canons and Chronologies', in Gary Taylor and John Lavagnino (eds.), *Thomas Middleton and Early Modern Textual Culture: A Companion to the Collected Works* (Oxford: Clarendon Press, 2007), pp. 80–97.

30. Thomas Middleton, *The Collected Works*, ed. Gary Taylor and John Lavagnino, 2 vols. (Oxford: Clarendon Press, 2007). On *The Family of Love*, see Gary Taylor, Paul Mulholland,

and MacD. P. Jackson, 'Thomas Middleton, Lording Barry, and The Family of Love', *Papers of the Bibliographical Society of America* 93 (1999), 213–42.

31. See the *ODNB* entry by David Gunby.
32. It is a great loss that Mark Eccles never completed his projected biographical dictionary of Elizabethan authors: see 'A Biographical Dictionary of Elizabethan Authors', *HLQ* 5 (1942), 281–302.
33. Katherine Duncan-Jones, *Ungentle Shakespeare: Scenes from His Life* (London: Thomson, 2001); Charles Nicholl, *Shakespeare the Lodger: His Life on Silver Street* (London: Penguin, 2007).
34. Most recently, see Germaine Greer, *Shakespeare's Wife* (London: Bloomsbury, 2007), ch. 19. For different interpretations, see Duncan-Jones, *Ungentle Shakespeare*, pp. 272–5; Peter Ackroyd, *Shakespeare: The Biography* (London: Chatto & Windus, 2005), pp. 485–6.
35. David Bevington, *Shakespeare and Biography* (Oxford: Oxford University Press, 2010), pp. 34–9.
36. Thomas Fuller, *The Worthies of England*, ed. John Freeman (London: Unwin, 1952), pp. 365–6.
37. Richard A. McCabe, 'Rhyme and Reason: Poetics, Patronage, and Secrecy in Elizabethan and Jacobean Ireland', in *Literary Milieux: Essays in Text and Context Presented to Howard Erskine-Hill* (Newark: University of Delaware Press, 2008), pp. 30–51, at pp. 37–8. See p. 236.
38. Alexander C. Judson, 'The Seventeenth-Century Lives of Edmund Spenser', *HLQ* 10 (1946), 35–48. See also G. L. Craik, *Spenser and His Poetry* (London: Charles Knight & Co., 1845), p. 39.
39. Richard Peterson, 'Laurel Crown and Ape's Tail: New Light on Spenser's Career from Sir Thomas Tresham', *Sp. St.* 12 (1989), 1–36.
40. See the *ODNB* article by W. B. Patterson.
41. Andrew Hadfield, 'Secrets and Lies: The Life of Edmund Spenser', in Kevin Sharpe and Steven Zwicker (eds.), *Writing Lives: Biography and Textuality, Identity and Representation in Early Modern England* (Oxford: Oxford University Press, 2008), pp. 55–73.
42. Linda Woodbridge, 'Jest Books, the Literature of Roguery, and the Vagrant Poor in Renaissance England', *ELR* 33 (2003), 201–10, at 206.
43. See e.g. *The Works of Edmond Spenser... Whereunto is added, an account of his life; with other new additions* (London, 1679); *The Works of Mr. Edmund Spenser*, 6 vols., ed. John Hughes (London, 1715), vol. i, p. vi; *A View of the State of Ireland as it was in the reign of Queen Elizabeth. Written by way of a Dialogue between Eudoxus and Ireneus: To which is prefix'd the Author's Life, and an Index added to the Work* (Dublin, 1763), pp. x–xi; *Poetical Works*, ed. Frances J. Child, 5 vols. (Boston: Little, Brown & Co., 1855), vol. i, p. xxix.
44. It is worth noting that even when extensive biographies of 17th-century figures do survive, as is the case with John Milton, they need to be treated with considerable caution: see Gordon Campbell and Thomas N. Corns, *John Milton: Life, Work and Thought* (Oxford: Oxford University Press, 2008), p. 2.
45. Kate Bennett, 'John Aubrey, Hint-Keeper: Life-Writing and the Encouragement of Natural Philosophy in the pre-Newtonian Seventeenth Century', *Seventeenth-Century* 22 (2007), 358–80.
46. *Aubrey's Brief Lives*, ed. Oliver Lawson Dick (1949; Harmondsworth: Penguin, 1962), p. 340.
47. See Judson, *Life*, p. 208 n. 19. On the Beestons see the *ODNB* lives by Andrew Gurr.
48. Tarnya Cooper, *Searching for Shakespeare* (London: National Gallery, 2006), pp. 180–1.
49. *Aubrey's Brief Lives*, p. 340.
50. On Andrewes, see *ODNB* entry by Peter McCullough; Lancelot Andrewes, *Selected Sermons & Lectures*, ed. Peter McCullough (Oxford: Oxford University Press, 2005), p. xv.
51. H. B. Wilson, *The History of Merchant Taylors' School* (London, 1814), pp. 557–62. See also the *ODNB* entries on Dove by Kenneth Fincham, and Watts by Brett Ussher.
52. See *Works* (1679); *View* (1763), pp. ii–iii. *The Faerie Queene. By Edmund Spenser. With an exact collation of the two original editions... To which are now added, a new Life of the Author [by Thomas Birch] and also a glossary. Adorn'd with thirty-two copper plates*, 3 vols. (London, 1751), vol. i, pp. iii–iv; Judson, 'Seventeenth-Century Lives', pp. 40–1. Birch's text and some of his notes are preserved as BL Add. MS 4235. On the illustrations, which were by William Kent, and their significance in developing the concept of the Gothic, see Andrew Hadfield, 'William Kent's Illustrations of *The Faerie Queene* (1751)', *Sp. St.* 14 (2000), 1–81.

53. W. H. Welply, 'Edmund Spenser: Being an Account of Some Recent Researches into His Life and Lineage, with Some Notice of His Family and Descendants', *N&Q* 162 (1932), 128–32, 146–50, 165–9, 182–7, 202–6, 220–4, 239–42, 256–60, at 166. See also Ray Heffner, 'Edmund Spenser's Family', *HLQ* 2 (1938), 79–84.

54. *Variorum*, vi. 220. On the Drydens in Northamptonshire, see James Winn, *John Dryden and His World* (New Haven: Yale University Press, 1987), pp. 4–8. I owe this reference to Paul Hammond.

55. Oliver Garnett, *Canons Ashby* (Swindon: National Trust, 2001), pp. 20–1.

56. On Dryden's interest in Spenser, see David Hill Radcliffe, *Edmund Spenser: A Reception History* (Columbia, SC: Camden House, 1996), pp. 27–9, *passim.*

57. *Aubrey's Brief Lives*, p. 340.

58. The house featured in *The Observer* weekend magazine, 26 July 2008, as one of three homes for sale 'with literary links' (p. 99).

59. Jane Hurst, 'Did Edmund Spenser Live Here?', *Alton Papers* 12 (2008), 3–12. I am extremely grateful to Ms Hurst for sending me her article.

60. Wallop's family estates were clearly substantial as the queen was prepared to visit Wallop in 1591: see *Victoria County History: Hampshire*, iii. 364.

61. Judson, *Life*, p. 151 n. 21, *passim*; *Chronology*, p. 54, *passim.* On Wallop, see the *ODNB* entry by Ronald H. Fritze.

62. Leicester Bradner, 'Spenser's Connections with Hampshire', *MLN* 60 (1945), 180–4. See pp. 238–9.

63. 'Dialogue between Eudoxus and Irenius on the history of Ireland, 1596', TCD MS 589. For a list of manuscripts of a *View*, see *Variorum*, x. 506–16.

64. *View 1997*, p. 6. On Ware's editing of *A View*, see Andrew Hadfield, 'Historical Writing, 1550–1660', in Raymond Gillespie and Andrew Hadfield (eds.), *The Oxford History of the Irish Book*, iii. *The Irish Book in English, 1550–1800* (Oxford: Oxford University Press, 2006), pp. 250–63, at pp. 255–60; Richard A. McCabe, *Spenser's Monstrous Regiment: Elizabethan Ireland and the Poetics of Difference* (Oxford: Oxford University Press, 2002), pp. 273–6; Bart Van Es, *Spenser's Forms of History* (Oxford: Oxford University Press, 2002), pp. 78–85. For more traditional views of how and why Ware altered a *View*, see Ciaran Brady, 'Spenser's Irish Crisis: Humanism and Experience in the 1590s', *P&P* 111 (1986), 17–49, at 25; David J. Baker, *Between Nations: Shakespeare, Spenser, Marvell, and the Question of Britain* (Stanford: Stanford University Press, 1997), pp. 120–3.

65. For details of Ussher's life and thought, see R. Buick Knox, *James Ussher, Archbishop of Armagh* (Cardiff: University of Wales Press, 1967); Jack Cunningham, *James Ussher and John Bramhall: The Theology and Politics of Two Irish Ecclesiastics of the Seventeenth Century* (Aldershot: Ashgate, 2007); Alan Ford, *James Ussher: Theology, History and Politics in Early-Modern Ireland and England* (Oxford: Oxford University Press, 2007). On Spenser and Arland Ussher, see pp. 192–3.

66. *Spenser Allusions*, pp. 226–7. Davenant claimed to be Shakespeare's illegitimate son: see S. Schoenbaum, *William Shakespeare: A Compact Documentary Life* (New York: Oxford University Press, 1977), pp. 224–7.

67. See the *ODNB* entries by W. H. Kelliher and Wilfrid Prest.

68. W. H. Welply, 'Some Spenser Problems', *N&Q* 180 (1941), 56–9, 74–6, 92–5, 104, 151, 224, 248, 436–9, 454–9, at 56.

69. Calton Younger, *Ireland's Civil War* (London: Muller, 1968), pp. 321–6. Welply notes at the end of one of his early articles, 'Final note—Most, if not all, of the documents cited as being in the Public Record Office, Dublin, no longer exist, having been burned in the recent destruction of the Four Courts' ('The Family and Descendants of Edmund Spenser', *JCHAS*, 2nd ser. 28 (1922), 22–34, 49–61, at 59).

70. See e.g. F. I. Carpenter, 'The Marriages of Edmund Spenser', *MP* 22 (1924), 97–8; Mark Eccles, 'Spenser's First Marriage', *TLS*, 31 Dec. 1931, p. 1053; Douglas Hamer, 'Spenser's Marriage', *RES* 27 (1931), 271–90; Raymond Jenkins, 'Spenser and the Clerkship in Munster', *PMLA* 47 (1932), 109–21; Raymond Jenkins, '*Newes out of Munster*, a Document in Spenser's Hand', *SP* 32

(1935), 125–30; A. C. Judson, 'Two Spenser Leases', *MLQ* 5 (1944), 143–7; Lee Piepho, '*The Shepheardes Calender* and Neo-Latin Pastoral: A Book Newly Discovered to Have Been Owned by Spenser', *Sp. St.* 16 (2002), 17–86; Lee Piepho, 'Edmund Spenser and Neo-Latin Literature: An Autograph Manuscript on Petrus Lotichius and His Poetry', *SP* 100 (2003), 123–34; Heffner, 'Spenser's Family'.

71. See the discussion in Robert D. Hume, *Reconstructing Contexts: The Aims and Principles of Archaeo-Historicism* (Oxford: Oxford University Press, 1999).

72. See Quentin Skinner, *Visions of Politics*, 3 vols. (Cambridge: Cambridge University Press, 2002), i. *Regarding Method*, in particular, chs. 5–7.

73. Jacques Derrida, 'Structure, Sign and Play in the Discourse of the Human Sciences', in *Writing and Difference*, trans. Alan Bass (London: Routledge, 1981), pp. 278–93.

74. See e.g. Beverley Southgate, *Postmodernism in History: Fear or Freedom* (London: Routledge, 2003), pt. 2; Alun Munslow, 'Biography and History: Criticism, Theory, Practice', in Alexander Lyon Macfie (ed.), *The Philosophy of History: Talks Given at the Institute of Historical Research, London, 2000–2006* (Basingstoke: Palgrave, 2000), pp. 226–36.

75. Frank Ankersmit, *Sublime Historical Experience* (Stanford: Stanford University Press, 2005), pp. 251–7, 275–80, *passim*; Marshall Sahlins, *Apologies to Thucydides: Understanding History as Culture and Vice Versa* (Chicago: University of Chicago Press, 2004).

76. See J. A. Downie, 'Marlowe, May 1593, and the "Must-Have" Theory of Biography', *RES* 58 (2007), 245–67, at 245. I am grateful to Ros Barber for bringing this article to my attention. See also Lukas Erne, 'Biography, Mythography and Criticism: The Life and Work of Christopher Marlowe', *MP* 103 (2005), 28–50.

77. For reflections on this problem, see Judith P. Zinsser, 'A Prologue for La Dame d'Esprit: The Biography of the Marquise Du Châtelet', in Alun Munslow and Robert A. Rosenstein (eds.), *Experiments in Rethinking History* (London: Routledge, 2004), pp. 195–208; Ray Monk, 'Getting Inside Heisenberg's Head', in Macfie (ed.), *Philosophy of History*, pp. 237–52; Mark Roseman, 'Surviving Memory: Truth and Inaccuracy in Holocaust Testimony', in Robert Perks and Alistair Thomson (eds.), *The Oral History Reader* (London: Routledge, 2nd edn., 2006), pp. 230–43.

78. Natalie Zemon Davis, *Trickster Travels: In Search of Leo Africanus, a Sixteenth-Century Muslim Between Worlds* (London: Faber, 2006), p. 13.

79. Downie has in mind such works as Charles Nicholl, *The Reckoning: The Murder of Christopher Marlowe* (London: Cape, 1992), and David Riggs, *The World of Christopher Marlowe* (London: Faber, 2004), ch. 15.

80. Fernand Braudel, *The Mediterranean and the Mediterranean World in the Age of Philip II*, trans. Siân Reynolds, 2 vols. (London: Collins, 1972).

81. On the Ottoman Empire and its presence in Europe, especially Britain, see Nabil Matar, *Islam in Britain, 1558–1685* (Cambridge: Cambridge University Press, 1998). For one series of approaches to the complexities of the Mediterranean world, see Matthew Dimmock and Andrew Hadfield (eds.), *Religions of the Book: Co-existence and Conflict, 1400–1660* (Basingstoke: Palgrave, 2008).

82. Recent overviews of Spenser's life includes: Ruth Mohl, 'Spenser, Edmund', in *Sp. Enc.*, pp. 668–71; Richard Rambuss, 'Spenser's Life and Career', in Andrew Hadfield (ed.), *The Cambridge Companion to Spenser* (Cambridge: Cambridge University Press, 2001), pp. 13–36; Andrew Hadfield, 'Spenser, Edmund', *ODNB* entry; Patrick Cheney, 'Life', in Bart Van Es (ed.), *A Critical Companion to Spenser Studies* (Basingstoke: Palgrave, 2006), pp. 18–41.

83. See Andrew Hadfield and Willy Maley, 'Introduction: Irish Representations and English Alternatives', in Brendan Bradshaw, Andrew Hadfield, and Willy Maley (eds.), *Representing Ireland: Literature and the Origins of Conflict, 1534–1660* (Cambridge: Cambridge University Press, 1993), pp. 1–23, at pp. 10–11.

84. The literature on this subject is now voluminous: for recent comment, see Thomas Herron, *Spenser's Irish Work: Poetry, Plantation and Colonial Reformation* (Aldershot: Ashgate, 2007).

85. On Spenser's literary heritage, see Wells (ed.), *Spenser Allusions*; Radcliffe, *Spenser: A Reception History*. On his impact on 17th-century identities, see Nicholas P. Canny, 'Edmund Spenser and

the Development of an Anglo-Irish Identity', *YES* 13 (1983), 1–19; Nicholas P. Canny, *Making Ireland British, 1580–1650* (Oxford: Oxford University Press, 2001), ch. 1, 'Spenser Sets the Agenda'; John Kerrigan, *Archipelagic English: Literature, History, and Politics, 1603–1707* (Oxford: Oxford University Press, 2008), pp. 3, 39, 45, *passim*.

86. For recent overviews, see Patrick Cheney, 'Life'; Rambuss, 'Spenser's Life and Career'.

87. See e.g. Park Honan, *Christopher Marlowe: Poet and Spy* (Oxford: Oxford University Press, 2005); Campbell and Corns, *Milton* (Oxford: Oxford University Press, 2008); John Stubbs, *Donne: The Reformed Soul* (London: Viking, 2006); Susanne Woods, *Lanyer: A Renaissance Woman Poet* (New York: Oxford University Press, 1999); Alan Haynes, *Walsingham: Elizabethan Spymaster & Statesman* (Stroud: Sutton, 2004); Peter C. Mancall, *Hakluyt's Promises: An Elizabethan's Obsession for an English America* (New Haven: Yale University Press, 2007); Mary S. Lovell, *Bess of Hardwick: First Lady of Chatsworth* (London: Abacus, 2006).

88. Judson's work was not always greeted enthusiastically by reviewers, principally because they felt that the life had not been defined clearly enough: W. L. Renwick felt that the portrait of an 'ambitious thruster' was inaccurate and this was not helped because Spenser 'is surrounded with very flat and faint shadows of his friends and associates' (*RES* 25 (1949), 261–2); B. E. C. Davis admitted that 'It is truly astonishing that no full-length life of Spenser should have appeared since the publication of Grosart's edition in 1884', but felt that, even so, 'There is still room for a full-length life of Spenser, historical and critical' (*MLR* 42 (1947), 494–5); the eminent historian Conyers Read was far more dismissive and asserted that Judson 'has given us neither a clear picture of Spenser nor a clear picture of the Elizabethan court circles nor anything approaching a clear picture of Munster' (*American Historical Review* 51 (1946), 538–9).

89. For comment, see Richard Rambuss, 'Spenser's Lives, Spenser's Careers', in Judith H. Anderson, Donald Cheney and David A. Richardson (eds.), *Spenser's Life and the Subject of Biography* (Amherst: University of Massachusetts Press, 1996), pp. 1–17, at p. 16; Gary Waller, *Edmund Spenser: A Literary Life* (Basingstoke: Palgrave, 1994), p. 25.

90. But see Patrick Cheney, 'Biographical Representations: Marlowe's Life of the Author', in Takashi Kozuka and J. R. Mulryne (eds.), *Shakespeare, Marlowe, Jonson: New Directions in Biography* (Aldershot: Ashgate, 2006), pp. 183–204, which makes a vigorous case that Marlowe's characters are often versions of the author.

91. This last section revises Hadfield, 'Secrets and Lies', p. 60.

92. A useful list of problems, some of which have not yet been solved, is given in Frederick Ives Carpenter, 'Desiderata in the Study of Spenser', *SP* 19 (1922), 238–43.

93. The most comprehensive recent overview is David Cressy, *Birth, Marriage & Death: Ritual, Religion, and the Life-Cycle in Tudor and Stuart England* (Oxford: Oxford University Press, 1997).

94. Fernand Braudel, *Civilization & Capitalism, 15th–18th. Century*, trans. Siân Reynolds, 3 vols. (London: Collins, 1981), i. 90; Sara Mendelson and Patricia Crawford, *Women in Early Modern England* (Oxford: Oxford University Press, 1998), pp. 194–200.

95. Lena Cowen Orlin, *Locating Privacy in Tudor London* (Oxford: Oxford University Press, 2007); Alan Stewart, *Close Readers: Humanism and Sodomy in Early Modern England* (Princeton: Princeton University Press, 1997), ch. 5.

96. Hadfield, ' "Secrets and Lies" ', p. 61. Alexandra Shepard, *Meanings of Manhood in Early Modern England* (Oxford: Oxford University Press, 2003), pp. 121–2. For a discussion of the Harvey–Spenser letters in the light of such issues, see Jonathan Goldberg, *Sodometries: Renaissance Texts, Modern Sexualities* (Stanford: Stanford University Press, 1992), pp. 63–101.

97. The literature on this subject is vast. For seminal discussions, see Lawrence Stone, *The Family, Sex and Marriage in England, 1500–1800* (London: Weidenfeld and Nicolson, 1977); Keith Wrightson, *English Society, 1580–1680* (London: Hutchinson, 1982), chs. 3–4. For a succinct overview, see Susan Brigden, *New Worlds, Lost Worlds: The Rule of the Tudors, 1485–1603* (London: Penguin, 2000), ch. 3.

98. Walter J. Ong, 'Latin Language Study as a Renaissance Puberty Rite', *SP* 56 (1959), 103–24.

99. See David Cressy, *Education in Tudor and Stuart England* (London: Arnold, 1975); Kenneth Charlton, *Education in Renaissance England* (London: Routledge, 1975); Helen M. Jewell, *Education in Early Modern England* (Basingstoke: Palgrave, 1998); T. W. Baldwin, *William Shakspere's Small Latine an Lesse Greeke*, 2 vols. (Urbana: University of Illinois Press, 1944); Juan Luis Vives, *Tudor School-Boy Life: The Dialogues of Juan Luis Vives* (1908; London: Frank Cass, 1970).

100. On the first issue, see Hume, *Reconstructing Contexts*, pp. 41, 47; on the second, see Andrew Hadfield (ed.), *Were Early Modern Lives Different?* (special issue), *Textual Practice* 23/2 (Apr. 2009).

101. See Francis Barker, *The Tremulous Private Body: Essays on Subjection* (London: Methuen, 1984); Catherine Belsey, *The Subject of Tragedy: Identity and Difference in Renaissance Drama* (London: Methuen, 1985). For a critical evaluation of such arguments, see David Aers, 'A Whisper in the Ear of Early Modernists; or, Reflections on Literary Critics Writing the "History of the Subject"', in David Aers (ed.), *Culture and History, 1350–1600: Essays on English Communities, Identities and Writing* (Hemel Hempstead, 1992), pp. 177–202; John Jeffries Martin, *Myths of Renaissance Individualism* (Basingstoke: Palgrave, 2004).

102. Stephen Greenblatt, 'Psychoanalysis and Renaissance Culture', in Patricia Parker and David Quint (eds.), *Literary Theory/Renaissance Texts* (Baltimore: Johns Hopkins University Press, 1986), pp. 210–24.

103. Natalie Zemon Davis, *The Return of Martin Guerre* (Cambridge, MA: Harvard University Press, 1983), pp. 21, 41, 44, 56.

104. Ibid. 83–4.

105. F. G. Emmison, *Elizabethan Life: Home, Work and Land* (Chelmsford: Essex County Council, 1976); Lawrence Stone, *The Crisis of the Aristocracy, 1558–1641* (rev. edn., Oxford: Clarendon Press, 1979); Helen Castor, *Blood and Roses: The Paston Family in the Fifteenth Century* (London: Faber, 2005); Craig Muldrew, *The Economy of Obligation: The Culture of Credit and Social Relations in Early Modern England* (Basingstoke: Palgrave, 1998).

106. *Le Retour de Martin Guerre*, dir. Martin Vigne (1982); *Sommersby*, dir. Jon Amiel (1993).

107. For a brief overview, see Debora Shuger, 'Life-Writing in Seventeenth-Century England', in Patrick Coleman, Jayne Lewis, and Jill Kowalik (eds.), *Representations of the Self from the Renaissance to Romanticism* (Cambridge: Cambridge University Press, 2000), pp. 63–78.

108. *The Autobiography of Thomas Whythorne*, ed. James M. Osborn (London: Oxford University Press, 1962); Andrew Mousley, 'Renaissance Selves and Life Writing: The Autobiography of Thomas Whythorne', *Forum for Modern Language Studies* 26 (1990), 222–30; Ronald Bedford, Lloyd Davis, and Philippa Kelly, *Early Modern English Lives, Autobiography and Self-Representation, 1500–1600* (Aldershot: Ashgate, 2007), pp. 15–21.

109. *The Diaries of Lady Anne Clifford*, ed. D. J. H. Clifford (Stroud: Sutton, 2003); Lucy Hutchinson, *Memoirs of the Life of Colonel Hutchinson: With a Fragment of Autobiography of Mrs Hutchinson*, ed. N. H. Keeble (London: Dent, 1995); Margaret Cavendish, *The Life of William Cavendish, Duke of Newcastle*, ed. C. H. Firth (2nd edn., London: Routledge, 1906); *The Memoirs of Anne, Lady Halkett and Ann, Lady Fanshawe*, ed. John Loftis (Oxford: Clarendon Press, 1979).

Chapter 1

1. Spenser, *Shorter Poems*, p. 424.

2. *Amoretti*, ed. Larsen, pp. 207–8.

3. Harvey had complained of Spenser's ignorance of astronomy in his copy of Dionysius Periegetes, *Surveye if the World* (1572): 'Pudet ipsum Spenserum, esti Sphaerae, astrolabiique non plane ignarum; suae in astronomicis Canonibus, tabulis, instrumentisque imperitiae' ('It is a shame that Spenser himself, while not entirely unaware of the Sphere [either a globe, or spherical map of the heavens] and the astrolabe, was unaware of his ignorance of astronomical principles, tables and instruments') (Harvey, *Marginalia*, p. 162) (I am extremely grateful to Norman Vance for help with this translation). Either Spenser had improved his knowledge by 1590 or Harvey was joking (*Amoretti*, ed. Larsen, p. 189); Stephen A. Barney, 'Reference Works, Spenser's', *Sp. Enc.*, pp. 590–3, at p. 592.

431

4. *Amoretti*, ed. Larsen, p. 189.
5. Welply, 'Edmund Spenser', pp. 165–6; *Chronology*, pp. 61–2; Jean R. Brink, 'Revising Spenser's Birth Date to 1554', *N&Q* 56 (2009), 523–7.
6. *Amoretti*, ed. Larsen, pp. 3–4. Pope Gregory XIII issued a papal bull on 24 Apr. 1582, decreeing that Catholic countries would adopt the Gregorian calendar which corrected the errors of the Julian calendar by omitting 10 days, and altering the rules for leap years. England, like most Protestant countries, preserved the Julian calendar so that Europe was now divided by time as well as religion. Spenser's mentor, Gabriel Harvey, was especially interested in calendars and almanacs, as his brothers, John and Richard, each wrote astrological discourses, works that Thomas Nashe ridiculed in their controversy. For comment on the astute awareness of time and dating in the late 16th century, and precedents for Spenser's keen interest, see Steve Sohmer, *Shakespeare's Mystery Play: The Opening of the Globe Theatre, 1599* (Manchester: Manchester University Press, 1999), pp. 17–24, *passim*; Anne Lake Prescott, 'The Thirsty Deer and the Lord of Life: Some Contexts for *Amoretti* 67–70', *Sp. St.* 6 (1985), 33–76. On the Harvey brothers, see Bernard Capp, *Astrology & The Popular Press: English Almanacs, 1500–1800* (London: Faber, 1979), p. 46, *passim*; Virginia F. Stern, *Gabriel Harvey: A Study of His Life, Marginalia, and Library* (Oxford: Clarendon Press, 1979), pp. 70–2, 91–2, *passim*; Nashe, *Works*, i. 167, iii. 72.
7. *Amoretti*, ed. Larsen, p. 190.
8. The New Year started on 25 March until England switched to the Gregorian calendar in 1752.
9. On Spenser's interest in numbers, see especially A. Kent Hieatt, *Short Time's Endless Monument: The Symbolism of the Numbers in Edmund Spenser's 'Epithalamion'* (New York: Columbia University Press, 1960); Alexander Dunlop, 'Calendar Symbolism in the "Amoretti"', *N&Q* 214 (1969), 24–6. More generally, see Tom W. N. Parker, *Proportional Form in the Sonnets of the Sidney Circle: Loving in Truth* (Oxford: Clarendon Press, 1998).
10. For a claim that Spenser was born in 1550, see Percy W. Long, 'Spenser's Birth Date', *MLN* 31 (1916), 178–80.
11. *Chronology*, p. 68.
12. John Stow locates the source in 'a village called *Winchcombe* in *Oxford*' (*A Survey of London*, ed. Charles Lethbridge Kingsford, 2 vols. (1908; Oxford: Clarendon Press, 2000), i. 11; William Harrison admits that the source has been disputed but feels able to solve the mystery: 'this famous streame hath his head or beginning out of the side of an hill, standing on the plaines of Cotswold, about one mile from Tetburie' ('An Historicall description of the Iland of Britaine', in Raphael Holinshed, *Chronicles of England, Scotland and Ireland*, 3 vols. (London, 1587), i. 45). See also William Camden, *Britain, or A chorographicall description of the most flourishing kingdomes, England, Scotland, and Ireland, and the ilands adioyning*, trans. Philemon Holland (London, 1610), p. 241.
13. See W. H. Herendeen, 'Rivers', *Sp. Enc.*, pp. 606–9; Alistair Fowler, *Spenser and the Numbers of Time* (London: Routledge, 1964), ch. 11; P. W. Joyce, 'Spenser's Irish Rivers', in *The Wonders of Ireland and Other Papers on Irish Subjects* (Dublin: Longman, 1911), pp. 72–114.
14. See F. C. Spenser, 'Locality of the Family of Edmund Spenser', *Gentleman's Magazine*, NS 18 (1842), 138–43, at 138; William Dugdale, *Antiquities of Warwickshire, illustrated from records, leiger-books, manuscripts, charters, evidences, tombes, and armes: Illustrated* (London: 1656), pp. 404–5, *passim*. On Althorp, see J. Alfred Gotch, *The Old Halls & Manor-Houses of Northamptonshire* (London: Batsford, 1936), pp. 68–71; John M. Steane, *The Northamptonshire Landscape: Northamptonshire and the Soke of Peterborough* (London: Hodder and Stoughton, 1974), p. 187. On Wormleighton, see Geoffrey Tyack, *Warwickshire Country Houses* (Chichester: Phillimore, 1994), pp. 273–4; Mary Dormer Harris, *Unknown Warwickshire* (London: John Lane, 1924), pp. 82–8.
15. Jeremy Wheeler, *Where Sheep Safely Graze: 1000 Years of Worship, 1000 Years of History: A Short History and Description of The Village of Wormleighton and the Church of St. Peter* (Wormleighton: Wormleighton PCC, 2011), p. 43.
16. Spenser, *Shorter Poems*, p. 234.
17. Ibid. 190.
18. See the *ODNB* entries on Alice Spenser (Louis A. Knalfa), Ferdinando Stanley (David Kathman), and Anne Clifford (Richard T. Spence); Campbell and Corns, *Milton*, p. 69; Cedric C.

Brown, *John Milton's Aristocratic Entertainments* (Cambridge: Cambridge University Press, 1985), pp. 13–26, 41–56. On Egerton, see pp. 336–8, 349.

19. Spenser, *Shorter Poems*, p. 290.

20. Studies of female patronage in early modern England are now legion: see Mendelson and Crawford, *Women in Early Modern England*, pp. 365–79; Jacqueline Pearson, 'Women Writers and Women Readers: The Case of Aemilia Lanier', in Kate Chedgzoy, Melanie Hansen, and Suzanne Trill (eds.), *Voicing Women: Gender and Sexuality in Early Modern Writing* (Keele: Keele University Press, 1996), pp. 45–54, at pp. 49–50. On Spenser's pursuit of female patronage elsewhere, see Ernest A. Strathmann, 'Lady Carey and Spenser', *ELH* 2 (1935), 33–57; Jon A. Quitslund, 'Spenser and the Patronesses of the *Fowre Hymnes*: "Ornaments of All True Love and Beautie"', in Margaret Hannay (ed.), *Silent but for the Word: Tudor Women as Patrons, Translators, and Writers of Religious Works* (Kent: Kent State University Press, 1985), pp. 184–202.

21. 'Edmund Spenser's Family: Two Notes and a Query', *N&Q* 44 (1997), 49–51, at 50.

22. Alan G. R. Smith, *Servant of the Cecils: The Life of Sir Michael Hickes* (London: Cape, 1977), p. 156.

23. See p. 267.

24. See e.g. the researches of Margaret Russell, countess of Cumberland (1560–1616), dedicatee of *Fowre Hymnes* (1596) and mother of Anne Clifford (1590–1676), who commissioned Spenser's funeral monument in 1620: Richard T. Spence, *Lady Anne Clifford: Countess of Pembroke, Dorset and Montgomery (1590–1676)* (Stroud: Sutton, 1997), pp. 164–8, *passim*.

25. J. Horace Round, *Studies in Peerage and Family History* (London: Constable, 1901), p. 281; Mary E. Finch, *The Wealth of Five Northamptonshire Families, 1540–1640* (Oxford: Northamptonshire Record Society, 1956), ch. 3.

26. On the continued rise of the Spencers in the early 17th century, see Linda Levy Peck, *Consuming Splendor: Society and Culture in Seventeenth-Century England* (Cambridge: Cambridge University Press, 2005), pp. 25–30.

27. Round, *Studies in Peerage*, pp. 289–90, 293; J. Horace Round, *Peerage and Pedigree: Studies in Peerage Law and Family History* (1910; London: Woburn, 1971), p. 188; Georgina Battiscombe, *The Spencers of Althorp* (London: Constable, 1984), p. 11.

28. Carpenter, *Reference Guide*, pp. 77–8; Carpenter, 'Marriages of Edmund Spenser'; Welply, 'Spenser: Recent Researches', p. 129; Douglas Hamer, 'Edmund Spenser: Some Further Notes', *N&Q* 162 (1932), 380–4, at 380; Mark Eccles, 'Elizabethan Edmund Spensers', *MLQ* 5 (1944), 413–27; Round, *Studies in Peerage*, p. 323.

29. The theory was most vociferously proposed by Grosart (see Appendix 1, p. 424), but was effectively demolished by W. H. Welply and Douglas Hamer: see e.g. Hamer, 'Spenser: Further Notes', pp. 380–1.

30. W. H. Welply, 'Edmund Spenser: Some New Discoveries and the Correction of Some Old Errors', *N&Q* 146 (1924), 445–7, at 446; 147 (1924), 35. For more details of the will, the legal dispute it generated, and its implications, see pp. 343–9.

31. Pauline Henley, *Spenser in Ireland* (Cork: Cork University Press, 1928), pp. 78–9. On the Spencers of Althorp, see Judson, *Life*, ch. 1. On marriages and family connections, see Stone, *Crisis*, ch. 11; Greer, *Shakespeare's Wife*, 67–8, *passim*.

32. Welply, 'Spenser: Recent Researches', p. 447; James Anderson Winn, *John Dryden and His World* (New Haven: Yale University Press, 1987), p. 4. On Canons Ashby, see Gotch, *Old Halls & Manor-Houses of Northamptonshire*, pp. 84–6.

33. Welply, 'Spenser: Recent Researches', p. 185.

34. Judson, *Life*, pp. 8–9.

35. Retha M. Warnicke, *William Lambarde: Elizabethan Antiquary, 1536–1601* (Chichester: Phillimore, 1973), p. 1.

36. A. S. W. Clifton, 'Edmund Spenser, His Connection with Northants', *N&Q* 154 (1928), 195.

37. Welply, 'Spenser: Recent Researches', p. 130; Brink, 'Spenser's Family', pp. 49–50.

38. Welply, 'Spenser: Recent Researches', p. 130, is dismissive. Maley, *Chronology*, p. 4, speculates that this John Spenser may have been Edmund's brother, as there was a John Spenser who

served as constable of Limerick in 1579. Maley also speculates that a James Spenser who worked in Ireland in the 1570s and 1580s may have been a relative, even a brother (*Chronology*, pp. 10, 38), but the name was common in the period and there is no useful evidence that makes either John or James a likely relative of the poet.

39. The marriage is well known: see Craik, *Spenser and His Poetry*, p. 250; H. J. S., 'Spenser and Travers', *N&Q*, 3rd ser. 4 (1863), 373; Welply, 'Spenser: Recent Researches', p. 130; W. H. Welply, 'Edmund Spenser's Brother-in-law, John Travers', *N&Q*, 179 (1940), 70–8, 92–7, 112–15.

40. Welply, 'Spenser's Brother-in-law, John Travers', p. 76. On Sylvanus Spenser, see pp. 408–9.

41. Welply, 'Spenser's Brother-in-law, John Travers', p. 93.

42. Ibid. 92.

43. John J. Fitzgerald, 'Documents Found at Castlewhite, Co. Cork', *JRSAI*, 6th ser. 20 (1930), 79–83, at 79.

44. Welply, 'Spenser's Brother-in-law, John Travers', p. 113.

45. Judson, *Life*, pp. 130–1; Henley, *Spenser in Ireland*, pp. 72–3; Welply, 'Spenser's Brother-in-law, John Travers', p. 95.

46. George Vertue, *Notebooks*, ed. K. Esdaile, earl of Ilchester and H. M. Hake, 6 vols., *Walpole Society* 18, 20, 22, 24, 26, 30 (1930–55), at 26. 99. On the portrait, see Appendix 2, pp. 413–14.

47. Vertue, *Notebooks*, 30. 193; 20. 79; Judson, 'Eighteenth-Century Lives', pp. 166–7. On Oldys and Winstanley, see the *ODNB* lives by Paul Baines and William E. Burns.

48. Henry A. Harber, *A Dictionary of London* (London: Jenkins, 1918), pp. 213–14.

49. Stow, *Survey*, i. 120–1.

50. Ian Grainger and Christopher Phillpotts, *The Royal Navy Victualling Yard, East Smithfield, London* (London: Museum of London, 2010), pp. 2, 9.

51. Ibid. 33.

52. Stow, *Survey*, i. 124; Ian Grainger, Duncan Hawkins, Lynne Coral, and Richard Mikulski, *The Black Death Cemetery, East Smithfield, London* (London: Museum of London, 2008), p. 10.

53. Andrew Pettegree, *Foreign Protestant Communities in Sixteenth-Century London* (Oxford: Clarendon Press, 1986), p. 18.

54. Pettegree, *Foreign Protestant Communities*, p. 108; Lien Bich Luu, *Immigrants and the Industries of London, 1500–1700* (Aldershot: Ashgate, 2005), ch. 4.

55. Pettegree, *Foreign Protestant Communities*, p. 21.

56. A useful, but rather fanciful, account of Spenser's journey to school is provided in Donald Bruce, 'Edmund Spenser: The Boyhood of a Poet', http://findarticles.com/p/articles/mi_m2242/is_n1537_v264/ai_15295932/pg_7/?tag=content;col1 (accessed 19 Feb. 2012). See also Walter Thornbury, *Old and New London: A Narration of Its People, and Its Places*, 2 vols. (London: Cassell 1879), ii. 28–41.

57. Fuller, *Worthies*, p. 367.

58. On grammar schools see Charlton, *Education in Renaissance England*, ch. 4; Jewell, *Education in Early Modern England*, pp. 80–3, 99–102. Invaluable details of the specific charters and practices of each grammar school are provided in Nicholas Carlisle, *A Concise Description of the Endowed Grammar Schools in England and Wales*, 2 vols. (London, 1818).

59. Carlisle, *Endowed Grammar Schools*, i. 49; F. W. M. Draper, *Four Centuries of Merchant Taylors' School, 1561–1961* (London: Oxford University Press, 1962), p. 1.

60. 'Ordinance Book, 1561–1667', London Metropolitan Archives, Merchants Taylors' School Records, MS 34270, p. 82.

61. Carlisle, *Endowed Grammar Schools*, i. 49; Stow, *Survey*, i. 237. The School statutes exist in the 'Ordinance Book', Merchants Taylors' School Records.

62. E. P. Hart (ed.), *Merchant Taylors' School Register*, 2 vols. (London: Merchant Taylors' Company, 1936); Rebekah Owens, 'The Career of Thomas Kyd Relating to His Attendance at Merchant Taylors' School', *N&Q* 254 (2009), 35–6; Mildred Campbell, *The English Yeoman under Elizabeth and the Early Stuarts* (1942; London: Merlin, 1960), p. 271.

63. 'Ordinance Book', Merchant Taylors' School Records.

64. On citizenship and London identity, see Philip Withington, *The Politics of Commonwealth: Citizens and Freemen in Early Modern England* (Cambridge: Cambridge University Press, 2005), pp. 10–15, *passim*; Mark Goldie, 'The Unacknowledged Republic: Officeholding in Early Modern England', in Tim Harris (ed.), *The Politics of the Excluded, c.1500–1850* (Basingstoke: Palgrave, 2001), pp. 153–94; Tracey Hill, *Pageantry and Power: A Cultural History of the Early Modern Lord Mayor's Show, 1585–1639* (Manchester: Manchester University Press, 2010), ch. 1.

65. On literature in the London merchant culture, see Ceri Sullivan, 'London's Early Modern Creative Industrialists', *SP* 103 (2006), 313–28. The article points out how many members of the Merchant Taylors' Company were involved in literary projects.

66. Lawrence Manley, *Literature and Culture in Early Modern London* (Cambridge: Cambridge University Press, 1995), ch 4. See pp. 303–5, 357–60.

67. On Spenser as a court poet see Stegner, 'Spenser's Biographers', *Sp. Handbook*, pp. 125–45, at p. 128.

68. Stow, *Survey*, i. 129–32; *The Map of Early Modern London*, http://mapoflondon.uvic.ca/render_page.php?id=TOWE3 (accessed 17 Mar. 2009).

69. Bruce, 'Spenser: Boyhood'.

70. Steve Rappaport, *Worlds Within Worlds: Structures of Life in Sixteenth-Century London* (Cambridge: Cambridge University Press, 1989), pp. 61–86; Ian W. Archer, *The Pursuit of Stability: Social Relations in Elizabethan London* (Cambridge: Cambridge University Press, 1991); John Pound, *Poverty and Vagrancy in Tudor England* (Harlow: Longman, 1971), *passim*; A. L. Beier, *Masterless Men: The Vagrancy Problem in England, 1560–1640* (London: Methuen, 1985), *passim*. On the population of England, see E. A. Wrigley and R. S. Schofield, *The Population History of England, 1541–1871* (1989; Cambridge: Cambridge University Press, 2002), p. 575.

71. Luu, *Immigrants*, ch. 2.

72. Paul Griffiths, *Lost Londons: Change, Crime and Control in the Capital City, 1550–1660* (Cambridge: Cambridge University Press, 2008), pp. 1–3.

73. On the influx of Dutch settlers and refugees into England in the 16th century, and their economic and cultural impact, see W. J. B. Pienaar, *English Influences in Dutch Literature and Justus Van Edden as Intermediary: An Aspect of Eighteenth-Century Achievement* (Cambridge: Cambridge University Press, 1929), pp. 8–12.

74. Luu, *Immigrants*, p. 4; Stephen Porter, *Shakespeare's London: Everyday Life in London, 1580–1616* (Stroud: Amberley, 2009), ch. 2.

75. Alan R. H. Baker, 'Changes in the Later Middle Ages', in Darby (ed.), *New Historical Geography of England*, pp. 186–247, at p. 244.

76. Bruce, 'Spenser: Boyhood'.

77. Nicholas Pevsner, *The Buildings of England: London*, i. *The Cities of London & Westminster* (Harmondsworth: Penguin, 1957), p. 33.

78. Cressy, *Education in Tudor and Stuart England*, pp. 71–2.

79. See William Kempe, *The Education of Children in learning declared by the dignitie, vtilitie, and method thereof. Meete to be knowne, and practised aswell of parents as schoolmaisters* (London, 1588), sig. F2ᵛ. I owe this reference to Sean B. Palmer. On 'petty schools', see Jewell, *Education in Early Modern England*, pp. 27–8; Singman, *Daily Life in Elizabethan England*, p. 42. Richard Mulcaster was a noted enthusiast for pre-school education and worries about the problem of the age at which children should start school in his educational treatises: Richard De Molen, *Richard Mulcaster (c.1531–1611) and Educational Reform in the Renaissance* (Nieuwkoop: De Graaf, 1991), pp. 54–5; Richard Mulcaster, *Positions, wherein those primitive circumstances be examined, which are necessarie for the training vp of children* (London, 1581), ed. Robert Herbert Quick (London: Longman, 1881), pp. 17–24, 222, 256.

80. Jewell, *Education in Early Modern England*, pp. 94–5.

81. Stephen K. Galbraith, 'Edmund Spenser and the History of the Book, 1569–1679', unpublished PhD dissertation, Ohio State University, 2006, p. 11. Galbraith's account of Spenser's education in terms of his exposure to typeface is excellent and I am grateful to Dr Galbraith for sharing his work with me in advance of publication and for many illuminating conversations.

82. Carlisle, *Endowed Grammar Schools*, i. 55; see also Wilson, *History of the Merchant Taylors' School*, pp. 11–21.
83. Carlisle, *Endowed Grammar Schools*, i. 75, 418, 425. On Colet, see the *ODNB* entry by J. B. Trapp; comments from Douglas Gray, *Later Medieval English Literature* (Oxford: Oxford University Press, 2008), p. 85. On the importance of grammar schools in 16th-century England, see J. W. Binns, *Intellectual Culture in Elizabethan and Jacobean England: The Latin Writings of the Age* (Leeds: Francis Cairns, 1990), p. 4.
84. Peter Mack, *A History of Renaissance Rhetoric, 1380–1620* (Oxford: Oxford University Press, 2011), pp. 7, 80.
85. Carlisle, *Endowed Grammar Schools*, i. 101, 408, 425, 627. On Nowell, see the *ODNB* entry by Stanford Lehmberg; Draper, *Four Centuries of Merchant Taylors' School*, pp. 6, 13–14, *passim*; Mark Eccles, 'Brief Lives: Tudor and Stuart Authors', *SP* 79/4, Texts and Studies (Autumn 1982), 1–135, at 100–1.
86. Carlisle, *Endowed Grammar Schools*, i. 75.
87. Ibid. On candles, see Singman, *Daily Life in Elizabethan England*, p. 80.
88. Vives, *Tudor School-Boy Life*; Joel B. Altman, *The Tudor Play of Mind: Rhetorical Inquiry and the Development of Elizabethan Drama* (Berkeley and Los Angeles: University of California Press, 1978), ch. 1; Ronald Knowles, *Shakespeare's Arguments with History* (Basingstoke: Palgrave, 2002), ch. 1.
89. Stow, *Survey*, i. 74. On Stow's dedication to Spenser, see Barrett L. Beer, *Tudor England Observed: The World of John Stow* (Stroud: Sutton, 1998), p. 17.
90. Mulcaster, *Positions*, p. 185.
91. The best short outline is Peter Mack, *Elizabethan Rhetoric: Theory and Practice* (Cambridge: Cambridge University Press, 2002), ch. 1. See also Cressy, *Education in Tudor and Stuart England*, especially part 5, and the compendious Baldwin, *Shakspere's Small Latine*. On Spenser's use of what he would have learned at school in his poetry, see David Herbert Rix, *Rhetoric in Spenser's Poetry* (State College, PA: Pennsylvania State College, 1940).
92. William Lily, *A short introduction of grammar generallie to be vsed. Compiled and set forth, for the bringing vp of all those that intend to attaine the knovvledge of the Latine* tongue (London, 1557) (although there were numerous reprints throughout the 16th century); Carol V. Kaske, *Spenser and Biblical Poetics* (Ithaca, NY: Cornell University Press, 1999), pp. 9–11; Galbraith, 'Spenser and the History of the Book', p. 13.
93. Mack, *Elizabethan Rhetoric*, pp. 13–14; Cressy, *Education in Tudor and Stuart England*, pp. 83–4. See also Andrew Wallace, *Virgil's Schoolboys: The Poetics of Pedagogy in Renaissance England* (Oxford: Oxford University Press, 2010), p. 40.
94. Peter Mack, 'Spenser and Rhetoric', *Sp. Handbook*, pp. 420–36, at pp. 425–6; Lesley B. Cormack, 'Maps as Educational Tools in the Renaissance', in David Woodward. (ed.), *The History of Cartography*, iii. *Cartography in the European Renaissance* (Chicago: University of Chicago Press, 2007), pt. 1 pp. 622–36, at pp. 622–3.
95. Galbraith, 'Spenser and the History of the Book', p. 16; R. T. D. Sayle, 'Annals of the Merchant Taylors' School Library', *The Library*, 4th ser. 15 (1935), 457–80, at 459. On Spenser's use of such works throughout his career, see De Wilt T. Starnes and Ernest William Talbert, *Classical Myth and Legend in Renaissance Dictionaries: A Study of Renaissance Dictionaries in Relation to the Classical Learning of Contemporary English Writers* (Chapel Hill: North Carolina University Press, 1955), ch. 4. A catalogue of 1773 reveals many of the same books: London Metropolitan Archives, Merchants Taylors' School Records, MS 34334.
96. Cressy, *Education in Tudor and Stuart England*, pp. 24–5; Skinner, *Visions of Politics*, vol. ii, ch. 12; Quentin Skinner, *Reason and Rhetoric in the Philosophy of Thomas Hobbes* (Cambridge: Cambridge University Press, 1996), p. 288.
97. Riggs, *World of Christopher Marlowe*, ch. 3.
98. For discussion of Spenser as a secretary, see Richard Rambuss, *Spenser's Secret Career* (Cambridge: Cambridge University Press, 1993).
99. Elaine V. Beilin, *Redeeming Eve: Women Writers of the English Renaissance* (Princeton: Princeton University Press, 1987), pp. 11–14.
100. Hill, *Pageantry and Power*, pp. 36–7.

101. John Wesley, 'Mulcaster's Boys: Spenser, Andrewes, Kyd', unpublished dPhil thesis, University of St Andrews, 2008, p. 82; Mulcaster, *Positions*, p. 124.

102. Mulcaster, *Positions*, pp. 276–7. Other educationalists also argued for the importance of corporal punishment: see Kempe, *Education of children*, sig. H2^r; Ong, 'Latin Language Study', pp. 111–13. The most famous case of enthusiastic caning was that of Nicholas Udall (1504–56), headmaster of Eton: see the *ODNB* entry by Matthew Steggle.

103. Fuller, *Worthies*, p. 600.

104. Mulcaster, *Positions*, ch. 35.

105. Rebecca W. Bushnell, *A Culture of Teaching: Early Modern Humanism in Theory and Practice* (Ithaca, NY: Cornell University Press, 1996), pp. 25–6.

106. Barker, 'Mulcaster', *ODNB*.

107. Victor Morgan, with Christopher Brooke, *A History of the University of Cambridge*, ii. *1546–1750* (Cambridge: Cambridge University Press, 2004), pp. 6–7.

108. Thomas M. Greene, 'Antique world', *Sp. Enc.*, pp. 42–6.

109. I am especially grateful to Neil Rhodes for discussing Spenser's relationship to Greek with me.

110. Sir James Whitelock (1570–1632), later to be a prominent judge, writes of his gratitude to Mulcaster for teaching him Latin, Greek, and Hebrew at the school: James Oliphant (ed.), *The Educational Writings of Richard Mulcaster (1532–1611)* (Glasgow: MacLehose, 1903), p. xv; G. Lloyd Jones, *The Discovery of Hebrew in Tudor England: A Third Language* (Manchester: Manchester University Press, 1983), pp. 225–6, 230–2.

111. Wallace, *Virgil's Schoolboys*, pp. 18–34, 50–7.

112. De Molen, *Mulcaster*, p. 37. On Andrewes's acknowledgement of his debt to Mulcaster, see the *ODNB* entry by Peter E. McCullough, p. 1.

113. Richard Mulcaster, *The Passage of our Most Drad Soueraigne Lady Quene Elyzabeth through the citie of London to westminster the daye before her coronacion Anno 1558* (London, 1558); Gabriel Heaton, *Writing and Reading Royal Entertainments: From George Gascoigne to Ben Jonson* (Oxford: Oxford University Press, 2010), p. 92.

114. Alexander B. Grosart (ed.), *The Townley MSS: The Spending of the Money of Robert Nowell of Reade Hall, Lancashire: Brother of Dean Alexander Nowell, 1568–1580* (Manchester: privately printed, 1877), pp. 28–9. On the spelling of Downhall's name, see A. F. Pollard and Marjorie Blatcher, 'Hayward Townshend's Journals', *HR* 12 (1934), 1–31, at 21. I am especially grateful to Henry Woudhuysen, who has given me access to an unpublished paper of his on Robert Willis and Gregory Downhall.

115. *Alumni Oxonienses: The Members of Oxford University, 1500–1714*, ed. Joseph Foster, 2 vols. (Oxford: Parker and Co., 1891) i. 420.

116. Leslie Hotson, *Shakespeare's Sonnets Dated and Other Essays* (London: Hart-Davies, 1949), p. 208.

117. Downhall's relationship with one of his students, Richard Willis, is recorded in Willis's *Mount Tabor or Private Exercises of a Penitent Sinner* (London, 1639), pp. 97–105.

118. A. E. B. Coldiron, 'Watson's *Hekatompathia* and Renaissance Lyric Translation', *Translation and Literature* 5 (1996), 3–25.

119. T. E. Hartley (ed.), *Proceedings in the Parliament of Elizabeth I*, iii. *1593–1601* (Leicester: Leicester University Press, 1995), pp. 376–7.

120. Willis, *Mount Tabor*, p. 98.

121. R. C. Bald, *John Donne: A Life* (Oxford: Clarendon Press, 1970), p. 97. On Egerton and Puckering see p. 349.

122. *ODNB* entry on 'Sir John Bennett (1552/3–1627)' by Sheila Doyle; *House of Commons*, ii. 45–6.

123. Paul E. J. Hammer, *The Polarisation of Elizabethan Politics: The Political Career of Robert Devereux, 2nd Earl of Essex, 1585–1597* (Cambridge: Cambridge University Press, 1999), pp. 184, 278, 364; *House of Commons*, ii. 45.

124. Draper, *Four Centuries of Merchant Taylors' School*, ch. 1; De Molen, *Mulcaster*, p. 146; *ODNB* entry on Alexander Nowell; *Robert Nowell*, ed. Grosart. On the influence of Nowell's catechism, see William P. Haugaard, *Elizabeth and the English Reformation: The Struggle for a Stable Settlement of Religion* (Cambridge: Cambridge University Press, 1968), pp. 277–90; Norman Jones, *The English Reformation: Religion and Cultural Adaptation* (Oxford: Blackwell,

2002), p. 172. Nowell was also well known for having spoken too bluntly to the queen about the corrosive power of images and been publicly rebuked by her at court, an incident which took place in 1565 while Spenser was still at school: Peter E. McCullough, *Sermons at Court: Politics and Religion in Elizabethan and Jacobean Preaching* (Cambridge: Cambridge University Press, 1998), p. 47. Robert Nowell may have had a connection to the Dudley family and it has been suggested that he might have introduced Spenser to them: C. M. Webster, 'Robert Nowell', *N&Q* 167 (1934), 116. A cousin, Laurence Nowell (1530–c.1570), produced the map of Britain and Ireland that Lord Burghley always carried with him; see *ODNB* entry by Reitha M. Warnicke; George Tolias, 'Maps in Renaissance Libraries and Collections', in Woodward (ed.), *History of Cartography*, iii/1. 637–60, at p. 643. The map is BL Add. 62540.

125. Alexander Nowell, *A Catechism or First Instruction and Learning of Christian Religion*, trans. Thomas Norton (1570; London: Parker Society, 1868); Michael Graves, *Thomas Norton: The Parliament Man* (Oxford: Blackwell, 1994), pp. 55, 322–4, 326–7, *passim*; Diarmaid MacCulloch, *Thomas Cranmer: A Life* (New Haven: Yale University Press, 1996), pp. 610–12; Thomas S. Freeman, ' "The Reformation of the Church in this Parliament": Thomas Norton, John Foxe and the Parliament of 1571', *Parliamentary History* 16 (1997), 131–47.

126. J. S., *Certaine worthye manuscript poems of great antiquitie reserued long in the studie of a Northfolke gentleman. And now first published by I.S. 1 The statly tragedy of Guistard and Sismond. 2 The northren mothers blessing. 3 The way to thrifte* (London, 1597); Williams, *Index of Dedications*, pp. 174–5. For comment, see Andrew Hadfield, 'Spenser and John Stow', *N&Q* 56 (2009), 538–40. On Wolfe, see the *ODNB* entry by Andrew Pettegree; Pettegree, *Foreign Protestant Communities*, pp. 93–4; McCullough, *Cranmer*, pp. 66, 524–5, 609–10. On William Smith, see *Chloris, or The Complaint of the Passionate Despised Shepheard* (London, 1596); *ODNB* entry by Jean R. Brink; *Spenser Allusions*, pp. 52–3; McCabe, 'Rhyme and Reason', p. 47.

127. Nowell was not necessarily an ideal channel for advancement in this period, as he was out of favour with Lord Burghley: see C. M. Webster, 'A Note on Alexander Nowell', *N&Q* 168 (1934), 58–9.

128. C. Bowie Millican, 'The Northern Dialect of *The Shepheardes Calender*', *ELH* 6 (1939), 211–13. Millican points out that the teachers were characterized as speaking with a northern pronunciation, which might have had an impact on Spenser's own language.

129. Philip Edgcumbe Hughes, 'Preaching, Homilies, and Prophesyings in Sixteenth Century England', *The Churchman* 89 (1975), 7–32, at 16–17.

130. Patrick Collinson, *Archbishop Grindal, 1519–1583: The Struggle for a Reformed Church* (London: Cape, 1979), pp. 125–52, 221–2, *passim*; Patrick Collinson, 'The Monarchical Republic of Elizabeth I', in Collinson, *Elizabethans* (London: Hambledon, 2003), pp. 31–57, at p. 44; James P. Bednarz, 'Grindal, Edmund', in *S. Enc.*, pp. 342–3.

131. Wilson, *History of the Merchant Taylors' School*, pp. 25–30; *ODNB* entry by David Daniell.

132. A. C. Judson, *A Biographical Sketch of John Young, Bishop of Rochester, with emphasis on his relations with Edmund Spenser* (Bloomington: Indiana University Studies, 1934); Percy W. Long, 'Spenser and the Bishop of Rochester', *PMLA* 31 (1916), 713–35; *Variorum*, x. 7, 16; *ODNB* entry by R. W. McConchie.

133. Byrom, 'Singleton'.

134. Richard Mulcaster, *The First Part of the Elementarie vvhich entreateth chefelie of the right writing of our English tung* (London, 1582), sig. Ai^v–Aii^r.

135. Homer, *Iliad*, trans. Stanley Lombardo (Indianapolis: Hackett, 1997), book 19, lines 90–158. Agamemnon explains his actions against Achilles in terms of the malign influence of Ate. On Ate, see Michael Grant and John Hazel, *Who's Who in Classical Mythology* (1973; London: Dent, 1993), p. 54.

136. *Variorum*, x. 147–8. For Mulcaster's probable influence on *The Faerie Queene*, see Hester Lees-Jeffries, *England's Helicon: Fountains in Early Modern Literature and Culture* (Oxford: Oxford University Press, 2007), pp. 182–3.

137. See e.g. Edward Said, *Culture and Imperialism* (1993; London: Vintage, 1994), p. 268; Eamon Grennan, 'Language and Politics: A Note on Some Metaphors in Spenser's *A View of the*

Present State of Ireland', *Sp. St.* 3 (1982), 99–110; Andrew Hadfield, *Spenser's Irish Experience: Wilde Fruit and Salvage Soyl* (Oxford: Clarendon Press, 1997), pp. 60–5.

138. Joan Heiges Blythe, 'Ate', *Sp. Enc.*, p. 76.

139. The process may well have been reciprocal: see Smith, 'Spenser's Scholarly Script', at p. 93. On the impact of humanist educational methods on poetry in the 16th century, especially Spenser, see Jeff Dolven, *Scenes of Instruction in Renaissance Romance* (Chicago: University of Chicago Press, 2007), pp. 3–4.

140. *Chronology*, p. 2; Bruce, 'Spenser: Boyhood'; Charles Bowie Millican, 'Mulcaster and Spenser', *ELH* 6 (1939), 214–16; Welply, 'Some Spenser Problems', p. 57. For other Elizabethans named Sylvanus, see B. H. Newdigate, 'Some Spenser Problems: Sylvanus Spenser', *N&Q* 180 (1941), 120.

141. The name Sylvanus was distinctive enough for it to be used in a dialogue presented to the earl of Essex in 1599, deliberately marking the work out as one that paid homage to the recently deceased poet: 'The Dialogue of Perergynne and Silvvynnus, by H. C., SP 63/203, 119, transcribed by Hiram Morgan, http://www.ucc.ie/celt/contents/online/E590001-001/nav.html.

142. *ODNB* entry on Mulcaster by William Barker.

143. *The Shepheardes Calender*, Dec., lines 37–48; Spenser, *Shorter Poems*, pp. 150–1. On Spenser as Colin Clout, see John D. Bernard, *Ceremonies of Innocence: Pastoralism in the Poetry of Edmund Spenser* (Cambridge: Cambridge University Press, 1989).

144. As Harvey signs his commendatory verse to *The Faerie Queene* as 'Hobbinol', as well as several letters, the identification cannot be in doubt: Virginia F. Stern, 'Harvey, Gabriel', in *Sp. Enc.*, pp. 347–8; McLane, *Spenser's Shepheardes Calender*, pp. 237–61, 'Gabriel Harvey as Hobbinol'.

145. For paradigmatic examples of an older method, which led to the reaction against such studies after the Second World War, see Edwin Greenlaw, 'Spenser and the Earl of Leicester'; Edwin Greenlaw, 'Spenser and British Imperialism', *MP* 60 (1911–12), 347–70. For analysis, see Radcliffe, *Spenser: Reception History*, ch. 4.

146. See Andrew Hadfield, 'Spenser's Rosalind', *MLR* 104 (2009), 935–46.

147. G. C. Moore Smith, 'Spenser and Mulcaster', *MLR* 8 (1913), 368; McLane, *Spenser's Shepheardes Calender*, p. 348. On the pronunciation, which strengthens the case, see Roland M. Smith, 'Spenser's Scholarly Script and "Right Writing"', in D. C. Allen (ed.), *Studies in Honor of T. W. Baldwin* (Urbana: University of Illinois Press, 1958), pp. 66–111, at p. 67. Francis Beaumont, *The Knight of the Burning Pestle*, ed. Michael Hattaway (1969; London: Black, 1995), I.i, lines 96–7. For a more sceptical analysis, which suggest that the identification is more complex than has generally been assumed, see John Wesley, 'Spenser's "Wrenock" and Anglo-Welsh Latimer', *N&Q* 56 (2009), 527–30. I am grateful to Dr Wesley for sending me this note in advance of publication.

148. De Molen, *Mulcaster*, p. 23. Financial issues appear to have followed Mulcaster around: see the *ODNB* entry.

149. Jan Van Dorsten, *Poets, Patrons, and Professors: Sir Philip Sidney, Daniel Rogers and the Leiden Humanists* (Leiden: Leiden University Press, 1962), pp. 79, 92, 167; *ODNB* entries on 'Alexander Neville', by Elizabeth Leedham-Green, 'Andrew Melville' by James Kirk. See also Abrahami Ortelii, *Epistulae*, ed. J. H. Hessels, 4 vols. (Cambridge: Ecclesiae Londino-Batavae Archivum, 1887), i. 178–9, 20–1, 249–52, *passim*. I owe this last reference to Nick Popper.

150. The main study of the individual Marian exiles remains Christina Garrett, *The Marian Exiles, 1553–1559* (Cambridge: Cambridge University Press, 1938). Coverdale, Alexander Nowell, his brother, Laurence (d. 1576), were all exiles.

151. Richard L. De Molen, 'Richard Mulcaster: An Elizabethan Savant,' *Sh. Stud.* 8 (1975), 29–82, at 60.

152. On Rogers's antiquarian labours, which were of great significance for Spenser, see Angus Vine, *In Defiance of Time: Antiquarian Writing in Early Modern England* (Oxford: Oxford University Press, 2010), pp. 29–37.

153. Nicholl, *A Cup of News*, pp. 130–1; Harvey, *Fovre Letters*, pp. 10–11; Stern, *Harvey*, pp. 94–5. It is also worth noting that Gabriel Harvey's mentor, Sir Thomas Smith, and Mulcaster appear to

have known each other, suggesting a further possible link between Spenser and Harvey: see pp. 109–10.

154. *ODNB* entries on 'John Rogers' by David Daniell, 'Daniel Rogers' by Mark Loudon, and 'Laurence Nowell' by Retha M. Warnicke; Pettegree, *Foreign Protestant Communities*, pp. 173–5; De Molen, *Mulcaster*, p. 146; Stern, *Harvey*, pp. 31, 39. On Daniel Rogers see James E. Phillips, 'Daniel Rogers: A Neo-Latin Link Between the Pléiade and Sidney's "Areopagus" ', in *Neo-Latin Poetry of the Sixteenth and Seventeenth Centuries* (Los Angeles: Clark Memorial Library, 1965), pp. 5–28, at p. 8; Roger Howell, *Sir Philip Sidney: The Shepherd Knight* (London: Hutchinson, 1968), pp. 158–62; Van Dorsten, *Poets, Patrons, and Professors*, pp. 39, 42; Jan Van Dorsten, *The Radical Arts: First Decade of an Elizabethan Renaissance* (Leiden: Leiden University Press, 1970), p. 75; John S. Nolan, *Sir John Norreys and the Elizabethan Military World* (Exeter: University of Exeter Press, 1997), p. 16; F. J. Levy, 'Daniel Rogers as Antiquary', *Bibliotèque d'Humanisme et Renaissance* 27 (1965), 444–62, at 446; H. R. Wilton Hall (ed.), *Records of the Old Archdeaconry of St. Albans: A Calender of Papers, AD 1575 to AD 1637* (St Albans: St Alban's and Hertfordshire Architectural and Archaeological Society, 1908), pp. 45, 47. I owe this reference to Natalie Mears. On Buchanan, Rogers, and Spenser, see Paul E. McLane, 'James VI in the "Shepheardes Calender" ', *HLQ* 16 (1953), 273–85; and p. 229.

155. De Molen, *Mulcaster*, p. 120; Van Dorsten, *Poets, Patrons, and Professors*, p. 28; Anne Lake Prescott, *French Poets and the English Renaissance: Studies in Fame and Transformation* (New Haven: Yale University Press, 1978), pp. 91–5.

156. W. L. Renwick, 'Mulcaster and Du Bellay', *MLR* 17 (1922), 282–7; Joachim Du Bellay, *The Regrets, with The Antiquities of Rome, Three Latin Elegies, and The Defense and Enrichment of the French Language: A Bilingual Edition*, ed. and trans. Richard Helgerson (Philadelphia: University of Pennsylvania Press, 2006), introd., p. 35. See also Albert C. Baugh and Thomas Cable, *A History of the English Language* (3rd edn.; London: Routledge, 1978), p. 203.

157. Alfred W. Satterthwaite, *Spenser, Ronsard, and Du Bellay: A Renaissance Comparison* (Princeton: Princeton University Press, 1960), pp. 30–1. Mulcaster was a pioneer, as was Spenser: see W. D. Elcock, 'English Indifference to Du Bellay's "Regrets" ', *MLR* 46 (1951), 175–84.

158. Leonard Foster, 'The Translator of the "Theatre for Worldlings" ', *ES* 48 (1967), 27–34, at 33.

159. As Joshua Scodel points out, 'Of the great sonneteers, only Spenser has close renditions of foreign sonnets': 'Non-Dramatic Verse: Lyric', in Gordon Braden, Robert Cummings, and Stuart Gillespie (eds.), *The Oxford History of Literary Translation in English*, ii. *1550–1660*, (Oxford: Oxford University Press, 2010), pp. 201–47, at p. 239.

160. Jan van der Noot, *A Theatre wherein be represented as wel the miseries & calamities that follow the voluptuous worldlings as also the greate ioyes and plesures which the faithfull do enioy. An argument both profitable and delectable, to all that sincerely loue the word of God. Deuised by S. Iohn van-der Noodt. Seene and allowed according to the order appointed* (London, 1569), sig. D7^r.

161. For comment, see Werner Waterschoot, 'On Ordering the "Poetische Werken" of Jan van der Noot', *Quaerendo* 1 (1971), 242–63, at 242–5; Van Dorsten, *Radical Arts*, *passim*; Bas Jongenelen and Ben Parsons, 'The Sonnets of *Het Bosken* by Jan Van Der Noot', *Sp. St.* 23 (2008), 235–55, at 235–6.

162. *The Olympic Epics of Jan Van Der Noot: A facsimile edition of 'Das Buch Extasis', 'Een Cort Begryp Der XII. Bocken Olympiados' and 'Abrege Des Douze Livres Olympiades'*, ed. C. A. Zaalberg (Assen: Van Gorcum, 1956).

163. Jongenlen and Parsons, 'Sonnets of *Het Bosken*', p. 236; Laura Hunt Yungblut, *Strangers Settled Here amongst Us: Politics, Perceptions and the Presence of Aliens in Elizabethan England* (London: Routledge, 1996), p. 18.

164. Jan Van Der Noot, *The Gouerance and Preseruation of them that Feare the Plage* (London, 1569); Ben Parsons and Bas Jongnelen, 'Jan Van Der Noot: A Mistaken Attribution in the Short-Title Catalogue?', *N&Q* 250 (Dec. 2006), 427.

165. Judson refers to his 'ardent Calvinism' (Judson, *Life*, p. 20). A more nuanced discussion is provided in John N. King, *Spenser's Poetry and the Reformation Tradition* (Princeton: Princeton University Press, 1990), pp. 233–4, *passim*.

166. Van Dorsten, *Radical Arts*, pp. 29–30; Waterschoot, 'ordering the "Poeticsche Werken" ', p. 243; Karen L. Bowen and Dirk Imhof, *Christopher Plantain and Engraved Book Illustrations*

in Sixteenth-Century Europe (Cambridge: Cambridge University Press, 2008), pp. 32, 286. Plantain's relationship to the Family may have been simply based on business concerns: Paul Valkema Blouw, 'Was Plantin a Member of the Family of Love? Notes on His Dealings with Hendrik Niclaes', *Quaerendo* 23 (1993), 3–23. Ortelius' religious beliefs undoubtedly had an impact on his published work: see Pauline Moffitt Watts, 'The European Religious Worldview and Its Influence on Mapping', in Woodward (ed.), *History of Cartography*, iii/1. 382–400, at pp. 392–3.

167. A history of the family is provided in Alastair Hamilton, *The Family of Love* (Cambridge: Clark, 1981). For their impact in England, see Christopher W. Marsh, *The Family of Love in English Society, 1550–1630* (Cambridge: Cambridge University Press, 1994); Jean Dietz Moss, 'The Family of Love and English Critics', *SCJ* 6 (1975), 35–52; Peter Lake, *The Boxmaker's Revenge: 'Orthodoxy', 'Heterodoxy' and the Politics of the Parish in Early Stuart London* (Stanford: Stanford University Press, 2001).

168. Van Dorsten, *Radical Arts*, pp. 30–2; Pettegree, *Foreign Protestant Communities*, pp. 90, 170.

169. Michael Srigley, 'The Influence of Continental Familism in England after 1570', in Gunnar Sorelius and Michael Srigley (eds.), *Cultural Exchange between European Nations during the Renaissance* (Uppsala: Uppsala University Press, 1994), pp. 97–110; David Wootton, 'Reginald Scot/Abraham Fleming/The Family of Love', in Stuart Clark (ed.), *Languages of Witchcraft: Narrative, Ideology and Meaning in Early Modern Culture* (Basingstoke: Palgrave, 2001), pp. 119–38.

170. Jean Dietz Moss, 'Variations on a Theme: The Family of Love in Renaissance England', *RQ* 31 (1978), 186–95, at 186. Tracts which explain how the Family functioned include Tobias, *Mirabilia Opera Dei Certaine Wonderfull Works of God which hapned to H.N. even from his youth: and how the God of heaven hath united himself with him, and raised up his gracious word in him, and how he hath chosen and sent him to be a minister of his gracious word* (London, 1650); Hendrik Niclaes, *An Apology for the Service of Love, and the people that own it, commonly called, the family of love. Being a plain, but groundly discourse, about the right and true Christian religion* (London, 1656).

171. Van Dorsten, *Radical Arts*, p. 75. On the earl of Northampton, see the *ODNB* entry by Pauline Croft. On Surrey's influence on Spenser, see William A. Ringler, Jr, 'Tudor Poetry', *Sp. Enc.*, pp. 702–4, at p. 703; W. A. Sessions, *Henry Howard, the Poet Earl of Surrey: A Life* (Oxford: Oxford University Press, 1999), pp. 135–6.

172. Werner Waterschoot, 'Jan Van Der Noot's *Het Bosken* Re-Examined', *Quarendo* 22 (1992), 28–45, at 39.

173. Waterschoot, 'Ordering the "Poeticsche Werken" ', pp. 243, 245.

174. Waterschoot, '*Het Bosken* Re-Examined', pp. 29–30.

175. Ibid. 41.

176. W. J. B. Pienaar, 'Edmund Spenser and Jonker Jan Van Der Noot', *ES* 8 (1926), 33–44, 67–76, at 67–8. see also *Poems of Sir Arthur Gorges*, introd., pp. xiii–xix.

177. Freidland, 'Illustrations in *The Theatre for Worldlings*', p. 111.

178. On Bynemann, see *ODNB* entry by Maureen Bell; H. R. Plomer, 'Henry Bynemann, Printer, 1566–83', *The Library*, NS 9 (1908), 225–44; *Printers*, pp. 59–60.

179. Eric St John Brooks, *Sir Christopher Hatton: Queen Elizabeth's Favourite* (London: Cape, 1946), pp. 135–7, 140–2, 316–23.

180. On the complex nature of late Elizabethan patronage, see Simon Adams, *Leicester and the Court: Essays on Elizabethan Politics* (Manchester: Manchester University Press, 2002), especially chs. 1, 3; John Guy (ed.), *The Reign of Elizabeth I: Court and Culture in the Last Decade* (Cambridge: Cambridge University Press, 1995), chs. 1–4.

181. Michael Bath, *Speaking Pictures: English Emblem Books and Renaissance Culture* (London: Longman, 1994), p. 109; Stewart Mottram, 'Spenser's Dutch Uncles: The Family of Love and the four translations of *A Theatre for Worldlings*', in José Maria Pérez Fernández and Edward Wilson-Lee (eds.), *Translation and the Book Trade in Early Modern Europe* (forthcoming). I am extremely grateful to Dr Mottram for allowing me to see this article in advance of publication.

182. Richard A. McCabe, 'Edmund Spenser, Poet of Exile', *PBA* 80 (1993), 73–103.

183. Pienaar, 'Spenser and van der Noot', p. 71.

184. On Day, see Elizabeth Evenden, *Patents, Pictures and Patronage: John Day and the Tudor Book Trade* (Aldershot: Ashgate, 2008); *ODNB* entry by Andrew Pettegree; Pettegree, *Foreign Protestant Communities, passim*; J. F. Mozley, *John Foxe and His Book* (New York: Macmillan, 1940). Day was the key publisher of Dutch texts and published one of the most significant tracts on the Dutch revolt, *A Defence and True Declaration of the Things Lately done in the Low Country* (1571): see van Gelderen (ed.), *The Dutch Revolt* (Cambridge: Cambridge University Press, 1993), pp. 1–77. He also had a number of connections to Spenser, including having been patronized by Cecil and imprisoned with John Rogers.

185. See Satterthwaite, *Spenser, Ronsard, and Du Bellay*, app. 1. Satterthwaite is sceptical that Spenser translated van der Noot's sonnets. See also Jan Van Dorsten, '*A Theatre for Worldlings*', *Sp. Enc.*, p. 685; Pienaar, 'Spenser and van der Noot', p. 38; Stein, *Studies in Spenser's Complaints*, pt. 4.

186. Forster, 'Translator of the *Theatre*', pp. 28–30.

187. Ibid. 33.

188. Johnson, *Critical Bibliography*, pp. 1–2. On the fonts see Steven K. Galbraith, ' "English" Black-Letter Type and Spenser's *Shepheardes Calender*', *Sp. St.* 23 (2008), 13–40; Lotte Hellinga, 'Printing', in Hellinga and Trapp (eds.), *Cambridge History of the Book in Britain*, iii. 65–108, at pp. 75–6; Nicholas Barker, 'Old English Letter Foundries', in Barnard, McKenzie, and Bell (eds.), *Cambridge History of the Book in Britain*, iv. 602–19, at pp. 604–5.

189. Louis S. Friedland, 'The Illustrations in *The Theatre for Worldlings*', *HLQ* 19 (1956), 107–20. Friedland corrects the commonly repeated error that the illustrations were the work of Marcus Gheeraerts the elder (*c.*1520/1–*c.*1586).

190. On De Heere, see Van Dorsten, '*Theatre*'; *ODNB* entry by Susan Bracken; van Dorsten, *Radical Arts*, pp. 53–61, *passim*; Michael Bath, 'Verse Form and Pictorial Space in van der Noot's *Theatre for Worldlings*', in Höltgen et al. (eds.), *Word and Visual Imagination*, pp. 73–105, at p. 78; Margaret Aston, *The King's Bedpost: Reformation and Iconography in a Tudor Group Portrait* (Cambridge: Cambridge University Press, 1993), pp. 167–8; Evenden, *John Day*, pp. 97–100.

191. Bath, 'Verse Form and Pictorial Space'. Marot's poetry had an impact on the work of Barnaby Googe (1540–94), whose work had a significant impact on Spenser: see Judith M. Kennedy, 'Googe, Barnabe', *Sp. Enc.*, pp. 336–7; Barnabe Googe, *Eclogues, Epitaphs and Sonnets*, ed. Judith M. Kennedy (Toronto: University of Toronto Press, 1989), introd., pp. 19–20.

192. John B. Bender, *Spenser and Literary Pictorialism* (Princeton: Princeton University Press, 1972), p. 153; S. K. Heninger, Jr, 'The Typographical Layout of Spenser's *Shepheardes Calender*', in Höltgen et al. (eds.), *Word and Visual Imagination*, pp. 33–71; Gilman, *Iconoclasm and Poetry*, pp. 63–70.

193. Bender, *Spenser and Literary Pictorialism*, pp. 4–22; W. B. C. Watkins, *Shakespeare and Spenser* (Princeton: Princeton University Press, 1950), ch. 7; Rosamund Tuve, 'Spenser and Some Pictorial Conventions: with Particular Reference to Illuminated Manuscripts (1940)', in *Essays by Rosamund Tuve: Spenser, Herbert, Milton*, ed. Thomas P. Roche, Jr (Princeton: Princeton University Press, 1970), pp. 112–38.

194. A case strongly argued in Patrick Cheney, *Spenser's Famous Flight: A Renaissance Idea of a Literary Career* (Toronto: University of Toronto Press, 1993), ch. 1.

195. The genre became popular as the 16th century drew to a close. It is worth noting that Spenser's fellow pupil at Merchant Taylors', Thomas Lodge, was the co-author of a bleak vision of London's sins, with Robert Greene, *A Looking Glass for London and England (1594)*, ed. W. W. Greg (London: Malone Society, 1932). For comment, see Darryl Grantley, *London in Early Modern English Drama: Representing the Built Environment* (Basingstoke: Palgrave, 2008), pp. 52–6.

196. Tom McFaul, '*A Theatre For Worldlings* (1569),' *Sp. Handbook*, pp. 149–59, at pp. 153–4.

197. Du Bellay, *Un Songe ou Vision* in *The Regrets*, trans. Helgerson, p. 281.

198. On the French and English adaptations of Petrarch, see Stephen Minta, *Petrarch and Petrarchanism: The English and French Traditions* (Manchester: Manchester University Press, 1980), pp. 143–79. On the more general issue of translations of the sonnet into English, see John Fuller, *The Sonnet* (London: Methuen, 1972), chs. 1–2.

199. Bath, 'Verse Form and Pictorial Space', p. 79.

200. Early modern interest in Egypt is not always emphasized as strongly as it should be: for an exception to the general rule, see Philip Schwyzer, *Archaeologies of English Renaissance Literature* (Oxford: Oxford University Press, 2007), ch. 5.

201. For a recent discussion of Spenser's interest in ruins, see Thomas Russell James Muir, 'Ruins and Oblivion in the Sixteenth Century', unpublished DPhil thesis, University of Sussex, 2005, ch. 5.

202. Richard A. McCabe, *The Pillars of Eternity: Time and Providence in The Faerie Queene* (Dublin: Irish Academic Press, 1989), ch. 6.

203. This moral could have been taken from a number of sources, perhaps the most obvious of which is Polybius, *The Rise of the Roman Empire*, trans. Ian Scott-Kilvert (Harmondsworth: Penguin, 1979), bk. 6.

204. On the development of Dutch resistance theory against Spanish invasion, see Martin van Gelderen, *The Political Thought of the Dutch Revolt, 1555–1590* (Cambridge: Cambridge University Press, 1992). Ch. 4 describes the development of ideas of resistance during the period of van der Noot's exile. See also Wyger R. E. Velema, ' "That a Republic is Better than a Monarchy": Anti-monarchism in Early Modern Dutch Political Thought', in Martin van Gelderen and Quentin Skinner (eds.), *Republicanism: A Shared European Heritage*, 2 vols. (Cambridge: Cambridge University Press, 2002), i. 9–25.

205. Van der Noot, *Theatre*, sigs. F5$^{r–v}$, G4$^{r–v}$, *passim*.

206. On Spenser and republicanism, see Andrew Hadfield, 'Was Spenser a Republican?', *English* 47 (1998), 169–82; David Scott Wilson-Okamura, 'Republicanism, Nostalgia and the Crowd', *Sp. St.* 17 (2003), 253–73; Andrew Hadfield, 'Was Spenser a Republican After All? A Response to David Scott Okamura-Wilson', *Sp. St.* 17 (2003), 275–90; Louis Adrian Montrose, 'Spenser and the Elizabethan Political Imaginary', *ELH* 69 (2002), 907–46.

207. Since A. Kent Hieatt's pioneering *Short Time's Endless Monument*, the literature on Spenser's interest in numerology has become extensive: see the overview in Alexander Dunlop, 'Number symbolism, modern studies of', *Sp. Enc.*, pp. 512–13.

208. Prescott, *French Poets*, p. 47. On Augustine's influence on Spenser's conception of numerology, see also Harold L. Weatherby, *Mirrors of Celestial Grace: Patristic Theology in Spenser's Allegory* (Toronto: University of Toronto Press, 1994), pp. 88–90.

209. John Wesley, 'Acting and *Actio* in the Sermons of Lancelot Andrewes', *RS* 23 (2009), 678–93; Lukas Erne, *Beyond The Spanish Tragedy: A Study of the Works of Thomas Kyd* (Manchester: Manchester University Press, 2001).

210. Pactol, 'The Libyan river whose sand was turned to gold by the touch of King Midas' (Du Bellay, *Un Songe ou Vision* in *The Regrets*, trans. Helgerson, p. 291).

211. Michael Holohan, '*Iamque opus exegi*: Ovid's Changes and Spenser's Brief Epic of Mutability', *ELR* 6 (1976), 244–70.

212. The most comprehensive survey of English iconoclasm is Margaret Aston, *England's Iconoclasts: Laws Against Images* (Oxford: Clarendon Press, 1988); on Spenser, see Ernest B. Gilman, *Iconoclasm and Poetry in the English Reformation: Down Went Dagon* (Chicago: University of Chicago Press, 1986), ch. 3. On the eye and delusive imagination, see Stuart Clark, *Vanities of the Eye: Vision in Early Modern European Culture* (Oxford: Oxford University Press, 2007); on Spenser, see Abigail Shinn, 'Spenser and Popular Culture', unpublished DPhil thesis, University of Sussex, 2009, ch. 3.

213. Nevertheless, they are important as the culmination of the sequence: see Carl J. Rasmussen, ' "Quietnesse of Minde": *A Theatre for Worldlings* as a Protestant Poetics', *Sp. St.* 1 (1980), 3–27, at 14.

214. Florence Sandler, '*The Faerie Queene*: An Elizabethan Apocalypse', in C. A. Patrides and Joseph Wittreich (eds.), *The Apocalypse in English Renaissance Thought and Literature*

(Manchester: Manchester University Press, 1984), pp. 148–74; King, *Spenser's Poetry and the Reformation Tradition*, *passim*; Richard Mallette, *Spenser and the Discourses of Reformation England* (Lincoln: University of Nebraska Press, 1997), *passim*; Andrew Escobedo, *Nationalism and Historical Loss in Renaissance England: Foxe, Dee, Spenser, Milton* (Ithaca, NY: Cornell University Press, 2004).

215. Prescott, *French Poets*, p. 46.

216. See e.g. Anthea Hume, *Edmund Spenser: Protestant Poet* (Cambridge: Cambridge University Press, 1984).

217. Spenser, *Shorter Poems*, p. 452. On Lady Margaret and Lady Anne, see pp. 352–6.

218. See Andrew Hadfield, 'Spenser's Reference to Censorship', *N&Q* 56/4 (Dec. 2009), 532–3.

219. Peterson, 'Laurel Crown and Ape's Tail'. See also Cyndia Clegg, *Press Censorship in Elizabethan England* (Cambridge: Cambridge University Press, 1997), p. 223; D. M. Loades, 'The Theory and Practice of Censorship in Sixteenth-Century England', *TRHS*, 5th ser. 24 (1974), 141–57.

220. Rambuss, *Spenser's Secret Career*, introd.

221. See pp. 182, 244. The best conjectural study of what Spenser may have revised is Josephine Waters Bennett, *The Evolution of 'The Faerie Queene'* (Chicago: University of Chicago Press, 1942). See also W. J. B. Owen, 'The Structure of *The Faerie Queene*', *PMLA* 68 (1953), 1079–1100.

222. See Elizabeth Bieman, '*Fowre Hymnes*', *Sp. Enc.*, pp. 315–17. For discussion, see Ayesha Ramachandran, 'Edmund Spenser, Lucrecian Neoplatonist: Cosmology in the *Fowre Hymnes*', in Kenneth Borris, Jon Quitslund, and Carol Kaske (eds.), *Spenser and Platonism* (special issue), *Sp. S* 24 (2009), 373–411.

223. Not everyone has taken this declaration at face value. Robert Ellrodt, in what is still the longest single analysis of the intellectual provenance of the poems, confesses: 'I incline to disbelieve Spenser when he says that the first two *Hymnes* were written in his youth' (*NeoPlatonism in the Poetry of Spenser* (Geneva: Droz, 1960), p. 59).

224. Corinne Saunders (ed.), *Chaucer* (Oxford: Blackwell, 2001), pp. 96–7, 129.

225. Clare R. Kinney, 'Marginal Presence: Lyric Resonance, Epic Absence: *Troilus and Criseyde* and/in *The Shepheardes Calender*', *Sp. St.* 18 (2004), 25–39; John A. Burrow, 'Chaucer, Geoffrey', *Sp. Enc.*, pp. 144–8.

226. Although it should be noted that C. S. Lewis asserted that 'nothing could show more clearly how imperceptively [Spenser] read the Chaucer whom he so revered' (*English Literature in the Sixteenth Century Excluding Drama* (Oxford: Oxford University Press, 1954), p. 369); Burrow, 'Chaucer', p. 145.

227. On the influence of Castiglione see Catherine Bates, *The Rhetoric of Courtship in Elizabethan Language and Literature* (Cambridge: Cambridge University Press, 1992), *passim*; Jennifer Richards, *Rhetoric and Courtliness in Early Modern Literature* (Cambridge: Cambridge University Press, 2003), ch. 2; on the influence of Ficino, see Brian P. Copenhaver, 'Astrology and Magic', in Schmitt and Skinner (eds.), *Cambridge History of Renaissance Philosophy*, pp. 264–300, at pp. 274–85.

228. See Margaret Healy, *Shakespeare, Alchemy and the Creative Imagination* (Cambridge: Cambridge University Press, 2011), chs. 1, 5. On the challenge to Platonic ideas, see Michael J. B. Allen, 'Renaissance Neoplatonism', in Norton (ed.), *Cambridge History of Literary Criticism*, iii. *The Renaissance*, pp. 435–41.

229. Healy, *Shakespeare, Alchemy*, p. 55; Jessica Woolf, *Humanism, Machinery, and Renaissance Literature* (Cambridge: Cambridge University Press, 2004), ch. 4.

230. On Neoplatonism see Paul O. Kristellar, *Renaissance Thought: The Classic, Scholastic, and Humanist Strains* (New York: Harper, 1961), ch. 3; Brian Vickers, 'Rhetoric and Poetics', in Charles B. Schmitt et al. (eds.), *The Cambridge History of Renaissance Philosophy* (Cambridge: Cambridge University Press, 1988), pp. 715–45, at pp. 738–40. See pp. 351–2.

231. See pp. 352–6.

232. 'An Hymn in Honour of Love', lines 113–19, Spenser, *Shorter Poems*, p. 456.

233. 'An Hymne in Honour of Beautie', lines 141–2, Spenser, *Shorter Poems*, p. 467.

234. It is also worth noting that *A Theatre* also had significant Neoplatonic elements: see Rasmussen, ' "Quietnesse of Minde" ', p. 8.

235. Hamilton, *Family of Love*, p. 73.
236. Ibid. 6–7.
237. Frances A. Yates, *The Rosicrucian Enlightenment* (London: Routledge, 1972), pp. 106, 259–60; Frances A. Yates, *Astrea: The Imperial Theme in the Sixteenth Century* (London: Routledge, 1975), pp. 191–4;
238. David Wootton, 'John Donne's Religion of Love', in John Brooke and Ian Maclean (eds.), *Heterodoxy in Early Modern Science and Religion* (Oxford: Oxford University Press, 2005), pp. 31–58.
239. Wootton, 'Reginald Scott', p. 131; Hamilton, *Family of Love*, pp. 114–15.
240. Wootton, 'Reginald Scott', pp. 124, 132.
241. Pico Della Mirandola, *Oration on the Dignity of Man* in Paul Oskar Kristellar (ed.), *The Renaissance Philosophy of Man* (Chicago: University of Chicago Press, 1948), pp. 213–54; Jon A. Quitslund, *Spenser's Supreme Fiction: Platonic Natural Philosophy and The Faerie Queene* (Toronto: University of Toronto Press, 2001), pp. 84–7, *passim*.

Chapter 2

1. See A. L. Rowse, *The England of Elizabeth* (1950; London: Macmillan, 1953), pp. 552–8.
2. Grosart (ed.), *Spending of the Money of Robert Nowell*, p. 28; Douglas Hamer, 'Edmund Spenser's Gown and Shilling', *RES* 23 (1947), 218–25, at 219–21; Judson, *Life*, pp. 18–19. On the importance of funerals and other public ceremonies and events in the London of Spenser's boyhood, as recorded by someone Spenser or his family might have known as he was clerk of Holy Trinity-the-less, a few hundred yards closer to the centre of London than the Merchant Taylors' School, see *The Diary of Henry Machin, Citizen and Merchant-Taylor of London, from AD 1550 to AD 1563*, ed. John Gough Nicholls (London: Camden Society, 1848); *ODNB* entry on Machin by Ian Mortimer.
3. Hamer, 'Spenser's Gown and Shilling', p. 225.
4. Grosart (ed.), *Spending of the Money of Robert Nowell*, p. 160.
5. Judson, *Life*, pp. 15, 18–19.
6. *The Statutes of Queen Elizabeth for the University of Cambridge*, appended to *Collection of the Statutes for the University and the Colleges of Cambridge* (London: Clowes, 1840), p. 34. Other scholarships established in the period include many by people connected to Spenser: Alexander Nowell later endowed Queen Elizabeth's Free School, Middleton, Lancashire; Edmund Grindal did the same for his old school, St Bees, Cumberland: Morgan and Brooke, *History of the University of Cambridge*, ii. 189–90.
7. Rappaport, *Worlds Within Worlds*, p. 85; Singman, *Daily Life in Elizabethan England*, pp. 35–6; *Statutes*, pp. 37–8.
8. Camden, *Britannia*, p. 486.
9. Morgan and Brooke, *History of the University of Cambridge*, ii. 247–8. For descriptions of outbreaks, see Charles Henry Cooper and John William Cooper, *Annals of Cambridge*, 5 vols. (Cambridge: Warwick, 1842–1908), ii. 233, 322–4. See also Ralph Houlbrooke, *Death, Religion and the Family in England, 1480–1750* (Oxford: Oxford University Press, 1998), p. 14.
10. Pembroke College, Cambridge, Archives, College MS M alpha x, fos. 55, 58, 66.
11. See Judson, *Life*, p. 42; *Complete Works*, ed. Grosart, i. 36; Judson, *John Young*, p. 12; Long, 'Spenser and the Bishop of Rochester', p. 717.
12. Aubrey Attwater, *A Short History of Pembroke College, Cambridge* (1936; Cambridge: Pembroke College, 1973), pp. 48–9.
13. For details of the Watts scholars, see Pembroke College, Cambridge, College MS A gamma (Richard Drake's book), p. 92; Pembroke College, Cambridge, College MS A alpha (Matthew Wren's notebook), pp. 92, 93. I owe these references to Jayne Ringrose, archivist at Pembroke College, Cambridge. On Spenser's connection to Watts, see pp. 114–15.
14. A. J. Magill, 'Spenser's Guyon and the Mediocrity of the Elizabethan Settlement', *SP* 67 (1970), 167–77, at 170–1.

15. For details, see Collinson, *Elizabethan Puritan Movement*, pt. 2; Haugaard, *Elizabeth and the English Reformation*, ch. 5; M. M. Knappen, *Tudor Puritanism* (1939; Chicago: University of Chicago Press, 1970), ch. 10; Claire Cross, *Church and People, England, 1450–1660* (2nd edn., Oxford: Blackwell, 1999), pp. 119–20; A. F. Scott Pearson, *Thomas Cartwright and Elizabethan Puritanism, 1535–1603* (Cambridge: Cambridge University Press, 1925), pp. 17–19. For earlier exchanges see Hastings Robinson (ed.), *The Zurich Letters*, 2 vols. (Cambridge: Cambridge University Press, 1845), ii. 119–26, *passim*. One of the authors is Miles Coverdale, another figure connected to Spenser through the Merchant Taylors' School.

16. Pearson, *Cartwright*, pp. 28–9.

17. Ibid., ch. 2. on the concept of 'adiaphora', derived from the writings of Thomas Starkey, see John N. Wall, 'Godly and Fruitful Lessons: *The English Bible*, Erasmus'; *Paraphrases* and *The Book of Homilies*', in Booty (ed.), *Godly Kingdom of Tudor England*, pp. 45–135, at pp. 63–4.

18. *ODNB* article on Thomas Cartwright by Patrick Collinson; Pearson, *Thomas Cartwright*, pp. 39–42; Cooper and Cooper, *Annals of Cambridge*, ii. 257–61.

19. Cooper and Cooper, *Annals of Cambridge*, ii. 250.

20. Ibid. 238, 243–4, 250. On Cambridge as an especially 'Puritan' university, see Collinson, *Elizabethan Puritan Movement*, ch. 3; H. C. Porter, *Reformation and Reaction in Tudor Cambridge* (Cambridge: Cambridge University Press, 1958); Morgan and Brooke, *History of the University of Cambridge*, vol. ii, ch. 13.

21. Pearson, *Cartwright*, p. 121; James Heywood and Thomas Wraight (eds.), *Cambridge University Transactions during the Puritan Controversies of the Sixteenth and Seventeenth Centuries*, 2 vols. (London: Bohn, 1854), *passim*.

22. Cited in Caius, *Works*, introd., p. 37.

23. *ODNB* article.

24. Judson, *Life*, pp. 35–6. On the impact of the massacre throughout Europe, see Robert M. Kingdon, *Myths about the St. Bartholomew's Day Massacres, 1572–1576* (Cambridge, MA: Harvard University Press, 1988), esp. ch. 7.

25. Cooper and Cooper, *Annals of Cambridge*, ii. 278; John Nichols, *The Progresses and Public Processions of Queen Elizabeth*, 3 vols. (London, 1823), ii. 280–1.

26. See e.g. Diarmaid MacCulloch, *Reformation: Europe's House Divided, 1490–1700* (Harmondsworth: Penguin, 2003), ch. 8.

27. Brink, 'Revising Spenser's Birth Date', pp. 525, 527.

28. Collinson, *Grindal*, ch. 2; Attwater, *Pembroke College*, pp. 37–43.

29. Attwater, *Pembroke College*, p. 37; Collinson, *Grindal*, p. 38.

30. Attwater, *Pembroke College*, pp. 31, 34–9; Wall, 'Godly and Fruitful Lessons', at p. 72.

31. Morgan and Brooke, *History of the University of Cambridge*, ii. 120. Statistics for the 1570s are hard to obtain: in the early 1620s, Trinity was the largest with 440 members and Trinity Hall the smallest with 56. King's, along with Pembroke, had 140 members.

32. Judson, *Life*, p. 30; Cooper and Cooper, *Annals of Cambridge*, ii. 269, 316. On Caius, see *The Works of John Caius, M.D . . . . with a memoir of his life by John Venn* (Cambridge: Cambridge University Press, 1912); *ODNB* entry by Vivian Nutton. Harvey acquired at least one of Caius' manuscripts after his death.

33. Robert Willis and John Willis Clark, *The Architectural History of the University of Cambridge, and of the Colleges of Cambridge and Eton*, 4 vols. (Cambridge: Cambridge University Press, 1886), i. 121–5; Attwater, *Pembroke College*, ch. 1; Nicholas Pevsner, *The Buildings of England: Cambridgeshire* (Harmondsworth: Penguin, 1970), pp. 123–9.

34. Alexander Judson, *Thomas Watts, Archdeacon of Middlesex (and Edmund Spenser)* (Bloomington: Indiana University Press, Indiana University Publications Series, Humanities Division, 1939), p. 16; *ODNB* entry on Thomas Watts by Brett Ussher.

35. J. and J. A. Venn (eds.), *Alumni Cantabrigienes*, 4 vols. (Cambridge: Cambridge University Press, 1922–7), iv. 132.

36. Judson, *Life*, p. 31. William Shakespeare, *King Lear*, ed. R. A. Foakes (London: Nelson, 1997), II.ii, line 15.

37. Judson, *Life*, p. 31; Elizabeth Burton, *The Elizabethans at Home* (1958; London: Arrow Books, 1970), p. 86. Schoolmasters and their pupils also often slept in the same room. See Willis, *Mount Tabor*, p. 97, where he notes that his teacher, Gregory Downhall, 'made me his bedfellow (my fathers house being next of all to the schoole). This bedfellowship begat in him familiaritie and gentlenesse towards mee, and in mee towards him, reverence and love'.

38. On the relative poverty of sizars see Nicholl, *Cup of News*, p. 23.

39. Thomas Middleton, *The Black Book* (1604), ed. G. B. Shand, in Middleton, *Collected Works*, i. 204–18, at p. 218; Nicholl, *Cup of News*, p. 23.

40. Hugh Kearney, *Scholars and Gentlemen: Universities and Society in Pre-industrial Britain* (Ithaca, NY: Cornell University Press, 1970), p. 33.

41. Campbell, *English Yeoman*, p. 271.

42. Stern, *Harvey*, pp. 11–12.

43. Gabriel Harvey and Edmund Spenser, *Three proper, and wittie, familiar letters: lately passed betvveene tvvo vniuersitie men: touching the earthquake in Aprill last, and our English refourmed versifying With the preface of a wellwiller to them both* (London, 1580), p. 6.

44. For further comment, see pp. 86–7.

45. Mark H. Curtis, *Oxford and Cambridge in Transition, 1558–1642: An Essay on the Changing Relations between the English Universities and English Society* (Oxford: Clarendon Press, 1959), ch. 10.

46. Curtis, *Oxford and Cambridge in Transition*, p. 86; Cressy, *Education in Tudor and Stuart England*, pp. 132–5; J. M. Fletcher, 'The Faculty of Arts', in James McConica (ed.), *The History of the University of Oxford*, iii. *The Collegiate University* (Oxford: Clarendon Press, 1986), pp. 157–212, at pp. 171–81; Binns, *Intellectual Culture*, pp. 5–6.

47. Mordechai Feingold, *The Mathematicians' Apprenticeship: Science, Universities and Society in England, 1560–1640* (Cambridge: Cambridge University Press, 1984), pp. 26–7; Cormack, 'Maps as Educational Tools', pp. 630–1.

48. See the description of Cambridge examinations in *The Diary of Baron Waldstein: A Traveller in Elizabethan England*, trans. G. W. Groos (London: Thames and Hudson, 1981), pp. 93–101.

49. Mack, *Elizabethan Rhetoric*, p. 58.

50. Mack, 'Spenser and Rhetoric', *Sp. Handbook*, p. 427.

51. William T. Costello, SJ, *The Scholastic Curriculum at Early Seventeenth-Century Cambridge* (Cambridge, MA: Harvard University Press, 1958), p. 146.

52. *Statutes, passim*. The statutes were unpopular and were formally opposed by a great number of fellows for providing the university authorities with what they saw as excessive powers: Heywood and Wraight (eds.), *Cambridge University Transactions*, i. 1–82; Cooper and Cooper, *Annals of Cambridge*, ii. 260–1. Of course, not every law or statute was followed, especially Sumptuary Laws: Ann Rosalind Jones and Peter Stallybrass, *Renaissance Clothing and the Materials of Memory* (Cambridge: Cambridge University Press, 2000), pp. 187–8.

53. A. F. Scott Pearson, *Thomas Cartwright and Elizabethan Puritanism, 1535–1603* (Cambridge: Cambridge University Press, 1925), p. 5.

54. Fletcher, 'Faculty of Arts', p. 173.

55. Curtis, *Oxford and Cambridge in Transition*, pp. 88–9; Fletcher, 'Faculty of Arts', pp. 167–9; *Collection of Statutes*, pp. 294–9.

56. Curtis, *Oxford and Cambridge in Transition*, pp. 137–9; Warren Boutcher, '"A French Dexterity, & an Italian Confidence": New Documents on John Florio, Learned Strangers and Protestant Humanist Study of Modern Languages in Renaissance England from *c.*1547 to *c.*1625', *Reformation* 2 (1997), 39–110.

57. Fletcher, 'Faculty of Arts', p. 172.

58. Galbraith, 'Spenser and the History of the Book', pp. 22–8. Spenser would almost certainly also have read Plato and the commentaries of Ficino: see Valery Rees, 'Ficinian Ideas in the Poetry of Edmund Spenser', in Borris et al. (eds.), *Spenser and Platonism*, pp. 73–134, at pp. 98–124.

59. Clare Sargent, 'The Early Modern Library (to *c.*1640)', and Kristian Jensen, 'Universities and Colleges', in Leedham-Green and Webber (eds.), *Cambridge History of Libraries*, i. 51–65, 345–62.

60. Curtis, *Oxford and Cambridge in Transition*, pp. 134–7; Gabriel Harvey, *Letter-Book of Gabriel Harvey, 1573–1580*, ed. Edward John Long Scott (London: Camden Society, 1884), pp. 167–8.
61. Harvey, *Letter-Book*, pp. 79–80.
62. Stern, *Harvey*, pp. 226, 239, 246, 265, 268. The reference in the *Letter-Book* further suggests that Harvey is thinking how to present his evidence, and, in the process, effacing his own role, given the experimental character of this text. It is also worth noting that Gabriel's brother refers to Machiavelli in *Lamb of God*, and that John Wolfe, Harvey's friend and publisher, published Machiavelli's *Discourses* in 1584, and the *Art of War* in Italian in 1587: N. W. Bawcutt, 'The "Myth of Gentillet" Reconsidered: An Aspect of Elizabethan Machiavellianism', *MLR* 99 (2004), 863–74, at 870–1. See also Alessandra Petrina, *Machiavelli in the British Isles: Two Early Modern Translations of The Prince* (Aldershot: Ashgate, 2009), pp. 17–18, *passim*.
63. Curtis, *Oxford and Cambridge in Transition*, pp. 136–7.
64. *Variorum*, x. 121, 229; Edwin A. Greenlaw, 'The Influence of Machiavelli on Spenser', *MP* 7 (1909), 187–202; Ronald A. Horton, 'Aristotle and His Commentators', *Sp. Enc.*, pp. 57–60. Guicciardini's *History of Italy* was translated into English by Geoffrey Fenton (c.1539–1608), who, like Spenser, also married into the Boyle family. See Hadfield, *Spenser's Irish Experience*, p. 46; *ODNB* entry on Fenton by Andrew Hadfield; Rudolf Gottfried, *Geoffrey Fenton's Historie of Guicciardini* (Bloomington: Indiana University Press, Indiana University Publications Series, Humanities Division, 1940); Nicholas Canny, *The Upstart Earl: A Study of the Social and Mental World of Richard Boyle, First Earl of Cork, 1566–1643* (Cambridge: Cambridge University Press, 1982), pp. 6, 28.
65. See p. 97.
66. Jason Lawrence, 'Spenser and Italian Literature', *Sp. Handbook*, pp. 602–19, at p. 603.
67. These are now preserved in the Huntington Library. For discussion, see Joyce Boro, 'Multilingualism, Romance, and Language Pedagogy; or, Why Were So Many Sentimental Romances Printed as Polyglot Texts?', in Schurink (ed.), *Tudor Translation*, pp. 18–38.
68. Jason Lawrence, *'Who the Devil Taught Thee So Much Italian?': Italian Language Learning and Literary Imitation in Early Modern England* (Manchester: Manchester University Press, 2005), pp. 12–13, 28, 46.
69. On Aristotle's continuing intellectual dominance in the late 16th century, see E. Jennifer Ashworth, 'Logic in Late Sixteenth-Century England: Humanist Dialectic and the New Aristotelianism', *SP* 88 (1991), 224–36, at 227.
70. Costello, *Scholastic Curriculum*, especially ch. 3.
71. Nicholl, *Cup of News*, p. 34.
72. Howard Hotson, *Commonplace Learning: Ramism and Its German Ramifications, 1543–1630* (Oxford: Oxford University Press, 2007), p. 17; Kees Meerhoff, 'Logic and Eloquence: A Ramusian Revolution?', *Argumentation* 5 (1991), 357–74; Ashworth, 'Logic in Late Sixteenth-Century England', p. 233.
73. Jones, *English Reformation*, p. 178.
74. *The logike of the moste excellent philosopher P. Ramus martyr*, trans. M. Roll (London, 1574); *The Latine Grammar of P. Ramus: translated into English* (London, 1585); *Elementes of Geometrie. Written in Latin by that excellent scholler, P. Ramus*, trans. Thomas Hood (London, 1590); *The Art of Arithmeticke in whole numbers and fractions in a more readie and easie method then hitherto hath bene published, written in Latin by P. Ramus; and translated into English by William Kempe* (London, 1592).
75. Lisa Jardine, 'Humanistic Logic', in Schmitt and Skinner (eds.), *Cambridge History of Renaissance Philosophy*, pp. 173–98, at p. 185; Fletcher, 'Faculty of Arts', p. 178. Roll's translation of Ramus' *Logic* hails him as 'Martyr to God' (p. 12).
76. Walter J. Ong, *Ramus, Method, and the Decay of Dialogue: From the Art of Discourse to the Art of Reason* (Cambridge, MA: Harvard University Press, 1958); Frances A. Yates, *The Art of Memory* (London: Routledge, 1966), *passim*. For attempts to apply Ramus' logical methods to Calvinist theology, see Dudley Fenner, *The artes of logike and rethorike plainelie set foorth in the English tounge, easie to be learned and practised: togeather with examples for the practise of the same, for methode in the gouernment of the familie, prescribed in the word of God: and for the whole in the*

resolution or opening of certaine partes of Scripture, according to the same (Middleburg, 1584); *ODNB* entry on Dudley Fenner by Patrick Collinson.

77. Mordechai Feingold, 'English Ramism: A Reinterpretation', in Mordechai Feingold, Joseph S. Freedman, and Wolfgang Rother (eds.), *The Influence of Petrus Ramus: Studies in Sixteenth-Century and Seventeenth-Century Philosophy and Sciences* (Basle: Schwabe and Co., 2001), pp. 127–76.

78. Mack, *History of Renaissance Rhetoric*, p. 142.

79. Ramus, *Logike*, sig. B1^{r-v}.

80. Aston, *England's Iconoclasts*, pp. 457–8.

81. Alexander Richardson, *The Logicians School-Master* (London, 1629), sig. C1^r. On Richardson (d. *c.*1621), see the *ODNB* entry by Roland Hall.

82. Sidney, *Apology*, pp. 82–3.

83. Although one should be wary of underestimating the achievements of Renaissance logic, see Jardine, 'Humanistic Logic', pp. 173–4. On Ramism at Cambridge, see Kearney, *Scholars and Gentlemen*, p. 63.

84. E. J. Ashworth, 'Traditional Logic', in Schmitt and Skinner (eds.), *Cambridge History of Renaissance Philosophy*, pp. 143–72; D. P. Henry, *Medieval Logic and Metaphysics* (London: Hutchinson, 1972).

85. 'Syllogism', in Ted Honderich (ed.), *The Oxford Companion to Philosophy* (Oxford: Oxford University Press, 1995), p. 862; Costello, *Scholastic Curriculum*, p. 49. On the varieties of the syllogism, based on what Spenser was probably taught at Cambridge, see Richardson, *Logicians School-Master*, chs. 9–16.

86. Ramus, *Logike*, pp. 82–4; Lisa Jardine, 'Humanism and the Sixteenth Century Cambridge Arts Course', *History of Education* 4 (1975), 16–31, at 20–1; Ashworth, 'Traditional Logic', pp. 162–72.

87. Fenner, *Artes of Logike and Rethorike*, sig. C3^v.

88. Jean Calvin, *Institutes of the Christian Religion*, ed. and trans. John T. McNeill and Ford Lewis Battles, 2 vols. (Philadelphia: Westminster Press, 1965), ii. 968–70 (III.24, 4); François Wendel, *Calvin: The Origins and Development of His Religious Thought*, trans. Philip Mairet (London: Fontana, 1965), pp. 234–42.

89. On Cartwright, see *ODNB* entry on 'Thomas Cartwright' by Patrick Collinson; Pearson, *Thomas Cartwright*; Patrick Collinson, *The Elizabethan Puritan Movement* (Oxford: Clarendon Press, 1967), *passim*.

90. Kearney, *Scholars and Gentlemen*, p. 63.

91. Lisa Jardine, 'The Place of Dialectic Teaching in Sixteenth-Century Cambridge', *SR* 21 (1974), 31–62, pp. 38–40.

92. Jardine, 'Humanism and the Sixteenth Century Arts Course', p. 21.

93. Kearney, *Scholars and Gentlemen*, p. 51.

94. Jardine, 'Place of Dialectic Teaching', p. 59.

95. Stern, *Harvey*, pp. 15, 25; *ODNB* entry on 'Gabriel Harvey' by Jason Scott-Warren.

96. Mack, 'Spenser and Rhetoric', *Sp. Handbook*, pp. 428–30.

97. Gabriel Harvey, *Ciceronianus*, ed. and trans. Harold S. Wilson and Clarence A. Forbes (Lincoln: University of Nebraska Studies, 1945), pp. 45, 59, 71–3, *passim*; John Charles Adams, 'Gabriel Harvey's *Ciceronianus* and the Place of Peter Ramus' *Dialecticae libri duo* in the Curriculum', *RQ* 43 (1990), 551–69; Binns, *Intellectual Culture*, pp. 278–82.

98. Gabriel Harvey, *Rhetor* (1577), trans. Mark Reynolds (http://comp.uark.edu/~mreynold/rheteng.html); Stern, *Harvey*, pp. 28–9.

99. Richards, *Rhetoric and Courtliness*, ch. 5.

100. Stern, *Harvey*, pp. 10–11, 31, 39, 40. See also James E. Phillips, 'George Buchanan and the Sidney Circle', *HLQ* 12 (1948–9), 23–55.

101. R. W. Maslen, 'Magical Journeys in Sixteenth-Century Prose', *YES* (*Travel and Prose Fiction in Early Modern England*, ed. Nandini Das) 41/1 (2011), 35–50, at 43.

102. Stern, *Harvey*, pp. 12–13.

103. Harvey, *Letter-Book*, pp. 162–5, 168–70, 176–9; Harvey–Spenser, *Letters*, p. 32.

104. Sir Thomas Smith, *Literary and Linguistic Works*, 3 vols. (Stockholm: Almqvist & Wiksell, 1963–83), ii. *A Critical Edition of De Recta et Emendata Linguae Graecae Pronuntiatione* (1978). For analysis see Richards, *Rhetoric and Courtliness*, ch. 3.
105. Harvey, *Letter-Book*, p. 19.
106. See p. 89.
107. W. K. Jordan, *Edward VI: The Threshold of Power: The Dominance of the Duke of Northumberland* (London: Allen & Unwin, 1970), pp. 127, 172, *passim*; Jennifer Loach, *Edward VI* (New Haven: Yale University Press, 1999), pp. 84, 92.
108. Stephen Alford, *Burghley: William Cecil at the Court of Elizabeth I* (New Haven: Yale University Press, 2008), pp. 197–8, 212, *passim*; Conyers Read, *Mr. Secretary Cecil and Queen Elizabeth* (London: Cape, 1955), pp. 42, 55, 351, *passim*; Conyers Read, *Lord Burghley and Queen Elizabeth* (London: Cape, 1960), pp. 144–5.
109. On Cranmer and Smith, see MacCulloch, *Cranmer*, pp. 445–6, *passim*.
110. For an analysis of the political context of the work, which concludes that it is a 'Protestant apologetic', hostile to female rule, a view which resembles Spenser's perception of Elizabeth throughout his writing career, see Anne McLaren, 'Reading Sir Thomas Smith's *De Republica Anglorum* as Protestant Apologetic', *HJ* 42 (1999), 911–39.
111. Sir Thomas Smith, *De Republica Anglorum: A Discourse on the Commonwealth of England*, ed. L. Alston (1906; Shannon: Irish University Press, 1972), p. 48.
112. Andrew Hadfield, 'Was Spenser a Republican?', *English* 47 (1998), 169–82; Andrew Zurcher, *Spenser's Legal Language: Law and Poetry in Early Modern England* (Cambridge: Brewer, 2007), pp. 136–7.
113. Spenser, *Shorter Poems*, p. 38; Smith, *De Republica Anglorum*, pp. 18–19.
114. See pp. 122–3.
115. *Variorum*, x. 285, 374, 397.
116. Stern, *Harvey*, p. 39.
117. *ODNB* entry on 'Thomas Smith' by Ian Archer; Mary Dewar, *Sir Thomas Smith: A Tudor Intellectual in Office* (Cambridge: Cambridge University Press, 1964), p. 203.
118. On the equally grand ambitions of one of Smith's neighbours, see Dominique Goy-Blanquet, 'Lord Keeper Bacon and the Writing on the Wall', *Law and Humanities* 4 (2010), 211–28. On the architecture and design of Hill Hall, see pp. 90–1.
119. James Hankins, 'Humanism and the Origins of Modern Political Thought', in Kraye (ed.), *Cambridge Companion to Renaissance Humanism*, pp. 118–41, at p. 127.
120. Cited in Lisa Jardine, 'Encountering Ireland: Gabriel Harvey, Edmund Spenser, and English Colonial Ventures', in Brendan Bradshaw, Andrew Hadfield, and Willy Maley (eds.), *Representing Ireland: Literature and the Origins of Conflict, 1534–1660* (Cambridge: Cambridge University Press, 1993), pp. 60–75, at p. 63. Harvey was also using Anthony Cope's translation of Livy: see Fred Schurink, 'How Gabriel Harvey Read Anthony Cope's Livy: Translation, Humanism, and War in Tudor England', in Schurink (ed.), *Tudor Translation*, pp. 58–78. For Harvey's particular interest in Livy and extensive notes on his works, see Harvey, *Marginalia*, pp. 93–4, 117, 134, *passim*.
121. Jardine, 'Encountering Ireland', pp. 63–4.
122. On Gilbert, see William Gilbert Gosling, *The Life of Sir Humphrey Gilbert, England's First Empire Builder* (London: Constable, 1911); *ODNB* entry on Humphrey Gilbert by Rory Rapple.
123. Thomas Churchyard, *A Generall Rehearsall of Warres* (1579), sigs. Q1^r–R1^v. On the FitzGerald Uprising, see Steven Ellis, *Tudor Ireland: Crown Community and the Conflict of Cultures* (Harlow: Longman, 1985), pp. 259–61.
124. Humphrey Gilbert, *Queene Elizabethes Achademy*, ed. F. J. Furnivall, EETS extra ser. 8 (London: Routledge, 1869), pp. 1–12.
125. D. B. Quinn, 'Sir Thomas Smith (1513–1577) and the Beginnings of English Colonial Theory', *Proceedings of the American Philosophical Society* 89 (1945), 543–60; Hiram Morgan, 'The Colonial Venture of Sir Thomas Smith in Ulster, 1571–5', *HJ* 28 (1985), 261–78; Anthony Grafton and Lisa Jardine, '"Studied for Action"' p. 42. An Edwardian coin minted in Dublin was discovered in Hill Hall, probably deposited in the house the late 1560s or 1570s:

Paul Drury, with Richard Simpson, *Hill Hall: A Singular House Devised by a Tudor Intellectual* (London: Society of Antiquaries, 2009), p. 35.

126. See Philip Withington, *Society in Early Modern England* (Cambridge: Polity, 2010), pp. 207–15.

127. Thomas Smith, *A letter sent by I.B. Gentleman vnto his very frende Maystet [sic] R.C. Esquire vvherin is conteined a large discourse of the peopling & inhabiting the cuntrie called the Ardes, and other adiacent in the north of Ireland, and taken in hand by Sir Thomas Smith one of the Queenes Maiesties priuie Counsel, and Thomas Smith Esquire, his sonne* (London, 1572), sig. B3ᵛ. The best analysis of the state of colonial practice and knowledge immediately before Smith's venture, which shows how closely Henry Sidney and William Cecil were involved in debates and organization of plantations in Ireland is D. G. White, 'The Tudor Plantations in Ireland before 1571', unpublished PhD thesis, University of Dublin, 1967. On Smith, Cecil, and Sidney, see also David Armitage, *The Ideological Origins of the British Empire* (Cambridge: Cambridge University Press, 2000), pp. 47–51.

128. Cited in Andrew Hadfield and John McVeagh (eds.), *Strangers to that Land: British Perceptions of Ireland from the Reformation to the Famine* (Gerrards Cross: Colin Smythe, 1994), p. 99. According to Mark A. Hutchinson, the pamphlet probably underplays the punitive nature of Smith's enterprise: 'Sir Henry Sidney and His Legacy: Reformed Protestantism and the Government of Ireland and England, c.1558–1580', unpublished PhD thesis, University of Kent at Canterbury, 2010, pp. 115–17.

129. An ideal expressed most clearly in the life and work of Sir Philip Sidney, enabling his contemporaries to construct him as a legend after his premature death in 1586: Howell, *Sidney: Shepherd Knight*; Van Dorsten et al. (eds.), *Sidney: 1586 and the Creation of a Legend*.

130. Cited in *Chronology*, pp. 3–4. See also Carpenter, *Reference Guide*, p. 13.

131. Honan, *Marlowe*, ch. 5; Eccles, 'Elizabethan Edmund Spensers', p. 415.

132. Spenser, *Selected Letters*, ed. Burlinson and Zurcher, *passim*.

133. *ODNB* entry on Henry Norris by Susan Doran; Nolan, *Sir John Norreys*, p. 16. On Henry Norris's links to Cecil, see Read, *Secretary Cecil*, pp. 391–3; Alford, *Burghley*, pp. 153–9.

134. *ODNB* article on John Whitgift by Brett Ussher; Attwater, *Pembroke College*, p. 37.

135. Collinson, *Grindal*, pp. 37, 270–1, *passim*; Attwater, *Pembroke College*, pp. 41–50; Judson, *Watts*, pp. 6, 8, 17, 26. Judson also shows that Watts was close to Alexander Nowell, and mentions him in his will (p. 21).

136. Judson, *John Young*, pp. 6, 15–16.

137. *ODNB* entry on John Young by Brett Ussher; Attwater, *Pembroke College*, pp. 43–4.

138. See pp. 110–18.

139. Judson, *John Young*, pp. 10–11.

140. See pp. 115–17.

141. We cannot be absolutely sure that the letters in the *Letter-Book* were ever actually sent, and certainly many of the later ones look like writing experiments with the form rather than real epistles. But these first letters seem more genuine and it looks as if Harvey was practising to make sure that he expressed himself exactly as he wanted to: see H. R. Woudhuysen, 'Leicester's Literary Patronage: A Study of the English Court, 1578–1582', unpublished DPhil thesis, University of Oxford, 1980, pp. 140–78. See also the analysis in Josephine Waters Bennett, 'Spenser and Gabriel Harvey's "Letter-Book"', *MP* 29 (1931), 163–86.

142. *ODNB* entry on Thomas Neville by J. B. Mullinger, rev. Stanford Lehmberg; Stern, *Harvey*, pp. 17–19.

143. Harvey, *Letter-Book*, p. 4.

144. Ibid. 6.

145. Ibid. 8.

146. Stern, *Harvey*, p. 18.

147. For discussion, see Nashe, *Works*, v. 65–110; Donald J. McGinn, *Thomas Nashe* (Boston: Twayne, 1981), chs. 8–10; Lorna Hutson, *Thomas Nashe in Context* (Oxford: Clarendon Press, 1989), ch. 10; Hadfield, ' "Not without Mustard" '.

148. On Wolfe and Harvey, see Stern, *Harvey*, pp. 101–3; *ODNB* entry on John Wolfe by Ian Gadd.

149. See the *ODNB* entries on John Still by John Craig and Thomas Preston by Alexandra Shepard. Harvey later wrote to Robert Dudley, earl of Leicester, recommending Still for a bishopric: Stern, *Harvey*, p. 50.

150. Harvey–Spenser *Letters*, pp. 55, 24.

151. Nashe, *Works*, iii. 76, 79.

152. Ibid. 88–9.

153. Stern, *Harvey*, p. 80.

154. Grafton and Jardine, ' "Studied for Action" ', 56.

155. On Cheke and Smith see *ODNB* entry on John Cheke by Alan Bryson; Richards, *Rhetoric and Courtliness*, chs. 3–5; John F. McDiarmid, 'Common Consent, *Latinitas*, and the "Monarchical Republic" in Mid-Tudor Humanism', in John F. McDiarmid (ed.), *The Monarchical Republic of Early Modern England: Essays in Response to Patrick Collinson* (Aldershot: Ashgate, 2007), pp. 55–74.

156. Stern, *Harvey*, p. 48; Harvey, *Letter-Book*, pp. 168–9.

157. Harvey–Spenser, *Letters*, p. 27. See also Harvey, *Marginalia*, p. 157.

158. For more evidence of the popularity of modern language editions at the universities, see 'Private Libraries in Renaissance England,' http://plre.folger.edu/books.php. I owe this reference to Jennifer Richards.

159. Harvey–Spenser, *Letters*, p. 28.

160. Arthur Tilley, 'Greek Studies in England in the Early Sixteenth-Century', *EHR* 53 (1938), 221–39, 438–56, at 440–1.

161. Harvey–Spenser, *Letters*, p. 27.

162. The story is not in *The Golden Legend*, the principal source of saints' lives in the post-medieval period, but was easily available elsewhere (Jacobus de Voraigne, *The Golden Legend: Readings on the Saints*, ed. and trans. William Granger Ryan, 2 vols. (Princeton: Princeton University Press, 1993)). John Bale, an author Spenser and Harvey would have known, tells the story but transforms the conversion of the Angles into one of lustful paederasty and a means of oppressing an independent church: *The Pageant of Popes* (London, 1574), sig. 35^{r-v}.

163. Jardine, *Erasmus*, pp. 182–7; Alistair Fox, *Thomas More: History & Providence* (Oxford: Blackwell, 1982), pp. 36–45. See also Altman, *Tudor Play of Mind*, pp. 32–3; Douglas Duncan, *Ben Jonson and the Lucianic Tradition* (Cambridge: Cambridge University Press, 1979); Arthur F. Kinney, *Humanist Poetics: Thought Rhetoric, and Fiction in Sixteenth-Century England* (Amherst: University of Massachusetts Press, 1986).

164. See Harvey, *Marginalia*, pp. 113, 155.

165. T. Murner, *A Merye, A Merye Jest of a man called Howleglas* (London, 1528?), Bodleian Library, shelfmark 4°.Z.3 Art Seld. sig. M4^v; cited in Stern, *Harvey*, p. 228. The volume, which is a substantial quarto, consists of several miscellaneous books bound together in the 17th century, from the collection of John Selden, perhaps bound by him, but more likely by the library when it acquired the volume, given its size and the poverty of the Bodleian in that period (I owe this information to Sarah Wheale). The volume includes the 1637 quarto of *Hamlet*, Fletcher's *Knight of the Burning Pestle*, Lindsay's *Satire of the Three Estates*, some of John Cleveland's poems, and *Merry Jests of Robin Hood*.

166. Galbraith, 'Spenser and the History of the Book', pp. 17–20.

167. P. M. Zall (ed.), *A Hundred Merry Tales and Other Jestbooks of the Fifteenth and Sixteenth Centuries* (Lincoln: University of Nebraska Press, 1963). For comment, see Garrett Sullivan and Linda Woodbridge, 'Popular Culture in Print', in Arthur Kinney (ed.), *The Cambridge Companion to English Literature, 1500–1600* (Cambridge: Cambridge University Press, 2000), pp. 265–86, at pp. 273–9; Robert W. Maslen, 'The Afterlife of Andrew Borde', *SP* 100 (2003), 463–92; Woodbridge, 'Jest Books'; Anne Lake Prescott, 'The Ambivalent Heart: Thomas More's Merry Tales', *Criticism* 45 (2003), 417–33; Indira Ghose, *Shakespeare and Laughter: A Cultural History* (Manchester: Manchester University Press, 2008), pp. 60–2, 97–109. Peter Burke's comment that popular culture was everyone's culture occurs in *Popular Culture in Early Modern Europe* (London: Temple Smith, 1978), prologue. On Spenser and jestbooks, see Andrew Hadfield, 'Spenser and Jokes: The 2008 Kathleen Williams Lecture', *Sp. St.* 25 (2010), 1–19.

168. For descriptions of the copies of books, see Stern, *Harvey*, pp. 203, 240.

169. Alexander Samson, 'Lazarillo de Tormes and the Picaresque in Early Modern England', in Hadfield (ed.), *Oxford Handbook of Early Modern Prose* (forthcoming).

170. Bodleian 4°.Z.3 Art Seld., sigs. N3^r, N3^v.

171. Bodleian 4°.Z.3 Art Seld., sig. N3^v.

172. Peter Bayley, 'Braggadocchio', *Sp. Enc.*, pp. 109–10.

173. Harvey–Spenser, *Letters*, pp. 29–30.

174. Patrick Collinson, 'Perne the Turncoat: An Elizabethan Reputation', in *Elizabethans*, pp. 179–217, at p. 217.

175. Nashe, *Works*, iii. 58.

176. Judson, *Life*, p. 38.

177. Harvey, *Fovre Letters*, p. 31; Stern, *Harvey*, p. 58; Richard A. McCabe, ' "Thine owne nations frend/And Patrone": The Rhetoric of Petition in Harvey and Spenser', *Sp. St.* 22 (2007), 47–72, at 60.

178. See Warren B. Austen, 'William Withie's Notebook: Lampoons on John Lyly and Gabriel Harvey', *RES* 23 (1947), 297–309.

179. On Forsett, see the *ODNB* entry by Sean Kelsey.

180. Edward Forsett, *Pedanticus*, III.v, lines 47–51 (ed. and trans. Dana F. Sutton: http://www. philological.bham.ac.uk/forsett/contents.html, accessed 13 May 2009). All subsequent references to this edition in parentheses in the text. See also *Pedanticus*, ed. E. F. J. Tucker (Hildesheim: Georg Olms Verlag, 1989), and for evidence of Forsett's authorship, see G. C. Moore Smith, 'The Authorship of "Pedantius" ', *N&Q* 153 (1927), 427.

181. John Nichols, *The Progresses and Public Processions of Queen Elizabeth*, 3 vols. (London, 1823), ii. 110; Stern, *Harvey*, p. 42; Thomas Hugh Jameson, 'The *Gratulationes Valdinenses* of Gabriel Harvey', unpublished PhD dissertation, Yale University, 1938; Patrick Collinson, 'Pulling the Strings: Religion and Politics in the Progress of 1578', in Elizabeth Jayne Archer, Elizabeth Goldring, and Sarah Knight (eds.), *The Progresses, Pageants, & Entertainments of Queen Elizabeth I* (Oxford: Oxford University Press, 2007), pp. 122–41.

182. Nashe, *Works*, iii. 80.

183. Ong, *Ramus*, ch. 5.

184. *Spenser Allusions*, p. 4, notes this possibility.

185. Harvey charted his progress from addiction to Ciceronianism to a more balanced use of the style in *Ciceronianus*, pp. 77–83. See Kendrick W. Prewitt, 'Gabriel Harvey and the Practice of Method', *SEL* 39 (1999), 19–39, at 21. See also G. K. Hunter, *John Lyly: The Humanist as Courtier* (London: Routledge, 1962), pp. 263–81.

186. Tacitus, *On Imperial Rome*, trans. Micahel Grant (Harmondsworth: Penguin, 1956), pp. 327–8; *The Satires of Horace and Persius*, trans. Niall Rudd (Harmondsworth: Penguin, 1973), pp. 147–8, *passim*.

187. Nashe, *Works*, i. 323, iii. 35.

188. *The Three Parnassus Plays, 1598–1603*, ed. J. B. Leishman (London: Nicholson and Watson, 1949), pp. 35, 55, 79–80, 97, 102.

189. Nicholl, *Cup of News*, pp. 50, 122–3. Burby was active from 1592 to 1607. He later published Richard Lichfield's *The Trimming of Thomas Nashe* (1597), suggesting that he also had contacts with the Harvey camp, which might indicate that he was associated with Harvey's ally in the printing trade, John Wolfe. See *Printers*, p. 55. The tract was once attributed to Harvey (see *The Works of Gabriel Harvey*, ed. Alexander B. Grosart, 3 vols. (London: privately printed, 1885), iii. 1–72), but the author has now been identified as Lichfield: see Benjamin Griffin, 'Nashe's Dedicatees: William Beeston and Richard Lichfield', *N&Q* 44 (Mar. 1997), 47–9.

190. Alan H. Nelson, *Monstrous Adversity: The Life of Edward de Vere, 17th earl of Oxford* (Liverpool: Liverpool University Press, 2003), pp. 262–5; Heaton, *Writing and Reading Royal Entertainments*, p. 73.

191. Carl H. Pforzheimer, *English Literature, 1475–1700*, 3 vols. (New York: privately printed, 1940), iii. 997–8. On Ponsonby, see Michael G. Brennan, 'William Ponsonby: Elizabethan Stationer', *AEB: Analytical & Enumerative Bibliography* 7 (1984), 91–110; *ODNB* entry on William Ponsonby by Sidney Lee, rev. Anita McConnell; Wayne Erikson, 'William Ponsonby', in Bracken and Silver (eds.), *Book Trade*, pp. 204–12.

192. See the *ODNB* entry on Benedict Barnham by Sarah Bendall. Barnham's daughter, Elizabeth, married Mervyn Touchet, the notorious 2nd earl of Castlehaven (1593–1631) in 1611, which might suggest that the Barnham family had connections with the Munster Plantation where Touchet probably grew up and where his family had lands. See the *ODNB* entry on Mervyn Touchet and Andrew Hadfield, 'Edmund Spenser and Samuel Brandon', *N&Q* 56/4 (Dec. 2009), 536–8.

193. Bernard Freyd, 'Spenser or Anthony Munday?—A Note on the *Axiochus*', *PMLA* 50 (1935), 903–8, at 905; Frederick M. Padelford, 'Reply to Bernard Freyd', *PMLA* 50 (1935), 908–13, at 908.

194. It is likely that the author of the letter was Munday, given his relationship to Barnham, and the attention he draws to their connections. The author does not, significantly enough, claim that he was the translator, but commends the importance of the work. The dedicatory letter 'To the Reader' makes the attribution, following the title page, and, given the separate printing of the texts, it is not unreasonable to assume that the book was stitched together in an opportunistic fashion and need not be read as a coherent, planned whole.

195. See Edmund Spenser, *The 'Axiochus' of Plato Translated by Edmund Spenser*, ed. Frederick Morgan Padelford (Baltimore: Johns Hopkins University Press, 1934), and the reviews by Douglas Bush (*MLN* 50 (1935), 191–2), and Douglas Hamer (*RES* 12 (1936), 84–6). The case for Munday is made in Celestine Turner Wright, 'Young Anthony Munday Again', *SP* 56 (1959), 150–68; 'Anthony Munday, "Edward" Spenser, and E. K.', *PMLA* 76 (1961), 34–9; ' "Lazarus Pyott" and Other Inventions of Anthony Munday', *PQ* 42 (1963), 532–41. The parallels with *The Faerie Queene* are noted in Harold L. Weatherby, '*Axiochus* and the Bower of Bliss: Some Fresh Light on Sources and Authorship', *Sp. St.* 6 (1985), 95–113. A sceptical view of Spenser's authorship is expressed in Holger Nørgaard, 'Translations of the Classics into English Before 1600', *RES* 9 (1958), 164–72, at 168.

196. Marshall W. S. Swan, 'The Sweet Speech and Spenser's (?) *Axiochus*', *ELH* 11 (1944), 161–81, at 163–4.

197. Naomi C. Liebler, 'Elizabethan Pulp Fiction: The Example of Richard Johnson', *Critical Survey* 12 (2000), 71–87. I am grateful to Prof. Liebler for drawing my attention to this article.

198. *ODNB* entry on John Charlewood by H. R. Tedder, rev. Robert Faber; on John Danter, see *Printers*, pp. 83–4. See also Wright, 'Young Anthony Munday', p. 157; Swan, 'Sweet Speech', pp. 164–5.

199. Edmund Spenser, *Axiochus. A most excellent dialogue, written in Greeke by Plato the phylosopher: concerning the shortnesse and vncertainty of this life, with the contrary ends of the good and wicked./ Translated out of Greeke by Edw. [sic] Spenser; Heereto is annexed a sweet speech or oration spoken at the tryumphe at White-hall before her Maiestie, by the page to the right noble Earle of Oxenforde* (London, 1592); Swan, 'Sweet Speech', pp. 166–73; Wright, 'Young Anthony Munday', pp. 156–7.

200. Philippe du Plessis Mornay, *Six Excellent Treatises of Life and Death collected (and published in French) by Philip Mornay, sieur du Plessis; and now (first) translated into English* (London, 1607). On Lownes see Johnson, *Critical Bibliography*, pp. 21–2; *Printers*, p. 180.

201. Philippe du Plessis Mornay, *A Discourse of Life and Death. written in French by Ph. Mornay. Antonius, a tragoedie written also in French by Ro. Garnier. Both done in English by the Countesse of Pembroke* (London, 1592); Philippe du Plessis Mornay, *A Discourse of Life and Death: vvritten in French by Phil. Mornay. Done in English by the Countesse of Pembroke* (London, 1606). On Mary Sidney's translation, see *The Collected Works of Mary Sidney Herbert, Countess of Pembroke*, ed. Margaret P. Hannay, Noel J. Kinnamonn, and Michael G. Brennan, 2 vols. (Oxford: Clarendon Press, 1998), i. 208–54. On the importance of Mornay for the Sidneys, see Duncan-Jones, *Sidney, passim*.

202. *Axiochus* appears to have been translated principally from the Latin, with reference to the Greek original: see Spenser, *Axiochus*, ed. Padelford, introd., p. 17.

203. Ibid. 12.

204. Prewitt, 'Harvey and the Practice of Method', p. 22.

205. Isabel Rivers, *Classical and Christian Ideas in English Renaissance Poetry* (London: Routledge, 1975), ch. 4; Reid Barbour, *English Epicures and Stoics: Ancient Legacies in Early Stuart Culture* (Amherst: University of Massachusetts Press, 1998), *passim*; Joshua Scodel, *Excess and the Mean in Early Modern English Literature* (Princeton: Princeton University Press, 2002), *passim*.
206. Spenser, *Axiochus*, sig. C1^{r-v}.
207. Jill Kraye, 'Moral Philosophy', in Schmitt and Skinner (eds.), *Cambridge History of Renaissance Philosophy*, pp. 303–86, at pp. 356–9; Kristeller, *Renaissance Thought*, ch. 3.
208. Spenser, *Axoichus*, sig. C1^{v}.
209. On Bruno and Ficino, see Ernst Cassirer, Paul Oskar Kristeller, and John Herman Randall, Jr (eds.), *The Renaissance Philosophy of Man* (Chicago: University of Chicago Press, 1948), pp. 185–212; Alfonso Ingegno, 'The New Philosophy of Nature', and Charles H. Lohr, 'Metaphysics', in Schmitt, Charles, and Skinner (eds.), *Cambridge History of Renaissance Philosophy*, pp. 236–64, at pp. 254–6, and pp. 537–638, at pp. 568–81; Mary Davies, 'Bruno in England, 1583–1585: The Cultural Context for Bruno's *De Gli Eroici Furori*', unpublished PhD thesis, Swansea University, 2009. On Bruno and the Sidney circle, see John Buxton, *Sir Philip Sidney and the English Renaissance* (London: Macmillan, 1966), pp. 160–7. On *Axiochus*, see William Keith Chambers Guthrie, *A History of Greek Philosophy: The Later Plato and the Academy* (Cambridge: Cambridge University Press, 1986), pp. 394–6.
210. *ODNB* entry on 'Charlewood'. I owe this point to Jill Kraye.
211. *Axiochus* is generally described as a second-rate work, one of 'inferior merit' (Guthrie, *Later Plato*, p. 395).
212. As may have happened with *A View*: see p. 367.
213. Charles Bowie Millican, 'The Supplicats for Spenser's Degrees', *HLQ* 2 (1939), 467–70, at 467. The following paragraph owes much to Millican's research.
214. John Venn (ed.), *Grace Book, containing the Records of the University of Cambridge for the Years 1542–1589* (Cambridge: Cambridge University Press, 1910), p. 260.
215. Venn (ed.), *Grace Book*, p. 290.
216. Judson, *Life*, p. 43. Venn explains that it is uncertain when lists began to reflect accurately a ranking order instead of simply one of seniority, and suggests that there was always an element of merit involved (*Grace Book*, introd., pp. viii–x). See also J. R. Tanner (ed.), *The Historical Register of the University of Cambridge: Being a Supplement to the Calendar with a Record of University Offices, Honours and Distinctions to the Year 1910* (Cambridge: Cambridge University Press, 1917), pp. 355–7. I owe this explanation to Malcolm Underhill, archivist of St John's College, Cambridge.
217. Attwater, *Pembroke College*, pp. 48–9; Cooper and Cooper, *Annals of Cambridge*, ii. 322–3.
218. Judson, *Life*, p. 43.

Chapter 3
1. *The Shepheardes Calender*, June, lines 9–24, in Spenser, *Shorter Poems*, p. 88.
2. Spenser, *Shorter Poems*, p. 91.
3. Ibid. 92.
4. For comment, see Richard A. McCabe, 'Authorial Self-Presentation,' *Sp. Handbook*, pp. 462–82, at p. 463.
5. See Michael McCanles, '*The Shepheardes Calender* as Document and Monument', *SEL* 22 (1982), 5–19; and pp. 126, 131.
6. Spenser, *Shorter Poems*, pp. 126–7.
7. On Harvey's ambitions as a poet, see Stern, *Harvey*, pp. 39–46; Harvey, *Letter-Book*, pp. 101–38.
8. And, we need to be further aware of the need to refer across works, especially when reading the *Calender* and the *Letters*: see pp. 145–6.
9. The January eclogue sees Colin lamenting his love for Rosalind and bemoaning Hobbinol's naive attachment to him. The narrative has moved on by June and Hobbinol's stability seems more appealing to Colin.

10. *The Eclogues, Georgics and Aeneid of Virgil*, trans. C. Day Lewis (Oxford: Oxford University Press, 1966), eclogue I, lines 64–6. For comment, see Bernard, *Ceremonies of Innocence*, pp. 54–61; Nancy Jo Hoffman, *Spenser's Pastorals: The Shepheardes Calender and 'Colin Clout'* (Baltimore: Johns Hopkins University Press, 1977), introd.; Helen Cooper, *Pastoral: Medieval into Renaissance* (Ipswich: Brewer, 1977), pp. 152–65; Paul Alpers, *What Is Pastoral?* (Chicago: University of Chicago Press, 1996), pp. 179–80.

11. See p. 146.

12. Scott-Warren, *ODNB* entry.

13. Although, given that Harvey's last years were probably spent practising 'physic' and experimenting with plant breeding in his native Saffron Walden, the reference may have some substance, and be intended as a playful irony: Stern, *Harvey*, ch. 7. For other information on Harvey's post-academic career, see Irving Ribner, 'Gabriel Harvey in Chancery—1608', *RES* 2 (1951), 142–7; Nicholas Popper, 'The English Polydaedali: How Gabriel Harvey Read Late Tudor London', *Journal of the History of Ideas* 66 (2005), 351–81.

14. 'It is called by *Caesar*, and other auncient writers, *Cancium* and *Cancia* in latine, which name (as I make coniecture) was framed out of *Caine*, a woorde that (in the language of the *Britaines*, whom *Caesar* at his ariuall founde inhabiting there) signifyeth, *bowghes*, or woods, and was imposed, by reason that this Countrie, both at that time, and also longe after, was in manner wholly ouergrowne with *woode*, as it shall hereafter in syt place more plainly appeare' (William Lambarde, *A Perambulation of Kent conteining the description, hystorie, and customes of that shyre* (London, 1576), p. 7). Spenser would have known Lambarde's work and made use of it in *A View* (*Variorum*, x. 280, 310, 362–3, *passim*). Lambarde was a Londoner, had a number of connections to Spenser's wider circles, knowing the Nowell family (he worked on Anglo-Saxon manuscripts with Laurence Nowell, cousin of the dean of Lichfield), John Stow, Sir Henry Sidney, and William Cecil: *ODNB* entry on 'William Lambarde', by J. D. Alsop. Lambarde's text was published by Ralph Newberry who had business connections with Henry Bynemann, publisher of the Harvey–Spenser *Letters*; *Printers*, p. 199. Most significantly he wrote a prayer with John Young, bishop of Rochester in the late 1570s when Spenser worked as Young's secretary: Warnicke, *Lambarde*, p. 46.

15. An early sceptical account is Percy W. Long, 'Spenser's Visit to the North of England', *MLN* 32 (1917), 58–9. Henry Woudhuysen wonders whether there is substance to a possible visit once Spenser had left Cambridge: 'Leicester's Literary Patronage', p. 134.

16. David Scott Wilson-Okamura, 'Problems in the Virgilian Career', *Sp. St.* 26 (2011), 1–30, at 10.

17. Shepard, *Meanings of Manhood*, ch. 4; Cressy, *Birth, Marriage & Death*, chs. 10–11.

18. Shepard, *Meanings of Manhood*, pp. 73–86; Singman, *Daily Life in Elizabethan England*, p. 50; Cressy, *Birth, Marriage & Death*, p. 285. The mean age for men marrying was about 27, but, the higher the social class, the earlier people tended to get married. On Spenser's marriage, see pp. 140–8.

19. *The Firste Syxe Bokes of the Mooste Christian Poet Marcellus Palingenius, called the zodiake of life, Newly translated out of Latin into English by Barnabe Googe* (London, 1561); Googe, *Eclogues, Epitaphs and Sonnets*, ed. Kennedy.

20. George Turbervile, *Epitaphes, Epigrams, Songs and Sonets with a discourse of the friendly affections of Tymetes to Pyndara his ladie* (London, 1567); *The Eclogues of Mantuan*, trans. George Turbervile (1567), ed. Douglas Bush (New York: Scholars' Facsimiles & Reprints, 1937).

21. *ODNB* entry by Michael Brennan.

22. Spenser, *Shorter Poems*, p. 146. The story of Tereus and Philomena was one of the most frequently retold of Ovid's myths of transformation (see *Metamorphoses*, trans. Mary M. Innes (Harmondsworth: Penguin, 1955), 146–53), and was an important source for Shakespeare's *Titus Andronicus*, a decade later—a work that also owes much to Spenser: see Jonathan Bate, *Shakespeare and Ovid* (Oxford: Clarendon Press, 1993), pp. 171–3, *passim*. On Gascoigne's life and career, see George Gascoigne, *A Hundreth Sundrie Flowres*, ed. G. W. Pigman III (Oxford: Clarendon Press, 2000), biographical introd. *The Steele Glasse* was dedicated to Arthur Lord Grey de Wilton, later to be Spenser's employer in Ireland, who was a close friend of Gascoinge (pp. xxxi, xl, lix).

23. Harvey, *Letter-Book*, pp. 58–68; Woudhuysen, 'Leicester's Literary Patronage', pp. 153–60.
24. Stern, *Harvey*, chs. 6–7.
25. Harvey, *Fovre Letters*, pp. 101–2; Spenser, *Shorter Poems*, p. 500.
26. On the ways in which letters advertised and established friendship, see Joseph Campana, '*Letters* (1580)', *Sp. Handbook*, pp. 177–97, at pp. 180–3; Lynne Magnusson, *Shakespeare and Social Dialogue: Dramatic Language and Elizabethan Letters* (Cambridge: Cambridge University Press, 1999), ch. 4.
27. Stern, *Harvey*, pp. 3–7. On John Harvey's involvement in town life, see K. C. Newton (ed.), *A Calendar of Deeds Relating to Saffron Walden and Neighbouring Parishes, 13th–18th. Centuries*, 6 vols. (Saffron Walden: Essex County Library, 1950), i. 127, 131, 133, 255; ii. 113, 311, 321, *passim*.
28. Peter M. Daly and Bari Hooper, 'John Harvey's Carved Mantle-Piece (ca. 1570): An Early Instance of the Use of Alciato Emblems in England', in Daly (ed.), *Andrea Alciato and the Emblem Tradition* (Aldershot: Ashgate, 1989), pp. 177–204, at p. 178.
29. Stern, *Harvey*, pp. 5–6; Nashe, *Works*, i. 195, 197, *passim*.
30. Daly and Hooper, 'John Harvey's Carved Mantle-Piece', p. 181.
31. On Alciati in England, see Bath, *Speaking Pictures*, chs. 1–3. On Spenser and Alciati, see Michael Bath, 'Honey and Gall or: Cupid and the Bees. A Case of Iconographic Slippage', in Daly (ed.), *Andrea Alciato*, pp. 59–94, at pp. 70–2.
32. Daly and Hooper, 'John Harvey's Carved Mantle-Piece', pp. 186–7; Emma Marshall Denkinger, 'Some Renaissance References to *Sic Vos Non Vobis*', *PQ* 10 (1931), 151–62, at 156–7.
33. I am extremely grateful to Martyn Everrett for providing me with much information. In *Ciceronianus* Harvey recounts how he retired to Saffron Walden for nearly twenty weeks reading ancient and modern texts ready for his inaugural lectures as professor of rhetoric: Harvey, *Ciceronianus*, p. 71; Harvey, *Marginalia*, p. 14. On John Harvey's house in Hill Street, see Stern, *Harvey*, p. 7; Nicholas Pevsner, *The Building of England: Essex* (rev. edn., Harmondsworth: Penguin, 1976), p. 336.
34. Stern, *Harvey*, p. 5.
35. Harvey, *Letter-Book*, pp. 167–8; Virginia F. Stern, 'The Bibliotheca of Gabriel Harvey', *RS* 25 (1972), 1–62, at 10–11; Stern, *Harvey*, pp. 40–1, 65; Spenser, *Shorter Poems*, p. 146.
36. Daly and Hooper, 'John Harvey's Carved Mantle-Piece', p. 178.
37. Dewar, *Smith*, pp. 102–3.
38. Ibid. 192; Elisabeth Woodhouse, 'Spirit of the Elizabethan Garden', *Garden History* 27 (1999), 10–31, at 28; Drury, with Simpson, *Hill Hall*, pp. 1, 203.
39. Drury, with Simpson, *Hill Hall*, pp. 203–4, 208. For some details of the pictures at Écouen, see Hervé Oursel and Thierry Crépin-Leblond, *Musée National de la Renaissance: Château D'Écouen: Guide* (Paris: Éditions de la Réunion des musées nationaux, 1994), pp. 100–11. I am grateful to Maurice Howard for bringing this book to my attention.
40. Drury, with Simpson, *Hill Hall*, pp. 180–242. See also Tessa Watt, *Cheap Print and Popular Piety, 1550–1640* (Cambridge: Cambridge University Press, 1991), p. 192.
41. Tara Hamling, *Decorating the 'Godly' Household: Religious Art in Post-Reformation Britain* (New Haven: Yale University Press, 2010), p. 46.
42. Richard Simpson, 'Images and Ethics in Reformation Political Discourse: The Paintings at Sir Thomas Smith's Hill Hall', in Tara Hamling and Richard L. Williams (eds.), *Art Re-formed: Re-assessing the Impact of the Reformation on the Visual Arts* (Newcastle upon Tyne: Cambridge Scholars, 2007), pp. 127–36.
43. Edward VI was often compared to Hezikiah and the choice of subject reflects Smith's interests and shows that, like many reformers, Edward's reign was a formative experience: Drury, with Simpson, *Hill Hall*, p. 210; Natalie Mears, *Queenship and Political Discourse in the Elizabethan Realms* (Cambridge: Cambridge University Press, 2005), pp. 134–40; Hamling, *Decorating the 'Godly' Household*, pp. 237–8.
44. Drury, with Simpson, *Hill Hall*, pp. 225–6.
45. The most obvious and extensive telling of the story of Cupid and Psyche was Apuleius, *The Golden Ass*, a work which had considerable importance in the Renaissance. Smith had a copy in his library: see Drury, with Simpson, *Hill Hall*, p. 181; Apuleius, *The Golden Ass*, trans. Robert

Graves (Harmondsworth: Penguin, 1950), pp. 114–57; Supriya Chaudhuri, 'Lucius, thou art translated: Adlington's Apuleius', *RS* 22 (2008), 669–704; Robert Carver, *The Protean Ass: The 'Metamorphoses' of Apuleius from Antiquity to the Renaissance* (Oxford: Oxford University Press, 2007). On Spenser's representation of the story, see William A. Oram, 'Pleasure', *Sp. Enc.*, p. 548.

46. See Joan Henges Blythe, 'Sins, seven deadly', *Sp. Enc.*, pp. 659–70; Drury, with Simpson, *Hill Hall*, p. 262.

47. Bennett, *Evolution of 'The Faerie Queene'*, ch. 18. On Spenser's visual imagination, see Bender, *Spenser and Literary Pictorialism*; Lucy Gent, *Picture and Poetry, 1560–1620: Relations Between Literature and the Visual Arts in the English Renaissance* (Leamington Spa: James Hall, 1981), pp. 46–7; Richard Pindell, 'The Mutable Image: Man-in-Creation', in Kenneth John Atchity (ed.), *Eterne in Mutabilitie: The Unity of The Faerie Queene: Essays Published in Memory of Davis Philoon Harding* (Hamden, CT: Archon Books, 1972), pp. 158–79. More generally, see Clark, *Vanities of the Eye*.

48. Frederick Hard, 'Spenser's "Clothes of Arras and of Toure"', *SP* 27 (1930), 162–85; William J. Thomas, 'Pictures of the Great Earl of Leicester', *N&Q*, 3rd ser. 2 (1862), 201–2, 224–6.

49. Drury, with Simpson, *Hill Hall*, p. 217. Just as there were links between Dutch writers and intellectuals in exile, so were there links between artists and craftsmen (pp. 222, 233).

50. Robert Salter, *Wonderfull Prophecies from the beginning of the monarchy of this land hidden vnder the parables of: Three young noble-men in a fiary fornace. A chast wife, and two old fornicators. The idol Belus and his dragon. Daniel in a den amid lyons* (London, 1627), p. 42; C. Bowie Millican, 'A Friend of Spenser', *TLS*, 7 Aug. 1937, p. 576; Cummings, *Critical Heritage*, pp. 68, 145–6.

51. There is no trace of Salter as an Oxford or Cambridge alumn us, but he must have attended university somewhere.

52. *Leicester's Commonwealth: The Copy of a letter written by a Master of Art of Cambridge (1584) and Related Documents*, ed. D. C. Peck (Athens, OH: Ohio University Press, 1985), pp. 86–90. *Leicester's Commonwealth* was probably written by Robert Parsons, but was based in part on information supplied by Philip Howard, 13th earl of Arundel (1557–95), her cousin: see Mitchell Leimon and Geoffrey Parker, 'Treason and Plot in Elizabethan Diplomacy: The "Fame of Sir Edward Stafford" Reconsidered', *EHR* III (1996), 1134–58, at 1142–3. Spenser knew this work and was eager to defend those it attacked, notably Lord Grey: see Andrew Hadfield, 'Spenser's *View* and *Leicester's Commonwealth*', *N&Q* 48 (Sept. 2001), 256–9.

53. Thomas Rogers, *Leicester's Ghost*, ed. Franklin B. Williams, Jr (Chicago: University of Chicago Press, 1972), lines 641–51. The poem exists in a number of manuscripts, the most important of which is BL Add. MS 12132, the author's own copy. It was eventually published along with *Leicester's Commonwealth* in 1641, showing the close link between literature and polemic in establishing Leicester's reputation.

54. Arthur Collins, *Historical Collection of the Noble Families of Cavendishe, Holles, Vere, Harley, and Ogle* (London, 1572), pp. 77–8.

55. C. T. Prouty, *George Gascoigne: Elizabethan Courtier, Soldier and Poet* (New York: Columbia University Press, 1942), p. 193. It should, however, be remembered that Gascoigne was later commissioned by Leicester to produce an entertainment for the queen's progress to Kenilworth in the summer of 1575 (pp. 87–9).

56. *ODNB* entry on Douglas Sheffield by Simon Adams.

57. See p. 250.

58. It is also worth noting that Douglas Sheffield was a Howard and so was part of the premier Catholic family in England: she was close to Philip Howard, 13th earl of Arundel (1557–95), the alleged traitor, who was the great-grandson of her uncle, Thomas Howard, 3rd duke of Norfolk (1473–1554).

59. Nicholas Breton, *A Smale Handfull of Fragrant Flowers selected and gathered out of the louely garden of sacred scriptures* (London, 1575), sig. A1ʳ. On Breton see the *ODNB* entry by Michael Brennan.

60. Nicholas Breton, *Melancholike Humours, in verses of diuerse natures* (London, 1600), F3ʳ–F4ʳ. On Breton's funeral elegy for Spenser, see p. 394.

61. This paragraph is heavily indebted to the pioneering analysis of P. M. Buck, Jr, 'Add. MS 34064: And Spenser's *Ruines of Time* and *Mother Hubberds Tale*', *MLN* 22 (1907), 41–6.
62. BL Add. 34064, sigs. 27–55.
63. On the familiar motif of the pelican sacrificing herself for her children, see e.g. Stephen Bateman, *Batman Upon Bartholome* (London, 1582), ch. 29; Nicholas Breton, *Brittons Bovvre of Delights Contayning Many, Most Delectable and Fine Deuices, of Rare Epitaphes, Pleasant Poems, Pastorals and Sonets* (London, 1591), sig. B3ᵛ–B4ʳ.
64. Steven W. May, *The Elizabethan Courtier Poets: The Poems and Their Contexts* (Columbia: University of Missouri Press, 1999), *passim*.
65. On Rogers, see Franklin B. Williams, Jr, 'Thomas Rogers of Bryanston, an Elizabethan Gentleman-of-Letters', *HSNPL* 16 (1934), 253–67; id., 'Thomas Rogers as Ben Jonson's Dapper', *YES* 2 (1972), 73–7.
66. *House of Commons*, ii. 303.
67. Thomas Rogers, *Celestiall Elegies of the Goddesses and the Muses Deploring the Death of the Right Honourable and Vertuous Ladie the Ladie Fraunces Countesse of Hertford* (London, 1598). The volume owes much to *Daphnaïda*.
68. Franklin B. Williams, Jr, '*Leicester's Ghost*', *HSNPL* 18 (1935), 271–85, at 277. The poem also shows knowledge of Drayton and Kyd (p. 278).
69. Spenser, *Shorter Poems*, p. 30. For details, see Joseph Black and Lisa Celovsky, ' "Lost Works", Suppositious Pieces, and Continuations', *Sp. Handbook*, pp. 349–64, at pp. 350–5.
70. Spenser, *Shorter Poems*, pp. 128, 136.
71. *Variorum*, x. 6; Black and Celovsky, ' "Lost Works" ', p. 353.
72. *Variorum*, x. 459–60. See p. 272–3.
73. This would have been normal for an aspiring writer: see Nicholl, *Cup of News*, pp. 36–7.
74. Marjorie Plant, *The English Book Trade: An Economic History of the Making and Sale of Books* (3rd edn., London: Allen & Unwin, 1974), pp. 203–4.
75. Spenser, *Selected Letters*, introd., p. xxxi. On wages see Singman, *Daily Life in Elizabethan England*, p. 36.
76. Smith's extensive library was probably also an inspiration for Harvey: for details, see Dewar, *Smith*, pp. 15, 203; Drury, with Simpson, *Hill Hall*, pp. 206–7. It is possible that Spenser was able to make use of Smith's library too.
77. Stern, *Harvey*, p. 250.
78. Ibid. 248; Nashe, *Works*, iii. 89. For evidence see Elizabeth S. Leedham-Green, *Books in Cambridge Inventories: Book Lists from Vice-Chancellor's Court Probate Inventories in the Tudor and Stuart Periods*, 2 vols. (Cambridge: Cambridge University Press, 1986). See also R. J. Fehrenbach and E. S. Leedham-Green (eds.), *Private Libraries in Renaissance England: A Collection and Catalogue of Tudor and Stuart Book-Lists*, 5 vols. (Tempe, AZ: MRTS, 1992–8), especially vols. iii–v.
79. On Vautrollier, see John Corbett, 'The Prentise and the Printer: James VI and Thomas Vautrollier', in Kevin J. McGinley and Nicola Royan (eds.), *The Apparalling of Truth: Literature and Literary Culture in The Reign of James VI: A Festschrift for Roderick J. Lyall* (Newcastle upon Tyne: Cambridge Scholars, 2010), 80–93; Alastair F. Mann, *The Scottish Book Trade, 1500–1720: Print, Commerce and Print Control in Early Modern Scotland* (East Linton: Tuckwell, 2000), pp. 1, 14, 36, 73, *passim*. Corbett also shows that Vautrollier was linked to Buchanan and Daniel Rogers (p. 86).
80. Corbett, 'Prentise and the Printer', p. 92; Johnson, *Critical Bibliography*, p. 31.
81. See Jennifer Richards, 'Gabriel Harvey, James VI, and the Politics of Reading Early Modern Poetry', *HLQ* 71 (2008), 303–22.
82. For details, see Stern, *Harvey*, pp. 198–242; Harvey, *Marginalia*; G. C. Moore Smith, 'Printed Books with Gabriel Harvey's Autograph or MS Notes', *MLR* 28 (1933), 78–81; 29 (1934), 68–70; 30 (1935), 209.
83. Harvey undoubtedly established special relationships with particular booksellers, notably John Wolfe, with whom he later lived, the principal publisher of Italian books in late Elizabethan England. See Harry R. Hoppe, 'John Wolfe, Printer and Publisher', *The Library*, 4th ser. 14

(1933), 241–89; Clifford Chambers Huffman, 'John Wolfe', in Bracken and Silver (eds.), *Book Trade*, p. 326–9; Harry Sellers, 'Italian Books Printed in England Before 1640', *The Library*, 4th ser. 5 (1924), 105–28.

84. See Stern, *Harvey*, pp. 193–4, 250. On Dee's library see William H. Sherman, *John Dee: The Politics of Reading and Writing in the English Renaissance* (Amherst: University of Massachusetts Press, 1995). See also Peter J. French, *John Dee: The World of an Elizabethan Magus* (London: Routledge, 1972), ch. 3.

85. Queens' College, Cambridge, MS 49, fos. 70ʳ–78ʳ, available on-line http://scriptorium.english. cam.ac.uk/manuscripts/images/index.php?ms=Queens_49; John Strype, *The Life of the Learned Sir Thomas Smith* (Oxford: Clarendon Press, 1820), pp. 165, 274–81. For intellectual links between Smith and Harvey, see David Harris Sacks, 'The Prudence of Thrasymachus: Sir Thomas Smith and the Commonwealth of England', in Anthony Grafton and J. H. M. Salmon (eds.), *Historians and Ideologues: Essays in Honour of Donald R. Kelley* (Rochester: Rochester University Press, 2001), p. 89–122, at p. 91.

86. See John Leon Lievsay, *Stefano Guazzo and the English Renaissance* (Chapel Hill: University of North Carolina Press, 1961), pp. 96–9. It is also important to note that Lodowick Bryskett, Spenser's friend and predecessor as the clerk of the Munster Council, made extensive use of the work in his *Discourse of Civil Life* (1606).

87. On Olaus Magnus, see Matthew Woodcock, 'Spenser and Olaus Magnus: A Reassessment', *Sp. St.* 21 (2006), 181–204; Andrew Hadfield, 'The Idea of the North', *Journal of the Northern Renaissance* 1/1 (spring 2009), 1–18. On Buchanan, see Andrew Hadfield, 'Spenser and Buchanan', in Roger Mason (ed.), *Buchanan* (Aldershot: Ashgate, forthcoming); James Emerson Phillips, *Images of a Queen: Mary Stuart in Sixteenth-Century Literature* (Berkeley and Los Angeles: University of California Press, 1964), pp. 201–3; Richard A. McCabe, 'The Masks of Duessa: Spenser, Mary Queen of Scots, and James VI', *ELR* 17 (1987), 224–42.

88. Grafton and Jardine, ' "Studied for Action" '; Caroline Ruutz-Rees, 'Some Notes of Gabriel Harvey's in Hoby's Translation of Castiglione's *Courtier* (1561)', *PMLA* 25 (1910), 608–39.

89. Caroline Brown Bourland, 'Gabriel Harvey and the Modern Languages', *HLQ* 4 (1940), 85–106.

90. See pp. 72–3.

91. Harvey–Spenser, *Letters*, pp. 49–50. On the Nine Comedies, which Harvey exhorts Spenser to write—and so may not have existed yet, if at all, see Allan Gilbert, 'Were Spenser's Nine Comedies Lost?', *MLN* 73 (1958), 241–3.

92. Prouty, *Gascoigne*, p. 157.

93. On the Muses, see Grant and Hazel, *Who's Who in Classical Mythology*, pp. 225–6.

94. Gascoigne, *Hundreth Sundrie Flowres*, ed. Pigman, pp. 5–58; Harvey, *Marginalia*, pp. 165–73; Alan H. Nelson and John R. Elliott, Jr (eds.), *Inns of Court: Records of Early English Drama*, 3 vols. (Woodbridge: Brewer, 2010), ii. 732.

95. Jerome Turler, *The traueiler of Ierome Turler deuided into two bookes. The first conteining a notable discourse of the maner, and order of traueiling ouersea, or into straunge and forrein countreys. The second comprehending an excellent description of the most delicious realme of Naples in Italy. A woorke very pleasaunt for all persons to reade, and right profitable and necessarie vnto all such as are minded to traueyll* (London, 1575). Subsequent references appear in the text. For Harvey's marginalia, see Harvey, *Marginalia*, pp. 173–4. For comment on Turler see Vine, *In Defiance of Time*, pp. 144–6.

96. *Chronology*, p. 8; Stern, *Harvey*, p. 237. See also Israel Gollancz, 'Spenseriana', *PBA* 3 (1907), 99–105, at 103–4.

97. For analysis of Turler, see Melanie Ord, *Travel and Experience in Early Modern English Literature* (Basingstoke: Palgrave, 2007), pp. 3–4, 68–9.

98. Claudian, 'Of an old Man of Verona who never left his home', *Claudian*, with an English translation by Maurice Platnauer, 2 vols. (Cambridge, MA: Harvard University Press, 1922), lines 1–6 (ii. 194–5).

99. Garrett, *Marian Exiles*; John Bossy, *The English Catholic Community, 1570–1850* (Darnton: Longman and Todd, 1975), pp. 11–74; Arnold Pritchard, *Catholic Loyalism in Elizabethan England* (London: Scolar, 1979), ch. 3.

100. On the need for a licence to travel, see Thomas Palmer, *An Essay of the Meanes how to make our travails more profitable* (London, 1606), fo. 11; Clare Howard, *English Travellers of the Renaissance* (London: John Lane, 1914), ch. 6. On the relationship between exile and the experience of travel in a later period, see Christopher D'Addario, *Exile and Journey in Seventeenth-Century Literature* (Cambridge: Cambridge University Press, 2007).

101. Matthew Day, 'Hakluyt, Harvey, Nashe: The Material Text and Early Modern Nationalism', *SP* 104 (2007), 281–305, at 284; Woudhuysen, 'Leicester's Literary Patronage', pp. 136–7.

102. *Variorum*, x. 112.

103. *Carew, 1575–88*, p. 104. On Fitzmaurice's rebellion, see Ellis, *Tudor Ireland*, pp. 259–61; Colm Lennon, *Sixteenth-Century Ireland: The Incomplete Conquest* (New York: St Martin's, 1995), pp. 213–15. On executions and scaffold speeches, see John Bellamy, *The Tudor Law of Treason: An Introduction* (London: Routledge, 1979), ch. 5.

104. Andrew Hadfield, 'Spenser's Description of the Execution of Murrogh O'Brien: An Anti-Catholic Polemic?', *N&Q* 244 (June 1999), 195–7.

105. Woudhouysen, 'Leicester's Literary Patronage', ch. 6.

106. On Pelham see the *ODNB* entry by J. J. N. McGurk.

107. On Dorothy Pelham née Catesby, see the *ODNB* entry by Hugh Hanley.

108. *Chronology*, pp. 4, 10, 38; *Carew, 1575–88*, pp. 180, 239–40, 267, 269–70, 273–4, 276–7, 280, 283; Welply, 'Spenser: Being an Account of Some Recent Researches', pp. 147–8.

109. *Carew, 1575–88*, p. 105; *Chronology*, p. 7. On Drury's role in Ireland, see *ODNB* entry by Sean Kelsey; Spenser, *Selected Letters, passim.*

110. Mark Brayshay, 'Royal Post-Horse Routes in England and Wales: The Evolution of the Network in the Later-Sixteenth and Early-Seventeenth Century', *JHG* 17 (1991), 373–89, at 382–4. See also Mark Brayshay, Philip Harrison, and Brian Chalkley, 'Knowledge, Nationhood and Governance: The Speed of the Royal Post in Early-Modern England', *JHG* 24 (1998), 265–88. I owe these references to Natalie Mears. See also J. Crofts, *Packhorse, Waggon and Post: Land Carriage and Communications under the Tudors and Stuarts* (London: Routledge, 1967), chs. 12–17; James Daybell, *The Material Letter: Manuscript Letters and the Culture and Practices of Letter-Writing in Early Modern England, 1512–1635* (Basingstoke: Palgrave, 2012), ch. 5.

111. Eleanor Rosenberg, *Leicester, Patron of Letters* (New York: Columbia University Press, 1955), pp. 336–48.

112. The *Letters* are, for 'reasons never made clear, published in reverse chronology': the correct dating of the sequence is Spenser to Harvey from Leicester House (5 Oct. 1579) and Westminster (15–16 Oct.); Harvey's reply from Trinity Hall (23 Oct.); Spenser to Harvey from Westminster (2 Apr. 1580); Harvey's reply from Saffron Walden (7 Apr.); a final letter from Harvey from Saffron Walden (23 Apr.); the anonymous address 'To the Curious Buyer' (19 June 1580): Henry R. Woudhuysen, 'Letters, Spenser's and Harvey's', *Sp. Enc.*, pp. 434–5. See also Welply, 'Some Spenser Problems', 458.

113. Harvey–Spenser, *Letters*, p. 60. For a rigorous and meticulous analysis of the Harvey–Spenser letters which establishes a plausible chronology, showing that Spenser was planning to go abroad in 1579 but was eventually frustrated in his plans, see Woudhuysen, 'Leicester's Literary Patronage', pp. 190–1.

114. For one argument that suggests that we can take such statements at face value, see Rambuss, *Spenser's Secret Career.*

115. Alan Kendall, *Robert Dudley, Earl of Leicester* (London: Cassell, 1980), ch. 8; Rosenberg, *Leicester*, p. 331; Wallace T. McCaffrey, *Elizabeth I* (London: Arnold, 1993), ch. 16.

116. *John Stubbs's Gaping Gulf with Letters and Other Relevant Documents*, ed. Lloyd E. Berry (Charlottesville: University of Virginia Press, 1968); Duncan-Jones, *Sidney*, ch. 7.

117. See also Adams, *Leicester and the Court*, ch. 4. Stubbes was the brother-in-law of Michael Hicks, one of the key servants of Lord Burghley, which suggests that, while there were clear circles of

patronage and interest groups, politics was yet to be as clearly factionalized as it was in the 1590s: Smith, *Hickes*, pp. 93–6.

118. Kendall, *Leicester*, pp. 184–5.

119. Georgii Sabini Brande, *Poemata* (1563) and Petrilotichii Secundi Solitariensis, *Poemata* (1563). The British Library copy (shelfmark BL11403.aaa6(1)) retains the original binding and so shows us the volume that Spenser would have owned (I owe this information to Lee Piepho). The copy in the Folger Shakespeare Library that Spenser did own has been separated (shelfmarks V.d.341 (Sabinus) and PA 8547 L7 p& 1576 (Lotichins)).

120. The poems and letters are catalogued separately as Folger MS X.d.520. Lee Piepho, 'Edmund Spenser and Neo-Latin Literature: An Autograph Manuscript on Petrus Lotichius and His Poetry', *SP* 100 (2003), 123–34, at 124.

121. Piepho, 'Autograph Manuscript', p. 127.

122. For further discussion, see Shinn, 'Spenser and Popular Print Culture'.

123. Binns, *Intellectual Culture*, p. 113.

124. Stephen Zon, *Petrus Lotichius Secundus: Neo-Latin Poet* (New York: Peter Lang, 1983), pp. 103, 165–6, 232–3, *passim*.

125. Binns, *Intellectual Culture*, pp. 16, 113. On Spenser's interest in the *Heroides*, see Syrithe Pugh, *Spenser and Ovid* (Aldershot: Ashgate, 2005), pp. 128–30, 218–21; Michael Holahan, 'Ovid', *Sp. Enc.*, pp. 520–2.

126. Lee Piepho, 'Spenser and Neo-Latin Literature', *Sp. Handbook*, pp. 573–85, at pp. 579–81.

127. Text of the poem in *Letters*, H1r–H2v; translation cited from *Variorum*, x. 256–8.

128. *Variorum*, x. 258.

129. John Hale, *The Civilization of Europe in the Renaissance* (London: HarperCollins, 1993), p. 62.

130. Constance M. Furey, 'Bound by Likeness: Vives and Erasmus on Marriage and Friendship', in Daniel T. Lochman, Martiere López, and Lorna Hutson (eds.), *Discourses and Representations of Friendship in Early Modern Europe, 1500–1700* (Farnham: Ashgate, 2011), pp. 29–43.

131. Harvey–Spenser, *Letters*, p. 54.

132. Paul R. Sellin, ' "Souldiers of one army": John Donne and the Army of the States General as an International Protestant Crossroads', in Mary Arshagouni Papazian (ed.), *John Donne and the Protestant Reformation* (Detroit: Wayne State University Press, 2003), pp. 143–92, at p. 167; Paul R. Sellin, *'So Doth, So Is Religion': John Donne and Diplomatic Contexts in the Reformed Netherlands, 1619–1620* (Columbia: University of Missouri Press, 1988), pp. 17–21. See also Paul R. Sellin and Augustus J. Veenendaal, Jr, 'A "Pub Crawl" Through Old The Hague: Shady Light On Life and Art Among English Friends of John Donne in The Netherlands', *John Donne Journal* 6 (1987), 235–60. Conway wrote a commendatory sonnet for Geoffrey Fenton's *Certaine Tragicall Discourses* (1567): see the *ODNB* entry by M. A. Stevens.

133. Harvey–Spenser, *Letters*, p. 54.

134. Stephen Gosson, *The Schoole of Abuse conteining a plesaunt [sic] inuectiue against poets, pipers, plaiers, iesters, and such like caterpillers of a co[m]monwelth* (London, 1579), A2v–A6v. Sidney's response probably dates from 1582–3: Duncan-Jones, *Sidney*, pp. 230–9.

135. On Dyer, see the entry in the *ODNB* by Stephen W. May; May, *Elizabethan Courtier Poets*, pp. 287–316, *passim*.

136. Grafton and Jardine, ' "Studied for Action" ', pp. 35–40; Stern, *Harvey*, pp. 31, 39.

137. Jameson, '*Gratulationes Valdinenses* of Gabriel Harvey'; Stern, *Harvey*, pp. 39–40.

138. Harvey–Spenser, *Letters*, pp. 6–7.

139. Thomas Drant (*c.*1540–78), was at Cambridge at the same time as Spenser, and would have been known to Spenser: see the *ODNB* entry by R. W. McConchie; Eccles, 'Brief Lives', p. 46.

140. *Horace his Arte of Poetrie, Pistles, and Satyrs Englished* (London, 1567); Reavley Gair, 'Areopagus', *Sp. Enc.*, p. 55.

141. W. R. Gair, 'Literary Societies in England from Parker to Falkland', unpublished DPhil thesis, University of Oxford, 1968, pp. 61–2.

142. Gair, '*Areopagus*'.

143. Gair, 'Literary Societies', pp. 65, 68. See also Howard Maynadier, 'The Areopagus of Sidney and Spenser', *MLR* 4 (1909), 289–301; Frederick E. Faverty, 'A Note on the Areopagus', *PQ* 5 (1926), 278–80.

144. See Derek Attridge, *Well-Weighed Syllables: Elizabethan Verse in Classical Metres* (Cambridge: Cambridge University Press, 1974), pp. 130, 138; Kevin Pask, *The Emergence of the English Author: Scripting the Life of the Poet in Early Modern England* (Cambridge: Cambridge University Press, 1996), pp. 98–104.

145. Richard Stanihurst, *The First Foure Bookes of Virgils AEneis, translated into English heroicall verse, by Richard Stanyhurst: with other poëticll [sic] deuises thereto annexed* (London, 1583), A4ʳ. I owe this point to an unpublished paper by Margaret Tudeau-Clayton.

146. Harvey–Spenser, *Letters*, p. 56. The scansion is that of Derek Attridge, *Well-Weighed Syllables*, p. 190.

147. Attridge, *Well-Weighed Syllables*, p. 190.

148. Thomas Kyd, *The Spanish Tragedy*, ed. Philip Edwards (1959; Manchester: Manchester University Press, 1988), III.ii, lines 1–11.

149. De Molen, *Mulcaster*, chs. 2–3; Wesley, 'Mulcaster's Boys', ch. 4.

150. On Fraunce's significance, see Katherine Koller, 'Abraham Fraunce and Edmund Spenser', *ELH* 7 (1940), 108–20.

151. On Fraunce's Ramism, see Tamara A. Goeglein, 'Reading English Ramist Logic Books as Early Modern Emblem Books: The Case of Abraham Fraunce', *Sp. St.* 20 (2005), 225–52; Ralph S. Pomeroy, 'The Ramist as Fallacy-Hunter: Abraham Fraunce and *The Lawiers Logicke*', *RQ* 40 (1987), 224–46. On Fraunce's possible access to *The Faerie Queene*, see Steven W. May, 'Marlowe, Spenser, Sidney and—Abraham Fraunce', *RES* (forthcoming). I am extremely grateful to Professor May for sending this article to me in adance of its publication.

152. Abraham Fraunce, *The Arcadian Rhetorike, or The praecepts of rhetorike made plaine by examples Greeke, Latin, English, Italian, French, Spanish, out of Homers Ilias, and Odissea, Virgils Aeglogs, [. . .] and Aeneis, Sir Philip Sydnieis Arcadia, songs and sonnets* (London, 1588), sig. C4ʳ.

153. Harvey–Spenser, *Letters*, p. 63.

154. Ibid. 64.

155. De Molen, *Mulcaster*, p. 105. On the extent of experiments with quantitative metre, especially among Cambridge students, see May, 'Fraunce'.

156. Sir Thomas Smith, *Literary and Linguistic Works*, 3 vols. (Stockholm: Almqvist & Wiksell, 1963–83), iii. *A Dialogue of the Correct and Improved Writing of English* (1983), p. 13.

157. Attridge, *Well-Weighed Syllables*, p. 174.

158. Ussher, 'Young', *ODNB*.

159. *Chronology*, p. 9.

160. James P. Bednarz, 'Young, John', *Sp. Enc.*, p. 739.

161. Camden, *Britannia*, p. 326.

162. Thomas Wilson, *An Accurate Description of Bromley, in Kent* (London, 1797), p. 21. On Tudor Bromley, see Edward Halsted, *The History and Topographical Survey of the County of Kent*, 4 vols. (Canterbury, 1778–99), i. 80–97; E. L. S. Horsburgh, *Bromley, Kent from the Earliest Times to the Present Century* (London: Hodder and Stoughton, 1929), pp. 19–20, 82–3.

163. Unpublished paper by Andrew Foster, University of Chichester, 29 June 2011.

164. See p. 191.

165. Harvey, *Rhetor*, section 68.

166. *ODNB* entry on Harrison by Felicity Heal. I owe this point to Ralph Houlbrooke and Helen Parish.

167. David Colclough, 'Introduction: Donne's Professional Lives', in Colclough (ed.), *John Donne's Professional Lives* (Cambridge: Brewer, 2003), pp. 1–16.

168. Brian P. Levack, *The Civil Lawyers in England, 1603–1641: A Political Study* (Oxford: Clarendon Press, 1973), ch. 5.

169. W. S. Holdsworth, *A History of English Law*, 9 vols. (5th edn., London: Methuen, 1931), i. 592.

170. Levack, *Civil Lawyers in England*, pp. 167–8.

171. Holdsworth, *History of English Law*, i. 594–5.

172. Holdsworth, *History of English Law*, 614, 616, 619.
173. Ibid. 620–2.
174. Zurcher, *Spenser's Legal Language*, ch. 3.
175. Tim Stretton, 'Women, Property and Law', in Anita Pacheco (ed.), *A Companion to Early Modern Women's Writing* (Oxford: Blackwell, 2002), pp. 40–57, at pp. 46–8.
176. Warnicke, *Lambarde*, ch. 7.
177. Lambarde, *Perambulation of Kent*, pp. 293–314; Camden, *Britannia*, pp. 332–3.
178. Fowler, *Spenser and the Numbers of Time*, pp. 172–5; Thomas P. Roche, Jr, *The Kindly Flame: A Study of the Third and Fourth Books of Spenser's Faerie Queene* (Princeton: Princeton University Press, 1964), 167–84.
179. Leicester Bradner sees a reference to Bromley in the July eclogue: 'An Allusion to Bromley in *The Shepherds' Calender*', *MLN* 49 (1934), 443–5. See also Magill, 'Spenser's Guyon', pp. 174–5.
180. Ben Jonson, 'To Penshurst', line 31, in Jonson, *Poems*, p. 89; Camden, *Britannia*, p. 329.
181. A. M. Buchan, 'The Political Allegory of Book IV of *The Faerie Queene*', *ELH* 11 (1944), 237–48, at 242–3.
182. Jack B. Oruch, 'Spenser, Camden, and the Poetic Marriage of Rivers', *SP* 64 (1967), 606–24; Buchan, 'Political Allegory of Book IV', pp. 239–40. On Camden, see p. 360.
183. Hadfield, *Spenser's Irish Experience*, ch. 5.
184. Spenser made extensive use of Irish geography in the extant description of the river marriage: see Joyce, 'Spenser's Irish Rivers'; A. C. Judson, *Spenser in Southern Ireland* (Bloomington: Principia, 1933). See also Oruch, 'Spenser, Camden', pp. 622–3.
185. On Bateman and Parker, see the *ODNB* entries by Rivkah Zim and David J. Crankshaw and Alexandra Gillespie.
186. Timothy Graham, 'Matthew Parker's Manuscripts: An Elizabethan Library and Its Use', in Leedham-Green and Webber (eds.), *Cambridge History of Libraries*, i. 322–41, at p. 327.
187. Stephen Bateman, *The Trauayled Pylgrime* (London, 1569).
188. Anne Lake Prescott, 'Spenser's Chivalric Restoration: From Bateman's "Travayled Pylgrime" to the Redcrosse Knight', *SP* 86 (1989), 166–97, at 170–1. De La Marche's other known work in English was *The Resolved Gentleman*, adapted and translated by Lewes Lewkenor, another writer with a Spenser connection see p. 294).
189. Dorothy Atkinson, 'Edmund Spenser's Family and the Church', *N&Q* 170 (1936), 172–5. See also Edward Bensly, 'Edmund Spenser's Family and the Church', *N&Q* 170 (1936), 231–2.
190. Atkinson, 'Spenser's Family', p. 174.
191. Judson, *Watts*, p. 8.
192. Ibid. 11.
193. Ibid. 17.
194. Ibid. 21.
195. Ibid. 24–5.
196. Lambarde, *Perambulation of Kent*, p. 266.
197. Harvey, *Letter-Book*, pp. 1–20, 24–40, 44–54, 159–61; Henry Woudhuysen, 'Gabriel Harvey', in Andrew Hadfield (ed.), *The Oxford Handbook to English Prose, 1500–1640* (Oxford: Oxford University Press, forthcoming).
198. Stone, *Crisis of the Aristocracy*, pp. 446–8, 707–11, *passim*; Wrightson, *English Society*, pp. 57–61. Welply suggests that Watts may have helped send Spenser from school to university ('Spenser: Being an Account of Some Recent Researches', p. 147); Judson is sceptical (*Watts*, p. 26).
199. Spenser, *Shorter Poems*, p. 116. On 'Diggon Davie', a figure who can be related to 'Colin Clout' as a version of the honest English ploughman serving the people and the true church, see Scott Lucas, 'Diggon Davie and Davy Dicar: Edmund Spenser, Thomas Churchyard, and the Poetics of Public Protest', *Sp. St.* 16 (2001), 151–65.
200. On Roffyn as Rochester, see McLane, *Spenser's Shepheardes Calender*, ch. 10; King, *Spenser's Poetry and the Reformation Tradition*, p. 30. On Artegall and Talus, see Michael O'Connell, *Mirror and Veil: The Historical Dimension of Spenser's Faerie Queene* (Chapel Hill: University of North Carolina Press, 1977), ch. 5; James Nohrnberg, *The Analogy of The Faerie Queene* (Princeton: Princeton University Press, 1977), pp. 409–25.

201. William Lewin appears to have been chancellor from 1576 until his death in 1598, perhaps working alongside Hugh Lloyd (d. 1601). The archdeacon in this period was Ralph Pickover (1576–98). It is also worth noting that there was a Robert Lougher, who was chancellor in the Exeter diocese in the 1560s, but there is no obvious connection to Rochester. I am extremely grateful to Andrew Foster for help with this note.

202. William Caxton (trans), *The History of Reynard the Fox* (June 1481), ed. Edward Arber (Westminster: Constable, 1895), pp. 6–7; B. E. C. Davis, *Edmund Spenser: A Critical Study* (Cambridge: Cambridge University Press, 1933), pp. 22, 102.

203. See e.g. the assumption that the eclogue is anti-Catholic in Hoffman, *Spenser's Pastorals*, p. 114; Hume, *Edmund Spenser: Protestant Poet*, pp. 38–40; King, *Spenser's Poetry and the Reformation Tradition*, p. 20. A different reading is provided in Nancy Lindheim, 'Spenser's Virgilian Pastoral: The Case for September', *Sp. St.* 11 (1990, pub. 1994), 1–16. S. K. Heninger is also sceptical and comments, 'The precise identities of Lowder and of the wolf in sheep's clothing...remain hidden' ('*The Shepheardes Calender*', *Sp. Enc.*, pp. 645–51, at p. 649).

204. John Young, *A Sermon Preached Before the Queenes Maiestie, the second of March. An. 1575* (London, 1576); Kevin Sharpe, *Selling the Tudor Monarchy: Authority and Image in Sixteenth-Century England* (New Haven: Yale University Press, 2009), p. 442.

205. Jones, *English Reformation*, chs. 3, 5; Brian Cummings, *The Literary Culture of the Reformation: Grammar and Grace* (Oxford: Oxford University Press, 2002), *passim*; Greg Walker, *Writing Under Tyranny: English Literature and the Henrician Reformation* (Oxford: Oxford University Press, 2005), ch. 17.

206. Compare the beast fable Sidney told in Germany, which also suggests that the easy divisions between good Protestants and bad Catholics made by Protestant propagandists were misleading: Stewart, *Sidney*, p. 105; Karl Joseph Hölgen, 'Why Are There No Wolves in England? Philip Camerarius and a German Version of Sidney's Table Talk', *Anglia* 99 (1981), 60–82.

207. Pritchard, *Catholic Loyalism*, chs. 1–2; Michael C. Questier, 'Elizabeth and the Catholics', in Ethan Shagan (ed.), *Catholics and the Protestant Nation: Religious Politics and Identity in Early Modern England* (Manchester: Manchester University Press, 2005), pp. 69–94; J. J. Scarisbrick, *The Reformation and the English People* (Oxford: Blackwell, 1984), ch. 6; Adrian Morey, *The Catholic Subjects of Elizabeth I* (London: Allen and Unwin, 1978), ch. 5. Norfolk was attended in the Tower before his execution by Alexander Nowell and by his old tutor, John Foxe: Michael A. R. Graves, *ODNB* entry on 'Thomas Howard, fourth duke of Norfolk'.

208. On Catholics in the south-east, see Michael C. Questier, *Catholicism and Community in Early Modern England: Politics, Aristocratic Patronage and Religion, c.1550–1640* (Cambridge: Cambridge University Press, 2006); A. G. Dickens, *The English Reformation* (rev. edn., London: Fontana, 1986), pp. 50, 56, *passim*; Felicity Heal, *Reformation in Britain and Ireland* (Oxford: Oxford University Press, 2003), pp. 209, 215, *passim*.

209. For comment, see Hamilton, *Family of Love*, pp. 115–16, 121–2; Marsh, *Family of Love*, 120–6, *passim*.

210. *ODNB* entry on William Wilkinson by Christopher Marsh.

211. Marsh, *Family of Love*; Wotton, 'Scot/Fleming'.

212. William Wilkinson, *A Confutation of Certaine Articles Deliuered vnto the Familye of Loue with the exposition of Theophilus, a supposed elder in the sayd Familye vpon the same articles* (London, 1579), sigs. A1ᵛ–B2ᵛ.

213. Ibid., sigs. F2ᵛ, F3ʳ, T2ʳ–T3ᵛ.

214. Ibid., sigs. A3ʳ⁻ᵛ.

215. Marsh, *Family of Love*, p. 110.

216. Ibid., chs. 7, 9.

217. The link has been made before: see McLane, *Spenser's Shepheardes's Calender*, pp. 163–7. McLane thinks that Spenser endorses Young's attack on the Family.

Chapter 4

1. Harvey, *Letter-Book*, pp. 64, 68; *Chronology*, p. 9.
2. Spenser, *Shorter Poems*, p. 24; Judith Owens, *Enabling Engagements: Edmund Spenser and the Poetics of Patronage* (Montreal: McGill-Queen's University Press, 2002), p. 44.
3. Skelton's works were edited by John Stow and published by Thomas Marsh, a work that Spenser would have consulted: *Pithy, Pleasaunt and Profitable Workes of Maister Skelton, Poete Laureate. Nowe collected and newly published. Anno 1568* (London, 1568). In a poem preserved in his *Letter-Book* Harvey imagines Skelton meeting the recently deceased George Gascoigne (d. 1577) in Hades: Harvey, *Letter-Book*, p. 57; Stern, *Harvey*, p. 33. On Stow's edition of Skelton, see Jane Griffiths, 'Text and Authority: John Stow's 1568 Edition of Skelton's *Workes*', in Ian Gadd and Alexandra Gillespie (eds.), *John Stow (1525–1605) and the Making of the English Past* (London: British Library, 2004), pp. 127–34.
4. John Mullan, *Anonymity: A Secret History of English Literature* (London: Faber, 2007), pp. 477–9.
5. Sidney, *Apology*, p. 110. *Spenser Allusions* (pp. 1–26) indicates that some commentators, such as Abraham Fraunce, knew who Spenser was, but it was only after the first edition of *The Faerie Queene* announced his identity in 1590 that readers were certain of his identity.
6. George Whetstone, *Sir Phillip Sidney, his honorable life, his valiant death, and true vertues* (London, 1587), sig. B2ᵛ; *Spenser Allusions*, p. 10. On Whetstone, see the *ODNB* entry by Emma Smith.
7. Graham Parry, 'Patronage and the Printing of Learned Works for the Author', in Barnard and McKenzie, (eds.), *Cambridge History of the Book in Britain*, iv. 174–88, at pp. 175, 181.
8. Ruth Samson Luborsky, 'The Illustrations to *The Shepheardes Calender*', *Sp. St.* 2 (1981), 3–53, at 16.
9. H. J. Byrom, 'Edmund Spenser's First Printer, Hugh Singleton', *The Library*, 4th ser. 14 (1933), 121–56.
10. Galbraith, ' "English" Black-Letter Type'; Mark Bland, 'The Appearance of the Text in Early Modern England', *Text* 11 (1998), 91–154. Throughout his career, Spenser made use of paratexts for a variety of purposes: they were always used as an integral part of the text. See William Oram, 'Introduction: Spenser's Paratexts', in Wayne C. Erikson (ed.), *The 1590 Faerie Queene*, *SLI* 38/2 (Fall 2005), pp. vii–xviii.
11. Spenser, *Shorter Poems*, pp. 29–30.
12. Spenser, *Faerie Queene*, p. 716; Bennett, *Evolution of 'The Faerie Queene'*, pp. 11–12; Carol Schreier Rupprecht, 'Dreams', *Sp. Enc.*, pp. 226–7.
13. Spenser, *Shorter Poems*, p. 147.
14. Ibid. 30–1.
15. Gabriel Harvey, *Smithus; vel Musarum lachrymae pro obitu honoratissimi viri, atque hominis multis nominibus clarissime, Thomae Smithi, Equitis Britanni, Maiestatisque Regiae secretarij* (London, 1578); Gabriel Harvey, *Gratulationum Valdinensium* (London, 1578).
16. Harvey, *Letter-Book*, pp. 102–38.
17. T. and C. H. Cooper, 'Edward Kirke, the Commentator on Spenser's *Shepheardes Calender*', *N&Q*, 2nd ser. 9 (1860), 42; Douglas Hamer, 'Some Spenser Problems', *N&Q* 180 (1941), 183–4, 220–4, 238–41, at 221.
18. 'Here lyeth the body of M. Edward Kirke, P. so of Risby who departed this life the 10th daye of Novemb' Ano Dni 1613 y year of his age 60.' See *ODNB* entry by Andrew Hadfield; A. F. Webling, *Risby* (Leicester: Edmund Ward, 1945), pp. 98–145. A fragment of Kirk's will, with his Italianate signature, survives in Suffolk Record Office, FL 618/3/27/i.
19. Webling, *Risby*, pp. 107–8, 144–5, 154–5; *ODNB* entry on the Gawdy family by Joy Rowe. See also Victor Skretkowicz, *European Erotic Romance: Philhellene Protestantism, Renaissance Translation and English Literary Politics* (Manchester: Manchester University Press, 2010), pp. 41–2, 47.
20. Most of the people connected to the production of the book were at Cambridge at the same time as Kirk: see René Graziani, 'Verses by E. K.', *N&Q* 16 (1969), 21.

21. Other documents that link the Spensers to the Kytsons survive, mainly property deeds: Suffolk Record Office, E6/1/2; Ac. 527/1, 4; 449/4/1.
22. *ODNB* entry on Sir Thomas Kitson by Charles Welch, rev. Ian Archer; Webling, *Risby*, p. 55; Questier, *Catholicism and Community in Early Modern England, passim.*
23. Webling, *Risby*, ch. 6.
24. Harvey–Spenser, *Letters*, p. 55.
25. Spenser, *Shorter Poems*, p. 31.
26. See, pp. 84–5.
27. On the relationship between the *Calender* and humanist editions, see McCanles, 'Shepheardes *Calender* as Document and Monument'. More generally, see J. B. Trapp, 'The Humanist Book', in Hellinga and Trapp (eds.), *Cambridge History of the Book in Britain*, iii. 285–315; David R. Carlson, *English Humanist Books: Writers and Patrons, Manuscripts and Print, 1475–1525* (Toronto: University of Toronto Press, 1993). James Kearney reminds us that *the Calender*'s form also recalls that of the heavily glossed 1570s editions of the *Geneva Bible*: see 'Reformed Ventriloquism: *The Shepheardes Calender* and the Craft of Commentary', *Sp. St.* 26 (2011), 111–51. There is a relatively large body of work on the identity of E. K. and the question of whether Spenser wrote the notes himself. See e.g. Agnes D. Kuersteiner, 'E. K. is Spenser', *PMLA* 50 (1935), 140–55; C. Margaret Grieg, 'The Identity of E. K. of *The Shepheardes Calender*', *N&Q* 197 (1952), 332–4; McLane, *Spenser's Shepheardes Calender*, ch. 17; Goldberg, *Sodometries*, pp. 64–7; Theodore L. Steinberg, 'E. K.'s *Shepheardes Calender* and Spenser's', *Modern Language Studies* 3 (1973), 46–58; Louise Schleiner, 'Spenser's "E. K." as Edmund Kent (Kenned/of Kent: Kyth (Couth), Kissed, and Kunning-Coning', *ELR* 20 (2008), 374–407.
28. Spenser, *Shorter Poems*, p. 126.
29. Ibid. 133.
30. Richard Helgerson, *Self-Crowned Laureates: Spenser, Jonson, Milton and the Literary System* (Berkeley and Los Angeles: University of California Press, 1983); Stephen B. Dobranski, *Readers and Authorship in Early Modern England* (Cambridge: Cambridge University Press, 2005).
31. Andrew Hadfield, 'Michael Drayton's Brilliant Career', *PBA* 125 (2004), 119–47.
32. For discussion, see Lynn Staley Johnson, *The Shepheardes Calender: An Introduction* (University Park: Pennsylvania State University Press, 1990), *passim*; Andrew King, 'Spenser, Chaucer, and Medieval Romance,' *Sp. Handbook*, pp. 553–72.
33. Jane Griffiths, 'What's in a Name? The Transmission of "John Skelton, Laureate" in Manuscript and Print', *HLQ* 67 (2004), 215–35; McCabe, 'Authorial Self-Presentation', *Sp. Handbook*, p. 463; Edmund Kemper Broadaus, *The Laureateship: A Study of the Office of Poet Laureate in England with Some Account of the Poets* (Oxford: Clarendon Press, 1921), pp. 20–1.
34. Googe, *Eclogues, Epitaphs and Sonnets*; Turbervile, *Eclogues of Mantuan*; Johnson, *Shepheardes Calender*, pp. 12, 36, 45. In a volume attached to his *Tragicall Tales* (London, 1587), *Epytaphes and Sonnettes annexed to the Tragical histories*, dated 1569, although published in 1587, Turbervile includes three verse epistles to friends written while he was in Moscow as secretary to Thomas Randolph, on a state visit to meet the Russian emperor, Ivan the Terrible (June 1568–Sept. 1569). One is addressed 'To Spencer' (pp. 186–90), and it is plausible that this could have been Edmund Spenser. The main objection is that Turbervile was about ten years older than Spenser and nothing else links the two at this point. Two other poems in the volume also address Spenser. The first begins 'Viurtue ti comes invidia', and 'Spare to speake, Spare to speede', also address 'My Spencer', and read as if they are giving advice to a younger man or social inferior: 'My Spencer, spite of vertues deadly foe, | The best are euer sure to beare the blame, | And enuie next to virtue stil doth goe, | But virtue shines, when enuie shrinkes for shame' (p. 150); the second concludes, 'Experience hath no pere, | it passeth learning farre: | I speake it not without my booke, but like a man of ware. | Wherefore be bold to hold | The fairest first of all, | Aye Venus aides the forward man, | and Cupid helps his thrall' (p. 155). It is plausible that Turbervile is represented as 'good Harpalus, now woxen aged, | In faithfull seuice of faire Cynthia' (*Colin Clouts come home againe*, lines 380–1), as Turbervile represents himself as Harpalus in the poem, 'He sorrowes other to haue the fruites of his seruice.' Moreover, Spenser and Turbervile had numerous connections in common, including links to the Gorges family, closely connected

to the Turberviles, and Ambrose Dudley, earl of Warwick, Turbervile's patron, to whose wife, Anne Dudley, Spenser dedicated *Fowre Hymns* (John Erskine Hankins, *The Life and Works of George Turberville* (Lawrence: University of Kansas Publications, 1940)), p. 24.

35. Judith M. Kennedy, 'Googe, Barnabe', and William E. Sheidley, 'Turbervile, George', *Sp. Enc.*, pp. 336–7, 704; *The Eclogues of Alexander Barclay*, ed. Beatrice White (Oxford: EETS, 1928); Johnson, *Shepheardes Calender*, p. 61.

36. Galbraith, 'Spenser and the History of the Book', p. 56. See also Joseph A. Dane, *Out of Sorts: On Typography and Print Culture* (Philadelphia: University of Pennsylvania Press, 2011), pp. 168–71.

37. On Googe and Turbervile's eclogues, see Jessica Winston, 'Lyric Poetry at the Early Elizabethan Inns of Court: Forming a Professional Community', in Archer et al. (eds.), *Inns of Court*, pp. 223–44.

38. Spenser, *Shorter Poems*, p. 29. For comment, see Cheney, *Spenser's Famous Flight*; M. I. Donnelly, 'The Life of Vergil and the Aspiration of the "New Poet"', *Sp. St.* 17 (2003), 1–35. Marot, in particular, is acknowledged as a major influence on the eclogues: Spenser, *Shorter Poems*, pp. 185, 201.

39. Jacopo Sannazaro, *Arcadia and Piscatorial Eclogues*, ed. and trans. Ralph Nashe (Detroit: Wayne State University Press, 1966). For comment on the relationship between the editions, see Galbraith, '"English" Black-Letter Type'; Heninger, 'Typographical Layout'. See also Alpers, *What is Pastoral?*, pp. 349–51, *passim*; Duncan-Jones, *Sidney*, pp. 142–3; Heninger, *Sidney and Spenser*, pp. 309, 402; Johnson, *Shepheardes Calender*, p. 31.

40. Adam Smyth, *Autobiography in Early Modern England* (Cambridge: Cambridge University Press, 2010), ch. 1. There is now a large literature on almanacs and a number of articles detailing Spenser's use of them. In general see Capp, *Astrology and the Popular Press*; Louise Hill Curth, *English Almanacs, Astrology & Popular Medicine: 1550–1700* (Manchester: Manchester University Press, 2007); R. C. Simmons, 'ABCs, Almanacs, Ballads, Chapbooks, Popular Piety and Textbooks', in Barnard and McKenzie (eds.), *Cambridge History of the Book in Britain*, iv. 504–13. On Spenser see Anne Lake Prescott, 'Refusing Translation: The Gregorian Calendar and Early Modern English Writers', *YES* 36 (2006), 112–22; Alison Chapman, 'The Politics of Time in Edmund Spenser's English Calendar', *SEL* 42 (2002), 1–24; Alison Chapman, 'Marking Time: Astrology, Almanacs and English Protestantism', *RQ* 60 (2007), 1257–90; Abigail Shinn, '"Extraordinary Discourses of vnnecessarie matter": Spenser's Shepheardes Calender and the Almanac Tradition', in Matthew Dimmock and Andrew Hadfield (eds.), *Literature and Popular Culture in Early Modern England* (Aldershot: Ashgate, 2009), pp. 137–49.

41. *The zodiake of life, written by the excellent and Christian poet, Marcellus Palingenius Stellatus*, trans. Barnabe Googe (London, 1576). The first six books had been published in 1561. For comment, see S. K. Heninger, Jr, 'The Implications of Form for *The Shepheardes Calender*', *SR* 9 (1962), 309–21, at 310–11; Rosamund Tuve, 'Spenser and the *Zodiacke of Life*', *JEGP* 34 (1935), 1–19.

42. Adam Smyth, 'Almanacs, Annotators, and Life-Writing in Early-Modern England', *ELR* 38 (2008), 200–44.

43. Richard Harvey's analysis, *An Astrological Discourse Upon the Great and Notable Coniunction of the Tvvo Superiour Planets, Saturne & Iupiter, which shall happen the 28 day of April, 1583* (London, 1583), written at his father's house in Saffron Walden, published by Byneman, and addressed to Gabriel, predicted the imminent end of the world, was supported by Robert Tanner's *A Prognosticall Iudgement of the Great Coniunction of the Two Superiour Planets, Saturne and Iupiter, which shall happen the 8. day of Aprill. 1583* (London, 1583), and his brother, John's *An Astrologicall Addition, or Supplement to be Annexed to the Late Discourse Vpon the Great Coniunction of Saturne, and Iupiter* (London, 1583), also addressed to Gabriel, but disputed by Thomas Heath in *A Manifest and Apparent Confutation of an Astrological Discourse, lately published* (London, 1583). For comment, see Stern, *Harvey*, pp. 70–2; P. G. Maxwell-Stuart, 'Astrology, Magic and Witchcraft', in Hadfield (ed.), *The Oxford Handbook to English Prose, 1500–1640* (forthcoming).

44. John Harvey, *Leape Yeere: A Compendious Prognostication for the Yeere of our Lorde God. M.D.LXXXIIII* (London, 1584); John Harvey, *An Almanacke, or Annuall Calender with a Compendious Prognostication Thereunto Appendyng, Seruyng for the Yeere of our Lord. 1589* (London, 1589). On Harvey see the *ODNB* entry by Bernard Capp.

45. They were mocked elsewhere in the late 16th century, at the Inns of Court, for example: see Nelson and Elliott, Jr (eds.), *Inns of Court: Records*, ii. 453–4.

46. For an account of Harvey's defence of his brothers in the face of the attacks by Nashe, see Nashe, *Works*, v. 75–9.

47. Richard Harvey, *A Theologicall Discourse of the Lamb of God and His Enemies contayning a briefe commentarie of Christian faith and felicitie, together with a detection of old and new barbarisme, now commonly called Martinisme* (London, 1590), p. 159.

48. Greg Walker, *John Skelton and the Politics of the 1520s* (Cambridge: Cambridge University Press, 1988); Jane Griffiths, *John Skelton and Poetic Authority: Defining the Liberty to Speak* (Oxford: Oxford University Press, 2006).

49. Burrow, 'Chaucer', *Sp. Enc.*

50. On the style and neologisms coined, see Baugh and Cable, *History of the English Language*, p. 230.

51. See e.g. James Jackson Higginson, *Spenser's Shepheardes Calender in Relation to Contemporary Events* (New York: Columbia University Press, 1912); Greenlaw, 'Spenser and the Earl of Leicester'; Judson, *Life*, ch. 8.

52. Again, the source is the *Letters*: see Rosenberg, *Leicester*, pp. 329–36; Woudhuysen, 'Leicester's Literary Patronage', pp. 194–5; William A. Ringler, Jr, 'Spenser, Shakespeare, Honor, and Worship', *Renaissance News* 14 (1961), 159–61. Harvey later planned to present a poem to Sidney, an act undoubtedly prevented by his death: Eleanor Relle, 'Some New Marginalia and Poems of Gabriel Harvey', *RES* 23 (1972), 401–16, at 402.

53. William R. Orwen, 'Spenser's 'Stemmata Dudleiana', *N&Q* 190 (1946), 9–11; Joseph L. Black and Lisa Celovsky, ' "Lost Works", Suppositious Pieces, and Continuations', *Sp. Handbook*, pp. 349–64, at p. 353. See also Philo M. Buck, Jr, 'Spenser's Lost Poems', *PMLA* 23 (1908), 80–99; Helen E. Sandison, 'Spenser's "Lost" Works and Their Probable Relation to His *Faerie Queene*', *PMLA* 25 (1910), 134–51.

54. See pp. 91–2.

55. Alford, *Burghley*, p. 122.

56. Ibid., ch. 5. On Burghley, see also Stephen Alford, *The Early Elizabethan Polity: William Cecil and the British Succession Crisis, 1558–1569* (Cambridge: Cambridge University Press, 1998); Stephen Alford, *Kingship and Politics in the Reign of Edward VI* (Cambridge: Cambridge University Press, 2002), pp. 139–41. On Leicester, whose Protestant affinities have always been rather more obvious, see Alan Kendall, *Robert Dudley, Earl of Leicester* (London: Cassell, 1980), pp. 166–8; Adams, *Leicester and the Court*, p. 5; Collinson, *Elizabethan Puritan Movement, passim.*

57. Alford, *Burghley*, ch. 15; Adams, *Leicester and the Court*, pp. 145–6, *passim.*

58. George Buchanan, *Ane detectioun of the doingis of Marie Quene of Scottis tuiching the murther of hir husband, and hir conspiracie, adulterie, and pretensit mariage with the Erle Bothwell. And ane defence of the trew Lordis, mantenaris of the kingis grace actioun and authoritie. Translatit out of the Latine quhilke was writtin be M.G.B.* (St Andrews, 1572). For comment, see John D. Staines, *The Tragic Histories of Mary Queen of Scots, 1560–1690* (Aldershot: Ashgate, 2009), pp. 27–39, *passim.*

59. *John Stubbs' Gaping Gulf*, ed. Berry, introd., pp. xxxiv–viii; William Lambarde, who had helped draft government legislation on the regulation of seditious books, noted the event in his diary: Warnicke, *Lambarde*, pp. 80–1. See also John M. Adrian, *Local Negotiations of English Nationhood, 1570–1680* (Basingstoke: Palgrave, 2011), ch. 2.

60. Mears, *Queenship and Political Discourse*, pp. 199–201.

61. Natalie Mears, 'Counsel, Public Debate, and Queenship: John Stubbs's *The Discoverie of a Gaping Gulf*, 1579', *HJ* 44 (2001), 629–50.

62. Richard A. McCabe, ' "Little booke: thy selfe present": The Politics of Presentation in *The Shepheardes Calender*', in Howard Erskine-Hill and Richard A. McCabe (eds.), *Presenting*

Poetry: Composition, Publication, Reception: Essays in Honour of Ian Jack (Cambridge: Cambridge University Press, 1995), pp. 15–40, at pp. 22–3.

63. On Singleton's life, see *ODNB* entry by Natalie Mears; Byrom, 'Spenser's First Printer'. See also Katherine Walsh, 'Deliberate Provocation or Reforming Zeal? John Bale as First Church of Ireland Bishop of Ossory (1552/3–1563)', in Carey and Lotz-Heumann (eds.), *Taking Sides?*, pp. 42–60, at p. 51.

64. Byrom, 'Spenser's First Printer', p. 151.

65. Frank Isaac, *English Printers' Types of the Sixteenth Century* (Oxford: Oxford University Press, 1936), pp. 28–9; *The Vocacyon of Johan Bale*, ed. Peter Happé and John N. King (Binghamton, NY: MRTS, 1990).

66. King, *Spenser's Poetry and the Reformation Tradition*, pp. 125, 159, 191; James A. Knapp, ' "That moste barbarous nacion": John Derricke's *Image of Ireland* and the "delight of the wel disposed reader" ', *Criticism* 42 (2000), 415–50.

67. Isaac, *English Printers' Types*, p. 29.

68. Luborsky, 'Illustrations'; Ruth Samson Luborsky, 'The Allusive Presentation of *The Shepheardes Calender*', *Sp. St.* 1 (1980), 29–67.

69. Harvey–Spenser, *Letters*, p. 53. The full quotation is given on p. 149.

70. For comment, see Isabel G. MacCaffrey, *Spenser's Allegory: The Anatomy of Imagination* (Princeton: Princeton University Press, 1976), pp. 353–5; Andrew Hadfield, *Literature, Politics and National Identity: Reformation to Renaissance* (Cambridge: Cambridge University Press, 1994), pp. 190–2.

71. See below, pp. 130–1.

72. Harvey–Spenser, *Letters*, p. 8. It is also worth noting that E. K.'s comments on painting were read seriously in the 17th century, suggesting further that the text was written with the knowledge of what painting could achieve: see Frederick Hard, 'E. K.'s Reference to Painting: Some Seventeenth Century Adaptations', *ELH* 7 (1940), 121–9.

73. Harvey–Spenser, *Letters*, p. 54. On Gosson, see *Markets of Bawdrie: The Dramatic Criticism of Stephen Gosson*, ed. Arthur F. Kinney (Salzburg: Institut für Englische Sprache und Literatur, Universität Salzburg, 1974).

74. Sidney, *Apology*, p. 110.

75. Danielle Clarke, 'Translation and the English Language', in Braden, Cummings, and Gillespie (eds.), *Oxford History of Literary Translation*, pp. 17–23, at pp. 20–1.

76. Spenser, *Shorter Poems*, p. 27; *Spenser Allusions*, pp. 4–5. 'Gallimaufry' could be used to designate a miscellaneous collection of 'albums, letters, and other documents' (Peter Beal (ed.), *A Dictionary of English Manuscript Terminology, 1450–2000* (Oxford: Oxford University Press, 2008), p. 169).

77. *Spenser Allusions*, p. 7. Webbe probably graduated from St John's College, Cambridge in the same year as Spenser, so may well have known who Spenser was, which is why he was able to identify him as the author of the *Calender*: see the *ODNB* entry on 'William Webbe' by Elizabeth Heale.

78. 'To His Booke', lines 1–4, 11–12, in Spenser, *Shorter Poems*, p. 24; Geoffrey Chaucer, *Troilus and Criseyde*, v, lines 1786–92, in *Riverside Chaucer*, p. 584. Alice S. Miskimin, *The Renaissance Chaucer* (New Haven: Yale University Press, 1975), pp. 274–5.

79. Ringler, 'Spenser, Shakespeare'.

80. 'March', lines 19–24, in Spenser, *Shorter Poems*, p. 53.

81. See *ODNB* article on 'Lettice Knollys' by Simon Adams.

82. Kendall, *Dudley*, pp. 181–2; J. E. Neale, *Queen Elizabeth* (London: Cape, 1934), p. 245.

83. See pp. 91–2.

84. Duncan-Jones, *Sidney*, pp. 194–6; Alan Young, *Tudor and Jacobean Tournaments* (London: George Philip, 1987), p. 135.

85. See Charles E. Mounts, 'Spenser and the Countess of Leicester', in Mueller and Allen (eds.), *That Soueraine Light*, pp. 111–22.

86. Spenser, *Shorter Poems*, p. 57.

87. Ibid. 66.

88. Ibid.
89. It may be a reference to the queen's progress to Audley End, 26–31 Aug. 1578, referred to in the notes to September when E. K. apparently first realizes that Hobbinol is Gabriel Harvey (Spenser, *Shorter Poems*, p. 126), indicating that Harvey reads out what Spenser writes. See pp. 84–5.
90. Kendall, *Dudley*, pp. 185–6.
91. See Hadfield, *Literature, Politics and National Identity*, pp. 126–31; Judith Haber, *Pastoral and the Poetics of Self-Contradiction: Theocritus to Marvell* (Cambridge: Cambridge University Press, 1994); Susan Snyder, *Pastoral Process: Spenser, Marvell, Milton* (Stanford: Stanford University Press, 1998), ch. 1.
92. See Owens, *Enabling Engagements*, pp. 43–4.
93. It is likely that the August eclogue, with a sestina in imitation of Sannazaro, was a late addition, as there are no glosses to the text: see Heninger, 'Typographical Layout', p. 37; Luborsky, 'Illustrations', p. 41; Galbraith, 'Spenser and the History of the Book', p. 65.
94. See Mears, 'Counsel, Public Debate, and Queenship', pp. 645–7; Hadfield, *Literature, Politics, National Identity*, introd.
95. Mears, 'Counsel, Public Debate, and Queenship', p. 646; Anne N. McLaren, *Political Culture in the Reign of Elizabeth I: Queen and Commonwealth, 1558–1585* (Cambridge: Cambridge University Press, 1999), ch. 3.
96. King, *Spenser's Poetry and the Reformation Tradition*, p. 38.
97. Watt, *Cheap Print*, p. 215; Hume, *Spenser: Protestant Poet*, p. 22
98. Spenser, *Shorter Poems*, p. 31.
99. On female beauty, see the fascinating discussion in Naomi Baker, ' "To make love to a deformity": Praising Ugliness in Early Modern England', *RS* 22 (2008), 86–109.
100. Spenser, *Shorter Poems*, p. 68.
101. John Guy, *'My Heart is My Own': The Life of Mary Queen of Scots* (London: HarperCollins, 2004), pp. 158–9, 278.
102. Guy, *'My Heart is My Own'*, ch. 28.
103. George Puttenham, *The Arte of English Poesie* (London, 1589), book III, ch. 20. See also Elizabeth I, *Collected Works*, ed. Leah S. Marcus, Janel Mueller, and Mary Beth Rose (Chicago: University of Chicago Press, 2000), pp. 133–4; John D. Staines, 'Elizabeth, Mercilla, and the Rhetoric of Propaganda in Spenser's *Faerie Queene*', *JMEMS* 31 (2001), 283–312, at 285.
104. For a very different reading of the eclogue, see Thomas H. Cain, 'The Strategy of Praise in Spenser's "Aprill" ', *SEL* 8 (1968), 45–58.
105. McLane, *Spenser's Shepheardes Calender*, pp. 47–60; Hoffman, *Spenser's Pastorals*, pp. 90–2; Louis Adrian Montrose, ' "The Perfecte Paterne of a Poete": The Poetics of Courtship in *The Shepheardes Calender*', *TSLL: Texas Studies in Literature and Language* 21 (1979), 34–67, at 39–43.
106. On the *Calender* as a Protestant poem, see King, *Spenser's Poetry and the Reformation Tradition*, ch. 1; McLane, *Spenser's Shepheardes Calender*, chs. 7–14; Hume, *Spenser: Protestant Poet*, ch. 2. On Spenser and ruins, see Van Es, *Spenser's Forms of History*, ch. 2; Tom Muir, 'Specters of Spenser: Translating the *Antiquitez*', *Sp. St.* 25 (2010), 327–61.
107. Honor McCusker, *John Bale: Dramatist and Antiquary* (Bryn Mawr: Bryn Mawr University Press, 1942). On Bale's relationship to Spenser, see Sandler, '*The Faerie Queene*: An Elizabethan Apocalypse'. More generally, see Eamon Duffy, *The Stripping of the Altars: Traditional Religion in England, 1400–1580* (New Haven: Yale University Press, 1992); Christopher Haigh (ed.), *The English Reformation Revised* (Cambridge: Cambridge University Press, 1987); Jones, *English Reformation*.
108. Spenser, *Shorter Poems*, p. 50.
109. *FQ* II.iii.26, line 9. For comment, see Louis Adrian Montrose, 'The Elizabethan Subject and the Spenserian Text', in David Quint and Patricia Parker (eds.), *Literary Theory/Renaissance Texts* (Baltimore: Johns Hopkins University Press, 1986), pp. 303–40, at pp. 326–9; Elizabeth Jane Bellamy, 'Waiting for Hymen: Literary History as "Symptom" in Spenser and Milton', *ELH* 64 (1997), 391–414.
110. David G. Hale, 'Aesop in Renaissance England', *The Library*, 5th ser. 27 (1972), 116–25, at 116.

111. The most radical attempt is that in Thomas Philip Nelan, 'Catholic Doctrines in Spenser's Poetry', unpublished PhD dissertation, New York University, Graduate School of Arts and Science, 1944. See also Weatherby, *Mirrors of Celestial Grace*, pp. 3–4, 31–2. See pp. 259–60.

112. Duffy, *The Stripping of the Altars*, pp. 281–2, 465–6; Cressy, *Birth, Marriage and Death*, pp. 374. On Cranmer's involvement in shaping the Prayer Book, see McCulloch, *Cranmer*, pp. 505–12. On Norton, see pp. 33–4.

113. Spenser, *Shorter Poems*, p. 84. For comment, see King, *Spenser's Poetry and the Reformation Tradition*, pp. 34–43. Robert Crowley (1517/19–88), a Protestant clergyman, writer, printer, and bookseller, published *The Vision of Pierce Plowman* (London, 1550) as a Protestant work: see John N. King, *English Reformation Literature: The Tudor Origins of the Protestant Tradition* (Princeton: Princeton University Press, 1982), pp. 319–57, 473–7, *passim*; *ODNB* entry by Basil Morgan. It is possible that Piers is meant to represent John Piers, bishop of Salisbury (1522/3–94): see Paul E. McLane, 'Piers of Spenser's *Shepheardes Calender*, Dr. John Piers of Salisbury', *MLQ* 9 (1948), 3–9.

114. Spenser, *Shorter Poems*, p. 86.

115. For discussion of a related distinction in the *Calender*, see Harold Stein, 'Spenser and William Turner', *MLN* 51 (1936), 345–51.

116. For a discussion of Elizabeth's impossible position, see Susan Doran, *Monarchy and Matriarchy: The Courtships of Elizabeth I* (London: Routledge, 1996).

117. On Grindal and Young, see Collinson, *Grindal*, pp. 270–1, 274, *passim*; *ODNB* entry on 'John Young' by Brett Ussher; and pp. 67–8.

118. Collinson, *Elizabethan Puritan Movement*, pp. 33, 73–6; Collinson, *Grindal*, pp. 126–7.

119. Collinson, *Grindal*, p. 172.

120. Ibid. 233–76. See also Peter Lake, *Moderate Puritans and the Elizabethan Church* (Cambridge: Cambridge University Press, 1982), p. 149.

121. Collinson, *Grindal*, p. 257.

122. Spenser, *Shorter Poems*, p. 93.

123. McCabe, '"Little booke"', p. 32.

124. Kathleen Williams, *Spenser's Faerie Queene: The World of Glass* (London: Routledge, 1966), ch. 6.

125. Not that Grindal was mean and did not run an impressive household: see Collinson, *Grindal*, 'Appendix: Getting and Spending: Grindal's Stewardship', pp. 295–308.

126. 'Morrell' can be derived from 'Elmore', another spelling of 'Aylmer'. See McLane, *Spenser's Shepheardes Calender*, ch. 12; S. K. Henninger, Jr, '*The Shepheardes Calender*', *Sp. Enc.*, pp. 645–51, at p. 648. See also the *ODNB* entry on 'John Aylmer' by Brett Usher, which makes the same identification. Thomalin is assumed to be Thomas Cooper, bishop of Lincoln (c.1517–94), another cleric close to Grindal: see the *ODNB* entry on 'Thomas Cooper' by Margaret Bowker.

127. Melampode: black hellebore; terebinth: the turpentine tree. See *Variorum*, vii. 330.

128. Schleiner, 'Spenser's "E. K." as Edmund Kent', pp. 378–9. See also Jane K. Pettegree, *Foreign and Native on the English Stage, 1588–1611: Metaphor and National Identity* (Basingstoke: Palgrave, 2011), ch. 3.

129. In 'To Penshurst', Ben Jonson writes of 'high-swoll'n Medway' (line 31), a reference to James's favourite, Robert Carr (1585/6–1645), being made Viscount Rochester in 1611, showing that the town and the river were closely identified. Ben Jonson, *Poems*, ed. Ian Donaldson (Oxford: Oxford University Press, 1975), p. 89.

130. The general reference in the eclogue is to the parable of the sheep and the goats (Matthew 25: 31–46).

131. St Margaret's church, Westminster, Parish Registers, reel 1, marriages, 25 May 1572–6 March 1598; Arthur Meredyth Burke, *Memorials of St. Margaret's Church, Westminster: The Parish Registers, 1539–1660* (London: Eyre and Spottiswoode, 1914), p. 294; Welply, 'Some Spenser Problems', 56–9; Eccles, 'Spenser's First Marriage'.

132. Burke, *Memorials*, p. 295; Welply, 'Spenser: Recent Researches', p. 182.

133. Welply, 'Some Spenser Problems', pp. 56–7; Eccles, 'Spenser's First Marriage'. See also Eccles, 'Elizabethan Edmund Spensers', in which he revises his earlier opinion that Robert was probably Machabyas' father (p. 424).
134. For the former example, see Eccles, 'Elizabethan Edmund Spensers', p. 425.
135. On Coverdale, see p. 34.
136. Donald Bruce, for example, argues that 'Her bizarre name . . . suggests her strictly evangelical parentage' ('Spenser in Westminster: His Marriage and Death', *N&Q* 242 (1997), 51–3, at 52). Another claim is that her name was determined by her parents opening the Bible at random (Hamer, 'Some Spenser Problems', p. 184).
137. I am very grateful to the London Huguenot Library historian, Lucy Gwynn, and Saskia Verwey and C. A. Knook of the Dutch Church in London, for help with my research.
138. Calvin, *Institutes*, 1.8.10, 3.5.8; *Calvin's Commentaries*, 22 vols., ed. and trans. Revd John King (Grand Rapids: Baker Book House, 2005).
139. Peter Marshall, *Beliefs and the Dead in Reformation England* (Oxford: Oxford University Press, 2002), pp. 54, 76–7.
140. Harvey–Spenser *Letters*, p. 61. Donald Bruce suggests that this was the case and that she lived in King Street, where Ben Jonson claimed that Spenser died, on the grounds that 'Spenser hated change' ('Spenser in Westminster', p. 51).
141. Cressy, *Birth, Marriage & Death*, ch. 15.
142. Julia F. Merritt, *The Social World of Early Modern Westminster: Abbey, Court and Community, 1525–1640* (Manchester: Manchester University Press, 2005), pp. 17, 22, 57, 124–5.
143. Cressy, *Birth, Marriage & Death*, chs. 10–11; Diana O'Hara, *Courtship and Constraint: Rethinking the Making of Marriage in Tudor England* (Manchester: Manchester University Press, 2000), ch. 1.
144. Archer, *Pursuit of Stability*, chs. 2–4; Withington, *Politics of Commonwealth*, pt. 2.
145. Nashe boasted that he could have been a college fellow, had he so wished: Nicholl, *Cup of News*, p. 38.
146. Peter Laslett, *The World We Have Lost* (2nd edn., London: Methuen, 1971), p. 85; Mendelson and Crawford, *Women in Early Modern England*, pp. 108–23; Paul Griffiths, *Youth and Authority: Formative Experiences in England, 1560–1640* (Oxford: Clarendon Press, 1996), p. 5.
147. *ODNB* entry on Mulcaster. Welply suggests that Katherine may have been a family name but notes that 'Elizabeth Boyle's immediate ancestry does not contain this name': 'Spenser: Recent Researches', p. 182.
148. Willy Maley, 'Spenser's Life', *Sp. Handbook*, pp. 13–29, at p. 19; Welply, 'Some Spenser Problems', p. 57.
149. See p. 288.
150. Jean R. Brink, 'Documenting Edmund Spenser: A New Life Record', *American Notes & Queries* 7 (1994), 201–8, at 207.
151. Although childbirth mortality rates were nowhere near as high as might have been expected, a recent estimate suggests that they were about 10 in every 1,000 live births (1%) before 1750, whereas in 1980 they were 0.1 for every 1,000 live births: Roger Schofield, 'Did the Mothers Really Die? Three Centuries of Maternal Mortality in "The World We Have Lost"', in Bonfield et al. (eds.), *The World We Have Gained*, pp. 231–60, at p. 259. On Spenser's comments on childbirth see pp. 263–4.
152. See H. F. Westlake, *St. Margaret's Church, Westminster: The Church of the House of Commons* (London: Smith, Elder & Co., 1914), chs. 1–3; J. R., *Historical Curiosities relating to St. Margaret's Church, Westminster* (London: privately printed, 1838); *St. Margaret's Church, Westminster: A Souvenir Guide* (London: Barnard and Westwood, 2006). It is interesting to note that Spenser's marriage is not mentioned in any of the works on the church.
153. Merritt, *Social World of Early Modern Westminster*, p. 41; Charles Smyth, *Church and Parish: Studies in Church Problems, illustrated from the Parochial History of St. Margaret's, Westminster* (London: SPCK, 1955), pp. 42, 188; Eamon Duffy, *Fires of Faith: Catholic England under Mary Tudor* (New Haven: Yale University Press, 2009), pp. 118–19, 176.
154. *Diary of Henry Machin*, pp. 84–5.

155. Griffiths, *Youth and Authority*, p. 28; C. S. Lewis, *The Allegory of Love: A Study in Medieval Tradition* (1936; Oxford: Oxford University Press, 1958), ch. 7; Lawrence Lerner, 'Marriage', *Sp. Enc.*, pp. 454–5.

156. Harvey–Spenser *Letters*, p. 49. For comment, see Richard Mallette, 'Rosalind', *Sp. Enc.*, p. 622. See also Margaret Galway, 'Spenser's Rosalind', *TLS*, 19 July 1947, p. 372.

157. Woudhuysen, 'Letters, Spenser's and Harvey's', p. 435.

158. Spenser, *Shorter Poems*, 'Januarie', lines 57, 60.

159. Puttenham, *Arte of English Poesie*, I.18.

160. See the overview of early articles in *Variorum*, vii, app. V, pp. 651–5; In particular, see Welply, 'Spenser: Recent Researches'. On Spenser House, see *Victoria County History: Lancashire*, vi. 473–8. One candidate is Rose Daniel, sister of the poet who married John Florio: see N. J. Halpin, 'On Certain Passages in the Life of Edmund Spenser', *PRIA* 4 (1847–50), 445–51.

161. Judson, *Life*, 44.

162. See Mallette, 'Rosalind'; McLane, *Spenser's Shepheardes Calender*, ch. 3; Bernard, *Ceremonies of Innocence*, ch. 4. See also Willy Maley's ingenious reading: *Salvaging Spenser: Colonialism, Culture and Identity* (Basingstoke: Macmillan, 1997), pp. 30–1.

163. As, indeed, has already been noted: Theodore H. Banks, 'Spenser's Rosalind: A Conjecture', *PMLA* 52 (1937), 335–7; Leicester Bradner, *Edmund Spenser and The Faerie Queene* (Chicago: University of Chicago Press, 1948), pp. 64–5.

164. See pp. 86–7.

165. Hadfield, 'Spenser's Rosalind', p. 940. This chapter draws on material in this article.

166. A useful comparison might be drawn with John Donne, who probably addressed a number of poems to his wife: see Andrew Hadfield, 'Donne's *Songs and Sonnets* and Artistic Identity', in Patrick Cheney, Andrew Hadfield, and Garrett Sullivan (eds.), *Early Modern English Poetry: A Critical Companion* (Oxford: Oxford University Press, 2006), pp. 206–16. Companionable marriage was an ideal heavily promoted in the 16th century: see Wrightson, *English Society*, ch. 4; Anthony Fletcher, 'The Protestant Idea of Marriage in Early Modern England', in Fletcher and Roberts (eds.), *Religion, Culture, and Society*, pp. 161–81; Thomas, *The Ends of Life*, pp. 214–20.

167. Menalcas appears in eclogues 3 and 5.

168. Cressy, *Birth, Marriage and Death*, ch. 10.

169. On living in Westminster see Merritt, *Social World of Early Modern Westminster*, ch. 5.

170. For a different argument, see Rambuss, *Spenser's Secret Career*.

171. For discussion, see Helgerson, *The Elizabethan Prodigals*.

172. Jean Brink argues that had Spenser been connected to Leicester in 1578 Harvey would have promoted him in *Gratulationes Valdinenses*, which suggests that he had entered the Leicester–Sidney circle at some point just before April 1579, the date of the epistle in the *Calender*. ' "All His Minde on Honour Fixed": The Preferment of Edmund Spenser', in Anderson et al. (eds.), *Spenser's Life*, pp. 45–64, at pp. 59–60.

173. Angel Day, *The English Secretorie* (London, 1586); Mack, *History of Renaissance Rhetoric*, pp. 290–1.

174. *ODNB* entry on 'Angell Day' by S. P. Cerasano. See also Skretkowicz, *European Erotic Romance*, ch. 2; Eccles, 'Brief Lives', pp. 41–2.

175. Christopher Burlinson and Andrew Zurcher, 'Spenser's Secretarial Career,' in *Sp. Handbook*, pp. 65–85, at pp. 66–7.

176. *ODNB* entry on 'Henry Cuffe' by Paul E. J. Hammer; Alan Stewart, 'Instigating Treason: The Life and Death of Henry Cuffe, Secretary', in Erica Sheen and Lorna Hutson (eds.), *Literature, Politics and Law in Renaissance England* (Basingstoke: Palgrave, 2005), pp. 50–70. On the role and significance of secretaries, see Alan G. R. Smith, 'The Secretariats of the Cecils, circa 1580–1612', *EHR* 83 (1968), 481–504; Paul E. J. Hammer, 'The Uses of Scholarship: The Secretariat of Robert Devereux, c.1585–1601', *EHR* 109 (1994), 26–51.

177. Thomas Twyne, *A Shorte and Pithie Discourse, concerning the engendering, tokens, and effects of all Earthquakes in Generall* (London, 1580); Thomas Churchyard, *A warning for the wise, a feare to the fond, a bridle to the lewde, and a glasse to the good Written of the late earthquake chanced in London and other places, the. 6. of April 1580* (London, 1580); Arthur Golding, *A discourse vpon the earthquake that hapned throughe this realme of Englande, and other places of Christendom, the first of Aprill. 1580* (London, 1580); Abraham Fleming, *A bright burning beacon forewarning all wise virgins to trim their lampes against the comming of the Bridegroome. Conteining a generall doctrine of sundrie signes and wonders, specially earthquakes both particular and generall: a discourse of the end of this world: a commemoration of our late earthquake, the 6. of April* (London, 1580); *The order of prayer, and other exercises, vpon Wednesdays and Frydayes, to auert and turne Gods wrath from vs, threatned by the late terrible earthquake: to be vsed in all parish churches and housholdes throughout the realme* (London, 1580). Later works looked back to the event: see e.g. James Yates, *The Castell of Courtesie whereunto is adioyned the holde of humilitie: with the chariot of chastitie thereunto annexed* (London, 1582), sig. G3^{r-v}. For analysis, see Gerald Snare, 'Satire, Logic, and Rhetoric in Harvey's Earthquake Letter to Spenser', *Tulane Studies in English* 18 (1970), 17–33.

178. *Chronology*, p. 12.

179. See pp. 106–8.

180. Stern, *Harvey*, pp. 56–9.

181. Nelson, *Monstrous Adversity*, pp. 224–5.

182. Harvey–Spenser, *Letters*, pp. 53–4.

183. Woudhuysen, 'Leicester's Literary Patronage', pp. 153–9; Harvey, *Letter-Book*, p. 158. See also David McKitterick, 'Review of Stern, *Harvey*,' in *The Library*, 6th ser. 3 (1981), 348–53.

184. *Variorum*, x. 249. Anon., *The Kalender of Shepheardes* (1506). For comment, which shows how the work may have influenced Spenser, see Martha W. Driver, 'When is a Miscellany Not Miscellaneous? Making Sense of the *Kalender of Shepherds*', *YES* 33 (2003), 199–214. See also H. S. Bennett, *English Books and Readers, 1475 to 1557: Being a Study of the Book Trade from Caxton to the Incorporation of the Stationers' Company* (Cambridge: Cambridge University Press, 1970), p. 162.

185. Harvey–Spenser, *Letters*, pp. 38–40.

186. Rambuss, *Spenser's Secret Career*; Jameson, '*Gratulationes Valdinenses* of Gabriel Harvey'.

187. William Fulwood, *The Enimie of Idlenesse teaching the maner and stile how to endite, compose and write all sorts of epistles and letters* (London, 1568). Fulwood (d. 1593) was a member of the Merchant Taylors' Company and was patronized by Leicester in the 1560s: see the *ODNB* entry by Cathy Shrank. See also Alan Stewart and Heather Wolfe, *Letterwriting in Renaissance England* (Washington, DC: Folger Shakespeare Library, 2004), pp. 21–34.

188. Harvey–Spenser, *Letters*, p. 60.

189. On the circumstances of the possible journey, see James R. Caldwell, 'Dating a Spenser–Harvey Letter', *PMLA* 41 (1926), 568–74; James H. Hewlett, 'Interpreting a Spenser–Harvey Letter', *PMLA* 42 (1927), 1060–5; Greenlaw, 'Spenser and Leicester', pp. 537–8. Caldwell's attempt to argue that the letter is two sections spliced together further supports the notion that the published letters were revised from earlier versions. Jon A. Quitslund argues that the mention of the journey was only ever a form of advertising that Spenser was willing to travel in the earl's service: 'Questionable Evidence in the *Letters* of 1580 between Gabriel Harvey and Edmund Spenser', in Anderson et al. (eds.), *Spenser's Life*, pp. 81–98, at p. 92.

190. Stewart and Wolfe, *Letterwriting in Renaissance England*, p. 22; Jardine, *Erasmus*.

191. Harvey–Spenser, *Letters*, p. 36; Nelson, *Monstrous Adversity*, pp. 225–9. Harvey denied the charge but was undoubtedly guilty: Stern, *Harvey*, pp. 64–6. Harvey had earlier dedicated complimentary verses to Oxford in *Gratulationes Valdinenses*.

192. For an account of the quarrel, see *The Works of Thomas Nashe*, ed. R. B. McKerrow, 5 vols. (Oxford: Blackwell, 1958), v. 65–110, at p. 74; *ODNB* entry on 'Edward de Vere, seventeenth earl of Oxford' by Alan H. Nelson.

Chapter 5

1. *Acts of the Privy Council, 1580–1*, 75, 106–7; *CSPI 1547–80*, p. 234; *Carew, 1575–88*, p. 277. On the title of the chapter, see Paul Muldoon, *To Ireland, I* (Oxford: Oxford University Press, 2000), p. 35.
2. For details of the Lord Deputy's trials and tribulations, see Ciaran Brady (ed.), *A Viceroy's Vindication: Sir Henry Sidney's Memoir of Service in Ireland, 1556–78* (Cork: Cork University Press, 2002).
3. *ODNB* entry on 'Grey, Arthur, fourteenth Baron Grey of Wilton', by Julian Lock.
4. *ODNB* entry.
5. Sir Philip De Malpas Grey Egerton (ed.), *A Commentary of the Services and Charges of William Lord Grey de Wilton, K.G., by his son, Arthur Lord Grey de Wilton* (London: Camden Society, 1847); 'Grey, William, thirteenth Baron Grey of Wilton (1508/9–62)', *ODNB* entry, by Julian Lock; Andy Wood, *The 1549 Rebellions and the Making of Early Modern England* (Cambridge: Cambridge University Press, 2007), pp. 51–2, 74, *passim*.
6. On Grey's reputation for ruthless military action, see Richard A. McCabe, 'The Fate of Irena: Spenser and Political Violence', in Patricia Coughlan (ed.), *Spenser and Ireland* (Cork: Cork University Press, 1989), pp. 109–25. For details of Ireland, see Cyril Falls, *Elizabeth's Irish Wars* (London: Constable, 1950), chs. 9–10; Ellis, *Tudor Ireland*, ch. 9; G. A. Hayes-McCoy, 'The Completion of the Tudor Conquest and the Advance of the Counter-Reformation, 1571–1603', in Moody et al. (eds.), *New History of Ireland*, iii. 94–141, at pp. 104–9.
7. Anthony M. McCormack, *The Earldom of Desmond, 1463–1583: The Decline and Crisis of a Feudal Lordship* (Dublin: Four Courts, 2005), chs. 4–8.
8. Ellis, *Tudor Ireland*, ch. 6.
9. McCormack, *Earldom of Desmond*, pp. 193–7.
10. Ciaran Brady, 'Faction and the Origins of the Desmond Rebellion of 1579', *IHS* 22 (1981), 289–312.
11. Brady, *Chief Governors*, ch. 5.
12. *Chronology*, p. 12.
13. 'Gascoigne's Woodmanship' is a witty appeal for support from Grey: Gascoigne, *Hundreth Sundrie Flowres*, pp. 312–16.
14. Judith Barry, 'Sir Geoffrey Fenton and the Office of Secretary of State for Ireland, 1580–1608', *IHS* 35 (2006), 137–59. On the movement for reform in a wider historical perspective, see Jon G. Crawford, *Anglicizing the Government of Ireland: The Irish Privy Council and the Expansion of Tudor Rule, 1556–1578* (Dublin: Irish Academic Press, 1993).
15. See TNA PRO SP 63/83/45, 63/85/13, 63/86/51, 63/91/22; Spenser, *Letters*, pp. 76, 109, 122, 174.
16. Spenser, *Letters*, introd., p. xlviii; Christopher Burlinson and Andrew Zurcher, ' "Secretary to the Lord Grey Lord Deputy Here": Edmund Spenser's Irish Papers', *The Library*, 7th ser. 6 (2005), 30–69, at 51–2. See also Richard Berleth, *The Twilight Lords: An Irish Chronicle* (New York: Barnes and Noble, 1978), p. 155; *ODNB* entry on Fenton by Andrew Hadfield.
17. Burlinson and Zurcher, 'Spenser's Secretarial Career', *Sp. Handbook*, pp. 71–2.
18. Although Edwin Greenlaw's assumption that *Mother Hubberds Tale* circulated in manuscript in 1580 has long held sway, there is no evidence that it did, or that it came to the attention of Burghley himself: see Greenlaw, 'Spenser and the Earl of Leicester'. For opposing views of the reasons for Spenser's emigration to Ireland, see Bradbrook, 'No Room at the Top'; Brink, ' "All his minde on honour fixed" '.
19. William J. Smyth, *Map-Making, Landscapes and Memory: A Geography of Colonial and Early Modern Ireland, c.1530–1750* (Cork: Cork University Press, 2006), pp. 31–6; Peter Barber, 'Mapmaking in England, ca. 1470–1650', in Woodward (ed.), *History of Cartography*, iii/2. 1589–1669, at p. 1623.
20. Paul E. J. Hammer, 'The Earl of Essex, Fulke Greville and the Employment of Scholars', *SP* 91 (1994), 167–80, at 175 n. 40.
21. Katherine Duncan-Jones, *Shakespeare: Upstart Crow to Sweet Swan: The Evolution of His Image* (London: Black, 2011), p. 176.
22. Plant, *English Book Trade*, p. 42.

23. Campbell, *English Yeoman*, app. III, p. 398.
24. Alan Stewart, 'The Making of Writing in Renaissance England: Re-thinking Authorship through Collaboration', in Healy and Healy (eds.), *Renaissance Transformations*, pp. 81–96.
25. On Boyle, see Canny, *Upstart Earl*; Terence Ranger, 'Richard Boyle and the Making of an Irish Fortune, 1588–1614', *IHS* 10 (1956–7), 257–97.
26. SP 63, 92, fo. 20ʳ; Carpenter, *Reference Guide*, p. 48; Carpenter, 'Spenser in Ireland', pp. 415–16.
27. D. C. Coleman, *The British Paper Industry, 1495–1860: A Study in Industrial Growth* (Oxford: Clarendon Press, 1958), pp. 1–18; Daybell, *Material Letter*, ch. 2.
28. Mark Bland, *A Guide to Early Printed Books and Manuscripts* (Oxford: Blackwell, 2010), p. 31; Coleman, *British Paper Industry*, p. 123; Susan Flavin and Evan T. Jones (eds.), *Bristol's Trade with Ireland and the Continent: The Evidence of the Exchequer Customs Accounts* (Dublin: Four Courts, 2009), pp. 632, 633, 639, *passim*.
29. Berleth, *Twilight Lords*, pp. 154–5.
30. *Acts of the Privy Council, 1580–1*, 181.
31. Stuart Kinsella, *Christ Church Cathedral, Dublin: A Survey of Monuments* (Dublin: Christ Church Cathedral Publications, 2009), p. 7.
32. Chris Wilson, 'The Proximate Determinants of Marital Fertility in England, 1600–1799', in Bonfield, et al. (eds.), *The World We Have Gained*, pp. 203–30, at pp. 205, 227–8. I owe this reference to Naomi Tadmor. On the Irish climate, see R. A. Butlin, 'Land and People, c.1600', in Moody et al. (eds.), *New History of Ireland*, iii. 142–67, at pp. 145–6.
33. Christopher Maginn, *'Civilizing' Gaelic Leinster: The Extension of Tudor Rule in the O'Byrne and O'Toole Lordships* (Dublin: Four Courts, 2005), p. 159.
34. Falls, *Elizabeth's Irish Wars*, pp. 69–71; Katherine Simms, 'Gaelic Warfare in the Middle Ages', in Bartlett and Jeffrey (eds.), *Military History of Ireland*, pp. 99–115.
35. For accounts of the battle, see Maginn, *'Civilizing' Gaelic Leinster*, pp. 159–66; Berleth, *Twilight Lords*, pp. 157–61.
36. *The Annals of the Four Masters*, trans. Owen Connellan, 2 vols. (Kansas: Irish Genealogical Foundation, 2003), ii. 505. See also Philip O'Sullivan Bear, *Ireland under Elizabeth: Chapters towards a History of Ireland in the Reign of Elizabeth*, trans. Matthew J. Byrne (Dublin: Sealy, Bryers and Walker, 1903), p. 19.
37. *Variorum*, x. 171–2.
38. On Hugh McShane, see Hiram Morgan, *Tyrone's Rebellion: The Outbreak of the Nine Years War in Tudor Ireland* (Woodbridge: Boydell, 1993), pp. 94–7, *passim*. For other examples of puns as cross-references between *A View* and *The Faerie Queene*, see Hadfield, *Spenser's Irish Experience*, p. 107. On the likelihood that Spenser accompanied Grey, see Judson, *Life*, p. 88; *Variorum*, x. 393.
39. Spenser, *Letters*, pp. 3–6. On Spenser's handwriting, see Christopher Burlinson and Andrew Zurcher, ' "Secretary to the Lord Grey Lord Deputy Here" '; Henry R. Plomer, 'Edmund Spenser's Handwriting', *MP* 21 (1923), 201–7; Raymond Jenkins, 'Spenser's Hand', *TLS*, 7 Jan. 1932, p. 12; Jenkins, '*Newes out of Munster*'; Raymond Jenkins, 'Spenser with Lord Grey in Ireland', *PMLA* 52 (1937), 338–53; Raymond Jenkins, 'Spenser: The Uncertain Years, 1584–89', *PMLA* 53 (1938), 350–62.
40. For the relevant descriptions, see Butlin, 'Land and People, c.1600', and Aiden Clark, 'The Irish Economy, 1600–60', in Moody et al. (eds.), *New History of Ireland*, iii. 168–86; K. W. Nicholls, *Gaelic and Gaelicized Ireland in the Middle Ages* (2nd edn., Dublin: Lilliput, 2003), ch. 6.
41. Spenser, *Letters*, p. 3.
42. Herbert Wood, *A Guide to the Public Records Deposited in the Public Record Office of Ireland* (Dublin: HMSO, 1919), p. 198; Carpenter, *Reference Guide*, p. 47.
43. Carpenter, *Reference Guide*, p. 47.
44. On the effects of Pelham's policies see Rory Rapple, *Martial Power and Elizabethan Political Culture: Military Men in England and Ireland, 1558–1594* (Cambridge: Cambridge University Press, 2009), pp. 3–5, 207–9, *passim*; Anne Chambers, *Eleanor, Countess of Desmond* (1986; Dublin: Wolfhound, 2000), pp. 132–52. Pelham's 'A Plot for Munster' (28 July 1580) shows how

far he was prepared to use martial law to suppress the rebellion and it makes an instructive parallel to Spenser's recommendations in *A View*: *Carew, 1575–88*, pp. 284–7.

45. *Annals of the Four Masters*, ii. 503–4. On the transformation of the rules of warfare in 16th-century Ireland, see David Edwards, 'The Escalation of Violence in Sixteenth-Century Ireland', in David Edwards, Pádraig Lenihan, and Clodagh Tait (eds.), *Age of Atrocity: Violence and Political Conflict in Early Modern Ireland* (Dublin: Four Courts, 2007), pp. 34–78.

46. Berleth, *Twilight Lords*, p. 126.

47. *Carew, 1575–88*, pp. 299, 307, 311–14.

48. A female ancestor of the Spencers of Wormleighton and Althorp had married one of the Wallops in the reign of Henry VII, so there may have been a real or assumed family connection between Spenser and Wallop: see Anon., *Early History of the Spencer Family* (London: Mitre, 1931), pp. 21–2.

49. SP 63, 97, fos. 22–33, 32^{r-v}; transcribed in Carpenter, *Reference Guide*, p. 47.

50. *ODNB* entry.

51. This paragraph relies on Falls, *Elizabeth's Irish Wars*, ch. 2; John McGurk, *The Elizabethan Conquest of Ireland: The Burdens of the 1590s Crisis* (Manchester: Manchester University Press, 1997), ch. 9; Ciaran Brady, 'The Captains' Games: Army and Society in Elizabethan Ireland', in Bartlett and Jeffery (eds.), *Military History of Ireland*, pp. 136–59.

52. Beier, *Masterless Men*, pp. 93–9; A. V. B. Norman and Don Pottinger, *English Weapons and Warfare, 449–1660* (1966; London: Arms and Armour Press, 1979), p. 178.

53. The fort was first occupied during the rebellion after the landing of James Fitzmaurice Fitzgerald on 18 July 1579. Fitzmaurice was killed on 18 Aug. 1579: see *ODNB* article by Anthony M. McCormack.

54. Eric Klingelhofer, *Castles and Colonists: An Archaeology of Elizabethan Ireland* (Manchester: Manchester University Press, 2010), pp. 37–8.

55. Frederick M. Jones, 'The Plan of the Golden Fort at Smerwick, 1580', *Irish Sword* 2 (1954–6), 41–2, at 42; Colin Breen, *An Archaeology of South-West Ireland, 1570–1670* (Dublin: Four Courts, 2007), p. 145.

56. National Maritime Museum, Dartmouth Collection, vol. 8 (Irish Maps 1594–1685), P/49/31.

57. Pelham to the Privy Council, 9 July 1580, *Carew, 1575–88*, pp. 267–9, at p. 268.

58. Spenser, *Letters*, pp. 13–27; *Chronology*, pp. 11–13. See also Raymond Jenkins, 'Spenser at Smerwick', *TLS*, 11 May 1933, p. 331.

59. *Chronology*, p. 13.

60. McCabe, *Spenser's Monstrous Regiment*, pp. 90–3; Lennon, *Sixteenth-Century Ireland*, pp. 227–8.

61. *Variorum*, x. 158.

62. Berleth, *Twilight Lords*, p. 59; John Derricke, *The Image of Irelande with a discouerie of woodkarne* (1581). See also Patricia Palmer, 'Missing Bodies, Absent Minds: Spenser, Shake-speare and a Crisis in Criticism', *ELR* 36 (2006), 376–95, at 390.

63. Hadfield, *Spenser's Irish Experience*, chs. 2–3.

64. It is worth noting that in his retrospective account of Tyrone's career, Thomas Gainsford (1566–1624), *The True Exemplary, and Remarkable History of the Earle of Tirone* (London, 1619), immediately after a defence of Lord Grey that suggests that he has been reading *A View*, argues that Tyrone's actions show that he has not learned the meaning of Erasmus' wisdom (p. 33).

65. Desiderius Erasmus, *The Collected Works of Erasmus*, xxxv. *The Adages, III, iv.i–iv.ii.100*, ed. John N. Grant (Toronto: University of Toronto Press, 2005), pp. 399–440. On Erasmus' pacifism and the general understanding of this, see Bruce Mansfield, *Phoenix of His Age: Interpretations of Erasmus, c.1550–1750* (Toronto: University of Toronto Press, 1979), p. 246; Walter M. Gordon, *Humanist Play and Belief: The Seriocomic Art of Desiderius Erasmus* (Toronto: University of Toronto Press, 1990), pp. 104, 109, 119.

66. Arthur F. Marotti, *Manuscript, Print and the English Renaissance Lyric* (Ithaca, NY: Cornell University Press, 1985), p. 306.

67. On Gascoigne, *Hundreth Sundrie Flowres*, pp. 398–439, at p. 399. On the culture of military poetry, see D. J. B. Trim, 'The Art of War: Martial Poetics from Henry Howard to Philip Sidney', in Pincombe and Shrank (eds.), *Tudor Literature*, pp. 587–605.

68. Harvey, *Marginalia*, p. 165; Prouty, *George Gascoigne*, p. 228.

69. See esp. *Variorum*, x. 238–9.

70. Tom Glasgow, 'Elizabethan Ships Pictured on Smerwick Map, 1580: Background, Authentication and Evaluation', *Mariner's Mirror* 52 (1966), 157–66. One of the ships, the *Lion*, was commanded by Sir William Gorges (d. 1585), father of Sir Arthur Gorges (p. 160). The map is TNA PRO MPF 75 (SP 64/1).

71. Carey, 'Atrocity and History', pp. 88–9; Fenton to Walsingham, 11 Nov. 1580, TNA PRO SP 63/78/257. It is worth noting that the sons of both Smith and Cheke perished in Ireland within a decade of each other, a sign of how involved in Ireland major English humanists were.

72. See Colin Martin and Geoffrey Parker, *The Spanish Armada* (London: Guild, 1988), pp. 90–1.

73. The two most significant accounts of the episode are Alfred O'Rahilly, 'The Massacre at Smerwick (1580)', *JCHAS* 42 (1937), 1–15, 65–83; Vincent P. Carey, 'Atrocity and History: Grey, Spenser and the Slaughter at Smerwick (1580)', in Edwards et al. (eds.), *Age of Atrocity*, pp. 79–94.

74. TNA PRO SP 63/78/29. Spenser, *Letters*, pp. 18–19. All letters to the queen were copied out in italic or Italian hand, while secretary hand was used for most other correspondence.

75. O'Sullivan Bear, *Ireland under Elizabeth*, p. 25; Robert S. Miola (ed.), *Early Modern Catholicism: An Anthology of Primary Sources* (Oxford: Oxford University Press, 2007), pp. 431–6; John Copinger, *The Theatre of Catolique and Protestant Religion Diuided into Twelue Bookes* (Saint-Omer, 1620), pp. 578–9; for comment, see Carey, 'Atrocity and History', p. 85. See also *Annals of the Four Masters*, ii. 506.

76. A. M., *The True Reporte of the Prosperous Successe which God gaue vnto our English souldiours against the forraine bands of our Romaine enemies lately ariued, (but soone inough to theyr cost) in Ireland, in the yeare 1580* (London, 1581); William Cecil, Baron Burghley, *The Execution of Iustice in England for maintenaunce of publique and Christian peace, against certeine stirrers of sedition, and adherents to the traytors and enemies of the realme* (London, 1583).

77. O'Rahilly, 'Massacre at Smerwick', p. 71.

78. For discussion, see Carey, 'Atrocity and History', p. 87.

79. George Hill, *An Historical Account of the MacDonnells of Antrim: Including notices of some other septs, Irish and Scottish* (Belfast: Archer, 1873), pp. 183–7; Vincent P. Carey, 'Sir Henry Sidney, and the Massacre at Mullaghmast, 1578', *IHS* 31 (1999), 305–27.

80. Walter Devereux, earl of Essex to the Queen, 31 July 1575, *Carew, 1575–88*, pp. 16–17.

81. David Edwards, *The Ormond Lordship in County Kilkenny, 1515–1642: The Rise and Fall of Butler Feudal Power* (Dublin: Four Courts, 2003), p. 233. See also Pelham to the Queen, 4 Nov. 1579: *Carew, 1575–88*, p. 164.

82. McCormack, *Earldom of Desmond*, pp. 177–8.

83. Pelham to the earl of Leicester, 26 Dec. 1579, *Carew, 1575–88*, pp. 189–90.

84. *Carew, 1575–88*, pp. 197–8. See also Micheál Ó Siochrú, *God's Executioner: Oliver Cromwell and the Conquest of Ireland* (London: Faber, 2008), p. 20.

85. 'Instructions to Sir Warham St. Leger', 1 Aug. 1580, signed by Pelham: *Carew, 1575–88*, pp. 306–7. St Leger was later at Bryskett's symposium in Dublin and so would have known Spenser.

86. Anthony M. McCormack, 'The Social and Economic Consequences of the Desmond Rebellion of 1579–83', *IHS* 133 (2004), 1–15, at 13; Smyth, *Map-Making, Landscapes and Memory*, pp. 45–7.

87. Connolly, *Contested Island*, p. 176. See also Hutchinson, 'Sir Henry Sidney and His Legacy', pp. 191–2.

88. On the religious context in England see Peter Lake and Michael Questier, 'Agency, Appropriation and Rhetoric under the Gallows: Puritans, Romanists and the State in Early Modern England', *P&P* 153 (Nov. 1996), 64–107; 'Puritans, Papists, and the "Public Sphere" in Early Modern England: The Edmund Campion Affair in Context', *Journal of Modern History* 72 (2000), 587–627. On Irish confessional identities, see Vincent P. Carey and Ute Lotz-Heumann (eds.), *Taking Sides? Colonial and Confessional Mentalités in Early Modern Ireland: Essays in Honour of Karl Bottigheimer* (Dublin: Four Courts, 2003).

89. See H. S. V. Jones, *Spenser's Defense of Lord Grey* (Urbana: Illinois Studies in Language and Literature, 1919); McCabe, 'The Fate of Irena'.

90. *Variorum*, x. 161–2.
91. Spenser has a 'Segnior Ieffrey' entreating with Grey; Grey names the corresponding figure as 'Alexandro [Bartoni] their CampMaster', but there are various explanations for this difference (Spenser, *Letters*, pp. 24–5).
92. David Edwards, 'Ideology and Experience: Spenser's *View* and Martial Law in Ireland', in Hiram Morgan (ed.), *Political Ideology in Ireland, 1541–1641* (Dublin: Four Courts, 1999), pp. 127–57.
93. *Variorum*, x. 64.
94. *FQ* V.xii.35–43; Hadfield, *Spenser's Irish Experience*, pp. 168–9.
95. William Camden, *Annales the true and royall history of the famous empresse Elizabeth Queene of England France and Ireland*, trans. Abraham Darcie (London, 1625), p. 409; Cannio, 'Reconstructing Lord Grey's Reputation', pp. 4–6.
96. Hiram Morgan, ' "Never Any Realm Worse Governed": Queen Elizabeth and Ireland', *TRHS*, 6th ser. 14 (2004), 295–308, at 301. Grey admitted that he executed some 1,500 men through martial law, not counting those from the lower classes he had put to death.
97. McCabe, *Spenser's Monstrous Regiment*, p. 217; *CSPI, 1574–85*, pp. 399–400.
98. See *ODNB* entry on Grey by Julian Lock. On the early history of Tudor plantation in Ireland, see White, 'Tudor Plantations', and, more specifically on Munster, D. B. Quinn, 'The Munster Plantation: Its Problems and Opportunities', *JCHAS* 71 (1966), 19–40; Michael MacCarthy-Morrogh, *The Munster Plantation: English Migration to Southern Ireland, 1583–1641* (Oxford: Clarendon Press, 1986), pp. 41–2.
99. Edwards, *Ormond Lordship*, pp. 98–100.
100. Ibid. 202–3. In a palatinate, or liberty, the local lord was enabled to oversee crucial aspects of the judicial system: see Lennon, *Sixteenth-Century Ireland*, p. 17.
101. On the Ormond lands, see Smyth, *Map-Making, Landscapes and Memory*, ch. 8. On Ormond's achievements, see e.g. Paul Cockerham, ' "To mak a Tombe for the Earell of Ormon and to set it up in Iarland": Renaissance Ideals in Irish Funeral Monuments', in Thomas Herron and Michael Potterton (eds.), *Ireland in the Renaissance, c.1540–1660* (Dublin: Four Courts, 2007), pp. 195–230.
102. Cited in Edwards, *Ormond Lordship*, p. 231.
103. Ibid. 234.
104. Morgan, 'Queen Elizabeth and Ireland', p. 303.
105. See pp. 252–3.
106. Richard Beacon, *Solon His Follie, or A politique discourse touching the reformation of commonweales conquered, declined or corrupted* (1594), ed. Clare Carroll and Vincent Carey (Binghamton, NY: MRTS, 1996), p. 65.
107. *ODNB* entry on 'George Gascoigne' by G. W. Pigman III.
108. See, in particular, Grey's funeral sermon, preached by his client, Thomas Sparke, *A Sermon Preached at Whaddon in Buckinghamshyre the 22. of Nouember 1593. at the buriall of the Right Honorable, Arthur Lorde Grey of Wilton* (Oxford, 1593). Grey was well disposed to Cartwright and challenged Elizabeth on her support for the bishops during the 1589 debate in the House of Lords on the Pluralities Bill.
109. It is worth noting that a Spanish military treatise recovered from the fort was translated by Nicholas Lichfield and dedicated to Sir Philip Sidney, providing another link between literature and military affairs: see *A Compendious Treatise Entituled, De Re Militari containing principall orders to be obserued in martiall affaires. Written in the Spanish tongue, by that worthie and famous captaine, Luis Gutierres de la Vega*, trans. Nicholas Lichfield (London, 1582); Duncan-Jones, *Sidney*, p. 229. I owe this reference to Barbara Fuchs.
110. On Malengin, see Harold Skulsky, 'Malengin', *Sp. Enc.*, p. 450.
111. The term is James Shapiro's, based on an analysis of Shakespeare's *Henry V*: Shapiro, *1599: A Year in the Life of William Shakesphere* (London: Faber, 2005), pp. 98–118. I owe this point to Tom Healy.
112. See pp. 265–7.
113. See e.g. Lacey, *Raleigh*, pp. 155–9.
114. David B. Quinn, *Ralegh and the British Empire* (London: Hodder and Stoughton, 1947), pp. 33–4; John Pope Hennessy, *Sir Walter Ralegh in Ireland* (London: Kegan Paul, 1883), ch. 4. It is worth noting that Geoffrey Fenton, who came over to Ireland in 1580, and with

whom Spenser would have worked in Dublin, was also present at the massacre: TNA PRO SP 63/78/25 and 38; *CSPI, 1575–88*, pp. 267, 268.

115. Mark Nicholls and Penry Williams, *Sir Walter Raleigh: In Life and Legend* (London: Continuum, 2011), pp. 13–21.

116. MacCarthy-Morrogh, *Munster Plantation*, p. 42.

117. On Ralegh, see *ODNB* entry by Mark Nicholls and Penry Williams. On Ralegh's lands in Ireland, see Kim Sloan, *A New World: England's First View of America* (London: British Museum, 2007), pp. 46–9; Lacey, *Raleigh*, pp. 117–22.

118. Lord Grey's son, Thomas, 15th Baron of Wilton (1575–1614), was involved in the Bye Plot with Ralegh in 1603, suggesting that Ralegh and Spenser had sustained connections in common: *ODNB* entry on Thomas Grey by Mark Nicholls; Mark Nicholls, 'Two Winchester Trials: The Prosecution of Henry, Lord Cobham, and Thomas, Lord Grey of Wilson, 1603', *HR* 68 (1995), 26–48.

119. *The Letters of Sir Walter Ralegh*, ed. Agnes Latham and Joyce Younings (Exeter: University of Exeter Press, 1999); *The Poems of Sir Walter Ralegh: A Historical Edition*, ed. Michael Ruddick (Tempe, AZ: MRTS, 1999), pp. 2–3.

120. Nicholls and Williams, *Raleigh*, p. 91, referring to Raleigh's (non-)relationship with Marlowe.

121. Nicholls, 'Two Winchester Trials', p. 36.

122. See, p. 232.

123. Jenkins, 'Spenser with Lord Grey', p. 344.

124. *CSPI, 1575–84*, pp. 272–3. Grey finally writes from Dublin on 8 Dec.

125. F. F. Covington, Jr, 'Biographical Notes on Spenser', *MP* 22 (1924), 63–6, at 66; Atkinson, *Bibliographical Supplement*, p. 1.

126. Jenkins, 'Spenser with Lord Grey', p. 344.

127. Spenser, *Letters*, pp. 155–67, 173–80, *passim*. On the conspiracy, see Lennon, *Sixteenth-Century Ireland*, pp. 203–4; Jon G. Crawford, *A Star Chamber Court in Ireland: The Court of Castle Chamber, 1571–1641* (Dublin: Four Courts, 2005), pp. 237–8.

128. For a recent interpretation of the fall of the Kildares, see Vincent P. Carey, *Surviving the Tudors: The 'Wizard' Earl of Kildare and English Rule in Ireland, 1537–1586* (Dublin: Four Courts, 2002), ch. 8.

129. Anne Fogarty, 'Literature in English, 1550–1690', in Margaret Kelleher and Philip O'Leary (eds.), *The Cambridge History of Irish Literature*, 2 vols. (Cambridge: Cambridge University Press, 2006), i. 140–90, at p. 156; Richard Nugent, *Cynthia*, ed. Angelina Lynch (Dublin: Four Courts, 2010).

130. Spenser, *Letters*, p. 225; *Chronology*, p. 17.

131. Roger B. Manning, *An Apprenticeship in Arms: The Origins of the British Army, 1585–1702* (Oxford: Oxford University Press, 2006), p. 395.

132. Lennon, *Sixteenth-Century Ireland*, pp. 8–9.

133. On the Castle of Alma, see Walter R. Davis, 'Alma, castle of', *Sp. Enc.*, pp. 24–5. It is worth noting that the first chamber of the mind in the Castle, that of imagination, 'filled was with flies', showing that they also corrupt the mind (II.ix.51, line 1).

134. *Fiants*, iv. 511; Carpenter, *Reference Guide*, p. 16; Frederick Ives Carpenter, 'Spenser in Ireland', *MP* 19 (1922), 405–19, at 414–15; Wood, *Guide to the Public Records*, p. 58.

135. James Murray, *Enforcing the English Reformation in Ireland: Clerical Resistance and Political Conflict in the Diocese of Dublin, 1534–1590* (Cambridge: Cambridge University Press, 2009), ch. 8; Alan Ford, *The Protestant Reformation in Ireland, 1590–1641* (Dublin: Four Courts, 1997), pp. 31–5, *passim*; Hutchinson, 'Sir Henry Sidney and His Legacy,' pp. 110–12, 179.

136. On Loftus' life, see *ODNB* entry by Helga Hammerstein-Robinson; Brendan Kane, *The Politics and Culture of Honour in Britain and Ireland, 1541–1641* (Cambridge: Cambridge University Press, 2010), pp. 245–67.

137. Smyth, *Map-Making, Landscapes and Memory*, pp. 235–46.

138. Thomas Herron, 'Reforming the Fox: Spenser's "Mother Hubberds Tale", the Beast Fables of Barnabe Rich, and Adam Loftus, Archbishop of Dublin', *SP* 105 (2008), 336–87.

139. McCabe, 'Rhyme and Reason,' p. 39.

140. Carpenter, 'Spenser in Ireland', p. 410; *Chronology*, p. 18.

141. See Welply, 'Spenser: Recent Researches', p. 148.

142. Wood, *Guide to the Public Records*, p. 2.

143. H. R. Plomer and T. P. Cross, *The Life and Correspondence of Lodowick Bryskett* (Chicago: University of Chicago Press, 1927), p. 10.

144. James J. Ferguson, 'Memorials of Edmund Spenser the Poet, and His Descendants, from the Public Records of Ireland', *Gentleman's Magazine* 44 (1855), 605–9, at 605.

145. Hans Pawlisch, *Sir John Davies and the Conquest of Ireland: A Study in Legal Imperialism* (Cambridge: Cambridge University Press, 1985), p. 38. See also Wood, *Guide to the Public Records*, pp. 3–58.

146. Elizabeth Fowler, *Literary Character: The Human Figure in English Writing* (Ithaca, NY: Cornell University Press, 2003), p. 218; K. W. Nicholls (ed.), 'Some Documents on Irish Law and Custom in the Sixteenth Century', *Analecta Hibernica* 26 (1970), 103–29; *Variorum*, x. 47–8, 53.

147. *Variorum*, x. 47–8, 53.

148. Henry Horwitz, *Chancery Equity Records, 1600–1800: A Guide to Documents in the Public Record Office* (London: HMSO, 1995), pp. 45–71. I am grateful to Simon Healy for explaining many of the complexities of Chancery courts to me.

149. Anthony J. Sheehan, 'Provincial Grievance and National Revolt: Munster in the Nine Years War', unpublished MA thesis, University College Dublin, 1982, p. 16.

150. For analysis, see Baker, ' "Some Quirk, Some Subtle Evasion" '.

151. Crawford, *Star Chamber Court in Ireland*, p. 27; Darryl J. Gless, 'Law, Natural and Divine', *Sp. Enc.*, pp. 430–1.

152. Crawford, *Star Chamber Court in Ireland*, pp. 31, 38, 115.

153. Mary O'Dowd, 'Women and the Irish Chancery Court in the Late Sixteenth and Early Seventeenth Centuries', *IHS* 31 (1999), 470–87. See pp. 343–8.

154. Crawford, *Star Chamber Court in Ireland*, pp. 29–30.

155. Andrew Zurcher, *Spenser's Legal Language: Law and Poetry in Early Modern England* (Cambridge: Brewer, 2007), pp. 130–52. On the development of the concept in England and its literary representation, see Bradin Cormack, *A Power to Do Justice: Jurisdiction, English Literature, and the Rise of Common Law, 1509–1625* (Chicago: University of Chicago Press, 2007), pp. 102–14, *passim*.

156. Smyth, *Map-Making, Landscapes and Memory*, pp. 233–4. On the Old English, see Aidan Clarke, *The Old English in Ireland, 1625–42* (Dublin: MacGibbon & Kee, 1966); Nicholas P. Canny, *The Formation of the Old English Elite in Ireland* (Dublin: National University of Ireland, 1975).

157. John Speed, *The Theatre of the Empire of Great Britaine presenting an exact geography of the kingdomes of England, Scotland, Ireland, and the iles adioyning* (London, 1612), map of Leinster between pp. 141–2. See also Moody et al. (eds.), *New History of Ireland*, ix. 37.

158. Denis McCarthy, *Dublin Castle* (2nd edn., Dublin: Stationery Office, 2004), pp. 129–40.

159. Derricke, *Image of Irelande*, plates 6 and 10; Alan J. Fletcher, *Drama, Performance, and Polity in Pre-Cromwellian Ireland* (Cork: Cork University Press, 2000), p. 141.

160. Henry A. Jeffries, *The Irish Church and the Tudor Reformations* (Dublin: Four Courts, 2010), p. 188; Murray, *Enforcing the Reformation*, p. 261.

161. See Colm Lennon, *The Lords of Dublin in the Age of Reformation* (Dublin: Irish Academic Press, 1989), chs. 2–4. See also D. B. Quinn and K. W. Nicholls, 'Ireland in 1534', in Moody et al. (eds.), *New History of Ireland*, iii. 1–38, at pp. 4–5.

162. McCarthy, *Dublin Castle*, p. 37.

163. On the roles of Christ Church and St Patrick's cathedrals, see Murray, *Enforcing the English Reformation*, app. 1, pp. 322–3.

164. Smyth, *Map-Making, Landscapes and Memory*, pp. 230–1.

165. Christopher Morash, *A History of Irish Theatre, 1601–2000* (Cambridge: Cambridge University Press, 2002), ch. 1.

166. S. J. Connolly, *Contested Island: Ireland, 1460–1630* (Oxford: Oxford University Press, 2007), p. 31. On London and its civic culture, see David L. Smith, Richard Strier, and David Bevington (eds.), *The Theatrical City: Culture, Theatre and Politics in London, 1576–1649* (Cambridge: Cambridge University Press, 1995); Manley, *Literature and Culture in Early Modern London*, ch. 5.

167. McCarthy, *Dublin Castle*, p. 36.

168. Fletcher, *Drama, Performance, and Polity*, pp. 137–41. The legend of St George was important in Ireland: In Limerick on 6 Nov. 1579 Pelham decreed that every horseman in the army in Ireland should wear two red crosses on the front and back of their tunics. The evidence has been cited to claim that Spenser was in Ireland in 1579 immediately after his wedding: see *Carew, 1575–88*, pp. 166–7; Roland M. Smith, 'Origines Arthurianae: The Two Crosses of Spenser's Red Cross Knight', *JEGP* 54 (1955), 670–83; Paul E. McLane, 'Was Spenser in Ireland in Early November 1579?', *N&Q* 204 (1959), 99–101.

169. Fletcher, *Drama, Performance, and Polity*, pp. 148–53.

170. Brady (ed.), *Viceroy's Vindication*, pp. 19–20; Lennon, *Lords of Dublin*, p. 122; Ellis, *Tudor Ireland*, pp. 168–74. On the relationship between the Old and New English, see Willy Maley, *Salvaging Spenser: Colonialism, Culture and Identity* (Basingstoke: Palgrave, 1997), ch. 3.

171. See Stewart, *Philip Sidney*, p. 71. On Bryskett, see also Plomer and Cross, *Bryskett*; Deborah Jones, 'Lodowick Bryskett and His Family', in C. J. Sisson (ed.), *Thomas Lodge and Other Elizabethans* (Cambridge, MA: Harvard University Press, 1933), pp. 243–361.

172. Duncan-Jones, *Sidney*, p. 25.

173. Michael Questier and Simon Healy, ' "What's in a Name?" A Papist's Perception of Puritanism and Conformity in the Early Seventeenth Century', in Arthur F. Marotti (ed.), *Catholicism and Anti-Catholicism in Early Modern English Texts* (Basingstoke: Palgrave, 1999), pp. 137–53, at p. 141.

174. McCabe, 'Rhyme and Reason', pp. 33–4.

175. Bryskett to Burghley, 15 May 1581, TNA PRO SP 63/83/27.

176. Bryskett contributed two poems to the volume mourning Sir Philip Sidney's death centred around Spenser's *Astrophel*, and attached to *Colin Clouts Come Home Againe* (1595), in the first of which he represented himself as Thestylis: A. H. Bullen (ed.), *An English Garner: Some Longer Elizabethan Poems* (London: Constable, 1903), pp. 287–301.

177. Spenser, *Shorter Poems*, p. 404.

178. *ODNB* entry; Plomer and Cross, *Bryskett*, ch. 9.

179. Tobias Griffin, 'A Good Fit: Bryskett and the Bowre of Bliss', *Sp. St.* 25 (2010), 377–9.

180. Plomer and Cross, *Bryskett*, p. 80.

181. See the *ODNB* entries: 'Long, John' by Henry A. Jeffries; 'Dillon, Sir Robert' by Jon G. Crawford; 'Pelham, Dorothy' by Hugh Hanley; 'Carleill, Christopher' by D. J. B. Trim; 'Norris, Sir Thomas' by Judith Hudson Barry; 'St Leger, Sir Warham' by David Edwards; Plomer and Cross, *Bryskett*, p. 82.

182. John Erskine argues that the debate is a fiction: see 'The Virtue of Friendship in *The Faerie Queene*', *PMLA* 30 (1915), 831–50, at 837–42.

183. Thomas E. Wright, 'Bryskett, Lodowick', *Sp. Enc.*, p. 119.

184. Lodowick Bryskett, *A Discourse of Ciuill Life containing the ethike part of morall philosophie. Fit for the instructing of a gentleman in the course of a vertuous life* (London, 1606), p. 25. Subsequent references to this edition in parentheses in the text.

185. Hadfield, 'Spenser and Brandon'.

186. Murray, *Enforcing the English Reformation*, p. 310; Christopher Maginn, 'The Baltinglass Rebellion, 1580: English Dissent or a Gaelic Uprising?', *HJ* 47 (2004), 205–32; *ODNB* entry on 'Eustace, James, third Viscount Baltinglass (1530–1585)' by Colm Lennon; Ellis, *Tudor Ireland*, p. 281–7.

187. John Speed, *The Theatre of the Empire of Great Britaine* (London, 1612), map facing p. 142.

188. *ODNB* entry; Anon., *Rathfarnham Castle: Visitors' Guide* (Dublin: Office of Public Works, n.d.).

189. *CSPI, 1574–85*, pp. 344–5; Covington, 'Biographical Notes on Spenser'; Judson, *Life*, p. 103; Henley, *Spenser in Ireland*, p. 61.

190. Welply, 'Family and Descendants of Spenser', p. 25. Also cited in Henley, *Spenser in Ireland*, pp. 202–3. It is also worth noting that Richard Boyle established a number of family links with the Kildares in the early 17th century, suggesting another link that would explain Spenser's interest: Canny, *Upstart Earl*, pp. 49–51, *passim*.

191. On Sarsfield, see the entry by Anthony M. McCormack, *DIB* viii. 777; on Aylmer, see the entry by Robert Armstrong, *DIB* i. 202–3. Both gentlemen had been active against Baltinglass, and Aylmer had married his widow.

192. W. Maziere Brady, *Clerical and Parochial Records of Cork, Cloyne, and Ross*, 3 vols. (Dublin: Alexander Thorn, 1863–4), ii. 260; Henley, *Spenser in Ireland*, pp. 193–4; Welply, 'Spenser: Recent Researches', pp. 169, 204.

193. On Graney, see Aubrey Gwynn and R. Neville Hadcock, *Medieval Religious Houses: Ireland* (Dublin: Blackrock, 1970), pp. 311, 317–18; Lord Walter FitzGerald, 'The Priory or Nunnery of Graney, County Kildare', *JKAS* 7 (1912–14), 373–81; John MacKenna, *Castledermot and Kilkea: A Social History, with Notes on Ballytore, Graney, Moone and Mullaghmast* (Athy: Winter Wood Books, 1982), pp. 53–6.

194. See, p. 363.

195. Jenkins, '*Newes Out of Munster*', p. 30.

196. Jenkins, 'Spenser with Grey', p. 339.

197. *Fiants*, iii. 524 (3785); Alexander C. Judson, 'Two Spenser Leases', *MLQ* 50 (1944), 143–7.

198. Roland M. Smith, 'Spenser's "Stony Aubrian"', *MLN* 59 (1944), 1–5, at 5.

199. *Chronology*, p. 42; *Patent and Close Rolls*, ii. 319–20; Jenkins, 'Spenser and the Clerkship in Munster', p. 214.

200. Gwynn and Hadcock, *Medieval Religious Houses: Ireland*, p. 250. On Wallop's acquisition of property, see Bagwell, *Ireland under the Tudors*, 3 vols. (London: Longman, 1885–90) iii. 126–7, 146–7, *passim*; Vernon James Watney, *The Wallop Family and Their Ancestry*, 4 vols. (Oxford: John Johnson, 1928), vol. i, pp. xl–xliv; Hampshire Record Office, Wallop Papers, 15M84/2/4/1; 15M84/2/4/3.

201. Plomer and Cross, *Bryskett*, pp. 49–50; Colm Tóibín, 'The Dark Sixteenth Century', *Dublin Review* 43 (Summer 2011), 31–54, at 46–8.

202. Alison M. Deveson, *En Suivant La Vérité: A History of the Earls of Portsmouth and the Wallop Family* (Farleigh Wallop: Portsmouth Estates, 2008), pp. 7–8, 39–40.

203. Plomer and Cross, *Bryskett*, pp. 49, 61–2.

204. *Fiants*, iv. 260 (5963). Wallop did not actually possess the lands officially until 1595, but obviously occupied them long before this date.

205. Philip H. Hore, 'Enniscorthy Castle', *JRSAI* 35 (1905), 74–6; William H. Gratton Flood, 'Enniscorthy in the Thirteenth Century: Who Built the Castle?', *JRSAI*, 5th ser. 34 (1904), 380–3; William H. Gratton Flood, 'Enniscorthy', *JRSAI* 35 (1905), 177–8.

206. Ferguson, 'Memorials of Spenser', p. 606; Judson, 'Two Spenser Leases', pp. 146–7; Judson, *Life*, p. 102. On New Ross, see Gwynn and Hadcock, *Medieval Religious Houses: Ireland*, p. 301. There was also a Franciscan friary in New Ross (pp. 215, 257).

207. Smyth, *Map-Making, Landscapes and Memory*, p. 33.

208. Grey was well known for his ability to secure lands for his followers: MacCarthy-Morrogh, *Munster Plantation*, p. 54.

209. Brendan Bradshaw, *The Dissolution of the Religious Orders in Ireland under Henry VIII* (Cambridge: Cambridge University Press, 1974); Karl Bottigheimer, *English Money and Irish Land: The 'Adventures' in the Cromwellian Settlement of Ireland* (Oxford: Clarendon Press, 1971); Ranger, 'Richard Boyle'; Kane, *Politics and Culture of Honour*, pp. 233–4, *passim*.

210. It is worth comparing Spenser's productivity once he had acquired an estate and reached the rank of gentleman with the change in Shakespeare's writing in 1599 once he became a shareholder in the Globe: see Shapiro, *1599*, p. 369.

211. Singman, *Daily Life*, pp. 37–42; Mendelson and Crawford, *Women in Early Modern England*, pp. 154–65.

212. Hadfield, '"Not without Mustard"'; Honan, *Shakespeare*, pp. 155–62.

213. *Fiants*, ii. 549 (3969); P. M. Buck, 'New Facts Concerning the Life of Edmund Spenser', *MLN* 19 (1904), 237–8.

214. *Annals of the Four Masters*, pp. 306–7. The entry is the first recorded for 1486, a sign of the importance of the institution. See also Lord Walter Fitzgerald, 'New Abbey of Kilcullen,with a sketch of the founder, Sir Roland FitzEustace, Baron Portlester', *JKAS* 3 (1902), 301–17.
215. *Fiants*, ii. 480–1 (4150); Brady, 'Captains' Games', p. 145.
216. Falls, *Elizabeth's Irish Wars*, pp. 52, 60–1, *passim*; McGurk, *Elizabethan Conquest of Ireland*, chs. 2, 4; Lindsay Boynton, *The Elizabethan Militia, 1558–1638* (London: Routledge, 1967), pp. 13–50.
217. Interestingly enough, Ralph Byrchensha (*c.*1565?–1622?), sent to Ireland as controller of the musters in 1598, wrote a poem about the Battle of Kinsale, *A Discourse Occasioned upon the Late Defeat, Giuen to the Arch-Rebels, Tyrone and Odonnell, by the Right Honourable the Lord Mountioy, Lord Deputie of Ireland, the 24. of December, 1601*, published in 1602, which is heavily indebted to Spenser and which was published by Mathew Lownes, Spenser's principal publisher after the death of William Ponsonby in 1604, who tried to have *A View* published in 1598 (see, pp. 365–7). This suggests that Spenser had a readership among those connected to the military. For comment, see Andrew Hadfield, 'An Allusion to Spenser's Irish Writings: Matthew Lownes and Ralph Byrchensha's *A Discourse occasioned on the late defeat, given to the Arch-rebels, Tyrone and O'Donnell* (1602)', *N&Q* 242 (Dec. 1997), 478–80. On Byrchensha's family, see Christopher D. S. Field, *ODNB* entry on 'Birchensha, John (*c.*1605–1681?)'.
218. *Fiants*, ii. 630 (4464).
219. C. G. Cruickshank, *Elizabeth's Army* (2nd edn., Oxford: Oxford University Press, 1966), pp. 139–42. On Kyffin, see, pp. 294–5.
220. Bryskett was the son of an Italian merchant, Antonio Bruschetto (d. 1574), and Elizabeth (d. 1579). Antonio came to England in 1523 and was naturalized in 1536 (*ODNB* entry on Bryskett).
221. On Desmond, see *ODNB* entry by J. N. N. McGurk; Brady, 'Faction and the Origins of the Desmond Rebellion'.
222. MacCarthy-Morrogh, *Munster Plantation*, p. 43.
223. See, pp. 202–5.
224. Jenkins, 'Spenser and the Clerkship in Munster', p. 113; Plomer and Cross, *Bryskett*, p. 9; Judson, *Life*, p. 113.
225. See Sir Henry Sidney to the Privy Council, 27 Feb. 1576: *Carew, 1575–88*, pp. 38–44, at pp. 41–2; Connolly, *Contested Island*, p. 135.
226. Sheehan, 'Provincial Grievance and National Revolt', pp. 13–14.
227. Crawford, *Anglicizing the Government of Ireland*, pp. 140–3, 308–14.
228. Jenkins, 'Spenser and the Clerkship in Munster', p. 113; Sheehan, 'Provincial Grievance and National Revolt', p. 14.
229. Anthony J. Sheehan, 'The Killing of the Earl of Desmond, November 1583', *JCHAS* 88 (1983), 106–10.
230. Jenkins, 'Spenser and the Clerkship in Munster', pp. 113–14.
231. *Chronology*, p. 12.
232. Ibid. 39. Spenser may then have used a deputy to act as commissioner of the musters in Kildare that July.
233. See, p. 38; Nolan, *Norreys*, p. 16.
234. Josephine Waters Bennett, 'The Allegory of Sir Artegall in *F.Q.*, V, xi–xii', *SP* 37 (1940), 177–200. Few have been persuaded that Artegall is really based on Sir John Norris rather than Grey.
235. Hayes-McCoy, 'Completion of the Tudor Conquest', p. 112. On Bingham, see *ODNB* entry by Bernadette Cunningham; Rapple, *Martial Power*, pp. 250–300.
236. *Chronology*, pp. 39–40; Hill, *MacDonnells*, pp. 158–81.
237. Jenkins, 'Spenser: The Uncertain Years', p. 361.
238. Norris to the Privy Council, 7 Nov. 1585, *CSPI, 1574–85*, p. 554; *Chronology*, pp. 40–1.
239. Norris to Burghley, 31 Nov. 1585, *CSPI, 1574–85*, pp. 556–7; *Chronology*, p. 41.
240. Nolan, *Norreys*, p. 69.

241. Nolan, *Norreys*, ch. 6.
242. Judson, *Life*, p. 118. On Norris and Mallow Castle, see Henry F. Berry, 'The Manor and Castle of Mallow in the Days of the Tudors', *JCHAS* 11 (1893), 21–5, 41–5.
243. Jenkins, 'Spenser: The Uncertain Years', pp. 350–1.
244. Alexander C. Judson, 'Spenser and the Munster Officials', *SP* 44 (1947), 157–73.
245. *Chronology*, pp. 42–3; Judson, *Life*, pp. 118–19.
246. Harvey, *Fovre Letters*, p. 102. For comment, see Stern, *Harvey*, pp. 93–8.
247. 'Slumbering I lay in melancholy bed', line 11; Harvey, *New Letter*, sig. D3ᵛ.
248. May, 'Fraunce'. On Marlowe's echoes of *The Faerie Queene* in *Tamburlaine*, see Charles Crawford, 'Edmund Spenser, "Locrine", and "Selimus"', *N&Q*, 9th ser. 7 (1901), 61–3, 203–5, 261–3; *Spenser Allusions*, pp. 15–19. See also the discussion as to who borrowed from whom, which conclusively demonstrates that Marlowe imitated Spenser: T. W. Baldwin, 'The Genesis of Some Passages which Spenser borrowed from Marlowe', *ELH* 9 (1942), 157–87; W. B. C. Watkins, 'The Plagarist? Spenser or Marlowe?', *ELH* 11 (1944), 249–65.
249. Carpenter, *Reference Guide*, p. 32; Henley, *Spenser in Ireland*, pp. 45, 68.
250. *CSPI, 1586–88*, p. 22; Henley, *Spenser in Ireland*, p. 45; J. J. Scarisbrick, *Henry VIII* (1968; London: Methuen, 1988), pp. 303, 456.
251. Howard B. Clarke, 'Cult, Church and Collegiate Church before c.1220', in John Crawford and Raymond Gillespie (eds.), *St. Patrick's Cathedral, Dublin: A History* (Dublin: Four Courts, 2009), pp. 45–72, at pp. 58, 68–9.
252. Raymond Gillespie, 'Reform and Decay, 1500–1598', in Crawford and Gillespie (eds.), *St. Patrick's Cathedral*, pp. 151–73, at pp. 153–4. I am extremely grateful to Raymond Gillespie for advice on prebends.
253. *Chronology*, p. 44; Judson, *Life*, pp. 119–20; Carpenter, 'Spenser in Ireland', p. 409.
254. For a different case, see Jenkins, 'Spenser and the Clerkship in Munster', p. 119. see also Carpenter, 'Spenser in Ireland,' pp. 406–10.
255. The Queen to the Lord Deputy (Henry Sidney), 27 Sept. 1575: *Carew, 1575–88*, pp. 25–6.
256. For discussion, see Jean R. Brink, 'Who Fashioned Edmund Spenser? The Textual History of *Complaints*', *SP* 88 (1991), 153–68.
257. See MacCarthy-Morrogh, *Munster Plantation*, pp. 215–22; John C. Appleby, 'The Problem of Piracy in Ireland, 1570–1630', in Claire Jowitt (ed.), *Pirates? The Politics of Plunder, 1550–1650* (Basingstoke: Palgrave, 2007), pp. 41–55.
258. Denis Power, 'The Archaeology of the Munster Plantation', in Horning et al. (eds.), *Post-Medieval Archaeology of Ireland*, pp. 23–36, at p. 32.
259. Zurcher, *Spenser's Legal Language*, pp. 111–14.
260. *Carew, 1575–88*, p. 462.
261. *Chronology*, pp. 45, 47; Carpenter, 'Spenser in Ireland', p. 419.
262. Ford, *Ussher*, p. 32; *ODNB* entry on 'James Ussher' by Alan Ford.
263. See, pp. 8–9.
264. Martin and Parker, *Spanish Armada*, p. 243. See also T. P. Kilfeather, *Ireland: Graveyard of the Spanish Armada* (Dublin: Anvil, 1967). See also *Carew, 1575–88*, p. 472.
265. Judson, *Life*, p. 123; Martin and Parker, *Spanish Armada*, pp. 234–44.
266. Carew to Walsingham, 18 Sept. 1588, *Carew, 1575–88*, p. 471.
267. Martin and Parker, *Spanish Armada*, pp. 120–2; Phillips, *Images of a Queen*, pp. 195–6; Staines, *The Tragic Histories of Mary Queen of Scots*, pp. 106–7; R. B. Wernham, *After the Armada: Elizabethan England and the Struggle for Western Europe, 1588–1595* (Oxford: Clarendon Press, 1984); Carol Z. Weiner, 'The Beleaguered Isle: A Study of Elizabethan and Early Jacobean Anti-Catholicism', *P&P* 51 (May 1971), 27–62.
268. Elizabeth Fowler, 'The Failure of Moral Philosophy in the Work of Edmund Spenser', *Representations* 51 (1995), 47–76; McCabe, 'Masks of Duessa'.
269. 'Grey', *ODNB* entry; *CSPS, 1586–8*, p. 44.
270. McCabe, 'Fate of Irena'.
271. Sidney, *Apology*, pp. 89–94.

272. Judson, *Life*, p. 123; O'Connell, *Mirror and Veil*, pp. 148–50; Michael O'Connell, '*The Faerie Queene, Book V*', *Sp. Enc.*, pp. 280–3, at p. 282; Douglas A. Northrop, 'Spenser's Defense of Elizabeth', *University of Toronto Quarterly* 38 (1968–9), 27–94, at 283.

273. *Variorum*, vi. 226–8; René Graziani, 'Philip II's Impressa and Spenser's Souldan', *JWCI* 27 (1964), 322–4; Benedict S. Robinson, *Islam and Early Modern English Literature: The Politics of Romance from Spenser to Milton* (Basingstoke: Palgrave, 2007), pp. 36–43.

274. Martin and Parker, *Spanish Armada*, pp. 186–7, *passim*.

275. *Chronology*, p. 50. On Lyon, see *ODNB* entry by Alan Ford; Ford, *Protestant Reformation in Ireland*, pp. 39–40, 88–9, *passim*.

276. On Spenser's allegory, see the various approaches in A. C. Hamilton, *The Structure of Allegory in The Faerie Queene* (Oxford: Clarendon Press, 1961); Isabel G. MacCaffrey, *Spenser's Allegory: The Anatomy of Imagination* (Princeton: Princeton University Press, 1976); Kenneth Borris, *Allegory and Epic in English Renaissance Literature: Heroic Form in Sidney, Spenser and Milton* (Cambridge: Cambridge University Press, 2000), pt. 2.

Chapter 6

1. Some of the estate maps still survive (not the one for Kilcolman): see National Maritime Museum, Dartmouth Collection, P/49/28, 38, which show the survey of the lands to the east of Youghal.

2. Klingelhofer, *Castles and Colonists*, p. 67.

3. Colonel James Grove White, *Historical and Topographical Notes, etc, on Buttevant, Castletownroche, Doneraile, Mallow, and Places in their vicinity*, 4 vols. (Cork: Guy and Co., 1905–25), iii. 264; *Fiants*, iv. 121. Irish land was traditionally divided up into units called 'townlands', which 'retained their identity largely irrespective of the patterns of settlement and land-utilization at any given time'. Any method of assessing land for rent and taxation was imposed on these units which varied in size throughout Ireland: Nicholls, *Gaelic and Gaelicized Ireland*, pp. 138–9.

4. Henley, *Spenser in Ireland*, p. 60.

5. Walter A. Jones, 'Doneraile and Vicinity', *JCHAS*, 2nd ser. 7 (1901), 238–42, at 239. The Roches were also in dispute with Spenser's neighbour, Norris, early in the 17th century: Henry F. Berry, 'The English Settlement in Mallow under the Jephson Family', *JCHAS*, 2nd ser. 12 (1906), 1–26, at 9. On the Roche family in Munster, see Eithne Donnelly, 'The Roches, Lords of Fermoy: The History of a Norman-Irish Family', *JCHAS* 38 (1933), 86–91; 39 (1934), 38–40, 57–68; 40 (1935), 37–42, 63–73; 41 (1936), 20–8, 78–84; 42 (1937), 40–52.

6. For details, see Eric Klingelhofer, 'Edmund Spenser at Kilcolman Castle: The Archaeological Evidence', *Post-Medieval Archaeology* 39 (2005), 133–54; Eric Klingelhofer, 'Current Archaeological Excavations at Kilcolman Castle', *Bulletin of the Early Modern Ireland Committee* 1 (1994), 51–4. See also D. Newman Johnson, 'Kilcolman Castle', *Sp. Enc.*, pp. 417–22; James N. Healy, *The Castles of County Cork* (Cork: Mercier, 1988), pp. 343–4.

7. Herbert Francis Hore, 'Woods and Fastnesses in Ireland', *UJA*, 1st ser. 6 (1858), 145–61, at 145; Power, 'Archaeology of the Munster Plantation', p. 24.

8. *Chronology*, p. 40; *CSPI, 1574–85*, p. 533.

9. Breen, *Archaeology of South-West Ireland*, p. 119.

10. J. H. Andrews, 'Land and People, c.1685', in Moody et al. (eds.), *New History of Ireland*, iii. 454–77, at p. 470.

11. C. Litton Falkiner, 'The Woods in Ireland', in *Illustrations of Irish History, Topography, mainly of the seventeenth century* (London: Longman, 1904), pp. 143–59, at p. 157; Eileen McCracken, *The Irish Woods Since Tudor Times: Distribution and Exploitation* (Newton Abbot: David and Charles, 1971), pp. 37, 39, 45. On deforestation in Ireland, see Smyth, *Map-Making, Landscapes and Memory*, pp. 86–102.

12. Andrews, 'Land and People,' p. 460. On the Blackwater, see Mary Hickson, 'The Blackwater, Cappoquin, and the Barons of Burnchurch', *JRSAI* 20 (1890), 244–6.

13. See e.g. National Maritime Museum, Dartmouth Collection, P/49/20, 27. It was possible to travel at 12–19 miles per day in Munster, and 29 miles per day could be achieved if necessary: McCormack, *Earldom of Desmond*, p. 36. For the use of waterways more generally and their

representation in literary texts, see Andrew McRae, *Literature and Domestic Travel in Early Modern England* (Cambridge: Cambridge University Press, 2009), ch. 1.

14. Flavin and Jones (eds.), *Bristol's Trade with Ireland and the Continent*, *passim*.

15. David Dickson, *Old World Colony: Cork and South Munster, 1630–1830* (Cork: Cork University Press, 2005), p. 22. On the importance of bridges for understanding pre-industrial society, see David Harrison, *The Bridges of Medieval England: Transport and Society 400–1800* (Oxford: Clarendon Press, 2004), pp. 221–32.

16. TNA PRO MPF 1/273; Smyth, *Map-Making, Landscapes and Memory*, p. 46.

17. For an assessment of the impact of this role on Spenser's literary imagination, see Benjamin P. Myers, 'The Green and Golden World: Spenser's Rewriting of the Munster Plantation', *ELH* 76 (2009), 473–90.

18. Robert Dunlop, 'The Plantation of Munster', *EHR* 3 (1888), 250–69, at 267–8; MacCarthy-Morrogh, *Munster Plantation*, pp. 291–2. See also Louise Imogen Guiney, 'Sir Walter Raleigh of Youghal in the County of Cork', *Atlantic Monthly* 66 (1890), 779–86; Nicholls and Williams, *Raleigh*, pp. 36–8.

19. Dunlop, 'The Plantation of Munster', p. 255.

20. Berry, 'English Settlement in Mallow', p. 11.

21. Carew MS 631, fo. 10; Bradner, 'Spenser's Connections with Hampshire'; Ray Heffner, 'Spenser's Acquisition of Kilcolman', *MLN* 46 (1931), 493–8; Michael MacCarthy-Morrogh, 'The Munster Plantation, 1583–1641', unpublished PhD thesis, University of London, 1983, pp. 367–8. For details of Reade's Hampshire lands, see *Victoria County History: Hampshire*, Hants (1911), iv. 316, 325, 363, 507.

22. Reade's will, dated 24 Oct. 1623, makes no mention of Irish lands and shows him existing as a Hampshire landowner: TNA PROB 11/142.

23. Hadfield, 'Secrets and Lies', pp. 64–5.

24. *Carew, 1575–88*, p. 449.

25. Heffner, 'Spenser's Acquisition of Kilcolman', pp. 494–5.

26. *CSPI, 1588–92*, p. 198.

27. Robert Payne, *A Briefe Description of Ireland* (London, 1589); Ciaran Brady, 'Spenser, Plantation and Government Policy,' *Sp. Handbook*, pp. 86–105, at p. 101. On Payne, see the *ODNB* entry by Andrew Hadfield. On Munster's fertility, see Dickson, *Old World Colony*, p. 215.

28. Thomas Harriot, *A Briefe and True Report of the New Found Land of Virginia* (London, 1590). Michael MacCarthy-Morrogh has argued that migration to southern Ireland seemed similar to moving house within England and should be seen in these terms: 'The English Presence in Early Seventeenth-Century Munster', in Ciaran Brady and Raymond Gillespie (eds.), *Natives and Newcomers* (Dublin: Irish Academic Press), pp. 171–90.

29. W. H. Grattan Flood, 'Molana Abbey, Co. Waterford', *JCHAS* 22 (1916), 1–7; NLI MS 41, 985/ 1–2 (patent of grant of Molana Abbey to Sir Walter Ralegh and grant of Molana Abbey to Sir Thomas Harriot); John W. Shirley, 'Sir Walter Ralegh and Thomas Harriot', in James W. Shirley (ed.), *Thomas Harriot: Renaissance Scientist* (Oxford: Clarendon Press, 1974), pp. 16–35, at pp. 21–2; Nicholls and Williams, *Raleigh*, p. 39.

30. Harriot's involvement in the production of some local maps for Ralegh provides further evidence of his presence in Ireland: see Barber, 'Mapmaking in England, ca. 1470–1650', p. 1613. White was also involved in making maps for his patron. W. A. Wallace argues that White lived in Ballynoe (Newtown), also on the Ralegh estates, about 2 miles from Molana. David Beers Quinn argues that White was a client of Hugh Cuffe's and lived near Charleville about 10 miles north of Kilcolman. Either way, White lived in Spenser's orbit: see W. A. Wallace, *John White, Thomas Harriot and Walter Ralegh in Ireland* (London: Historical Association, 1985), pp. 7–10.

31. See the *ODNB* entry on Harriot, by J. J. Roche.

32. Shirley, 'Ralegh and Harriot'; Shohachi Fukada, 'Fanchin, Molanna', *Sp. Enc.*, p. 300.

33. It is possible, but unlikely, that Spenser was significantly misleading the commissioners, although we might be sceptical about some of the details in his answers to the Munster commission.

34. Spenser, *Letters*, pp. 213–14.
35. Carew MS 617, fo. 166; *Carew, 1589–1600*, pp. 61–2.
36. On Maurice Roche, see the *ODNB* entry on 'David Roche' by Robert Dunlop, rev. Bernadette Cunningham.
37. *CSPI, 1588–92*, pp. 14–26; Heffner, 'Spenser's Acquisition of Kilcolman', p. 496.
38. TNA PRO SP 63/147/14 and 15; *Chronology*, p. 51.
39. *Annals of the Four Masters*, ii. 670.
40. Wilson McLeod, *Divided Gaels: Gaelic Cultural Identities in Scotland and Ireland, c.1200–c.1650* (Oxford: Oxford University Press, 2004), pp. 117, 125, 182, *passim*.
41. Transcribed in *Chronology*, pp. 51–2.
42. Pawlisch, *Sir John Davies*, p. 109.
43. Andrew Zurcher, *Shakespeare and the Law* (London: Black, 2010), p. 82. See also B. J. Sokol and Mary Sokol, *Shakespeare's Legal Language: A Dictionary* (London: Athlone, 2000), pp. 408–10; Julia Reinhard Lupton, 'Mapping Mutability: or, Spenser's Irish Plot', in Bradshaw et al. (eds.), *Representing Ireland*, pp. 93–115; McRae, *God Speed the Plough*, pp. 158, 167.
44. Dunlop, 'Plantation of Munster', pp. 250, 252, 259.
45. TNA PRO SP 63/147/16; Spenser, *Letters*, p. 217.
46. Bernadette Cunningham, 'Native Culture and Political Change in Ireland, 1580–1640', in Brady and Gillespie (eds.), *Natives and Newcomers*, pp. 148–70.
47. *Variorum*, x. 65–6. Patricia Coughlan, 'The Local Context of Mutabilitie's Plea', *IUR: Spenser in Ireland, 1596–1996*, ed. Anne Fogarty (Autumn/Winter 1996), 320–41.
48. *Carew, 1575–88*, pp. 256–7.
49. *ODNB* entry on 'David Roche'. On Maurice Roche, see also Judson, *Life*, pp. 133–4; Richard Bagwell, *Ireland under the Tudors*, i. 76.
50. Ironically enough, although it was not unusual for late 16th-century Ireland, Maurice Roche's son, David, having been a rebel, then became a noted loyalist under James I, securing much land, the friendship of Richard Boyle and George Carew, and the hatred of his countrymen. Spenser's grandchildren fought on opposite sides in the Williamite Wars: *ODNB* entry on 'David Roche'; Henley, *Spenser in Ireland*, pp. 208–11.
51. MacCarthy-Morrogh, *Munster Plantation*, p. 131.
52. On the number of disputes in everyday life in England, see Emmisson, *Elizabeth Life: Home, Land & Work*, ch. 17; MacCarthy-Morrogh, *Munster Plantation*, ch. 1.
53. *Fiants*, iv. 121.
54. Lupton, 'Mapping Mutability', pp. 106–11. See also Coughlan, 'The Local Context of Mutabilitie's Plea'.
55. Spenser, *Letters*, p. 221; MacCarthy-Morrogh, *Munster Plantation*, pp. 290–1.
56. BL Add. MS 19869, transcribed in Spenser, *Letters*, p. 220.
57. Patricia Coughlan, 'Cross-Currents in Colonial Discourse: The Political Thought of Vincent and Daniel Gookin', in Jane Ohlmeyer (ed.), *Political Thought in Seventeenth-Century Ireland* (Cambridge: Cambridge University Press, 2000), pp. 56–82.
58. Jones, 'Doneraile and Vicinity', p. 234; Henley, *Spenser in Ireland*, p. 200.
59. Jones, 'Doneraile and Vicinity', pp. 233–4; Walter A. Jones and Mananaan Mac Lir, *The Synans of Doneraile* (Cork: Guy, 1909).
60. Transcribed in Carpenter, *Reference Guide*, p. 35; Judson, *Life*, p. 135. On the list of sheriffs, see Henry F. Berry, 'Sheriffs of the County of Cork: Henry III to 1660', *JRSAI* 15 (1905), 39–52, at 47.
61. Breen, *Archaeology of South-West Ireland*, pp. 123–4.
62. Anthony J. Sheehan, 'Official Reaction to Native Land Claims in the Plantation of Munster', *IHS* 23 (1983), 297–318, at 297.
63. Brady, (ed.), *Sidney's Memoir*, pp. 44, 46, *passim*.
64. Sokol and Sokol, *Shakespeare's Legal Language*, pp. 189–93; Horwitz, *Chancery Equity Prodceedings*, pp. 31–6.
65. Edward MacLysaght (ed.), 'Doneraile Papers', *Analecta Hibernica* 15 (1944), 335–62; 20 (1958), 56–91, at 57; MacCarthy-Morrogh, *Munster Plantation*, p. 168. See also Seamus Crowley, 'Some

of Spenser's Doneraile Neighbours', *North Cork Writers Journal*, 1 (1894), 71–5. Another contemporary, Nicholas Synan, was a prominent friar, 'probably the last Conventual Franciscan in Ireland': Fr. Candice Mooney, *The Friars of Broad Lane: The Story of a Franciscan Friary in Cork, 1229–1977* (Cork: Tower Books, 1977), p. 36.

66. Basil O'Connell, 'The Nagles of Ballygriffin and Nano Nagle', *Irish Genealogist* 3 (1957), 67–73, at 68, suggests the marriage took place c.1630. For further details, see Appendix One.

67. David Edwards, 'A Haven of Popery: English Catholic Migration to Ireland In the Age of Plantations', in Alan Ford and John McCafferty (eds.), *The Origins of Sectarianism in Early Modern Ireland* (Cambridge: Cambridge University Press), pp. 95–126, at p. 117.

68. See p. 342.

69. Jeffries, *Irish Church*, pp. 136–7.

70. Edwards, 'Have of Popery,' p. 121.

71. Conveyance of Lands of Rossagh and Kilcolman from Richard Nagle to Sylvanus Spenser, Doneraile Papers, TNA MS 32,867 (1); Bond of Arbitration between Sir William St Leger and William Spenser, Doneraile Papers, TNA MS 34,058 (1). See also MacLysaght (ed.), 'Doneraile Papers', *Analecta Hibernica* 15. 337, 339; 20. 59, 67–8, 70.

72. Berry, 'English Settlement in Mallow,' p. 2.

73. Power, 'Archaeology of the Munster Plantation', p. 28.

74. H. G. Leask, 'Mallow Castle, Co. Cork', *JCHAS* 49 (1944), 19–24. See also Tadhg O'Keefe and Sinéad Quirke, 'A House at the Birth of Modernity: Ightermurragh Castle, Co. Cork', in James Lyttleton and Colin Rynne (eds.), *Plantation Ireland* (Dublin: Four Courts, 2009), pp. 86–112, at p. 102; Tadhg O'Keefe, 'Plantation-era Great Houses in Munster: A Note on Sir Walter Ralegh's House and Its Context', in Herron and Potterton (eds.), *Ireland in the Renaissance*, pp. 274–88, at pp. 277–8; Healy, *Castles of Cork*, pp. 356–8; White, *Historical and Topographical Notes*, iv. 80–9.

75. Berry, 'English Settlement in Mallow', p. 14.

76. Sheehan, 'Official Reaction', p. 297.

77. Hammer, *Polarisation of Elizabethan Politics*, pp. 306–8.

78. A. L. Rowse, *Sir Walter Ralegh: His Family and Private Life* (London: Harper, 1962), pp. 62–3, 98, *passim*.

79. MacCarthy-Morrogh, 'Munster Plantation', pp. 375–8. See also Rolf Loeber and Terence Reeves-Smith, 'Lord Audley's Grandiose Building Schemes in the Ulster Plantation', in Brian Mac Curta, SJ (ed.), *Reshaping Ireland, 1550–1700: Colonization and Its Consequences: Essays Presented to Nicholas Canny* (Dublin: Four Courts, 2011), pp. 82–100.

80. TNA PRO SP 63/203, 119, fo. 1.

81. Andrew Hadfield and Willy Maley, 'Introduction: Irish Representations and English Alternatives', in Bradshaw et al. (eds.), *Representing Ireland*, pp. 1–23, at p. 3; *Amoretti* 22, line 10, Spenser, *Shorter Poems*, p. 398.

82. Personal communication by Kenneth Nicholls. I am extremely grateful to Prof. Nicholls for discussing the dialogue with me and sharing his knowledge and insights. Hiram Morgan has suggested that the author was Henry Chettle (http://www.ucc.ie/celt/contents/online/E590001-001/nav.html, introd.). On Chettle, see the *ODNB* entry by Emma Smith. There is no evidence that Chettle had any particular connection with Ireland. The dialogue appears in a 'Book on the State of Ireland' (c.1599), which has the signature of Thomas Wilson at the bottom of the opening page, presumably the Thomas Wilson (d. 1629), servant of and record keeper for the Cecils. Wilson claimed that he was writing a treatise on Ireland, but this has never materialized and is unlikely to be this dialogue, although Mark Netzloff makes a case that he could be the author: see *CSPI, 1598–9*, pp. 505–8; Sir Thomas Wilson, 'The State of England Anno. Dom. 1600', in *Camden Miscellany*, 3rd ser. 16 (London: Camden Society, 1936), pp. 1–47; Mark Netzloff, 'Forgetting the Ulster Plantation: John Speed's *The Theatre of Great Britain* (1611) and the Colonial Archive', *JMEMS* 31 (2001), 313–48, at 345 n. 76. The most plausible candidate, if the author is not Cuffe, is now thought to be Hugh Collier, a messenger and government spy (http://www.ucc.ie/celt/published/E590001-001/index. html). If so, the title needs to be explained: perhaps Collier met the brothers in London in 1599 and composed it as homage to their father. I am grateful to Hiram Morgan for discussing the text with me.

83. Berry, 'Sheriffs of the County Cork', p. 47. It is also worth noting that Sir Robert Tynte, the third husband of Elizabeth Boyle, served as sheriff from 1625 to 1626.

84. Judson, 'Spenser and the Munster Officials'; *Chronology*, pp. 85–108.

85. MacCarthy-Morrogh, *Munster Plantation*, pp. 289–92. Hatton, who died in 1591, was eager to be involved in plantation ventures, but never visited Ireland, and lost interest in his estate there. His seigniory of 12,880 acres was at Knocknamona: MacCarthy-Morrogh, *Munster Plantation*, p. 291; Brooks, *Hatton*, pp. 322–3.

86. See Christopher Butler, ' "Pricking" and Ambiguity at the Start of *The Faerie Queene*', *N&Q* 55 (2008), 159–61; Judith H. Anderson, ' "A Gentle Knight was pricking on the plaine": The Chaucerian Connection', *ELR* 15 (1985), 166–74; Hadfield, 'Spenser and Jokes', p. 9.

87. Beal (ed.), *Dictionary of English Manuscript Terminology*, p. 313.

88. For an overview of early modern horse riding, see Anthony Dent, *Horses in Shakespeare's England* (London: Allen, 1987). Spenser would undoubtedly have known the widely available horse manual, Thomas Blundeville's *The Foure Chiefest Offices Belonging to Horsemanship* (London, 1565), frequently reprinted afterwards. I am grateful to Donna Landry for advice on horses and horsemanship.

89. For discussion, see McRae, *Literature and Domestic Travel*, esp. ch. 2; Crofts, *Packhorse, Waggon and Post*; Richard Joyce, 'Irish Postal History—Part 1', *Cahir Na Mart* 26 (2008), 59–79. I am grateful to Natalie Mears for this last reference.

90. MacCarthy-Morrogh, *Munster Plantation*, p. 31; Nicholas Canny, *From Reformation to Restoration: Ireland, 1534–1660* (Dublin: Hellicon, 1987), p. 87; Myers, 'Green and Golden World', p. 477.

91. Richard W. Hoyle, 'Woad in the 1580s: Alternative Agriculture in England and Ireland', in *Landscape, People and Alternative Agriculture: Essays Celebrating Joan Thirsk at Eighty* (Agricultural History Rev., suppl. ser. 3, 2004), pp. 56–73.

92. Marcel Kocken and Etienne Rynne, 'A Belgian Bronze Mortar from Co. Cork', *JCHAS* 67 (1962), 80–1.

93. Nicholls, *Gaelic and Gaelicized Ireland*, pp. 144–5. See also Raymond Gillespie, 'The Problems of Plantations: Material Culture and Social Change in Early Modern Ireland', in Lyttleton and Rynne (eds.), *Plantation Ireland*, pp. 43–60.

94. Baptista Boazio and Robert Dunlop, 'Sixteenth-Century Maps of Ireland', *EHR* 20 (1905), 309–37; J. H. Andrews, 'Colonial Cartography in a European Setting: The Case of Tudor Ireland', in Woodward (ed.), *History of Cartography*, iii/2. 1670–83.

95. Michael MacCarthy-Morrogh points out that Edward Denny, the Kerry undertaker, was the first cousin of both Ralegh and Sir Humphrey Gilbert, and had served under Grey, to whom he was related by marriage (*Munster Plantation*, p. 49). Such evidence further suggests that Spenser's connections in the Irish civil service were crucial to his career advancement.

96. *ODNB* entry on 'Sir Edward Fitton' by Bernadette Cunningham.

97. Sheehan, 'Official Reaction', p. 301; Quinn, 'Munster Plantation', p. 24. 'Coyne and livery' was food and lodging for a superior's soldiers.

98. MacCarthy-Morrogh, *Munster Plantation*, pp. 81–3.

99. Ibid. 192–3. On Spenser's paranoia, see Thomas H. Cain, *Praise in The Faerie Queene* (Lincoln: University of Nebraska Press, 1978), chs. 4–7; Christopher Highley, *Shakespeare, Spenser and the Crisis in Ireland* (Cambridge: Cambridge University Press, 1997), ch. 5.

100. A handsome linen map on vellum (*c*.1595), by Francis Jobson, the surveyor employed by the Munster Commissioners, shows the estates of the planters: National Maritime Museum, Dartmouth Collection, P/49/20. There is an equally attractive, smaller colour copy, showing that it was widely known and used (27).

101. Thomas Herron, 'Early Modern Ireland and the New English Epic: Connecting Edmund Spenser and Sir George Carew', *Eolas* 1 (2006), 27–52, at 43. Sir Peter had served in France with Sir John Wallop, Henry Wallop's uncle, providing yet another link between the English gentry who went to Ireland in the 16th century, and suggesting how closely connected such figures and their clients were: John Wagner, *The Devonshire Gentleman: A Life of Sir Peter Carew* (Hull:

Hull University Press, 1998), pp. 66–70; *ODNB* entry on Sir John Wallop by Alan Bryson. On Spenser's knowledge of Holinshed, see *Variorum*, x. 266, 292–6, *passim*.

102. See the *ODNB* entry on Carew by Ute Lotz-Heumann; Standish O'Grady (ed.), *Pacata Hibernia: or a history of the Wars in Ireland during the reign of Queen Elizabeth especially within the Province of Munster under the government of Sir George Carew)* (London: Downey, 1896).

103. George Carew, *The Historie of Aravcana, written in verse by Don Alonso de Ercilla translated out of the spanishe into Englishe prose allmost to the Ende of the 16: Canto*, ed. Frank Pierce (Manchester: Manchester University Press, 1964). For comment, see David Armitage, 'Literature and Empire', in Nichoas P. Canny (ed.), *The Origins of Empire* (Oxford: Oxford University Press, 1998), pp. 99–123, at pp. 118–19; Palmer, *Language and Conquest*, p. 111; Barbara Fuchs, 'Travelling Epic: Translating Ercilla's *La Araucana* in the Old World', *JMEMS* 36 (2006), 379–95, at 387–92.

104. As is noted by Sidney Lysaght, 'Kilcolman Castle', *The Antiquary* 5 (1882), 153–6, at 155.

105. The opening pages of Barnabe Googe's translation of Conrad Heresbach's *Foure Bookes of Husbandry* (London, 1577), fos. 3ʳ–7ʳ, discuss the role of a bailiff in running an estate.

106. See White, *Historical and Topographical Notes*, ii. 120–7. On Castlepook Cave, see R. F. Scharff, H. J. Seymour, and E. T. Newton, 'The Exploration of Castlepook Cave, County Cork, Being the Third Report from the Committee Appointed to Explore Irish Caves', *PRIA*, sect. B, 34 (1917–19), 33–72.

107. *Colin Clout*, lines 92, 117, 130, 135; *FQ* VII.vi.40, line 4.

108. Chancery Bill A171, National Archives of Ireland (transcribed fully in Brink, 'Documenting Edmund Spenser'). I am especially grateful to Kenneth Nicholls for bringing this possible relationship to my attention and for discussing the sources with me.

109. Patricia Palmer, 'Interpreters and the Politics of Translation and Traduction in Sixteenth-Century Ireland', *IHS* 131 (2003), 257–77, at 259; Sir Thomas Browne, writing in 1610, cited in Canny, *Upstart Earl*, p. 127.

110. Pauline Henely, 'Notes on Irish Words in Spenser's *Viewe of Ireland*', *JCHAS* 57 (1952), 121–4.

111. John W. Draper, 'Linguistics in *The Present State of Ireland*', *MP* 17 (1919–20), 471–86, at 472. See also the excellent discussion in Patricia Palmer, *Language and Conquest in Early Modern Ireland: English Renaissance Literature and Elizabethan Imperial Expansion* (Cambridge: Cambridge University Press, 2001), pp. 78–9; Eiléan Ní Chuuilleanáin, 'Ireland, the cultural context', *Sp. Enc.*, pp. 403–4.

112. Draper, 'Spenser's Linguistics', p. 472.

113. Cited in Connolly, *Contested Island*, p. 33. See also Colm Lennon, *Richard Stanihurst, the Dubliner, 1547–1618* (Dublin: Irish Academic Press, 1981), p. 145; Vincent Carey, ' "Neither good English nor good Irish": Bi-lingualism and Identity Formation in Sixteenth-Century Ireland', in Morgan (ed.), *Political Ideology in Ireland*, pp. 45–61.

114. *Variorum*, x. 127.

115. Palmer, 'Interpreters and the Politics of Translation', pp. 260–3.

116. See Roland M. Smith, 'The Irish Background of Spenser's View', *JEGP* 42 (1943), 499–515; Roland M. Smith, 'More Irish Words in Spenser', *MLN* 59 (1944), 472–7; Clare Carroll, 'Spenser's Relation to the Irish Language: The Sons of Milesio in *A View*, *Faerie Queene* V, and the *Leabhar Gabhála*', in *Circe's Cup: Cultural Transformations in Early Modern Ireland* (Cork: Cork University Press, 2001), pp. 61–8.

117. McCabe, *Spenser's Monstrous Regiment*, p. 47.

118. See Palmer, *Language and Conquest in Early Modern Ireland*, p. 79; Henley, *Spenser in Ireland*, p. 103; Roland M. Smith, 'Spenser, Holinshed, and the Leabhar Gabhala', *JEGP* 43 (1944), 390–401. On Brehon Law, see Pawlisch, *Sir John Davies*, pp. 55–9, *passim*.

119. *Leabhar Gabhála: The Book of the Conquests of Ireland. The recension of Micheál Ó Cléirigh*, ed. R. A. Stewart Macalister and John MacNeill (Dublin: Hodges, Figgis, 1916).

120. Eusebius of Caesarea, *The Auncient Ecclesiasticall Histories of the first six hundred yeares after Christ*, trans. Meredith Hanmer (London, 1577). On some of Hanmer's multiple ecclesiastical positions, see James B. Leslie, *Ossory Clergy and Parishes: being an account of the clergy of the Church of Ireland in the Diocese of Ossory, from the earliest period* (Enniskillen: Fermanagh Times Office, 1933), pp. 193, 261, 284, 319, 349.

121. Calendar of the Lismore Manuscripts with Index of Matters, AD 1396–1974, 13 vols. (Chatsworth House Archives), i. 8.
122. Dr Meredith Hanmer's collection of historical notes and documents', SP 63/214, fo. 230^v.
123. Sir James Ware, *Ancient Irish Histories. The Works of Spencer, Campion, Hanmer, and Marleburrough* (Dublin, 1633).
124. See the *ODNB* entry on Hanmer by Alan Ford.
125. D. B. Quinn, *The Elizabethans and the Irish* (Ithaca, NY: Cornell University Press, 1966), pp. 14–15, 53–4, *passim*; Hadfield and McVeagh (eds.), *Strangers to that Land*, pp. 74–6.
126. Joan Thirsk, 'Farming Techniques', in Joan Thirsk (ed.), *The Agrarian History of England and Wales*, iv. *1500–1640* (Cambridge: Cambridge University Press, 1967), pp. 161–99, at p. 163; Myers, 'Green and Golden World', pp. 477–8.
127. *Variorum*, x. 97–8.
128. Andrew Hadfield, 'Briton and Scythian: Tudor Representations of Irish Origins', *IHS* 112 (1993), 390–408; Richard Hakluyt, *The Principall Nauigations, Voiages and Discoueries of the English Nation* (London, 1589), pp. 332–74; Giles Fletcher, *Of the Russe Commonwealt, or Maner of gouernement of the Russe emperour, (commonly called the Emperour of Moskouia) with the manners, and fashions of the people of that countrey* (London, 1591), fos. 65–75.
129. *Variorum*, x. 98.
130. Ann Rosalind Jones and Peter Stallybrass, 'Dismantling Irena: The Sexualising of Ireland in Early Modern England', in Andrew Parker, Mary Russo, Doris Sommer, and Patricia Yaeger (eds.), *Nationalisms and Sexualities* (London: Routledge, 1992), pp. 157–71.
131. See Mary O'Dowd, 'Gaelic Economy and Society', in Brady and Gillespie (eds.), *Natives and Newcomers*, pp. 120–47. O'Dowd notes that historians need to be careful of descriptions of Irish society from English observers, which have been used due to the absence of Gaelic sources, because 'such accounts were usually written with a particular political or propaganda end in view' (p. 120).
132. Nicholls, *Gaelic and Gaelicized Ireland*, p. 132.
133. Ibid. 132–5.
134. Thirsk, 'Farming Techniques', p. 99. For English agricultural practices in this period, see also Baker, 'Changes in the Later Middle Ages', p. 216; D. C. Coleman, *The Economy of England, 1450–1750* (Oxford: Oxford University Press, 1977), ch. 2.
135. See Connolly, *Contested Island*, pp. 16–18. Indeed, agriculture in northern Europe could be seen as part of a much larger and more coherent economic system: Aldo De Maddalena, 'Rural Europe, 1500–1750', in Carlo M. Cipolla (ed.), *The Fontana Economic History of Europe: The Sixteenth and Seventeenth Centuries* (London: Fontana, 1974), pp. 273–353.
136. Payne, *Briefe Description*, pp. 8–9.
137. See Hore, 'Woods and Fastnesses', p. 158.
138. Breen, *Archaeology of South-West Ireland*, p. 179; Robert Dunlop, 'An Unpublished Survey of the Plantation of Munster in 1622', *JRSAI* 54 (1924), 128–46, at 145.
139. Klingelhofer, *Castles and Colonists*, p. 19.
140. McCracken, *Irish Woods*, pp. 15–16; On Spenser's relationship to the destruction of woodland in his poetry, see Elizabeth M. Weixel, 'Squires of the Wood: The Decline of the Aristocratic Forest in Book VI of *The Faerie Queene*', *Sp. St.* 25 (2010), 187–213.
141. McCracken, *Irish Woods*, ch. 4.
142. Eileen McCracken, 'Charcoal Burning Ironworks in Seventeenth and Eighteenth-Century Ireland', *UJA* 20 (1957), 123–38, at 134.
143. See Colin Rynne, 'The Social Archaeology of Plantation-Period Ironworks in Ireland: Immigrant Industrial Communities and Technology Transfer, c.1560–1640', in Lyttleton and Rynne (eds.), *Plantation Ireland*, pp. 248–64, at pp. 253, 258; Seamus Crowley, 'Mallow Iron Mines', *MFCJ* 22 (2004), 21–32, at 29–32; Eileen McCracken, 'Supplementary List of Irish Charcoal Burning Iron Works', *UJA* 28 (1965), 132–6, at 132. On the excavations at Mogeely, see Eric Klingelhofer, 'Elizabethan Settlements: Mogeely Castle, Curraglass and Carrigeen, C. Cork (Part II)', *JCHAS* 105 (2000), 155–74; Klingelhofer, *Castles and Colonists*, pp. 73–8. See also Richard Caulfield, *The Council Book of the Corporation of Youghal, from 1610 to 1659, from 1666*

to 1687, and from 1690 to 1800 (Guildford: Billing and Sons, 1878), pp. xliv–vi; Denis Power et al. (eds.), *Archaeological Inventory of County Cork*, 4 vols., ii. *East and South Cork* (Dublin: Stationery Office), 1994, pp. 216–17.

144. On Munster, see McCormack, 'Social and Economic Consequences of the Desmond Rebellion'. On land in England see Thirsk, 'Farming Techniques', p. 177.

145. Thirsk, 'Farming Techniques', p. 171; Gervase Markham, *The English Housewife*, ed. Michael R. Best (Montreal: McGill-Queen's University Press, 1986), chs. 4, 9.

146. Nicholls, *Gaelic and Gaelicized Ireland*, p. 133. See also the description in Fynes Moryson, *An Itinerary Containing His Ten Yeeres Travell through the Twelve Dominions of Germany, Bohmerland, Sweitzerland, Netherland, Denmarke, Poland, Italy, Turky, France, England, Scotland, and Ireland* (1617), 4 vols. (Glasgow: MacLehose, 1908), iv. 192–203; Markham, *English Housewife*, ch. 8.

147. J. Tierney, 'Plant Remains', in Klingelhofer, 'Spenser at Kilcolman', pp. 147–8.

148. 'Doneraile Papers', pp. 59, 62.

149. *Colin Clout*, line 318; 'Two Cantos of Mutabilitie', VII.vi.55, line 8; *Epithalamion*, line 69.

150. Campbell, *English Yeoman*, pp. 197–204; Eileen M. Murphy, 'An Overview of Livestock, Husbandry, and Economic Practices', in Horning et al. (eds.), *Post-Medieval Archaeology of Ireland*, pp. 371–91, at pp. 377–81.

151. Breen, Archaeology of *South-West Ireland*, p. 171; Klingelhofer, *Castles and Colonists*, p. 13. See also Thomas Herron, 'Irish Archaeology and the Poetry of Edmund Spenser: Content and Context', in Lyttleton and Rynne (eds.), *Plantation Ireland*, pp. 229–47, at p. 243.

152. M. McCarthy, 'Appendix I: Faunal Remains Summary', in Klingelhofer, 'Spenser at Kilcolman', pp. 150–1.

153. Klingelhofer, *Castles and Colonists*, p. 123.

154. Nicholls, *Gaelic and Gaelicized Ireland*, p. 138. If such sheep were used, then this might be seen as a further example of the bad faith of *A View*, and Spenser's desire to disguise how Irish farms really worked. On English sheep breeds and breeding, see Thirsk, 'Farming Techniques', pp. 189–91.

155. Herron, Irish Archaeology and Spenser', p. 243; Nicholls, *Gaelic and Gaelicized Ireland*, pp. 144–5; McCormack, 'Social and Economic Consequences of the Desmond Rebellion', pp. 6–7.

156. See Gordon Batho, 'Noblemen, Gentlemen and Yeomen', in Thirsk (ed.), *Agrarian History*, pp. 276–305, at pp. 290–1, *passim*.

157. *The Private Life of an Elizabethan Lady: The Diary of Lady Margaret Hoby, 1599–1605* (Stroud: Sutton, 1998), p. 64.

158. Dickson, *Old World Colony*, p. 20.

159. See H. G. Leask, *Irish Castles and Castellated Houses* (Dundalk: Dundalgan Press, 1977), chs. 9–10.

160. See Terence Reeves-Smith, 'Community to Privacy: Late Tudor and Jacobean Manorial Architecture in Ireland, 1560–1640', in Horning et al. (eds.), *Post-Medieval Archaeology of Ireland*, pp. 269–326, at pp. 290–300. Evidence suggests that Ralegh developed Myrtle Grove in a similar fashion: O'Keefe, 'Plantation-Era Great Houses in Munster', p. 287.

161. Peck, *Consuming Splendor*, pp. 195–6; Stone, *Crisis of the Aristocracy*, p. 552.

162. Hamling, *Decorating the 'Godly' Household*, pp. 77–8, 221.

163. Catherine Richardson, *Domestic Life and Domestic Tragedy in Early Modern England: The Material Life of the Household* (Manchester: Manchester University Press, 2006), pp. 46–7.

164. Burton, *Elizabethans at Home*, pp. 98–101.

165. Klingelhofer, *Castles and Colonists*, pp. 154–5; Myrtle Grove, renovated at about the same time as Kilcolman, had all of these features: Goddard H. Orpen, 'Ralegh's House, Youghal,' *JRSAI*, 5th ser. 33 (1903), 310–12.

166. Hamling, *Decorating the 'Godly' Household*, pp. 30, 37.

167. Ibid. 105–8.

168. Hilary Jenkinson, 'English Wall-Paper of the Sixteenth and Seventeenth Centuries', *AJ* 5 (1925), 237–53. I owe this reference to Angus Vine.

169. As was the case, on a grander scale, with Hill Hall: see Drury with Simpson, *Hill Hall*, pp. 467–506. See also Maurice Howard, *The Early Tudor Country House: Architecture and Politics, 1490–1550* (London: George Philip, 1987), ch. 1. Compare also the architectural developments at Barryscourt Castle: Breen, *Archaeology of South-West Ireland*, p. 111.

170. Klingelhofer, *Castles and Colonists*, p. 121.

171. Parlours were often added to houses in late 16th-century England: Richardson, *Domestic Life and Domestic Tragedy*, p. 90.

172. Klingelhofer, 'Spenser at Kilcolman', pp. 137, 149; Breen, *Archaeology of South-West Ireland*, p. 109; Dunlop, 'Unpublished Survey', pp. 143–4.

173. Klingelhofer, 'Spenser at Kilcolman', p. 142; Klingelhofer, 'Current Archaeological Excavations at Kilcolman'; Newman Johnson, 'Kilcolman Castle', p. 422.

174. Klingelhofer, *Castles and Colonists*, p. 120.

175. Ibid. 95.

176. Ibid. 154.

177. Markham, *English Housewife*, ch. 2.

178. Murphy, 'An Overview of Livestock, Husbandry, and Economic Practices', pp. 382–4.

179. Klingelhofer, *Castles and Colonists*, p. 123.

180. Klingelhofer, 'Elizabethan Settlements', p. 169. On Spenser and music, see Bruce Pattison, *Music and Poetry of the English Renaissance* (2nd edn., London: Methuen, 1970), pp. 65–7, 142–4, *passim*. On the verse on the earl's lute, see Spenser, *Shorter Poems*, p. 779; David Lee Miller, 'The Earl of Cork's Lute', in Anderson et al. (eds.), *Spenser's Life*, pp. 146–77.

181. Peck, *Consuming Splendor*, p. 215; Muldrew, *Economy of Obligation*, pt. 2.

182. Breen, *Archaeology of South-West Ireland*, pp. 26, 133.

183. Klingelhofer, 'Spenser at Kilcolman', pp. 144–8.

184. Klingelhofer, *Castles and Colonists*, pp. 126–7.

185. Breen, *Archaeology of South-West Ireland*, pp. 171–6.

186. Ibid. 133.

187. Markham, *English Housewife*, pp. 60–2;

188. Klingelhofer, 'Spenser at Kilcolman', pp. 143–4. On English garden styles and fashions, see Roy Strong, *The Renaissance Garden in England* (London: Thames and Hudson, 1979), ch. 2; Burton, *Elizabethans at Home*, ch. 8.

189. Jane H. Ohlmeyer, ' "Civilizinge of those Rude Partes": Colonization within Britain and Ireland, 1580s–1640s', in Canny (ed.), *Origins of Empire*, pp. 124–47, at p. 140; Alexandra Walsham, *The Reformation of the Landscape: Religion, Identity, and Memory in Early Modern Ireland* (Oxford: Oxford University Press, 2011), pp. 313–16. For specific examples, see James Lyttleton, 'Gaelic Classicism in the Irish Midland Plantations: An Archaeological Reflection', in Herron and Potterton (eds.), *Ireland in the Renaissance*, pp. 231–54, at pp. 248–51; Breen, *Archaeology of South-West Ireland*, p. 126. On Italian garden design and its wider impact, see John Dixon Hunt (ed.), *The Italian Garden: Art, Design and Culture* (Cambridge: Cambridge University Press, 1996); and, for an account of an English Italianate garden, see *Diary of Baron Waldstein*, pp. 159–63.

190. Breen, *Archaeology of South-West Ireland*, p. 26; MacCarthy-Morrogh, *Munster Plantation*, p. 125; Dunlop, 'Unpublished Survey', p. 143.

191. Bate, *Soul of the Age*, ch. 3; John Dixon Hunt and Michael Leslie, 'Gardens', *Sp. Enc.*, pp. 323–5.

192. Wallace, *Virgil's Schoolboys*, ch. 3; Lees-Jeffries, *England's Helicon*, pt. 2; William A. Sessions, 'Spenser's Georgics', *ELR* 10 (1980), 202–38.

193. See, pp. 325–6.

194. See pp. 409–10; Macfarlane, *The Family Life of Ralph Josselin* (London: Cambridge University Press, 1970), pp. 146–8.

195. Macfarlane, *Family Life of Ralph Josselin*, app. B, pp. 205–10.

196. Michael Quiane, 'The Diocesan Schools, 1570–1870', *JCHAS* 66 (1961), 26–50.

197. Personal communication from Eric Klingelhofer. On the tutoring role of servants, see Sheila McIsaac Cooper, 'Servants as Educators in Early-Modern England', *Pedagogical History* 43 (2007), 457–63, at p. 550.

198. On the poverty of Irish ecclesiastical livings, see Ford, *Protestant Reformation*, ch. 5, 'Protestant Preachers in Munster and the Pale'.
199. Personal communication from Brian Cummings.
200. Personal communication from Eric Klingelhofer.
201. See Grove White, *Historical and Topographical Notes*, i. 334–49, 72–89.
202. Canny, *Upstart Earl*, p. 27.
203. See Appendix 1 for details.
204. *The Book of Common Prayer*, ed. Brian Cummings (Oxford: Oxford University Press, 2011), introd., pp. xxv–xxxiv.
205. Shohachi Fukuda, 'Bregog, Mulla', *Sp. Enc.*, p. 110.
206. For analysis, see Joyce, *Wonders of Ireland*, pp. 107–12; Henley, *Spenser in Ireland*, pp. 85–7; Roland M. Smith, 'Spenser's Irish River Stories', *PMLA* 50 (1935), 1047–56.
207. Anon., 'Spenser's Streams: The Mull and Arlo', *Dublin University Magazine* 38 (1851), 233–52.
208. R. W. Evans, 'Notes on River Bregog', *JCHAS* 18 (1912), 201–3, at 201.
209. Daniel Carey, 'Spenser, Purchas, and the Poetics of Colonial Settlement', in Fiona Bateman and Lionel Pilkington (eds.), *Studies in Settler Colonialism: Politics, Identity and Culture* (Basingstoke: Palgrave, 2011), pp. 28–46, at p. 29. On Spenser and the bards, see also Christopher Highley, 'Spenser and the Bards', *Sp. St.* 12 (1998), 77–103.
210. Carey, 'Spenser, Purchas', pp. 30–3. Carey points out that Spenser represents the Bregog, possibly as a metonymic self-portrait, as deceitful or lying in *Colin Clout*, line 118. For later reflections on the relationship between Spenser and this area, see Elizabeth Bowen, *Bowen's Court & Seven Winters* (London: Vintage, 1999), pp. 3–32.
211. Walsham, *Reformation of the Landscape*, ch. 4.
212. Eamon Duffy, 'Bare Ruined Choirs: Remembering Catholicism in Shakespeare's England', in Richard Dutton, Alison Findlay, and Richard Wilson (eds.), *Theatre and Religion: Lancastrian Shakespeare* (Manchester: Manchester University Press, 2003), pp. 40–57.
213. Alison Shell, *Oral Culture and Catholicism in Early Modern England* (Cambridge: Cambridge University Press, 2007), pp. 4–5.
214. Ben Jonson, 'Conversations with William Drummond', in *The Complete Poems*, ed. George Parfitt (Harmondsworth: Penguin, 1975), pp. 459–80, at p. 465.
215. Although it has been noted Jonson's judgement has had little impact on the general consensus about Spenser's religious leanings and has not often been connected to the destruction of religious houses in Britain and Ireland, see e.g. F. M. Padelford, 'Spenser and the Puritan Propaganda', *MP* 11 (1913), 85–106, at 106; King, *Spenser's Poetry and the Reformation Tradition*, pp. 237–8; James A. Riddell and Stanley Stewart, *Jonson's Spenser: Evidence and Historical Criticism* (Pittsburgh: Duquesne University Press, 1995), pp. 22–3. An exception is Merritt Y. Hughes, 'Spenser's "Blatant Beast"', *MLR* 13 (1918), 267–75, at 270–2, although Hughes describes Spenser's verses as a moment of 'rare tolerance' (270) and still sees Spenser as sympathetic to the fairly hot sort of Protestants.
216. Stewart, *Close Readers*, ch. 5.
217. A notorious modern misreading was the basis of a modern psychoanalytical study of Luther's conversion: see Erik H. Erikson, *Young Man Luther: A Study in Psychoanalysis and History* (1958; New York: Norton, 1962), pp. 204–6; Quentin Skinner, *The Foundations of Modern Political Thought*, 2 vols. (Cambridge: Cambridge University Press, 1978), ii. 7.
218. *FQ* I.iii.16–22; Darryl J. Gless, 'Abessa, Corceca, Kirkrapine', *Sp. Enc.*, pp. 3–4.
219. Claire McEachern, 'Spenser and Religion', *Sp. Handbook*, pp. 30–47, at p. 39.
220. F. L. Cross, *The Oxford Dictionary of the Christian Church*, rev. E. A. Livingstone (Oxford: Oxford University Press, 2005), p. 320; J. Charles Cox and Alfred Harvey, *English Church Furniture* (London: Methuen, 1907), chs. 2–4.
221. *Book of Common Prayer*, introd., p. xxiv.
222. See, Duffy, *Stripping of the Altars*, pt. 3; Aston, *England's Iconoclasts*, ch. 7; Gilman, *Iconoclasm and Poetry*, ch. 2.
223. On Stow's religious sympathies, see David Womersley, *Divinity and State* (Oxford: Oxford University Press, 2010), pp. 71–94.

224. *ODNB* entry on Edmund Campion by Michael A. R. Graves; *ODNB* entry on Richard Stanihurst by Colm Lennon.

225. Smith, *A Letter Sent by I. B. Gentleman*, sig. C2^{r-v}. I am grateful to Willy Maley for this reference.

226. Jeffries, *Irish Church*, pp. 242–3.

227. Henley, *Spenser in Ireland*, pp. 69–70.

228. Myrtle Grove had a library: Orpen, 'Ralegh's House'.

229. Thomas Kelly, *Early Public Libraries* (London: Library Association, 1966), ch. 2.

230. J. H. Baker, 'The Third University, 1450–1550: Law School or Finishing School?', in Archer et al. (eds.), *Inns of Court*, pp. 8–24, at p. 17.

231. Raymond Gillespie, 'The Book Trade in Southern Ireland, 1590–1640', in Gerard Long (ed.), *Books Beyond the Pale: Aspects of the Provincial Book Trade in Ireland Before 1850* (Dublin: Rare Books Group of the Library Association of Ireland, 1996), pp. 1–17, at p. 1.

232. Elizabethanne Boran, 'Libraries and Collectors, 1550–1700', in Gillespie and Hadfield (eds.), *Oxford History of the Irish Book*, iii. 91–110.

233. Plant, *English Book Trade*, pp. 238–47.

234. Hanmer was notorious for his acquisition of ecclesiastical livings. It is also worth noting that in London, he had been accused of melting down church brass in order to counterfeit coins: see *ODNB* entry.

235. Gearóid Mac Niocaill (ed.), *Crown Surveys of Lands, 1540–41, with the Kildare Rental begun in 1518* (Dublin: Irish Manuscripts Commission, 1992), pp. 312–14. I owe this reference to Willy Maley.

236. Spenser's library would certainly have been much more substantial than that constructed by Jonathan Bate as Shakespeare's small working library: *Soul of the Age: The Life, Mind and World of William Shakespeare* (London: Viking, 2008), pp. 141–57.

237. R. M. Fisher, 'William Crashawe's Library at the Temple', *The Library*, 5th ser. 30 (1975), 116–24. On Crashaw, see the *ODNB* entry by W. H. Kelliher.

238. David Pearson, 'English Book Owners in the Seventeenth Century: A Work in Progress Listing' (The Bibliographical Society: http://www.bibsoc.org.uk/electronic-publications. htm); David Pearson, 'The Libraries of English Bishops, 1600–40', *The Library*, 6th ser. 14 (1992), 221–57; Sears Jayne, *Library Catalogues of the English Renaissance* (rev. edn., Godalming: St Pauls, 1983), pp. 125–8, 131, *passim*.

239. Evidence from 'Catalogus Librorum Bibliotheca Petworthiana', the library catalogue of Petworth House made in 1694, suggests that books were lent out to readers (fos. 74–5). On the catalogue, see G. R. Batho, 'The Library of the "Wizard" Earl: Henry Percy, Ninth Earl of Northumberland (1564–1632)', *The Library*, 5th ser. 15 (1960), 246–61.

240. Fisher, 'William Crashaw's Library', p. 121.

241. On books imported into Ireland, see Flavin and Jones (eds.), *Bristol's Trade with Ireland and the Continent*, pp. 836, 841, 842, 895, 896. On the importance of the ports in south-west Ireland, the most important of which was Waterford, see Ada Kathleen Longfield, *Anglo-Irish Trade in the Sixteenth-Century* (London: Routledge, 1929), pp. 35–6, 39.

242. See 65, pp. 95–7.

243. Graham Pollard, 'Changes in the Style of Bookbinding, 1550–1830', *The Library*, 5th ser. 11 (1956), 71–94, at 72.

244. See Sears Jayne and Francis R. Johnson (eds.), *The Lumley Library: The Catalogue of 1609* (London: British Library, 1956); David J. McKitterick (ed.), *The Library of Sir Thomas Knyvett of Ashwellthorpe, c.1539–1618* (Cambridge: Cambridge University Library, 1978); Robert H. MacDonald (ed.), *The Library of Drummond of Hawthornden* (Edinburgh: Edinburgh University Press, 1971).

245. Nicholas Barker and David Quentin (eds.), *The Library of Thomas Tresham and Thomas Brudenell* (London: Roxburghe Club, 2006), introd., p. 98. The remnants of the library of Bishop Henry King (1592–1669), bought back by Chichester Cathedral after it was dispersed during the Civil War, is exclusively in Latin, obviously a choice made by the cathedral. Containing principally theological works, there are also copies of Buchanan's *History of Scotland*, Colet's Greek dictionary, various works by Erasmus and Petrarch, and John Bale's

Illustrium Maioris Britanniae Scriptorum (1548), his catalogue of British writers based on his extensive research into the libraries broken up after the dissolution of the monasteries, providing further evidence that Spenser was likely to have had some of these works: Mary Hobbs, John Fines, and Peter Atkinson (eds.), *Chichester Cathedral Library Catalogue*, 3 vols. (Chichester: Chichester Cathedral, 2001–2), ii, app. 9. On King, see the *ODNB* entry by Mary Hobbs.

246. Sir Thomas Knyvett possessed an impressive collection of French literature and history: McKitterick (ed.), *Library of Sir Thomas Knyvett*. Sir Thomas Browne, whose catalogue stretches to 2,448 titles, also had an impressive range of foreign language books in addition to his collection of Latin works: see Jeremiah S. Finch, 'Sir Thomas Browne's Library', *English Language Note* 19 (1982), 360–70.

247. McKitterick (ed.), *Library of Sir Thomas Knyvett*, introd., p. 30; Barney, 'Reference Works'.

248. There were other serious collectors of books of English poetry, such as the Anglo-Dutch merchant John Morris: see T. A. Birrell, *The Library of John Morris: The Reconstruction of a Seventeenth-Century Collection* (London: British Library, 1976), introd., pp. xiv–xv.

249. McKitterick (ed.), *Library of Sir Thomas Knyvett*, p. 8; Pollard, 'Changes in the Style of Bookbinding'; Cristina Dondi, 'The European Printing Revolution', in Michael F. Suarez, SJ, and H. R. Woudhuysen (eds.), *The Oxford Companion to the Book* 2 vols. (Oxford: Oxford University Press, 2010), pp. 53–61, at p. 56.

250. Fehrenbach and Leedham-Green (eds.), *Private Libraries in Renaissance England, passim*; David Scott Wilson-Okamura, *Virgil in the Renaissance* (Cambridge: Cambridge University Press, 2010), p. 27. For an argument that Spenser made special use of Cicero's *De Oratore*, see Judith H. Anderson, 'Spenser's *Faerie Queene* and Cicero's *De Oratore*', *Sp. St.* 25 (2010), 365–70.

251. Wilson-Okamura, *Virgil in the Renaissance*, p. 30.

252. Pearson, 'Libraries of English Bishops', p. 228.

253. Zurcher, *Spenser's Legal Language, passim*; Jayne and Johnson (eds.), *Lumley Library*, introd., pp. 28–9.

254. Googe, *Foure Bookes of Husbandry*, fo. 1ʳ⁻ᵛ; Thomas Tusser, *Fiue Hundreth Points of good husbandry* (London, 1573); Nicholas Malby, *A Plaine and Easie Way to Remedie a Horse that is Foundered in his Feete* (London, 1576); Nicholas Malby, *Remedies for Diseases in Horses* (London, 1576); Stern, *Harvey*, p. 237. See also Andrew McRae, *God Speed the Plough: The Representation of Agrarian England, 1500–1660* (Cambridge: Cambridge University Press, 1996), pp. 138–9, 146–51; Campbell, *English Yeoman*, p. 168.

255. Birrell, *Library of John Morris*, introd., p. xix; Wilson-Okamura, *Virgil in the Renaissance*, pp. 82–5.

256. Conversely, it would be unsafe to rely on the *Complaints* or the 1st edn. of *The Faerie Queene*.

257. McKitterick (ed.), *Library of Sir Thomas Knyvett*, introd., pp. 28–9; Humphrey Llwyd, *The Breviary of Britain, with selections from The History of Cambria*, ed. Philip Schwyzer (London: MHRA, 2011), introd., pp. 29–30.

258. On Spenser's use of Chaucer, see Wilson-Okamura, *Virgil in the Renaissance*, p. 26. On Dante, see Mathew Tosello, 'Spenser's Silence about Dante', *SEL* 17 (1977), 59–66. See also Robin Kirkpatrick, 'Dante Alighieri', *Sp. Enc.*, pp. 295–8; Hamilton, *Structure of Allegory*, pp. 30–43. As Tosello points out, although Dante is not mentioned in Spenser's works, there are numerous possible allusions and Dante was known to Harvey and was cited in van der Noot's *Theatre* (fos. 55–6), as a critic of the papacy. On Spenser and Boccaccio, see Rosamund Tuve, 'Spenser's Reading: The *De Claris Mulierbus*', in *Essays by Rosamund Tuve*, pp. 83–101. On Du Bartas's importance for both Spenser and Harvey, see Peter Augur, 'The Semaines' Dissemination in England and Scotland until 1641', *RS* (forthcoming).

259. Carlo M. Bajetta, *Sir Walter Ralegh: Poeta di corte elisabettiano* (Milan: Mursia, 1998), pp. 189–91; Steven W. May, *Sir Walter Ralegh* (Boston: Twayne, 1989), pp. 11, 43; H. R. Woudhuysen, *Sir Philip Sidney and the Circulation of Manuscripts, 1558–1640* (Oxford: Clarendon Press, 1996), pp. 153, 329; Koller, 'Spenser and Ralegh'.

260. Tuve, 'Some Pictorial Conventions'.

261. Definite conclusions must await the publication of Hugh Adlington's *John Donne's Books*. I am extremely grateful to Dr Adlington for sharing his research with me and advising me on early modern libraries.

Chapter 7

1. BL Add. MS 19837, fo. 79; Raymond Gillespie and Andrew Hadfield, 'Two References to Edmund Spenser in Chancery Disputes', *N&Q* 246 (Sept. 2001), 249–51.
2. Welply, 'Spenser: Recent Researches', p. 50.
3. *CSPI, 1586–8*, p. 403. Brysse was one a group of military men who signed a certificate to state that James FitzSimmons had served in Ireland for seven years.
4. *CSPI, 1588–92*, pp. 140, 341; Judson, *Life*, p. 137.
5. Caulfield, *Council Book of Youghal*, pp. xxii–xxiv; Hennessy, *Ralegh in Ireland*, pp. 114–16; Quinn, *Raleigh and the British Empire*, p. 146; Rowse, *Ralegh*, pp. 154–8; Judson, *Life*, p. 138; Guiney, 'Raleigh', pp. 780–2. On Ralegh and Myrtle Grove, see Klingelhofer, *Castles and Colonists*, pp. 144–5; Orpen, 'Ralegh's House'; Nicholls and Williams, *Raleigh*, p. 37. The story is so well known that it is often repeated in garbled forms, e.g., Simon Schama's statement that Spenser 'entertained Walter Raleigh at his house on the Blackwater River in Ireland' (*Landscape & Memory* (London: Fontana, 1995), p. 330).
6. Francis Allen to Anthony Bacon: Lambeth MS 647, fos. 247–8; Alexander M. Buchan, 'Ralegh's *Cynthia*—Facts or Legend', *MLQ* 1 (1940), 461–74, at 469–70.
7. See Nicholls and Williams, *Raleigh*, pp. 1, 16, 37, *passim*.
8. Walter Oakeshott, 'Carew Ralegh's Copy of Spenser', *The Library* 26 (1971), 1–21. It is also worth noting that outside these annotations, which make the odd claim that the lady, Rosalind, whom Colin serves in *Colin Clouts come home againe* is, in fact, herself (p. 5). Such comments suggest that the relationship between Spenser and the Raleghs was never really close. Lady Ralegh does not mention Spenser anywhere else: on her life, see Anna Beer, *Bess: The Life of Lady Ralegh, Wife to Sir Walter* (London: Constable and Robinson, 2004).
9. Oakeshott, 'Carew Ralegh's Copy of Spenser', pp. 5–6; Hadfield, 'Spenser's Rosalind', pp. 941–3.
10. May, *Ralegh*, p. 11.
11. On the literary relationship between Ralegh and Spenser, see Walter Oakeshott, *The Queen and the Poet* (London: Faber, 1960); Jerry Leath Mills, 'Raleigh, Walter', *Sp. Enc.*, pp. 584–5; Thomas Herron, 'Ralegh's Gold: Placing Spenser's Dedicatory Sonnets', *SLI* 38 (2005), 133–47.
12. Spenser, *Faerie Queene*, p. 716.
13. Ralegh, *Poems*, pp. 46–66; Oakeshott, *Queen and the Poet*, ch. 3; Jerome S. Dees, 'Colin Clout and the Shepherd of the Ocean', *Sp. St.* 15 (2001), 185–96; Georgia Brown, *Redefining Elizabethan Literature* (Cambridge: Cambridge University Press, 2004), pp. 29–30.
14. Jean R. Brink, 'Dating Spenser's "Letter to Raleigh"', *The Library*, 16 (1994), 219–24.
15. May, 'Abraham Fraunce'.
16. Joseph Loewenstein, 'Spenser's Retrography', in Anderson et al. (eds.), *Spenser's Life*, pp. 99–130, at p. 103.
17. Jason Scott-Warren, 'Unannotating Spenser', in Helen Smith and Louise Wilson (eds.), *Renaissance Paratexts* (Cambridge: Cambridge University Press, 2011), pp. 153–64. I am extremely grateful to Dr Scott-Warren for allowing me to see this important essay in advance of its publication. See also Jason Scott-Warren, *Sir John Harington and the Book as Gift* (Oxford: Oxford University Press, 2001).
18. On Field see the *ODNB* entry by David Kathman.
19. Owens, *Enabling Engagements*, pp. 70–5.
20. See, pp. 239–40, 305.
21. Richard A. McCabe, 'Introduction', *Sp. Handbook*, pp. 1–10, at p. 1.
22. Colin Burrow, *Epic Romance: Homer to Milton* (Oxford: Clarendon Press, 1993), ch. 5.
23. Altman, *Tudor Play of Mind*, chs. 1–2.

24. Darryl J. Gless, *Interpretation and Theology in Spenser* (Cambridge: Cambridge University Press, 1994), p. 48.

25. Zurcher, 'Spenser's Dedications', p. 173; Ty Buckman, 'Forcing the Poet into Prose: "Gealous Opinions and Misconstructions" and Spenser's Letter to Ralegh', in Erikson (ed.), *1590 Faerie Queene*, pp. 17–34, at p. 30.

26. The letter and the commendatory verses are to be found in Edmund Spenser, *The Faerie Queene* (London, 1590), pp. 591–600. The dedicatory sonnets are unpaginated, which indicates that they were hastily bound into the volume, as many commentators have noted, and which tells its own story of Spenser's problematic relationship with his potential patrons: see Johnson, *Critical Bibliography*, pp. 11–18; L. G. Black, '*The Faerie Queene*, commendatory verses and dedicatory sonnets', *Sp. Enc.*, pp. 291–3; Jean R. Brink, 'Precedence and Patronage: The Ordering of Spenser's Dedicatory Sonnets (1590)', in Erikson (ed.), *1590 Faerie Queene*, pp. 51–72.

27. See Jane Grogan, *Exemplary Spenser: Visual and Poetic Pedagogy in The Faerie Queene* (Aldershot: Ashgate, 2009), p. 30.

28. Grogan, *Exemplary Spenser*, p. 33.

29. Adams, *Leicester and the Court*, ch. 7, 'Elizabeth's Eyes at Court: The Earl of Leicester'.

30. See, pp. 327–8.

31. Brink, 'Precedence and Patronage', p. 60; James P. Bednarz, 'The Collaborator as Thief: Ralegh's (Re)Vision of *The Faerie Queene*', *ELH* 63 (1996), 279–307, at 279.

32. Richard Beacon, the Munster planter, dedicated his dialogue on Ireland, *Solon His Follie* (1594), to Elizabeth, presumably not because he was on good terms with his queen but because he wanted it to be read by those close to her: see Beacon, *Solon His Follie*, ed. Carroll and Carey; Sydney Anglo, 'A Machiavellian Solution to the Irish Problem: Richard Beacon's *Solon His Follie* (1594)', in Edward Chaney and Peter Mack (eds.), *England and the Continental Renaissance: Essays in Honour of J. B. Trapp* (Woodbridge: Boydell, 1990), pp. 153–64.

33. *Calendar of Patent Rolls 33 Elizabeth I (1590–1591)*, ed. Simon R. Neal (Kew: List and Index Society, 2005), p. 38.

34. Carpenter, *Reference Guide*, p. 70; Herbert Berry and E. K. Timings, 'Spenser's Pension', *RES* 11 (1960), 254–9, at 255.

35. *ODNB* entry on Churchyard by Raphael Lyne; Allan Griffith Chester, 'Thomas Churchyard's Pension', *PMLA* 50 (1935), 902.

36. Roger A. Geimer, 'Spenser's Rhyme or Churchyard's Reason: Evidence of Churchyard's First Pension', *RES* 20 (1969), 306–9.

37. Ernest A. Strathmann, 'Spenser's *Legends* and *Court of Cupid*', *MLN* 46 (1931), 498–501; Batho, 'Library of the "Wizard" Earl', p. 256; Edward Doughtie, 'John Ramsey's Manuscript as a Personal and Family Document', in W. Speed Hill (ed.), *New Ways of Looking at Old Texts: Papers of the Renaissance English Text Society, 1985–1991* (Binghamton, NY: MRTS, 1993), pp. 281–8.

38. Bodleian Library, Douce MS 280 (Commonplace Book of John Ramsey), fos. 56–81; Marotti, *Manuscript, Print and the English Renaissance Lyric*, pp. 189–93.

39. Duncan-Jones, *From Crow to Swan*, p. 105; Nashe, *Works*, iii. 128.

40. *ODNB* entry on Wolfe. For Wolfe's significance to the printing trade, see Joseph Loewenstein, 'For a History of Literary Property: John Wolfe's Reformation', *ELR* 18 (1988), 389–412.

41. Gabriel Harvey, *A New Letter of Notable Contents* (London, 1593).

42. Lawrence, '*Who the Devil Taught Thee So Much Italian?*', pp. 187–201.

43. Sir Philip Sidney, *The Countesse of Pembrokes Arcadia* (London, 1590); *ODNB* entry on Ponsonby by Sidney Lee, rev. Anita McConnell.

44. For comment, see Gordon Braden, 'Non-Dramatic Verse: Epic Kinds', in Braden, Cummings, and Gillespie (eds.), *Oxford History of Literary Translation*, pp. 188–9; Massimiliano Morini, *Tudor Translation in Theory and Practice* (Aldershot: Ashgate, 2006), pp. 118–28.

45. Edmund Spenser, *The Shepheardes Calender* (London, 1591); Mark Bland, 'John Windet', in Bracken and Silver (eds.), *Book Trade*, pp. 319–25, at p. 321; Johnson, *Critical Bibliography*, pp. 6–7.

46. *ODNB* entry on Hooker by S. Mendyk; Wagner, *Life of Peter Carew*, ch. 10.
47. Gosling, *Sir Humphrey Gilbert*, pp. 12–19; Rowse, *Ralegh*, *passim*.
48. Richard Carew, *The survey of Cornwall* (London, 1602); Torquato Tasso, *Godfrey of Bulloigne, or The Recouerie of Hierusalem*, trans. R. C. [Richard Carew] (London, 1594). On Carew, see *ODNB* entry by S. Mendyk; A. L. Rowse, *Tudor Cornwall: Portrait of a Society* (London: Cape, 1941), pp. 421–6, *passim*.
49. Camden, *Remains*, pp. 42–51, at p. 51; Baugh and Cable, *History of the English Language*, p. 207.
50. See p. 535 n. 199.
51. See May, 'Abraham Fraunce'.
52. Loewenstein, 'Spenser's Retrography', pp. 99–130, at p. 101.
53. See p. 265.
54. See p. 8.
55. On Farleigh Wallop, see *Victoria County History: Hampshire*, iii. 364–6.
56. *ODNB* entry.
57. Deveson, *En Suivant La Vérité*, pp. 1, 6–8.
58. Judson, *Life*, p. 151.
59. Ibid. 140; W. P. Williams, 'Bibliography, critical', *Sp. Enc.*, pp. 90–3, at p. 91; Johnson, *Critical Bibliography*, p. 27.
60. *Chronology*, p. 56.
61. F. P. Wilson, 'Spenser and Ireland', *RES* 2 (1926), 456–7. The detail is recorded in Wallop's Treasury Accounts for 1588–91 (Bodleian Library, MS Rawlinson A.317, fo. 351). On the provenance of the manuscript, see F. J. Routledge, 'Manuscripts at Oxford Relating to the Later Tudors, 1547–1603', *TRHS*, 3rd ser. 8 (1914), 119–59, at 151.
62. Spenser, *Shorter Poems*, p. 344; Zurcher, 'Getting It Back to Front', pp. 184–5.
63. On *Colin Clout*, see pp. 284–5, 311–12.
64. Scott-Warren, *Harington and the Book as Gift*, introd.; see also Patricia Wareh, 'Humble Presents: Pastoral and Gift-Giving in the Commendatory Verses and Dedicatory Sonnets', in Erikson (ed.), *1590 Faerie Queene*, pp. 119–32.
65. See Montrose, 'Elizabethan Subject and the Spenserian Text'.
66. On Stanley, see the *ODNB* entry by David Kathman. On Alice Spenser, see the *ODNB* entry by Louis A. Knalfa; Paul E. McLane, 'Spenser's Chloris: The Countess of Derby', *HLQ* 24 (1961), 145–50; May, *Courtier Poets*, pp. 369–76.
67. Strathmann, 'Lady Carey and Spenser', pp. 52–3; Sam Meyer, *An Interpretation of Edmund Spenser's Colin Clout* (Cork: Cork University Press, 1969), pp. 150–1.
68. For other possible revisions, see Kathrine Koller, 'Spenser and Ralegh', *ELH* 1 (1934), 37–60, at 55–9.
69. David W. Burchmore, 'The Image of the Centre in *Colin Clouts come home againe*', *RES* 28 (1977), 393–406.
70. *ODNB* entry on Ralegh by Mark Nicholls and Penry Williams; Rowse, *Ralegh*, chs. 9–10; Beer, *Bess*, ch. 2.
71. Koller, 'Spenser and Ralegh', pp. 44–5. For attempts to reconstruct the possible revisions of Ralegh's poem, see also Buchan, 'Ralegh's "Cynthia"'; *Poems of Ralegh*, ed. Rudick, introd., pp. xlvii–li.
72. Cited in *ODNB* entry. More generally, see Stephen Greenblatt, *Sir Walter Raleigh: The Renaissance Man and His Roles* (New Haven: Yale University Press, 1973).
73. Although the *OED* suggests that this usage became possible only in the late 17th century.
74. Daniel Javitch, *Poetry and Courtliness in Renaissance England* (Princeton: Princeton University Press, 1978); Albert H. Tricomi, *Anti-Court Drama in England, 1603–42* (Charlottesville: University Press of Virginia, 1989).
75. *FQ* VI.i.3, line 8; I.i.35, line 7.
76. See Hadfield, *Spenser's Irish Experience*, pp. 13–17; Nicholas Canny and Andrew Carpenter (eds.), 'The Early Planters: Spenser and His Contemporaries', in Seamus Deane (ed.), *The Field Day Anthology of Irish Writing*, 3 vols. (Derry: Field Day Publications, 1991), i. 171–234.

77. Canny, *Upstart Earl*, pp. 6, 19; MacCarthy-Morrogh, *Munster Plantation*, pp. 141–3. It was a common complaint that undertakers spent little time in Munster, perhaps one reason why Spenser so vociferously stated his allegiance to the area: see Dunlop, 'Unpublished Survey', p. 146.
78. Quinn, *Raleigh and the British Empire*, ch. 5.
79. See, pp. 265–7.
80. *FQ* IV.vii.36, line 3.
81. *FQ* IV.viii.18, line 2. On Spenser's comments on Ralegh in *FQ* IV, see A. Leigh DeNeef, 'Timias', *Sp. Enc.*, pp. 690–1; James P. Bednarz, 'Ralegh in Spenser's Historical Allegory', *Sp. St.* 4 (1984), 49–70; Cheney, *Spenser's Famous Flight*, pp. 133–43; Graham Atkin, 'Raleigh, Spenser, and Elizabeth: Acts of Friendship in *The Faerie Queene*, Book IV', in J. B. Lethbridge (ed.), *Edmund Spenser: New and Renewed Directions* (Madison: Fairleigh Dickinson University Press), pp. 195–213.
82. Koller, 'Spenser and Ralegh', p. 49. For the case against, see Jeffrey Knapp, *An Empire Nowhere: England, America, and Literature from Utopia to The Tempest* (Berkeley and Los Angeles: University of California Press, 1992), ch. 3, which argues that Spenser was at least as keen to encourage readers to study his poetry as to speculate in New World voyages.
83. Hadfield, 'Spenser's Rosalind', pp. 941–3.
84. Burchmore, 'Image of the Centre', p. 399.
85. Thomas Watson, *An Eglogue upon the Death of the Right Honorable Sir Francis Walsingham* (London, 1590), sig. C4ʳ; *Spenser Allusions*, pp. 20–1.
86. On Watson, see the *ODNB* entry by Albert Chatterley.
87. Ibid.
88. Thomas Watson, *Hekatompathia, or Passionate Centurie of Love* (London, 1582), sig. A3ʳ⁻ᵛ. On Oxford as a patron of poetry, see Nelson, *Monstrous Adversity*, pp. 236–9, 380–4, *passim*.
89. Stern, *Harvey*, p. 108; Harvey, *Marginalia*, pp. 166, 233; Stephen Clucas, 'Thomas Watson's *Hekatompathia* and European Petrarchanism', in Martin McLaughlin, Letizia Panizza, and Peter Hainsworth (eds.), *Petrarch in Britain: Interpreters, Imitators and Translators over 700 Years* (Oxford: Oxford University Press/British Academy, 2007), pp. 217–27.
90. Watson, *Hekatompathia*, sonnets 15, 16, 20.
91. Carpenter, *Reference Guide*, p. 86; Mark Eccles, 'Watson, Thomas', *Sp. Enc.*, pp. 727–8; *Spenser Allusions*, pp. 25, 28, 51, 61, 73; Joseph Warren Beach, 'A Sonnet of Watson and a Stanza of Spenser', *MLN* 18 (1903), 218–20.
92. Joseph Black, ' "Pan is Hee": Commending *The Faerie Queene*', *Sp. St.* 15 (2001), 121–34; D. Allen Carroll, 'Thomas Watson and the 1588 MS Commendation of *The Faerie Queene*: Reading the Rebus', *Sp. St.* 16 (2002), 105–23.
93. Spenser, *Letters*, nos. 10, 12, 14, 16, *passim*; Plomer, 'Spenser's Handwriting', p. 203. On Walsingham and Ireland, see Haynes, *Walsingham*, pp. 83–4.
94. Jean R. Brink, 'Materialist History of the Publication of Spenser's *Faerie Queene*', *RES* 54 (2001), 1–26, at 2–7.
95. Brink, 'Materialist History', p. 7; Plant, *English Book Trade*, p. 69.
96. This explanation was first suggested by Israel Gollancz, but has held considerable sway over commentators, substituting 'biographical supposition for textual analysis', as Brink has argued: see Gollancz, 'Spenseriana', pp. 104–5; Johnson, *Critical Bibliography*, p. 15; Brink, 'Materialist History', p. 10; Zurcher, 'Spenser's Dedications', p. 174.
97. Nashe, *Works*, i. 244.
98. This claim might also explain Spenser's omission and Nashe's desire to embarrass Spenser: see Kelsie Harder, 'Nashe's Rebuke of Spenser', *N&Q* 198 (1953), 145–6.
99. See the *ODNB* entry on George Chapman by Mark Thornton Burnett.
100. Nicholl, *Cup of News*, pp. 109–10. Nashe satirized Ralegh and his circle, including Chapman, in *Pierce Penilesse* (pp. 107–9).
101. Sukanta Chaudhuri, 'Amyntas', *Sp. Enc.*, pp. 38–9, at p. 38.
102. This provides yet more evidence that *Colin Clout* was revised between 1591 and its publication in 1595.

103. On Nashe's family, see Nicholl, *Cup of News*, ch. 2.
104. Nicholl, *Cup of News*, pp. 89–90.
105. Ibid. 90, 110.
106. Nashe, *Works*, iii. 96.
107. Nicholl, *Cup of News*, pp. 184–5.
108. Ronald A. Tumelson II, 'Robert Greene, "Author Playes"', in Melinkoff and Gieskes (eds.), *Writing Robert Greene*, pp. 95–114.
109. For a modern judgement that accords with that of Nashe, see Kingsley Amis, 'Oxford and After', in Anthony Thwaite (ed.), *Larkin at Sixty* (London: Faber, 1982), pp. 23–30, recording Larkin's comment: 'First I thought Troilus and Criseyde was the most *boring* poem in English. Then I thought Beowulf was. Then I thought Paradise Lost was. Now I *know* that The Faerie Queene is the *dullest thing out. Blast* it' (cited on p. 25).
110. Nashe, *Works*, i. 244. For comment, see Brink, 'Materialist History', pp. 15–16; Zurcher, 'Getting It Back to Front in 1590'.
111. Oakeshott, 'Carew Ralegh's Copy of Spenser', p. 4.
112. Ralegh, *Poems*, p. 140; Bednarz, 'Collaborator as Thief', pp. 291–2.
113. Bajetta, *Ralegh*, pp. 287–8.
114. Andrew Zurcher, *Edmund Spenser's The Faerie Queene: A Reading Guide* (Edinburgh: Edinburgh University Press, 2011), p. 163.
115. A. D. Cousins, 'Ralegh's "A Vision upon this Conceipt of *The Faerie Queene*"', *The Explicator* 41/3 (spring 1983), 14–16; Bednarz, 'Collaborator as Thief', pp. 280–1.
116. For a different reading, see Bednarz, 'Collaborator as Thief', pp. 282–3.
117. See William A. Oram, 'What Did Spenser Really Think of Sir Walter Ralegh When He Published the First Instalment of *The Faerie Queene*', *Sp. St.* 15 (2001), 165–74; Owens, *Enabling Engagements*, p. 116.
118. Does the reference hint at more than this, suggesting that Spenser may have had clerical ambitions once? Or is it a sly reference to his ecclesiastical livings in Ireland? For comment, see Jeffrey Knapp, 'Spenser the Priest', *Representations* 81 (Winter 2003), 61–78.
119. For analysis of the strategies that those dealing with the court had to adopt, see Bates, *Rhetoric of Courtliness*, chs. 1–2; Richards, *Rhetoric and Courtliness*, ch. 1.
120. Black, '*The Faerie Queene*, commendatory verses and dedicatory sonnets', p. 292. Charles Crawford claims that 'Ignoto' was Nicholas Breton ('*Greene's Funeralls*, 1594, and Nicholas Breton', *SP* 26, extra ser. 1 (1929), 1–39, at 7), but Ignoto was a commonly used pseudonym: Marcey North, 'Ignoto in the Age of Print: The Manipulation of Anonymity in Early Modern England', *SP* 91 (1994), 390–416, at 412–16.
121. W. I., 'When stout *Achilles* heard of *Helens* rape', line 15. For analysis, see Wendy Wall, *The Imprint of Gender: Authorship and Publication in the English Renaissance* (Ithaca, NY: Cornell University Press, 1993), pp. 227–9, at pp. 241–2.
122. Michael Leslie, *Spenser's 'Fierce Warres and Faithfull Loves': Martial and Chivalric Symbolism in 'The Faerie Queene'* (Cambridge: Brewer, 1983); Paul Stevens, 'Spenser and the End of the British Empire', *Sp. St.* 22 (2007), 5–26; Young, *Tudor and Jacobean Tournaments*, pp. 168, 170, *passim.*
123. Ignoto, 'To looke vpon a worke of rare deuise', line 19.
124. For details, see Black, '*The Faerie Queene*, commendatory verses and dedicatory sonnets'; for comment, see Owens, *Enabling Engagements*, chs. 3–4.
125. See Simon Adams, 'Court', *Sp. Enc.*, pp. 193–4. The most conspicuous absentee from those we know to have been Spenser's patrons is Sir Henry Wallop.
126. Black, '*The Faerie Queene*, commendatory verses and dedicatory sonnets'.
127. Franklin B. Williams, Jr, *Index of Dedications and Commendatory Verses in English Books Before 1641* (London: Bibliographical Society, 1962).
128. Arthur F. Marotti, '"Love Is Not Love": Elizabethan Sonnet Sequences and the Social Order', *ELH* 49 (1982), 396–428.
129. May, *Elizabethan Courtier Poets*.

130. For comments, see Stephen Greenblatt, 'Murdering Peasants: Status, Genre and the Representation of Rebellion', *Representations* 1 (1983), 1–29; Andrew Hadfield, 'Sidney's "Poor Painter" and John Stubbs's *Gaping Gulf*', *SJ* 15/2 (Fall 1997), 45–8.

131. Sidney, *Apology*, p. 85.

132. Nolan, *Norreys and the Elizabethan Military World*.

133. For a more general analysis, see Ian Maclean, *The Renaissance Notion of Woman: A Study in the Fortunes of Scholasticism and Medical Science in European Intellectual Life* (Cambridge: Cambridge University Press, 1980).

134. 'To the right noble Lord and most valiaunt Captaine Sir Iohn Norris knight, Lord President of Mounster', lines 9–12.

135. William S. Maltby, *The Black Legend in England: The Development of Anti-Spanish Sentiment, 1558–1660* (Durham, NC: University of North Carolina Press, 1971).

136. George Gascoigne, *The spoyle of Antwerpe. Faithfully reported, by a true Englishman, who was present at the same* (London, 1576). Spenser would surely have read this work, given the obvious connections they had.

137. 'To the right Honourable the Earle of Ormond and Ossory', lines 2, 7, 13–14. For comment, see Hadfield, *Spenser's Irish Experience*, pp. 4–6.

138. Howard, *Early Tudor Country House*, pp. 88–93, *passim*.

139. Jane Fenlon, *Ormond Castle: Visitor's Guide* (Dublin: Office of Public Works, 2008).

140. See p. 167.

141. 'To the most renowned and valiant Lord, the Lord Grey of Wilton', lines 1–5.

142. Johnson, *Critical Bibliography*, p. 17; Hiroshi Yamashita, Haruo Sato, Toshiyuki Suzuki, and Akira Takano, *A Textual Companion to The Faerie Queene 1590* (Tokyo: Kenyusha, 1993). William Proctor Williams, 'Bibliography, critical', *Sp. Enc.*, pp. 90–3.

143. For analysis see Dorothy Stephens, 'Spenser's Language(s)' and Jeff Dolven, 'Spenser's Metrics', *Sp. Handbook*, pp. 367–84, 385–402.

144. Cummings, *Critical Heritage*, p. 294. For recent analyses of the poem's style, see Catherine Addison, 'Rhyming Against the Grain: A New Look at the Spenserian Stanza', in Lethbridge (ed.), *Spenser: New and Renewed Directions*, pp. 337–51; David Scott Wilson-Okamura, 'The Formalist Tradition', *Sp. Handbook*, pp. 718–32, at pp. 718–23.

145. Wilson-Okamura, *Virgil in the Renaissance*, p. 124.

146. Ibid. 93.

147. John Dixon, *The First Commentary on 'The Faerie Queene', being an analysis of the annotations in Lord Bessborough's copy of the first edition of 'The Faerie Queene'*, ed. Graham Hough (privately printed, 1964); Alastair Fowler, 'Oxford and London Marginalia to the *Faerie Queene*', *N&Q* 8 (1961), 416–19; John Manning, 'Notes and Marginalia in Bishop Percy's Copy of *The Faerie Queene*', *N&Q* 31 (1984), 225–7; Fleck, 'Early Modern Marginalia in Spenser's *Faerie Queene* at the Folger'.

148. Harvey–Spenser *Letters*, p. 50; Bennett, *Evolution of 'The Faerie Queene'*, ch. 1.

149. See p. 155.

150. Miskimin, *Renaissance Chaucer*, ch. 7.

151. Robert Cummings, 'Translation and Literary Innovation', in Braden, Cummings, and Gillespie (eds.), *Oxford History of Literary Translation*, pp. 32–44, at pp. 38–9.

152. Spenser, *Faerie Queene*, p. 715; O'Connell, *Mirror and Veil*, pp. 5–6, 23–31; Cheney, *Spenser's Famous Flight*, pp. xi–iii, *passim*; Burrow, *Epic Romance*, pp. 100–46; John Watkins, *The Specter of Dido: Spenser and Virgilian Epic* (New Haven: Yale University Press, 1995).

153. Robert Cummings, 'Mirrors for Policy', in Braden, Cummings, and Gillespie (eds.), *Oxford History of Literary Translation*, pp. 408–17, at pp. 413–14.

154. *The bookes of Xenophon contayning the discipline, schole, and education of Cyrus the noble kyng of Persie. Translated out of Greeke into Englyshe, by M. Wylliam Barkar* (London, 1552?). Spenser probably consulted the later edition: *The VIII. bookes of Xenophon, containinge the institutio[n], schole, and education of Cyrus, the noble Kynge of Persye also his ciuill and princelye estate, his expedition into Babylon, Syria and Aegypt, and his exhortation before his death, to his children* (London, 1567). The modern translation is Xenophon, *Cyropaedia*, trans. Walter Miller (1914;

Cambridge, MA: Harvard University Press, 1968). For commentary, see Grogan, *Exemplary Spenser*, ch. 1. On Barker, see *ODNB* entry by Kenneth R. Bartlett.

155. See e.g. H. S. V. Jones, *A Spenser Handbook* (New York: Crofts, 1930), ch. 13; Graham Hough, *A Preface to The Faerie Queene* (London: Duckworth, 1962), ch. 14; William Nelson, *The Poetry of Edmund Spenser* (New York: Columbia University Press, 1963), pp. 116–46; Peter Bayley, *Edmund Spenser: Prince of Poets* (London: Hutchinson, 1971), ch. 5; Robin Headlam Wells, *Spenser's Faerie Queene and the Cult of Elizabeth* (London: Croom Helm, 1983). For an overview, see Radcliffe, *Spenser: Reception History*, pp. 178–97.

156. Elizabeth's decision not to marry was not necessarily a foolish one, given the problems she faced whether she married a foreign prince or an English subject. For discussion, see Doran, *Monarchy and Matriarchy*.

157. See pp. 209–10.

158. Sharpe, *Selling the Tudor Monarchy*, pp. 426–8; McRae, *God Speed the Plough*, pp. 201–4.

159. See Paul J. Alpers, 'How to Read *The Faerie Queene*', *Essays in Criticism* 18 (1968), 429–43; Martha Craig, 'The Secret Wit of Spenser's Language', in Paul J. Alpers (ed.), *Elizabethan Poetry: Modern Essays in Criticism* (London: Oxford University Press, 1967), pp. 447–72.

160. For discussion, see King, *Spenser's Poetry and the Reformation Tradition*, pp. 50–3, 73–6, *passim*.

161. Geneva translation (1560).

162. Douglas Brooks-Davies, *Spenser's Faerie Queene: A Critical Commentary on Books I and II* (Manchester: Manchester University Press, 1977), p. 23.

163. See the excellent—and witty—discussion in Victoria Coldham-Fussell, 'Spenser's Divine Comedy: Humour and Humanity in *The Faerie Queene*', unpublished PhD dissertation, University of Cambridge, 2010, ch. 4.

164. R. W. Southern, *Western Society and the Church in the Middle Ages* (Harmondsworth: Penguin, 1970), p. 18.

165. Bale, *Pageant of Popes*; King, *English Reformation Literature*, pp. 425–43; King, *Spenser's Poetry and the Reformation Tradition*, *passim*.

166. Zall (ed.), *Hundred Merry Tales*, pp. 332, 334.

167. On Protestant conceptions of marriage, see MacCulloch, *Reformation*, chs. 15–16; Cressy, *Birth, Marriage and Death*, chs. 12–16; Dickens, *English Reformation*, pp. 336–9, *passim*.

168. Martin Luther, *The Pagan Servitude of the Church* (1520), in Martin Luther, *Selections from his Writings*, ed. John Dillenberger (New York: Doubleday, 1961), pp. 249–359, at pp. 326–40. See also Jean Calvin, *Commentaries: The First Epistle of Paul the Apostle to the Corinthians*, ed. John W. Fraser (Edinburgh: Oliver, 1960), pp. 134–69.

169. On the ways in which the narrative of romances, such as *Orlando Furioso*, inevitably move sideways, or 'dilate', see Patricia Parker, *Inescapable Romance: Studies in the Poetics of a Mode* (Princeton: Princeton University Press, 1979); Patricia Parker, 'Romance', *Sp. Enc.*, pp. 609–18. See also Burrow, *Epic Romance*, ch. 5.

170. John M. Steadman, 'Una and the Clergy: The Ass Symbol in *The Faerie Queene*', *JWCI* 21/1–2 (Winter–Spring 1958), 134–7.

171. See the analysis of the picture of the young daughter of the Picts by Jacques Le Morne de Morgues in Juliet Fleming, *Graffiti and the Writing Arts of Early Modern England* (London: Reaktion, 2001), p. 101.

172. *Riverside Chaucer*, I, line 151 (p. 25).

173. For further discussion, see Andrew Hadfield, 'Spenser and Religion—Yet Again', *SEL* 51 (2011), 21–46.

174. Aristotle, *Nicomachean Ethics*, pp. 4–6.

175. For the significance of Una, see Douglas Brooks-Davies, 'Una', *Sp. Enc.*, pp. 704–5.

176. Haugaard, *Elizabeth and the English Reformation*.

177. Morey, *Catholic Subjects*, pp. 94–5.

178. Robert Stillman has made a persuasive case that Philip Sidney was influenced by the ideals of moderation espoused by Philip Melanchthon and his followers, the Philippists: see *Philip Sidney and the Poetics of Renaissance Cosmopolitanism* (Aldershot: Ashgate, 2008). Spenser may

have had similar intellectual inclinations, but there is no obvious evidence that he was influenced by Melanchthon's ideas. On reactions to the threat of persecution throughout the 16th century, see Cummings, *Literary Culture of the Reformation, passim.*

179. Andrew King, *The Faerie Queene and Middle English Romance: The Matter of Just Memory* (Oxford: Clarendon Press, 2000), ch. 6.

180. D. Douglas Walters, *Duessa as Theological Satire* (Columbia: University of Missouri Press, 1970); Richard F. Hardin, 'Adicia, Souldan', *Sp. Enc.*, pp. 7–8.

181. For arguments about Spenser's syncretism, see James E. Phillips, 'Spenser's Syncretistic Religious Imagery', *ELH* 36 (1969), 110–30; Ramachandran, 'Spenser, Lucretian Neoplatonist', pp. 396–402.

182. Waetherby, *Mirrors of Celestial Grace*, p. 31. See also Tom Muir, 'Without Remainder: Ruins and Tombs in Shakespeare's *Sonnets*', *Textual Practice* 24 (2010), 21–49.

183. One early reader suggests that Spenser's poem was ambiguous in its religious affiliation, possibly Catholic: see Guillaume Coatalen, '"Lô a Timorous Correction": Unrecorded Extracts from Spenser and Harrington and Nagative Criticism of *The Faerie Queene* in a Folio from the Bodleian Library', *RES* 56/227 (2005) 730–48. I owe this reference to Sara Trevisan.

184. On Guyon's obvious relationship to a romance hero, Guy of Warwick, and how this literary relationship qualifies and complicates the Red-Cross Knight's quest in Book I, see King, 'Spenser, Chaucer, and Medieval Romance', *Sp. Handbook*, pp. 566–7.

185. See Christopher Tilmouth, *Passion's Triumph Over Reason: A History of the Moral Imagination from Spenser to Rochester* (Oxford: Oxford University Press, 2007), ch. 2, to which this paragraph is indebted. Aristotle, *The Nicomachean Ethics*, trans. David Ross (1925; Oxford: Oxford University Press, 1980), pp. 72–8, 159–91.

186. Aristotle, *Nicomachean Ethics*, pp. 172–5; Tilmouth, *Passion's Triumph Over Reason*, pp. 20–1, *passim.*

187. Fogarty, 'Literature in English', p. 151.

188. James Lyndon Shanley, 'Spenser's Temperance and Aristotle', *MP* 43 (1946), 170–4, at 172.

189. Mary Villeponteaux, '"Not as women wonted be": Spenser's Amazon Queen', in Julia M. Walker (ed.), *Dissing Elizabeth: Negative Representations of Gloriana* (Durham, NC: Duke University Press, 1998), pp. 209–25.

190. Scodel, *Excess and Mean in Early Modern English Literature*, pp. 143–6; Hadfield, *Literature, Politics and National Identity*, pp. 194–201; Claire McEachern, *The Poetics of English Nationhood, 1590–1612* (Cambridge: Cambridge University Press, 1996), ch. 2.

191. O'Connell, *Mirror and Veil*, ch. 1; David Norbrook, *Poetry and Politics in the English Renaissance* (rev. edn., Oxford: Oxford University Press, 2002), pp. 125–8.

192. For comment, see Lauren Silberman, *Transforming Desire: Erotic Knowledge in Books III and IV of The Faerie Queene* (Berkeley and Los Angeles: University of California Press, 1995), ch. 3.

193. Yates, *Art of Memory*, p. 43.

194. The name 'Scudamore' may be a compliment to the Scudamore family of Kentchurch and Holme Lacy, Herefordshire. The head of the family when Spenser was writing *The Faerie Queene* was Sir John Scudamore (*c.*1542–1623), whose wife, Mary, was a Boleyn. Sir John was a gentleman usher to the queen and Mary was a lady of the queen's bedchamber. Mary was beaten by Elizabeth when they were secretly married, but later restored to favour. Spenser may well be drawing a pointed contrast between the treatment of the Scudamores and the Raleghs. John Dowland openly praised the Scudamores in his *First Book of Songs or Ayres* (1597), using a distinctly Spenserian phrase, which suggests that there were indeed links between Spenser and the Scudamores, perhaps through the Careys who were close to the Scudamores and whom Spenser cultivated at this time (see p. 282). See Linda R. Galyon, 'Scudamore, family', *Sp. Enc.*, pp. 634–5; Ian Atherton, 'Scudamore family, per. 1520–1800', *ODNB*; Simon Adams, 'Scudamore [nee Shelton], Mary, Lady Scudamore (*c.*1550–1603)', *ODNB*; Kirsten Gibson, 'The Order of the Book: Materiality, Narrative and Authorial Voice in John Dowland's *First Book of Songes or Ayres*', *RS* 26 (2012), 13–33, at 22–3, 32; Elizabeth Eva Leach, 'The Unquiet Thoughts of Edmund Spenser's Scudamore and John Dowland's *First Book of Songs*', in M. Jennifer Bloxham, Gioia Filcamo, and Leofranc Holford-Stevens (eds.), *Uno Gentile et Subtile Ingenio: Studies in Music in Honour of Bonnie J. Blackburn* (Turnhout, Belgium: Brepols, 2009), pp. 513–20.

195. *Epithalamion*, in Spenser, *Shorter Poems*, lines 372–89, pp. 447–8. The Latmian shepherd was Endymion who seduced the goddess with a fleece and was condemned to perpetual sleep. This may be a reference to Leicester, whom Elizabeth had nearly married (d. 1588), or Alençon (d. 1584). For further discussion, see pp. 323–4.
196. Anne Shaver, 'Diana', *Sp. Enc.*, pp. 217–18.
197. On the numerological significance of the canto, see Michael Baybak, Paul Delaney, and A. Kent Hieatt, 'Placement "In the Middest" in *The Faerie Queene*', *Papers in Language and Literature* 5 (1969), 227–34.
198. Louis Schwartz, *Milton and Maternal Mortality* (Cambridge: Cambridge University Press, 2009), pp. 2, 148.
199. Mendelson and Crawford, *Women in Early Modern England*, p. 152.
200. Alan Macfarlane, *Family Life of Ralph Josselin*, pp. 84–6; *The Diary of Ralph Josselin, 1616–1683*, ed. Alan Macfarlane (Oxford: Oxford University Press, 1976), pp. 415–16.
201. Linda A. Pollack, 'Embarking on a Rough Passage: The Experience of Pregnancy in Early-Modern Society', in Valerie Fildes (ed.), *Women as Mothers in Pre-industrial England* (London: Routledge, 1990), pp. 39–67, at pp. 47–9; Schwartz, *Milton and Maternal Mortality*, ch. 2.
202. Adrian Wilson, 'The Ceremony of Childbirth and Its Interpretation', in Fildes (ed.), *Women as Mothers*, pp. 68–107; Schwartz, *Milton and Maternal Mortality*, pp. 22–3; Cross, *Oxford Dictionary of the Christian Church*, p. 355; Mendelson and Crawford, *Women in Early Modern England*, p. 153–4.
203. Pollack, 'Embarking on a Rough Passage', p. 47.
204. See p. 288.
205. I am grateful to Naomi Tadmor for discussing these issues with me. See pp. 324–5.

Chapter 8

1. Bernard E. C. Davis, 'The Text of Spenser's "Complaints"', *MLR* 20 (1925), 18–24, at 22; Plant, *English Book Trade*, pp. 144–5. Davis suggests that the whole volume was suppressed, as 'no expurgated quarto has come to light'. See also Stein, *Studies in Spenser's Complaints*, pp. 13–14.
2. The whole volume is copied out in BL MS Harley 6910, along with other poems by Chapman, Drayton, Sidney, Southwell, Sylvester, and others, as well as an extract from *Colin Clout* and the greater part of the *Hymne in Honour of Beautie* and the *Hymne of Heauenly Beautie* copied from the printed texts. For comment, see Katherine K. Gottschalk, 'Discoveries Concerning British Library Harley 6910', *MP* 77 (1979), 121–31; Ernest H. Strathmann, 'A Manuscript Copy of Spenser's *Hymnes*', *MLN* 48 (1933), 217–21. Selections from *Complaints* are also found in BL Add. MS 34064; and BL Add. MS 68942, copied out in the early 17th century, contains most of *Mother Hubberds Tale* (1,362 lines of 1,388). Bodleian Library, Douce MS 280, John Ramsey's Commonplace Book, contains complete texts of *Mother Hubberds Tale*, *Teares of the Muses*, and *Visions of Petrarch*, showing that he wanted copies of these proscribed poems.
3. Woudhuysen, *Sidney*, pp. 175–6.
4. *Stationers*, ii. 268.
5. Edmund Spenser, *Complaints* (London, 1591), BL 239 i I; Peterson, 'Laurel Crown and Ape's Tail', p. 10; Harold Stein, *Studies in Spenser's Complaints* (New York: Oxford University Press, 1934), p. 10. On Henry Cocke, see Duncan-Jones, *Sidney*, p. 227.
6. Berry and Timings, 'Spenser's Pension', p. 255; Peterson, 'Laurel Crown and Ape's Tail', p. 12.
7. Richard Verstegan, *A Declaration of the True Causes of the Great Troubles, presupposed to be intended against the realme of England* (Antwerp, 1592), p. 68. Subsequent references in parentheses in the text.
8. On Verstegan (Rowland), see *ODNB* entry by Paul Arblaster. On the importance of Verstegan and Catholic perceptions of Burghley, see Christopher Highley, *Catholics Writing the Nation in Early Modern Britain and Ireland* (Oxford: Oxford University Press, 2008), *passim*; Morey, *Catholic Subjects*, *passim*.

9. Alford, *Burghley*, p. 316.
10. Thomas Lodge, *Catharos: Diogenes in his Singularitie* (London, 1591); Eliane Cuvelier, 'Renaissance Catholicism in the Work of Thomas Lodge', in Charles C. Whitney (ed.), *Thomas Lodge* (Aldershot: Ashgate, 2011), pp. 502–17.
11. On the Treshams, see Finch, *Wealth of Five Northamptonshire Families*, ch. 4; Pritchard, *Catholic Loyalism*, pp. 49–57.
12. 'The Tresham Papers belonging to T. B. Clarke-Thornhill Esq., of Rushton Hall, Northants', in *Report on Manuscripts in Various Collections*, 8 vols. (London: HMC, 1901–13), iii. 1–154, at pp. 136–7.
13. See W. D. Sweeting, *Architectural Description of the Triangular Lodge at Rushton* (Northampton: Taylor and Son, 1881); J. Alfred Gotch et al., *Rushton and Its Owners* (Northampton: Taylor and Son, 1896), pp. 17–24; Gerard Kilroy, 'Sir Thomas Tresham: His Emblem', *Emblematica* 17 (2009), 149–79. Tresham's building was perhaps inspired by Pythagorean and Neoplatonic ideas, as well as Catholicism: Healy, *Shakespeare, Alchemy*, pp. 77–88.
14. Transcribed in Peterson, 'Laurel Crown and Ape's Tail', pp. 22–3.
15. *MHT*, lines 1381–2. See Kent T. Van Den Berg, ' "The Counterfeit in Personation": Spenser's *Prosopopoia, or Mother Hubberds Tale*', in Louis L. Martz and Aubrey Williams (eds.), *The Author in His Work: Essays on a Problem in Criticism* (New Haven: Yale University Press, 1978), pp. 85–102, at pp. 97–8.
16. Transcribed in Peterson, 'Laurel Crown and Ape's Tail', p. 23.
17. Spenser, *Shorter Poems*, p. 190.
18. Harvey, *Foure Letters*, p. 15.
19. John Weever, *Epigrammes in the Oldest Cut, and Newest Fashion* (London, 1599), sig. G3^r. On Weever (1575/6–1632), see the *ODNB* entry by David Kathman.
20. Hoyt H. Hudson, 'John Hepworth's Spenserian Satire upon Buckingham: With Some Jacobean Analogies', *Huntington Library Bulletin* 6 (1934), 39–71.
21. One reader who was not offended by the poem and who did not notice anything satirical about it was Henry Gurney (1549–1616): see Steven W. May, 'Henry Gurney, A Norfolk Farmer, Reads Spenser and Others', *Sp. St.* 20 (2005), 183–223, at 192–3.
22. Josephine Waters Bennett, 'A Bibliographical Note on *Mother Hubberds Tale*', *ELH* 4 (1937), 60–1.
23. For comment, see Einar Bjorvand, '*Complaints: Prosopopoia, or Mother Hubberds Tale*', *Sp. Enc.*, pp. 184–5; Kenneth John Atchity, 'Spenser's *Mother Hubberds Tale*: Three Themes of Order', *PQ* 52 (1973), 161–72.
24. Jill Mann, *Chaucer and Medieval Estates Satire: The Literature of Social Classes and the 'General Prologue' to The Canterbury Tales* (London: Cambridge University Press, 1973); Shinn, 'Spenser and Popular Print Culture', ch. 3; John Desmond Peter, *Complaint and Satire in Early English Literature* (Oxford: Clarendon Press, 1956).
25. Richard A. McCabe, 'Elizabethan Satire and the Bishops' Ban of 1599', *YES* 11 (1981), 188–93; Richard A. McCabe, ' "Right Puisante and Terrible Priests": The Role of the Anglican Church in Elizabethan State Censorship', in Andrew Hadfield (ed.), *Literature and Censorship in Renaissance England* (Basingstoke: Palgrave, 200), pp. 75–94. Spenser's place in the vogue for satire in the 1590s is often only perfunctorily acknowledged, especially as Spenser adopted the persona of John Skelton: see e.g. Ejner J. Jensen, 'Verse Satire in the English Renaissance', in Ruben Quintero (ed.), *A Companion to Satire* (Oxford: Blackwell, 2007), pp. 101–17, at pp. 108–9.
26. Richards, *Rhetoric and Courtliness*, pp. 115–20; Neil Rhodes, *Elizabethan Grotesque* (London: Routledge, 1980), pt. 1.
27. See p. 468 n. 39. For comment, see Capp, *Astrology and the Popular Press*, pp. 141, 143, 166, *passim*.
28. John Harvey, *A Discoursiue Probleme Concerning Prophesies* (London, 1588), pp. 80–1.
29. Harvey–Spenser *Letters*, pp. 37–40; Richards, *Rhetoric and Courtliness*, pp. 121, 131, 134, 137; Stern, *Harvey*, p. 108; Harvey, *Pierces Supererogation*, sigs. E2^r, Gg1^r.
30. First argued in J. E. Neale, *The Elizabethan Political Scene* (London: J. Cumberlege, 1949).

31. Natalie Mears, '*Regnum Cecilianum*? A Cecilian Perspective of the Court', in Guy (ed.), *Reign of Elizabeth I*, pp. 46–64, at p. 46; McCabe, 'Rhyme and Reason', p. 35.
32. Rebecca Bushnell, *Tragedies of Tyrants: Political Thought and Theater in the English Renaissance* (Ithaca, NY: Cornell University Press, 1990), introd.
33. Bruce Harris, 'The Ape in "Mother Hubberds Tale"', *HLQ* 4 (1941), 191–203; Mears, '*Regnum Cecilianum*?'; Adams, *Leicester and the Court, passim.*
34. Davis, 'Text of Spenser's "Complaints"', pp. 23–4.
35. Edmund Spenser, *The Faerie Queene, The Shepheardes Calender, together with the other works of Edmund Spenser* (London, 1611), Cambridge University Library, shelfmark, Keynes S.6.9. The title page, the headnote devices for the first two books of *The Faerie Queene*, and the woodcuts in the *Calender* have all been coloured in by the owner in the 17th or 18th century.
36. Edmund Spenser, *The Faerie Queene, The Shepheardes Calender, together with the other works of Edmund Spenser* (London, 1611), Cambridge University Library, shelfmark, O*.9.27 (C). See also Johnson, *Critical Bibliography*, pp. 33–4.
37. Richard Niccols, *The Begger's Ape* (London, 1627); Harris, 'The Ape in "Mother Hubberds Tale"', p. 201. Niccols (1583/4–1616), who re-edited *A Mirror for Magistrates* in 1610, makes use of Spenser's work elsewhere and acknowledges his importance for a later generation of poets: see the *ODNB* entry by Andrew Hadfield.
38. Spenser also attacks Burghley for his extravagant building projects, especially Theobalds, for which he was well known: see Frederick Hard, 'Spenser and Burghley', *SP* 28 (1931), 219–34.
39. Harris, 'The Ape in "Mother Hubberds Tale"', pp. 198–200.
40. Judson, *Life*, pp. 153–5.
41. Spenser, *Shorter Poems*, p. 165.
42. See, pp. 93–5.
43. Spenser, *Shorter Poems*, p. 581. For an alternative view, see Brink, 'Who Fashioned Edmund Spenser?'.
44. Spenser, *Shorter Poems*, p. 166. The fact that one of the scribes of BL Add. MS 34064 copied out 'only those portions of the *Ruins of Time*...which have to do with the Dudley family' only strengthens this suspicion: Buck, 'Add. MS. 34064', p. 43.
45. Battiscombe, *Spencers of Althorp*, pp. 11–12.
46. Greenlaw, 'Spenser and the Earl of Leicester'; John Kerrigan (ed.), *Motives of Woe: Shakespeare & 'Female Complaint': A Critical Anthology* (Oxford: Clarendon Press, 1991), pp. 139–40; Satterthwaite, *Spenser, Ronsard, and Du Bellay*, ch. 5.
47. In England authors and publishers were expected to cooperate on producing the text: see Elizabeth Evenden and Thomas S. Freeman, *Religion and the Book in Early Modern England: The Making of John Foxe's 'Book of Martyrs'* (Cambridge: Cambridge University Press, 2011), p. 24.
48. Edmund Spenser, *Complaints* (London, 1591), Cambridge University Library, Syn. 7.59.77.
49. Amanda Rogers Jones, 'Orderly Disorder: Rhetoric and Imitation in Spenser's Three Beast Poems from the *Complaints* volume', unpublished MA thesis, Virginia Polytechnic Institute, 2001, p. 3.
50. See p. 127.
51. The most thorough examination of the possible reasons for Spenser's animus against Burghley is Bruce Danner, *Furious Muse: Edmund Spenser's War on Lord Burghley* (Basingstoke: Palgrave, 2011).
52. See p. 33.
53. Although Scudamore would appear to refer to a real courtier: see p. 506 n. 194.
54. *The Ruines of Time* in Spenser, *Shorter Poems*, lines 253–9; A. Leigh Deneef, *Spenser and the Motives of Metaphor* (Durham, NC: Duke University Press, 1982), p. 31.
55. Alford, *Burghley*, pp. 243–4, 260–5, *passim*; Read, *Lord Burghley*, pp. 314–17.
56. Camden, *Britannia*, p. 51.
57. Hannibal Hamlin, *Psalm Culture in Early Modern English Literature* (Cambridge: Cambridge University Press, 2004), p. 225.
58. Weiner, 'The Beleaguered Isle'.

59. See pp. 91–4.
60. Curtis Perry, *Literature and Favortism in Early Modern England* (Cambridge: Cambridge University Press, 2006), ch. 2.
61. Nashe, *Works*, i. 221–6; Nicholl, *Cup of News*, pp. 112–14, 118–19.
62. Rogers, *Leicester's Ghost*, ed. Williams, lines 1–7. On Rogers see above, p. 94.
63. Williams, '*Leicester's Ghost*', p. 277.
64. Wernham, *After the Armada*, ch. 1. See also Knapp, *An Empire Nowhere*, chs. 1–3.
65. For comment, see Anne Lake Prescott, 'Spenser (Re)Reading Du Bellay', in Anderson et al. (eds.), *Spenser's Life and the Subject of Biography*, pp. 131–45, at pp. 135–40.
66. Fowler, *Spenser and the Numbers of Time*; Alexander Dunlop, 'Number symbolism, modern studies in', *Sp. Enc.*, pp. 512–13.
67. Michael Questier, *Conversion, Politics and Religion in England, 1580–1625* (Cambridge: Cambridge University Press, 1996), p. 204.
68. See Richard Danson Brown, '*The New Poet*': *Novelty and Tradition in Spenser's Complaints* (Liverpool: Liverpool University Press, 1999), ch. 4.
69. William A. Oram, 'Spenser's Audiences, 1589–91', *SP* 100 (2003), 514–33, at 524–5.
70. On Wolsey, see Walker, *Skelton*, chs. 5–6.
71. On Spenser's calculated rudeness, see Bruce Danner, 'Retrospective Fiction-Making and the "Secrete" of the 1591 *Virgils Gnat*', *Sp. St.* 25 (2010), 215–45, at 224.
72. *ODNB* entry on Conway; see p. 106.
73. For another reading, see Rambuss, *Spenser's Secret Career*, pp. 19–21.
74. Danner, 'Retrospective Fiction-Making', p. 238.
75. Henry G. Lotspeich, 'Spenser's *Virgils Gnat* and its Latin Original', *ELH* 2 (1935), 235–41; Oliver Farrar Emerson, 'Spenser's *Virgils Gnat*', *JEGP* 17 (1918), 94–118.
76. Gordon Braden, 'Non-Dramatic Verse', pp. 185–6; William Weaver, 'Paraphrase and Patronage in *Virgils Gnat*', *Sp. St.* 25 (2010), 247–61, at 250.
77. Gordon Braden, '*Complaints: Virgils Gnat*', *Sp. Enc.*, pp. 183–4.
78. Readings of the poem relate Spenser's complaint to his attack on Lettice Knollys (Mounts, 'Spenser and the Countess of Leicester'); or to his warning the court against the Alençon match (Greenlaw, 'Spenser and the Earl of Leicester'; Rosenberg, *Leicester*, pp. 338–40; Doris Adler, 'Imaginary Toads in Real Gardens', *ELR* 11 (1981), 235–60, at 257–8).
79. See Hadfield, 'Michael Drayton's Brilliant Career'.
80. For comment on these, see Helgerson, *Du Bellay*, introd., pp. 34–6; Lawrence Manley, 'Spenser and the City: The Minor Poems', *MLQ* 43 (1982), 203–27; Scodel, 'Non-Dramatic Verse', pp. 239–40.
81. Bellay, *Regrets*, trans. Helgerson, pp. 324–34.
82. A. E. B. Coldiron, 'How Spenser Excavates Du Bellay's *Antiquitez*: Or, The Role of the Poet, Lyric Historiography, and the English Sonnet', *JEGP* 101 (2002), 41–67.
83. Spenser, *Shorter Poems*, p. 275. The original is in Du Bellay, *Regrets*, trans. Helgerson, p. 255.
84. See McCabe, *Pillars of Eternity*, pp. 62–4.
85. Herron, *Spenser's Irish Work*, pt. 2.
86. See the *ODNB* entry on Elizabeth Carey by Eliane V. Beilin; Strathmann, 'Lady Carey and Spenser'; Judson, *Life*, pp. 4, 142, *passim*.
87. Comment on the poem has been relatively substantial: for an overview see Judith Dundas, '*Complaints: Muiopotmos, or The Fate of the Butterflie*', *Sp. Enc.*, pp. 186–7. On the Minerva–Arachne contest, see Robert A. Brinkley, 'Spenser's *Muiopotmos* and the Politics of Metamorphosis', *ELH* 48 (1981), 668–76. See also William Wells, ' "To Make a Milde Construction": The Significance of the Opening Stanzas of *Muiopotmos*', *SP* 42 (1945), 544–54.
88. Don Cameron Allen, 'On Spenser's "Muiopotmos"', *SP* 53 (1956), 141–58; Franklin E. Court, 'The Theme and Structure of Spenser's *Muiopotmos*', *SEL* 10 (1970), 1–15.
89. Allegorical readings have often been forced and not been widely accepted: see e.g. Brice Harris, 'The Butterfly in Spenser's *Muiopotmos*', *JEGP* 43 (1944), 302–16. For comment on the process of reading the poem allegorically, see Andrew D. Weiner, 'Spenser's *Muiopotmos* and the Fates of Butterflies and Men', *JEGP* 84 (1985), 203–20.

90. For comment on the ekphrasis in the poem, see Bender, *Spenser and Literary Pictorialism*, pp. 162–8; Judith Dundas, ' "Muiopotmos": A World of Art', *YES* 5 (1975), 30–8.

91. For a different reading, see Cheney, *Spenser's Famous Flight*, p. 3, where he argues that the *Complaints* and *Colin Clouts come home againe* 'do not belong to the generic progression organizing the fiction of the New Poet's career'.

92. On this last point, see Spenser, *Shorter Poems*, p. 592.

93. On Stubbes, see pp. 127–8; G. P. V. Akrigg, *Shakespeare and the Earl of Southampton* (London: Hamilton, 1968).

94. Edmund Spenser, *The Yale Edition of the Shorter Poems of Edmund Spenser*, ed. William A. Oram, Einar Bjorvand, Ronald Bond, Thomas H. Cain, Alexander Dunlop, and Richard Schell (New Haven: Yale University Press, 1989), pp. 487–91; William A. Oram, '*Daphnaïda* and Spenser's Later Poetry', *Sp. St.* 4 (1983), 33–47.

95. See e.g. Jonathan Gibson, 'The Legal Context of Spenser's *Daphnaïda*', *RES* 55 (2004), 24–44, at 27–8.

96. Gibson, 'Legal Context of *Daphnaïda*', p. 28 (my discussion is significantly indebted to Gibson's excellent article). See also see the *ODNB* entry by Colin Burrow, and *The Poems of Sir Arthur Gorges*, ed. Helen Estabrook Sandison (Oxford: Clarendon Press, 1953), introd., pp. xiii–xxvii; Bajetta, *Ralegh*, *passim*.

97. Pienaar, 'Spenser and Jonker van der Noot', p. 67. On Parr, see *ODNB* entry by Susan E. James. On Helena Snakenborg, see *ODNB* entry by Paul Harrington; Charles Angell Bradford, *Helena, Marchioness of Northampton* (London: Allen & Unwin, 1936); Gunnar Sjören, 'Helena, Marchioness of Northampton: A Swedish lady at the Court of Elizabeth I', *History Today* 28 (1978), 597–604; Tracy Borman, *Elizabeth's Women: The Hidden Story of the Virgin Queen* (London: Cape, 2009), pp. 277–82, *passim*.

98. On Thomas Gorges, see *ODNB* entry by Paul Harrington.

99. See p. 479 n. 70.

100. It is also worth noting that the Wraxall, Nailsea, and Tynte deeds held in the Somerset Archives provide details of a number of land deals between the Tynte and Gorges family branches in the West Country: see TNA PRO DD\S\WH/47, 48, 96. Elizabeth Boyle's third husband was Robert Tynte, whom she married in 1612, providing further evidence of the links between the families, especially if, as Judson suggests, the marriages were arranged by Robert Boyle (Judson, *Life*, p. 168). For (not very convincing) speculations of a Howard link through Spenser's grandfather, see Welply, 'Some Spenser Problems', pp. 58–9. The subsequent exchange shows how difficult it is to establish any clear link to branches of the Spenser family with any certainty, but does provide a great deal of information about the Spensers in Northamptonshire and Warwickshire: J. B. Whitmore, 'Reader's Reply', *N&Q* 180 (1941), 120; Hamer, 'Some Spenser Problems: John and Giles Spenser', pp. 165–7.

101. Gorges' poems are collected in fair copy in BL Egerton 3165; Gorges, *Poems*, ed. Sandison, introd., *passim*.

102. Helen E. Sandison, 'Arthur Gorges, Spenser's Alcyon and Raleigh's Friend', *PMLA* 43 (1928), 645–74; Helen E. Sandison, 'Spenser's Manilla', *TLS*, 8 Sept. 1927, p. 608; Kathrine Koller, 'Identifications in *Colin Clouts come home againe*', *MLN* 50 (1935), 155–8, at 156.

103. Gibson, 'Legal Context of *Daphnaïda*', p. 26.

104. Ibid. 27; *ODNB* entry; Sandison, 'Arthur Gorges', pp. 647–55.

105. See G. W. Pigman III, *Grief and the English Elegy* (Cambridge: Cambridge University Press, 1985), pp. 75–81; Oram, '*Daphnaïda* and Spenser's Later Poetry'; Deneef, *Spenser and the Motives of Metaphor*, pp. 41–50. For the latter reading see Patrick Cheney, 'Dido to Daphne: Early Modern Death in Spenser's Shorter Poems', *Sp. St.* 18 (2003), 143–63.

106. Norman Berlin, 'Chaucer's *The Book of the Duchess* and Spenser's *Daphnaïda*: A Contrast', *Studia Neophilologica* 38 (1966), 282–9; Dennis Kay, *Melodious Tears: The English Funeral Elegy from Spenser to Milton* (Oxford: Clarendon Press, 1990), pp. 51–2. For a more general context for Chaucer's poem, see James Simpson, *Reform and Cultural Revolution: The Oxford English Literary History*, ii. *1350–1547* (Oxford: Oxford University Press, 2003), pp. 162–4.

107. Ardis Butterfield, 'Chaucer's French Inheritance', in Piero Boitani and Jill Mann (eds.), *The Cambridge Companion to Chaucer* (2nd edn., Cambridge: Cambridge University Press, 2003), pp. 20–35, at p. 28.
108. Gibson, 'Legal Context of *Daphnaïda*', p. 31; Kerrigan (ed.), *Motives of Woe*, pp. 139–63; Susan Wiseman and Alison Thorne (eds.), *The Rhetoric of Complaint: Ovid's Heroides in the Renaissance and Restoration, RS*, special issue, 22/3 (June 2008).
109. Gibson, 'Legal Context of *Daphnaïda*', p. 35.
110. Zurcher, *Spenser's Legal Language*, pp. 130–8; James Lydon, 'The Expansion and Consolidation of the Colony, 1215–54', in Moody et al. (eds.), *New History of Ireland*, ii. 156–78, at p. 173.
111. Jonathan Gibson, 'Sir Arthur Gorges (1557–1625) and the Patronage System', unpublished PhD thesis, University of London, 1998, p. 187.
112. Gibson, 'Gorges', pp. 146, 187–99.
113. Ibid. 80–2.
114. A brass rubbing of Gorges with his second wife, Lady Elizabeth Clinton, with their eleven children, seven of whom survived into adulthood, is preserved in BL Add. MS 32486, fos. 11–12.

Chapter 9
1. *CSPI, 1592–6*, p. 58.
2. See p. 297.
3. *CSPI 1592–6*, pp. 56–7.
4. Ibid. 60.
5. Judson, 'Two Spenser Leases'. See p. 202.
6. It is possible that earlier versions of some of the *Amoretti* existed: see L. Cummings, 'Spenser's *Amoretti* VIII: New Manuscript Versions', *SEL* 4 (1964), 125–35.
7. Klingelhofer, *Castles and Colonists*, ch. 5.
8. Frederick Hard, 'Princelie Pallaces: Spenser and Elizabethan Architecture', *Sewanee Review* 42 (1934), 293–310. More generally, see James J. Yoch, 'Architecture as Virtue: The Luminous Palace from Homeric Dream to Stuart Propaganda', *SP* 75 (1978), 403–29.
9. Roche's petition to Loftus would support Thomas Herron's claim that Spenser saw Loftus as a personal enemy: 'Reforming the Fox'.
10. Curtis to Robert Cecil, Feb. 1598/9, *CSPI, 1598–9*, pp. 484–5. See also John Norris to Burghley, 11 Oct. 1597, *CSPI, 1596–7*, p. 415.
11. Welply, 'Spenser: Some New Discoveries', p. 150.
12. The document, destroyed in the fire of 1922, is cited in James Hardiman, *Irish Minstrelsy, or Bardic Remains of Ireland; with English Poetical Translations*, 2 vols. (London, 1831), i. 320. Also cited in *Chronology*, p. 60. See also Carpenter, *Reference Guide*, p. 22; Judson, *Life*, p. 160.
13. *Chronology*, p. 60; MacCarthy-Morrogh, *Munster Plantation*, chs. 1–3. The Roches did fight a number of legal battles with other Irish families, such as their local rivals, the Condons: McCormack, *Earldom of Desmond*, p. 165.
14. Cited in Carpenter, *Reference Guide*, p. 34.
15. Craig Muldrew, 'The Culture of Reconciliation: Community and the Settlement of Economic Disputes in Early Modern England', *HJ* 39/4 (1996), 915–42.
16. Franklin B. Williams, Jr, 'Commendatory Verses: The Rise of the Art of Puffing', *SB* 19 (1966), 1–14, at 1; id., 'Commendatory sonnets', *Sp. Enc.*, p. 177.
17. Giovanni Battista Nenna, *Nennio, or A Treatise of Nobility*, trans. William Jones (Jerusalem: Israel Universities Press, 1967), p. 11, lines 1–2, 13–14.
18. Justus Lipsius, *Sixe Bookes of Politickes or Ciuil Doctrine, written in Latine by Iustus Lipsius: which doe especially concerne principalitie; Done into English by William Iones Gentleman* (London, 1594).
19. See the *ODNB* article by Christopher W. Brooks.
20. On Lipsius, see Kraye, 'Moral Philosophy', pp. 370–3. On Spenser and Lipsius, see Merritt Y. Hughes, 'Spenser's Palmer', *ELH* 2 (1935), 151–64, at 159.
21. *The Historie of George Castriot, surnamed Scanderbeg, King of Albanie Containing his famous actes, his noble deedes of armes, and memorable victories against the Turkes, for the faith of Christ.*

Comprised in twelue bookes: by Iaques de Lauardin, Lord of Plessis Bourrot, a nobleman of France. Newly translated out of French into English by Z. I. Gentleman (London, 1596). For comment, see Vine, *In Defiance of Time*, pp. 127–8.

22. Franklin B. Williams, Jr, 'Spenser, Shakespeare, and Zachary Jones', *Shakespeare Quarterly* 19 (1968), 205–12.

23. Lauardin, *Scanderbeg*, sig. ¶7ʳ. On Spenser's representation of Saracens, see Robinson, *Islam and Early Modern English Literature*, ch. 1.

24. John H. Astington, 'Sir John Astley and Court Culture', *Sh. Stud.* 30 (2002), 106–10.

25. For analysis, see Hadfield, 'Was Spenser a Republican?', pp. 171–2; John Gillies, *Shakespeare and the Geography of Difference* (Cambridge: Cambridge University Press, 1994), pp. 123–4.

26. Gaspar Contarini, *The Commonwealth and Gouernment of Venice*, trans. Lewis Lewkenor (London, 1599), sig. ¶3ᵛ.

27. For details of Lewkenor's life, see Marco Nievergelt's Early English Books Online (EEBO) introd. to *The Resolved Gentleman*; Questier, *Catholicism and Community*, pp. 58–9.

28. Lewis Lewkenor, *A Discourse of the Usage of the English Fugitiues, by the Spaniard* (London, 1595), later expanded as *The Estate of English Fugitiues under the King of Spaine and his Ministers* (London, 1596); Williams, 'Commendatory sonnets'. Both works were immediately reprinted. For comment, see Andrew Hadfield, *Literature, Travel, and Colonial Writing in the English Renaissance, 1545–1625* (Oxford: Clarendon Press, 1998), p. 48.

29. Lewis Lewkenor, *The Resolved Gentleman* (London, 1594), fo. 45; *Spenser Allusions*, p. 36.

30. *ODNB* entry on Kyffin by Glanmor Williams.

31. *Andria the First Comoedie of Terence, in English. A furtherance for the attainment vnto the right knowledge, & true proprietie, of the Latin tong. And also a commodious meane of help, to such as haue forgotten Latin, for their speedy recouering of habilitie, to vnderstand, write, and speake the same. Carefully translated out of Latin, by Maurice Kyffin* (London, 1588).

32. Maurice Kyffin, *The Blessednes of Brytaine* (London, 1588); Lewkenor, *Resolved Gentleman*, sig. A2ʳ.

33. Gabriel Harvey, *Pierces Supererogation* (London, 1593), p. 191; Frederick Hard, 'Notes on John Eliot and His *Ortho-epia Gallica*', *HLQ* 1 (1938), 169–87, at 170–4.

34. Hard, 'Notes on John Eliot'.

35. See also the entry on Kyffin in John Edward Lloyd and R. T. Jenkins (eds.), *The Dictionary of Welsh Bibliography Down to 1940* (London: Honourable Society of Cymmrodorian, 1959) p. 538.

36. Rudolf B. Gottfried, 'Spenser and *The Historie of Cambria*', *MLN* 72 (1957), 9–13; Donald Williams Bruce, 'Spenser's Welsh', *N&Q* 32 (1985), 465–7.

37. For comment on the quarrel, see Nashe, *Works*, v. 65–110; Hadfield, ' "Not without Mustard" '.

38. Nashe, *Works*, i. 282, 299; ii. 108, 323, *passim*.

39. The last recoded work is *The Trimming of Thomas Nashe* (London, 1597), once attributed to Harvey, but now known to be the work of Richard Lichfield: see Griffin, 'Nashe's Dedicatees'.

40. The Marprelate quarrel (1588–9) saw the publication of scurrilous anti-episcopal tracts on a secret portable press, answered by writers—including Lyly and Nashe—who defended the ecclesiology of the established church. In their quarrel, Nashe associated Harvey with the Marprelates.

41. Joseph L. Black (ed.), *The Martin Marprelate Tracts: A Modernized and Annotated Edition* (Cambridge: Cambridge University Press, 2008), introd., p. lxxiii.

42. Hadfield, ' "Not without Mustard" ', p. 74.

43. Welply, 'Spenser: Recent Researches', p. 165.

44. See pp. 407–8.

45. Mary Anne Hutchinson, 'Boyle family', *Sp. Enc.*, p. 109; Townshend, *Earl of Cork*, pp. 32–3, 206–9.

46. Welply, 'More Notes on Spenser', p. 111.

47. Philip G. Lee, 'The Ruined Monuments of Sir Robert Tynte and Sir Edward Harris in Kilcredan Church, Balycrenane, near Ladysbridge', *JCHAS*, 2nd ser. 31 (1926), 86–7, at 86. The quotation is from W. N. Brady, who saw the monument before it was mutilated.

48. Amy Louise Harris, 'The Tynte Monument, Kilcredan, Co. Cork: A Reappraisal', *JCHAS* 104 (1999), 137–44, at 139.

49. Judson, 'Notes on the Life of Spenser', p. 28.
50. Ralph A. Houlbrooke, *The English Family, 1450–1700* (London: Longman, 1984), p. 39.
51. Heffner, 'Spenser's Family', p. 82.
52. Richard Boyle, 'Memoir', BL Add. MS 19832, 23 June 1632.
53. *ODNB* entry on Fenton by Andrew Hadfield.
54. An opposite explanation is given by Ray Heffner who assumes that Spenser met Elizabeth in England and that her family moved to Ireland because of him.
55. Dorothea Townshend, *The Life and Letters of the Great Earl of Cork* (London: Duckworth, 1904), p. 8; Welply, 'Spenser: Recent Researches', p. 166.
56. Welply, 'Spenser: Some New Discoveries', pp. 446–7; Welply, 'More Notes on Spenser', p. 116.
57. On Kilcoran, see Samuel Hayman, *Memorials of Youghal, Ecclesiastical and Civil* (Youghal: John Lindsay, 1879), p. 29.
58. Richard Boyle, *The Lismore Papers: Autobiographical Notes, Remembrances, and Diaries,* ed. Alexander B. Grosart, 2nd ser., 5 vols. (London: privately printed, 1886), vol. i, introd., p. xv.
59. Houlbrooke, *English Family*, p. 19; Robert Day, 'Notes on Youghal', *JRSAI*, 5th ser. 33 (1903), 319–25, at 325.
60. Welply, 'Spenser's Brother-in-law, John Travers'.
61. Townshend, *Earl of Cork*, p. 38; Dickson, *Old World Colony*, p. 10.
62. Caulfield, *Council Book of Youghal*, p. xxv; Flavin and Jones (eds.), *Bristol's Trade with Ireland and the Continent, passim.*
63. Camden, *Britannia* (Ireland), p. 78.
64. Dickson, *Old World Colony*, ch. 4; Mark McCarthy, 'Geographical Change in an Early Modern Town: Urban Growth and Cultural Politics in Cork, 1600–41', *JCHAS* 106 (2001), 53–78; MacCarthy-Morrogh, 'English Presence in Munster', p 175; Andy Halpin and Conor Newman, *Ireland: An Oxford Archaeological Guide* (Oxford: Oxford University Press, 2006), pp. 536–9.
65. Dickson, *Old World Colony*, pp. 8, 18–19, 22; Berry, 'English Settlement in Mallow', p. 17. A study of a particular Youghal family which bears out this analysis, is found in Henry F. Berry, 'The Old Youghal Family of Stout', *JCHAS* 23 (1917), 19–29. Youghal was by no means exclusively Protestant, however, and maintained a Jesuit School: see Jeffries, *Irish Church*, p. 166.
66. McCormack, *Earldom of Desmond*, pp. 146–8.
67. Niall O'Brien, 'Bristol Apprentices from Youghal, 1532–1565', *JCHAS* 115 (2010), 109–14.
68. Welply, 'More Notes on Spenser', p. 114.
69. *Chronology*, p. 85.
70. Welply, 'Spenser: Some New Discoveries', p. 446.
71. TNA PROB 11/64.
72. Boyle, *Lismore Papers*, 2nd ser., vol. i, introd., pp. xv–xvi; Hamer, 'Spenser's Marriage', p. 276.
73. Chatsworth House, 1st earl of Cork's Journals, 3 Mar. 1612, Cork MSS, vol. 25, fo. 11; transcribed in Boyle, *Lismore Papers*, 2nd ser., vol. i, introd., p. xvi; Hamer, 'Spenser: Some Further Notes', p. 383. See also J. Coleman, 'The Poet Spenser's Wife', *JCHAS*, 2nd ser. 1 (1895), 131–3. 'Kinswoman' probably meant cousin, a flexible and rather vague term in this period: Houlbrooke, *English Family*, p. 40.
74. Hamer, 'Spenser's Marriage', p. 276.
75. Horace T. Fleming, 'Some Notes on the Tynte Family', *JCHAS* 9 (1903), 156–7; Caulfield, *Council Book of Youghal*, pp. 162, 219–20.
76. M. J. C. Buckley, 'The Burgh or "Ville" of Youghal', *JRSAI*, 5th ser. 33 (1903), 326–32, at 328–9; Caulfield, *Council Book of Youghal*, pp. 131, 300.
77. See David Cressy, *Literacy and the Social Order: Reading and Writing in Tudor and Stuart England* (Cambridge: Cambridge University Press, 1980), pp. 144–5. We do not know whether Machabyas was literate.
78. Chatsworth House, Cork MSS, vol. 6, no. 132; transcribed in Boyle, *Lismore Papers*, 2nd ser. ii. 12–13; Berry, 'Sheriffs of the County Cork', pp. 42, 51–2.
79. Chatsworth House, Cork MSS, vol. 7, no. 184; transcribed in Boyle, *Lismore Papers*, 2nd ser. ii. 60. On Richard Seckerstone, see the correspondence between H. W. Garrod and

W. H. Welply, 'Spenser and Elizabeth Boyle', *TLS*, 24 May 1923. Garrod raises the possibility that Elizabeth was a widow when she met Spenser but is refuted by Welply. On the children of Robert and Elizabeth Tynte, see Hamer, 'Spenser: Some Further Notes', p. 383; Douglas Hamer, 'Robert Tynte's Sons', *N&Q* 162 (1932), 62–3. Hamer argues that they had only one child, not seven as was often claimed. On the Tynte family, see also Welply, 'More Notes on Spenser', pp. 111–16; W. H. Welply, 'Spenser–Tynte Genealogy', *N&Q* 187 (1944), 128–9.

80. Welply, 'Spenser: Recent Researches', p. 183.
81. For England, see Wrightson, *English Society*, ch. 3.
82. On Freckleton, see Douglas Hamer, 'Captain Sir Ferdinando Freckleton', *N&Q* 162 (1932), 209–10, 231, although Hamer is sceptical that this is the right Freckleton. See also R. Bingham Adams, 'Ferdinando Freckleton', *N&Q* 162 (1932), 88, 265–6; Ernest H. Strathmann, 'Ferdinando Freckleton and the Spenser Circle', *MLN* 58 (1943), 542–4.
83. Welply, 'Spenser's Brother-in-Law, John Travers'; Judson, *Life*, pp. 130–1. On Spenser's family, see also Welply, 'Family and Descendants of Spenser'.
84. Hamer, 'Spenser: Some Further Notes', p. 383.
85. Hamer, 'Spenser's Marriage', p. 280.
86. Maley, *Salvaging Spenser*, ch. 3.
87. *ODNB* entry on Boyle by Toby Barnard. The link to the Cliffords suggests a further network to which Spenser belonged: see pp. 352–3.
88. Herron, 'Reforming the Fox'; Barnard, *ODNB* entry; Canny, *Upstart Earl*, ch. 2.
89. Welply, 'Spenser: Some New Discoveries', p. 169; Hamer, 'Spenser's Marriage', pp. 274, 280. See pp. 408–9.
90. Muldrew, 'Culture of Reconciliation', pp. 922–3. On the other Boyle disputes, see pp. 343–8.
91. Spenser, *Shorter Poems*, p. 670.
92. Welply, 'Spenser: Recent Researches', p. 184.
93. Spenser, *Shorter Poems*, p. 386.
94. Rudolf Gottfried, 'The "G. W. Senior" and "G. W. I." of Spenser's *Amoretti*', *MLQ* 3 (1942), 543–6, at 545; Welply, 'Spenser: Recent Researches', p. 184. Frederick Ives Carpenter suggests that George Wilkins and his son are the most likely authors: 'G. W. Senior and G. W. I.', *MP* 22 (1924), 67–8.
95. Other—less likely—candidates are the playwrights George Wilkins, senior and junior: see Anthony Parr, 'Wilkins, George (d. 1618)', *ODNB*.
96. See the *ODNB* entry on Geoffrey Whitney by Andrew King.
97. See the *ODNB* entry on Isabella Whitney by Betty S. Travitsky; Beilin, *Redeeming Eve*, pp. 88–101.
98. Paul Salzman, *Reading Early Modern Women's Writing* (Oxford: Oxford University Press, 2006), p. 45. See also Lorna Hutson, 'The "Double Voice" of Renaissance Equity and the Literary Voices of Women', in Danielle Clarke and Elizabeth Clarke (eds.), *'This Double Voice': Gendered Writing in Early Modern England* (Basingstoke, Palgrave, 2000), pp. 142–63.
99. Geoffrey Whitney, *A Choice of Emblemes, and other Devises, for the moste parte gathered out of sundrie writers, Englished and moralized* (Leiden, 1586), pp. 86–7, 194–5; Gottfried, '"G. W. Senior"', p. 544.
100. John Manning, 'Emblems', *Sp. Enc.*, pp. 247–8; R. J. Manning, '"Deuicefull Sights": Spenser's Emblematic Practice in *The Faerie Queene*, V, 1–3', *Sp. St.* 5 (1984), 65–89.
101. 'G. W. Senior, to the Author', lines 1–4.
102. Maurice Evans (ed.), *Elizabethan Sonnets* (London: Dent, 1977); J. W. Lever, *The Elizabethan Love Sonnet* (London: Methuen, 1956), ch. 5; Reed Way Dasenbrock, 'The Petrarchan Context of Spenser's *Amoretti*', *PMLA* 100 (1985), 38–50.
103. Michael R. G. Spiller, *The Development of the Sonnet: An Introduction* (London: Routledge, 1992), p. 143. On Spenser's sources, see L. E. Kastner, 'Spenser's "Amoretti" and Desportes', *MLR* 4 (1908), 65–9; Janet C. Scott, 'The Sources of Spenser's "Amoretti"', *MLR* 22 (1927), 189–95.
104. See Robert S. Miola, 'Spenser's Anacreontics: A Mythological Metaphor', *SP* 77 (1980), 50–66; Carol V. Kaske, 'Spenser's *Amoretti* and *Epithalamion* of 1595: Structure, Genre, and

Numerology', *ELR* 8 (1978), 271–95; Anne Lake Prescott, 'Spenser and French Literature', *Sp. Handbook*, pp. 620–34, at p. 628.

105. Thomas M. Greene, 'Spenser and the Epithalamic Convention', *CL* 9 (1957), 215–28, at 222. See also Enid Welsford, *Spenser: Fowre Hymnes, Epithalamion: A Study of Edmund Spenser's Doctrine of Love* (Oxford: Blackwell, 1967), p. 70.

106. On Spenser's stanza see A. C. Partridge, *The Language of Renaissance Poetry* (London: Andre Deutsch, 1971), p. 86; for classical precedents, see *Claudian*, ii. 242–67; Statius, 'Epithalamion in Honour of Stella and Violentilla', *Silvae*, Bk. 1, no. 2, in *Statius*, ed. and trans. D. R. Shackleton Bailey, 2 vols. (Cambridge, MA: Harvard University Press, 2003), i. 14-37; Germaine Warkentin, 'Amoretti, Epithalamion', *Sp. Enc.*, pp. 30–8, at p. 35.

107. *Edmund Spenser's Amoretti and Epithalamion: A Critical Edition*, ed. Kenneth J. Larsen (Tempe, AZ: MRTS, 1997), introd., p. 3. See also Dunlop, 'Calendar Symbolism in the *Amoretti*', 24–6; William C. Johnson, 'Spenser's *Amoretti* and the Art of the Liturgy', *SEL* 14 (1974), 47–61.

108. Spenser, *Shorter Poems*, p. 394; Jones, *Spenser Handbook*, p. 338.

109. Sir Philip Sidney, *Astrophil and Stella*, sonnet 9 (Evans (ed.), *Elizabethan Sonnets*, p. 5).

110. Christopher Warley, *Sonnet Sequences and Social Distinction in Renaissance England* (Cambridge: Cambridge University Press, 2005), pp. 110–12.

111. Knapp, *Empire Nowhere*, ch. 1. Nashe had a similar view: see Andrew Hadfield, '*Lenten Stuff*: Thomas Nashe and the Fiction of Travel', *YES* 41 (2011), 68–83.

112. For a related argument, see Herron, 'Ralegh's Gold'.

113. On the blazon, see Nancy Vickers, 'Diana Described: Scattered Woman and Scattered Rhyme', *Critical Inquiry* 8 (1981), 265–79.

114. Spenser, *Shorter Poems*, p. 419. On the relationship between Spenser's sequence and the Song of Songs, see *Amoretti and Epithalamion*, ed. Larsen, pp. 194–5; Noam Flinker, *The Song of Songs in English Renaissance Literature: Kisses of Their Mouths* (Woodbridge: Boydell, 2000), pp. 76–9; Isabel Baroway, 'The Imagery of Spenser and the *Song of Songs*', *JEGP* 33 (1934), 23–44, at 39–40. Baroway argues that Spenser has effectively translated the biblical text in scattered fragments throughout his poems (pp. 24, 44).

115. Flinker, *Song of Songs*, pp. 12–19.

116. See e.g. A. R. Cirillo, 'Spenser's *Epithalamion*: The Harmonious Universe of Love', *SEL* 8 (1968), 19–34, at 32.

117. Yates, *Astrea*, p. 72; Helen Hackett, *Virgin Mother, Maiden Queen: Elizabeth I and the Cult of the Virgin Mary* (Basingstoke: Macmillan, 1995), pp. 174–80.

118. As Donne's poem is about the poet-narrator and his wife in bed, he may have been influenced by reading Spenser's poem, especially as he did later write an epithalamion based on Spenser's poem, and they had connections in common, notably through Alice Stanley, countess of Derby, to whom Spenser dedicated *The Teares of the Muses*: Bald, *John Donne*, p. 77; Stubbs, *Donne*, p. 127.

119. For a splendid reading of the complex politics of the poem, see Warley, *Sonnet Sequences*, pp. 116–22.

120. McLane, *Spenser's Shepheardes Calender*, ch. 2.

121. Silberman, *Transforming Desire*, ch. 3.

122. Van Es, *Spenser's Forms of History*, pp. 37–48.

123. Bednarz, 'Ralegh in Spenser's Historical Allegory'; Borman, *Elizabeth's Women*, ch. 15.

124. Julia M. Walker, 'Bones of Contention: Posthumous Images of Elizabeth and Stuart Politics', in Walker (ed.), *Dissing Elizabeth*, pp. 252–76.

125. On the precise nature of the numerology, see Hieatt, *Short Time's Endless Monument*; J. C. Eade, 'The Pattern in the Astronomy of Spenser's *Epithalamion*', *RES* 23 (1972), 173–8. On the *Epithalamion* as an expression of harmony, see e.g. Welsford, *Spenser: Fowre Hymnes, Epithalamion*, pp. 83–91; Alastair Fowler, *Time's Purpled Masquers: Stars and the Afterlife in Renaissance English Literature* (Oxford: Clarendon Press, 1996), pp. 59–61.

126. On the anxieties in the *Amoretti* and *Epithalamion*, see also Scott Wilson, *Cultural Materialism: Theory and Practice* (Oxford: Blackwell, 1995), pp. 64–82.

127. Sidney, *Astrophil and Stella*, sonnets 30, 24. For further links between the sequences, see Jacqueline T. Miller, '"Love Doth Hold My Hand": Writing and Wooing in the Sonnets of Sidney and Spenser', *ELH* 46 (1979), 541–58.
128. Marotti, *Manuscript, Print, and the English Renaissance Lyric*, p. 229.
129. For comment, see Ted Brown, 'Metapoetry in Edmund Spenser's *Amoretti*', *PQ* 82 (2003), 401–17, at 412–13. See p. 179.
130. Robert G. Benson, 'Elizabeth as Beatrice: A Reading of Spenser's "Amoretti"', *South Central Bulletin* 32 (1972), 184–8.
131. For the first point, see Myron Turner, 'The Imagery of Spenser's *Amoretti*', *Neophilologus* 72 (1988), 284–99, at 295; for the second, William C. Johnson, 'Gender Fashioning and the Dynamics of Mutuality in Spenser's *Amoretti*', *ES* 74 (1993), 503–19.
132. On spring love poems, see e.g. Theodore Silverstein (ed.), *Medieval English Lyrics* (London: Arnold, 1971), pp. 85–8.
133. *Amoretti and Epithalamion*, ed. Larsen, p. 233.
134. Hamer, 'Spenser's Marriage', p. 271. The story that Spenser was married in Cork is often repeated, even though no evidence supports it and it is implausible that the marriage party would have travelled into Cork: see e.g. Michael Shine, 'Spenser and Kilcolman', *MFCJ* 22 (2004), 139–54, at 146.
135. M. J. C. Buckley, 'Notes on St. Mary's Church, Youghal', *JRSAI*, 5th ser. 33 (1903), 333–44; Raymond Gillespie, 'An Age of Modernization, 1598–1690', in Crawford and Gillespie (eds.), *St. Patrick's Cathedral*, pp. 174–96, at pp. 183–4; Halpin and Newman, *Ireland*, p. 538.
136. On Baxter, see *ODNB* entry by Andrew Hadfield; Eccles, 'Brief Lives', pp. 11–12.
137. Halpin and Newman, *Ireland*, p. 539.
138. Carpenter, *Reference Guide*, p. 84, citing Edith Rickert.
139. *Georgics*, I, lines 373–8. Spenser has the forlorn Belge fear that her lot might 'Yeeld [her] an hostry [dwelling] mongst the croking frogs' (*FQ* V.x.23, line 8), indicating that he found them a nuisance in Ireland. See also Joseph Loewenstein, 'Echo's Ring: Orpheus and Spenser's Career', *ELR* 16 (1986), 287–302, at 296–8.
140. On Elizabeth as a reader of the poems, see Brown, 'Metapoetry in Spenser's *Amoretti*', p. 402; Cheney, *Spenser's Famous Flight*, p. 148.
141. Cited in Gollancz, 'Spenseriana', p. 100. Gollancz is the only scholar to have seen this copy and to have written about it. Its current whereabouts are not known, but it exists in a private collection.
142. Although, see Cummings, 'Spenser's *Amoretti* VIII: New Manuscript Versions'.
143. See also Cain, *Praise in The Faerie Queene*, chs. 6–7.
144. See Gollancz, 'Spenseriana', p. 101, who makes a similar point.
145. *The Booke of common prayer and administration of the sacraments, and other rites and ceremonies in the Church of England* (London, 1580), 'The forme of the solemnization of Matromonie'. See also Cressy, *Birth, Marriage & Death*, ch. 15.
146. Raymond Jenkins, 'Rosalind in *Colin Clouts come home againe*', *MLN* 67 (1952), 1–5.
147. On the poem's relation to Spenser's own life, see David R. Shore, '*Colin Clouts come home againe*', *Sp. Enc.*, pp. 173–7; Meyer, *Colin Clout*, ch. 6.
148. On the Graces in the poem, see Stella P. Revard, 'Graces', *Sp. Enc.*, pp. 338–9; Gerald Snare, 'Spenser's Fourth Grace', *JWCI* 34 (1971), 350–5.
149. Edwin Greenlaw, 'Spenser's Fairy Mythology', *SP* 15 (1918), 105–22, at 108–9.
150. For details, see Johnson, *Critical Bibliography*, pp. 30–1; Patrick Cheney, '*Colin Clouts come home againe, Astrophel*, and *The Doleful Lay of Clorinda* (1595)', *Sp. Handbook*, pp. 237–55.
151. *ODNB* entry on Essex by Paul E. J. Hammer.
152. Spenser, *Shorter Poems*, p. 166.
153. Raphael Falco, 'Spenser's "Astrophel" and the Formation of Elizabethan Literary Genealogy', *MP* 91 (1993), 1–25, at 4–5.
154. This might explain the unusual dedicatory letter to the *Fowre Hymnes*.
155. Edmund Spenser, *Colin Clouts come home againe* (London, 1595), sigs. E3ʳ–K4ʳ. On Roydon, see the *ODNB* entry by B. J. Sokol. On the order of the poems see Danielle Clarke, '"In Sort As

She It Sung": Spenser's "Doleful Lay" and the Construction of Female Authorship', *Criticism* 42 (2000), 451–68, at 451.

156. Cheney, '*Colin Clouts come home againe*', *Sp. Handbook*, p. 239.

157. Marotti, *Manuscript, Print, and the English Renaissance Lyric*, pp. 234–5.

158. R. S. (ed.), *The Phoenix Nest* (London, 1595), pp. 1–11; Nicholl, *Cup of News*, p. 120. On the poems in the volume, by Raleigh, Breton, and others, see Michael Rudick, 'The "Ralegh Group" in *The Phoenix Nest*', *SB* 24 (1971), 131–7. Other contributors may have been William Herbert, the Munster planter who held lands to the west of Spenser in Kerry and Thomas Watson, another likely acquaintance: *The Phoenix Nest, 1593*, ed. Hyder Edward Rollins (Cambridge, MA: Harvard University Press, 1931), introd., pp. xviii–ix.

159. Charles Whitworth, 'Thomas Lodge', in Charles C. Whitney (ed.), *Thomas Lodge* (Aldershot: Ashgate, 2011), pp. 23–36, at p. 32.

160. *Collected Works of Mary Sidney Herbert*, i. 123–4; Frederic B. Tromly, 'Lodowick Bryskett's Elegies on Sidney in Spenser's *Astrophel* Volume', *RES* 147 (1986), 384–8, assumes that Bryskett wrote the elegy alone but provides evidence of his collaboration with Spenser.

161. Michael Brennan, *Literary Patronage in The English Renaissance: The Pembroke Family* (London: Routledge, 1988), p. 86.

162. Katherine Duncan-Jones, '*Astrophel*', *Sp. Enc.*, pp. 74–6, at p. 74.

163. Cheney, '*Colin Clouts come home againe*', *Sp. Handbook*, p. 252.

164. L. B., 'A Pastorall Aeglogue Vpon the Death of Sir Philip Sidney Knight', *Colin Clout*, sig. H2ᵛ.

165. Danielle Clarke, '"Signifying, but not sounding": Gender and Paratext in the Complaint Genre', in Smith and Wilson (eds.), *Renaissance Paratexts*, pp. 133–50, at p. 145.

166. Appropriately enough, the poem can now be found in both the works of Mary Sidney and Spenser; Spenser, *Shorter Poems*, pp. 380–4; Spenser, *Shorter Poems*, ed. Oram et al., pp. 578–81; *Variorum*, vii. 186–8; *Collected Works of Mary Sidney Herbert*, i. 119–35. The poem does appear as 'disputed work' in Sidney, but not in Spenser. For arguments for Mary Sidney's authorship, see Beilin, *Redeeming Eve*, pp. 137–9; Kay, *Melodious Tears*, pp. 58–61; Jonathan Goldberg, 'Between Men: Literary History and the Work of Mourning', in Karen Weisman (ed.), *The Oxford Handbook of the Elegy* (Oxford: Oxford University Press, 2010), pp. 498–517, at p. 514; Patricia Pender, 'The Ghost and the Machine in the Sidney Family Corpus', *SEL* 51 (2011), 65–85, at 77.

167. Diane Watt, *Medieval Women's Writing: Works by and for Women in England, 1100–1500* (Cambridge: Polity, 2007), p. 14, *passim*; Elizabeth D. Harvey, *Ventriloquized Voices: Feminist Theory and English Renaissance Texts* (London: Routledge, 1992), ch. 3; Pender, 'Ghost and the Machine', pp. 65–6.

168. William W. Barker, 'Erasmus, Desiderius', *Sp. Enc.*, pp. 251–2; Sidney, *Apology*, p. 101. On the tradition of male appropriation of the female voice, see Harvey, *Ventriloquized Voices*, ch. 2.

169. Wall, *Imprint of Gender*, pp. 260–3; Roy Tommy Eriksen, 'Gascoigne, George', *Sp. Enc.*, p. 325; Louis S. Friedland, 'A Source of Spenser's "The Oak and the Briar"', *PQ* 33 (1954), 222–4 (but see the sceptical assessment of the evidence in Waldo F. McNeir, 'Ariosto's Sospetto, Gascoigne's Suspicion, and Spenser's Malbecco', in Horst Oppel (ed.), *Festschrift Für Walther Fischer* (Heidelberg: Carl Winter, 1959), pp. 34–48).

170. Nelson, *Poetry of Edmund Spenser*, pp. 75, 325; Roy T. Erikson, 'Two into One: The Unity of George Gascoigne's Companion Poems', *SP* 81 (1984), 275–98.

171. *The Works in Verse and Prose of Nicholas Breton*, ed. Alexander B. Grosart, 2 vols. (1879; New York: AMS Press, 1966), i. 21–8, 2–15; Beilin, *Redeeming Eve*, p. 127; Jean Robertson, 'Nicholas Breton's Authorship of "Marie Magdalens Loue" and "The Passion of a Discontented Minde"', *MLR* 36 (1941), 449–59.

172. Jean Robertson, '*The Passions of the Spirit* (1599) and Nicholas Breton', *HLQ* 3 (1939), 69–75; Michael G. Brennan, 'Nicholas Breton's *The Passions of the Spirit* and the Countess of Pembroke', *RES* 38 (1987), 221–5.

173. Herbert David Rix, 'Spenser's Rhetoric and the "Doleful Lay"', *MLN* 53 (1938), 261–5; Percy W. Long, 'Spenseriana: The Lay of Clorinda', *MLN* 31 (1916), 79–82; Charles G. Osgood, 'The "Doleful Lay of Clorinda"', *MLN* 35 (1920), 90–6.

174. Pamela Coren, 'Edmund Spenser, Mary Sidney, and the *Doleful Lay*', *SEL* 42 (2002), 25–41, at 39. For a claim that the two writers did cooperate, see Gary F. Waller, *Mary Sidney, Countess of Pembroke: A Critical Study of Her Writings and Literary Milieu* (Salzburg: Salzburg University Press, 1979), p. 92.

175. L. B., 'The Mourning Muse of Thestylis', *Colin Clout*, sig. H1^r.

176. Clarke, '"In Sort As She It Sung"', p. 451.

177. *Collected Works of Mary Sidney Herbert*, i. 125. On Mary Sidney's role in publishing her brother's works, see Duncan-Jones, *Sidney*, pp. 277–8; Marion Wynne-Davies, '"For *Worth*, Not Weakness, Makes in Use but One": Literary Dialogues in an English Renaissance Family', in Clarke and Clarke (eds.), *'This Double Voice'*, pp. 164–84.

178. Anne Lake Prescott, 'The Countess of Pembroke's Ruins of Rome', *SJ* 23 (2005), 1–17; Beilin, *Redeeming Eve*, p. 141.

179. Kerrigan (ed.), *Motives of Woe*.

180. Clarke, '"In Sort As She It Sung"', p. 461.

181. Marotti, *Manuscript, Print, and the English Renaissance Lyric*, pp. 312–13; Germaine Warkentin, 'Patrons and Profiteers: Thomas Newman and the "Violent Enlargement" of *Astrophil and Stella*', *Book Collector* 34 (1985), 461–87, at 464–5.

182. Kay, *Melodious Tears*, p. 54.

183. Cheney, '*Colin Clouts come home againe*', *Sp. Handbook*, p. 248.

184. Quintilian, *The Orator's Education*, trans. Donald A. Russell, 4 vols. (Cambridge, MA: Harvard University Press, 2001), IV.i.63, at i.41; Jonathan Culler, 'Apostrophe', in *The Pursuit of Signs: Semiotics, Literature, Deconstruction* (London: Routledge, 1981), pp. 135–54, at p. 135.

185. Brian Vickers, *In Defence of Rhetoric* (Oxford: Clarendon Press, 1988), p. 493.

186. Montrose, 'Spenser and the Elizabethan Political Imaginary'.

187. On Sidney's reputation, see Falco, 'Spenser's "Astrophel"'; Raphael Falco, 'Instant Artefacts: Vernacular Elegies for Philip Sidney', *SP* 89 (1992), 1–19. More generally, see Jan Van Dorsten, Domini Baker-Smith, and Arthur F. Kinney (eds.), *Sir Philip Sidney: 1586 and the Creation of a Legend* (Leiden: Brill, 1986); Alexander, *Writing After Sidney*.

188. Clarke, '"In Sort As She It Sung"', p. 460.

189. Falco, 'Instant Artefacts', p. 1.

190. On the poem's ambivalent assessment of Sidney's achievements, see Lisa M. Klein, 'Spenser's *Astrophel* and the Sidney Legend', *SJ* 12/2 (1993), 42–55; Theodore L. Steinberg, 'Spenser, Sidney, and the Myth of Astrophel', *Sp. St.* 18 (1990, pub. 1994), 187–201. On Spenser's use of Adonis, see Alexander, *Writing After Sidney*, p. 70.

191. For evidence of specific responses to each other's work, see Patrick Cheney, 'Perdita, Pastorella, and the Romance of Literary Form: Shakespeare's Counter-Spenserian Authorship', in J. B. Lethbridge (ed.), *Shakespeare and Spenser: Attractive Opposites* (Manchester: Manchester University Press, 2008), pp. 121–42; Hadfield, 'Spenser's Rosalind'.

192. On the concept of 'waste', see pp. 202–3.

193. See Hadfield, *Spenser's Irish Experience*, ch. 5.

194. R. B. Wernham, *Before the Armada: The Growth of English Foreign Policy, 1485–1588* (London: Cape, 1966), p. 193; Manning, *Apprenticeship in Arms*, p. 35.

195. Anne Lake Prescott, 'Belge', *Sp. Enc.*, pp. 82–3.

196. In contrast to the representation of Sidney as a martial hero in Roydon's poem: Spenser, *Colin Clout*, I4^v; Falco, 'Instant Artefacts', pp. 17–18.

197. Falco, 'Spenser's "Astrophel"', p. 12.

198. On Spenser's later reputation and identity, see, in particular, Michelle O'Callaghan, *The 'Shepheardes Nation': Jacobean Spenserians and Early Stuart Political Culture, 1612–1625* (Oxford: Clarendon Press, 2000).

199. On Penelope Devereux, see the *ODNB* entry by Alison Wall; Freedman, *Poor Penelope*, chs. 9–15.

200. Walter G. Friedrich, 'The Stella of *Astrophel*', *ELH* 3 (1936), 114–39.
201. Kerrigan (ed.), *Motives of Woe*, chs. 5–7.
202. Falco, 'Spenser's "Astrophel"', p. 20.

Chapter 10

1. Attempts have been made to suggest that Spenser's authorship of *A View* is in doubt, as there is no manuscript that bears his name, only the initials 'E. S.': see Jean R. Brink, 'Constructing the *View of the Present State of Ireland*', *Sp. St.* 11 (1994), 203–28, at 216–23; Cannio, 'Reconstructing Lord Grey's Reputation'. However, the volume of evidence that Spenser wrote the dialogue is overwhelming. To cite just part of the case: Spenser's grandson thought that he wrote it, as he argued to Cromwell (see pp. 410–11); a contemporary, William Scott, also attributed *A View* to Spenser in his manuscript treatise, *The Modell of Poesye* (*c.*1599) (BL Add. MS 81083, fo. 10ʳ, where he cites Spenser as an authority on bards in Ireland (I am extremely grateful to Gavin Alexander for pointing this out to me)); it was entered into the Stationers' Register by Matthew Lownes, who also had access to other Spenser manuscripts, as he published 'Two Cantos of Mutabilitie'; the first print edition by Sir James Ware was almost certainly based on a manuscript he acquired from Archbishop James Ussher, whose father worked with Spenser in Dublin; the 'Dialogue of Sylvanus and Peregrine', which might have been written by Spenser's neighbour in Munster, Hugh Cuffe, would then have to be seen as a case of mistaken identity with its author falsely imagining that Spenser wrote *A View*; and, perhaps most important of all, *A View* looks as if it were written by Spenser as it contains a number of characteristic puns (e.g., savage/salvage) also found elsewhere in his work, and its argument resembles that of parts of *The Faerie Queene*, as well as the documents he brought over from Ireland in Dec. 1598. See Andrew Hadfield, 'Certainties and Uncertainties: By Way of Response to Jean Brink', *Sp. St.* 12 (1995), 197–202.
2. Alan Bliss, 'The English Language in Early Modern Ireland', in Moody et al. (eds.), *New History of Ireland*, ii. 546–60, at p. 557.
3. Anne Laurence, 'The Cradle to the Grave: English Observations of Irish Social Customs in the Seventeenth Century', *Seventeenth Century* 3 (1988), 63–84, at 75–8.
4. Valerie Fildes, *Wet Nursing: A History from Antiquity to the Present* (Oxford: Blackwell, 1988), pp. 73–4; Patricia Crawford, '"The Sucking Child": Adult Attitudes to Child Care in the First Year of Life in Seventeenth-Century England', *Continuity and Change* 1 (1986), 23–51, at 31–2.
5. See Hadfield and McVeagh (eds.), *Strangers to that Land*, ch. 3.
6. Nicholas Canny argues that the earl of Cork sent his children out to be suckled by Irish wet nurses, which is why they spoke such good Irish: *Upstart Earl*, pp. 126–7. It is possible that English families were more prepared to do this in the early 17th century.
7. Mendelson and Crawford, *Women in Early Modern England*, pp. 154–6.
8. Fildes, *Wet Nursing*, pp. 79–81. This was a European phenomenon: see e.g. John A. Najemy, *A History of Florence, 1200–1575* (Oxford: Blackwell, 2006), pp. 239–41.
9. Linda Campbell, 'Wet-Nurses in Early Modern England: Some Evidence from the Thownshed Archive', *Medical History* 33 (1989), 360–70, at 364.
10. Ibid. 365, 369. See also Fiona Newell, 'Wet Nursing and Child Care in Aldenham, Hertfordshire, 1595–1726: Some Evidence on the Circumstances and Effects of Seventeenth-Century Child Rearing Practices', in Fildes (ed.), *Women as Mothers*, pp. 122–38.
11. Ralph Josselin's wife, Jane, breastfed her children, a factor which influenced her fertility cycle: Macfarlane, *Family Life of Ralph Josselin*, app. A, pp. 199–204.
12. Alison Sim, *The Tudor Housewife* (Stroud: Sutton, 1996), p. 26; Robert Cleaver, *A Godly Form of Household Gouernment* (London, 1598), pp. 231–5. I owe this last reference to Amy Kenny. See also Fildes, *Wet Nursing*, p. 68; Crawford, '"The Sucking Child"', p. 31.
13. Fildes, *Wet Nursing*, pp. 83–4; Campbell, 'Wet-Nurses in Early Modern England', p. 367.
14. Houlbrooke, *English Family*, p. 134.
15. See pp. 219–20.

16. Hoby, *The Private Life of an Elizabethan Lady*; *Diaries of Lady Anne Clifford*. See also Greer, *Shakespeare's Wife*, chs. 7–10.
17. Descriptions of marriage can be found in Houlbrooke, *English Family*, ch. 5; Mendelson and Crawford, *Women in Early Modern England*, pp. 126–48. See also Tusser, *Fiue Hundred Points of Good Husbandrie*, pp. 65–77, 'The points of Huswiferie, vnited to the comfort of Husbandrie', an account that includes general and specific advice, including recipes for cakes.
18. Cleaver, *Household Gouernment*, pp. 243–6.
19. Houlbrooke, *English Family*, p. 96.
20. On Spenser and marriage, see Laurence Lerner, 'Marriage', *Sp. Enc.*, pp. 454–5; Hadfield, 'Secrets and Lies', pp. 72–3. Spenser does discuss the relationship between children, continuity, and fame: see Cheney, *Spenser's Famous Flight*, p. 194; Ricardo J. Quinones, *The Renaissance Discovery of Time* (Cambridge, MA: Harvard University Press, 1972), pp. 245–6.
21. Carol V. Kaske, 'Amavia, Mortdant, Ruddymane', *Sp. Enc.*, pp. 25–7; Carol V. Kaske, '"Religious Reuerence Doth Buriall Teene": Christian and Pagan in *The Faerie Queene*, II, 1–3', *RES* 30 (1979), 129–43; Brooks-Davies, *Spenser's Faerie Queene*, pp. 118–33.
22. Houlbrooke, *English Family*, p. 111.
23. Carol V. Kaske, 'Bible', *Sp. Enc.*, pp. 87–90.
24. *Chronology*, p. 67; *Stationers*, iii. 34.
25. Bennett, *Evolution of 'The Faerie Queene'*, ch. 14.
26. Spenser, *Faerie Queene*, p. 716; Maurice Hunt, 'Hellish Work in *The Faerie Queene*, *SEL* 41 (2001), 91–108, at 96.
27. For discussion, see Edmund Spenser, *The Faerie Queene: Book Six and Mutabilitie Cantos*, ed. Andrew Hadfield and Abraham Stoll (Indianapolis: Hackett, 2007), introd., pp. vii–x.
28. Hadfield, *Spenser's Irish Experience*, ch. 5.
29. Spenser, *Faerie Queene*, p. 714.
30. See Richard Neuse, 'Book VI as Conclusion to *The Faerie Queene*', *ELH* 35 (1968), 329–53.
31. Bednarz, 'Ralegh in Spenser's Historical Allegory'; Jerry Leath Mills, 'Raleigh, Walter', *Sp. Enc.*, pp. 584–5; O'Connell, *Mirror and Veil*, pp. 110–22.
32. Spenser, *Faerie Queene*, p. 27.
33. Armitage, *Ideological Origins of the British Empire*, p. 53.
34. Johnson, *Critical Bibliography*, p. 19; Edmund Spenser, *The Faerie Queene Disposed into twelue bookes, fashioning XII. morall vertues* (London, 1596), pp. 589–90.
35. Johnson, *Critical Bibliography*, pp. 13–18; Scott-Warren, 'Unannotating Spenser'; Edmund Spenser, *The Faerie Queene Disposed into twelue books, fashioning XII. morall vertues* (London, 1590).
36. Frank B. Evans, 'The Printing of Spenser's *Faerie Queene* in 1596', *SB* 18 (1965), 50–69, esp. 65–7.
37. For a summary of the 2nd edition of the poem, see Andrew Hadfield, '*The Faerie Queene*, Books IV–VII', in Hadfield (ed.), *Cambridge Companion to Spenser*, pp. 124–42.
38. Danner, *Furious Muse*, ch. 1. See also Anne K. Tuell, 'The Original End of *Faerie Queene*, Book III', *MLN* 36 (1921), 309–11.
39. An analytical overview can be found in James Norhnberg, '*The Faerie Queene*, Book IV', *Sp. Enc.*, pp. 273–80, and a reading of the book in Jonathan Goldberg, *Endlesse Worke: Spenser and the Structures of Discourse* (Baltimore: Johns Hopkins University Press, 1981). See also David R. Pichaske, '*The Faerie Queene* IV. ii and iii: Spenser and the Genesis of Friendship', *SEL* 17 (1977), 81–93.
40. As Frank Covington pointed out, Spenser may have been indebted to a Latin poem by Alexander Neckham for his representation of the Irish rivers. Neckham's work was known to Camden: see 'Spenser and Alexander Neckham', *SP* 22 (1925), 222–5.
41. On Spenser's rivers, see Joyce, 'Spenser's Irish Rivers'; Judson, *Spenser in Southern Ireland*; W. H. Grattan Flood, 'Identification of the Spenserian "Aubrian" River', *JCHAS* 22 (1916), 143–4; Smith, 'Spenser's "Stony Aubrian"'.
42. Norhnberg, '*Faerie Queene*, Book IV', p. 273.
43. Ibid.

44. Patrick Cheney, 'Spenser's Completion of *The Squire's Tale*: Love, Magic, and Heroic Action in the Legend of Cambell and Triamond', *Journal of Medieval and Renaissance Studies* 15 (1985), 135–55.

45. Harry Berger, Jr, 'Two Spenserian Retrospects: The Antique Temple of Venus and the Primitive Marriage of Rovers', in *Revisionary Play: Studies in the Spenserian Dynamics* (Berkeley and Los Angeles: University of California Press, 1988), pp. 195–214.

46. Silberman, *Transforming Desire*, pp. 117–24; Susumu Kawanishi, 'Lust', *Sp. Enc.*, pp. 442–3.

47. Hadfield, *Spenser's Irish Experience*, pp. 138–40.

48. Lewis, *Allegory of Love*, p. 347.

49. McCabe, *Spenser's Monstrous Regiment*, pp. 90–3.

50. McCabe, 'The Fate of Irena'.

51. For discussion, see Humphrey Tonkin, *Spenser's Courteous Pastoral: Book VI of The Faerie Queene* (Oxford: Oxford University Press, 1972), ch. 3. For a different reading, which compares Calidore's stay to that of the Red-Cross Knight in the House of Holiness, see Arnold Williams, *Flower on a Lowly Stalk: The Sixth Book of The Faerie Queene* (East Lansing: Michigan State University Press, 1967), p. 57.

52. Jane Aptekar, *Icons of Justice: Iconography and Thematic Imagery in Book V of The Faerie Queene* (New York: Columbia University Press, 1969), pp. 80, 114, 155. For the general context, see William Palmer, *The Problem of Ireland in Tudor Foreign Policy, 1485–1603* (Woodbridge: Boydell, 1994), chs. 7–8.

53. Although Book VI also provides some important qualifications of the brutal, potentially tyrannical, masculine military world in Book V, reminding readers of the importance of virtues associated with women, such as mercy and pity: see John D. Staines, 'Pity and the Authority of Feminine Passions in Books V and VI of *The Faerie Queene*', *Sp. St.* 25 (2010), 129–61.

54. See further analysis of these stanzas, p. 171.

55. Falls, *Elizabeth's Irish Wars*, pp. 72, 182; Morgan, *Tyrone's Rebellion*, pp. 173–4.

56. Moody et al. (eds.), *New History of Ireland*, viii. 217–18.

57. Ibid. 218.

58. On the Babington Plot, see John Guy, *Tudor England* (Oxford: Oxford University Press, 1988), pp. 334–5; Jayne Elizabeth Lewis, *The Trial of Mary Queen of Scots: A Brief History with Documents* (Boston: Bedford/St Martin's, 1999), pp. 93–107.

59. *CSPS, 1595–7*, p. 288.

60. Ibid. 291.

61. On the process of licensing books in England, see Clegg, *Press Censorship in Elizabethan England*, pt. 1. James falsely imagines that texts were all approved by the crown authorities.

62. *CSPS, 1589–1603*, p. 747.

63. Andrew Hadfield, '"Bruited Abroad": John White's and Thomas Harriot's Colonial Representations of Ancient Britain', in David Baker and Willy Maley (eds.), *British Identities and English Renaissance Literature* (Cambridge: Cambridge University Press, 2002), pp. 159–77, at p. 174.

64. For analysis, see McCabe, 'Masks of Duessa'; Andrew Hadfield, 'Spenser and the Stuart Succession', *Literature and History* 13/1 (Spring 2004), 9–24.

65. For analysis, see, pp. 194–5.

66. Jeffries, *Irish Church*, p. 276. Such opposition may have been aimed at James's Protestantism rather than his Catholic origins.

67. Maley, *Salvaging Spenser*, ch. 7; Nicholas Canny, 'Poetry as Politics: A View of the Present State of *The Faerie Queene*', in Morgan (ed.), *Political Ideology in Ireland*, pp. 110–26, at pp. 122–3.

68. Spenser, *Shorter Poems*, p. 452; Welply, 'Spenser: Recent Researches', pp. 184–5.

69. Rudolf Gottfried, 'The Date of Spenser's *View*', *MLN* 52 (1937), 176–80; Ray Heffner, 'Spenser's *View of Ireland*: Some Observations', *MLQ* 3 (1942), 507–15; *Variorum*, x. 503–5.

70. *CSPI, 1592–5*, p. 421; *CSPI, 1596–7*, pp. 230, 233, 480.

71. For analysis, see W. C. Martin, 'The Date and Purpose of Spenser's *View*', *PMLA* 47 (1932), 137–43; Rudolf B. Gottfried, 'Spenser's *View* and Essex', *PMLA* 52 (1937), 645–51.

72. Robert Lacey, *Robert, Earl of Essex: An Elizabethan Icarus* (London: Weidenfeld and Nicolson, 1970), pp. 150–64.
73. *Variorum*, x. 228.
74. Paul E. J. Hammer, 'Patronage at Court, Faction and the Earl of Essex', in Guy (ed.), *Reign of Elizabeth I*, pp. 65–86, at p. 83.
75. Hammer, *Polarisation of Elizabethan Politics*, ch. 7.
76. Lacey, *Ralegh*, pp. 249–60.
77. Nicholls and Williams, *Ralegh*, pp. 121–3.
78. On Essex's disastrous campaign, see Lennon, *Sixteenth-Century Ireland*, pp. 297–9; Ellis, *Tudor Ireland*, pp. 306–7.
79. *Variorum*, x. 43–4.
80. Andrew Hadfield, 'The Name "Eudoxus" in Spenser's *View*', *N&Q* 242 (Dec. 1997), 477–8; Fogarty, 'Literature in English', p. 154.
81. Bodleian Library, MS Rawlinson B.478. This was the manuscript used in W. L. Renwick's edition of *A View* (1934; Oxford: Clarendon Press, 1970).
82. *The Records of the Honourable Society of Lincoln's Inn: The Black Books*, 6 vols. (London: Lincoln's Inn, 1897–2001), ii. 39; Galbraith, 'Spenser and the History of the Book', p. 188.
83. Elizabeth Fowler, '*A Vewe of the Present State of Ireland* (1596, 1633)', *Sp. Handbook*, pp. 314–32, at p. 325.
84. Louis A. Knalfa, 'Mr. Secretary Donne: The Years with Sir Thomas Egerton', in Colclough (ed.), *John Donne's Professional Lives*, pp. 37–72, at pp. 44, 51–2.
85. Nicholl, *Cup of News*, p. 207.
86. BL Add. MS 22022; *Variorum*, x. 514.
87. TNA PRO SP 63, 202, pt. 4, item 58; *CSPI, 1598–9*, p. 431.
88. *Variorum*, x. 506. On Egerton, see *ODNB* entry by J. H. Baker.
89. TCD MS 589, fos. 68, 69. There are a number of discrepancies between the manuscript and the printed text which indicate that this text may not have been the one Ware used to print *A View* in 1633, pointing us to another copy, which may or may not be extant: *Variorum*, x. 516–17; Johnson, *Critical Bibliography*, pp. 49–53.
90. Lambeth Palace, MS 510.
91. Bruce Avery, 'Mapping the Irish Other: Spenser's *A View of the Present State of Ireland*', *ELH* 57 (1990), 263–79; John Breen, 'The Empirical Eye: Edmund Spenser's *A View of the Present State of Ireland*', *Irish Review* 16 (Autumn/Winter 1994), 44–52; Henry S. Turner, 'Literature and Mapping in Early Modern England, 1520–1688', in Woodward (ed.), *History of Cartography*, iii/1. 412–26, at p. 415; Pauline Moffitt Watts, 'The European Religious Worldview and Its Influence on Mapping', in Woodward (ed.), *History of Cartography*, iii/1. 382–400.
92. *Variorum*, x. 512.
93. NLI MS 661 (Gurney MS); Gonville and Caius College, Cambridge, MS 188.221; Beinecke Library, Yale, Osborn MS fa.12; TNA PRO SP 63, 202, 4, 58. The Beinecke copy is in six hands. It belonged to the herald Sir Henry St George (1581–1644), who had a link to William Camden (see *ODNB* entry by Thomas Woodcock) (personal communication from Kathryn James).
94. Folger MS V.b.214. *A View* is copied out from sig. 136^r–193^r. For comment, see James McManaway, 'Elizabeth, Essex, and James', in Herbert Davis and Helen Gardner (eds.), *Elizabethan and Jacobean Studies: Presented to Frank Percy Wilson in Honour of His Seventieth Birthday* (Oxford: Clarendon Press, 1959), pp. 219–30; Pierre Lefranc, 'Ralegh in 1596 and 1603: Three Unprinted Letters in the Huntington Library', *HLQ* 29 (1966), 337–45.
95. For comment, see Heaton, *Writing and Reading Royal Entertainments*, pp. 86–9.
96. McManaway, 'Elizabeth, Essex, and James', p. 221. The Folger text appears to have been copied from the Beinecke text, which, in turn, derives from the Gonville and Caius manuscript.
97. 'A View of the Present State of Ireland', Castle Howard archives. A study of the manuscript, and how it passed into the hands of the northern branch of the Howard family, is currently being prepared by the Castle curator, Dr Christopher Ridgway. I am extremely grateful to Dr Ridgway for sharing his findings with me.

98. Vine, *In Defiance of Time*, pp. 72–3.
99. Bodleian Library, MS Gough Ireland 2, fos. 16ʳ, 17ʳ, 30ʳ.
100. Heffner, 'Spenser's *View*', pp. 509–11; Joseph Loewenstein, 'Spenser's Textual History', *Sp. Handbook*, pp. 637–63, at p. 646.
101. BL MS Sloane 1695.
102. BL MS Harley 1932.
103. BL MS Harley 7388.
104. Other copies include the two in Cambridge University Library, Dd.10.60 and Dd.14.28.1, the first in a number of hands following on from each other, suggesting that this was another copy produced in a scriptorium, produced in relay; the second bound together with a number of 17th-century texts, including a treatise by Sir Robert Cotton, a journal of the House of Commons for July 1643, and several parliamentary speeches, suggesting that a reader in the 1640s wanted to read *A View* alongside events in England, undoubtedly connected to the trial of the earl of Strafford.
105. See e.g. Anon., 'The Supplication of the blood of the English, most lamentably murdred in Ireland, Cryeng out of the yearth for revenge, *c*.1598' [BL Add. MS 34313, fos. 85–121], ed. Willy Maley, *Analecta Hibernica*, 36 (1994), 3–91, a work that may have been composed in one sitting.
106. *Variorum*, x. 230–1. On the nature of a dialogue's conclusion, see Virginia Cox, *The Renaissance Dialogue: Literary Dialogue in Its Social and Political Contexts, Castiglione to Galileo* (Cambridge: Cambridge University Press, 1992), pp. 99–113; Jon R. Snyder, *Writing the Scene of Speaking: Theories of Dialogue in the Late Italian Renaissance* (Stanford: Stanford University Press, 1989), pp. 1–38.
107. See e.g. Smith, 'Irish Background of Spenser's View'; Clare Carroll, 'Spenser and the Irish Language: The Sons of Milesio in *A View of the Present State of Ireland, The Faerie Queene*, Book V, and the *Leabhar Gabhála*', *IUR: Spenser in Ireland, 1596–1996*, ed. Anne Fogarty (Autumn/Winter 1996), 281–90.
108. Brink, 'Constructing the *View of the Present State of Ireland*', p. 223.
109. Ware (ed.), *Historie of Ireland*; Hadfield, 'Historical Writing, 1550–1660', pp. 255–7. See also Alan Ford, 'The Irish Historical Renaissance and the Shaping of Protestant History', in Ford and McCafferty (eds.), *Origins of Sectarianism*, pp. 127–57.
110. *Variorum*, x. 155–6.
111. Canny, *Making Ireland British*, ch. 4. See also Herbert F. Hore, 'Woods and Fastnesses, and Their Denizens, in Ancient Leinster', *Journal of the Kilkenny and South-East of Ireland Archaeological Society*, NS 1 (1856), 229–40, at 232; A. C. Forbes, 'Some Legendary and Historical References to Irish Woods, and Their Significance', *PRIA*, sect. B, 41 (1932–3), 15–36, at 26–7.
112. Anon., '"A Discourse of Ireland" (circa 1599): A Sidelight on English Colonial Policy', *PRIA* 47 (1941–2), 151–66, at 166; see also Smyth, *Map-Making, Landscapes and Memory*, p. 126.
113. *Variorum*, x. 158.
114. For another version of Spenser's logic in *A View*, see Willy Maley, '"This ripping of auncestours": The Ethnographic Present in Spenser's *A View of the State of Ireland*', in Philippa Berry and Margaret Tudeau-Clayton (eds.), *Textures of Renaissance Knowledge* (Manchester: Manchester University Press, 2003), pp. 117–34.
115. Brady, 'Spenser's Irish Crisis', p. 41; Avery, 'Mapping the Irish Other', pp. 263, 277; Hadfield, *Spenser's Irish Experience*, ch. 2.
116. *Variorum*, x. 138; McEachern, 'Spenser and Religion', *Sp. Handbook*, pp. 30–47, at p. 40.
117. Hadfield and McVeagh (eds.), *'Strangers to that Land'*, pp. 44–7.
118. Canny, *Making Ireland British*, ch. 1.
119. Brian Jackson, 'The Construction of Argument: Henry Fitzsimon, John Rider and Religious Controversy in Dublin, 1599–1614', in Ciaran Brady and Jane Ohlmeyer (eds.), *British Interventions in Early Modern Ireland* (Cambridge: Cambridge University Press, 2005), pp. 97–115.
120. Fraunce, *Arcadian Rhetorike*. Trinity College Dublin, founded in 1592, was notable for the Ramist character of its curriculum: Alan Ford, '"That Bugbear Armenianism": Archbishop Laud and Trinity College, Dublin', in Brady and Ohlmeyer (eds.), *British Interventions in Early Modern Ireland*, pp. 135–60, at p. 154.

121. For analysis, see David J. Baker, '"Some Quirk, Some Subtle Evasion": Legal Subversion in Spenser's *A View of the Present State of Ireland*', *Sp. St.* 6 (1986), 147–63; Ciaran Brady, 'The Road to the View: On the Decline of Reform Thought in Tudor Ireland', in Coughlan (ed.), *Spenser and Ireland*, pp. 25–45; Fowler, 'Failure of Moral Philosophy'.

122. See also Fowler, *Literary Character*, p. 190.

123. *Variorum*, x. 149. For analysis of Spenser's military proposals, see Brendan Bradshaw, 'Robe and Sword in the Conquest of Ireland', in Clare Cross, David Loades, and J. J. Scarisbrick (eds.), *Law and Government under the Tudors: Essays Presented to Sir Geoffrey Elton on His Retirement* (Cambridge: Cambridge University Press, 1988), pp. 139–62; Brady, 'Spenser's Irish Crisis'.

124. Phil Withington, '"For This Is True Or Els I Do Lye": Thomas Smith, William Bullein, and Mid-Tudor Dialogue', in Michael Pincombe and Cathy Shrank (eds.), *The Oxford Handbook of Tudor Literature, 1485–1603* (Oxford: Oxford University Press, 2009), pp. 455–71; Richards, *Rhetoric and Courtliness*.

125. Spenser, *Faerie Queene*, pp. 716–17.

126. Much of the following paragraphs rely on work I did with Mr Simon Healy of the History of Parliament Trust. I am extremely grateful to Mr Healy for his cooperation with me and for his expertise about Chancery records in particular.

127. Will of Stephen Boyle, gentleman of Bradden, Northamptonshire, 8 Oct. 1582 (TNA PROB 11/64); Welply, 'Spenser: Some New Discoveries', pp. 445–6.

128. On the Lucies, see the *ODNB* entry on Thomas Lucy (*c.*1532–1600), by Robert Bearman; on Knightley, see *Alumni Oxonienses*, ii. 864; Dugdale, *Antiquities of Warwickshire*, pp. 210, 291, 403.

129. TNA PRO C2 Eliz. S1/40; recorded in *Calendars of the Proceedings in Chancery in the Reign of Queen Elizabeth*, iii (1832), p. 4.

130. TNA PROB 11/64.

131. *Alumni Oxonienses*, ii. 462.

132. TNA PRO, IPM for Thomas Emelye, 15 Sept. 1608.

133. Joseph Foster, *The Register of Admissions to Gray's Inn, 1521–1889, together with the register of marriages in Gray's Inn Chapel, 1695–1754* (London: privately printed, 1889), p. 45.

134. Reginald J. Fletcher (ed.), *The Pension Book of Gray's Inn*, 2 vols. (London: Chiswick Press, 1901–10), i. *1569–1669*, pp. 63, 99.

135. *Acts of the Privy Council, 1591–2*, p. 299.

136. *Acts of the Privy Council, 1590–1*, p. 224.

137. Horwitz, *Chancery Equity Records*, pp. 31–6.

138. BL Add. MS 19837, fo. 70; Welply, 'Spenser: Recent Researches', pp. 149–50.

139. Welply, 'Spenser: Recent Researches', pp. 149–50.

140. *CSPI, 1588–92*, pp. 554, 568, 578.

141. Pilip Ó Mórdha, 'Early History of Modern Clones', *Clogher Record* 16 (1997), 95–100, at 95; Ranger, 'Richard Boyle', p. 277.

142. *Variorum*, x. 163.

143. For further discussion, see Gillespie and Hadfield, 'Edmund Spenser in Chancery Disputes'.

144. Huntington Library, Ellesmere MS 7014. Panton, appears to have owned both this copy and Bodleian Library, MS Rawlinson B.478, further demonstrating Egerton's links to that work: *Variorum*, x. 511–12.

145. For details of the case, see Welply, 'Spenser: Recent Researches', pp. 184–6.

146. Felicity Heal and Clive Holmes, *The Gentry in England and Wales, 1500–1700* (Basingstoke: Macmillan, 1994), pp. 81–91.

147. Brink, 'Documenting Edmund Spenser'; Henley, *Spenser in Ireland*, pp. 194–5.

148. The Ferdinando Freckleton who was buried in Bermondsey, Surrey, on 2 May 1596, must have been a minor, as the record in the church register indicates: 'ffernando the sonne of James Freckleton'. He was undoubtedly a relative of Spenser's father-in-law: Adams, 'Ferdinando Freckleton'; Anon., *The Registers of Saint Mary Magdalene, Bermondsey, 1548–1609* (London, 1894), p. 157. See also Douglas Hamer, 'Captain Sir Ferdinando Freckleton', p. 231.

149. TNA PROB 11/109; Hamer, 'Captain Sir Ferdinando Freckleton', p. 209; Erne, *Beyond The Spanish Tragedy*, pp. 127–8. On Puckering see the *ODNB* entry by N. G. Jones. The will of John Freckleton confirms the relationship, as Puckering's son, also Sir Thomas, proved the document, and, once his familial and charity obligations were discharged, John left the remainder of his goods to Sir Thomas: TNA PROB 11/143 fos. 130ᵛ–131. The will further confirms that the family had means.

150. Hamer, 'Captain Sir Ferdinando Freckleton', p. 209.

151. Richard Tarlton, *Tarleton's Tragical Treatises, contaynyng sundrie discourses and pretty conceytes, both in prose and verse* (London, 1578), sig. A4ᵛ. The volume, which survives in a single copy in the Folger Shakespeare Library, is incomplete, only the prefatory sections surviving. Freckleton's reference to his ability to keep a secret in the last line suggests that he may have been eager to secure a position as a secretary: Rambuss, *Spenser's Secret Career*, ch. 1.

152. On Tarlton, see the *ODNB* entry by Peter Thomson. On Tarlton and the Nashe–Harvey quarrel, see Stern, *Harvey*, pp. 70, 93–4; Nashe, *Works*, i. 188, 197, 215, *passim*.

153. *Acts of the Privy Council* (1596–7), pp. 242, 252.

154. Hamer, 'Captain Sir Ferdinando Freckleton', pp. 209–10.

155. See *Carew, 1601–3*, pp. 93, 397. I owe this reference to John McGurk.

156. Dugdale, *Antiquities of Warwickshire*, p. 479; *Victoria County History: Warwickshire*, iii. 82.

157. Hamer, 'Captain Sir Ferdinando Freckleton', p. 210.

158. Jospeh Hunter, cited in Strathmann, 'Freckleton', p. 543.

159. Heffner, 'Spenser's Family', p. 82; Battiscombe, *The Spencers of Althorp*, pp. 11–14.

160. *ODNB* entry.

161. Stubbes, *Donne*, pp. 89–91.

162. On Greenwich Palace, see Young, *Tudor and Jacobean Tournaments*, pp. 108–9; Judson, *Life*, p. 187.

163. Nichols, *Progresses*, iii. 398–407.

164. Anne Lake Prescott, 'Burbon', *Sp. Enc.*, p. 121; Bennett, *Evolution of 'The Faerie Queene'*, ch. 15; James Emerson Phillips, 'Renaissance Concepts of Justice and the Structure of *The Faerie Queene*', *HLQ* 33 (1969–70), 103–20.

165. Sears Jayne, 'Ficino and the Platonism of the English Renaissance', *CL* 4 (1952), 214–38; Jefferson B. Fletcher, 'Benivieni's "Ode of Love" and Spenser's "Fowre Hymnes"', *MP* 8 (1911), 545–60. See also Edgar Wind, *Pagan Mysteries in the Renaissance* (London: Faber, 1967), pp. 27–35.

166. It is worth noting that Harvey was 'one of the few Elizabethans who remembered Dante for the *Commedia* rather than for the conveniently anti-papal *De Monarchia*': 'Some New Marginalia', p. 403.

167. Philip B. Rollinson, 'A Generic View of Spenser's *Four Hymns*', *SP* 68 (1971), 292–304.

168. See esp. Cheney, *Spenser's Famous Flight*, ch. 5. See also Elizabeth Bieman, '*Fowre Hymnes*', *Sp. Enc.*, pp. 315–17; Josephine Waters Bennett, 'The Theme of Spenser's *Fowre Hymnes*', *SP* 28 (1931), 18–57; Frederick Morgan Padleford, 'Spenser's *Fowre Hymnes*: A Resurvey', *SP* 29 (1932), 207–32; Jon Quitslund, 'Thinking About Thinking in the *Fowre Hymnes*', in Borris et al (eds.), *Spenser and Platonism*, pp. 499–517.

169. *FQ*, Book IV, proem, i; McCabe, 'Authorial Self-Presentation', p. 478.

170. Alison Shell, *Catholicism, Controversy and the English Literary Imagination, 1558–1660* (Cambridge: Cambridge University Press, 1999), pp. 74–6.

171. Terry Comito, 'A Dialectic of Images in Spenser's *Fowre Hymnes*', *SP* 74 (1977), 301–21, at 301.

172. See p. 47.

173. Edmund Spenser, *Fowre Hymnes* (London, 1596).

174. Einar Bjorvand, 'Spenser's Defence of Poetry: Some Structural Aspects of the *Fowre Hymnes*', in Maren-Sofie Røstvig (ed.), *Fair Forms: Essays in English Literature from Spenser to Jane Austen* (Cambridge: Brewer, 1975), pp. 13–53, at p. 26; Johnson, *Critical Bibliography*, pp. 31–2.

175. For speculations about the revision of the *Hymns*, see Bennett, 'Theme of Spenser's *Fowre Hymnes*', pp. 49–57, who takes the letter at face value, as I do; for an argument for a late date, see Bjorvand, 'Spenser's Defence of Poetry', at p. 13. On the links between the poems, see Paula

Johnson, *Form and Transformation in Music and Poetry of the English Renaissance* (New Haven: Yale University Press, 1972), pp. 125–31.

176. Evans (ed.), *Elizabethan Sonnets*, pp. 31–2.
177. Bruno dedicated two works to Sidney and they probably met at an Ash Wednesday supper at Fulke Greville's house: Duncan-Jones, *Sidney*, p. 271.
178. John Donne, 'The Ecstasy', lines 69–76, in *The Complete English Poems*, ed. A. J. Smith (Harmondsworth: Penguin, 1971), pp. 55–6. On 'The Extasie', see Wilbur Sanders, *John Donne's Poetry* (Cambridge: Cambridge University Press, 1971), pp. 94–106. Elsewhere Donne is much more serious about Neoplatonsim and alchemy: see Healy, *Shakespeare, Alchemy*, p. 55.
179. Giovanni Dall'Orto, ' "Socratic Love" as a Disguise for Same-Sex Love in the Italian Renaissance', in Kent Gerard and Gert Hekma (eds.), *The Pursuit of Sodomy: Male Homosexuality in Renaissance and Enlightenment Europe* (New York: Harrington Park Press, 1989), pp. 33–65. I owe this reference to Elizabeth Pallitto.
180. See Gordon Teskey, 'A Retrograde Reading of Spenser's *Fowre Hymnes*', in Borris et al. (eds.), *Spenser and Platonism*, pp. 481–97; Hadfield, 'Spenser and Religion'.
181. On Russell, see the *ODNB* entry by John McGurk.
182. On Margaret Russell, see the *ODNB* entry by Richard T. Spence; Quitsland, 'Spenser and the Patronesses of the *Fowre Hymnes*'.
183. See the *ODNB* entry by Peter Holmes.
184. Martin Holmes, *Proud Northern Lady: Lady Anne Clifford, 1590–1676* (Chichester: Phillimore, 1975), p. 130; Spence, *Lady Anne Clifford*, pp. 67–8.
185. Spence, *Lady Anne Clifford*, pp. 8, 12–13.
186. Woods, *Lanyer*, pp. 42–71; Beilin, *Redeeming Eve*, p. 192.
187. Holmes, *Lady Anne Clifford*, pp. 138–9; Spence, *Lady Anne Clifford*, 66.
188. *Diaries of Lady Anne Clifford*, pp. 15, 24, 26, 50, 61.
189. Spenser, *Shorter Poems*, p. 656.
190. Rosamund Tuve, ' "Spenserus" ', in *Essays by Rosamund Tuve*, pp. 139–62, at pp. 140–3. On Malby, who was secretary to the earl of Warwick in the early 1560s, see the *ODNB* entry by Bernadette Cunningham.
191. See the *ODNB* entry by Simon Adams; Jeremiah Wiffen, *Historical Memoirs of the House of Russell*, 2 vols. (London, 1833), i. 272, 396; ii. 61.
192. MS Bodley 902, fo. 184ʳ. Anne Russell's signature is on fo. 80ᵛ. For comment, see Tuve, ' "Spenserus" ', p. 139. Ovid, *Tristia*, 1.9, lines 5–6 (trans. from Ovid, *Sorrows of an Exile*, trans. A. D. Melville (1995; Oxford: Oxford University Press, 1995), p. 19).
193. See the gloss to July, line 177. On Spenser and Gower, see Tuve, ' "Spenserus" ', pp. 141–2; R. F. Yeager, 'Gower, John', *Sp. Enc.*, pp. 337–8; Nohrnberg, *Analogy*, pp. 271, 318, 383, 641. Spenser would have seen Gower's tomb in Southwark Cathedral: Guy Rowston, *Southwark Cathedral: The Authorized Guide* (Bromley: Robert James, 2006), p. 25; Nicholas Pevsner, *The Buildings of England: London except The Cities of London & Westminster* (Harmondsworth: Penguin, 1952), ii. 395–6.
194. M. St Clare Byrne and Gladys Scott Thomson, ' "My Lord's Books": The Library of Francis, Second Earl of Bedford in 1584', *RES* 28 (1931), 385–405.
195. On Francis Russell, see Wiffen, *Historical Memoirs*, i, ch. 10; Gladys Scott Thomson, *Two Centuries of Family History: A Study in Social Development* (London: Longman, 1930), ch. 4; *ODNB* entry by Wallace T. MacCaffrey. On dedications to the earl see Byrne and Thomson, 'My Lord's Books', pp. 390–1.
196. Tuve, ' "Spenserus" ', pp. 143–4.
197. Cited in Beilin, *Redeeming Eve*, p. 192.
198. Bjorvand, 'Spenser's Defence of Poetry', pp. 27–8. See also Wind, *Pagan Mysteries*, ch. 3.
199. Dan S. Norton, 'The Background of Spenser's *Prothalamion*', unpublished PhD dissertation, Princeton University, 1940, pp. 37, 73.
200. For details of their history, see Norton, 'Background of Spenser's *Prothalamion*', pp. 40–93.
201. Ibid. 1.

202. Norton, 'Background of Spenser's *Prothalamion*', pp. 85–7.
203. Sylvia Freedman, *Poor Penelope: Lady Penelope Rich, An Elizabethan Woman* (Abbotsbrook: Kensal, 1983), pp. 86–7.
204. Leicester/Essex House was one of the grand houses on the Strand built by Elizabeth's chief courtiers. The inventory of Leicester's possessions survives: Charles Lethbridge Kingsford, 'Essex House, formerly Leicester House and Exeter Inn', *Archaeologica, or Miscellaneous Tracts Relating to Antiquity* 73 (1903), 1–54.
205. Manolo Guerci, 'Salisbury House in London, 1599–1694: The Strand Palace of Sir Robert Cecil', *Architectural History* 52 (2009), 31–78. On the competition between the owners of grand houses, see Manolo Guerci, 'The Construction of Northumberland House and the Patronage of Its Original Builder, Lord Henry Howard, 1603–14', *AJ* 90 (2010), 341–400, at 345–9.
206. Hammer, *Polarisation of Elizabethan Politics*, p. 286; *ODNB* entry on 'Somerset, Edward, fourth earl of Worcester', by Pauline Croft; Dan S. Norton, 'Queen Elizabeth's "Brydale Day"', *MLQ* 5 (1944), 149–54, at 149–50; Norton, 'Background of Spenser's *Prothalamion*', p. 42.
207. Helena Shire, *A Preface to Spenser* (London: Longman, 1978), p. 175. On the innovative nature of the poem, see also J. Norton Smith, 'Spenser's *Prothalamion*: A New Genre', *RES* 10 (1959), 173–8; Michael West, 'Prothalamia in Propertius and Spenser', *CL* 26 (1974), 346–53.
208. Norton, 'Background of Spenser's *Prothalamion*', pp. 74–85, 92.
209. Norton, 'Queen Elizabeth's "Brydale Day"', p. 149.
210. On Essex in the poem, see Judith Owens, 'Commerce and Cadiz in Spenser's *Prothalamion*', *SEL* 47 (2007), 79–106, at 90–7.
211. Paul E. J. Hammer, 'Myth-Making: Politics, Propaganda and the Capture of Cadiz in 1596', *HJ* 40 (1997), 621–42, at 623; Owens, 'Commerce and Cadiz', p. 92.
212. Spenser, *Shorter Poems*, p. 733; Hammer, *Polarisation of Elizabethan Politics*, p. 70.
213. Edmund Spenser, *Prothalamion, or A Spousall Verse* (London, 1596); Johnson, *Critical Bibliography*, pp. 32–3.
214. Einar Bjorvand, '*Prothalamion*', *Sp. Enc.*, pp. 561–2.
215. M. L. Wine, 'Spenser's "Sweete Themmes": Of Time and the River', *SEL* 2 (1962), 111–17, at 117; Harry Berger, 'Spenser's *Prothalamion*: An Interpretation', *Essays in Criticism* 15 (1965), 363–80, at 364–5.
216. See Owens, 'Commerce and Cadiz', p. 90.
217. See Daniel H. Woodward, 'Some Themes in Spenser's *Prothalamion*', *ELH* 29 (1962), 34–46, at 35.
218. Manley, *Literature and Culture in Early Modern London*, p. 209.
219. William Vallans, *A Tale of Two Swans, wherein is comprehended the original and increase of the riuer Lee* (London, 1590), sig. A2^r; Oruch, 'Spenser, Camden'.
220. On Vallans, see the *ODNB* entry by Nick de Somogyi.
221. Vallans, *Tale of Two Swans*, sig. B4^r.

Chapter 11

1. Falls, *Elizabeth's Irish Wars*, p. 192.
2. Ellis, *Tudor Ireland*, p. 302.
3. Moody et al. (eds.), *New History of Ireland*, viii. 218.
4. Guy, *Tudor Ireland*, pp. 350, 365.
5. Falls, *Elizabeth's Irish Wars*, p. 206. On the fort, see Klingelhofer, *Castles and Colonists*, pp. 43–6.
6. Hayes-McCoy, 'Tudor Conquest and Counter-Reformation', p. 124.
7. Ellis, *Tudor Ireland*, p. 303.
8. On the position of the Old English, see Patrick Corish, *The Irish Catholic Experience: A Historical Survey* (Dublin: Gill and Macmillan, 1985), ch. 3; McGurk, *Elizabethan Conquest*, chs. 8–9.
9. Welply 'Edmund Spenser: Recent Researches', p. 169; Ferguson, 'Memorials of Spenser', p. 607; *Chronology*, p. 70; White, *Historical and Topographical Notes*, iv. 170–5. The Chancery case which provides the evidence for Peregrine's right to Renny was destroyed in 1922.

10. On the status of professions and the general levels of salaries, which rarely exceeded £20 per anum, see Wilfrid R. Prest (ed.), *The Professions in Early Modern England* (Beckenham: Croom Helm, 1987).

11. Ralph Josselin, writing in the third quarter of the 17th century, provides details which show that in his later years he spent about a fifth of his income on dowries for his daughters. Overall, Josselin spent a quarter of his substantial income on purchasing land; a third on his children; and a quarter on maintaining his household: Macfarlane, *Family Life of Ralph Josselin*, pp. 42, 54.

12. J. R. O'Flanagan, *The Blackwater in Munster* (London, 1844), p. 118. White, *Historical and Topographical Notes*, iii. 172–3, shows that the tree was still standing in the early 20th century, 'situated in the S. W. of the townland of Renny Lower, on the bank of the River Blackwater, about 10 chains S. of the road leading from Fermoy to Castletownroche'.

13. Gwynn and Hadcock, *Medieval Religious Houses: Ireland*, pp. 161–2; Halpin and Newman, *Ireland*, pp. 508–10; *Patent and Close Rolls*, ii. 158.

14. Henley, *Spenser in Ireland*, p. 70; Newman Johnson, 'Kilcolman Castle', p. 418; Gwynn and Hadcock, *Medieval Religious Houses: Ireland*, pp. 161–2; *Fiants* (Elizabeth 5911).

15. Henley, *Spenser in Ireland*, p. 68; Ferguson, 'Memorials of Spenser', p. 608; James S. Ferguson, 'Memorials of Edmund Spenser the Poet, and His Descendants, from the Public Records of Ireland', *JCHAS* 14 (1908), 39–43, at 41. Henley appears to have mistranscribed Ferguson's figure of 395 as 365.

16. Judson, *Spenser in Southern Ireland*, p. 31; Shohachi Fukuda, 'Bregog, Mulla', *Sp. Enc.*, p. 110.

17. On the Barry family's acquisition of religious property after the dissolution, see Bradshaw, *Dissolution*, pp. 166–7; Gwynn and Hadcock, *Medieval Religious Houses: Ireland*, p. 243.

18. Ferguson, 'Memorials of Spenser', p. 608; Henley, *Spenser in Ireland*, p. 68.

19. *Chronology*, p. 70; Ferguson, 'Memorials of Spenser', p. 606. The original document was destroyed in 1922.

20. Henley, *Spenser in Ireland*, pp. 67–8; *Fiants*, i. 35 (Henry VIII, 304). On Katherine Spenser, see Appendix 1.

21. Ferguson, 'Memorials of Spenser', *JCHAS* pp. 14, 41.

22. *Chronology*, p. 71; Ferguson, 'Memorials of Spenser', p. 606.

23. Anthony J. Sheehan, 'The Overthrow of the Plantation of Munster in October 1598', *Irish Sword* 15 (1982), 11–22, at 11; Klingelhofer, *Castles and Colonists*, p. 26.

24. Brink, 'Documenting Edmund Spenser', pp. 206–7.

25. Roger A. Mason, 'George Buchanan, James VI and the Presbyterians', in Roger A. Mason (ed.), *Scots and Britons: Scottish Political Thought and the Union of 1603* (Cambridge: Cambridge University Press, 1994), pp. 112–37.

26. Alan Stewart, *The Cradle King: A Life of James VI and I* (London: Chatto and Windus, 2003), p. 93.

27. Susan Doran, '"Revenge her most foul and unnatural murder": The Impact of Mary Stuart's Execution on Anglo-Scottish Relations', *History* 85 (2000), 589–612.

28. *Chronology*, p. 72; *Stationers*, iii. 34.

29. Avery, 'Mapping the Irish Other'; John Breen, '"Imaginative Groundplot": *A Vewe of the Present State of Ireland*', *Sp. St.* 12 (1991; pub. 1998), 151–68; Andrew Hadfield, 'Censoring Ireland in Elizabethan England', in Hadfield (ed.), *Literature and Censorship*, pp. 149–64, at p. 153.

30. Galbraith, 'Spenser and the History of the Book', p. 184. The following account is much indebted to Dr Galbraith's excellent analysis, which substantially corrects earlier accounts, including my own.

31. *Spenser Allusions*, pp. 48, 50, 56–8; Bartholomew Griffin, *Fidessa, More Chaste Then Kinde* (1602).

32. See John Izon, 'Bartholomew Griffin and Sir Thomas Lucy', *TLS*, 19 Apr. 1957, p. 245; *ODNB* entry on 'Griffin, Bartholomew', by B. J. Sokol.

33. On the court case, see pp. 343–8.

34. *The Records of the Honourable Society of Lincoln's Inn: The Black Books*, 6 vols. (London: Lincoln's Inn, 1897–2001), ii. 39; Galbraith, 'Spenser and the History of the Book', p. 188.
35. See p. 336.
36. Galbraith, 'Spenser and the History of the Book', p. 192.
37. Ibid. 201.
38. Hadfield, *Spenser's Irish Experience*, pp. 81–2.
39. Peter Blayney, 'The Publication of Playbooks', in John D. Cox and David Scott Kastan (eds.), *A New History of Early English Drama* (New York: Columbia University Press, 1997), pp. 383–422, at p. 398; Galbraith, 'Spenser and the History of the Book', p. 201.
40. On Holinshed, see Annabel Patterson, *Reading Holinshed's Chronicles* (Chicago: University of Chicago Press, 1994), p. 13. On Derricke, see *ODNB* entry by Andrew Hadfield. James I, inspecting documents at Whitehall early in his reign, commented, 'We had more ado with Ireland than all the world besides', cited in Hadfield and Maley, 'Introduction: Irish Representations and English Alternatives', p. 6.
41. Hadfield, 'Censoring Ireland in Elizabethan England', pp. 155–8. On Beacon, see Beacon, *Solon His Follie*, ed. Carey and Carroll, introd., pp. xiii–xxv.
42. On Byrchensa see Hadfield, 'Allusion to Spenser's Irish Writings'.
43. *Printers*, p. 180.
44. For details of the work of the Lownes brothers, see *A Short-Title Catalogue of Books Printed in England, Scotland & Ireland and of English Books Printed Abroad, 1475–1640*, comp. A. W. Pollard and G. R. Redgrave, 3 vols. (London: Bibliographical Society, 1976–91), iii. 109–10.
45. Andrew Zurcher, 'The Printing of the *Cantos of Mutabilitie* in 1609', in Jane Grogan (ed.), *Celebrating Mutabilitie* (Manchester: Manchester University Press, 2010), pp. 40–60.
46. See Johnson, *Critical Bibliography*, pp. 21–3.
47. On paper quality, see Bland, *Guide to Early Printed Books*, pp. 29–32.
48. Lodovico Ariosto, *Orlando Furioso*, trans. Sir John Harington, ed. Graham Hough (Carbondale: Southern Illinois University Press, 1962); Sir Philip Sidney, *The Countesse of Pembrokes Arcadia* (London, 1593); Samuel Daniel, *The Works of Samuel Daniel, newly augmented* (London, 1601). I am grateful to David Scott Kastan for advice on this point.
49. Scott-Warren, *Harington and the Book as Gift*, pp. 34–5.
50. Spenser, *Faerie Queene*, p. 715.
51. Johnson, *Critical Bibliography*, pp. 33–48.
52. *ODNB* entry; *Stationers*, iii. 274; Zurcher, 'Printing of the *Cantos of Mutabilitie*', p. 41; Colin Burrow, *Edmund Spenser* (Plymouth: Northcote House, 1996), p. 41.
53. *ODNB* entry on Richard Field by David Kathman; Johnson, *Critical Bibliography*, pp. 18, 20, 31.
54. George Walton Williams, 'The Printer of the First Folio of Sidney's *Arcadia*', *The Library*, 5th ser. 12 (1957), 274–5; Bland, 'Windet', p. 324; Huffman, 'Wolfe', p. 329.
55. Sheldon P. Zitner, '*The Faerie Queene, Book VII*', *Sp. Enc.*, pp. 287–9, at p. 289; Shire, *Preface to Spenser*, p. 187; Julian Lethbridge, 'Spenser's Last Days', in Lethbridge (ed.), *Spenser: New and Renewed Directions*, pp. 302–36, at pp. 306–8, 312–13. Commentators have generally been sceptical of arguments for an early date, but for such claims, see Evelyn May Albright, 'Spenser's Reasons for Rejecting the Cantos of Mutability', *SP* 25 (1928), 93–127; Evelyn May Albright, 'On the Dating of Spenser's "Mutability" Cantos', *SP* 26 (1926), 482–98; J. M. Purcell, 'The Date of Spenser's Mutabilitie Cantos', *PMLA* 50 (1935), 914–17. On Spenser and Ovid, see William P. Cumming, 'The Influence of Ovid's *Metamorphoses* on Spenser's "Mutabilitie" Cantos', *SP* 28 (1931), 241–56.
56. Russell J. Meyer, '"Fixt in heauens hight": Spenser, Astronomy, and the Date of the *Cantos of Mutabilitie*', *Sp. St.* 4 (1983), 115–29; Hugh De Lacy, 'Astrology in the Poetry of Edmund Spenser', *JEGP* 33 (1934), 520–43; J. C. Eade, 'Astronomy, astrology', *Sp. Enc.*, pp. 72–4.
57. Heffner, 'Did Spenser Die in Poverty?', p. 222.
58. *Variorum*, x. 531; Jack B. Oruch, 'Works, lost', *Sp. Enc.*, pp. 737–8.
59. Spenser, *Faerie Queene*, p. 691.
60. Zurcher, 'Printing of the *Cantos of Mutabilitie*', p. 58; Hadfield, 'Spenser and Samuel Brandon'; Lethbridge, 'Spenser's Last Days', pp. 328–31.
61. Zurcher, 'Printing of the *Cantos of Mutabilitie*', p. 45.

62. Gordon Teskey, 'Night Thoughts on Mutability', in Grogan (ed.), *Celebrating Mutabilitie*, pp. 24–39, at pp. 30–1. See also Richard A. McCabe, *The Pillars of Eternity: Time and Providence in The Faerie Queene* (Dublin: Irish Academic Press, 1989), pp. 199–210.

63. Spenser, *Faerie Queene*, p. 712.

64. Two essays that argues for a late date based on the preponderance of feminine rhymes in the poem, as well as other issues, are Edwin Greenlaw, 'Spenser's "Mutabilitie"', *PMLA* 45 (1930), 684–703, at 695–703; Frederick M. Padelford, 'The Cantos of Mutabilitie: Further Considerations Bearing on the Date', *PMLA* 45 (1930), 704–11.

65. On the first two points see pp. 394–9; on Spenser's poetic disciples, see William B. Hunter, Jr (ed.), *The English Spenserians: The Poetry of Giles Fletcher, George Wither, Michael Drayton, Phineas Fletcher and Henry More* (Salt Lake City: University of Utah Press, 1977); Joan Grundy, *The Spenserian Poets: A Study in Elizabethan and Jacobean Poetry* (London: Arnold, 1969); O'Callaghan, '*Shepheardes Nation*'.

66. On Arthur in the poem, see Gordon Teskey, 'Arthur in *The Faerie Queene*', *Sp. Enc.*, pp. 69–72; Nohrnberg, *Analogy*, pp. 35–58; King, *The Faerie Queene and Middle English Romance*, pp. 72–7, 117–25; Sheila T. Cavanagh, *Wanton Eyes and Chaste Desires: Female Sexuality in The Faerie Queene* (Bloomington: Indiana University Press, 1994), ch. 1.

67. Andrew Hadfield, '"The Sacred Hunger of Ambitious Minds": Spenser's Savage Religion', in Donna Hamilton and Richard Strier (eds.), *Religion, Literature and Politics in Post-Reformation England, 1540–1688* (Cambridge: Cambridge University Press, 1996), pp. 27–45.

68. Marshall, *Beliefs and the Dead*, pp. 227–8.

69. See e.g. Marcia B. Hall (ed.), *Michelangelo's Last Judgement* (Cambridge: Cambridge University Press, 2005), introd., pp. 15–16.

70. See pp. 42–6, 342.

71. Ayesha Ramachandran, 'Mutabilitie's Lucretian Metaphysics: Scepticism and Cosmic Process in Spenser's *Cantos*', in Grogan (ed.), *Celebrating Mutabilitie*, pp. 220–45. Ramachandran associates Mutability with Lucretius, whereas I would argue that nature's speech also sounds Lucretian in substance. On Lucretius in early modern Europe, see Kraye, 'Moral Philosophy', pp. 376–7.

72. Lucretius, *On The Nature of the Universe*, trans. Ronald Latham (Harmondsworth: Penguin, 1951), pp. 31–5.

73. Lucretius, *Nature of the Universe*, pp. 121–9.

74. Justus Lipsius, *Two bookes of constancie. Written in Latine, by Justus Lipsius. Containing, principallie, A comfortable conference, in common calamities. And will serve for a singular consolation to all that are privately distressed, of afflicted, either in body or mind. Englished by John Stradling* (London, 1595); Glyn P. Norton, 'Introduction', in Norton (ed.), *The Cambridge History of Literary Criticism*, iii. *The Renaissance* (Cambridge: Cambridge University Press, 1999), pp. 1–22, at p. 17.

75. Although the case is often made. For recent restatements, see e.g. Richard J. Berleth, 'Fraile Woman, Foolish Gerle: Misogyny in Spenser's "Mutabilitie Cantos"', *MP* 93 (1995), 37–53, at 52–3; E. A. F. Porges Watson, 'Mutabilitie's Debateable Land: Spenser's Ireland and the Frontiers of Faerie', in Lethbridge (ed.), *Spenser: New and Renewed Directions*, pp. 286–301, at pp. 300–1; Robert Lanier Reid, 'Spenser's Mutability Song: Conclusion or Transition?', in Grogan (ed.), *Celebrating Mutabilitie*, pp. 61–84, at p. 79.

76. Sandler, '*Faerie Queene*: An Elizabethan Apocalypse', pp. 169–71; King, *Spenser Poetry and the Reformation Tradition*, pp. 146–7.

77. Spenser, *Faerie Queene*, p. 716.

78. McCabe, 'Masks of Duessa'; Hadfield, 'Spenser and the Stuart Succession'. Mary K. Woodworth makes a case that Mutability is Arbella Stuart: 'The Mutability Cantos and the Succession', *PMLA* 59 (1944), 985–1002.

79. On Mutability's arguments, see Rix, *Rhetoric in Spenser's Poetry*, pp. 82–4.

80. Anne Lake Prescott, 'Titans', *Sp. Enc.*, p. 691; Aptekar, *Icons of Justice*, pp. 27–38.

81. Michael O'Connell, 'Giant with the Scales', pp. 331–2; Annabel Patterson, 'The Egalitarian Giant: Representations of Justice in History/Literature', *Journal of British Studies* 31 (1992), 97–132.

82. Fowler, 'Failure of Moral Philosophy'; Bellamy, *Tudor Law of Treason*, ch. 5.

83. Maurice Evans, *Spenser's Anatomy of Heroism* (Cambridge: Cambridge University Press, 1970), pp. 202–3.

84. Glenn A. Steinberg, 'Chaucer's Mutability in Spenser's *Mutabilitie Cantos*', *SEL* 46 (2006), 27–42; Edmund Spenser, *The Mutabilitie Cantos*, ed. S. P. Zitner (London: Nelson, 1968), introd., pp. 29–30; Fowler, *Literary Character*, pp. 240–1.

85. On the suspicion of nature and the lack of interest in walking and climbing in the Renaissance, see Hale, *Civilization of Europe*, p. 42; Keith Thomas, *Man and the Natural World: Changing Attitudes in England, 1500–1800* (1983; Harmondsworth: Penguin, 1984), p. 258.

86. For discussion of the local setting, see Coughlan, 'Local Context of Mutabilitie's Plea'; Lethbridge, 'Spenser's Last Days', pp. 317–21; Judson, *Spenser in Southern Ireland*.

87. Pugh, *Spenser and Ovid*, p. 273.

88. On the relationship between Milton and Spenser, see, in particular, Maureen Quilligan, *Milton's Spenser: The Politics of Reading* (Ithaca, NY: Cornell University Press, 1983); David Mikics, *The Limits of Moralizing: Pathos and Subjectivity in Spenser and Milton* (Lewisburg: Bucknell University Press, 1994), ch. 5.

89. Pugh, *Spenser and Ovid*, ch. 7. On Spenser's knowledge of the area and its myths, see Joyce, *Wonders of Ireland*, pp. 72–114.

90. Richard N. Ringler, 'The Faunus Episode', *MP* 43 (1966), 12–19; Holahan, '*Iamque Opus Exegi*'.

91. *Variorum*, x. 145.

92. Richard D. Jordan, 'Faunus, fauns', *Sp. Enc.*, p. 304; Thomas Herron, 'Native Irish Property and Propriety in the Faunus Episode and *Colin Clouts come home again*', in Grogan (ed.), *Celebrating Mutabilitie*, pp. 136–77, at p. 141.

93. On Faunus and Pan, see Jane Davidson Reid (ed.), *The Oxford Guide to Classical Mythology in the Arts, 1300–1990s* (Oxford: Oxford University Press, 1993), p. 802. Patricia Merivale, in her entry 'Pan', fails to mention this vital link: *Sp. Enc.*, p. 527.

94. Perhaps following Ovid, who may have represented himself as Actaeon: see Patrick Cheney, *Marlowe's Counterfeit Profession: Ovid, Spenser, Counter-Nationhood* (Toronto: Toronto University Press, 1997), p. 165.

95. See pp. 266–8.

96. Joyce, 'Spenser's Irish Rivers', pp. 98–105.

97. The episode has been read as a direct allegory of events in Ireland, to my mind, erroneously: see e.g. Shire, *Preface to Spenser*, p. 187; Herron, *Spenser's Irish Work*, pp. 161–2.

98. Joyce, 'Spenser's Irish Rivers', p. 104.

99. Edwards, *Ormond Lordship*, pp. 15–16, 39, *passim*.

100. For a reading of Spenser's thinking about the environment in the Mutability Cantos, see Richard Chamberlain, *Radical Spenser: Pastoral, Politics and the New Aestheticism* (Edinburgh: Edinburgh University Press, 2005), ch. 6.

101. See e.g. the maps of late 16th-century Munster in the Dartmouth Collection: (National Maritime Museum) P/49, 20, 22, 27, 29.

102. Richard Helgerson, 'The Land Speaks', in *Forms of Nationhood: The Elizabethan Writing of England* (Chicago: University of Chicago Press, 1992), pp. 105–47.

103. Falls, *Elizabeth's Irish Wars*, pp. 210–11.

104. Ibid. 213.

105. 'William Farmer's Chronicles of Ireland from 1594 to 1613', ed. C. Litton Falkiner, *EHR* 22 (1907), 104–30, 527–52, at 108–9; Falls, *Elizabeth's Irish Wars*, p. 217; McGurk, *Elizabethan Conquest of Ireland*, 227.

106. Sheehan, 'Overthrow of the Plantation of Munster', p. 12.

107. Bagwell, *Ireland under the Tudors*, vol. iii, ch. 48; McGurk, *Elizabethan Conquest of Ireland*, pp. 200–1.

108. BL Harley MS 286, fo. 272, transcribed in *Chronology*, p. 72; Mananaan Mac Lir, 'Spenser as High Sheriff of Cork County', *JCHAS* 7 (1901), 249–50, at 249.

109. MacCarthy-Morrogh, *Munster Plantation*, p. 268. See also Brady, 'Captains' Games', p. 155. On martial law, see David Edwards, 'Martial Law and the Tudor Reconquest of Ireland',

History Ireland 5 (Summer 1997), 16–21; Edwards, 'Spenser's *View* and Martial Law'. On sheriffs in England, see Penry Williams, *The Tudor Regime* (Oxford: Clarendon Press, 1979), pp. 407–8.

110. Vincent P. Carey, 'The Irish Face of Machiavelli: Richard Beacon's *Solon His Follie* (1594) and Republican Ideology in the Conquest of Ireland', in Morgan (ed.), *Political Ideology in Ireland*, pp. 83–109, at p. 88.

111. *CSPI, 1598–9*, p. 395; Sheehan, 'Provincial Grievance and National Revolt', p. 15. See also the criticisms of sheriffs in the anonymous 'Discourse on the Mere Irish of Ireland', Exeter College, Oxford, MS 154, ff.55–74 (transcribed by Hiram Morgan, CELT, http://www.ucc.ie/celt/published/E600001-004/index.html). I owe this reference to Brendan Kane.

112. Berry, 'Sheriffs of the County Cork', pp. 48, 51–2.

113. Ibid. 47.

114. Welply, 'Spenser: Recent Researches', p. 186.

115. *CSPI, 1598–9*, p. 398.

116. Sheehan, 'Overthrow of the Plantation of Munster', p. 16; Sheehan, 'Political Grievance and National Revolt', pp. 83–4; 'Farmer's Chronicles', pp. 110–11.

117. Bagwell, *Ireland under the Tudors*, iii. 302–3.

118. James Goold to Sir Robert Cecil, 6 Oct. 1598, *CSPI, 1598–9*, p. 282.

119. *CSPI, 1598–9*, p. 291. On Ormond's resolute military tactics, see Sheehan, 'Political Grievance and National Revolt', pp. 92–5.

120. *CSPI, 1598–9*, p. 292.

121. Sheehan, 'Political Grievance and National Revolt', pp. 100–2.

122. Edwards, 'Spenser's *View* and Martial Law', pp. 154–5.

123. Berry, 'Sheriffs of the County Cork', p. 40.

124. MacCarthy-Morrogh, *Munster Plantation*, p. 269.

125. Sheehan, 'Overthrow of the Plantation of Munster', pp. 11–12.

126. *CSPI, 1598–9*, p. 280.

127. Sheehan, 'Overthrow of the Plantation of Munster', pp. 14–15.

128. *Chronology*, p. 73; Hayes-McCoy, 'Tudor Conquest and Counter-Reformation', in Moody et al. (eds.), *New History of Ireland*, iii. 94–141, at p. 128; Sheehan, 'Political Grievance and National Revolt', p. 78.

129. *CSPI, 1598–9*, p. 281.

130. *CSPI, 1588–9*, p. 299; Sheehan, 'Official Reaction', p. 314.

131. On the Barry lands, which stretched from Fermoy down to the south coast, see the map in Nicholls and Quinn, 'Ireland in 1534', in Moody et al. (eds.), *New History of Ireland*, iii. 1–38, at pp. 2–3.

132. Sheehan, 'Official Reaction', pp. 314–15.

133. Canny, *Making Ireland British*, ch. 8; Brian Mac Curta (ed.), *Ulster 1641: Aspects of the Rising* (Belfast: Institute of Irish Studies, 1993).

134. *CSPI, 1588–9*, p. 300.

135. See also the descriptions of atrocities in Anon., '*The Supplication of the blood of the English*', ed. Maley. It is worth noting that this English family has a wet nurse.

136. *CSPI, 1598–9*, p. 290.

137. See also the accounts in *Annals of the Four Masters*, pp. 624–41; Moryson, *Itinerary*, ii. 218–20.

138. *CSPI, 1588–9*, p. 300.

139. Roy Harvey Pearce, 'Primitivistic Ideas in *The Faerie Queene*', *JEGP* 44 (1945), 138–51; Waldo F. McNeir, 'The Sacrifice of Serena: *The Faerie Queene*, VI, viii. 31–51', in Bernhard Fabian and Ulrich Suerbaum (eds.), *Festschrift für Edgar Mertner* (Munich: Wilhelm Fink, 1968), pp. 117–56.

140. Hadfield, *Spenser's Irish Experience*, ch. 5.

141. Maley, *Salvaging Spenser*, ch. 3.

142. *Chronology*, p. 73; *CSPI, 1598–9*, pp. 291, 293–4.

143. Klingelhofer, 'Spenser at Kilcolman Castle', pp. 137–40.

144. Sheehan, 'Overthrow of the Plantation of Munster', p. 16.

145. Stone, *Crisis of the Aristocracy*, pp. 135–6.

146. Jonson, *Poems*, ed. Parfitt, p. 465.
147. I am extremely grateful to Charles and Catherine Harold Barry for showing me this map. See also *Chronology*, p. 73.
148. King, 'Spenser, Chaucer, and Medieval Romance', *Sp. Handbook*, pp. 568, 570. Klingelhofer is sceptical, calling the story 'fanciful' and pointing out that the story is modelled on Aeneas' flight from Troy: Klingelhofer, *Castles and Colonists*, p. 111.
149. *CSPI, 1598–9*, p. 399.
150. In a letter to the Privy Council dated 21 Dec. Norris writes 'Since my last letter of the 9th of this month, and sent by Mr Spenser' (*CSPI, 1598–9*, p. 414).
151. SP 63/202, pt. 4/59.
152. See the *ODNB* entry on Carleton by L. J. Reeve.
153. All Souls College, Oxford, MS 155, fo. 58^{r-v}; BL Harleian 3787, no. 21; Marotti, *Manuscript, Print, and the English Renaissance Lyric*, p. 37.
154. Heaton, *Writing and Reading Royal Entertainments*, pp. 197–8. On the Yelvertons, see the *ODNB* entries on Sir Christopher by David Ibbetson and Sir Henry by S. R. Gardiner, rev. Louis A. Knalfa. On Yelverton's epilogue for *Jocasta*, see Gascoigne, *Hundreth Sundrie Flowres* ed. Pigman, pp. 515–16, *passim*; Nelson and Elliott (eds.), *REED: Inns of Court*, ii. 732.
155. *Variorum*, x. 533.
156. The best discussion is Ciaran Brady, '*A Brief Note of Ireland*', *Sp. Enc.*, pp. 111–12.
157. *Variorum*, x. 235.
158. Morgan, 'Elizabeth and Ireland', p. 305.
159. *Variorum*, x. 236.
160. '"A Discourse of Ireland" (circa 1599)'; Hadfield and McVeagh (eds.), *Strangers to that Land*, pp. 49–50.
161. *Supplication*, p. 12.
162. Ibid. 8. The work, which is neatly copied out in secretary hand, exists as a small quarto as part of an early 17th-century compilation of tracts on Ireland, alongside Thomas Blenerhasset's work on the Plantation of Ulster, Captain Thomas Lee's treatise on Ireland, and others, and looks as if it was assembled for use by an important, busy official working in Ireland, perhaps Sir Arthur Chichester, the long-serving Lord Deputy (1605–16), whose copy of *A View* also survives in the British Library.
163. Brady, '*Brief Note*', p. 112.
164. Morgan suggests that Spenser might have written a *Supplication*: 'Queen Elizabeth and Ireland', p. 306. See also Hiram Morgan, 'Spenser's Supplication' (http://ucc-ie.academia.edu/HiramMorgan/Papers/107464/Spensers_Supplication_of_the_Blood_of_the_English).
165. Byrchensha, *Discourse Occasioned Upon the Late Defeat*, sig. B4^v; Hiram Morgan (ed.), *The Battle of Kinsale* (Bray: Wordwell, 2004), p. 393.
166. *Variorum*, x. 237–8. For the history of Norris's feud with Russell, see Nolan, *Norreys and the Elizabethan Military World*, pp. 224–37.
167. V. B. Hulbert, 'Spenser's Relation to Certain Documents on Ireland', *MP* 34 (1936–7), 345–53, at 349–50.
168. Brady, '*Brief Note*', p. 111.
169. *Variorum*, x. 243.
170. Ibid. 244.
171. Ibid. 244–5.
172. F. V. Emery, 'England circa 1600', in Darby (ed.), *New Historical Geography*, pp. 248–301, at pp. 288–9.
173. Brayshay, 'Royal Post-Horse Routes', p. 276.
174. Jonson, *Poems*, p. 465. A manuscript note in the 2nd edition of *The Faerie Queene*, discovered by the antiquary John Brand (1744–1806), also states that Spenser died in King Street: Welply, 'Spenser: Recent Researches', p. 186.
175. Stow, *Survey*, ii. 102, 374.
176. Merritt, *Social World of Early Modern Westminster*, pp. 149–53.
177. Welply, 'Spenser: Recent Researches', p. 186.

178. Judson, *Life*, p. 201; *Chronology*, p. 75.
179. TNA E. 351/543, fo. 40ʳ, cited in *Chronology*; *Chronology*, pp. 75–6; Bennett, 'Did Spencer Starve?'.
180. Judson, *Life*, p. 200.
181. On the Elizabethan climate, see Singman, *Daily Life in Elizabethan England*, pp. 81, 94; on disease see Rappaport, *Worlds Within Worlds*, pp. 71–6.
182. Archer, *Pursuit of Stability*, pp. 9–10; Beier, *Masterless Men*, pp. 29–32, 36–7.
183. Shapiro, *1599*, pp. 70–1.
184. On Shakespeare and Spenser, see the essays in J. B. Lethbridge (ed.), *Shakespeare and Spenser: Attractive Opposites* (Manchester: Manchester University Press, 2008); Hadfield, 'Spenser's Rosalind'. For a visual representation of their imagined meeting, see Henry Wallis, 'Shakespeare and Spenser' (1864) (Spenser files, National Portrait Gallery).
185. Berry and Timings, 'Spenser's Pension', p. 255.
186. *Chronology*, pp. 76–9; *Spenser Allusions*, pp. 56–63; Hadfield, 'Spenser and Samuel Brandon'.
187. Thomas Lodge, *A Fig for Momus* (London, 1595), sig. B4ʳ–C2ʳ.
188. *Spenser Allusions*, p. 60.
189. See the *ODNB* entry by David Kathman.
190. *The Workes of Our Antient and Learned English Poet, Geffrey Chaucer, newly printed* [ed. Thomas Speght] (London, 1598), sig. Ciiiʳ⁻ᵛ; *Spenser Allusions*, p. 62.
191. See the *ODNB* entry by David Matthews.
192. Bennett, 'Did Spenser Starve?'.
193. Berry and Timings, 'Spenser's Pension', pp. 257–8; Brink, 'Spenser's Family', p. 51.
194. Berry and Timings, 'Spenser's Pension', p. 259; Maley, 'Spenser's Life', *Sp. Handbook*, p. 27.
195. *Letters by John Chamberlain, written during the reign of Elizabeth*, ed. Sarah Walters (London: Camden Society, 1861), p. 41. On Chamberlain, see the *ODNB* entry by P. J. Finkelpearl.
196. W. I. Zeitler, 'The Date of Spenser's Death', *MLN* 43 (1928), 233–4.
197. Heffner, 'Did Spenser Die in Poverty?', p. 233.
198. William Camden, *The History of the Most Renowned and Victorious Princess Elizabeth*, trans. Anon. (London, 1688), p. 565. For comment, see Judson, 'Seventeenth-Century Lives of Spenser', pp. 35–7.
199. Richard S. Peterson, '*Enuies Scourge, and Vertues Honour*: A Rare Elegy for Spenser', *Sp. St.* 25 (2010), 287–325; *The Poems of Charles FitzGeoffrey, 1593–1636*, ed. Alexander B. Grosart (Manchester: privately printed, 1881), introd., pp. xix–x, xxiii, 21–2; Carpenter, *Reference Guide*, p. 237; Cummings, *Critical Heritage*, pp. 109–11. Fitzgeoffrey, who had family connections in Northamptonshire, later became a clergyman in Cornwall and knew Richard Carew, translator of Tasso: see the *ODNB* entry by Anne Duffin; Rowse, *Tudor Cornwall*, pp. 425–6.
200. Breton, *Works*, ed. Grosart, i. 15–16.
201. Cited in Carpenter, *Reference Guide*, p. 229. Translation by Paul Shorey. On Alabaster, see *ODNB* entry by Francis J. Bremer; Eccles, 'Brief Lives', pp. 4–5.
202. Weever, *Epigrammes*, sig. G3ʳ.
203. E. A. J. Honigmann, *John Weever: A Biography of a Literary Associate of Shakespeare and Jonson, together with a photographic facsimile of Weever's Epigrammes (1599)* (Manchester: Manchester University Press, 1987), pp. 22–3, 25–6.
204. For a list of some other possible elegies thrown into the grave, see Judson, *Life*, p. 206 n. 12.
205. See the list in Carpenter, *Reference Guide*, pp. 85–7.
206. Anthony Copley, *A Fig for Fortune* (London, 1596). Copley's poem, 'a barely concealed plea for Catholic toleration', is a reworking of the last four cantos of Book I of *The Faerie Queene*, suggesting that Elizabeth has been misled by supporters of the Church of England into diluting and distorting the true faith. He was later exiled after the Bye Plot, when he turned evidence against Ralegh, which might suggest a link to Spenser, especially as Arthur Lord Grey de Wilton's son, Thomas, was also involved: on Copley see the *ODNB* entry by Michael A. R. Graves; Shell, *Catholicism, Controversy and the English Literary Imagination*, p. 136.
207. Roderick L. Eagle, 'The Search for Spenser's Grave', *N&Q* 201 (1956), 282–3.
208. Richard Jenkyns, *Westminster Abbey* (London: Profile, 2004), pp. 79–80.

209. John Dart, *Westmonasterium, or The History and Antiquities of the Abbey Church of St. Peter's Westminster . . . A survey of the Church and Cloysters, taken in the year 1723*, 2 vols. (London, 1742), i. 71.

210. Heffner, 'Did Spenser Die in Poverty?', pp. 233–4. On Lane, see the *ODNB* entry by Verne M. Underwood. Lloyd was a friend of Christopher Carleil, who had been present at the debate at Bryskett's house in Ireland: Eccles, 'Brief Lives', p. 79.

211. On Lloyd, see the *ODNB* entry by Andrew Hadfield.

212. Three poems are attributed to 'E. S.': 'Being trapped in Loue he complayneth' (No. 38); 'Being forsaken of his frend he complaineth' (50); and 'Requirying the fauour of his loue: She aunswereth thus', all of which clearly belong to the mid-century (Edwards died in 1566). The claim that they might have been by Spenser is given short shrift in Richard Edwards (ed.), *The Paradise of Dainty Devises*, ed. Hyder Edward Rollins (Cambridge, MA: Harvard University Press, 1927), introd., p. lxii. The anthology did not meet with universal approval; see Koller, 'Fraunce and Spenser', p. 118.

213. John Lane, 'Triton's Trumpet' (1621), BL MS Royal 17.B.XV, fo. 172$^{r–v}$; Heffner, 'Did Spenser Die in Poverty?', p. 233.

214. The laureateship was not officially established until 1668, when Dryden was made Poet Laureate, but pre-eminent poets, notably Chaucer, Skelton, and Spenser, were often afforded the unofficial title: see Broadus, *Laureateship*, pp. 17, 20–3, 33–7.

215. National Portrait Gallery 776 (Michael Drayton by unknown artist, oil on panel, 1599).

216. William Browne, *Britannia's Pastorals: The Second Book* (London, 1616; Menston: Scolar Press, 1969), p. 27, p. 36; *Spenser Allusions*, p. 146; Judson, *Life*, pp. 206–7. On Browne (1590/1–1645?), see O'Callaghan, 'Shepherdes Nation', pp. 21–2, *passim*; *ODNB* entry by Michelle O'Callaghan.

217. Curtis Perry, *The Making of Jacobean Culture* (Cambridge: Cambridge University Press, 1997), p. 80.

218. On Anne Clifford as a patron, see Woudhuysen, *Sidney*, 327–31.

219. 'The Notebook and Accounts of Nicholas Stone', *Walpole Society*, 7 (1918–19), p. 54.

220. Pevsner, *Buildings of England: Essex*, p. 43; *ODNB* entry on Stone by Adam White. See also Llewellyn, *Funeral Monuments in Post-Reformation England*, pp. 166–7.

221. Peck, *Consuming Splendor*, p. 280; Stone, 'Notebook and Accounts', pp. 170–1.

222. Dart, *Westmonasterium*, ii. 74; Judson, *Life*, p. 207.

223. On Dart see the *ODNB* entry by Gordon Goodwin, rev. Nicholas Doggett.

224. Dart, *Westmonasterium*, ii. 75.

225. Ibid.; Cummings, *Critical Heritage*, p. 315; Scott L. Newstock, *Quoting Death in Early Modern England: The Poetics of Epitaphs Beyond the Tomb* (Basingstoke: Palgrave, 2009), p. 54.

226. Long, 'Spenser's Birth-Date', p. 179. Dart also notes that the date must be wrong: *Westmonasterium*, ii. 75.

227. Hughes's edition did not meet with universal approval: see Loewenstein, 'Spenser's Textual History', *Sp. Handbook*, pp. 646–7.

228. *The Works of Mr Edmund Spenser*, ed. John Hughes (London, 1715), vol. i, opposite p. xxii. On the illustrations, see Rachel E. Hile, 'Louis du Guernier's Illustrations for the John Hughes Edition of the *Works of Mr Edmund Spenser* (1715)', *Sp. St.* 23 (2008), 181–213, at 196.

229. Pask, *Emergence of the English Author*, chs. 2, 5; Radcliffe, *Spenser: Reception History*, pp. 26, 29, 31, 41, *passim*.

230. *ODNB* entry on Mason by Jules Smith; Judson, *Life*, pp. 207–8.

231. Attwater, *Pembroke College*, p. 102.

Afterword

1. Richard A. McCabe, 'Edmund Spenser', in Claude Rawson (ed.), *The Cambridge Companion to English Poets* (Cambridge: Cambridge University Press, 2011), pp. 53–71, at p. 53.

2. Lewis, *Allegory of Love*, p. 359; Gordon Teskey, 'Thinking Moments in *The Faerie Queene*', *Sp. St.* 22 (2007), 103–25.

3. Alpers, 'How to Read *The Faerie Queene*'.

4. Brendan Kennelly, 'Delight', in *Cromwell* (Newcastle: Bloodaxe Books, 1983), p. 110.

5. Sidney, *Apology*, p. 86.
6. W. B. Yeats, 'Edmund Spenser', in *Essays and Introductions* (London: Macmillan, 1961), pp. 356–83.
7. Cited in Norbrook, *Poetry and Politics in the English Renaissance*, p. 311.
8. Campbell, *English Yeoman*, ch. 2.
9. Hiram Morgan, 'Mid Atlantic Blues', *Irish Review* 11 (Winter 1991), 50–5; Nicholas Canny, 'The Ideology of English Colonisation: From Ireland to America', *William and Mary Quarterly* 30 (11973), 575–98; Armitage, *Ideological Origins of the British Empire*, pp. 48–9, *passim*.
10. Fowler, 'Failure of Moral Philosophy'.
11. Gascoigne, 'Dulce Bellum Inexpertis', st. 12 (p. 401).
12. McCabe, 'Fate of Irena', pp. 120–2.

Appendix 1

1. Hugh Cuffe to Sir Robert Cecil, Feb. 1600–1, *Calendar of the Manuscripts of . . . the Marquis of Salisbury . . . preserved at Hatfield House, Hertfordshire*, 18 vols. (London: HMC, 1883–1971) xi. 94–7. Henley, *Spenser in Ireland*, p. 193, erroneously cites Cuffe's letter as evidence that Elizabeth had 'returned to Ireland'.
2. MacCarthy-Morrogh, *Munster Plantation*, pp. 136–9.
3. MacCarthy-Morrogh, 'English Presence in Early Seventeenth-Century Munster'.
4. Mary Hickson, 'The Seggerson or Seckerston Family', *Journal of the Historical and Archaeological Association of Ireland*, 4th ser. 8 (1887–8), 340–1; Deposition of Therlagh Kelly, undated, MS 823, fo. 170^{r–v}, http://1641.tcd.ie/deposition.php?depID=823170r156.
5. Welply, 'Spenser: Recent Researches', p. 202.
6. Power, 'Archaeology of the Munster Plantation', p. 27.
7. Klingelhofer, *Castles and Colonists*, p. 81.
8. George Bennett, *The History of Bandon and the Principal Towns in the West Riding, County Cork* (Cork: Guy, 1869), pp. 94–5.
9. On escheats, see Holdsworth, *History of English Law*, iv. 437, 446.
10. Henley, *Spenser in Ireland*, p. 204.
11. Will of William Wiseman, 17 Feb. 1635, NAI RC 5, 'Transcripts of Deeds and Wills recited in Inquisitions (Chancery)', xviii. 362–74. Wiseman left some money to his nephew, Edmund Spenser.
12. Bennett, *History of Bandon*, pp. 25–7.
13. Welply, 'Spenser: Recent Researches', p. 182; Henley, *Spenser in Ireland*, pp. 204.
14. Welply, 'Spenser: Some New Discoveries', p. 447; Atkinson, *Bibliographical Supplement*, p. 30.
15. Hamer, 'Spenser's Marriage', p. 276.
16. Mary Anne Hutchinson, 'Boyle family', *Sp. Enc.*, p. 109.
17. Mendelson and Crawford, *Women in Early Modern England*, p. 182.
18. Caufield, *Council Book of Youghal*, p. 276; Welply, 'Spenser: Recent Researches', p. 169.
19. Henley, *Spenser in Ireland*, p. 199.
20. *Lismore Papers*, 2nd ser., vol. ii, pp. 12–3.
21. *The Complete Works of Edmund Spenser*, ed. Alexander Grosart, 9 vols. (London: privately printed, 1882–4), i. 556–7; Hamer, 'Spenser's Marriage', p. 224; Henley, *Spenser in Ireland*, pp. 194–5.
22. Stretton, 'Women, Property and Law', p. 49; Wrightson, *English Society*, pp. 101–2.
23. *CSPI, 1603–6*, p. 116.
24. On Heriot, see H. S. Bennett, *Life on the English Manor: A Study of Peasant Conditions, 1150–1400* (1937; Cambridge: Cambridge University Press, 1948), pp. 143–50.
25. Hamer, 'Spenser's Marriage', pp. 274–5; Spenser, *Works*, ed. Grosart, i. 558.
26. Henley, *Spenser in Ireland*, pp. 200–1; Welply, 'Spenser: Recent Researches', p. 202; Spenser, *Works*, ed. Grosart, i. 558–9.
27. *CSPI, 1611–14*, p. 221; Welply, 'Spenser: Recent Researches', p. 202.
28. Klingelhofer, *Castles and Colonists*, p. 122.
29. Ibid. 109, 117; Dunlop, 'Unpublished Survey', pp. 143–4.

30. O'Connell, 'The Nagles of Ballygriffin', p. 68; TCD MS 1216 (c.1703), fo. 52. On the provenance of this manuscript, a substantial collection of genealogies of prominent Irish families and its relationship to other manuscripts, see William O'Sullivan, 'John Mullan's Manuscripts', in Vincent Kinane and Anne Walsh (eds.), *Essays on the History of Trinity College Library* (Dublin: Four Courts, 2000), pp. 104–15. Other genealogies of the Nagles exist: see NLI MS GO 87, fo. 87; NLI MS GO 96, fos. 185–7; NLI MS GO 165, fos. 119–21.
31. On Monanimy and the Nagles, see Samuel Lewis, *A Topographical Dictionary of Ireland*, 2 vols. (1837; Baltimore: Clearfield, 2000), ii. 384–5.
32. Welply, 'Spenser: Recent Researches', p. 202.
33. Ibid. 203.
34. Hazel Maynard, entry on Sir Richard Nagle, *DIB* vi. 849–52. Richard was the son of James, brother of Elinor: O'Sullivan, 'Nagles of Ballygriffin', p. 67. Sylvanus's wife was also the great aunt of Edmund Burke: Thomas B. Gibson, 'Spenser and Kilcolman', *Dublin University Review* 3/1 (Mar. 1887), 82–92, at 91.
35. Henley, *Spenser in Ireland*, pp. 195–9.
36. MacCarthy-Morrogh, 'Munster Plantation', app. II, 'Biographies of the Undertakers'.
37. Henley, *Spenser in Ireland*, p. 199.
38. *Lismore Papers*, 2nd ser., vol. ii, pp. 139–40. See also ibid., 1st ser., vol. ii, p. 143.
39. Ibid., 2nd ser., vol. ii, p. 60.
40. Welply, 'Spenser: Recent Researches', p. 169.
41. Ibid. 203–4.
42. Ibid. 204.
43. Henley, *Spenser in Ireland*, pp. 203–4.
44. 'Edward Deering's Minutes of Trials Before the Court of Claims in Ireland—Book Marked C from 12 August 1660 to 26 Febr. 1663/4', Bodleian Library, Carte MS 67, fo. 29ᵛ.
45. Welply, 'Spenser: Recent Researches', p. 204.
46. Ibid. 203. The gravestones do not survive, and the overgrown graveyard, the church having been deconsecrated, contains very few gravestones dating before 1750: see Anon., *Memorial Inscriptions From St. James's Graveyard, Dublin* (Dublin: National Archives, 1988).
47. Henley, *Spenser in Ireland*, p. 205; Welply, 'Spenser: Recent Researches', p. 221.
48. 27 Mar. 1657, Letters of Lord Protector and Council, A/28, 26, fo. 118, PRO (Ireland). The document was destroyed in 1922, but is transcribed in Robert Dunlop (ed.), *Ireland under the Commonwealth: Being a Selection of Government Documents Relating to the Government of Ireland from 1651 to 1659*, 2 vols. (Manchester: Manchester University Press, 1913), ii. 659. See also Henley, *Spenser in Ireland*, pp. 206–7.
49. Welply, 'Spenser: Recent Researches', p. 221.
50. Thomas Eliot, Deputy Surveyor-General, 'Lands Set Out To The Transplanted Irish in the Province of Connaught' (c.1660), NLI MS 2515 (Ormond Family Papers), p. 151. For comment, see John Cunningham, 'Oliver Cromwell and the "Cromwellian" Settlement of Ireland', *HJ* 53 (2010), 919–37, at 933–4; Welply, 'Spenser: Recent Researches', p. 222.
51. Breandán Mac Giolla Choille (ed.), *Books of Survey and Distribution*, iii. *Co. Galway* (Dublin: HMC, 1962), pp. 129–30; Robert A. Simington (ed.), *Books of Survey and Distribution*, i. *Co. Roscommon* (Dublin: HMC, 1949), pp. 60–1.
52. See also the analysis in McCabe, *Spenser's Monstrous Regiment*, p. 285.
53. McCabe, *Spenser's Monstrous Regiment*, pp. 284–5; Fowler, '*A View of the Present State of Ireland*', *Sp. Handbook*, p. 326.
54. Houlbrooke, *English Family*, p. 111.
55. Deposition of Richard Gettings, 10 May 1642, MS 824, fo. 112ʳ⁻ᵛ, http://1641.tcd.ie/deposition.php?depID=824112r100a.
56. Deposition of John Petters, 19 Aug. 1642, MS 824, fo. 40ʳ⁻ᵛ, http://1641.tcd.ie/deposition.php?depID=824040r044; Deposition of William Merryfield, 19 Aug. 1642, MS 824, fo. 40ʳ⁻ᵛ, http://1641.tcd.ie/deposition.php?depID=825033r027.

57. Willy Maley, 'How Milton and Some Contemporaries Read Spenser's *View*'; Norah Carlin, 'Extreme of Mainstream? The English Independents and the Cromwellian Reconquest of Ireland, 1649–1651', in Bradshaw et al. (eds.), *Representing Ireland*, pp. 191–208, 209–26.

58. Henley, *Spenser in Ireland*, pp. 207–8; Welply, 'Spenser: Recent Researches', p. 221.

59. Atkinson, *Bibliographical Supplement*, p. 24.

60. Indenture between Hugolin Spenser and Pierce Power, National Archives of Ireland RC5, vol. 19, pp. 343–53; Andrew Hadfield, 'A Mortgage Agreement of Hugolin Spenser, Edmund Spenser's Grandson', *Sp. St.* (forthcoming).

61. Deposition of Hugh Hide, 14 Mar. 1653 who stated 'That there was of English Liuinge neere this deponent Viz Hughline Spencer now Liuinge att Renny': MS 827, fos. 118ʳ–119ᵛ (http://1641.tcd.ie/deposition.php?depID=8271181131).

62. Welply, 'Spenser: Recent Researches', p. 239.

63. J. G. Simms, 'The War of the Two Kings, 1685–91', in Moody et al. (eds.), *New History of Ireland*, iii. 478–508.

64. Henley, *Spenser in Ireland*, pp. 208–10; Welply, 'Spenser: Recent Researches', p. 223.

65. Welply, 'Spenser: Recent Researches', pp. 166, 240.

66. Henley, *Spenser in Ireland*, pp. 210–11; Welply, 'Spenser: Recent Researches', p. 239.

67. Herbert Wood, 'Spenser's Great-Grandson', *TLS*, 14 Feb. 1929, p. 118.

68. Welply, 'Spenser: Recent Researches', pp. 240–1.

69. Ibid. 240.

Appendix 2

1. Stephen Orgel, *Imagining Shakespeare* (Basingstoke: Palgrave, 2003), pp. 69–84.

2. Robert Tittler, *The Face of the City: Civic Portraiture and Civic Identity in Early Modern England* (Manchester: Manchester University Press, 2007).

3. Cooper, *Searching for Shakespeare*, pp. 175–91.

4. John Cotgrave, *Wits Interpreter, the English Parnassus, or A sure guide to those admirable accomplishments that compleat our English gentry* (London, 1655); Edward Phillips, *The New World of English Words, or A General English Dictionary* (London, 1658). On Cotgrave (1611?–1655?), see the *ODNB* entry by W. H. Kelliher. It is worth noting that some of the other portraits in the frontispiece to Phillips's dictionary are based on real portraits, such as Camden, Chaucer, and Bacon; others, notably Sidney, are clearly not.

5. Vertue, *Notebooks*, xviii. 25, 58. On Vertue's links to the Kit-Cat Club and Kneller, see Brian Cowman, 'An Open Elite: The Peculiarities of Connoisseurship in Early Modern England', *Modern Intellectual History* 1 (2004), 151–83, at 177.

6. 'There was no painting in Guise's collection when it came to Christ Church, Oxford, that was identified to be Spenser. Guise seems to have changed his collection quite a lot over the years and many of the paintings mentioned by Vertue were not in the collection anymore by the time it was bequeathed to Christ Church in 1765. It would also have been an unusual painting for Guise to have (or hold on to) as his interest as a collector were Italian old masters (very little portraiture). Should a portrait of Spenser have been in his collection it would have been not unlikely that he would have sold it to "streamline" his collection' (personal communication from Jacqueline Thalmann (Curator, Picture Gallery, Christ Church, Oxford).

7. For a list of copies of the Chesterfield portrait, see Freeman O'Donoghue, *Catalogue of Engraved British Portraits Preserved in the Department of Prints and Drawings in the British Museum*, 6 vols. (London: British Museum, 1908–25), iv. 166–7.

8. David Piper, 'The Chesterfield House Library Portraits', in René Wellek and Alvaro Ribeiro (eds.), *Evidence in Literary Scholarship: Essays in Memory of James Marshall Osborn* (Oxford: Clarendon Press, 1979), pp. 179–95, at p. 187. On Vertue, see *ODNB* entry by Martin Myrone; Alexander C. Judson, 'The Eighteenth-Century Lives of Spenser', *HLQ* 16 (1953), 161–81, at

164–8. The Director of the National Portrait Gallery, Sir Henry Hake, advised Alexander Judson and Lord Ilchester, who had both asked for his advice, against trusting Vertue as a reliable source (letters 10 Sept. (to Ilchester) and 6 Oct. (to Judson) 1948) (Spenser files, National Portrait Gallery).

9. Attwater, *Pembroke College*, p. 102. On Benjamin Wilson and William Mason, see the *ODNB* articles by E. I. Carlyle (rev. John A. Hargreaves) and Jules Smith.

10. Cooper (ed.), *Searching for Shakespeare*, pp. 70–1

11. Judson, *Life of Spenser*, pp. 208–9. Parts of this paragraph were written by Tarnya Cooper and I am extremely grateful for her advice on early modern portraiture.

12. *ODNB* entry by Raymond N. MacKenzie; Ophelia Field, *The Kit-Cat Club* (London: Harper-Collins, 2009), pp. 12–13.

13. Field, *Kit-Cat Club*, pp. 262–3.

14. John Somers, Baron Somers by Sir Godfrey Kneller, Bt. (1715–16), National Portrait Gallery 3223.

15. See the *ODNB* entry on Horace Walpole by Paul Langford; J. H. Plumb, *Sir Robert Walpole: The Making of a Statesman* (London: Cresset, 1956), p. 115. Betty Kemp points out that Vertue visited the Walpole family home and commented on its decor, designed by William Kent: *Sir Robert Walpole* (London: Weidenfeld and Nicolson, 1976), pp. 67–8.

16. *The Faerie Queene . . . with an exact Collation of the two Original Editions . . . to which are now added a new Life of the Author and also a glossary. Adorn'd with thirty-two copper plates from the original drawings of the late W. Kent*, ed. Thomas Birch, 3 vols. (London, 1751), vol. i, p. xviii.

17. H. M., Letter, 4 Feb. 1818, *Gentleman's Magazine* 88 (Jan.–June 1818), 224.

18. Hadfield, 'William Kent's Illustrations of *The Faerie Queene*'.

19. Gilbert White, *The Natural History of Selbourne*, ed. Richard Mabey (Harmondsworth: Penguin, 1977); information at the Gilbert White House, The Wakes, Selbourne.

20. Radcliffe, *Spenser: Reception History*, ch. 4; Wurtsbaugh, *Two Centuries of Spenserian Scholarship*, ch. 4.

21. Edmund Spenser, *Faery Queene, Book I*, ed. G. W. Kitchin (1864; Oxford: Clarendon Press, 1964), introd., p. x. Kitchin (1827–1912) was a friend of Charles Dodgson, another fellow at Christ Church who took a number of pictures of Kitchin's daughter. The interest in photography probably inspired Kitchin to read a great deal into portraits: see the *ODNB* entry by M. C. Curthoys.

22. On ruffs and hairstyles, see Jeffrey L. Singman, *Daily Life in Elizabethan England* (London: Greenwood, 1995), pp. 104–9.

23. Thomas Pennant, *A Tour in Scotland; MDCCLXIX* (London, 1776), p. 85. The edition in which the details are announced is the fourth, the first having been published in 1772; Piper, 'Chesterfield House Portraits', p. 187; Spenser files, National Portrait Gallery. On Thomas Pennant, see the *ODNB* entry by Charles W. J. Withers. I am grateful to Tarnya Cooper for advice on this paragraph.

24. Samuel Redgrave (ed.), *Catalogue of the Special Exhibition of Portrait Miniatures On Loan at The South Kensington Museum, June 1865* (London: Whittingham and Wilkins, 1865), p. 133; Judson, *Life*, p. 210. Other attributions in the Fitzhardinge collection also look fanciful: item 1476 states, 'Portrait, called Queen Elizabeth, but most probably that of Anne of Denmark, Queen of James I'.

25. On the history of a portrait surviving in Spenser's family in Ireland, see Welply, 'Edmund Spenser: Life and Lineage', pp. 241–2. There are other spurious relics of Spenser's life in Ireland 'discovered' in the early 18th century, indicating an appetite for material connected to the poet: see e.g. the clearly faked *A Canto of The Faerie Queene written by Spenser never before published* (1738).

26. Welply, 'Spenser: Recent Researches', p. 241.

27. Varro, 'Spenser's Age at His Death', *N&Q*, 1st ser. 4 (1851), 74.

28. E. M. B., 'Spenser's Monument', *N&Q*, 1st ser. 1 (1850), 481–2; E. M. B., 'Portraits of Spenser', *N&Q*, 1st ser. 3 (1851), 301; E. M. B., 'Spenser's Portrait', *N&Q*, 1st ser. 4 (1851), 101.

29. A. C. Judson, 'Spenser: Two Portraits', *N&Q* 182 (1942), 64.

30. Alexander C. Judson, 'Another Spenser Portrait', *HLQ* 6 (1943), 203–4.

Appendix 3

1. Cummings, *Critical Heritage*, p. 319. Edward Phillips, *Theatrum Poetarum Anglicanorum* (London, 1675), pt. II, pp. 34–6; subsequent references in parentheses in the text.
2. See *ODNB* entry by Gordon Campbell.
3. The author may have been Brooke Bridges: see Judson, 'Seventeenth-Century Lives', p. 45.
4. *Works* (1679), A1ʳ⁻ᵛ. The author's folio copy of *The Faerie Queene*, with extensive annotations is in the Folger Shakespeare Library: see Andrew Fleck, 'Early Modern Marginalia in Spenser's *Faerie Queene* at the Folger', *N&Q* 55 (2008), 165–70.
5. The story is first told in Phillips's version, although he has Spenser returning from Ireland to read *The Faerie Queene* to Sir Philip, having been secretary to Philip's brother, Sir Henry.
6. Hadfield, 'Kent's Illustrations', pp. 46–7; Greg Kucich, *Keats, Shelley, and Romantic Spenserianism* (University Park: Pennsylvania State University Press, 1991), pp. 302–11.
7. *Aubrey's Brief Lives*, p. 337.
8. However, it should also be noted that, while the other stories that Aubrey tells about Spenser have a clear source, this lacks one, which arouses some suspicion. Katherine Duncan-Jones asserts, 'Aubrey himself had his doubts about this story' (Duncan-Jones, *Sidney*, p. 120).
9. Sir Philip Sidney, *An Apology for Poetry*, ed. Geoffrey Shepherd, rev. Robert Maslen (Manchester: Manchester University Press, 2002), p. 110. For more sustained and sceptical discussion, see S. K. Heninger, Jr, *Sidney and Spenser: The Poet as Maker* (University Park: Pennsylvania State University Press, 1989).
10. The lines probably do refer to Burghley, as revisions to remove personal references to the 1611 folio indicate (Spenser, *Shorter Poems*, pp. 180, 590, 750).
11. This is true of Sean Lysaght's recent collection of lyric poems, which imaginatively reconstructs Spenser's life, *Spenser* (Westport: Stonechat Editions, 2011). I am extremely grateful to Jane Grogan for sending me a copy.
12. The defining life of an English reformer was Lawrence Humphrey's life of Bishop John Jewel: see Pritchard, *English Biography*, pp. 33–5.
13. Hile, 'Louis du Guernier's Illustrations'.
14. For analysis of Hughes's work, see *ODNB* entry by Thomas N. McGeary; Jewel Wurtsbaugh, *Two Centuries of Spenserian Scholarship (1609–1805)* (1936; Port Washington: Kennikat, 1970), ch. 2; Radcliffe, *Spenser, Reception History*, pp. 43–5; Ray Heffner, 'The Printing of John Hughes' Edition of Spenser, 1715', *MLN* 50 (1935), 151–3; Judson, 'Eighteenth-Century Lives', pp. 162–4. On Hughes's criticism of Spenser, see also Herbert E. Cory, *The Critics of Edmund Spenser* (1911; New York: Haskell, 1964), pp. 71–4; William R. Mueller, *Spenser's Critics: Changing Currents in Literary Taste* (Syracuse: Syracuse University Press, 1959), pp. 18–31.
15. *Works*, ed. John Hughes, vol. i, p. ii; subsequent references in parentheses in the text.
16. Wurtsbaugh, *Two Centuries*, p. 49, points out that Hughes was the 'best critic' among the 18th-century editors of Spenser, even though his edition is 'Largely dependent upon the accounts given by Camden and upon the summary of the last folio' and 'adds little new information'.
17. National Library of Wales MSS 3580Ci (Puleston 20). In a letter to Francis Price, 10 Oct. 1745, Edmund Spenser remarks, rather sadly, that events in Scotland have been 'a great damp for people must think of other things than Books'.
18. There is a life in Latin, written by John Ball (d. 1739), as a preface to his edition of a Latin translation of *The Shepheardes Calender* by Theodore Bathurst, which is sceptical of stories of Burghley's animus against Spenser, as well as the loss of the last books of *The Faerie Queene* by the unfortunate servant: *The Shepherds Calender, containing twelve aeglogues, proportionable to the twelve months. By Edmund Spencer, Prince of English Poets—Calendarium Pastorale, sive aeglogae duodecim, totidem anni mensibus accommodatae. Anglice olim scriptae ab Edmundo Spensero ... nunc autem elegante Latino carmine donatae a Theodoro Bathurst. Eng. & Lat.*, ed. John Ball (London, 1732). For comment, see Judson, 'Eighteenth-Century Lives', pp. 168–70. On Birch see the *ODNB* entry by David Philip Miller.
19. *The Faerie Queene ... with an exact Collation of the two Original Editions ... to which are now added a new Life of the Author and also a glossary. Adorn'd with thirty-two copper plates from the*

original drawings of the late W. Kent, ed. Thomas Birch, 3 vols. (London, 1751), vol. i, p. iii; subsequent references in parentheses in the text.

20. Cited in Cummings, *Critical Heritage*, pp. 56–9.

21. See pp. 284–5.

22. *The Works of Edmund Waller, Esq. in verse and prose. Published by Mr Fenton. (Observations on some of Mr Waller's poems)* (London, 1729), pp. xxix–xxx; Judson, 'Seventeenth-Century Lives', p. 164; Wurtsbaugh, *Two Centuries*, p. 55.

23. C. Suetonius Tranquillis, *Collections*, trans. J. C. Rolfe, 2 vols. (Cambridge, MA: Harvard University Press, 1914), ii. 461.

24. For analysis of different aspects of this widespread phenomenon, see Aaron Gurevich, *The Origins of European Individualism*, trans. Katherine Judelson (Oxford: Blackwell, 1995), ch. 5; Backus, *Life Writing*, ch. 2; Leslie P. Fairfield, '*The vocacyon of Johan Bale* and Early English Autobiography', *RQ* 24 (1971), 327–40.

25. On wordplay in the antiquarian sections of *A View*, see Anne Fogarty, 'The Colonization of Language: Narrative Strategies in *A View of the Present State of Ireland* and *The Faerie Queene*, Book VI', in Coughlan (ed.), *Spenser and Ireland, pp. 75–108; Baker,* '"Some Quirk, Some Subtle Evasion"'; Judith H. Anderson, 'The Antiquities of Fairyland and Ireland', JEGP *86 (1987), 199–214.*

26. *The Works of Edmund Spenser*, ed. H. J. Todd, 8 vols. (London, 1805); *The Works of Edmund Spenser, with observations on his life and writings*, ed. J. C. (London, 1840); Craik, *Spenser and His Poetry*; *Poetical Works*, ed. Child; *The Works of Edmund Spenser*, ed. J. Payne Collier, 5 vols. (London: Bell and Daldy, 1862); J. W. Hales, 'Edmund Spenser', in *Complete Works of Edmund Spenser*, ed. R. Morris (London: Macmillan, 1869), pp. xi–lv; R. W. Church, *Spenser* (London: Macmillan, 1879); *The Life of Edmund Spenser*, in *Works*, ed. Grosart, i (1882). See also Charles Henry Cooper and Thompson Cooper, *Athenae Cantabrigienses*, 2 vols. (Cambridge: Macmillan, 1858), ii. 258–67.

27. See e.g. Bruce, 'Spenser: Boyhood'; Donald Bruce, 'Spenser's Birth and Birthplace', *N&Q* 42 (1995), 283–5.

28. Rather more unkindly, Charles Eliot Norton dismissed Grosart's edition of Donne's poetry as marred 'by blunders proceeding from carelessness and lack of intelligence'. Both quotations are cited in the *ODNB* entry by Arthur Sherbo.

29. Craik, *Spenser and his Poetry*, pp. 11–12; *Poetical Works*, ed. Child, p. ix; F. C. Spenser, 'Locality of the Family of Edmund Spenser', *Gentleman's Magazine*, NS 18 (1842), 138–43; Anon., 'Edmund Spenser—The State Papers', *Dublin University Magazine* 58 (Aug. 1861), 132–44, at 131. See also F., 'Spenser's Lancashire Home', *N&Q*, 9th ser. 3 (1899), 481–3; A. J. Hawks, 'An Edmund Spenser in Lancashire in 1566', *N&Q* 196 (1951), 336.

30. See the criticisms in Welply, 'Spenser: Recent Researches', pp. 128–30.

31. *Works*, ed. Grosart, vol. i, pp. xiii; vol. iii, pp. civ–vii; subsequent references in parentheses in the text For another far-fetched reading, see Halpin, 'On Certain Passages in the Life of Edmund Spenser'.

32. *Variorum*, x. 11, line 223; trans., p. 257. Interestingly enough, William Camden refers to the mountains of Snowdonia as the British Alps (*Britannia*, p. 667).

33. J. B. Bullen, *The Myth of the Renaissance in Nineteenth-Century Writing* (Oxford: Oxford University Press, 1994). For one typical example, that emerged out of the same intellectual culture as Grosart, see Walter Ralegh, *Some Authors: A Collection of Literary Essays, 1896–1916* (Oxford: Clarendon Press, 1923), which contains essays on Boccaccio, Sir Thomas Hoby, Sir John Harington, and John Dryden, among others.

34. See p. 430 n. 88.

35. Lorna Reynolds, 'Review of Alexander C. Judson, *Life of Spenser*', *Dublin Magazine* (Apr./June 1947), 51–3, at 53.

36. Maley, 'Spenser's Life', *Sp. Handbook*, p. 28.

37. For an overview, see Stegner, 'Spenser's Biographers'.

Bibliography

PRIMARY SOURCES

Manuscript
Beinecke Library, Yale
  Osborn MS fa.12 (*View*)

British Library
  Add. MS 4235 (John Birch, 'Life of Spenser')
  Add. MS 12132 (Thomas Rogers, 'Leicester's Ghost')
  Add. MS 19832 (Richard Boyle, 'Memoir', 23 June 1632)
  Add. MS 19837 (Irish Chancery Recognizances)
  Add. MS 19869 (Grant to MacHenry)
  Add. MS 22022 (*View*)
  Add. MS 32486
  Add. MS 34313, fos. 85–121 ('The Supplication of the blood of the English, most lamentably murdred in Ireland, Cryeng out of the yearth for revenge, *c.*1598')
  Add. MS 34064 (Poetic miscellany attributed to Nicholas Breton)
  Add. MS 62540 (Laurence Nowell, Map of Britain and Ireland)
  Add. MS 68942 (manuscript version of *Mother Hubberds Tale*)
  Add. MS 81083 (William Scott, 'The Modell of Poesye', *c.*1599)
  MS Egerton 3165 (Arthur Gorges's poems)
  MS Harley 286
  MS Harley 1932 (*View*)
  MS Harley 3787, no. 21, fo. 184 ('Brief Note')
  MS Harley 6910
  MS Harley 7388 (*View*)
  MS Royal 17. B.XV (John Lane, 'Triton's Trumpet', 1621)
  MS Sloane 1695 (*View*)

Cambridge, Gonville and Caius College
  MS 188.221 (*View*)

Cambridge, Pembroke College
  College MS A alpha (Matthew Wren's notebook)
  A gamma (Richard Drake's book)
  M alpha x (Matthew Wren's notebook)

Cambridge, Queens' College
  MS 49

Cambridge University Library
Dd.10.60 (*View*)
Dd.14.28.1 (*View*)

Castle Howard Archives
'A View of the Present State of Ireland'

Chatsworth House
Calendar of the Lismore Manuscripts with Index of Matters, AD 1396–1974, 13 vols.
Cork MSS, vol. 6, no. 132; vol. 7, no. 184; vol. 25 (1st earl of Cork's Journals)

Folger Shakesepeare Library, Washington, DC
MS V.b.214 (contains a *View*)
MS X.d.520

Hampshire Record Office
Wallop Papers, 15M84/2/4/1; 15M84/2/4/3

Huntington Library
Ellesmere MS 7014 (*View*)

Lambeth Palace Library
MS 510 (*View*)
Carew MS 617
MS 631
MS 647

London Metropolitan Archives
MS 34270 (Merchant Taylors' School 'Ordinance Book, 1561–1667')
MS 34334 (Merchants Taylors' School Records)

The National Archives
PRO C2 Eliz. S1/40
PRO MPF 1/273
PRO SP 63 (Ireland: Elizabeth I)
MS 32,867 (1) (Doneraile Papers)
MS 34,058 (1)
TNA. PRO DD\S\SH/47, 48, 96
PRO MPF 75 (SP 64/1) ('Smerwick Harbour Map, 1580')
PRO IPM for Thomas Emelye, 15 September 1608
PROB 11/64 (Stephen Boyle, will, 8 October 1582)
PROB 11/109 (Walter Freckleton, will, 13 April 1607)
PROB 11/142 (Andrew Reade, will, 24 October 1623)
PROB 11/143 (John Freckleton, will, 3 February 1623/4)

National Archives of Ireland (NAI)
Chancery Bill A171
RC5, 'Transcripts of Deeds and Wills recited in Inquisitions (Chancery)', vol. 19, pp. 343–53
('Indenture between Hugolin Spenser and Pierce Power', 9 August 1673)
RC5, vol. 18, pp. 362–74 (William Wiseman, will 17, February 1635)

National Library of Ireland (NLI)
 MS 41, 985/1–2 (patent of grant of Molana Abbey to Sir Walter Ralegh and grant of Molana
  Abbey to Sir Thomas Harriot)
 MS 661 (Gurney MS) (*View*)
 MS 2515 (Ormond Family Papers) (Thomas Eliot, Deputy Surveyor-General, 'Lands Set Out To
 The Transplanted Irish in the Province of Connaught', *c.*1660)
 MS GO 87
 MS GO 96
 MS GO 165

National Library of Wales
 MSS 3580Ci (Puleston 20)
 National Maritime Museum
 Dartmouth Collection, vol. 8 (Irish Maps 1594–1685)

National Portrait Gallery
 Spenser files

Oxford, All Souls College
 MS 155, 58 ('Brief Note')

Oxford, Bodleian Library
 MS Bodley 902 (John Gower, *Confessio Amantis*)
 Carte MS 67 ('Edward Deering's Minutes of Trials Before the Court of Claims in Ireland—
  Book Marked C from 12 August 1660 to 26 Febr. 1663/4')
 Douce MS 280 (Commonplace Book of John Ramsey)
 MS Gough Ireland 2 (*View*)
 MS Rawlinson B.478 (*View*)
 MS Rawlinson A.317 (Wallop's Irish Treasury Accounts, 1588–91)

Petworth House
 '*Catalogus Librorum Biblotheca Petworthiana*' (1694)

St Margaret's Church, Westminster
 Parish Registers, reel 1, vol. 1, baptisms, 2 January 1539 to 15 May 1572;
 reel 1, vol. 2, marriages, 25 May 1572 to 6 March 1598

Suffolk Record Office
 E6/1/2
 Ac. 527/1, 4
 449/4/1
 FL 618/3/27/i (Edward Kirk, will (fragment))

Trinity College Dublin
 MS 1216 (*c.*1703)
 MS 589 (Edmund Spenser, 'Dialogue between Eudoxus and Irenius on the history of
 Ireland, 1596')

Printed

Andrewes, Lancelot, *Selected Sermons & Lectures*, ed. Peter McCullough (Oxford: Oxford University Press, 2005).

Anon., *The Annals of the Four Masters*, trans. Owen Connellan, 2 vols. (Kansas: Irish Genealogical Foundation, 2003).

Anon., *Calendars of the Proceedings in Chancery in the Reign of Queen Elizabeth*, vol. iii (1832).

Anon., *A Canto of The Faerie Queene written by Spenser never before published* (1738).

Anon., *Collection of the Statutes for the University and the Colleges of Cambridge* (London: Clowes, 1840).

Anon., '"A Discourse of Ireland" (circa 1599): A Sidelight on English Colonial Policy', ed. D. B. Quinn, *PRIA* 47 (1941–2), 151–66.

Anon., *Here beginneth a merye iest of a man that was called Howleglas* (London, 1565?).

Anon., *The Kalender of Shepheardes* (1506).

Anon., *Leabhar Gabhála: The Book of the Conquests of Ireland. The Recension of Micheál Ó Cléirigh*, ed. R. A. Stewart Macalister and John MacNeill (Dublin: Hodges, Figgis, 1916).

Anon., *Leicester's Commonwealth: The Copy of a Letter Written by a Master of Art of Cambridge (1584) and Related Documents*, ed. D. C. Peck (Athens, OH: Ohio University Press, 1985).

Anon., *The order of prayer, and other exercises, vpon Wednesdays and Frydayes, to auert and turne Gods wrath from vs, threatned by the late terrible earthquake: to be vsed in all parish churches and housholdes throughout the realme* (London, 1580).

Anon., *The Records of the Honourable Society of Lincoln's Inn: The Black Books*, 6 vols. (London: Lincoln's Inn, 1897–2001).

Anon., *The Registers of Saint Mary Magdalene, Bermondsey, 1548–1609* (1894).

Anon., '*The Supplication of the blood of the English, most lamentably murdred in Ireland, Cryeng out of the yearth for revenge*, c.1598', ed. Willy Maley, *Analecta Hibernica* 36 (1994), 3–91.

Anon., *The Three Parnassus Plays, 1598–1603*, ed. J. B. Leishman (London: Nicholson and Watson, 1949).

Apuleius, *The Golden Ass*, trans. Robert Graves (Harmondsworth: Penguin, 1950).

Ariosto, Lodovico, *Orlando Furioso*, trans. Sir John Harington, ed. Graham Hough (Carbondale: Southern Illinois University Press, 1962).

Aristotle, *The Nicomachean Ethics*, trans. David Ross (1925; Oxford: Oxford University Press, 1980).

Aubrey, John, *Aubrey's Brief Lives*, ed. Oliver Lawson Dick (1949; Harmondsworth: Penguin, 1962).

Bale, John, *The Vocacyon of Johan Bale*, ed. Peter Happé and John N. King (Binghamton, NY: MRTS, 1990).

—— *The Pageant of Popes* (London, 1574).

Barclay, Alexander, *The Eclogues of Alexander Barclay*, ed. Beatrice White (Oxford: EETS, 1928).

Bateman, Stephen, *The Trauayled Pylgrime* (London, 1569).

—— *Batman Upon Bartholome* (London, 1582).

Beacon, Richard, *Solon His Follie, or A politique discourse touching the reformation of common-weales conquered, declined or corrupted* (1594), ed. Clare Carroll and Vincent Carey (Binghamton, NY: MRTS, 1996).

Beaumont, Francis, *The Knight of the Burning Pestle*, ed. Michael Hattaway (1969; London: Black, 1995).

Bellay, Joachim Du, *The Regrets, with The Antiquities of Rome, Three Latin Elegies, and The Defense and Enrichment of the French Language: A Bilingual Edition*, ed. and trans. Richard Helgerson (Philadelphia: University of Pennsylvania Press, 2006).

Black, Joseph L. (ed.) *The Martin Marprelate Tracts: A Modernized and Annotated Edition* (Cambridge: Cambridge University Press, 2008).

Blundeville, Thomas, *The Foure Chiefest Offices Belonging to Horsemanship* (London, 1565).

The Book of Common Prayer, ed. Brian Cummings (Oxford: Oxford University Press, 2011).

The Booke of common prayer and administration of the sacraments, and other rites and ceremonies in the Church of England (London, 1580).

Boyle, Richard, *The Lismore Papers: Autobiographical Notes, Remembrances, and Diaries*, ed. Alexander B. Grosart, 2nd ser., 5 vols. (London: privately printed, 1886).

Brady, Ciaran (ed.) *A Viceroy's Vindication: Sir Henry Sidney's Memoir of Service in Ireland, 1556–78* (Cork: Cork University Press, 2002).

Brady, W. Maziere, *Clerical and Parochial Records of Cork, Cloyne, and Ross*, 3 vols. (Dublin: Alexander Thorn, 1863–4).

Breton, Nicholas, *The Works in Verse and Prose of Nicholas Breton*, ed. Alexander B. Grosart, 2 vols. (1879; New York: AMS Press, 1966).

——*A Smale Handfull of Fragrant Flowers selected and gathered out of the louely garden of sacred scriptures* (London, 1575).

—— *Brittons Bowvre of Delights Contayning Many, Most Delectable and Fine Deuices, of Rare Epitaphes, Pleasant Poems, Pastorals and Sonets* (London, 1591).

——*Melancholike Humours, in verses of diuerse natures* (London, 1600).

Browne, William, *Britannia's Pastorals* (London, 1616; Menston: Scolar Press, 1969).

Bryskett, Lodowick, *A Discourse of Ciuill Life containing the ethike part of morall philosophie. Fit for the instructing of a gentleman in the course of a vertuous life* (London, 1606).

Buchanan, George, *Ane detectioun of the doingis of Marie Quene of Scottis tuiching the murther of hir husband, and hir conspiracie, adulterie, and pretensit mariage with the Erle Bothwell. And ane defence of the trew Lordis, mantenaris of the kingis grace actioun and authoritie. Translatit out of the Latine quhilke was writtin be M.G.B.* (St Andrews, 1572).

Bullen, A. H. (ed.), *An English Garner: Some Longer Elizabethan Poems* (London: Constable, 1903).

Burke, Arthur Meredyth, *Memorials of St. Margaret's Church, Westminster: The Parish Registers, 1539–1660* (London: Eyre and Spottiswoode, 1914).

Byrchensha, Ralph, *A Discourse Occasioned Upon the Late Defeat, Giuen to the Arch-Rebels, Tyrone and Odonnell, by the right Honourable the Lord Mountioy, Lord Deputie of Ireland, the 24. of December, 1601* (London, 1602).

Caius, John, *The Works of John Caius, M.D. . . . with a Memoir of his Life by John Venn* (Cambridge: Cambridge University Press, 1912).

Calendar of Patent Rolls 33 Elizabeth I (1590–1591), ed. Simon R. Neal (Kew: List and Index Society, 2005).

Calvin, Jean, *Institutes of the Christian Religion*, ed. and trans. John T. McNeill and Ford Lewis Battles, 2 vols. (Philadelphia: Westminster Press, 1965).

——*Commentaries: The First Epistle of Paul the Apostle to the Corinthians*, ed. John W. Fraser (Edinburgh: Oliver, 1960).

Camden, William, *Britain, or A chorographicall description of the most flourishing kingdomes, England, Scotland, and Ireland, and the ilands adioyning*, trans. Philemon Holland (London, 1610).

—— *Annales the true and royall history of the famous empresse Elizabeth Queene of England France and Ireland*, trans. Abraham Darcie (London, 1625).

—— *The History of the Most Renowned and Victorious Princess Elizabeth*, trans. anon. (London, 1688).

Carew, George, *The Historie of Aravcana, written in verse by Don Alonso de Ercilla translated out of the spanishe into Englishe prose allmost to the Ende of the 16: Canto*, ed. Frank Pierce (Manchester: Manchester University Press, 1964).

Carew, Richard, *The survey of Cornwall* (London, 1602).

Cassirer, Ernst, Paul Oskar Kristeller, and John Herman Randall, Jr. (eds.), *The Renaissance Philosophy of Man* (Chicago: University of Chicago Press, 1948).

Caulfield, Richard, *The Council Book of the Corporation of Youghal, from 1610 to 1659, from 1666 to 1687, and from 1690 to 1800* (Guildford: Billing and Sons, 1878).

Cavendish, Margaret, *The Life of William Cavendish, Duke of Newcastle*, ed. C. H. Firth (2nd edn., London: Routledge, 1906).

Caxton, William (trans.) *The History of Reynard the Fox* (June 1481), ed. Edward Arber (Westminster: Constable, 1895).

Cecil, William, Baron Burghley, *The Execution of Iustice in England for maintenaunce of publique and Christian peace, against certeine stirrers of sedition, and adherents to the traytors and enemies of the realme* (London, 1583).

Chamberlain, John, *Letters by John Chamberlain, written during the reign of Elizabeth*, ed. Sarah Walters (London: Camden Society, 1861).

Chaucer, Geoffrey, *The Workes of Our Antient and Learned English Poet, Geffrey Chaucer, newly printed* [ed. Thomas Speght] (London, 1598).

—— *The Riverside Chaucer*, ed. Larry D. Benson et al. (1987; Oxford: Oxford University Press, 1988).

Chettle, Henry, and Thomas Greene (attrib.), *Greene's Groatsworth of Wit, Bought with a Million of Repentance (1592)*, ed. D. Allen Carroll (Binghamton, NY: MRTS, 1994).

Churchyard, Thomas, *A Generall Rehearsall of Warres* (1579).

—— *A warning for the wise, a feare to the fond, a bridle to the lewde, and a glasse to the good Written of the late earthquake chanced in London and other places, the. 6. of April 1580* (London, 1580).

Claudian, with an English trans. by Maurice Platnauer, 2 vols. (Cambridge, MA: Harvard University Press, 1922).

Cleaver, Robert, *A Godly Form of Household Gouernment* (London, 1598).

Clifford, Lady Ann, *Diaries of Lady Anne Clifford*, ed. D. J. H. Clifford (Stroud: Sutton, 2003).

Collins, Arthur, *Historical Collection of the Noble Families of Cavendishe, Holles, Vere, Harley, and Ogle* (London, 1572).

Contarini, Gaspar, *The Commonwealth and Gouernment of Venice*, trans. Lewis Lewkenor (London, 1599).

Copinger, John, *The Theatre of Catolique and Protestant Religion Diuided into Twelue Bookes* (Saint-Omer, 1620).

Copley, Anthony, *A Fig for Fortune* (London, 1596).

Cotgrave, John, *Wits Interpreter, the English Parnassus, or A sure guide to those admirable accomplishments that compleat our English gentry* (London, 1655).

Daniel, Samuel, *The Works of Samuel Daniel, newly augmented* (London, 1601).

Dart, John, *Westmonasterium, or The History and Antiquities of the Abbey Church of St. Peter's Westminster . . . A survey of the Church and Cloysters, taken in the year 1723*, 2 vols. (London, 1742).

Day, Angel, *The English Secretorie Wherin is contayned, a perfect method, for the inditing of all manner of epistles and familiar letters, together with their diuersities, enlarged by examples vnder their seuerall tytles* (London, 1586).

Derricke, John, *The Image of Irelande with a discouerie of woodkarne* (1581).

Dixon, John, *The First Commentary on 'The Faerie Queene', being an analysis of the annotations in Lord Bessborough's copy of the first edition of 'The Faerie Queene'*, ed. Graham Hough (privately printed, 1964).

Donne, John, *The Complete English Poems*, ed. A. J. Smith (Harmondsworth: Penguin, 1971).

Drant, Thomas, *Horace his Arte of Poetrie, Pistles, and Satyrs Englished* (London, 1567).

Dugdale, William, *Antiquities of Warwickshire, illustrated from records, leiger-books, manuscripts, charters, evidences, tombes, and armes: Illustrated* (London, 1656).

Dunlop, Robert (ed.), *Ireland under the Commonwealth: Being a Selection of Government Documents Relating to the Government of Ireland from 1651 to 1659*, 2 vols. (Manchester: Manchester University Press, 1913).

—— 'An Unpublished Survey of the Plantation of Munster in 1622', *JRSAI* 54 (1924), 128–46.

Edwards, Richard (ed.), *The Paradise of Dainty Devisese*, ed. Hyder Edward Rollins (Cambridge, MA: Harvard University Press, 1927).

Egerton, Sir Philip De Malpas Grey (ed.), *A Commentary of the Services and Charges of William Lord Grey de Wilton, K.G., by his son, Arthur Lord Grey de Wilton* (London: Camden Society, 1847).

Elizabeth I, *Collected Works*, ed. Leah S. Marcus, Janel Mueller, and Mary Beth Rose (Chicago: University of Chicago Press, 2000).

Erasmus, Desiderius, *The Collected Works of Erasmus*, xxxv. *The Adages, III, iv.i–iv.ii.100*, ed. John N. Grant (Toronto: University of Toronto Press, 2005).

Eusebius of Caesarea, *The Auncient Ecclesiasticall Histories of the first six hundred yeares after Christ*, trans. Meredith Hanmer (London, 1577).

Evans, Maurice (ed.), *Elizabethan Sonnets* (London: Dent, 1977).

Fanshaw, Ann, *The Memoirs of Anne, Lady Halkett and Ann, Lady Fanshawe*, ed. John Loftis (Oxford: Clarendon Press, 1979).

Farmer, William, 'William Farmer's Chronicles of Ireland from 1594 to 1613', ed. C. Litton Falkiner, *EHR* 22 (1907), 104–30, 527–52.

Fenner, Dudley, *The artes of logike and rethorike plainelie set foorth in the English tounge, easie to be learned and practised: togeather with examples for the practise of the same, for methode in the gouernment of the familie, prescribed in the word of God: and for the whole in the resolution or opening of certaine partes of Scripture, according to the same* (Middleburg, 1584).

Fenton, Elijah, *The Works of Edmund Waller, Esq. in verse and prose. Published by Mr. Fenton. (Observations on some of Mr. Waller's poems.)* (London, 1729).

Fitzgeoffrey, Charles, *The Poems of Charles FitzGeoffrey, 1593–1636*, ed. Alexander B. Grosart (Manchester: privately printed, 1881).

Fleming, Abraham, *A bright burning beacon forewarning all wise virgins to trim their lampes against the comming of the Bridegroome. Conteining a generall doctrine of sundrie signes and wonders, specially earthquakes both particular and generall: a discourse of the end of this world: a commemoration of our late earthquake, the 6. of April* (London, 1580).

Fletcher, Giles, *Of the Russe Commonwealt, or Maner of gouernement of the Russe emperour, (commonly called the Emperour of Moskouia) with the manners, and fashions of the people of that countrey* (London, 1591).

Forsett, Edward, *Pedantius*, ed. E. F. J. Tucker (Hildesheim: Georg Olms Verlag, 1989).

Fraunce, Abraham, *The Arcadian Rhetorike, or The praecepts of rhetorike made plaine by examples Greeke, Latin, English, Italian, French, Spanish, out of Homers Ilias, and Odissea, Virgils Aeglogs, . . . and Aeneis, Sir Philip Sydnieis Arcadia, songs and sonnets* (London, 1588).

Fuller, Thomas, *The Worthies of England*, ed. John Freeman (London: Unwin, 1952).

Fulwood, William, *The Enimie of Idlenesse teaching the maner and stile how to endite, compose and write all sorts of epistles and letters* (London, 1568).

Gainsford, Thomas, *The True Exemplary, and Remarkable History of the Earle of Tirone* (London, 1619).

Gascoigne, George, *The spoyle of Antwerpe. Faithfully reported, by a true Englishman, who was present at the same* (London, 1576).

——*A Hundreth Sundrie Flowres*, ed. G. W. Pigman III (Oxford: Clarendon Press, 2000).

Gelderen, Martin van (ed.), *The Dutch Revolt* (Cambridge: Cambridge University Press, 1993).

Gilbert, Humphrey, *Queene Elizabethes Achademy*, ed. F. J. Furnivall, EETS extra ser. 8 (London: Routledge, 1869), pp. 1–12.

Golding, Arthur, *A discourse vpon the earthquake that hapned throughe this realme of Englande, and other places of Christendom, the first of Aprill. 1580* (London, 1580).

Googe, Barnabe, *The Firste Syxe Bokes of the Mooste Christian Poet Marcellus Palingenius, called the zodiake of life, Newly translated out of Latin into English by Barnabe Googe* (London, 1561).

——*Eclogues, Epitaphs and Sonnets*, ed. Judith M. Kennedy (Toronto: University of Toronto Press, 1989).

——*Foure Bookes of Husbandry, collected by M. Conradus Heresbachius* (London, 1577).

Gorges, Sir Arthur, *The Poems of Sir Arthur Gorges*, ed. Helen Estabrook Sandison (Oxford: Clarendon Press, 1953).

Gosson, Stephen, *The Schoole of Abuse conteining a plesaunt [sic] inuectiue against poets, pipers, plaiers, iesters, and such like caterpillers of a co[m]monwelth* (London, 1579).

——*Markets of Bawdrie: The Dramatic Criticism of Stephen Gosson*, ed. Arthur F. Kinney (Salzburg: Institut fur Englische Sprache und Literatur, Universitat Salzburg, 1974).

Greene, Robert, *Greenes vision vvritten at the instant of his death. Conteyning a penitent passion for the folly of his pen* (London, 1592).

——*The Repentance of Robert Greene Maister of Artes. Wherein by himselfe is laid open his loose life, with the manner of his death* (London, 1592).

Greville, Fulke, 'A Dedication to Sir Philip Sidney', in *The Prose Work of Fulke Greville, Lord Brooke*, ed. John Gouws (Oxford: Oxford University Press, 1986), pp. 3–135.

Griffin, Bartholomew, *Fidessa, More Chaste Then Kinde* (1602).

Grosart, A. B., *The Townley MSS: The Spending of the Money of Robert Nowell of Reade Hall, Lancashire: Brother of Dean Alexander Nowell, 1568–1580* (Manchester: privately printed, 1877).

Hadfield, Andrew, and John McVeagh (eds.), *Strangers to that Land: British Perceptions of Ireland from the Reformation to the Famine* (Gerrards Cross: Colin Smythe, 1994).

Hakluyt, Richard, *The Principall Nauigations, Voiages and Discoueries of the English Nation* (London, 1589).

Halkett, Anne, *see* Fanshawe, Ann.

Halsted, Edward, *The History and Topographical Survey of the County of Kent*, 4 vols. (Canterbury, 1778–99).

Harriot, Thomas, *A Briefe and True Report of the New Found Land of Virginia* (London, 1590).

Hartley, T. E. (ed.), *Proceedings in the Parliament of Elizabeth I*, iii. *1593–1601* (Leicester: Leicester University Press, 1995).

Harvey, Gabriel, *The Works of Gabriel Harvey*, ed. Alexander B. Grosart, 3 vols. (London: privately printed, 1885).

—— *Letter-Book of Gabriel Harvey, 1573–1580*, ed. Edward John Long Scott (London: Camden Society, 1884).

—— *Ciceronianus*, ed. and trans. Harold S. Wilson and Clarence A. Forbes (Lincoln: University of Nebraska Studies, 1945).

—— *Fowre Letters and certaine Sonnets, especially touching Robert Greene and other parties by him abused (1592)*, ed. G. B. Harrison (1922; Edinburgh: Edinburgh University Press, 1966).

—— *Gratulationum Valdinensium* (London, 1578).

—— *A New Letter of Notable Contents* (London, 1593).

Harvey, Gabriel, *Pierces Supererogation, or A new prayse of the old asse, a preparatiue to certaine larger discourses, intituled Nashes fame* (London, 1593).

—— *Smithus; vel Musarum lachrymae pro obitu honoratissimi viri, atque hominis multis nominibus clarissime, Thomae Smithi, Equitis Britanni, Maiestatisqúe Regiae secretarij* (London, 1578).

Harvey, John, *An Astrologicall Addition, or Supplement to be Annexed to the Late Discourse Vpon the Great Coniunction of Saturne, and Iupiter* (London, 1583).

—— *Leape Yeere: A Compendious Prognostication for the Yeere of our Lorde God. M.D.LXXXIIII* (London, 1584).

—— *A Discoursiue Probleme Concerning Prophesies how far they are to be valued, or credited, according to the surest rules, and directions in diuinitie, philosophie, astrologie, and other learning* (London, 1588).

—— *An Almanacke, or Annuall Calender with a Compendious Prognostication Thereunto Appendyng, Seruyng for the Yeere of our Lord. 1589* (London, 1589).

Harvey, Richard, *An Astrological Discourse Upon the Great and Notable Coniunction of the Tvvo Superiour Planets, Saturne & Iupiter, which shall happen the 28 day of April, 1583* (London, 1583).

—— *A Theologicall Discourse of the Lamb of God and His Enemies contayning a briefe commentarie of Christian faith and felicitie, together with a detection of old and new barbarisme, now commonly called Martinisme* (London, 1590).

Heath, Thomas, *A Manifest and Apparent Confutation of an Astrological Discourse, lately published* (London, 1583).

Heywood, James, and Thomas Wraight (eds.), *Cambridge University Transactions during the Puritan Controversies of the Sixteenth and Seventeenth Centuries*, 2 vols. (London: Bohn, 1854).

Hoby, Margaret, *The Private Life of an Elizabethan Lady: The Diary of Lady Margaret Hoby, 1599–1605* (Stroud: Sutton, 1998).

Holinshed, Raphael, *Chronicles of England, Scotland and Ireland*, 3 vols. (London, 1587).

Homer, *Illiad*, trans. Stanley Lombardo (Indianapolis: Hackett, 1997).

Horace, *The Satires of Horace and Persius*, trans. Niall Rudd (Harmondsworth: Penguin, 1973).

Hunter, William B., Jr (ed.), *The English Spenserians: The Poetry of Giles Fletcher, George Wither, Michael Drayton, Phineas Fletcher and Henry More* (Salt Lake City: University of Utah Press, 1977).

Hutchinson, Lucy, *Memoirs of the Life of Colonel Hutchinson: With a Fragment of Autobiography of Mrs Hutchinson*, ed. N. H. Keeble (London: Dent, 1995).

Jonson, Ben, *Poems*, ed. Ian Donaldson (Oxford: Oxford University Press, 1975).

—— *The Complete Poems*, ed. George Parfitt (Harmondsworth: Penguin, 1975).

Josselin, Ralph, *The Diary of Ralph Josselin, 1616–1683*, ed. Alan Macfarlane (Oxford: Oxford University Press, 1976).

Kempe, William, *The Education of Children in learning declared by the dignitie, vtilitie, and method thereof. Meete to be knowne, and practised aswell of parents as schoolmaisters* (London, 1588).

Kristellar, Paul Oskar (ed.), *The Renaissance Philosophy of Man* (Chicago: University of Chicago Press, 1948).

Kyd, Thomas, *The Spanish Tragedy*, ed. Philip Edwards (1959; Manchester: Manchester University Press, 1988).

Kyffin, Maurice, *The Blessednes of Brytaine* (London, 1588).

Lambarde, William, *A Perambulation of Kent conteining the description, hystorie, and customes of that shyre* (London, 1576).

Lauardin, Jaques de, *The Historie of George Castriot, surnamed Scanderbeg, King of Albanie Containing his famous actes, his noble deedes of armes, and memorable victories against the Turkes, for the faith of Christ. Comprised in twelue bookes: by Iaques de Lauardin, Lord of Plessis Bourrot, a nobleman of France. Newly translated out of French into English by Z.I. Gentleman* (London, 1596).

Lewkenor, Lewis, *The Resolved Gentleman* (London, 1594).

—— *A Discourse of the Usage of the English Fugitiues, by the Spaniard* (London, 1595).

—— *The Estate of English Fugitiues under the King of Spaine and his Ministers* (London, 1596).

Lichfield, William, *The Trimming of Thomas Nashe Gentleman, by the high-tituled patron Don Richardo de Medico campo, barber chirurgion to Trinitie Colledge in Cambridge* (London, 1597).

Lily, William, *A short introduction of grammar generallie to be vsed. Compiled and set forth, for the bringing vp of all those that intend to attaine the knovvledge of the Latine tongue* (London, 1557).

Lipsius, Justus, *Two bookes of constancie. Written in Latine, by Justus Lipsius. Containing, principallie, A comfortable conference, in common calamities. And will serue for a singular consolation to all that are privately distressed, of afflicted, either in body or mind. Englished by John Stradling* (London, 1595).

Llwyd, Humphrey, *The Breviary of Britain, with selections from 'The History of Cambria'*, ed. Philip Schwyzer (London: MHRA, 2011).

Lodge, Thomas, *Catharos: Diogenes in his Singularitie* (London, 1591).

—— *A Fig for Momus* (London, 1595).

—— and Robert Greene, *A Looking Glass for London and England (1594)*, ed. W. W. Greg (London: Malone Society, 1932).

Lucretius, *On The Nature of the Universe*, trans. Ronald Latham (Harmondsworth: Penguin, 1951).

Luther, Martin, *Selections from His Writings*, ed. John Dillenberger (New York: Doubleday, 1961).

Mac Giolla Choille, Breandán (ed.) *Books of Survey and Distribution*, iii. *Co. Galway* (Dublin: HMC, 1962).

Machin, Henry, *The Diary of Henry Machin, Citizen and Merchant-Taylor of London, from A.D. 1550 to A.D. 1563*, ed. John Gough Nicholls (London: Camden Society, 1848).

MacLysaght, Edward (ed.), 'Doneraile Papers', *Analecta Hibernica* 15 (1944), 335–62; 20 (1958), 56–91.

Mac Niocaill, Gearóid, ed., *Crown Surveys of Lands, 1540–41, with the Kildare Rental begun in 1518* (Dublin: Irish Manuscripts Commission, 1992).

Malby, Nicholas, *A Plaine and Easie Way to Remedie a Horse that is Foundered in his Feete* (London, 1576).

—— *Remedies for Diseases in Horses* (London, 1576).

Markham, Gervase, *The English Housewife*, ed. Michael R. Best (Montreal: McGill-Queen's University Press, 1986).

Middleton, Thomas, *The Collected Works*, ed. Gary Taylor and John Lavagnino, 2 vols. (Oxford: Clarendon Press, 2007).

Miola, Robert S. (ed.), *Early Modern Catholicism: An Anthology of Primary Sources* (Oxford: Oxford University Press, 2007).

Mornay, Philippe du Plessis, *A Discourse of Life and Death: written in French by Ph. Mornay. Antonius, a tragoedie written also in French by Ro. Garnier. Both done in English by the Countesse of Pembroke* (London, 1592).

——*A Discourse of Life and Death: written in French by Phil. Mornay. Done in English by the Countesse of Pembroke* (London, 1606).

——*Six Excellent Treatises of Life and Death collected (and published in French) by Philip Mornay, sieur du Plessis; and now (first) translated into English* (London, 1607).

Moryson, Fynes, *An Itinerary Containing His Ten Yeeres Travell through the Twelve Dominions of Germany, Bohmerland, Sweitzerland, Netherland, Denmarke, Poland, Italy, Turky, France, England, Scotland, and Ireland* (1617), 4 vols. (Glasgow: MacLehose, 1908).

Mulcaster, Richard, *The Passage of our Most Drad Soueraigne Lady Quene Elyzabeth through the citie of London to westminster the daye before her coronacion Anno 1558* (London, 1558).

——*Positions, wherein those primitive circumstances be examined, which are necessarie for the training vp of children* (London, 1581); ed. Robert Herbert Quick (London: Longman, 1881).

——*The First Part of the Elementarie vvhich entreateth chefelie of the right writing of our English tung* (London, 1582).

——*The Educational Writings of Richard Mulcatser (1532–1611)*, ed. James Oliphant (Glasgow: MacLehose, 1903).

Munday, Anthony [A. M.], *The True Reporte of the Prosperous Successe which God gaue vnto our English souldiours against the forraine bands of our Romaine enemies lately ariued, (but soone inough to theyr cost) in Ireland, in the yeare 1580* (London, 1581).

Murner, T., *A Merye Jest of a man called Howleglas* (London, 1528?), Bodleian Library, shelfmark 4°.Z.3 Art Seld.

Nashe, Thomas, *The Works of Thomas Nashe*, ed. R. B. McKerrow, 5 vols. (Oxford: Blackwell, 1958).

Nelson, Alan H., and John R. Elliott, Jr (eds.), *Inns of Court: Records of Early English Drama*, 3 vols. (Woodbridge: Brewer, 2010).

Nenna, Giovanni Battista, *Nennio, or A Treatise of Nobility*, trans. William Jones (Jerusalem: Israel Universities Press, 1967).

Newton, K. C. (ed.), *A Calendar of Deeds Relating to Saffron Walden and Neighbouring Parishes, 13th–18th. Centuries*, 6 vols. (Saffron Walden: Essex County Library, 1950).

Niccols, Richard, *The Begger's Ape* (London, 1627).

Nicholls, K. W. (ed.), 'Some Documents on Irish Law and Custom in the Sixteenth Century', *Analecta Hibernica* 26 (1970), 103–29.

Nichols, John, *The Progresses and Public Processions of Queen Elizabeth*, 3 vols. (London, 1823).

Niclaes, Hendrik, *An Apology for the Service of Love, and the people that own it, commonly called, the family of love. Being a plain, but groundly discourse, about the right and true Christian religion* (London, 1656).

Noot, Jan van der, *A Theatre wherein be represented as wel the miseries & calamities that follow the voluptuous worldlings as also the greate ioyes and plesures which the faithfull do enioy. An argument both profitable and delectable, to all that sincerely loue the word of God. Deuised by S. Iohn van-der Noodt. Seene and allowed according to the order appointed* (London, 1569).

——*The Olympic Epics of Jan van der Noot: A facsimile edition of 'Das Buch Extasis', 'Een Cort Begryp Der XII Bocken Olympiados' and 'Abrege Des Douze Livres Olympiades'*, ed. C. A. Zaalberg (Assen: Van Gorcum, 1956).

——(misattributed), *The Gouerance and Preseruation of them that Feare the Plage* (London, 1569).

Nowell, Alexander, *A Catechism or First Instruction and Learning of Christian Religion*, trans. Thomas Norton (1570; London: Parker Society, 1868).

Nowell, Robert, *The Spending of the Money of Robert Nowell*, ed. Alexander B. Grosart (Manchester: privately printed, 1877).

Nugent, Richard, *Cynthia*, ed. Angelina Lynch (Dublin: Four Courts, 2010).

O'Grady, Standish, (ed.), *Pacata Hibernia, or A history of the Wars in Ireland during the reign of Queen Elizabeth especially within the Province of Munster under the government of Sir George Carew)* (London: Downey, 1896).

Ortelii, Abrahami, *Epistulae*, ed. J. H. Hessels, 4 vols. (Cambridge: Ecclesiae Londino-Batavae Archivum, 1887).

O'Sullivan Bear, Philip, *Ireland under Elizabeth: Chapters towards a History of Ireland in the Reign of Elizabeth*, trans. Matthew J. Byrne (Dublin: Sealy, Bryers and Walker, 1903).

Ovid, *Metamorphoses*, trans. Mary M. Innes (Harmondsworth: Penguin, 1955).

——*Sorrows of an Exile*, trans. A. D. Melville (1992; Oxford: Oxford University Press, 1995).

Palmer, Thomas, *An essay of the meanes how to make our travails more profitable* (London, 1606).

Payne, Robert, *A Briefe Description of Ireland* (London, 1589).

Pennant, Thomas, *A Tour in Scotland; MDCCLXIX* (London, 1776).

Petrilotichii, Secundi Solitariensis, *Poemata* (1576).

Phillips, Edward, *The New World of English Words, or A General English Dictionary* (London, 1658).

——*Theatrum Poetarum Anglicanorum* (London, 1675).

Pollard, A. F., and Marjorie Blatcher, 'Hayward Townshend's Journals', *HR* 12 (1934), 1–31.

Polybius, *The Rise of the Roman Empire*, trans. Ian Scott-Kilvert (Harmondsworth: Penguin, 1979).

Puttenham, George, *The Arte of English Poesie* (London, 1589).

Quintilian, *The Orator's Education*, trans. Donald A. Russell, 4 vols. (Cambridge, MA: Harvard University Press, 2001).

Ralegh, Sir Walter, *The Letters of Sir Walter Ralegh*, ed. Agnes Latham and Joyce Younings (Exeter: University of Exeter Press, 1999).

——*The Poems of Sir Walter Ralegh: A Historical Edition*, ed. Michael Rudick (Tempe, AZ: MRTS, 1999).

Ramus, Peter, *The logike of the moste excellent philosopher P. Ramus martyr*, trans. M. Roll (London, 1574).

——*The Latine Grammar of P. Ramus: translated into English* (London, 1585).

——*Elementes of Geometrie. Written in Latin by that excellent scholler, P. Ramus*, trans. Thomas Hood (London, 1590).

——*The Art of Arithmeticke in whole numbers and fractions in a more readie and easie method then hitherto hath bene published, written in Latin by P. Ramus; and translated into English by William Kempe* (London, 1592).

Richardson, Alexander, *The Logicians School-Master* (London, 1629).

Robinson, Hastings (ed.), *The Zurich Letters*, 2 vols. (Cambridge: Cambridge University Press, 1845).

Rogers, Thomas, *Celestiall Elegies of the Goddesses and the Muses Deploring the Death of the Right Honourable and Vertuous Ladie the Ladie Fraunces Countesse of Hertford* (London, 1598).

——*Leicester's Ghost*, ed. Franklin B. Williams, Jr (Chicago: Chicago University Press, 1972).

Sabini, Georgii Brande, *Poemata* (1563).

Salter, Robert, *Wonderfull Prophecies from the beginning of the monarchy of this land hidden vnder the parables of: Three young noble-men in a fiary fornace. A chast wife, and two old fornicators. The idol Belus and his dragon. Daniel in a den amid lyons* (London, 1627).

Sannazaro, Jacopo, *Arcadia and Piscatorial Eclogues*, ed. and trans. Ralph Nashe (Detroit: Wayne State University Press, 1966).

Shakespeare, William, *King Lear*, ed. R. A. Foakes (London: Nelson, 1997).

Sidney, Mary, *The Collected Works of Mary Sidney Herbert, Countess of Pembroke*, ed. Margaret P. Hannay, Noel J. Kinnamonn, and Michael G. Brennan, 2 vols. (Oxford: Clarendon Press, 1998).

Sidney, Sir Philip, *The Countesse of Pembrokes Arcadia* (London, 1590).

Sidney, Sir Philip, *The Countesse of Pembrokes Arcadia* (London, 1593).

——*An Apology for Poetry*, ed. Geoffrey Shepherd, rev. Robert Maslen (Manchester: Manchester University Press, 2002).

Silverstein, Theodore (ed.), *Medieval English Lyrics* (London: Arnold, 1971).

Simington, Robert A. (ed.), *Books of Survey and Distribution*, i. *Co. Roscommon* (Dublin: HMC, 1949).

Skelton, John, *Pithy, Pleasaunt and Profitable Workes of Maister Skelton, Poete Laureate. Nowe collected and newly published. Anno 1568* (London, 1568).

Smith, Sir Thomas, *De Republica Anglorum: A discourse on the commonwealth of England*, ed. L. Alston (1906; Shannon: Irish University Press, 1972).

—— *A letter sent by I.B. Gentleman vnto his very frende Maystet [sic] R.C. Esquire vvherin is conteined a large discourse of the peopling & inhabiting the cuntrie called the Ardes, and other adiacent in the north of Ireland, and taken in hand by Sir Thomas Smith one of the Queenes Maiesties priuie Counsel, and Thomas Smith Esquire, his sonne* (London, 1572).

—— *Literary and Linguistic Works*, 3 vols. (Stockholm: Almqvist & Wiksell, 1963–83).

Smith, William, *Chloris, or The Complaint of the Passionate Despised Shepheard* (London, 1596).

Sparke, Thomas, *A Sermon Preached at Whaddon in Buckinghamshyre the 22. of Nouember 1593. at the buriall of the Right Honorable, Arthur Lorde Grey of Wilton* (Oxford, 1593).

Speed, John, *The Theatre of the Empire of Great Britaine* (London, 1612).

Spenser, Edmund, *The Works of Edmond Spenser . . . Whereunto is added, an account of his life; with other new additions* (London, 1679).

—— *The Works of Mr. Edmund Spenser,* ed. John Hughes, 6 vols. (London, 1715).

—— *The Works of Edmund Spenser,* ed. H. J. Todd, 8 vols. (London, 1805).

—— *The Works of Edmund Spenser, with observations on his life and writings,* ed. J. C. (London, 1840).

—— *Poetical Works,* ed. Frances J. Child, 5 vols. (Boston: Little, Brown & Co., 1855).

—— *The Works of Edmund Spenser,* ed. J. Payne Collier, 5 vols. (London: Bell and Daldy, 1862).

—— *Complete Works of Edmund Spenser,* ed. R. Morris (London: Macmillan, 1869).

—— *The Complete Works of Edmund Spenser,* ed. Alexander Grosart, 9 vols. (London: privately printed, 1882–4).

—— *The Yale Edition of the Shorter Poems of Edmund Spenser,* ed. William A. Oram, Einar Bjorvand, Ronald Bond, Thomas H. Cain, Alexander Dunlop, and Richard Schell (New Haven: Yale University Press, 1989).

—— *Edmund Spenser's Amoretti and Epithalamion: A Critical Edition,* ed. Kenneth J. Larsen (Tempe, AZ: MRTS, 1997).

—— *Axiochus. A most excellent dialogue, written in Greeke by Plato the phylosopher: concerning the shortnesse and vncertainty of this life, with the contrary ends of the good and wicked. / Translated out of Greeke by Edw. [sic] Spenser; Heereto is annexed a sweet speech or oration spoken at the tryumphe at White-hall before her Maiestie, by the page to the right noble Earle of Oxenforde* (London, 1592).

—— *The 'Axiochus' of Plato Translated by Edmund Spenser,* ed. Frederick Morgan Padleford (Baltimore: Johns Hopkins University Press, 1934).

—— *Colin Clouts come home againe* (London, 1595).

—— *Complaints* (London, 1591), BL shelfmark 239 i I.

—— *Complaints* (London, 1591), Cambridge University Library, shelfmark Syn. 7.59.77.

—— *The Faerie Queene Disposed into twelue books, fashioning XII. morall vertues* (London, 1590).

—— *The Faerie Queene Disposed into twelue bookes, fashioning XII. morall vertues* (London, 1596).

—— *The Faerie Queene, The Shepheardes Calender, together with the other works of Edmund Spenser* (London, 1611), Cambridge University Library, shelfmark Keynes S.6.9.

—— *The Faerie Queene, The Shepheardes Calendar, together with the other works of Edmund Spenser* (London, 1611), Cambridge University Library, shelfmark O*.9.27 (C).

—— *The Faerie Queene. By Edmund Spenser. With an exact Collation of the two Original Editions . . . to which are now added, a new Life of the Author [by Thomas Birch] and also a glossary. Adorn'd with thirty-two copper plates from the original drawings of the late W. Kent,* ed. Thomas Birch, 3 vols. (London, 1751).

—— *The Faerie Queene: Book Six and Mutabilitie Cantos,* ed. Andrew Hadfield and Abraham Stoll (Indianapolis: Hackett, 2007).

—— *Faery Queene, Book I,* ed. G. W. Kitchin (1864; Oxford: Clarendon Press, 1964).

—— *Fowre Hymnes* (London, 1596).

—— *The Mutabilitie Cantos*, ed. S. P. Zitner (London: Nelson, 1968).

—— *Prothalamion or A Spousall Verse* (London, 1596).

—— *The Shepheardes Calender* (London, 1591).

—— *The Shepherds Calender, containing twelve æglogues, proportionable to the twelve months. By Edmund Spencer, Prince of English Poets.-Calendarium Pastorale, sive æglogæ duodecim, totidem anni mensibus accommodatæ. Anglice olim scriptæ ab Edmundo Spensero . . . nunc autem elegante Latino carmine donatæ a Theodoro Bathurst. Eng. & Lat.*, ed. John Ball (London, 1732).

——*A View of the State of Ireland as it was in the reign of Queen Elizabeth. Written by way of a Dialogue between Eudoxus and Ireneus: To which is prefix'd the Author's Life, and an Index added to the Work* (Dublin, 1763).

—— *A View of the Present State of Ireland*, ed. W. L. Renwick (1934; Oxford: Clarendon Press, 1970).

Stanihurst, Richard, *The First Foure Bookes of Virgils AEneis, translated into English heroicall verse, by Richard Stanyhurst: with other poëticll [sic] deuises thereto annexed* (London, 1583).

Stapleton, Richard [R. S.] (ed.), *The Phoenix Nest* (London, 1595).

—— *The Phoenix Nest, 1593*, ed. Hyder Edward Rollins (Cambridge, MA: Harvard University Press, 1931).

Statius, *Statius*, ed. and trans. D. R. Shackleton Bailey, 2 vols. (Cambridge, MA: Harvard University Press, 2003).

Stellatus, Marcellus Palingenius, *The Zodiake of Life, written by the excellent and Christian poet, Marcellus Palingenius Stellatus*, trans. Barnabe Googe (London, 1576).

Stone, Nicholas, 'The Notebook and Accounts of Nicholas Stone', *Walpole Society*, vol. 7 (1918–19).

Stow, John, *A Survey of London*, ed. Charles Lethbridge Kingsford, 2 vols. (1908; Oxford: Clarendon Press, 2000).

—— *Certaine worthye manuscript poems of great antiquitie reserued long in the studie of a Northfolke gentleman. And now first published by I.S. 1 The statly tragedy of Guistard and Sismond. 2 The northren mothers blessing. 3 The way to thrifte* (London, 1597).

Stubbs, John, *John Stubbs's Gaping Gulf with Letters and Other Relevant Documents*, ed. Lloyd E. Berry (Charlottesville: University of Virginia Press, 1968).

Suetonius Tranquillis, C., *Collections*, trans. J. C. Rolfe, 2 vols. (Cambridge, MA: Harvard University Press, 1914).

Tacitus, *On Imperial Rome*, trans. Michael Grant (Harmondsworth: Penguin, 1956).

Tanner, Robert, *A Prognosticall Iudgement of the Great Coniunction of the Two Superiour Planets, Saturne and Iupiter, which shall happen the 8. day of Aprill. 1583* (London, 1583).

Tarlton, Richard, *Tarleton's Tragical Treatises, contaynyng sundrie discourses and pretty conceytes, both in prose and verse* (London, 1578).

Tasso, Torquato, *Godfrey of Bulloigne, or The Recouerie of Hierusalem*, trans. R. C. [Richard Carew] (London, 1594).

Terence, *Andria the First Comoedie of Terence, in English. A furtherance for the attainment vnto the right knowledge, & true proprietie, of the Latin tong. And also a commodious meane of help, to such as haue forgotten Latin, for their speedy recouering of habilitie, to vnderstand, write, and speake the same. Carefully translated out of Latin, by Maurice Kyffin* (London, 1588).

Tobias, *Mirabilia Opera Dei Certaine Wonderfull Works of God which hapned to H.N. even from his youth: and how the God of heaven hath united himself with him, and raised up his gracious word in him, and how he hath chosen and sent him to be a minister of his gracious word* (London, 1650).

Tresham, Thomas (and others), 'The Tresham Papers belonging to T. B. Clarke-Thornhill Esq., of Rushton Hall, Northants', in *Report on Manuscripts in Various Collections*, 8 vols. (London: HMC, 1901–13), iii. 1–154.

Turbervile, George, *Epitaphes, Epigrams, Songs and Sonets with a discourse of the friendly affections of Tymetes to Pyndara his ladie* (London, 1567).

Turbervile, George, *The Eclogues of Mantuan*, trans. George Turbervile (1567), ed. Douglas Bush (New York: Scholars' Facsimiles & Reprints, 1937).

—— *Tragicall Tales translated by Turberville* (London, 1587).

Turler, Jerome, *The Traueiler of Ierome Turler deuided into two bookes. The first conteining a notable discourse of the maner, and order of traueiling ouersea, or into straunge and forrein countreys. The second comprehending an excellent description of the most delicious realme of Naples in Italy. A woorke very pleasaunt for all persons to reade, and right profitable and necessarie vnto all such as are minded to traueyll* (London, 1575).

Tusser, Thomas, *Fiue Hundreth Points of good husbandry vnited to as many of good huswiferie first deuised* (London, 1573).

Twyne, Thomas, *A Shorte and Pithie Discourse, concerning the engendering, tokens, and effects of all Earthquakes in Generall* (London, 1580).

Vallans, William, *A Tale of Two Swans, wherein is comprehended the original and increase of the riuer Lee* (London, 1590).

Vega, Luis Gutierres de la, *A Compendious Treatise Entituled, De Re Militari containing principall orders to be obserued in martiall affaires. Written in the Spanish tongue, by that worthie and famous captaine, Luis Gutierres de la Vega*, trans. Nicholas Lichfield (London, 1582).

Venn, John (ed.), *Grace Book, containing the Records of the University of Cambridge for the Years 1542–1589* (Cambridge: Cambridge University Press, 1910).

Verstegan, Richard, *A Declaration of the True Causes of the Great Troubles, presupposed to be intended against the realme of England* (Antwerp, 1592).

Vertue, George, *Notebooks*, ed. K. Esdaile, earl of Ilchester and H. M. Hake, 6 vols., *Walpole Society*, 18, 20, 22, 24, 26, 30 (1930–55).

Virgil, Publius Maro, *The Eclogues, Georgics and Aeneid of Virgil*, trans. C. Day Lewis (Oxford: Oxford University Press, 1966).

Vives, Juan Luis, *Tudor School-Boy Life: The Dialogues of Juan Luis Vives* (1908; London: Frank Cass, 1970).

Voraigne, Jacobus de, *The Golden Legend: Readings on the Saints*, ed. and trans. William Granger Ryan, 2 vols. (Princeton: Princeton University Press, 1993).

Waldstein, Baron, *The Diary of Baron Waldstein: A traveller in Elizabethan England*, trans. G. W. Groos (London: Thames and Hudson, 1981).

Ware, Sir James, *Ancient Irish Histories. The Works of Spencer, Campion, Hanmer, and Marleburrough* (Dublin, 1633).

Watson, Thomas, *Hekatompathia, or Passionate Centurie of Love* (London, 1582).

——*An Eglogue upon the Death of the Right Honorable Sir Francis Walsingham* (London, 1590).

Weever, John, *Epigrammes in the Oldest Cut, and Newest Fashion* (London, 1599).

Whetstone, George, *Sir Phillip Sidney, his honorable life, his valiant death, and true vertues* (London, 1587).

White, Gilbert, *The Natural History of Selbourne*, ed. Richard Mabey (Harmondsworth: Penguin, 1977).

Whitney, Geoffrey, *A Choice of Emblemes, and other Deuises, for the moste parte gathered out of sundrie writers, Englished and moralized* (Leiden, 1586).

Whythorne, Thomas, *The Autobiography of Thomas Whythorne*, ed. James M. Osborn (London: Oxford University Press, 1962).

Wilkinson, William, *A Confutation of Certaine Articles Deliuered vnto the Familye of Loue with the exposition of Theophilus, a supposed elder in the sayd Familye vpon the same articles* (London, 1579).

Willis, Richard, *Mount Tabor, or Private Exercises of a Penitent Sinner* (London, 1639).

Wilson, Sir Thomas, 'The State of England Anno. Dom. 1600', in *Camden Miscellany*, 3rd ser. 16 (London: Camden Society, 1936), 1–47.

Wilson, Thomas, *An Accurate Description of Bromley, in Kent* (London, 1797).

Wilton Hall, H. R. (ed.), *Records of the Old Archdeaconry of St. Albans: A Calender of Papers, AD 1575 to AD 1637* (St Albans: St Alban's and Hertfordshire Architectural and Archaeological Society, 1908).

Xenophon, *The bookes of Xenophon contayning the discipline, schole, and education of Cyrus the noble kyng of Persie. Translated out of Greeke into Englyshe, by M. Wylliam Barkar* (London, 1552?).

——*The VIII. bookes of Xenophon, containinge the institutio[n], schole, and education of Cyrus, the noble Kynge of Persye also his ciuill and princelye estate, his expedition into Babylon, Syria and Aegypt, and his exhortation before his death, to his children* (London, 1567).

BIBLIOGRAPHY

—— *Cyropaedia*, trans. Walter Miller (1914; Cambridge, MA: Harvard University Press, 1968).

Yates, James, *The Castell of Courtesie whereunto is adioyned the holde of humilitie: with the chariot of chastitie thereunto annexed* (London, 1582).

Young, John, *A Sermon Preached before the Queenes Maiestie, the second of March. An. 1575* (London, 1576).

Zall, P. M. (ed.), *A Hundred Merry Tales and Other Jestbooks of the Fifteenth and Sixteenth Centuries* (Lincoln, NB: University of Nebraska Press, 1963).

SECONDARY SOURCES

Printed

Ackroyd, Peter, *Shakespeare, The Biography* (London: Chatto & Windus, 2005).

Adams, John Charles, 'Gabriel Harvey's *Ciceronianus* and the Place of Peter Ramus' *Dialecticae libri duo in the Curriculum*', *RQ* 43 (1990), 551–69.

Adams, R. Bingham, 'Ferdinando Freckleton', *N&Q* 162 (1932), 88, 265–6.

Adams, Simon, *Leicester and the Court: Essays on Elizabethan Politics* (Manchester: Manchester University Press, 2002).

Addison, Catherine, 'Rhyming Against the Grain: A New Look at the Spenserian Stanza', in Lethbridge (ed.), *Edmund Spenser: New and Renewed Directions*, pp. 337–51.

Adler, Doris, 'Imaginary Toads in Real Gardens', *ELR* 11 (1981), 235–60.

Adrian, John M., *Local Negotiations of English Nationhood, 1570–1680* (Basingstoke: Palgrave, 2011).

Aers, David, 'A Whisper in the Ear of Early Modernists; or, Reflections on Literary Critics Writing the "History of the Subject"', in David Aers (ed.), *Culture and History, 1350–1600: Essays on English Communities, Identities and Writing* (Hemel Hempstead: Harvester, 1992), pp. 177–202.

Akrigg, G. P. V., *Shakespeare and the Earl of Southampton* (London: Hamilton, 1968).

Albright, Evelyn May, 'Spenser's Reasons for Rejecting the Cantos of Mutability', *SP* 25 (1928), 93–127.

—— 'On the Dating of Spenser's "Mutability" Cantos', *SP* 26 (1926), 482–98.

Alexander, Gavin, *Writing After Sidney: The Literary Response to Sir Philip Sidney, 1586–1640* (Oxford: Clarendon Press, 2006).

Alford, Stephen, *Burghley: William Cecil at the Court of Elizabeth I* (New Haven: Yale University Press, 2008).

Allen, Don Cameron, 'On Spenser's "Muiopotmos"', *SP* 53 (1956), 141–58.

Allen, Michael J. B., 'Renaissance Neoplatonism', in Norton (ed.), *Cambridge History of Literary Criticism*, iii. *The Renaissance*, pp. 435–41.

Alpers, Paul J., 'How to Read *The Faerie Queene*', *Essays in Criticism* 18 (1968), 429–43.

—— *What Is Pastoral?* (Chicago: University of Chicago Press, 1996).

Altman, Joel B., *The Tudor Play of Mind: Rhetorical Inquiry and the Development of Elizabethan Drama* (Berkeley and Los Angeles: University of California Press, 1978).

Amis, Kingsley, 'Oxford and After', in Anthony Thwaite (ed.), *Larkin at Sixty* (London: Faber, 1982), pp. 23–30.

Anderson, Judith H., '"A Gentle Knight was pricking on the plaine": The Chaucerian Connection', *ELR* 15 (1985), 166–74.

—— 'The Antiquities of Fairyland and Ireland', *JEGP* 86 (1987), 199–214.

—— 'Spenser's *Faerie Queene* and Cicero's *De Oratore*', *Sp. St.* 25 (2010), 365–70.

—— Donald Cheney, and David A. Richardson (eds.), *Spenser's Life and the Subject of Biography* (Amherst: University of Massachusetts Press, 1996).

Andrews, J. H., 'Colonial Cartography in a European Setting: The Case of Tudor Ireland' in Woodward (ed.), *History of Cartography*, iii/2. 1670–83.

Anglo, Sydney, 'A Machiavellian Solution to the Irish Problem: Richard Beacon's *Solon His Follie* (1594)', in Edward Chaney and Peter Mack (eds.), *England and the Continental Renaissance: Essays in Honour of J. B. Trapp* (Woodbridge: Boydell, 1990), pp. 153–64.

Ankersmit, Frank, *Sublime Historical Experience* (Stanford: Stanford University Press, 2005).

Anon., *Early History of the Spencer Family* (London: Mitre, 1931).

Anon., 'Edmund Spenser—The State Papers', *Dublin University Magazine* 58 (Aug. 1861), 132–44.

Anon., *Memorial Inscriptions From St. James's Graveyard, Dublin* (Dublin: National Archives, 1988).

Anon., *Rathfarnham Castle: Visitors' Guide* (Dublin: Office of Public Works, n.d.).

Anon., *St. Margaret's Church, Westminster: A Souvenir Guide* (London: Barnard and Westwood, 2006).

Anon., 'Spenser's Streams: The Mull and Arlo', *Dublin University Magazine* 38 (1851), 233–52.

Appleby, John C., 'The Problem of Piracy in Ireland, 1570–1630', in Claire Jowitt (ed.), *Pirates? The Politics of Plunder, 1550–1650* (Basingstoke: Palgrave, 2007), pp. 41–55.

Aptekar, Jane, *Icons of Justice: Iconography and Thematic Imagery in Book V of The Faerie Queene* (New York: Columbia University Press, 1969).

Archer, Elisabeth Jayne, Elizabeth Goldring, and Sarah Knight (eds.), *The Intellectual and Cultural World of the Early Modern Inns of Court* (Manchester: Manchester University Press, 2011).

Archer, Ian W., *The Pursuit of Stability: Social Relations in Elizabethan London* (Cambridge: Cambridge University Press, 1991).

Armitage, David, *The Ideological Origins of the British Empire* (Cambridge: Cambridge University Press, 2000).

—— 'Literature and Empire', in Canny (ed.), *Origins of Empire*, pp. 99–123.

Ashworth, E. J., 'Traditional Logic', in Schmitt and Skinner (eds.), *Cambridge History of Renaissance Philosophy*, pp. 143–72.

—— 'Logic in Late Sixteenth-Century England: Humanist Dialectic and the New Aristotelianism', *SP* 88 (1991), 224–36.

Astington, John H., 'Sir John Astley and Court Culture', *Sh. Stud.* 30 (2002), 106–10.

Aston, Margaret, *England's Iconoclasts: Laws Against Images* (Oxford: Clarendon Press, 1988).

—— *The King's Bedpost: Reformation and Iconography in a Tudor Group Portrait* (Cambridge: Cambridge University Press, 1993).

Atchity, Kenneth John, 'Spenser's *Mother Hubberds Tale*: Three Themes of Order', *PQ* 52 (1973), 161–72.

Atkin, Graham, 'Raleigh, Spenser, and Elizabeth: Acts of Friendship in *The Faerie Queene*, Book IV', in Lethbridge (ed.), *Spenser: New and Renewed Directions*, pp. 195–213.

Atkinson, Dorothy, 'Edmund Spenser's Family and the Church', *N&Q* 170 (1936), 172–5.

Attridge, Derek, *Well-weighed Syllables: Elizabethan Verse in Classical Metres* (Cambridge: Cambridge University Press, 1974).

Attwater, Aubrey, *A Short History of Pembroke College Cambridge* (1936; Cambridge: Pembroke College, 1973).

Augur, Peter, 'The Semaines' Dissemination in England and Scotland until 1641', *RS* (forthcoming).

Austen, Warren B., 'William Withie's Notebook: Lampoons on John Lyly and Gabriel Harvey', *RES* 23 (1947), 297–309.

Avery, Bruce, 'Mapping the Irish Other: Spenser's *A View of the Present State of Ireland*', *ELH* 57 (1990), 263–79.

Bachelor, John (ed.), *The Art of Literary Biography* (Oxford: Clarendon Press, 1995).

Bagwell, Richard, *Ireland under the Tudors*, 3 vols. (London: Longman, 1885–90).

Bajetta, Carlo M., *Sir Walter Ralegh: Poeta di corte elisabettiano* (Milan: Mursia, 1998).

Baker, Alan R. H., 'Changes in the Later Middle Ages', in Darby (ed.), *New Historical Geography of England*, pp. 186–247.

Baker, David J., '"Some Quirk, Some Subtle Evasion": Legal Subversion in Spenser's *A View of the Present State of Ireland*', *Sp. St.* 6 (1986), 147–63.

—— *Between Nations: Shakespeare, Spenser, Marvell, and the Question of Britain* (Stanford: Stanford University Press, 1997).

Baker, J. H., 'The Third University, 1450–1550: Law School or Finishing School?', in Archer et al. (eds.), *Inns of Court*, pp. 8–24.

Baker, Naomi, '"To make love to a deformity": Praising Ugliness in Early Modern England', *RS* 22 (2008), 86–109.

Bald, R. C., *John Donne: A Life* (Oxford: Clarendon Press, 1970).

Baldwin, T. W., 'The Genesis of Some Passages which Spenser Borrowed from Marlowe', *ELH* 9 (1942), 157–87.

——— *William Shakspere's Small Latine and Lesse Greeke*, 2 vols. (Urbana: University of Illinois Press, 1944).

Banks, Theodore H., 'Spenser's Rosalind: A Conjecture', *PMLA* 52 (1937), 335–7.

Barber, Peter, 'Mapmaking in England, ca. 1470–1650', in Woodward (ed.), *History of Cartography*, iii/2. 1589–1669.

Barbour, Reid, *English Epicures and Stoics: Ancient Legacies in Early Stuart Culture* (Amherst: University of Massachusetts Press, 1998).

Barker, Francis, *The Tremulous Private Body: Essays on Subjection* (London: Methuen, 1984).

Barker, Nicholas, 'Old English Letter Foundries', in Barnard, McKenzie, and Bell (eds.), *Cambridge History of the Book in Britain*, iv. 602–19.

———and David Quentin (eds.), *The Library of Thomas Tresham and Thomas Brudenell* (London: Roxburghe Club, 2006).

Barnard, John, and Don McKenzie (eds.), with the assistance of Maureen Bell, *The Cambridge History of the Book in Britain*, iv. *1557–1695* (Cambridge: Cambridge University Press, 2002).

Barry, Judith, 'Sir Geoffrey Fenton and the Office of Secretary of State for Ireland, 1580–1608', *IHS* 35 (2006), 137–59.

Bartlett, Thomas, and Keith Jeffrey (eds.), *A Military History of Ireland* (Cambridge: Cambridge University Press, 1996).

Bate, Jonathan, *Shakespeare and Ovid* (Oxford: Clarendon Press, 1993).

——— *Soul of the Age: The Life, Mind and World of William Shakespeare* (London: Viking, 2008).

Bate, Walter Jackson, *Samuel Johnson* (New York: Harcourt Brace, 1977).

Bates, Catherine, *The Rhetoric of Courtship in Elizabethan Language and Literature* (Cambridge: Cambridge University Press, 1992).

Bath, Michael, 'Verse Form and Pictorial Space in van der Noot's *Theatre for Worldlings*', in Höltgen et al. (eds.), *Word and Visual Imagination*, pp. 73–105.

——— 'Honey and Gall or: Cupid and the Bees. A Case of Iconographic Slippage', in Daly (ed.), *Andrea Alciato*, pp. 59–94.

——— *Speaking Pictures: English Emblem Books and Renaissance Culture* (London: Longman, 1994).

Batho, Gordon, 'The Library of the "Wizard" Earl: Henry Percy, Ninth Earl of Northumberland (1564–1632)', *The Library*, 5th ser. 15 (1960), 246–61.

——— 'Noblemen, Gentlemen and Yeomen', in Thirsk (ed.), *Agrarian History*, p. 276–305.

Battiscombe, Georgina, *The Spencers of Althorp* (London: Constable, 1984).

Baugh, Albert C., and Thomas Cable, *A History of the English Language* (3rd edn., London: Routledge, 1978).

Bawcutt, N. W., 'The "Myth of Gentillet" Reconsidered: An Aspect of Elizabethan Machiavellianism', *MLR* 99 (2004), 863–74.

Bayley, Peter, *Edmund Spenser: Prince of Poets* (London: Hutchinson, 1971).

Beach, Joseph Warren, 'A Sonnet of Watson and a Stanza of Spenser', *MLN* 18 (1903), 218–20.

Beal, Peter, *A Dictionary of English Manuscript Terminology, 1450–2000* (Oxford: Oxford University Press, 2008).

——— (ed.), *Index of English Literary Manuscripts*, i/2. *Douglas to Wyatt* (London: Mansell, 1980).

Bedford, Ronald, Lloyd Davis, and Philippa Kelly, *Early Modern English Lives: Autobiography and Self-Representation, 1500–1660* (Aldershot: Ashgate, 2007).

Bednarz, James P., 'Ralegh in Spenser's Historical Allegory', *Sp. St.* 4 (1984), 49–70.

Bednarz, James P., 'The Collaborator as Thief: Ralegh's (Re)Vision of *The Faerie Queene*', *ELH* 63 (1996), 279–307.

Beer, Anna, *Bess: The Life of Lady Ralegh, Wife to Sir Walter* (London: Constable and Robinson, 2004).

Beer, Barrett L., *Tudor England Observed: The World of John Stow* (Stroud: Sutton, 1998).

Beier, A. L., *Masterless Men: The Vagrancy Problem in England, 1560–1640* (London: Methuen, 1985).

Beilin, Elaine V., *Redeeming Eve: Women Writers of the English Renaissance* (Princeton: Princeton University Press, 1987).

Bellamy, Elizabeth Jane, 'Waiting for Hymen: Literary History as "Symptom" in Spenser and Milton', *ELH* 64 (1997), 391–414.

Bellamy, John, *The Tudor Law of Treason: An Introduction* (London: Routledge, 1979).

Belsey, Catherine, *The Subject of Tragedy: Identity and Difference in Renaissance Drama* (London: Methuen, 1985).

Bender, John B., *Spenser and Literary Pictorialism* (Princeton: Princeton University Press, 1972).

Bennett, George, *The History of Bandon and the Principal Towns in the West Riding, County Cork* (Cork: Guy, 1869).

Bennett, H. S., *Life on the English Manor: A Study of Peasant Conditions, 1150–1400* (1937; Cambridge: Cambridge University Press, 1948).

——*English Books and Readers, 1475 to 1557: Being a Study of the Book Trade from Caxton to the Incorporation of the Stationers' Company* (Cambridge: Cambridge University Press, 1970).

Bennett, Josephine Waters, 'Spenser and Gabriel Harvey's "Letter-Book"', *MP* 29 (1931), 163–86.

——'The Theme of Spenser's *Fowre Hymnes*', *SP* 28 (1931), 18–57.

——'Did Spenser Starve?', *MLN* 52 (1937), 400–1.

——'A Bibliographical Note on *Mother Hubberds Tale*', *ELH* 4 (1937), 60–1.

——'The Allegory of Sir Artegall in *F.Q.*, V, xi–xii', *SP* 37 (1940), 177–200.

——*The Evolution of 'The Faerie Queene'* (Chicago: University of Chicago Press, 1942).

Bennett, Kate, 'John Aubrey, Hint-Keeper: Life-Writing and the Encouragement of Natural Philosophy in the Pre-Newtonian Seventeenth Century', *Seventeenth Century* 22 (2007), 358–80.

Bensly, Edward, 'Edmund Spenser's Family and the Church', *N&Q* 170 (1936), 231–2.

Benson, Robert G., 'Elizabeth as Beatrice: A Reading of Spenser's "Amoretti"', *South Central Bulletin* 32 (1972), 184–8.

Berger, Harry, Jr, 'Two Spenserian Retrospects: The Antique Temple of Venus and the Primitive Marriage of Rovers', in *Revisionary Play: Studies in the Spenserian Dynamics* (Berkeley and Los Angeles: University of California Press, 1988), pp. 195–214.

Berleth, Richard, *The Twilight Lords: An Irish Chronicle* (New York: Barnes and Noble, 1978).

——'Fraile Woman, Foolish Gerle: Misogyny in Spenser's "Mutabilitie Cantos"', *MP* 93 (1995), 37–53.

Berlin, Norman, 'Chaucer's *The Book of the Duchess* and Spenser's *Daphnaida*: A Contrast', *Studia Neophilologica* 38 (1966), 282–9.

Bernard, John D., *Ceremonies of Innocence: Pastoralism in the Poetry of Edmund Spenser* (Cambridge: Cambridge University Press, 1989).

Berry, Henry F., 'The Manor and Castle of Mallow in the Days of the Tudors', *JCHAS* 11 (1893), 21–5, 41–5.

——'Sheriffs of the County of Cork: Henry III to 1660', *JRSAI* 15 (1905), 39–52.

——'The English Settlement in Mallow under the Jephson Family', *JCHAS*, 2nd ser. 12 (1906), 1–26.

——'The Old Youghal Family of Stout,' *JCHAS* 23 (1917), 19–29.

Berry, Herbert, and E. K. Timings, 'Spenser's Pension', *RES* 11 (1960), 254–9.

Bevington, David, *Shakespeare and Biography* (Oxford: Oxford University Press, 2010).

Binns, J. W., *Intellectual Culture in Elizabethan and Jacobean England: The Latin Writings of the Age* (Leeds: Francis Cairns, 1990).

Birrell, T. A., *The Library of John Morris: The Reconstruction of a Seventeenth-Century Collection* (London: British Library, 1976).

Bjorvand, Einar, 'Spenser's Defence of Poetry: Some Structural Aspects of the *Fowre Hymnes*', in Maren-Sofie Røstvig (ed.), *Fair Forms: Essays in English Literature from Spenser to Jane Austen* (Cambridge: Brewer, 1975), pp. 13–53.

Black, Joseph L., '"Pan is Hee": Commending *The Faerie Queene*', *Sp. St.* 15 (2001), 121–34.

——and Lisa Celovsky, '"Lost Works", Suppositious Pieces, and Continuations', *Sp. Handbook*, pp. 349–64.

Bland, Mark, 'John Windet', in Bracken and Silver (eds.), *Book Trade*, pp. 319–25.

—— 'The Appearance of the Text in Early Modern England', *Text* 11 (1998), 91–154.

—— *A Guide to Early Printed Books and Manuscripts* (Oxford: Blackwell, 2010).

Blayney, Peter, 'The Publication of Playbooks', in John D. Cox and David Scott Kastan (eds.), *A New History of Early English Drama* (New York: Columbia University Press, 1997), pp. 383–422.

Blouw, Paul Valkema, 'Was Plantin a Member of the Family of Love? Notes on His Dealings with Hendrik Niclaes', *Quaerendo* 23 (1993), 3–23.

Boazio, Baptista, and Robert Dunlop, 'Sixteenth-Century Maps of Ireland', *EHR* 20 (1905), 309–37.

Bonfield, Lloyd, Richard M. Smith, and Keith Wrightson (eds.), *The World We Have Gained: Histories of Population and Social Structure* (Oxford: Blackwell, 1986).

Booty, John E. (ed.), *The Godly Kingdom of Tudor England: Great Books of the English Reformation* (Wilton, CT: Morehouse-Barlow, 1981).

Boran, Elizabethanne, 'Libraries and Collectors, 1550–1700', in Gillespie and Hadfield (eds.), *Oxford History of the Irish Book*, iii. 91–110.

Borman, Tracy, *Elizabeth's Women: The Hidden Story of the Virgin Queen* (London: Cape, 2009).

Boro, Joyce, 'Multilingualism, Romance, and Language Pedagogy; or, Why Were So Many Sentimental Romances Printed as Polyglot Texts?', in Schurink (ed.), *Tudor Translation*, pp. 18–38.

Borris, Kenneth, *Allegory and Epic in English Renaissance Literature: Heroic Form in Sidney, Spenser and Milton* (Cambridge: Cambridge University Press, 2000).

—— Jon Quitslund, and Carol Kaske (eds.), *spenser and platonism (special issue)*, *Sp. St.* 24 (2009).

Bossy, John, *The English Catholic Community, 1570–1850* (Darnton: Longman and Todd, 1975).

Bottigheimer, Karl, *English Money and Irish Land: The 'Adventurers' in the Cromwellian Settlement of Ireland* (Oxford: Clarendon Press, 1971).

Bourland, Caroline Brown, 'Gabriel Harvey and the Modern Languages', *HLQ* 4 (1940), 85–106.

Boutcher, Warren, ' "A French Dexterity, & an Italian Confidence": New Documents on John Florio, Learned Strangers and Protestant Humanist Study of Modern Languages in Renaissance England from c.1547 to c.1625', *Reformation* 2 (1997), 39–110.

Bowen, Elizabeth, *Bowen's Court & Seven Winters* (London: Vintage, 1999).

Bowen, Karen L., and Dirk Imhof, *Christopher Plantain and Engraved Book Illustrations in Sixteenth-Century Europe* (Cambridge: Cambridge University Press, 2008).

Boynton, Lindsay, 'The Tudor Provost-Marshal', *EHR* 77 (1962), 437–55.

—— *The Elizabethan Militia, 1558–1638* (London: Routledge, 1967).

Bradbrook, Muriel, 'No Room at the Top: Spenser's Pursuit of Fame', in John Russell Brown and Bernhard Harris (eds.), *Elizabethan Poetry* (London: Arnold, 1980), pp. 90–109.

Braden, Gordon, 'Non-Dramatic Verse: Epic Kinds', in Braden, Cummings, and Gillespie (eds.), *Oxford History of Literary Translation*, pp. 167–93.

—— Robert Cummings, and Stuart Gillespie (eds.), *The Oxford History of Literary Translation in English*, ii. *1550–1660* (Oxford: Oxford University Press, 2010).

Bradford, Charles Angell, *Helena, Marchioness of Northampton* (London: Allen & Unwin, 1936).

Bradner, Leicester, 'An Allusion to Bromley in the *Shepherds' Calender*', *MLN* 49 (1934), 443–5.

—— 'Spenser's Connections with Hampshire', *MLN* 60 (1945), 180–4.

—— *Edmund Spenser and The Faerie Queene* (Chicago: University of Chicago Press, 1948).

Bradshaw, Brendan, *The Dissolution of the Religious Orders in Ireland under Henry VIII* (Cambridge: Cambridge University Press, 1974).

—— 'Robe and Sword in the Conquest of Ireland', in Clare Cross, David Loades, and J. J. Scarisbrick (eds.), *Law and Government under the Tudors: Essays Presented to Sir Geoffrey Elton on His Retirement* (Cambridge: Cambridge University Press, 1988), pp. 139–62.

Bradshaw, Brendan, Andrew Hadfield, and Willy Maley (eds.), *Representing Ireland: Literature and the Origins of Conflict, 1534–1660* (Cambridge: Cambridge University Press, 1993).

Brady, Ciaran, 'Faction and the Origins of the Desmond Rebellion of 1579', *IHS* 22 (1981), 289–312.

—— 'Spenser's Irish Crisis: Humanism and Experience in the 1590s', *P&P* 111 (1986), 17–49.

Brady, Ciaran, 'The Road to the View: On the Decline of Reform Thought in Tudor Ireland', in Coughlan (ed.), *Spenser and Ireland*, pp. 25–45.

—— *The Chief Governors: The Rise and Fall of Reform Government in Tudor Ireland, 1536–1588* (Cambridge: Cambridge University Press, 1994).

——'The Captains' Games: Army and Society in Elizabethan Ireland', in Bartlett and Jeffrey (eds.), *Military History of Ireland*, pp. 136–59.

——and Raymond Gillespie (eds.), *Natives and Newcomers: The Making of Irish Colonial Society, 1534–1641* (Dublin: Irish Academic Press, 1986).

——and Jane Ohlmeyer (eds.), *British Interventions in Early Modern Ireland* (Cambridge: Cambridge University Press, 2005).

Braudel, Fernand, *The Mediterranean and the Mediterranean World in the Age of Philip II*, trans. Siân Reynolds, 2 vols. (London: Collins, 1972).

—— *Civilization & Capitalism, 15th.–18th. Century*, trans. Siân Reynolds, 3 vols. (London: Collins, 1981).

Brayshay, Mark, 'Royal Post-Horse Routes in England and Wales: The Evolution of the Network in the Later-Sixteenth and Early-Seventeenth Century', *JHG* 17 (1991), 373–89.

——Philip Harrison, and Brian Chalkley, 'Knowledge, Nationhood and Governance: The Speed of the Royal Post in Early-Modern England', *JHG* 24 (1998), 265–88.

Breen, Colin, *An Archaeology of South-West Ireland, 1570–1670* (Dublin: Four Courts, 2007).

Breen, John, '"Imaginative Groundplot": *A Vewe of the Present State of Ireland*', *Sp. St.* 12 (1991; pub. 1998), 151–68.

——'The Empirical Eye: Edmund Spenser's *A View of the Present State of Ireland*', *Irish Review* 16 (autumn/winter 1994), 44–52.

Brennan, Michael G., 'William Ponsonby: Elizabethan Stationer', *AEB: Analytical & Enumeral Bibliography* 7 (1984), 91–110.

——'Nicholas Breton's *the Passions of the Spirit* and the Countess of Pembroke,' *RES* 38 (1987), 221–5.

—— *Literary Patronage in the English Renaissance: The Pembroke Family* (London: Routledge, 1988).

Brigden, Susan, *New Worlds, Lost Worlds: The Rule of the Tudors, 1485–1603* (London: Penguin, 2000).

Brink, Jean R., 'Who Fashioned Edmund Spenser? The Textual History of *Complaints*', *SP* 88 (1991), 153–68.

——'Dating Spenser's "Letter to Raleigh', *The Library* 16 (1994), 219–24.

——'Constructing the *View of the Present State of Ireland*', *Sp. St.* 11 (1994), 203–28.

——'Documenting Edmund Spenser: A New Life Record', *American Notes & Queries* 7 (1994), 201–8.

——'"All His Minde on Honour Fixed": The Preferment of Edmund Spenser', in Anderson et al. (eds.), *Spenser's Life*, pp. 45–64.

——'Edmund Spenser's Family: Two Notes and a Query', *N&Q* 44 (1997), 49–51.

—— 'Materialist History of the Publication of Spenser's *Faerie Queene*', *RES* 54 (2001), 1–26.

——'Precedence and Patronage: The Ordering of Spenser's Dedicatory Sonnets (1590)', in Erikson (ed.), *The 1590 Faerie Queene: Paratexts and Publishing*, pp. 51–72.

——'Revising Spenser's Birth Date to 1554', *N&Q* 56 (2009), 523–7.

Brinkley, Robert A., 'Spenser's *Muiopotmos* and the Politics of Metamorphosis', *ELH* 48 (1981), 668–76.

Broadus, Edmund Kemper, *The Laureateship: A Study of the Office of Poet Laureate in England with Some Account of the Poets* (Oxford: Clarendon Press, 1921).

Brooks, Eric St John, *Sir Christopher Hatton: Queen Elizabeth's Favourite* (London: Cape, 1946).

Brooks-Davies, Douglas, *Spenser's Faerie Queene: A Critical Commentary on Books I and II* (Manchester: Manchester University Press, 1977).

Brown, Cedric C., *John Milton's Aristocratic Entertainments* (Cambridge: Cambridge University Press, 1985).

Brown, Georgia, *Redefining Elizabethan Literature* (Cambridge: Cambridge University Press, 2004).

Brown, Richard Danson, *'The New Poet': Novelty and Tradition in Spenser's Complaints* (Liverpool: Liverpool University Press, 1999).

Brown, Ted, 'Metapoetry in Edmund Spenser's *Amoretti*', *PQ* 82 (2003), 401–17.

Bruce, Donald, 'Spenser's Welsh', *N&Q* 32 (1985), 465–7.
——'Edmund Spenser: The Boyhood of a Poet', http://findarticles.com/p/articles/mi_m2242/is_n1537_v264/ai_15295932/pg_7/?tag=content;col1 (accessed 19 Feb. 2012).
——'Spenser's Birth and Birthplace', *N&Q* 42 (1995), 283–5.
——'Spenser in Westminster: His Marriage and Death', *N&Q* 242 (1997), 51–3.
Buchan, Alexander M., 'Ralegh's *Cynthia*—Facts or Legend', *MLQ* 1 (1940), 461–74.
——'The Political Allegory of Book IV of *The Faerie Queene*', *ELH* 11 (1944), 237–48.
Buck, P. M., Jr, 'New Facts Concerning the Life of Edmund Spenser', *MLN* 19 (1904), 237–8.
——'Add. MS 34064 and Spenser's *Ruins of Time* and *Mother Hubberds Tale*', *MLN* 22 (1907), 41–6.
——'Spenser's Lost Poems', *PMLA* 23 (1908), 80–99.
Buckley, M. J. C., 'Notes on St Mary's Church, Youghal', *JRSAI*, 5th ser. 33 (1903), 333–44.
Buckman, Ty, 'Forcing the Poet into Prose: "Gealous Opinions and Misconstructions" and Spenser's Letter to Ralegh', in Erikson (ed.), *The 1590 Faerie Queene: Paratexts and Publishing*, pp. 17–34.
Bullen, J. B., *The Myth of the Renaissance in Nineteenth-Century Writing* (Oxford: Oxford University Press, 1994).
Burchmore, David W., 'The Image of the Centre in *Colin Clouts come home againe*', *RES* 28 (1977), 393–406.
Burke, Peter, *Popular Culture in Early Modern Europe* (London: Temple Smith, 1978).
Burlinson, Christopher, and Andrew Zurcher, '"Secretary to the Lord Grey Lord Deputy Here": Edmund Spenser's Irish Papers', *The Library*, 7th series, 6 (2005), 30–69.
Burrow, Colin, *Epic Romance: Homer to Milton* (Oxford: Clarendon Press, 1993).
——*Edmund Spenser* (Plymouth: Northcote House, 1996).
Burton, Elizabeth, *The Elizabethans at Home* (1958; London: Arrow Books, 1970).
Bush, Douglas, 'Review of Spenser, *Axiochus*, ed. Padelford', *MLN* 50 (1935), 191–2.
Bushnell, Rebecca, *Tragedies of Tyrants: Political Thought and Theater in the English Renaissance* (Ithaca, NY: Cornell University Press, 1990).
——*A Culture of Teaching: Early Modern Humanism in Theory and Practice* (Ithaca, NY: Cornell University Press, 1996).
Butler, Christopher, '"Pricking" and Ambiguity at the Start of *The Faerie Queene*', *N&Q* 55 (2008), 159–61.
Butterfield, Ardis, 'Chaucer's French Inheritance', in Piero Boitani and Jill Mann (eds.), *The Cambridge Companion to Chaucer* (2nd edn., Cambridge: Cambridge University Press, 2003), pp. 20–35.
Buxton, John, *Sir Philip Sidney and the English Renaissance* (London: Macmillan, 1966).
Byrne, M. St Clare, and Gladys Scott Thomson, '"My Lord's Books": The Library of Francis, Second Earl of Bedford in 1584', *RES* 28 (1931), 385–405.
Byrom, H. J., 'Edmund Spenser's First Printer, Hugh Singleton', *The Library*, 4th ser. 14 (1933), 121–56.
Cain, Thomas H., 'The Strategy of Praise in Spenser's "Aprill"', *SEL* 8 (1968), 45–58.
——*Praise in The Faerie Queene* (Lincoln: University of Nebraska Press, 1978).
Caldwell, James R., 'Dating a Spenser–Harvey Letter', *PMLA* 41 (1926), 568–74.
Campbell, Gordon, and Thomas N. Corns, *John Milton: Life, Work, and Thought* (Oxford: Oxford University Press, 2008).
Campbell, Linda, 'Wet-Nurses in Early Modern England: Some Evidence from the Townshend Archive', *Medical History* 33 (1989), 360–70.
Campbell, Mildred, *The English Yeoman under Elizabeth and the Early Stuarts* (1942; London: Merlin, 1960).
Cannio, Catherine G., 'Reconstructing Lord Grey's Reputation: A New View of the *View*', *SCJ* 29/1 (1998), 3–18.
Canny, Nicholas P., 'The Ideology of English Colonisation: From Ireland to America', *William and Mary Quarterly* 30 (1973), 575–98.
——*The Formation of the Old English Elite in Ireland* (Dublin: National University of Ireland, 1975).
——*The Upstart Earl: A Study of the Social and Mental World of Richard Boyle, First Earl of Cork, 1566–1643* (Cambridge: Cambridge University Press, 1982).

Canny, Nicholas P., 'Edmund Spenser and the Development of an Anglo-Irish Identity', *YES* 13 (1983), 1–19.

——*From Reformation to Restoration: Ireland, 1534–1660* (Dublin: Hellicon, 1987).

——'Poetry as Politics: A View of the Present State of *The Faerie Queene*', in Morgan (ed.), *Political Ideology in Ireland*, pp. 110–26.

——*Making Ireland British, 1580–1650* (Oxford: Oxford University Press, 2001).

——(ed.), *The Origins of Empire: The Oxford History of the British Empire*, i (Oxford: Oxford University Press, 1998).

——and Andrew Carpenter (eds.), 'The Early Planters: Spenser and His Contemporaries', in Seamus Deane (ed.), *The Field Day Anthology of Irish Writing*, 3 vols. (Derry: Field Day Publications, 1991), i. 171–234.

Capp, Bernard, *Astrology & The Popular Press: English Almanacs, 1500–1800* (London: Faber, 1979).

Carey, Daniel, 'Spenser, Purchas, and the Poetics of Colonial Settlement', in Fiona Bateman and Lionel Pilkington (eds.), *Studies in Settler Colonialism: Politics, Identity and Culture* (Basingstoke: Palgrave, 2011), pp. 28–46.

Carey, Vincent P., 'Sir Henry Sidney, and the Massacre at Mullaghmast, 1578', *IHS* 31 (1999), 305–27.

——'The Irish Face of Machiavelli: Richard Beacon's *Solon his Follie* (1594) and Republican Ideology in the Conquest of Ireland', in Morgan (ed.), *Political Ideology in Ireland*, pp. 83–109.

——'"Neither good English nor good Irish": Bi-lingualism and Identity Formation in Sixteenth-Century Ireland', in Morgan (ed.) *Political Ideology in Ireland*, pp. 45–61.

——*Surviving the Tudors: The 'Wizard' Earl of Kildare and English Rule in Ireland, 1537–1586* (Dublin: Four Courts, 2002).

——'Atrocity and History: Grey, Spenser and the Slaughter at Smerwick (1580)', in Edwards et al. (eds.), *Age of Atrocity*, pp. 79–94.

——and Ute Lotz-Heumann (eds.), *Taking Sides? Colonial and Confessional Mentalités in Early Modern Ireland: Essays in Honour of Karl Bottigheimer* (Dublin: Four Courts, 2003).

Carlin, Norah, 'Extreme of Mainstream? The English Independents and the Cromwellian Reconquest of Ireland, 1649–1651', in Bradshaw et al. (eds.), *Representing Ireland*, pp. 209–26.

Carlisle, Nicholas, *A Concise Description of the Endowed Grammar Schools in England and Wales*, 2 vols. (London, 1818).

Carlson, David R., *English Humanist Books: Writers and Patrons, Manuscripts and Print, 1475–1525* (Toronto: University of Toronto Press, 1993).

Carpenter, Frederick Ives, 'Desiderata in the Study of Spenser', *SP* 19 (1922), 238–43.

——'Spenser in Ireland', *MP* 19 (1922), 405–19.

——'The Marriages of Edmund Spenser', *MP* 22 (1924), 97–8.

——'G. W. Senior and G. W. I.', *MP* 22 (1924), 67–8.

Carroll, Clare, 'Spenser and the Irish Language: The Sons of Milesio in *A View of the Present State of Ireland*, *The Faerie Queene*, Book V, and the *Leabhar Gabhála*', *IUR: Spenser in Ireland, 1596–1996*, ed. Anne Fogarty (Autumn/Winter 1996), 281–90.

——*Circe's Cup: Cultural Transformations in Early Modern Ireland* (Cork: Cork University Press, 2001).

Carroll, D. Allen, 'Thomas Watson and the 1588 MS Commendation of *The Faerie Queene*: Reading the Rebus', *Sp. St.* 16 (2002), 105–23.

Carver, Robert, *The Protean Ass: The 'Metamorphoses' of Apuleius from Antiquity to the Renaissance* (Oxford: Oxford University Press, 2007).

Castor, Helen, *Blood and Roses: The Paston Family in the Fifteenth Century* (London: Faber, 2005).

Cavanagh, Sheila T., *Wanton Eyes and Chaste Desires: Female Sexuality in The Faerie Queene* (Bloomington: Indiana University Press, 1994).

Chamberlain, Richard, *Radical Spenser: Pastoral, Politics and the New Aestheticism* (Edinburgh: Edinburgh University Press, 2005).

Chambers, Anne, *Eleanor, Countess of Desmond* (1986; Dublin: Wolfhound, 2000).

Chapman, Alison, 'The Politics of Time in Edmund Spenser's English Calendar', *SEL* 42 (2002), 1–24.
——'Marking Time: Astrology, Almanacs and English Protestantism', *RQ* 60 (2007), 1257–90.
Charlton, Kenneth, *Education in Renaissance England* (London: Routledge, 1975).
Chaudhuri, Supriya, 'Lucius, thou art translated: Adlington's Apuleius', *RS* 22 (2008), 669–704.
Cheney, Donald, 'Spenser's Fortieth Birthday and Related Fictions', *Sp. St.* 4 (1984), 3–31.
Cheney, Patrick, 'Spenser's Completion of *The Squire's Tale*: Love, Magic, and Heroic Action in the Legend of Cambell and Triamond', *Journal of Medieval and Renaissance Studies* 15 (1985), 135–55.
——*Spenser's Famous Flight: A Renaissance Idea of a Literary Career* (Toronto: University of Toronto Press, 1993).
——*Marlowe's Counterfeit Profession: Ovid, Spenser, Counter-Nationhood* (Toronto: Toronto University Press, 1997).
——'Life', in Van Es (ed.), *Critical Companion*, pp. 18–41.
——'Dido to Daphne: Early Modern Death in Spenser's Shorter Poems', *Sp. St.* 18 (2003), 143–63.
——'Biographical Representations: Marlowe's Life of the Author', in Takashi Kozuka and J. R. Mulryne (eds.), *Shakespeare, Marlowe, Jonson: New Directions in Biography* (Aldershot: Ashgate, 2006), pp. 183–204.
——'Perdita, Pastorella, and the Romance of Literary Form: Shakespeare's Counter-Spenserian Authorship', in Lethbridge (ed.), *Shakespeare and Spenser*, pp. 121–42.
Chester, Allan Griffith, 'Thomas Churchyard's Pension', *PMLA* 50 (1935), 902.
Church, R. W., *Spenser* (London: Macmillan, 1879).
Cirillo, A. R., 'Spenser's *Epithalamion*: The Harmonious Universe of Love', *SEL* 8 (1968), 19–34.
Clark, Stuart, *Vanities of the Eye: Vision in Early Modern European Culture* (Oxford: Oxford University Press, 2007).
Clarke, Aidan, *The Old English in Ireland, 1625–42* (Dublin: MacGibbon & Kee, 1966).
Clarke, Howard B., 'Cult, Church and Collegiate Church before c.1220', in Crawford and Gillespie (eds.), *St. Patrick's Cathedral*, pp. 45–72.
Clarke, Danielle, '"In Sort As She It Sung": Spenser's "Doleful Lay" and the Construction of Female Authorship', *Criticism* 42 (2000), 451–68.
——'Translation and the English Language', in Braden, Cummings, and Gillespie (eds.), *Oxford History of Literary Translation*, pp. 17–23.
——'"Signifying, but not sounding": Gender and Paratext in the Complaint Genre', in Smith and Wilson (eds.), *Renaissance Paratexts*, pp. 133–50.
——and Elizabeth Clarke (eds.), *'This Double Voice': Gendered Writing in Early Modern England* (Basingstoke: Palgrave, 2000).
Clegg, Cyndia, *Press Censorship in Elizabethan England* (Cambridge: Cambridge University Press, 1997).
Clifton, A. S. W., 'Edmund Spenser, His Connection with Northants', *N&Q* 154 (1928), 195.
Clucas, Stephen, 'Thomas Watson's *Hekatompathia* and European Petrarchanism', in Martin McLaughlin, Letizia Panizza, and Peter Hainsworth (eds.), *Petrarch in Britain: Interpreters, Imitators and Translators over 700 years* (Oxford: Oxford University Press/British Academy, 2007), pp. 217–27.
Coatalen, Guillaume, '"Lô A Timorous Correction": Unrecorded Extracts From Spenser and Harrington and Negative Criticism of *The Faerie Queene* in a Folio from the Bodleian Library', *RES* 56 (2005), 730–48.
Cockerham, Paul, '"To mak a Tombe for the Earell of Ormon and to set it up in Iarland": Renaissance Ideals in Irish Funeral Monuments', in Herron and Potterton (eds.), *Ireland in the Renaissance*, pp. 195–230.
Colclough, David (ed.), *John Donne's Professional Lives* (Cambridge: Brewer, 2003).
——'Introduction: Donne's Professional Lives', in Colclough (ed.), *John Donne's Professional Lives*, pp. 1–16.
Coldiron, A. E. B., 'Watson's *Hekatompathia* and Renaissance Lyric Translation', *Translation and Literature* 5 (1996), 3–25.

Coldiron, A. E. B., 'How Spenser Excavates Du Bellay's *Antiquitez*: Or, The Role of the Poet, Lyric Historiography, and the English Sonnet', *JEGP* 101 (2002), 41–67.

Coleman, D. C., *The British Paper Industry, 1495–1860: A Study in Industrial Growth* (Oxford: Clarendon Press, 1958).

—— *The Economy of England, 1450–1750* (Oxford: Oxford University Press, 1977).

Coleman, J., 'The Poet Spenser's Wife', *JCHAS*, 2nd ser. 1 (1895), 131–3.

Collinson, Patrick, *The Elizabethan Puritan Movement* (Oxford: Clarendon Press, 1967).

—— *Archbishop Grindal, 1519–1583: The Struggle for a Reformed Church* (London: Cape, 1979).

—— *Elizabethans* (London: Hambledon, 2003).

Comito, Terry, 'A Dialectic of Images in Spenser's *Fowre Hymnes*', *SP* 74 (1977), 301–21.

Connolly, S. J., *Contested Island: Ireland, 1460–1630* (Oxford: Oxford University Press, 2007).

Cooper, Charles Henry, and John William Cooper, *Annals of Cambridge*, 5 vols. (Cambridge: Warwick, 1842–1908).

—— and Thompson Cooper, *Athenae Cantabrigienses*, 2 vols. (Cambridge: Macmillan, 1858).

Cooper, Helen, *Pastoral: Medieval into Renaissance* (Ipswich: Brewer, 1977).

Cooper, Sheila McIsaac, 'Servants as Educators in Early-Modern England', *Pedagogical History* 43 (2007), 457–63.

Cooper, T., and C. H. Copper 'Edward Kirke, the Commentator on Spenser's *Shepheardes Calender*', *N&Q*, 2nd ser. 9 (1860), 42.

Cooper, Tarnya, *Searching for Shakespeare* (London: National Gallery, 2006).

Copenhaver, Brian P., 'Astrology and Magic', in Schmitt and Skinner (eds.), *Cambridge History of Renaissance Philosophy*, pp. 264–300.

Corbett, John, 'The Prentise and the Printer: James VI and Thomas Vautrollier', in Kevin J. McGinley and Nicola Royan (eds.), *The Apparelling of Truth: Literature and Literary Culture in The Reign of James VI: A Festscchrift for Roderick J. Lyall* (Newcastle upon Type: Cambridge Scholars, 2010), 80–93.

Coren, Pamela, 'Edmund Spenser, Mary Sidney, and the *Doleful Lay*', *SEL* 42 (2002), 25–41.

Corish, Patrick, *The Irish Catholic Experience: A Historical Survey* (Dublin: Gill and Macmillan, 1985).

Cormack, Bradin, *A Power to Do Justice: Jurisdiction, English Literature, and the Rise of Common Law, 1509–1625* (Chicago: University of Chicago Press, 2007).

Cormack, Lesley B., 'Maps as Educational Tools in the Renaissance', in Woodward (ed.), *History of Cartography*, iii/1. 622–36.

Cory, Herbert E., *The Critics of Edmund Spenser* (1911; New York: Haskell, 1964).

Costello, William T., SJ, *The Scholastic Curriculum at Early Seventeenth-Century Cambridge* (Cambridge, MA: Harvard University Press, 1958).

Coughlan, Patricia (ed.), *Spenser and Ireland: An Interdisciplinary Perspective* (Cork: Cork University Press, 1989).

—— 'The Local Context of Mutabilitie's Plea', *IUR: Spenser in Ireland, 1596–1996*, ed. Anne Fogarty (Autumn/Winter 1996), 320–41.

—— 'Cross-Currents in Colonial Discourse: The Political Thought of Vincent and Daniel Gookin', in Jane Ohlmeyer (ed.), *Political Thought in Seventeenth-Century Ireland* (Cambridge: Cambridge University Press, 2000), pp. 56–82.

Court, Franklin E., 'The Theme and Structure of Spenser's *Muiopotmos*', *SEL* 10 (1970), 1–15.

Cousins, A. D., 'Ralegh's "A Vision upon this Conceipt of *The Faerie Queene*", *The Explicator* 41/3 (spring 1983), 14–16.

Covington, F. F., Jr, 'Biographical Notes on Spenser', *MP* 22 (1924), 63–6.

—— 'Spenser and Alexander Neckham', *SP* 22 (1925), 222–5.

Cowman, Brian, 'An Open Elite: The Peculiarities of Connoisseurship in Early Modern England', *Modern Intellectual Hsitory* 1 (2004), 151–83.

Cox, J. Charles, and Alfred Harvey, *English Church Furniture* (London: Methuen, 1907).

Cox, Virginia, *The Renaissance Dialogue: Literary Dialogue in Its Social and Political Contexts, Castiglione to Galileo* (Cambridge: Cambridge University Press, 1992).

Craig, Martha, 'The Secret Wit of Spenser's Language', in Paul J. Alpers (ed.), *Elizabethan Poetry: Modern Essays in Criticism* (London: Oxford University Press, 1967), pp. 447–72.

Craik, G. L., *Spenser and his Poetry* (London: Charles Knight & Co., 1845).

Crawford, Charles, 'Edmund Spenser, "Locrine", and "Selimus"', *N&Q*, 9th ser. 7 (1901), 61–3, 203–5, 261–3.

——'*Greene's Funeralls*, 1594, and Nicholas Breton', *SP* 26, extra ser. 1 (1929), 1–39.

Crawford, John, and Raymond Gillespie (eds.), *St. Patrick's Cathedral, Dublin: A History* (Dublin: Four Courts, 2009).

Crawford, Jon G., *Anglicizing the Government of Ireland: The Irish Privy Council and the Expansion of Tudor Rule, 1556–1578* (Dublin: Irish Academic Press, 1993).

——*A Star Chamber Court in Ireland: The Court of Castle Chamber, 1571–1641* (Dublin: Four Courts, 2005).

Crawford, Patricia, '"The Sucking Child": Adult Attitudes to Child Care in the First Year of Life in Seventeenth-Century England,' *Continuity and Change* 1 (1986), 23–51.

Cressy, David, *Education in Tudor and Stuart England* (London: Arnold, 1975).

——*Literacy and the Social Order: Reading and Writing in Tudor and Stuart England* (Cambridge: Cambridge University Press, 1980).

——*Birth, Marriage & Death: Ritual, Religion, and the Life-Cycle in Tudor and Stuart England* (Oxford: Oxford University Press, 1997).

Crofts, J., *Packhorse, Waggon and Post: Land Carriage and Communications under the Tudors and Stuarts* (London: Routledge, 1967).

Cross, Claire, *Church and People, England, 1450–1660* (2nd edn., Oxford: Blackwell, 1999).

Cross, F. L., *The Oxford Dictionary of the Christian Church*, rev. E. A. Livingstone (Oxford: Oxford University Press, 2005).

Crowley, Seamus, 'Some of Spenser's Doneraile Neighbours', *North Cork Writers Journal*, 1 (1984), 71–5.

——'Mallow Iron Mines', *MFCJ* 22 (2004), 21–32.

Cruickshank, C. G., *Elizabeth's Army* (2nd edn., Oxford: Oxford University Press, 1966).

Culler, Jonathan, 'Apostrophe', in *The Pursuit of Signs: Semiotics, Literature, Deconstruction* (London: Routledge, 1981), pp. 135–54.

Cumming, William P., 'The Influence of Ovid's *Metamorphoses* on Spenser's "Mutabilitie" Cantos', *SP* 28 (1931), 241–56.

Cummings, Brian, *The Literary Culture of the Reformation: Grammar and Grace* (Oxford: Oxford University Press, 2002).

Cummings, L., 'Spenser's *Amoretti* VIII: New Manuscript Versions', *SEL* 4 (1964), 125–35.

Cummings, Robert, 'Mirrors for Policy' in Braden, Cummings, and Gillespie (eds.), *Oxford History of Literary Translation*, pp. 408–17.

——'Translation and Literary Innovation,' in Braden, Cummings, and Gillespie (eds.), *Oxford History of Literary Translation*, pp. 32–44.

Cunningham, Bernadette, 'Native Culture and Political Change in Ireland, 1580–1640', in Brady and Gillespie (eds.), *Natives and Newcomers*, pp. 148–70.

Cunningham, Jack, *James Ussher and John Bramhall: The Theology and Politics of Two Irish Ecclesiastics of the Seventeenth Century* (Aldershot: Ashgate, 2007).

Cunningham, John, 'Oliver Cromwell and the "Cromwellian" Settlement of Ireland', *HJ* 53 (2010), 919–37.

Curth, Louise Hill, *English Almanacs, Astrology & Popular Medicine: 1550–1700* (Manchester: Manchester University Press, 2007).

Curtis, Mark H., *Oxford and Cambridge in Transition, 1558–1642: An Essay on the Changing Relations between the English Universities and English Society* (Oxford: Clarendon Press, 1959).

Cuvelier, Eliane, 'Renaissance Catholicism in the Work of Thomas Lodge', in Whitney (ed.), *Thomas Lodge*, pp. 502–17.

D'Addario, Christopher, *Exile and Journey in Seventeenth-Century Literature* (Cambridge: Cambridge University Press, 2007).

Dall'Orto, Giovanni, '"Socratic Love" as a Disguise for Same-Sex Love in the Italian Renaissance', in Kent Gerard and Gert Hekma (eds.), *The Pursuit of Sodomy: Male Homosexuality in Renaissance and Enlightenment Europe* (New York: Harrington Park Press, 1989), pp. 33–65.

Daly, Peter M. (ed.), *Andrea Alciato and the Emblem Tradition: Essays in Honor of Virginia Woods Callahan* (Aldershot: Ashgate, 1989).

——and Bari Hooper, 'John Harvey's Carved Mantle-Piece (ca. 1570): An Early Instance of the Use of Alciato Emblems in England', in Daly (ed.), *Andrea Alciato*, pp. 177–204.

Dane, Joseph A., *Out of Sorts: On Typography and Print Culture* (Philadelphia: University of Pennsylvania Press, 2011).

Danner, Bruce, 'Retrospective Fiction-Making and the "Secrete" of the 1591 *Virgils Gnat*', *Sp. St.* 25 (2010), 215–45.

——*Furious Muse: Edmund Spenser's War on Lord Burghley* (Basingstoke: Palgrave, 2011).

Darby, H. C. (ed.), *A New Historical Geography of England Before 1600* (Cambridge: Cambridge University Press, 1973).

Dasenbrock, Reed Way, 'The Petrachan Context of Spenser's *Amoretti*', *PMLA* 100 (1985), 38–50.

Davis, Bernard E. C., 'The Text of Spenser's "Complaints"', *MLR* 20 (1925), 18–24.

Davis, Harold H., 'The Military Career of Thomas North', *HLQ* 12 (1949), 315–21.

——*Edmund Spenser: A Critical Study* (Cambridge: Cambridge University Press, 1933).

——'Review of Alexander C. Judson, *Life of Spenser*', *MLR* 42 (1947), 494–5.

Davis, Natalie Zemon, *The Return of Martin Guerre* (Cambridge, MA: Harvard University Press, 1983).

——*Trickster Travels: In Search of Leo Africanus, a Sixteenth-Century Muslim Between Worlds* (London: Faber, 2006).

Day, Matthew, 'Hakluyt, Harvey, Nashe: The Material Text and Early Modern Nationalism', *SP* 104 (2007), 281–305.

Day, Robert, 'Notes on Youghal', *JRSAI*, 5th ser. 33 (1903), 319–25.

Daybell, James, *The Material Letter: Manuscript Letters and the Culture and Practices of Letter-Writing in Early Modern England, 1512–1635* (Basingstoke: Palgrave, 2012).

Dees, Jerome S., 'Colin Clout and the Shepherd of the Ocean', *Sp. St.* 15 (2001), 185–96.

De Lacy, Hugh, 'Astrology in the Poetry of Edmund Spenser', *JEGP* 33 (1934), 520–43.

De Molen, Richard L., 'Richard Mulcaster: An Elizabethan Savant', *Sh. Stud.* 8 (1975), 29–82.

——*Richard Mulcaster (c.1531–1611) and Educational Reform in the Renaissance* (Nieuwkoop: De Graaf, 1991).

Deneef, A. Leigh, *Spenser and the Motives of Metaphor* (Durham, NC: Duke University Press, 1982).

Denkinger, Emma Marshall, 'Some Renaissance References to *Sic Vos Non Vobis*', *PQ* 10 (1931), 151–62.

Dent, Anthony, *Horses in Shakespeare's England* (London: Allen, 1987).

Derrida, Jacques, 'Structure, Sign and Play in the Discourse of the Human Sciences', in *Writing and Difference*, trans. Alan Bass (London: Routledge, 1981).

Deveson, Alison M., *En Suivant La Vérité: A History of the Earls of Portsmouth and the Wallop Family* (Farleigh Wallop: Portsmouth Estates, 2008).

Dewar, Mary, *Sir Thomas Smith: A Tudor Intellectual in Office* (Cambridge: Cambridge University Press, 1964).

Dickens, A. G., *The English Reformation* (rev. edn., London: Fontana, 1986).

Dickson, David, *Old World Colony: Cork and South Munster, 1630–1830* (Cork: Cork University Press, 2005).

Dobranski, Stephen B., *Readers and Authorship in Early Modern England* (Cambridge: Cambridge University Press, 2005).

Dolven, Jeff, *Scenes of Instruction in Renaissance Romance* (Chicago: University of Chicago Press, 2007).

Donaldson, Ian, *Ben Jonson: A Life* (Oxford: Oxford University Press, 2011).

Donnelly, Eithne, 'The Roches, Lords of Fermoy: The History of a Norman-Irish Family', *JCHAS* 38 (1933), 86–91; 39 (1934), 38–40, 57–68; 40 (1935), 37–42, 63–73; 41 (1936), 20–8, 78–84; 42 (1937), 40–52.

Donnelly, M. I., 'The Life of Vergil and the Aspiration of the "New Poet"', *Sp. St.* 17 (2003), 1–35.

Doran, Susan, *Monarchy and Matriarchy: The Courtships of Elizabeth I* (London: Routledge, 1996).

—— '"Revenge her most foul and unnatural murder": The Impact of Mary Stuart's Execution on Anglo-Scottish Relations', *History* 85 (2000), 589–612.

Dorsten, Jan Van, *Poets, Patrons, and Professors: Sir Philip Sidney, Daniel Rogers and the Leiden Humanists* (Leiden: Leiden University Press, 1962).

—— *The Radical Arts: First Decade of an Elizabethan Renaissance* (Leiden: Leiden University Press, 1970).

—— Dominic Baker-Smith, and Arthur F. Kinney (eds.), *Sir Philip Sidney: 1586 and the Creation of a Legend* (Leiden: Brill, 1986).

Doughtie, Edward, 'John Ramsey's Manuscript as a Personal and Family Document', in W. Speed Hill (ed.), *New Ways of Looking at Old Texts: Papers of the Renaissance English Text Society, 1985–1991* (Binghamton, NY: MRTS, 1993), pp. 281–8.

Downie, J. A., 'Marlowe, May 1593, and the "Must-Have" Theory of Biography', *RES* 58 (2007), 245–67.

Draper, F. W. M., *Four Centuries of Merchant Taylors' School, 1561–1961* (London: Oxford University Press, 1962).

Draper, John W., 'Linguistics in *The Present State of Ireland*', *MP* 17 (1919–20), 471–86.

Driver, Martha W., 'When is a Miscellany Not Miscellaneous? Making Sense of the *Kalender of Shepherds*', *YES* 33 (2003), 199–214.

Drury, Paul, with Richard Simpson, *Hill Hall: A Singular House Devised by a Tudor Intellectual* (London: Society of Antiquaries, 2009).

Duffy, Eamon, *The Stripping of the Altars: Traditional Religion in England, 1400–1580* (New Haven: Yale University Press, 1992).

—— 'Bare Ruined Choirs: Remembering Catholicism in Shakespeare's England', in Richard Dutton, Alison Findlay, and Richard Wilson (eds.), *Theatre and Religion: Lancastrian Shakespeare* (Manchester: Manchester University Press, 2003), pp. 40–57.

—— *Fires of Faith: Catholic England under Mary Tudor* (New Haven: Yale University Press, 2009).

Duncan, Douglas, *Ben Jonson and the Lucianic Tradition* (Cambridge: Cambridge University Press, 1979).

Duncan-Jones, Katherine, *Sir Philip Sidney, Courtier Poet* (London: Hamish Hamilton, 1991).

—— *Ungentle Shakespeare: Scenes from His Life* (London: Thomson, 2001).

—— *Shakespeare: Upstart Crow to Sweet Swan: The Evolution of His Image* (London: Black, 2011).

Dundas, Judith, '"Muiopotmos": A World of Art', *YES* 5 (1975), 30–8.

Dunlop, Alexander, 'Calendar Symbolism in the "Amoretti"', *N&Q* 214 (1969), 24–6.

Dunlop, Robert, 'The Plantation of Munster', *EHR* 3 (1888), 250–69.

Eade, J. C., 'The Pattern in the Astronomy of Spenser's *Epithalamion*', *RES* 23 (1972), 173–8.

Eagle, Roderick L., 'The Search for Spenser's Grave', *N&Q* 201 (1956), 282–3.

Eccles, Mark, 'Spenser's First Marriage', *TLS*, 31 Dec. 1931, p. 1053.

—— 'A Biographical Dictionary of Elizabethan Authors', *HLQ* 5 (1942), 281–302.

—— 'Elizabethan Edmund Spensers', *MLQ* 5 (1944), 413–27.

—— 'Brief Lives: Tudor and Stuart Authors', *SP* 79/4, Texts and Studies (Autumn 1982), 1–135.

Edel, Leon, *The Life of Henry James*, 5 vols. (London: Hart-Davies, 1953–72).

Edwards, David, 'Martial Law and the Tudor Reconquest of Ireland', *History Ireland* 5 (Summer 1997), 16–21.

—— 'Ideology and Experience: Spenser's *View* and Martial Law in Ireland', in Morgan (ed.), *Political Ideology in Ireland*, pp. 127–57.

Edwards, David, *The Ormond Lordship in County Kilkenny, 1515–1642: The Rise and Fall of Butler Feudal Power* (Dublin: Four Courts, 2003).

—— 'A Haven of Popery: English Catholic Migration to Ireland In the Age of Plantations', in Ford and McCafferty (eds.), *Origins of Sectarianism*, pp. 95–126.

—— 'The Escalation of Violence in Sixteenth-Century Ireland', in Edwards et al. (eds.), *Age of Atrocity*, pp. 34–78.

—— Pádraig Lenihan, and Clodagh Tait (eds.), *Age of Atrocity: Violence and Political Conflict in Early Modern Ireland* (Dublin: Four Courts, 2007).

Elcock, W. D., 'English Indifference to Du Bellay's "Regrets"', *MLR* 46 (1951), 175–84.

Ellis, Steven, *Tudor Ireland: Crown, Community and the Conflict of Cultures, 1470–1603* (Harlow: Longman, 1985).

Ellrodt, Robert, *Neoplatonism in the Poetry of Spenser* (Geneva: Droz, 1960).

E. M. B., 'Spenser's Monument', *N&Q*, 1st ser. 1 (1850), 481–2.

——'Portraits of Spenser', *N&Q*, 1st ser. 3 (1851), 301.

——'Spenser's Portrait', *N&Q*, 1st ser. 4 (1851), 101.

Emerson, Oliver Farrar, 'Spenser's *Virgils Gnat*', *JEGP* 17 (1918), 94–118.

Emery, F. V., 'England circa 1600', in Darby (ed.), *New Historical Geography*, pp. 248–301.

Emmison, F. G., *Elizabethan Life: Home, Work and Land* (Chelmsford: Essex County Council, 1976).

Erikson, Erik H., *Young Man Luther: A Study in Psychoanalysis and History* (1958; New York: Norton, 1962).

Erikson, Roy T., 'Two Into One: The Unity of George Gascoigne's Companion Poems', *SP* 81 (1984), 275–98.

Erikson, Wayne C. (ed.), *The 1590 Faerie Queene: Paratexts and Publishing*, *SLI* 38/2 (Fall 2005).

Erne, Lukas, *Beyond The Spanish Tragedy: A Study of the Works of Thomas Kyd* (Manchester: Manchester University Press, 2001).

——'Biography, Mythography and Criticism: The Life and Work of Christopher Marlowe', *MP* 103 (2005), 28–50.

Erskine, John, 'The Virtue of Friendship in *The Faerie Queene*', *PMLA* 30 (1915), 831–50.

Escobedo, Andrew, *Nationalism and Historical Loss in Renaissance England: Foxe, Dee, Spenser, Milton* (Ithaca, NY: Cornell University Press, 2004).

Evans, Frank B., 'The Printing of Spenser's *Faerie Queene* in 1596', *SB* 18 (1965), 50–69.

Evans, Maurice, *Spenser's Anatomy of Heroism* (Cambridge: Cambridge University Press, 1970).

Evans, R. W., 'Notes on River Bregog', *JCHAS* 18 (1912), 201–3.

Evenden, Elizabeth, *Patents, Pictures and Patronage: John Day and the Tudor Book Trade* (Aldershot: Ashgate, 2008).

——— and Thomas S. Freeman, *Religion and the Book in Early Modern England: The Making of John Foxe's 'Book of Martyrs'* (Cambridge: Cambridge University Press, 2011).

F., 'Spenser's Lancashire Home', *N&Q*, 9th ser. 3 (1899), 481–3.

Fairfield, Leslie P., '*The Vocacyon of Johan Bale* and Early English Autobiography', *RQ* 24 (1971), 327–40.

Falco, Raphael, 'Instant Artefacts: Vernacular Elegies for Philip Sidney', *SP* 89 (1992), 1–19.

——'Spenser's "Astrophel" and the Formation of Elizabethan Literary Genealogy', *MP* 91 (1993), 1–25.

Falkiner, C. Litton, *Illustrations of Irish History, Topography, Mainly of the Seventeenth Century* (London: Longman, 1904).

Falls, Cyril, *Elizabeth's Irish Wars* (London: Constable, 1950).

Faverty, Frederick E., 'A Note on the Areopagus', *PQ* 5 (1926), 278–80.

Fehrenbach, R. J., and E. S. Leedham-Green (eds.), *Private Libraries in Renaissance England: A Collection and Catalogue of Tudor and Stuart Book-Lists*, 5 vols. (Tempe, AZ: MRTS, 1992–8).

Feingold, Mordechai, *The Mathematicians' Apprenticeship: Science, Universities and Society in England, 1560–1640* (Cambridge: Cambridge University Press, 1984).

——'English Ramism: A Reinterpretation', in Mordechai Feingold, Joseph S. Freedman, and Wolfgang Rother (eds.), *The Influence of Petrus Ramus: Studies in Sixteenth-Century and Seventeenth-Century Philosophy and Sciences* (Basle: Schwabe and Co., 2001), pp. 127–76.

Fenlon, Jane, *Ormond Castle: Visitor's Guide* (Dublin: Office of Public Works, 2008).

Ferguson, James J., 'Memorials of Edmund Spenser the Poet, and His Descendants, from the Public Records of Ireland', *Gentleman's Magazine* 44 (1855), 605–9.

——'Memorials of Edmund Spenser the Poet, and His Descendants, from the Public Records of Ireland', *JCHAS* 14 (1908), 39–43.

Field, Ophelia, *The Kit-Cat Club* (London: HarperCollins, 2009).

Fildes, Valerie, *Wet Nursing: A History from Antiquity to the Present* (Oxford: Blackwell, 1988).

——(ed.), *Women as Mothers in Pre-Industrial England* (London: Routledge, 1990).

Finch, Jeremiah S., 'Sir Thomas Browne's Library', *English Language Notes* 19 (1982), 360–70.

Finch, Mary E., *The Wealth of Five Northamptonshire Families, 1540–1640* (Oxford: Northamptonshire Record Society, 1956).

Fisher, R. M., 'William Crashawe's Library at the Temple', *The Library*, 5th ser. 30 (1975), 116–24.

Fitzgerald, John J., 'Documents Found at Castlewhite, Co. Cork', *JRSAI*, 6th ser. 20 (1930), 79–83.

Fitzgerald, Lord Walter, 'New Abbey of Kilcullen, with a Sketch of the Founder, Sir Roland FitzEustace, Baron Portlester', *JKAS* 3 (1902), 301–17.

——'The Priory or Nunnery of Graney, County Kildare,' *JKAS* 7 (1912–14), 373–81.

Flavin, Susan, and Evan T. Jones (eds.), *Bristol's Trade with Ireland and the Continent: The Evidence of the Exchequer Customs Accounts* (Dublin: Four Courts, 2009).

Fleck, Andrew, 'Early Modern Marginalia in Spenser's *Faerie Queene* at the Folger', *N&Q* 55 (2008), 165–70.

Fleming, Horace T., 'Some Notes on the Tynte Family', *JCHAS* 9 (1903), 156–7.

Fleming, Juliet, *Graffiti and the Writing Arts of Early Modern England* (London: Reaktion, 2001).

Fletcher, Alan J., *Drama, Performance, and Polity in Pre-Cromwellian Ireland* (Cork: Cork University Press, 2000).

Fletcher, Anthony, and Peter Roberts (eds.), *Religion, Culture, and Society in Early Modern Britain: Essay in Honour of Patrick Collinson* (Cambridge: Cambridge University Press, 1994).

——'The Protestant Idea of Marriage in Early Modern England', in Fletcher and Roberts (eds.), *Religion, Culture, and Society*, pp. 161–81.

Fletcher, J. M., 'The Faculty of Arts', in James McConica (ed.), *The History of the University of Oxford*, iii. *The Collegiate University* (Oxford: Clarendon Press, 1986), pp. 157–212.

Fletcher, Jefferson B., 'Benivieni's "Ode of Love" and Spenser's "Fowre Hymnes"', *MP* 8 (1911), 545–60.

Fletcher, Reginald J. (ed.), *The Pension Book of Gray's Inn*, 2 vols. (London: Chiswick Press, 1901–10).

Flinker, Noam, *The Song of Songs in English Renaissance Literature: Kisses of Their Mouths* (Woodbridge: Boydell, 2000).

Fogarty, Anne, 'The Colonization of Language: Narrative Strategies in *A View of the Present State of Ireland* and *The Faerie Queene*, Book VI', in Coughlan (ed.), *Spenser and Ireland*, i. 75–108.

——'Literature in English, 1550–1690', in Margaret Kelleher and Philip O'Leary (eds.), *The Cambridge History of Irish Literature*, 2 vols. (Cambridge: Cambridge University Press, 2006), i. 140–90.

Forbes, A. C., 'Some Legendary and Historical References to Irish Woods, and Their Significance', *PRIA*, sect. B, 41 (1932–3), 15–36.

Ford, Alan, *The Protestant Reformation in Ireland, 1590–1641* (Dublin: Four Courts, 1997).

——'"That Bugbear Armenianism": Archbishop Laud and Trinity College, Dublin', in Brady and Ohlmeyer (eds.), *British Interventions in Early Modern Ireland*, pp. 135–60.

——*James Ussher: Theology, History and Politics in Early-Modern Ireland and England* (Oxford: Oxford University Press, 2007).

——and John McCafferty (eds.), *The Origins of Sectarianism in Early Modern Ireland* (Cambridge: Cambridge University Press, 2005).

——'The Irish Historical Renaissance and the Shaping of Protestant History', in Ford and McCafferty (eds.), *Origins of Sectarianism*, pp. 127–57.

Foster, Joseph, *The Register of Admissions to Gray's Inn, 1521–1889, Together with the Register of Marriages in Gray's Inn Chapel, 1695–1754* (London: privately printed, 1889).

Foster, Leonard, 'The Translator of the "Theatre for Worldlings"', *ES* 48 (1967), 27–34.

Fowler, Alistair, *Spenser and the Numbers of Time* (London: Routledge, 1964).

——*Time's Purpled Masquers: Stars and the Afterlife in Renaissance English Literature* (Oxford: Clarendon Press, 1996).

Fowler, Elizabeth, 'The Failure of Moral Philosophy in the Work of Edmund Spenser', *Representations* 51 (1995), 47–76.

——*Literary Character: The Human Figure in English Writing* (Ithaca, NY: Cornell University Press, 2003).

Fox, Alistair, *Thomas More: History & Providence* (Oxford: Blackwell, 1982).

Freedman, Sylvia, *Poor Penelope: Lady Penelope Rich, An Elizabethan Woman* (Abbotsbrook: Kensal, 1983).

Freeman, Thomas S., '"The Reformation of the Church in this Parliament": Thomas Norton, John Foxe and the Parliament of 1571', *Parliamentary History* 16 (1997), 131–47.

French, Peter J., *John Dee: The World of an Elizabethan Magus* (London: Routledge, 1972).

Freyd, Bernard, 'Spenser or Anthony Munday?—A Note on the *Axiochus*', *PMLA* 50 (1935), 903–8.

Friedland, Louis S., 'A Source of Spenser's "The Oak and The Briar"', *PQ* 33 (1954), 222–4.

—— 'The Illustrations in *The Theatre for Worldlings*', *HLQ* 19 (1956), 107–20.

Friedrich, Walter, G., 'The Stella of *Astrophel*', *ELH* 3 (1936), 114–39.

Fuchs, Barbara, 'Travelling Epic: Translating Ercilla's *La Araucana* in the Old World', *JMEMS* 36 (2006), 379–95.

Fuller, John, *The Sonnet* (London: Methuen, 1972).

Furey, Constance M., 'Bound by Likeness: Vives and Erasmus on Marriage and Friendship', in Daniel T. Lochman, Martiere López, and Lorna Hutson (eds.), *Discourses and Representations of Friendship in Early Modern Europe, 1500–1700* (Farnham: Ashgate, 2011), pp. 29–43.

Galbraith, Steven K., '"English" Black-Letter Type and Spenser's *Shepheardes Calender*', *Sp. St.* 23 (2008), 13–40.

Galway, Margaret, 'Spenser's Rosalind', *TLS*, 19 July 1947, p. 372.

Garnett, Oliver, *Canons Ashby* (Swindon: National Trust, 2001).

Garrett, Christina, *The Marian Exiles, 1553–1559* (Cambridge: Cambridge University Press, 1938).

Garrod, H. W., and W. H. Welply, 'Spenser and Elizabeth Boyle', *TLS*, 24 May 1923, p. 321.

Geimer, Roger A., 'Spenser's Rhyme or Churchyard's Reason: Evidence of Churchyard's First Pension', *RES* 20 (1969), 306–9.

Gelderen, Martin van, *The Political Thought of the Dutch Revolt, 1555–1590* (Cambridge: Cambridge University Press, 1992).

Gent, Lucy, *Picture and Poetry, 1560–1620: Relations Between Literature and the Visual Arts in the English Renaissance* (Leamington Spa: James Hall, 1981).

Ghose, Indira, *Shakespeare and Laughter: A Cultural History* (Manchester: Manchester University Press, 2008).

Gibson, Jonathan, 'The Legal Context of Spenser's *Daphnaïda*', *RES* 55 (2004), 24–44.

Gibson, Kirsten, 'The Order of the Book: Materiality, Narrative and Authorial Voice in John Dowland's *First Book of Songes or Ayres*', *RS* 26 (2012), 13–33.

Gibson, Thomas B., 'Spenser and Kilcolman', *Dublin University Review* 3/1 (Mar. 1887), 82–92.

Gilbert, Allan, 'Were Spenser's Nine Comedies Lost?', *MLN* 73 (1958), 241–3.

Gillespie, Raymond, 'The Book Trade in Southern Ireland, 1590–1640', in Gerard Long (ed.), *Books Beyond the Pale: Aspects of the Provincial Book Trade in Ireland Before 1850* (Dublin: Rare Books Group of the Library Association of Ireland, 1996).

—— 'The Problems of Plantations: Material Culture and Social Change in Early Modern Ireland', in Lyttleton and Rynne (eds.), *Plantation Ireland*, pp. 43–60.

—— 'Reform and Decay, 1500–1598', in Crawford and Gillespie (eds.), *St. Patrick's Cathedral*, pp. 151–73.

—— 'An Age of Modernization, 1598–1690', in Crawford and Gillespie (eds.), *St. Patrick's Cathedral*, pp. 174–96.

—— and Andrew Hadfield, 'Two References to Edmund Spenser in Chancery Disputes', *N&Q* 246 (Sept. 2001), 249–51.

—— and Andrew Hadfield (eds.), *The Oxford History of the Irish Book*, iii. *The Irish Book in English, 1550–1800* (Oxford: Oxford University Press, 2006).

Gillies, John, *Shakespeare and the Geography of Difference* (Cambridge: Cambridge University Press, 1994).

Gilman, Ernest B., *Iconoclasm and Poetry in the English Reformation: Down Went Dagon* (Chicago: University of Chicago Press, 1986).

Glasgow, Tom, 'Elizabethan Ships Pictured on Smerwick Map, 1580: Background, Authentication and Evaluation', *Mariner's Mirror* 52 (1966), 157–66.

Gless, Darryl J., *Interpretation and Theology in Spenser* (Cambridge: Cambridge University Press, 1994).

Goeglein, Tamara A., 'Reading English Ramist Logic Books as Early Modern Emblem Books: The Case of Abraham Fraunce', *Sp. St.* 20 (2005), 225–52.

Goldberg, Jonathan, *Endlesse Worke: Spenser and the Structures of Discourse* (Baltimore: Johns Hopkins University Press, 1981).

——*Sodometries: Renaissance Texts, Modern Sexualities* (Stanford: Stanford University Press, 1992).

——'Between Men: Literary History and the Work of Mourning', in Karen Weisman (ed.), *The Oxford Handbook of the Elegy* (Oxford: Oxford University Press, 2010), pp. 498–517.

Goldie, Mark, 'The Unacknowledged Republic: Officeholding in Early Modern England', in Tim Harris (ed.), *The Politics of the Excluded, c.1500–1850* (Basingstoke: Palgrave, 2001), pp. 153–94.

Gollancz, Israel, 'Spenseriana', *PBA* 3 (1907), 99–105.

Gordon, Walter M., *Humanist Play and Belief: The Seriocomic Art of Desiderius Erasmus* (Toronto: University of Toronto Press, 1990).

Gosling, William Gilbert, *The Life of Sir Humphrey Gilbert, England's First Empire Builder* (London: Constable, 1911).

Gotch, J. Alfred, *The Old Halls & Manor-Houses of Northamptonshire* (London: Batsford, 1936).

——et al., *Rushton and Its Owners* (Northampton: Taylor and Son, 1896).

Gottfried, Rudolf, 'The Date of Spenser's *View*', *MLN* 52 (1937), 176–80.

——'Spenser's *View* and Essex', *PMLA* 52 (1937), 645–51.

——'The "G. W. Senior" and "G. W. I." of Spenser's *Amoretti*', *MLQ* 3 (1942), 543–6.

——*Geoffrey Fenton's Historie of Guicciardini* (Bloomington: Indiana University Press, Indiana University Publications Series, Humanities Division, 1940).

——'Spenser and *The Historie of Cambria*', *MLN* 72 (1957), 9–13.

Gottschalk, Katherine K., 'Discoveries Concerning British Library Harley 6910', *MP* 77 (1979), 121–31.

Goy-Blanquet, Dominique, 'Lord Keeper Bacon and the Writing on the Wall', *Law and Humanities* 4 (2010), 211–28.

Grafton, Anthony, and Lisa Jardine, ' "Studied for Action": How Gabriel Harvey Read His Livy', *P&P* 129 (1990), 30–78.

Graham, Timothy, 'Matthew Parker's Manuscripts: An Elizabethan Library and Its Use', in Leedham-Green and Webber (eds.), *Cambridge History of Libraries*, i. 322–41.

Grainger, Ian, Duncan Hawkins, Lynne Coral, and Richard Mikulski, *The Black Death Cemetery, East Smithfield, London* (London: Museum of London, 2008).

——and Christopher Phillpotts, *The Royal Navy Victualling Yard, East Smithfield, London* (London: Museum of London, 2010).

Grant, Michael, and John Hazel, *Who's Who in Classical Mythology* (1973; London: Dent, 1993).

Grantley, Darryl, *London in Early Modern English Drama: Representing the Built Environment* (Basingstoke: Palgrave, 2008).

Gratton Flood, William H., 'Enniscorthy in the Thirteenth Century: Who Built the Castle?' *JRSAI*, 5th ser. 34 (1904), 380–3.

——'Enniscorthy', *JRSAI* 35 (1905), 177–8.

——'Molana Abbey, Co. Waterford', *JCHAS* 22 (1916), 1–7.

——'Identification of the Spenserian "Aubrian" River', *JCHAS* 22 (1916), 143–4.

Graves, Michael, *Thomas Norton: The Parliament Man* (Oxford: Blackwell, 1994).

Gray, Douglas, *Later Medieval English Literature* (Oxford: Oxford University Press, 2008).

Graziani, René, 'Philip II's Impressa and Spenser's Souldan', *JWCI* 27 (1964), 322–4.

——'Verses by E. K.', *N&Q* 16 (1969), 21.

Greenblatt, Stephen, *Sir Walter Raleigh: The Renaissance Man and His Roles* (New Haven: Yale University Press, 1973).

——'Murdering Peasants: Status, Genre and the Representation of Rebellion', *Representations* 1 (1983), 1–29.

Greenblatt, Stephen, 'Psychoanalysis and Renaissance Culture', in Patricia Parker and David Quint (eds.), *Literary Theory/Renaissance Texts* (Baltimore: Johns Hopkins University Press, 1986), pp. 210–24.

Greene, Thomas M., 'Spenser and the Epithalamic Convention', *CL* 9 (1957), 215–28.

Greenlaw, Edwin, 'The Influence of Machiavelli on Spenser', *MP* 7 (1909), 187–202.

——'Spenser and the Earl of Leicester', *PMLA* 26 (1910), 535–61.

——'Spenser and British Imperialism', *MP* 60 (1911–12), 347–70.

——'Spenser's Fairy Mythology', *SP* 15 (1918), 105–22.

——'The Cantos of Mutabilitie: Further Considerations Bearing on the Date', *PMLA* 45 (1930), 704–11.

Greer, Germaine, *Shakespeare's Wife* (London: Bloomsbury, 2007).

Grennan, Eamon, 'Language and Politics: A Note on Some Metaphors in Spenser's *A View of the Present State of Ireland*', *Sp. St.* 3 (1982), 99–110.

Grieg, C. Margaret, 'The Identity of E. K. of *The Shepheardes Calender*', *N&Q* 197 (1952), 332–4.

Griffin, Benjamin, 'Nashe's Dedicatees: William Beeston and Richard Lichfield', *N&Q* 44 (Mar. 1997), 47–9.

Griffin, Tobias, 'A Good Fit: Bryskett and the Bowre of Bliss', *Sp. St.* 25 (2010), 377–9.

Griffiths, Jane, 'Text and Authority: John Stow's 1568 Edition of Skelton's *Workes*', in Ian Gadd and Alexandra Gillespie (eds.), *John Stow (1525–1605) and the Making of the English Past* (London: British Library, 2004), pp. 127–34.

——'What's in a Name? The Transmission of "John Skelton, Laureate" in Manuscript and Print', *HLQ* 67 (2004), 215–35.

——*John Skelton and Poetic Authority: Defining the Liberty to Speak* (Oxford: Oxford University Press, 2006).

Griffiths, Paul, *Youth and Authority: Formative Experiences in England, 1560–1640* (Oxford: Clarendon Press, 1996).

——*Lost Londons: Change, Crime and Control in the Capital City, 1550–1660* (Cambridge: Cambridge University Press, 2008).

Grogan, Jane, *Exemplary Spenser: Visual and Poetic Pedagogy in The Faerie Queene* (Aldershot: Ashgate, 2009).

——(ed.), *Celebrating Mutabilitie: Essays on Edmund Spenser's Mutabilitie Cantos* (Manchester: Manchester University Press, 2010).

Grundy, Joan, *The Spenserian Poets: A Study in Elizabethan and Jacobean Poetry* (London: Arnold, 1969).

Guerci, Manolo, 'Salisbury House in London, 1599–1694: The Strand Palace of Sir Robert Cecil', *Architectural History* 52 (2009), 31–78.

——'The Construction of Northumberland House and the Patronage of Its Original Builder, Lord Henry Howard, 1603–14', *AJ* 90 (2010), 341–400.

Guiney, Louise Imogen, 'Sir Walter Raleigh of Youghal in the County of Cork', *Atlantic Monthly* 66 (1890), 779–86.

Gurevich, Aaron, *The Origins of European Individualism*, trans. Katherine Judelson (Oxford: Blackwell, 1995).

Guthrie, William Keith Chambers, *A History of Greek Philosophy: The Later Plato and the Academy* (Cambridge: Cambridge University Press, 1986).

Guy, John, *Tudor England* (Oxford: Oxford University Press, 1988).

——(ed.), *The Reign of Elizabeth I: Court and Culture in the Last Decade* (Cambridge: Cambridge University Press, 1995).

——*'My Heart is My Own': The Life of Mary Queen of Scots* (London: HarperCollins, 2004).

Gwynn, Aubrey, and R. Neville Hadcock, *Medieval Religious Houses: Ireland* (Dublin: Blackrock, 1970).

Haber, Judith, *Pastoral and the Poetics of Self-Contradiction: Theocritus to Marvell* (Cambridge: Cambridge University Press, 1994).

Hackett, Helen, *Virgin Mother, Maiden Queen: Elizabeth I and the Cult of the Virgin Mary* (Basingstoke: Macmillan, 1995).

Hadfield, Andrew, 'Briton and Scythian: Tudor Representations of Irish Origins', *IHS* 112 (1993), 390–408.

——*Literature, Politics and National Identity: Reformation to Renaissance* (Cambridge: Cambridge University Press, 1994).

——'Certainties and Uncertainties: By Way of Response to Jean Brink', *Sp. St.* 12 (1995), 197–202.

——'"The Sacred Hunger of Ambitious Minds": Spenser's Savage Religion', in Donna Hamilton and Richard Strier (eds.), *Religion, Literature and Politics in Post-Reformation England, 1540–1688* (Cambridge: Cambridge University Press, 1996), pp. 27–45.

——*Spenser's Irish Experience: Wilde Fruit and Salvage Soyl* (Oxford: Clarendon Press, 1997).

——'Sidney's "poor painter" and John Stubbs's *Gaping Gulf*', *SJ* 15/2 (Fall 1997), 45–8.

——'An Allusion to Spenser's Irish Writings: Matthew Lownes and Ralph Byrchensa's *A Discourse occasioned on the late defeat, given to the Arch-rebels, Tyrone and O'Donnell* (1602)', *N&Q* 242 (Dec. 1997), 478–80.

——'The Name "Eudoxus" in Spenser's *View*', *N&Q* 242 (Dec. 1997), 477–8.

——*Literature, Travel, and Colonial Writing in the English Renaissance, 1545–1625* (Oxford: Clarendon Press, 1998).

——'Was Spenser a Republican?', *English* 47 (1998), 169–82.

——'Spenser's Description of the Execution of Murrogh O'Brien: An Anti-Catholic Polemic?', *N&Q* 244 (June 1999), 195–7.

——'William Kent's Illustrations of *The Faerie Queene* (1751)', *Sp. St.* 14 (2000), 1–81.

——'Spenser's *View* and *Leicester's Commonwealth*', *N&Q* 48 (Sept. 2001), 256–9.

——'*The Faerie Queene*, Books IV-VII', in Hadfield (ed.), *Cambridge Companion to Spenser*, pp. 124–42.

——'Censoring Ireland in Elizabethan England', in Hadfield (ed.), *Literature and Censorship in Renaissance England* (Basingstoke: Palgrave, 2001), pp. 149–64.

——'"Bruited Abroad": John White's and Thomas Harriot's Colonial Representations of Ancient Britain', in David Baker and Willy Maley (eds.), *British Identities and English Renaissance Literature* (Cambridge: Cambridge University Press, 2002), pp. 159–77.

——'Was Spenser a Republican After All? A Response to David Scott Okamura-Wilson', *Sp. St.* 17 (2003), 275–90.

——'Spenser and the Stuart Succession', *Literature and History* 13/1 (Spring 2004), 9–24.

——'Michael Drayton's Brilliant Career', *PBA* 125 (2004), 119–47.

——'Historical Writing, 1550–1660', in Gillespie and Hadfield (eds.), *Oxford History of the Irish Book*, iii. 250–63.

——'Donne's *Songs and Sonnets* and Artistic Identity', in Patrick Cheney, Andrew Hadfield, and Garrett Sullivan (eds.), *Early Modern English Poetry: A Critical Companion* (Oxford: Oxford University Press, 2006), pp. 206–16.

——'Secrets and Lies: The Life of Edmund Spenser', in Kevin Sharpe and Steven Zwicker (eds.), *Writing Lives: Biography and Textuality, Identity and Representation in Early Modern England* (Oxford: Oxford University Press, 2008), pp. 55–73.

——'The Fair Rosalind: What's in a Literary Name: Disguise and the Absent Beloved in Spenser and Shakespeare', *TLS*, 12 Dec. 2008, pp. 13–14.

——'The Idea of the North', *Journal of the Northern Renaissance* 1/1 (Spring 2009), 1–18.

——'Spenser's Rosalind', *MLR* 104/4 (Oct. 2009), 935–46.

——'"Not without Mustard": Self-Publicity and Polemic in Early Modern Literary London', in Healy and Healy (eds.), *Renaissance Transformations*, pp. 64–78.

——'Spenser and Buchanan', in Roger Mason (ed.), *Buchanan* (Aldershot: Ashgate, forthcoming).

——'Spenser's Reference to Censorship', *N&Q* 56/4 (Dec. 2009), 532–3.

Hadfield, Andrew, 'Edmund Spenser and Samuel Brandon', *N&Q* 56 (Dec. 2009), 536–8.

——'Spenser and John Stow', *N&Q* 56 (Dec. 2009), 538–9.

——'Spenser and Jokes: The 2008 Kathleen Williams Lecture', *Sp. St.* 25 (2010), 1–19.

——'*Lenten Stuff*: Thomas Nashe and the Fiction of Travel', *YES* 41 (2011), 68–83.

——'Spenser and Religion—Yet Again', *SEL* 51/1 (2011), 21–46.

——'A Mortgage Agreement of Hugolin Spenser, Edmund Spenser's Grandson', *Sp. St.* (forthcoming).

Hadfield, Andrew, and Willy Maley, 'Introduction: Irish Representations and English Alternatives', in Bradshaw et al. (eds.), *Representing Ireland*, pp. 1–23.

——(ed.), *The Cambridge Companion to Spenser* (Cambridge: Cambridge University Press, 2001).

——(ed.), *Literature and Censorship in Renaissance England* (Basingstoke: Palgrave, 2001).

——(ed.), (special issue), *Textual Practice: Were Early Modern Lives Different?* 23/2 (Apr. 2009).

——(ed.), *The Oxford Handbook to English Prose, 1500–1640* (Oxford: Oxford University Press, forthcoming).

——and Matthew Dimmock (eds.), *Religions of the Book: Co-existence and Conflict, 1400–1660* (Basingstoke: Palgrave, 2008).

——and Raymond Gillespie (eds.), *The Oxford History of the Irish Book*, iii. *The Irish Book in English, 1550–1800* (Oxford: Oxford University Press, 2006).

Haigh, Christopher (ed.), *The English Reformation Revised* (Cambridge: Cambridge University Press, 1987).

Hale, David G., 'Aesop in Renaissance England', *The Library*, 5th ser. 27 (1972), 116–25.

Hale, John, *The Civilization of Europe in the Renaissance* (London: HarperCollins, 1993).

Hales, J. W., 'Edmund Spenser', in Morris (ed.), *Complete Works*, pp. xi–lv.

Hall, Marcia B. (ed.), *Michelangelo's Last Judgement* (Cambridge: Cambridge University Press, 2005).

Halpin, Andy, and Conor Newman, *Ireland: An Oxford Archaeological Guide* (Oxford: Oxford University Press, 2006).

Halpin, N. J., 'On Certain Passages in the Life of Edmund Spenser', *PRIA* 4 (1847–50), 445–51.

Hamer, Douglas, 'Spenser's Marriage', *RES* 27 (1931), 271–90.

——'Robert Tynte's Sons', *N&Q* 162 (1932), 62–3.

——'Captain Sir Ferdinando Freckleton', *N&Q* 162 (1932), 209–10, 231.

——'Edmund Spenser: Some Further Notes', *N&Q* 162 (1932), 380–4.

——'Review of Spenser, *Axiochus*, ed. Padelford', *RES* 12 (1936), 84–6.

——'Some Spenser Problems', *N&Q* 180 (1941), 165–7, 183–4, 220–24, 238–41.

——'Edmund Spenser's Gown and Shilling', *RES* 23 (1947), 218–25.

Hamilton, A. C., *The Structure of Allegory in The Faerie Queene* (Oxford: Clarendon Press, 1961).

Hamilton, Alastair, *The Family of Love* (Cambridge: Clark, 1981).

Hamlin, Hannibal, *Psalm Culture in Early Modern English Literature* (Cambridge: Cambridge University Press, 2004).

Hamling, Tara, *Decorating the 'Godly' Household: Religious Art in Post-Reformation Britain* (New Haven: Yale University Press, 2010).

Hammer, Paul E. J., 'The Uses of Scholarship: The Secretariat of Robert Devereux, c.1585–1601', *EHR* 109 (1994), 26–51.

——'The Earl of Essex, Fulke Greville and the Employment of Scholars', *SP* 91 (1994), 167–80.

——'Patronage at Court, Faction and the Earl of Essex', in Guy (ed.), *Reign of Elizabeth I*, pp. 65–86.

——*The Polarisation of Elizabethan Politics: The Political Career of Robert Devereux, 2nd Earl of Essex, 1585–1597* (Cambridge: Cambridge University Press, 1999).

Hankins, James, 'Humanism and the Origins of Modern Political Thought', in Kraye (ed.), *Cambridge Companion to Renaissance Humanism*, pp. 118–41.

Hankins, John Erskine, *The Life and Works of George Turberville* (Lawrence: University of Kansas Publications, 1940).

Harber, Henry A., *A Dictionary of London* (London: Jenkins, 1918).

Hard, Frederick, 'Spenser's "Clothes of Arras and of Toure"', *SP* 27 (1930), 162–85.

——'Spenser and Burghley', *SP* 28 (1931), 219–34.

——'Princelie Pallaces: Spenser and Elizabethan Architecture', *Sewanee Review* 42 (1934), 293–310.

——'Notes on John Eliot and His *Ortho-epia Gallica*', *HLQ* 1 (1938), 169–87.

——'E. K.'s Reference to Painting: Some Seventeenth Century Adaptations', *ELH* 7 (1940), 121–9.

Harder, Kelsie, 'Nashe's Rebuke of Spenser', *N&Q* 198 (1953), 145–6.

Hardiman, James, *Irish Minstrelsy, or Bardic Remains of Ireland; with English Poetical Translations*, 2 vols. (London, 1831).

Harman, Edward George, *Edmund Spenser and the Impersonations of Francis Bacon* (London: Constable, 1915).

Harris, Amy Louise, 'The Tynte Monument, Kilcredan, Co. Cork: A Reappraisal', *JCHAS* 104 (1999), 137–44.

Harris, Brice, 'The Ape in "Mother Hubberds Tale"', *HLQ* 4 (1941), 191–203.

—— 'The Butterfly in Spenser's *Muiopotmos*', *JEGP* 43 (1944), 302–16.

Harris, Mary Dormer, *Unknown Warwickshire* (London: John Lane, 1924).

Harrison, David, *The Bridges of Medieval England: Transport and Society 400–1800* (Oxford: Clarendon Press, 2004).

Hart, E. P. (ed.), *Merchant Taylors' School Register*, 2 vols. (London: Merchant Taylors' Company, 1936).

Harvey, Elizabeth D., *Ventriloquized Voices: Feminist Theory and English Renaissance Texts* (London: Routledge, 1992).

Haugaard, Wiiliam P., *Elizabeth and the English Reformation: The Struggle for a Stable Settlement of Religion* (Cambridge: Cambridge University Press, 1968).

Hawkes, A. J., 'An Edmund Spenser in Lancashire in 1566', *N&Q* 196 (1951), 336.

Hayman, Samuel, *Memorials of Youghal, Ecclesiastical and Civil* (Youghal: John Lindsay, 1879).

Haynes, Alan, *Walsingham: Elizabethan Spymaster & Statesman* (Stroud: Sutton, 2004).

Headlam Wells, Robin, *Spenser's Faerie Queene and the Cult of Elizabeth* (London: Croom Helm, 1983).

Heal, Felicity, *Reformation in Britain and Ireland* (Oxford: Oxford University Press, 2003).

—— and Clive Holmes, *The Gentry in England and Wales, 1500–1700* (Basingstoke: Macmillan, 1994).

Healy, James N., *The Castles of County Cork* (Cork: Mercier, 1988).

Healy, Margaret, *Shakespeare, Alchemy and the Creative Imagination* (Cambridge: Cambridge University Press, 2011).

—— and Thomas Healy (eds.), *Renaissance Transformations: The Making of English Writing, 1500–1650* (Edinburgh: Edinburgh University Press, 2009).

Heaton, Gabriel, *Writing and Reading Royal Entertainments: From George Gascoigne to Ben Jonson* (Oxford: Oxford University Press, 2010).

Heffner, Ray, 'Spenser's Acquisition of Kilcolman', *MLN* 46 (1931), 493–98.

—— 'Did Spenser Die in Poverty?', *MLN* 48 (1933), 221–6.

—— 'The Printing of John Hughes' Edition of Spenser, 1715', *MLN* 50 (1935), 151–3.

—— 'Edmund Spenser's Family', *HLQ* 2 (1938), 79–84.

—— 'Spenser's *View of Ireland*: Some Observations', *MLQ* 3 (1942), 507–15.

Helgerson, Richard, *The Elizabethan Prodigals* (Berkeley and Los Angeles: University of California Press, 1976).

—— *Self-Crowned Laureates: Spenser, Jonson, Milton and the Literary System* (Berkeley and Los Angeles: University of California Press, 1983).

—— *Forms of Nationhood: The Elizabethan Writing of England* (Chicago: University of Chicago Press, 1992).

Hellinga, Lotte, 'Printing', in Hellinga and Trapp (eds.), *Cambridge History of the Book in Britain*, iii. 65–108.

—— and J. B. Trapp (eds.), *The Cambridge History of the Book in Britain*, iii. *1400–1557* (Cambridge: Cambridge University Press, 1999).

Heninger, S. K., 'The Implications of Form for *The Shepheardes Calender*', *SR* 9 (1962), 309–21.

Heninger, S. K., 'The Typographical Layout of Spenser's *Shepheardes Calender*', in Höltgen et al. (eds.), *Word and Visual Imagination*, pp. 33–71.

—— *Sidney and Spenser: The Poet as Maker* (University Park: Pennsylvania State University Press, 1989).

—— 'Spenser and Sidney at Leicester House', *Sp. St.* 8 (1990), 239–49.

Henley, Pauline, *Spenser in Ireland* (Cork: Cork University Press, 1928).

—— 'Notes on Irish Words in Spenser's *Viewe of Ireland*', *JCHAS* 57 (1952), 121–4.

Hennessy, John Pope, *Sir Walter Ralegh in Ireland* (London: Kegan Paul, 1883).

Henry, D. P., *Medieval Logic and Metaphysics* (London: Hutchinson, 1972).

Herron, Thomas, 'Ralegh's Gold: Placing Spenser's Dedicatory Sonnets', in Erikson (ed.), *1590: Faerie Queene*, 133–47.

——'Early Modern Ireland and the New English Epic: Connecting Edmund Spenser and Sir George Carew', *Eolas* 1 (2006), 27–52.

—— *Spenser's Irish Work: Poetry, Plantation and Colonial Reformation* (Aldershot: Ashgate, 2007).

——and Michael Potterton (eds.), *Ireland in the Renaissance, c.1540–1660* (Dublin: Four Courts, 2007).

—— 'Reforming the Fox: Spenser's "Mother Hubberds Tale", the Beast Fables of Barnabe Rich, and Adam Loftus, Archbishop of Dublin', *SP* 105 (2008), 336–87.

Herron, Thomas, 'Irish Archaeology and the Poetry of Edmund Spenser: Content and Context', in Lyttleton and Rynne (eds.), *Plantation Ireland*, pp. 229–47.

——'Native Irish Property and Propriety in the Faunus Episode and *Colin Clouts come home again*', in Grogan (ed.), *Celebrating Mutabilitie*, pp. 136–77.

Hewlett, James H., 'Interpreting a Spenser–Harvey Letter', *PMLA* 42 (1927), 1060–5.

Hickson, Mary, 'The Seggerson or Seckerston Family', *Journal of the Historical and Archaeological, Association of Ireland*, 4th ser. 8 (1887–8), 340–1.

—— 'The Blackwater, Cappoquin, and the Barons of Burnchurch', *JRSAI* 20 (1890), 244–6.

Hieatt, A. Kent, *Short Time's Endless Monument: The Symbolism of the Numbers in Edmund Spenser's 'Epithalamion'* (New York: Columbia University Press, 1960).

Higginson, James Jackson, *Spenser's Shepheardes Calender in Relation to Contemporary Events* (New York: Columbia University Press, 1912).

Highley, Christopher, *Shakespeare, Spenser and the Crisis in Ireland* (Cambridge: Cambridge University Press, 1997).

——Spenser and the Bards', *Sp. St.* 12 (1998), 77–103.

—— *Catholics Writing the Nation in Early Modern Britain and Ireland* (Oxford: Oxford University Press, 2008).

Hile, Rachel, 'Louis du Guernier's Illustrations for the John Hughes Edition of the *Works of Mr. Edmund Spenser* (1715)', *Sp. St.* 23 (2008), 181–213.

Hill, George, *An Historical Account of the MacDonnells of Antrim: Including Notices of Some Other Septs, Irish and Scottish* (Belfast: Archer, 1873).

Hill, Tracey, *Pageantry and Power: A Cultural History of the Early Modern Lord Mayor's Show, 1585–1639* (Manchester: Manchester University Press, 2010).

H. J. S., 'Spenser and Travers', *N&Q*, 3rd ser. 4 (1863), 373.

H. M., Letter, 4 February 1818, *Gentleman's Magazine* 88 (Jan.–June 1818), 224.

Hobbs, Mary, John Fines, and Peter Atkinson (eds.), *Chichester Cathedral Library Catalogue*, 3 vols. (Chichester: Chichester Cathedral, 2001–2).

Hoffman, Nancy Jo, *Spenser's Pastorals: The Shepheardes Calender and 'Colin Clout'* (Baltimore: Johns Hopkins University Press, 1977).

Holdsworth, W. S., *A History of English Law*, 9 vols. (5th edn., London: Methuen, 1931).

Holmes, Martin, *Proud Northern Lady: Lady Anne Clifford, 1590–1676* (Chichester: Phillimore, 1975).

Holohan, Michael, '*Iamque opus exegi*: Ovid's Changes and Spenser's Brief Epic of Mutability', *ELR* 6 (1976), 244–70.

Holroyd, Michael, *Bernard Shaw*, 4 vols. (London: Chatto and Windus, 1988–92).

Höltgen, Karl Josef, 'Why Are There No Wolves in England? Philip Camerarius and a German version of Sidney's Table Talk', *Anglia* 99 (1981), 60–82.

—— Peter M. Daly, and Wolfgang Lottes (eds.), *Word and Visual Imagination: Studies in the Interaction of English Literature and the Visual Arts* (Erlangen: Universitätsbibliothek, 1988).

Honan, Park, *Christopher Marlowe: Poet and Spy* (Oxford: Oxford University Press, 2005).

Honderich, Ted (ed.), *The Oxford Companion to Philosophy* (Oxford: Oxford University Press, 1995).

Honigmann, E. A. J., *John Weever: A Biography of a Literary Associate of Shakespeare and Jonson, together with a Photographic Facsimile of Weever's Epigrammes (1599)* (Manchester: Manchester University Press, 1987).

Hoppe, Harry R., 'John Wolfe, Printer and Publisher', *The Library*, 4th ser. 14 (1933), 241–89.

Hore, Herbert Francis, 'Woods and Fastnesses, and Their Denizens, in Ancient Leinster', *Journal of the Kilkenny and South-East of Ireland Archaeological Society*, NS 1 (1856), 229–40.

—— 'Woods and Fastnesses in Ireland,' *UJA*, 1st ser. 6 (1858), 145–61.

Hore, Philip H., 'Enniscorthy Castle', *JRSAI* 35 (1905), 74–6.

Horning, Audrey, Ruari Ó Baoll, Colm Donnelly, and Paul Logue (eds.), *The Post-Medieval Archaeology of Ireland, 1550–1850* (Dublin: Wordwell, 2007).

Horsburgh, E. L. S., *Bromley, Kent from the Earliest Times to the Present Century* (London: Hodder and Stoughton, 1929).

Horwitz, Henry, *Chancery Equity Records, 1600–1800: A Guide to Documents in the Public Record Office* (London: HMSO, 1995).

Hotson, Howard, *Commonplace Learning: Ramism and Its German Ramifications, 1543–1630* (Oxford: Oxford University Press, 2007).

Hotson, Leslie, *Shakespeare's Sonnets Dated and Other Essays* (London: Hart-Davies, 1949).

Hough, Graham, *A Preface to The Faerie Queene* (London: Duckworth, 1962).

Houlbrooke, Ralph A., *The English Family, 1450–1700* (London: Longman, 1984).

—— *Death, Religion and the Family in England, 1480–1750* (Oxford: Oxford University Press, 1998).

Howard, Clare, *English Travellers of the Renaissance* (London: John Lane, 1914).

Howard, Maurice, *The Early Tudor Country House: Architecture and Politics, 1490–1550* (London: George Philip, 1987).

Howell, Roger, *Sir Philip Sidney: The Shepherd Knight* (London: Hutchinson, 1968).

Hoyle, Richard W., 'Woad in the 1580s: Alternative Agriculture in England and Ireland', in *Landscape, People and Alternative Agriculture: Essays Celebrating Joan Thirsk at Eighty* (*Agricultural History Rev.*, supp. ser. 3, 2004), pp. 56–73.

Hudson, Hoyt H., 'John Hepworth's Spenserian Satire upon Buckingham: With Some Jacobean Analogies', *Huntington Library Bulletin* 6 (1934), 39–71.

Huffman, Clifford Chambers, 'John Wolfe', in Bracken and Silver (eds.), *Book Trade*, pp. 326–9.

Hughes, Merritt Y., 'Spenser's "Blatant Beast"', *MLR* 13 (1918), 267–75.

—— 'Spenser's Palmer', *ELH* 2 (1935), 151–64.

Hughes, Philip Edgcumbe, 'Preaching, Homilies, and Prophesyings in Sixteenth Century England', *The Churchman* 89 (1975), 7–32.

Hulbert, V. B., 'Spenser's Relation to Certain Documents on Ireland', *MP* 34 (1936–7), 345–53.

Hume, Anthea, *Edmund Spenser: Protestant Poet* (Cambridge: Cambridge University Press, 1984).

Hume, Robert D., *Reconstructing Contexts: The Aims and Principles of Archaeo-Historicism* (Oxford: Oxford University Press, 1999).

Hunt, John Dixon (ed.), *The Italian Garden: Art, Design and Culture* (Cambridge: Cambridge University Press, 1996).

Hunt, Maurice, 'Hellish Work in *The Faerie Queene*', *SEL* 41 (2001), 91–108.

Hunter, G. K., *John Lyly: The Humanist as Courtier* (London: Routledge, 1962).

Hurst, Jane, 'Did Edmund Spenser Live Here?', *Alton Papers* 12 (2008), 3–12.

Hutson, Lorna, *Thomas Nashe in Context* (Oxford: Clarendon Press, 1989).

—— 'The "Double Voice" of Renaissance Equity and the Literary Voices of Women', in Clarke and Clarke (eds.), *'This Double Voice'*, pp. 142–63.

Ingegno, Alfonso, 'The New Philosophy of Nature', in Schmitt and Skinner (eds.), *Cambridge History of Renaissance Philosophy*, pp. 236–64.

Isaac, Frank, *English Printers' Types of the Sixteenth Century* (Oxford: Oxford University Press, 1936).

Izon, John, 'Bartholomew Griffin and Sir Thomas Lucy', *TLS*, 19 Apr. 1957, p. 245.

Jackson, Brian, 'The Construction of Argument: Henry Fitzsimon, John Rider and Religious Controversy in Dublin, 1599–1614', in Brady and Ohlmeyer (eds.), *British Interventions in Early Modern Ireland*, pp. 97–115.

Jackson, MacDonald P., 'Early Modern Authorship: Canons and Chronologies', in Gary Taylor and John Lavagnino (eds.), *Thomas Middleton and Early Modern Textual Culture: A Companion to the Collected Works* (Oxford: Clarendon Press, 2007), pp. 80–97.

James, Brenda, and William D. Rubinstein, *The Truth Will Out: Unmasking the Real Shakespeare* (Harlow: Longman, 2005).

Jardine, Lisa, 'The Place of Dialectic Teaching in Sixteenth-Century Cambridge', *SR* 21 (1974), 31–62.

——'Humanism and the Sixteenth Century Cambridge Arts Course', *History of Education* 4 (1975), 16–31.

——'Humanistic Logic', in Schmitt and Skinner (eds.), *Cambridge History of Renaissance Philosophy*, pp. 173–98.

——'Encountering Ireland: Gabriel Harvey, Edmund Spenser, and English colonial ventures', in Brendan Bradshaw, Andrew Hadfield, and Willy Maley (eds.), *Representing Ireland: Literature and the Origins of Conflict, 1534–1660* (Cambridge: Cambridge University Press, 1993), pp. 60–75.

——and William Sherman, 'Pragmatic Readers: Knowledge Transactions and Scholarly Services in Late Elizabethan England', in Fletcher and Roberts (eds.), *Religion, Culture, and Society*, pp. 102–24.

Javitch, Daniel, *Poetry and Courtliness in Renaissance England* (Princeton: Princeton University Press, 1978).

Jayne, Sears, 'Ficino and the Platonism of the English Renaissance', *CL* 4 (1952), 214–38.

——*Library Catalogues of the English Renaissance* (rev. edn., Godalming: St Pauls, 1983).

—— and Francis R. Johnson (eds.), *The Lumley Library: The Catalogue of 1609* (London: British Library, 1956).

Jeffries, Henry A., *The Irish Church and the Tudor Reformations* (Dublin: Four Courts, 2010).

Jenkins, Raymond, 'Spenser and the Clerkship in Munster', *PMLA* 47 (1932), 109–21.

——'Spenser's Hand', *TLS*, 7 Jan. 1932, p. 12.

——'Spenser at Smerwick', *TLS*, 11 May 1933, p. 331.

—— '*Newes out of Munster*, a Document in Spenser's Hand', *SP* 32 (1935), 125–30.

——'Spenser with Lord Grey in Ireland', *PMLA* 52 (1937), 338–53.

——'Spenser: The Uncertain Years, 1584–89', *PMLA* 53 (1938), 350–62.

—— 'Two Spenser Leases', *MLQ* 50 (1944), 143–7.

——'Spenser and the Munster Officials', *SP* 44 (1947), 157–73.

——'Rosalind in *Colin Clouts come home againe*', *MLN* 67 (1952), 1–5.

Jenkinson, Hilary, 'English Wall-Paper of the Sixteenth and Seventeenth Centuries', *AJ* 5 (1925), 237–53.

Jenkyns, Richard, *Westminster Abbey* (London: Profile, 2004).

Jensen, Ejner J., 'Verse Satire in the English Renaissance', in Ruben Quintero (ed.), *A Companion to Satire* (Oxford: Blackwell, 2007), pp. 101–17.

Jensen, Kristian, 'Universities and Colleges', in Leedham-Green and Webber (eds.), *Cambridge History of Libraries*, i. 345–62.

Jewell, Helen M., *Education in Early Modern England* (Basingstoke: Palgrave, 1998).

Johnson, Lynn, *The Shepheardes Calender: An Introduction* (University Park: Pennsylvania State University Press, 1990).

Johnson, Paula, *Form and Transformation in Music and Poetry of the English Renaissance* (New Haven: Yale University Press, 1972).

Johnson, William C., 'Spenser's *Amoretti* and the Art of the Liturgy', *SEL* 14 (1974), 47–61.

——'Gender Fashioning and the Dynamics of Mutuality in Spenser's *Amoretti*', *ES* 74 (1993), 503–19.

Jones, Ann Rosalind, and Peter Stallybrass, 'Dismantling Irena: The Sexualising of Ireland in Early Modern England', in Andrew Parker, Mary Russo, Doris Sommer, and Patricia Yaeger (eds.), *Nationalisms and Sexualities* (London: Routledge, 1992), pp. 157–71.

—— *Renaissance Clothing and the Materials of Memory* (Cambridge: Cambridge University Press, 2000).

Jones, Deborah, 'Lodowick Bryskett and His Family', in C. J. Sisson (ed.), *Thomas Lodge and Other Elizabethans* (Cambridge, MA: Harvard University Press, 1933), pp. 243–361.

Jones, Frederick M., 'The Plan of the Golden Fort at Smerwick, 1580', *Irish Sword* 2 (1954–6), 41–2.

Jones, H. S. V., *Spenser's Defense of Lord Grey* (Urbana: Illinois Studies in Language and Literature, 1919).

——*A Spenser Handbook* (New York: Crofts, 1930).

Jones, Norman, *The English Reformation: Religion and Cultural Adaptation* (Oxford: Blackwell, 2002).

Jones, Walter A., 'Doneraile and Vicinity', *JCHAS*, 2nd ser. 7 (1901), 238–42; 8 (1902), 232–48.

——and Mananaan Mac Lir, *The Synans of Doneraile* (Cork: Guy, 1909).

Jongenelen, Bas, and Ben Parsons, 'The Sonnets of *Het Bosken* by Jan van der Noot', *Sp. St.* 23 (2008), 235–55.

Jordan, W. K., *Edward VI: The Threshold of Power: The Dominance of the Duke of Northumberland* (London: Allen & Unwin, 1970).

Joyce, P. W., 'Spenser's Irish Rivers', in *The Wonders of Ireland and Other Papers on Irish Subjects* (Dublin: Longman, 1911), pp. 72–114.

Joyce, Richard, 'Irish Postal History—Part 1', *Cahir Na Mart* 26 (2008), 59–79.

Judson, Alexander C., *Spenser in Southern Ireland* (Bloomington: Principia, 1933).

——*A Biographical Sketch of John Young, Bishop of Rochester, with Emphasis on His Relations with Edmund Spenser* (Bloomington: Indiana University Studies, 1934).

——*Thomas Watts, Archdeacon of Middlesex (and Edmund Spenser)* (Bloomington: Indiana University Press, Indiana University Publications Series, Humanities Division, 1939).

——'Spenser: Two Portraits', *N&Q* 182 (1942), 64.

——'Another Spenser Portrait', *HLQ* 6 (1943), 203–4.

——'Two Spenser Leases', *MLQ* 5 (1944), 143–7.

——'The Seventeenth-Century Lives of Edmund Spenser', *HLQ* 10 (1946), 35–48.

——'The Eighteenth-Century Lives of Spenser', *HLQ* 16 (1953), 161–81.

Kane, Brendan, *The Politics and Culture of Honour in Britain and Ireland, 1541–1641* (Cambridge: Cambridge University Press, 2010).

Kaske, Carol V., 'Spenser's *Amoretti* and *Epithalamion* of 1595: Structure, Genre, and Numerology', *ELR* 8 (1978), 271–95.

——'"Religious Reuerence Doth Buriall Teene": Christian and Pagan in *The Faerie Queene*, II, 1–3', *RES* 30 (1979), 129–43.

——*Spenser and Biblical Poetics* (Ithaca, NY: Cornell University Press, 1999).

Kastner, L. E., 'Spenser's "Amoretti" and Desportes', *MLR* 4 (1908), 65–9.

Kay, Dennis, *Melodious Tears: The English Funeral Elegy from Spenser to Milton* (Oxford: Clarendon Press, 1990).

Kearney, Hugh, *Scholars and Gentlemen: Universities and Society in Pre-Industrial Britain* (Ithaca, NY: Cornell University Press, 1970).

Kearney, James, 'Reformed Ventriloquism: *The Shepheardes Calender* and the Craft of Commentary', *Sp. St.* 26 (2011), 111–51.

Kelly, Thomas, *Early Public Libraries* (London: The Library Association, 1966).

Kemp, Betty, *Sir Robert Walpole* (London: Weidenfeld and Nicolson, 1976).

Kendall, Alan, *Robert Dudley, Earl of Leicester* (London: Cassell, 1980).

Kennelly, Brendan, *Cromwell* (Newcastle: Bloodaxe Books, 1983).

Kerrigan, John, *Archipelagic English: Literature, History, and Politics, 1603–1707* (Oxford: Oxford University Press, 2008).

——(ed.), *Motives of Woe: Shakespeare & 'Female Complaint': A Critical Anthology* (Oxford: Clarendon Press, 1991).

Kilfeather, T. P., *Ireland: Graveyard of the Spanish Armada* (Dublin: Anvil, 1967).

Kilroy, Gerard, 'Sir Thomas Tresham: His Emblem', *Emblematica* 17 (2009), 149–79.

King, Andrew, *The Faerie Queene and Middle English Romance: The Matter of Just Memory* (Oxford: Clarendon Press, 2000).

King, John N., *English Reformation Literature: The Tudor Origins of the Protestant Tradition* (Princeton: Princeton University Press, 1982).

—— *Spenser's Poetry and the Reformation Tradition* (Princeton: Princeton University Press, 1990).

Kingdon, Robert M., *Myths about the St. Bartholomew's Day Massacres, 1572–1576* (Cambridge, MA: Harvard University Press, 1988).

Kingsford, Charles Lethbridge, 'Essex House, formerly Leicester House and Exeter Inn', *Archaeologica, or Miscellaneous Tracts Relating to Antiquity* 73 (1903), 1–54.

Kinney, Arthur F., *Humanist Poetics: Thought Rhetoric, and Fiction in Sixteenth-Century England* (Amherst: University of Massachusetts Press, 1986).

Kinney, Clare R., 'Marginal Presence: Lyric Resonance, Epic Absence: *Troilus and Criseyde* and/in *The Shepheardes Calender*', *Sp. St.* 18 (2004), 25–39.

Kinsella, Stuart, *Christ Church Cathedral, Dublin: A Survey of Monuments* (Dublin: Christ Church Cathedral Publications, 2009).

Kintgen, Eugene R., *Reading in Tudor England* (Pittsburgh: University of Pittsburgh Press, 1996).

Klein, Lisa M., 'Spenser's *Astrophel* and the Sidney Legend', *SJ* 12/2 (1993), 42–55.

Klingelhofer, Eric, 'Current Archaeological Excavations at Kilcolman Castle', *Bulletin of the Early Modern Ireland Committee* 1 (1994), 51–4.

—— 'Elizabethan Settlements: Mogeely Castle, Curraglass and Carrigeen, C. Cork (Part II)', *JCHAS* 105 (2000), 155–74.

—— 'Edmund Spenser at Kilcolman Castle: The Archaeological Evidence', *Post-Medieval Archaeology* 39 (2005), 133–54.

—— *Castles and Colonists: An Archaeology of Elizabethan Ireland* (Manchester: Manchester University Press, 2010).

Knalfa, Louis A., 'Mr. Secretary Donne: The Years with Sir Thomas Egerton', in Colclough (ed.), *John Donne's Professional Lives*, pp. 37–72.

Knapp, James A., '"That moste barbarous nacion": John Derricke's *Image of Ireland* and the "delight of the wel disposed reader"', *Criticism* 42 (2000), 415–50.

Knapp, Jeffrey, *An Empire Nowhere: England, America, and Literature from Utopia to The Tempest* (Berkeley and Los Angeles: University of California Press, 1992).

—— 'Spenser the Priest', *Representations* 81 (Winter 2003), 61–78.

Knappen, M. M., *Tudor Puritanism* (1939; Chicago: University of Chicago Press, 1970).

Knowles, Ronald, *Shakespeare's Arguments with History* (Basingstoke: Palgrave, 2002).

Knox, R. Buick, *James Ussher, Archbishop of Armagh* (Cardiff: University of Wales Press, 1967).

Kocken, Marcel, and Etienne Rynne, 'A Belgian Bronze Mortar from Co. Cork', *JCHAS* 67 (1962), 80–1.

Koller, Kathrine, 'Spenser and Ralegh', *ELH* 1 (1934), 37–60.

—— 'Identifications in *Colin Clouts come home againe*', *MLN* 50 (1935), 155–8.

—— 'Abraham Fraunce and Edmund Spenser', *ELH* 7 (1940), 108–20.

Kraye, Jill, 'Moral Philosophy', in Schmitt and Skinner (eds.), *Cambridge History of Renaissance Philosophy*, pp. 303–86.

—— (ed.), *The Cambridge Companion to Renaissance Humanism* (Cambridge: Cambridge University Press, 1996).

Kristellar, Paul O., *Renaissance Thought: The Classic, Scholastic, and Humanist Strains* (New York: Harper, 1961).

Kucich, Greg, *Keats, Shelley, and Romantic Spenserianism* (University Park: Pennsylvania State University Press, 1991).

Kuersteiner, Agnes D., 'E. K. is Spenser', *PMLA* 50 (1935), 140–55.

Lacey, Robert, *Robert, Earl of Essex: An Elizabethan Icarus* (London: Weidenfeld and Nicolson, 1970).

—— *Sir Walter Raleigh* (London: Sphere, 1975).

Lake, Peter, *Moderate Puritans and the Elizabethan Church* (Cambridge: Cambridge University Press, 1982).

—— *The Boxmaker's Revenge: 'Orthodoxy', 'Heterodoxy' and the Politics of the Parish in Early Stuart London* (Stanford: Stanford University Press, 2001).

——and Michael Questier, 'Agency, Appropriation and Rhetoric under the Gallows: Puritans, Romanists and the State in Early Modern England', *P&P* 153 (Nov. 1996), 64–107.

—— and Michael Questier, 'Puritans, Papists, and the "Public Sphere" in Early Modern England: The Edmund Campion Affair in Context', *Journal of Modern History* 72 (2000), 587–627.

Laslet, Peter, *The World We Have Lost* (2nd edn., London: Methuen, 1971).

Laurence, Anne, 'The Cradle to the Grave: English Observations of Irish Social Customs in the Seventeenth Century', *Seventeenth Century* 3 (1988), 63–8.

Lawrence, Jason, *'Who the Devil Taught Thee So Much Italian?' Italian Language Learning and Literary Imitation in Early Modern England* (Manchester: Manchester University Press, 2005).

Leach, Elizabeth Eva, 'The Unquiet Thoughts of Edmund Spenser's Scudamore and John Dowland's *First Book of Songs*', in M. Jennifer Bloxham, Gioia Filcamo, and Leofranc Holford-Stevens (eds.), *Uno Gentile et Subtileingenio: Studies in Music in Honour of Bonnie J. Blackburn* (Turnhout, Belgium: Brepols, 2009), pp. 513–20.

Leask, H. G., 'Mallow Castle, Co. Cork', *JCHAS* 49 (1944), 19–24.

——*Irish Castles and Castellated Houses* (Dundalk: Dundalgan Press, 1977).

Lee, Hermione, *Virginia Woolf* (New York: Knopf, 1997).

Lee, Philip G., 'The Ruined Monuments of Sir Robert Tynte and Sir Edward Harris in KIlcredan Church, Balycrenane, near Ladysbridge', *JCHAS*, 2nd ser. 31 (1926), 86–7.

Leedham-Green, Elizabeth S., *Books in Cambridge Inventories: Book Lists from Vice-Chancellor's Court Probate Inventories in the Tudor and Stuart Periods*, 2 vols. (Cambridge: Cambridge University Press, 1986).

——and Teresa Webber (eds.), *The Cambridge History of Libraries in Britain and Ireland*, i. *To 1640* (Cambridge: Cambridge University Press, 2006).

Lees-Jeffries, Hester, *England's Helicon: Fountains in Early Modern Literature and Culture* (Oxford: Oxford University Press, 2007).

Lefranc, Pierre, 'Ralegh in 1596 and 1603: Three Unprinted Letters in the Huntington Library', *HLQ* 29 (1966), 337–45.

Leimon, Mitchell, and Geoffrey Parker, 'Treason and Plot in Elizabethan Diplomacy: The "Fame of Sir Edward Stafford" Reconsidered', *EHR* 111 (1996), 1134–58.

Lennon, Colm, *Richard Stanihurst, the Dubliner, 1547–1618* (Dublin: Irish Academic Press, 1981).

—— *Sixteenth-Century Ireland: The Incomplete Conquest* (New York: St Martin's, 1995).

—— *The Lords of Dublin in the Age of Reformation* (Dublin: Irish Academic Press, 1989).

——'The Changing Face of Dublin, 1550–1750', in Peter Clark and Raymond Gillespie (eds.), *Two Capitals: London and Dublin, 1500–1840* (Oxford: Oxford University Press, 2001), pp. 39–52.

Leslie, James B., *Ossory Clergy and Parishes: Being an Account of the Clergy of the Church of Ireland in the Diocese of Ossory, from the Earliest Period* (Enniskillen: Fermanagh Times Office, 1933).

Leslie, Michael, *Spenser's 'Fierce Warres and Faithfull Loves': Martial and Chivalric Symbolism in 'The Faerie Queene'* (Cambridge: Brewer, 1983).

Lethbridge, J. B., 'Spenser's Last Days', in Lethbridge (ed.), *Spenser: New and Renewed Directions*, pp. 302–36.

——(ed.), *Edmund Spenser: New and Renewed Directions* (Madison: Fairleigh Dickinson University Press, 2006).

—— (ed.), *Shakespeare and Spenser: Attractive Opposites* (Manchester: Manchester University Press, 2008).

Levack, Brian P., *The Civil Lawyers in England, 1603–1641: A Political Study* (Oxford: Clarendon Press, 1973).

Lever, J. W., *The Elizabethan Love Sonnet* (London: Methuen, 1956).

Levy, F. J., 'Daniel Rogers as Antiquary', *Bibloteque d'Humanisme et Renaissance* 27 (1965), 444–62.

Lewis, C. S., *The Allegory of Love: A Study in Medieval Tradition* (1936; Oxford: Oxford University Press, 1958).

Lewis, C. S., *English Literature in the Sixteenth Century Excluding Drama* (Oxford: Oxford University Press, 1954).

Lewis, Jayne Elizabeth, *The Trial of Mary Queen of Scots: A Brief History with Documents* (Boston: Bedford/St Martin's, 1999).

Lewis, Samuel, *A Topographical Dictionary of Ireland*, 2 vols. (1837; Baltimore: Clearfield, 2000).

Liebler, Naomi C., 'Elizabethan Pulp Fiction: The Example of Richard Johnson', *Critical Survey* 12 (2000), 71–87.

Lievsay, John Leon, *Stefano Guazzo and the English Renaissance* (Chapel Hill: University of North Carolina Press, 1961).

Lindheim, Nancy, 'Spenser's Virgilian Pastoral: The Case for September', *Sp. St.* 11 (1990, pub. 1994), 1–16.

Lloyd Jones, G., *The Discovery of Hebrew in Tudor England: A Third Language* (Manchester: Manchester University Press, 1983).

Loach, Jennifer, *Edward VI* (New Haven: Yale University Press, 1999).

Loades, D. M., 'The Theory and Practice of Censorship in Sixteenth-Century England', *TRHS*, 5th ser. 24 (1974), 141–57.

Loeber, Rolf, and Terence Reeves-Smith, 'Lord Audley's Grandiose Building Schemes in the Ulster Plantation,' in Brian Mac Curta, SJ (ed.), *Reshaping Ireland, 1550–1700: Colonization and Its Consequences: Essays Presented to Nicholas Canny* (Dublin: Four Courts, 2011), pp. 82–100.

Loewenstein, Joseph, 'Echo's Ring: Orpheus and Spenser's Career', *ELR* 16 (1986), 287–302.

——'For a History of Literary Property: John Wolfe's Reformation', *ELR* 18 (1988), 389–412.

——'Spenser's Retrography', in Anderson et al. (eds.), *Spenser's Life*, pp. 99–130.

Lohr, Charles H., 'Metaphysics', in Schmitt and Skinner (eds.), *Cambridge History of Renaissance Philosophy*, pp. 537–638.

Long, Percy W., 'Spenser and the Bishop of Rochester', *PMLA* 31 (1916), 713–35.

——'Spenser's Birth Date', *MLN* 31 (1916), 178–80.

——'Spenseriana: The Lay of Clorinda', *MLN* 31 (1916), 79–82.

——'Spenser's Visit to the North of England', *MLN* 32 (1917), 58–9.

Longfield, Ada Kathleen, *Anglo-Irish Trade in the Sixteenth-Century* (London: Routledge, 1929).

Lotspeich, Henry G., 'Spenser's *Virgils Gnat* and its Latin Original', *ELH* 2 (1935), 235–41.

Lovell, Mary S., *Bess of Hardwick: First Lady of Chatsworth* (London: Abacus, 2006).

Luborsky, Ruth Samson, 'The Alusive Presentation of *The Shepheardes Calender*', *Sp. St.* 1 (1980), 29–67.

——'The Illustrations to *The Shepheardes Calender*', *Sp. St.* 2 (1981), 3–53.

Lucas, Scott, 'Diggon Davie and Davy Dicar: Edmund Spenser, Thomas Churchyard, and the Poetics of Public Protest', *Sp. St.* 16 (2001), 151–65.

Lupton, Julia Reinhard, 'Mapping Mutability: or, Spenser's Irish Plot', in Bradshaw et al. (eds.), *Representing Ireland*, pp. 93–115.

Luu, Lien Bich, *Immigrants and the Industries of London, 1500–1700* (Aldershot: Ashgate, 2005).

Lydon, James, 'The Expansion and Consolidation of the Colony, 1215–54', in Moody et al. (eds.), *New History of Ireland*, ii. 156–78.

Lysaght, Sean, *Spenser* (Westport: Stonechat Editions, 2011).

Lysaght, Sidney, 'Kilcolman Castle', *The Antiquary* 5 (1882), 153–6.

Lyttleton, James, 'Gaelic Classicism in the Irish Midland Plantations: An Archaeological Reflection', in Herron and Potterton (eds.), *Ireland in the Renaissance*, pp. 231–54.

—— and Colin Rynne (eds.), *Plantation Ireland: Settlement and Material Culture, c.1550–c.1700* (Dublin: Four Courts, 2009).

McCabe, Richard A., 'Elizabethan Satire and the Bishops' Ban of 1599', *YES* 11 (1981), 188–93.

——'The Masks of Duessa: Spenser, Mary Queen of Scots, and James VI', *ELR* 17 (1987), 224–42.

——'The Fate of Irena: Spenser and Political Violence', in Coughlan (ed.), *Spenser and Ireland*, pp. 109–25.

——'Edmund Spenser, Poet of Exile', *PBA* 80 (1993), 73–103.

—— *The Pillars of Eternity: Time and Providence in The Faerie Queene* (Dublin: Irish Academic Press, 1989).

—— '"Little booke: thy selfe present": The Politics of Presentation in *The Shepheardes Calender*', in Howard Erskine-Hill and Richard A. McCabe (eds.), *Presenting Poetry: Composition, Publication, Reception: Essays in Honour of Ian Jack* (Cambridge: Cambridge University Press, 1995), pp. 15–40.

—— '"Right Puisante and Terrible Priests": The Role of the Anglican Church in Elizabethan State Censorship', in Hadfield (ed.), *Literature and Censorship*, pp. 75–94.

—— *Spenser's Monstrous Regiment: Elizabethan Ireland and the Poetics of Difference* (Oxford: Oxford University Press, 2002).

—— '"Thine owne nations frend / And Patrone": The Rhetoric of Petition in Harvey and Spenser', *Sp. St.* 22 (2007), 47–72.

—— 'Rhyme and Reason: Poetics, Patronage, and Secrecy in Elizabethan and Jacobean Ireland', in *Literary Milieux: Essays in Text and Context Presented to Howard Erskine-Hill* (Newark: University of Delaware Press, 2008).

—— 'Edmund Spenser', in Claude Rawson (ed.), *The Cambridge Companion to English Poets* (Cambridge: Cambridge University Press, 2011), pp. 53–71.

MacCaffrey, Isabel G., *Spenser's Allegory: The Anatomy of Imagination* (Princeton: Princeton University Press, 1976).

McCaffrey, Wallace T., *Elizabeth I* (London: Arnold, 1993).

McCanles, Michael, '*The Shepheardes Calender* as Document and Monument', *SEL* 22 (1982), 5–19.

McCarthy, Denis, *Dublin Castle* (2nd edn., Dublin: Stationery Office, 2004).

McCarthy, Mark, 'Geographical Change in an Early Modern Town: Urban Growth and Cultural Politics in Cork, 1600–41', *JCHAS* 106 (2001), 53–78.

MacCarthy-Morrogh, Michael, *The Munster Plantation: English Migration to Southern Ireland, 1583–1641* (Oxford: Clarendon Press, 1986).

—— 'The English Presence in Early Seventeenth-Century Munster', in Brady and Gillespie (eds.), *Natives and Newcomers*, pp. 171–90.

McCormack, Anthony M., 'The Social and Economic Consequences of the Desmond Rebellion of 1579–83', *IHS* 133 (2004), 1–15.

—— *The Earldom of Desmond, 1463–1583: The Decline and Crisis of a Feudal Lordship* (Dublin: Four Courts, 2005).

McCracken, Eileen, 'Charcoal Burning Ironworks in Seventeenth and Eighteenth-Century Ireland', *UJA* 20 (1957), 123–38.

—— 'Supplementary List of Irish Charcoal Burning Iron Works', *UJA* 28 (1965), 132–6.

—— *The Irish Woods Since Tudor Times: Distribution and Exploitation* (Newton Abbot: David and Charles, 1971).

McCrea, Scott, *The Case for Shakespeare: The End of the Authorship Question* (Westport, CT: Praeger, 2005).

MacCulloch, Diarmaid, *Thomas Cranmer: A Life* (New Haven: Yale University Press, 1996).

—— *Reformation: Europe's House Divided, 1490–1700* (Harmondsworth: Penguin, 2003).

McCullough, Peter E., *Sermons at Court: Politics and Religion in Elizabethan and Jacobean Preaching* (Cambridge: Cambridge University Press, 1998).

Mac Curta, Brian (ed.), *Ulster 1641: Aspects of the Rising* (Belfast: Institute of Irish Studies, 1993).

McCusker, Honor, *John Bale: Dramatist and Antiquary* (Bryn Mawr: Bryn Mawr University Press, 1942).

McDiarmid, John F., 'Common Consent, Latinitas, and the "Monarchical Republic" in Mid-Tudor Humanism', in John F. McDiarmid (ed.), *The Monarchical Republic of Early Modern England: Essays in Response to Patrick Collinson* (Aldershot: Ashgate, 2007), pp. 55–74.

MacDonald, Robert H. (ed.), *The Library of Drummond of Hawthornden* (Edinburgh: Edinburgh University Press, 1971).

McEachern, Claire, *The Poetics of English Nationhood, 1590–1612* (Cambridge: Cambridge University Press, 1996).

Macfarlane, Alan, *The Family Life of Ralph Josselin, a Seventeenth-Century Clergyman: An Essay in Historical Anthropology* (London: Cambridge University Press, 1970).

Macfie, Alexander Lyon (ed.), *The Philosophy of History: Talks Given at the Institute of Historical Research, London, 2000–2006* (Basingstoke: Palgrave, 2006).

McGinn, Donald J., *Thomas Nashe* (Boston: Twayne, 1981).

McGurk, John, *The Elizabethan Conquest of Ireland: The Burdens of the 1590s Crisis* (Manchester: Manchester University Press, 1997).

Mack, Peter, *Elizabethan Rhetoric: Theory and Practice* (Cambridge: Cambridge University Press, 2002).

—— *A History of Renaissance Rhetoric, 1380–1620* (Oxford: Oxford University Press, 2011).

MacKenna, John, *Castledermot and Kilkea: A Social History, with Notes on Ballytore, Graney, Moone and Mullaghmast* (Athy: Winter Wood Books, 1982).

McKitterick, David J. (ed.), *The Library of Sir Thomas Knyvet of Ashwellthorpe, c.1539–1618* (Cambridge: Cambridge University Library, 1978).

—— 'Review of Stern, *Harvey*', in *The Library*, 6th ser. 3 (1981), 348–53.

McLane, Paul E., 'Piers of Spenser's *Shepheardes Calender*, Dr. John Piers of Salisbury', *MLQ* 9 (1948), 3–9.

—— 'James VI in the "Shepheardes Calender"', *HLQ* 16 (1953), 273–85.

—— 'Was Spenser in Ireland in Early November 1579?', *N&Q* 204 (1959), 99–101.

—— *Spenser's Shepheardes Calender: A Study in Elizabethan Allegory* (Notre Dame: University of Notre Dame Press, 1961).

—— 'Spenser's Chloris: The Countess of Derby', *HLQ* 24 (1961), 145–50.

McLaren, Anne, 'Reading Sir Thomas Smith's *De Republica Anglorum* as Protestant Apologetic', *HJ* 42 (1999), 911–39.

—— *Political Culture in the Reign of Elizabeth I: Queen and Commonwealth, 1558–1585* (Cambridge: Cambridge University Press, 1999).

Maclean, Ian, *The Renaissance Notion of Woman: A Study in the Fortunes of Scholasticism and Medical Science in European Intellectual Life* (Cambridge: Cambridge University Press, 1980).

McLeod, Wilson, *Divided Gaels: Gaelic Cultural Identities in Scotland and Ireland, c.1200–c.1650* (Oxford: Oxford University Press, 2004).

Mac Lir, Manananan, 'Spenser as High Sheriff of Cork County', *JCHAS* 7 (1901), 249–50.

McManaway, James, 'Elizabeth, Essex, and James', in Herbert Davis and Helen Gardner (eds.), *Elizabethan and Jacobean Studies: Presented to Frank Percy Wilson in Honour of His Seventieth Birthday* (Oxford: Clarendon Press, 1959), pp. 219–30.

McNeir, Waldo F., 'Ariosto's Sospetto, Gascoigne's Suspicion, and Spenser's Malbecco', in Horst Oppel (ed.), *Festschrift Für Walther Fischer* (Heidelberg: Carl Winter, 1959), pp. 34–48.

—— 'The Sacrifice of Serena: *The Faerie Queene*, VI, viii. 31–51', in Bernhard Fabian and Ulrich Suerbaum (eds.), *Festschrift für Edgar Mertner* (Munich: Wilhelm Fink, 1968), pp. 117–56.

McRae, Andrew, *God Speed the Plough: The Representation of Agrarian England, 1500–1660* (Cambridge: Cambridge University Press, 1996).

—— *Literature and Domestic Travel in Early Modern England* (Cambridge: Cambridge University Press, 2009).

Maddalena, Aldo De, 'Rural Europe, 1500–1750', in Carlo M. Cipolla (ed.), *The Fontana Economic History of Europe: The Sixteenth and Seventeenth Centuries* (London: Fontana, 1974), pp. 273–353.

Magill, A. J., 'Spenser's Guyon and the Mediocrity of the Elizabethan Settlement', *SP* 67 (1970), 167–77.

Maginn, Christopher, 'The Baltinglass Rebellion, 1580: English Dissent or a Gaelic Uprising?', *HJ* 47 (2004), 205–32.

—— *'Civilizing' Gaelic Leinster: The Extension of Tudor Rule in the O'Byrne and O'Toole Lordships* (Dublin: Four Courts, 2005).

Magnusson, Lynne, *Shakespeare and Social Dialogue: Dramatic Language and Elizabethan Letters* (Cambridge: Cambridge University Press, 1999),.

Maley, Willy, 'How Milton and Some Contemporaries Read Spenser's *View*', in Bradshaw et al. (eds.), *Representing Ireland*, pp. 191–208.

—— *Salvaging Spenser: Colonialism, Culture and Identity* (Basingstoke: Macmillan, 1997).

—— '"This ripping of auncestours": The Ethnographic Present in Spenser's *A View of the State of Ireland*', in Philippa Berry and Margaret Tudeau-Clayton (eds.), *Textures of Renaissance Knowledge* (Manchester: Manchester University Press, 2003), pp. 117–34.

Mallette, Richard, *Spenser and the Discourses of Reformation England* (Lincoln: University of Nebraska Press, 1997).

Maltby, William S., *The Black Legend in England: The Development of Anti-Spanish Sentiment, 1558–1660* (Durham, NC: University of North Carolina Press, 1971).

Von Maltzahn, Nicholas von, 'John Milton: The Later Life (1641–1674)', in Nicholas McDowell and Nigel Smith (eds.), *The Oxford Handbook of Milton* (Oxford: Oxford University Press, 2009), pp. 26–47.

Mancall, Peter C., *Hakluyt's Promises: An Elizabethan's Obsession for an English America* (New Haven: Yale University Press, 2007).

Manley, Lawrence, 'Spenser and the City: The Minor Poems', *MLQ* 43 (1982), 203–27.

—— *Literature and Culture in Early Modern London* (Cambridge: Cambridge University Press, 1995).

Mann, Alastair F., *The Scottish Book Trade, 1500–1720: Print, Commerce and Print Control in Early Modern Scotland* (East Linton: Tuckwell, 2000).

Mann, Jill, *Chaucer and Medieval Estates Satire: The Literature of Social Classes and the 'General Prologue' to the 'Canterbury Tales'* (London: Cambridge University Press, 1973).

Manning, R. J., '"Deuicefull Sights": Spenser's Emblematic Practice in *The Faerie Queene*, V, 1–3', *Sp. St.* 5 (1984), 65–89.

Manning, Roger B., *An Apprenticeship in Arms: The Origins of the British Army, 1585–1702* (Oxford: Oxford University Press, 2006).

Mansfield, Bruce, *Phoenix of His Age: Interpretations of Erasmus, c.1550–1750* (Toronto: University of Toronto Press, 1979).

Marcus, Laura, *Auto/biographical Discourses: Theory, Criticism, Practice* (Manchester: Manchester University Press, 1994).

Marotti, Arthur F., '"Love Is Not Love": Elizabethan Sonnet Sequences and the Social Order', *ELH* 49 (1982), 396–428.

—— *Manuscript, Print and the English Renaissance Lyric* (Ithaca, NY: Cornell University Press, 1985).

Marsh, Christopher W., *The Family of Love in English Society, 1550–1630* (Cambridge: Cambridge University Press, 1994).

Marshall, H. E., *English Literature for Boys and Girls* (London: T. C. and E. C. Jack, 1910).

Marshall, Peter, *Beliefs and the Dead in Reformation England* (Oxford: Oxford University Press, 2002).

Martin, Colin, and Geoffrey Parker, *The Spanish Armada* (London: Guild, 1988).

Martin, John Jeffries, *Myths of Renaissance Individualism* (Basingstoke: Palgrave, 2004).

Martin, W. C., 'The Date and Purpose of Spenser's *View*', *PMLA* 47 (1932), 137–43.

Mascuch, Michael, *Origins of the Individualist Self: Autobiography and Self-Identity in England, 1591–1791* (Cambridge: Polity, 1997).

Maslen, Robert W., 'The Afterlife of Andrew Borde', *SP* 100 (2003), 463–92.

—— 'Magical Journeys in Sixteenth-Century Prose', *YES* (*Travel and Prose Fiction in Early Modern England*, ed. Nandini Das) 41/1 (2011), 35–50.

Mason, Roger A., 'George Buchanan, James VI and the Presbyterians', in Roger A. Mason (ed.), *Scots and Britons: Scottish Political Thought and the Union of 1603* (Cambridge: Cambridge University Press, 1994), pp. 112–37.

Matar, Nabil, *Islam in Britain, 1558–1685* (Cambridge: Cambridge University Press, 1998).

Maxwell-Stuart, P. G., 'Astrology, Magic and Witchcraft', in Andrew Hadfield (ed.), *The Oxford Handbook to English Prose, 1500–1640* (Oxford: Oxford University Press, forthcoming).

May, Steven W., *Sir Walter Ralegh* (Boston: Twayne, 1989).

—— *The Elizabethan Courtier Poets: The Poems and Their Contexts* (Columbia: University of Missouri Press, 1999).

—— 'Henry Gurney, A Norfolk Farmer, Reads Spenser and Others', *Sp. St.* 20 (2005), 183–223.

May, Steven W., 'Marlowe, Spenser, Sidney and—Abraham Fraunce', *RES* (forthcoming).

Maynadier, Howard, 'The Areopagus of Sidney and Spenser', *MLR* 4 (1909), 289–301.

Mears, Natalie, '*Regnum Cecilianum*? A Cecilian Perspective of the Court', in Guy (ed.), *Reign of Elizabeth I*, pp. 46–64.

——'Counsel, Public Debate, and Queenship: John Stubbs's *The Discoverie of a Gaping Gulf*, 1579', *HJ* 44 (2001), 629–50.

——*Queenship and Political Discourse in the Elizabethan Realms* (Cambridge: Cambridge University Press, 2005).

Meerhoff, Kees, 'Logic and Eloquence: A Ramusian Revolution?', *Argumentation* 5 (1991), 357–74.

Melnikoff, Kirk, and Edward Gieskes (eds.), *Writing Robert Greene: Essays on England's First Notorious Professional Writer* (Aldershot: Ashgate, 2008).

Mendelson, Sara, and Patricia Crawford, *Women in Early Modern England* (Oxford: Oxford University Press, 1998).

Merritt, Julia F., *The Social World of Early Modern Westminster: Abbey, Court and Community, 1525–1640* (Manchester: Manchester University Press, 2005).

Meyer, Michael, *Ibsen: A Biography* (London: Hart-Davies, 1967–71).

Meyer, Russell J., '"Fixt in heauens hight": Spenser, Astronomy, and the Date of the *Cantos of Mutabilitie*', *Sp. St.* 4 (1983), 115–29.

Meyer, Sam, *An Interpretation of Edmund Spenser's Colin Clout* (Cork: Cork University Press, 1969).

Mikics, David, *The Limits of Moralizing: Pathos and Subjectivity in Spenser and Milton* (Lewisburg: Bucknell University Press, 1994).

Miller, David Lee, 'The Earl of Cork's Lute', in Anderson et al. (eds.), *Spenser's Life*, pp. 146–77.

Miller, Jacqueline T., '"Love Doth Hold My Hand": Writing and Wooing in the Sonnets of Sidney and Spenser', *ELH* 46 (1979), 541–58.

Millican, Charles Bowie, 'A Friend of Spenser', *TLS*, 7 Aug. 1937, p. 576.

——'Mulcaster and Spenser', *ELH* 6 (1939), 214–16.

——'The Supplicats for Spenser's Degrees', *HLQ* 2 (1939), 467–70.

——'The Northern Dialect of *The Shepheardes Calender*', *ELH* 6 (1939), 211–13.

Minta, Stephen, *Petrarch and Petrarchanism: The English and French Traditions* (Manchester: Manchester University Press, 1980).

Miola, Robert S., 'Spenser's Anacreontics: A Mythological Metaphor', *SP* 77 (1980), 50–66.

Miskimin, Alice S., *The Renaissance Chaucer* (New Haven: Yale University Press, 1975).

Monk, Ray, 'Getting Inside Heisenberg's Head', in Macfie (ed.), *Philosophy of History*, pp. 237–52.

Montrose, Louis Adrian, '"The Perfecte Paterne of a Poete": The Poetics of Courtship in *The Shepheardes Calender*', *TSLL: Texas Studies in Literature and Language* 21 (1979), 34–67.

——'The Elizabethan Subject and the Spenserian Text', in David Quint and Patricia Parker (eds.), *Literary Theory/Renaissance Texts* (Baltimore: Johns Hopkins University Press, 1986), pp. 303–40.

——'Spenser and the Elizabethan Political Imaginary', *ELH* 69 (2002), 907–46.

Moody, T. W., F. X. Martin, and F. J. Byrne (eds.), *A New History of Ireland*, viii. *A Chronology of Irish History to 1976* (Oxford: Clarendon Press, 1982).

Mooney, Fr. Candice, *The Friars of Broad Lane: The Story of a Franciscan Friary in Cork, 1229–1977* (Cork: Tower Books, 1977).

Moore Smith, G. C., 'Spenser and Mulcaster', *MLR* 8 (1913), 368.

——'Printed Books with Gabriel Harvey's Autograph or MS Notes', *MLR* 28 (1933), 78–81; 29 (1934), 68–70; 30 (1935), 209.

Morash, Christopher, *A History of Irish Theatre, 1601–2000* (Cambridge: Cambridge University Press, 2002).

Morey, Adrian, *The Catholic Subjects of Elizabeth I* (London: Allen and Unwin, 1978).

Morgan, Hiram, 'The Colonial Venture of Sir Thomas Smith in Ulster, 1571–5', *HJ* 28 (1985), 261–78.

——'Mid Atlantic Blues', *Irish Review* 11 (Winter 1991), 50–5.

——— *Tyrone's Rebellion: The Outbreak of the Nine Years War in Tudor Ireland* (Woodbridge: Boydell, 1993).

——— (ed.), *Political Ideology in Ireland, 1541–1641* (Dublin: Four Courts, 1999).

——— (ed.), *The Battle of Kinsale* (Bray: Wordwell, 2004).

——— '"Never Any Realm Worse Governed": Queen Elizabeth and Ireland', *TRHS*, 6th ser. 14 (2004), 295–308.

Morgan, Victor, with Christopher Brooke, *A History of the University of Cambridge*, ii. *1546–1750* (Cambridge: Cambridge University Press, 2004).

Morini, Massimiliano, *Tudor Translation in Theory and Practice* (Aldershot: Ashgate, 2006).

Moss, Jean Dietz, 'The Family of Love and English Critics', *SCJ* 6 (1975), 35–52.

——— 'Variations on a Theme: The Family of Love in Renaissance England', *RQ* 31 (1978), 186–95.

Mottram, Stewart, 'Spenser's Dutch Uncles: The Family of Love and the four translations of *A Theatre for Worldlings*', in José María Pérez Fernández and Edward Wilson-Lee (eds.), *Translation and the Book Trade in Early Modern Europe* (forthcoming).

Mounts, Charles E., 'Spenser and the Countess of Leicester', in Mueller and Allen (eds.), *That Soueraine Light*, pp. 111–22.

Mousley, Andrew, 'Renaissance Selves and Life Writing: *The Autobiography of Thomas Whythorne*', *Forum for Modern Language Studies* 26 (1990), 222–30.

Mozley, J. F., *John Foxe and His Book* (New York: Macmillan,, 1940).

Mueller, William R., *Spenser's Critics: Changing Currents in Literary Taste* (Syracuse: Syracuse University Press, 1959).

——— and Don Cameron Allen (eds.), *That Soueraine Light: Essays in Honor of Edmund Spenser, 1552–1952* (Baltimore: Johns Hopkins University Press, 1952).

Muir, Tom, 'Without Remainder: Ruins and Tombs in Shakespeare's *Sonnets*', *Textual Practice* 24 (2010), 21–49.

——— 'Specters of Spenser: Translating the *Antiquitez*', *Sp. St.* 25 (2010), 327–61.

Muldoon, Paul, *To Ireland, I* (Oxford: Oxford University Press, 2000).

Muldrew, Craig, 'The Culture of Reconciliation: Community and the Settlement of Economic Disputes in Early Modern England', *HJ* 39/4 (1996), 915–42.

——— *The Economy of Obligation: The Culture of Credit and Social Relations in Early Modern England* (Basingstoke: Palgrave, 1998).

Mullan, John, *Anonymity: A Secret History of English Literature* (London: Faber, 2007).

Munslow, Alun, 'Biography and History: Criticism, Theory, Practice', in Macfie (ed.), *Philosophy of History*, pp. 226–36.

Murphy, Eileen M., 'An Overview of Livestock, Husbandry, and Economic Practices', in Horning et al. (eds.), *Post-Medieval Archaeology of Ireland*, pp. 371–91.

Murray, James, *Enforcing the English Reformation in Ireland: Clerical Resistance and Political Conflict in the Diocese of Dublin, 1534–1590* (Cambridge: Cambridge University Press, 2009).

Myers, Benjamin P., 'The Green and Golden World: Spenser's Rewriting of the Munster Plantation', *ELH* 76 (2009), 473–90.

Myers, James P., Jr, '"Murdering heart . . . Murdering hand": Captain Thomas Lee of Ireland, Elizabethan Assassin', *SCJ* 22 (1991), 47–60.

Najemy, John A., *A History of Florence, 1200–1575* (Oxford: Blackwell, 2006).

Neale, J. E., *Queen Elizabeth* (London: Cape, 1934).

——— *The Elizabethan Political Scene* (London: J. Cumberlege, 1949).

Nelson, Alan H., *Monstrous Adversity: The Life of Edward de Vere, 17th Earl of Oxford* (Liverpool: Liverpool University Press, 2003).

Nelson, William, *The Poetry of Edmund Spenser* (New York: Columbia University Press, 1963).

Netzloff, Mark, 'Forgetting the Ulster Plantation: John Speed's *The Theatre of Great Britain* (1611) and the Colonial Archive', *JMEMS* 31 (2001), 313–48.

Neuse, Richard, 'Book VI as Conclusion to *The Faerie Queene*', *ELH* 35 (1968), 329–53.

Newdigate, B. H., 'Some Spenser Problems: Sylvanus Spenser', *N&Q* 180 (1941), 120.

Newell, Fiona, 'Wet Nursing and Child Care in Aldenham, Hertfordshire, 1595–1726: Some Evidence on the Circumstances and Effects of Seventeenth-Century Child Rearing Practices', in Fildes (ed.), *Women as Mothers*, pp. 122–38.

Newstock, Scott L., *Quoting Death in Early Modern England: The Poetics of Epitaphs Beyond the Tomb* (Basingstoke: Palgrave, 2009).

Nicholl, Charles, *A Cup of News: The Life of Thomas Nashe* (London: Routledge, 1984).

—— *The Reckoning: The Murder of Christopher Marlowe* (London: Cape, 1992).

——, *Shakespeare the Lodger: His Life on Silver Street* (London: Penguin, 2007).

Nicholls, K. W., *Gaelic and Gaelicized Ireland in the Middle Ages* (2nd edn., Dublin: Lilliput, 2003).

Nicholls, Mark, 'Two Winchester Trials: The Prosecution of Henry, Lord Cobham, and Thomas, Lord Grey of Wilson, 1603', *HR* 68 (1995), 26–48.

——and Penry Williams, *Sir Walter Raleigh: In Life and Legend* (London: Continuum, 2011).

Nichols, John, *The Progresses and Public Processions of Queen Elizabeth*, 3 vols. (London, 1823).

Nohrnberg, James, *The Analogy of The Faerie Queene* (Princeton: Princeton University Press, 1977).

Nolan, John S., *Sir John Norreys and the Elizabethan Military World* (Exeter: University of Exeter Press, 1997).

Norbrook, David, *Poetry and Politics in the English Renaissance* (rev. edn., Oxford: Oxford University Press, 2002).

Nørgaard, Holger, 'Translations of the Classics into English Before 1600', *RES* 9 (1958), 164–72.

Norman, A. V. B., and Don Pottinger, *English Weapons and Warfare, 449–1660* (1966; London: Arms and Armour Press, 1979).

North, Marcey, 'Ignoto in the Age of Print: The Manipulation of Anonymity in Early Modern England', *SP* 91 (1994), 390–416.

Northrop, Douglas A., 'Spenser's Defense of Elizabeth', *University of Tononto Quarterly* 38 (1968–9), 27–94.

Norton, Dan S., 'Queen Elizabeth's "Brydale Day"', *MLQ* 5 (1944), 149–54.

Norton, Glyn P. (ed.), *The Cambridge History of Literary Criticism*, iii. *The Renaissance* (Cambridge: Cambridge University Press, 1999).

Oakeshott, Walter, *The Queen and the Poet* (London: Faber, 1960).

—— 'Carew Ralegh's Copy of Spenser', *The Library* 26 (1971), 1–21.

O'Brien, Niall, 'Bristol Apprentices from Youghal, 1532–1565', *JCHAS* 115 (2010), 109–14.

O'Callaghan, Michelle, *The 'Shepheardes Nation': Jacobean Spenserians and Early Stuart Political Culture, 1612–1625* (Oxford: Clarendon Press, 2000).

O'Connell, Basil, 'The Nagles of Ballygriffin and Nano Nagle', *Irish Genealogist* 3 (1957), 67–73.

O'Connell, Michael, *Mirror and Veil: The Historical Dimension of Spenser's Faerie Queene* (Chapel Hill: University of North Carolina Press, 1977).

O'Donoghue, Freeman, *Catalogue of Engraved British Portraits Preserved in the Department of Prints and Drawings in the British Museum*, 6 vols. (London: British Museum, 1908–25).

O'Dowd, Mary, 'Gaelic Economy and Society', in Brady and Gillespie (eds.), *Natives and Newcomers*, pp. 120–47.

—— 'Women and the Irish Chancery Court in the Late Sixteenth and Early Seventeenth Centuries', *IHS* 31 (1999), 470–87.

O'Flanagan, J. R., *The Blackwater in Munster* (London, 1844).

O'Hara, Diana, *Courtship and Constraint: Rethinking the Making of Marriage in Tudor England* (Manchester: Manchester University Press, 2000).

Ohlmeyer, Jane H., '"Civilizinge of those Rude Partes": Colonization within Britian and Ireland, 1580s–1640s', in Canny (ed.), *Origins of Empire*, pp. 124–47.

O'Keefe, Tadgh, 'Plantation-era Great Houses in Munster: A Note on Sir Walter Ralegh's House and Its Context', in Herron and Potterton (eds.), *Ireland in the Renaissance*, pp. 274–88.

——and Sinéad Quirke, 'A House at the Birth of Modernity: Ightermurragh Castle, Co. Cork', in Lyttleton and Rynne (eds.), *Plantation Ireland*, pp. 86–112.

Ó Mórdha, Pilip, 'Early History of Modern Clones', *Clogher Record* 16 (1997), 95–100.

Ong, Walter J., *Ramus, Method and the Decay of Dialogue* (Cambridge, MA: Harvard University Press, 1958).

——'Latin Language Study as a Renaissance Puberty Rite', *SP* 56 (1959), 103–24.

O'Rahilly, Alfred, 'The Massacre at Smerwick (1580)', *JCHAS* 42 (1937), 1–15, 65–83.

Oram, William, '*Daphnaïda* and Spenser's Later Poetry', *Sp. St.* 4 (1983), 33–47.

——'What Did Spenser Really Think of Sir Walter Ralegh When He Published the First Instalment of *The Faerie Queene*', *Sp. St.* 15 (2001), 165–74.

——'Spenser's Audiences, 1589–91', *SP* 100 (2003), 514–33.

——'Introduction: Spenser's Paratexts', in Erikson (ed.), *1590: Faerie Queene*, pp. vii–xviii.

Ord, Melanie, *Travel and Experience in Early Modern English Literature* (Basingstoke: Palgrave, 2007).

Orgel, Stephen, *Imagining Shakespeare* (Basingstoke: Palgrave, 2003).

Orlin, Lena Cowen, *Locating Privacy in Tudor London* (Oxford: Oxford University Press, 2007).

Orpen, Goddard H., 'Ralegh's House, Youghal', *JRSAI*, 5th ser. 33 (1903), 310–12.

Oruch, Jack B., 'Spenser, Camden, and the Poetic Marriage of Rivers', *SP* 64 (1967), 606–24.

Orwen, William R., 'Spenser's 'Stemmata Dudleiana', *N&Q* 190 (1946), 9–11.

Osgood, Charles G., 'The "Doleful Lay of Clorinda"', *MLN* 35 (1920), 90–6.

Ó Siochrú, Micheál, *God's Executioner: Oliver Cromwell and the Conquest of Ireland* (London: Faber, 2008).

O'Sullivan, William, 'John Mullan's Manuscripts', in Vincent Kinane and Anne Walsh (eds.), *Essays on the History of Trinity College Library* (Dublin: Four Courts, 2000), pp. 104–15.

Oursel, Hervé, and Thierry Crépin-Leblond, *Musée National de la Renaissance: Château D'Écouen: Guide* (Paris: Éditions de la Réunion des musées nationaux, 1994).

Owen, W. J. B., 'The Structure of *The Faerie Queene*', *PMLA* 68 (1953), 1079–1100.

Owens, Judith, *Enabling Engagements: Edmund Spenser and the Poetics of Patronage* (Montreal: McGill-Queen's University Press, 2002).

——'Commerce and Cadiz in Spenser's *Prothalamion*', *SEL* 47 (2007), 79–106.

Owens, Rebekah, 'The Career of Thomas Kyd Relating to His Attendance at Merchant Taylors' School', *N&Q* 254 (2009), 35–6.

Padelford, Frederick M., 'Spenser and the Puritan Propaganda', *MP* 11 (1913), 85–106.

——'The Cantos of Mutabilitie: Further Considerations Bearing on the Date', *PMLA* 45 (1930), 704–11.

——'Spenser's *Fowre Hymnes*: A Resurvey', *SP* 29 (1932), 207–32.

——'Reply to Bernard Freyd', *PMLA* 50 (1935), 908–13.

Palmer, Patricia, *Language and Conquest in Early Modern Ireland: English Renaissance Literature and Elizabethan Imperial Expansion* (Cambridge: Cambridge University Press, 2001).

——'Interpreters and the Politics of Translation and Traduction in Sixteenth-Century Ireland', *IHS* 131 (2003), 257–77.

——'Missing Bodies, Absent Minds: Spenser, Shakespeare and a Crisis in Criticism', *ELR* 36 (2006), 376–95.

Palmer, William, *The Problem of Ireland in Tudor Foreign Policy, 1485–1603* (Woodbridge: Boydell, 1994).

Parker, Patricia, *Inescapable Romance: Studies in the Poetics of a Mode* (Princeton: Princeton University Press, 1979).

Parker, Tom W. N., *Proportional Form in the Sonnets of the Sidney Circle: Loving in Truth* (Oxford: Clarendon Press, 1998).

Parry, Graham, 'Patronage and the Printing of Learned Works for the Author', in Barnard and McKenzie (eds.), *Cambridge History of the Book in Britain*, iv. 174–88.

Parsons, Ben, and Bas Jongnelen, 'Jan van der Noot: A Mistaken Attribution in the Short-Title Catalogue?', *N&Q* 250 (Dec. 2006), 427.

Partridge, A. C., *The Language of Renaissance Poetry* (London: Andre Deutsch, 1971).

Pask, Kevin, *The Emergence of the English Author: Scripting the Life of the Poet in Early Modern England* (Cambridge: Cambridge University Press, 1996).

Patterson, Annabel, 'The Egalitarian Giant: Representations of Justice in History/Literature', *Journal of British Studies* 31 (1992), 97–132.

—— *Reading Holinshed's Chronicles* (Chicago: University of Chicago Press, 1994).

Pattison, Bruce, *Music and Poetry of the English Renaissance* (2nd edn., London: Methuen, 1970).

Pawlisch, Hans, *Sir John Davies and the Conquest of Ireland: A Study in Legal Imperialism* (Cambridge: Cambridge University Press, 1985).

Pearce, Roy Harvey, 'Primitivistic Ideas in *The Faerie Queene*', *JEGP* 44 (1945), 138–51.

Pearson, A. F. Scott, *Thomas Cartwright and Elizabethan Puritanism, 1535–1603* (Cambridge: Cambridge University Press, 1925).

Pearson, David, 'The Libraries of English Bishops, 1600–40', *The Library*, 6th ser. 14 (1992), 221–57.

Pearson, Jacqueline, 'Women Writers and Women Readers: The Case of Aemilia Lanier', in Kate Chedgzoy, Melanie Hansen, and Suzanne Trill (eds.), *Voicing Women: Gender and Sexuality in Early Modern Writing* (Keele: Keele University Press, 1996), pp. 45–54.

Peck, Linda Levy, *Consuming Splendor: Society and Culture in Seventeenth-Century England* (Cambridge: Cambridge University Press, 2005).

Pender, Patricia, 'The Ghost and the Machine in the Sidney Family Corpus', *SEL* 51 (2011), 65–85.

Perry, Curtis, *The Making of Jacobean Culture* (Cambridge: Cambridge University Press, 1997).

—— *Literature and Favouritism in Early Modern England* (Cambridge: Cambridge University Press, 2006).

Peter, John Desmond, *Complaint and Satire in Early English Literature* (Oxford: Clarendon Press, 1956).

Peterson, Richard, 'Laurel Crown and Ape's Tail: New Light on Spenser's Career from Sir Thomas Tresham', *Sp. St.* 12 (1989), 1–36.

—— '*Enuies Scourge, and Vertues Honour*: A Rare Elegy for Spenser', *Sp. St.* 25 (2010), 287–325.

Petrina, Alessandra, *Machiavelli in the British Isles: Two Early Modern Translations of The Prince* (Aldershot: Ashgate, 2009).

Pettegree, Andrew, *Foreign Protestant Communities in Sixteenth-Century London* (Oxford: Clarendon Press, 1986).

Pettegree, Jane K., *Foreign and Native on the English Stage, 1588–1611: Metaphor and National Identity* (Basingstoke: Palgrave, 2011).

Pevsner, Nicholas, *The Buildings of England, London, i.: The Cities of London & Westminster* (Harmondsworth: Penguin, 1957).

—— *The Buildings of England, London except The Cities of London & Westminster ii.* (Harmondsworth: Penguin, 1952).

—— *The Buildings of England: Cambridgeshire* (Harmondsworth: Penguin, 1970).

—— *The Buildings of England: Essex* (rev. edn., Harmondsworth: Penguin, 1976).

Phillips, James E., 'George Buchanan and the Sidney Circle', *HLQ* 12 (1948–9), 23–55.

—— *Images of a Queen: Mary Stuart in Sixteenth-Century Literature* (Berkeley and Los Angeles: University of California Press, 1964).

—— 'Daniel Rogers: A Neo-Latin Link Between the Pléiade and Sidney's "Areopagus"', in *Neo-Latin Poetry of the Sixteenth and Seventeenth Centuries* (Los Angeles: Clark Memorial Library, 1965), pp. 5–28.

—— 'Spenser's Syncretistic Religious Imagery', *ELH* 36 (1969), 110–30.

—— 'Renaissance Concepts of Justice and the Structure of *The Faerie Queene*', *HLQ* 33 (1969–70), 103–20.

Pichaske, David R., '*The Faerie Queene* IV. ii and iii: Spenser and the Genesis of Friendship', *SEL* 17 (1977), 81–93.

Pienaar, W. J. B., 'Edmund Spenser and Jonker Jan van der Noot', *ES* 8 (1926), 33–44, 67–76.

—— *English Influences in Dutch Literature and Justus Van Edden as Intermediary: An Aspect of Eighteenth-Century Achievement* (Cambridge: Cambridge University Press, 1929).

Piepho, Lee, '*The Shepheardes Calender* and Neo-Latin Pastoral: A Book Newly Discovered to Have Been Owned by Spenser', *Sp. St.* 16 (2002), 17–86.

——'Edmund Spenser and Neo-Latin Literature: An Autograph Manuscript on Petrus Lotichius and His Poetry', *SP* 100 (2003), 123–34.

Pigman, G. W. III, *Grief and the English Elegy* (Cambridge: Cambridge University Press, 1985).

Pincombe, Michael and Cathy Shrank (eds.), *The Oxford Handbook of Tudor Literature, 1485–1603* (Oxford: Oxford University Press, 2009).

Pindell, Richard, 'The Mutable Image: Man-in-Creation', in Kenneth John Atchity (ed.), *Eterne in Mutabilitie: The Unity of The Faerie Queene: Essays Published in Memory of Davis Philoon Harding* (Hamden, CT: Archon Books, 1972), pp. 158–79.

Piper, David, 'The Chesterfield House Library Portraits', in René Wellek and Alvaro Ribeiro (eds.), *Evidence in Literary Scholarship: Essays in Memory of James Marshall Osborn* (Oxford: Clarendon Press, 1979), pp. 179–95.

Plant, Marjorie, *The English Book Trade: An Economic History of the Making and Sale of Books* (3rd edn., London: Allen & Unwin, 1974).

Plomer, Henry R., 'Henry Bynemann, Printer, 1566–83', *The Library*, NS 9 (1908), 225–44.

——'Edmund Spenser's Handwriting', *MP* 21 (1923), 201–7.

——and T. P. Cross, *The Life and Correspondence of Lodowick Bryskett* (Chicago: University of Chicago Press 1927).

Plumb, J. H., *Sir Robert Walpole: The Making of a Statesman* (London: Cresset, 1956).

Pollack, Linda A., 'Embarking on a Rough Passage: The Experience of Pregnancy in Early-Modern Society', in Fildes (ed.), *Women as Mothers*, pp. 39–67.

Pollard, Graham, 'Changes in the Style of Bookbinding, 1550–1830', *The Library*, 5th ser. 11 (1956), 71–94.

Pomeroy, Ralph S., 'The Ramist as Fallacy-Hunter: Abraham Fraunce and *The Lawiers Logicke*', *RQ* 40 (1987), 224–46.

Popper, Nicholas, 'The English Polydaedali: How Gabriel Harvey Read Late Tudor London', *Journal of the History of Ideas* 66 (2005), 351–81.

Porges Watson, E. A. F., 'Mutabilitie's Debateable Land: Spenser's Ireland and the Frontiers of Faerie', in Lethbridge (ed.), *Spenser: New and Renewed Directions*, pp. 286–301.

Porter, H. C., *Reformation and Reaction in Tudor Cambridge* (Cambridge: Cambridge University Press, 1958).

Porter, Stephen, *Shakespeare's London: Everyday Life in London, 1580–1616* (Stroud: Amberley, 2009).

Pound, John, *Poverty and Vagrancy in Tudor England* (Harlow: Longman, 1971).

Power, Denis, 'The Archaeology of the Munster Plantation', in Horning et al. (eds.), *Post-Medieval Archaeology of Ireland*, pp. 23–36.

——et al. (eds.), *Archaeological Inventory of County Cork*, 4 vols. (Dublin: Stationery Office, 1992–2000).

Prescott, Anne Lake, *French Poets and the English Renaissance: Studies in Fame and Transformation* (New Haven: Yale University Press, 1978).

——'The Thirsty Deer and the Lord of Life: Some Contexts for *Amoretti* 67–70', *Sp. St.* 6 (1985), 33–76.

——'Spenser's Chivalric Restoration: From Bateman's "Travayled Pylgrime" to the Redcrosse Knight', *SP* 86 (1989), 166–97.

——'Spenser (Re)Reading Du Bellay', in Anderson et al. (eds.), *Spenser's Life and the Subject of Biography*, pp. 131–45.

——'The Ambivalent Heart: Thomas More's Merry Tales', *Criticism* 45 (2003), 417–33.

——'The Countess of Pembroke's Ruins of Rome', *SJ* 23 (2005), 1–17.

——'Refusing Translation: The Gregorian Calendar and Early Modern English Writers', *YES* 36 (2006), 112–22.

Prest, Wilfrid R. (ed.), *The Professions in Early Modern England* (Beckenham: Croom Helm, 1987).

Prewitt, Kendrick W., 'Gabriel Harvey and the Practice of Method', *SEL* 39 (1999), 19–39.

Pritchard, Alan, *English Biography in the Seventeenth Century: A Critical Survey* (Toronto: University of Toronto Press, 2005).

Pritchard, Arnold, *Catholic Loyalism in Elizabethan England* (London: Scolar, 1979).

Prouty, C. T., *George Gascoigne: Elizabethan Courtier, Soldier and Poet* (New York: Columbia University Press, 1942).

Pugh, Syrithe, *Spenser and Ovid* (Aldershot: Ashgate, 2005).

Purcell, J. M., 'The Date of Spenser's Mutabilitie Cantos', *PMLA* 50 (1935), 914–17.

Quaine, Michael, 'The Diocesan Schools, 1570–1870', *JCHAS* 66 (1961), 26–50.

Questier, Michael C., *Conversion, Politics and Religion in England, 1580–1625* (Cambridge: Cambridge University Press, 1996).

——'Elizabeth and the Catholics', in Ethan Shagan (ed.), *Catholics and the 'Protestant Nation': Religious Politics and Identity in Early Modern England* (Manchester: Manchester University Press, 2005), pp. 69–94.

——*Catholicism and Community in Early Modern England: Politics, Aristocratic Patronage and Religion, c.1550–1640* (Cambridge: Cambridge University Press, 2006).

Questier, Michael C., and Simon Healy, '"What's in a Name?": A Papist's Perception of Puritanism and Conformity in the Early Seventeenth Century', in Arthur F. Marotti (ed.), *Catholicism and Anti-Catholicism in Early Modern English Texts* (Basingstoke: Palgrave, 1999), p. 137–53.

Quilligan, Maureen, *Milton's Spenser: The Politics of Reading* (Ithaca, NY: Cornell University Press, 1983).

Quiniones, Ricardo J., *The Renaissance Discovery of Time* (Cambridge, MA: Harvard University Press, 1972).

Quinn, D. B., 'Sir Thomas Smith (1513–1577) and the Beginnings of English Colonial Theory', *Proceedings of the American Philosophical Society* 89 (1945), 543–60.

——*Ralegh and the British Empire* (London: Hodder and Stoughton, 1947).

——*The Elizabethans and the Irish* (Ithaca, NY: Cornell University Press, 1966).

——'The Munster Plantation: Its Problems and Opportunities', *JCHAS* 71 (1966), 19–40.

Quitslund, Jon A., 'Spenser and the Patronesses of the *Fowre Hymnes*: "Ornaments of All True Love and Beautie"', in Margaret Hannay (ed.), *Silent but for the Word: Tudor Women as Patrons, Translators, and Writers of Religious Works* (Kent: Kent State University Press, 1985), pp. 184–202.

——'Questionable Evidence in the *Letters* of 1580 between Gabriel Harvey and Edmund Spenser', in Anderson et al. (eds.), *Spenser's Life*, pp. 81–98.

——*Spenser's Supreme Fiction: Platonic Natural Philosophy and The Faerie Queene* (Toronto: University of Toronto Press, 2001).

——'Thinking About Thinking in the *Fowre Hymnes*', in Borris et al. (eds.), *Spenser and Platonism*, pp. 499–517.

Radcliffe, David Hill, *Edmund Spenser: A Reception History* (Columbia, SC: Camden House, 1996).

Raleigh, Walter, *Some Authors: A Collection of Literary Essays, 1896–1916* (Oxford: Clarendon Press, 1923).

Ramachandran, Ayesha, 'Edmund Spenser, Lucrecian Neoplatonist: Cosmology in the *Fowre Hymnes*', in Borris et al. (eds.), *Spenser and Platonism*, pp. 373–411.

——'Mutabilitie's Lucretian Metaphysics: Scepticism and Cosmic Process in Spenser's *Cantos*', in Grogan (ed.), *Celebrating Mutabilitie*, pp. 220–45.

Rambuss, Richard, *Spenser's Secret Career* (Cambridge: Cambridge University Press, 1993).

——'Spenser's Lives, Spenser's Careers', in Anderson et al. (eds.), *Spenser's Life*, pp. 1–17.

——'Spenser's Life and Career', in Hadfield (ed.), *Cambridge Companion to Spenser*, pp. 13–36.

Ranger, Terence, 'Richard Boyle and the Making of an Irish Fortune, 1588–1614', *IHS* 10 (1956–7), 257–97.

Rappaport, Steve, *Worlds Within Worlds: Structures of Life in Sixteenth-Century London* (Cambridge: Cambridge University Press, 1989).

Rapple, Rory, *Martial Power and Elizabethan Political Culture: Military Men in England and Ireland, 1558–1594* (Cambridge: Cambridge University Press, 2009).

Rasmussen, Carl J., '"Quietnesse of Minde": *A Theatre for Worldlings* as a Protestant Poetics', *Sp. St.* 1 (1980), 3–27.

Read, Conyers, 'Review of Alexander C. Judson, *Life of Spenser*', *American Historical Review* 51 (1946), 538–9.

——*Mr. Secretary Cecil and Queen Elizabeth* (London: Cape, 1955).

——*Lord Burghley and Queen Elizabeth* (London: Cape, 1960).

Redgrave, Samuel (ed.), *Catalogue of the Special Exhibition of Portrait Miniatures On Loan at The South Kensington Museum, June 1865* (London: Whittingham and Wilkins, 1865).

Rees, Valery, 'Ficinian Ideas in the Poetry of Edmund Spenser', in Borris et al. (eds.), *Spenser and Platonism*, pp. 73–134.

Reid, Jane Davidson (ed.), *The Oxford Guide to Classical Mythology in the Arts, 1300–1990s* (Oxford: Oxford University Press, 1993).

Reid, Robert Lanier, 'Spenser's Mutability Song: Conclusion or Transition?', in Grogan (ed.), *Celebrating Mutabilitie*, pp. 61–84.

Renwick, W. L., 'Mulcaster and Du Bellay', *MLR* 17 (1922), 282–7.

——'Review of Alexander C. Judson, *Life of Spenser*', *RES* 25 (1949), 261–2.

Reeves-Smith, Terence, 'Community to Privacy: Late Tudor and Jacobean Manorial Architecture in Ireland, 1560–1640', in Horning et al. (eds.), *Post-Medieval Archaeology of Ireland*, pp. 269–326.

Relle, Eleanor, 'Some New Marginalia and Poems of Gabriel Harvey', *RES* 23 (1972), 401–16.

Reynolds, Lorna, 'Review of Alexander C. Judson, *Life of Spenser*', *Dublin Magazine* (Apr./June 1947), 51–3.

Rhodes, Neil, *Elizabethan Grotesque* (London: Routledge, 1980).

Ribner, Irving, 'Gabriel Harvey in Chancery—1608', *RES* 2 (1951), 142–7.

Richards, Jennifer, *Rhetoric and Courtliness in Early Modern Literature* (Cambridge: Cambridge University Press, 2003).

—— 'Gabriel Harvey, James VI, and the Politics of Reading Early Modern Poetry', *HLQ* 71 (2008), 303–22.

Richardson, Catherine, *Domestic Life and Domestic Tragedy in Early Modern England: The Material Life of the Household* (Manchester: Manchester University Press, 2006).

Rickman, John, 'Historical Curiosities relating to St. Margaret's Church', (London: Privately printed, 1838).

Riddell, James A., and Stanley Stewart, *Jonson's Spenser: Evidence and Historical Criticism* (Pittsburgh: Duquesne University Press, 1995).

Riggs, David, *The World of Christopher Marlowe* (London: Faber, 2004).

Ringler, Richard N., 'The Faunus Episode', *MP* 43 (1966), 12–19.

Ringler, William A., Jr, 'Spenser, Shakespeare, Honor, and Worship', *Renaissance News* 14 (1961), 159–61.

Rivers, Isabel, *Classical and Christian Ideas in English Renaissance Poetry* (London: Routledge, 1975).

Rix, Herbert David, 'Spenser's Rhetoric and the "Doleful Lay"', *MLN* 53 (1938), 261–5.

—— *Rhetoric in Spenser's Poetry* (State College: Pennsylvania State College, 1940).

Robertson, Jean, '*The Passions of the Spirit* (1599) and Nicholas Breton', *HLQ* 3 (1939), 69–75.

—— 'Nicholas Breton's Authorship of "Marie Magdalens Loue" and "The Passion of a Discontented Minde"', *MLR* 36 (1941), 449–59.

Robinson, Benedict S., *Islam and Early Modern English Literature: The Politics of Romance from Spenser to Milton* (Basingstoke: Palgrave, 2007).

Roche, Thomas P., Jr, *The Kindly Flame: A Study of the Third and Fourth Books of Spenser's Faerie Queene* (Princeton: Princeton University Press, 1964).

Rollinson, Philip B., 'A Generic View of Spenser's *Four Hymns*', *SP* 68 (1971), 292–304.

Roseman, Mark, 'Surviving Memory: Truth and Inaccuracy in Holocaust Testimony', in Robert Perks and Alistair Thomson (eds.), *The Oral History Reader* (2nd edn., London: Routledge, 2006), pp. 230–43.

Rosenberg, Eleanor, *Leicester, Patron of Letters* (New York: Columbia University Press, 1955).

Round, J. Horace, *Studies in Peerage and Family History* (London: Constable, 1901).

—— *Peerage and Pedigree: Studies in Peerage Law and Family History* (1910; London: Woburn, 1971).

Routledge, F. J., 'Manuscripts at Oxford Relating to the Later Tudors, 1547–1603', *TRHS*, 3rd ser. 8 (1914), 119–59.

Rowse, A. L., *Tudor Cornwall: Portrait of a Society* (London: Cape, 1941).

—— *The England of Elizabeth* (1950; London: Macmillan, 1953).

—— *Sir Walter Ralegh: His Family and Private Life* (London: Harper, 1962).

Rowston, Guy, *Southwark Cathedral: The Authorized Guide* (Bromley: Robert James, 2006).

Rudick, Michael, 'The "Ralegh Group" in *The Phoenix Nest*', *SB* 24 (1971), 131–7.

Ruutz-Rees, Caroline, 'Some Notes of Gabriel Harvey's in Hoby's Translation of Castiglione's *Courtier* (1561)', *PMLA* 25 (1910), 608–39.

Rynne, Colin, 'The Social Archaeology of Plantation-Period Ironworks in Ireland: Immigrant Industrial Communities and Technology Transfer, *c.*1560–1640', in Lyttleton and Rynne (eds.), *Plantation Ireland*, pp. 248–64.

Sacks, David Harris, 'The Prudence of Thrasymachus: Sir Thomas Smith and the Commonwealth of England', in Anthony Grafton and J. H. M. Salmon (eds.), *Historians and Ideologues: Essays in Honour of Donald R. Kelley* (Rochester: Rochester University Press, 2001), pp. 89–122.

Sahlins, Marshall, *Apologies to Thucydides: Understanding History as Culture and Vice Versa* (Chicago: University of Chicago Press, 2004).

Said, Edward, *Culture and Imperialism* (1993; London: Vintage, 1994).

Salzman, Paul, *Reading Early Modern Women's Writing* (Oxford: Oxford University Press, 2006).

Samson, Alexander, 'Lazarillo de Tormes and the Picaresque in Early Modern England', in Hadfield (ed.), *Oxford Handbook of Early Modern Prose* (forthcoming).

Sanders, Wilbur, *John Donne's Poetry* (Cambridge: Cambridge University Press, 1971).

Sandison, Helen E., 'Spenser's "Lost" Works and Their Probable Relation to His *Faerie Queene*', *PMLA* 25 (1910), 134–51.

——'Arthur Gorges, Spenser's Alcyon and Raleigh's Friend', *PMLA* 43 (1928), 645–74.

——'Spenser's Manilla', *TLS*, 8 Sept. 1927, p. 608.

Sandler, Florence, '*The Faerie Queene*: An Elizabethan Apocalypse', in C. A. Patrides and Joseph Wittreich (eds.), *The Apocalypse in English Renaissance Thought and Literature* (Manchester: Manchester University Press, 1984), pp. 148–74.

Sargent, Clare, 'The Early Modern Library (to c.1640)', in Leedham-Green and Webber (eds.), *Cambridge History of Libraries*, i. 51–65.

Satterthwaite, Alfred W., *Spenser, Ronsard, and Du Bellay: A Renaissance Comparison* (Princeton: Princeton University Press, 1960).

Saunders, Corinne (ed.), *Chaucer* (Oxford: Blackwell, 2001).

Sayle, R. T. D., 'Annals of the Merchant Taylors' School Library', *The Library*, 4th ser. 15 (1935), 457–80.

Scarisbrick, J. J., *Henry VIII* (1968; London: Methuen, 1988).

—— *The Reformation and the English People* (Oxford: Blackwell, 1984).

Schama, Simon, *Landscape & Memory* (London: Fontana, 1995).

Scharff, R. F., H. J. Seymour, and E. T. Newton, 'The Exploration of Castlepook Cave, County Cork, Being the Third Report from the Committee Appointed to Explore Irish Caves', *PRIA*, sect. B, 34 (1917–19), 33–72.

Schleiner, Louise, 'Spenser's "E. K." as Edmund Kent (Kenned/of Kent: Kyth (Couth), Kissed, and Kunning-Coning', *ELR* 20 (2008), 374–407.

Schmitt, Charles B., and Quentin Skinner (eds.), *The Cambridge History of Renaissance Philosophy* (Cambridge: Cambridge University Press, 1988).

Schoenbaum, S., *William Shakespeare: A Compact Documentary Life* (New York: Oxford University Press, 1977).

Schofield, Roger, 'Did The Mothers Really Die? Three Centuries of Maternal Mortality in "The World We Have Lost"', in Bonfield et al. (eds.), *The World We Have Gained*, pp. 231–60.

Schurink, Fred (ed.), *Tudor Translation* (Basingstoke: Palgrave, 2011).

——'How Gabriel Harvey Read Anthony Cope's Livy: Translation, Humanism, and War in Tudor England', in Schurink (ed.), *Tudor Translation*, pp. 58–78.

Schwartz, Louis, *Milton and Maternal Mortality* (Cambridge: Cambridge University Press, 2009).

Schwyzer, Philip, *Archaeologies of English Renaissance Literature* (Oxford: Oxford University Press, 2007).

Scodel, Joshua, *Excess and the Mean in Early Modern English Literature* (Princeton: Princeton University Press, 2002).

—— 'Non-Dramatic Verse: Lyric', in Braden, Cummings, and Gillespie (eds.), *Oxford History of Literary Translation*, pp. 201–47.

Scott, Janet C., 'The Sources of Spenser's "Amoretti"', *MLR* 22 (1927), 189–95.

Scott-Warren, Jason, *Sir John Harington and the Book as Gift* (Oxford: Oxford University Press, 2001).

—— 'Unannotating Spenser', in Smith and Wilson (eds.), *Renaissance Paratexts*, pp. 153–64.

Sellers, Harry, 'Italian Books Printed in England Before 1640', *The Library*, 4th ser. 5 (1924), 105–28.

Sellin, Paul R., *'So Doth, So Is Religion': John Donne and Diplomatic Contexts in the Reformed Netherlands, 1619–1620* (Columbia: University of Missouri Press, 1988).

—— '"Souldiers of one army": John Donne and the Army of the States General as an International Protestant Crossroads', in Mary Arshagouni Papazian (ed.), *John Donne and the Protestant Reformation* (Detroit: Wayne State University Press, 2003), pp. 143–92.

—— and Augustus J. Veenendaal, Jr, 'A "Pub Crawl" through Old The Hague: Shady Light on Life and Art among English Friends of John Donne in the Netherlands', *John Donne Journal* 6 (1987), 235–60.

Sessions, W. A., 'Spenser's Georgics', *ELR* 10 (1980), 202–38.

—— *Henry Howard, the Poet Earl of Surrey: A Life* (Oxford: Oxford University Press, 1999).

Shanley, James Lyndon, 'Spenser's Temperance and Aristotle', *MP* 43 (1946), 170–4.

Shapiro, James, *1599: A Year in the Life of William Shakespeare* (London: Faber, 2005).

—— *Contested Will: Who Wrote Shakespeare?* (London: Faber, 2010).

Sharpe, Kevin, *Selling the Tudor Monarchy: Authority and Image in Sixteenth-Century England* (New Haven: Yale University Press, 2009).

Sheehan, Anthony J., 'The Overthrow of the Plantation of Munster in October 1598', *Irish Sword* 15 (1982), 11–22.

—— 'The Killing of the Earl of Desmond, November 1583', *JCHAS* 88 (1983), 106–10.

—— 'Official Reaction to Native Land Claims in the Plantation of Munster', *IHS* 23 (1983), 297–318.

Shell, Alison, *Catholicism, Controversy and the English Literary Imagination, 1558–1660* (Cambridge: Cambridge University Press, 1999).

—— *Oral Culture and Catholicism in Early Modern England* (Cambridge: Cambridge University Press, 2007).

Shepard, Alexandra, *Meanings of Manhood in Early Modern England* (Oxford: Oxford University Press, 2003).

Sherman, William H., *John Dee: The Politics of Reading and Writing in the English Renaissance* (Amherst: University of Massachusetts Press, 1995).

Shine, Michael, 'Spenser and Kilcolman', *MFCJ* 22 (2004), 139–54.

Shinn, Abigail, '"Extraordinary Discourses of vnnecessarie matter": Spenser's *Shepheardes Calender* and the Almanac Tradition', in Matthew Dimmock and Andrew Hadfield (eds.), *Literature and Popular Culture in Early Modern England* (Aldershot: Ashgate, 2009), pp. 137–49.

Shire, Helena, *A Preface to Spenser* (London: Longman, 1978).

Shirley, John W., 'Sir Walter Ralegh and Thomas Harriot', in James W. Shirley (ed.), *Thomas Harriot: Renaissance Scientist* (Oxford: Clarendon Press, 1974), pp. 16–35.

Shuger, Debora, 'Life-Writing in Seventeenth-Century England', in Patrick Coleman, Jayne Lewis, and Jill Kowalik (eds.), *Representations of the Self from the Renaissance to Romanticism* (Cambridge: Cambridge University Press, 2000), pp. 63–78.

Silberman, Lauren, *Transforming Desire: Erotic Knowledge in Books III and IV of The Faerie Queene* (Berkeley and Los Angeles: University of California Press, 1995).

Sim, Alison, *The Tudor Housewife* (Stroud: Sutton, 1996).

Simmons, R. C., 'ABCs, Almanacs, Ballads, Chapbooks, Popular Piety and Textbooks', in Barnard and McKenzie (eds.), *Cambridge History of the Book in Britain*, iv. 504–13.

Simms, Katherine, 'Gaelic Warfare in the Middle Ages', in Bartlett and Jeffrey (eds.), *Military History of Ireland*, pp. 99–115.

Simpson, James, *Reform and Cultural Revolution: The Oxford English Literary History*, ii. *1350–1547* (Oxford: Oxford University Press, 2003).

Simpson, Richard, 'Images and Ethics in Reformation Political Discourse: The Paintings at Sir Thomas Smith's Hill Hall', in Tara Hamling and Richard L. Williams (eds.), *Art Re-formed: Re-assessing the Impact of the Reformation on the Visual Arts* (Newcastle upon Tyne: Cambridge Scholars, 2007), pp. 127–45.

Singman, Jeffrey L., *Daily Life in Elizabethan England* (London: Greenwood, 1995).

Sjören, Gunnar, 'Helena, Marchioness of Northampton: A Swedish Lady at the Court of Elizabeth I', *History Today* 28 (1978), 597–604.

Skinner, Quentin, *The Foundations of Modern Political Thought*, 2 vols. (Cambridge: Cambridge University Press, 1978).

—— *Reason and Rhetoric in the Philosophy of Thomas Hobbes* (Cambridge: Cambridge University Press, 1996).

—— *Visions of Politics*, 3 vols. (Cambridge: Cambridge University Press, 2002).

Skretkowicz, Victor, *European Erotic Romance: Philhellene Protestantism, Renaissance Translation and English Literary Politics* (Manchester: Manchester University Press, 2010).

Sloan, Kim, *A New World: England's First View of America* (London: British Museum, 2007).

Smith, Alan G. R., *Servant of the Cecils: The Life of Sir Michael Hickes* (London: Cape, 1977).

—— 'The Secretariats of the Cecils, circa 1580–1612', *EHR* 83 (1968), 481–504.

Smith, David L., Richard Strier, and David Bevington (eds.), *The Theatrical City: Culture, Theatre and Politics in London, 1576–1649* (Cambridge: Cambridge University Press, 1995).

Smith, G. C. Moore, 'The Authorship of "Pedantius"', *N&Q* 153 (1927), 427.

Smith, Helen, and Louise Wilson (eds.), *Renaissance Paratexts* (Cambridge: Cambridge University Press, 2011).

Smith, J. Norton, 'Spenser's *Prothalamion*: A New Genre', *RES* 10 (1959), 173–8.

Smith, Roland M., 'Spenser's Irish River Stories', *PMLA* 50 (1935), 1047–56.

—— 'The Irish Background of Spenser's View', *JEGP* 42 (1943), 499–515.

—— 'Spenser, Holinshed, and the *Leabhar Gabhala*', *JEGP* 43 (1944), 390–401.

—— 'More Irish Words in Spenser', *MLN* 59 (1944), 472–7.

—— 'Spenser's "Stony Aubrian"', *MLN* 59 (1944), 1–5.

—— 'Origines Arthurianae: The Two Crosses of Spenser's Red Cross Knight', *JEGP* 54 (1955), 670–83.

—— 'Spenser's Scholarly Script and "Right Writing"', in D. C. Allen (ed.), *Studies in Honor of T. W. Baldwin* (Urbana: University of Illinois Press, 1958), pp. 66–111.

Smyth, Adam, 'Almanacs, Annotators, and Life-Writing in Early-Modern England', *ELR* 38 (2008), 200–44.

—— *Autobiography in Early Modern England* (Cambridge: Cambridge University Press, 2010).

Smyth, Charles, *Church and Parish: Studies in Church Problems, illustrated from the Parochial History of St. Margaret's, Westminster* (London: SPCK, 1955).

Smyth, William J., *Map-Making, Landscapes and Memory: A Geography of Colonial and Early Modern Ireland, c.1530–1750* (Cork: Cork University Press, 2006).

Snare, Gerald, 'Satire, Logic, and Rhetoric in Harvey's Earthquake Letter to Spenser', *Tulane Studies in English* 18 (1970), 17–33.

—— 'Spenser's Fourth Grace', *JWCI* 34 (1971), 350–5.

Snyder, Jon R., *Writing the Scene of Speaking: Theories of Dialogue in the Late Italian Renaissance* (Stanford: Stanford University Press, 1989).

Snyder, Susan, *Pastoral Process: Spenser, Marvell, Milton* (Stanford: Stanford University Press, 1998).

Sohmer, Steve, *Shakespeare's Mystery Play: The Opening of the Globe Theatre, 1599* (Manchester: Manchester University Press, 1999).

Sokol, B. J., and Mary Sokol, *Shakespeare's Legal Language: A Dictionary* (London: Athlone, 2000).

Southern, R. W., *Western Society and the Church in the Middle Ages* (Harmondsworth: Penguin, 1970).

Southgate, Beverley, *Postmodernism in History: Fear or Freedom* (London: Routledge, 2003).

Spence, Richard T., *Lady Anne Clifford: Countess of Pembroke, Dorset and Montgomery (1590–1676)* (Stroud: Sutton, 1997).

Spenser, F. C., 'Locality of the Family of Edmund Spenser', *Gentleman's Magazine*, NS 18 (1842), 138–43.

Spiller, Michael R. G., *The Development of the Sonnet: An Introduction* (London: Routledge, 1992).

Srigley, Michael, 'The Influence of Continental Familism in England after 1570', in Gunnar Sorelius and Michael Srigley (eds.), *Cultural Exchange between European Nations during the Renaissance* (Uppsala: Uppsala University Press, 1994), pp. 97–110.

Staines, John D., 'Elizabeth, Mercilla, and the Rhetoric of Propaganda in Spenser's *Faerie Queene*', *JMEMS* 31 (2001), 283–312.

—— *The Tragic Histories of Mary Queen of Scots, 1560–1690* (Aldershot: Ashgate, 2009).

—— 'Pity and the Authority of Feminine Passions in Books V and VI of *The Faerie Queene*', *Sp. St.* 25 (2010), 129–61.

Starnes, De Wilt T., and Ernest William Talbert, *Classical Myth and Legend in Renaissance Dictionaries: A Study of Renaissance Dictionaries in Relation to the Classical Learning of Contemporary English Writers* (Chapel Hill: North Carolina University Press, 1955).

Steadman, John M., 'Una and the Clergy: The Ass Symbol in *The Faerie Queene*', *JWCI* 21/1–2 (Winter/Spring 1958), 134–7.

Steane, John M., *The Northamptonshire Landscape: Northamptonshire and the Soke of Peterborough* (London: Hodder and Stoughton, 1974).

Stein, Harold, *Studies in Spenser's Complaints* (New York: Oxford University Press, 1934).

—— 'Spenser and William Turner', *MLN* 51 (1936), 345–51.

Steinberg, Glenn A., 'Chaucer's Mutability in Spenser's *Mutabilitie Cantos*', *SEL* 46 (2006), 27–42.

Steinberg, Theodore L., 'E. K.'s *Shepheardes Calender* and Spenser's', *Modern Language Studies*, 3 (1973), 46–58.

—— 'Spenser, Sidney, and the Myth of Astrophel', *Sp. St.* 18 (1990, pub. 1994), 187–201.

Stern, Virginia, F., 'The Bibliotheca of Gabriel Harvey', *RS* 25 (1972), 1–62.

—— *Gabriel Harvey: A Study of His Life, Marginalia, and Library* (Oxford: Clarendon Press, 1979).

Stevens, Paul, 'Spenser and the End of the British Empire', *Sp. St.* 22 (2007), 5–26.

Stewart, Alan, *Close Readers: Humanism and Sodomy in Early Modern England* (Princeton: Princeton University Press, 1997).

—— *Philip Sidney: A Double Life* (London: Pimlico, 2001).

—— 'The Making of Writing in Renaissance England: Re-thinking Authorship through Collaboration', in Healy and Healy (eds.), *Renaissance Transformations*, pp. 81–96.

—— *The Cradle King: A Life of James VI and I* (London: Chatto and Windus, 2003).

—— 'Instigating Treason: The Life and Death of Henry Cuffe, Secretary', in Erica Sheen and Lorna Hutson (eds.), *Literature, Politics and Law in Renaissance England* (Basingstoke: Palgrave, 2005), pp. 50–70.

—— and Heather Wolfe, *Letterwriting in Renaissance England* (Washington, DC: Folger Shakespeare Library, 2004).

Stillman, Robert E., *Philip Sidney and the Poetics of Renaissance Cosmopolitanism* (Aldershot: Ashgate, 2008).

Stone, Lawrence, *An Elizabethan: Sir Horatio Palavicino* (Oxford: Clarendon Press, 1956).

—— *The Crisis of the Aristocracy, 1558–1641* (rev. edn., Oxford: Clarendon Press, 1979).

—— *The Family, Sex and Marriage in England, 1500–1800* (London: Weidenfeld and Nicolson, 1977).

Strathmann, Ernest A., 'Spenser's *Legends* and *Court of Cupid*', *MLN* 46 (1931), 498–501.

—— 'A Manuscript Copy of Spenser's *Hymnes*', *MLN* 48 (1933), 217–21.

—— 'Lady Carey and Spenser', *ELH* 2 (1935), 33–57.

—— 'Ferdinando Freckleton and the Spenser Circle', *MLN* 58 (1943), 542–4.

Stretton, Tim, 'Women, Property and Law', in Anita Pacheco (ed.), *A Companion to Early Modern Women's Writing* (Oxford: Blackwell, 2002), pp. 40–57.

Strong, Roy, *The Renaissance Garden in England* (London: Thames and Hudson, 1979).

Strype, John, *The Life of the Learned Sir Thomas Smith* (Oxford: Clarendon Press, 1820).

Stubbs, John, *Donne: The Reformed Soul* (London: Viking, 2006).

Sullivan, Ceri, 'London's Early Modern Creative Industrialists', *SP* 103 (2006), 313–28.

Sullivan, Garrett, and Linda Woodbridge, 'Popular Culture in Print', in Arthur Kinney (ed.), *The Cambridge Companion to English Literature, 1500–1600* (Cambridge: Cambridge University Press, 2000), pp. 265–86.

Swan, Marshall W. S., 'The Sweet Speech and Spenser's (?) *Axiochus*', *ELH* 11 (1944), 161–81.

Sweeting, W. D., *Architectural Description of the Triangular Lodge at Rushton* (Northampton: Taylor and Son, 1881).

Tanner, J. R. (ed.), *The Historical Register of the University of Cambridge: Being a Supplement to the Calendar with a Record of University Offices, Honours and Distinctions to the Year 1910* (Cambridge: Cambridge University Press, 1917).

Taylor, Gary, Paul Mulholland, and MacD. P. Jackson, 'Thomas Middleton, Lording Barry, and The Family of Love', *Papers of the Bibliographics Society of America* 93 (1999), 213–42.

Teskey, Gordon, 'Thinking Moments in *The Faerie Queene*', *Sp. St.* 22 (2007), 103–25.

Teskey, Gordon, 'A Retrograde Reading of Spenser's *Fowre Hymnes*', in Borris et al. (eds.), *Spenser and Platonism*, pp. 481–97.

—— 'Night Thoughts on Mutability', in Grogan (ed.), *Celebrating Mutabilitie*, pp. 24–39.

Thirsk, Joan (ed.), *The Agrarian History of England and Wales*, iv. *1500–1640* (Cambridge: Cambridge University Press, 1967).

—— 'Farming Techniques', in Joan Thirsk (ed.), *Agrarian History*, pp. 161–99.

Thomas, Keith, *Man and the Natural World: Changing Attitudes in England, 1500–1800* (1983; Harmondsworth: Penguin, 1984).

—— *The Ends of Life: Roads to Fulfilment in Early Modern England* (Oxford: Oxford University Press, 2009).

Thomas, William J., 'Pictures of the Great Earl of Leicester,' *N&Q*, 3rd ser. 2 (1862), 201–2, 224–6.

Thomson, Gladys Scott, *Two Centuries of Family History: A Study in Social Development* (London: Longman, 1930).

Thornbury, Walter, *Old and New London: A Narration of Its People, and Its Places*, 2 vols. (London: Cassell, 1879).

Tilley, Arthur, 'Greek Studies in England in the Early Sixteenth-Century', *EHR* 53 (1938), 221–39, 438–56.

Tilmouth, Christopher, *Passion's Triumph Over Reason: A History of the Moral Imagination from Spenser to Rochester* (Oxford: Oxford University Press, 2007).

Tittler, Robert, *The Face of the City: Civic Portraiture and Civic Identity in Early Modern England* (Manchester: Manchester University Press, 2007).

Tóibín, Colm, 'The Dark Sixteenth Century', *Dublin Review* 43 (Summer 2011), 31–54.

Tolias, George, 'Maps in Renaissance Libraries and Collections', in Woodward (ed.), *History of Cartography*, iii/1. 637–60.

Tonkin, Humphrey, *Spenser's Courteous Pastoral: Book VI of The Faerie Queene* (Oxford: Oxford University Press, 1972).

Tosello, Mathew, 'Spenser's Silence about Dante', *SEL* 17 (1977), 59–66.

Townshend, Dorothea, *The Life and Letters of the Great Earl of Cork* (London: Duckworth, 1904).

Trapp, J. B., 'The Humanist Book', in Hellinga and Trapp (eds.), *Cambridge History of the Book in Britain*, iii. 285–315.

Tricomi, Albert H., *Anti-Court Drama in England, 1603–42* (Charlottesville: University Press of Virginia, 1989).

Trim, D. J. B., 'The Art of War: Martial Poetics from Henry Howard to Philip Sidney', in Pincombe and Shrank (eds.), *Tudor Literature*, pp. 587–605.

Tromly, Frederic B., 'Lodowick Bryskett's Elegies on Sidney in Spenser's *Astrophel* Volume', *RES* 147 (1986), 384–8.

Tuell, Anne K., 'The Original End of *Faerie Queene,* Book III', *MLN* 36 (1921), 309–11.

Tumelson, Ronald A., II, 'Robert Greene, "Author Playes"', in Melinkoff and Gieskes (eds.), *Writing Robert Greene,* pp. 95–114.

Turner, Henry S., 'Literature and Mapping in Early Modern England, 1520–1688', in Woodward (ed.), *History of Cartography,* iii/1. 412–26.

Turner, Myron, 'The Imagery of Spenser's *Amoretti*', *Neophilologus* 72 (1988), 284–99.

Tuve, Rosamund, 'Spenser and the *Zodiacke of Life*', *JEGP* 34 (1935), 1–19.

—— *Essays by Rosamund Tuve: Spenser, Herbert, Milton,* ed. Thomas P. Roche, Jr (Princeton: Princeton University Press, 1970).

Tyack, Geoffrey, *Warwickshire Country Houses* (Chichester: Phillimore, 1994).

Van Den Berg, Kent T., '"The Counterfeit in Personation": Spenser's *Prosopopoia, or Mother Hubberds Tale*', in Louis L. Martz and Aubrey Williams (eds.), *The Author in His Work: Essays on a Problem in Criticism* (New Haven: Yale University Press, 1978), pp. 85–102.

Van Es, Bart, *Spenser's Forms of History* (Oxford: Oxford University Press, 2002).

—— (ed.), *A Critical Companion to Spenser Studies* (Basingstoke: Palgrave, 2006).

Varro, 'Spenser's Age at His Death', *N&Q,* 1st ser. 4 (1851), 74.

Velema, Wyger R. E., '"That a Republic is Better than a Monarchy": Anti-monarchism in Early Modern Dutch Political Thought', in Martin van Gelderen and Quentin Skinner (eds.), *Republicanism: A Shared European Heritage,* 2 vols. (Cambridge: Cambridge University Press, 2002), i. 9–25.

Vickers, Brian, *In Defence of Rhetoric* (Oxford: Clarendon Press, 1988).

—— 'Rhetoric and Poetics', in Charles B. Schmitt et al. (eds.), *The Cambridge History of Renaissance Philosophy* (Cambridge: Cambridge University Press, 1988), pp. 715–45.

Vickers, Nancy, 'Diana Described: Scattered Woman and Scattered Rhyme', *Critical Inquiry* 8 (1981), 265–79.

Villeponteaux, Mary, '"Not as women wonted be": Spenser's Amazon Queen', in Walker (ed.), *Dissing Elizabeth,* pp. 209–25.

Vine, Angus, *In Defiance of Time: Antiquarian Writing in Early Modern England* (Oxford: Oxford University Press, 2010).

Wagner, John, *The Devonshire Gentleman: A life of Sir Peter Carew* (Hull: Hull University Press, 1998).

Walker, Greg, *John Skelton and the Politics of the 1520s* (Cambridge: Cambridge University Press, 1988).

—— *Writing under Tyranny: English Literature and the Henrician Reformation* (Oxford: Oxford University Press, 2005).

Walker, Julia M., 'Bones of Contention: Posthumous Images of Elizabeth and Stuart Politics', in Walker (ed.), *Dissing Elizabeth,* pp. 252–76.

—— (ed.), *Dissing Elizabeth: Negative Representations of Gloriana* (Durham, NC: Duke University Press, 1998).

Wall, John N., 'Godly and Fruitful Lessons: *The English Bible,* Erasmus' *Paraphrases* and *The Book of Homilies*', in Booty (ed.), *Godly Kingdom of Tudor England,* pp. 45–135.

Wall, Wendy, *The Imprint of Gender: Authorship and Publication in the English Renaissance* (Ithaca, NY: Cornell University Press, 1993).

Wallace, Andrew, *Virgil's Schoolboys: The Poetics of Pedagogy in Renaissance England* (Oxford: Oxford University Press, 2010).

Wallace, W. A., *John White, Thomas Harriot and Walter Ralegh in Ireland* (London: Historical Association, 1985).

Waller, Gary F., *Mary Sidney, Countess of Pembroke: A Critical Study of Her Writings and Literary Milieu* (Salzburg: Salzburg University Press, 1979).

—— *Edmund Spenser: A Literary Life* (Basingstoke: Palgrave, 1994).

Walsh, Katherine, 'Deliberate Provocation or Reforming Zeal? John Bale as First Church of Ireland Bishop of Ossory (1552/3–1563)', in Carey and Lotz-Heumann (eds.), *Taking Sides?,* pp. 42–60.

Walsham, Alexandra, *The Reformation of the Landscape: Religion, Identity, and Memory in Early Modern Ireland* (Oxford: Oxford University Press, 2011).

Walters, D. Douglas, *Duessa as Theological Satire* (Columbia: University of Missouri Press, 1970).

Wareh, Patricia, 'Humble Presents: Pastoral and Gift-Giving in the Commendatory Verses and Dedicatory Sonnets', in Erikson (ed.), *1590: Faerie Queene*, pp. 119–32.

Warkentin, Germaine, 'Patrons and Profiteers: Thomas Newman and the "Violent Enlargement" of *Astrophil and Stella*', *Book Collector* 34 (1985), 461–87.

Warley, Christopher, *Sonnet Sequences and Social Distinction in Renaissance England* (Cambridge: Cambridge University Press, 2005).

Warnicke, Retha M., *William Lambarde: Elizabethan Antiquary, 1536–1601* (Chichester: Phillimore, 1973).

Waterschoot, Werner, 'On Ordering the "Poetische Werken" of Jan van der Noot', *Quaerendo* 1 (1971), 242–63.

—— 'Jan van der Noot's *Het Bosken* Re-Examined', *Quarendo* 22 (1992), 28–45.

Watkins, John, *The Specter of Dido: Spenser and Virgilian Epic* (New Haven: Yale University Press, 1995).

Watkins, W. B. C., 'The Plagarist? Spenser or Marlowe?', *ELH* 11 (1944), 249–65.

—— *Shakespeare and Spenser* (Princeton: Princeton University Press, 1950).

Watney, Vernon James, *The Wallop Family and Their Ancestry*, 4 vols. (Oxford: John Johnson, 1928).

Watt, Teresa, *Cheap Print and Popular Piety, 1550–1640* (Cambridge: Cambridge University Press, 1991).

Watts, Pauline Moffitt, 'The European Religious Worldview and Its Influence on Mapping', in Woodward (ed.), *History of Cartography*, iii/1. 382–400.

Weatherby, Harold L., '*Axiochus* and the Bower of Bliss: Some Fresh Light on Sources and Authorship', *Sp. St.* 6 (1985), 95–113.

—— *Mirrors of Celestial Grace: Patristic Theology in Spenser's Allegory* (Toronto: University of Toronto Press, 1994).

Weaver, William, 'Paraphrase and Patronage in *Virgils Gnat*', *Sp. St.* 25 (2010), 247–61.

Webling, A. F., *Risby* (Leicester: Edmund Ward, 1945).

Webster, C. M., 'Robert Nowell', *N&Q* 167 (1934), 116.

—— 'A Note on Alexander Nowell', *N&Q* 168 (1934), 58–9.

Weiner, Andrew D., 'Spenser's *Muiopotmos* and the Fates of Butterflies and Men', *JEGP* 84 (1985), 203–20.

Weiner, Carol Z., 'The Beleaguered Isle: A Study of Elizabethan and Early Jacobean Anti-Catholicism', *P&P* 51 (May 1971), 27–62.

Weixel, Elizabeth M., 'Squires of the Wood: The Decline of the Aristocratic Forest in Book VI of *The Faerie Queene*', *Sp. St.* 25 (2010), 187–213.

Wells, William, '"To Make a Milde Construction": The Significance of the Opening Stanzas of *Muiopotmos*', *SP* 42 (1945), 544–54.

Welply, W. H., 'The Family and Descendants of Edmund Spenser', *JCHAS*, 2nd ser. 28 (1922), 22–34, 49–61.

—— 'Edmund Spenser: Some New Discoveries and the Correction of Some Old Errors', *N&Q* (1924), 146, 445–7; 147 (1924), 35.

—— 'Edmund Spenser: Being an Account of Some Recent Researches into His Life and Lineage, with Some Notice of His Family and Descendants', *N&Q* 162 (1932): 128–32, 146–50, 165–9, 182–7, 202–6, 220–4, 239–42, 256–60.

—— 'More Notes on Edmund Spenser', *N&Q* 165 (1933), 92–4, 111–16.

—— 'Edmund Spenser's Brother-in-Law, John Travers', *N&Q* 179 (1940), 70–8, 92–7, 112–15.

—— 'Some Spenser Problems', *N&Q* 180 (1941), 56–9, 74–6, 92–5, 104, 151, 224, 248, 436–9, 454–9.

—— 'Spenser–Tynte Genealogy', *N&Q* 187 (1944), 128–9.

Welsford, Enid, *Spenser: Fowre Hymnes, Epithalamion: A Study of Edmund Spenser's Doctrine of Love* (Oxford: Blackwell, 1967).

Wendel, François, *Calvin: The Origins and Development of His Religious Thought*, trans. Philip Mairet (London: Fontana, 1965).

Wernham, R. B., *Before the Armada: The Growth of English Foreign Policy, 1485–1588* (London: Cape, 1966).

—— *After the Armada: Elizabethan England and the Struggle for Western Europe, 1588–1595* (Oxford: Clarendon Press, 1984).

Wesley, John, 'Spenser's "Wrenock" and an Anglo-Welsh Latimer', *N&Q* 56 (2009), 527–30.

—— 'Acting and *Actio* in the Sermons of Lancelot Andrewes', *RS* 23 (2009), 678–93.

West, Michael, 'Prothalamia in Propertius and Spenser', *CL* 26 (1974), 346–53.

—— 'Spenser's Art of War: Chivalric Allegory, Military Technology, and the Elizabethan Mock-Heroic Sensibility', *RQ* 41 (1988), 654–704.

Westlake, H. F., *St. Margaret's Church, Westminster: The Church of the House of Commons* (London: Smith, Elder & Co., 1914).

Wheeler, Jeremy, *Where Sheep Safely Graze: 1000 Years of Worship, 1000 Years of History: A Short History and Description of The Village of Wormleighton and the Church of St. Peter* (Wormleighton: Wormleighton PCC, 2011).

White, Colonel James Grove, *Historical and Topographical Notes, etc, on Buttevant, Castletownroche, Doneraile, Mallow, and Places in their vicinity*, 4 vols. (Cork: Guy and Co., 1905–25).

White, T. H., *The Age of Scandal: An Excursion through a Minor Period* (London: Cape, 1950).

Whitmore, J. B., 'Reader's Reply,' *N&Q* 180 (1941), 120.

Whitney, Charles C. (ed.), *Thomas Lodge* (Aldershot: Ashgate, 2011).

Whitworth, Charles, 'Thomas Lodge', in Whitney (ed.), *Thomas Lodge*, pp. 23–36.

Wiffen, Jeremiah, *Historical Memoirs of the House of Russell*, 2 vols. (London, 1833).

Wilkes, Roger, *Scandal! A Scurrilous History of Gossip, 1700–2000* (London: Atlantic Books, 2002).

Williams, Arnold, *Flower on a Lowly Stalk: The Sixth Book of The Faerie Queene* (East Lansing: Michigan State University Press, 1967).

Williams, Franklin B., Jr, 'Thomas Rogers of Bryanston, An Elizabethan Gentleman-of-Letters', *HSNPL* 16 (1934), 253–67.

—— '*Leicester's Ghost*', *HSNPL* 18 (1935), 271–85.

—— *Index of Dedications and Commendatory Verses in English Books Before 1641* (London: Bibliographical Society, 1962).

—— 'Commendatory Verses: The Rise of the Art of Puffing', *SB* 19 (1966), 1–14.

—— 'Spenser, Shakespeare, and Zachary Jones', *Shakespeare Quarterly* 19 (1968), 205–12.

—— 'Thomas Rogers as Ben Jonson's Dapper', *YES* 2 (1972), 73–7.

Williams, George Walton, 'The Printer of the First Folio of Sidney's *Arcadia*', *The Library*, 5th ser. 12 (1957), 274–5.

Williams, Kathleen, *Spenser's Faerie Queene: The World of Glass* (London: Routledge, 1966).

Williams, Penry, *The Tudor Regime* (Oxford: Clarendon Press, 1979).

Willis, Robert, and John Willis Clark, *The Architectural History of the University of Cambridge, and of the Colleges of Cambridge and Eton*, 4 vols. (Cambridge: Cambridge University Press, 1886).

Wilson, Adrian, 'The Ceremony of Childbirth and Its Interpretation, in Fildes (ed.), *Women as Mothers*, pp. 68–107.

Wilson, Chris, 'The Proximate Determinants of Marital Fertility in England, 1600–1799', in Bonfield et al. (eds.), *The World We Have Gained*, pp. 203–30.

Wilson, F. P., 'Spenser and Ireland', *RES* 2 (1926), 456–7.

Wilson, H. B., *The History of Merchant Taylors' School* (London, 1814).

Wilson, Scott, *Cultural Materialism: Theory and Practice* (Oxford: Blackwell, 1995).

Wilson-Okamura, David Scott, 'Republicanism, Nostalgia and the Crowd', *Sp. St.* 17 (2003), 253–73.

—— *Virgil in the Renaissance* (Cambridge: Cambridge University Press, 2010).

—— 'Problems in the Virgilian Career', *Sp. St.* 26 (2011), 1–30.

Wind, Edgar, *Pagan Mysteries in the Renaissance* (London: Faber, 1967).

Wine, M. L., 'Spenser's "Sweete Themmes": Of Time and the River', *SEL* 2 (1962), 111–17.

Winn, James Anderson, *John Dryden and His World* (New Haven: Yale University Press, 1987).

Winston, Jessica, 'Lyric Poetry at the Early Elizabethan Inns of Court: Forming a Professional Community', in Archer et al. (eds.), *Inns of Court*, pp. 223–44.

Wiseman, Susan, and Alison Thorne (eds.), *The Rhetoric of Complaint: Ovid's Heroides in the Renaissance and Restoration* (special issue), *RS* 22/3 (June 2008).

Withington, Philip, *The Politics of Commonwealth: Citizens and Freemen in Early Modern England* (Cambridge: Cambridge University Press, 2005).

——'"For This Is True Or Els I Do Lye": Thomas Smith, William Bullein, and Mid-Tudor Dialogue', in Pincombe and Shrank (eds.), *Oxford Handbook of Tudor Literature*, pp. 455–71.

—— *Society in Early Modern England* (Cambridge: Polity, 2010).

Womersley, David, *Divinity and State* (Oxford: Oxford University Press, 2010).

Wood, Andy, *The 1549 Rebellions and the Making of Early Modern England* (Cambridge: Cambridge University Press, 2007).

Wood, Herbert, *A Guide to the Public Records Deposited in the Public Record Office of Ireland* (Dublin: HMSO, 1919).

—— 'Spenser's Great-Grandson', *TLS*, 14 Feb. 1929, p. 118.

Woodbridge, Linda, 'Jest Books, the Literature of Roguery, and the Vagrant Poor in Renaissance England', *ELR* 33 (2003), 201–10.

Woodcock, Matthew, 'Spenser and Olaus Magnus: A Reassessment', *Sp. St.* 21 (2006), 181–204.

Woodhouse, Elisabeth, 'Spirit of the Elizabethan Garden', *Garden History* 27 (1999), 10–31.

Woods, Susanne, *Lanyer: A Renaissance Woman Poet* (New York: Oxford University Press, 1999).

Woodward, Daniel H., 'Some Themes in Spenser's *Prothalamion*', *ELH* 29 (1962), 34–46.

Woodward, David (ed.), *The History of Cartography*, iii. *Cartography in the European Renaissance*, 2 parts (Chicago: University of Chicago Press, 2007).

Woodworth, Mary K., 'The Mutability Cantos and the Succession', *PMLA* 59 (1944), 985–1002.

Woolf, Jessica, *Humanism, Machinery, and Renaissance Literature* (Cambridge: Cambridge University Press, 2004).

Wootton, David, 'Reginald Scot/Abraham Fleming/The Family of Love', in Stuart Clark (ed.), *Languages of Witchcraft: Narrative, Ideology and Meaning in Early Modern Culture* (Basingstoke: Palgrave, 2001), pp. 119–38.

——'John Donne's Religion of Love', in John Brooke and Ian Maclean (eds.), *Heterodoxy in Early Modern Science and Religion* (Oxford: Oxford University Press, 2005), pp. 31–58.

Woudhuysen, H. R., *Sir Philip Sidney and the Circulation of Manuscripts, 1558–1640* (Oxford: Clarendon Press, 1996).

——'Gabriel Harvey', in Hadfield (ed.), *Oxford Handbook of Early Modern Prose* (forthcoming).

Wraight, A. D., *In Search of Christopher Marlowe: A Pictorial Biography* (1965; Chichester: Hart, 1993).

Wright, Celestine Turner, 'Young Anthony Munday Again', *SP* 56 (1959), 150–68.

——'Anthony Munday, "Edward" Spenser, and E. K.', *PMLA* 76 (1961), 34–9.

—— '"Lazarus Pyott" and Other Inventions of Anthony Munday', *PQ* 42 (1963), 532–41.

Wrightson, Keith, *English Society, 1580–1680* (London: Hutchinson, 1982).

Wrigley, E. A., and R. S. Schofield, *The Population History of England, 1541–1871* (1989; Cambridge: Cambridge University Press, 2002).

Wurtsbaugh, Jewel, *Two Centuries of Spenserian Scholarship (1609–1805)* (1936; Port Washington: Kennikat, 1970).

Wynne-Davies, Marion, '"For *Worth*, Not Weakness, Makes in Use but One": Literary Dialogues in an English Renaissance Family', in Clarke and Clarke (eds.), *'This Double Voice'*, pp. 164–84.

Yamashita, Hiroshi, Haruo Sato, Toshiyuki Suzuki, and Akira Takano, *A Textual Companion to The Faerie Queene 1590* (Tokyo: Kenyusha, 1993).

Yates, Frances A., *The Art of Memory* (London: Routledge, 1966).

—— *The Rosicrucian Enlightenment* (London: Routledge, 1972).

—— *Astrea: The Imperial Theme in the Sixteenth Century* (London: Routledge, 1975).

Yeats, W. B., 'Edmund Spenser', in W. B. Yeats, *Essays and Introductions* (London: Macmillan, 1961), pp. 356–83.

Yoch, James J., 'Architecture as Virtue: The Luminous Palace from Homeric Dream to Stuart Propaganda', *SP* 75 (1978), 403–29.

Young, Alan, *Tudor and Jacobean Tournaments* (London: George Philip, 1987).

Younger, Calton, *Ireland's Civil War* (London: Muller, 1968).

Yungblut, Laura Hunt, *Strangers Settled Here amongst Us: Politics, Perceptions and the Presence of Aliens in Elizabethan England* (London: Routledge, 1996).

Zeitler, W. I., 'The Date of Spenser's Death', *MLN* 43 (1928), 233–4.

Zinsser, Judith P., 'A Prologue for La Dame d'Esprit: The Biography of the Marquise Du Châtelet', in Alun Munslow and Robert A. Rosenstein (eds.), *Experiments in Rethinking History* (London: Routledge, 2004), pp. 195–208.

Zon, Stephen, *Petrus Lotichius Secundus: Neo-Latin Poet* (New York: Peter Lang, 1983).

Zurcher, Andrew, 'Getting it Back to Front in 1590: Spenser's Dedications, Nashe's Insinuations, and Raleigh's Equivocations', in Erikson (ed.), *1590: Faerie Queene*, pp. 173–98.

—— *Spenser's Legal Language: Law and Poetry in Early Modern England* (Cambridge: Brewer, 2007).

—— 'The Printing of the *Cantos of Mutabilitie* in 1609', in Grogan (ed.), *Celebrating Mutabilitie*, pp. 40–60.

—— *Shakespeare and the Law* (London: Black, 2010).

—— *Edmund Spenser's The Faerie Queene: A Reading Guide* (Edinburgh: Edinburgh University Press, 2011).

UNPUBLISHED

Coldham-Fussell, Victoria, 'Spenser's Divine Comedy: Humour and Humanity in *The Faerie Queene*', unpublished PhD dissertation, University of Cambridge, 2010.

Davies, Mary, 'Bruno in England, 1583–1585: The Cultural Context for Bruno's *De Gli Eroici Furori*', unpublished PhD thesis, Swansea University, 2009.

Gair, W. R., 'Literary Societies in England from Parker to Falkland', unpublished DPhil thesis, University of Oxford, 1968.

Galbraith, Stephen K., 'Edmund Spenser and the History of the Book, 1569–1679', unpublished PhD dissertation, Ohio State University, 2006.

Gibson, Jonathan, 'Sir Arthur Gorges (1557–1625) and the Patronage System', unpublished PhD thesis, University of London, 1998.

Hutchinson, Mark A., 'Sir Henry Sidney and His Legacy: Reformed Protestantism and the Government of Ireland and England, c.1558–1580', unpublished PhD thesis, University of Kent at Canterbury, 2010.

Jameson, Thomas Hugh, 'The *Gratulationes Valdinenses* of Gabriel Harvey', unpublished PhD dissertation, Yale University, 1938.

Jones, Amanda Rogers, 'Orderly Disorder: Rhetoric and Imitation in Spenser's Three Beast Poems from the *Complaints* Volume', unpublished MA thesis, Virginia Polytechnic Institute, 2001.

MacCarthy-Morrogh, Michael, 'The Munster Plantation, 1583–1641', unpublished PhD thesis, University of London, 1983.

Muir, Thomas Russell James, 'Ruins and Oblivion in the Sixteenth Century', unpublished DPhil thesis, University of Sussex, 2005.

Nelan, Thomas Philip, 'Catholic Doctrines in Spenser's Poetry', unpublished PhD dissertation, New York University, Graduate School of Arts and Science, 1944.

Norton, Dan S., 'The Background of Spenser's *Prothalamion*', unpublished PhD dissertation, Princeton University, 1940.

Richardson, Brenda E., 'Studies in Related Aspects of the Life and Thought of Robert Greene, with Particular Reference to the Material of His Prose Pamphlets', unpublished DPhil thesis, University of Oxford, 1976.

Sheehan, Anthony Joseph, 'Provincial Grievance and National Revolt: Munster in the Nine Years War', unpublished MA thesis, University College Dublin, 1982.

Shinn, Abigail, 'Spenser and Popular Print Culture', unpublished DPhil thesis, University of Sussex, 2009.

Wesley, John, 'Mulcaster's Boys: Spenser, Andrewes, Kyd', unpublished DPhil thesis, University of St Andrews, 2008.

White, D. G., 'The Tudor Plantations in Ireland before 1571', unpublished PhD thesis, University of Dublin, 1967.

Woudhuysen, H. R., 'Leicester's Literary Patronage: A Study of the English Court, 1578–1582', unpublished DPhil thesis, University of Oxford, 1980.

ONLINE RESOURCES

Anon., 'Discourse on the Mere Irish of Ireland', Exeter College, Oxford, MS 154, fos. 55–74, transcribed by Hiram Morgan, CELT, http://www.ucc.ie/celt/published/E600001–004/index.html.

H.C., 'The Dialogue of Perergynne and Silvvynnus', TNA, PRO SP 63/203, 119, transcribed by Hiram Morgan, CELT, http://www.ucc.ie/celt/contents/online/E590001–001/nav.html.

On-Line Depositions Website, Trinity College Dublin, http://1641.tcd.ie/index.php?state=loggedin &cookie=false.

Forsett, Edward, *Pedantius*, ed. Dana F. Sutton, http://www.philological.bham.ac.uk/forsett/contents.html.

Harvey, Gabriel, *Rhetor* (1577), trans. Mark Reynolds, http://comp.uark.edu/~mreynold/rheteng.html.

The Map of Early Modern London, http://mapoflondon.uvic.ca/section.php?id.

Morgan, Hiram, 'Spenser's Supplication', http://ucc-ie.academia.edu/HiramMorgan/Papers/107464/Spensers_Supplication_of_the_Blood_of_the_English.

Pearson, David, 'English Book Owners in the Seventeenth Century: A Work in Progress Listing', The Bibliographical Society, http://www.bibsoc.org.uk/electronic-publications.htm.

Private Libraries in Renaissance England, (http://plre.folger.edu/books.php).

Queens' College, Cambridge, MS 49, http://scriptorium.english.cam.ac.uk/manuscripts/images/index.php?ms =Queens_49.

Index